Patron: Her Majesty the Queen
Established 2002
Incorporated by Royal Charter 1898

CILIP: the Chartered Institute of Library and Information Professionals

YEARBOOK 2014–15

Compiled by

Kathryn Beecroft and Simon Edwards

D1103298

facet publishing

90721 000 009 505

Published by Facet Publishing
7 Ridgmount Street, London WC1E 7AE

Facet Publishing is wholly owned by CILIP: the Chartered Institute of Library and Information Professionals. CILIP was formed in April 2002 following the unification of the Institute of Information Scientists and The Library Association.

British Library Cataloguing in Publication Data
A cataloguing record for this book is available from the British Library.

ISBN 978-1-85604-709-8
ISSN 1746-9929

First published 2015

Text printed on FSC accredited material.

Typeset by Facet Publishing Production in 10/13 pt Nimbus Sans.
Printed and made in Great Britain by CPI Group (UK) Ltd, Croydon CR0 4YY.

Contents

CONTENTS

Note on the 2014–15 edition

CILIP underwent a major reorganisation during the course of 2012–14. It was therefore felt to be more helpful to delay publication of the *Yearbook* until the major part of the restructuring was in place. However, information of record for 2011–13 is included .

CILIP's vision and mission

Vision

A fair and economically prosperous society is underpinned by literacy, access to information and the transfer of knowledge.

Mission

CILIP exists to:

- Promote and support the people who work to deliver this vision
- Be the leading voice for information, library and knowledge practitioners, working to advocate strongly, provide unity through shared values and develop skills and excellence

CILIP is a professional body, a chartered institute, charity and membership body. We are committed to delivering public good to society through the work of our members. Our members deliver the highest standards of professional practice, demonstrated through their commitment to continuing professional development, professional registration and revalidation.

We aim to be the voice of the profession in a changing society, where information and knowledge are currency and commodity, and where the ability to be information and digitally literate makes the difference to success and prosperity. Access to information is a right for all citizens as is their right to freedom of expression.

Our members work in all sectors of society, underpinning further and higher education, supporting local communities, ensuring effective knowledge dissemination in business and government, building literacies in schools and supporting health practitioners and patients to make informed choices.

Strategic plan

CILIP are currently developing a new Str ategic Plan for 2016-2020. The 2015 business plan will use the four strategic goals currently identified for the new Strategic Plan:

- **Build membership:** through the best possible offers: recognised as the lead membership body for librarians, information and knowledge workers
- **Inspire our members to develop their skills and professionalism:** recognised as providing the best possible professional development and member networks that meet our members' needs and deliver high value for members
- **Build value with employers:** recognised as promoting excellence in the workforce and responding to employers' needs for skilled and value-driven employees with high ethical standards
- **Build influence through research and evidence-based advocacy and campaigning:** recognised as the strong clear voice of the profession as contributors to society and promoters of change for the good of the informed citizen.

CILIP equal opportunities and diversity statement

Our vision is an informed society in which everyone has ready access to the knowledge, information and works of imagination appropriate to their needs, wants and aspirations. This is the distinctive contribution of library and information professionals to developing a society where:

- All groups are empowered;
- Attitudes and prejudices that hinder the progress of individuals and groups are confronted and tackled;
- Cultural, racial, and societal diversity is respected and celebrated;
- Individuals and communities live together in mutual respect and tolerance;
- Discrimination is challenged and tackled robustly.

In affirming this vision CILIP will seek:

- To achieve recognisable excellence as an organisation that values and puts into practice equal opportunities and diversity
- To work towards establishing an LIS workforce that is representative of the diversity within UK society
- To facilitate an awareness and appreciation of the value and importance of diversity and equal opportunities to LIS work amongst our members and staff
- To collaborate with other interested parties in the encouragement and mainstreaming of best practice in service delivery so that the values of diversity and equal opportunities are embodied in the services provided by our members
- To tackle prejudice wherever it is found in the LIS domain.

Part 1
THE ORGANISATION

Part 1

THE INFORMATION

CILIP offices

CILIP: the Chartered Institute of Library and Information Professionals

7 Ridgmount Street, London WC1E 7AE
Telephone: 020 7255 0500*
Fax: 020 7255 0501
E-mail: info@cilip.org.uk.
Website: www.cilip.org.uk
Office hours: Monday–Friday 09.00–17.00.
Switchboard hours: Monday–Friday 08.30–17.00. An electronic queuing system is in operation: calls are answered in sequence.

CILIP in Scotland

126 West Regent Street, Glasgow, G2 2RQ
Telephone: 0141 222 5785
Email: admin@cilips.org.uk
Website: www.cilips.org.uk

CILIP Cymru/Wales

Head of CILIP Cymru/Wales
Email: mandy.powell@cilip.org.uk
Email: wales@cilip.org.uk
Telephone: 07837 032536
Bute Library, Cardiff University, PO Box 430
Cardiff CF24 ODE
Website: www.cilip.org.uk/wales

CILIP in Ireland

Development Officer, CILIP Ireland
Email: louisa.costelloe@cilip.org.uk
Telephone: 07837082566
Website: www.cilip.org.uk/ireland

Statutory information

Registered Charity Number: 313014
VAT Number: GB 233 1573 87
Solicitors: Bates, Wells and Braithwaite
Bankers: Bank of Scotland
Auditors: Kingston Smith (to September 2014)
Haysmacintyre (from September 2014)

---

* Note To call UK numbers from abroad, start with the international dialling code from your country (for example: 00). Next, dial the country code for the UK, which is 44. Finally, dial the UK number, without the first 0.

Structure

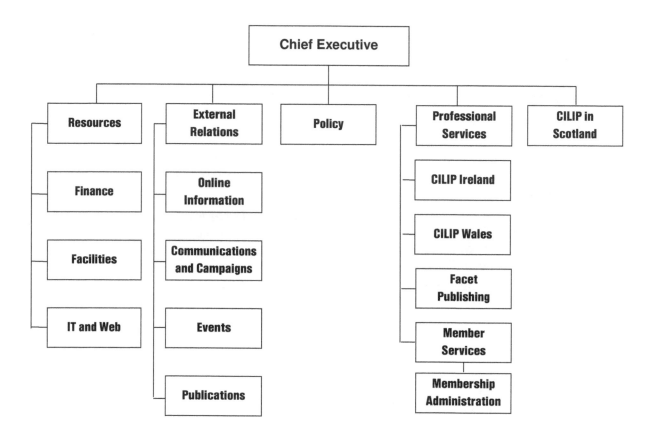

Chief Executive

The Chief Executive is responsible for the overall management of the Institute.

Chief Executive

until 31 January 2015: **Annie Mauger**
after 31 January 2015: **Jill Colbert**
(Interim Chief Executive)

CILIP Cymru/Wales

Head of CILIP Cymru/Wales:
Mandy Powell mandy.powell@cilip.org.uk

CILIP in Ireland

Development Officer, CILIP in Ireland:
Louisa Costelloe
louisa.costelloe@cilip.org.uk

CILIP in Scotland

Director of CILIP in Scotland:
Cathy Kearney
catherine.kearney@cilips.org.uk
Policy and Digital Officer
Sean McNamara
sean.mcnamara@cilips.org.uk

[Further Devolved Nations contact details may be found on page 88.]

Policy

Develops policy messages that define the professional interests of CILIP, engages members and reflect the values of the profession.

Head of Policy:
Guy Daines guy.daines@cilip.org.uk

Professional Services

The focus of the directorate is on member services, creating community and active recruitment by bringing together all areas of activity that relate directly to members.
Director of Professional Services:
Simon Edwards
simon.edwards@cilip.org.uk

Member Services Team

The Member Services Team is responsible for many of CILIP's frontline services to members including membership administration and engagement, member advice, Regional Member Networks, Special Interest Groups, Professional Registration (Certification, Chartership, Fellowship and Revalidation), Accreditation of Academic and Vocational Qualifications, Onsite Training, CPD and the Virtual Learning Environment.

Head of Business Development (Member Services):
Luke Stevens-Burt luke.stevens-burt@cilip.org.uk

Facet Publishing

The leading publisher of books for library and information professionals worldwide, Facet Publishing has an internationally established list of over 200 specialist titles in print which cover all the major aspects of professional LIS activity.

It publishes books for library, museum, archive, records management and publishing communities, as well as students on information, media, business and communications courses. CILIP members receive a 20% discount.

Publishing Director, Facet Publishing:
Helen Carley
helen.carley@facetpublishing.co.uk

Online shop: www.facetpublishing.co.uk

To order Facet Publishing books: contact
Bookpoint Ltd,
Mail Order Department,
130 Milton Park, Abingdon,
Oxon OX14 4SB.
Telephone: 01235 827702
Fax: 01235 827703
E-mail: facet@bookpoint.co.uk

External Relations

The team lead on developing and delivering communications and raising CILIP's profile. Areas of work including managing social media, email marketing, public relations, advocacy, digital content, media relations and public affairs.

Director of External Relations:
Mark Taylor mark.taylor@cilip.org.uk

CILIP Events

The events team organise conferences, briefings and supplier showcases on a range of topics for the library, information and knowledge community.

Head of Events and Marketing:
Jason Russell jason.russell@cilip.org.uk

CILIP Update

Update is the leading publication for the library, information and knowledge management community. An essential read for all information professionals, it contains news, interviews with key figures in the information world and in-depth features on topics across the sectors. Members and subscribers can access a print and digital edition of the magazine, and it is also available as an app. As well as an important benefit for members *Update* is also available on paid subscription.

Head of Publications:
      Gary Allman gary.allman@cilip.org.uk
www.cilip.org.uk/update

Resources

Responsible for providing all support services for the organisation.

Director of Resources:
      Jill Colbert jill.colbert@cilip.org.uk

Facilities

Responsible for buildings management, health and safety, room bookings and catering.

Reception: reception@cilip.org.uk
Room bookings:
      roombookings@cilip.org.uk

Finance

Provides an effective financial management service to CILIP and Member Networks. Ensures compliance with statutory and other financial regulations. Also responsible for the accurate processing of all subscriptions sent to CILIP.

Head of Finance:
      Bose Dada bose.dada@cilip.org.uk

Human Resources

Responsible for employment matters, staff recruitment and training.

HR Administrator:
      Iona Khan
      personneldepartment@cilip.org.uk

IT & Web

Responsible for support and maintenance of all equipment, software/hardware upgrades including all databases. Also responsible for development and maintenance of the website.

Telephone: 020 7255 0660

I T & Web Manager:
      Chris Bacon chris.bacon@cilip.org.uk

Subject directory

academic and vocational qualifications	memberservices@cilip.org.uk	020 7255 0613
accreditation	memberservices@cilip.org.uk	020 7255 0613
advertising (Update, Lisjobnet and Buyers' Guide)	advertising@cilip.org.uk	020 7255 0553
advocacy	policy@cilip.org.uk	020 7255 0632
books (purchasing)	info@facetpublishing.co.uk	020 7255 0590
Buyers' Guide	advertising@cilip.org.uk	020 7255 0550
careers advice	memberservices@cilip.org.uk	020 7255 0574
Carnegie/Greenaway (www.carnegiegreenaway.org.uk/)	ckg@cilip.org.uk	020 7255 0650
Certification	memberservices@cilip.org.uk	020 7255 0613
Chartership	memberservices@cilip.org.uk	020 7255 0613
Chief Executive	annie.mauger@cilip.org.uk	020 7255 0691
CILIP in Ireland	louisa.costelloe@cilip.org.uk	028 7181 2680
CILIP in Scotland	admin@cilips.org.uk	0141 222 5785
CILIP Wales/CILIP Cymru	wales@cilip.org.uk	07837 032536
conferences, exhibitions and special events	events@cilip.org.uk	020 7255 0544
corporate marketing	marketing@cilip.org.uk	020 7255 0650
courses	memberservices@cilip.org.uk	020 7255 0560

editorial
    Facet Publishing
    CILIP Update
	
	damien.mitchell@facetpublishing.co.uk
	update@cilip.org.uk
		
		020 7255 0593
		020 7255 0585

events	events@cilip.org.uk	020 7255 0544
exhibitions	events@cilip.org.uk	020 7255 0544
Facet Publishing(www.facetpublishing.co.uk)	info@facetpublishing.co.uk	020 7255 0590
Fellowship	memberservices@cilip.org.uk	020 7255 0613
finance	financedepartment@cilip.org.uk	020 7255 0673
governance	jill.colbert@cilip.org.uk	020 7255 0512
information	memberservices@cilip.org.uk	020 7255 0620
international activities	guy.daines@cilip.org.uk	020 7255 0642
LACA: Libraries & Archives Copyright Alliance	policy@cilip.org.uk	020 7255 0624
LIBEX job exchange	libex@cilip.org.uk	020 7255 0616
Libraries in the UK and the Republic of Ireland directory	info@facetpublishing.co.uk	020 7255 0590

mailing lists	membership@cilip.org.uk	020 7255 0600
marketing 　CILIP 　Facet Publishing	 marketing@cilip.org.uk james.williams@facetpublishing.co.uk	 020 7255 0650 020 7255 0597
media	media@cilip.org.uk	020 7255 0650
membership	membership@cilip.org.uk	020 7255 0600
policy	policy@cilip.org.uk	020 7255 0632
press releases and media	marketing@cilip.org.uk	020 7255 0650
professional registration	memberservices@cilip.org.uk	020 7255 0610
publications 　books from Facet Publishing 　purchasing books: 　www.facetpublishing.co.uk 　*Buyer's Guide* 　*CILIP Update*	 info@facetpublishing.co.uk facet@bookpoint.co.uk advertising@cilip.org.uk update@cilip.org.uk	 020 7255 0590 01235 827702 020 7255 0550 020 7255 0580
reception (Ridgmount Street)	reception@cilip.org.uk	020 7255 0500
recruitment: lisjobnet.com	lisjobnet@cilip.org.uk	020 7255 0550
room bookings (Ridgmount Street)	roombookings@cilip.org.uk	020 7255 0500
switchboard (Ridgmount Street)	reception@cilip.org.uk	020 7255 0500
Update magazine	update@cilip.org.uk	020 7255 0580
website	web@cilip.org.uk	020 7255 0623

Facet Publishing books published 2010–2014

Barbara Allan *The No-nonsense Guide to Training in Libraries*; May 2013; 978-1-85604-828-6

Mohamed Ally and Gill Needham *M-Libraries 3: transforming libraries with mobile technology*; Jan. 2012; 978-1-85604-776-0

Mohamed Ally and Gill Needham *M-Libraries 4: from margin to mainstream – mobile technologies transforming lives and libraries*; Sep. 2013; 978-1-85604-944-3

Paige G. Andrew and Mary Lynette Larsgaard *RDA and Cartographic Resources*; Oct. 2014; 978-1-85604-772-2

David Bawden and Lyn Robinson *Introduction to Information Science*; Jul. 2012; 978-1-85604-810-1

Michael Bemis *Library and Information Science: guide to key literature and sources*; Mar. 2014; 978-1-78330-002-0

Sidney Berger *Rare Books and Special Collections*; Jul. 2014; 978-1-78330-015-0

Amanda Bielskas and Kathleen M. Drey *IM and SMS Reference Services for Libraries* (Tech Set 19); Jun. 2012; 978-1-85604-844-6

Helen Blanchett, Chris Powis and Jo Webb *A Guide to Teaching Information Literacy: 101 practical tips*; Oct. 2011; 978-1-85604-659-6

Phil Bradley *Expert Internet Searching* 4th edn; Aug. 2013; 978-1-85604-605-3

Marshall Breeding *Cloud Computing for Libraries* (Tech Set 11); Jun. 2012; 978-1-85604-847-7

Alison Brettle and Christine Urquhart *Changing Roles and Contexts for Health Library and Information Professionals*; Nov. 2011; 978-1-85604-740-1

Karl Bridges, editor *Customer-based Collection Development: an overview*; Jul. 2014; 978-1-85604-931-3

Vanda Broughton *Essential Library of Congress Subject Headings*; Nov. 2011; 978-1-85604-618-3

Caroline Brown *Archives and Recordkeeping: theory into practice*; Dec. 2013; 978-1-85604-825-5

Adrian Brown *Practical Digital Preservation: a how-to guide for organizations of any size*; May 2013; 978-1-85604-755-5

Karen Calhoun *Exploring Digital Libraries: foundations, practice, prospects*; Jan. 2014; 978-1-85604-820-0

Kay Ann Cassell and Uma Hiremath *Reference and Information Services: an introduction* 3rd edn; Dec. 2012; 978-1-85604-839-2

Kay Ann Cassell and Uma Hiremath *Reference and Information Services in the 21st Century: an introduction* 2nd edn rev; Jun. 2011; 978-1-85604-778-4

Sally Chambers *Catalogue 2.0: the future of the library catalogue*; Jul. 2013; 978-1-85604-716-6

G. G. Chowdhury *Sustainability of Scholarly Information*; Jul. 2014; 978-1-85604-956-6

G. G. Chowdhury and Sudatta Chowdhury *Information Users and Usability in the Digital Age*; Oct. 2011; 978-1-85604-597-1

G. G. Chowdhury and Schubert Foo *Digital Libraries and Information Access: research perspectives*; September 2012; 978-1-85604-821-7

Jason A. Clark *Building Mobile Library Applications* (Tech Set 12); Jun. 2012; 978-1-85604-845-3

Lynn Coleman, Victoria L. Lemieux, Rod Stone and Geoffrey Yeo *Managing Records in Global Financial Markets: ensuring compliance and mitigating risk*; Aug. 2011; 978-1-85604-663-3; £64.95

Edward M. Corrado and Heather Lea Moulaison *Getting Started with Cloud Computing*: a LITA guide; Jul. 2011; 978-1-85604-807-1

Joy Court *Read to Succeed: strategies to engage children and young people in reading for pleasure*; Aug. 2011; 978-1-85604-747-0

Alison Cullingford *Special Collections Handbook*; Feb. 2011; 978-1-85604-757-9

Emma Dadson *Emergency Planning and Response for Libraries, Archives and Museums*; Aug. 2012; 978-1-85604-808-8

Heather Dawson *Know It All, Find it Fast for Academic Libraries*; Oct. 2011; 978-1-85604-759-3

Janet Delve and David Anderson, editors *Preserving Complex Digital Objects*; Jun. 2014; 978-1-85604-958-0

Martin de Saulles *Information 2.0: new models of information production, distribution and consumption*; May 2012; 978-1-85604-754-8

Kevin C. Desouza and Scott Paquette *Knowledge Management: an introduction*; Aug. 2011; 978-1-85604-735-7

Lorcan Dempsey and Kenneth J. Varnum *The Network Reshapes the Library: Lorcan Dempsey on libraries, services, and networks*; Aug. 2014; 978-1-78330-041-9

Jane Devine and Francine Egger-Sider *Going Beyond Google Again: strategies for using and teaching the invisible web*; Oct. 2013; 978-1-85604-838-5

Milena Dobreva, Andy O'Dwyer and Pierluigi Feliciati *User Studies for Digital Library Development*; Jun. 2012; 978-1-85604-765-4

Christinea Donnelly *Know It All, Find It Fast for Youth Librarians and Teachers*; Nov. 2011; 978-1-85604-761-6

Daniel G. Dorner, G E Gorman and Philip J. Calvert *Information Needs Analysis: principles and practice in information organizations*; Dec. 2014; 978-1-85604-484-4

Mike Ellis *Managing and Growing a Cultural Heritage Web Presence: a strategic guide*; Apr. 2011; 978-1-85604-710-4

Magda El-Sherbini *RDA: strategies for implementation*; Jul. 2013; 978-1-85604-834-7

Nicole C. Engard, editor *More Library Mashups: exploring new ways to deliver library data*; Oct. 2014; 978-1-78330-035-8

G. Edward Evans and Camila A. Alire *Management Basics for Information Professionals* 3rd edn; September 2013; 978-1-85604-954-2

Robin M. Fay and Michael P. Sauers *Semantic Web Technologies and Social Searching for Librarians* (Tech Set 20); Jun. 2012; 978-1-85604-842-2

John P. Feather *The Information Society* 6th edn; Mar. 2013; 978-1-85604-818-7

Maggie Fieldhouse and Audrey Marshall *Collection Development in the Digital Age*; Dec. 2011; 978-1-85604-746-3

Helen Forde and Jonathan Rhys-Lewis *Preserving Archives* 2nd edn; Mar. 2013; 978-1-85604-823-1

Allen Foster and Pauline Rafferty *Innovations in Information Retrieval: perspectives for theory and practice*; Jul. 2011; 978-1-85604-697-8

Patricia C. Franks *Records and Information Management*; Jun. 2013; 978-1-85604-836-1

Masha Garibyan, Simon McLeish and John Paschoud *Access and Identity Management for Libraries: controlling access to online information*; Oct. 2013; 978-1-85604-588-9

Peter Godwin and Jo Parker *Information Literacy Beyond Library 2.0*; Mar. 2012; 978-1-85604-762-3

Maria J. Grant, Barbara Sen and Hannah Spring *Research, Evaluation and Audit: key steps in demonstrating your value*; Oct. 2013; 978-1-85604-741-8

Samantha K. Hastings, editor *Annual Review of Cultural Heritage Informatics 2012–2013*; Jul. 2014; 978-1-78330-026-6

Peter Hernon and Joseph R. Matthews *Reflecting on the Future of Academic and Public Libraries*; Mar. 2013; 978-1-85604-948-1

Philip Hider *Information Resource Description: creating and managing metadata*; Nov. 2012; 978-1-85604-667-1

Lorna M. Hughes *Evaluating and Measuring the Value, Use and Impact of Digital Collections*;

Nov. 2011; 978-1-85604-720-3

Peggy Johnson *Fundamentals of Collection Development and Management*, 3rd edn; Mar. 2014; 978-1-85604-937-5

Joint Steering Committee for the Development of RDA; *RDA: Resource Description and Access 2014 Revision*; Oct. 2014; 978-1-78330-042-6

Ed Jones *RDA and Serials Cataloguing*; Jul. 2013; 978-1-85604-950-4

Joint Steering Committee for the Development of RDA *RDA: Resource Description and Access 2013 Revision*; looseleaf with ringbinder; Nov. 2013; 978-1-85604-966-5

Richard Kaplan *Building and Managing E-book Collections: a how to do it manual for librarians*; Aug. 2012; 978-1-85604-837-8

Joan R. Kaplowitz *Transforming IL Instruction Using Learner-centred Teaching*; Jan. 2012; 978-1-85604-835-4

Marie R. Kennedy and Cheryl LaGuardia *Marketing Your Library's Electronic Resources: a how-to-do-it-manual*; Apr. 2013; 978-1-85604-942-9

Michael Lascarides *Next-Gen Library Redesign* (Tech Set 16); Jun. 2012; 978-1-85604-849-1

Libraries & Information Services in the UK and the Republic of Ireland 2015, 38th edn; Dec. 2014; 978-1-85604-801-9

Alison Mackenzie and Lindsey Martin *Mastering Digital Librarianship: strategy, networking and discovery in academic libraries*; Nov. 2013; 978-1-85604-943-6

Thomas P. Mackey and Trudi E. Jacobson *Metaliteracy: reinventing information literacy to empower learners*; Apr. 2014; 978-1-78330-012-9

Thomas P. Mackey and Trudi E. Jacobson *Teaching Information Literacy Online*; Feb. 2011; 978-1-85604-767-8

Alan MacLennan *Information Governance and Assurance: reducing risk, promoting policy*; Jun. 2014; 978-1-85604-940-5

Sharon Markless and David Streatfield *Evaluating the Impact of Your Library* 2nd edn; Dec. 2012; 978-1-85604-812-5

Freda Matassa *Museum Collections Management: a handbook*; May 2011; 978-1-85604-701-2

Freda Matassa *Organizing Exhibitions: a handbook for museums, libraries and archives*; Apr. 2014; 978-1-85604-945-0

Robert Maxwell *Maxwell's Handbook for RDA*; Feb. 2014; 978-1-85604-832-3

Maxine Melling and Margaret Weaver *Collaboration in Libraries and Learning Environments*; Dec. 2012; 978-1-85604-858-3

Stephen J. Miller *Metadata for Digital Collections: a how-to-do-it manual*; Jun. 2011; 978-1-85604-771-5

Richard Moniz, Joe Eshleman and Jo Henry *Fundamentals for the Academic Liaison*; Mar. 2014; 978-1-78330-005-1

Joe Murphy *Location-Aware Services and QR Codes for Libraries* (Tech Set 13); Jun. 2012; 978-1-85604-846-0

Greg Notess *Screencasting for Libraries* (Tech Set 17); Jun. 2012; 978-1-85604-848-4

Gillian Oliver and Fiorella Foscarini *Records Management and Information Culture: tackling the people problem*; Jan. 2014; 978-1-85604-947-4

Charles Oppenheim *The No-nonsense Guide to Legal Issues in Web 2.0 and Cloud Computing*; Jul. 2012; 978-1-85604-804-0

Tim Buckley Owen *Successful Enquiry Answering Every Time* 6th edn; May 2012; 978-1-85604-811-8

Paul Pedley *The E-copyright Handbook*; Aug. 2012; 978-1-85604-827-9

Paul Pedley *Essential Law for Information Professionals* 3rd edn; Jan. 2012; 978-1-85604-769-2

Cheryl Ann Peltier-Davis *The Cybrarian's Web: an A–Z guide to 101 free Web 2.0 tools and other resources*; Feb. 2012; 978-1-85604-829-3

Alison Jane Pickard *Research Methods in Information* 2nd edn; Jan. 2013; 978-1-85604-813-2

Sue Polanka *No Shelf Required 2: use and management of electronic books*; Feb. 2012; 978-1-85604-830-9

Ned Potter *The Library Marketing Toolkit*; Jun. 2012; 978-1-85604-806-4

Kate Price and Virginia Havergal *E-Books in Libraries: a practical guide*; Feb. 2011; 978-1-85604-572-8

Graham Pryor Managing Research Data; Jan. 2012; 978-1-85604-756-2

Graham Pryor, Sarah Jones and Angus Whyte *Delivering Research Data Management Services: fundamentals of good practice*; Dec. 2013; 978-1-85604-933-7

Carolynn Rankin and Avril Brock *Library Services for Children and Young People: challenges and opportunities in the digital age*; Nov. 2012; 978-1-85604-712-8

Bethan Ruddock *The New Professional's Toolkit*; May 2012; 978-1-85604-768-5

Ian Ruthven and Diane Kelly *Interactive Information Seeking, Behaviour and Retrieval*; Aug. 2011; 978-1-85604-707-4

Aaron Schmidt and Amanda Etches *User Experience (UX) Design for Libraries* (Tech Set 18); Jun. 2012; 978-1-85604-843-9

Katharine Schopflin *A Handbook for Corporate Information Professionals*; Dec. 2014; 978-1-85604-968-9

Jane Secker and Emma Coonan *Rethinking Information Literacy: a practical framework forsupporting learning*; Dec. 2012; 978-1-85604-822-4

Sue Shaper, editor *CILIP Guidelines for Secondary School Libraries*, 3rd edn; Apr. 2014; 978-1-85604-969-6

Debbie Shorley and Michael Jubb *The Future of Scholarly Communication*; Mar. 2013; 978-1-85604-817-0

Carol A. Singer *Fundamentals of Managing Reference Collections*; Jul. 2012; 978-1-85604-831-6

Sarah K. Steiner *Strategic Planning for Social Media in Libraries* (Tech Set 15); Jun. 2012; 978-1-85604-841-5

David Stuart *Facilitating Access to the Web of Data: a guide for librarians*; Jul. 2011; 978-1-85604-745-6

David Stuart *Web Metrics for Library and Information Professionals*; Jan. 2014; 978-1-85604-874-3

Beth C. Thomsett-Scott *Marketing with Social Media: a LITA guide*; Dec. 2013; 978-1-78330-001-3

Seth van Hooland and Ruben Verborgh *Linked Data for Libraries, Archives and Museums: how to clean, link and publish your metadata*; Jun. 2014; 978-1-85604-964-1

Kenneth J. Varnum *Drupal in Libraries* (Tech Set 14); Jun. 2012; 978-1-85604-840-8

Kenneth J. Varnum, editor *The Top Technologies Every Librarian Needs to Know: a LITA guide*; Jul. 2014; 978-1-78330-033-4

Andrew Walsh *Using Mobile Technology to Deliver Library Services: a handbook*; Aug. 2012; 978-1-85604-809-5

Claire Warwick, Melissa Terras and Julianne Nyhan *Digital Humanities in Practice*; Oct. 2012; 978-1-85604-766-1

Les Watson *Better Library and Learning Space: projects, trends and ideas*; Oct. 2013; 978-1-85604-763-0

Mary Beth Weber and Fay Angela Austin *Describing Electronic, Digital, and Other Media Using AACR2 and RDA: a how-to-do-it manual and CD-ROM for librarians*; Jan. 2011; 978-1-85604-684-8

Anne Welsh and Sue Batley *Practical Cataloguing: AACR, RDA and MARC21*; Mar. 2012; 978-1-85604-695-4

Martin White *The Intranet Management Handbook*; Feb. 2011; 978-1-85604-734-0

Paul Younger and Peter Morgan *Using Web 2.0 for Health Information*; Apr. 2011; 978-1-85604-731-9

Part 2
GOVERNANCE

Council/Board

CILIP's governing body is its Council, which manages the affairs of the Institute.

Council is comprised of 12 Councillors elected directly by the Membership in accordance with the Bye-laws and General Regulations. Councillors are also the Trustees of CILIP so the terms may be used interchangeably. There is provision for up to three-co-options on Council. Please note that from 1 April 2015 CILIP Council will be replaced by CILIP Board

David Byrne
(To serve until 31 December 2015)
E-mail: david.byrne@cilip.org.uk

Maria Cotera
(To serve until 31 March 2015)
Email: maria.cotera@cilip.org.uk

Mike Hosking (Honorary Treasurer)
(To serve until 31 March 2015)
E-mail: mike.hosking@cilip.org.uk

Emma McDonald
(To serve until 31 December 2015)
E-mail: emma.mcdonald@cilip.org.uk

Liz McGettigan
(To serve until 31 March 2015)
E-mail: liz.mcgettigan@cilip.org.uk

Karen McFarlane
(To serve until 31 December 2016)
E-mail: karen.mcfarlane@cilip.org.uk

David McMenemy
(To serve until 31 December 2016)
E-mail: david.mcmenemy@cilip.org.uk

Nick Poole
(Served until 30 November 2014)
E-mail: nick.poole@cilip.org.uk

David Stewart
(To serve until 31 December 2016)
E-mail: david.stewart@cilip.org.uk

Martyn Wade
(To serve until 31 December 2015)
E-mail: martyn.wade@cilip.org.uk

Keith Wilson
(To serve until 31 March 2015)
E-mail: keith.wilson@cilip.org.uk

Honorary Officers

Chair of Council
Martyn Wade (until 31 March 2015)

Honorary Treasurer
Mike Hosking (until 31 March 2015)

2014 President/2015 Immediate Past President
Barbara Band

2014 Vice-President/2015 President
Jan Parry

2015 Vice-President
Dawn Finch

Presidents and Secretaries of CILIP

Presidents

2015 Jan Parry
2014 Barbara Band
2013 Phil Bradley
2012 Phil Bradley
2011 Brian Hall
2010 Biddy Fisher
2009 Peter Griffiths
2008 Bruce Madge
2007 Ian Snowley
2006 Martin Molloy
2005 Debby Shorley
2004 Margaret Haines
2003 Margaret Watson
2002 Sheila Corrall

Secretaries

2002–2010	Bob McKee (until 31 October 2010)
2010–2015	Annie Mauger (31 October 2010–31 January 2015)
2015–	To be announced

Governance Structure

This is the new Governance Structure that will be implemented as of 1 April 2015.

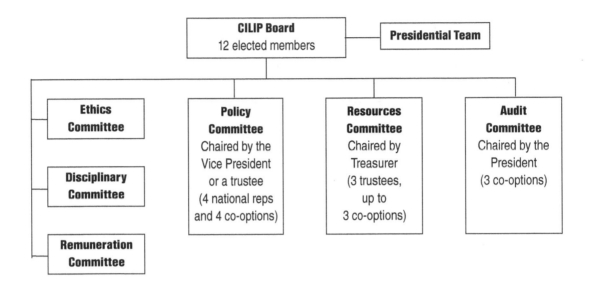

In addition to the Governance Structure, there is also the Professional Registration and Accreditation Board:

- Professional Registration and Accreditation Board works on behalf of Council to:
  — Maintain a strategic overview of the provision of Library and Information Science related academic and vocational qualifications
  — Maintain a strategic overview of Professional Registration
  — To Assess all applications for admission to the Register of Practitioners.

CILIP Royal Charter

The text of the Royal Charter was approved by the Privy Council and by the CILIP AGM on 18 October 2007.

The 1986 Royal Charter

ELIZABETH THE SECOND by the Grace of God of the United Kingdom of Great Britain and Northern Ireland and of Our other Realms and Territories Queen, Head of the Commonwealth, Defender of the Faith:

TO ALL TO WHOM THESE PRESENTS SHALL COME, GREETINGS!

WHEREAS Her Majesty Queen Victoria in the year of our Lord One thousand eight hundred and ninety eight by Royal Charter (hereinafter called 'the Original Charter') dated the seventh day of February in the sixty first year of Her Reign constituted a Body Corporate by the name of The Library Association (hereinafter called 'the Association') with perpetual succession and with power to sue and to be sued by this name and to use a Common Seal:

AND WHEREAS the Original Charter was amended by an Order in Council dated the sixteenth day of December One Thousand Nine Hundred and Eighty Six:

AND WHEREAS it has been represented unto Us that the Association seeks with others to unite all persons engaged or interested in library work and information science for the purpose of promoting the development of libraries and information services and the advancement of information science for the public benefit and to that end the Association has resolved to change its name to the Chartered Institute of Library and Information Professionals:

WHEREAS it has been represented unto Us by the Association that it is expedient to revise the objects and powers of the Association and that the provisions of the Original Charter, except in so far as they incorporate the Association, should be replaced:

NOW, THEREFORE, KNOW YE that We, by virtue of Our Prerogative Royal and of all other powers enabling Us so to do, have, of Our especial grace, certain knowledge and mere motion, granted and declared and by these Presents for Us, Our Heirs and Successors, grant and declare as follows:

Interpretation

1.   In this Our Charter unless the context otherwise requires:

(i)   'the Institute' shall mean the Chartered Institute of Library and Information Professionals;

(ii)   'the Charter' means the Charter of Incorporation of the Institute;

(iii)   'the Byelaws' shall mean the Byelaws set out in the Schedule below as amended from time to time as provided below;

(iv)   'a Member' means a member of the Institute in any category of membership established in accordance with Regulations;

(v)   'Individual Member' means an individual who is admitted as a Member in accordance with Regulations;

(vi)   'Organisation Member' means a corporate body, society or other non-corporate organisation which maintains or is interested in libraries or information services and is admitted as a Member in accordance with the Byelaws;

(vii) 'the Board means the Board of Trustees for the time being appointed pursuant to the Charter and the Byelaws;

(viii) 'Board Member means a member of the Board, whether elected or appointed;

(ix)   'Duly Appointed Body' means any person or body of people to whom or to which powers are reserved or properly delegated under the Charter or Byelaws;

(x)   'Regulations' means regulations made and publicised by the Board in accordance with the Byelaws;

(xi)   'Registered Practitioner' means an Individual Member who is entitled under the Byelaws and Regulations to use after his or her name the letters "MCLIP", "FCLIP", or "ACLIP" and is respectively entitled to describe himself or herself as "Chartered Member of the CILIP", "Chartered Fellow of the CILIP", or "Certified Member of the CILIP".

(xii) Words denoting the singular number include the plural and vice versa;

(xiii) Words importing the masculine gender include the feminine gender; and

(xiv) Words importing persons include corporations.

Objects and powers

2.   The objects of the Institute shall be to work for the benefit of the public to promote education and knowledge through the establishment and development of libraries and information services and to advance information science (being the science and practice of the collection, collation, evaluation and organised dissemination of information) and for that purpose the

Institute shall have power to do all or any of the following things:

(a) to foster and promote education, training, invention and research in matters connected with information science and libraries and information services and to collect, collate and publish information, ideas, data and research relating thereto;

(b) to unite all persons engaged or interested in information science and libraries and information services by holding conferences and meetings for the discussion of questions and matters affecting information science and libraries and information services or their regulation or management and any other questions or matters relating to the objects of the Institute;

(c) to promote the improvement of the knowledge, skills, position and qualifications of librarians and information personnel;

(d) to promote study and research in librarianship and information science and to disseminate the results;

(e) to promote and encourage the maintenance of adequate and appropriate provision of library and information services of various kinds throughout the United Kingdom, the Channel Islands and the Isle of Man;

(f) to scrutinise any legislation affecting the provision of library and information services and to promote such further legislation as may be considered necessary to that end;

(g) to represent and act as the professional body for persons working in or interested in library and information services;

(h) to maintain a register of Registered Practitioners;

(i) to ensure the effective dissemination of appropriate information of interest to Members;

(j) to work with similar institutes overseas and with appropriate international bodies to promote the widespread provision of adequate and appropriate library and information services;

(k) to provide appropriate services to Members in furtherance of these objectives;

(l) to form and promote the formation of branches, regional member networks, sections or groups of the Institute in any part of the world and to dissolve branches, regional member networks, sections or groups so established;

(m) to print and publish and to sell, lend and distribute any communications, papers or treatises which are relevant to the objects of the Institute;

(n) to raise funds and to invite and receive contributions provided that the Institute shall in raising funds not undertake any substantial trading activities and shall conform to any relevant statutory regulations;

(o) to invest the monies of the Institute not immediately required for the furtherance of its objects in or upon such investments, securities or property as may be thought fit;

(p) to purchase, take on lease or in exchange, hire, or otherwise acquire any real or personal property necessary for or conducive to the objects of the Institute and to maintain and equip the same for use in furtherance thereof;

(q)   to borrow or raise money with or without security for the objects of the Institute provided that no money shall be raised by mortgage of any real or leasehold property of the Institute situate in Our United Kingdom without such consent or approval (if any) as may be by law required;

(r)   to sell, manage, lease, mortgage or dispose of all or any part of the property of the Institute, provided that no disposition of any real or leasehold property situate in our United Kingdom shall be made without such consent or approval (if any) as may be by law required;

(s)   to make and give effect to any arrangements for the joint working or co-operation with any other society or body, whether incorporated or not, carrying on work which is within the objects of the Institute;

(t)   to undertake, execute and perform any trusts or conditions affecting any real or personal property of any description acquired by the Institute;

(u)   generally to do all other lawful acts whatsoever that are conducive or incidental to the attainment of the objects of the Institute.

Income and property

3.   The income and property of the Institute wheresoever derived shall be applied solely towards the promotion of the objects of the Institute as set forth in this Our Charter, and no portion thereof shall be paid or transferred directly or indirectly by way of dividend, bonus or otherwise howsoever by way of profit to any Member and save as hereinafter provided no Board Member shall be appointed to any office of the Institute paid by salary or fees or receive remuneration from the Institute: provided that nothing herein contained shall prevent the payment in good faith by the Institute:

(a)   of fees to any person (not being a Board Member) in return for services actually rendered or reasonable and proper pensions to former employees of the Institute or their dependants;

(b)   of fees to any Board Member who possesses specialist skills or knowledge required by the Institute for its proper administration of reasonable fees for work of that nature done by the Board Member when instructed by the Institute to act on its behalf but on condition that:
         (i) at no time may a majority of the Board benefit under this provision; and
         (ii) a Board Member must withdraw from any meeting whilst his or her appointment or remuneration is being discussed and may not vote or count in the quorum in respect of that matter;

(c)   of reasonable and proper rent for premises demised or let by any Member or Board Member;

(d)   of reasonable and proper interest on money borrowed by the Institute from a Member or Board Member for the objects of the Institute;

(e)   of reasonable and proper out of pocket expenses incurred by any Member or Board Member on behalf of the Institute;

(f)   of all reasonable and proper premiums in respect of trustees' indemnity insurance effected in accordance with Article 8 of this Our Charter.

If the Institute is registered with the Office of the Scottish Regulator the additional requirements under section 67 of the Charities And Trustees Investment (Scotland) Act 2005 must be complied with.

Members

4.   The Members shall consist of such persons and shall have such rights and privileges as may be prescribed by or under the Byelaws for the time being to be framed in pursuance of this Our Charter.

5.   There shall be such classes of Organisation and Individual Members as may be prescribed pursuant to the Byelaws. The qualifications, method and terms of admission, rights, privileges and obligations of each such class of membership and the disciplinary arrangements to which Members shall be subject shall be as the Byelaws and Regulations prescribe. Members may be designated as belonging to the Institute by such abbreviations as the Byelaws and Regulations shall prescribe. No other abbreviation to indicate a class of membership may be used.

Board

6.   The powers of the Institute shall be vested in a Board elected or appointed in accordance with the Byelaws and which may in respect of the affairs of the Institute exercise all such powers and do all such things as may lead to the furtherance of the objects of the Institute including all such powers and things as may be exercised or done by the Institute and are not by this Our Charter or the Byelaws expressly directed or required to be exercised or done by any other person or by the Institute in general meeting.

7.   In the execution of their powers under this Our Charter, no Board Member or other office holder shall be liable for any loss to the property of the Institute arising by reason of any improper investment made in good faith (so long as where appropriate advice shall have been sought before making such investment) or for the negligence or fraud of any other Board Member or other office holder or by reason of any mistake or omission made in good faith by any Board Member or other office holder or by reason of any other matter or thing whatsoever except wilful and individual fraud, wrongdoing or omission on the part of the Board Member or other office holder.

8.   The Board may pay out of the funds of the Institute the cost of any premium in respect of insurance or indemnities to cover any liability of the Board (or any Board Member) and any other office holder which by virtue of any rule of law would otherwise attach to them in respect of any negligence, default, breach of duty or breach of trust of which they may be guilty in relation to the Institute; provided that any such insurance or indemnity shall not extend to any claim arising from criminal or wilful or deliberate neglect or default on the part of the Board (or Board Member) or other office holder.

Delegation of the Board's Powers

9.   The Council may delegate its powers in such manner as is permitted by the Bye-laws.

President

10.   A President may be appointed in accordance with the Byelaws with such powers and functions as are prescribed by the Byelaws.

General meetings

11.   Meetings of the Institute shall be convened and the proceedings there regulated in accordance with the Byelaws.

Byelaws

12.   The affairs of the Institute shall be managed and regulated in accordance with the Byelaws which shall remain in force until revoked, amended or added to as provided below.

Supplementary provisions

13.   The provisions of the Original Charter, except in so far as they incorporate the Institute and confer upon it perpetual succession and a Common Seal, are hereby revoked, but nothing in this revocation shall affect the legality or validity of any act, deed or thing lawfully done or executed under the provisions of the Original Charter.

14.   The Byelaws scheduled in the Original Charter as amended from time to time shall be deemed to be and shall continue to be the Byelaws. Any of the Byelaws may from time to time be revoked, amended or added to by a resolution passed by a majority of not less than two thirds of the Individual Members voting in person or by proxy at a duly convened general meeting of the Institute provided that no new Byelaw and no such revocation, amendment or addition as aforesaid shall have any force or effect if it be repugnant to any of the provisions of this Our Charter or the laws of Our Realm, nor until it shall have been approved by Our Privy Council of which approval a certificate under the hand of the Clerk of Our Privy Council shall be conclusive evidence. This provision shall apply to the Byelaws as revoked, altered or added to in manner aforesaid.

15.   The Institute may by resolution in that behalf passed by a majority of not less than two-thirds of the Individual Members voting in person or by proxy on the question at a duly convened general meeting of the Institute alter, amend or add to any of the provisions of this Our Charter and such alteration, amendment or addition shall, when approved by Us, Our Heirs or Successors in Council become effectual so that this Our Charter shall thenceforward continue and operate as though it had been originally granted and made accordingly. This provision shall apply to this Our Charter as altered, amended or added to in manner aforesaid.

16.   The Institute may by resolution passed by a majority of not less than two-thirds of the Individual Members voting in person or by proxy on the question at a duly convened general meeting of the Institute surrender this Our Charter subject to the sanction of Us, Our Heirs or Successors in Council and upon such terms as We or They may consider fit and wind up or otherwise deal with the affairs of the Institute in such manner as they shall be directed by the special resolution having due regard to the liabilities of the Institute for the time being and if on the winding up or dissolution of the Institute there shall remain after satisfaction of debts and liabilities any property whatsoever, that property shall

not be paid or distributed among the Members or any of them but shall subject to any special trust affecting the same be given and transferred to some other charitable institute or institutes having objects similar to the objects of the Institute to be determined by the Individual Members at or before the time of dissolution.

17.   Nothing in this Charter shall authorise an application of the property of the Institute for purposes which are not charitable in accordance with section 7 of the Charities and Trustee Investment (Scotland) Act 2005.

IN WITNESS whereof We have caused these Our Letters to be made Patent.

WITNESS Ourself at Westminster the Twenty-first day of May in the Fifty-first Year of Our Reign.

CILIP Bye-laws

Made by Council 16 June 1986, as approved by the Annual General Meeting on 10 September 1986 and as allowed by Her Majesty's Privy Council on 15 December 1986. Revised in 1987, 1989, 1997, 2001, 2005, 2007, 2008 and 2014.

SECTION 1
Interpretation

1. In the event of any inconsistency between the provisions of the Charter and the provisions of the Bye-laws the provisions of the Charter shall prevail.

2. In these Bye-laws, unless the context otherwise requires: expressions or words used in the Charter shall have the meanings there defined;

2.1 The expressions "Individual Member", "Organisation Member", "President", "Vice-President", "Honorary Treasurer", and Chief Executive Officer shall be read and construed as if the words "of the Institute" were inserted thereafter;

2.2 The following expressions have the following meanings:

"**Annual General Meeting**" the General Meeting held further to Bye-law 20;

"**Audit Committee**" means the Audit Committee established in accordance with Bye-law 56(c);

"**Ballot**" means a Full Ballot or a Written Ballot;

"**Board**" means the Board of Trustees for the time being appointed pursuant to the Charter and these Bye-laws;

"**Board Member**" means a member of the Board, whether elected or appointed;

"**Chair**" means the chair of the Board appointed in accordance with Bye-law 41

"**Charter**" means the Charter of Incorporation of the Institute;

"**Chief Executive Officer**" means the person appointed to that post in accordance with Bye-law 74;

"**Devolved Nation**" means Wales, Northern Ireland and Scotland;

"**Disciplinary Committee**" means the Disciplinary Committee established in accordance with Bye-law 56(e)

"**Duly Appointed Body**" means any person or body of people to whom or to which powers are reserved or properly delegated under the Charter or these Bye-Laws;

"**Full Ballot**" means a ballot of all the Individual Members conducted in accordance with Regulations and not taken at a General Meeting;

"**General Meeting**" means a general meeting in which the Individual Members assemble including the Annual General Meeting;

"**governance year**" means the period from 1 January to 31 December;

"**Honorary Fellows**" means those individuals admitted to be Honorary Fellows in accordance with Bye-law 14;

"**Honorary Officers**" means the President, the Vice-President, and the Honorary Treasurer;

"**Individual Member**" means an individual who is admitted as a Member in accordance with the Regulations;

"**Member**" means a member of the Institute in any category of membership established in accordance with the Regulations;

"**Organisation Member**" means a corporate body, society or other non-corporate organisation which maintains or is interested in libraries or information services and is admitted as a Member in accordance with the Regulations;

"**Regional Member Network**" means a body of Members associated with a geographical area as defined from time to time by the Board;

"**Registered Practitioner**" means an Individual Member who is entitled under these Bye-laws and the Regulations to use after his or her name the letters "MCLIP", "FCLIP", or "ACLIP" and is respectively entitled to describe himself or herself as "Chartered Member of the CILIP", "Chartered Fellow of the CILIP", or "Certified Member of the CILIP";

"**Regulations**" means regulations made and published by the Board in accordance with Bye-law 28;

"**Special Interest Group or SIG**" means a group established with the approval of the Board to further specialist interests within the Institute;

"**Written Ballot**" means a poll taken at or after a General Meeting or otherwise in accordance with the Regulations.

3. Where these Bye-laws confer any power to make Regulations that power shall be construed as including power to rescind, revoke, amend or vary any Regulations made in pursuance of that power.

SECTION 2
Categories and Privileges of Membership

4. The categories of Membership and the privileges and obligations applicable to each category shall be established by Regulations provided that Organisation Members shall not be entitled to vote at General Meetings nor on the election of Board Members, nor to hold office in the Institute.

5. Membership shall not be transferable and shall cease on death. All the privileges of membership shall be enjoyed by a Member for his or her own benefit and the Member shall not be entitled to transfer such privileges or any of the benefits derived therefrom to any other person, firm, company or body.

Subscriptions

6. The Institute in General Meeting shall have power to determine the amount of all subscriptions, entrance, registration, admission and other fees (except for examination fees) payable by the Members. The Board, however, shall have the power to make Regulations for the payment of subscriptions (including payment by instalment) and for suspension and expulsion from the Institute in the case of a Member failing to pay. The Board may also make Regulations admitting persons to membership or continuing Members in membership at reduced subscriptions. Members paying reduced subscriptions shall enjoy all the privileges of membership applicable to their category of membership, including voting and the receipt of publications usually distributed

to Members. The amount of examination fees shall be determined from time to time by the Board.

Admission, Removal and Reinstatement of Members

7. Members shall be admitted by the Board and may be removed in accordance with the procedures prescribed in Regulations.

8. The Board shall have power to reinstate any Member whose membership has been cancelled for any reason, and may cause reinstatement to be subject to previous compliance with such conditions as it may determine, including the payment of subscriptions in arrears.

9. There shall be maintained at the offices of the Institute a Register of Members containing the names of all Members identifying their category of membership and identifying those who are Registered Practitioners. Copies of the Register of Members shall be published in such manner and at such intervals as the Board shall decide.

SECTION 3
Professional Registration

10. The Board shall from time to time make Regulations for the purpose of establishing the rights and responsibilities of Registered Practitioners, testing the proficiency of Members desiring to be admitted as Registered Practitioners and testing the continuing proficiency of Members so admitted.

11. The Board shall have power to grant exemption from the provisions contained in the Regulations or parts thereof to Members who are considered by the

Board to have satisfied criteria equivalent to those contained in the Regulations.

12. The Board shall issue to each Registered Practitioner a certificate indicating his or her respective Registered Practitioner status. Such certificates shall remain the property of the Institute. Any Registered Practitioner ceasing to be a Member or otherwise ceasing to hold the relevant Registered Practitioner status shall immediately cease to describe himself or herself as a Registered Practitioner.

13. The Board shall have power to cancel the registration of any Registered Practitioner whose membership is terminated for any reason and to reinstate the registration when such Registered Practitioner has been reinstated to membership under Bye-law 8. The Board may specify the conditions under which reinstatement may be made, including the payment of a further registration fee. Any Registered Practitioner whose registration is so cancelled shall immediately cease to describe himself or herself as a Registered Practitioner.

SECTION 4
Honorary Awards

14. The Board shall have power to admit as Honorary Fellows individuals who in the opinion of the Board have rendered distinguished service in promoting the objects of the Institute. Honorary Fellows shall be entitled to use after their names the letters "HonFCLIP" and to describe themselves as "Honorary Fellow of the CILIP".

15. The Board may remove any person's Honorary Fellow status, in which case that person shall cease to describe himself or

herself as an Honorary Fellow of the CILIP and cease to use the letters "HonFCLIP".

SECTION 5
Conduct of Members

16. The Board shall have power to issue a set of Ethical Principles and Code of Professional Practice setting out the standards of professional behaviour expected of Members and may from time to time amend the ethical principles and code or any part or parts thereof.

17. Every Member (including every Organisation Member and its representatives) shall observe the provisions of the Charter, the Bye-laws and the Regulations and shall conduct him or herself in such a manner as shall not prejudice his or her professional status or the reputation of the Institute and without prejudice to the generality of the foregoing shall, in particular, comply at all times with the Ethical Principles and Code of Professional Practice prescribed and published by the Board under the provisions of the last preceding Bye-law.

18. The Board shall make and publish Regulations for the conduct of the disciplinary proceedings in respect of any complaint made against a Member and such Regulations may establish a range of sanctions including the suspension or expulsion of a Member.

19. Disciplinary proceedings shall be conducted by the Disciplinary Committee as prescribed by these Bye-laws and Regulations.

SECTION 6
General Meetings

20. The Annual General Meeting of the Institute shall be held once in every year at such place and at such time as the Board may determine, provided that no more than sixteen months shall elapse between such meetings.

21. The Board may whenever it thinks fit convene a General Meeting and the Chief Executive Officer shall convene a General Meeting within one calendar month of receiving a requisition from any one hundred Individual Members, provided that the purpose for which the meeting is to be called is stated in the requisition.

22. The Board may make and publish Regulations for the management and conduct of General Meetings.

23. The proceedings at any General Meeting or on the conduct of a Ballot shall not be invalidated by reason of any accidental informality or irregularity (including any accidental omission to give or any non-receipt of notice) or any want of qualification in any of the persons present or voting or by reason of any business being considered which is not specified in the notice unless such specification is a requirement of the Bye-laws or Regulations.

24. The business of the Annual General Meeting shall be to receive and consider the annual report of the Institute, the Honorary Treasurer's report and the balance sheet and accounts of the Institute with the auditor's report thereon; to determine the amount of subscriptions and other fees in accordance with Bye-law 6, to

appoint auditors in accordance with Bye-law 66; any motions of which notice shall have been given in the notice of the meeting; and to consider any questions submitted to the meeting in accordance with Regulations. The minutes of the preceding Annual General Meeting containing a transcript of all resolutions passed shall be read or submitted to the Annual General Meeting. All other business transacted at any Annual General Meeting and all business transacted at any other General Meeting shall be deemed special business.

25. No business shall be transacted at any General Meeting unless a quorum is present. Save as herein otherwise provided fifty Individual Members present in person shall constitute a quorum for an Annual General Meeting and twenty Individual Members present in person shall constitute a quorum for any other General Meeting.

26. If within half an hour from the time appointed for the holding of a General Meeting a quorum is not present the meeting, if convened on the requisition of Individual Members, shall be dissolved. For other General Meetings, if a quorum is not present within 30 minutes, the meeting must be adjourned to a date, time and place determined by the chair of the meeting and notified to Individual Members. If at the adjourned meeting a quorum is not present within half an hour from the time appointed for holding the meeting then the Individual Members present will constitute a quorum.

SECTION 7
The Board

27. The management of the affairs of the Institute shall be vested in the Board, which, in addition to the powers and authority expressly conferred on it by these Bye-laws or otherwise, may in respect of the affairs of the Institute exercise all such powers and do all such things as may lead to the furtherance of the objects of the Institute including all such powers and things as may be exercised or done by the Institute and are not by these Bye-laws expressly directed or required to be exercised or done by any other person or by the Institute in General Meeting.

Regulations

28. The Board shall have power from time to time to make, repeal or alter Regulations as to the admission of Members, as to the management of the Institute and its affairs, as to the duties of any officers or employees of the Institute, as to the conduct of business of the Institute, the Board or any other Duly Appointed Body and as to any other matters or things within the powers or under the control of the Board provided that such Regulations shall not be inconsistent with the Charter or these Bye-laws and any Regulations (including any repeal or alteration) affecting or made in accordance with the provisions of the following Bye-laws shall not have effect unless approved by a simple majority vote at a General Meeting or by Ballot:

- Bye-law 4: categories, privileges and obligations of Members
- Bye-law 7: admission and removal of Members (but not, for the avoidance of doubt, Bye-law 6)

- Bye-law 18: disciplinary proceedings.

Composition of the Board

29. Subject to any transitional provisions in the Regulations, the Board shall consist of not more than fifteen Board Members and shall comprise the following persons:

   a. Twelve Board Members, all of whom must be Individual Members, elected by the Individual Members in accordance with Bye-laws 31-35.
   b. Up to Three Board Members, all of whom must be Individual Members, appointed by the Board in accordance with Bye-Laws 36-39.

30. Any person who is a Board Member may not serve during his or her term in office on any Regional Member Network or Special Interest Group.

Election of Board Members

31. At the annual election to be held each year for the ensuing year commencing 1 January, the Individual Members shall elect three Board Members to serve for four years. The election shall be held in accordance with Regulations and will be overseen by the Audit Committee.

32. If the Institute, for any reason, fails to fill a vacant Board Member post through the election process, then the vacancy shall be filled by the Board through the appointment process. The person filling the vacancy shall be an Individual Member and shall serve from the date appointed for the remainder of the four year term for that vacant post.

33. No Board Member shall be elected for a term of more than four years, but shall be eligible for re-election on ceasing to be a Board Member. Provided that a Board Member who has held office for eight consecutive years will not be eligible for re-election until one further full governance year has elapsed.

34. The Board shall make and publish Regulations prescribing who is eligible to vote and the requirements and procedures for the nomination of candidates for election.

35. Voting in annual elections shall be by Full Ballot.

Appointment of Board Members

36. The Board may appoint up to three Board Members, who must be Individual Members of CILIP.

37. No Board Member shall be appointed for a term of more than four years, but shall be eligible for re-appointment on ceasing to be a Board Member. Provided that a Board Member who has held office for eight consecutive years will not be eligible for re-appointment until one further full governance year has elapsed.

38. Appointed Board Members shall have the same rights and responsibilities as elected Board Members.

39. The Board shall make and publish Regulations prescribing the requirements and procedures for the appointment of Board Members.

Election of Vice-President

40. The Vice-President and President shall be appointed as follows:

40.1 At the annual election to be held each year for the ensuing year commencing 1 January, the Individual Members shall elect a Vice-President to serve for one year. The election shall be held in accordance with Regulations and will be overseen by the Audit Committee.

40.2 The Vice-President shall be appointed as the President at the end of his or her year in office as Vice-President with effect from the date of appointment until 31 December in the year of appointment.

40.3 If the Institute, for any reason, fails to elect a Vice-President then the Audit Committee may (with the agreement of the Board) determine how the vacancy shall be filled.

40.4 Any person who is appointed President or Vice-President may not serve during his or her term in office on any Regional Member Network or Special Interest Group.

40.5 The Board shall make and publish Regulations prescribing the requirements and procedures for the nomination of candidates for election.

40.6 Voting in annual elections shall be by Full Ballot.

Honorary Officers

41. The Board shall appoint from among their number the Chair of the Board and Honorary Treasurer and may at any time remove them from those offices with the agreement of the Audit Committee. Appointments to those offices shall commence on the date of appointment and end on 31 December in the year of appointment, but may be renewed for subsequent terms of 1 year.

Termination of office and filling of vacancies

42. A Board Member shall vacate office and cease to be a member of the Board if he or she:

    (a) ceases to be a Member of CILIP;
    (b) is suspended from membership of the Institute;
    (c) is absent from meetings of the Board for three consecutive meetings without the consent of the Board and the Board resolves that his or her office be vacated;
    (d) becomes bankrupt or makes any arrangement or composition with his or her creditors;
    (e) becomes in the view of the Board, incapable by reason of mental disorder;
    (f) becomes prohibited by law from holding office as a charity trustee;
    (g) is removed by a resolution passed by a two thirds majority of the Individual Members voting at a General Meeting;
    (h) is removed by a resolution passed by a two thirds majority decision of the total number of Board Members in the case of an infringement of the Code of Conduct for Trustees. The Board may also suspend a Board Member pending investigation of any allegations of misconduct.

43. A Board Member may at any time give notice in writing or by email of his or her resignation from the Board with effect from such date as the Board Member indicates (but only if at least three Board members remain in office when such resignation takes effect).

44. The Board shall determine in Regulations the method by which casual vacancies among elected Board Members shall be filled.

Proceedings of the Board

45. The Board may meet together for the despatch of business and adjourn or otherwise regulate their meetings and proceedings as they think fit and may hold meetings in person or by suitable electronic means.

46. Meeting of the Board shall be held at least four times in every year at such place and at such time as the Board may determine.

47. The quorum necessary for the transaction of business at Board meetings shall be eight Board Members or such higher number as the Board may determine provided that if the number of Board Members falls below this they may meet to deal with the appointment of new Board Members.

48. The Chair of the Board shall preside at meetings of the Board but in his or her absence the chair shall be taken by the Honorary Treasurer or in the absence of the Honorary Treasurer by another Board Member chosen by the Board Members present.

49. Every question at meetings of the Board shall be determined by a majority of the votes of the Board Members present in person or by electronic means and if there is an equality of votes the chair of the meeting shall have a second or casting vote.

50. All acts done by any meeting of the Board or by any Duly Appointed Body shall, notwithstanding that it shall afterwards be discovered that there were defects in the appointment of all or any of the members of the Board or of such other duly Appointed Body or that any such person was disqualified from holding office or had vacated office, be as valid as if every such person had been duly appointed and was qualified and had continued in office.

51. A resolution in writing passed in such manner as may be prescribed by Regulations shall be as valid and effectual as if it had been passed at a meeting duly convened and held.

52. A resolution approved by electronic communication in such manner as may be prescribed by Regulations shall be as valid and effectual as if it had been passed at a meeting duly convened and held.

53. Whenever a Board Member has a personal interest in a matter to be discussed at a meeting, and whenever a Board Member has an interest in another organisation whose interests are reasonably likely to conflict with those of the Institute in relation to a matter to be discussed at a meeting, he or she must:

   (a) declare an interest before discussion begins on the matter;
   (b) withdraw from that part of the meeting unless expressly invited to remain;
   (c) in the case of personal interests not be counted in the quorum for that part of the meeting; and
   (d) in the case of personal interests withdraw during the vote and have no vote on the matter.

provided that this shall not apply to decisions regarding trustee indemnity insurance or general benefits available to Members or categories of Members of the Institute.

Delegation of the Board's powers

54. The Board may by power of attorney or otherwise appoint any person to be the agent of the Institute for such purposes and on such conditions as they determine.

55. The Board may delegate any of its powers or functions in accordance with the conditions set out in these Bye-laws, and may delegate day to day management of the affairs of the Institute to the Chief Executive Officer or other staff.

Delegation to Committees

56. The Board shall establish the following Committees, each of which shall be chaired by a Board Member:

    (a) Policy
    (b) Resources
    (c) Audit
    (d) Ethics
    (e) Disciplinary
    (f) Remuneration

57. The Board shall make Regulations in respect of each Committee prescribing:

    (a) its powers and functions (including any powers of delegation);
    (b) its composition, appointment and removal processes;
    (c) the requirements for calling and holding of meetings;
    (d) the requirements for reporting back to the Board
    (e) such other matters as the Board thinks fit.

Delegation of Investment Management

58. The Board may delegate to one or more investment managers, for such period and upon such terms as it may think fit, power at the discretion of the investment manager to buy and sell investments on behalf of the Institute. Where the Board makes such a delegation it shall ensure that the investment manager is given clear instructions as to investment policy;

59. Except to the extent that the Board has exercised its power of delegation, the Board shall arrange that the investments are kept under review by one or more independent professional advisers, who shall be required to inform the Board promptly about any changes in investments which appear to them to be desirable;

60. Without prejudice to any other of its powers, the Board may if it thinks fit invest in the name of or under the control of any corporation or corporations as nominees of the Board the whole or such part of the investments and income arising from those investments as the Board may determine;

61. The Board may pay reasonable remuneration to the investment managers, independent professional advisers or nominees for services rendered under the above provisions.

SECTION 8
Financial Matters

62. Subject to the authority of the Board the Honorary Treasurer shall supervise the financial affairs of the Institute and in particular the procedures for dealing with receipts, payments, assets and liabilities.

The Honorary Treasurer shall submit a report to the Annual General Meeting of the Institute. In the absence of the Honorary Treasurer the report shall be submitted by the President of the Board. The Board may make such Regulations as it sees fit as regards the payment of accounts and the signature of cheques and other financial documents.

63. The Board may borrow money for the purposes of the Institute and secure the repayment thereof or the fulfilment of any contract or engagement of the Institute in any manner, upon any security, and issue any debentures to secure the same.

64. The Board may, out of the monies of the Institute, by way of reserve fund from time to time reserve or set apart such sums as in its judgement are necessary or expedient to be applied at the discretion of the Board to meet the claims on or liabilities of the Institute, or to be used as a sinking fund to pay off debentures or encumbrances of the Institute, or for any other purpose of the Institute.

Expenses

65. Members of any Duly Appointed Body shall be paid out of the funds of the Institute all reasonable out of pocket expenses properly and necessarily incurred by them on behalf of the Institute.

Audit, Accounts and Reports

66. At each Annual General Meeting an auditor or auditors of the Institute shall be appointed by resolution of the members. No person shall be appointed auditor of the Institute who is employed by or otherwise holds office in the Institute nor unless he or she is qualified for

appointment as auditor of a company (other than an exempt private company) under the provisions of the Companies Act 2006 or any statutory re-enactment or modification thereof.

67. The Board shall comply with the requirements of the Charities Act 2011 (or any statutory re-enactment or modification thereof) as to keeping financial records, the audit or examination of accounts and the preparation and submission to the Charity Commission of:

   (a) annual reports;
   (b) annual returns;
   (c) annual statements of accounts.

SECTION 9
Devolved Nations

68. The Board may establish offices or branches in each of the Devolved Nations and shall devolve governance, function and financing or other arrangements by agreement. CILIP in Scotland has its own governance arrangements and a separate agreement with CILIP.

SECTION 10
Regional Member Networks

69. The Board may establish Regional Member Networks and shall prescribe Regulations for their membership, establishment, constitution, functions, financing, merger, dissolution and procedures. The Board may from time to time alter the boundaries of any region served by a Regional Member Network. For the avoidance of doubt, Regional Member Networks are not separate legal entities but part of the Institute.

70. The officers of the committee of the

Regional Member Network shall deliver a business plan on the proposed work of the Regional Member Network each year and report on the work of the Regional Member Network during each year for the scrutiny of the Board.

SECTION 11
Special Interest Groups

71. The Board may establish Special Interest Groups and shall prescribe Regulations for their membership, establishment, constitution, functions, financing, merger, dissolution and procedures.

72. The officers of the committee of each Special Interest Group shall deliver a business plan on the proposed work of the Special Interest Group each year and report on the work of the Special Interest Group during each year for the scrutiny of the Board.

Organisations in Liaison

73. The Board may from time to time recognise independent organisations which have objects similar to the objects of the Institute and whose membership includes a significant number of Members of the Institute as Organisations in Liaison with the Institute and may determine the rights and obligations of such Organisations in Liaison.

SECTION 12
Chief Executive Officer

74. The Chief Executive Officer shall be appointed by the Board for such term, upon such conditions and by such process as the Board may think fit. The Chief Executive Officer shall keep a record of all proceedings, shall draft reports, issue notices, and conduct correspondence and

shall have charge of all books, papers and other property belonging to the Institute and shall have general day to day conduct of the management of the Institute under the supervision of the Board. The Chief Executive Officer may not be on the Board.

Seal

75. The Seal of the Institute shall only be used by the authority of the Board. Any instrument to which the Seal is affixed may be signed by:

   • any two Board Members; or
   • a Board Member and the Chief Executive Officer; or
   • by such other persons as the Board may authorise.

Notices etc.

76. All notices, voting papers and circulars and other documents required by these Bye-laws to be given or sent may be given personally or by sending the same by post to the registered address of the Member, (or, as appropriate, to the principal office of the Institute) or by email or such other suitable means as the Board may prescribe, provided always that publication of a notice in the official journal of the Institute shall constitute good service of any notice to be served upon all Members.

77. Any such notice, voting paper, circular or other document sent through the post to the registered address of any Member shall have been deemed to have been served on the Member on the third day after the day it is posted if sent by first class post and on the fifth day after posting if sent by second class post, and in proving such service it shall be sufficient to prove that such notice, voting paper or circular was properly addressed and

posted. Any such document sent by email shall be deemed served on the day after transmission and in proving service it shall be sufficient to prove that the document was transmitted by the Institute's email server and was addressed to an email address provided by the Member to the Institute for the receipt of notices.

Indemnity

78. Every Board Member, other officer and every employee of the Institute carrying out the proper business of the Institute shall be indemnified by the Institute against, and it shall be the duty of the Board out of the funds of the Institute to pay, all costs, losses and expenses which any such person may incur or become liable to by reason of any contract entered into, or act or thing done or omitted to be done by him or her as such Board Member, officer or employee or in any other way in the proper discharge of his or her duty, including reasonable travelling expenses.

SECTION 13
Office of the President

79. The Office of the President, shall be controlled by the President, assisted by the Vice-President and any other person (being an Individual Member, but not being a Board Member) as the Board may decide.

80. The Office of the President shall be provided by the Board with such resources as it may reasonably require (but at the discretion of the Board) in order to perform the functions reserved to it in these Bye-laws.

81. The Vice-President shall be elected and a President appointed in accordance with Bye-law 40. Neither shall be Board Members. A President or Vice-President may be removed by a resolution passed by a two thirds majority of the Individual Members voting at a General Meeting.

82. The Vice-President shall:

   (a) chair the Policy Committee established under Bye-law 56;
   (b) attend meetings of the Board as an observer with a right to speak but not to vote;
   (c) assist the President in the running of the Office of the President and in the performance of the President's functions.

83. The President shall:

   (a) represent the Institute at functions and may delegate this role to any other appropriate Individual Member;
   (b) chair the Audit Committee and the Ethics Committee established under Bye-law 56;
   (c) sit ex-officio on each of the Committees established under Bye-law 56 except the Disciplinary Committee;
   (d) perform such functions as may be established by Regulations made by the Board in relation to the hearing of appeals from the decisions of hearing groups established by the Disciplinary Committee.

General Regulations
CILIP Regulations 2014

Drawn up under the Provisions of CILIP Bye-law 28
Adopted by CILIP Board 20th September 2014 and amended 26th November 2014

Index

Under the provisions of Bye-Law 28, the CILIP Board has the power to make regulations on any matters relevant to CILIP, provided the regulations are not inconsistent with the Charter and Bye-Laws. In addition, certain Bye-laws oblige the Board to make regulations to give effect to their provisions. As at 20th September 2014, the Board has made regulations on the following matters:

*Note: Appendix D and Appendix E are no longer in use.

General Regulations

Definitions

1. Words and phrases defined in the Institute's Royal Charter and Bye-laws shall have the same meanings when used in these Regulations.

Categories and privileges of Members – Bye-law 4

Regulations made under Bye-law 4 require the approval of a simple majority vote at a General Meeting or by Ballot

2. There shall be the following categories of Member:

2.1 Individual Members comprising:

2.1.1 Ordinary Members, being individuals who are eligible for admission as Certified Members, Chartered Members or Chartered Fellows but who have not been so admitted;

2.1.2 Certificated Members, being Registered Practitioners admitted to ACLIP status in accordance with these Regulations;

2.1.3 Chartered Members, being Registered Practitioners admitted to MCLIP status in accordance with these Regulations;

2.1.4 Chartered Fellows, being Registered Practitioners admitted to FCLIP status in accordance with these Regulations;

2.1.5 Honorary Fellows, being individuals admitted to Hon FCLIP status in accordance with these Regulations; and

2.2 Organisation Members, being corporate bodies, societies and other organisations which maintain, or are interested in, libraries and/or information services.

3. The privileges attached to each category of Member are as follows:

3.1 Certificated Members, Chartered Members, Chartered Fellows and Honorary Fellow have full membership of the Institute with all rights and privileges including the right to vote and the right to use the post-nominals applicable to their status;

3.2 Ordinary Members have full membership of the Institute with all rights and privileges including the right to vote; but excluding the right to use post-nominals;

3.3 Organisation Members have the right to appoint one or more named representatives nominated by the Organisation Member and approved by the Board of the Institute. Such representatives shall enjoy all the privileges of a Member except that they shall not be entitled to be elected onto or to remain on the Register of Registered Practitioners unless they are themselves Certificated Members, Chartered Members or Chartered Fellows. Nor shall they, by virtue only of their appointment as a nominated representative, be entitled to vote, to hold office within the Institute, or to use post-nominals.

Subscriptions – Bye-law 6

4. Date of payment

4.1 Annual subscriptions shall be due and payable in advance each year on the anniversary of the Member joining. If a Member's subscription is not paid within 60 days of the due date for payment then his, her or its membership shall be deemed to have lapsed and the Member shall not be entitled to vote on any matter in respect of which he or she (if an Individual Member) would otherwise be entitled to vote.

4.2 If an Individual Member whose right to vote has lapsed under Regulation 4.1 pays his or her subscription within a further 60 days then his or her rights to vote shall be restored.

4.3 A Member whose subscription is not paid within 120 days of the due date for payment shall be deemed to have resigned and shall automatically cease to be a Member.

5. Payment by instalment

5.1 Where any resolution adopted by the Annual General Meeting of the Institute permits subscriptions, entrance, registration, admission and other fees to be paid by instalments, the provisions of Regulation 4 regarding suspension and termination of membership shall not apply provided each instalment is paid by its due date.

5.2 In the event of an instalment not being paid by the due date, the full subscription or other payment shall fall due immediately and the provisions of Regulation 4 shall apply as if in the case of non-payment.

5.3 The Chief Executive Officer shall have the power to suspend the operation of Regulation 4 if a payment is received after the due date as a result of circumstances outside the Member's control or in cases of hardship.

5.4 Where voting rights are suspended or membership terminated under Regulation 4, no instalment already received shall be refunded to the Member.

Admission and reinstatement of Members – Bye-laws 7–8

Regulations made under Bye-law 7 require the approval of a simple majority vote at a General Meeting or by Ballot

6. Names of individuals or institutions seeking membership of the Institute will be placed before a meeting of the Board.

7. Admission will be by the majority vote of those Board Members present.

8. The decision on the admission of any candidate may be deferred if agreed by a majority vote of those Board Members present.

9. The Board may also by majority vote reinstate Members whose memberships have been terminated, including reinstatement to the Register of Registered Practitioners.

10. In the event of an application for reinstatement by a person who resigned from his/her former membership of the Institute (or whose membership terminated for any other reason) whilst subject to complaint under consideration under the Institute's disciplinary Procedure, the Board may require such person to co-operate in the completion of the outstanding disciplinary process before considering his/her reinstatement as a Member or as a condition of that re-instatement.

11. The decision of the Board as to the admission or reinstatement of a Member and as to the category of membership to which a person is admitted shall be final and binding.

12. The Board may delegate decisions on the admission and reinstatement of Members on such terms as it thinks fit provided that the decision of any non-admitted person or body shall be subject to appeal to the Board.

Publication of the Registers of Members and Registered Practitioners – Bye-law 9

13. The current Registers of Members and Registered Practitioners will be made available either in print or electronic form or both.

Professional Registration – Bye-law 10

Regulations made under Bye-law 10 require full consultation with the membership

14. The Regulations for professional registration, by which Individual Members are admitted to the Register of Registered Practitioners, are given at Appendix A.

Exemption from provisions of Bye-law 10 – Bye-law 11

15. The Board will ensure that the terms of reference of the Professional Registration and Accreditation Board include the responsibility of the Board to draw attention to any need for the use of these powers of exemption, and for any subsequent changes to Regulations.

Power to admit Honorary Fellows – Bye-law 14

16. Nominations for the award of an honorary fellowship may be made by Members, Devolved Nations, Regional Member Networks, Special Interest Groups or the Board.

17. Nominations may be made for individuals who have made a significant contribution to the profession. Nominees need not be Members of the Institute. The criteria for

nominations shall be published by the Institute when the call for nominations is made.

18. Nominations for the award of honorary fellowships will be considered in the first instance by an Honorary Awards Panel (established annually by Board), which will propose to the Board such of the nominations as it thinks fit.

19. Decisions on the award of honorary fellowships will be made by the Board, and the Board's Board decision shall be final.

Ethical Principles and Code of Professional Practice – Bye-laws 16–17

20. The Ethical Principles and Code of Professional Practice are given at Appendix B.

Disciplinary proceedings – Bye-laws 18–19

Regulations made under Bye-law 18 require the approval of a simple majority vote at a General Meeting or by Ballot

21. These Regulations are given at Appendix B.

General Meetings – Bye-law 22
Notice

22. 28 days' notice in writing at the least of every Annual General Meeting and twenty-one days' notice in writing at the least of every other General Meeting (exclusive in every case both of the day on which it is served or deemed to be served and of the day for which it is given) specifying the place, the day and the hour of the meeting

and in the case of special business the nature of that business, shall be given to the Individual Members and to the auditors of the Institute.

23. Every General Meeting shall be held at a place determined by the Board.

Chairing a General Meeting

24. The President shall chair each General Meeting. If the President is unable or unwilling to act then the chair shall be taken by the Vice-President and failing him or her by the Chair. If none of those office holders is able or willing to act then the Individual Members present shall choose one of their number to chair the meeting.

25. The President, though present at a General Meeting, may if he or she sees fit yield the chair to the Vice-President or a Board Member or to such other person as the Individual Members present may choose.

Adjournment of a General Meeting

26. The chair of any general meeting may, with the consent of the meeting, adjourn the meeting from time to time, and from place to place as the meeting may determine, but no business shall be transacted at any adjourned meeting other than the business left unfinished at the meeting from which the adjournment took place. No notice need be given of any adjourned meeting unless it is so directed in the resolution for adjournment.

Voting

27. At every General Meeting a resolution put to the vote of the meeting shall be decided on a show of hands, unless a Ballot is demanded in accordance with the Regulations. Unless otherwise specified in the Charter, Bye-laws or Regulations; a resolution of the Individual Members must be passed by a simple majority of votes cast.

28. Unless a Ballot is demanded, a declaration by the chair of the meeting that a resolution has been carried or carried by a particular majority, or lost or not carried by a particular majority shall be conclusive, and an entry to that effect in the minutes of the proceedings of the meeting shall be sufficient evidence of the fact so declared, without proof of the number or proportion of the votes given for or against such resolution.

Eligibility to Vote

29. No Individual Member present in person or by proxy is entitled to vote at General Meetings or in Ballots if their subscriptions are in arrears (as defined in Regulations).

Votes on a show of hands

30. On a vote which is carried out by a show of hands, each Individual Member present in person or by proxy has one vote (subject to Regulations 29 and 50).

Votes on a Ballot

31. On a vote on a resolution which is carried out by Written Ballot, the following persons shall (subject to Regulation 29) have one vote each:

31.1 Every Individual Member present in person; and

31.2 Every Individual Member present by proxy (subject to Regulation 50)

32. On a vote on a resolution which is carried out by Full Ballot every Individual Member

shall have one vote (subject to Regulation 29).

Written Ballot

33. A Written Ballot may be demanded :

33.1 in advance of the General Meeting where it is to be put to the vote; or

33.2 at the General Meeting, either before a show of hands on that resolution or immediately after the result of a show of hands on that resolution is declared.

34. A Written Ballot may be demanded by:

34.1 the chair of the meeting or

34.2 at least twenty Individual Members present in person or by proxy.

35. A demand for a Written Ballot may be withdrawn if:

35.1 the Written Ballot has not yet been taken; and

35.2 the chairman of the meeting consents to the withdrawal.

36. If a Written Ballot is demanded it shall be taken at such time and place and in such a manner as the chair of the meeting shall direct provided always that no Written Ballot shall be taken on:

    a)   the election of the chair
    b)   the appointment of scrutineers or
    c)   the adjournment of the meeting.

37. Notwithstanding a demand for a Ballot on any resolution, the meeting may continue for the transaction of any other business in respect of which a Ballot has not been demanded.

38. The Individual Members or the chair, as the case may be, demanding a Written Ballot may nominate up to three persons, who need not be Members, to act as scrutineers. If a Written Ballot is demanded it shall be taken in such manner as the chair of the meeting directs, and the result of the Written Ballot shall be deemed the resolution of the General Meeting at which the Written Ballot was demanded unless a Full Ballot is demanded in accordance with the Regulations.

Casting vote on a show of hands or Written Ballot

39. In the case of an equality of votes, whether on a show of hands or in a Written Ballot, the chair of the meeting shall be entitled to a second or casting vote.

Full Ballot

40. A Full Ballot on a resolution may be demanded:

40.1 in advance of the General Meeting where it is to be put to the vote by the Board; or

40.2 at the General Meeting if a Written Ballot is demanded by Individual Members the chair of the meeting may instead direct that the resolution is put to a Full Ballot instead of a Written Ballot; or

40.3 at the General Meeting immediately after the result of a Written Ballot is declared by one quarter of the Individual Members present in person or by proxy and entitled to vote

41. The decision of a Full Ballot shall be deemed to be the decision of the meeting.

42. The chair shall direct the manner in which the Full Ballot shall be conducted (which may for example be online or by other electronic means) provided that the result of the vote shall be declared not later than forty-eight days after the meeting.

43. The Audit Committee shall act as scrutineers of the Full Ballot and its report shall be conclusive as to the result of the voting and the result shall take effect from the date of that report. In the event of a tie on a Full Ballot conducted under these Regulations, the resolution shall be declared not carried.

Proxy votes

44. An Individual Member who is entitled to be present and to vote at a General Meeting may appoint a proxy to vote on his or her behalf. A proxy must be an Individual Member who is entitled to vote.

45. A proxy appointment must be in writing and signed by the Individual Member appointing the proxy or in an electronic form as determined by the Board. To be valid a proxy appointment must use the form prescribed by the Board and shall be delivered to the registered office of the Institute not less than forty-eight hours before the date on which the meeting or adjourned meeting to which it relates fall. A proxy appointment shall be valid only for the meeting named on the form and any adjournment of that meeting to which it relates.

46. When two or more valid proxy appointments are delivered or received in respect of the same Individual Member for use at the same General Meeting, the one which was received last is treated as replacing and revoking the others for that Individual Member. Any question as to whether a proxy appointment has been validly delivered or received which is unresolved at the beginning of a General Meeting must be referred to the chair of the meeting whose decision shall be final and conclusive.

47. The proceedings at a General Meeting are not invalidated where an appointment of a proxy in respect of that meeting is sent in electronic form as provided in these Regulations, but because of a technical problem it cannot be read by the recipient.

48. The proxy appointment shall be deemed to confer authority to:

    a) vote on any amendment of a resolution put to the meeting for which it is given as the proxy thinks fit if no specific instructions have been given by the Individual Member concerning the amendment; and

    b) demand or join in demanding a Ballot.

49. A proxy must vote in accordance with any instructions given by the Individual Member by whom the proxy is appointed.

50. A person entitled to vote at a General Meeting remains so entitled even though a valid proxy form has been delivered to the Institute in respect of that person. If the person casts a vote in such circumstance, any vote cast on their behalf by the proxy is not valid.

Submissions of Resolutions to the AGM or to a General Meeting – Bye-law 24

51. Notice of a resolution proposed by an Individual Member shall be made in writing and shall be served on the Chief Executive Officer not less than 60 days before the date of the meeting.

52. Any Individual Member who desires to move an amendment to a notice of resolution may:

    a) serve on the Chief Executive Officer a notice in writing of such amendment at least one week before the meeting

    b) propose an amendment from the floor of the meeting in order to resolve some differences that have emerged at the meeting

    providing always that the proposed amendment does not, in the reasonable opinion of the chair of the meeting, materially alter the scope of the resolution.

53. If the chair of the meeting, acting in good faith, wrongly decides that an amendment to a resolution is out of order, their error does not invalidate the vote on that resolution.

Minutes of meetings of Board, and other Duly Appointed Bodies – Bye-law 45

54. Proper minutes shall be recorded of all resolutions and proceedings of meetings of the Board and other Duly Appointed Bodies, and every minute signed by the chair of the meeting to which it relates or by the chair of a subsequent meeting shall be sufficient evidence of the facts therein

stated. Minutes shall be distributed in a timely fashion.

Nominations for elections of Vice-President and Board Members and election process – Bye-laws 31–35 and 40

55. A notice of election and call for nominations for the post of Board Member and Vice-President shall be published in the journal and on the Institute's website.

56. Full details of how to stand, the requirements of the roles and the prescribed format for nominations shall be made available on the website.

57. All candidates and nominators must be Individual Members of the Institute whose subscriptions are not in arrears.

58. Candidates seeking election must submit an application in the prescribed format, giving evidence of how they meet the requirements of the role specification. Candidates may not stand for election as both Vice President and Board Member.

59. All candidates must be supported by two eligible Individual Members who will confirm, in the prescribed format, how they know the candidate and that to the best of their knowledge the candidate meets the requirements of the role specification.

60. All required submissions must be received by the Chief Executive Officer by such time as has been specified in the notice of election in order to be valid.

61. The Board will appoint three of its Board Members to review all nominations for election as a Board Member to confirm

that evidence has been provided that candidates meet the requirements of the role specification.

62. All candidates standing for election as a Board Member that are so confirmed shall go forward to the election. All nominations received for the role of Vice-President shall go forward to election.

63. If the number of candidates is the same as or less than the number of vacancies then the candidates shall be declared elected without a Full Ballot and the results shall be published on the Institutes website. If the number of candidates exceeds the number of vacancies then the election shall be conducted by Full Ballot by whatever means is prescribed by the Board which may include electronic or postal voting.

64. Not less than 14 days before the opening of voting, a notice will be published in the journal of the Institute, or otherwise despatched (including by email or post) to Individual Members qualified to vote, stating:

   a) the date on which the voting will begin;
   b) that any qualified Individual Member failing to receive notification of how to vote must notify the Chief Executive Officer of that fact within 7 days after the date for the commencement of voting.

65. The application forms of candidates and the supporting statements shall be available to Individual Members entitled to vote on the Institute's website.

66. The voting communication will include details of how to vote and the latest date for receipt of votes.

67. The result of the count shall be published on the Institute's website within twenty-four hours of the result being known and will include:

   a) the number of votes cast for each candidate for contested places and the candidates declared elected;
   b) the number of voting papers issued and returned or the number of participants if the Full Ballot is held electronically.

68. The entire election process shall be overseen and scrutinised by the Audit Committee and any procedural issues that arise will be referred to and decided by the Audit Committee.

Appointment of Board Members – Bye-laws 36–39

69. Following the election of Board Members, the Board will identify what additional skills, experience or representation may be required to ensure its effective operation and decision making.

70. Up to three Board Members may then be appointed to fulfil these requirements (subject to the transitional provisions in Regulations 107–108).

71. The appointment process will be agreed by the Audit Committee and will follow an open application process.

Filling Casual Vacancies among Elected Board Members – Bye-law 44

72.   If an elected Board Member ceases to hold office before the expiry of their term then the casual vacancy may be filled by the Board through the appointment process or the Board may decide to fill the vacancy as part of the annual elections. In either case, the replacement Board Member must be an Individual Member and shall serve from the date appointed for the remainder of the four year term for that vacant post.

Board written resolutions and electronic communications – Bye-laws 51–52

73.   A resolution of the Board without holding a meeting may be passed by a majority of not less than six Board Members approving the resolution provided a copy of the Resolution has been circulated to all Board Members. Evidence of approval may be the signature of the relevant Board Members on a copy of the resolution returned to the Chief Executive Officer by post or by fax or approval given by email received from any email address of the Board Members registered with the Institute for the purpose of sending and receiving notices.

Regulations for committees – Bye-law 57

Policy Committee

74.   The Policy Committee will develop professional policy for the Board and will advise on policy matters in accordance with any terms of reference issued by the Board from time to time.

74.1   The Policy Committee will comprise the President ex-officio together with up to ten members appointed by the Board including:

a)   three Board Members
b)   three representatives from the Devolved Nations, nominated by CILIPS Board and the Committees in Northern Ireland and Wales
c)   four co-opted members from CILIP Special Interest Groups and Regional Member Networks dependent upon the experience and expertise required in policy priority areas
d)   additional expertise may be co-opted on to the Committee on a time-limited advisory basis.

74.2   Appointment of Board Members to the Committee will be for three years, renewable for a further term of three years. A Board Member who has held office on the Policy Committee for six consecutive years will not be eligible for re-appointment until one further full governance year has elapsed.

74.3   Representatives of Devolved Nations will be appointed for three years, subject to the continued approval of their nominating body.

74.4   All other appointments will be for a time agreed by the Board according to the prevailing policy priorities.

74.5   Meetings of the Policy Committee will be held at least four times a year.

Resources Committee

75.   The Resources Committee will assist the Board by overseeing CILIP's financial

management and control and the use of its resources in accordance with any term of reference issued by the Board from time to time.

75.1 Membership of the Resources Committee will be appointed by the Board and will comprise:

a) three Board Members including the Treasurer who will Chair the Committee

b) up to two co-opted members, who may not be Members, with the required skills.

c) the President ex officio.

75.2 Appointment of Board Members to the Committee will be for three years, renewable for a further term of three years. A Board Member who has held office for six consecutive years on the Resources Committee will not be eligible for re-appointment until one further full governance year has elapsed.

75.3 Meetings of the Resources Committee will be held at least four times a year.

Audit Committee

76. The Audit Committee will act in accordance with any terms of reference issued by the Board from time to time and will monitor the integrity of CILIP's financial statements and activities, and its annual report. The Committee will also monitor and oversee CILIP's elections and appointment processes.

76.1 Membership of the Audit Committee will be appointed by the Board and will comprise:

a) at least three Board Members

b) up to two co-opted members with the required skills.

c) the President ex-officio

76.2 Appointment of Board Members to the Committee will be for three years, renewable for a further term of three years. A Board Member who has held office on the Audit Committee for six consecutive years will not be eligible for re-appointment until one further full governance year has elapsed.

76.3 The President shall chair the Audit Committee.

76.4 Meetings of the Audit Committee will be held at least four times a year.

Ethics Committee

77. The Ethics Committee will provide advice to the Board on ethical issues and promote a better understanding of professional ethics among Members in accordance with any terms of reference issued by the Board from time to time.

77.1 Membership of the Ethics Committee will be appointed by the Board and will comprise:

a) two Board Members

b) two Members drawn from the wider membership

c) the President ex officio.

77.2 Appointment of Board Members to the Committee will be for three years, renewable for a further term of three years. A Board Member who has held office for six consecutive years on the Ethics Committee will not be eligible for re-appointment until one further full governance year has elapsed

77.3 The Ethics Committee will be chaired by the President.

77.4 Meetings of the Ethics Committee will be held once a year. The chair of the Committee can call additional meetings as necessary.

Disciplinary Committee

78. The Disciplinary Committee will operate under the Regulations at Appendix B.

Remuneration Committee

79. The Remuneration Committee will determine the framework and policy for remuneration of the Chief Executive and Senior Management Team and will oversee any major changes to organisational structure or benefits affecting CILIP staff in accordance with any terms of reference issued by the Board from time to time.

79.1 Membership of the Remuneration Committee will be appointed by the Board and will comprise at least three Board Members and the President ex-officio.

79.2 Appointment of to the Committee will be for three years, renewable for a further term of three years. A Committee member who has held office for six consecutive years will not be eligible for re-appointment until one further full governance year has elapsed.

79.3 The Board will appoint a chair from the Remuneration Committee membership.

79.4 Meetings of the Remuneration Committee will be held once a year or more frequently if circumstances require.

Further Provisions regarding Committees

80. All committees will report to the Board and the Board will receive minutes from all committee meetings.

81. The Board may establish any sub-boards as it may from time to time think fit in order to carry out its functions, duties and responsibilities or to implement any of its resolutions, including the Professional Registration and Accreditation Board and the International Board.

82. The Board will approve the remit and operations of each of the committees and sub-boards, including the quorum, terms of reference and reporting mechanisms and will review these from time to time.

Process of appointment to committees – Bye-law 57

83. The process of making appointments to committees shall be established by the Board and shall be compatible with the standards and processes for making appointments to the boards of non-departmental public bodies.

Expenses

84. Reasonable expenses incurred by members of duly appointed bodies in attending meetings shall be reimbursed by the Institute. Expenses incurred by Institute representatives on joint and external committees may also be reimbursed. Expenses incurred by observers shall not normally be reimbursed by the Institute, but the Board may authorise reimbursement if it is satisfied that the interests of the Institute make it appropriate to do so.

Open meetings

85. Individual Members and the nominated representatives of Organisation Members may attend and observe as visitors meetings and other forms of debate of duly appointed bodies (other than those of the Disciplinary Panel). Visitors shall be excluded from any part of a meeting at which a duly appointed body is discussing confidential business.

Payment of accounts and signature of cheques – Bye-law 62

86. Payment of accounts

86.1 Heads of a department shall be responsible for managing their department's budget and authorising expenditure.

86.2 Invoices and other requests for payments must be signed by the head of the relevant department, or by another member of the department specifically authorised to do so.

86.3 In exceptional circumstances, payments may be authorised by the Chief Executive Officer, a director or the head of finance.

87. Signature of cheques

87.1 Cheques must be signed by two authorised signatories, at least one of whom must come from the A list.

87.2 The lists of cheque signatories are:

A List (finance staff):
    Director of Resources and
    Head of Finance
B List (non-finance staff):
    Chief Executive Officer, directors,

and other senior members of staff determined from time to time by the director of finance and notified to the Institute's bankers.

Regional Member Networks – Bye-law 69

88. A Regional Member Network shall appoint a chair, an honorary secretary or honorary secretaries, an honorary treasurer, and such other members as required to form a committee to manage its affairs.

89. A Regional Member Network shall not take any action, other than by recommendation to the Board, which affects other Regional Member Networks, the general conduct of the Institute or the external relations of the Institute.

90. The funds and facilities of a Regional Member Network shall not be employed to promote the candidature of any candidate for election to office of the Institute; but this shall not prevent the provision of factual information on a non-discriminatory basis.

91. Subject to approval by the Board, Regional Member Networks may create and dissolve sub-regions to facilitate provision of services to Members.

92. Individual Members will be assigned to an appropriate Regional Membership Network. Individual Members may pay the Institute an additional fee to be a corresponding member of any Regional Member Network of which they are not a member.

93. The form of Regional Member Network rules, which may be amended for any Regional Member Network with the

approval of the Board is set out in Appendix F.

Special Interest Groups – Bye-law 71

94. The procedure as set out in the Special Interest Group Rules in Appendix F, shall be used by the Board when considering the creation, merger or dissolution of Special Interest Groups.

95. Individual Members may join one or more SIGs by notice to the Chief Executive Officer. The Board shall determine whether and in what circumstances an additional subscription is to be levied in respect of membership of SIGs and the level of any such additional subscription.

96. A SIG shall appoint a chair, an honorary secretary or honorary secretaries, an honorary treasurer, and such other members as required to form a committee to manage its affairs.

97. A SIG shall not take any action, other than by recommendation to the Board, which affects other SIGs, the general conduct of the Institute or the external relations of the Institute.

98. The funds and facilities of a SIG shall not be employed to promote the candidature of any candidate for election to office of the Institute; but this shall not prevent the provision of factual information on a non-discriminatory basis.

99. Subject to approval by the Board, SIGs may create and dissolve sub-groups to facilitate provision of services to Members.

Group-only Members of SIGs

100. The Institute recognises that there are people who are interested in the work of one or more of the Institute's SIGs but who would not wish to become Members of the Institute. The Institute is therefore willing to allow such people to become 'Group-only' members of a SIG. Group-only members are entitled to the advantages of membership of the SIG. Subscription charges will be set annually by the Board. Whilst Group-only membership is administered by the Institute, Group-only members are not Members of the Institute.

101. Group-only members may become members of the SIGs committee, but not in the office of chair, honorary secretary or honorary treasurer, nor in the roles of mentor support officer or candidate support officer. Group-only members may not form the majority of members of the committee.

102. Group-only members may vote on matters internal to the SIG.

103. Group-only members cannot comprise more than 25% of the total membership of a SIG.

Member network forum

104. The member networks forum, attended by representatives of Regional Member Networks and Special Interest Groups, shall be held at least twice each year. The forum will always be attended by at least one Board Member.

105. A policy seminar will be held on an annual basis with the member networks forum to assist in the setting of policy priorities for the following year.

Regulations for the Retired Members' Guild – Bye-law 28

106.   The Regulations are given at Appendix C.

Regulation for the Retirement of the transitional Board – Bye-Law 29

107.   The following provisions shall apply to the transitional Board:

107.1   The Board Members to serve from 1 January 2015 shall be those eight individuals elected as Councillors at the annual elections in 2012 and 2013. The four Councillors elected in 2011 and due to retire on 31 December 2014 shall remain in office until 31 March 2015 when three shall retire (if those to retire cannot be agreed then the decision shall be decided by lot).

107.2   At the annual election for 2014, the Individual Members shall elect three Board Members to serve, commencing 1 April 2015 for a term ending on 31 December 2018.

107.3   In 2015, 2016 and 2017:

107.3.1 On the 31 December three elected Board Members shall retire. The Board Members to retire shall be those who have been in office longest since their last appointment or reappointment. As between persons who became or were last reappointed as Board Members on the same day those to retire shall (unless otherwise agreed amongst themselves) be decided by lot.

107.3.2 the Individual Members shall elect three Board Members to serve for four years from the following 1 January.

107.   During the transitional period the Board may appoint Board Members in accordance with Bye-laws 36–39.

107.5   The provisions for filling casual vacancies in the Bye-laws shall apply to the transitional period as shall the provision that no Board Member may serve for a period of more than eight consecutive years without taking a break from office for a full governance year.

108.   Any question about implementation of these transitional provisions shall be decided by the Board.

Appendix A
Regulations for Professional Registration and Revalidation

Established in December 2013.
Relating to bye-laws 11, 12 and 15

NOTE: These Regulations were approved by CILIP Council in September 2013. They are explained in a set of handbooks for members interested in working towards Certification (ACLIP), Chartered Membership (MCLIP) and Fellowship (FCLIP) and revalidation. All of these are available on the CILIP website. References to appendices etc. are to additional documents that are available as separate documents on the website. The Regulations apply from 1 December 2013

Section 1: Gaining CILIP Certification

2013 Regulations drawn up under Bye-law 11

1 Registration

All applicants must be current members of CILIP.
Members are able to enrol online via the CILIP website at: www.cilip.org.uk/professionalregistration

2 Application

Each applicant will submit a portfolio including:

*   Evaluative statement (Maximum 1,000 words)
*   Evidence to support evaluative statement
*   Curriculum Vitae
*   Job description
*   Initial PKSB assessment
*   Current PKSB assessment
*   Mentor/Mentee Agreement Form
*   Mentor/Mentee Completion Form

The evaluative statement must address the assessment criteria outlined in Section 3.

2.1 Notes on submission

*   All applications should be made via the CILIP Virtual Learning Environment. Hardcopy applications will be accepted where reasonable adjustments need to be made. Candidates should discuss this in advance with CILIP staff.
*   All applications must be in the English or Welsh language
*   All supporting evidence should be word processed

2.2 Confidentiality

All applications (electronic and hard copy) will be stored and treated in a confidential manner by the Professional Registration and Accreditation Board.

3 Assessment

All applications are assessed by the CILIP Professional Registration and Accreditation Board that is appointed by CILIP Council.
Assessment will be carried out against clearly identified criteria to ensure transparency and consistency of practice to all candidates.
All applicants will be notified of the outcome within ten working days of the date of the Professional Registration and Accreditation

Board meeting.

3.1 Assessment criteria

Members need to demonstrate they have:

1. Identified areas for improvement in their personal performance and undertaken activities to develop skills and enhance knowledge
2. Considered the organisational context of their service and examined their role within the organisation
3. Enhanced their knowledge of information services in order to understand the wider professional context within which they work

3.2 Form of assessment

The Professional Registration and Accreditation Board will determine an appropriate method for the additional assessment of any application, where necessary, which may include one or more of the following:

(a) a request for additional written information
(b) a professional interview of the candidate (where the Board is making reasonable adjustments for the candidate)

3.3 Admission to the Register of Certified Members

The date of admission to the register will normally be that on which the CILIP Professional Registration and Accreditation Board accepts the application.

Once admitted to the Register you must remain in membership of CILIP to retain the use of the post nominal letters ACLIP and to describe yourself as a Certified Member.

4 Appeals

Candidates whose applications are rejected have a right of Appeal, according to procedures approved by Council. A copy of the Appeals Procedures will be sent to unsuccessful candidates. (See Appendix 1 to these Regulations).

5 Reinstatement to the register

Any member re-joining CILIP who has previously achieved certification will be eligible to be reinstated onto the register of practitioners.

Members will be asked to revalidate in order to demonstrate that they have been maintaining their Continuing Professional Development whilst not in membership.

On successful completion, members will be re-instated and will be able to use their postnominals again.

6 Fees and charges

The fees for enrolment and submission will be determined annually by CILIP AGM.

7 Appendices

Appendix 1 Appeals procedure

1) An appeal may be made against a decision of the Professional Registration and Accreditation Board not to accept a candidate's Application for Certification.

2) A candidate whose submission is not accepted will be sent the following documents:-

(a) A letter informing the candidate of the decision and the date of the Professional Registration and Accreditation Board meeting at which it was made.

(b)   A copy of the assessment feedback from Board members, setting out the reasons for rejection.

(c)   A copy of this Appeals Procedure.

3)   A candidate who wishes to appeal against the decision of the Assessment Panel must do so within six weeks of the date of receipt of the letter referred to in 2. The Appeal must be made in writing to the Director of Professional Services and should state the grounds and reasons for the appeal.

4)   The only grounds on which an Appeal may be made are:

(a)   That all or part of the information used by the Assessment Panel was biased or incorrect due to no fault of the candidate and that the Panel did not know this at the time it took its decision.

(b)   That the Assessment Panel failed to follow its own published procedures and that this materially affected its decision.

(c)   The candidate wishes to challenge the decision of the Professional Registration and Accreditation Board; believing they fully meet the assessment criteria

5)   In the case of an appeal based on grounds stated in 4(a) and 4(b) above, the Director of Professional Services will decide whether there is a case for appeal. Where there is not s/he will inform the candidate of the reason for his ruling. In such cases there will be no further appeal.

6)   Where there is a case for appeal the Director of Professional Services will instruct a reassessment of the application by the Professional Registration and Accreditation Board. .

7)   In the case of an appeal based on grounds stated in 4(c), the Director of Professional Services will ask the external examiners to review the appeal to decide whether there is a case. Where there is not, the Director of Professional Services will inform the candidate of the reason for the decision. In such cases there will be no further appeal.

8)   Where external examiners have agreed there is a case for appeal the Director of Professional Services will instruct a reassessment of the application by the Professional Registration and Accreditation Board.

9)   Where the Professional Registration and Accreditation Board have been asked to reassess an application, the Director of Professional Services will inform the candidate of the final Board decision.

10)   All candidates are eligible to reapply.

Section 2: Gaining Chartered Membership

Regulations drawn up under Bye-law 11

1 Registration

All applicants must be current members of CILIP.
Members are able to enrol online via the CILIP website at www.cilip.org.uk/ professionalregistration

2 Application

Each applicant will submit a portfolio including:

- Evaluative statement (Maximum 1,000 words)
- Evidence to support evaluative statement
- Curriculum Vitae
- Job description
- Initial PKSB assessment
- Current PKSB assessment
- Mentor/Mentee Agreement Form
- Mentor/Mentee Completion Form

The evaluative statement must address the assessment criteria outlined in Section 3.

2.1 Notes on submission

- All applications should be made via the CILIP Virtual Learning Environment. Hardcopy applications will be accepted where reasonable adjustments need to be made. Candidates should discuss this in advance with CILIP staff.
- All applications must be in the English or Welsh language
- All supporting evidence should be word processed

2.2 Confidentiality

All applications (electronic and hard copy) will be stored and treated in a confidential manner by the Professional Registration and Accreditation Board.

3 Assessment

All applications are assessed by the CILIP Professional Registration and Accreditation Board that is appointed by CILIP Council.
Assessment will be carried out against clearly identified criteria to ensure transparency and consistency of practice to all candidates.
All applicants will be notified of the outcome within ten working days of the date of the Professional Registration and Accreditation Board meeting.

3.1 Assessment criteria

Members need to demonstrate they have:

1. Identified areas for improvement in their personal performance, undertaken activities to develop skills, applied these in practice, and reflected on the process and outcomes

2. Examined the organisational context of their service, evaluated service performance, shown the ability to implement or recommend improvement, and reflected on actual or desired outcomes

3. Enhanced their knowledge of the wider professional context and reflected on areas of current interest

3.2 Forms of assessment

The Professional Registration and Accreditation Board will determine an appropriate method for the additional assessment of any application, where necessary, which may include one or more of the following:

(a) a request for additional written information
(b) a professional interview of the candidate (where the Board is making reasonable adjustments for the candidate)

4.3 Admission to the Register of Chartered Members

The date of admission to the register will normally be that on which the Professional Registration and Accreditation Board accepts the application.

Once admitted to the Register you must remain in membership of CILIP to retain the use of the post nominal letters MCLIP and to describe yourself as a Chartered Member.

5 Reinstatement to the register

Any member re-joining CILIP who has previously achieved chartership will be eligible to be reinstated onto the register of practitioners.

Members will be asked to revalidate in order to demonstrate that they have been maintaining their Continuing Professional Development whilst not in membership.

On successful completion, members will be re-instated and will be able to use their postnominals again.

6 Fees and charges

The fees for enrolment and submission will be determined annually by CILIP AGM.

7 Appendices

Appendix 1 Appeals procedure

1) An appeal may be made against a decision of the Professional Registration and Accreditation Board not to accept a candidate's Application for Chartership.

2) A candidate whose submission is not accepted will be sent the following documents:-

(a) A letter informing the candidate of the decision and the date of the Professional Registration and Accreditation Board meeting at which it was made.
(b) A copy of the assessment feedback from Board members, setting out the reasons for rejection.
(c) A copy of this Appeals Procedure.

3) A candidate who wishes to appeal against the decision of the Assessment Panel must do so within six weeks of the date of receipt of the letter referred to in 2. The Appeal must be made in writing to the Director of Professional Services and should state the grounds and reasons for the appeal.

4) The only grounds on which an Appeal may be made are:

(a) That all or part of the information used by the Assessment Panel was biased or incorrect due to no fault of the candidate and that the Panel did not know this at the time it took its decision.
(b) That the Assessment Panel failed to follow its own published procedures and that this materially affected its decision.
(c) The candidate wishes to challenge the decision of the Professional Registration and Accreditation

Board; believing they fully meet the assessment criteria

5) In the case of an appeal based on grounds stated in 4(a) and 4(b) above, the Director of Professional Services will decide whether there is a case for appeal. Where there is not s/he will inform the candidate of the reason for his ruling. In such cases there will be no further appeal.

6) Where there is a case for appeal the Director of Professional Services will instruct a reassessment of the application by the Professional Registration and Accreditation Board. .

7) In the case of an appeal based on grounds stated in 4(c), the Director of Professional Services will ask the external examiners to review the appeal to decide whether there is a case. Where there is not, the Director of Professional Services will inform the candidate of the reason for the decision. In such cases there will be no further appeal.

8) Where external examiners have agreed there is a case for appeal the Director of Professional Services will instruct a reassessment of the application by the Professional Registration and Accreditation Board.

9) Where the Professional Registration and Accreditation Board have been asked to reassess an application, the Director of Professional Services will inform the candidate of the final Board decision.

10) All candidates are eligible to reapply.

Section 3: Chartered Fellow

Regulations drawn up under Bye-law 11

1 Registration

All applicants must be current members of CILIP. Members are able to enrol online via the CILIP website at www.cilip.org.uk/ professionalregistration

2 Application

Each applicant will submit a portfolio including:

- Evaluative statement (Maximum 1,000 words)
- Evidence to support evaluative statement
- Curriculum Vitae
- Job description
- Initial PKSB assessment
- Current PKSB assessment
- Supporting letters of which one must be from the mentor

The evaluative statement must address the assessment criteria outlined in Section 3.

2.1 Notes on submission

- All applications should be made via the CILIP Virtual Learning Environment. Hardcopy applications will be accepted where reasonable adjustments need to be made. Candidates should discuss this in advance with CILIP staff.
- All applications must be in the English or Welsh language
- All supporting evidence should be word processed

2.2 Confidentiality

All applications (electronic and hard copy) will be stored and treated in a confidential manner by the Professional Registration and Accreditation Board.

3 Assessment

All applications are assessed by the CILIP Professional Registration and Accreditation Board that is appointed by CILIP Council.

Assessment will be carried out against clearly identified criteria to ensure transparency and consistency of practice to all candidates.

All applicants will be notified of the outcome within ten working days of the date of the Professional Registration and Accreditation Board meeting.

3.1 Assessment Criteria

Members need to demonstrate they have:

1. Identified areas for improvement in their personal performance, undertaken activities to develop skills, applied these in practice, and reflected on the process and outcomes
2. Examined the organisational context of their work and evidenced substantial achievement in professional practice
3. Established their commitment to, and enhanced their knowledge of, the information professions in order to have made a significant contribution to all or part of the profession(s)

4.2 Forms of Assessment

The Professional Registration and Accreditation Board will determine an appropriate method for the additional assessment of any application, where necessary, which may include one or more of the following:

(a) a request for additional written information from either the candidate or a referee

(b) a professional interview of the candidate (where the Board is making reasonable adjustments for the candidate)

4.3 Admission to the Register

Date of Registration as a Fellow will normally be that on which the Professional Registration and Accreditation Board accepts the application.

Once admitted to the Register you must remain in membership of CILIP in order to retain your post-nominal letters and to describe yourself as a Chartered Fellow.

5 Reinstatement to the register of Chartered Fellows

Any member re-joining CILIP who has previously achieved fellowship will be eligible to be reinstated onto the register of practitioners.

Members will be asked to revalidate in order to demonstrate that they have been maintaining their Continuing Professional Development whilst not in membership.

On successful completion, members will be re-instated and will be able to use their postnominals again.

6 Fees and charges

The fees for enrolment and submission will be determined annually by CILIP AGM.

7 Appendices

Appendix 1 Appeals procedure

1) An appeal may be made against a decision of the Professional Registration and Accreditation Board not to accept a candidate's Application for Chartership.

2) A candidate whose submission is not accepted will be sent the following documents:-

(a) A letter informing the candidate of the decision and the date of the Professional Registration and Accreditation Board meeting at which it was made.

(b) A copy of the assessment feedback from Board members, setting out the reasons for rejection.

(c) A copy of this Appeals Procedure.

3) A candidate who wishes to appeal against the decision of the Assessment Panel must do so within six weeks of the date of receipt of the letter referred to in 2. The Appeal must be made in writing to the Director of Professional Services and should state the grounds and reasons for the appeal.

4) The only grounds on which an Appeal may be made are:

(a) That all or part of the information used by the Assessment Panel was biased or incorrect due to no fault of the candidate and that the Panel did not know this at the time it took its decision.

(b) That the Assessment Panel failed to follow its own published procedures and that this materially affected its decision.

(c) The candidate wishes to challenge the decision of the Professional Registration and Accreditation

Board; believing they fully meet the assessment criteria

5) In the case of an appeal based on grounds stated in 4(a) and 4(b) above, the Director of Professional Services will decide whether there is a case for appeal. Where there is not s/he will inform the candidate of the reason for his ruling. In such cases there will be no further appeal.

6) Where there is a case for appeal the Director of Professional Services will instruct a reassessment of the application by the Professional Registration and Accreditation Board. .

7) In the case of an appeal based on grounds stated in 4(c), the Director of Professional Services will ask the external examiners to review the appeal to decide whether there is a case. Where there is not, the Director of Professional Services will inform the candidate of the reason for the decision. In such cases there will be no further appeal.

8) Where external examiners have agreed there is a case for appeal the Director of Professional Services will instruct a reassessment of the application by the Professional Registration and Accreditation Board.

9) Where the Professional Registration and Accreditation Board have been asked to reassess an application, the Director of Professional Services will inform the candidate of the final Board decision.

10) All candidates are eligible to reapply.

Section 4: CILIP Revalidation Scheme

Regulations drawn up under Bye-law 11

1 Registration

All applicants must be current members of CILIP.
   Members are able to enrol online via the CILIP website at
www.cilip.org.uk/professionalregistration

2 Application

2.1 Form of application

Each applicant will submit:

a. A CPD log
b. A statement reflecting on how development activities have contributed to their professional practice for the level being revalidated (Maximum 250 words)

2.2 Notes on Submission

* All applications should be made via the CILIP Virtual Learning Environment. Hardcopy applications will be accepted where reasonable adjustments need to be made. Candidates should discuss this in advance with CILIP staff.
* All applications must be in the English or Welsh language

2.2 Confidentiality

All applications (electronic and hard copy) will be stored and treated in a confidential manner by the Professional Registration and Accreditation Board.

3 Assessment

All applications are assessed by the CILIP Professional Registration and Accreditation Board that is appointed by CILIP Council.
   Assessment will be carried out against clearly identified criteria to ensure transparency and consistency of practice to all candidates.
   All applicants will be notified of the outcome immediately following assessment.

3.1 Criteria of assessment

Members need to demonstrate they have:

1. Spent a minimum of 20 hours per year on personal and professional development

2. Reflected on how development activities have contributed to their professional practice for the level being revalidated

Appendix B
Ethical Principles
Code of Professional Practice
CILIP Disciplinary Regulations

Introduction

Library and information professionals are frequently the essential link between information users and the information or piece of literature which they require. They therefore occupy a privileged position which carries corresponding responsibilities. In addition, whether they are self-employed or employed, their position is sometimes a sensitive one, which may impose a need to balance conflicting requirements.

The purpose of the Principles and Code which follow this introduction is to provide a framework to help library and information professionals, who are members of CILIP, to manage the responsibilities and sensitivities which figure prominently in their work. There is a statement of *Ethical Principles* and a more extended *Code of Professional Practice*, which applies these principles to the different groups and professionals to which our members must relate. The *Code* also makes some additional points with regard to professional behaviour. Given the diversity of the information profession, it is inevitable that not every statement in the *Code of Professional Practice* will be equally applicable to every member of CILIP. However, the *Ethical Principles* ought to command more general support, even though some members may not feel the force of each one of them to the same extent in their day-to-day experience. The *Principles* and *Code* assume that respect for duly enacted law is a fundamental responsibility for everybody.

By the terms of its Royal Charter, CILIP has a responsibility to 'the public good'. It is therefore anticipated that our *Ethical Principles* and our *Code of Professional Practice* may be of interest well beyond the immediate limits of the membership of CILIP, both to those whose work bears close comparison with ours, and also to those who may, from time to time, want a clear statement of our ethical principles and what we consider to be good professional practice.

Associated with these *Principles* and *Code*, there is a growing collection of practical examples, illustrating how information professionals and others can use the *Principles* and *Code* to help them cope with ethical dilemmas they may face. In further support of the *Principles* and *Code*, CILIP has established an Ethics Panel of experienced members of the profession, and they and the professional staff of CILIP are available to members who may need additional help in resolving ethical issues.

CILIP's Disciplinary Regulations provide that a Member will be guilty of professional misconduct if he/she has acted contrary to the aims, objects and interests of CILIP or in a manner unbecoming or prejudicial to the profession. In reaching decisions under the Disciplinary Procedure, regard will be had to the *Statement of Ethical Principles* and the *Code of Professional Practice* and Members should therefore be aware that failure to comply with the *Principles* and *Code* may, depending on the circumstances, be a ground for disciplinary action.

Ethical Principles

The conduct of members should be characterised by the following general principles, presented here in no particular order of priority:

1. Concern for the public good in all professional matters, including respect for diversity within society, and the promoting of equal opportunities and human rights.

2. Concern for the good reputation of the information profession.

3. Commitment to the defence, and the advancement, of access to information, ideas and works of the imagination.

4. Provision of the best possible service within available resources.

5. Concern for balancing the needs of actual and potential users and the reasonable demands of employers.

6. Equitable treatment of all information users.

7. Impartiality, and avoidance of inappropriate bias, in acquiring and evaluating information and in mediating it to other information users.

8. Respect for confidentiality and privacy in dealing with information users.

9. Concern for the conservation and preservation of our information heritage in all formats.

10. Respect for, and understanding of, the integrity of information items and for the intellectual effort of those who created them.

11. Commitment to maintaining and improving personal professional knowledge, skills and competences.

12. Respect for the skills and competences of all others, whether information professionals or information users, employers or colleagues.

Code of Professional Practice

This Code applies the ethical principles to the different groups and interests to which CILIP members must relate. The Code also makes some additional points with regard to professional behaviour. The principles and values will differ in their relative importance according to context.

A Personal Responsibilities

People who work in the information profession have personal responsibilities which go beyond those immediately implied by their contract with their employers or clients. Members should therefore:

1. strive to attain the highest personal standard of professional knowledge and competence

2. ensure they are competent in those branches of professional practice in which qualifications and/or experience entitle them to engage by keeping abreast of developments in their areas of expertise

3. claim expertise in areas of library and information work or in other disciplines only where their skills and knowledge are adequate

B Responsibilities to Information and its Users

The behaviour of professionals who work with information should be guided by a regard for the interests and needs of information users. People working in the information profession also need to be conscious that they have responsibility for a growing heritage of information and data, irrespective of format. This includes works of the imagination as well as factual data. Members should therefore:

1. ensure that information users are aware of the scope and remit of the service being provided

2. make the process of providing information, and the standards and procedures governing that process, as clear and open as possible

3. avoid inappropriate bias or value judgements in the provision of services

4. protect the confidentiality of all matters relating to information users, including their enquiries, any services to be provided, and any aspects of the users' personal circumstances or business

5. deal fairly with the competing needs of information users, and resolve conflicting priorities with due regard for the urgency and importance of the matters being considered

6. deal promptly and fairly with any complaints from information users, and keep them informed about progress in the handling of their complaints.

7. ensure that the information systems and

services for which they are responsible are the most effective, within the resources available, in meeting the needs of users

8. ensure that the materials to which they provide access are those which are most appropriate to the needs of legitimate users of the service

9. defend the legitimate needs and interests of information users, while upholding the moral and legal rights of the creators and distributors of intellectual property

10. respect the integrity of information sources, and cite sources used, as appropriate

11. show an appropriate concern for the future information needs of society through the long term preservation and conservation of materials as required, as well as an understanding of proper records management.

C Responsibilities to Colleagues and the Information Community

The personal conduct of information professionals at work should promote the profession in the best possible manner at all times. Members should therefore:

1. act in ways that promote the profession positively, both to their colleagues and to the public at large

2. afford respect and understanding to other colleagues and professionals and acknowledge their ideas, contributions and work, wherever and whenever appropriate

3. refer to colleagues in a professional manner and not discredit or criticise their

work unreasonably or inappropriately

4. when working in an independent capacity, conduct their business in a professional manner that respects the legitimate rights and interests of others

5. encourage colleagues, especially those for whom they have a line-management responsibility, to maintain and enhance their professional knowledge and competence

6. refrain from ascribing views to, or speaking on behalf of, CILIP, unless specifically authorised to do so

7. report significant breaches of this Code to the appropriate authorities[1]

8. refrain from any behaviour in the course of their work which might bring the information profession into disrepute.

D Responsibilities to Society

One of the distinguishing features of professions is that their knowledge and skills are at the service of society at large, and do not simply serve the interests of the immediate customer. Members should therefore:

1. consider the public good, both in general and as it refers to particular vulnerable groups, as well as the immediate claims arising from their employment and their professional duties

---

1 The appropriate authority will vary depending on the context of the case. It may be CILIP, the employer, a regulatory body or an officer managing the 'whistle-blowing' procedure or some other body. It is not possible to be prescriptive.

2. promote equitable access for all members of society to public domain information of all kinds and in all formats

3. strive to achieve an appropriate balance within the law between demands from information users, the need to respect confidentiality, the terms of their employment, the public good and the responsibilities outlined in this Code

4. encourage and promote wider knowledge and acceptance of, and wider compliance with, this Code, both among colleagues in the information professions and more widely among those whom we serve.

E Responsibilities as Employees

Members who are employed have duties that go beyond the immediate terms of their employment contract. On occasion these may conflict with the immediate demands of their employer but be in the broader interest of the public and possibly the employer themselves.[2] Members should therefore:

1. develop a knowledge and understanding of the organisation in which they work and use their skills and expertise to promote the legitimate aims and objectives of their employer

2. avoid engaging in unethical practices during their work and bring to the attention of their employer any concerns they may have concerning the ethics or legality of specific decisions, actions or behaviour at work.

---

2 It is recognised that sometimes Members, acting as a representative of employers, have to make decisions that may impact adversely on levels of service or the employment of staff. This is not in itself unethical behaviour but there might be circumstances in which it could be – the lawfulness of the action or the way it is managed, for instance.

CILIP Disciplinary Regulations

Preamble

Professional practice is shaped by two key elements: knowledge and skills; ethics and conduct. As the regulatory body for library and information practice in the uk, CILIP provides a framework of qualification and accreditation to benchmark the knowledge and skills of professional practitioners. CILIP also prescribes a set of ethical principles and a code of professional conduct to benchmark the behaviour of professional practitioners. These disciplinary regulations set out the procedures to be followed when a complaint is made about the professional conduct of a cilip member.

Introduction

84. These regulations were made by the Council on 22 September 2011. They came into force on that date, superseding all previous disciplinary regulations.

    1. These regulations set out the procedures to be followed in the investigation and adjudication of any complaint that a Member may have acted in a manner contrary to the aims, objects and interests of CILIP or otherwise contrary to its Charter, Bye-Laws or Regulations, or in a manner prejudicial to his/her professional status or the reputation of CILIP. They are intended therefore to cover issues relating to the professional conduct of a Member. It will not normally be within the scope of these regulations to consider alleged grievances against a Member which are of an employment or contractual nature.

    2. Members are required to comply at all times with the ethical principles and Code of Professional Practice prescribed and published by CILIP. At all stages of these disciplinary procedures, regard will be had to any such ethical principles and/or Code of Professional Practice in force at the time of the conduct which is the subject of the complaint. Failure to comply with any such ethical principles or Code may be a ground for disciplinary action.

    3. These regulations relate to the conduct of Individual Members (but not Organisation Members) of CILIP.

    4. There are broadly four stages to these Regulations: (1) a complaint is made and investigated; (2) if there is a case to answer, a consent order may be offered or a disciplinary hearing is held; (3) there is a right of appeal against the outcome of a disciplinary hearing; and (4) a decision to suspend or expel a Member must also be endorsed by the Council.

Invoking the Disciplinary Procedure

5. A member of CILIP or any other person may make a formal complaint in writing to CILIP (by email or letter to the Chief Executive) concerning the professional conduct of a Member.

6. The Chief Executive (or his/her nominee) shall if possible acknowledge a formal complaint within seven working days of receipt.

7. Where the Chief Executive (in consultation with the President) deems it appropriate, the complaint will be investigated under these regulations provided that it is made within six months from the time when it arose.

8. CILIP can itself initiate a complaint where the Chief Executive becomes aware of any fact or matter concerning the professional conduct of a Member which in his/her opinion (in consultation with the President) warrants investigation under these regulations.

Grounds for Disciplinary Action

9. It shall be a ground for disciplinary action if a Member is guilty of professional misconduct. This is defined as a Member having acted:

    (i)   contrary to the aims, objects and interests of CILIP, or otherwise contrary to its Charter, Bye-Laws or Regulations or
    (ii) in a manner prejudicial to his/her professional status or the reputation of CILIP.

Stage I – Disciplinary Investigation

Appointment of an Investigating Officer

10. Where a complaint or matter is to be investigated, the President shall appoint an Investigating Officer to consider the matter further.

11. The Investigating Officer shall be a member of the Disciplinary Panel (other than the President and Chair) who has no interest in the matter and has received appropriate training in the role.

12. Notwithstanding the requirement for the annual appointment of members to the Disciplinary Panel, an Investigating Officer shall continue in that role until the matter he/she was appointed to deal with has been concluded.

Duties and powers of the Investigating Officer

13. The Investigating Officer shall consider the matter and decide whether or not in his/her opinion there is a case to be answered, and if there is then whether to proceed under paragraph 20(ii) or (iii) below.

14. In considering the matter, the Investigating Officer shall make such inquiries as he/she considers necessary to establish the facts and circumstances by whatever means he/she considers appropriate, including requesting a response from the Member within a specified period of not less than ten working days.

15. The Member shall be informed, upon the raising of any questions with him/her, that such questions are asked in connection with possible disciplinary proceedings.

16. The Member is expected to comply with the reasonable requirements of the Investigating Officer.

17. The identity of the complainant shall be made known to the Member unless the Investigating Officer determines that there are compelling reasons why the complainant should not be identified taking into account, amongst other things, the need for the Member to fully understand the nature of the complaint against him/her.

18. The Investigating Officer shall seek to complete his/her inquiries within thirty working days of the matter being referred to him/her. CILIP will keep the complainant and the Member informed of the timetable.

19. Upon completion of the investigation, the Investigating Officer shall decide whether in his/her opinion:

    (i)   there is no case to answer; or
    (ii)   there is a case to answer and the Member to be invited to consent to a disciplinary order imposing a written warning and/or written reprimand under paragraph 30 below; or
    (iii) there is a case to answer and the matter to proceed to a disciplinary hearing under paragraph 31 below.

The Investigating Officer's Decision – No case to answer

20. If the Investigating Officer decides that there is no case to answer, the complainant (if applicable) will be informed, giving him/her brief written reasons for the decision and notifying him/her in writing of his/her right to request a review of the decision.

21. CILIP shall at the same time inform the Member of the decision in writing with brief written reasons, advising him/her that the complainant has the right to ask for a review of the decision, and therefore that the matter may be reviewed.

Review of decision

22. Provided the complainant makes his/her request for a review in writing and within twenty working days from the date of the notification sent to him/her under paragraph 21 above, the Investigation Officer's decision will be reviewed by the Vice-President or if he/she is not available, by a Past President ("the reviewer").

23. The Investigation Officer's decision will be reviewed on the basis of the written request for the review together with the papers that were before the Investigating Officer when he/she reached his/her decision. If possible, the review will be carried out within thirty working days of receipt of the request for a review.

24. The outcome of the review will be:

    (i)   To confirm the decision of the Investigating Officer that there is no case to answer; or
    (ii)   To remit the matter back to the Investigating Officer for reconsideration if the reviewer is of the opinion that one or more of the following apply:
           (a) Fresh evidence of a material nature has become available to the complainant since the Investigation Officer's decision; or
           (b) The Investigating Officer's decision was not one which could reasonably have been arrived at upon due consideration of the

facts and matters before him/her; or

(c) The Investigating Officer was biased; or

(d) The Investigating Officer did not adequately investigate the complaint in accordance with these regulations.

25. CILIP shall inform both the Member and the complainant of the review decision. There shall be no right of appeal by any party against the review decision.

26. Where the reviewer remits the matter for reconsideration under paragraph 25(ii)c above, the President shall appoint a different Investigating Officer to reconsider the matter.

27. In reconsidering any matter, the Investigating Officer must have regard to any written reasons given by the reviewer for remitting the matter.

28. If, after reconsideration of the matter, the Investigating Officer decides again that there is no case to answer, there shall be no further right of review.

The Investigating Officer's decision – Case to answer (with offer of Consent Order)

29. If the Investigating Officer decides that there is a case to answer under paragraph 20(ii) above:

29.1 CILIP will write to the Member outlining the alleged conduct or circumstances alleged to amount to professional misconduct with brief written reasons for the decision, inviting him/her to respond in writing within 20 working days consenting to a disciplinary order imposing a written warning and/or a written reprimand (but no other form of disciplinary action).

29.2 If the Member gives his/her written consent within 20 working days, CILIP will make the disciplinary order as proposed by CILIP and consented to by the Member.

29.3 If the Member either refuses consent or does not reply within 20 working days, the matter will proceed to a hearing under paragraph 31 below.

29.4 CILIP will keep the complainant informed of actions taken under this paragraph with brief written reasons for any disciplinary order made under paragraph 30.2 above.

The Investigating Officer's decision – Case to answer (at disciplinary hearing)

30. If the Investigating Officer decides that there is a case to answer under paragraph 20(iii) above (or if paragraph 30.3 applies):

30.1 CILIP will inform the Member and the complainant in writing that the matter will proceed to a disciplinary hearing.

30.2 The matter will be referred to the Chair of the Disciplinary Panel.

Stage II – Disciplinary Hearing

31. Upon receiving a referral under paragraph 31.2 above, the Chair of the Disciplinary Panel shall appoint a Disciplinary Hearing Group (DHG) to hear the matter.

Composition of the disciplinary hearing group (DHG)

32. In each case, the DHG shall comprise any three members of the Disciplinary Panel, including the Chair of the Disciplinary Panel, who have not served in the same

matter and who have no interest in the matter.

33. The Chair of the Disciplinary Panel shall chair the DHG. If the Chair of the Disciplinary Panel has an interest in the matter or if for any other reason he/she is unable to sit on the DHG, he/she will nominate a third member of the DHG in his/her place (from among the members of the Disciplinary Panel) and will then nominate one of the three members of the DHG to serve as Chair.

34. Notwithstanding the requirement for the annual appointment of members to the Disciplinary Panel, a DHG shall continue with its original membership until it has concluded the matter it was appointed to deal with.

The parties in the proceedings before the DHG

35. The Investigating Officer shall, on behalf of CILIP, present the case before the DHG, and for this purpose may instruct a representative (who may be legally qualified). Any costs incurred are to be borne by CILIP.

36. The Member shall be entitled to be represented by any person (who may be legally qualified). Any costs incurred are to be borne by the Member.

Procedure of the DHG

37. The hearing of the case shall be conducted as outlined below except where to do so would be unjust or inconvenient, in which case the Chair of the DHG may modify the procedure to the extent that he/she deems necessary, provided that

the result is fair to the Member under complaint.

Procedure before the DHG
Notification of hearing and exchange of information

38. Following the appointment of the DHG, CILIP shall serve on the Member at least fifteen working days' written notice of the date, time and place of the hearing.

39. The notice referred to at paragraph 39 above shall include

(i) particulars of the conduct or circumstances alleged by the Investigating Officer to amount to professional misconduct;

(ii) a summary of the facts and matters relied upon by the Investigating Officer, including copies of any written statement and other document that it is proposed to put before the DHG;

(iii) the names and addresses of any witnesses whom the Investigating Officer intends to call in person and an outline of what each witness is expected to say;

(iv) an invitation to the Member to attend the hearing and/or to submit written representations for consideration by the DHG.

40. At least five working days prior to the date of the hearing, the Member shall:

(i) confirm whether or not he/she intends to attend the hearing and, if so, the name of any person who will be accompanying or representing him/her.

(ii) submit:
(a) brief particulars of any defence

intended to be made;

(b) a summary of the facts and matters that will be relied upon in that defence, including copies of any written statement and other document that he/she intends to refer to; and

(c) the names and addresses of any witnesses whom he/she intends to call in person and an outline of what each witness is expected to say.

41. Neither party shall, without the consent of the other or the permission of the DHG, rely on any statement or document or call any witness other than those provided or identified under paragraphs 40 and 41 above.

Adjournment

42. At the request of either party or at his/her own volition, the Chair of the DHG may, at any time, adjourn the hearing if satisfied that it is in the interests of justice so to do. An application for the adjournment of a hearing that has not begun may be agreed between the parties.

43. In the event that any member of the DHG (sitting at the hearing of a case) is unwilling or unable to hear an entire case and the matter cannot be dealt with by adjournment of the hearing, then the Chair of the Disciplinary Panel shall appoint a new DHG and the case shall be re-heard. Members of the DHG who sat previously and were not the member unable or unwilling to continue shall be eligible to be appointed to the new DHG.

The absence of the Member

44. If at the hearing the Member is not present in person or represented, the DHG may proceed to consider the matter in the Member's absence if it is satisfied that notice was properly served upon him/her in accordance with paragraphs 39 and 40 above.

Joinder of cases

45. The DHG may hear two or more complaints against a Member at the same time.

Joinder of members

46. The DHG may also hear complaints against two or more Members at the same time if it considers it just to do so.

Proof and evidence

47.

(i) The burden of proving the alleged professional misconduct shall lie upon the Investigating Officer

(ii) The professional misconduct shall be proved by the Investigating Officer on a balance of probabilities

(iii) The DHG shall not be bound by strict rules of evidence

Private hearing

48. The hearing shall be conducted in private unless the Member requests otherwise (such request to be decided by the Chair of the DHG at his /her sole discretion) save that the complainant (where applicable) shall be permitted to attend unless the Chair of the DHG decides otherwise at his/her sole discretion.

49. The Chief Executive of CILIP or his/her nominee and such other persons as are reasonably required by CILIP for secretarial/recording purposes may also be in attendance at the hearing.

Order of proceedings

50. The order of proceedings for the hearing, unless the Chair of the DHG otherwise directs, will be as follows:

    (I) submissions by, or on behalf of, the investigating officer;

    (ii) hearing of any witnesses called by the investigating officer followed by cross-examination of such witnesses by, or on behalf, of, the member;

    (iii) submissions by, or on behalf of, the member;

    (iv) hearing of any witnesses called by the member followed by cross-examination of such witnesses by, or on behalf, of the investigating officer;

    (v) closing submissions by, or on behalf, of the investigating officer;

    (vi) closing submissions by, or on behalf, of the member;

    (vii) after retiring as necessary, the DHG shall advise the parties (if present) whether or not it finds any allegation of professional misconduct proven.

51. Members of the DHG may themselves at any stage question witnesses, parties or representatives as they think fit.

Order of proceedings following a finding of professional misconduct

52. The Investigating Officer shall, following a finding of professional misconduct, inform the DHG of any further circumstances known to CILIP, whether favourable or adverse to the Member that might be relevant to any course of action which the DHG might take.

53. The Member shall then be entitled to respond on the matter of disciplinary action.

Decision

54. The DHG may, following a finding of professional misconduct, order any one or more courses of disciplinary action in accordance with paragraph 57 below.

55. Decisions of the DHG at all stages shall made by a simple majority.

Disciplinary action

56. Any one or more of the following courses of disciplinary action may be ordered by the DHG as is considered appropriate (and on such terms and conditions and for such period as is considered appropriate) having regard to the nature and seriousness of the professional misconduct, the Member's character and past record, and to any other relevant circumstances:

    (i) a written warning and/or written reprimand; and/or

    (ii) a requirement for the member to give a written undertaking as to future conduct; and/or

    (iii) a requirement for the member to undertake specific training and/or to report regularly to or to seek guidance from a senior colleague; and/or

    (iv) suspension or removal of the member from any office within cilip, its groups and/or branches; and/or

    (v) alteration of the membership status of the member; and/or

    (vi) a recommendation to the council that the member be suspended from membership for a fixed period of time; or

    (vii) a recommendation to the council that the member be expelled from membership of CILIP.

57. If, notwithstanding its finding that the Member is guilty of professional misconduct, the DHG is of the opinion that in all the circumstances, no such order is appropriate, it may make no order.

58. The DHG may also, wherever it considers appropriate and whether or not it decides to order any disciplinary action, communicate to the Member its advice as to his/her future conduct.

59. Where the DHG determines to recommend to the Council that the Member be suspended or expelled from membership of CILIP, the Member shall be suspended from membership on an interim basis pending the Council's resolution in the matter, and during such interim suspension is entitled to no privileges of membership.

Notification of decision

60. CILIP shall serve on the Member written notice of the decision of the DHG together with any disciplinary action ordered as promptly as is practicable after the conclusion of the hearing, and whether or not the Member attended the hearing. Where there has been a finding of professional misconduct, the notice shall inform the Member of his/her right of appeal.

61. CILIP shall also inform the complainant of the decision of the DHG.

Reasons

62. The DHG shall also provide the Member with brief written reasons for the decision as soon as is practicable.

Recording

63. The proceedings before the DHG shall be recorded and a copy of the recording shall be provided to the Member upon written request by him/her and upon payment by him/her of the costs involved in making the copy.

Stage III – Appeal
Right of appeal

64. A Member may, on the grounds set out at paragraph 70 below, appeal to the Appeal Hearing Group against a finding of the DHG that he/she is guilty of professional misconduct and/or against any disciplinary action ordered by the DHG.

65. There is no right of appeal by a complainant against any aspect of a decision by the DHG.

Notice of intention to appeal

66. Notice of intention to appeal shall be lodged with the CILIP Chief Executive in writing within five working days of service of the DHG's decision.

67. If notice of intention to appeal is lodged within the time permitted, the order of the DHG shall not take effect until the determination of the matter on appeal.

Grounds of appeal

68. The Member shall be permitted a further ten working days to submit a written statement setting out the grounds upon which the appeal is brought and any facts and matters relied upon by him/her, including, where applicable, a description of any fresh evidence upon which the Member intends to rely.

69.   An appeal may be made on the following grounds:

(i)   that the disciplinary hearing did not follow due process and/or

(ii)   there is fresh evidence of a material nature which for good reason was unavailable to the DHG, which might cause the Appeal Hearing Group to reconsider the DHG's finding of professional misconduct and/or the disciplinary action ordered by the DHG.

70.   CILIP shall inform the complainant where a notice of intention to appeal/grounds of appeal are lodged by the Member.

Appointment and composition of the appeal hearing group (AHG)

71.   When an appeal is made on grounds set out at paragraph 70 above, the President shall establish an AHG of three persons to hear the appeal and shall appoint one of those three persons as the Chair of the AHG.

72.   The three persons shall be drawn from the members of the Disciplinary Panel who have had no previous involvement with the disciplinary case which is under appeal, and have no interest in the matter.

73.   Notwithstanding the requirement for the annual appointment of members to the Disciplinary Panel, an AHG shall continue with its original membership until the appeal of the matter it was appointed to deal with has been concluded.

The parties in proceedings before the AHG

74.   The Member shall be the Appellant at this stage and he/she shall be entitled to be represented by any person (who may be legally qualified). Any costs are to be borne by the Member.

75.   The Investigating Officer shall act on behalf of CILIP as respondent to the Appeal and for this purpose may instruct a representative (who may be legally qualified). Any costs will be borne by CILIP.

Procedure before the AHG

76.   On an appeal, the AHG shall consider the Member's Grounds of Appeal together with any fresh evidence of a material nature which for good reason was unavailable to the DHG; and such other material as the Chair of the AHG considers appropriate, which will usually include the record of the hearing before the DHG, and the documents, statements and other evidence produced to the DHG.

77.   The hearing of an appeal before the AHG shall be conducted as outlined below except where to do so would be unjust, in which case Chair of the AHG may modify the procedure to the extent that he/she deems necessary provided the result is fair to the Member.

Procedure for an Appeal
Notification of hearing and exchange of information

78.   Following the appointment of an AHG, CILIP shall serve on the Member (at this stage the Appellant) at least fifteen working days' written notice of the date, time and place of the appeal hearing. Normally the appeal hearing should be held if possible within forty working days of receipt of the Member's Notice of Intention to Appeal.

79. At least ten working days prior to the date of the hearing, the Appellant shall:

    (i) confirm whether or not he/she intends to attend the hearing and, if so, the name of any person who will be accompanying or representing him/her.

    (ii) if he/she wishes to adduce fresh written evidence or to call any fresh witness evidence, submit (with an explanation as to why such evidence was previously unavailable):
        (a) any such fresh written evidence that he/she wishes to rely upon;
        (b) the names and addresses of any witnesses whom he/she wishes to call in person to give any fresh evidence, and an outline of what each witness is expected to say.

80. At least five working days prior to the date of the hearing, the Investigating Officer shall provide the Appellant with any fresh evidence which he/she wishes to rely upon in light of the appeal, together with the names and addresses of any witnesses which he/she wishes to call in person and an outline of what each witness is expected to say.

Adjournment

81. At the request of a party or at his/her own volition, the Chair of the AHG may at any time adjourn the appeal hearing if satisfied that it is in the interests of justice to do so. An application for the adjournment of an appeal hearing that has not begun may be agreed between the parties.

82. In the event that any member of the AHG (sitting at the hearing of a case) is unwilling or unable to hear an entire case and the matter cannot be dealt with by adjournment of the hearing, then the President shall appoint a new AHG and the case shall be re-heard. Members of the AHG who sat previously and were not the member unable or unwilling to continue shall be eligible to be appointed to the new AHG.

The absence of the appellant

83. If at the appeal hearing, the Appellant is not present in person or represented, the AHG may proceed to consider the matter in the Appellant's absence if it is satisfied that notice was properly served upon him/her in accordance with paragraph 79 above.

Private Hearing

84. The hearing shall be conducted in private unless the Appellant requests otherwise (such request to be decided by the Chair of the AHG at his /her sole discretion) save that the complainant (where applicable) shall be permitted to attend unless the Chair of the AHG decides otherwise at his/her sole discretion.

85. The Chief Executive of CILIP or his/her nominee and such other persons as are reasonably required by CILIP for secretarial/recording purposes may also be in attendance at the hearing.

Order of proceedings

86. The order of proceedings for the Appeal hearing, unless the Chair of the AHG otherwise directs, will be as follows:

    (i) The Appellant shall outline the grounds of his/her appeal, citing (with the agreement of the AHG) any fresh evidence;

(ii) Hearing of any witnesses called by the Appellant (limited to fresh evidence with the agreement of the AHG) followed by a cross-examination of such witnesses by, or on behalf of the Investigating Officer;

(iii) Response by, or on behalf of the Investigating Officer;

(iv) Hearing of any witnesses called by the Investigating Officer (with the agreement of the AHG) followed by a cross-examination of such witnesses by, or on behalf of the Appellant;

(v) Closing submissions by, or on behalf of the Appellant.

87. Members of the AHG may themselves at any stage question witnesses, parties or representatives as they think fit.

Decision

88. The AHG may affirm, vary or rescind any finding or order of the DHG and may substitute any other finding or order (on such terms and conditions, if any) as it considers appropriate which the DHG might have made.

89. All decisions of the AHG shall be reached by a simple majority.

Notification of decision by the AHG

90. CILIP shall serve on the Member written notice of the decision of the AHG as promptly as is practicable after the conclusion of the hearing, and whether or not the Member attended the hearing. CILIP will also inform the complainant of the outcome of the appeal.

Final decision

91. A decision of the AHG is final.

Reasons

92. The AHG shall also provide the Member with brief written reasons for its decision as soon as is practicable.

Recording

93. The proceedings before the AHG shall be recorded and a copy of the recording shall be provided to the Member upon written request by him/her and upon payment by him/her of the costs involved in making the copy.

Stage IV – Endorsement by Council of recommendation to suspend or expel member

94. A recommendation that the Member be suspended or expelled from membership of CILIP shall not take effect without being endorsed by the CILIP Council.

95. The Member shall be advised of the date of the meeting of the Council at which the recommendation will be proposed for endorsement. Whenever possible, the matter will be resolved at the next meeting of the Council.

96. The Council shall meet in private to consider the recommended suspension or expulsion of a Member and shall receive from the President a paper summarizing the disciplinary proceedings in the matter, to include the alleged professional misconduct, a summary of the Member's defence and drawing attention to any aspects of the matter which are particularly complex or important, and the reasons for the recommended suspension or expulsion.

97. The Council shall decide either:

(a)   to endorse the recommended suspension or expulsion; or

(b)   to refer the matter back to the DHG (or AHG as appropriate), with a brief summary of its reasons for the referral and an instruction that the matter be reconsidered.

98.   The Council shall reach its decision by a simple majority of those present and entitled to vote. Any Council member who has had a prior involvement in the case (whether as a member of the Disciplinary Panel or otherwise) shall not be entitled to participate in the Council's discussion or vote on the recommendation.

99.   The Member shall be notified of the Council's decision as soon as practicable after the meeting.

General provisions

Publication of findings

100.   The President shall report to the next meeting of CILIP Council on any completed disciplinary case (save for a case which Council has already considered). Unless otherwise recommended by the DHG (or AHG as appropriate), any such report shall be anonomised.

101.   Following the report of each disciplinary case to the Council (or a decision by Council under paragraph 98(a) above, CILIP shall

(i)   publish the outcome of the matter in such form and manner and to such extent as the Chief Executive in consultation with the President shall deem necessary (taking into account any recommendations made by the

DHG, AHG or Council regarding publication of the matter) save that there will be no publication where no disciplinary action is taken unless the Member so requests (and the Chief Executive in consultation with the President agrees to publish the matter).

(ii)   inform the complainant (if applicable, and if not previously informed) in writing of the outcome of the complaint.

102.   If a Member subject to a complaint resigns his/her membership, or if for any other reason his/her membership terminates whilst the matter remains unresolved under these Disciplinary Regulations, the Chief Executive may at his/her discretion and in consultation with the President, cause to be published such resignation/termination of membership and inform the complainant in the manner set out above.

Time limits

103.   All time limits set out in these regulations shall be doubled when the correspondence address held by CILIP for the Member concerned is outside the UK.

Service of notices/documents

104.   Save as provided for at paragraph 106 below, any notice or other documents required by these regulations to be sent to or served on a Member or a complainant may be delivered either personally or electronically or by first class post.

105.   Any notice required to be sent to the member under paragraphs 30(i) (offer of consent order), 39 (notice of disciplinary

hearing), 61 (notice of disciplinary decision and right to appeal), 79 (notice of appeal hearing), 91 (notice of appeal decision) and 100 (notice of Council decision) shall be delivered personally (by handing to the member) or by recorded delivery post.

106. Save as provided for at paragraph 106 above, any such notice or document shall:

    (a) If delivered personally, be handed to the Member (or complainant as appropriate) or left at the last address of the Member or complainant concerned which is recorded by him/her with CILIP;

    (b) If served by post or electronically, be sent to the last address (postal or email as appropriate) of the Member or complainant concerned which is recorded by him/her with CILIP.

107. Service shall be deemed to have taken place:

    (a) If delivered personally, when handed to the Member (or complainant as appropriate) or left at the relevant address;

    (b) If sent by first class post on the second day following that on which it was posted unless at the place of receipt that latter day is a Sunday or a public holiday in which case service shall be deemed to have occurred on the first day thereafter which is not one of such exceptional days;

    (c) If sent by recorded delivery, on the date of delivery as confirmed by the Royal Mail;

    (d) If sent electronically, on the same day it was sent.

Archiving

108. The written record of each Disciplinary Case shall be kept on file by the CILIP Governance Unit for five years after the conclusion of that case. In any Case where a Member has been expelled from membership of CILIP, the written record shall be kept indefinitely except that, in the event of re-instatement to membership, such record shall be kept only for five years thereafter.

Retrospection

109. These regulations supersede all previous disciplinary regulations. They cannot be applied retrospectively to any Disciplinary Case heard under previous regulations.

UK law

UK law shall apply in resolving any disputes regarding the application of this procedure.

Appendix C
Regulations for the Retired Members Guild

Bye-law 42

Objects

The objects of the Retired Members Guild are to encourage Members of the Chartered Institute of Library and Information Professionals to remain in membership after retirement, to foster their social interaction, and to afford them the opportunity of making a positive contribution to librarianship and information science.

Activities

1. To support the efforts of the Chartered Institute of Library and Information Professionals for the improvement of libraries of all types.

2. To keep Members in touch with one another by arranging meetings and conferences and by the publication of a newsletter.

3. To seek out and make known, further benefits available for retired members.

4. To assist in the work of appropriate voluntary organizations by publicizing their activities and maintaining a register of expertise.

5. To undertake historical research and the conservation of records relating to the history of the Institute and its Branches and Groups.

Membership

Membership of the Guild is open to all personal Members of the Chartered Institute of Library and Information Professionals and to representatives of institutional members appointed in accordance with the bye-laws of the Institute. Persons and institutions shall become members of the Guild on notifying a desire to do so to the Secretary of the Guild and on of payment of the additional subscription.

The Guild shall be able to admit, at the discretion of the National Committee, persons who cannot be Fellows or Members of the Chartered Institute of Library and Information Professionals, as Personal Affiliates. Such members will not have the right to vote and will not be entitled to hold office. They will pay such annual subscriptions as may be determined by the National Committee.

Subordinate Bodies

The Guild Committee shall have authority to establish subordinate bodies on a regional or subject basis. The Committee shall require the Chair or Secretary of any such subordinate body to report regularly on its activities. The National Committee shall lay down such provisions for the conduct of business of subordinate bodies as it sees fit.

Officers

The Officers of the Guild shall be:

Chair
Secretary
Treasurer
Editor

Guild Committee

The affairs of the Guild shall be governed by a committee comprising the officers of the Guild and six elected members of the Guild. In addition the committee may co-opt up to three members of the Guild to the committee.

The Guild Year

The Year for all Guild activities, including terms of office and accounts shall be the calendar year.

Terms of Office

Officers of the Guild shall hold office for two years. Other committee members shall hold office for two years. In both cases terms shall commence on 1 January following election.

Elections

The election of officers and committee members shall be conducted in accordance with the regulations set out in Annex A (available upon application).

Committee Procedure

The Guild Committee shall meet not less frequently than twice a year. Meetings shall be called by the Chair or the Secretary. The Chair or Secretary shall call a meeting whenever required to do so by one third of the members of the committee and at other times at their discretion.

Each member of the committee, including co-opted members, shall exercise one vote. Observers invited to attend committee meetings shall have no vote. In the event of a tie, the chair shall have a casting vote irrespective of whether he/she has exercised his/her initial vote on the same issue. No decisions shall be taken by the committee if fewer than one quarter of the members are present but the committee may continue to sit despite the lack of that quorum.

The committee shall have authority to establish sub-committees and working parties as appropriate to deal with matters within the responsibilities of the Guild.

Accounts and Treasurer

The Treasurer of the Guild shall be responsible for the receipt of all monies due to the Guild and shall make such payments as the committee shall direct and shall maintain accounts of all receipts, payments, assets and liabilities of the Guild. In discharging his/her duties the Treasurer of the Guild shall adhere to the requirements of the bye-laws of the Chartered Institute of Library and Information Professionals and shall abide by such guidance as the Chartered Institute of Library and Information Professionals issues with regard to the keeping of accounts.

Two honorary auditors shall be appointed at the annual general meeting of the Guild. The honorary auditors shall not be members of the Guild committee and need not be members of the Guild. They shall be required to sign a certificate in respect of the adequacy of the accuracy of the accounts as presented to the annual general meeting.

The audited accounts, in addition to being presented to the annual general meeting, shall be communicated to members of the Guild either in the Guild's newsletter or otherwise.

Secretary

The Secretary of the Guild shall maintain a record of all proceedings and shall be responsible for preparing reports, issuing notices, conducting correspondence, giving notice of impending elections, circulating ballot papers in accordance with the election regulations in Annex A, and the safe keeping of ballot papers. She/he shall forward to the Secretary of the Chartered Institute of Library and Information Professionals any reports and records required under the bye-laws of the Institute and shall submit regularly to the Institute copies of the minutes of the Guild Committee meetings and general meetings of the Guild.

Annual General Meeting

A general meeting of the members of the Guild shall be held each year before 30 June. Preliminary notice of the date of the meeting and the business to be considered shall be given to all members of the Guild not less than five weeks before the date of the meeting. Notice of further business proposed by the members shall be given to all members of the Guild not less than three weeks before the date of the meeting. Notice of the dates of meetings and of the business to be transacted shall be provided to members either by notice in the Chartered Institute of Library and Information Professionals Update or in the Guild newsletter or by other direct postal communication to members of the Guild.

At the annual general meeting there shall be distributed to every member present a copy of the audited accounts and the annual report of the Guild committee for the previous year. The texts of the annual report and accounts shall be communicated to all members of the Guild either in the Guild's newsletter or otherwise.

Special General Meeting

The Secretary of the Guild shall convene a special general meeting of the Guild when required to do so either by the Guild committee or by any 20 members of the Guild. Any demand for a special meeting shall state the business proposed to be conducted at the meeting. A special general meeting shall be held not later than 10 weeks after the receipt of the demand. A notice of the meeting and of the business to be conducted shall be given to all members of the Guild not less than three weeks before the date fixed for the meeting. It shall contain the words of any motion which has been submitted for the meeting. All members of the Guild shall be entitled to vote on any such motion whether present at the special meeting or not and for this purpose ballot papers shall be circulated with the notice of the meeting. The notice shall specify that ballot papers are to be returned not later than the day before the date of the special meeting.

No business shall be conducted at a special meeting unless 30 members of the Guild are present, irrespective of the number of ballot papers which have been returned by post.

Votes at general meetings shall be by show of hands unless the meeting decides otherwise by simple majority. Only those persons entitled to vote in elections of the Guild as detailed above shall be entitled to vote. In the event of a tie the chair of the meeting shall exercise a casting vote irrespective of whether he/she has exercised an initial vote on the issue.

Procedure at General Meetings

The chair of a general meeting shall conduct its business as far as possible in accordance with the rules of procedure adopted by the Chartered Institute of Library and Information Professionals for its general meetings mutatis mutandis.

Accidental omissions

Any accidental omission to give notice to or the non-receipt of notice by any member of the Guild shall not invalidate any resolution passed or proceedings held at any meeting.

Amendment of these rules

These rules may be amended only by decision of a general meeting of the Guild. No amendment shall be adopted unless it has been approved by two-thirds of the members voting in person or by postal ballot as detailed above. No amendment shall take effect until it has been approved by the Council of the Chartered Institute of Library and Information Professionals.

Appendix F*
Regional Member Network and Special Interest Group Rules

Regional Member Network and Special Interest Group rules are currently being reviewed and are due to be approved in Spring 2015.

For the latest version of the rules, please visit www.cilip.org.uk/cilip/how-cilip-works/constitutional-documents.

---

*Note: Appendix D and Appendix E are no longer in use.

Part 3
GENERAL INFORMATION

CILIP's Devolved Nations and Member Networks

CILIP's Devolved Nations

CILIP in Scotland (CILIPS)

Supporting the development of members with networking and learning opportunities through the Branch and Group network and events such as the annual conference, Autumn Gathering and CPD programme. Recognition and reward through awards and bursaries. A regular newsletter to keep members informed of advocacy and policy work in devolved matters.

CILIP in Scotland (formerly Scottish Library Association) was set up in 1908 and affiliated with CILIP (Library Association) in 1931, retaining its own constitution and separate governance arrangements. As a devolved nation, CILIPS funds its own office in Glasgow, is registered as a Scottish charity and within CILIP is responsible for all policy, financial and operational matters relating to its internal affairs and for those professional matters solely affecting the operation, development and promotion of library and information services in Scotland

For information on the Governance structure for Scotland, please see the CILIPS website.

Website: www.cilips.org.uk
Email: admin@cilips.org.uk
Geographical coverage: Scotland.
Regional sub-branches: Central, East, North, North East, Tayside and West Branch.

CILIP Cymru/Wales

Supporting the development of members with networking and learning opportunities in the form of conferences, events and training. Recognition and reward for members comes through awards, bursaries and area-specific advocacy and policy work.

Website: www.cilip.org.uk/wales
E-mail: mandy.powell@cilip.org.uk
Geographical coverage: Wales.

CILIP Ireland

Working on behalf of members to improve and support library and information services throughout the island of Ireland. Committee members represent the public, academic, government and schools sectors.

Website: www.cilip.org.uk/ireland
Email: louisa.costelloe@cilip.org.uk
Geographical coverage: Northern and Southern Ireland.

CILIP's Member Networks

Regional Member Networks and Special Interest Groups are an essential part of CILIP's value to its members and are fundamental in creating a vibrant sense of community within the profession.

They are strong advocates and are the voice of CILIP both at a local level and within their specialist fields. They provide CILIP Council and staff with knowledge of the concerns and needs of members and with expert advice on policy and developments in the different parts of the profession.

CILIP's Member Networks provide excellent opportunities for members to engage in continuing professional development and to get involved in professional activities. Being active in Member Networks is key to growing future leaders in the profession.

CILIP's website has further information about Member Networks including social media contacts, events, resources, training, awards, grants and bursaries.

Regional Member Networks

There are nine Regional Member Networks in England. Each Regional Member Network provides the following core offers to CILIP members:

- To identify and meet the needs for local members; providing support for members in their continuing professional development throughout their career
- To support those that are undertaking Professional Registration
- To develop a sense of community amongst members in the region
- To support CILIP membership recruitment and retention
- To ensure that CILIP has a presence at a local level

East Midlands

Website: www.cilip.org.uk/east-midlands
Twitter: @CILIPEastMids
Email: CILIPEMBranch@gmail.com
Geographical coverage: Derbyshire, Leicestershire, Lincolnshire, Northamptonshire, Nottinghamshire and the non-metropolitan districts of Derby, Leicester, Nottingham and Rutland.

East Midlands Member Network supports members through opportunities for professional and personal development and networking. It is the regional voice for library and information workers on a local regional and national stage acting as a conduit for CILIP both to disseminate information and send comment back.

East of England

Website: www.cilip.org.uk/east-England
Twitter: @cilipeoe
Email: cilipeast@gmail.com
Geographical coverage: Bedfordshire, Cambridgeshire, Essex, Hertfordshire, Norfolk and Suffolk.

East of England Member Network's aims are to promote continuing professional development, to encourage networking and to represent members in this area. Regular events and courses are held throughout the year.

London

Website: www.cilip.org.uk/london
Twitter: @ciliplndn
Email: cilipinlondon@gmail.com
Geographical coverage: CILIP members living or working in London.

CILIP in London is the largest of CILIP's Member Networks. CILIP in London is a network for CILIP members living or working in Greater London. It runs a variety of events throughout the year, including professional development talks, discussions and social events.

North East

Website: www.cilip.org.uk/north-east
Twitter: @CILIPNE
Email: (via website): Secretary (liaison) – Louise.gordon@newcastle.ac.uk
Geographical coverage: Durham and Northumberland, Gateshead, Newcastle-upon-Tyne, North and South Tyneside, Sunderland, Darlington, Hartlepool, Middlesbrough, Redcar and Cleveland, and Stockton-on-Tees.

CILIP North East Member Network's mission is to:

- Set, maintain, monitor and promote standards of excellence in the creation, management, evaluation, exploitation and sharing of information and knowledge resources.
- Support the principle of equality of access to information, ideas and works of the imagination which it affirms is fundamental to a thriving economy, democracy, culture and civilisation.
- Support, represent and assist in the continuing professional development needs of new, students and existing members of the profession, enabling them to achieve and maintain the highest professional standards.
- Be a forum to effectively engage with members, potential members and stakeholders.

North West

Website: www.cilip.org.uk/north-west
Twitter: @CILIPNW
Email: Andrew.Taylor, Honorary Secretary: taylora@hope.ac.uk
Geographical coverage: Cheshire, Cumbria, Lancashire and Isle of Man, Bolton, Bury,

Knowsley, Liverpool, Manchester, Oldham, Rochdale, St Helens, Salford, Sefton, Stockport, Tameside, Trafford, Wigan and Wirral. Blackburn, Darwen, Blackpool, Halton and Warrington.

North West Member Network's purpose is to represent and support all the members of CILIP in the North West of England. Its primary aim is to be the regional voice for members, representing views and opinions on a local and national level. It also acts as a channel between different Member Networks and Groups, ensuring regional voices are heard.

South East

Website: www.cilip.org.uk/south-east
Twitter: By sub-regions: @CILIPHW; @CILIPinKent; @CILIPinSurrey; @CILIPSussex; @CILIPTV
Email: via website
Geographical coverage: South East Member Network runs around the southern side of London from Kent in the south east corner, through Sussex and Surrey to Hampshire and the Isle of Wight then up through Berkshire and Oxfordshire to Buckinghamshire.

South East Member Network's purpose is to represent and support all the members of CILIP who live or work in the South East of England. It covers a large area and the region is divided into five active sub-regions: CILIP in Hants and Wight, CILIP in Kent, CILIP in Surrey, CILIP in Sussex and CILIP in the Thames Valley. There is a committee for the region and each sub-region also has a committee that organises a varied and ambitious programme of events and activities. The main aim of the South East Member Network is to encourage, fund and support their work.

South West

Website: www.cilip.org.uk/south-west
Twitter: @CILIPSW
Email: cilipsw@googlemail.com
Geographical coverage: Bristol, Channel Islands, Cornwall (including Isles of Scilly), Devon, Dorset Gloucestershire, Somerset (including Bath and North East Somerset, North Somerset) and Wiltshire.

The South West Members Network aims to provide information, networking opportunities and relevant courses for all existing and potential members of CILIP living and working in the South West of the UK.

West Midlands

Website: www.cilip.org.uk/west-midlands
Twitter: @CILIPWM
Email: via website
Geographical coverage: Herefordshire, Shropshire, Staffordshire, Warwickshire and Worcestershire, the metropolitan districts of Birmingham, Coventry, Dudley, Sandwell, Solihull, Walsall and Wolverhampton and the non-metropolitan districts of Stoke-on-Trent and Telford and Wrekin.

West Midlands Member Network represents library and information professionals living or working in the West Midlands. It runs a variety of events throughout the year, including professional development talks and a members' day.

Yorkshire and Humberside

Website: www.cilip.org.uk/yorkshire
Twitter: @cilip_yh
Email: cilipyh@gmail.com
Geographic coverage: The districts of Barnsley, Bradford, Calderdale, Doncaster, Kirklees, Leeds, Rotherham, Sheffield and

Wakefield; the East Riding of Yorkshire, Kingston upon Hull, North East Lincolnshire, North Lincolnshire and York and the southern part of the county of North Yorkshire.

The Yorkshire & Humberside Member Network aims to provide members with access to training and networking events, professional registration support and continuing professional development opportunities.

Special Interest Groups

Special Interest Groups provide CILIP members with access to events, training and other networking and continuing professional development opportunities within a shared area of professional interest. For even greater involvement members can join the committee itself and play a part in how they operate. Membership of two Groups is included in the CILIP subscription and members may join as many others as they wish on payment of a nominal charge for each.

Academic and Research Libraries Group (ARLG)
Cataloguing and Indexing Group (CIG)
Commercial, Legal and Scientific Information Group (CLSIG)
Community, Diversity and Equality Group (CDEG)
Information Group (GIG)
Health Libraries Group (HLG)
Information Literacy Group (ILG)
Information Services Group (ISG)
International Library and Information Group (ILIG)
Library and Information History Group (LIHG)
Library and Information Research Group (LIRG)
Local Studies Group (LSG)
Multimedia Information and Technology Group (MmIT)
Patent and Trademark Group (PATMG)
Prison Libraries Group (PrLG)
Public and Mobile Libraries Group (PMLG)
Publicity and Public Relations Group (PPRG)
Rare Books and Special Collections Group (RBSCG)
School Libraries Group (SLG)
UK eInformation Group (UKeiG)
Youth Libraries Group (YLG)

Academic and Research Libraries Group (ARLG)

Website: www.cilip.org.uk/arlg
Twitter: @ CILIP_ARLG
Email: arlg@cilip.org.uk

The Academic and Research Libraries Group (ARLG) aims to provide a focus and forum for the professional concerns and interests of everyone working in academic or research libraries, linking those with current and emerging issues and developments and the overall direction of CILIP's corporate plan. ARLG is made up of regional divisions providing a local focus for its activities.

Through its national committee, its regional divisions and especially its membership as a whole, ARLG has the following aims and objectives:

- Ensure opportunities for individual, personal and professional development through involvement in the group's activities as a whole as well as participation in its formal structures.
- Engage proactively with national issues and debates, contributing to the formulation of CILIP initiatives and responses, and ensuring appropriate linkages, participation and communication with CILIP.
- Encourage and facilitate the exchange of information and experience within the group and with other organisations.
- Support, develop and publicise innovative services, best practice and staff development, through bursaries, awards and other initiatives.
- Develop and sustain a strong regional structure which optimises members' active participation in the group and engagement with regional agenda.
- Develop and sustain international links to widen awareness of overseas developments and facilitate visits, exchanges etc.

Cataloguing and Indexing Group (CIG)

Website: www.cilip.org.uk/cig
Twitter: @CILIPCIG
Email: CIGcommittee@gmail.com

Cataloguing and Indexing Group (CIG) is a forum for CILIP members interested in the organisation of knowledge to enable resource discovery and collection management. CIG believes that the storage, organisation and retrieval of information in any form and by any means is a central and fundamental concern of librarianship and information science. This provides a means of exploiting that information (whether printed or electronic) for the maximum benefit of all users.

CIG promotes best practice, contributes to the development of metadata, national and international standards and formats and provides opportunities for learning and professional development. CIG members are active in all areas of library and information science and the publishing sector.

The Group:

- is actively engaged in the development and maintenance of metadata standards, including RDA, seeking to work in partnership with the organisations and groups responsible for their advancement.
- unites all those with an interest in bibliographic control, including not only librarians but also colleagues from the book trade.
- holds an annual residential seminar and other meetings and workshops throughout the year.
- publishes a quarterly journal *Catalogue & Index* and other specialist publications.
- advises CILIP on matters concerning bibliographic control.

Commercial, Legal and Scientific Information Group (CLSIG)

Website: www.cilip.org.uk/clsig
Twitter: @clsig
Email: secretary@clsig.org.uk

The Commercial, Legal & Scientific Information Group (CLSIG) supports and promotes the professional interests of members in commercial, legal and scientific workplace libraries and information services. This is facilitated by providing professional development training, networking opportunities for members and representing their interests within CILIP and the wider information community.

CLSIG aims to further develop an already active programme of events to facilitate professional development; to encourage and support greater activity in our regional Groups, and always to represent and support the commercial information sector on national and topical issues. Professional development is promoted through an active programme of events and visits. Joint events with other groups have been actively promoted for several years, and since CLSIG membership covers the whole UK as well as abroad, efforts are now being made to hold more CLSIG events outside the South-East and to provide remote attendance where possible.

CLSIG Journal is published four times a year electronically, with an aim to publish in-depth articles on themes of interest to information professionals working in the commercial sector. Members receive a regular news bulletin by email to keep them up to date with Group activities and personnel changes.

Community, Diversity and Equality Group (CDEG)

Website: www.cilip.org.uk/cdeg
Twitter: @CDEGroup
Email: cdeg.cilip@gmail.com

The Community, Diversity and Equality Group (CDEG) believes that libraries transform lives. CDEG wants to develop a diverse library and information workforce that supports communities to achieve sustainable needs-based services.

CDEG's objectives:

- Provide a forum for progressive, socially responsible views on library and information issues.
- Support and advocate on behalf of library workers who believe that libraries are agents of social change, with the power to transform the lives of individuals and communities.
- Develop partnerships and strategic alliances with voluntary and statutory organizations, nationally and internationally, engaged with libraries and the struggle for social justice.
- Conduct campaigns and raise wider awareness of library and information activities that promote social justice.
- Monitor, evaluate and challenge our professional values, with special emphasis on embedding diversity and equality across all aspects of CILIP's work.
- Promote and work to improve freedom of access to information.
- Promote and work to improve accessibility of information in all formats.

Government Information Group (GIG)

Website: www.cilip.org.uk/gig
Twitter: @gig_cilip
Email: via the website

The Government Information Group (GIG) represents the professional interests of librarians and information workers in government departments and agencies, parliamentary and national libraries. GIG welcomes members from any sector of the profession, particularly those with an interest in government information and documentation.

The Group organises professional training for its members on topical subjects such as freedom of information, mentoring, electronic publishing and information handling. It promotes professional registration – CILIP's framework of qualifications – in government departments.

Visits are arranged to government libraries and other national collections. As part of its policy of fostering contacts between members, the Group organises social activities. The Government Information Group journal is a joint journal between GIG and NGLIS. GIG is represented on a number of other professional bodies, including SCOOP and the Special Libraries Committee and regularly comments on CILIP's policies and initiatives.

Health Libraries Group (HLG)

Website: www.cilip.org.uk/hlg
Twitter: @CILIPHLG
Email: hlg@cilip.org.uk

Health Libraries Group (HLG) is a UK based network of individuals working in or professionally interested in health and social care information. Its strength is a diverse and active membership covering all health and social sectors, and geographical areas in the UK. Members work for the health service, the academic sector, the independent sector, government departments, professional associations, charities and public libraries. Students with an interest in health and social care information are also welcome.

HLG works to a business plan and has a journal, newsletters, two subject groups – Libraries for Nursing and HLG Wales, runs CPD events and jointly publishes HLISD, a directory of health library and information services. Health Information and Libraries Journal (HILJ) is published by Wiley and is available free to Group members. An electronic newsletter is published quarterly and each subject group has its own newsletter. The Health Library and Information Services Directory in the UK and the Republic of Ireland (HLISD) is published in partnership with the NHS England Library Leads (SHaLL).

Study days and other meetings are held throughout the year. The HLG Conference is held biannually and HLG contributes to the CILIP Umbrella conference. HLG also supports members professional development by offering bursaries to attend CPD activities.

Information Literacy Group (ILG)

Website: www.cilip.org.uk/ilg
Twitter: @infolitgroup
Email: cilipilg@gmail.com

Information Literacy Group (ILG) encourages debate and the exchange of knowledge in all aspects of Information Literacy. ILG aims to:

- provide a forum for discussion
- disseminate information about local, national and international initiatives
- encourage the publication of articles, both nationally and internationally, which share new ideas, initiatives and experience
- encourage collaboration and support across all sectors of the profession
- highlight and promote good practice

ILG achieves this by:

- maintaining an active email list, lis-infoliteracy
- organising the Librarians' Information Literacy Annual Conference (LILAC)
- publishing the Journal of Information Literacy (JIL)
- maintaining the Information Literacy website
- highlighting effective practice through the Information Literacy Practitioner of the Year Award
- organising meetings, seminars and training events
- responding to initiatives where appropriate
- working in partnership with other relevant organisations and agencies

Information Services Group (ISG)

Website: www.cilip.org.uk/isg
Twitter: @ISGCILIP
Email: ISGHonSecretary@cilip.org.uk
The Information Services Group supports members' interests in the provision of information services by promoting activities that improve the effectiveness of information provision to all sectors of society. The Group welcomes members from all areas of the information library world. Regional ISG Committees run their own events and visits and are represented on the National ISG committee.

ISG's annual Reference Awards are held in October with nominations open to all from February to August. As well as the Group's web pages and the Journal *Refer*, ISG now has a *Referplus* web page, with expanded articles, links and a growing set of recommended Reference websites. ISG has representation at Umbrella and on the IFLA Reference & Information Services Section Committee.

International Library and Information Group (ILIG)

Website: www.cilip.org.uk/ilig
Twitter: @CILIP_ILIG
Email: ilig@cilip.org.uk
The International Library and Information Group's special interest is the international aspect of library and information science and knowledge management. As a result ILIG has members in the UK and all over the world.

ILIG offers informal but informative early evening meetings and more formal half, or full day, seminars and courses that look at in detail at an aspect of the profession. ILIG's journal, Focus, is published three times a year. ILIG welcomes all those interested in the international aspects of library and information science to join ILIGlist. ILIG has also relaunched the Hosts directory – a list of CILIP members and international colleagues who are willing to host, for a day or two, a fellow library and information worker who is visiting their city or region.

Through the International Award ILIG acknowledges the achievements of those whose work overseas has helped their community and ILIG manages, for CILIP, the Anthony Thompson Award.

Library and Information History Group (LIHG)

Website: www.cilip.org.uk/lihg
Twitter: @CILIP_LIHG
Email: via the website

The Library and Information History Group (LIHG) was formed in 1962. It is one of CILIP's oldest Special Interest Groups and is the only Group in the UK specifically devoted to the history of libraries and librarianship. The Group welcomes anyone with an interest in library and information history. The LIHG includes and supports professional researchers, but most members are simply interested in the subject. Membership offers opportunities to receive and share news and information, to attend and contribute to lectures and events, and to help promote the value of library and information resources.

The LIHG publishes a regular newsletter, and a scholarly journal, Library & Information History, appears under its aegis. The LIHG also organises seminars, conferences and visits, and seeks to support action for the preservation of library records, artefacts and buildings. The Group holds regular meetings around the country which consist of a committee meeting, followed by a visit or lecture or both. LIHG is strongly committed to increasing access to resources for the library historian whether textual or artefactual. Indeed, it is often said that the LIHG represents the historical conscience of librarianship.

Library and Information Research Group (LIRG)

Website: www.cilip.org.uk/lirg
Twitter: @ciliplirg
Email: via the website

The Library and Information Research Group (LIRG) promotes the value of information research and links research with practice. The activities of the Group are co-ordinated by an elected committee of researchers, research students, lecturers and practitioners in the library and information profession.

LIRG aims to raise awareness of information research by:

- Increasing its profile and influencing its direction
- Promoting the dissemination of sound research methodology and results
- Assisting in the development of emerging researchers
- Enabling networking between researchers

LIRG's portfolio of activities includes:

- publishing LIS research in its open access journal, *Library and Information Research* (*LIR*)
- running UK-wide research-related courses
- running, when appropriate, conferences on special research topics
- contributing sessions on research to Umbrella
- offering four different research awards

Local Studies Group (LSG)

Website: www.cilip.org.uk/lsg
Twitter: @CILIP_LSG
Email: via website

The Local Studies Group (LSG) supports people working in local studies librarianship by promoting standards, lobbying, discussing matters of interest in The Local Studies Librarian and in its electronic newsletter, holding meetings, workshops and conferences.

LSG produces an annual journal and regular newsletters with articles of interest to the library, information and knowledge community, whilst regional sub-groups organise events at a local level.

Multimedia and information Technology Group (MmiT)

Website: www.cilip.org.uk/mmit
Twitter: @MultiMedialT
Email: MmITcommittee@gmail.com.
The Multimedia Information and Technology (MmIT) Group aims to unite CILIP members engaged in, or interested in, multimedia information and technology developments in library and information science. It is a means of sharing experience and ideas, and promoting common professional interests. Members are drawn from all information service sectors, and have in common an interest in the delivery of information based on modern media, including graphic forms, streaming video, film clips, sometimes animation, and sound – alongside traditional text.

The Group acts as a forum for explaining and reflecting on the exploitation of technology in information provision. It deals with the integration and management of all the forms in which information is presented, the use of a range of electronic delivery systems, now including web-based applications, and innovation; all in the interests of communicating information.

The Multimedia Information & Technology Journal is a central feature of the Group's activities. The regularly updated blog can be used by anyone with a useful contribution to make, whether it is an event, a research report, opinion piece, or anything else relevant to multimedia. A conference, usually oversubscribed, covers a key topic of the moment, and invariably boasts highly respected speakers.

Patent and Trademark Group (PATMG)

Website: www.cilip.org.uk/patmg
Twitter: @UKPATMG
Email: via the website
The Patent and Trade Mark Group (PATMG) is a Special Interest Group of CILIP, whose members are information professionals specialising in patent and trade mark information. PATMG holds lectures, meetings and discussions to share expertise on patent and trademark searching and analysis. PATMG is based in the UK but open to members anywhere in the world. Members are drawn from industry, patent agencies, freelance search firms, database producers, patent/trademark information suppliers, academic institutions, patent and trademark offices and libraries.

Membership of the Group is a useful way of interacting with others to exchange ideas and information techniques. PATMG runs useful regular events covering various aspects of patent and trademark information work, as well as an occasional Patent Information Jamboree event, held in London. Searcher Newsletter is issued six times a year to help members stay up to date with developments in the field.

Prison Libraries Group (PLG)

Website: www.cilip.org.uk/prlg
Twitter: @PrisonLibraries
Email: prlg@hotmail.co.uk
The Prison Libraries Group serves the interest of all members concerned with the provision of library services to prison communities. The Group is committed to improving the quality of the service whilst raising the profile of prison libraries.

The Group aims to:

- share and develop ideas through training and publications
- be of benefit and support to all members concerned with library services to prisoners, prison and education staff
- liaise with the Prison Service
- encourage contracts between local library authorities and Prison Service establishments
- be an active part of CILIP

The committee meets a minimum of four times a year and the Group holds its AGM during the spring Training Day.

Public and Mobile Libraries Group (PMLG)

Website: www.cilip.org.uk/pmlg
Twitter: @CILIPPMLG
Email: Honorary Secretary –
Dianne.Hird@kirklees.gov.uk
The Public and Mobile Library Group (PMLG) exists to provide information, training, development and networking opportunities to staff working in public and mobile libraries and to act as advocates for public library services. So it is for absolutely anyone whose library service is either public or mobile.

The Group encompasses all levels of member, both front-line and backroom staff, from first job to senior management in the public library field, as well as mobile library staff from all fields.

PMLG also provides members with training, professional development opportunities, support and advice.

Publicity and Public Relations Group (PPRG)

Website: www.cilip.org.uk/pprg
Twitter: @pprg
Email: pprg09@yahoo.com
Libraries need to actively communicate and demonstrate their value, now more than ever, to current and potential users as well as key stakeholders. The Publicity and Public Relations Group (PPRG) is committed to promoting marketing excellence, introducing new techniques and theories, and sharing best practice amongst our membership. PPRG's interests cover the marketing and promotion of library services, creating user engagement, implementing effective communication strategies and developing dialogue with customers.

PPRG activities:

- Annual Marketing Excellence Awards to recognise and celebrate marketing successes across all library sectors
- A national conference and other seminars throughout the year, so members can find out more about new and innovative ways to promote their service
- Publish a quarterly eBulletin to share ideas and best practice
- Provide networking opportunities with other library staff working in this area

PPRG welcomes membership from individuals from all library sectors who are actively working in or professionally interested in marketing their services.

Rare Books and Special Collections Group (RBSCG)

Website: www.cilip.org.uk/rbscg
Twitter: @CILIPRareBooks
Email: Honorary Secretary:
lucy.grace.evans@gmail.com

The Rare Books and Special Collections Group unites librarians responsible for collections of rare books, manuscripts and special materials, with other interested individuals. The Group promotes the study and exploitation of rare books, encourages awareness of preservation, conservation and digitisation issues, and fosters training opportunities related to the maintenance, display and use of collections.

Three or four times a year, a talk and accompanying exhibition or library visit are held in different parts of the country to cater for a geographically diverse membership. These meetings attract an international audience, particularly to the residential study conference held annually in the second week of September. The Group also publishes an online newsletter three times a year, including articles, news and reviews, and the texts of papers delivered at the Group's meetings and conferences.

School Libraries Group (SLG)

Website: www.cilip.org.uk/slg
Twitter: @CILIPSLG
Email: susan.staniforth@gloucestershire.gov.uk

The School Libraries Group (SLG) offers help and support to members. It holds a conference every two years which provides a forum for discussion and debate on current issues in school librarianship. SLG runs regional training courses on a wide range of topics concerned with school librarianship and campaigns in support of school libraries, school librarians and schools library services. SLG publishes the journal *School Libraries in View*, circulates a monthly enewsletter to members and produce publications such as CILIP's *Guidelines for Secondary School Libraries*.

SLG aims to:

- promote and support the development of well-resourced and professionally managed library resource centres in schools.
- promote the development of reading for pleasure, of information literacy, and of e-learning
- enhance and promote the status of school librarians.
- promote and support the role of schools library services
- provide appropriate advice, information, guidance and training opportunities relevant to school libraries
- liaise with local, national and international organisations in order to promote the role of school libraries, school library staff and schools library services.

UK eInformation Group (UKeiG)

Website: www.cilip.org.uk/ukeig
Twitter: @ukeig
Email: val.skelton@ukeig.org.uk

UKeiG is a respected and well-established forum for all information professionals, users and developers of electronic information resources. UKeiG promotes and advances the effective exploitation and management of electronic information and offers a wide range of resources including seminars and workshops, our e-journal eLucidate, publications and a popular series of Factsheets.

UKeiG aims to:

- Stimulate communication and the exchange of knowledge about electronic information.
- Disseminate high quality advice, information and publications about e-industry news and developments.
- Raise awareness of existing and new technologies that retrieve, manage and process electronic information.
- Support continuing professional development by delivering a high quality portfolio of practical and affordable training programmes and seminars.
- Encourage innovation in electronic information retrieval, management and processing
- Support and stimulate the information industry through a range of awards and bursaries.

Youth Libraries Group (YLG)

Website: http://www.cilip.org.uk/ylg
Twitter: @youthlibraries
Email: via website

The Youth Libraries Group of CILIP is the organisation of choice for librarians, information professionals and all those working with or interested in children's and young people's books, reading development, the promotion of libraries and reading for pleasure.

YLG members come from a wide range of workplaces – public libraries, schools, school library services, colleges, universities and early years settings. YLG also welcomes and has many student, non-working and international members. With twelve regional groups across the United Kingdom, YLG is one of the largest and liveliest Special Interest Groups in CILIP.

The Group:

- Promotes excellence in children and young people's literature by organising, judging and publicising the most prestigious children's book award in the UK – the CILIP Carnegie and Kate Greenaway medals.
- Advocates quality provision of public and schools library services to children and young people by disseminating best practice on professional issues.
- Inspires, supports and represents all those working in or with library services for children and young people through its publications, annual conference, meetings, training courses and events.
- Provides specialist expertise, knowledge and advice to CILIP, the Government, the book trade and related professions on issues relating to books, reading and library services for children and young people.
- Creates opportunities to network with colleagues and those in related professions.

National committees

CPD Forum

The CPD Forum is a national CILIP meeting which brings together the National Offers Group and the Professional Registration Support Network which supports Candidate Support Officers (CSOs) and Mentor Support Officers (MSOs).

Together these groups work to provide development opportunities for CILIP members, no matter what stage of their career.

The CPD Forum:

- Provides a forum for CSOs and MSOs to meet together with a member of the Professional Registration Board and CILIP officers to share information, knowledge and best practice and receive training
- Ensures quality control across the delivery of Professional Registration training and support (including Mentor training and support)
- Supports the development and delivery of online training to support Professional Registration which will supplement face to face training
- Contributes to CILIP policy development (where appropriate)
- Develops and delivers national core offers to support all members in their CPD.

National Offers Group

CDG and PTEG national committees have now merged to become the National Offers Group. The focus of the group is to develop career development opportunities for all CILIP members throughout their career.

Professional Registration Support Network

The Professional Registration Support Network brings together all Candidate Support Officers (CSOs) and Mentor Support Officers (MSOs) with CILIP staff and a representative from the Professional Registration and Accreditation Board.

Thes group consolidates training, information, advice and knowledge sharing for all those supporting Professional Registration. Working closely with the National Offers Group, they provide excellent support and training to candidates and mentors

Retired Members Guild (RMG)

Website: www.cilip.org.uk/rmg
E-mail: alison.hall6@btinternet.com
The Guild enables retired librarians to keep in touch with each other, to participate in activities and to assist CILIP in its promotion of libraries of all types.

Activities

Amongst its activities, the Guild arranges meetings and visits to libraries and places of interest to librarians both at home and overseas. Partners are welcome at all of these events.

The Guild publishes a lively and informative journal, *Post-Lib* which details the many varied activities that retired librarians pursue and also makes comments on the current library scene.

The Guild also seeks out additional financial and other benefits available for retired and older people and makes these known. It assists CILIP with the organisation of its elections by the provision of scrutineers and the development of guidelines.

It helps the Library Campaign to maintain and improve library services. It also responds to requests from voluntary societies and charities for assistance with their library services where this complies with the CILIP Guidelines for voluntary work.

Suppliers Network

CILIP works across the whole library and information domain and recognises the importance of partnerships with the vendor community. Its Suppliers Network offers companies that sell products and services, systems and software to the library and information sector the opportunity to have a closer association with CILIP, the only chartered body for library and information professionals. This involvement generates better awareness of both sides' needs and expectations for the future and lends a louder voice for our lobbying activities.

Suppliers Network Contact:
Gary Allman
gary.allman@cilip.org.uk
0207 255 0552

Companies in membership
2CQR
3M UK PLC
Access IT
Amlib UK and 247lib.com
Axiell
Better World Books
Bibliographic Data Services Ltd (BDS)
Bibliotheca Ltd
Bruynzeel Storage Systems Ltd
Capita
Civica
Copyright Licensing Agency Limited (CLA)
Clio Software Ltd
CredoD-Tech
Demco Interiors
EOS International

EX Libris (UK)
FG Library Products Ltd
Finnmade Furniture Solutions Ltd
Gresswell
Infor
Ingram/Coutts
Innovative Interfaces
Insight Media Internet Ltd
Intrepid Security Systems
IS Oxford
Lorensbergs
LFC
Nielsen BookData
OCLC
Opening the Book
Oxford University Press
Premier Moves
Proquest
PTFS
Read How You Want.com Ltd
SerotaLibrary Furniture
SirsiDynix
Softlink Europe
Soutron Ltd
Sydney Plus
The Book Rescuers
theDesignConcept
Thomson Reuters
UK Pressonline

CILIP Benevolent Fund

The Benevolent Fund was established in the last century and became a registered charity in 1964. In 2002, when The Library Association and the Institute of Information Scientists merged to form CILIP, it changed its name to the CILIP Benevolent Fund and its Trust Deed was amended to enable it to provide help to all Members of CILIP and former members of The Library Association and The Institute of Information Scientists, together with their dependents.

The Fund is able to provide emergency assistance by means of grants to help in meeting any unusual or unexpected expenses that are causing anxiety and hardship. Its income derives principally from CILIP Members' donations, plus interest on invested capital. The Fund is a registered charity, separate from CILIP and its finances do not form part of those of CILIP. It is administered by seven Trustees, all of whom have considerable library/information experience, appointed by CILIP Council, who usually meet three times a year. However, between meetings most requests for help can be promptly met as the Chair, advised by two Trustees, is authorised to take action when necessary.

Two leaflets – *What is the CILIP Benevolent Fund?* and *A Will to Help: an opportunity to remember the CILIP Benevolent Fund when making your will* – are readily available from the Secretary of the Fund. All enquiries should be addressed to the Secretary in the first instance.

Trustees
Graham Cornish (Chair)
Mary Auckland
Biddy Fisher
Bernard Naylor
Gillian Pentelow
Michael Saich
(One vacancy)

Secretary
Eric Winter
CILIP Benevolent Fund,
7 Ridgmount Street,
London WC1E 7AE
Telephone: 07977 910492 (mobile)
Fax: 020 7255 0501
E-mail: eric.winter@cilip.org.uk

Registered Charity number
237352

Advocacy and campaigning

The leading voice for the sector, CILIP promotes the importance of the library, information and knowledge management community. We work to ensure that members' voices are heard and value is recognised by politicians, the media, the public and key organisations. We do this through advocacy and campaigns.

As many issues relating to libraries, information and knowledge are the responsibility of devolved governments across the UK, CILIP carries out advocacy and campaigns activity on a UK-basis and specifically in the devolved nations.

We put the value of library, information and knowledge staff at the heart of our advocacy and campaigns. We highlight the contributions staff make to end-users, individuals, communities, the economy and wider society.

We advocate across a range of sectors and policy interests including information management; information literacy; library and information services in the public, health, academic, government and school sectors; ebooks and copyright.

Consultations

CILIP responses to a range of consultations from governments and a range of organisations, making sure our voice is heard by key decision makers.

Libraries APPG

CILIP provides the secretariat for the Libraries All Party Parliamentary Group. The Libraries APPG provides MPs and Peers with information and opportunities for debate about the important role libraries play in society and their future; highlights the contribution that a wide variety of library and information services make, promotes and discusses themes in the wider information and knowledge sector including the impact of technology, skills and training, professional standards and broader issues.

Campaigns

Between 2012 and 2014 we ran a campaign to Shout About the importance of school libraries and librarians. Activity to engage key stakeholders included supporting a mass lobby of Parliament; meeting Ofsted, the Department for Education and Parliamentarians; working with partners such as the School Library Association and National Union of Teachers to raise the profile of school librarians; commissioning YouGov to poll attitudes to information children find online; using UK-wide events such as National Libraries Day to raise the profile of school libraries; and supporting the Libraries All Party Parliamentary

Group's report *The Beating Heart of the School*.

In 2014 we campaigned to Let Libraries Lend Ebooks. The campaign asked for clear European copyright law that allows libraries to fulfil their mission of providing everyone with the opportunity to read, and access information and knowledge and provides reasonable payment for authors and publishers. Over 200 individuals, organisations and politicians signed up in support of the campaign and over ten thousand people signed the European-wide campaign.

2014 also saw the successful result of twenty years of lobbying for copyright laws to be updated to be fit for the digital age. CILIP convenes the Libraries and Archives Copyright Alliance (LACA), which lobbies in the UK and Europe about copyright and related rights on behalf of UK users of copyright works through library, archive and information services and its member organisations.

Since its inception in 2012 CILIP has played a key role organising National Libraries Day, a celebration of all types of library service and staff. In 2014 over 600 events took place across the country and support came from a range of politicians and celebrities.

Medals and Awards

CILIP Awards

The CILIP Carnegie and Kate Greenaway Medals

The CILIP Carnegie and Kate Greenaway Medals are the UK's most prestigious children's book awards. The Carnegie Medal is awarded for outstanding writing and The Kate Greenaway Medal is awarded for outstanding illustration, in a book for children and young people.

Nominations are invited from all Members of CILIP either personally, through their local authority or through their regional Branch or Special Interest Group or via the dedicated nomination form available on the awards website during the nomination period: www.ckg.org.uk. Eligible titles must be written in English; be published originally for children and young people and have received their first publication in the United Kingdom between the preceding 1 September–31 August period, or have had co-publication elsewhere within a three month time lapse.

The selection process is organised by CILIP's Youth Libraries Group (YLG), which appoints 12 regional judges who are experienced children's librarians.

A shortlist for each medal is announced in March each year and the winners are announced and presented at a London ceremony in June. The winning author and illustrator receive a golden medal, a certificate and £500 worth of books to donate to a library of their choice. Since 2000 the winner of the Kate Greenaway Medal has also received the Colin Mears Award, which is a cash prize of £5,000.

The accompanying shadowing scheme for children and young people has 5,000 registered reading groups in schools and public libraries in the UK and overseas. An estimated 100,000 children 'shadowed' the judging process in 2014, reading the shortlisted titles, getting involved in literacy activities and posting their book reviews on a dedicated award shadowing website.

For further information on the Carnegie and Kate Greenaway Medals including past winners, criteria and information on the shadowing scheme visit www.ckg.org.uk or contact the CILIP Marketing Team: ckg@cilip.org.uk.

In 2006/7 it was agreed to change the year of the medals from the date of publication to the date of presentation.

Medal winners 2014:
Jon Klassen – CILIP Kate Greenaway Medal (left)
Kevin Brooks – CILIP Carnegie Medal (right)

Carnegie Medal winners

2014 Kevin Brooks, *The Bunker Diary*, Puffin Books

2013 Sally Gardner, *Maggott Moon*, Hot Key Books

2012 Patrick Ness, *A Monster Calls*, Walker Books

2011 Patrick Ness, *Monsters of Men*, Walker Books

2010 Neil Gaiman, *The Graveyard Book*, Bloomsbury

2009 Siobhan Dowd, *Bog Child*, David Fickling

2008 Philip Reeve, *Here Lies Arthur*, Scholastic

2007 Meg Rosoff, *Just in Case,* Penguin

2005 Mal Peet, *Tamar*, Walker Books

Kate Greenaway Medal winners

2014 Jon Klassen, *This Is Not My Hat,* Walker Books

2013 Levi Pinfold, *Black Dog*, Templar

2012 Jim Kay, *A Monster Calls*, Walker Books

2011 Grahame Baker-Smith, *FArTHER*, Templar

2010 Freya Blackwood, *Harry and Hopper*, Scholastic

2009 Catherine Rayner, *Harris Finds His Feet*, Little Tiger Press

2008 Emily Gravett, Little Mouse's Big Book of Fears, Macmillan

2007 Mini Grey, The Adventures of the Dish and the Spoon, Jonathan Cape

2005 Emily Gravett, *Wolves*, Macmillan

The CILIP Libraries Change Lives Award

The Libraries Change Lives Award highlights and rewards library, information and knowledge partnership work that changes lives, brings people together and demonstrate innovation and creativity. The Award is run by CILIP and its Community Diversity and Equality Group (CDEG) who promote social justice through the use of library, information and knowledge services to empower people and improve their quality of life.

A trophy, a certificate and £5,000 prize are presented to the winning project. The winning project should be a partnership between a library or information service and one or more community agencies. It should be an example of good practice, have started in the past three years and be ongoing. Applications are invited from any type of library or information service throughout the UK. An opening announcement and call for entries is made in February via CILIP Update and the CILIP weekly enewsletter and social media channels.

Further information and an electronic entry form are available on the CILIP website www. cilip.org.uk/lcla. Entries close at the end of April.

Winners of the 2014 CILIP Libraries Change Lives Award: Northamptonshire Library and Information Service and the Northamptonshire Local Enterprise Partnership – Enterprise Hubs

Winners

2014 Northamptonshire Library and Information Service and the Northamptonshire Local Enterprise Partnership – Enterprise Hubs

2013 Surrey County Council Libraries – Domestic Abuse: how Surrey libraries can help

2012 North Yorkshire County Council & North Yorkshire Youth Music Action Zone

2011 Making the Difference: Opportunities for Adults with Learning Disabilities – Kent Libraries and Archives

2010 HMP Edinburgh Library Partnership – The City of Edinburgh Council

2009 Across the Board: Autism support for families – Leeds Library and Information Service

2008 Bradford / Care Trust Libraries Partnership Project – Bradford Libraries and Archive Information Service

2007 Welcome to Your Library – London Libraries Development Agency

2006 Sighthill Library Youth Work – Edinburgh City Libraries and Information Service

2005 Northamptonshire Black History Project – Northamptonshire Libraries and Information Service and the Northamptonshire Racial Equality Council

CILIP Aspire Award

The CILIP Aspire Award helps new professionals with their development by attending leading library and information events.

The award is for CILIP members who have recently joined the profession. It provides an annual bursary to attend a library and information conference.

The award is in memory of Bob McKee who was Chief Executive of CILIP.

www.cilip.org.uk/aspireaward

Winners

2014 Victoria Killington
2013 Katherine Grigsby
2012 Sarah Childs
2011 Carly Miller

The CILIP/ESU Travelling Librarian Award

Each year, the English-Speaking Union (ESU) and CILIP invite applications for the Travelling Librarian Award, from qualified librarians working in UK libraries or information centres. The Travelling Librarian Award is intended to encourage UK/US/Commonwealth contacts in the library world and the establishment of permanent links through a professional development study tour. The visit is for two weeks and normally takes place in the autumn.

Applicants must be: (a) qualified librarians and; (b) in membership of CILIP at time of application.

For further information see: http://www.cilip.org.uk/cilip/membership/membership-benefits/careers-advice-and-support/grants-and-bursaries/travelling

Winners

2014 Elizabeth Williams
2013 Kirsten McCormick
2012 Goorgo Roo
2011 Jane Rawson
2010 David Clover
     Jo McCausland

The CILIP Robinson Award for Innovation in Library Administration by Para-Professional Staff

The Robinson Award is one of the ways in which CILIP recognises the contribution of and promotes the value of para-professional staff.

Following closure of the Affiliated Member's National Committee, CILIP are reviewing how this award will be administered in future.

Devolved Nation Awards

CILIP Cymru Wales

- **Welsh Librarian of the Year**
  The Welsh Librarian of the Year Award recognises and celebrates the contribution of librarians and information professionals to contemporary society in Wales and beyond.

Further information: www.cilip.org.uk/cilip-cymru-wales/cilip-cymru-wales-welsh-librarian-year-award

CILIP in Scotland

- **Student Awards**
  Each year two CILIP medals for achievement are awarded to students completing library related courses at Strathclyde University and Robert Gordon University. Students are nominated by the University and the awards presented at Annual Conference.

Regional Member Network Awards

North East

- **Viki Lagus Award for LIS students**
  The Viki Lagus prize is awarded by the North East Member Network every year to a Northumbria University Library and Information Science (LIS) undergraduate and apostgraduate student who have demonstrated commitment to continuing professional development. To be nominated, the students have to be CILIP members and write an article for the Member Network's journal NE Links.

Further information: www.cilip.org.uk/north-east/viki-lagus-award-lis-students

Special Interest Group Awards

Awards are defined here as prizes for work or projects completed or the winner's contribution to the profession/sector. This list does not include grants 'awarded' for projects/research or bursaries to attend conferences. Further information on individual Member Network's bursaries, grants and other awards can be found on CILIP's website.

Academic & Research Libraries Group

- **Innovation Award**
  The Award is intended to reward and support an individual, group or team pursuing innovation and excellence in the broad area of learning and teaching, and learner support, within academic, national or research libraries. The Award is open to any member of staff employed in academic, national or research libraries in the UK, and to students hoping to work in these institutions. Bids for funding of up to £1000 will be considered.

Further information: www.cilip.org.uk/academic-and-research-libraries-group/awards/innovation-award-academic-and-research-libraries-group

Cataloguing & Indexing Group

- **Alan Jeffreys Award**
  The Alan Jeffreys Award is awarded to recognise those who have made significant contributions to the understanding and development of cataloguing, indexing and related fields of librarianship. The recipient of the award should have made a substantive

contribution to the development, teaching or practice of cataloguing or indexing. Nominations should provide evidence of exceptional achievement in one or more of the following categories: teaching or professional development; leadership in a changing environment; delivery of a project.

Further information: www.cilip.org.uk/cataloguing-and-indexing-group/alan-jeffreys-award

Community, Diversity and Equality Group

- **The Diversity Award**
  The Diversity Award aims to recognise outstanding achievement in the promotion of diversity. It is given to an individual or team who has shown commitment to the advancement of diversity within a library or information setting.

Further information: www.cilip.org.uk/community-diversity-and-equality-group/awards/diversity-award-community-diversity-and-equality-group

Government Information Group

- **GIG Award**
  The award is granted to mark a major contribution to the work of government libraries.

Further information:
www.cilip.org.uk/government-information-group/gig-award

Health Libraries Group

- **Cyril Barnard Memorial Prize**
  Established in 1962, this prize is awarded in

recognition of outstanding services to medical librarianship and is awarded every three years. Award recipients are nominated by the Health Library Group committee.

Further information: www.cilip.org.uk/health-libraries-group/awards/cyril-barnard-memorial-prize

Information Literacy Group

- **Information Literacy Practitioner of the Year Award**
  This is an award for achievement in the field of Information Literacy in the United Kingdom. The award is open to an individual working in the Information Literacy arena, and in any sector, in the UK.

Further information: www.cilip.org.uk/information-literacy-group/about/information-literacy-practitioner-year-award

Information Services Group

- **Reference Awards**
  Running since 1970, the annual ISG Reference Awards - Besterman/McColvin Medals - acknowledge the importance of both print and electronic sources by recognising and rewarding the work of those who create important reference works. Since 2012 there has also been a category for special interest reference items. The Group also presents the Walford Award to an individual who has made a significant contribution to the information world.

Further information:
www.cilip.org.uk/information-services-group/isg-reference-awards

International Library and Information Group

- **International Award**
  This is an annual prize, awarded to a person, group or committee, that has made a real difference to a community through their work in library and information services in countries outside the United Kingdom of Great Britain and Northern Ireland. Any CILIP member may make a nomination. The nominee may be of any nationality and need not be a professionally trained librarian or information scientist.

Further information: www.cilip.org.uk/international-library-and-information-group/awards/ilig-international-award

Library and Information Research Group

- **LIRG Student Prize**
  Typically entries will be a postgraduate dissertation or a final year undergraduate project. Each type will be given appropriate consideration. Every Department of Library and Information Studies is encouraged to nominate one of their students' projects.

Further information: www.cilip.org.uk/library-and-information-research-group/contact-us

Local Studies Group

The Local Studies Group awards the Dorothy McCulla Memorial Prize each year and also supports the Alan Ball Award.

- **McCulla Memorial Prize**
  Nominations are sought each year for a member of the Group who has made an outstanding contribution to local studies work. The panel looks in particular for good overall

service provision, innovation and promotional work and the winner receives a cash award and hand-written certificate.

Further information: www.cilip.org.uk/local-studies-group/awards/mcculla-memorial-prize

- **Alan Ball Local History Awards**
  The Alan Ball Local History Awards were established in 1985 to encourage local history publishing by public libraries and local authorities.

Further information: www.cilip.org.uk/local-studies-group/awards/alan-ball-local-history-awards

Prison Libraries Group

- **Prison Library of the Year**
  The Prison Library of the Year award aims to recognise the outstanding work of prison librarians, library assistants and orderlies. Each year the PrLG committee welcomes nominations from any prison library in the United Kingdom.

Further information: www.cilip.org.uk/prison-libraries-group/about/prison-library-year

Public & Mobile Libraries Group

The annual awards recognise the outstanding contribution that staff make to their customers, the communities they serve and the wider public library profession. The awards are:

- **Public Library Champion of the Year**
  Recognises the achievements of outstanding frontline public library staff that make a real difference to the people who use their library.

- **Mobile Library Champion of the Year**
  Recognises the achievements of outstanding mobile library assistants, drivers or librarians who make a real difference to the lives of the people who use their services.

- **Public Librarian of the Year**
  Recognises the achievements of outstanding library and information professionals working in a public library service that make a real difference to the communities they serve and the wider public library profession.

Further information: www.cilip.org.uk/public-and-mobile-libraries-group/awards

Publicity & Public Relations Group

- **Marketing Excellence Awards**
  Across the UK, CILIP members and others are producing increasingly sophisticated marketing and publicity material and running innovative promotional campaigns, often with limited resources. The Awards aim to recognise and reward this valuable work. Gold, silver and bronze awards are made for a marketing campaign that includes several promotional elements, which are co-ordinated and presented in an integrated way to increase their impact.

Further information: www.cilip.org.uk/publicity-and-public-relations/marketing-excellence-awards

UK eInformation Group

- **Jason Farradane Award**
  The Award is made to an individual or a group of people for outstanding work in the information field. It is an international award, open to all, although nominations must be made by a CILIP member. The winner receives a commemorative plaque.

Further information: www.cilip.org.uk/uk-einformation-group/awards-and-bursaries/jason-farradane-award

- **Tony Kent Strix Award**
  The Award is given in recognition of an outstanding practical innovation or achievement in the field of information retrieval. The Award is open to individuals or groups from anywhere in the world. The Award is managed by UKeiG in conjunction with a group of experts in the field of information retrieval.

Further information: www.cilip.org.uk/uk-einformation-group/awards-and-bursaries/tony-kent-strix-award

CILIP Honorary Fellows

Every year CILIP invites nominations for Honorary Fellowship (HonFCLIP). This award is made by Council to recognise distinguished service in promoting the purpose and objects of CILIP as laid out in CILIP's Royal Charter.

Nominations may be made by current individual members of CILIP or by any of the Regional Member Networks and Special Interest Groups of CILIP or any of the Committees, Boards and Panels of CILIP. Individual members can make only one nomination in each annual round.

Nominees may come either from within the library and information community or from associated professions or disciplines. Fellows of the Institute may be nominated for Honorary Fellowship but it is not necessary to be a Fellow in order to be eligible for Honorary Fellowship. Nominations are made in confidence and are considered in confidence by the Honorary Awards Panel and the Council.

Contact: Chief Executive, CILIP
Tel: 020 7255 0690
Annie.Mauger@cilip.org.uk

2014	Danny Budzak
	Janene Cox
	Lloyd Ellis
	Jennifer Housego
	John Vincent
	Philip Wark
2013	Alastair Allan
	Norman Briggs
	Peter Griffiths
	Jan Parry
2012	Professor Sheila Corrall
	Susan Shaper
2011	Alan Gibbons
	John Lake
	Judith Lehmann
2010	Toby Bainton
	Professor David Baker
	Sue Cook
	Eric Davies
	Premilla Gamage
	Linda Houston
	Stephanie Kenna
	Kathryn Sheard
	Keith Wilson

Ridgmount Street facilities

Ridgmount Street offers Members a range of facilities in London's West End. The building is conveniently located near to several tube stations, and within 10 minutes of King's Cross and Euston main line stations.

Ewart Room

Monday–Friday 9 am–5 pm
Members, and non-members visiting Ridgmount Street for meetings or events, are welcome to use the Ewart Room, situated on the ground floor, as a meeting point. Please check availability in advance. A vending machine is available.

Rooms for hire

All our rooms offer natural light and are fully equipped with air conditioning and audio-visual and presentation equipment. Induction loops are available in Charter East and West. Furniture can be adapted for a range of room layouts. Our friendly staff will ensure that you have an anxiety free meeting or event.

The Charter Suite

A double-glazed, air-conditioned room which seats up to 100 people and can be divided into two smaller areas (Charter East and West).

The Lorna Paulin Room

A double-glazed, air-conditioned room which seats up to 40 people. Equipped with full audiovisual facilities and 11 internet-enabled multimedia PCs. Most CILIP Training and Development Events are held in this room.

The Farradane Room

A double-glazed, air-conditioned room which seats up to 32 people. Equipped with audiovisual facilities.

Catering facilities

CILIP provides a wide range of high quality catering services for meetings, courses and seminars held at Ridgmount Street.

Disabled access

There is full disabled access to all public areas of the building.

Further information and bookings

Please contact Room Bookings for further information and bookings. Telephone 0207 255 0500; e-mail: roombookings@cilip.org.uk

The CILIP archive

The CILIP archive incorporates the archives of The Library Association and the Institute of Information Scientists. It consists of such items as:

- FLA theses
- photographs
- slides
- artefacts
- Council and Committee Papers
- Branch and Group publications and journals
- leaflets
- major project/event files
- the Thorne Papers
- some Group/Branch archives.

Most of the archive is now housed with University College London, who provide a controlled environment in which to store the archive and facilities for researchers to view selected material.

CILIP retains on site at Ridgmount Street a complete set of bound *Library Association Records*, *Library Association Yearbooks*, back copies of *CILIP Update* and *Gazette*, Council minutes for the last five years, , FLA theses and essays and a collection of Library Association Publishing and Facet Publishing books.

In the first instance, all enquiries about the archives should be made to the CILIP Member Services Team team by one of the following methods:

- telephone: 020 7255 0620, Monday to Friday, 9:00– 17:00
- e-mail: memberservices@cilip.org.uk.

Part 4
CILIP Members

List of Members of CILIP

Professional Register

Personal Members
Organisation Members
Overseas Organisation Members
Note: This list of members reflects the membership
of CILIP at 18 November 2014.

Personal Members

The date shown after the square-bracketed
Membership number indicates when a member
joined the Institute.

Dates of Revalidation are preceded by **RV**.

At the end of each entry, the following
abbreviations (in bold) for membership type are
given. These are followed by the date of
attainment of qualifications (also in bold) where
appropriate.

- **CM**: Chartership
- **FE**: Fellowship
- **HFE**: Honorary Fellowship (without other CILIP
  qualification)
- **ACL**: Certification
- **AF**: Affiliated membership
- **ME**: Associate membership.

Lists of members by country are held at CILIP
Ridgmount Street and are available to members on
request.

Members' personal addresses are confidential
and are in no circumstances sold to outside
agencies. However, if members wish to contact
one another and the information provided here is
insufficient for that purpose, Membership may be
able to provide assistance.

Further information

E-mail: membership@cilip.org.uk
Telephone: 020 7255 0600

Abbreviations

For ease of use, abbreviations are being phased out in the Personal Members section. However, you may still find some of the following abbreviations in designations and addresses.

Admin.	Administration or Administrative	Estab.	Establishment		
		Exec.	Executive	N.	North
Arch.	Archives or Archivist			Nat.	National
Asst.	Assistant	F.E.	Further Education		
Assoc.	Associate or Association	Fed.	Federation	Off.	Office
		Form.	Formerly	Offr.	Officer
Auth.	Authority				
		Grp.	Group	Poly.	Polytechnic
Bibl.	Bibliographer			Postgrad.	Postgraduate
Bor.	Borough	H.E.	Higher Education	Prof.	Professor
Br.	Branch	Hist.	Historical or History	p./t.	Part time
Brit.	British	Hon.	Honorary		
		Hosp.	Hospital(s)	Ref.	Reference
Catg.	Cataloguing	HQ	Headquarters	Reg.	Region or Regional
Catr.	Cataloguer			Rep.	Representative
CC	County Council or City Council	Ind.	Industry or Industries	Res.	Research
		Inf.	Information		
Cent.	Central or Centre	Inst.	Inst. or Institution	S.	South
Ch.	Chief	Internat.	International	Sch.	School(s)
Child.	Children('s)			Sci.	Science or Scientific
Circ.	Circulation	L.	Library(ies)	Sec.	Secretary
Co.	Company or County	LB	London Borough	Sect.	Section
Co. L.	County Library(ies)	Lab.	Laboratory	Sen.	Senior
Coll.	College	Lect.	Lecturer	Serv.	Service(s)
Comm.	Commerce or Commercial	Lend.	Lending	Soc.	Society
		Lib.	Librarian or Librarianship	Stud.	Student
Comp.	Comprehensive			Super.	Supervisor
Dep.	Deputy	MBC.	Metropolitan Borough Council	Tech.	Technical, Technology or Technological
Dept.	Department				
Devel.	Development	MDC	Metropolitan District Council	Temp.	Temporary
Dir.	Director				
Dist.	District	Mgmnt.	Management	Univ.	University
Div.	Division or Divisional	Mgr.	Manager		
		Med.	Medical	W.	West
E.	East	Met.	Metropolitan		
Educ.	Education(al)	Min.	Ministry	Yth.	Youth
Elect.	Electrical	Mob.	Mobile		
Eng.	Engineering	Mus.	Museum		

A

Aabryn, Ms J, BA, Student, Victoria University of Wellington.
[10032560]   16/12/2013   **ME**
Abbas, Mr Z, BSc (Hons) MSc, Student, City University London.
[10035519]   16/10/2014   **ME**
Abbay, Miss O J, PhD BA (Hons) FCLIP, Retired.
[16487]   20/01/1951   **FE07/04/1980**
Abbott, Ms K J, BSc DipLib MCLIP, Retired.
[23406]   06/01/1975   **CM04/03/1977**
Abbott, Mr P A B, BA DipLib MCLIP, Head of Libraries and Archives, Royal Armouries, Leeds.
[9268]   12/01/1986   **CM24/06/1992**
Abbott, Mr R, MA BSc MCLIP, Retired. Former member of Intute, Health and Life Sciences, University of Nottingham.
[60125]   21/04/1975   **CM01/06/1981**
Abbott, Miss S J, BA (Hons), E-Resources Librarian, The National Archives, Kew.
[38097]   08/01/1985   **ME**
Abbott, Miss S K M, Msc BA PgDipLib MCLIP, Digital Library Manager, University of Exeter, Exeter.
[53666]   27/08/1996   **CM07/09/2005**
Abbott, Mr W R, BA DipLib MCLIP, Retired. CILIP representative on BRICMICS.
[21107]   05/10/1973   **CM30/10/1975**
Abbs, Mr C R, BA (Hons) MA MCLIP, Assistant Librarian, Department of Health, Leeds.
[55551]   20/10/1997   **CM15/10/2002**
Abdirahman, Mr A M, BA MLIS Msc MCLIP, Director of Library Resources, American Intercontinental University, London.
[59632]   05/07/2001   **CM21/06/2006**
Abel, Ms Y C, BTech MCLIP, Head of Information Resources, Civil Aviation Authority.
[60077]   11/01/1977   **CM20/05/1980**
Abell, Ms J, BA (Hons) FA Dip (Hons) Land. Arc MCLIP, Library Assistant, City University.
[59484]   09/04/2001   **CM12/09/2012**
Abernethy, Miss S H, BA DipLib MCLIP, Librarian, Wansbeck Hospital, Northumbria Healthcare NHS Trust.
[37791]   26/10/1984   **CM15/02/1989**
Abney, Ms A, Graduate Assistant, University of Maryland.
[10032621]   20/12/2011   **ME**
Abou Mattar, Mrs M, Master student – ENSSIB France.
[10018432]   18/01/2011   **ME**
Abrahaley-Mebrahtu, Mrs M T, BSc MSc MCLIP, Evening and Weekend Library Manager.
[46079]   01/10/1991   **CM23/06/2004**
Abraham, Mr J M, BLib MCLIP, Operations Manager, Yate Library, South Gloucestershire Council.
[30576]   03/02/1979   **CM05/10/1984**
Abraham-Araya, Miss R, Library Assistant, Royal Society of Chemistry.
[10031823]   08/10/2013   **ME**
Abrams, Mrs K, BA (Hons) MA, Librarian, Croydon High School.
[10011368]   16/10/2008   **ME**
Abrams, Miss L, BARCH, Assistant Librarian, HMP Grendon & Springhill.
[10022863]   30/04/2013   **AF**
Acham, Ms K, BSc DipInfSc MCLIP, L. Manager, Preston College.
[60701]   24/02/1983   **CM14/07/1988**
Ackerman, Miss G S, BA MCLIP, Academic Liaison Librarian, University of Westminster.
[34255]   09/10/1981   RV01/10/2008   **CM24/02/1986**

Ackrill, Dr U, MCLIP, Librarian, Beeston, Nottinghamshire County Council.
[64576]   03/03/2005   **CM06/05/2009**
Ackroyd, Miss M C, BA (Hons) MSc, Customer Services Assistant, Health Sciences Library.
[10022291]   05/02/2013   **ME**
Acreman, Mrs P, MCLIP, Retired.
[30]   06/12/1966   **CM01/01/1970**
Acum, Mrs T A, BA (Hons), Librarian Connecting Communities, Hull City Council.
[42477]   18/11/1988   **CM17/01/2001**
Adair, Ms H W, BA DipLib MCLIP, Learning Development Manager, Aberdeen City Council.
[32836]   09/10/1980   **CM31/10/1983**
Adair, Ms M A, BA (Hons) MPhil PgDipLIS MCLIP, Assistant Director Libraries NI.
[37332]   09/07/1984   **CM16/05/1990**
Adair, Miss R K, BSc (Hons) DipIM MCLIP, Head of Learning Resources, Lincoln College.
[47516]   22/09/1992   **CM21/05/1997**
Adal, Miss S, Unwaged.
[56920]   04/11/1998   **ME**
Adam, Miss J M, BA MSc MCLIP, Children's Librarian, Aberdeen City Libraries.
[30593]   26/02/1979   **CM26/02/1981**
Adam, Mr R, BSc MA MCLIP, Retired.
[60127]   22/10/1975   **CM22/10/1975**
Adamiec, Miss B, BA (Hons), Librarian/Knowledge and Information Resources Manager Ministry of Defence.
[65996]   11/08/2006   **ME**
Adams, Mrs A, Student, Aberystwyth University.
[10010695]   21/08/2008   **ME**
Adams, Ms A C, BA (Hons), Librarian, Brooke Weston, Northamptonshire.
[65811]   10/05/2006   **AF**
Adams, Mrs A M, MA DipLib MCLIP, Editor, Bronte Studies
[35]   10/10/1967   **CM01/01/1970**
Adams, Mrs C A, BA DipLib MCLIP, Unemployed.
[38054]   17/01/1985   **CM15/11/1988**
Adams, Mrs D, BA MSc DipM DipMgmt MCLIP, Learning Resource Centre Manager, Sydenham School.
[32540]   24/04/1980   **ME**
Adams, Mrs H, BA (Hons) MA MCLIP, Career Break.
[49897]   07/01/1994   **CM16/07/2003**
Adams, Mrs J, BA (Hons) ACLIP, Assistant Library Manager, Retford Library.
[10032324]   19/11/2013   **ACL13/05/2014**
Adams, Miss J, Business Information and Research Assistant, Derbyshire and Nottinghamshire Chamber of Commerce.
[10031610]   11/09/2013   **ME**
Adams, Mrs J R, BA MSc MCLIP, Retired.
[40697]   01/01/1962   **CM01/01/1966**
Adams, Ms K D, BA (Hons) PgDipLib FHEA, Academic Liaison Librarian, London Metropolitan University.
[10021295]   18/07/2014   **ME**
Adams, Mrs P, BA MCLIP, Director, School Library Association.
[18087]   03/10/1972   **CM28/02/1977**
Adams, Mr P K, BLib MCLIP, Senior Assistant Librarian, Content Delivery, De Montfort University Library, Leicester.
[32249]   10/03/1980   **CM12/03/1986**
Adams, Mr P M, MA MCLIP HonFCLIP, Employment not known.
[60128]   14/05/1968   **HFE29/06/2005**
Adams, Mrs R A, MBE BA DipLib MCLIP HonFCLIP, Retired.
[11354]   01/01/1968   **HFE23/10/2003**

Adams, Mr R E, BA MCLIP, Life Member.
[58]   06/10/1960   **CM01/01/1962**
Adams, Miss R L, BA (Hons) MBIS (LARS), Student, Monash
University.
[10033110]   11/02/2014   **ME**
Adams, Mr R S, MCLIP, Vol. Librarian, Terence Higgins Trust L.
[61]   01/01/1950   **CM01/01/1955**
Adams, Ms S L, BA MA MA, Librarian, Selwyn College, University of
Cambridge.
[64136]   19/01/2005   **ME**
Adams, Mr S R, BSc MSc MRSC MCLIP, Managing Director, Magister
Ltd, Cornwall.
[60141]   28/02/1982   **CM29/12/1986**
Adams-Fielding, Mrs K A H, ACLIP BA (Hons) PgDip, L. & Learning
Resources Centre Assistant, Halesowen College, West Mids.
[10009512]   03/06/2008   **ACL17/06/2009**
Adamson, Ms E, BA (Hons) MA, Head of Library Division, Cardiff
Metropolitan University, Cardiff.
[58506]   08/03/2000   **ME**
Adamson, Mr T L, MA, Programmes Executive, The Manufacuring
Institute.
[10002899]   10/05/2007   **ME**
Adderley, Miss C A, MCLIP, Retired.
[70]   01/01/1968   **CM01/01/1971**
Addis, Mrs F E, MCLIP, Retired.
[73]   01/01/1956   **CM01/01/1962**
Addison, Ms J F, BA DipLib MCLIP, Retired.
[11390]   10/05/1968   **CM01/01/1971**
Addy, Miss C E, BSc (Hons) PgDipLIM MCLIP, Librarian, BAE Systems,
Preston.
[58091]   27/10/1999   **CM29/03/2004**
Addy, Mrs M A S, BA MCLIP, Retired.
[1907]   01/01/1970   **CM30/09/1973**
Adebajo, Miss O, BA (Hons) MSc, Subject Liaison Librarian.
[10008531]   01/04/2008   **ME**
Adejumo, Mrs F, BLS PGDM MBA, Deputy Institute Librarian, National
Institute For Policy and Strategic Studies.
[10025021]   03/12/2013   **ME**
Adekaiyaoja, Mrs L B, LLB (Hons) ICSA MCLIP, Training & Information
Manager – TRL Pharmacy Locum Agency.
[62153]   03/03/2003   **CM23/06/2004**
Adelberg, Miss A A C, BA MCLIP, Life Member.
[76]   01/01/1949   **CM01/01/1955**
Adeloye, Mr A, MA MPhil MSc MCLIP, Chief Librarian, Nigeria High
Commission, London.
[45491]   16/01/1991   **CM18/11/1993**
Adetoro, Dr A A, DipLib BEd (Hons) MLS PhD, Associate Professor, Tai
Solarin Univiversity of Education.
[10008313]   19/03/2008   **ME**
Adewuyi, Miss M, BSc, student, City University, London.
[10021964]   06/11/2012   **ME**
Adey, Mrs H, BA MSc MCLIP, Resource Acquisitions & Supply Team
Manager, Nottingham Trent University, Nottingham.
[39602]   17/03/1986   **CM23/03/1993**
Adil, Mr S A, MLiSc,
[10008299]   19/03/2008   **ME**
Adiyadorj, Mrs O, Student.
[10017089]   22/06/2010   **ME**
Adlem, Mrs A M, BA DipLib MCLIP MSc, Cataloguer, Coutts Information
Ser., Ringwood.
[36324]   06/10/1983   **CM15/09/1993**
Adnum, Mrs V B, BA MCLIP, Life Member.
[16499]   01/01/1941   **CM01/01/1948**

Adupa, Mr S, MLISc MPhil, Student – Pd. D.
[10032137]   29/10/2013   **ME**
Afghan, Ms A P, MCLIP, Head Librarian, Whitgift School, South
Croydon.
[65718]   23/02/2006   **CM06/05/2009**
Agarwal, Mrs S, University of Bristol.
[10019445]   04/07/2011   **ME**
Agate, Miss C, BA MCLIP, Community Librarian, Norfolk & Norwich
Millennium Library, Norfolk L. & Information Servs.
[24930]   27/10/1975   **CM02/07/1979**
Agboola, Ms T, BSc MSc PgDip,
[53528]   09/07/1996   **ME**
Ager, Miss B J, BA (Hons) MA, Student, Robert Gordon University.
[10032633]   23/12/2013   **ME**
Ager, Mrs C R, BA (Hons) PGCE MCLIP, Retired.
[53013]   24/01/1996   **CM22/07/1998**
Ager, Miss N D, BA (Hons), Service Dev. Librarian, Sandwell and West
Birmingham Hospitals NHS Trust.
[64173]   14/01/2005   **ME**
Agheda, Ms R, MSc, Child. Librarian, Battersea Park Library, London.
[10001690]   06/03/2007   **ME**
Agunloye, Mr B, Student, Robert Gordon University.
[10022277]   11/06/2013   **ME**
Agus, Mrs J, BA BMus MCLIP, Librarian, Royal Welsh College of Music
& Drama, Cardiff.
[93]   19/09/1967   **CM01/01/1972**
Ah Fat, Miss P F, BLib MA MCLIP, Head of Learning Resource Centre
for, Open University of Mauritius Reduit, Mauritius.
[28469]   19/01/1978   **CM14/10/1981**
Ahmad, Mr N, E-Learning & Systems manager, Tower Hamplets
College, London.
[10022087]   05/12/2012   **ME**
Ahmad, Dr N, PhD MPhil DipLib MCLIP, Researcher-Freelance.
[10687]   01/01/1970   **CM20/06/1974**
Ahmed, Mrs L A, BA (Hons) PgDip ILM, Knowledge Centre Manager,
BSI, London.
[10015709]   05/10/1995   **ME**
Ahmed, Miss M, LRC Assistant, Sir George Monoux College.
[10031579]   04/09/2013   **ME**
Ahmed, Mr M, Mohamed Ahmed Mohamed, Student, Cairo University.
[10025057]   18/02/2014   **ME**
Ahmed, Mrs N, Librarian, St Mary's College.
[10014099]   25/06/2009   **ME**
Ahmed, Ms S, BSc PGCE DipLIS MA, Subject Librarian, London
Metropolitan University, North Campus.
[47577]   02/10/1992   **ME**
Ahmed, Mr S M, MSc, Information Systems Officer, DIA HQ Abuja
Nigeria.
[10021954]   05/11/2012   **ME**
Aiken, Mrs J D, BA (Hons) PGCE MCLIP, Assistant Director (Collections
& Resources) Teesside University Library & Information Services.
[33680]   03/02/1981   **CM14/08/1985**
Ainscough, Mr P J, MA DMS FCLIP, Retired.
[104]   01/01/1954   **FE21/07/1989**
Ainsley, Mrs T A, FHEA PgCertHELT BSc, Collection Development
Librarian, The University Library, Northumbria University, Newcastle.
[58064]   22/10/1999   **ME**
Ainsworth, Mrs A L, BA (Hons) MCLIP,
[10009295]   08/02/1993   **CM24/07/1996**
Ainsworth, Mrs F H S, BA (Hons) DipLib MCLIP, College Manager,
Royal Botanic Gardens Kew, Richmond.
[46184]   14/10/1991   **CM06/04/2005**
Aird, Mrs C D, MA MCLIP, Life Member.
[109]   01/01/1963   **CM01/01/1966**

Aird, Ms L P, BA DipLib MCLIP, School Librarian, St Christopher School Letchworth, Herts.
[36906]   13/01/1984   CM07/10/1986

Aird, Mr R C, BSc (Hons), Libraries, Archives & Customer Services Manager, Stirling Council.
[10006293]   05/10/2007   ME

Aitchison, Dr B, MA (Hons) MLITT PhD, Student, Robert Gordon University.
[10018064]   09/11/2010   ME

Aitchison, Mrs J, BA FCLIP, Retired.
[118]   01/01/1948   FE01/01/1953

Aitchison, Miss M J, MSc MPhil MCLIP, Retired.
[119]   01/01/1963   CM01/01/1968

Aitchison, Mr T M, OBE BSc HonFCLIP, Retired.
[120]   01/01/1950   FE01/04/2002

Aitken, Mrs C, BA DipIS MCLIP, Librarian, Schlumberger Cambridge Research, Cambridgeshire.
[59791]   03/10/2001   RV24/04/2009   CM21/05/2003

Aitken, Mr D A, BSc PgDip ACLIP, Systems and Acquisitions Librarian, Scottish Government, Edinburgh.
[66058]   13/09/2006   ACL05/10/2007

Aitken, Mrs J, MA (Hons) MCLIP, Principal Librarian, Mitchell Library, Glasgow.
[32706]   04/07/1980   CM26/07/1982

Aitken, Miss J L, BA (Hons), Librarian, West Yorkshire Police, Wakefield.
[61732]   30/10/2002   ME

Aitken, Mrs K B, BSc MSc MCLIP, RDSM Librarian, Long Eaton L.
[10013436]   24/04/2009   CM06/07/2011

Aitken, Miss K V, MA (Hons) DipILS,
[58093]   27/10/1999   ME

Aitken, Mrs P A, MA DipLib MCLIP, Lib. (Job Share), Hyndland Secondary School, Glasgow.
[34092]   01/10/1981   CM26/05/1993

Aitkins, Ms J U, BA MSc DMS MCLIP, Head of Public Serv., University Of Leicester. Leicester.
[31622]   08/10/1979   CM25/02/1983

Aiton, Mr S, International Benefits Researcher, Towers Watson, London.
[63229]   22/03/2004   ME

Ajai-Ajagbe, Ms K F B, BA (Hons) PgCE MIfL QTLS PgDip, Currently Student.
[57800]   02/08/1999   ME

Ajibade, Miss B A I A, BA (Hons) MSc MCLIP, Unwaged.
[50843]   21/10/1994   CM10/07/2002

Akehurst, Ms Y, BA, LRC Manager, Burgess Hill School.
[10015919]   05/04/2013   ME

Akeroyd, Mr J, MPhil BSc MCLIP, Information Management Consultant.
[31533]   20/10/1979   CM10/10/1983

Akers, Ms J M, Subject Librarian, Oxford Brookes University, Oxford.
[10001554]   23/10/1992   ME

Akhtar, Mrs K, BA, Student, Robert Gordon University.
[10034201]   20/06/2014   ME

Akhtar, Mr M, BSc DipIST MIET, Unwaged.
[60811]   31/10/1989   CM31/10/1989

Akinade-Ahmadou, Mrs S, BA MSc, Area Services Coordinator (Librarian), Eltham Centre Library.
[10032029]   22/10/2013   ME

Akinfe, Ms A O, BA (Hons) MA, Sch. Librarian, Archbishop Tenison's School, London.
[54906]   06/05/1997   ME

Akinlade, Mrs R O, MA, Learning & Teaching Librarian, OU, Milton Keynes.
[10000581]   14/10/2006   ME

Akintunde, Dr S A, PhD PgCert MSc BSc (Hons) Dip Lib, University Librarian, University of Jos, Jos, Plateau State 930001, Nigeria.
[10017420]   19/08/2010   ME

Akroyd, Mrs S K, BA (Hons) MA MCLIP, Librarian, Nottingham City Council.
[51791]   01/07/1995   CM12/03/2003

Alabi, Dr G A, BSc MiSLS PhD, Retired Professor of Library & Information Science.
[10033392]   07/03/2014   ME

Alayo, Mrs A, BA MSc MCLIP, Assistant Librarian, Barts Health NHS Trust.
[10001029]   14/12/2006   CM15/01/2013

Albin, Mrs L E, BA (Hons) DipLib MCLIP, Subject Librarian – Arts University Bournemouth (AUB).
[47035]   06/04/1992   CM22/11/1995

Albrandt, Ms V J, MA, Assistant Researcher, Hogan Lovells LLP, London.
[65370]   12/01/2006   ME

Albrow, Mr A J, BA MCLIP, L. & Information Manager, Medical Protection Society, Leeds.
[10000687]   11/01/1977   CM31/01/1979

Alcock, Miss J E, BSc (Hons) MScEcon MCLIP, Evidence Based Researcher, Evidence Base, Birmingham City University.
[65335]   11/01/2006   RV27/03/2014   CM19/10/2012

Alcock, Mrs J M D, MA MCLIP, Self-employed, now retired.
[11343]   01/01/1970   CM11/09/1972

Alcock, Ms R J, BA MCLIP, Sch. Librarian, Ballakermeen High School, Isle of Man.
[38080]   08/01/1985   CM10/05/1988

Aldenton, Ms S J, ALA MSc, Associate Director information Management, Curtin University, Perth, Western Australia.
[10019758]   06/09/2011   ME

Alderman, Mrs L A, BA (Hons) DipLIS MCLIP,
[47959]   28/10/1992   CM22/05/1996

Alderton, Miss S M, BA MCLIP, Life Member.
[142]   28/09/1950   CM01/01/1957

Aldrich, Ms E, MLib MCLIP, Retired.
[7998]   16/01/1969   CM19/07/1973

Aldrich, Mrs E J, BA (Hons) MA MCLIP, Head of Library & Knowledge Services, Maidstone & Tunbridge Wells NHS T.
[55991]   12/01/1998   CM21/03/2001

Aldridge, Ms L M, BA (Hons) MA MCLIP, Senior Lib. – Child. Serv., Cambs. L.
[47923]   26/10/1992   CM17/03/1999

Aldridge, Mrs S, ACLIP, School Librarian, Aldwickbury School, /Working 12 Hours Per Week.
[10010105]   07/07/2008   ACL04/03/2009

Ale, Mrs V F, Student, University of the West of England.
[10032960]   30/01/2014   ME

Aleksandrowicz, Miss F E, MCLIP, Learning Resource Center Co-ordinator, Boroughmuir High School, Edinburgh.
[63122]   11/02/2004   CM10/11/2010

Alencar-Brayner, Dr A, BA MA PhD, Graduate Trainee, City University, London.
[10014552]   02/11/2001   ME

Alexander, Ms C M K, BA MSc, Subject Librarian, UWS.
[10032266]   12/11/2013   ME

Alexander, Miss G, MA (Hons) MSc, Early Years Gifting Programme Co-ordinator, Aberdeen Central Library.
[65616]   01/03/2006   ME

Alexander, Mr N S, BA MA, Learning Support Librarian, Queen's Park Library, London.
[10007702]   21/02/2008   ME

Alfonsin Rosales, Miss C G, MSc, Unknown.
[10031589]   11/09/2013   ME
Allan, Mr A J, BLib MCLIP HonFCLIP, Senior Liaison Librarian,
Sheffield University Library, South Yorks.
[164]   01/01/1968   **HFE30/09/2013**
Allan, Mrs C, Senior Information Officer, Knight Frank LLP.
[10031692]   24/09/2013   ME
Allan, Mrs C A, BA (Hons) MSc, Senior Information Officer, Bank of
England, London.
[49201]   12/10/1993   ME
Allan, Ms C M, BSc (Hons) MSc, Subject Lib. Natural Sci., University of
Stirling.
[49534]   09/11/1993   **CM22/07/1998**
Allan, Mr J G, MCLIP, Librarian, Falkirk Community Trust.
[22273]   21/03/1974   **CM23/08/1976**
Allan, Mrs J M, BA (Hons),
[49778]   06/12/1993   ME
Allan, Rev J R, BA Dip Lib MCLIP MBA, Retired.
[34578]   15/01/1982   **CM16/02/1988**
Allan, Mrs L, MSc MCLIP,
[10012368]   29/01/2009   **CM20/06/2012**
Allan, Mrs M M, MA MCLIP, Life Member.
[12248]   01/01/1950   **CM01/01/1953**
Allan, Miss S L, MA (Hons) DipLIS MCLIP, Comm. Librarian, Dunblane
Library, Stirlingshire.
[58725]   01/07/2000   **CM15/01/2003**
Allan, Miss V, Community and Information Officer, North Yorks. County
Council.
[63230]   22/03/2004   ME
Allard, Ms M, MA DipLib MCLIP, L. Resource Centre Manager,
Aberdeen Grammar School.
[39865]   01/10/1986   **CM15/05/1989**
Allardice, Ms C M, BA HDipLib BA (Hons) MA MBA FCLIP, Head of
Knowledge and Information Management, Foreign & Commonwealth
Office.
[44598]   02/11/1990   **FE21/05/2003**
Allardice, Mrs E C, BSc (Hons) MA, L. Assistant, Woodhall Library,
Welwyn Garden City.
[10009708]   02/06/2008   AF
Allbon, Mrs E, BA (Hons) MSc DipLaw ILTM MCLIP, Law Librarian, City
University Library, London.
[62136]   28/02/2003   **CM07/09/2005**
Allchin, Mr O, Student.
[10022065]   28/11/2012   ME
Allchin, Mr P W M, BA MSc MCILIP, Reference Information Specialist,
British Library, London.
[10013404]   29/04/2009   **CM09/11/2011**
Allcock, Mrs J V, BA MCLIP, Senior Library Assistant, Knowsley
Metropolitan Borough Council, Whiston Library.
[42750]   16/02/1989   **CM20/03/1996**
Allcock, Mrs K J, BA (Hons) MA MCLIP, Part-time Librarian, Shropshire
Arch.
[50621]   01/10/1994   **CM18/03/1998**
Allcock, Mrs L W, BA (Hons), Tax Librarian, Ernst & Young, London.
[41862]   27/04/1988   ME
Allden, Ms A, BA MSc MBCS MCLIP, Director or Information Serv. &
University Librarian, University of Bristol.
[60778]   31/03/1988   **CM31/03/1988**
Allen, Ms A J, BA MCLIP, Locality Librarian, West, Hinckley Library,
Leics.
[25945]   06/05/1976   **CM28/11/1980**
Allen, Mr D E, MSC, L. Collections Coordinator, Royal Society of
Chemistry.
[62521]   31/07/2003   ME

Allen, Mr D W, BScSoc MCLIP, Retired.
[197]   01/01/1968   **CM01/01/1971**
Allen, Mr G C, MCILIP, Consultant, Ottimamente Ltf.
[25711]   23/02/1976   **CM01/07/1994**
Allen, Mr G R, BA BSc MRSC MCLIP, Retired.
[60129]   13/06/1975   **CM13/06/1975**
Allen, Mr I C, BA, Libraries & Publications Manager, Slaughter and May,
London.
[34457]   04/11/1981   ME
Allen, Mr J, Library Technician, West Suffolk Hospital NHS Trust.
[10031928]   15/10/2013   ME
Allen, Mr J E R, BA Dip Lib, Assistant Acquisitions and Metadata
Librarian, University of the Arts.
[10013854]   07/05/1988   ME
Allen, Mr J N, BA FCLIP, Life Member.
[207]   01/01/1952   **FE01/01/1964**
Allen, Mrs J W, MCLIP, Retired.
[208]   20/01/1964   **CM01/01/1969**
Allen, Miss L A, BA (Hons), Deputy L. Servs. Manager, Birmingham
Community Healthcare NHS Trust, Birmingham.
[37038]   31/01/1984   ME
Allen, Mr P N, MCLIP, Retired.
[219]   01/01/1961   **CM01/01/1965**
Allen, Mr R, BA (Hons) MCLIP, Team Leader Children's Services, West
Sussex Lib. Serv.
[59107]   16/11/2000   **CM29/11/2006**
Allen, Mr T, BLib, Unwaged.
[10033592]   01/04/2014   ME
Allen, Ms Y, BA (Hons) MA, Subject Librarian, University of
Roehampton London.
[56122]   03/03/1998   ME
Allery, Miss J C, BA DipLib, Institutional Repository Cataloguing
Assistant, University of Greenwich.
[38348]   11/03/1985   ME
Allington-Smith, Mr D, Student, City University London.
[10032098]   08/10/2014   ME
Allison, Miss F I, BA MCLIP, Shared Reading Facilitator.
[34684]   28/01/1982   **CM04/08/1987**
Allister, Mrs S, BA (Hons) MSc, Information Officer, Diabetes Res. Unit,
Llandough Hospital, Penarth.
[57401]   05/03/1999   ME
Allred, Mr J R, FCLIP MPhil, Retired.
[237]   01/01/1953   **FE01/01/1964**
Allsop, Mrs J, BA DipLib MCLIP, Part-time Night Clerk, Short Loans,
Lancaster University Library, Lancs.
[32799]   10/09/1980   **CM01/09/1987**
Allsop, Mrs P, BA DipLib, Corporate Web Manager, Isle of Anglesey
County Council.
[33008]   22/10/1980   **CM19/01/1984**
Allsopp, Dr D, BSc PhD CBiol FSB MCLIP, Retired.
[60130]   21/04/1975   **CM21/06/1979**
Allum, Mr D N, BA MCLIP, Retired.
[19462]   01/01/1966   **CM01/01/1970**
Allwood, Ms A, BA, Robert Gordon University.
[10021081]   29/05/2012   ME
Alman, Mrs M, BA BCom MCLIP, Life Member.
[242]   01/01/1937   **CM01/01/1941**
Almustapha, Mr A H, Head of Virtual Library, Federal College of
Education (Technical).
[10032496]   10/12/2013   ME
Al-Othaimeen, Dr E, Phd, Assistant Professor, College of Basic
Education.
[10031938]   15/10/2013   ME

Al-Shabibi, Mrs A M R, BA DipLib MCLIP, Unwaged Chartered
Librarian, London.
[33970]   01/07/1981   CM10/05/1985
Al-Shiba, Ms S H, BA, Student, UCL.
[10035414]   13/10/2014   ME
Al-Shorbaji, Dr N M A, BA DipDOC MLib PhD, Director, Knowledge
Management and Sharing, World Heatlh Organisation, Geneva.
[34941]   14/05/1982   ME
Al-Talal, Dr G, BSc Mphil PHd, Head of Res. & Information Serv.,
Federation of Master Builders, London.
[10008574]   08/12/2000   ME
Altaner, Mrs A, BA MLS, Librarian, London Borough of Harrow.
[61022]   01/02/2002   ME
Alvey, Mrs K J, BA (Hons) MCLIP, Stock Manager, Bath Central Library,
Bath & North East Somerset.
[39445]   28/01/1986   CM21/12/1988
Amador, Dr V, BA MA PhD, Teaching Fellow, Heriot-Watt University,
Edinburgh.
[65075]   24/10/2005   ME
Amaeshi, Prof B O, BA MA MCLIP, Retired.
[24309]   07/02/1962   CM01/01/1966
Amatt, Mr L K, BA FCLIP, Retired.
[251]   01/01/1963   FE05/11/1973
Amdurer, Mr D, BA (Hons), Librarian and Literacy Co-ordinator, The
Crossley Heath School.
[10025152]   05/09/2014   ME
Ameen, Prof K, PhD, Professor and Chairperson, Department of
Information Managment, University of the Punjab, Lahore, PK.
[10033232]   21/02/2014   ME
Ameen, Prof K, PhD, Professor and Chairperson, Department of
Information Managment, University of the Punjab, Lahore, PK.
[10033232]   03/10/2006   ME
Ames, Mrs D E, BA (Hons), High School Librarian, Benjamin Britton
High School, Suffolk.
[61592]   02/10/2002   ME
Ames, Miss J M, BA (Hons), Student, Aberystwyth University.
[10032682]   03/01/2014   ME
Ames, Dr S, MA MScR PhD, Student, Robert Gordon University.
[10034448]   14/07/2014   ME
Amies, Mr P S, BA (Hons) DipLIS MCLIP, Cataloguer, University
College, London.
[50659]   05/10/1994   CM20/09/2000
Ammaccapane, Miss T, Student, RGU.
[10032306]   14/11/2013   ME
Ammon, Dr M R, MA PhD, Library Services Administrator, Engineering
Department, University of Cambridge.
[10031466]   13/08/2013   AF
Ananda, Miss A, Student, Coleg Llandrillo.
[10032512]   11/12/2013   ME
Anders, Mrs J H S, BSc (Hons) MSc MCLIP, SHERPA Serv.
Development Officer, Centre for Res. Development (CRC), University
of Nottingham.
[59090]   13/11/2000   CM17/09/2008
Andersen, Mrs A P, BA PGCE, Library Assistant, International School
of Lund (ISLK).
[10033163]   18/02/2014   ME
Anderson, Mrs A, MCLIP, Comm. Librarian, North Lanarkshire Council,
Lanarkshire.
[21293]   01/10/1973   CM12/07/1976
Anderson, Mrs C A, BA MCLIP, Research Librarian: Latin American &
Caribbean Studies and Commonwealth Studies, Senate House
Library, University of London.
[29038]   09/03/1978   CM06/04/1981

Anderson, Ms C J, BA (Hons) MCLIP, Senior Information & Research
Manager, Linklaters LLP, London.
[48073]   04/11/1992   CM19/07/2000
Anderson, Mrs D, MA DipLib HonFLA, Director, IFLA Office for U BC
[267]   01/01/1953   HFE12/06/1986
Anderson, Mr G, BA MCLIP, Senior Lib and Cultural Venues Manager,
The Mitchell Library, Culture and Sport Glasgow.
[37434]   14/09/1984   CM15/02/1989
Anderson, Mr G P J, BA (Hons),
[10000923]   28/11/2006   ME
Anderson, Mrs H, BA (Hons) MSc (Econ) MCLIP, Assistant Librarian
(Acquisitions and Metadata Support), University Ulster,
Newtownabbey, County Antrim.
[63745]   01/10/2004   CM11/07/2012
Anderson, Miss J, MA MCLIP, UWS University of the West of Scotland,
Crichton Library, Dumfries Campus.
[32771]   25/08/1980   CM03/11/1983
Anderson, Mrs J C, BA (Hons) MA MCLIP, Service Improvement
Manager, Integreon Managed Solutions Ltd, Bristol.
[53894]   09/10/1996   CM17/01/2001
Anderson, Mr J D, MA, Student, Robert Gordon University.
[10032508]   10/12/2013   ME
Anderson, Mr J E, BA MLib NDipM MCLIP, Enquiry Serv. Manager,
Cambridgeshire County Council, Cambridge Central Library.
[43050]   03/07/1989   CM24/04/1991
Anderson, Mrs J E, BA DipLib MCLIP, Retired.
[759]   01/01/1970   CM01/01/1972
Anderson, Miss L, Admin Assistant/ Student.
[10032084]   24/10/2013   ME
Anderson, Mrs L B, BA, Part-time School Librarian, West Lothian
Council.
[10000833]   09/11/2006   ME
Anderson, Ms L C, BA MSc MCLIP, Librarian, Downside Abbey.
[10009526]   02/06/2008   CM14/03/2012
Anderson, Ms L E, BA (Hons) MCLIP, Knowledge Management
Specialist, Pennine Care NHS Foundation Trust.
[58431]   11/02/2000   CM21/08/2009
Anderson, Mr M C,
[10033398]   07/03/2014   ME
Anderson, Ms M E, BA MCLIP, Information Serv. Advisor, Napier
University, Edinburgh.
[30082]   06/12/1978   CM20/10/1981
Anderson, Ms M L, BSc (Hons), Delivery Manager, Integreon.
[10002004]   20/10/1994   ME
Anderson, Ms S A, Student.
[10032142]   29/10/2013   ME
Anderson, Mr S C, BA (Hons), Research and Information Worker.
[10015057]   09/10/2009   ME
Anderson, Mrs T, DipILS MCLIP, LRC Co-ord., Aberdeen C. C.,
Aberdeen.
[50094]   21/03/1994   CM15/09/2004
Anderson, Mr T J B, BA MCLIP, Retired.
[16539]   01/01/1948   CM01/01/1954
Anderton, Mrs J F, BA Dip Lib, Librarian, Monmouth Sch.
[10008445]   12/01/1979   ME
Anderton, Miss M F, BSc MSc FCLIP, Information Consultant, Self-
employed.
[60517]   18/01/1978   FE01/04/1984
Andrew, Miss E L, BA (Hons) MA MCLIP, Senior Information Assistant,
Northumbria University, Newcastle-Upon-Tyne.
[66143]   03/10/2006   CM08/03/2013
Andrew, Miss S M, BA PGCE DipLib MCLIP, Customer Services
Supervisor, Purley Library, London Borough of Croydon.
[38600]   25/07/1985   CM12/12/1990

Andrews, Mr D M, BSc MA, Principal Librarian, Balham & Northcote, London Borough of Wandsworth.
[62030]   22/01/2003   ME

Andrews, Mrs G E, FRSA MCLIP, Life Member.
[308]   01/01/1951   CM01/01/1971

Andrews, Mr J M, BA DipInfLib MCLIP, Subject Advisor, University of Birmingham.
[42624]   24/01/1989   CM19/03/2008

Andrews, Dr J S, MA PhD MCLIP, Life Member.
[16540]   01/01/1951   CM01/01/1954

Andrews, Mrs P C S, BSc, Student, University of Sheffield.
[10020674]   22/03/2012   AF

Andrews, Mrs R C, BA, LR Co-ordinator, Richard Huish College, Taunton.
[10019879]   28/04/1994   ME

Angel, Mrs J, ACLIP, LRC Manager, Kings Priory School.
[10019487]   08/07/2011   ACL16/01/2014

Angier, Miss L E, BA, Library Assistant, Skadden.
[10018537]   03/02/2011   ME

Anglim, Mrs A L, BA (Hons) MCLIP, Principal Librarian (Schools), The Mitchell Library.
[37395]   06/08/1984   CM24/07/1996

Angus, Mrs R F, BA (Hons) PGCE,
[10015535]   11/12/2009   ME

Annis, Mr M, BSc (Hons) DipLib MCLIP, Children's Librarian Bedlington Library.
[10017350]   01/10/1981   CM18/07/1985

Ansell, Mrs D, Information Manager, Civil Service.
[10034310]   02/07/2014   ME

Ansell, Mrs J M, MCLIP, Retired.
[321]   01/01/1958   CM25/02/1977

Anson, Mrs J M, BA DipLib MCLIP, Librarian, Dallam School, Cumbria.
[33365]   04/11/1980   CM07/10/1986

Anson, Miss S, Teaching Assistant, Alumwell Junior School.
[10034243]   21/07/2014   ME

Ansorge, Mrs C A, MA MCLIP, Head of Near Eastern Department, Cambridge University Library.
[1760]   01/01/1969   CM01/01/1971

Anstead, Mrs A H, BSc (Hons) DipLib DipTrans MCIL, Freelance.
[37400]   09/08/1984   ME

Anstey, Mrs K A, MCLIP BA (Hons),
[22153]   21/02/1974   CM12/07/1976

Anstis, Ms P L, Learning Res. Assistant, Luther King Hse. Library, Partnership for Theological Ed., Manchester.
[56924]   06/11/1998   ME

Anthony, Mr R L, BA DipLib MA, Senior Assistant Librarian (Library Web Services), House of Lords Library, London.
[45494]   20/02/1991   ME

Anthony, Ms S G, BSc DipLib, Librarian, Cwmbran Library, Torfaen County Borough Council, Gwent.
[39409]   27/01/1986   ME

Anthony-Edwards, Mr J, MA MA, Associate University Librarian (Library Services), University of Salford.
[59295]   31/01/2001   ME

Antill, Mr J K, FCLIP, Life Member.
[16544]   01/01/1953   FE01/01/1968

Anton, Mrs L M, MA MCLIP BCS,
[22133]   28/01/1974   CM01/01/1976

Anuar, Mrs H, BA HonFLA FCLIP, Resident in Singapore.
[16545]   01/01/1952   HFE01/01/1985

Apperley, Mrs M, ACLIP, Lib. Sch. Holmwood House Prep. Sch. Colchester.
[10018499]   28/01/2011   ACL08/03/2013

Appleby, Mrs S, MA (Hons) MCLIP, Network Librarian, Inverness Royal Academy, Inverness.
[61101]   25/02/2002   CM21/06/2006

Appleton, Mr L, BA (Hons) MA PGCE MEd, Associate Director, Library Services, University of the Arts, London.
[59163]   04/12/2000   ME

Appleyard, Sir R, HonFCLIP, Hon. Fellow.
[60135]   18/11/1987   FE18/11/1987

Appleyard, Miss S C, BA (Hons) MSc ACLIP, Library Operations Manager, Franklin Wilkin's Library, King's College London.
[10008128]   20/03/2008   ACL17/06/2009

Applin, Mrs J F, Learning & Teaching Support Supervisor, Universityof Sussex, Brighton.
[10009989]   05/11/2010   ME

Archer, Mrs A L, MCLIP, L. & Information Officer, Newcastle Libraries.
[60947]   15/01/2002   CM13/08/2010

Archer, Ms B A, BA, Librarian, Word & Image Department, Victoria & Albert Museum, London.
[43382]   16/10/1989   ME

Archer, Mr D, BA MA, Reader Services Librarian, London School of Hygiene & Tropical Medicine.
[10007990]   18/06/2008   ME

Archer, Mr M K, BSc BA MCLIP, Consultant.
[60608]   01/01/1983   CM01/01/1983

Archer, Mr S, MA MA (Cantab), Sub-Librarian, Parker Library and Digital Projects Librarian.
[10001228]   03/02/2007   ME

Archibald, Ms G, Content Manager, UKBA, Easingwold, York.
[38806]   08/10/1985   ME

Archibald, Mrs J, MCLIP, Service Support Librarian, Teesside University Library.
[10018416]   14/01/2011   CM13/11/2013

Archibald, Mrs P V, MSc DipEd, L. Assistant, Scotish Police Serv. Authority, Scottish Police College L.
[61265]   13/05/2002   ME

Archibald, Mrs R, Library Manager, Danderhall Library.
[54147]   07/11/1996   ME

Archinard, Ms V, Information Scientist, ThinkAnalytics.
[10031783]   04/10/2013   ME

Ardener, Mrs M, MCLIP, Retired.
[357]   01/01/1949   CM01/01/1970

Ardizzone, Ms J T, MA MCLIP, Librarian, Deutsch-Franzosisches Inst., Ludwigsburg, Germany.
[44083]   25/04/1990   CM25/09/1996

Ardley, Mrs A G, BSc (Hons) MCLIP, Librarian, The Hazeley Academy. Milton Keynes.
[63231]   22/03/2004   CM21/03/2007

Arens, Mrs E A, MCLIP, Assistant Systems Librarian, University of Leicester.
[65798]   03/05/2006   CM13/04/2011

Arfa, Mrs J A, BA (Hons), Unwaged.
[51183]   23/11/1994   ME

Argent, Mrs H S, BSc,
[36102]   27/05/1983   ME

Argent, Mrs L, Team Organiser, Interfleet Tech. Ltd, Derby.
[64881]   02/09/2005   AF

Arif, Ms S, Subject Liaison Librarian, Brunel University.
[10013853]   23/04/2013   ME

Arisco, Ms F, BA (Hons) LLM, Student, London Metropolitan University.
[10019345]   09/06/2011   ME

Arlow, Ms C, BA MA, Student, Queens University Belfast.
[10034294]   01/07/2014   ME

Armitage, Miss P A M, BA,
[10011463]   21/10/2008   ME

Armitage, Mrs S J, BA (Hons) PgDip, Director of L. Sales, Bibliographic
Data Serv. Ltd, Dumfries.
[62169]   01/04/2003   ME
Armitage, Mr T R, BA MCLIP, Researcher, Self-Employed.
[29364]   03/07/1978   CM19/07/1983
Armsby, Mr A F, BA MCLIP, Retired.
[377]   01/01/1962   CM01/01/1967
Armson, Mr P, MCLIP, Life Member.
[380]   01/01/1947   CM01/01/1953
Armston, Mrs H S, MA,
[10021038]   17/05/2012   ME
Armstrong, Miss A, BA (Hons) DipILM MCLIP, Audit & Evaluation
Officer, Durham University, Teeside.
[49738]   29/11/1993   CM22/05/1996
Armstrong, Mr C J, BLib FIAP FCLIP, Director, Information Automation
Ltd, Bronant, Aberystwyth SY23 4TJ.
[48480]   21/01/1993   FE01/04/2002
Armstrong, Mrs D M, MCLIP, Retired.
[384]   06/03/1963   CM01/01/1968
Armstrong, Ms E, BA (Hons) DipILM MCLIP, Learning Res. Manager,
Cramlington Learning Village, Northumberland.
[47702]   19/10/1992   CM23/09/1998
Armstrong, Miss E K, Sales Assistant, Home Bargains, Leek.
[49757]   02/12/1993   ME
Armstrong, Ms F A, BA MA DipLIS MScEcon, Assistant Librarian, Cwm
Taf LHB Library, Prince Charles Hospital.
[61306]   20/05/2002   ME
Armstrong, Ms H, MA (Hons) DipLib MCLIP, Higher Library Executive,
House of Commons Library.
[31742]   25/11/1979   CM17/12/1982
Armstrong, Ms H D, MCLIP, Retired.
[28776]   11/02/1978   CM17/06/1980
Armstrong, Ms J, BA (Hons) MCLIP, School Librarian, St Edmund's
College, Hertfordshire.
[41818]   21/04/1988   CM18/03/1998
Armstrong, Mrs J L, MCLIP, Retired.
[16462]   17/03/1967   CM01/01/1971
Armstrong, Mrs K M P, BA MA MCLIP, Libraries Manager, Central
Library, South Shields.
[33613]   22/01/1981   CM10/03/1983
Armstrong, Miss L, BA MA, Team Librarian for Fiction, Reading
Libraries.
[64188]   31/01/2005   ME
Armstrong, Miss L E, BA (Hons) MCLIP, Acquisitions Librarian, South
Ayrshire Council.
[41575]   25/01/1988   CM14/09/1994
Armstrong, Miss R J, MCLIP, Life Member.
[395]   01/01/1951   CM01/01/1957
Armstrong, Miss T, BA (Hons) MCLIP, Information Manager, City of
London.
[52553]   07/11/1995   CM17/01/2001
Armstrong Viner, Mr R F, MA BSc (Hons) MCLIP, Head of Collection
Management, University of Kent, Canterbury.
[56761]   08/10/1998   CM06/04/2005
Arnfield, Mr A, Knowledge Manager, Lynfield Mount Hospital, Bradford.
[10016809]   01/04/2011   ME
Arnold, Dr B P, MA MSt DPhil, Student.
[10022812]   23/04/2013   ME
Arnold, Miss B W, MCLIP, Life Member.
[399]   01/01/1950   CM01/01/1955
Arnold, Mr G, Information Centre Assistant, Ministry of Defence,
Fareham.
[10012435]   10/02/2010   AF

Arnold, Ms K L, BA (Hons) MSc, Career break.
[39858]   29/08/1986   ME
Arnold, Mrs S, Information Specialist, Nat Collaborating Centre for
Cancer, Cardiff.
[52999]   14/02/1996   ME
Arnold, Mr T, BA MA, Librarian, Plymouth Hospitals NHS Trust.
[10009140]   05/09/2014   ME
Arnot, Dr J, MA (Hons) PhD PgDip, Librarian, NHS Health Scotland.
[61784]   05/11/2002   ME
Arnott, Mr G, BA (Hons) PgDip LIS MA PgDip HETL, Unemployed.
[10022328]   11/02/2013   ME
Arrington, Ms A, Student, Simmons College.
[10034764]   14/08/2014   ME
Arscott, Mr T, Student.
[10032135]   29/10/2013   ME
Arthur, Miss C, Librarian, Sch. L. Serv. Hounslow.
[62780]   22/10/2003   ME
Arthur, Mrs R E, BA FCLIP, Senior Manager (Information and Culture),
North Ayrshire Council.
[29559]   01/10/1978   RV10/03/2010   FE21/11/2001
Arunachalam, Mr S, FCLIP HonFCLIP, Hon. Fellow.
[60105]   07/12/2001   FE01/04/2002
Asamoah-Okyere, Mr E, BSc MSc, Student University of Strathclyde.
[10032422]   03/12/2013   ME
Ascough, Miss C, BA (Hons), Student.
[10032474]   09/12/2013   ME
Asgarali, Mrs S, MSc, Student, City University, London.
[10019279]   20/05/2011   ME
Ash, Mr C S, LLB (Hons) PgDip MCLIP, Library Manager, Sandwell
Council.
[65501]   09/02/2006   CM09/11/2011
Ash, Mrs E, BA (Hons), Assistant Librarian, Radley College.
[10035270]   03/10/2014   ME
Ash, Mr T M, BA (Hons) ACLIP, Systems and Communications
Librarian, Croydon College.
[10008636]   16/04/2009   ACL04/08/2010
Ashbey, Mrs K, MCLIP, Retired.
[15067]   29/12/1970   CM07/08/1974
Ashby, Ms K E, BA (Hons), Unemployed.
[41331]   02/11/1987   ME
Ashby, Miss M M, MA DipEdTech MCLIP, Retired.
[431]   01/01/1959   CM01/01/1963
Ashdown, Mr S, Information Manager, Civil Service.
[10034301]   02/07/2014   ME
Ashdown, Mr S T, ALIB ACLIP, Lib. Assistant, Brighton College,
Brighton.
[10017335]   29/07/2010   ACL12/09/2012
Asher, Ms M I, MA, Bookshop Assistant/Student, Strathclyde University.
[10033587]   01/04/2014   ME
Ashford, Miss L, MA,
[10012019]   10/12/2008   ME
Ashill, Mr C G, BA MLib MCLIP, Library Assistant, Institute of Classical
Studies, London.
[49271]   20/10/1993   CM20/11/2002
Ashley, Mr B L, BA DipLib MCLIP, Senior Manager (East Midlands),
Arts Council England.
[29564]   04/10/1978   CM11/12/1981
Ashley, Mrs E, BA MCLIP, Library Assistant, University Hospital of
South Manchester.
[35297]   06/10/1982   CM19/01/1988
Ashley, Mrs J, BA (Hons) PGCE MSc MCLIP FHEA, Academic Liaison
Librarian, Durham University.
[57376]   17/02/1999   CM15/09/2004

129

Ashley, Ms K, ACLIP, Assistant in Charge, Clay Cross Library,
Derbyshire County Council.
[10010861]   02/09/2008 **ACL28/01/2009**
Ashley, Mrs K, BA (Hons) MCLIP, Sch. Librarian, Post 16 Learning
Resource Centre for Manager.
[45390]   23/11/1990 **CM18/03/1998**
Ashman, Mrs R, BA (Hons) MCLIP, Bibliographical Servs. Assistant.
[30577]   27/01/1979 **CM16/04/1984**
Ashman, Mr R A, BA MCLIP DMS, Central Library Manager,
Southampton Central Library.
[32729]   13/08/1980 **CM24/07/1984**
Ashmore, Miss D, BA, Community Library Assistant, Huntingdon
Library & Archives.
[10033818]   02/05/2014 **ME**
Ashmore, Mr W S H, BA FCLIP, Life Member.
[444]   01/01/1941 **FE01/01/1954**
Ashraf, Ms F M, BSc MA, Learning Facilitator. Westminster Kingsway
College.
[58782]   20/07/2000 **ME**
Ashton, Mrs H C, BSc, Head of Library Services, Newcastle College.
[40393]   28/01/1987 **ME**
Ashton, Mrs L, BSc MA MSc MCLIP, Digital Content Officer, Ashridge
Business School.
[10021830]   18/10/2012 **CM13/11/2013**
Ashwell, Miss C, BA (Hons), Student, University of Oxford.
[10035493]   16/10/2014 **ME**
Ashworth, Mrs L, BA DipLib MCLIP, Community Child. Librarian,
Salford Community Leisure.
[33087]   08/10/1980 **CM08/10/1982**
Ashworth, Mr N P, BEd,
[10033089]   10/02/2014 **ME**
Asiimwe, Miss G, BLIS MCLIP, Lib. Officer, African Prisons Project,
Uganda.
[10015550]   14/12/2009 **CM15/07/2014**
Askham, Mrs A S, MCLIP, Part-time Information Librarian, University of
Bath.
[62500]   29/07/2003 **CM10/07/2009**
Aslett, Mrs A M, BA MCLIP, Librarian, St Paul's School, Barnes,
London.
[2116]   09/05/1972 **CM11/08/1977**
Asquith, Mr P, BA, College Librarian, Dearne Valley College.
[10001981]   07/11/1991 **ME**
Astall, Mr H R, FCLIP, Life Member.
[476]   01/01/1953 **FE18/05/1973**
Astbury, Mr R G, FCLIP, Life Member.
[477]   01/01/1949 **FE01/01/1958**
Aston, Mr M, BSc (Hons) MCLIP, Local History Manager, Islington Local
History Centre and Museum, Finsbury Library, London Borough of
Islington.
[46212]   01/10/1991 **CM20/05/1998**
Atanassova, Dr R I, BA (Hons) DPhil, Curator, British Library, London.
[10015659]   08/01/2010 **ME**
Atherton, Ms L H, BA (Hons) MA MCLIP, Head Librarian, Wellington
College, Berkshire.
[46355]   30/10/1991 **RV27/08/2014   CM23/07/1997**
Atherton, Mr N E, BSc (Hons) MCLIP, Learning Resources Team
Leader, Riverside College Halton.
[53179]   01/04/1996 **CM22/08/2012**
Athreya, Mrs K, BBM MBA MA, Unwaged (Volunteer).
[10018283]   13/12/2010 **ME**
Atiogbe, Miss P K, BSc (Hons) MSc (Dist) MCLIP, Library Services
Manager, Epsom and St Helier University Hospitals NHS Trust.
[59529]   26/04/2001 **CM23/06/2004**

Atkins, Mr C, BA (Hons) MCLIP, Librarian: Local Information & Studies,
Royal Borough of Windsor & Maidenhead.
[44854]   01/01/1991 **CM31/01/1996**
Atkins, Mrs P K, BSc DipLib MCLIP,
[34776]   11/02/1982 **CM16/05/1985**
Atkins, Ms R L, BA MSc, Subject Librarian & Repository Manager.
[10001218]   02/02/2007 **ME**
Atkins, Miss S, BA (Hons) MA, Academic Support Officer, Department
of Info Studies.
[10022298]   05/02/2013 **ME**
Atkinson, Mrs A L, BA (Hons) MCLIP, History Services Development
Manager, Kent County Council.
[26767]   23/11/1976 **CM14/10/1980**
Atkinson, Miss E J,
[10020199]   17/11/2011 **ME**
Atkinson, Mrs F, BA (Hons) MA MCLIP, Community Services Manager,
Bracknell Forest Libraries.
[46094]   01/10/1991 **CM23/03/1994**
Atkinson, Mrs J, BSc BA MCLIP, Retired.
[8425]   17/01/1967 **CM01/01/1969**
Atkinson, Ms J C E, BA (Hons) PgDipILS MA MCLIP, Assistant
Librarian, University of Ulster at Coleraine, Co. Londonderry.
[44588]   31/10/1990 **CM21/05/2008**
Atkinson, Ms J D, BA MA DipLib MCLIP, Retired.
[27875]   12/10/1977 **CM29/11/1979**
Atkinson, Mrs J E, Information Officer, North Yorks. Co. Council,
Northallerton.
[63404]   28/04/2004 **ME**
Atkinson, Mrs J M, BA (Hons) PGILM, Unwaged.
[56679]   01/10/1998 **ME**
Atkinson, Mr J T, BA, Information Asssitant & MA Student.
[10025258]   25/04/2014 **ME**
Atkinson, Miss L, MSc BA AKC MCLIP, Librarian, Camden PL, London.
[10016430]   24/01/1973 **CM01/08/1976**
Atkinson, Mrs L A, BA MA MCLIP, Cataloguer/Liaison Support
Librarian, University of Reading.
[51909]   04/08/1995 **CM23/06/2004**
Atkinson, Mrs L S, BSc MSc MCLIP, Reader Serv. Manager, Bodleian
Health Care Library, University of Oxford.
[26080]   16/07/1976 **CM28/09/1978**
Atkinson, Miss N P, MCLIP, Retired.
[509]   01/01/1957 **CM01/01/1962**
Atkinson, Mr P J, BSc MPhil MCLIP, Retired.
[20485]   01/04/1973 **CM25/09/1975**
Atkinson, Mr R G, BA (Hons) MA MCLIP, Director of Library & Media
Services, Birkbeck, University of London.
[43670]   22/11/1989 **CM14/09/1994**
Atkinson, Mrs S, BA MCLIP, Librarian, Brookfield Comm. School,
Chesterfield.
[28873]   20/01/1978 **CM21/10/1982**
Atkinson, Mr S, BSc DipLib MCLIP, Tech. Serv. Librarian, University
College Falmouth.
[39973]   07/10/1986 **CM15/03/1989**
Atkinson, Mr S B, BA, Central Enquiry Unit Officer, Essex Libraries.
[10021999]   15/11/2012 **ME**
Atlass, Mrs H J, MCLIP, Retired.
[7698]   01/11/1970 **CM16/12/1974**
Atlee, Mr I H N, MCLIP, Life Member.
[512]   01/01/1962 **CM01/01/1969**
Attar, Dr K, BA PhD MA, Rare Books Librarian, Senate House London,
University of London.
[56653]   01/10/1998 **ME**
Aubertin-Potter, Miss N A R, BA PhD MCLIP, Retired.
[43664]   21/11/1989 **CM24/09/1997**

Auchinvole, Miss R, BA MCLIP, Res. Librarian, Turnbull High School, Bishopbriggs.
[38988]   22/10/1985   **CM22/05/1991**

Auckland, Ms M J, OBE BSc MSc MCLIP HonFCLIP, Independent Consultant & Trainer.
[522]   01/01/1969   **HFE24/10/2002**

Aucock, Miss J, MA DipLib, Head of Cataloguing and Repository Services, LIS, University of St Andrews, Fife.
[36265]   12/09/1983   **ME**

Audelan, Miss C N C, Degree, Student, Ecole Nationale Des Chartes.
[10034378]   09/07/2014   **ME**

Audsley, Miss E, MCLIP, Retired.
[523]   01/01/1971   **CM22/04/1975**

Auger, Mr C P, FCLIP, Life Member.
[525]   01/01/1949   **FE01/01/1965**

Aurelio, Mr M, BA (Hons) MA MSc, NHS Management Trainee, Health Informatics.
[10019900]   29/09/2011   **ME**

Austin, Miss K, MSc, Information Officer, Olswang LLP.
[10011805]   14/11/2008   **ME**

Austin, Mrs M E, BA (Hons) MA MCLIP, Library and Learning Officer, Gateshead College.
[10012469]   10/02/2009   **RV**16/01/2014   **CM22/08/2012**

Austin, Mrs R J, Y Bont Support Librarian, Welsh Assembly Gov., Aberystwyth.
[10012465]   10/02/2009   **ME**

Austin, Mrs S M, BA (Hons) DipILM MCLIP, Libray Manager, South Tyneside NHS Foundation Trust.
[47771]   14/10/1992   **CM19/07/2000**

Auty, Miss C C, BA (Hons) MSc MCLIP, Deputy Pictab Secretary, UK Parliament.
[56267]   23/04/1998   **CM23/01/2002**

Avafia, Mr K E, FCLIP, Retired.
[22518]   15/03/1962   **FE29/01/1992**

Avent-Gibson, Ms D J, BScEcon (Hons) MCLIP, Subject Lib. /Assistant Librarian, University of Bristol.
[48824]   21/06/1993   **CM19/11/2003**

Averill, Miss L J, BA MSc MCLIP, Unwaged.
[56869]   29/10/1998   **CM08/08/2008**

Avery, Ms A J, BA (Hons), Librarian, Netherbrook Primary School.
[37593]   05/10/1984   **ME**

Avery, Ms N, BA (Hons) MCLIP, Principal Librarian, Information Serv., Bedford Central Library, Beds. County Council.
[42129]   04/10/1988   **CM23/03/1993**

Awre, Mr C L, BSc MSc, Head of Information Management, L. & Learning Innovation, Brynmor Jones Library, University of Hull.
[60821]   04/12/1989   **ME**

Awwad, Miss N, PGdip, Principal Lib. Assistant, Harold Cohen L. University of Liverpool.
[10006605]   15/11/2007   **ME**

Axelsson, Miss F H, Study Librarian at Södertälje Public Library, Sweden.
[10000627]   18/10/2006   **ME**

Axford, Mr J A, Information Manager, Ministry of Defence.
[10016565]   14/04/2010   **ME**

Axford, Mrs W, MA MCLIP, Retired.
[544]   01/01/1955   **CM01/01/1959**

Ayling, Ms S M, BA DipLib MA MCLIP, Part-time Librarian, Linslade Lower School, Beds. County Council.
[30306]   19/01/1979   **CM08/02/1983**

Aynsley, Miss S E, MA MCLIP, Deputy Library Services Manager, Lewisham and Greenwich NHS Trust.
[10012652]   03/03/2009   **CM27/03/2013**

Ayoola, Mrs B B E, MSc, Assistant Learning Resource Manager, Lewisham College, London.
[10000539]   01/10/1993   **ME**

Ayre, Mrs C I, BA (Hons) MA MCLIP, Web Programme Admin., Global Care.
[58118]   03/11/1999   **CM19/11/2003**

Ayre, Mr S M, BA (Hons) MA (Dist) MCLIP, Library Services Manager, George Eliot Hospital NHS Trust.
[57487]   06/04/1999   **RV**14/12/2012   **CM06/04/2005**

Ayres, Miss C A, BSc DipLib MCLIP, Head of Systems & Services, University of Reading Library.
[36003]   11/04/1983   **CM14/04/1987**

Ayris, Mr D A, BA MCLIP, Life Member.
[553]   01/01/1956   **CM01/01/1967**

Azubike, Mrs M, BA MEd MCLIP, LRC Manager /Subject Specialist, University of East London.
[32915]   03/10/1980   **CM29/04/1986**

B

Baah, Mr K A, MA MCLIP, Customer Services Manager, London Borough of Hackney.
[10020395]   27/10/1989   **CM15/11/2000**

Baalham, Rev G R, BSc, Teaching Assistant, Gusford Primary School.
[35478]   25/10/1982   **CM21/01/1986**

Baalham, Mr M C, BA (Hons) MA, Assistant Librarian/Rare Books Cataloguer, Longleat House, Warminster.
[10000991]   12/05/2004   **ME**

Baatsvik-Miller, Miss L, Student, City University London.
[10035598]   22/10/2014   **ME**

Babalola, Mr S, MLS, Student, University of Sheffield.
[10035513]   16/10/2014   **ME**

Babbs, Mrs C, BA MCLIP, Sch. L. Resource Centre Co-ordinator, Liberton High School, Edinburgh.
[32997]   17/10/1980   **CM18/03/1998**

Babcock, Mr C J, BA DipLib PGCE MCLIP, Part-time Supervisor, Croydon College Library.
[50244]   13/05/1994   **CM24/07/1996**

Babicz, Miss J, Student.
[10035285]   03/10/2014   **ME**

Bacca, Miss S, Student, Aberystwyth University.
[10017332]   23/07/2014   **ME**

Bachell, Mr A J, BSc MSc, N/A.
[10034023]   21/05/2014   **ME**

Back, Ms C L, BSc, Development Officer (Digital) Plymouth Libraries.
[64514]   22/04/2005   **ME**

Backhouse, Ms K L, Special Collections Librarian.
[10006562]   15/11/2007   **ME**

Bacon, Ms A R, MCLIP,
[31555]   18/10/1979   **CM08/04/1986**

Bacon, Mrs D E, MA MCLIP, Retired.
[27880]   11/10/1977   **CM29/11/1979**

Bacon, Mrs H A, BA MCLIP, Unemployed (made redundant Jul. 2013).
[26650]   30/09/1976   **CM25/09/1981**

Bacon, Mr N, BEd DipLib MCLIP, Retired.
[46882]   21/02/1992   **CM18/11/1993**

Badahdah, Mr M A, PhD Student, CEM, University of Brighton.
[10015114]   13/10/2009   **ME**

Badcock, Mrs J, MCLIP, Learning Resource Centre Manager, Worksop Post.
[10007710]   20/03/2008   **CM19/10/2012**

Bader, Miss H V, MSc BA (Hons) PgCert MCLIP, Assistant Librarian, Royal Welsh College of Music & Drama, Cardiff.
[63015]   15/12/2003   **CM11/11/2009**

Badger, Mr I E, BA (Hons) PgDipLIM MCLIP, Learning & Teaching Librarian, University for the Creative Arts.
[62907]   18/11/2003   **CM29/03/2006**

Badisang, Miss B E G, MA, Librarian.
[45569]   15/03/1991   **ME**

Badock, Miss A, BA, Student, University of Sheffield.
[10035546]   17/10/2014   **ME**

Baffour-Awuah, Mrs M, BEd PGLib MLIS FCLIP, Retired Principal Librarian, Botswana National Library Service; Volunteer at Infomatrix, Botswana.
[34371]   23/10/1981   **FE08/09/2005**

Bagley, Mr D E, MA FCLIP, Retired Polytechnic librarian (Life Member).
[571]   25/09/1948   **FE01/01/1966**

Bagley, Mr S P, BA (Hons) MCLIP, Information Officer, Highways Agency, Leeds.
[48861]   05/07/1993   **CM22/01/1997**

Bagshaw, Mrs J A, BA MCLIP, Advisory Librarian, School Library Service, Essex County Council.
[38551]   02/07/1985   **CM09/08/1988**

Baguma, Mr S D, BSc, Student, Loughborough University.
[10035333]   16/10/2014   **ME**

Baig, Mrs Q A, BSc MCLIP, Unwaged.
[577]   17/10/1971   **CM08/08/1974**

Bailas-Ferry, Mrs M L, Assistant Librarian, Boston University.
[10022036]   20/11/2012   **ME**

Baildam, Mrs L J, BEd (Hons) MA, Associate Librarian, Roy Graham Library, Newbold College of Higher Education, Bracknell, Berkshire.
[57234]   14/01/1999   **ME**

Bailes, Mrs L C, Librarian, St James Independent School for Senior Boys.
[63262]   23/03/2004   **ME**

Bailes-Collins, Mrs R A, BLib MCLIP, School Librarian.
[42151]   10/10/1988   **CM18/07/1991**

Bailey, Ms A J, BA MA, Curator, Printed Historical Sources 1914, British Library, London.
[35221]   07/10/1982   **ME**

Bailey, Mrs A J, BA (Hons) MA MCLIP, Information Officer, Derbys. County Council, Matlock.
[53007]   14/02/1996   **CM19/11/2003**

Bailey, Mrs D A, BA (Hons), LRC Manager, Sheffield.
[61205]   08/04/2002   **ME**

Bailey, Mrs F F, BA MCLIP, Children and Families Librarian, Pembrokeshire County Council.
[38345]   28/03/1985   **CM17/01/1990**

Bailey, Mr I, MSc MCLIP, Admissions Adminstrator, University of Greenwich, Woolwich.
[43017]   16/06/1989   **CM27/02/1991**

Bailey, Miss J, LLB MA, Senior Information Assistant, University of Nottingham.
[10011895]   26/11/2008   **ME**

Bailey, Miss J, Student, Manchester Metropolitan University.
[10034550]   21/07/2014   **ME**

Bailey, Ms L, BA (Hons) MLib MCLIP, Lib. – Faculty of Classics, University of Cambridge.
[49281]   20/10/1993   **CM24/07/1996**

Bailey, Ms L, BA (Hons),
[10012781]   26/10/1981   **ME**

Bailey, Miss L G, BSc, MSc Student, University of Sheffield.
[10031868]   10/10/2013   **ME**

Bailey, Ms M B, MCLIP, Retired.
[591]   18/01/1946   **CM01/01/1951**

Bailey, Ms P, BA MCLIP MIOD FRSA, Managing Director, Bailey Solutions Ltd, Hove.
[10011882]   05/10/1983   **CM16/12/1986**

Bailey, Mrs R, BA MCLIP, Part-time Stock Librarian, Southampton City College.
[26917]   15/12/1976   **CM10/08/1983**

Bailey, Miss V L, BA (Hons), Working part time in a public library.
[10015104]   23/10/2009   **ME**

Baillie, Ms E M, MTh DipTheol Msc MCLIP, Librarian, Goethe Institute, Glasgow.
[64009]   02/12/2004   **CM10/07/2009**

Bailyes, Mr D J, BA (Hons),
[10022419]   26/02/2013   **ME**

Bain, Mr J R, BA MCLIP, Librarian, Berwickshire High School.
[28259]   02/11/1977   **CM08/06/1982**

Bain, Mrs L M, BA MCLIP, Network Librarian, Turriff Academy, Aberdeenshire.
[21875]   05/02/1974   **CM19/11/1979**

Baines, Ms J C, BA (Hons), Library Assistant, University of Sussex.
[10023127]   11/06/2013   **AF**

Bains, Miss A, BA (Hons) MSc MCLIP, Sure Start Librarian, Chesterfield Library, Derbyshire County Council.
[55963]   02/01/1998   **CM04/10/2013**

Bains, Miss N K, BA (Hons),
[10011612]   29/10/2008   **AF**

Baird, Mrs B I,
[65307]   19/12/2005   **AF**

Baird, Mr I S, MA DipLib MCLIP, Academic Librarian (Health & Social Care), Teesside University, Middlesbrough.
[36259]   04/09/1983   **CM24/03/1987**

Baird, Mrs J S M, MCLIP, Life Member.
[16569]   06/02/1959   **CM01/01/1966**

Baird, Mr T H, MA (Hons) MLitt, Student (PhD), University Strathclyde, Glasgow.
[59492]   09/04/2001   **ME**

Bairstow, Mrs M, BA MCLIP, Librarian, Health & Safety Executive, Sheffield, & Information Advisor, Sheffield Hallam University, South Yorks.
[25498]   25/01/1976   **CM08/07/1980**

Baisden, Miss J, Student, Wayne State University.
[10032882]   22/01/2014   **ME**

Bajwa, Ms R, BA (Hons) MCLIP, Library Assistant, John Laing Integrated Services.
[10022255]   01/07/1996   **CM12/09/2001**

Baker, Miss A J, Senior Library Assistant – Community Information Service, Dudley Metropolitan Borough Council.
[10017731]   30/09/2010   **AF**

Baker, Mrs A L, BLib MCLIP, Learning Res. Centre Manager, Suffolk One.
[36835]   04/01/1984   **CM16/02/1988**

Baker, Mr A S J, BA DipLib MCLIP, Librarian, Haddon L. of Arch. & Anthropology, Cambridge University.
[34411]   05/11/1981   **RV06/02/2008**   **CM23/06/1986**

Baker, Ms C A, HonFCLIP, Hon. Fellow.
[61176]   26/03/2002   **FE26/03/2002**

Baker, Mrs C J, BSc (Hons) DipLib, Information and Content Developer, CMI.
[10015088]   08/10/1986   **ME**

Baker, Prof D M, MA MMus MLS PhD MBA FCMI FCLIP HonFCLIP, Emeritus Professor.
[22964]   31/08/1974   **HFE02/09/2010**

Baker, Mr D T H, MA MPhil, PhD Student, University of Cambridge.
[10031587]   04/09/2013   **ME**

Baker, Mr J, MA MCLIP, Librarian, East Kent Hospitals NHS Trust, Margate.
[44610]   06/11/1990   **RV**18/01/2012   **CM15/05/2002**

Baker, Miss J, BSc (Hons) PgDipILS MCLIP, Senior Librarian, Lending Servs., Jersey L.
[59729]   10/09/2001   **CM01/02/2006**

Baker, Mrs J K, BLib MCLIP, Librarian, Telford L.
[32410]   01/04/1980   **CM25/11/1985**

Baker, Miss J K, BA MCLIP, Retired.
[633]   16/10/1966   **CM01/01/1970**

Baker, Mrs J M, MLS MCLIP, Information Specialist, BASF Plc, Cheadle.
[12366]   08/10/1969   **CM07/01/1974**

Baker, Miss K, BA MA, Student, University of Chester.
[10035115]   16/09/2014   **ME**

Baker, Mrs K L, BA MA MCLIP, Librarian, National Railway Museum, York.
[59985]   15/11/2001   **CM13/06/2007**

Baker, Mrs K M, BA (Hons), LRC Manager, Brentford School for Girls, Middx.
[46363]   30/10/1991   **ME**

Baker, Mr L W, FCLIP, Life Member.
[637]   15/03/1948   **FE01/01/1958**

Baker, Mr O A, MCLIP, Retired.
[641]   01/01/1963   **CM01/01/1969**

Baker, Miss S, BA (Hons), Senior Library Assistant, University of Southampton.
[10035165]   15/10/2014   **ME**

Baker, Mr S J, BA MCLIP, Principal Librarian Information an E Services – Nottinghamshire Libraries.
[39271]   01/01/1986   **CM21/07/1993**

Baker, Ms T A, BA DipLib MCLIP, Librarian, Warwickshire County Council, Leamington Spa.
[38622]   12/08/1985   **CM10/05/1988**

Bakewell, Miss G M, MEd MCLIP, Retired.
[651]   19/08/1964   **CM01/01/1969**

Bakshi, Mrs S, MLISc, Student, University of Burdwan.
[10035070]   23/09/2014   **ME**

Balaam, Miss A J, BSc (Hons) MCLIP, School Librarian, Copleston High School, Ipswich.
[49432]   27/10/1993   **CM21/01/1998**

Balazs, Ms M, BSc MA, Head of Learning Resources & ILT, K College.
[10022620]   05/04/2013   **ME**

Balchin, Ms J M, BA (Hons) MA MCLIP, Learning Res. Centre Manager, The Sixth Form College, Farnborough.
[50956]   31/10/1994   **CM17/03/1999**

Baldock, Miss S C, BA, Student.
[10032095]   24/10/2013   **ME**

Baldwin, Mrs B W, BA MCLIP, Retired.
[656]   02/10/1960   **CM01/01/1964**

Baldwin, Mr D R, MCLIP, Lib. Arts & Heritage Manager, Civic Centre, Southampton.
[23504]   02/01/1975   **CM03/09/1979**

Baldwin, Mrs J, MCLIP, Retired.
[660]   20/01/1969   **CM01/01/1971**

Baldwin, Mrs R J, BA DipHE MCLIP DipLib, Library Assistant, University of Southampton.
[37472]   01/10/1984   **CM06/10/1987**

Baldwin, Mrs S H, BA (Hons) MA, Team Librarian, Shrewsbury Library, Shropshire.
[10015435]   18/11/2009   **ME**

Bales, Mrs L M, BA, Student/Graduate Trainee, Northumbria University.
[10022249]   29/01/2013   **ME**

Ball, Mr A J, BA (Hons), Research Officer, University of Bath.
[61771]   05/11/2002   **ME**

Ball, Mr A W, BA FCLIP FSA FRHistS FRSA, Life Member.
[670]   01/01/1954   **FE01/01/1958**

Ball, C F, Esq BA MCLIP, Life Member.
[672]   29/08/1958   **CM01/01/1963**

Ball, Mr D, MA DipLib MLitt FCLIP, Owner and Consultant, David Ball Consulting, Bournemouth.
[26222]   06/09/1976   **FE01/04/2002**

Ball, Mr G R, BA (Hons) FCLIP, Retired.
[675]   01/02/1951   **FE01/01/1965**

Ball, Mrs H C, BA MCLIP, Genealogist, Probate & Information Researcher.
[34690]   26/01/1982   **CM31/10/1984**

Ball, Mrs J E, BLib PGCE MCLIP, Reading Engagement Manager, Bristol Libraries, Bishopsworth Library.
[10017418]   18/02/1986   **CM21/12/1988**

Ball, Ms J E, BA (Hons) MA MCLIP, Res. Liaison Manager, University of Sussex.
[51150]   24/11/1994   **RV**09/06/2005   **CM23/09/1998**

Ball, Mrs M J, MA DipLib MCLIP, E-Learning Librarian, Richmond Upon Thames College, Middx.
[31724]   12/11/1979   **CM10/11/1987**

Ball, Mr M S, MA, Library Student, Northumbria University.
[10035451]   14/10/2014   **ME**

Ball, Miss R, BA (Hons), Learning Resources Centre Assistant/Student, Northumbria University.
[10031676]   10/10/2013   **ME**

Ball, Miss S E, BBibl, Temporary Project Cataloguer, King's College, London.
[57741]   19/07/1999   **ME**

Ball, Ms S F, MSc, Freelance Information Management Provider.
[10034025]   21/05/2014   **ME**

Ball, Mrs S G, BA MCLIP, Libraries Service Development Manager, Staffordshire County Council.
[37778]   09/10/1984   **CM05/07/1988**

Ball, Miss S J, BA, Assistant Librarian, GCHQ, Library, Cheltenham.
[35916]   24/01/1983   **ME**

Ballantyne, Mr J J, BA DipLib MCLIP, Retired.
[686]   01/01/1969   **CM01/01/1971**

Ballard, Ms H, BLib MCLIP DCMS, Business Services Manager, Medway Council.
[37641]   10/10/1984   **CM09/08/1988**

Ballard, Mrs J, BLS MCLIP, Lib. Hockerill Anglo-European College, Bishops Stortford, Herts.
[27983]   03/10/1977   **CM01/07/1982**

Ballardini, Ms E L, BA (Hons),
[10031969]   16/10/2013   **ME**

Balmforth, Mr C J, MSc BA (Hons), College Librarian, Dearne Valley College, Rotherham.
[59244]   15/01/2001   **ME**

Balmforth, Mr J J, BSc, Student.
[10033712]   16/04/2014   **ME**

Balmforth, Mrs L D, BA (Hons) MCLIP, Information Officer & Librarian, National Childbirth Trust, London.
[3718]   13/01/1971   **CM15/09/1974**

Balnaves, Dr F J, PhD MA MLitt BA FLAA MCLIP, Life Member.
[16579]   27/08/1951   **CM01/01/1954**

Bamber, Mr A L, BA FCLIP, Life Member.
[694]   22/01/1954   **FE11/12/1989**

Bamborough, Ms S C, BA MCLIP,
[29921]   01/11/1978   **CM09/06/1983**

Bamford, Miss A C, BA, Assistant Librarian, Education Library Service, Winsford.
[64987]   06/10/2005   ME
Bamford, Mr P, BA MCLIP, Honorary Cathedral Librarian, Chester Cathedral.
[697]   01/01/1972   CM19/09/1989
Bamhare, Mr H, MA,
[10034719]   07/10/2014   ME
Bamkin, Dr M R, Student.
[64959]   03/10/2005   ME
Bampton, Mrs C E, MA, Knowledge Support Librarian, North Cumbria University Hospitals.
[10015359]   12/11/2009   ME
Band, Mrs B, BSc (Econ) MCLIP, Librarian, Emmbrook School, Berks.
[54582]   30/01/1997   CM10/07/2009
Banfi, Mrs A F, Information Specialist, NBS, Newcastle upon Tyne.
[63117]   11/02/2004   ME
Banfield, Mrs C, BA (Hons) MCMI LRCM, ALIS – Lisburn.
[10015811]   29/01/2010   ME
Banham, Miss C R, MCLIP, Career Break.
[22243]   18/03/1974   CM19/09/1978
Banister, Mrs K J, BA (Hons) MCLIP, Front Line Officer, Lancs. Co. Library, Harris Central Library.
[42258]   13/10/1988   CM20/05/1998
Banks, Mrs J N, BA (Hons) MCLIP PGCE, Unemployed.
[36903]   01/02/1984   CM15/03/1989
Banks, Mr P R, MA, Information & L. Manager, Courts & Tribunals Serv., London.
[41193]   15/10/1987   CM15/08/1990
Bannister, Ms E L, MCLIP, Senior Librarian: Stock.
[64249]   22/02/2005   CM27/08/2014
Bannister, Ms N, MA PgDipILS PGCE (LL), Subject Lib., South Thames College, London.
[57047]   30/11/1998   ME
Bansal, Mrs R, MLIB BLIB MCLIP, Unwaged.
[10014809]   16/09/2009   CM14/11/2012
Banting, Miss V A, DipLib MCLIP, Stock Development Officer.
[32010]   28/01/1980   CM05/05/1982
Barbalet, Ms S, BA (Hons) AALIA, Survey Resources Network Officer, UK Data Archive, Uni of Essex.
[65483]   24/02/2006   ME
Barbarino, Mrs P, MA MA MCLIP, CEO, Life, London.
[48409]   05/01/1993   CM17/11/1999
Barber, Mrs C E, MCLIP, Community Librarian, Holywell L.
[23121]   05/11/1974   CM12/12/1978
Barber, Mr G, MSc BA (Hons) DipLib MCLIP, Deputy UniversityLibrarian, Southampton Solent University.
[27509]   01/05/1977   CM24/11/1981
Barber, Miss J M, BA DipLib MCLIP, Co. Director (IT Bureau), Self-employed.
[32857]   03/10/1980   CM04/03/1983
Barber, Miss L J, BA (Hons) MCLIP, Locality Librarian, Leics. L. Serv., Hinckley (part time).
[35299]   11/10/1982   CM14/09/1994
Barber, Mrs M C, BA DipLib MCLIP, Head of Libraries & Information, The University of Law.
[31840]   07/01/1980   CM18/01/1982
Barclay, Mr J, Assistant Librarian, British School of Osteopathy, London.
[10015730]   19/01/2010   ME
Barclay, Mrs J M, BA MA MCLIP, Horticultural Database Administrator, Royal Horticultural Society.
[60844]   10/03/1993   CM01/03/1993
Barclay, Mrs J M T, BA (Hons), Librarian, King's College, Somerset.
[10018553]   01/02/2011   ME

Barclay, Mr N J, BA, Student, City University London.
[10032409]   03/12/2013   ME
Barclay, Mr T, BA, Information /Local Studies. Librarian, Carnegie Library, South Ayrshire Council, Ayr.
[20430]   15/03/1973   CM02/09/1976
Barclay, Mrs Y, BSc (Hons) PgDip MCLIP, Young People's Librarian Aberdeen City Council, Aberdeen.
[64482]   31/03/2005   CM14/12/2012
Barden, Mrs H P, ACLIP, Library Assistant, St Austell Library, Cornwall.
[64240]   22/02/2005   ACL05/10/2007
Bardill, Ms A, Student, Aberystwyth University.
[65302]   15/12/2005   ME
Barefoot, Mrs A L, BA MSc CertMgmt MCLIP, Information Specialist, Cranfield University, Swindon.
[57081]   04/12/1998   CM28/01/2009
Barengo, Miss M, MA,
[10012000]   09/12/2008   ME
Barette, Mrs H M, BA MCLIP, Senior Lib. -Cataloguing, States of Jersey L. Serv.
[39199]   04/01/1986   CM12/12/1990
Barker, Mr A C, BA (Hons) DipILM MCLIP, Head of L. Academic Serv., University of East Anglia.
[54189]   30/10/1996   CM15/11/2000
Barker, Ms C A, BA (Hons) CertEd MSc MCLIP, Senior Assistant Librarian, Bibliographic Services, De Montfort University, Leicester.
[50350]   04/07/1994   CM21/03/2001
Barker, Mrs C K, BA (Hons) DipILM MCLIP, Librarian, Howes Percival, Norwich.
[52007]   07/09/1995   CM19/01/2000
Barker, Mrs C M, BA (Hons) MSc (Econ), Deputy Librarian, Quincentenary Library, Jesus College, Cambridge.
[63014]   12/12/2003   ME
Barker, Mr D C, BA MCLIP, Retired.
[751]   23/10/1967   CM01/01/1971
Barker, Mrs E J, BSc (Hons) MSc (Econ) MCLIP, Unwaged.
[55708]   06/11/1997   CM12/03/2003
Barker, Miss H, MSc, Senior L. Assistant, University of Surrey.
[10001629]   15/12/2003   ME
Barker, Miss J M, BA DipLib MCLIP, Librarian Kingswood and Hanham Lib. South Glos.
[38026]   14/01/1985   CM14/03/1990
Barker, Mr L A, BA PGCE DipLib MCLIP DMS, Archivist, Essex Record Office.
[40976]   02/10/1987   CM22/05/1991
Barker, Miss M A, BA (Hons) MCLIP, Learning Resources Officer, Thomas Rotherham College, Rotherham.
[44570]   29/10/1990   CM21/01/1998
Barker, Mr M C, BA (Hons), Community Librarian, Wigmore Library, Luton.
[65882]   16/06/2006   ME
Barker, Ms M G H, MA DipLib MCLIP, Library Services Manager, University of Salford.
[30578]   06/02/1979   CM01/07/1994
Barker, Mr P D, BA, Student, Aberystwyth University.
[10015489]   14/12/2009   ME
Barker, Mr P H, MA MCLIP, Retired.
[764]   16/02/1964   CM01/01/1967
Barker, Mr R F S, Library & Information Assistant, Hawick Library.
[10031647]   17/09/2013   AF
Barker, Mr T, MA MSc, Librarian, Serco Group PLC.
[10025369]   18/07/2014   ME
Barker-Ottley, Mrs K, MA, Prison Librarian, HMP Bure, Norfolk C. C.
[10000737]   13/11/2006   ME

Barksby, Mr D W, MA,
[10014280]   13/07/2009   **ME**
Barkway, Mrs J A, BA DipLib MCLIP, Library Services Manager, Wirral Council.
[40110]   16/10/1986   **CM18/01/1989**
Barkworth, Ms A, Student at Robert Gordon University.
[10032421]   03/12/2013   **ME**
Barlow, Mrs H C, BSc MCLIP FSocInd, Self-employed indexer.
[44295]   20/08/1990   **CM27/05/1992**
Barlow, Mrs J, BA (Hons) MSc MCLIP, Trust Library Services Manager, SWBH NHS Trust.
[59758]   19/09/2001   **CM13/06/2007**
Barlow, Mrs J B, MA DipLib MCLIP, HRNet Manager, Cranfield Trust, Romsey.
[44399]   04/10/1990   **CM18/11/1993**
Barlow, Ms J K, BA (Hons) MLIS, LRC Manager, Bournemouth & Poole College.
[10015291]   30/10/2009   **ME**
Barlow, Miss L C, BA (Hons) MA MCLIP, Librarian, Francis Holland School, Regent's Park.
[56667]   01/10/1998   **CM20/11/2002**
Barlow, Ms R, BA DipLib, Information Officer, Reynolds Porter Chamberlain LLP, London.
[49497]   05/11/1993   **ME**
Barnabas, Mrs S M, MCLIP, Life Member.
[779]   06/03/1961   **CM01/01/1969**
Barnard, Mrs F E K, LLB MCLIP, School Librarian, Bishops Hatfield Girls School, Herts.
[781]   04/02/1972   **CM01/09/1974**
Barnard, Mrs G R, BMus DipLib MCLIP, Employment not known.
[34437]   23/10/1981   **CM16/12/1986**
Barnard, Miss K, MA, Student, UCL.
[10031872]   10/10/2013   **ME**
Barnard, Mrs N E, BA DipLIS MCLIP, Sub-Librarian, Oxford Brookes University.
[46484]   12/11/1991   **CM22/05/1996**
Barnoo, Mr A,
[10032119]   29/10/2013   **ME**
Barnes, Mr C I, CEng MCLIP MBCS, Retired.
[31035]   01/01/1966   **CM14/03/1980**
Barnes, Mr C J, BA MA MCLIP, Retired.
[19579]   26/10/1972   **CM09/02/1976**
Barnes, Mrs D, BA MCLIP, Retired from Hampshire Libraries Outreach Team.
[20193]   01/01/1973   **CM01/02/1976**
Barnes, Mrs D J, BA DipLib MSc, DMICP Issue & Problem Manager, MOD, Corsham.
[38370]   01/04/1985   **ME**
Barnes, Mr D L, BSc (Hons) MSc MCLIP, Librarian, South Dartmoor Community College, Ashburton.
[53362]   20/05/1996   **CM01/04/2002**
Barnes, Mrs J, BA (Hons) MCLIP, Children &Young Peoples Librarain, Northumberland (Job Share).
[54363]   25/11/1996   **CM21/05/2003**
Barnes, Dr J J, BA (Hons) MSc DipRSA EdD MCLIP,
[61171]   26/03/2002   **CM26/03/2002**
Barnes, Miss J M, BA (Hons) PgDipLIM MCLIP, Load2Learn Assistant, RNIB, Peterborough.
[47595]   05/10/1992   **RV**08/03/2013 **CM07/09/2005**
Barnes, Mrs J N, Library and Information Services Administrator, Foster Wheeler Energy Ltd.
[10032394]   03/12/2013   **ME**
Barnes, Mrs L, Librarian, Redmoor High School, Leics.
[64788]   05/07/2005   **ME**

Barnes, Mrs M A, Resource Centre Manager/Team Librarian, Suffolk County Council, Lowestoft.
[10011807]   14/11/2008   **AF**
Barnes, Miss M J, BA (Hons) MSc MCLIP, Gloucestershire County Council.
[43678]   22/11/1989   **CM21/11/2001**
Barnes, Mr M P K, OBE DMA MCLIP, Retired.
[805]   01/01/1960   **CM01/01/1965**
Barnes, Mrs N M, Locality Team leader, Cornwall Council.
[10000667]   25/10/2006   **AF**
Barnes, Ms S M, BA (Hons) DipLIS, Information & Archives Manager, Westminster Library, London.
[51291]   05/01/1995   **ME**
Barnes, Miss W I L, BA MCLIP, Library Systems Officer (Circulations), Oxfordshire County Council.
[38414]   17/04/1985   **CM24/06/1992**
Barnett, Mr C, MA FInsAM MCLIP, Retired.
[810]   01/01/1966   **CM01/01/1970**
Barnett, Mrs E M, MCLIP, Retired.
[10562]   18/01/1963   **CM01/01/1967**
Barnett, Mr G, FCLIP, Urdu Team Manager, Foreign & Commonwealth Office.
[811]   11/12/1963   **FE21/02/1974**
Barnett, Mr J, BA MPhil, eResources and Serials Information Assistant, Main Library, University of Birmingham.
[10021819]   16/04/2013   **AF**
Barnett, Miss J, Information Assistant, Institute of Chartered Accountants of England and Wales.
[10032574]   17/12/2013   **ME**
Barnett, Miss K L, BA (Hons) MSc (Econ) MCLIP, Assistant Librarian, Educ. L. & Res. Serv., Port Talbot.
[53397]   03/06/1996   **CM21/05/2003**
Barney, Miss D J, BA (Hons) MA, Lib. /Information Specialist, Foreign & Commonwealth Office, London.
[49563]   11/11/1993   **ME**
Barney, Dr T H, MA PhD, Research Fellow, Department of Linguistics, University of Lancaster.
[40500]   25/02/1987   **ME**
Barnicoat, Mr K, Student, UCL.
[10020102]   01/11/2011   **ME**
Baron, Miss L, BA (Hons), Information Specialist, FCO, London.
[55526]   20/10/1997   **ME**
Baron, Mrs L M, BA DipLib MCLIP, School Librarian, Sutton High School, Surrey.
[29951]   16/11/1978   **CM27/11/1981**
Barontini, Ms C, MA, User Support Manager, Birkbeck.
[47557]   01/10/1992   **CM20/11/2002**
Barr, Mr C B L, MA FSA MCLIP, Life Member.
[826]   02/05/1958   **CM01/01/1962**
Barr, Mr P, MCLIP, College Librarian, Britannia Royal Naval College.
[10016442]   23/03/2010   **CM13/11/2013**
Barr, Mrs R A, BA, Student, Aberystwyth University.
[10011157]   29/09/2008   **ME**
Barr, Mrs W, BSc MCLIP, Librarian, Denny High School, Falkirk.
[61263]   13/05/2002   **CM06/04/2005**
Barraclough, Miss C E, BA MCLIP, Area Librarian, Mid Herts, Hertfordshire.
[38753]   04/10/1985   **CM14/11/1989**
Barraclough, Mr P M, BA PGCE, MA Librarianship student, University of Sheffield.
[10032038]   22/10/2013   **ME**
Barranco Garcia, Ms I, MA BA MCLIP,
[10012266]   26/01/2009   **CM13/05/2014**

Barratt, Ms M M, BA MCLIP DipLaw, L. Strategy + Performance Manager, London Borough of Enfield.
[28778]   19/01/1978   **CM22/01/1981**

Barratt, Miss P M, MCLIP, Life Member.
[839]   02/03/1943   **CM01/01/1946**

Barrett, Mr B J, MA BTh CTh DipLib MCLIP ALAI, Information Scientist, Child & Family Agency, Republic of Ireland.
[41115]   08/10/1987   **CM12/12/1990**

Barrett, Miss C E, BA DipLib MCLIP, Librarian, NHS Scotland Cent. Legal Office, Edinburgh.
[10001379]   04/10/1988   **CM14/09/1994**

Barrett, Mr D, BA (Hons), Student, University of the West of England.
[10031842]   08/10/2013   **ME**

Barrett, Mr D A, BA, Customer Serv. Officer, Ashford Library, Kent County Council.
[41048]   05/10/1987   **ME**

Barrett, Miss E A, BA (Hons) MSc, Evidence Specialist, NHS Evidence, National Institutefor Health & Clinical Excellence.
[42589]   13/01/1989   **ME**

Barrett, Mrs H, BA MA, Health Sciences Lib.
[10006754]   10/12/2007   **ME**

Barrett, Miss I M R, BA, Unwaged.
[33265]   27/10/1980   **ME**

Barrett, Mrs L M, BA MLS MCLIP HonFCLIP,
[44405]   05/10/1990   **HFE21/10/2004**

Barrett, Mrs P A, BA MA (Ed) MCLIP, LRC Manager, Oakmeeds Community College, West Sussex.
[62349]   07/05/2003   **CM04/10/2006**

Barringer, Mrs N J, BA MA MCLIP,
[65854]   06/06/2006   **CM05/05/2010**

Barron, Mrs F M, BSc (Hons) MCLIP, Retired.
[4428]   20/01/1970   **CM18/12/1972**

Barrow, Mrs B M, MCLIP, Life Member.
[858]   09/01/1951   **CM01/01/1958**

Barrow, Mr T, Learning Res. Centre Manager, Hornsey School for Girls, London.
[65444]   24/02/2006   **AF**

Barry, Mrs G R, BA MSc MCLIP, Retired.
[24964]   24/10/1975   **CM07/11/1978**

Barry, Ms J A, BA (Hons) MCLIP, School Librarian, Beardsen Academy, Glasgow.
[45301]   04/10/1990   **CM27/11/1996**

Barry, Ms R, MappSc, Unwaged.
[10032264]   12/11/2013   **ME**

Barson, Ms A J, BSc MSc MCLIP, Acquisition Serv. Manager, University of the West of England.
[61234]   17/04/2002   **CM15/09/2004**

Barson, Mrs J M, BA FCLIP, Retired.
[2720]   04/02/1960   **FE01/01/1963**

Barstow, Ms C, BSc (Hons) MA DipLS MCLIP, Librarian, Bromley House Library, Nottingham.
[39684]   21/05/1986   **CM15/10/2002**

Barter, Mrs E K, Part-time typist.
[48169]   11/11/1992   **ME**

Bartholomew, Mr J, BSc BA (Hons) PgDip, Assistant Librarian, Sainsburys Res. Unit, University of East Anglia, Centre for Visual Arts, Norwich.
[58466]   24/02/2000   **ME**

Bartholomew, Mrs J M, MA DipLib MCLIP, Unwaged.
[34914]   19/04/1982   **CM26/11/1997**

Bartholomew, Mrs M L, ACLIP, Learning Resource Centre Manager, Sussex Coast College Hastings.
[64397]   14/03/2005   **ACL10/01/2006**

Bartle, Dr D G, BA DipLib Phd MCLIP, Archivist, Haberdashers Company.
[36302]   01/10/1983   **CM20/01/1987**

Bartlett, Mr D A, Library Assistant, Greenwich Sch. of Management, London.
[59498]   11/04/2001   **ME**

Bartlett, Miss J, BA, Lbrary & Open Access IT Assistant, Camberwell College of Arts.
[10032076]   24/10/2013   **ME**

Bartlett, Mrs J, BA (Hons) PgDip, Learning Resources Manager, The Fashion Retail Academy, London.
[10016067]   12/02/2010   **ME**

Bartlett, Mrs M K, BA (Hons) QTS, Librarian/ Learning Resources Manager, Portsmouth High School.
[10032604]   19/12/2013   **ME**

Bartlett, Mrs R, BA MCLIP, Life Member.
[876]   11/09/1956   **CM01/01/1960**

Bartlett, Mrs S J V, BA (Hons) DipLib MCLIP, Web Training Consultant.
[26865]   28/12/1976   **CM06/09/1979**

Bartlett, Mrs W M, BA (Hons),
[52315]   25/10/1995   **ME**

Bartley, Mrs V J, BSc DipLib MCLIP, Manager of Content Development, Dialog, London.
[31557]   03/11/1979   **CM03/11/1981**

Barton, Ms C, BA MA MCLIP, Comm. Learning & Information Librarian, Derbyshire County Council.
[10002005]   28/03/2007   **CM16/12/2010**

Barton, Mrs E, BSc MCLIP, Retired.
[8776]   01/02/1972   **CM01/07/1974**

Barton, Mrs H E B, BSc (Hons) MSc MCLIP, Patent Support.
[47730]   15/10/1992   **CM26/11/1997**

Barton, Miss S E, BA MCLIP, Head of Information, McCann Erickson, London.
[34773]   09/02/1982   **CM04/04/1985**

Barton, Ms V, MA MCLIP, Locality Librarian, West Leicestershire.
[10001314]   15/01/2007   **CM05/05/2010**

Barwell, Miss E R, BA (Hons) MCLIP, Library And Heritage Manager, Rutland Library Service.
[59901]   26/10/2001   **CM21/06/2006**

Barwick, Mrs M S, Resource Information Officer, University of Warwick.
[10035556]   20/10/2014   **ME**

Bashforth, Mr S F, BA MCLIP, Retired.
[886]   29/05/1970   **CM18/02/1974**

Basing, Miss H, BA MSc, Library Manager.
[62847]   17/11/2003   **ME**

Basinger, Mrs E C, MCLIP, Librarian, LiveWire Warrington.
[20238]   13/02/1973   **CM01/09/1976**

Basini, Miss L M, MSc BA (Hons) ACLIP, Senior Library Assistant, Princess Royal Hospital, Telford Health Library.
[10020189]   15/11/2011   **ACL14/11/2012**

Basker, Mr A J, BSc MA MCLIP, Retired.
[33668]   01/01/1968   **CM01/01/1972**

Baskerville, Miss R J, BSc (Hons), Library Assistant, Overton Library.
[10022895]   07/05/2013   **AF**

Basra, Miss A, BA, MLIS Candidate, University of Western Ontario.
[10031613]   08/10/2013   **ME**

Bass, Miss J, MCLIP, Retired.
[891]   02/01/1960   **CM01/01/1969**

Bass, Mrs P, BA MCLIP, Retired.
[892]   12/10/1960   **CM01/01/1962**

Bassant, Mr R, Librarian, Carnegie Free Library, Trinidad, West Indies.
[58422]   07/02/2000   **ME**

Bassett, Ms L, Know How Officer, Slaughter & May, London.
[64937]   27/09/2005   **ME**

Bassett, Mr T S, Student.
[10009110]   30/04/2008   ME
Bastable, Ms D, BA (Hons), Community Library Manager, Sandwell
MBC.
[62518]   30/07/2003   ME
Bastable, Mrs L M, MCLIP, Retired.
[15400]   06/11/1971   **CM01/09/1974**
Bastiampillai, Miss M A, BA MA MCLIP, Deputy Learning Resources
Manager, Uxbridge College, Middlesex.
[39299]   15/01/1986   **CM19/08/1992**
Bastone, Mrs S C, MCLIP, Head of Learning Resources, LVS Ascot,
Berkshire.
[51099]   15/11/1994   **CM21/11/2007**
Batchelor, Ms E J, BA DipILS MCLIP, Deputy Librarian, Faculty of
Education, University of Cambridge.
[47024]   02/04/1992   **CM23/07/1997**
Batchelor, Mrs K M, BA DipLib MCLIP, Customer Serv. Manager,
Oxfordshire County Libraries.
[32242]   11/02/1980   **CM05/05/1982**
Batchelor, Mrs S C, BA DipLib MCLIP, Librarian, Cambridgeshire
County Council, St Neots, Cambridgeshire.
[35810]   24/01/1983   **CM01/04/1986**
Batcock, Miss C, MCLIP, Retired.
[902]   10/02/1959   **CM07/09/1972**
Bate, Mrs K A, Libr., Crewe Library, Cheshire.
[63365]   20/04/2004   ME
Bate, Mr S, BSc MSc, MAP Librarian.
[10032981]   03/02/2014   ME
Bater, Mr R, MCLIP MBCS, Retired.
[19858]   01/01/1973   **CM02/11/1984**
Bates, Ms C A, BA (Hons) MCLIP, Librarian, Nottingham University,
Samworth Academy.
[52352]   26/10/1995   **CM17/09/2003**
Bates, Mr D J, Employed.
[10000966]   17/01/1983   ME
Bates, Mrs H M, MCLIP, Learning Res. Centre Manager, Brockenhurst
College, Hants.
[27449]   01/04/1977   **CM19/06/1984**
Bates, Miss K F, BA (Hons) MA, Library Manager (Manchester &
Liverpool), BPP Professional Education.
[10006708]   21/11/2007   ME
Bates, Ms S E, BSc MSc MCLIP, Patent Analyst, Shell, London.
[44211]   09/07/1990   **CM01/04/2002**
Bates-Hird, Mrs S B, FCLIP, Information Manager, Sandwell Lib. &
Information Serv., West Bromwich.
[6828]   27/01/1969   **FE17/11/1999**
Bathgate, Ms W, BA (Hons) MA MSc MCLIP, Librarian, Bannockburn
High School, Stirling.
[43302]   17/10/1989   **CM27/01/1993**
Batley, Miss P, MA MCLIP, Life Member.
[929]   05/02/1958   **CM01/01/1961**
Batt, Mr C, OBE BA FCLIP HonFLA, Retired.
[930]   17/03/1966   **HFE01/01/1998**
Battersby, Mrs M, BA MCLIP, School Librarian, St George's Academy,
Harpenden.
[37796]   28/10/1984   **CM27/07/1994**
Battersby, Mr R, BA DipLib MCLIP, Head of Library Academic Support,
User Services Division, Information Services, University of
Edinburgh.
[32630]   30/06/1980   **CM23/11/1982**
Battye, Ms J E, BA MCLIP, Former Head of Library & Information Serv.,
Central Library, Royal Borough of Kensington & Chelsea;
independent consultant.
[32392]   31/03/1980   **CM01/07/1984**

Baud, Mrs A, MA DipLib MCLIP, Director of Library & Learning Services
Bath Spa University.
[36540]   19/10/1983   **CM10/02/1987**
Baum, Mrs B, BA MLIS MCLIP DipLib HDipEd, Research. Officer, Idox,
Glasgow.
[29607]   17/10/1978   **CM20/01/1982**
Baveystock, Mrs G Y, BA DipLib MCLIP, Principal Librarian, Slough
Borough Council, Berks. Slough.
[41214]   16/10/1987   **CM16/05/1990**
Bawden, Mr B, MA PgDip, Children's & Young People's Librarian,
Tooting Library.
[10021576]   03/09/2012   ME
Baxendale, Mrs M, BA MCLIP, Life Member.
[941]   14/04/1952   **CM01/01/1956**
Baxter, Mr P B, BMus (Hons) DipLib MCLIP, Senior Librarian, Surrey
Performing Arts Library.
[33477]   05/01/1981   **CM30/05/1985**
Baxter, Mr P J, MA, Senior Officer: Learning, Reader Development &
Bibliographic Services.
[10025412]   16/04/2014   ME
Bayjoo, Miss J, BA MA, Graduate Trainee.
[10025415]   24/10/2013   ME
Bayley, Miss A, BA MCLIP, Retired.
[953]   01/07/1972   **CM01/09/1976**
Bayley, Miss D J, MBE BA DipLib MCLIP, Life Member.
[954]   01/01/1949   **CM01/01/1952**
Baylis, Ms J I, BA DipLib MCLIP, Manager, Dementia Knowledge
Centre, Alzheimer's Society, London.
[31359]   11/10/1979   **CM06/10/1982**
Bayliss, Mrs J A, BLib MCLIP, Assistant Librarian, Ipswich Hospital
NHS Trust.
[37922]   22/11/1984   **CM21/12/1989**
Bayliss, Mrs J A, ACLIP, Serv. Development /Supporting Families,
Dudley Library, Dudley.
[10015373]   10/11/2009   **ACL20/06/2012**
Bayliss, Miss N, MCLIP,
[10015190]   23/10/2009   **CM11/07/2012**
Baynes, Mr D, MCLIP, Retired.
[965]   01/04/1965   **CM01/01/1968**
Baynes, Mrs J, MCLIP, Retired.
[38322]   01/01/1964   **CM01/07/1994**
Bazely, Mrs J H, BA DipLib MCLIP, Branch Library Manager,
Southchurch Library, Southend-on-Sea.
[33594]   24/01/1981   **CM01/07/1984**
Beach, Miss S,
[10012165]   08/01/2009   ME
Beahan, Miss K T, HNC BA, Principal L. Assistant, Mary Seacole
Library, Birmingham City University.
[10006764]   03/12/2007   ME
Beale, Mrs H E, BA MCLIP, Librarian, Morgan Cole Solicitors, Swansea.
[34548]   06/01/1982   **CM06/11/1985**
Bean, Dr E, BSc (Hons) MSc PhD DIC, Librarian, HMP The Verne.
[10031923]   15/10/2013   ME
Beards, Mr S P R, BA MCLIP, Retired.
[29880]   17/10/1978   **CM16/07/1982**
Beardsley, Ms H R, MA (Hons) MLib MCLIP, Senior Subject Librarian
(Arts and Humanities).
[49287]   20/10/1993   **CM27/11/1996**
Beardsmore, Mrs J M, BLib MCLIP, Head of Service Libraries, Dudley
Metropolitan Borough Council.
[10001137]   09/10/1979   **CM01/07/1994**
Bearne, Miss V, MCLIP, Retired.
[993]   20/08/1969   **CM22/08/1974**

Beasley, Mr D A, BA MCLIP, Librarian, The Goldsmiths' Company, London.
[32253]   17/03/1980   **CM19/03/1984**

Beasley, Mr M A, MCLIP, Unemployed.
[32013]   30/01/1980   **CM19/06/1986**

Beattie, Mr G, BEng (Hons) MSc MCLIP, Associate Director – Training & Skills, Library Services, King's College London.
[55955]   24/12/1997   **CM21/03/2001**

Beauchamp, Mr P J, MCLIP, Unwaged.
[1004]   15/02/1967   **CM01/01/1969**

Beaufoy, Mrs M E, FCLIP, Life Member.
[1005]   06/10/1938   **FE01/01/1958**

Beaumont, Mrs A M, BA MScEcon MCLIP, Knowledge & L. Serv. Manager, Royal Preston Hospital, Lancs. Teaching Hospital NHS Foundation Trust.
[46780]   22/01/1992   **RV**16/07/2008   **CM08/12/2004**

Beaumont, Mrs D, BA (Hons) MA, Access Development Manager, Coventry Library & Information Service, Coventry.
[57511]   14/04/1999   **ME**

Beaumont, Ms M J, MCLIP, Life Member.
[16599]   12/02/1964   **CM01/01/1967**

Beautemps, Mrs V, MCLIP, Deputy Librarian, Oxford Union Society, Oxford.
[65586]   23/02/2006   **CM07/07/2010**

Beavan, Dr I M, BA PhD FCLIP, Emeritus Keeper of Rare Books, Historic Collections, University of Aberdeen.
[1018]   01/10/1970   **FE23/03/1994**

Beaven, Mr A R, BSc (Hons) MCLIP,
[60793]   03/01/1989   **CM15/05/1990**

Beaven, Mrs O J, BSc (Hons) MSc, Information Specialist, BMJ Publ. Group, London.
[47709]   13/03/1992   **ME**

Beaver, Miss W J, BA MCLIP, Comm. Librarian, Devizes Library, Wilts. County Council.
[41207]   19/10/1987   **CM16/11/1994**

Bebbington, Mr L W, MA (Hons) MSc, Deputy Lib. & Head of L. Serv., University of Aberdeen.
[10015773]   01/04/1987   **ME**

Beck, Miss N, BA (Hons), Assistant Librarian, Manchester Metropolitan University.
[63806]   01/10/2004   **ME**

Beckett, Ms E S, BSc (Hons) MCLIP, Stock Management Librarian, North Bristol NHS Trust, Southmead Hospital, L. & Information Serv.
[44323]   06/09/1990   **CM26/11/1997**

Beckett, Mrs H L, BA (Hons) MCLIP, Community Serv. Librarian, Bracknell L.
[38208]   27/01/1985   **CM20/11/2002**

Beckles, Ms Z, BSc MA MCLIP, Information Scientist.
[10010529]   01/08/2008   **CM16/05/2012**

Beckwith, Mrs J A, BA MCLIP MSc, Library, archive & museum Serv. Manager, Royal College of Physicians, London.
[30956]   05/08/1992   **CM04/02/1985**

Beddard, Ms A F M, MCLIP, User Serv. Manager, Arup, London.
[18077]   02/10/1972   **CM11/11/1976**

Beddard, Miss V L, BA (Hons) MSc MCLIP, Lib. Sandwell Academy, West Midlands.
[60865]   13/12/2001   **CM12/05/2011**

Beddows, Mrs E A, BA MCLIP, L. Assistant, Burntwood Library, Staffordshire County Council.
[48190]   16/11/1992   **CM15/01/2003**

Bedford, Mr D D, MA PgDip Lib, Academic Support Librarian (Health), Drill Hall Library, Universities at Medway, University of Greenwich.
[10013694]   22/05/2009   **ME**

Bedford, Ms S C, BSc (Hons) MCLIP, Librarian, Bournemouth & Poole College.
[58926]   05/10/2000   **RV**13/05/2014   **CM20/04/2012**

Bedigan, Dr K M, MA MPhil PhD, Student, University of Strathclyde.
[10035613]   23/10/2014   **ME**

Beduz, Miss L C, BA (Hons), Information Officer, Institution of Mechanical Engineers, London.
[10001373]   07/10/2004   **ME**

Bedwell, Mr M, BA, Student, University of Bristol.
[10032530]   12/12/2013   **ME**

Bee, Ms C L, MSc, Academic Subject Librarian at the University of Lincoln.
[10019496]   11/07/2011   **ME**

Bee, Miss E A, BEd DipLib MCLIP, Job Seeking.
[32015]   12/02/1980   **CM16/02/1983**

Beebee, Mr S R, BA (Hons) MA MSc, Part-time Student, Aberystwyth University, Castlepoint Library, Bournemouth.
[66160]   04/10/2006   **ME**

Beeby, Miss K, BA (Hons) MA, Trainee Librarian/ Student.
[10016428]   24/03/2010   **AF**

Beecher, Ms D, BA (HONS) MSc (ECON), Trials Search Co-ordinator, Cochrane Injuries Group, LSHTM.
[10013869]   04/06/2009   **ME**

Beedle, Mrs F J, Librarian, University of Cambridge, Local Exam. Syndicate, Cambridge.
[57273]   29/01/1999   **ME**

Beeftink, Miss J, BA MCLIP,
[10014975]   08/10/1979   **CM30/12/1981**

Beeley, Mrs C, MCLIP, Information Librarian, Kingston University.
[671]   01/04/1967   **CM01/01/1971**

Beeley, Mrs J E, MCLIP, Operations Manager, Library & Knowledge Services, Maidstone & Tunbridge Wells NHS Trust.
[11869]   29/08/1969   **CM10/09/1973**

Beer, Mrs D M, MA BA MCLIP, Information Systems Manager, Instituteof Development Studies, Brighton.
[31360]   05/10/1979   **CM11/02/1982**

Beer, Mrs H, BA, LIbrary Assistant, Queen Mary's College.
[10033094]   10/02/2014   **ME**

Beer, Miss N J, BA (Hons) MSc MCLIP, Learning and Teaching Librarian, The Open University, Milton Keynes.
[10017910]   26/10/2010   **CM04/10/2013**

Beeson, Mrs H, BA (Hons) MA MCLIP PGCTHE FHEA, Academic Practice Tutor, University of Northampton.
[59111]   17/11/2000   **CM06/04/2005**

Beeson, Mr M L, BA (Hons) DipIS MCLIP, Teaching and Learning Support Manager, Queen Mary University of London.
[50561]   16/09/1994   **CM21/11/2001**

Beever, Mrs P A, MA DipLib MCLIP, Reader Serv. Librarian, Oakham Library, Rutland.
[40717]   05/05/1987   **CM14/02/1990**

Beevers, Mr C J, BSc (Hons) PgDipLIM, Document Delivery Supervisor, University of Huddersfield.
[58357]   19/01/2000   **ME**

Begg, Miss R E, BSc (Hons) MA MCLIP, Information Professional.
[64818]   20/07/2005   **CM10/03/2011**

Beharrell, Mr W, BA (Hons) MSt, Graduate Trainee, All Souls College, Oxford.
[10022040]   20/11/2012   **ME**

Beighton, Mrs T, Area Community Manager, Hinckley Library, Leicestershire.
[10018893]   25/03/2011   **ME**

Belch, Mrs A L, BA (Hons) MCLIP, Assistant Librarian, Lancashire Teaching Hospitals NHS Foundation Trust.
[62704]   07/10/2003   **CM07/07/2010**

Belger, Mrs S J, BA (Hons) MSc, Library Supervisor.
[10016993]   16/06/2010   **ME**
Bell, Mrs A H, BA DipLib MCLIP, Service Development Leader, Central
Library, Edinburgh.
[28851]   26/01/1978   **CM06/04/1981**
Bell, Miss C, Library and LRC Assistant, Halesowen College.
[10012537]   05/09/2014   **ME**
Bell, Ms C E, BA MA, Part-time Librarian, Balshaw's C E High School,
Leyland.
[10017919]   26/10/2010   **ME**
Bell, Mrs C S, BA MCLIP,
[27511]   26/04/1977   **CM24/05/1979**
Bell, Mr D J, MCLIP, Academic Liaison Librarian, Oxford Brookes
University.
[19619]   24/10/1972   **CM22/11/1976**
Bell, Ms D L, BA (Hons) MA MCLIP, Research Librarian, City University,
London.
[52074]   02/10/1995   **RV**19/10/2006   **CM15/03/2000**
Bell, Dr E M, BA (Hons) MA MCLIP MSc PhD, Unwaged.
[55393]   09/10/1997   **CM15/10/2002**
Bell, Miss F, BA, Library and Information Assistant, Bond Dickinson LLP.
[10025451]   06/12/2013   **ME**
Bell, Mrs H C, BA DipLib MCLIP, Librarian, Barrow, Cumbria County
Council.
[35733]   17/01/1983   **CM01/02/1986**
Bell, Mrs J, MCLIP, County L. Manager, Lancs CC.
[30774]   04/04/1979   **CM25/11/1983**
Bell, Mr K E, BA M Phil DipLib MCLIP, Retired.
[1081]   03/02/1970   **CM22/02/1988**
Bell, Mr K W, MBE MInstE MCLIP, Retired.
[60519]   03/04/1966   **CM03/04/1966**
Bell, Mrs L, ACLIP, Assistant Locality Librarian, Halesowen Library,
Dudley.
[10017735]   30/09/2010   **ACL18/12/2013**
Bell, Mrs M, BA DIP LIB MCLIP, Information Manager, Scottish
Enterprise, Glasgow.
[35236]   04/10/1982   **CM29/11/1986**
Bell, Mrs M A, BA DipLib MCLIP, Retired.
[21716]   31/12/1973   **CM01/07/1990**
Bell, Mr M J, BA, English Instructor/Library Intern (Voluntary), Lakeland
College, Japan.
[10022293]   05/02/2013   **ME**
Bell, Mrs M S, BLS MCLIP, Operational Manager, Area D, Ls. NI.
[40524]   25/02/1987   **CM26/05/1993**
Bell, Mrs N J, MA,
[10017888]   21/10/2010   **ME**
Bell, Mrs S, BA MCLIP, Service Development Manager Aberdeen City
Libraries.
[22990]   07/10/1974   **CM01/08/1978**
Bell, Ms S, BAppSc, Team Leader, Shire of Kalamunda Library
Services, Australia.
[10021092]   29/05/2012   **ME**
Bell, Mrs V N, BSc (Hons) MLIS MCLIP, Primary Care Librarian,
Defence Medical Library Service, MOD.
[48426]   04/01/1993   **CM04/02/2004**
Bell, Miss W J, BA (Hons) DipLib MCLIP, Unwaged.
[31511]   18/10/1979   **CM24/01/1984**
Bellamy, Mr P D, BA MCLIP, Senior Librarian, Falkirk Community Trust.
[30597]   01/03/1979   **CM06/07/1981**
Bellamy, Ms P D, BSc PGCE, Senior Library Manager, Royal Greenwich
Libraries.
[10022295]   05/02/2013   **ME**

Bellamy, Mr P R, BA DipLib MCLIP, Senior Information Assistant,
University of Nottingham.
[38044]   10/01/1985   **CM17/10/1990**
Belle, Ms J, RVN BSc MSc, Library Volunteer at RCVS
Knowledge/Veterinary Nurse.
[10033634]   07/04/2014   **AF**
Bellinger, Mr R P, BLib MSc MCLIP, Principal Officer, Libraries,
Bridgend County Borough Council.
[46314]   28/10/1991   **CM25/05/1994**
Bellingham, Ms M, BA, Student, UCL.
[10032650]   22/01/2014   **ME**
Bellingham, Mrs R A, MCLIP, Part-time. Librarian, Bentleys Stokes &
Lowless, Solicitors, London.
[24716]   07/10/1975   **CM26/11/1980**
Bellis, Mr R, L. Assistant, DWP Library, London.
[10007234]   25/01/2008   **AF**
Bello, Mr S A, Student, University of Pretoria.
[10032657]   23/12/2013   **ME**
Bello, Mr T M, BSc, Student, Information School, The University of
Sheffield.
[10034260]   27/06/2014   **ME**
Belsham, Mrs C T, LLB Honours, LLB Honours, Head of Library and
Archivst, Streatham and Clapham High School for Girls Girls Day
School Trust.
[47504]   14/09/1992   **ME**
Belsham, Ms J K, BA DipLib MCLIP, Senior Information Advisor,
Kingston University, Kingston.
[37422]   30/08/1984   **CM15/08/1990**
Belsham, Mrs S R, MCLIP, Assistant Librarian, Thomas Plume Library,
Maldon.
[1108]   08/11/1967   **CM01/01/1972**
Belton, Mrs M P, BA MCLIP, Librarian, Long Eaton Library, Derbys.
[34658]   21/01/1982   **CM01/07/1990**
Bendall, Dr A S, MA MCLIP, Fellow & Development Director, Emmanuel
College, Cambridge.
[35001]   23/11/1982   **CM17/09/1986**
Benjafield, Miss J A, ACLIP, Library Assistant, Worksop Library, Notts.
[65581]   22/02/2006   **ACL29/03/2007**
Benjamin, Dr C, BA (Hons) Dip CG PhD, Student, Robert Gordon
University.
[10035228]   22/10/2014   **ME**
Bennet, Mr M C, BSc, PT Student/Library Assistant, University of Surrey
Library, Guildford.
[64648]   11/05/2005   **ME**
Bennett, Miss A L C, BA (Hons) MA MCLIP, Chief Librarian, Priaulx
Library, St Peter Port, Guernsey.
[52312]   23/10/1995   **CM26/11/1997**
Bennett, Mrs C, BA (Hons) MA, Assistant Librarian, Office for National
Statistics, Library and Information Services, Titchfield.
[60875]   18/12/2001   **ME**
Bennett, Ms C P, BA (Hons), Librarian, St Helens College, Merseyside.
[34361]   26/10/1981   **ME**
Bennett, Mrs D A, BA (Hons) DipLib MCLIP,
[10011622]   21/10/1976   **CM29/02/1980**
Bennett, Mr D E, BSc MSc MCLIP, Assistant Librarian (Promotions).
[65202]   17/11/2005   **CM21/08/2009**
Bennett, Mrs E P, BSc MCLIP, Unwaged.
[35105]   03/09/1982   **CM10/05/1988**
Bennett, Miss F J, MA DipLib,
[40715]   06/05/1987   **ME**
Bennett, Mr G M, BSc MA, Assistant Librarian, University of Essex,
Southend.
[10005907]   01/10/2004   **ME**

Bennett, Mrs H R, BA (Hons) MA MCLIP, Assistant Librarian, Guildford College.
[10001222]   02/02/2007   **CM06/07/2011**

Bennett, Mrs J, BA MCLIP, Part-time Senior Information Serv. Assistant, Leeds Metropolitan University Part-time, w/e Customer Serv. Office Birkby L.
[36757]   09/11/1983   **CM18/07/1990**

Bennett, Mrs J T, BA (Hons), Information Servs. Manager, Lazard. London.
[65721]   30/01/2006   **ME**

Bennett, Miss K, BA (Hons) MA MCLIP, Liaison Librarian, Newman University, Birmingham.
[10011897]   26/11/2008   **CM11/04/2013**

Bennett, Mrs K L, LIC Admin Officer, Royal Society of Chemistry, London.
[10018886]   25/03/2011   **AF**

Bennett, Mrs M R, BA (Hons) QTS, Library Assistant, Graham School.
[10034530]   18/07/2014   **ME**

Bennett, Mr M R, MCLIP, Retired.
[1141]   25/04/1963   **CM01/01/1967**

Bennett, Mr M S, BA MA MCLIP, Knowledge & Information Manager, HM Gov. Communications Centre, Milton Keynes.
[43234]   10/10/1989   **CM23/03/1993**

Bennett, Mrs R, BA (Hons) MA MCLIP, Business Research Analyst, KBR, Leatherhead.
[63215]   16/03/2004   **CM30/04/2014**

Bennett, Mr S E, BA, Customer Serv. Officer, Kirklees Cult. & Leisure Serv., Huddersfield.
[40496]   10/02/1987   **ME**

Bennett, Mrs W, BA MCLIP, Lending Services Manager, CultureNL Ltd.
[29474]   29/07/1978   **CM18/03/1981**

Benoy, Mrs K, BA MCLIP, Librarian The Thomas Alleyne Academyl, Stevenage.
[34982]   25/05/1982   **CM06/05/1985**

Benson, Miss J E, BLib MCLIP, Retired.
[1156]   24/10/1968   **CM26/09/1973**

Benson, Miss J M, BA MCLIP, Retired.
[1157]   28/09/1965   **CM01/01/1968**

Benson, Ms M T, BA MA, PhD student, University of Sheffield.
[10032130]   29/10/2013   **ME**

Benson, Mrs P, Prof. Librarian, Office of the Prime Minister L. Div., Trinidad.
[55721]   11/11/1997   **ME**

Benstead, Miss K, BA (Hons) MA, Information Services Manager, Royal College of Defence Studies.
[59845]   16/10/2001   **ME**

Bent, Mrs M J, MA BSc PgDip MCLIP FHEA FRSA, Faculty Liaison Librarian, Robinson Library, University Newcastle, Newcastle.
[29170]   29/03/1978   **CM30/06/1981**

Ben-Tahir, Mr I, BA MS MCASI MCLIP ARAeS RCAF, Information Scientist, Canada. Joined Institute of Information Scientists 20/06/1986.
[60082]   20/06/1986   **CM20/06/1986**

Bentley, Mrs E A, BA MCLIP DipEd, Librarian, Addey & Stanhope School.
[29008]   08/03/1978   **CM23/03/1981**

Bentley, Miss R B, BA (Hons), Student, Manchester Metropolitan University.
[10031766]   01/10/2013   **ME**

Bentley, Mr S R, MSc, Assistant Librarian, University of Hull.
[65863]   09/06/2006   **ME**

Benton, Mr E, MA (Hons) MA MCLIP, Libr., Godolphin & Latymer School, London.
[59054]   06/11/2000   **CM02/02/2005**

Berberovic, Mr D, Student, Robert Gordon University.
[10033295]   28/02/2014   **ME**

Berendse, Mrs S, MLIS, Information Specialist, National Collaborating Centre for for Cancer.
[62948]   21/11/2003   **ME**

Bergen, Ms C L, MA MCLIP DipRSA CertEd FRSA, Freelance.
[26034]   01/07/1976   **CM09/03/1978**

Bergeron, Ms A N J, ACLIP, Learning Resources Assistant, City Lit.
[10020014]   25/10/2011   **ACL16/01/2014**

Berkmen, Mrs M, MCLIP, Retired.
[17039]   30/01/1960   **CM01/01/1964**

Berman, Mrs A, BEd CTHIC ACLIP, Enquiry Team Librarian, Welwyn Garden City Central Library and Information Service, Hertfordshire.
[10018789]   10/03/2011   **ACL16/05/2012**

Bernard, Ms F J F, BA (Hons) MSc (Hons), Student, Robert Gordon University, Aberdeen.
[10016165]   19/02/2010   **ME**

Bernard, Miss M A, BA DipLib MCLIP, Service & Strategy Manager Bournemouth Borough Council.
[32254]   22/02/1980   **CM11/11/1982**

Bernstein, Mrs A J, MA, Senior Library Assistant, University of Sheffield, Main L.
[58654]   04/05/2000   **ME**

Berridge, Mrs J J, BA MCLIP, Part-time Library Assistant, Nailsea Group, North Somerset.
[27154]   03/02/1977   **CM02/11/1979**

Berridge, Mrs V, BEd (Hons), Senior Library Assistant, Education L. Serv., Winsford.
[10013812]   29/05/2009   **AF**

Berrington, Mr M, BA (Hons) MA DipLib, Deputy University Librarian, Boots Library, Nottingham Trent University, Nottingham.
[10017249]   04/10/1984   **ME**

Berrisford, Mrs A J, BSc (Econ), Sch. Librarian, Portland Place School, Westminster. W1B 1NJ.
[10005236]   27/06/2007   **ME**

Berry, Ms B L, BA MSc (Econ), Library and Information Services Manager, Royal College of Psychiatrists, London.
[46311]   28/10/1991   **ME**

Berry, Miss E J, BA, Library Assistant, Stratford-upon-Avon College.
[10021194]   21/06/2012   **ME**

Berry, Mrs H M, BA PGCE MSc MCLIP, Development Librarian, Leeds City L.
[42412]   30/10/1988   **CM26/02/1992**

Berry, Miss J P, BA (Hons) MBA MCLIP, Librarian, BMA, London.
[22833]   12/10/1974   **CM28/07/1977**

Berry, Ms K, BA DMS MCLIP, Unwaged.
[30539]   13/03/1979   **CM27/07/1983**

Berry, Mrs N J, BA MSc, Resident in France.
[10012024]   10/12/2008   **ME**

Berry, Ms S, BA DipLib MCLIP, Information Resources Manager, Evalueserve UK Limited.
[34235]   15/10/1981   **CM14/11/1989**

Berry, Mr T J, MCLIP, Special Serv. Librarian, Hounslow.
[1188]   01/10/1971   **CM07/11/1974**

Bertenshaw, Mr C W, BA (HONS) MA, Assistant in Charge, Bakenwell Library, Derbyshire.
[10020806]   18/04/2012   **AF**

Bertuzzo, Mrs M J, BA (Hons), Assistant Librarian, Capel Manor College.
[10020061]   28/10/2011   **ME**

Berute, Miss K, Librarian.
[10018818]   15/03/2011   **ME**

Berwick, Ms J, BA MCLIP, L. & Information Serv. Manager, CMS
Cameron McKenna, London.
[32634]   01/07/1980   CM08/12/1982
Besag, Mr D, BA (Hons) MA,
[10022090]   25/01/2001   ME
Best, Mrs A C, MCLIP, Senior Librarian, Warwick School, Warwick.
[5088]   28/09/1971   CM19/08/1976
Best, Mrs H,
[10001330]   08/03/2007   ME
Best, Mr K R, BA MSc, Collection Access Officer, Library Support
Services, Lincoln.
[57671]   01/07/1999   ME
Best, Mr K W, MBE FCLIP, Life Member.
[1198]   17/01/1949   FE01/01/1959
Best, Miss S, MA, Student, University of Strathclyde.
[10035695]   29/10/2014   ME
Beswick, Mrs S, BA (Hons) MCLIP, Senior Assistant (Request &
Projects) ELS, Education L. Serv., Reading.
[49784]   06/12/1993   CM23/09/1998
Beton, Miss H, BA (Hons) MA MCLIP, Resources Information Specialist,
Library, Cranfield University.
[56651]   01/10/1998   CM15/05/2002
Bett, Miss N K, BA (Hons) MSc MCLIP, Librarian, Dunfermline High
School.
[54066]   22/10/1996   CM02/02/2005
Betteridge, Ms H, BA (Hons) MA, Student, University of Chichester.
[10025496]   21/10/2014   ME
Betteridge, Mr R L, BA (Hons) MSc MCLIP, Curator, National Library of
Scotland, Edinburgh.
[64842]   01/08/2005   CM14/12/2011
Bettles, Mrs A, BA (Hons) MCLIP, Global Information Centre Leader,
Infineum UK Ltd, Oxon.
[23148]   06/11/1974   CM02/08/1978
Betts, Mrs A M, BSc (Hons) MA MCLIP, Information Res. Officer, EON
UK, Notts.
[01229]   18/04/2002   CM13/06/2007
Betts, Mr D A, BA FCLIP, Retired.
[1208]   26/02/1958   FE01/01/1970
Betts-Gray, Mrs M J F, MA MCLIP, Business Information Specialist,
Cranfield University, Bedfordshire.
[33285]   28/10/1980   CM10/11/1983
Bevan, Miss C, ACLIP, Senior Lib. Assistant, University of Sunderland,
St Peter's Library, Sunderland.
[10008686]   09/04/2008   ACL04/03/2009
Bevan, Mr S J, BSc (Econ) (Hons) MA MCLIP, University Librarian.
[40294]   14/01/1987   CM18/04/1989
Beveridge, Ms K, BA (Hons) PgDipLIS, Assistant Librarian, Dundee
University Library.
[48327]   26/11/1992   ME
Beveridge, Miss L, BA (Hons) MCLIP, Student.
[10000651]   19/10/2006   CM18/01/2012
Beverley, Mrs E F, BA, Reader Development Officer, Young People &
Families, Wokingham Borough Council.
[58133]   04/11/1999   ME
Bevin, Dr D J, MA PhD MCLIP, Librarian, Chawton House Library.
[10013519]   01/01/1996   RV16/05/2012   CM17/05/2000
Bevin, Mrs P J, MA MCLIP, Retired.
[1213]   13/09/1951   CM01/01/1958
Bevington, Mr R D G, BA (Hons) DipLib,
[37895]   15/11/1984   CM18/07/1990
Bevis, Mrs J, BA (Hons) MSc MCLIP, Volunteer Librarian, Collections
Team at Bursledon Brickworks Industrial Museum.
[49582]   19/11/1993   CM17/03/1999

Beyer, Mrs F R, BSc (Hons) PgDip MCLIP, Information Specialist,
University of York.
[51401]   06/02/1995   CM28/01/2009
Bhadhal, Miss I, BA DipLib MCLIP, Reader Dev. Manager JLIS
Hounslow Contract.
[40074]   25/10/1986   CM14/02/1990
Bhandol, Mrs J M, BSc MCLIP, Academic Liaison Librarian, University
of Bedfordshire.
[62479]   10/07/2003   CM05/05/2010
Bhatti, Mrs K, Learning Res. Centre Manager, Stockeley Academy School.
[10001281]   14/02/2007   ACL17/06/2009
Bhimani, Ms N, MA MLS MCLIP FHEA, Special Collections Librarian,
Institute of Education, University of London.
[39120]   20/11/1985   CM21/05/2003
Bianchini, Mrs F A, Data Quality Officer, University of Creative Arts.
[10032187]   05/11/2013   ME
Bibb, Mrs A, BA MCLIP, Retired.
[567]   06/01/1964   CM01/01/1968
Bibi, Ms K, Lib. Asst/Librarian, Tower Hamlets Sch. Serv., London.
[10015083]   12/10/2009   AF
Bick, Miss L V, Student, University of Strathclyde.
[10035322]   08/10/2014   ME
Bickerton, Mrs D N, BA MA MCLIP, Life Member.
[28204]   27/08/1977   CM05/05/1982
Bickley, Miss A L, BA (Hons) MA MCLIP, Librarian, Peter Symonds
College, Winchester.
[56794]   16/10/1998   CM18/09/2002
Bickley, Ms R, BA MA MCLIP AFHEA, Academic Liaison Librarian.
[10015085]   12/10/2009   CM14/11/2012
Bicknell, Miss S S, MA (Hons), Trainee Research Librarian, Baker Tilly.
[10022334]   11/02/2013   ME
Biddle, Miss R, BSc, Senior Library Assistant.
[10033768]   25/04/2014   ME
Bide, Mrs R A C, Learning Resources Manager, Teddington School,
Middlesex.
[54985]   03/06/1997   AF
Biggins, Mr A, BSc MCLIP, Retired.
[1233]   18/01/1972   CM05/12/1974
Biggs, Miss P E, BSc DipLib MCLIP, Deputy Librarian, National Institute
Medical Res., London.
[36331]   05/10/1983   CM04/10/1988
Biggs, Ms S M, BA DipLib MCLIP, Unwaged.
[26937]   12/01/1977   CM16/07/1979
Biglou, Mrs L S, OBE MA DIPlib MCLIP, Director, British Council,
Ghana.
[10008668]   31/01/1986   CM16/10/1989
Bignell, Mr A P, BA DipLib MCLIP, Hd. of Libraries, Culture and
Learning, Hertfordshire County Council, Hertford.
[31564]   20/11/1979   CM16/06/1982
Bignold, Mrs H, BLib MCLIP MA, Librarian, Claysmore Prep School.
[38331]   08/03/1985   RV19/08/2011   CM16/02/1988
Bihet, Miss F E, BA (Hons) MA PGCE ACLIP, Information Assistant, St
Luke's Campus, Exeter.
[10023358]   02/07/2013   ACL18/12/2013
Bilgen, Mr D, MSc MCLIP, Information Specialist, Aston University.
[10013510]   30/04/2009   CM30/04/2014
Bilkhu, Mrs P K, BA MCLIP, Information Officer, ERA Tech.,
Leatherhead.
[29528]   28/07/1978   CM04/06/1981
Billing, Mrs C, MCLIP, Prison Librarian, H. M. P. Haverigg, Cumbria.
[6127]   01/01/1972   CM01/12/1974
Billingham, Ms C, BScEcon, Child. Librarian, City & County of
Swansea.
[64069]   15/12/2004   ME

Billingham, Miss J A, MCLIP, Retired.
[1246]   14/03/1963   **CM01/01/1967**
Billings, Ms K A, BSc MCLIP, Unwaged.
[34685]   26/01/1982   **CM12/10/1984**
Billot, Miss M M, BA, Retired.
[1251]   01/01/1966   **ME**
Bilton, Ms R A, BLib MA MCLIP, District Librarian, Borehamwood
Library, Herts.
[39422]   24/01/1986   **CM14/11/1989**
Bimpeh-Segu, Mr A, BSc,
[10001687]   06/03/2007   **ME**
Bingham, Miss H E, BSc MSc MCLIP, L. and E-Learning Lead, Health
Education, Wessex.
[39256]   12/01/1986   **CM14/11/1990**
Bingley, Mr C H, MA HonFLA, Publisher.
[31194]   30/09/1971   **HFE10/09/1986**
Binnie, Mrs J G, MA (Hons) DipLib,
[35583]   03/11/1982   **ME**
Birbeck, Mr V P, BA (Hons) MPhil MCLIP, Library & Information
Management, European Monitoring Centre for Drugs & Drug
Addiction.
[34645]   21/01/1982   **CM24/09/1997**
Birch, Mrs P A, MCLIP, Retired.
[15968]   10/08/1970   **CM01/01/1973**
Birch, Mrs S M, MCLIP, Life Member.
[1270]   17/10/1944   **CM01/01/1968**
Birch, Mrs V H, BLib MCLIP, Information & Services Librarian, Herts. C.
C.
[34934]   29/04/1982   **CM05/05/1987**
Bird, Mrs B, BEd DipLIS MCLIP, Library Development Officer, Solihull
Central Library, Solihull MBC.
[49392]   21/10/1993   **CM21/07/1999**
Bird, Mrs E M, MCLIP, Life Member.
[1282]   27/09/1949   **CM01/01/1953**
Bird, Miss J V, BSc DipLib MCLIP, Content Coordinator, NERC Library
Service.
[31728]   05/11/1979   **CM19/05/1982**
Bird, Ms S M, BA (Hons) MSc MCLIP AlfL, Learning Resources
Manager, Henley College Coventry.
[42681]   09/02/1989   **RV**20/06/2014   **CM12/12/1991**
Bird, Ms V, MSc MCLIP, Subject Librarian (Politics, Economics, Finance
& Management Studies), SOAS, University of London.
[64362]   08/03/2005   **CM28/01/2009**
Birdi, Dr B K, BA (Hons) MA PhD MCLIP, Lecturer in Librarianship,
Information School, University of Sheffield.
[51811]   06/07/1995   **CM08/12/2004**
Birkby, Mrs A E, BA FCLIP, Life Member.
[1292]   03/10/1957   **FE01/01/1962**
Birkenhead, Mr G, BA (Hons) MSc MCLIP, Improvement Adviser.
[10009994]   03/08/1993   **CM19/01/2000**
Birkinshaw, Miss A D, BA DipLib MCLIP, Team Leader, Piershill L.,
Edinburgh City L.
[39147]   12/11/1985   **CM15/11/1988**
Birkwood, Miss K I, MA (Hons), Rare Books and Special Collections
Librarian, Royal College of Physicians, London.
[66130]   02/10/2006   **ME**
Birley, Ms C M, MSc, Library Services Assistant, Leeds Beckett
University.
[10018845]   21/03/2011   **AF**
Birse, Ms S D, BSc (Hons) MLIM MCLIP, Development Librarian (East
Perthshire), Loch Leven Community Library.
[53478]   01/07/1996   **CM15/03/2000**

Birt, Mrs H T, MCLIP, Principal Lib. Children & Young People, Dudley
Library, St James Road, Dudley.
[10001183]   03/02/2007   **CM11/08/1976**
Birtwhistle, Mrs J M, BA (Hons) MA DipIM MCLIP, Unwaged.
[55664]   07/11/1997   **CM16/05/2001**
Birtwistle, Mrs J L, BA MCLIP, Deputy Library Manager, High Wycombe
Lib, Bucks. County Council.
[27876]   12/10/1977   **CM30/04/1982**
Bishop, Mr G B A, MCLIP, Retired.
[1305]   08/11/1966   **CM14/08/1972**
Bishop, Freeman J, BSc (Hons) MSc MScEcon LLM, Chief Executive
Officer, Crocels Community Media Group.
[10019522]   04/08/2011   **ME**
Bishop, Mrs J H, BLS (Hons) MCLIP, Information and Archives Officer,
Barnabas Fund.
[33462]   01/01/1981   **CM17/09/2003**
Bishop, Mr P J, BSc (Hons) MCLIP, Backlog Reduction Proj. Co-
ordinator, British Library, Boston Spa.
[49429]   27/10/1993   **CM24/09/1997**
Bisset, Mr D W, MCLIP FSA, Retired.
[1316]   05/02/1957   **CM01/01/1961**
Bisset, Mr J M, MA, Librarian, Academic L. Serv., University of the West
of England.
[10001147]   12/01/2007   **ME**
Bithell, Miss C J, BSc MSc (Econ) MCLIP, Principal Librarian, Young
People's Servs., Jersey L.
[54630]   12/02/1997   **CM16/05/2001**
Bitner, Mrs I K, MA MCLIP, Life Member.
[16617]   15/01/1953   **CM01/01/1956**
Black, Mr A D L, LLB DipLib MCLIP, Head Librarian, Forest School.
[40398]   22/01/1987   **CM18/11/1992**
Black, Prof A M, BA MA DipLib PhD, Prof., Graduate Sch. of LIS,
University of Illinois at Ubana-Champaign, USA.
[35918]   25/02/1983   **ME**
Black, Miss C, MSCi, Student.
[10020020]   25/10/2011   **ME**
Black, Ms E P, BA MCLIP, Community Librarian.
[52971]   06/02/1996   **CM17/09/2003**
Black, Dr F A, BEd MLIS PhD HonFCLIP, Associate Vice-President
Academic, Dalhousie University, Nova Scotia.
[61294]   14/05/2002   **HFE12/12/2007**
Black, Mrs F J, BA DipEdTech DipCG (HE) MCLIP, Librarian, Language
Centre Library, University. of Glasgow, Glasgow.
[32779]   23/08/1980   **CM18/06/1985**
Black, Mrs G I, LLB (Hons) PgDip, Quality Assurance Manager, DWF
Biggart Baillie, Glasgow.
[59287]   29/01/2001   **CM29/03/2004**
Black, Ms J, MCLIP, Lifelong Learning Librarian, Carnegie Library, Ayr.
[10006257]   26/09/2007   **CM17/09/2008**
Black, Mrs K C, BA (Hons), Student.
[10015241]   29/10/2009   **ME**
Black, Miss K J, BA (Hons) MSc, Librarian, Scottish Media Group,
Glasgow.
[59467]   03/04/2001   **ME**
Black, Ms M A, MLib MCLIP, Retired.
[1331]   18/02/1966   **CM01/01/1971**
Black, Miss V, BA (Hons) PgDip, School Librarian.
[10017184]   11/07/2010   **ME**
Blackbourn, Mrs S E, BLib MCLIP, Librarian, Hampshire County
Council.
[39504]   11/02/1986   **CM13/06/1990**
Blackburn, Mrs E C, BEng (Hons) MSc MIET RN, Royal Navy Air
Engineer Officer.
[10022944]   14/05/2013   **ME**

Blackburn, Mrs H M, BA (Hons) MCLIP Msc, L. Manager, Alder Hey Children's, NHS Found. Trust, Liverpool.
[52755]   06/12/1995   **CM18/09/2002**

Blackett, Mrs S, BA (Hons) MCLIP PGCE, Information Services Coordinator, Durham University.
[48814]   07/06/1993   **CM20/03/1996**

Blackhurst, Mrs J K, MA (Hons) MA MCLIP, Assistant Librarian, Girton College, University of Cambridge.
[53983]   15/10/1996   **CM19/07/2000**

Blackledge, Ms P J, BSc (HONS), Learning Centre Assistant, Sussex Downs College.
[10013200]   16/04/2009   **AF**

Blackler, Miss F, ACLIP, Library Service Advisor, Arnold Library.
[10022215]   22/01/2013   **ACL16/01/2014**

Blackley, Mrs I, MCLIP, Information Delivery Coordinator, Enquiries Direct, C/O Guildford Library, Surrey.
[22099]   29/01/1974   **CM21/09/1977**

Blackman, Mr M J R, BSc CChem MRSC MCLIP, Retired.
[60791]   20/12/1988   **CM12/12/2001**

Blackshaw, Mr L R, Resources Officer, Nottinghamshire Co. Teaching PCT, Rainworth.
[43900]   15/02/1990   **ME**

Blackwell, Mrs J C, BA ACLIP, Community Librarian, Worthing Library, West Sussex.
[10015372]   09/11/2009   **ACL22/08/2012**

Blagbrough, Miss S, BA (Hons) DipILS MCLIP MSc, Research Assistant, Liverpool Hope University.
[44535]   23/10/1990   **CM22/11/1995**

Blagden, Mr J F, MA MCLIP, Retired: Former University Librarian, Cranfield University.
[1359]   28/02/1955   **CM01/01/1958**

Blagden, Mrs P E, BA MA DipLib CertEd FCLIP, Library Service Manager, Hampshire Healthcare Library Service.
[26970]   10/01/1977   **RV**17/06/2011   **FE13/06/2007**

Blair, Mrs C L, BA (Hons) MA MCLIP, Assistant Librarian, University of Winchester, Winchester.
[44868]   02/01/1991   **CM20/03/1996**

Blair, Ms C M, BA DipLib MCLIP, Enquiry Executive, Business and Transport Section, House of Commons Library.
[38952]   21/10/1985   **CM15/08/1989**

Blake, Mr A T, BA (Hons), Service Manager Customer Service, Dorset County Council.
[10034193]   18/06/2014   **ME**

Blake, Mr D S, BA MSc DipLib MCLIP, Head of L. & Archives, Society of Friends (Quakers).
[30108]   15/01/1979   **CM17/07/1984**

Blake, Mrs J E, BA MCLIP, Service Design and Development Manager, Somerset CC.
[29144]   20/04/1978   **CM14/05/1981**

Blake, Mrs J M, Learning resource Co-ordinator, Lealands High School, Luton.
[10021782]   11/10/2012   **AF**

Blake, Ms M, BA DipInfSc FCLIP MA, Information Consultant, Self-employed.
[57480]   06/04/1999   **FE01/04/2002**

Blake, Mrs M E, BA MCLIP, Unemployed.
[28284]   07/11/1977   **CM26/10/1982**

Blake, Mr N A C,
[10020125]   07/11/2011   **ME**

Blakeman, Ms K H, BSc DipInfSc FCLIP HonFCLIP, RBA Information Services, Reading.
[60146]   10/12/2001   **HFE01/10/2006**

Blakeway, Ms A J, MA DipLib, Archives & Local Studies Assistant, Hampshire Record Office, Winchester.
[25221]   05/01/1976   **ME**

Blakeway, Miss J, BA MCLIP, Data Support Officer, South Lanarkshire Council, Hamilton.
[21397]   01/11/1973   **CM16/06/1976**

Blakey, Mrs N R M, BA MCLIP, Librarian, The Magnet, East Sussex.
[1376]   29/09/1971   **CM28/02/1974**

Blanchett, Mrs H, BA (Hons) MSc MCLIP, Assistant Liaison Librarian, Robinson Library, Newcastle University.
[48135]   11/11/1992   **CM27/11/1996**

Blandford, Dr L, PhD MA BA, Student at Northumbria University and Lending Services Liaison Officer at the University of Kent.
[10031576]   03/09/2013   **ME**

Blandford, Miss S L, MCLIP, Retired.
[1384]   14/09/1949   **CM01/01/1955**

Blatchford, Miss B R, MA, Student.
[10006698]   21/11/2007   **ME**

Blaxter, Mrs E, BA (Hons) MA MCLIP FHEA, Head of Information Management, University of Strathclyde.
[41096]   06/10/1987   **CM16/11/1994**

Bleakley, Mrs C, MCLIP, Collections Care Assistant.
[20551]   02/04/1973   **CM05/07/1976**

Bleasdale, Dr C H, MA AIRT MCLIP, Retired.
[1387]   03/09/1950   **CM01/01/1959**

Blenkinsop, Mrs H, BSc (Hons) MSc, Library Assistant, University of Sunderland.
[10015611]   17/12/2009   **ME**

Blewer, Miss E, ACLIP, Resources Assistant & Library Assistant, Warwickshire Schools Library Service.
[10022089]   05/12/2012   **ACL16/01/2014**

Blewett, Mrs C A, DipLib MCLIP, Hook Infant School.
[32147]   16/01/1980   **CM25/04/1984**

Bley, Mr R S, BA DipLib MCLIP, Managing Director, Ex Libris Group.
[41447]   01/01/1988   **CM15/09/1993**

Bliss, Miss A M, MA MCLIP, Retired.
[16622]   07/10/1963   **CM01/01/1968**

Bliss, Mrs M M, MCLIP, Life Member.
[1392]   11/02/1948   **CM01/01/1952**

Blomfield, Ms H, BA, Graduate Trainee, The London Library.
[10032572]   17/12/2013   **ME**

Blondiaux-Ding, Mrs E, MA, Systems & Acquisitions Librarian, New College Nottingham / NCN.
[10007133]   18/01/2008   **ME**

Bloom, Miss A J, BA (Hons), Reader and Information Serv. Librarian, Wimbledon College of Art, University of the Arts, London.
[61948]   16/12/2002   **ME**

Bloomfield, Mrs G M N, BA, Librarian, St Catherine's School.
[41689]   08/02/1988   **ME**

Bloomfield, Mrs S A, BSc Dip Lib MCLIP, Senior Librarian, Hertfordshire County Council.
[22272]   01/03/1974   **CM13/02/1978**

Bloomfield, Mrs S J, Librarian, Southend High School for Boys.
[10025571]   19/11/2013   **ME**

Blott, Mrs J S, MCLIP, Unemployed.
[30292]   05/12/1978   **CM24/06/1983**

Blow, Miss J A, BA MCLIP, Life Member.
[1404]   20/09/1954   **CM01/01/1962**

Blower, Mr A V, BA (Hons) DipHE MCLIP, Key Documents Editor (Web), MOD, London.
[39212]   01/01/1986   **CM20/03/1996**

Blows, Ms K, BA (Hons) MSc, Information Executive, ICAEW, London.
[10008520]   26/11/2010   **ME**

Blows, Ms S, DipIS MCLIP, Librarian, Diss Library, Norfolk.
[46210]   10/10/1991   **CM15/03/2000**
Bloxham, Ms H A, MCLIP, L. Manager, UK Atomic Energy Authority, Fusion Library, Oxon.
[21861]   04/02/1974   **CM01/01/1978**
Bloxham, Mrs J, MA, Part-time Student /LRC. Assistant, Thames Valley/West Thames College, London.
[64130]   18/01/2005   **ME**
Bloxsidge, Mrs E L, MSc, Unwaged.
[10021240]   29/06/2012   **ME**
Blumenthal, Mr K R, BA,
[10031921]   14/10/2013   **ME**
Blundell, Miss C J, BA (Hons), Customer Serv. Team Leader, Shire Hall Library, Staffordshire.
[65774]   01/05/2006   **AF**
Blundell, Mrs P M, Unwaged.
[51528]   28/03/1995   **ME**
Blundell, Mr S R A, BA DipLib MCLIP, Librarian, The Reform Club, London.
[39785]   12/07/1986   **CM19/08/1992**
Blunden, Mr D, BA (Hons) MA, Local Studies Librarian, Barnsley Metropolitan Borough Council.
[61814]   11/11/2002   **ME**
Blunk, Mrs R, MLIS, Academic Liaison Librarian, University Campus Suffolk.
[10023117]   19/11/2013   **ME**
Blunt, Mr M G, Student, Aberystwyth University.
[10025574]   08/05/2014   **ME**
Blysniuk, Mrs J A, BA MCLIP, Senior Manager Lancashire School Library Service LCC.
[32195]   25/01/1980   **CM17/05/1985**
Blyth, Mr J M, BA (Hons) MCLIP,
[10007705]   05/03/1974   **CM01/01/1977**
Blyth, Mrs K A, BA (Hons) MA MCLIP PgDip PSM, Team Manager Reading & Programmes, County L. Hq., Nottinghamshire County Council.
[55685]   04/11/1997   **CM17/01/2001**
Boag, Ms I, BA (Hons), Student.
[10019926]   04/10/2011   **ME**
Boal, Mrs C, BA MCLIP, Res. Centre Manager, Leith Academy, City of Edinburgh Council.
[34605]   19/01/1982   **CM05/06/1986**
Boal, Miss H M, BSc (Hons) DipLIS MCLIP, Stock and Reading Library, Bristol Central Library, Bristol C. C.
[43375]   16/10/1989   **CM25/01/1995**
Boanas, Mrs A E, BA MCLIP, Librarian (Bibl. Serv.), Carcroft L. Headquarters, Doncaster Metropolitan Borough Council.
[38475]   26/04/1985   **CM05/07/1988**
Boardman, Mr R, Student, Robert Gordon University.
[10021965]   06/11/2012   **ME**
Boateng, Miss A K, BA PgCert MSc MCLIP, Head of Information Services, University of East London.
[61482]   14/08/2002   RV22/09/2010   **CM04/10/2006**
Boateng, Mr K A, Student.
[10031956]   15/10/2013   **ME**
Boateng, Mrs R M, BA FCLIP, Life Member.
[16625]   01/01/1961   **FE04/09/1978**
Boateng, Mrs S, MCLIP,
[10010896]   28/01/2009   **CM30/04/2014**
Bobbette, Mrs N, BA (Hons), Library Supervisor, North Somerset Council.
[10025579]   10/02/2014   **ME**
Bocking, Miss M, BSc (Econ) MCLIP, Life Member.
[1427]   15/03/1955   **CM01/01/1962**

Boddington, Miss S K, BA MCLIP, Retired.
[1428]   01/01/1968   **CM01/01/1970**
Bode, Mrs R S, BA MA MCLIP, Not Known.
[10032106]   28/10/2013   **CM15/09/2004**
Bodian, Mrs M T, BSc MCLIP, Information Specialist, Bre Global, Bre, Watford.
[60561]   28/03/1980   **CM04/07/1986**
Bodin, Mrs P D, Enquiry Officer, Clacton Library, Essex.
[59960]   12/11/2001   **AF**
Boeg, Mr N P, BA MA MCLIP,
[46581]   20/11/1991   **CM25/01/1995**
Boespflug, Ms K, MA MAS, Academic Librarian, University of Zurich, Institute of Geography, Library, Zurich, Switzerland.
[10006140]   11/09/2007   **ME**
Boffa, Mr J M, FCLIP, Retired, Part-time, Sch. L. Serv., Malta.
[21759]   07/01/1974   **FE15/12/1981**
Bogard, Mrs D, BA (Hons), Information and Systems Officer, Careers & Employability Service, University of Chichester.
[10022645]   05/04/2013   **ME**
Bogie, Mrs E R, Metadata Specialist, Western Bank Library, University of Sheffield.
[10021035]   11/03/2013   **ME**
Bogle, Mrs A R, MA DipLib MCLIP, Librarian, NHS National Serv. Scotland, Health Management Library, Edinburgh.
[40112]   18/10/1986   RV30/04/2014   **CM11/12/1989**
Bohle, Miss S, BA MLIS COS AHIP FRAS, Director of the Library, University of Northwestern Ohio.
[10034164]   11/06/2014   **ME**
Bohm, Mr J C, MA MSc, Library and Information Officer, Health Services Management Centre, University of Birmingham.
[10007225]   25/01/2008   **ME**
Boland, Ms D, Learning Assistant, the Manchester College.
[10013143]   02/04/2009   **AF**
Bolsover, Mrs L, MSc MCLIP, Senior Information Assistant, Brunel University, Uxbridge.
[64366]   14/03/2005   **CM09/09/2013**
Bolton, Mr D C, BA (Hons) MA MCLIP, Faculty Librarian, University of Gloucestershire.
[52331]   30/10/1995   **CM17/01/2001**
Bolton, Mr L, BA (Hons) PgDip MCLIP, Strategic Manager, Swindon Libraries.
[10022001]   18/10/1994   **CM19/03/1997**
Bolton, Mrs R, BA (Hons) MLib MCLIP, Outreach Services Manager, Wiltshire Libraries, Wiltshire Council.
[48099]   09/11/1992   **CM24/07/1996**
Bomford, Mrs H B, BA MCLIP, School Librarian, Westonbirt School, Gloucestershire.
[40184]   01/11/1986   **CM30/01/1991**
Bonansea-Ryan, Mrs S, BA MCLIP, Asset Data Manager, Genesis Housing Association.
[21904]   24/01/1974   **CM19/12/1980**
Bond, Mr A, BA (Hons) MA, Senior Librarian, Luton Borough Council.
[56537]   12/08/1998   **ME**
Bond, Mr C E, FCLIP, Life Member.
[1450]   01/01/1944   **FE01/01/1954**
Bond, Miss J, BA (Hons) MA, Information Centre Manager, Mayer Brown International LLP.
[57385]   24/02/1999   **ME**
Bond, Ms M A, Faculty Librarian, Liverpool Hope University.
[10018178]   01/12/2010   **ME**
Bond, Mr N J, MCLIP, Retired.
[1459]   01/01/1961   **CM01/01/1964**

Bond, Ms R, BA MA MPhil, College Librarian, Eton College Library, Windsor.
[64978]   04/10/2005   **ME**

Bond McNally, Mrs A, BA (Hons) PgDip, Reader Development Lib., Bury MBC.
[59124]   21/11/2000   **ME**

Bone, Mr D, BA, Senior Administrator & Librarian, British Museum.
[10011930]   24/10/2013   **ME**

Boneham, Dr J, BD (Hons) MTh MScEcon PhD, Reference Specialist (News) at the British Library.
[10017826]   11/10/2010   **ME**

Bonham, Mrs A O, BA MCLIP, Bookstart plus dev. worker, Southend-on-Sea Library, Essex.
[35593]   15/11/1982   **CM15/09/1993**

Bonnell, Miss J L, Liaison Librarian, Nottingham Trent University, Clifton Campus.
[64677]   25/05/2005   **ME**

Bonner, Mr A R, MA MCLIP, Life Member.
[1467]   29/10/1951   **CM01/01/1955**

Bonnett, Mrs P, BA FCLIP, Assistant Editor, Health Information & Libraries Journal.
[9518]   20/02/1962   **FE17/11/1999**

Bonsall, Mrs S M, BA (Hons) DipLIS MCLIP, Librarian, Library Support Services, Oxfordshire County Council.
[44603]   05/11/1990   **CM18/09/2002**

Boodt, Ms D V, BSc, Teacher, Uknow Better School of English.
[10033473]   17/03/2014   **ME**

Booker, Mrs S A, ACLIP, Library Assistant, Cambridgeshire County Council.
[63519]   16/06/2004   **ACL08/06/2005**

Boon, Mr J M, BA (Hons) MA MSc MPhil, Senior Information Specialist, Infotrieve Inc.
[10011715]   01/11/2008   **ME**

Booth, Dr A, BA DipLib MSc MCLIP PhD, Reader – Evidence Based Info Practice, Sch. of Health & Related Research, University of Sheffield.
[35227]   01/10/1982   **CM30/01/1991**

Booth, Dr B K W, MA PLD FBCS FRSA FMA, Chief Information Officer, IPSOS, London.
[60805]   06/07/1989   **CM06/07/1989**

Booth, Ms C, BA (Hons), User Services Assistant, Liverpool School of Tropical Medicine.
[10020378]   10/02/2012   **ME**

Booth, Mrs C M, MA, Sci. Curator, National Library of Scotland.
[22706]   17/09/1974   **CM28/02/1977**

Booth, Miss E E, BA MA MA, Library Assistant (Cataloguing and Metadata).
[10017994]   01/11/2010   **ME**

Booth, Ms P, MED BA MCLIP, Retired.
[1485]   12/09/1955   **CM01/01/1962**

Booth, Miss S J, BA (Hons) PgDip, Neighbourhood Librarian.
[66110]   25/09/2006   **ME**

Boothroyd, Mrs A, BA MA, Fundraising Research Officer, Cambridge University, Development Office.
[58308]   06/01/2000   **ME**

Boothroyd, Mrs K M, BA (Hons) MCLIP, Service Development Manager, Libraries Management Team, St Helens.
[47867]   22/10/1992   **CM27/11/1996**

Booty, Mr C J, MCLIP, Information and Learning Services Development Manager, Essex County Council.
[10020392]   01/01/1972   **CM02/11/1984**

Boraston, Ms J A, MA F. iFI BA (Lib),
[29588]   24/10/1978   **ME**

Borchgrevink, Mrs H, DipLib MCLIP, Librarian, Oslo International School, Norway.
[26066]   20/05/1976   **CM16/02/1979**

Borcsok, Mrs N, MR, Information Officer, BSRIA.
[10031941]   15/10/2013   **ME**

Borland, Miss M C, MCLIP, Life Member.
[1494]   12/01/1943   **CM01/01/1949**

Borri, Miss A, BA MA, Assistant Academic Support Librarian, University of the Arts London.
[10014359]   17/07/2009   **ME**

Borst-Boyd, Mrs R R, BA DipLib MCLIP, Librarian, Oakville Public Library, Oakville.
[30818]   08/05/1979   **CM11/05/1981**

Borthwick, Miss A, MA PgDip, University of Aberdeen.
[10011216]   02/10/2008   **ME**

Borthwick, Mrs F, BA (Hons) MCLIP, Customer Services Consultant.
[54330]   21/11/1996   **CM20/09/2000**

Borthwick, Mrs H E, BSc MCLIP, Librarian, National Records of Scotland.
[43257]   13/10/1989   **CM16/07/2003**

Borymchuk, Dr O, BA MA DPHIL,
[10012033]   10/12/2008   **ME**

Bosch, Ms A S, BSc PgDipLIS, Information Specialist, Ashridge Business School.
[54759]   01/04/1997   **ME**

Bosher, Mrs C, BA FCLIP, Retired.
[20246]   01/01/1940   **FE01/01/1951**

Boss, Ms L C, MA (Hons) DipLIS MCLIP, Unemployed/ Weekly Volunteer Fairhavens Hospice Library, Southend, Essex.
[51344]   24/01/1995   **CM12/03/2003**

Bossons, Ms K J, BA (Hons) MCLIP, Lib. & Info Officer (Heritage), Newcastle Lib. & Information Service.
[48744]   04/05/1993   **CM26/11/1997**

Bostock, Mrs G, BA (Hons) MA MCLIP, Retired.
[50189]   27/04/1994   **CM12/03/2003**

Boston, Mrs J, BA (Hons) MSc, Subject Librarian, University of the West of Scotland, Ayr.
[63667]   12/08/2004   **ME**

Boswarthack, Ms C A, BA MCLIP, Head of Barbican and Community Libraries, City of London Corporation.
[34295]   23/10/1981   **CM26/07/1984**

Bottomley, Mrs J, ACLIP, Library Assistant/Officer, The British School in the Netherlands.
[10021366]   25/07/2012   **ACL09/09/2013**

Botwright, Miss S, BA MSc, EUscreenXL Cataloguer – Screen Archive South East.
[10021248]   02/07/2012   **ME**

Boucher, Mrs C M, BA MPhil MA, Deputy Health Sci. Librarian, LIC, Swansea University.
[56758]   09/10/1998   **ME**

Boughton, Mr G G, Assistant Librarian (MCLIP), Defence Geographic Centre, Middlesex.
[65915]   04/07/2006   **CM19/10/2012**

Boughton, Ms L C W, BA DipLib MCLIP, Freelancer.
[30364]   29/01/1979   **CM13/06/1989**

Boulton, Mr G H, BA MCLIP, Lead Officer, Library Operations, Royal Borough of Kingston upon Thames.
[29928]   27/10/1978   **CM31/10/1980**

Boulton, Mr K G, MA MCLIP, Information Systems Librarian, University of York.
[19792]   22/11/1972   **CM22/10/1975**

Boulton, Miss M C, BA DipLib MCLIP, Librarian, Royal College of Veterinary Surgeons.
[45629]   08/04/1991   **CM21/07/1993**

Bourelle, Ms J N, BA ACLIP, Library Assistant, Strahearn Community Library.
[10020493]   21/02/2012   **ACL13/11/2013**

Bourne, Mrs E M, MCLIP, Librarian, Redcliffe College, Gloucester.
[6794]   15/01/1961   **CM01/01/1966**

Bourne, Mr R M, BA FCLIP, Retired.
[1527]   01/08/1961   **FE18/11/1993**

Bourton, Mrs C M, MCLIP, School Librarian, Village School, Brent.
[32648]   19/07/1980   **CM10/11/1982**

Boutal, Mrs H J, BSc ACLIP, Part Time, Library Assistant, Sunninghill Library, RBWM.
[10018491]   27/01/2011   **ACL18/01/2012**

Boutland, Mr M T, Admin. Assistant, Hertfordshire County Council, Hemel Hempstead.
[59939]   08/11/2001   **ME**

Bovington, Ms J H, BA (Hons), Library Manager, Chipping Norton School.
[10012689]   04/09/2013   **ME**

Bowden, Mrs J, BSc PgC, Unwaged.
[10006491]   07/09/2005   **ME**

Bowden, Prof R G, MLS FCLIP HonFLA, Life Member.
[16634]   03/07/1961   **HFE01/01/1994**

Bowe, Mrs C B, BA MCLIP, Access and Outcomes Librarian Gloucester, Gloucestershire County Council.
[30321]   10/01/1979   **RV22/06/2007   CM06/08/1981**

Bowen, Mr D K, BA MCLIP, Child. and Sch. Librarian, Area Library, Carmarthen.
[26686]   08/11/1976   **CM30/10/1979**

Bowen, Mr D M, BA (Hons) DipInf MCLIP, Library Assistant, Carmarthen L.
[56413]   06/07/1998   **CM19/11/2008**

Bowen, Mr G P, MCLIP, Life Member.
[1540]   15/09/1950   **CM01/01/1958**

Bowen, Miss L, BA DipLib MCLIP, Librarian, University of Westminster.
[26286]   01/10/1976   **CM12/01/1979**

Bowen, Mr M, Cataloguer, Natural History Museum.
[10001136]   15/10/1986   **ME**

Bowen, Ms S V, BA DipLib MCLIP, Community Librarian Weston Librarian, Weston-super-Mare.
[35268]   03/10/1982   **CM05/05/1987**

Bowers, Ms G E, BA (Hons) MCLIP, Information Serv. Manager, Bedford Borough L.
[61599]   03/10/2002   **CM09/11/2005**

Bowers, Mrs M, MTheol MCLIP MSc, Relief Library Assistant, Highland Council.
[26872]   01/01/1977   **CM18/12/1978**

Bowers, Ms N R, BA MRES, Library Assistant, Kedleston Road Library, University Of Derby.
[10019395]   20/06/2011   **AF**

Bowers, Mrs Z D, Unwaged.
[37539]   03/10/1984   **ME**

Bowers Sharpe, Ms K, BA MA, Reference Librarian, Western Illinois University Library, USA.
[56009]   16/01/1998   **ME**

Bowie, Miss J E, BA MCLIP, Self-employed/retired at home.
[25223]   05/01/1976   **CM09/01/1978**

Bowl, Miss C L, BSc MCLIP, Information Officer, Travers Smith, London.
[39767]   01/07/1986   **CM08/03/1989**

Bowler, Ms V C, BA (Hons), Student, Aberystwyth University.
[10032007]   21/10/2013   **ME**

Bowles, Mr D H, BA (Hons) MA DipLIS MCLIP, Librarian, Information & Learning Team, Shared Services (Bexley & Bromley).
[46234]   18/10/1991   **CM22/05/1996**

Bowley, Mrs M S, MCLIP, Unemployed.
[25725]   23/09/1975   **CM08/12/1978**

Bowlt, Ms H, BA (Hons) MCLIP, Library Customer Service Manager, Central Library Service, Milton Keynes Council.
[41788]   08/04/1988   **CM22/07/1992**

Bowman, Miss C H, BA MA, Library Assistant & Student, University of the West of England.
[10035692]   29/10/2014   **ME**

Bowman, Dr J H, JP MA PhD MCLIP FRSA FSA, Retired.
[24476]   08/09/1975   **CM28/09/1977**

Bowman, Mrs R C, ACLIP, Self-employed.
[65877]   14/06/2006   **ACL05/10/2007**

Bowman, Mr S, BA (Hons) MA MSc FCLIP FHEA, Deputy Librarian, University of Chichester.
[42457]   16/11/1988   **RV13/05/2014   FE01/06/2005**

Bown, Mrs S J, Lib. Mgr, Balderton Cluster.
[10013402]   23/04/2009   **AF**

Bowring, Mr J R, BA MCLIP, Retired.
[1559]   16/03/1965   **CM01/01/1969**

Bowtell, Mrs F L, MCLIP, Learning & Teaching Lib. - Techn., Open University, Milton Keynes.
[62302]   17/04/2003   **CM19/11/2008**

Bowtell, Ms S M, MCLIP, TwoSues Training for Sch. Libraries.
[1561]   07/09/1964   **CM01/01/1968**

Bowyer, Ms S E, BA (Hons) DipLib MCLIP, Assistant Archivist, National Library of Wales, Aberystwyth.
[45427]   19/02/1991   **CM20/11/2002**

Boxall, Mr J A, BA (Hons) MA ACLIP, Learning Resource Advisor, Vision West Nottinghamshire College, Mansfield.
[10006939]   17/12/2007   **ACL09/11/2011**

Boxall, Mrs R C, BA (Hons), Learning Resource Advisor, West Nottinghamshire College.
[65278]   12/12/2005   **ME**

Boxford, Miss A J, BA (Hons) MA MCLIP, District Library Manager, Cambs CC.
[53942]   11/10/1996   **CM12/03/2003**

Boyce, Miss J M, MCLIP, Librarian, Colston's School, Bristol.
[1565]   19/03/1972   **CM10/11/1975**

Boyce, Mr L E, BA DipLib MCLIP, Retired.
[24403]   08/08/1975   **CM31/08/1978**

Boyd, Ms D, BA (Hons) PgDip MCLIP, Librarian, Central Library, Manchester.
[43715]   06/12/1989   **CM04/10/2006**

Boyd, Mr D H, MCLIP, Retired.
[1569]   09/10/1965   **CM01/01/1968**

Boyd, Mr G, BA (Hons) MSc MCLIP, Unwaged.
[61648]   15/10/2002   **CM01/02/2006**

Boyd, Ms H, BA, Graduate Trainee Library Assistant, Stanmore College.
[10033071]   16/09/2014   **ME**

Boyd, Miss L A, MA (Hons) DipLib MCLIP, Library Resource Centre Manager, North Lanarkshire Council.
[10001133]   05/10/1990   **CM23/01/1993**

Boyd, Mrs M B, BA MA MCLIP, Retired.
[42112]   01/10/1988   **CM18/07/1990**

Boyd, Mr N, BA (Hons) MCLIP, Training & Quality Coordinator, Anglia Ruskin University, Chelmsford.
[49296]   20/10/1993   **CM18/09/2002**

Boyde, Miss S J, MA DipLib MCLIP, Retired.
[1577]   14/10/1971   **CM22/12/1982**

Boydell, Ms L, BA (Hons) MA, Senior Knowledge Manager, DLA Piper UK LLP, London.
[49163]   08/10/1993   **CM23/07/1997**

Boyd-Moss, Miss S A L, BSc (Hons) MA, L. Executive, House of Commons Library, London.
[59486]   09/04/2001   **ME**

Boyer, Mrs B, MCLIP, Life Member.
[1578]   03/10/1941   **CM01/01/1944**

Boyes, Mrs D, BA DipLib MCLIP, The University of Northampton, Library and Learning Services, Information Assistant (Cataloguing).
[35811]   17/01/1983   **CM18/02/1986**

Boylan, Ms S, Librarian, Young People's Serv., East Lothian Council.
[64445]   30/03/2005   **ME**

Boyle, Ms G A, MCLIP, User Serv. Librarian, Dudley Group of Hospitals NHS Trust, West Midlands.
[56900]   02/11/1998   **CM16/05/2012**

Boyle, Mrs J, BA DipILS DipEIM MCLIP, Information and Records Manager, Highlands & Islands Enterprise.
[57473]   01/04/1999   **CM12/03/2003**

Boyle, Mrs J V S, BA (Hons), L. Manager, Trafford College, Altrincham.
[49324]   22/10/1993   **ME**

Boynton, Miss J, BA (Hons), Senior Information Specialist, National Institute for Health & Clinical Excellence, Manchester.
[48650]   01/04/1993   **ME**

Boyton, Mr J, Library Assistant, Uxbridge High School.
[10034447]   09/09/2014   **ME**

Bozic, Ms A C, BSc (Hons) PgDip, Library Assistant, The RSA.
[10019764]   16/11/1994   **ME**

Brabazon, Mr C R, BA DipLib MCLIP, Library and Information Services Manager, North Lincolnshire Council.
[38683]   01/10/1985   **CM15/03/1989**

Brace, Mr P J, BA DipLib MCLIP, Assistant Librarian, MOD, London.
[33274]   21/11/1980   **CM01/07/1990**

Bracher, Mr T N, BA MSc DipLib MCLIP, Archives & Local Studies Manager, Wiltshire & Swindon History Centre.
[46167]   07/10/1991   **CM15/09/1993**

Brack, Miss K L, MA (Hons) PgDip, Librarian, Monifieth Hight School, Dundee.
[10011819]   17/11/2008   **ME**

Brackenbury, Mrs H L, BA (Hons) (Oxon) MA, Librarian, Withington Girl's School, Manchester.
[10006809]   10/12/2007   **ME**

Bradburn, Mrs J, MCLIP, Retired.
[20134]   01/01/1967   **CM14/11/1974**

Bradbury, Mr D, MA MCLIP, Retired.
[21747]   10/01/1974   **CM12/08/1976**

Bradbury, Mrs L, BA MCLIP, Retired.
[8043]   22/07/1969   **CM19/02/1974**

Braddock, Mrs C H, BLIB MCLIP, District Manager, Staffordshire County Council, Leek L.
[37287]   01/06/1984   **CM06/09/1988**

Bradford, Miss C, MA MCLIP, Academic Support Librarian, University of Warwick.
[42607]   18/01/1989   **RV**13/05/2014   **CM18/11/1992**

Bradley, Miss A, BA MCLIP, Life Member.
[1594]   21/03/1950   **CM01/01/1956**

Bradley, Mrs C, Student, Robert Gordon University.
[10025644]   22/10/2013   **ME**

Bradley, Ms F, BA MA MIM, Manager Member Services and Development, IFLA.
[10018102]   16/11/2010   **ME**

Bradley, Mr G, FCLIP, Life Member.
[1600]   17/02/1948   **FE01/01/1963**

Bradley, Mr I G, MCLIP, Life Member.
[1602]   09/01/1962   **CM01/01/1966**

Bradley, Mrs L, Knowledge Services Manager, Western Isles Hospital Library, Isle of Lewis.
[10019850]   23/09/2011   **ME**

Bradley, Mr P, BA (Hons) MCLIP, Internet Consultant.
[10016762]   01/11/1979   **CM13/11/1984**

Bradley, Mr P G, BA MA MCLIP, Subject Librarian, Health and Social & Policy Sciences University of Bath.
[58242]   24/11/1999   **RV**27/08/2014   **CM29/11/2006**

Bradley, Miss S, BA, Primary Care Librarian, North Bristol NHS Trust.
[10013856]   04/06/2009   **ME**

Bradley, Miss S J, BSc MSc MCLIP, Enterprise Content Manager, Anglian Water.
[44957]   23/01/1991   **CM01/04/1992**

Bradly, Mrs J E, BA MCLIP,
[4160]   02/02/1969   **CM30/07/1973**

Bradnock, Mrs A M, MA DipLib MCLIP, Retired. School Librarian.
[49886]   07/01/1994   **CM25/09/1996**

Bradshaw, Mrs E C, BA DipLib MCLIP, Team Librarian, Reading Library, Reading.
[25786]   02/03/1976   **CM11/05/1979**

Bradshaw, Mrs K, BSc (Hons) DipLIS, Subject Librarian, University of Bath.
[47057]   08/04/1992   **CM21/05/1997**

Bradshaw, Ms W A, MCLIP, BA(Hons) MA, Librarian, London Borough of Haringey.
[61557]   01/10/2002   **CM14/12/2012**

Bradwell, Mr A, BA CertEd DipLib MCLIP, Academic Liaison Librarian, Anglia Polytechnic University, Chelmsford, Essex.
[43606]   09/11/1989   **CM27/07/1994**

Brady, Ms A E, BA (Hons) MCLIP, Assistant Director, Aston University, Birmingham.
[30298]   17/01/1979   **CM29/01/1985**

Brady, Mrs A P, BA DipLib MCLIP, Research Analyst.
[28050]   04/10/1977   **CM18/02/1980**

Brady, Ms D, MRES BSocSc MCLIP, Librarian, St Christophers Hospice, Sydenham.
[28270]   31/10/1977   **CM31/12/1979**

Bragg, Mr J H R, MSC MCLIP, Life Member.
[16640]   28/01/1965   **CM01/01/1970**

Bragg, Mrs J M, BA (Hons) MCLIP, Retired.
[59934]   07/11/2001   **CM13/06/2007**

Bragg, Lord M, HonFLA, Hon. Fellow.
[50582]   22/09/1994   **HFE22/09/1994**

Brain, Mr D, Information Support Administrator, Ministry of Defence.
[10034541]   21/07/2014   **ME**

Brain, Mrs M E, BA MCLIP, Librarian, Dr. J. H. Burgoyne & Partners, Ilkley, West Yorks.
[1622]   19/10/1971   **CM03/12/1976**

Brain, Mrs S H, BA (Hons) MScILM MCLIP, Senior Assistant Librarian, University West of England, Bristol.
[58583]   04/04/2000   **RV**16/01/2014   **CM12/03/2003**

Brall, Mr R J, BA DipLib MCLIP, Librarian, HM Crown Prosecution Service.
[33559]   16/01/1981   **CM07/03/1985**

Bramall, Mrs H D, BEd DipLib BA (Hons), Comm. Librarian Ref, Walsall MBC.
[34421]   05/11/1981   **ME**

Bramhall, Mr P, BA MA, Student, University of the West of England.
[10035607]   23/10/2014   **ME**

Bramley, Mrs A W, MCLIP, L. &Information Specialist.
[7269]   06/01/1965   **CM01/01/1970**

Bramley, Mrs C L, BA (Hons) MSc MCLIP, Unwaged.
[55484]   17/10/1997   **CM20/09/2000**

Bramley, Ms R A, BA MA, Library Manager, Varndean College,
Brighton.
[10001698]   01/10/1998   **ME**

Bramwell, Mrs V, BA (Hons) MA MCLIP, Library Manager, Cheshire &
Wirral Partnership NHS.
[58907]   03/10/2000   **CM09/07/2008**

Brand, Ms S J, MA PgDP MCLIP, School Librarian, Notre Dame High
School, Glasgow.
[10000705]   26/10/2006   **CM10/07/2009**

Branigan, Ms J, BA (Hons) DipLib MCLIP, Information Services
Executive, NEPIA.
[43177]   14/09/1989   **CM18/11/1992**

Branney, Ms C, BA (Hons) MSc MCLIP, Information Specialist, Foreign
& Commonwealth Office, London.
[35836]   21/01/1983   **CM10/05/1988**

Brasier, Mrs M E, MA DipLib MCLIP, Partner, Melchior Telematics,
Nottingham.
[34056]   21/08/1981   **CM29/07/1986**

Brassington, Mrs J C, MCLIP, L. Serv. Manager, Bath & North East
Somerset Council.
[10013097]   12/09/1974   **CM18/07/1977**

Brassington, Mrs M, BA MCLIP, Cataloguing Librarian, Spalding
Gentlemen's Society.
[1648]   17/01/1966   **CM01/01/1971**

Brathwaite, Mrs A S, Library Assistant II (AG), The National Library of
Trinidad & Tobago / Student, Aberystwyth University.
[10033877]   08/05/2014   **ME**

Brathwaite, Miss T, BA (Lis) PgDip (IR) MA (ECP), Librarian, Institute of
International Relations.
[10013115]   03/04/2009   **ME**

Bratt, Miss C, MCLIP,
[64945]   03/10/2005   **CM19/10/2012**

Brattset-Hodson, Mrs T, BA (Hons), Assistant Librarian, DWP Library,
Sheffield.
[10020841]   01/11/1995   **ME**

Bravin, Mrs K B, BA MCLIP, Teacher, British School of Brussels,
Tervuren, Belgium.
[26302]   01/10/1976   **CM12/12/1979**

Bray, Mr G, BA,
[10032533]   12/12/2013   **ME**

Bray, Mrs J G, BA FCLIP, Retired.
[1655]   19/12/1966   **FE09/09/2009**

Braybrooks, Miss D A, BA (Hons), Sch Librarian, Stratton Upper
School, Bedfordshire.
[10020606]   12/03/2012   **ME**

Brayshaw, Mrs K, BA (Hons) MA, Student, Aberystwyth University.
[10008804]   23/04/2008   **ME**

Brazendale, Mrs E H, MA PGCE MCLIP, Librarian, Robert Gordons
College, Aberdeen.
[29315]   26/05/1978   **CM05/07/1982**

Brazier, Mrs C, MA DipLib MA, Director Collections, British Library.
[34131]   08/10/1981   **ME**

Brazier, Ms H, MA MCLIP,
[32881]   06/10/1980   **CM01/12/1982**

Brazier, Ms J L, MA MPhil, Assistant L. Resources Manager, Stafford
College, Stafford.
[10018300]   14/12/2010   **ME**

Brazier, Mrs J M, BA MCLIP, Librarian, High School for Girls, Gloucester.
[25549]   21/01/1976   **CM24/04/1986**

Brbre, Mr I, MSc, Information Manager (Library & e-Learning Systems),
NHS.
[65054]   14/10/2005   **ME**

Breag, Mrs L R, BA (Hons) MA, Librarian, Oakham Sch.
[58280]   07/12/1999   **CM15/01/2003**

Brear, Miss C A, BA MA, User Services Libr., Totton College,
Southampton.
[63120]   11/02/2004   **ME**

Brebner, Mrs J, BA (Hons), Senior Library Assistant, Inverurie Library,
Aberdeenshire.
[49368]   29/10/1993   **ME**

Breckon, Mr G J, DipLib MCLIP, Librarian, Wirral Hospital NHS Trust,
Arrowe Park Hospital.
[57787]   05/08/1999   **CM13/05/2014**

Bredgaard, Miss S V, BSc, School Librarian, Kirk Hallam ommunity
Technology & Sports College.
[10022564]   26/03/2013   **ME**

Breeden, Miss S B, MCLIP, Life Member.
[1667]   01/10/1953   **CM01/01/1966**

Breedon, Mrs K T, Senior Information Assistant, University of
Nottingham, Nottingham.
[10021141]   12/06/2012   **AF**

Breen, Miss G, Student.
[10020877]   19/04/2012   **ME**

Breen, Ms S, MLIS BA (International), Assistant Librarian, King's
College London.
[10020228]   02/12/2011   **ME**

Breheny, Mrs T, BA (Hons) MA MA, Academic Support Librarian,
University of Salford.
[10018787]   10/03/2011   **ME**

Bremner, Ms J M, BA DipLib MCLIP, Library Central Services Manager,
Bristol City Council.
[32882]   06/10/1980   **CM11/04/1984**

Brennan, Miss A, MA PgDip, Academic Librarian, Abertay University.
[10021497]   23/08/2012   **ME**

Brennan, Miss E C, Lib. /Head of Res., Beacon Comm. College,
Crowborough.
[55510]   20/10/1997   **ME**

Breslin, Mrs J, BA (Hons) MA MCLIP, Research Services Manager,
Europe, Morrison & Foerster(UK) LLP.
[53633]   19/08/1996   **CM10/07/2002**

Breslin, Mrs T R, MCLIP, Self-employed writer.
[1675]   13/10/1967   **CM31/03/1981**

Breslin Davda, Mrs F, BA (Hons) MSc MCLIP, Doctoral Researcher,
Computer and Information Sciences, Livingstone Tower, University of
Strathclyde.
[63941]   18/11/2004   **CM12/05/2011**

Brett, Miss A S, BA (HONS) MA, Information Literacy Lead, Dixons
Trinity Academy, Bradford.
[10021729]   05/10/2012   **ME**

Brett, Ms J, BLib MCLIP, Assistant Librarian, Robinson Library,
Newcastle University.
[37234]   08/05/1984   **CM08/12/1987**

Brett, Ms R, BA (Hons) MSc, Senior Research Librarian, Berwin
Leighton Paisner LLP, London.
[65541]   21/02/2006   **ME**

Brettle, Dr A J, Research Fellow (Information), University of Salford,
Inst. Health & Social Care Res.
[10001620]   12/11/1991   **ME**

Brett-Michaels, Mrs S, Library Assistant, Lancashire Care NHS
Foundation Trust.
[10031623]   12/09/2013   **ME**

Brevitt, Mrs B, BA (Hons) MSc MCLIP, Freelance Clerk, Project
Manager and Education specialist.
[48658]   02/04/1993   **CM22/03/1995**

Brewer, Mrs A, BSc DipInfSci MCLIP, Senior Information Specialist
(Science), Medicines and Healthcare Products Regulatory Agency,
NIBSC, Herts.
[10000181]   28/01/1998   **CM11/12/2001**

Brewer, Miss J A, MCLIP, Retired.
[2216]   20/07/1962   **CM01/01/1966**
Brewer, Mrs M J, BA DipLib MCLIP, Secondary School Librarian, Doha
    Montessori & British School, Doha, Qatar.
[31975]   10/01/1980   **CM28/05/1982**
Brewer, Miss P M S J, MBIM MCLIP, Life Member.
[1684]   03/09/1946   **CM01/01/1952**
Brewerton, Mr A W, MA DipLib FCLIP DipM ACIM, Head of Academic
    Serv., University of Warwick.
[42415]   21/10/1988   **FE20/05/1998**
Brewster, Mr B P, BA (Hons) MA, Information Executive, ICAEW,
    London.
[63733]   06/09/2004   **ME**
Brewty, Miss C A, BA MCLIP, L. Res. Manager, Greig City Academy,
    Hornsey.
[38693]   01/10/1985   **CM23/03/1994**
Brice, Mrs A, MA DipLib MCLIP, Associate Director, NHS National
    Knowledge Service.
[35248]   05/10/1982   **CM04/10/1988**
Brick, Ms C L, BA (Hons) MSc (Econ) MCLIP, College Librarian, Lews
    Castle College, University of the Highland and Islands, Stornoway.
[51445]   14/02/1995   **CM13/06/2007**
Briddock, Miss R M, MA MA C TEFLA MCLIP, Retired.
[31208]   16/10/1979   **CM10/11/1981**
Briddon, Mr J M, BSc PGCE PgCert (HE) MA MCLIP, Director of
    Library Services, University of the West of England.
[53190]   25/03/1996   **CM08/12/2004**
Bridge, Mrs E H, PgDip LIS, Senior Librarian, Schools Library Service,
    West Sussex County Council.
[10008412]   21/08/1987   **ME**
Bridge, Mrs L E, MCLIP, Lib. Manager, Bolton Metropolitan Borough
    Council.
[21773]   10/01/1974   **CM23/02/1977**
Bridge, Mrs M A, OBE MA MCLIP, Retired.
[12544]   30/10/1971   **CM13/02/1975**
Bridgen, Mr R G, BLib MCLIP, Library and Knowledge Services'
    Manager, United Lincoln Hospitals NHS Trust.
[44264]   31/07/1990   **CM13/06/2007**
Bridle, Mr O, BSC MA, Subject Librarian for Biology and Forestry,
    Radcliffe Science Library, Oxford.
[10006799]   13/12/2007   **ME**
Bridson, Mrs P A, MCLIP, Res. Centre Manager, Maricourt High
    School, Sefton Metropolitan Borough Council.
[3285]   06/01/1969   **CM01/01/1972**
Brierley, Miss J, DipLib MCLIP, Lib. -Leisure L., Central Library,
    Nottingham Central Library.
[37995]   01/01/1985   **CM10/11/1987**
Brierley, Mr R J, BA MA MCLIP, Librarian, Derby City Council.
[45444]   06/02/1991   **CM04/02/2004**
Briers, Mrs S C, BA MCLIP, Information Professional.
[30516]   29/01/1979   **CM14/09/1982**
Briggs, Mr C A, BA DipLib MCLIP, Curator F, British Library, Boston
    Spa, West Yorks.
[37455]   01/10/1984   **CM14/03/1990**
Briggs, Ms G R, BA MA, Library Customer Development Manager,
    University of West London Library.
[10004796]   06/06/2007   **ME**
Briggs, Mrs S A, MCLIP, School Lib. & Information Mngr, Wilsthorpe
    Business & Enterprise College, Long Eaton, Derbyshire.
[10010326]   22/07/2008   **CM14/11/2012**
Briggs, Miss T J, BA (Hons) MCLIP,
[49011]   27/08/1993   **CM20/05/1998**
Bright, Mrs J A, BA MCLIP, Serv. Development Librarian, Dudley Ls.
[10006242]   13/06/1979   **CM13/09/1984**

Bright, Mrs M, MCLIP, Sch. L. & Community Serv. Manager, London
    Borough of Enfield.
[5111]   05/10/1971   **CM14/07/1975**
Brill, Mrs L, MCLIP, Part-time Librarian, The Pilgrims Sch. + Part-time
    Librarian, St Swithin's Junior School, Winchester, Hants.
[49051]   20/09/1993   **CM22/11/1995**
Brimble, Miss S, Information Manager.
[10034313]   02/07/2014   **ME**
Brimlow, A E, MA DipLib MCLIP, Social Inclusion Manager, Essex
    County Council Library, Chelmsford.
[27901]   02/10/1977   **CM28/04/1981**
Brindley, Mr G D, Assistant College Librarian, Tresham Institute,
    Kettering.
[59975]   14/11/2001   **ME**
Brindley, Dame L J, MA FCLIP, master, pembroke college, oxford.
[22909]   03/10/1974   **FE18/04/1990**
Brindley, Mrs M, Learning Spaces Manager, Walsall College, Walsall.
[10018167]   01/12/2010   **AF**
Brine, Dr A C, BA MSc MCLIP PhD, Head of Archives and Resource
    Management, De Montfort University.
[40215]   17/11/1986   **CM30/01/1991**
Brine, Mrs A M, BA DipLib MCLIP, Information Professional.
[43195]   02/10/1989   **CM22/04/1992**
Brine, Dr J J, BA PhD MCLIP, Subject Lib. Health & Medicine Lancaster
    University Library.
[1729]   03/01/1972   **CM04/03/1974**
Brisley, Mr A J, BLib MCLIP, Library &. Information Manager, North
    Somerset Council.
[23614]   17/01/1975   **CM04/09/1979**
Britcher, Miss H M, BSc MSc, Team Leader Procurement & Metadata,
    University of Portsmouth.
[10018706]   01/03/2011   **ME**
Britchford, Mrs H C, MCLIP, Retired.
[5100]   05/09/1963   **CM12/08/1976**
Britland, Miss I, MCLIP, Life Member.
[1749]   17/07/1961   **CM01/01/1967**
Britnell, Mrs L J, Unwaged.
[63506]   15/06/2004   **ME**
Britt, Mr R, BSc MIL MITI MCLIP, Translator, Boehringer Ingelheim Ltd,
    Bracknell.
[60158]   18/12/1974   **CM19/07/1979**
Brittan, Miss S O, Knowledge and Library Services Manager, Public
    Health England.
[55203]   13/08/1997   **ME**
Brittin, Mrs M E, BA MCLIP, Life Member.
[1752]   02/01/1970   **CM21/08/1972**
Broad, Mrs J M, BEd DipLib MCLIP, Customer Serv. & Site Liaison
    Manager, StaffordshireUniversity, Stoke on Trent.
[46530]   18/11/1991   **CM26/05/1993**
Broadbent, Miss A Y, BA MCLIP, L. Systems Officer, Oxon. Support
    Serv., Oxford.
[27903]   17/10/1977   **CM11/02/1980**
Broadbent, Miss H A, BA MCLIP, Life Member.
[1762]   21/03/1971   **CM22/05/1974**
Broadbent, Mrs K J, BA (Hons), Senior Librarian, The Henley College.
[44981]   24/01/1991   **ME**
Broadbent, Mrs L R, BA FCLIP, Life Member.
[13945]   01/01/1957   **FE01/01/1962**
Broadbent, Mrs R, BA (Hons) MSc MCLIP, Account Manager, Capita
    Software Services.
[61303]   16/05/2002   **CM17/09/2008**
Broadfoot, Ms N M, BA MA, Librarian.
[10021299]   06/07/2012   **ME**

Broadfoot, Mr S, MSc, Lib. Information Serv., Hamilton Townhouse Library, Scotland.
[10021006]   04/05/2012   **ME**

Broadley, Miss A, LLB, Student, University of Edinburgh.
[10025697]   03/12/2013   **ME**

Broadley, Ms R F, BA (Hons) MCLIP, Librarian, Sacred Heart High School.
[10011493]   22/10/2008   **CM20/06/2014**

Broady-Preston, Dr J E, BA (Hons) MA PhD MCLIP FHEA, Reader in Information Management, Institute of Management, Law and Information Science, Aberystwyth University.
[35476]   13/10/1982   **CM01/04/2002**

Brock, Miss E J, BLS MCLIP, Community Librarian, Norfolk L. & Information Serv.
[27904]   07/10/1977   **CM30/04/1982**

Brock, Miss S A, BA DipLib MA MCLIP, Customer Service Manager (Lending Services), Kings College, London.
[46135]   07/10/1991   **CM27/07/1994**

Brocklebank, Mrs J, BA DipLib MIL MCLIP,
[37482]   01/10/1984 **RV13/12/2006 CM19/08/1992**

Brocklehurst, Mrs M C, BA (Hons) Dip Lib MCLIP, Bookshop Owner, Norfolk Children's Book Centre, Norwich.
[10019918]   04/02/1975   **CM28/06/1977**

Brocklehurst, Mrs M L, BSc (Hons) MA MCLIP, Reference Librarian, Hendrick Hudson Free Library, Montrose, NY, USA.
[50047]   21/02/1994   **CM15/09/2004**

Brocklesby, Mr M, BA MA, Student, University of Wales Aberystwyth.
[10032649]   23/12/2013   **ME**

Brockley, Mrs J M, BA (Hons) MCLIP, Learning Resource Centre Manager, Newport High School.
[64439]   30/03/2005   **CM21/11/2007**

Broderick, Mr N, BA, Information Knowledge Management and Communications, Civil Service.
[10034299]   02/07/2014   **ME**

Brodie, Mrs A H, MCLIP, Life Member.
[1772]   19/04/1944   **CM01/01/1948**

Brodie, Mr C J, BA PgDip MCLIP, L. Serv. Manager, North Manchester Primary Care Trust, Chorlton.
[50106]   28/03/1994   **CM07/09/2005**

Brodin, Ms K M, BA (Hons) MSc MCLIP, Library Manager, Glasgow Life, Glasgow.
[62624]   01/10/2003   **CM21/06/2006**

Brodrick, Mr J N R, BA, Student.
[10022761]   17/04/2013   **ME**

Broekmann, Mrs E P, BA HED HDipLib MCLIP, Librarian and School Archivist, Notting Hill and Ealing High School.
[61522]   04/09/2002   **CM29/03/2006**

Broggi, Mrs C, BA (Hons) MCLIP, Library Manager, West Sussex County Council.
[46774]   22/01/1992   **CM22/05/1996**

Brolly, Mrs A M, BA MCLIP, Reader Development Librarian, Herts County Council, Bishops Stortford Library.
[32104]   28/01/1980   **CM25/02/1985**

Bromage, Miss S, BA (Hons)PgDip MLitt MSc MCLIP, Archivist, Scottish Political Archive.
[10001770]   22/02/2007   **CM12/09/2012**

Bromley, Mr D W, JP MA FCLIP, Life Member.
[1780]   03/03/1953   **FE01/01/1960**

Brook, Mrs M, BA MSc, Training and Documentation Team Member (Collection Processing), British Library.
[10009463]   20/05/2008   **ME**

Brook, Mr M J, BA (Hons) DipLib MCLIP, Library Service Manager, West. Berkshire. Council.
[30369]   13/01/1979   **CM01/07/1984**

Brook, Ms S J, GCIS, Student, Robert Gordon University.
[10032585]   17/12/2013   **ME**

Brooke, Mr J D, BA, Lib. /Information Officer, Lib & Know Serv, GMW Mental Health Trust.
[42408]   21/10/1988   **ME**

Brooke, Miss P E M O, MCLIP, Life Member.
[1797]   08/03/1949   **CM01/01/1954**

Brooker, Miss D J, BA MCLIP, Online Serv. Manager, Devon L. Serv. L. Headquarters, Exeter.
[32883]   06/10/1980   **CM10/08/1984**

Brooker, Mrs J C, MCLIP, Librarian, Maidstone Girls Grammar School, Kent.
[22933]   01/10/1974   **CM23/01/1978**

Brookes, Miss H L, BA, Assistant Library Graduate Trainee.
[10035530]   16/10/2014   **ME**

Brookes, Mrs J, BSc MA MCLIP, Team Leader, North Yorkshire County Council.
[59935]   07/11/2001   **CM10/07/2009**

Brookes, Miss K, BA (Hons) PGCE MCLIP, Childrens Librarian, Chichester Library, Chichester, WestSussex.
[10001449]   14/02/2007   **CM27/01/2010**

Brookes, Mrs Y M, BA (Hons) MCLIP, Electronic Res. Librarian, HEFT, West Mids.
[28992]   30/01/1978   **CM01/10/1986**

Brooking, Mrs A J, BA MCLIP, Parish Administrator, Waltham Abbey Parochial Church Council.
[37548]   10/10/1984   **CM18/09/1991**

Brooks, Mrs C, TD BA PgCertPSM FCLIP HonFCLIP, Learning & Development Officer, Health & Communities Department, Derbyshire.
[27143]   31/01/1977   **HFE07/12/2007**

Brooks, Miss C L, MA MSc, Central Librarian, Aberdeen City Council.
[10033167]   18/02/2014   **ME**

Brooks, Mrs J, BA MCLIP, Retired.
[25404]   06/01/1976   **CM05/07/1978**

Brooks, Ms K, Library and Learning Resources Assistant, Barton Peveril Sixth Form College.
[10035736]   31/10/2014   **ME**

Brooks, Mrs L G, BA DipLib MCLIP FLS, Librarian, The Linnean Society Of London.
[26962]   19/01/1977   **CM21/09/1981**

Brooks, Mr P C, BA (Hons) PGCE MA MCLIP, Head of Library Services, Royal Agricultural University, Cirencester.
[51873]   21/07/1995   **CM18/09/2002**

Brooks, Ms R, BA (Hons) MA PgDip PGCE (FE),
[10001776]   10/02/1995   **ME**

Brooks, Ms S A, MA MCLIP, Librarian, Museum of London.
[50681]   10/10/1994   **CM17/05/2000**

Brooks-Belo, Mrs P, Librarian.
[10007218]   18/05/2009   **ME**

Brophy, Prof P, OBE JP BSc HonFCLIP FHEI FRSA, Retired.
[24063]   14/04/1975   **FE06/09/2000**

Broster, Mr T A, FCLIP, Life Member.
[19469]   08/01/1954   **FE01/01/1966**

Brotherton, Miss J, BA (Hons) MA, Customer Services Librarian, University of Wolverhampton.
[10014287]   14/07/2009   **ME**

Broughton, Mrs D V, BA DipLib MA MCLIP, Assistant Librarian, Gray's Inn Library.
[43865]   05/02/1990   **CM25/01/1995**

Broughton, Miss S C, BA DipLib PgCert MCLIP, Information Officer, West Berks. Council, Newbury.
[30118]   11/01/1979   **CM06/07/1981**

Broughton, Ms V D, MA DipLib, Lecturer, UCL.
[44471]   11/10/1990   ME
Brown, Mrs A, BA MCLIP, Deputy Learning Resources. Manager,
Harrow College.
[32640]   10/07/1980   CM15/12/1983
Brown, Mrs A, ACLIP, District Manager – West Lancashire Libraries,
Lancashire County Council.
[10007753]   21/02/2008   ACL04/03/2009
Brown, Mr A, BSc PGCE, Student.
[10020490]   21/02/2012   ME
Brown, Mr A A, MA (Hons) FCLIP, Retired.
[1935]   01/01/1958   FE09/11/1973
Brown, Mr A D, BSc (Hons) MA MCLIP, L. Systems Liaison Officer,
Bury Metropolitan Borough Council.
[49932]   25/01/1994   CM18/11/1998
Brown, Ms A J, BA MA MCLIP, Cebis Specialist, University Hospitals
Coventry & Warwickshire NHS Trust, Coventry.
[59599]   26/06/2001   CM15/09/2004
Brown, Mrs A M, BA (Hons), Service advisor, Support and information
zone, University of Chichester.
[10007996]   05/03/2003   ME
Brown, Dr A S, BA (Hons) MPhil MCLIP, Library Assistant, Birmingham.
[65160]   03/11/2005   CM23/01/2008
Brown, Mrs B M, MA MSc MCLIP, Services Development Lib. - Music &
Fine Art Collections, Edinburgh City Library.
[39195]   05/01/1986   CM17/01/1990
Brown, Mrs C, BA (Hons), Lib/Work Related Coordinator, Balshaws CE
High School.
[10020759]   03/04/2012   ME
Brown, Mr C, MCLIP, Retired.
[1845]   01/01/1969   CM20/12/1972
Brown, Miss C A, MA MCLIP, Library & Information Manager, Collyer
Bristow, London.
[49656]   23/11/1993   CM22/09/1999
Brown, Ms C E, BA (Hons) MA MCLIP, Staff Development Manager,
Nottinghamshire L. Serv.
[42640]   30/01/1989   CM04/02/2004
Brown, Mr D B, MA MCLIP, Academic Liaison Librarian, University of
York.
[10010660]   19/08/2008   CM12/05/2011
Brown, Mr D J, BA MA MCLIP, Retired.
[1854]   26/02/1965   CM01/01/1968
Brown, Miss E, Student, Robert Gordon University.
[10025721]   04/12/2013   ME
Brown, Mrs F J L, BScEcon ILS MA (Hons), Liaison Librarian,
Veterinary Medicine, Veterinary Librarian, University of Edinburgh.
[49134]   07/10/1993   ME
Brown, Miss G, BA, Graduate Library Trainee, St Hilda's College
(Library).
[10032483]   09/12/2013   ME
Brown, Mr G, BA (Hons) MCLIP, Librarian, Bournemouth Borough
Council.
[59128]   21/11/2000   CM28/01/2009
Brown, Mr G, PGD, Library Assistant, University of the West of England.
[10034325]   04/07/2014   ME
Brown, Mrs H J, School Administrator, Ombersley Endowed First
School.
[44696]   28/11/1990   ME
Brown, Miss J, BA (Hons) MCLIP, Librarian: Young People's Services,
Hertfordshire County Council.
[44829]   10/12/1990   CM23/03/1994
Brown, Ms J A, MA, Librarian, Impington Village College.
[63239]   22/03/2004   ME

Brown, Mrs J E, BA MCLIP, Retired formally Business/Management
Librarian, University Chester.
[22904]   02/10/1974   CM04/07/1978
Brown, Mrs J M, MCLIP, Prison Librarian, HMP Gloucester,
[10011505]   23/10/2008   CM11/07/2012
Brown, Miss J O, FCLIP, Life Member.
[1889]   11/10/1946   FE01/01/1960
Brown, Miss J R, BA (Hons), Student, Robert Gordon University.
[65092]   25/10/2005   ME
Brown, Miss J T, BA (Hons) MCLIP, Part-time Information Advisor,
University of Wales Inst., Cardiff, Cyncoed Site.
[44580]   30/10/1990   CM21/05/2003
Brown, Mr J W, BA DipILM MCLIP, LRC Manager, Heaton Manor
School, Newcastle upon Tyne.
[48906]   15/07/1993   CM25/01/1995
Brown, Miss K, ACLIP, Library Assistant, Hemel Hempstead Library,
Herts.
[66109]   01/10/2006   ACL23/09/2009
Brown, Mrs K, MA, Senior Library Assistant/IT Support, Cardiff
University, Arts and Social Studies Library.
[10032703]   07/01/2014   ME
Brown, Ms K B, MA (Hons) PgDip,
[10005723]   26/07/2007   ME
Brown, Miss K I, BA (Hons) MCLIP, Head of L. Serv., Dentons UKMEA
LLP, London.
[49833]   16/12/1993   CM21/05/1997
Brown, Ms L, BA (Hons) MCLIP, Literacy Development Officer, Central
Library, Blackburn.
[62904]   18/11/2003   CM12/05/2011
Brown, Ms L, MCLIP, Prison Librarian, HMP Dovegate.
[10000755]   06/10/1973   CM01/04/1977
Brown, Ms L, Student, Pratt Institute.
[10032694]   06/01/2014   ME
Brown, Mrs L, BA MCLIP, Unwaged.
[26882]   16/12/1976   CM29/11/1979
Brown, Ms L D, MA, Library Support Advisor, Anglia Ruskin University.
[10034198]   19/06/2014   ME
Brown, Mr L S, MRSC FEI FRSH MCMI MCLIP GrIMF, Retired.
[60160]   05/06/1975   CM02/05/1980
Brown, Miss M, MCLIP, Retired.
[1900]   09/01/1968   CM01/01/1971
Brown, Miss M A, FCLIP, Life Member.
[1906]   28/03/1957   FE01/01/1963
Brown, Ms M E, BSc MCLIP, District Manager, Burnley Central Library.
[23166]   07/10/1974   CM01/03/1977
Brown, Mr M P, BA (Hons) MSc, Deputy Information Serv. Manager,
Lazard, London.
[57082]   04/12/1998   ME
Brown, Mrs N, BA DipLib MCLIP, Reading & Learning Part-time,
Weymouth Library, Dorset.
[41718]   22/02/1988   CM27/01/1993
Brown, Mrs N J, Assistant Librarian, Samuel Whitbread Academy.
[10031695]   24/09/2013   ME
Brown, Miss R J, MA BA (Hons), Deputy Head Library and Information
Services, Prince Consort's Library, Aldershot.
[64627]   29/04/2005   ME
Brown, Mr R W, BA (Hons) MCLIP, Children & Young People's Lib. Serv.
Manager, NLC.
[43658]   16/11/1989   CM23/03/1994
Brown, Miss S, BA (Hons) MA MCLIP, Employment not known.
[58156]   09/11/1999   CM23/01/2002
Brown, Mrs S, MA, Librarian, Lord Wandsworth College, Hook.
[10016304]   05/03/2010   ME

Brown, Miss S, MA (Hons) MSc MCLIP, Young People's Servs Officer.
[57982]   08/10/1999   **CM04/10/2006**

Brown, Mrs S A, BA MCLIP, Senior Librarian, Huntingdon Library,
Cambridge.
[24619]   07/10/1975   **CM05/04/1978**

Brown, Mrs S J, Student.
[10018253]   01/01/2011   **ME**

Brown, Miss S J, BA, Student.
[10023211]   18/06/2013   **ME**

Brown, Ms S L, BA, Librarian, Trinity College, Bristol.
[35719]   21/01/1983   **ME**

Brown, Ms S L, BA (Hons) DipLIS MCLIP, Senior Officer, Libraries
Information Service, London Borough of Camden, London.
[47641]   09/10/1992   **CM18/11/1998**

Brown, Miss S M, BA (Hons) DipInfMgt MCLIP, Information Specialist,
House of Commons.
[46101]   02/10/1991   **CM21/11/2001**

Brown, Ms S M, MCLIP, Self-employed.
[22349]   09/04/1974   **CM13/07/1977**

Brown, Mrs S M E, MCLIP, Retired.
[4614]   26/03/1970   **CM01/07/1974**

Brown, Mr T, Res. Centre Manager, North Chadderton School, Oldham.
[61033]   01/02/2002   **ME**

Brown, Miss T M, BLib MCLIP, Unwaged.
[29601]   23/10/1978   **CM05/04/1985**

Brown, Mr T W B, BSc DipLib MCLIP, Retired.
[28265]   24/10/1977   **CM16/09/1980**

Brown, Ms V A, BA (Hons) DipLib MCLIP, Information and Enquiry
Officer.
[44007]   05/04/1990   **CM18/11/1993**

Brown, Mrs V F G, MCLIP,
[6476]   21/03/1963   **CM01/01/1967**

Brown Jensen, Ms R P, BA MA PhD, Librarian, Allenbourn Middle
School.
[10001067]   12/01/2007   **AF**

Browne, Miss J H, ACLIP, Learning Res. Assistant, Preston College,
Preston.
[10018882]   24/03/2011   **ACL09/09/2013**

Brownhill, Mrs H K, BA (Hons) DipIM MCLIP, Senior Librarian, Health
Library, York Hospital.
[52241]   18/10/1995   **RV22/06/2007**   **CM17/11/1999**

Browning, Mrs D A, BA DipLib MCLIP, Business Implementation Oficer,
Bath & North East Somerset Council.
[38008]   04/01/1985   **CM18/04/1989**

Brownlee, Mrs A C, BA MCLIP, School L. Resource Centre for
Coordinator, Wester Hailes Educ. Centre for, Edinburgh.
[28622]   09/01/1978   **CM22/09/1981**

Brownlee, Mr S C, BA (Hons) DipLib MCLIP, Retired.
[24329]   07/07/1975   **CM21/06/1978**

Brownlie, Mr I M, Student.
[10005360]   05/07/2007   **ME**

Brownson, Miss R M, BA (Hons), Library Customer Service Assistant,
Newcastle College.
[10035158]   22/09/2014   **ME**

Bruce, Mrs A M, BA MCLIP, Information Serv. Librarian, Aberdeenshire
L. & Information Serv.
[34229]   14/10/1981   **CM12/05/1987**

Bruce, Miss J, BA (Hons) MCLIP, School Librarian, Oriel High School,
Crawley.
[50147]   12/04/1994   **CM23/09/1998**

Bruce, Mr N M, MA DipLib FCLIP LLM, Service Manager, Culture,
Aberdeen.
[29370]   26/06/1978   **FE18/09/2003**

Bruce, Mrs R M, BA MCLIP, Additional Support for Learning Librarian,
North Lanarkshire Council.
[41134]   24/09/2013   **CM16/11/1994**

Bruce, Miss S M A, Library Assistant, Fortrose Community Library.
[10035099]   15/09/2014   **ME**

Bruce-Cudjoe, Miss E E, BLS DipLib MSc, Librarian/ Head of Office,
Bank of Ghana.
[60922]   10/01/2002   **ME**

Brugnoli, Mrs C A, BA (Hons), Library Assistant, Thurleigh Lower
School.
[10021657]   20/09/2012   **AF**

Brumfit, Mr T C, BA MA MCLIP, Information Librarian (Document
Delivery), University of Bath.
[10011671]   06/11/2008   **CM20/06/2014**

Brumpton, Mrs C, MSc Econ BA (Hons), Research & Resources
Manager, Old palace of John Whitgift School, Croydon.
[10016484]   30/07/1998   **ME**

Brumwell, Ms A D, BA (Hons) MA, Educational Consultant, Kirklees
Council.
[10013721]   22/05/2009   **ME**

Brumwell, Ms J A, MCLIP, Retired.
[21778]   09/01/1974   **CM02/07/1976**

Brunel Cohen, Mr R S, BA DCC DipLib, Unwaged.
[41524]   15/01/1988   **ME**

Brunning, Ms L, eLearning Content Developer, Hopwood Hall College.
[64871]   22/08/2005   **ME**

Bryan, Mr A D, MA, Student, Aberystwyth University.
[10034742]   12/08/2014   **ME**

Bryan, Miss S, Assistant Librarian, Foreign & Commonwealth Office,
London.
[10007382]   13/02/2008   **ME**

Bryan, Mr T D B, BA MCLIP, Service Manager – Libraries, Sport and
Leisure, London Borough of Harrow.
[40980]   01/10/1987   **RV19/11/2008**   **CM30/01/1991**

Bryant, Mrs D, Teaching Assistant /Sch. L., Hayward's Primary School,
Crediton.
[10011560]   27/10/2008   **AF**

Bryant, Miss J E, MA (Hons) MA MSc MCLIP, Librarian.
[63784]   06/10/2004   **RV12/09/2012**   **CM06/05/2009**

Bryant, Miss M C, BA MA MCLIP, Unwaged.
[43860]   05/02/1990   **CM18/11/1993**

Bryant, Mr M E N, BA DipLib DM, Outreach Librarian, Ridgeway NHS
Trust.
[29316]   10/05/1978   **CM10/05/1980**

Bryant, Mr P, HonFLA, Senior Research Fellow, Centre for Bibl.
Management, University of Bath.
[1986]   01/02/1950   **HFE01/01/1992**

Bryce, Mrs K, MCLIP, President, Andornot Consulting Inc., Vancouver,
Canada.
[2158]   19/01/1970   **CM01/01/1973**

Bryceland, Mrs M, BA (Hons) MCLIP, SeniorLibrary Assistant, South
Leicestershire College.
[22197]   27/02/1974   **RV15/07/2014**   **CM25/01/1977**

Bryder, Ms J, BA (Hons) DipLIM MCLIP, Collections Development
Librarian, UCA, Farnham, GU9 7DS.
[46646]   02/12/1991   **CM15/01/2003**

Bryer, Mr L A, BA (Hons) MA, Research & Development Manager,
CITB, Norfolk.
[63119]   11/02/2004   **ME**

Bryn Jones, Mrs L K, BSc, Learning Centre Assistant.
[4680]   26/03/1969   **CM15/08/1972**

Bryon, Mrs J, PhD MCLIP, Retired.
[1992]   17/03/1961   **CM01/01/1966**

Bryson, Mrs A V, BA DipLib MCLIP, Assistant Director, Libraries NI.
[32526]   16/05/1980   **CM27/07/1982**
Brzozowska-Szczecina, Mrs E, MA, Librarian, London College of Contemporary Arts.
[10034767]   14/08/2014   **ME**
Buchan, Miss M L T, MA DipLib MCLIP, Associate Director Acad. and Reader Serv., Robert Gordon University, Aberdeen.
[38549]   01/07/1985   **CM18/07/1990**
Buchanan, Miss A, MA (Hons) MPhil, Local Studies Librarian, Bath & North East Somerset Council, Bath.
[55810]   19/11/1997   **ME**
Buchanan, Mr A J, Unwaged.
[63793]   06/10/2004   **ME**
Buchanan, Mrs C A, BA (Hons) PgDip MCLIP,
[58161]   09/11/1999   **CM09/11/2005**
Buchanan, Mrs C M, MCLIP, Principal L. Officer, Cornwall County Library, Truro.
[21263]   03/10/1973   **CM17/10/1975**
Buchanan, Mr D S, MA MCLIP, Life Member.
[1997]   14/10/1955   **CM01/01/1958**
Buchanan, Ms H V, BA, Head of Stock Maintenance, Imperial College, University of London.
[44666]   21/11/1990   **ME**
Buchanan, Miss K L, Comm. L. Manager, Maindee and Carnegie Libraries.
[10000756]   02/12/1989   **ME**
Buchanan, Mr N T, BA (Hons) PgDip MCLIP, Campus Library, University of the West of Scotland, Ayr.
[57538]   21/04/1999   **CM23/01/2008**
Buchanan, Ms S, MCLIP, LRC Manager, Chessington Community College, Surrey.
[7212]   30/07/1970   **CM05/06/1974**
Buck, Ms E M, BA (Hons) MA MCLIP, Head of Learning Services, University Campus Suffolk.
[56135]   05/03/1998   **CM01/06/2005**
Buckland, Ms J M, BSc MSc, Librarian, NHS, Dorchester.
[10013458]   27/04/2009   **ME**
Buckland, Mrs R M, BA (Hons), Librarian, Ripley St Thomas Sch. & Information Officer, University of Cumbria, Lancaster.
[10015055]   09/10/2009   **ME**
Buckle, Mr D G R, BA, Retired.
[31116]   17/08/1979   **ME**
Buckle, Mrs E W, BA MCLIP, Retired.
[23029]   16/10/1974   **CM09/09/1977**
Buckle, Mrs L K, BA MCLIP AI, Freelance Indexer.
[32629]   06/07/1980   **CM11/12/1989**
Buckle, Mr T, BA (Hons),
[10022466]   05/03/2013   **AF**
Buckley, Miss L J, BA MSc SRAD Dip, PhD Student.
[10022168]   15/01/2013   **ME**
Buckley Owen, Mr T K, BA DipLib MCLIP, Information industry commentator & trainer, Self-Employed.
[11110]   01/01/1972   **CM26/11/1974**
Buckman, Mrs E A, MCLIP, Life Member.
[11750]   03/09/1959   **CM01/01/1969**
Buckman, Mr T, ACLIP, Customer Serv. Supervisor, Morden Library, London.
[10019441]   04/07/2011   **ACL09/07/2013**
Budd, Mr M, BA (Bris), Student, Lincoln's Inn Library.
[10035415]   13/10/2014   **ME**
Budden, Mrs Y C, BA (Hons) MSc, Academic Support Manager (Research), University of Warwick.
[63292]   07/04/2004   **ME**

Budgen, Mrs P M, BA MA MCLIP, Lib. Servs. Assistant Manager, University of Birmingham.
[28329]   15/11/1977   **CM19/11/1979**
Bugden, Ms R J, BEd DipLIS MCLIP PgDipEd (SEN), Retired.
[43190]   01/10/1989   **CM23/03/1994**
Bugden, Mrs S, Unwaged.
[57470]   01/04/1999   **ME**
Buick, Mrs L, BLib MCLIP, Operational Manager, LibrariesNI, Central Library, Ballymena.
[30856]   03/05/1979   **CM31/08/1982**
Bukumunhe, Ms L P R, BSc MA MCLIP, Senior Librarian, Luton Borough Council, Leagrave Library.
[61350]   13/06/2002   **CM31/01/2007**
Bukunola, Mrs C A, MCLIP, Retired.
[2031]   01/01/1970   **CM11/12/1981**
Bulbrook, Mrs L, LRC Manager, Neal Wade Community College, Cambridgeshire.
[10012231]   03/02/2009   **AF**
Buley, Mr C G, Unemployed.
[42784]   08/03/1989   **ME**
Bull, Mrs E J, BA (Hons) DipInf MCLIP, Director of L. Serv., Queen Mary University, London.
[48010]   02/11/1992   **CM24/05/1995**
Bull, Ms I, BA (Hons), Student, University of Strathclyde.
[10035520]   16/10/2014   **ME**
Bull, Miss K R, BSc (Hons) MSc MCLIP, Information Sci., KIR., Oxford University.
[47479]   01/09/1992   **CM27/11/1996**
Bull, Ms S, BA (Hons), Learning Resources Assistant, Brompley College of Further and Higher Education.
[10022375]   19/02/2013   **AF**
Bullas, Miss S, BMus (Hons) MSc, Coordinator: Child. & Young People's Serv., Central Library, Halifax.
[10014169]   07/07/2009   **ME**
Bullimore, Mr A M, BA DipLib MCLIP, Assistant Librarian, University of Bedfordshire.
[41823]   19/04/1988   **CM14/03/1990**
Bullivant, Mrs E M, MCLIP, Life Member.
[2044]   10/02/1944   **CM01/01/1951**
Bullock, Mrs J A, MCLIP, Librarian, Wilmslow Library, Cheshire County Council.
[24896]   20/10/1975   **CM11/09/1979**
Bullock, Miss J P, MA FCLIP, Life Member.
[2047]   31/10/1940   **FE01/01/1966**
Bullough, Mrs N C, BA, Librarian – Lycee Resources, British Section Lycee International.
[10031748]   01/10/2013   **ME**
Bulman, Mrs M J, MA MCLIP, Librarian, Medical Res. Council, Harwell, Didcot.
[16109]   10/11/1971   **CM01/02/1975**
Bulpitt, Mr G, MA CertEd MCLIP FRSA, Retired.
[2051]   07/10/1967   **CM01/01/1971**
Bunch, Mr A J, BA (Hons) DMS MCLIP, Retired.
[2054]   25/03/1957   **CM01/01/1964**
Bunch, Ms A J, OBE MA FCLIP FSA Scot FRSA, Retired.
[2053]   01/10/1953   **FE06/06/1973**
Bundy, Ms C M, BSc (Econ) MSc MCLIP, ICT Consultant.
[56614]   18/09/1998   **CM21/03/2001**
Bundy, Mr D E, BA MCLIP, Retired.
[2055]   14/09/1970   **CM16/10/1973**
Bunn, Miss R M, ISO, Life Member.
[2058]   29/07/1960   **ME**
Bunt, Mrs M A, Retired.
[38088]   08/01/1985   **ME**

Bunting, Miss C A, BA (Hons) DipLib, Senior Bibliographic Servs.
Librarian, Leeds Metropolitan University.
[39939]   02/10/1986   ME
Bunton, Ms L, MA MSc MCLIP,
[10015468]   15/07/2002   CM16/01/2014
Bunyan, Ms S A, MA MSc, Project Manager, Jisc.
[10006342]   10/10/2007   ME
Burbage, Mr B E, MRSC MCLIP, Retired.
[19884]   01/01/1973   CM01/04/1976
Burch, Mr B, OBE MA MCLIP, Retired.
[2064]   01/01/1959   CM01/01/1961
Burch, Mrs G E, BA MCLIP, Librarian, West Sussex County Council.
[32941]   01/10/1980   CM05/10/1984
Burchell, Mr M T, Corporate Records Officer, Foreign & Commonwealth
Office.
[10032980]   03/02/2014   ME
Burchett-Vass, Miss J, BSc MCLIP, Assistant Information Specialist,
National Institute for Health and Clinical Excellence.
[10011194]   30/09/2008   CM14/03/2012
Burden, Ms L, BA, KM Team Lead, Department For Environment Food
& Rural Affairs (DEFRA).
[37150]   06/03/1984   ME
Burford, Miss P H, ACLIP, Information Librarian, Sandwell Library, West
Bromwich.
[64103]   17/01/2005   ACL29/03/2007
Burge, Ms S M, BA (Hons) FCLIP HonFCLIP, Retired.
[21247]   08/10/1973   HFE23/10/2003
Burgess, Miss A F, BA MLib DipLib MCLIP, Business Manager,
Contracts (Dorset Library Service).
[26944]   19/01/1977   CM15/03/1979
Burgess, Miss C, BA (Hons) MCLIP, Archivist.
[10003982]   23/05/2007   CM27/01/2010
Burgess, Ms C A, MA MSc, Library Assistant, Portishead Library.
[10017772]   11/09/2013   ME
Burgess, Mrs D H, Part-time Library Assistant, North Somerset District
Council.
[2431]   15/04/1970   ME
Burgess, Mrs H M, MCLIP, Life Member.
[2078]   03/03/1942   CM01/01/1946
Burgess, Mrs J, ACLIP, Senior Library Assistant, Guille-Alles Library,
Guernsey.
[10015980]   04/07/2011   ACL11/07/2012
Burgess, Mrs L, BSc PGDiP MCLIP, Assistant Librarian, Department of
Health, Social Services & Public Safety, Belfast.
[10011704]   12/11/2008   CM09/11/2011
Burgess, Mr M, BSc (Hons) MA MSc, Assistant Librarian, Manchester
Metropolitan University.
[10019028]   12/04/2011   ME
Burgess, Miss R P, BLib MCLIP, Head of L., Arts & Heritage, Bracknell
Forest Borough Council.
[27910]   04/10/1977   CM03/08/1983
Burgess, Mrs S, BA MCLIP, Librarian, City of Salford, Cultural Serv.
[33685]   05/02/1981   CM10/12/1985
Burgess, Miss S C, BA (Hons) PgDip MCLIP, Head Librarian, Great
Western Hospital NHS Foundation, Gt. Western Hospital.
[52357]   26/10/1995   RV27/03/2014   CM16/05/2001
Burgess, Miss V J, BA MA MCLIP,
[39731]   04/06/1986   CM15/09/1993
Burgess, Mr V W, MCLIP, Unemployed.
[2088]   06/03/1967   CM15/12/1972
Burgum, Miss S J, BA DipLib MCLIP, School Librarian, Erith School,
Kent.
[34233]   15/10/1981   CM18/07/1990

Burke, Miss E, Library Assistant, University of the Arts London.
[10034965]   17/09/2014   ME
Burmajster, Mrs A, MA MCLIP, Head of Information & Advisory
Services, Institute of Directors.
[51803]   04/07/1995   CM18/03/1998
Burman, Mrs J, BSc (Econ) MCLIP, Librarian, Newark L.
[65377]   09/01/2006   CM21/03/2007
Burn, Miss L, BA (Hons), Student, Aberystwyth University.
[10020210]   23/11/2011   ME
Burnett, Miss A, Library Assistant, Robert Gordon University,
Aberdeen.
[64761]   30/06/2005   AF
Burnett, Miss A, MA MSc, Network Librarian, Aberdeenshire Council.
[10019053]   13/04/2011   ME
Burnett, Mr A D, MA FIAP MCLIP, Retired.
[2109]   15/08/1959   CM01/01/1964
Burnett, Ms C F, BA MPhil MCLIP, Lead for Library Services; Queens
Hospital, Romford.
[37318]   02/07/1984   CM04/10/1988
Burnett, Mrs J C, BA MCLIP, Information & People's Network Librarian,
Hertfordshire County Council, Bishops Stortford L.
[28286]   06/11/1977   CM09/01/1980
Burnett, Mrs S,
[10013987]   15/06/2009   AF
Burns, Mrs E, MCLIP, Librarian, Macmillan Academy.
[65502]   10/02/2006   CM09/07/2013
Burns, Mrs H, BA (Hons) MSc, Librarian, Perth High School.
[10012470]   10/02/2009   ME
Burns, Mr J E, BA (Hons) MSc (Econ) MCLIP, Library Manager,
Worthing Area, West Sussex CC.
[52799]   15/12/1995   CM19/01/2000
Burns, Ms M, BA PgDipILS MCLIP, Primary Librarian, Falkirk Library
Services, Falkirk.
[62357]   09/05/2003   CM09/11/2005
Burns, Ms R A, BA DipLib MCLIP, Librarian, Trinity Grammar School,
Melbourne.
[26909]   10/01/1977   CM17/01/1979
Burnside, Mrs E L, BA (Hons) HAAD, Children's Librarian, Surbiton &
Tolworth Library.
[10000766]   14/11/2006   ME
Burrell, Mrs J W, BA DipLib MCLIP AFHEA, Academic Liaison
Librarian, Liverpool John Moores University.
[40900]   16/08/1987   CM27/01/1993
Burrell, Mrs K A, MCLIP, Retired.
[23980]   01/01/1958   CM01/01/1964
Burrell, Miss P J, Library & Information Assistant.
[10008013]   03/03/2008   ACL16/06/2010
Burrington, Dr G A, OBE MA FCLIP, Life Member.
[2139]   01/01/1962   FE01/01/1965
Burrough, Mrs P J, MCLIP, Life Member.
[6591]   15/08/1949   CM01/01/1967
Burrows, Mrs C, MCLIP, Retired.
[4897]   09/01/1967   CM01/01/1970
Burrows, Mr J B S, Library Assistant, Music Department Library,
Cambridge University Library.
[42878]   06/04/1989   ME
Burrows, Mr K, BA DipLib MCLIP, Library Manager, Lancs. County
Council, Nelson.
[37967]   01/01/1985   CM15/02/1989
Burry, Mrs K M, BA MCLIP, Information Assistant, National Union of
Teachers, London.
[38356]   25/03/1985   CM27/03/1991

Burscheidt, Ms L, MA MALIS, Assistant Librarian, North East London NHS Foundation Trust.
[10010125]   04/07/2008   **ME**

Burt, Miss J H, Life Member.
[2150]   16/12/1946   **ME**

Burton, Miss A E,
[10020716]   29/03/2012   **ME**

Burton, Ms A J, ACLIP, Librarian, Rastrick High School, West Yorkshire.
[10012561]   24/02/2009   **ACL17/06/2011**

Burton, Mr J C, Student, University of Sheffield.
[10032599]   18/12/2013   **ME**

Burton, Mr L A, BA (Hons) MSc MA, L. & Information Officer, City Library, Newcastle.
[10006927]   17/12/2007   **ME**

Burton, Miss L J, MA (Hons), Knowledge Support Officer, NHS Education for Scotland.
[10017528]   01/09/2010   **ME**

Burton, Mr M E, BA DipLib MCLIP, Community Cultural Services Manager, South Gloucestershire Council.
[34744]   16/02/1982   **CM18/06/1985**

Burton, Ms S, BA (Hons) MA MCLIP, Learning Centre Services Manager, Richard Huish College, Richard Huish College.
[27519]   29/04/1977   **CM09/09/1981**

Burton, Mr S, BA (Hons), Student, University of Sheffield.
[10017877]   21/10/2010   **ME**

Burton, Miss S A, Lib. and Information Assistant, Judge Business School, Cambridge.
[10016015]   10/02/2010   **AF**

Burtonshaw, Miss B E, MCLIP, Life Member.
[2169]   01/02/1948   **CM01/01/1963**

Burtrand, Mrs D C, Bsc (Hons) MCLIP, Central Enquiry Unit Officer, Essex County Council Libraries.
[1851]   12/10/1970   **CM17/07/1973**

Bury, Mr N J, BA MCLIP, District Manager, Rossendale Library, Lancs.
[31795]   02/01/1980   **CM30/11/1983**

Bury, Mr R S, MA MCLIP, Employment not known.
[39098]   05/11/1985   **CM05/07/1988**

Bury, Dr S J, MA MA PhD DipLib FCLIP, Andrew W Melton, Chief Librarian, Frick Art Reference Library, NYC.
[24407]   30/07/1975   **FE18/04/1989**

Busby, Mr N, BA MA, Library & Information Manager and Moodle Administrator.
[10006111]   17/06/2009   **ME**

Busby, Mr R J, FCLIP FSA, Retired.
[2174]   30/01/1962   **FE29/07/1974**

Bushell, Mr J M, BA (Hons) MA, Senior Information Executive, Inst. of Chartered Accountants Library, London.
[50207]   04/05/1994   **ME**

Bushnell, Mr I W, BA MCLIP, Retired.
[2182]   01/01/1971   **CM01/01/1974**

Bussey, Ms J, PgDip, Library Advisor, University for the Creative Arts Rochester.
[10013715]   22/05/2009   **ME**

Bussey, Mrs S J M, L. Res. Manager, Derby High School.
[56317]   13/05/1998   **ME**

Bussey, Mrs S M, BA MCLIP, Retired.
[2183]   07/02/1963   **CM01/01/1967**

But, Ms K, BSc (Hons), Librarian, Hong Kong Maritme Museum.
[52816]   19/12/1995   **ME**

Butchart, Mr I C, BA MSc MCLIP PGCE, Retired.
[2185]   01/01/1969   **CM01/01/1971**

Butcher, Miss A L, BMus DipLib, Music Cataloguer, BBC Information & Arch., London.
[38936]   17/10/1985   **ME**

Butcher, Mrs D, MCLIP, Freelance Registered Indexer.
[1035]   21/07/1969   **CM31/08/1973**

Butcher, Mrs D P E, MCLIP, Retired.
[2186]   01/01/1936   **CM01/01/1941**

Butcher, Mr D R, BA MCLIP, Lecturer, School of Information Studies, University of Central England in Birmingham.
[2187]   15/01/1965   **CM01/01/1967**

Butcher, Miss F D, BA MCLIP, Librarian, Renfrew Div. Sch. L. Serv.
[29606]   15/10/1978   **CM16/02/1983**

Butcher, Mr J R, BSc (Hons) MSc (Econ) MCLIP, Res. Librarian, (Cataloguing & Acquisitions), Plymouth Central Library.
[56098]   12/02/1998   **CM18/09/2002**

Butcher, Miss K L, MA, Library Acquisitions Assistant, British Library for Development Studies, Institute of Development Studies, Brighton.
[10012946]   17/03/2009   **ME**

Butchers, Miss T A M, BA (Hons) MA MCLIP, Customers Services Manager (Face to Face): Communities, Warwickshire County Council.
[50588]   26/09/1994   **CM22/09/1999**

Butler, Ms A, BA (Hons) DipILM MCLIP, Librarian, Hillsborough College, Sheffield.
[52457]   02/11/1995   **CM20/01/1999**

Butler, Mrs C, BA (Hons), Student, Aberystwyth University.
[10020305]   11/01/2012   **ME**

Butler, Mrs C E, MBE MCLIP, Retired.
[32233]   01/01/1960   **CM28/08/1981**

Butler, Miss E, BA MA MCLIP, Faculty Support Team Manager, University of Derby.
[59194]   13/12/2000   **CM07/09/2005**

Butler, Miss F J, BA (Hons) MA, Book Selection Specialist, Askews & Holts Library Services Ltd, Preston, Lancashire.
[10001333]   06/02/2007   **ME**

Butler, Miss J, Msc econ, Student.
[10006299]   10/10/2007   **ME**

Butler, Ms J C, BA DipLib MCLIP, Global Master Data Manager, Unilever plc, London.
[35197]   01/10/1982   **CM01/09/1987**

Butler, Miss K, BA (Hons), KCollege, Kent.
[65778]   27/04/2006   **AF**

Butler, Miss K, MSc BA (Hons) MCLIP,
[10006214]   26/09/2007   **CM27/03/2014**

Butler, Mrs L L, BA MBA MCLIP, Retired.
[24667]   18/10/1975   **CM16/12/1977**

Butler, Mrs L M, BA MCLIP, Customer Services and Site Manager, Harold Cohen Library, Liverpool.
[28234]   26/10/1977   **CM10/08/1982**

Butler, Mr M, BA, Student, Manchester Metropolitan University.
[10016084]   16/02/2010   **ME**

Butler, Miss S, S A Recruitment, Isle of Man.
[64632]   27/04/2005   **ME**

Butler, Ms S C, BA (Hons) MA MCLIP, Librarian, Bader International Study Centre.
[49188]   11/10/1993   **CM19/03/1997**

Butler, Mr T, BA (Hons), L. Operations Manager, Croydon College, Surrey.
[56028]   28/01/1998   **ME**

Butler, Ms W F, MA DipLib MCLIP, Librarian, Newcastle under Lyme Sch.
[27308]   01/03/1977   **CM11/05/1979**

Butt, Mrs H M, BA MCLIP, Retired.
[4121]   18/01/1971   **CM01/03/1976**

Butt, Mrs L, BA MA MCLIP, Retired.
[51531]   01/04/1995   **CM21/11/2001**

Butterfield, Mr D, BA FCLIP, Retired.
[2218]   29/07/1952   **FE01/01/1957**
Butterworth, Mrs J M, BA MCLIP, Retired.
[20508]   14/01/1973   **CM08/07/1977**
Butterworth, Mrs S, BA MCLIP, Freelance Indexer.
[15752]   21/01/1969   **CM03/12/1976**
Buttle, Mrs F A, BSc (Hons) MSc MCLIP, Hon. Lib. (Volunteer), Child.
English. Library, Stuttgart, Germany.
[55649]   31/10/1997   **CM20/11/2002**
Button, Mrs A, BA (Hons), Faculty Outreach Librarian, Heart of England
NHS Foundation Trust.
[49389]   21/10/1993   **ME**
Button, Mr A J, BA MCLIP, Virtual Library Officer. Warwickshire Co. L.
[40275]   09/12/1986   **CM14/11/1990**
Button, Ms H J, DipLib MCLIP, College Library Manager, City College
Plymouth.
[33556]   19/01/1981   **CM16/05/1985**
Butts, Ms S C, MA (Hons) DipLib MCLIP, Senior Librarian, Moray
Council Library, Moray.
[33836]   24/03/1981   **CM20/01/1986**
Buxton, Mrs C N, MCLIP, Senior Network Librarian, Highland Council,
Grantown Grammar School.
[36437]   12/10/1983   **CM27/01/2010**
Buxton Collins, Mrs T,
[10020401]   11/02/2012   **AF**
Byatt, Ms D R, BSc DipLib MCLIP, Academic Liaison Librarian,
University of Southampton.
[31761]   29/11/1979   **CM10/01/1983**
Byatt, Mrs R, BSc (Hons) Diploma LIS, Library Assistant, Barberry
Library, Birmingham & Solihull Mental Health NHS Foundation Trust.
[10010884]   01/04/1995   **ME**
Bye, Mr D J, BA (Hons) MCLIP, Information Adviser, Sheffield Hallam
University.
[43415]   18/10/1989   **CM23/06/2004**
Bye, Mr G F C, BA MCLIP, Retired.
[24617]   01/10/1975   **CM25/06/1979**
Byers, Mrs F M, Assistant Librarian, (Chil. & Y.), Upper Norwood Joint
Library, London Borough of Croydon & London Borough of Lambeth.
[62824]   05/11/2003   **ME**
Byers, Mr L, Librarian/Student.
[10025831]   24/03/2014   **ME**
Byfield, Mr P A, LLB (Hons) MA, Legal Knowledge Manager, EBRD,
London.
[56448]   06/07/1998   **ME**
Byford, Mr A J, BA, Retired.
[10008409]   19/10/1970   **ME**
Byford, Miss K J, PgCPSM BA MCLIP, Unemployed.
[26695]   27/10/1976   **CM11/08/1980**
Byford, Mrs R L, BLS MCLIP, Information Officer, Warner Library, Mid
Essex Hospitals Trust.
[33463]   01/12/1980   **CM13/11/1984**
Byrnand, Ms P M, BA MCLIP, Librarian, St Dominic's VI Form College,
Harrow, Middlesex.
[10002756]   27/04/2007   **CM05/05/2010**
Byrne, Mrs B M, BA DipEd DipLib MCLIP, Principle Consultant, BLIS
Byrne Lang. & Information Serv.
[23356]   09/12/1974   **CM31/12/1989**
Byrne, Miss C A, MA Mmus Bmus (Hons) DipABRSM, Assistant
Librarian, Christ's College, Cambridge.
[10019722]   31/08/2011   **ME**
Byrne, Ms D, Unemployed.
[10019965]   12/10/2011   **ME**

Byrne, Mr D F, BA MLib MCLIP, Senior Business Support Manager –
BT.
[34202]   10/10/1981   **CM18/02/1986**
Byrne, Mrs H M, BA MCLIP, Retired.
[28535]   10/01/1978   **CM04/02/1980**
Byrne, Mrs M M, Senior L. Assistant, Manchester Metropolitan
University Library, Manchester.
[10018539]   03/02/2011   **ME**
Byron, Mrs A H E, MCLIP, Unemployed.
[21541]   29/10/1973   **CM04/08/1977**

C

C, Miss S, Research Scholar, Research Scholar, Pondicherry University.
[10025838]   12/12/2013   **ME**
Cabey, Mr J, BA MA, Assistant Librarian, University of Brighton.
[10012512]   23/02/2009   **ME**
Cable, Miss E, MSc MCLIP, Library Assistant.
[10019997]   20/10/2011   **CM13/05/2014**
Cable, Mr P J, BA MSc, Res., Hogan Lovells International LLP, London.
[61157]   15/03/2002   **ME**
Cabrera Perez, Miss E, BA (Hons) PgDip, Librarian, Stockport Library,
Adv. & Information Serv., Cheshire.
[10006597]   11/01/1985   **ME**
Caddy, Miss E A, MA, Senior Information Assistant, Tribal Group.
[10013144]   02/04/2009   **ME**
Cadney, Mr D L J, BA FCLIP, Retired.
[2254]   21/01/1953   **FE01/01/1968**
Cafferkey, Mr S, BSc, Library Assistant, Glucksman Library, University
of Limerick.
[10022250]   29/01/2013   **ME**
Cahill, Mr J, BA MSc, Student, University of Wales Aberystwyth.
[10032638]   23/12/2013   **ME**
Cahill, Mrs R, Learning Advisor, Gower College, Swansea.
[10020613]   16/03/2012   **ME**
Cain, Ms C F, MA MSc Dip Psych, Head Librarian, Sabhal Mor Ostaig,
Isle of Skye.
[41906]   16/05/1988   **ME**
Caine, Mrs S J, BSc MCLIP, Retired.
[56609]   14/09/1998   **CM01/04/2002**
Caird, Ms S M, BSc MA, Senior Librarian, Ashurst LLP, London.
[55417]   10/10/1997   **ME**
Cairns, Ms A M,
[65061]   24/10/2005   **ME**
Cairns, Mrs J, BA MCLIP, Sch. Librarian, Canon Slade School, Bolton,
Lancs.
[39864]   01/10/1986   **CM18/07/1990**
Cairns, Mrs M, BA (Hons) DipLib MScEdTech, Student, CILIP Scotland.
[10035268]   03/10/2014   **ME**
Cairns, Mr R J, Enquiries Assistant, SPICE, The Scottish Parliament,
Edinburgh.
[10013712]   22/05/2009   **ME**
Caldwell, Ms A, BA MCLIP, Lib. & Information Officer, Dundee C. C.
[31218]   05/10/1979   **CM21/09/1983**
Caley, Mr R J, BA DipLib, Research & Learner Support Officer,
Liverpool John Moores University.
[33624]   29/01/1981   **ME**
Callaghan, Ms S, MLIS,
[10019482]   07/07/2011   **ME**
Callanan, Mrs E D, BA MCLIP, Retired.
[2279]   24/03/1955   **CM01/01/1960**
Callander, Mrs A J, Library Assistant, Wirral MBC.
[10034760]   14/08/2014   **ME**

Callear, Mrs J, Head of Bibliographic Services, Birmingham Libraries.
[10002569]   24/05/1986   **ME**
Callegari, Mr L, BA (Hons) MA MSc MCLIP, Learning Support Lib.
[54475]   20/12/1996   **CM07/09/2005**
Caller, Mrs A, BA (Hons) PGCE, Library Assistant, Walkden Library, Salford.
[10015247]   29/10/2009   **ME**
Calles-Cartas, Ms B A, BA (Hons) MRes PgCLIS, Student, Robert Gordon University.
[10035516]   16/10/2014   **ME**
Callow, Mr S D, BA (Hons) ACMI, Library Assistant, Weoley Castle Library, Birmingham.
[10020227]   02/12/2011   **AF**
Calver, Mrs M, MCLIP, Retired Knowledge Systems Librarian, Western Sussex Hospitals NHS Trust.
[23336]   31/10/1974   **CM07/12/1977**
Camann, Mrs N, MEd, Student, Queen Elizabeth Hospital NHS Trust.
[10032623]   20/12/2013   **ME**
Cameron, Mrs A M, MA (Hons) DipILS MCLIP, Librarian, Scottish Screen Arch., Glasgow.
[55230]   05/09/1997   **CM18/09/2002**
Cameron, Mrs H M, BA (Hons) MSc MCLIP, Research Officer, IDOX.
[65695]   01/04/2006   **CM22/02/2010**
Cameron, Mrs H M, BA MCLIP, Unwaged.
[23236]   16/11/1974   **CM30/04/1980**
Cameron, Miss I M M, MA MCLIP, Librarian, Retired.
[2301]   18/09/1968   **CM18/02/1974**
Cameron, Miss L, MA BA (Hons), Librarian, Clifford Chance, London.
[47823]   14/10/1992   **ME**
Cameron, Mrs M, Cataloguer, Mitchell Library, Glasgow.
[10002121]   24/08/2007   **AF**
Cameron, Miss N, BA (Hons) MCLIP, Reader Development Librarian, Aberdeen City Council.
[64749]   01/07/2005   **CM14/11/2012**
Cameron, Mr W H M, BA DipLib MCLIP, Librarian, Highland Theological College, Dingwall
[31220]   02/10/1979   **CM10/11/1981**
Camosso-Stefinovic, Mrs J, BA (Hons) MA MSc MCLIP, Information Consultant Healthcare Research.
[59938]   08/11/2001   **CM11/03/2009**
Camp, Mrs S A, MA,
[10033088]   10/02/2014   **ME**
Campbell, Mrs C J, BA MCLIP, Assistant Librarian (Counter Serv.), Oxford Brookes University.
[33045]   16/10/1980   **CM02/07/1984**
Campbell, Mr G A, MA BCom Dip Lib MCLIP, Lib. & Mus. Manager, The Moray Council.
[25499]   09/02/1976   **CM07/02/1978**
Campbell, Mrs J, BSc (Hons) PgDip, Faculty Liaison Librarian, Newcastle University, Robinson Library.
[10016536]   01/04/2010   **ME**
Campbell, Mrs K, ACLIP, Librarian, Buro Happold, Bath.
[57574]   10/05/1999   **ACL23/01/2007**
Campbell, Ms L, MITG MCLIP, Retired.
[2326]   28/01/1970   **CM01/08/1972**
Campbell, Ms L A, Library Team Leader, Kensington and Chelsea College, London.
[10018754]   29/01/2013   **ME**
Campbell, Ms L G, BA MA, Unwaged.
[10011282]   07/10/2008   **ME**
Campbell, Miss O, BA (Hons) PGCE, Student, Belfast Central Library.
[10035572]   20/10/2014   **ME**

Campbell, Mrs S A, MCLIP, Principal Lib. (Cent. Servs.), Moray Council.
[3833]   18/03/1972   **CM01/07/1975**
Campbell, Mrs S C C, MCLIP, Senior Librarian, Falkirk Council.
[40246]   18/11/1986   **CM24/05/1995**
Campbell, Mr W A, MA MCLIP MA (LIB), Retired.
[20459]   21/03/1973   **CM09/08/1976**
Campey, Mrs M D K, BA (Hons) DipHE, Student, Anglia Ruskin University.
[10032502]   10/12/2013   **ME**
Camps, Mrs P M, MCLIP, Retired.
[1920]   13/02/1960   **CM01/01/1964**
Camroux-Mclean, Mrs E M, BA (Hons), Assistant Librarian, Foreign & Commonwealth Office, London.
[56430]   06/07/1998   **ME**
Canaway, Mr N S, MBA MCLIP, Retired.
[21824]   07/02/1974   **CM03/03/1977**
Canessa, Mrs J Y, MCLIP, LRC Manager, Esher College, Surrey.
[63531]   17/06/2004   **CM09/07/2008**
Cann, Mrs A J, BA MA, Subject Liaison Librarian (Business, Economics and Finance), Brunel University.
[62823]   05/11/2003   **ME**
Canning, Mrs A, Librarian, Department for Communities and Local Government.
[64230]   21/02/2005   **ME**
Canning, Miss R, BA (Hons) MA ACLIP, Senior Library Assistant, North Middlesex UniversityHospital NHS Trust, London.
[10015325]   10/11/2009   **ACL03/11/2010**
Cannings, Miss C E, BA (Hons) MCLIP, Cataloguing and Liaison Support Librarian, University of Reading, Reading.
[62871]   17/11/2003   **CM09/11/2011**
Cannon, Ms C J, BA MPhil MA MCLIP, Associate Director, Collection Support, University of Oxford.
[50616]   01/10/1994   **CM23/07/1997**
Cannon, Mrs C S, BA DipLib AKC MCLIP, Teaching Assistant, St Wilfrid's School, Burgess Hill.
[40169]   06/11/1986   **CM27/03/1991**
Cannon, Miss M G, MCLIP, Norton Rose Fulbright LLP.
[10018701]   24/02/2011   **CM15/07/2014**
Cannon, Mr P, BA MSc, Subject Librarian: Social Sciences, University of the West of Scotland.
[65458]   23/02/2006   **ME**
Cannon, Miss T, Student, Northumbria University.
[10035529]   16/10/2014   **ME**
Cantoni, Mr S, BSc, Student, Kings College.
[10033464]   14/03/2014   **ME**
Cantrell, Mrs A J, BA MA MCLIP, Information Officer, University of Sheffield.
[61550]   11/09/2002   **CM03/10/2007**
Canzonieri, Miss M, Student, UCL.
[10025872]   29/01/2014   **ME**
Cape, Mr B E M, BA (Hons) MA MCLIP, Library Contracts and Performance Manager, London Borough of Southwark.
[59475]   04/04/2001   **CM02/02/2005**
Card, Mr R M, BA MA, Branch Supervisor, Whitegrove Library.
[58200]   16/11/1999   **ME**
Carden, Mrs K J, Acquisitions Librarian, Robert Gordon University.
[58623]   19/04/2000   **ME**
Carder, S J, BA (Hons), Retired.
[43459]   26/10/1989   **ME**
Cardnell, Mrs J A, BA DipLib MCLIP, School Librarian, Colfe's School, London.
[26623]   26/10/1976   **CM09/12/1979**

Care, Mrs R, MEng MSc MCLIP,
[10006819]   17/12/2007   **CM09/11/2011**
Carey, Mrs A J, BSc MCLIP, L. & Information Manager, Bond Pearce, Plymouth.
[60444]   11/12/2001   **CM11/12/2001**
Carey, Miss E M, BFA MLIS, Student, McGill University.
[10033951]   13/05/2014   **ME**
Carey, Miss G G, BA MCLIP,
[34314]   14/10/1981   **CM16/10/1989**
Carey, Mr N, BA (Hons) MSc, College Library Support Team Supervisor, University of Glasgow.
[61961]   19/12/2002   **ME**
Cargill Thompson, Dr H E C, BSc PhD FSA MCLIP, Retired.
[2370]   01/01/1966   **CM01/01/1971**
Carl, Mr M, BA (Hons) MA, Student, University of Sheffield.
[10031815]   07/10/2013   **ME**
Carle, Mrs A, BA (Hons) MCLIP, School Librarian, St Columba's High School.
[48071]   04/11/1992   **CM23/01/2002**
Carle, Miss C A, MCLIP, Life Member.
[2371]   09/09/1951   **CM01/01/1957**
Carlisle, Miss A, BA (Hons) MCLIP, Library Acess and Development Officer, Dumfries and Galloway Libraries, Dumfries.
[39444]   29/01/1986   **CM27/05/1992**
Carlton, Mr S,
[10017717]   29/09/2010   **ME**
Carlyle, Dr E R, PhD MA (Cantab) MA MSc MRes MCLIP, Head of Support and Well-being, Macmillan Cancer Support, London.
[42046]   18/08/1988   **CM01/04/2002**
Carmel, Mr M J, BA MSc FCLIP, Life Member.
[18545]   01/01/1966   **FE16/10/1989**
Carnson, Miss S F, BA DipLib MIIS MCLIP, Retired.
[26468]   05/10/1976   **CM30/11/1978**
Carpenter, Mr C, BA MA MCLIP, Liaison Lib, University of Reading.
[10000666]   25/10/2006   **CM07/07/2010**
Carpenter, Miss E, MA MSc, Assistant Librarian, LSHTM, London.
[10016149]   19/02/2010   **AF**
Carpenter, Mrs P J, BSc MA MCLIP, Community Library, Bracknell L.
[57430]   01/04/1999   **CM29/08/2007**
Carr, Mrs E M, Senior Library & Information Assistant, MOD, Hohne Library.
[10034377]   09/07/2014   **ME**
Carr, Miss G E, MA BA, Collections Access Officer, Lincolnshire CC.
[10033400]   07/03/2014   **ME**
Carr, Ms J, BA Int MA, Student.
[10022002]   16/11/2012   **ME**
Carr, Mr M G, MBiochem (Hons) MA MCLIP BD,
[58943]   05/10/2000   **CM29/03/2006**
Carr, Ms N E, BA (Hons) PgDip, Librarian, Accrington & Rossendale College, Accrington.
[10007920]   28/02/2008   **ME**
Carr, Mr S J, BA (Hons) MCLIP, Information Specialist, Health & Safety Executive, Bootle.
[43475]   26/10/1989   **CM26/07/1995**
Carrette, Mrs S E, BSc MCLIP, Information Servcices Officer, Joseph Rowntree Foundation.
[60156]   07/12/1988   **CM04/05/1993**
Carrick, Mrs E J, BA MCLIP, Library Area Team Leader, Stony Stratford and Wolverton.
[40296]   20/01/1987   **CM18/07/1991**
Carrick, Mr G, MA MCLIP, Learning Support Librarian, Maida Vale Librarian, Sutherland Avenue, London.
[40190]   03/11/1986   **CM13/06/1989**

Carrington, Ms R J, BSc (Hons) MA, Keeper: Live Art Archives, University of Bristol Theatre Collection.
[58864]   18/09/2000   **ME**
Carritt, Ms A S, MA MCLIP, User Education Librarian, Bodleian Library, Oxford.
[10007704]   01/10/1994   **CM19/07/2000**
Carroll, Mrs A, BA (Hons) MSc, Internal Communications Officer, National Child. Bureau, London.
[59804]   03/10/2001   **ME**
Carroll, Mrs J, ACLIP, Stock Team Leader, Bedford Borough Council.
[10008748]   21/06/2010   **ACL14/12/2012**
Carroll, Mr R A, BA FCLIP, Life Member.
[16736]   12/02/1948   **FE01/01/1963**
Carroll, Ms S, BA, Student, University of Strathclyde.
[10025897]   04/09/2013   **ME**
Carson, Mrs C, Learning Resources Facilitator (Systems), New College Stamford.
[10035013]   05/09/2014   **ME**
Carson, Mrs C M, BSc (Econ) MCLIP, User Services Manager, University College Falmouth.
[61682]   21/10/2002   **CM17/09/2008**
Carson, Mrs S, Student, University of Ulster.
[10033291]   28/02/2014   **ME**
Carson, Mr W R H, MBE HonFLAI HonFCILIP FCILIP, Life Member.
[2425]   01/01/1949   **HFE01/01/1989**
Carter, Mr A, MA FCLIP FSAScot, Life Member.
[2426]   24/03/1949   **FE01/01/1968**
Carter, Mrs A J, BSc Econ (Hons), Learning Resources Manager, John of Gaunt School, Trowbridge, Wilts.
[63475]   14/05/2004   **ME**
Carter, Ms A M, BA (Hons) MCLIP, Librarian, Central Sussex 6th Form Haywards Heath.
[10016434]   24/03/2010   **CM29/05/2013**
Carter, Miss B, BA (Hons) MSc MCLIP, Des Imoc Ihub Info Assure, Ministry of Defence.
[61200]   08/04/2002   **CM29/08/2007**
Carter, Ms B, Student, Glyndwr University, Wrexham.
[10017825]   11/10/2010   **ME**
Carter, Mrs C J, MA MCLIP, Academic Liaison Librarian.
[10001289]   21/02/2005   **CM09/09/2009**
Carter, Miss D, BLib MSc MCLIP, Director, Dcision Consult Sarl.
[39682]   06/05/1986   **CM27/05/1992**
Carter, Mrs E, Relief Librarian, HMP Sudbury.
[8350]   23/03/1971   **ME**
Carter, Mrs E R, MCLIP, Life Member.
[2433]   29/01/1932   **CM01/01/1944**
Carter, Ms G, Unwaged.
[65179]   07/11/2005   **AF**
Carter, Mrs H, BA MCLIP, information and Research Manager, Derbyshire & Nottinghamshire Chamber of Commerce.
[32871]   07/10/1980   **CM30/07/1985**
Carter, Mrs J, Subject Lib. /University Archivist/Lib. Acquisitions Assistant.
[46867]   13/02/1992   **ME**
Carter, Mrs K, BA MCLIP, School Librarian, West Park School, Derby.
[10014929]   01/05/1984   **CM09/08/1988**
Carter, Miss K J, BA MA,
[10007999]   03/03/2008   **ME**
Carter, Ms L D, BA Cert CE, Student, Strathclyde University.
[10020012]   25/10/2011   **ME**
Carter, Mr L J, BSc MSc PhD MCLIP, Retired.
[48288]   24/11/1992   **CM26/01/1994**
Carter, Mrs M E, BA FCLIP, Life Member.
[2448]   01/01/1940   **FE01/01/1946**

Carter, Mrs P R, BSc (Hons) BSc (Econ) MCLIP, Assistant Librarian, Barbican Library, City of London.
[53225]   04/04/1996   CM25/07/2001

Carter, Mr R C, BA (Hons) PgDip MCLIP, Lib, Department of Geography, University of Cambridge.
[53926]   11/10/1996   CM17/09/2008

Carter, Mr R O, BSc, Information Assistant, Newcastle University, Newcastle Upon Tyne.
[10005033]   01/12/1980   ME

Carter, Miss S, MSc BSc MCLIP, Subject Librarian, Leeds City College.
[10012349]   05/02/2009   CM22/08/2012

Carter, Mr S, BA (Hons) MA, Unwaged.
[38932]   21/10/1985   ME

Carter, Ms S E, BA (Hons) MA MCLIP, Various Temporary Librarian Roles.
[46893]   28/02/1992   CM18/03/1998

Carter, Mrs S L, L. Manager, Cefas, Lowestoft.
[59508]   18/04/2001   CM09/07/2008

Carter, Ms V I, BSc (Hons) MCLIP, Assistant Librarian, Learning Centre, South Thames College.
[58980]   16/10/2000   CM07/09/2005

Carty, Ms C J, BA (Hons) MA MCLIP, English Cataloguing, University of Cambridge,
[56985]   18/11/1998   CM29/03/2006

Carty, Mrs L M, BA (Hons), Lib. Asst (Volunteer), Royal Wolverhampton NHS Bell Library.
[10020830]   18/04/2012   ME

Carvell, Mrs P A, BA MCLIP, Collection Management Librarian, Bermuda National Library, Hamilton.
[26772]   26/11/1976   CM06/10/1980

Carver, Ms K, BA MA PGCHE SFHEA MCLIP, Subject Librarian, J B Priestley Library, Bradford.
[10013811]   21/01/1998   CM04/02/2004

Cascant Ortolano, Ms L, B. Lib. I. Sc BS., Clinical Outreach Librarian, Buckinghamshire Healthcare NHS Trust, Aylesbury.
[10016134]   17/02/2010   ME

Case, Mr M L, BSc (Hons) PgDipIM MCLIP, Subject Librarian, Anglia Ruskin, Chelmsford.
[52243]   18/10/1995   CM16/07/2003

Case, Ms V P, MCLIP, University of Law.
[10015079]   12/10/2009   CM13/11/2013

Caseley, Mrs E, MCLIP, Deputy Director of Library Services, Kings College.
[63066]   27/01/2004   CM19/11/2008

Casey, Miss M E, BSc (Hons) PgDip MCLIP, Assistant Information Specialist, NICE.
[65935]   23/06/2006   CM20/04/2009

Cashman, Mr J M, BA DipLib MCLIP, Lib. /Arch., Foreign Exchange Co., Killorglin.
[41120]   09/10/1987   CM18/11/1992

Casimir, Mrs H S, MCLIP, Life Member.
[2478]   02/09/1947   CM01/01/1952

Cass, Miss E J, BA (Hons) MSc MCLIP, Licensing Manager, British Library, Boston Spa, West Yorkshire.
[52453]   02/11/1995   CM20/01/1999

Casselden, Ms B, BA (Hons) PGCE MA FHEA MCLIP, Senior Lecturer, Northumbria University, Newcastle.
[49768]   06/12/1993   CM20/05/1998

Cassells, Mrs A T S, MA MCLIP CERT Gen Studies, School Librarian, Boclair Academy, Bearsden.
[28167]   06/10/1977   CM27/11/1980

Cassels, Mrs A F, BA MCLIP, Library Officer: Reading, Wakefield Council.
[32519]   20/04/1980   CM30/09/1985

Cassels, Mr A M, MA MSc MSc MBCS MCLIP, Information Centre Manager, Fera, York.
[38099]   17/01/1985   CM16/05/1990

Cassettari, Ms G, MA MCLIP, Information & Knowledge Manager, Metropolitan Police Serv, London.
[52975]   07/02/1996   CM20/01/1999

Cassidy, Ms A E, BA MSc DipInfSc MCLIP, Lead Programme Manager for Information Security and Cloud Computing, BSI Group, London.
[60137]   23/04/1981   CM01/05/1985

Cassidy, Mrs A M, MCLIP, Learning Centre Facilitator, York College.
[21145]   04/10/1973   CM01/07/1977

Cassidy, Ms J, BA DipLIS, Librarian, Chief State Solicitor's Office, Dublin, Ireland.
[57497]   06/04/1999   ME

Cassidy, Mrs J, BA DipLib, Senior L. Assistant, Lancashire C. C.
[49972]   31/01/1994   ME

Cassidy, Miss R, BA, Graduate Trainee Librarian, Leeds University Library.
[10020636]   14/03/2012   ME

Casteleyn, Mrs M T, FCLIP, Life Member.
[2483]   18/10/1963   FE27/11/1984

Castens, Mrs L D, LLB (Hons) PgDip MSc MCLIP FLF, Head of Library & Information Services, University of Gloucestershire.
[56278]   20/04/1998   CM15/02/2012

Castens, Ms M E, BSc MA DMS MCLIP, Retired, April 2012.
[2484]   18/06/1969   CM18/11/1974

Castle, Ms C M, BA (Hons) MCLIP, Lib. i/c., Department of Zoology, University of Cambridge.
[52425]   25/10/1995   RV29/03/2007   CM23/09/1998

Castle, Mrs E M, BA MCLIP, Unwaged.
[23323]   27/11/1974   CM10/01/1977

Castle, Mrs J, MA (Hons) DipILS MCLIP, L. & Heritage Serv. Manager, West Lothian Council.
[38902]   14/10/1985   CM05/07/1988

Castle, Mr J D, BA (Hons) MA, Information Management Consultant, Statoil (U. K.) Ltd.
[56844]   26/10/1998   ME

Castle, Mrs S, BA BSc (Econ), Community Librarian, Medway Libraries.
[10002772]   10/05/2007   ME

Castle, Ms S, BA (Hons) MA MCLIP FHEA, Library Liaison Manager: Learning & Teaching, King's College London.
[60034]   29/11/2001   CM16/07/2003

Castle-Smith, Mr D, BA (Hons) MCLIP, College Team Leader, Fife C., Dunfermline.
[54377]   29/11/1996   CM17/05/2000

Caston, Ms L P, MA (Hons) DipLib MCLIP, External Funding Officer, Angus Council.
[30126]   17/01/1979   CM12/11/1981

Cater, Mr M, BA (Hons) MCLIP, Knowlege Services Professional – Access, Dudley Office of Public Health.
[49400]   21/10/1993   CM20/11/2002

Cater, Mrs S, BA DipLIS, Unwaged.
[10019847]   14/02/1995   ME

Catt, Mr B J, MA, Professionally qualified Serials and E-Resources Assistant at The University of York Library.
[10022576]   26/03/2013   ME

Catto, Mr D B, MA DipEd DipMan MCLIP, Local Studies Librarian, Aberdeenshire Libraries.
[10001057]   19/10/1976   CM30/10/1979

Cavanagh, Mr M J, MA, Head of Cultural Services, Pembrokeshire County Council.
[10013551]   05/05/2009   ME

Cavanagh, Mrs M S, MA DipLib MCLIP, Head of Local Studies, West Lothian Council.
[26696]   27/10/1976   **CM29/11/1979**

Cavanagh, Mr P, BA (Hons) MSciLM MCLIP, Assistant Librarian, Kimberlin Library, De Montfort University, Leicester.
[61927]   05/12/2002   **CM23/01/2008**

Cavaroli, Miss A, MA,
[10012098]   17/12/2008   **ME**

Cave, Mr R J, MA FCLIP MRSC, Freelancer.
[60168]   12/04/1962   **FE01/12/1976**

Cave, Mrs Z T, MLib BA MCLIP, Support/Study Mentor and Mental Health Mentor, University of Wales: Trinity Saint David.
[26922]   13/12/1976   **CM08/07/1980**

Cavender, Mr N J R, BA, Student, Northumbria University.
[10035100]   15/09/2014   **ME**

Cavorsi, Ms L, MA, Student, City University London.
[10021866]   31/01/2014   **ME**

Cawkwell, Miss J A, BA MA,
[10005602]   25/07/2007   **ME**

Cawood, Mrs A L, BA (Hons) DipLIS MCLIP, Information Officer, Agriculture & Development Board, Stoneleigh Park.
[48917]   21/07/1993   **CM25/09/1996**

Cawsey, Mrs P M, Librarian, International Sch. of Lausanne, Switzerland.
[60905]   09/01/2002   **ME**

Cawthorne, Mr D J, BA MCLIP, Public Library Consultant, Exertis MSE Library Multimedia.
[2518]   24/09/1970   **CM28/08/1973**

Cawthorne, Ms W A, BSc (Hons) DipLib MCLIP, Assistant Librarian, The Geological Society.
[26310]   30/09/1976   **CM29/11/1979**

Cefai, Mrs J A, MCLIP, Staff Learning & Dev. Manager, Anglia Ruskin University, Cambridge.
[18069]   21/09/1972   **CM11/12/1989**

Ceiriog-Hughes, Mrs S M T, BA MA MCLIP, Assistant Librarian, Moberly Library, Winchester College.
[10016585]   11/10/1989   **RV13/11/2013**   **CM27/01/1993**

Celac, Miss V, MSc, Unwaged.
[10016916]   08/06/2010   **ME**

Celik, Mrs M A R F, BA MCLIP, Law Librarian, Winston & Strawn, London.
[33293]   12/11/1980   **CM10/06/1986**

Centio, Ms J, Information Assistant, BLM, London.
[10016042]   10/02/2010   **AF**

Centrone, Ms M C, PgDip PhD MCLIP, Lending Services Supervisor, Templeman Library, University of Kent.
[10013430]   16/07/2010   **CM13/11/2013**

Chachu, Mrs N, Head Librarian, Ashesi University College, Accra, Ghana.
[30581]   12/12/1978   **ME**

Chad, Mr K, MA MCLIP, Director, Ken Chad Consulting Ltd, Brentwood.
[10011375]   30/11/1973   **CM16/12/1976**

Chadder, Miss J E, BA MCLIP, Life Member.
[2522]   01/01/1954   **CM01/01/1960**

Chadwick, Miss L K, Chief Information Officer, MOD.
[10033534]   24/03/2014   **ME**

Chafey, Mr K G, MCLIP, Retired.
[2532]   01/01/1959   **CM01/01/1963**

Chai, Miss Y X, LLB, Student, City University London.
[10035452]   14/10/2014   **ME**

Chakrabarty, Mrs E, BA MCLIP, Life Member.
[12187]   17/10/1967   **CM01/01/1970**

Chalk-Birdsall, Mrs D, MCLIP, Academic Liaison Librarian, Architecture & Interior Design for The Cass   LMU.
[29017]   13/03/1978   **CM21/08/1981**

Challinor, Dr C, Resources Officer, Library & Health Promotion Resources, Lynfield Mount Hospital.
[10019537]   22/07/2011   **ME**

Challinor, Miss H L, BA (Hons) MCLIP, Information Standards Librarian, Department for Education, Sheffield.
[42638]   20/01/1989   **CM19/03/2008**

Challinor, Ms J, BA (Hons) DipLib, Careers Information Manager, Careers Serv., University of Edinburgh.
[10015675]   21/10/1985   **ME**

Challis, Mrs C E, MA (OXON) MSc, Unwaged.
[10021930]   01/11/2012   **ME**

Challis, Mr R A, BA MA, Student, University of the West of England.
[10032151]   29/10/2013   **ME**

Chalmers, Miss E C M, BSc (Hons) PGCE MCLIP, Library and Knowledge Service Manager, Stenhouse Library, Kingston Hospital.
[10007784]   20/11/2003   **CM19/08/2011**

Chalmers, Mrs I C L, BA MCLIP, Retired.
[42162]   12/10/1988   **CM01/04/2002**

Chalmers, Miss J E S, MCLIP, Retired.
[2541]   01/01/1958   **CM01/01/1965**

Chaloner, Ms L, Msc, Unemployed.
[10001586]   15/01/2003   **ME**

Chamberlain, Mrs E J, MA MCLIP, Systems & Research Librarian, Buckinghamshire New University, High Wycombe.
[37048]   02/02/1984   **CM14/11/1989**

Chamberlain, Mrs H E, BA MCLIP, Ls. Operations & Staff Development Manager, Bath & North East Somerset Council, Somerset.
[36133]   14/06/1983   **CM26/11/1997**

Chambers, Miss C, BA (Hons) MA MCLIP,
[58599]   11/04/2000   **CM19/11/2003**

Chambers, Mrs L, BA (Hons) MInfSci MCLIP, Schools Lib. Serv., LB Tower Hamlets.
[31848]   08/01/1980   **CM27/07/1982**

Chambers, Mr M W, MA MA DipLib, Unemployed.
[36406]   05/10/1983   **ME**

Chambers, Mrs N E, BA MCLIP, School Librarian, Evesham High School, Evesham, Worcs.
[28743]   23/01/1978   **CM30/07/1982**

Chambers, Mr R, BA, Information Assistant, Leeds Trinity University college.
[10021976]   08/11/2012   **ME**

Chambers, Ms S E, BA MA, Project Medewerker, Koninklijke Bibl., The Hague.
[54796]   02/04/1997   **ME**

Chambers, Mrs W M, BA Dip LIS, Duty Librarian, Edinburgh University, Edinburgh.
[57897]   01/10/1999   **ME**

Chamley, Miss J S, MA MCLIP, Skills Plus and Self Service Assistant, University of Northumbria, Newcastle Upon Tyne.
[10015078]   12/10/2009   **CM27/03/2014**

Champion, Mrs M M, MCLIP, Life Member.
[2566]   04/07/1950   **CM01/01/1962**

Champion, Ms O J, BA (Hons) MSc MCLIP, Career Break,
[51312]   11/01/1995   **CM26/11/1997**

Champion, Mrs P M, MCLIP, Teaching Assistant, Prestwood Jnr. School, Great Missenden.
[23392]   11/01/1975   **CM09/12/1977**

Champion, Mrs S P, MA, Unwaged.
[51045]   09/11/1994   **ME**

Champion, Mrs Y, BA DipLib MCLIP, Employment not known.
[31607]   15/11/1979   **CM07/12/1982**

Chan, Ms A K Y, Technical Serv., University of Sydney, NSW Australia.
[42840]   16/03/1989   ME
Chan, Mr B E, MSc FRSA MCLIP MinstLM, Old War Office Information
Centre Manager, MOD, London.
[55876]   27/11/1997   CM11/03/2009
Chan, Mr G K L, MSc MCLIP, Trials Search Co-ordinator, Cochrane
Epilepsy Group.
[2569]   30/08/1969   CM31/05/1973
Chandler, Miss L, Know-How Officer, Slaughter & May, London.
[63243]   22/03/2004   ME
Chandler, Miss M, BA (Hons) MCLIP, Subject Librarian, University of
Liverpool.
[46390]   31/10/1991   CM16/07/2003
Chandler, Mr P J, Assistant Librarian, Royal College of Defence
Studies, London.
[51294]   04/01/1995   ME
Chandler, Ms P S, BLS MA PGCE MCLIP, Librarian, St Peter's School,
York.
[30129]   05/12/1978   CM17/08/1982
Chandler, Mrs S, Library Assistant, Huddersfield R. I.
[10022420]   26/02/2013   ME
Chaney, Ms A E P, BA (Hons) MA MCLIP, Cataloguer, Newsam Library
and Archives, Institute of Education, University of London.
[29783]   01/10/1978   CM28/01/1983
Chaney, Mrs K V, MCLIP, Librarian, Canterbury Christ Church
University, Southborough, Kent.
[2579]   07/02/1972   CM13/02/1976
Channell, Mr B F, L. Manager.
[10007738]   21/02/2008   ME
Chapman, Miss A, BA (Hons), Student, The Unversity of Sheffield.
[10031901]   11/02/2014   ME
Chapman, Mrs A D, MA FCLIP, Retired.
[2589]   08/09/1967   FE09/07/1981
Chapman, Mrs A D, Volunteer, Citizen's Advice Bureau.
[31560]   01/11/1979   ME
Chapman, Mrs A V, BA (Open) MCLIP, Retired.
[2590]   04/02/1959   CM01/01/1964
Chapman, Ms E A, BA MA DipLib FCLIP, Director of L. Serv., BLPES,
London School of Economics.
[18409]   30/09/1972   FE18/01/1989
Chapman, Mr E J, MA FRSA MCLIP, Retired.
[19471]   19/10/1954   CM01/01/1963
Chapman, Mr J E M, BSc, Information Assistant, Kingston University.
[10020695]   26/03/2012   ME
Chapman, Miss K, BA MA MSc, Principal Librarian, Amgueddfa Cymru
– National Museum of Wales, Cardiff.
[10019604]   03/08/2011   ME
Chapman, Mrs M, MCLIP, Retired.
[8884]   01/01/1956   CM01/01/1970
Chapman, Mr M M, MA, Retired.
[2609]   16/10/1970   CM05/12/1972
Chapman, Ms N J, BA (Hons) MSc, Senior Researcher, Hogan Lovells
International LLP, London.
[55398]   09/10/1997   ME
Chapman, Mr P, Managing Director, Evolve Business Consultancy,
Farnham.
[10008390]   19/03/2008   ME
Chapman, Mr R E, MSc BSc MCLIP, 1 Sussex Keep, Sussex Close,
Slough, SL1 1NY.
[60171]   23/03/1970   CM31/07/1980
Chapman, Mrs S, BLib (Hons) MLib MCLIP, Library Assistant (Cardiff
University) & Casual Library Assistant (Vale of Glamorgan Council).
[43866]   30/01/1990   CM21/05/1997

Chapman, Mrs S, MCLIP, Life Member.
[2610]   01/01/1957   CM01/01/1966
Chapman, Mrs S M, MA MLib MCLIP, Unemployed.
[22584]   04/07/1974   CM20/09/1995
Chapman, Mrs S P, BA MCLIP, Assistant School Librarian, King
James's School, Knaresborough.
[45514]   26/02/1991   CM15/10/2002
Chapman, Mr V S, BLib (Hons) MCLIP, Central Librarian LB of
Lewisham.
[31586]   20/10/1979   CM15/04/1988
Chapman-Daniel, Mrs A, BA, Director /Owner, Minesoft Ltd, London.
[10009811]   12/12/2001   ME
Chappell, Mr D L, BA (Hons) MSc MCLIP, Academic Liaison Librarian,
Glasgow School of Art.
[56513]   04/08/1998   CM10/07/2009
Chappelle, Mrs C A, BA MCLIP, Collection Management Assistant,
University of Manchester.
[2614]   10/09/1970   CM17/06/1974
Charillon, Miss A, Library & Information Officer : Business & IP Centre
Newcastle, Newcastle Libraries.
[10018690]   01/03/2011   ME
Charin, Ms S, Lib. & Information Serv. Manager.
[63244]   22/03/2004   ME
Charles, Ms E E, BA MSc MCLIP, Assistant Director: E-Services, Media
Services and Systems, Birkbeck, University of London.
[37713]   17/10/1984   CM15/03/1989
Charles, Mrs J Y, BA (Hons) MSc MRQA, Quality & Compliance
Manager, Global. Information Serv.
[51040]   09/11/1994   ME
Charles, Ms S, BA MA, Student, UCL.
[10035621]   24/10/2014   ME
Charles, Ms S, Student, UCL.
[10021893]   25/10/2012   ME
Charlesworth, Miss A D, BA (Hons) MA, Library Operations Manager,
Kings College London.
[56799]   19/10/1998   ME
Charlesworth, Mrs M K, MSc BA (Hons), Librarian.
[10017891]   21/10/2010   ME
Charlton, Mrs H M, BA MCLIP,
[36883]   13/01/1984   CM21/12/1988
Charnley, Ms C, BA MSc MCLIP, L. and Knowledge Serv. Manager,
South Staffordshire & Shropshire Healthcare NHS Foundation Trust,
Stafford.
[46457]   07/11/1991   CM26/01/1994
Charwat, Mrs E, MA Msc, Deputy Librarian, The Linnean Society of
London.
[64891]   07/09/2005   ME
Chase, Mr B J, FCLIP, Retired.
[2626]   01/01/1959   FE01/01/1964
Chase, Ms S A, BA (Hons) DipInf, Head of Library and Info Services,
Weil, Gotshal & Manges, London.
[49506]   08/11/1993   ME
Chatfield, Mr B R,
[10021100]   29/05/2012   AF
Chatten, Mrs J, Knowledge Assistant, Nabarro, London.
[10007182]   25/01/2008   AF
Chatten, Mrs Z, BA (Hons) MA MCLIP, Liaison Librarian, University of
Liverpool.
[57975]   07/10/1999   CM08/12/2004
Chatterton, Miss C J, MCLIP, Tech. Librarian, Cormac Solutions Ltd.
[64823]   20/07/2005   CM12/05/2011
Chatwin, Mrs L, BA MA, Student.
[10018008]   03/11/2010   ME

Chau, Miss C W C, MLib MCLIP, Senior Assistant Librarian (Information Management), Hong Kong Institute of Education.
[42202]   13/10/1988   **CM16/09/1992**

Chaudhry, Ms R Y, BA (Hons) MCLIP, Librarian, Rugby High School Academy Trust.
[37656]   13/10/1984   **CM14/03/1990**

Chaudhury, Mr M, BSC (Hons) MA MBA PGCE, Head of Learning Resource Services, Barking & Dagenham College.
[58525]   10/03/2000   **ME**

Chavez, Mrs R, BAHons MCLIP, Information Advisor (Resources and Content), Kingston College.
[65375]   10/01/2006   **CM11/06/2010**

Cheale, Miss J, ACLIP, LRC Manager, Stour Valley Community School, Clare.
[10020015]   25/10/2011   **ACL27/08/2014**

Chedgzoy, Mr J N, BA (Hons) DipLis MCLIP, Library Service Manager, Herefordshire Council.
[46986]   20/03/1992   **CM24/07/1996**

Cheeseborough, Mrs J, BA (Hons) DipLib FCLIP, Retired.
[33034]   17/10/1980   **FE19/03/2008**

Cheeseman, Mrs N, MCLIP, Assistant Librarian, Parmiter's School, Watford.
[10011450]   23/10/2009   **CM13/11/2013**

Cheesman, Mr B, MA MCLIP, Life Member.
[2643]   01/10/1956   **CM01/01/1959**

Cheesman, Miss D A, BA DipLib MCLIP, System Consultant, Ex Libris.
[43572]   09/11/1989   **CM15/09/1993**

Cheetham, Mrs L M, BA MCLIP, School Librarian, Hitchin Girls School, Herts.
[30196]   08/01/1979   **CM08/01/1981**

Chelin, Ms J A, BA DipLib PGC (HE) FCLIP, Deputy Librarian, University of the West of England, Bristol.
[39406]   29/01/1986   **FE11/04/2013**

Chell, Mrs J E, ACLIP, Lib. Assistant, Tremough Library, Penryn.
[10008302]   20/03/2008   **ACL22/09/2010**

Chen, Mrs X, Student, University of Strathclyde.
[10017766]   06/10/2010   **ME**

Cheney, Ms C R, BA MCLIP, Biomedical Team Leader, UCL.
[36530]   17/10/1983   **CM09/07/1987**

Cherpeau, Ms C M, BSc (Hons) MCLIP, Senior Librarian: Information and Archive Services, Knowsley L. Serv., Huyton L.
[45304]   04/10/1990   **CM09/09/2009**

Cherry, Mr M, BSc BA (Hons), Librarian, Library & Museum of Freemasonry, London.
[62125]   21/02/2003   **ME**

Cherry, Mrs S, BA (Hons), Market Dir & Info Mgmt Adv., A I Cherry Chartered Accountants.
[10020781]   04/04/2012   **ME**

Cherry, Mrs S A, ACLIP, Senior Lib. Assistant, L. Serv., Medway NHS Foundation Trust, Gillingham.
[10016567]   14/04/2010   **ACL22/09/2010**

Chesney, Mrs A R, BA MCLIP,
[34617]   19/01/1982   **CM16/12/1983**

Chesworth, Mr S, MCLIP, Library Manager, South Cheshire College, Crewe.
[62906]   18/11/2003   **CM29/11/2006**

Chetwood, Ms R L,
[63599]   05/07/2004   **AF**

Chevalier, Mrs S J, Senior Library Assistant, London Borough of Sutton.
[10034129]   09/06/2014   **ME**

Chevallot, Ms I C, BA (Hons) Dip InfServ MCLIP,
[10016887]   01/06/2010   **CM09/11/2011**

Cheyney, Mr K G, MCLIP, Life Member.
[2666]   13/03/1951   **CM01/01/1957**

Chibnall, Miss M I, BA MCLIP, Retired, Former Assistant Librarian, Royal Astronomical Society, London.
[18422]   21/10/1972   **CM07/11/1975**

Chidzey, Mr P, BSc (Hons), KIM Professional, MOD.
[10035261]   02/10/2014   **ME**

Child, Ms A, BA (Hons) MA,
[10026000]   21/07/2014   **ME**

Child, Miss E, Clinical Information Specialist, Edge Hill University.
[10017993]   01/11/2010   **ME**

Child, Ms R, BA MA, Student, Robert Gordon University.
[10026001]   29/10/2013   **ME**

Child, Mrs R, BSc (Hons) MA,
[10013358]   16/04/2009   **ME**

Childs, Mr A D, BA FCLIP, Life Member.
[2677]   04/03/1948   **FE01/01/1960**

Childs, Mrs E, DipILM, Information Special, Government Communications HQ.
[64319]   02/03/2005   **ME**

Childs Smith, Ms K E, BA MCLIP, Head of L. & Information Serv., NSPCC, London.
[30895]   05/05/1979   **CM18/06/1984**

Chiles, Ms S J B, BA (Hons) PgDipLib, Freelancer; Copy Editor and Proof Reader.
[10034102]   09/06/2014   **ME**

Chilmaid, Mrs D J, MBA DipLib MCLIP, Business Manager, Kent Libraries, Registration & Archives.
[32148]   21/01/1980   **CM27/09/1982**

Chilton, Mrs S, MCLIP, Information Manager, Northumbria University, Newcastle.
[10001148]   12/01/2007   **CM22/02/2010**

Chilvers, Dr A H, BA (Hons) DipLib MA PhD MCLIP, Career break.
[43982]   20/03/1990   **CM16/12/1992**

Chilvers, Mrs I, MSc, Library Manager, University of Cambridge.
[10016683]   26/04/2010   **ME**

Chinn, Ms M, MCLIP, Retired.
[21810]   15/01/1974   **CM21/01/1976**

Chinnery, Miss C, BLib MCLIP, L. Manager, Peterborough Regional College.
[21992]   18/01/1974   **CM19/12/1978**

Chirgwin, Mr F J, BA MSc FCLIP, Life Member.
[2685]   21/05/1959   **FE01/01/1965**

Chirgwin, Mrs T M D W, MA (Oxon) MMus DipLIM MCLIP, Chester University Library.
[55321]   01/10/1997   **CM17/01/2001**

Chivas, Mrs G, BSc MCLIP, Librarian, Cox Green Library, Maidenhead.
[23816]   31/01/1975   **CM12/01/1979**

Chivers, Mr S, Def Comrcl-Comms-IM-2, Ministry of Defence.
[10034748]   12/08/2014   **ME**

Cho, Miss J, Student, Open Polytechnic of New Zealand.
[10026009]   12/05/2014   **ME**

Choi, Mr P H L, MA MSc, Student, University of Glasgow.
[10033610]   03/04/2014   **ME**

Chojna, Mrs A, MA, Faculty Information Adviser, London South Bank University, London.
[10019440]   04/07/2011   **ME**

Choolhun, Mrs N, BA (Hons) Pg DipLib, Library Co-ordinator, College of Law, London.
[60976]   22/01/2002   **ME**

Choong, Mrs C L, BA MTh MSc MCLIP, Senior Lib Assistant, Bibliographic & User Services, Canterbury Christ Church University.
[59846]   16/10/2001   **CM09/09/2009**

Chopra, Mr V, Learning Centre Assistant (management information & reports), Southampton City College.
[10006182]   18/09/2007   **AF**

Choudhury, Mr S K, BSc (BZC) BLISc MBA MSc MLISc, Senior Technical Assistant 'B', Information Centre, RCI, Defence R&D, Hyderabad, India.
[10019510]   12/07/2011   **ME**

Chouglay, Mrs L A, BSc (Hons) DipLib MCLIP, Midday meals supervisor, St Peter's School, Rochester, Kent.
[39216]   01/01/1986   **CM24/05/1995**

Choules, Ms J E, BA (Hons) MA MCLIP, Stock Dev. Manager, Bristol L.,
[49237]   14/10/1993   **CM19/03/1997**

Chowdory, Miss N, BA MA, Library Assistant, University of Robert Gordon.
[10023383]   09/07/2013   **ME**

Chrimes, Mr M M, MBE BA MLS MCLIP, Librarian, Inst. of Civil Engineers, London.
[26211]   20/08/1976   **CM20/08/1978**

Chrisp, Mr P S, BA MCLIP, Retired.
[2696]   09/10/1965   **CM01/07/1988**

Christensen, Ms E, BA MA, Library and Information Administrator, G C U London Ltd.
[10026019]   28/02/2014   **ME**

Christie, Miss P M, BA MCLIP, Director of Libraries & Academic Support Services, University of the Arts London.
[25018]   02/11/1975   **CM22/03/1983**

Christine, Miss R, MA MCLIP, Librarian, Mary Erskine Sch.
[53834]   03/10/1996   **RV**29/03/2007   **CM20/09/2000**

Christison, Mrs A, BSc (Hons) MSc MCLIP, Librarian, National Coal Mining Museum, Wakefield.
[54523]   14/01/1997   **CM18/09/2002**

Christophers, Mr R A, MA PhD FCLIP, Part-time L. Consultant.
[2700]   14/02/1958   **FE01/01/1963**

Christophorou, Mr G M, BSc, Student, Manchester Metropolitan University.
[10032486]   09/12/2013   **ME**

Chryssanthopoulos, Mrs P, BSc DipLib MA, Unemployed.
[46082]   01/10/1991   **ME**

Chuah, Miss M, BA MCLIP, Librarian, University of Malaya Library, Kuala Lumpur.
[24410]   29/07/1975   **CM14/01/1980**

Chudasama, Miss S, BSc MSc, Business & Management Information Specialist.
[65099]   01/11/2005   **ME**

Church, Miss J, Part-time Student, University of Wales, Aberystwyth, Montrose Library, Angus.
[65457]   23/02/2006   **ME**

Church, Mrs J C,
[10020785]   04/04/2012   **AF**

Cieciura, Mrs E K, BA MLib MCLIP, Research & Knowledge Exchange Officer, RKEOps, Bournemouth University.
[39291]   07/01/1986   **CM26/05/1993**

Cingi, Miss A, BA PGDIP CELTA, Library Assistant at Bridgend Library.
[10031480]   15/08/2013   **ME**

Cinnamond, Mrs J, MCLIP, Life Member.
[2712]   03/03/1960   **CM01/01/1965**

Cipkin, Mr C B, BA (Hons) MA ARCO MCLIP, Assistant Director for Library Academic Engagement at the University of Birmingham.
[51805]   04/07/1995   **RV**25/01/2011   **CM17/03/1999**

Ciubotaru, Miss C E, MA, Library Assistant, Oxfordshire County Council.
[10032031]   22/10/2013   **ME**

Clackson, Mrs A M, BMus (Hons) DipLib, Librarian, University of Strathclyde.
[34247]   13/10/1981   **ME**

Clague, Mr P, BA FCLIP, Life Member.
[2713]   29/03/1955   **FE01/01/1967**

Clapham, Ms J, BA (Hons)Hum, Librarian (Job Share), National Coal Mining Museum, Wakefield.
[62743]   14/10/2003   **ME**

Clapham, Ms L, BA MCLIP, Sch. Librarian, Sidney Stringer Academy, Coventry.
[36716]   11/11/1983   **CM10/12/1986**

Clapp, Mrs F C, MCLIP, Unwaged.
[26516]   13/10/1976   **CM25/01/1980**

Clare, Ms H M, BA MA MCLIP, Co-ordinator, Kingston University, Kingston, Surrey.
[61743]   31/10/2002   **CM10/07/2009**

Clare, Mrs J B, BA (Hons) MCLIP, E-Learning/Resources Manager, The Billericay School, Essex.
[26807]   07/11/1976   **CM15/02/1980**

Claridge, Miss C, Metadata Librarian, University of Warwick Library.
[58129]   04/11/1999   **ME**

Claridge, Mr J, Dip, Team Leader Acquisitions.
[64969]   05/10/2005   **AF**

Clark, Mr A, BA, Reference and Information Librarian City of York.
[10017882]   21/10/2010   **ME**

Clark, Mr A, MA (Hons), School Librarian, Kincorth Academy.
[10002514]   01/05/2007   **ME**

Clark, Mr A J, BSocSci MCLIP, Retired. Continuing interest in library design. Member Designing Libraries Advisory Board.
[22092]   09/01/1974   **CM17/03/1976**

Clark, Ms B, BA (Hons) MA PgCert, L. Res. Manager, Notre Dame R. C. Girls School, London.
[10016708]   29/04/2010   **ME**

Clark, Mr B F, BLib MCLIP, Chief Librarian, Sandwell MBC.
[29937]   09/11/1978   **CM09/11/1980**

Clark, Ms B L, BA (Hons) PgDip IM, Head of Electronic Services and Deputy Head Teaching & Research Support, University of London.
[10035683]   29/10/2014   **ME**

Clark, Miss C, MA MCLIP,
[10013345]   16/04/2009   **CM09/11/2011**

Clark, Ms C J, BEd MLib MCLIP, Upper School Librarian, American International School of Budapest, Hungary. (Retired!).
[26089]   21/07/1976   **CM09/10/1979**

Clark, Mr D, MCLIP, Sci. & Tech. Librarian, University of Derby.
[29019]   21/03/1977   **CM21/03/1980**

Clark, Mr D A, BA DipLib MCLIP, School Librarian, Tarbert/Argyll, Argyll & Bute Council.
[36722]   10/11/1983   **CM23/03/1994**

Clark, Mr D H, MCLIP, Life Member.
[2725]   12/10/1944   **CM01/01/1952**

Clark, Mrs D W, MCLIP, Head Reference Serv., House of Commons L. London.
[780]   23/09/1968   **CM02/03/1973**

Clark, Miss E E, BA (Hons) MSc (Econ),
[10006527]   30/10/2007   **ME**

Clark, Mrs F, BA, Unwaged.
[10023320]   01/04/1996   **ME**

Clark, Mrs F H, BA MCLIP, L. & Information Serv. Mgr, Central Library, Aberdeen City L.
[30394]   07/02/1979   **CM31/08/1983**

Clark, Mr H G, MCLIP, Retired.
[2728]   11/10/1941   **CM01/01/1952**

Clark, Miss H K, Student.
[10031764]   01/10/2013   **ME**

Clark, Mr H M, Academic Liaison Librarian, Bradford College.
[49269]   20/10/1993   **ME**

Clark, Miss J E, MSc BA MCLIP, Retired.
[2737]   13/10/1970   **CM01/10/1972**

Clark, Mrs J M, MCLIP, Local Studies & Archives Assistant, Oldham
Council.
[28988]   20/02/1978   CM31/08/1983
Clark, Mrs K, BLib MCLIP, Information Manager, Royal College of
Nursing, London.
[22511]   13/05/1974   CM24/11/1977
Clark, Miss K R, MA BA (Hons), School Librarian/LRC Manager, Castle
Hill High School.
[10017039]   18/06/2010   ME
Clark, Miss L, MA, Student, Leeds Beckett University.
[10033407]   22/10/2014   ME
Clark, Mrs L C, MBA PgD BA (Hons), Student, CILIP Scotland.
[10035267]   03/10/2014   ME
Clark, Mrs L J, BA (Hons) DipLib Dip MCLIP, Senior Health
Improvement Specialist: Knowledge Management, Stoke-on-Trent
City Council.
[34570]   04/01/1982   CM09/03/1985
Clark, Mrs L M, BA MCLIP, Customer Services Librarian, Stockport
College, Stockport.
[40421]   22/01/1987   CM15/08/1990
Clark, Mrs L M, BA MCLIP, Resource Development Librarian,
Motherway Library, North Lanarkshire Ls.
[31261]   12/10/1979   CM01/07/1989
Clark, Mrs M E, MCLIP, Life Member.
[2741]   01/01/1957   CM01/01/1961
Clark, Miss P, MA, Student, University of Strathclyde.
[10019055]   13/04/2011   ME
Clark, Mrs R E, MA (Hons) DipLIS MCLIP,
[54353]   26/11/1996   CM20/09/2000
Clark, Mr R M, BA DipLib MCLIP, External Research Database
Manager, Slaughter & May, London.
[37702]   19/10/1984   CM02/06/1987
Clark, Mr R M, BA (Hons), Student.
[10017883]   21/10/2010   ME
Clark, Mrs S, MA (Hons) PgDip MCLIP, Assistant Librarian, University of
the West of England, Bristol.
[63154]   13/02/2004   CM10/07/2009
Clark, Mrs S A, BA (Hons) DipLib MCLIP, L. Manager, Cornwall CC.
[56357]   16/06/1998   CM21/05/2008
Clark, Mrs S C, Student, Cornwall Library Service.
[10032509]   10/12/2013   ME
Clark, Miss S C, BA (Hons) MA, Student, Robert Gordon University.
[10017771]   06/10/2010   ME
Clark, Mrs S E, BA (Hons) MCLIP, Retired.
[2751]   16/07/1968   CM26/06/1974
Clark, Mr T J, MA (Hons) MSc,
[65014]   05/10/2005   ME
Clark, Miss W, BA (Hons) MCLIP, Audience Development Officer, Essex
County Council, Brentwood Library.
[49119]   06/10/1993   CM18/11/1998
Clarke, Mr A, BA (Hons) MA MSc, Repository Support Librarian,
University of Bath.
[10011203]   02/10/2008   ME
Clarke, Mrs A, MCLIP, Retired.
[2752]   08/02/1962   CM01/01/1966
Clarke, Miss A, Student, Aberystwyth University.
[10032437]   04/12/2013   ME
Clarke, Miss C J, MCLIP, Systems Librarian, NWHC, Nuneaton.
[63507]   16/06/2004   CM27/01/2010
Clarke, Ms D A, BA DipLib MCLIP, Joint Digital Content Manager and
Metadata Librarian, Oxford Brookes University Library, Oxford.
[51784]   01/07/1995   CM09/07/2013
Clarke, Rev F A, DMS MCMI PgDipTheol MCLIP, Unwaged.
[2765]   20/01/1964   CM01/01/1967

Clarke, Ms F E, BA PgDip, Assistant Subject Librarian (BELL)/Weekend
Supervisor, University of Chester.
[61731]   29/10/2002   ME
Clarke, Mrs G J, BA, Open Learning Centre Mgr, Gillotts School,
Henley-on-Thames, Oxon.
[37056]   12/01/1984   ME
Clarke, Mrs G L, ACLIP,
[10012546]   19/12/2008   ACL22/08/2012
Clarke, Miss J, BA DMS MCLIP, Career Break.
[25021]   01/11/1975   CM27/06/1980
Clarke, Mrs J L, MCLIP, Head of L. & Information Serv., Holman,
Fenwick Willan, London.
[23042]   23/10/1974   CM27/10/1977
Clarke, Mrs J M, BA (Hons), Librarian, Altrincham Grammar School for
Boys, Altrincham, Cheshire.
[52726]   28/11/1995   ME
Clarke, Mrs L A, BA (Hons) PGCE MCLIP, School Librarian, Lea Forest
Primary Academy, Birmingham.
[42268]   13/10/1988   CM26/11/1997
Clarke, Mrs L E, BA (Hons) MCLIP, Employed (Part-time), Cheshire
County Council Bibliographical Serv., Chester.
[10001631]   11/10/1984   CM15/11/1988
Clarke, Mr M E, BA MCLIP, Tri-Borough Director of Libraries and
Archives, Royal Borough of Kensington & Chelsea.
[39336]   17/01/1986   CM18/07/1991
Clarke, Miss M E, BA (Hons) MSc MA MCLIP,
[56916]   04/11/1998   CM15/05/2002
Clarke, Ms P M, BA MCLIP, Group Child. Librarian, Redcar Central
Library, Redcar & Cleveland Borough Council.
[19882]   01/01/1973   CM18/01/1979
Clarke, Mr P R, BSc MCLIP, Consultant.
[2788]   12/08/1968   CM20/07/1972
Clarke, Mrs R, LRC Manager, St Edwards College, Liverpool.
[64299]   23/02/2005   ME
Clarke, Mrs R M, BA (Hons) MCLIP,
[38199]   28/01/1985   CM24/05/1995
Clarke, Mrs S B, MA DipLib MCLIP, School Librarian, Tormead School,
Guildford.
[35411]   03/10/1982   CM07/07/1987
Clarke, Mrs S D, BSc (Hons) MCLIP, Senior Researcher, Warren
Partners.
[59852]   17/10/2001   CM10/03/2011
Clarke, Mrs S P, BA FCLIP, Retired.
[2793]   03/10/1949   FE20/01/1999
Clarke, Mr T, MBA CITP FRSA, Branch Assistant, Stoke Community
Librarian, Ipswich.
[10017173]   11/07/2010   AF
Clarke, Ms Z A, BA MA MCLIP, Academic Liaison Manager (Arts &
Sciences), Edge Hill University.
[40320]   10/01/1987   CM13/06/1990
Clarkson, Mr J A J, BA MCLIP, School Librarian, Trinity Academy,
Edinburgh.
[39761]   01/07/1986   CM13/06/1990
Clarkson, Ms M, PgDip, Lib & Know Serv Manager, Croydon Health
Services Library.
[10020764]   03/04/2012   ME
Clarkson, Mrs M A, BA (Hons) MCLIP, Service Development Manager,
Manchester City Council.
[39789]   04/07/1986   CM23/03/1994
Clary, Ms S, Information Assistant, Natural History Museum.
[10022228]   22/01/2013   AF

Clausen, Dr H, Dr. Hist. Ecc. PhD MA MLSc FCLIP, Retired. Chairman of Board of Directors (St Andrew's Roman Catholic Diocesan Library, Copenhagen).
[46818]   05/02/1992   FE21/07/1993

Clavel-Merrin, Ms G M, MLib MCLIP, International Relations, Swiss National Library, Bern, Switzerland.
[27544]   28/04/1977   CM02/03/1983

Clay, Mrs A J, BA (Hons) MCLIP, Bibl. Serv. Officer, Warrington Borough Council Ls., Warrington, Cheshire.
[48955]   02/08/1993   CM27/11/1996

Claydon, Mr T, BA (Hons) MA, Library Assistant, UCL.
[10014076]   18/02/2012   ME

Clayton, Dr D J, BA MA PhD FRSHistS FSA, Hon. Research Fellow, Faculty of Humanities, University of Manchester.
[10015656]   02/10/1974   ME

Clayton, Ms G M, BA DipLib MCLIP, Librarian, Emersons Green, South Glos. Council.
[30310]   16/01/1979   CM24/03/1981

Clayton, Miss J E, BA MCLIP, Retired.
[18169]   04/10/1972   CM03/04/1975

Clayton, Miss J M, BA DLIS MCLIP, Employment not known.
[25242]   03/01/1976   CM17/01/1979

Clayton, Mr P A, FSA FRNS FCLIP DipArch, Retired.
[2817]   14/03/1955   FE01/01/1964

Clayton, Mr R E, BA (Hons) MA MCLIP, County Librarian, Rutland County Council, Oakham.
[48366]   08/12/1992   CM31/01/1996

Clayton, Mrs S M, BA MCLIP,
[34061]   02/09/1981   CM15/09/1983

Clayton, Mrs S P, BA (Hons) MCLIP, Outreah Librarian.
[10006653]   08/01/1979   CM23/09/1982

Clayton, Mrs V A, BA (Hons) MCLIP, Resources & Skills Manager, Sherborne School, Sherborne.
[41294]   30/10/1987   CM14/02/1990

Clear, Mrs F C, BA DipLib MCLIP, Business Manager, Family Information Link, Stockport
[34575]   12/01/1982   CM11/04/1985

Clear, Mrs R L, BA (Hons) MA MCLIP, Librarian, Clifton College Preparatory School, Clifton Bristol.
[56519]   03/08/1998   CM10/07/2002

Cleaver, Mrs A V, MSC MCLIP, Manager, Know-How, Maitland Advisory LLP.
[26991]   05/01/1977   CM30/05/1979

Cleaves, Ms H, BA (Hons) MA, School Librarian, Kingston Grammar School.
[10006658]   11/09/2007   ME

Cleeve, Mr A G, BMus (Hons) MSc, Layclerk and Choir Librarian at Durham Cathedral. Also Library Assistant (Part time), Durham University Library.
[10012051]   12/12/2008   ME

Cleeve, Mrs M L, BA MCLIP, Information Consultant.
[2825]   01/01/1965   CM01/01/1969

Clegg, Mrs A, MA FCLIP, Retired.
[2827]   10/03/1960   FE01/01/1968

Clegg, Mr D, BA (Hons), Group Manager Plymouth.
[10008256]   15/05/1985   ME

Clegg, Ms S J, BA MCLIP, General Serv. Co-ordinator, Glasgow City Council, Mitchell L.
[33964]   15/06/1981   CM22/08/1984

Cloggett, Mrs L A, BA (Hons) MA MCLIP, Reference Librarian, Southampton Central Reference Library.
[55219]   20/08/1997   CM23/01/2002

Cleghorn, Ms F A, MSc,
[21971]   17/01/1974   ME

Clemens, Miss S, MA ACLIP, Project Development Officer, Royal Institution of Cornwall.
[10021947]   05/11/2012   ACL16/01/2014

Clement, Mr A C, MA MCLIP, Information Officer, IMECHE, London.
[62008]   16/01/2003   CM04/10/2006

Clement, Ms E, BA MA MCLIP, Subject Librarian (Peace, Development & Economics, University of Bradford.
[56935]   06/11/1998   RV17/10/2006   CM25/07/2001

Clement, Mrs G E G, FCLIP, Life Member.
[2835]   11/10/1942   FE01/01/1957

Clements, Mrs E R, MCLIP, Retired.
[7670]   15/07/1955   CM01/01/1969

Clements, Mr F A, FCLIP, Retired.
[2838]   15/07/1965   FE27/10/1975

Clements, Mrs G F, BA (Hons) MCLIP, Information & Lifelong Learning Librarian, Hertfordshire County Council.
[40471]   09/02/1987   CM29/03/2004

Clements, Mrs S A, BA (Hons), Service Development Manager, Coventry City Council.
[37050]   04/02/1984   ME

Clemow, Mrs H L, BA (Hons) DipLib, Administrator.
[46083]   01/10/1991   CM14/09/1994

Clemson, Mrs J A, BSc MCLIP, School Librarian, Great Sankey High School, Warrington.
[57645]   14/06/1999   CM09/07/2008

Cleveland, Ms J J, BA (Hons) MSc, PG Student.
[10020402]   11/02/2012   ME

Clifford, Mr B E, BA MA HonFCLIP, Deputy Librarian, University of Leeds.
[25965]   12/04/1976   FE01/04/2002

Clifford, Mrs K M L, BSc (Hons) MSc MCLIP, Senior Information Advisor (Bibliographic & Metadata) Library & Learning Servs., Kingston University, London.
[62714]   03/10/2003   CM21/03/2007

Clifford, Miss S K, MCLIP, Retired.
[2854]   25/08/1948   CM01/01/1967

Clifford-Smith, Mrs A E, BA (Hons) MA, Librarian/ Resource Manager, Plashet Comprehensive School.
[10032634]   23/12/2013   ME

Clift, Mrs C, BA (Hons) MA MCLIP, Librarian, Rutlish School, Merton.
[2855]   14/02/1964   CM01/01/1968

Clift, Mrs G, BA, LRC Manager part-time. Jobshare, Ashville College, Harrogate.
[10012964]   17/03/2009   ME

Cliftlands, Mr A D, BA (Hons) DipLib, Senior Information Specialist, MHRA, London.
[43241]   13/10/1989   ME

Climpson, Mr D G, MA MCLIP, Retired.
[2857]   01/10/1968   CM01/01/1971

Clinton, Ms P, BA (Hons) PgDip MCLIP, School Librarian.
[10020200]   17/08/1990   CM25/01/1995

Clipsham, Mrs G, BA MCLIP, Reading Development Coordinator, Bucks CC, Aylesbury HQ.
[27488]   25/02/1977   CM12/06/1979

Clitheroe, Mr F R, BA MCLIP, Literary Editor, The Lymes Press, Staffordshire.
[2862]   07/06/1963   CM01/01/1971

Clogg, Ms M J, BSc DipLib MCLIP, Retired.
[31587]   01/11/1979   CM13/10/1982

Cloke, Mr N, Information Professional, Ministry of Defence.
[10034153]   10/06/2014   ME

Close, Ms S, BLib MCLIP, Lib. & Information Serv. Manager, BT Group, Ipswich.
[27929]   01/10/1977   CM10/08/1988

165

Clough, Miss H, MCLIP, Learning and Teaching Librarian, The Open University, Milton Keynes.
[59843]   16/10/2001   **CM11/03/2009**

Clouston, Mr R W, BSc MCLIP, Retired.
[2870]   03/11/1967   **CM01/01/1971**

Clover, Mr D C, BCom DipLib MA MCLIP, Associate Director, Modern Collections, Senate House Library, University of London.
[57646]   14/06/1999   **CM17/09/2008**

Clower, Mrs M J, BA DIPLIB MCLIP, Librarian, Royal Russell School, Croydon.
[24692]   06/10/1975   **CM26/11/1982**

Clucas, Mrs M G, BA DipLib MCLIP, Retired.
[2873]   27/02/1970   **CM01/11/1972**

Cluer, Mrs M, Assistant Librarian, Part-time.
[10001244]   03/02/2007   **ME**

Cluett, Mr A R, BA (Hons) MA,
[10033395]   07/03/2014   **ME**

Cluley, Mrs J, MA (Hons), Library Assistant, Heriot Watt University.
[10033903]   12/05/2014   **AF**

Coady, Miss E, MCLIP, Performing Arts Librarian, Dorking, Surrey CC.
[65464]   23/02/2006   **CM07/07/2010**

Coast-Smith, Ms C T, PgDipIM BA (Hons) MCLIP, Librarian, Surrey County Council.
[10007010]   19/08/1985   **CM27/02/1991**

Coates, Dr A E, MA DPhil DipLib MCLIP, Assistant Librarian – Rare Books, University of Oxford, Bodleian Library.
[37575]   08/10/1984   **CM25/05/1994**

Coates, Miss C, BA (Hons), Library Cluster Manager, West Sussex County Council.
[10031929]   15/10/2013   **ME**

Coates, Ms C M, MA MCLIP, Reitred.
[2884]   28/01/1969   **CM01/07/1972**

Coates, Mr E J, HonFLA FCLIP, Retired.
[2885]   14/05/1934   **FE01/01/1943**

Coates, Mr M J, BSc MA, Information Specialist, Cabinet Office, London.
[10000888]   20/11/2006   **ME**

Cobb, Mrs A, BA MCLIP, Sch. Lib., East Barnet School, Hertfordshire.
[39897]   06/10/1986   **CM17/10/1990**

Cobb, Miss A J, BA (Hons) MCLIP, Customer Services Manager: Customer Relations, University of Leeds.
[46828]   15/01/1985   **CM24/07/1996**

Cobb, Miss J, BA (Hons) MPHIL, Student, Aberystwyth University.
[10034147]   10/06/2014   **ME**

Cobb, Ms J L, BA DipLib MCLIP, Information Scientist.
[31770]   02/01/1980   **CM29/04/1983**

Cobb, Mrs L V, MCLIP, Learning Resource Manager, Selby High School.
[63247]   22/03/2004   **CM17/09/2008**

Cobb, Mrs M, BA (Hons) DipLIS, Librarian.
[49266]   20/10/1993   **ME**

Cobb, Mr W P C, MCLIP, Life Member.
[2899]   29/03/1948   **CM01/01/1960**

Cobine, Miss L, MLIS, Researcher.
[10018562]   07/02/2011   **ME**

Coburn, Mr A, BA MCLIP, Acquisitions & Cataloguing Librarian, Essex County Council.
[22640]   27/07/1974   **CM24/09/1979**

Cochrane, Mr F, ISO DGA FCLIP, Life Member.
[2903]   19/02/1948   **FE01/01/1956**

Cochrane, Miss F J, BA (Hons) MSc, Information Centre Manager, Weil Gotshal & Manges, London.
[10001507]   23/07/1999   **ME**

Cochrane, Mrs S E, BSc (Hons), Librarian, Preston Lodge High School, Prestonpans.
[10015819]   28/01/2010   **ME**

Cockburn, Miss M, MA (HONS), Library Assistant, Scottish Borders Council.
[10021594]   06/09/2012   **AF**

Cocking, Mrs Y M, MCLIP, Life Member.
[5158]   31/01/1963   **CM01/01/1966**

Cockrill, Mr I W, BA (Hons) MCLIP, Unwaged.
[44802]   05/12/1990   **CM24/05/1995**

Cockroft, Mrs S, ACLIP, Team Leader, Brighouse Library, West Yorkshire.
[10009522]   03/06/2008   **ACL03/12/2008**

Codd, Mr F M, BA (Hons) MSc (Econ) MCLIP, Higher Library Executive, House of Commons Library.
[54387]   02/12/1996   **CM15/01/2003**

Codina, Mrs A, Librarian, Herbert Smith LLP.
[10006404]   17/10/2007   **ME**

Coe, Mrs C E, BA GDL,
[10032321]   18/11/2013   **ME**

Coe, Ms S L, BA (Hons) MCLIP, Information Specialist, Foreign & Commonwealth Office, London.
[38800]   09/10/1985   **CM09/11/2005**

Coffer, Mr J P, BSc (Hons) PgDipIS, Information Specialist, Tobacco Documentation Centre, Brentford.
[48418]   04/01/1993   **ME**

Coffey, Mrs B Z, BSc (Hons) MSc MCLIP, Information Specialist (Customer Services), Royal Society of Medicine.
[43736]   13/12/1989   **CM22/07/1998**

Coffey, Mr M, BA (Hons), Information Manager, HM Courts & Tribunals Service.
[10031826]   08/10/2013   **ME**

Cohen, Ms A, MA, Student, Bar Ilan University School of Information studies, Israel.
[10031955]   15/10/2013   **ME**

Cohen, Ms C, Graduate.
[10018988]   04/04/2011   **ME**

Cohen, Mrs C J, BA DipLib MCLIP, Librarian, Charter Academy, Portsmouth.
[33249]   14/10/1980   **CM08/12/1982**

Cohen, Ms J E, BA (Hons) MSc MCLIP, S02 ALIS Online, Prince Consort's Library, Aldershot.
[43884]   08/02/1990   **CM27/07/1994**

Cohen, Mr M J, BA (Hons) MSc MCLIP, Team Leader – Collections, Queen Mary, University of London.
[57018]   25/11/1998   **CM23/06/2004**

Cohen, Dr P M, BA PhD DipLib MCLIP, Head L. Serv., Dublin Inst. Tech.
[34668]   21/01/1982   **CM16/02/1988**

Cohen, Mrs S, BA (HONS) PGCE PgDip,
[10021660]   24/09/2012   **ME**

Coker, Mrs G, Unwaged.
[10019404]   16/10/1985   **ME**

Coker, Mrs S M,
[65977]   09/08/2006   **AF**

Colborne, Ms T, BA (Hons) MA MCLIP, Assistant Librarian, Rutherford Appleton Laboratory, Harwell.
[46131]   07/10/1991   **CM31/01/1996**

Colbourn, Dr P, BSc PhD MSc (Econ) MCLIP, Retired.
[51195]   23/11/1994   **CM28/10/2004**

Colbourne, Mrs G M, BA MCLIP, Area Librarian, Warwickshire Library & Information Service, Warwick.
[60903]   09/01/2002   **CM22/08/2012**

Colbron, Mrs G E, BA (Hons) MSc MCLIP, School Librarian, Port Glasgow Shared Campus, Port Glasgow.
[10017911]   26/10/2010   **CM16/01/2014**

Cole, Mrs B J, BA MCLIP, Retired health librarian.
[25001]   20/11/1975   **CM14/02/1980**

Cole, Mrs C A, MA MCLIP,
[36420]   05/10/1983   **CM20/01/1987**

Cole, Ms C E, BA MCLIP, Serv. Quality Librarian, NorthamptonshireC. C.
[32409]   27/03/1980   **CM19/10/1984**

Cole, Miss E, BA (Hons) MA, Scholarly Publications Librarian, University Library, Northumbra University, Newcastle.
[10011286]   09/10/2008   **ME**

Cole, Mr G P, BA FHEA MCLIP, Community Engagement & School Support Librarian, University of the West of England, Bristol.
[28277]   09/11/1977   **CM17/04/1980**

Cole, Miss P V M, BA DipLib MCLIP, Policy Officer, Pub. & Comm. Serv. Union, London.
[29616]   16/10/1978   **CM21/12/1981**

Cole, Dr R A, BA (Hons) MLITT PhD MA, Trainee L. & Information Officer, Newcastle City Library, Newcastle.
[10018565]   07/02/2011   **ME**

Cole, Miss W E, BA (Hons) MCLIP, Librarian, Sch. & Related Serv., Rhondda-Cynon-Taf Co. Borough Council.
[45456]   11/02/1991   **CM20/09/2000**

Colehan, Mr P, FCLIP, Life Member.
[2956]   01/01/1941   **FE01/01/1950**

Coleman, Miss A H, BA (Hons) MCLIP, Senior Researcher, Hogan Lovells, London.
[53973]   15/10/1996   **CM18/09/2002**

Coleman, Mrs C, BA MA MCLIP, Assistant Learning Resources Manager, Andover College.
[43528]   01/12/1989   **CM20/11/2002**

Coleman, Mrs C R, BSc (Hons) MSc MCLIP, Clinical Outreach Librarian, Bucks Healthcare NHS Trust, Stoke Mandeville Hospital.
[56909]   04/11/1998   **CM21/05/2003**

Coleman, Mrs G, Information Professional, Ministry of Defence.
[10034745]   12/08/2014   **ME**

Coles, Mrs A M, BA (Hons) DipHE MPhil MCLIP, Tutor Librarian (Goschen Centre). City College, Saltash Rd, Keyham, Plymouth. PL2 2DP.
[25243]   02/01/1976   **CM27/11/1979**

Coles, Mrs I, BA MCLIP, School Librarian, Buckinghamshire County Council, Milton Keynes.
[18127]   03/10/1972   **CM02/10/1975**

Coles, Miss K L, BA, Student, Robert Gordon University.
[10032990]   03/02/2014   **ME**

Coles, Miss L A M, Office Management. Mod, Ministry of Defence.
[10033917]   12/05/2014   **ME**

Coles, Mrs P E, BSc MA MCLIP, Senior Information Scientist.
[10007267]   03/03/2004   **CM08/09/2010**

Coletti, Mrs E, MSc, Library Assistant, Gray's Inn Library.
[10020949]   27/04/2012   **ME**

Coley, Mrs A N M, BA DipLib MCLIP, Librarian, Ravenswood House, Southern Health NHS Foundation Trust.
[40058]   20/10/1986   **CM15/05/2002**

Coley, Mrs C, MLib FCLIP, Retired.
[18435]   16/10/1972   **RV**20/02/2014   **FE03/10/2007**

Colhoun, Ms N A, BA (Hons) BSc (Hons) PGCE, Student, University of Sheffield.
[10035155]   22/09/2014   **ME**

Colinese, Mr P E, BSc AKC FCIS FCLIP, Retired.
[60175]   01/04/1963   **FE02/08/1966**

Collacott, Mrs S M, BLib MCLIP PGCE, Supply Teacher, Cheltenham Bournside School.
[30503]   14/02/1979   **CM13/11/1981**

Collas, Mr S A, BSc DipLib MCLIP FRSA, Lib. & Information Officer, Guille-Alles Library, St Peter Port, Guernsey.
[27267]   15/01/1977   **CM09/01/1981**

Colley, Mr R P G, BA (Hons) DipLIS MCLIP, Unemployed.
[42559]   04/01/1989   **CM17/11/1999**

Collier, Ms D V, BA (Hons), Information & Welfare Officer, British Polio Fellowship, South Ruislip.
[42029]   07/08/1988   **ME**

Collier, Mrs E A, MCLIP, Learning Centre Manager, Northenden Campus, City College Manchester.
[2405]   13/01/1967   **CM05/07/1972**

Collier, Mrs J L, BA MCLIP, Librarian, The William Allitt School, Derbyshire County Council.
[33451]   09/01/1981   **CM17/01/1985**

Collier, Mrs R, BSc (Hons) MA, Information Manager, David Lock Associates, Milton Keynes, Bucks.
[53924]   10/10/1996   **ME**

Collier, Mr R N, Learning Res. Supervisor, Oxford & Cherwell College, Oxford.
[62581]   03/09/2003   **ME**

Collin, Dr M Y C, BA PhD MCLIP, Employment not known.
[4970]   04/03/1964   **CM01/01/1968**

Collinge, Miss N, BSc (Hons), Librarian, Grt Yarmouth College.
[10020728]   29/03/2012   **ME**

Collingwood, Ms L, BA DipLib MCLIP, L. /Res. Centre Manager, Finham Park School, Coventry.
[48945]   02/08/1993   **CM20/09/1995**

Collins, Mr B, BA MCLIP, Retired.
[2992]   23/09/1969   **CM05/02/1973**

Collins, Ms D B, MA, Librarian, Hurstpierpoint College, West Sussex (independent mixed secondary school).
[55469]   14/10/1997   **ME**

Collins, Mrs J, MA (Hons) MSc, Unwaged.
[58370]   31/01/2000   **ME**

Collins, Ms J E L, BA (Hons), Student.
[10017723]   29/09/2010   **ME**

Collins, Mrs N C, BA (Hons), on sabbatical.
[47878]   23/10/1992   **ME**

Collins, Mr P, BA (Hons) MA MCLIP, Librarian, King Ecgbert School, Sheffield.
[58940]   09/10/2000   **CM01/02/2006**

Collins, Mrs P, Medical Librarian, NHS.
[47120]   08/05/1992   **ME**

Collins, Mrs P L, BA MCLIP, ISS Business Change, MOD, London.
[42913]   19/04/1989   **CM16/10/1991**

Collins, Mr S N, BA (Hons) MA MCLIP, Information Specialist, Kingston University.
[52702]   22/11/1995   **CM21/11/2001**

Collins, Miss T A, Student, Aberystwyth University.
[10034435]   11/07/2014   **ME**

Collins, Mrs V, ACLIP, Library Service Adviser, Kirkby in asfield Library.
[10021012]   04/05/2012   **ACL11/04/2013**

Collinson, Mr T, BA (Hons) FRGS FHEA ILTM, Faculty Librarian, University of Portsmouth.
[39496]   07/02/1986   **CM14/09/1994**

Collis, Miss A E, BA MA MCLIP, Librarian, St Antony's College Library, St Antony's College, Oxford.
[10007816]   28/02/2008   **CM16/05/2012**

Collis, Mr R J, DL HonFLA, Deputy Lieutenant of Buckinghamshire, Trustee, Buckinghamshire Community Foundation.
[3009]   06/03/1963   **HFE01/01/1999**

Collison, Mrs A M, DipLib MCLIP, Retired.
[35774]   24/01/1983   **CM02/07/1987**
Collman, Mr S P, BSc,
[10007964]   03/03/2008   **ME**
Colquhoun, Mr H A, FCLIP, Life Member.
[3015]   24/09/1954   **FE01/01/1967**
Colquhoun, Mr J W, LLB MSc, Knowledge Management Manager,
Brodies LLP, Edinburgh.
[60239]   09/04/1990   **ME**
Colquhoun (nee Powell), Mrs G, BA (Hons) MCLIP, Librarian, Uplands
Community College Wadhurst East Sussex.
[37553]   05/10/1984   **CM18/04/1989**
Colson, Miss C, BLS DUT MCLIP, School Librarian, Monkton Senior
School, Bath.
[65346]   12/01/2006   **CM19/11/2008**
Coltart, Mrs I C, MCLIP, Life Member.
[3016]   01/01/1969   **CM26/01/1973**
Colver, Ms L A, BA (Hons), Learning Centre Supervisor,
Wolverhampton University.
[56798]   19/10/1998   **ME**
Comben, Mrs C, BSc DipLib MCLIP, Librarian, RPS Energy, Goldvale
House, 27-41 Church St West, Woking, Surrey. GU21 6DH.
[29155]   17/03/1978   **CM12/05/1981**
Comben, Miss H, BA MA MCLIP, Learning Centre Manager, University
Gloucestershire.
[58104]   27/10/1999   **CM10/07/2002**
Comissiong, Miss B L W, BA DipLib MCLIP, Life Member.
[16785]   01/01/1950   **CM01/01/1961**
Comley, Mr W R, BA DipLib MCLIP, Retired.
[31054]   06/08/1979   **CM22/03/1985**
Common, Miss D J, BSc MCLIP, Retired.
[3024]   20/03/1964   **CM01/01/1967**
Compston, Mrs J L, BA (Hons), Lib. -Educ. Serv., S. E. L. B., Armagh.
[50410]   19/07/1994   **ME**
Compton, Mrs F D, BA MCLIP, Librarian, London Studio Centre,
London.
[38846]   14/10/1985   **CM05/11/1987**
Compton, Miss P J, BA MCLIP, Retired.
[3025]   25/09/1963   **CM01/01/1966**
Compton, Ms R H,
[10009322]   15/05/2008   **ME**
Compton, Mrs S S, BA MCLIP, School Librarian, Dame Alice Owen's
School, Potter's Bar, Herts.
[3199]   01/07/1972   **CM12/01/1976**
Conboy, Ms C M, BEd MCLIP, Librarian, Beds L Serv.
[40297]   19/01/1987   **CM16/10/1989**
Conboy, Miss L, BA (Hons) PgDip, Student.
[10018691]   24/02/2011   **ME**
Concannon, Mr J G, BA (Hons) PgDip MA, Academic Support Librarian
for the London School of Hospitality and Tourism.
[50188]   27/04/1994   **ME**
Condell, Mrs M I, MCLIP, Classroom Assistant, Brighton & Hove
Council.
[12577]   04/10/1971   **CM22/07/1974**
Condon, Mrs J I, BA MCLIP, Retired: Former Learning Resources
Manager.
[3027]   26/09/1969   **CM18/09/1972**
Condon, Mr P, BA MCLIP, Unemployed.
[41792]   08/04/1988   **CM16/10/1991**
Conkey, Miss J M, BEd, Deputy Librarian, Presbyterian Church in
Ireland, Union Theological College.
[10021904]   29/10/2012   **ME**

Conlon, Mrs C, BA (Hons) DipInf, L. Executive, House of Commons
Library, London.
[47976]   29/10/1992   **ME**
Conlon, Mrs K, BSc GradIPM, Sch. Librarian, Palmers Green High
School, London.
[10001328]   06/02/2007   **ME**
Conn, Mrs S, BA (Hons) MSc MCLIP, Information Professional.
[63984]   22/11/2004   **CM10/03/2011**
Connell, Ms M A, MA BSc MCLIP, Information Officer, TWI Ltd,
Cambridge.
[59135]   22/11/2000   **CM10/03/2011**
Connell, Rev M G, MA (Hons) MSc MCLIP, LiaisonTeam Manager,
University of Reading, Berks.
[46296]   24/10/1991   **CM22/03/1995**
Connell, Mr R, BA (Hons) MA PgDip DipILM MCLIP, Business & Social
Sciences Team Leader, Liaison Librarian for Law/Politics &
International Relations, University of Reading.
[59006]   20/10/2000   **CM29/08/2007**
Connell, Miss S, BA MCLIP, Unwaged.
[29157]   05/04/1978   **CM21/11/1982**
Connell, Ms S E, BA DipLib MCLIP, Librarian, Lister Community School.
[37684]   19/10/1984   **CM05/07/1988**
Connelly, Mr J,
[10034776]   14/08/2014   **ME**
Connelly, Mr T J, LLB MSc, Special Collections Reading Room
Manager, National Library of Scotland, Edinburgh.
[10012934]   20/03/2009   **ME**
Conner, Mrs A C, Stock & Web Manager, Flitwick Library, Bedfordshire.
[63920]   03/11/2004   **ME**
Connery, Ms H, ACLIP, Library Services at Home, Birmingham.
[10001478]   26/02/2007   **ACL16/04/2008**
Connick, Mrs H, Development Officer, Plymouth City Council.
[10035302]   07/10/2014   **ME**
Connolly, Miss J, MA BA (HONS), Birth to Five Development Manager
Cultural Services.
[10021900]   31/01/2005   **ME**
Connolly, Mr T M, BA PgDip, Volunteer, Rose Bruford College.
[10012580]   19/02/2009   **ME**
Connor, Mr A J, BSc (Hons), Student, Cranfield University.
[10033292]   28/02/2014   **ME**
Connor, Mrs C A, BA MCLIP, Taxonomies Product Manager,
LexisNexis, London.
[27618]   01/06/1977   **CM22/10/1980**
Connor, Ms H R, Student, Northumbria University.
[10032477]   09/12/2013   **ME**
Connor, Mrs K D, PgCert, Library Team Leader, Perth College.
[10012893]   19/03/2009   **ME**
Connor, Mrs L A, MCLIP, Sch. Lib.
[10012684]   05/03/2009   **CM16/05/2012**
Constable, Mrs C, MA BA (Hons) MCLIP, Information Resources Co-
ordinator, Royal College of Nursing Library, London.
[56815]   20/10/1998   **CM17/09/2008**
Constable, Mrs L, BA (Hons) MCLIP, Senior Manager, Dorset Library
Service, Dorset County Council.
[18116]   02/10/1972   **CM01/07/1975**
Constance-Hughes, Dr R M, BA (Hons) PhD, Blackbrook Estate,
Monmouthshire.
[62533]   06/08/2003   **ME**
Conway, Mrs K J, BA MA MCLIP, Help Services Team Manager,
Sheffield Hallam University.
[42963]   10/05/1989   **CM15/09/1993**
Conway, Mrs M A, BA MCLIP, Librarian Glasgow Life Glasgow
Libraries.
[35262]   07/10/1982   **CM27/05/1992**

Conway, Mr P S, OBE BA MIMgt MILAM FCLIP FRSA, Retired.
[3048]   02/05/1968   **FE21/11/2001**

Conyers, Dr A D, MA MCLIP, Retired.
[3049]   11/10/1965   **CM01/01/1969**

Cook, Ms A, BA (Hons) MLitt PgDip, Assistant Liaison Librarian, Arts &
Humanities Liaison, Newcastle University Library.
[10011828]   18/11/2008   **ME**

Cook, Miss A C, BA PgDip, Senior Assistant Librarian, Kings College.
[10014739]   07/09/2009   **ME**

Cook, Miss B A, BA MCLIP, L. & Information Officer, Dundee City
Council.
[25861]   01/04/1976   **CM15/01/1981**

Cook, Ms C, School Librarian, Park View School: The Academy of
Mathematics & Science.
[10013591]   08/05/2009   **ME**

Cook, Mrs C C, BA MCLIP, Retired.
[18230]   04/10/1972   **CM22/12/1974**

Cook, Mr D, BA DipLib MCLIP, Global Intranet Content Manager,
Huntsman Pigments, Billingham to 2011.
[34787]   11/02/1982   **CM11/11/1986**

Cook, Mrs E F, Area Super. for North and East Wiltshire Libraries,
Chippenham Library, Wiltshire.
[64852]   25/07/2005   **AF**

Cook, Ms F S, MCLIP, Librarian, Cheney School, Oxford.
[30899]   12/06/1979   **CM09/07/1981**

Cook, Mr G C, BSc MSc, Unwaged.
[10018776]   09/03/2011   **ME**

Cook, Mrs H J, BA MCLIP, Librarian, Angus Council, Forfar.
[29860]   08/10/1978   **CM15/08/1983**

Cook, Mr I N, MCLIP, Information Manager, Communication Workers
Union, London.
[3058]   01/01/1972   **CM03/04/1975**

Cook, Mrs J A, Unwaged.
[44758]   15/11/1990   **ME**

Cook, Mrs K M, ACLIP, Part-time Library Assistant, Scone Library,
Perth, Scotland.
[10020498]   21/02/2012   **ACL09/09/2013**

Cook, Mrs K S M, BSc (Econ) MCLIP, Retired.
[50152]   01/04/1994   **CM06/04/2005**

Cook, Mrs L J, Unemployed.
[45328]   10/10/1990   **AF**

Cook, Miss M, MA, Graduate Library Trainee, The Codrington Library.
[10035276]   03/10/2014   **ME**

Cook, Mr M, BA (Hons) MCLIP, Public Health Specialist (Evidence,
Knowledge, Cancer).
[10013666]   15/05/2009   **CM12/09/2012**

Cook, Mrs M M, BA, Team Leader (Children's Literacies and Arts)
Springvale Resource Centre, Saltcoats.
[10019280]   23/11/1993   **CM24/09/1997**

Cook, Ms N, BA, Library Assistant.
[10022034]   20/11/2012   **AF**

Cook, Mrs R L, BA (Hons) MLib MCLIP, Career Break.
[49375]   01/11/1993   **CM21/05/1997**

Cook, Mr S, BA (Hons) MA, Assistant Librarian, Royal College of
Obstetricians & Gynaecologists.
[57867]   01/10/1999   **ME**

Cook, Mrs S, MCLIP HonFCLIP, Customer Serv. Manager, Central
Library, Sheffield.
[18577]   23/09/1968   **HFE02/09/2010**

Cook, Mrs S, BSc Econ MCLIP, E-Learning Advisor, Swansea University
/ JISC RSC Wales.
[65231]   25/11/2005   **CM09/07/2013**

Cook, Miss V C, BA (Hons), O C L C Account Manager, Scotland,
Ireland, Wales.
[38156]   24/01/1985   **ME**

Cooke, Ms A J, e-learning Manager, Blackburn College.
[10002941]   31/01/2007   **CM06/05/2009**

Cooke, Mrs C, BAHons DipLib PGCE MCLIP PGCer, Systems Librarian,
Anglo European College of Chiropractic, Bournemouth.
[47749]   16/10/1992   **CM31/01/2007**

Cooke, Miss C D, MCLIP, Retired.
[3075]   26/03/1960   **CM16/03/1965**

Cooke, Miss C M, MA ALCM FCLIP, Senior Business Systems Analyst,
Marylebone Library, Westminster City Council.
[29617]   02/10/1978   **RV12/09/2012   FE29/03/2006**

Cooke, Miss F, MA (Hons) PgDip, Careers Information Adviser,
University of Edinburgh.
[10032035]   22/10/2013   **ME**

Cooke, Mr I C, BA (Hons) MA, Curator, politics & International Studies,
The British Library.
[55515]   16/10/1997   **ME**

Cooke, Mrs J S, BA (Hons), L. and Information Co-ordinator, Isle of
Wight Council L. Serv., Newport, Isle of Wight.
[58535]   24/03/2000   **ME**

Cooke, Dr L, PhD MA MCLIP FHEA CLTHE, Senior Lecturer in
Information & Knowledge Mgmt, Loughborough University.
[28533]   19/01/1978   **CM22/04/1992**

Cooke, Mr P, BA, Junior Library Assistant, Aberystwyth University.
[10021716]   03/10/2012   **ME**

Cooke, Mrs R, MCLIP,
[10007028]   27/04/2001   **CM15/07/2014**

Cooke Holmes, Mrs F, BA MCLIP, Sch. Librarian, Valley Park School,
Maidstone.
[43266]   12/10/1989   **CM14/11/1991**

Cookey, Mrs E, BSc, Director, The Grove Library Services.
[10031580]   04/09/2013   **ME**

Cook-Mcanoy, Mrs P M, BA MLib DMS MIMgt, Events & Comm.
ManagementTeam GCHQ, Cheltenham.
[28280]   01/10/1977   **CM13/02/1980**

Cooksey, Ms J, BA (Hons) DipILS MCLIP, Subject Lib. :Languages, Film
Studies, English Studies & Sociology, Oxford Brookes University.
[48655]   02/04/1993   **CM20/09/2000**

Cooksley, Mrs H C, MA (Cantab) MSc MCLIP, Subject Librarian,
University of Bath.
[65139]   03/11/2005   **CM10/11/2010**

Coombe, Mrs A R, BScEcon MSc, Information Specialist, West
Midlands Deanery, Birmingham Res. Pk.
[51259]   12/12/1994   **ME**

Coombes, Miss T, BSc MCLIP, Prison Librarian, Wormwood Scrubs,
London Borough of Hammersmith & Fulham.
[32506]   07/05/1980   **CM21/03/1984**

Coombs, Ms J, BA MA MCLIP, Academic Team Manager, De Montfort
University.
[10023160]   30/01/2014   **ME**

Coombs, Miss L, MA MCLIP, Librarian, Tresham college, Kettering.
[10015289]   30/10/2009   **CM27/03/2014**

Cooper, Mr A, MSc DipLib, Retired.
[3105]   01/01/1970   **CM01/01/1972**

Cooper, Mr A B, MLS MCLIP, Retired.
[3106]   05/02/1962   **CM01/01/1965**

Cooper, Mrs A L, BA MCLIP, Outreach Officer, Enfield Library and
Museum Service.
[37327]   02/07/1984   **CM23/03/1993**

Cooper, Mrs C M, BA DipLib MCLIP, Community & Sch. Librarian,
Ullapool.
[60698]   03/02/1983   **CM04/04/1986**

Cooper, Mrs E, BA DipLIS MCLIP, College Librarian, New College, Telford.
[10010643]   01/10/1974   **CM30/04/1994**
Cooper, Mrs E, MCLIP, Life Member.
[3113]   07/10/1959   **CM01/01/1964**
Cooper, Mr E, FCLIP, Retired.
[18578]   01/01/1954   **FE06/11/1975**
Cooper, Ms G M M, BA (Hons) MLIS, Department of Information Services, House of Commons, London.
[10013852]   04/06/2009   **ME**
Cooper, Ms G S, PgDipLib MCLIP, Cataloguer, British Library, Boston Spa.
[33600]   22/01/1981   **CM26/01/1984**
Cooper, Ms H A, LLB PGCE, Librarian, King Henry VIII School.
[10035245]   01/10/2014   **ME**
Cooper, Mrs H M, MA MCLIP, Life Member.
[7164]   08/03/1953   **CM01/01/1956**
Cooper, Mr J B, MA MCLIP, Retired.
[3121]   01/01/1949   **CM01/01/1954**
Cooper, Mrs J C, BA (Hons) PGCE PgDipIS, Librarian, TWI Ltd, Cambridge.
[47794]   19/10/1992   **ME**
Cooper, Mrs J H, BA (Hons) DipIS MCLIP, Careers Information Officer, School of Oriental & African Studies (SOAS).
[51004]   08/11/1994   **CM23/07/1997**
Cooper, Mrs J M, BA MA MCLIP, Librarian, West Berkshire Council.
[31300]   11/10/1979   **CM12/02/1982**
Cooper, Mrs K, BA MCLIP, Librarian, Cornish Studies Library, Cornwall County Council.
[40276]   29/11/1986   **CM18/07/1991**
Cooper, Mr K R, HonFCLIP, Hon. Fellow.
[60774]   24/03/1988   **HFE24/03/1988**
Cooper, Miss L A, FCLIP, Retired.
[3125]   08/11/1969   **FE09/11/2005**
Cooper, Mrs L D, MPhil MCLIP, Retired.
[3126]   10/01/1968   **CM01/01/1971**
Cooper, Mrs L J, BA (Hons) MA MCLIP, Deputy Librarian, The Institution of Structural Engineers.
[56821]   23/10/1998   **CM25/01/2011**
Cooper, Miss M I, BA FCLIP MBA, Life Member.
[3128]   26/09/1949   **FE01/01/1961**
Cooper, Mr M R, BA ACLIP, Senior Library Assistant, Health Servs. Library, Royal Hallamshire Hospital, Sheffield.
[10019636]   12/08/2011   **ACL09/09/2013**
Cooper, Ms N F, BA (Hons) PgDipLib, Stock and Distribution Coordinator, Cambridgeshire C. C.
[43945]   28/02/1990   **ME**
Cooper, Miss O F, MCLIP, Life Member.
[3129]   29/03/1946   **CM01/01/1952**
Cooper, Miss P I, MCLIP, Retired.
[3131]   16/02/1949   **CM01/01/1955**
Cooper, Mrs S J, BA (Hons) DipLib MCLIP, Res. Centre Librarian, Brighouse High School.
[32269]   12/01/1980   **CM22/03/1995**
Cooper, Mrs S W, BA (Hons) DipLIM MCLIP, Child. Librarian, Wrexham Library.
[54156]   07/11/1996   **CM19/05/1999**
Cope, Mr A, BA (Hons), Repository Officer, De Montfort University.
[61865]   22/11/2002   **ME**
Cope, Mr B E, MCLIP DMS, Retired.
[20187]   01/02/1973   **CM18/07/1975**
Cope, Mrs E C, BA MCLIP, Content Delivery Manager, Leeds Beckett University.
[64928]   13/09/2005   **RV30/04/2014**   **CM10/03/2011**

Cope, Mrs Y M, MCLIP, Retired.
[18382]   18/10/1972   **CM18/07/1975**
Copeland, Mr C, Digital Development Officer, Central Library.
[10021680]   27/09/2012   **AF**
Copeland, Mrs K A, BA (Hons) ACLIP, Assistant in Charge, New Mills Library.
[10022221]   22/01/2013   **ACL09/07/2013**
Copeland, Dr S M, MA MPhil PhD DipLib MCLIP, Information Resource Manager, Robert Gordon University, Aberdeen.
[34167]   08/10/1981   **CM17/11/1985**
Copland, Mr I C, MCLIP, Retired.
[3145]   26/09/1963   **CM01/01/1970**
Coppendale, Ms L M, BA (Hons) DipIS MCLIP, Librarian, Danum Academy, Doncaster.
[52131]   05/10/1995   **CM17/03/1999**
Coppins, Mr M, Job Seeking.
[50155]   13/04/1994   **ME**
Copsey, Mr D J, MA DipLib FCLIP, Independent Consultant.
[3149]   05/10/1971   **RV27/08/2014**   **FE07/09/2005**
Corben, Miss L M, BA MCLIP, Team Librarian, Nottingham City L. and Information Serv., Nottingham.
[24411]   07/08/1975   **CM30/01/1978**
Corbett, Miss A, BSc, Student.
[10033412]   11/03/2014   **ME**
Corbett, Mrs F, MSc, Digital Resources Officer, Northumberland County Council.
[10006804]   10/12/2007   **ME**
Corbett, Miss H L, BLib MCLIP, Librarian, Department of Health & Social Services & Public Safety, Belfast.
[38512]   07/05/1985   **CM20/09/1995**
Corbett, Mrs P C, MLib MCLIP, Principal Libraries & Arts Officer, Library H. Q Flintshire County Council.
[23607]   20/01/1975   **CM24/07/1978**
Corbett, Mr S J, BA DipLib MCLIP, Content Management Librarian, Chartered Inst. of Personnel & Devel London.
[30140]   15/01/1979   **CM14/05/1981**
Corble, Ms A R, BA MA, Student, Goldsmiths, University of London.
[10021348]   19/07/2012   **ME**
Corby, Mrs R J, BA MCLIP, Branch Librarian, Torbay L. Serv., Paignton, Devon.
[36199]   04/07/1983   **CM11/12/1989**
Corcoran, Mrs J, BSc, L. Assistant, L. Support Unit, Inverness.
[10006782]   13/12/2007   **ME**
Cordell, Miss H, BA MA MSc MCLIP, Retired.
[3154]   11/10/1971   **CM14/11/1973**
Cordes, Mr C, MCLIP, Strategic Manager Library Operations, Walsall Metropolitan Borough Council.
[3156]   01/01/1971   **CM29/07/1974**
Cordiner, Miss M, BSc MCLIP, Head of Library Services, University of London.
[24332]   12/07/1975   **CM03/10/1977**
Corea, Mrs I, BA MCLIP, Retired.
[18925]   12/08/1950   **CM01/01/1963**
Cork, Miss L J, BA (Hons), Senior Library Assistant, Shoreham Library.
[10032267]   12/11/2013   **AF**
Cormie, Ms V H, MSc MCLIP, Senior Academic Liaison Librarian, University of St Andrews.
[43578]   09/11/1989   **CM22/01/1997**
Cornell, Ms E, BEd DipLib MCLIP, Retired.
[38415]   15/04/1985   **CM09/08/1988**
Cornhill, Mrs J, BA (Hons) MA MCLIP, Self-employed.
[10006302]   10/10/2007   **CM12/09/2012**
Cornick, Mrs R, BA (Hons) MCLIP, Grad. Librarian,
[48246]   17/11/1992   **CM21/05/1997**

Cornish, Mr A L, BA DipLib MCLIP, Senior Librarian, Luton Central
Library.
[10001567]   01/06/1979   **CM08/07/1983**
Cornish, Rev G P, BA FCLIP, Copyright Consultant/Life member.
[3174]   24/05/1968   **FE27/07/1994**
Cornish, Mrs J, MCLIP, Stock & Reader Development Librarian.,
Hertfordshire County Council., Hemel Hempstead Library.
[64440]   30/03/2005   **CM28/01/2009**
Cornish, Mrs S R, BA DipLib MCLIP, Serv. Development Manager –
Social Inclusion, Royal Borough of Kensington & Chelsea.
[36306]   01/10/1983   **CM20/01/1987**
Cornmell, Mrs S, BA (Hons) PgDipLib LLB (Hons), Information
Specialist, Health & Safety Executive, Bootle.
[35444]   11/10/1982   **ME**
Coroon, Mrs J, BA (HONS) PgDip, Learner Support Tutor,
Aberdeenshire Libraries.
[10020761]   03/04/2012   **ME**
Corp, Miss F A N, BA MCLIP, Life Member.
[3176]   14/03/1963   **CM01/01/1968**
Corr, Mr S, Library Assistant, Enniskillen Library, Enniskillen.
[10022137]   08/01/2013   **AF**
Corrales Siodor, Mr F R, DipHE, Lib. Shelver.
[63798]   04/10/2004   **ME**
Corrall, Prof S M, MA DipLib MBA MSc FCLIP FCMI HonFCLIP, Prof. &
Chair, Lib. & Information Science, University of Pittsburgh, USA.
[24068]   19/04/1975   **HFE30/09/2012**
Correia, Prof A M R, PhD HonFCLIP, Prof., ISEGI/UNL, Lisbon.
[53437]   01/07/1996   **HFE09/04/1991**
Corrigan, Mrs M, BA (Hons) MA MCLIP, Assistant Lib, University of
Ulster.
[50687]   10/10/1994   **CM19/05/1999**
Corrigan, Mrs M, LLCM (TD) MCLIP, Retired.
[3183]   19/01/1967   **CM01/01/1970**
Cosgrove, Mrs C M, BSc (Hons) BA MCLIP FEi, Knowledge and
Information Manager, Energy Institute, London.
[28471]   09/12/1977   **CM08/12/1982**
Costas, Miss V, BA (Hons) MA MCLIP, Information Professional.
[59696]   08/08/2001   **CM21/06/2006**
Costello, Mrs H, MSc, Information Officer, Scotish Parliament.
[10022318]   05/02/2013   **ME**
Costello, Mrs M, BA (Hons) MCLIP, L. Resource Centre Manager,
Coatbridge High School, North Lanarkshire.
[56986]   18/11/1998   **CM12/09/2001**
Costello, Mrs P, BA (Hons) MCLIP, R&D Senior Policy Analyst, Welsh
Government.
[53560]   22/07/1996   **CM18/03/1998**
Costelloe, Ms L, BA PgDip MSc MCLIP, Development Officer, CILIP
Ireland.
[10001584]   26/02/2007   **CM11/04/2013**
Costigan, Ms A T, BSc (Hons) MSc, Librarian, J B Priestley Library,
University of Bradford.
[10005075]   02/09/1982   **ME**
Cotera, Ms M, BA MCLIP, Executive Assistant – Americas, ACCA
Global.
[56698]   05/10/1998   **CM15/05/2002**
Coton, Ms R L, BA (Hons) MA MCLIP, Deputy Head of Serv., Western
Sussex Hospitals NHS Trust, Worthing.
[51960]   21/08/1995   **CM09/11/2011**
Cotsell, Miss A R, BA (Hons) MCLIP, Senior Lib. Children & Young
People Team, Oxfordshire County Council.
[47772]   14/10/1992   **CM06/04/2005**
Cottam, Ms S, MA BA (HONS), Learning and Teaching Services
Assistant, University of Leicester.
[10020862]   19/04/2012   **ME**

Cotterell, Mr L, Def Comrcl-Comms-IM-1, Ministry of Defence.
[10034746]   12/08/2014   **ME**
Cotterell, Mrs M, Information Manager, Ministry of Defence.
[10035066]   09/09/2014   **ME**
Cotterill, Ms A, BSc MA MCLIP, Transparency and Open Data Lead,
Home Office.
[27941]   02/10/1977   **RV27/06/2006**   **CM31/07/1984**
Cotterill, Mrs L P, BA (Hons) Mclip, Library Manager, East Cheshire
NHS Trust.
[28155]   12/10/1977   **CM18/01/1982**
Cottle, Mr M E, MSc (Econ), Relief Librarian, Crickhowell Library,
Powys.
[10008398]   19/03/2008   **AF**
Coulbeck, Mrs S, BA (Hons) MA, Progression Coach, Grimsby Institute.
[10006645]   11/09/2007   **ME**
Coulling, Ms K R, BA (Hons) DipLib MCQI CQP MCLIP, Retired.
[41915]   18/05/1988   **CM22/07/1998**
Coulshed, Mr N J, BA DipLib, Librarian, Gtr. Manchester West Mental
Health, NHS Found. Trust, Prestwich Hospital.
[39499]   10/02/1986   **ME**
Coulson, Ms K V, BSocSc (Hons) MSc PGCTHE MCLIP FHEA, Head
of the Centre for Achievement and Performance, The University of
Northampton.
[57992]   11/10/1999   **CM15/09/2004**
Coupe, Ms M T, MCLIP, Owner of Child. Day Nursery.
[24635]   01/10/1975   **CM28/12/1977**
Coupland, Mrs C, Student, Aberystwyth Universlty.
[10022483]   11/03/2013   **ME**
Courage, Ms F P, MA, Special Collections Manager, University of
Sussex Library, Brighton.
[57707]   05/07/1999   **ME**
Court, Mrs J E, BA DipLib FRSA FEA, Chair, CILIP CKG Working Party.
Reviews Editor, The School Librarian. Freelance.
[30141]   17/01/1979   **ME**
Court, Mrs R, BA (Hons) MA MCLIP, Information Specialist, University
of Warwick.
[58099]   29/10/1999   **CM15/10/2002**
Courtney, Mrs E M, BA DipLib MCLIP, Part-time Librarian, Richmond
American International University in London, Richmond.
[32151]   01/02/1980   **CM09/08/1983**
Cousins, Mrs A, MCLIP, Retired.
[8839]   12/01/1967   **CM01/01/1970**
Cousins, Mr P C, BA MCLIP, Retired.
[3224]   10/10/1968   **CM01/01/1971**
Coutts, Miss M M, MA MA MCLIP, Retired.
[29941]   24/10/1978   **CM15/01/1981**
Cove, Mr M A, BA (Hons) MCLIP, Library Assistant, Cambridge Central
L.
[64152]   19/01/2005   **CM14/03/2012**
Coveney, Mrs C A, MA MCLIP MCMI, Library Services Manager
Library, the Open University, Milton Keynes.
[53271]   12/04/1996   **CM16/07/2003**
Cowan, Miss L M, BA (HONS) PGCE MA, Senior Library Assistant, St
Hugh's College Library, Oxford.
[10020706]   27/03/2012   **ME**
Cowan, Miss M A, MCLIP, Retired.
[18080]   01/10/1972   **CM14/07/1975**
Cowan, Mr P F, BEd DipLib MCLIP, Libraries & Culture Officer, North
Ayrshire Council.
[37685]   19/10/1984   **CM10/05/1988**
Cowan, Mrs R M E, MA MCLIP, Senior Librarian, Cambs. L., Central
Library.
[42959]   05/05/1989   **CM16/11/1994**

Cowdrey, Mrs A P, School Librarian, Bangor Grammar School.
[59819]   10/10/2001   ME
Cowell, Mrs J F, BSc MA MCLIP, Research Services Manager.
[65350]   01/01/2006   CM13/04/2011
Cowen, Miss N, BA (Hons) MSc MCLIP, Societe Generale, London.
[58195]   16/11/1999   CM09/11/2005
Cowie, Mr C F, BA MCLIP, Retired.
[60180]   10/12/2001   CM01/04/2002
Cowin, Ms P, BA MA MCLIP, Broadcast Media Co-ord. BBC Information
and Archives.
[42243]   17/10/1988   CM22/07/1992
Cowley, Mr J, BA FCLIP, Life Member.
[3254]   10/10/1947   FE01/01/1959
Cowling, Mrs I L, MCLIP, Life Member.
[3258]   16/07/1957   CM01/01/1962
Cowling, Miss J C, BA (Hons), Assistant Librarian, North East Wales
Schools Library Service, Flintshire.
[59651]   12/07/2001   ME
Cowling, Miss N, Sch. Lib. Adviser., Devon County Council, Exeter.
[39503]   12/02/1986   ME
Cowmeadow, Dr N, Local History Officer, AK Bell Library.
[10033635]   07/04/2014   ME
Cowsill, Mrs A C, BA DIP LIB MCLIP, Senior Librarian, Cheshire Educ.
Library, Cheshire.
[31743]   01/01/1956   CM04/10/2004
Cox, Dr A M, FCLIP, Senior Lecturer, Information School, University of
Sheffield.
[10000937]   04/02/1994   FE13/11/2013
Cox, Miss C M, BA, Unemployed.
[39485]   02/02/1986   ME
Cox, Mrs H C, BA DipLib MCLIP, Part-time Team Librarian, Sch. L.
Serv., Norfolk.
[33227]   01/10/1980   CM03/08/1983
Cox, Mrs H J, Learning Resources Facilitator, New College, Stamford.
[10020707]   27/03/2012   AF
Cox, Ms J, BLib MCLIP HonFCLIP, Commissioner for Tourism and
Cultural County Staffordshire County Council.
[34953]   14/05/1982   CM07/02/1986
Cox, Miss J, BA ACLIP, Library User Support Assistant, University of
Surrey.
[10022296]   05/02/2013   ACL27/08/2014
Cox, Miss J C, BA MCLIP, Library Customer Advisor, Wythall Library,
Worcestershire County Council.
[47981]   29/10/1992   CM06/04/2005
Cox, Mr J G E, MCLIP, Retired.
[3281]   18/01/1959   CM01/01/1964
Cox, Mr J J, MA DipLib MCLIP, University Librarian, National University
of Ireland, Galway.
[35183]   04/10/1982   CM20/01/1986
Cox, Mrs J L, BSc (Econ) MCLIP, Stock & Reader Development
Manager, Bexley & Bromley Shared Service.
[45357]   25/10/1990   CM25/07/2001
Cox, Miss J M, BA MCLIP, Stock and Information Services Librarian,
Jubilee Library. Brighton & Hove Council.
[40360]   12/01/1987   CM27/05/1992
Cox, Mrs K A, BA (Hons) MSc MCLIP, Career Break.
[55729]   10/11/1997   CM29/03/2004
Cox, Ms K L, BA (Hons) MA, Assistant Librarian, House of Lords
Library.
[59369]   06/02/2001   ME
Cox, Mrs K L, BA (Hons) DipMS MCLIP, School Librarian, Kings
Monkton School, Cardiff.
[46589]   20/11/1991   CM17/11/1999

Cox, Ms L A, BA DipLib MCLIP, Head of Internal Communications &
Information Mgmnt, Becta.
[40941]   08/09/1987   CM18/07/1990
Cox, Mrs L A, MSc MCLIP, Librarian, ARRB Group Ltd, Australia.
[23190]   05/11/1974   CM12/06/1979
Cox, Miss M, BA (Hons) PGCE, Reading Room Services Co-ordinator,
Shakespeare Centre Library & Arch., Stratford-Upon-Avon.
[10015731]   19/01/2010   AF
Cox, Miss M J, Part-time Student, University of Wales, Aberystwyth,
City of Bristol College.
[64854]   03/08/2005   ME
Cox, Mrs P, ACLIP, Assistant Locality Manager, Dudley Library, Dudley.
[10017533]   02/09/2010   ACL22/08/2012
Cox, Mrs R, BSc DipLib MCLIP, Business Analyst, NISE.
[20011]   06/01/1973   CM31/12/1989
Cox, Mr R D J, MCLIP, Head of Lib & Arch., Faculty of Dance, Trinity
Laban Conservatoire of Music and Dance, London.
[31810]   02/01/1980   CM28/04/1982
Cox, Mrs S E, MA MCLIP, Journals Librarian, St George's Library, St
George's University of London.
[65874]   07/06/2006   CM09/09/2009
Cox, Miss S J, BA (Hons) DipILS MCLIP, Senior Information Officer,
Mayer Brown International LLP.
[49438]   27/10/1993   CM26/11/1997
Cox, Mrs T L, BLS MCLIP, Head of L., Solihull Metropolitan Borough
Council., West Midlands.
[34733]   22/01/1982   CM10/05/1988
Coxall, Mr O, BA (Hons) MA, Outreach Librarian, University of Oxford,
Bodleian Health Care L. s.
[66013]   21/08/2006   ME
Coyle, Mrs M E M, MCLIP, Retired.
[3470]   01/01/1971   CM30/09/1985
Coysh, Miss C A, Reader development & Stock Mgmnt/CCI Lib.
[62186]   10/03/2003   ME
Coyte, Miss J, BA MCLIP, L. Serv. Manager, Lewisham Hospital,
Lewisham Healthcare NHS Trust.
[25740]   03/03/1976   CM21/02/1978
Crabb, Mrs J M, FCLIP, Life Member.
[29118]   23/01/1950   FE01/01/1958
Crabtree, Mrs S A, BSc (Hons) CPhys MCLIP, Knowledge Manager –
Australia, Egon Zehnder International, Melbourne.
[18324]   10/10/1972   CM07/05/1975
Cracknell, Mrs L S, Librarian, Pembroke College, University of Oxford.
[64225]   21/02/2005   ME
Craddock, Mr S M, BA Lib MCLIP, Unwaged.
[39222]   01/01/1986   CM20/03/1996
Cradock, Mrs E W, BA DipLib MCLIP, Library Manager, Cheshire
County Council.
[33492]   13/01/1981   CM09/09/2009
Craig, Mrs A, BLib MSc MCLIP, Team Leader: Community and
Partnerships, University of Worcester.
[23673]   23/01/1975   CM08/08/1980
Craig, Mr A N, MA PgDip, Electronic Resources Officer, Royal Preston
Hospital.
[10021892]   25/10/2012   ME
Craig, Mrs C M, Early Years Librarian., Central Library, Tyne & Wear.
[10020646]   19/03/2012   ME
Craig, Mr J S, Student, University of Strathclyde, Glasgow.
[10011960]   19/03/2009   ME
Craig, Mr R, OBE BA MA MCLIP HonFCLIP, Director, CILIP Scotland.
[18587]   06/05/1966   HFE24/10/2002
Craig, Miss T A, PgDip, Library Assistant, The Mitchell Library,
Glasgow.
[10020687]   26/03/2012   ME

Crane, Mr D P, BA, Grad. Trainee Librarian, Middlesex University.
[10019372]   16/06/2011   **ME**

Crane, Miss K A, BA (Hons), Student, University of Essex.
[10032678]   03/01/2014   **ME**

Crane, Ms R, BA, Student.
[10009221]   06/05/2008   **ME**

Cranmer, Mr C I A, MCLIP, Lib. and Information Officer, City Chambers, Dundee.
[3320]   17/02/1968   **CM01/01/1972**

Cranmer, Mrs J S J, BSc MLS MCLIP, Unwaged.
[28205]   12/10/1977   **CM05/11/1979**

Craven, Mrs E A, BA MA MCLIP, Cataloguer, Literary & Philosophical Society, Newcastle upon Tyne.
[20755]   26/06/1973   **CM28/07/1975**

Craven, Mrs J E, BA (Hons) MA MCLIP, Information Specialist, National Institutefor Health & Care Excellence.
[48521]   02/02/1993   **CM17/11/1999**

Craven, Mr N, MA FSA (SCOT) FCLIP, Retired.
[3331]   30/06/1950   **FE01/01/1972**

Crawford, Dr A, PhD MA MCLIP, Digital Humanities Research Librarian, University of St Andrews.
[34178]   07/10/1981   **CM18/01/1985**

Crawford, Mrs A, MA (Hons), Librarian, West Dunbartonshire Council, Clydebank High School.
[61179]   03/04/2002   **ME**

Crawford, Mr D, MA DipLib MCLIP, School Librarian, Notre Dame H. School, Greenock.
[29159]   13/03/1978   **CM22/03/1984**

Crawford, Mr D S, BA DipLib FCLIP, Emeritus Librarian, McGill University, Montreal, Canada.
[16802]   23/10/1966   **FE26/11/1997**

Crawford, Dr J C, BA MA PhD FCLIP FSA (Scot), Retired.
[3337]   02/10/1963   **FE21/12/1988**

Crawforth, Mrs T M,
[65006]   06/10/2005   **ME**

Crawley, Ms J A, BH MMus MSc MCLIP, Assistant Librarian, University of West of England.
[40323]   05/01/1987   **CM15/09/2004**

Crawshaw, Mr K, BA DLIS MCLIP, Voluntary Sector Trusts for Libraries & Museums and School Governance.
[19644]   30/10/1972   **CM05/09/1975**

Creamer, Mrs L, MA DipLib MCLIP, Data Manager, BDS Ltd, Dumfries.
[24642]   01/10/1975   **CM07/10/1977**

Creaser, Mrs C, BSc CStat, LISU, Loughborough University.
[10000462]   10/10/2006   **ME**

Creasey, Mr J C, MA DipLib MCLIP, Life Member.
[3351]   06/10/1961   **CM01/01/1964**

Creasey, Mr J O, MA MCLIP, Retired.
[3352]   03/10/1956   **CM01/01/1962**

Creaven, Ms T, Unwaged.
[52342]   30/10/1995   **ME**

Creber, Mr J K, BA MCLIP, Retired.
[3354]   28/10/1970   **CM02/08/1973**

Creech, Mr J W, Merlin IHUB Manager, Agusta Westlands.
[10034205]   20/06/2014   **ME**

Cregg, Miss C L, BA (Hons) MCIPD MCLIP, HR Manager, British Nuclear Group, Romney Marsh.
[45589]   02/04/1991   **CM16/11/1994**

Crellin, Ms C J, BA MA MCLIP, Head of Cataloguing, Archives Management Team, Foreign & Commonwealth Office.
[43430]   26/10/1989   **CM29/01/1992**

Crellin, Mr M, BA, Researcher, Grant Thornton UK LLP.
[10035104]   15/09/2014   **ME**

Crennell, Miss C J, BA (Hons) MRes MSc, Collections Assistant, Trade Lit. Collection, Science Museum Library, Swindon.
[10000740]   01/11/2006   **ME**

Cressey, Mr J, BA, Graduate Trainee Library Assistant, University of Reading.
[10035145]   08/10/2014   **ME**

Cresswell, Ms L A, BA DipLib MCLIP, Children's & Young People's Librarian.
[36363]   01/10/1983   **CM19/01/1988**

Creswick, Miss H M, MCLIP, Toy Lib. Manager, Emmanuel Chursh, Northwood.
[28797]   07/02/1978   **CM06/07/1981**

Crew, Mr J R, BSc (Hons) MSc MA MCLIP, Information Services Librarian (Systems), Royal College of Surgeons of England, London.
[66042]   12/09/2006   **CM27/03/2014**

Crickard, Miss M, Bsc Dip, Student, University of Ulster.
[10026221]   13/10/2014   **ME**

Crilley, Ms K, MSc MCLIP, Knowledge Manager, Ministry of Defence, London.
[10006208]   26/09/2007   **CM11/03/1977**

Crilly, Ms J F, BA (Hons) MSc MCLIP, Associate Director and Head of Resources, library services, University of the Arts London.
[32473]   21/04/1980   **CM28/04/1982**

Crimp, Ms J K, MCLIP, Librarian, International School of Aberdeen.
[62805]   24/10/2003   **CM23/01/2008**

Crinnion, Mrs K A, BSc MA MCILIP, Assistant Librarian, Robinson Library, Newcastle University.
[64730]   08/06/2005   **CM11/03/2009**

Cripps, Mrs A E, MA DipLib MCLIP,
[27864]   30/09/1977   **CM01/01/1980**

Critchley, Mr D A, BA (Hons) MCLIP, Senior Librarian – Home Office.
[39035]   29/10/1985   **CM24/03/1992**

Critchley, Mr S M, BA (Hons) MA FHEA, Principal Hill Field Projects, Editor in Chief Ilegedly, Joint Editor ETiC (English Teaching in China).
[46439]   06/11/1991   **CM01/07/1993**

Crocker, Miss T, BSc (Hons) ACLIP, Knowledge Officer, Nabarro LLP, London.
[10007179]   25/01/2008   **ACL18/01/2012**

Crofts, Miss S J, BA DipLib MA MCLIP, Senior Academic Serv. Librarian, University of Greenwich, London.
[44185]   02/07/1990   **CM26/01/1994**

Crofts, Mrs S M Q, BA (Hons) PGCE MCLIP, Lib. -Senior L., Pates Grammar School, Cheltenham.
[20875]   27/08/1973   **CM01/10/1975**

Croghan, Mr A, MA FCLIP, Life Member.
[3392]   01/01/1951   **FE01/01/1966**

Croll, H, MA MCLIP, Retired.
[3396]   19/09/1966   **CM01/01/1969**

Croll, Ms K J, BA (Hons) MSc MCLIP,
[51292]   06/01/1995   **CM20/05/1998**

Crombie, Mr M N, BA (Hons) MSc, Senior/Systems Librarian Edinburgh College.
[10000232]   26/11/2010   **ME**

Cromey, Miss S, MA MA DipLib MCLIP, Oxford Brokes University., Headington Library.
[31238]   02/10/1979   **CM02/10/1981**

Crompton, Miss J H, BA MCLIP, Self-employed.
[32509]   28/04/1980   **CM02/11/1984**

Cromwell, Mr D J, BA (Hons), Student Aberystwyth University.
[10032277]   13/11/2013   **ME**

Cronin, Mrs G, BA (Hons) MSc, User Experience Librarian, Cambridge Judge Business School.
[10031529]   29/11/2013   **ME**

Cronin, Mrs H, BA DipLIS MCLIP, L. Manager, Molesey Library, Surrey. County Council.
[44531] 22/10/1990 **CM24/09/1997**

Cronin, Mr P M, BA DipLIS, Librarian/information officer at British Gas plc, later BG Group plc, 1989-2014.
[10006119] 11/09/2007 **ME**

Cronin, Mr R, MA (Cantab), Student, Northumbria University.
[10018926] 30/01/2014 **ME**

Crook, Rev C, JP BSc DMS FCLIP, Retired.
[3400] 03/09/1964 **FE18/11/1993**

Crook, Miss C M, BA MCLIP, User Services Lib., University of Brighton.
[33549] 20/01/1981 **CM04/07/1986**

Crook, Mr D M, MCLIP, Retired.
[3402] 07/03/1955 **CM01/01/1961**

Crook, Miss L H, BA (Hons) MA, Library Assistant, John Rylands University Library of Manchester.
[58879] 29/09/2000 **ME**

Crookall, Miss D M, MA BA AFHEA, Academic Liaison Librarian, Avril Robarts Library, City Campus, Liverpool John Moores University.
[10017063] 21/06/2010 **AF**

Crookes, Mr R K, BA (Hons) MA MCLIP, Senior Training Specialist (UK, Ireland & Nordic Countries), EBSCO Information Services.
[52382] 26/10/1995 **CM18/11/1998**

Crooks, Miss C, MA (Hons) MA, Assistant Librarian, Royal College of Defence Studies, MOD.
[61571] 02/10/2002 **ME**

Cropley, Mrs J G, BA (Hons) DipLib MCLIP, Managing Consultant, Mouchel Managment Consulting, London.
[18100] 30/09/1972 **CM08/12/1975**

Cropp, Mrs V, MA BA MCLIP, Sixth Form Librarian, The Woodroffe School, Lyme Regis.
[29270] 03/05/1978 **CM18/07/1980**

Cropper, Mr B, MA DipLib MCLIP HonFCLIP, Retired.
[18442] 19/10/1972 **HFE21/10/2004**

Cropper, Miss J L, MCLIP, Stock Librarian, Bibliographical Serv., Chichester WSCC.
[3410] 01/01/1971 **CM31/08/1977**

Crosier, Miss P A, BSc (Hons) DipIS MCLIP MSc, Assistant Academic Librarian, Teesside University.
[48333] 27/11/1992 **RV27/08/2014 CM21/03/2001**

Cross, Mrs A, BLib PGCE FHEA MCLIP, Assistant Head (Information Serv.), Learning & Corporate Support Serv., University of Glamorgan.
[33689] 04/02/1981 **CM28/10/1985**

Cross, Ms E, BA (Hons) MA MCLIP, Senior Assistant Librarian, University of West England.
[54143] 31/10/1996 **CM17/09/2003**

Cross, Mrs F J, BA MCLIP, Information Specialist, Irwin Mitchell.
[65566] 28/02/2006 **CM13/10/2010**

Cross, Miss J A, Documentalist, Amnesty International, London.
[56960] 13/11/1998 **ME**

Cross, Ms S, PgDip MCLIP, School Librarian, Falkirk council.
[10010713] 29/08/2008 **CM10/03/2010**

Cross, Miss S A, BA (Hons) MCLIP, Librarian, Information & Lifelong Learning, Northumberland Co. L. Serv.
[34116] 01/10/1981 **CM16/10/1989**

Cross, Miss S L, BA (Hons), L. Assistant, 5 Boroughs Partnership NHS Trust, Warrington.
[10006121] 11/09/2007 **ME**

Crossen, Dr C E, BA MA PhD, Student, Manchester Metropolitan University.
[10035522] 16/10/2014 **ME**

Crossey, Mr C, BSSc MSc, Assistant Librarian, St Mary's University College.
[10022042] 20/11/2012 **ME**

Crossland, Miss S L, BA (Hons) MA, Site Librarian; Univesity Centre Doncaster.
[59921] 02/11/2001 **ME**

Crossley, Mr L A, Programme Team Senior Officer, Surrey Libraries.
[10020639] 14/03/2012 **AF**

Crossley, Mrs R, ACLIP, Team Library, Calderdale MBC.
[10009537] 03/06/2008 **ACL03/12/2008**

Cross-Menzies, Ms A, BA (Hons) MA ACLIP, LIS Resources Assistant, The University of Chester.
[10020624] 14/03/2012 **ACL27/03/2014**

Crosthwaite, Mrs J E, BScEcon MCLIP, Librarian, Braes High School, Falkirk.
[59654] 13/07/2001 **CM09/11/2005**

Crouch, Miss A L, BA (Hons) MCLIP, Senior Special Collections Cataloguer, Lancs. Co. L. Serv., Preston.
[49752] 01/12/1993 **CM21/03/2001**

Crouch, Ms K E, BA (Hons) MSc MCLIP, Information Officer, College of Law, London.
[10002549] 17/08/1993 **CM19/01/2000**

Croucher, Dr B C, BA (Hons) DipIS, Information Serv. Helpdesk Manager, University Edinburgh.
[50650] 06/10/1994 **ME**

Croucher, Miss M M, BA DipEd MCLIP, Retired.
[3423] 17/02/1972 **CM29/10/1974**

Crow, Mrs E, BA (Hons) DipILS MCLIP, Information Specialist, Wood Mackenzie, Guildford.
[53980] 15/10/1996 **CM20/01/1999**

Crow, Ms U, BA (Hons) PgDipILM, Library Services Manager, Buckinghamshire New University.
[58193] 16/11/1999 **ME**

Crowe, Mrs N J, BA MCLIP, Part-time Local Studies Librarian, Medway Arch. & Local Studies Centre, Medway Council.
[34402] 29/10/1981 **CM07/10/1986**

Crowley, Mrs A V, BA, Library Assistant, Woodhall Library.
[10033593] 01/04/2014 **ME**

Crowley, Miss C, BA (Hons) Dip MA MCLIP, Interloans/Training Support, St Georges Library, London.
[62224] 24/03/2003 **CM10/07/2009**

Crowley, Ms E, BSc (Hons) MSc, Senior Academic Serv. Lib, University of Greenwich Dreadnought Library, London.
[10006327] 02/12/2004 **ME**

Crowley, Mr J, BA, Assistant Librarian, Department of Information Studies.
[10032091] 24/10/2013 **ME**

Crowley, Mrs S A, BLib MCLIP, Library Services Manager, The Library, Binford Place, Somerset CC.
[29562] 01/01/1978 **CM28/09/1984**

Crowley, Mrs S J, MSc, Community L & I Librarian, Chesterfield Library.
[10021078] 29/05/2012 **ME**

Crowther, Ms H M, Learning Resources Manager, Blackpool VI Form College, Blackpool.
[42683] 06/02/1989 **ME**

Crudge, Dr S E, BSc (Hons) MSc MCLIP, Library and Learning Resources Manager, Tresham College of Further and Higher Education.
[57862] 14/09/1999 **RV27/03/2014 CM08/08/2008**

Crumplin, Mr J D, MA MLitt, Cataloguer, Royal Institute of British Architects.
[59299] 31/01/2001 **ME**

Cruse, Ms J E, BA (Hons) Dip Lib, Information Assistant, The University of Law.
[37581] 09/10/1984 ME

Crush, Miss L M, BA, Information Assistant, Student at Aberystwyth University.
[10022853] 30/04/2013 ME

Cruz De Carvalho, Miss N, BA, Student.
[10019738] 02/09/2011 ME

Cryer, Miss N C, BA (Hons), Librarian, English Heritage, Swindon.
[64017] 02/12/2004 ME

Cuadrado Mendez, Mr A, Student.
[10020105] 02/11/2011 ME

Cuff, Mr R H, British Aerospace (Dynamics) Ltd, Filton, Bristol.
[3450] 05/05/1966 ME

Culbertson, Mrs K B, MA DipLib MCLIP, Unemployed.
[36356] 03/10/1983 **CM04/08/1987**

Cull, Ms S E, BA MA, Acquisitions Librarian, Serials, Royal College of Nursing, London.
[37753] 13/10/1984 ME

Cullen, Mrs J R, ACLIP, School Librarian, Ludgrove School, Wokingham.
[61843] 18/11/2002 **ACL06/02/2008**

Cullen, Mr M S, BA, Graduate Library Trainee, Tust Library, Torbay.
[10022108] 18/12/2012 ME

Cullen, Mrs N, BA (Hons) PgDipLIS, Senior Library Assistant, Home L. Serv., North Ayrshire L. Headquarters.
[65336] 11/01/2006 ME

Cullen, Mrs S, BA MSc MCLIP, Senior Library Adviser (Collections).
[64722] 03/06/2005 **CM29/11/2006**

Cullingford, Ms A, BA MA MCLIP, Special Collections Librarian, University of Bradford, J. B. Priestley L.
[46475] 11/11/1991 **CM27/07/1994**

Cumming, Mrs L J, BA MCLIP, Retired.
[23544] 03/01/1975 **CM22/05/1978**

Cummings, Miss A J, MA, Learning Res. Centre Assistant, Derwentside College, Co. Durham.
[55709] 10/11/1997 ME

Cummings, Mr G K, MLS MSc MCLIP, Reader Serv. Librarian, Co. of Los Angeles.
[30609] 27/02/1979 **CM27/02/1981**

Cummings, Ms H K, BSc (Hon) PgDip, Librarian.
[49772] 06/12/1993 ME

Cummings, Miss P D, Information Support Assistant.
[10034744] 12/08/2014 ME

Cummins, Ms S, BEd MCLIP, Lib. /L. Advisor, Sch. L. Serv., London Borough of Tower Hamlets.
[35982] 03/03/1983 **CM23/06/1986**

Cunnea, Mr P A, MA (Hons) PgDipLis, Digital Assets Manager, National Library of Scotland, Edinburgh.
[44929] 18/01/1991 ME

Cunningham, Ms A J, BA, Student, Manchester Metropolitan University.
[10032495] 10/12/2013 ME

Cunningham, Mr G, BA BSc (Econ) FCLIP, Hon. Fellow.
[47152] 01/01/1992 **FE01/01/1992**

Cunningham, Mrs J C, BA (Hons) DipPG (with dist.),
[10015355] 10/11/2009 ME

Cunningham, Mr J P, BA MCLIP, Library Systems Administrator, North Lanarkshire Council.
[29626] 05/10/1978 **CM09/08/1982**

Cunningham, Mrs K A A, MA DipLib, Cataloguing and Metadata Manager, University of Strathclyde Library.
[41589] 25/01/1988 ME

Cunningham, Ms M, MA, Student, Robert Gordon University.
[10035416] 13/10/2014 ME

Cunningham, Mr P, BA MCLIP, Schools Library Service Manager, Suffolk Libraries IPS.
[37491] 01/10/1984 **CM18/07/1991**

Cunningham, Mr R, BA (Hons) MA PgDip, Education Faculty Librarian.
[10020615] 05/04/2013 ME

Curbbun, Mrs C M B, BA MCLIP, Teaching Assistant /Sch. Librarian, Thorley Hill Sch. Hertfordshire.
[36142] 01/07/1983 **CM10/05/1988**

Curley, Mr F A, BA MA, Student, Manchester Metropolitan University.
[10034756] 13/08/2014 ME

Curran, Mrs E R M, BA DipLib MCLIP, Librarian, James Allen's Girls' School, London.
[37342] 06/07/1984 **CM15/05/1989**

Curran, Miss J S, Student, Robert Gordon University.
[10032488] 10/12/2013 ME

Curran, Ms S N K, BA Grad Dip Lib Studies MIT, Librarian, Ministry of Justice, London.
[10006850] 28/01/2011 ME

Currie, Ms A, BA MLIS MSc, Student, University of Glasgow.
[10033958] 14/05/2014 ME

Currie, E, BA, e-government Librarian, LAI, Suffolk C. C., Ipswich.
[44062] 23/04/1990 **CM21/10/1992**

Currie, Mrs J S, BA (Hons), Area Manager, Devon County Council: Devon Libraries.
[57566] 05/05/1999 ME

Currie, Mrs K R, MA DipLib MCLIP, Assistant Learning Centre Manager, City & Islington College, Centre for Lifelong Learning.
[31299] 11/10/1979 **CM10/02/1982**

Currie, Ms P, MA (Hons) MSc Dip IOL, Project Librarian, British School at Athens.
[10008749] 23/04/2008 ME

Currie James, Mrs L A, MCLIP, Librarian, Falkirk Community Trust, Falkirk.
[10000503] 16/10/2006 **CM01/05/2011**

Currington, Mrs H M, BA MCLIP, Retired.
[7216] 02/09/1970 **CM22/08/1973**

Curry, Miss D, FCLIP, Retired.
[3499] 19/03/1942 **FE01/01/1966**

Curry, Mr R J, BA (Hons) MA MCLIP, Head of Academic Development and Delivery, Oxford Brookes University.
[62666] 01/10/2003 **CM29/11/2006**

Curry, Ms S, Inspire support and L. Collab. Specialist (Self-employed).
[3503] 03/07/1969 ME

Curtis, Mrs D J, BA MCLIP DipRSA, L. Serv. Manager, Glos. Hospital NHS Trust.
[22588] 05/07/1974 **RV**22/09/2010 **CM22/08/1977**

Curtis, Mr J, BA, Librarian, Holland Park School.
[10021140] 11/06/2012 ME

Curtis, Ms J A, BA (Hons) DipILS MCLIP, Sub. Librarian, Doncaster College.
[41507] 11/01/1988 **CM21/05/2003**

Curtis, Mr J P, BSc (Hons) DipIM MCLIP, Site Librarian, Shrewsbury and Telford Hospt., NHS Trust, Shrewsbury.
[50389] 13/07/1994 **CM06/04/2005**

Curtis, Mr R, BA MA, Eservices Librarian. Ministry of Justice, London.
[59807] 04/10/2001 ME

Curtis, Mrs R, BA (Hons) MCLIP MEd, Faculty Team Librarian, University of Nottingham, Greenfield Medical Lib.
[41386] 17/11/1987 **CM22/09/1999**

Curtis-Brown, Miss L A, BA (Hons) MA,
[52201] 12/10/1995 ME

Cusack, Mrs K J, DipLIS MCLIP, Unwaged.
[53047] 19/02/1996 **CM24/09/1997**

Cusack, Mrs N, Library Assistant, Cardiff University.
[10032169]   14/01/2014   ME
Cushion, Miss J, BA MA MCLIP, Subject Librarian, Anglia Ruskin
University, Cambridge.
[10006936]   17/12/2007   CM14/11/2012
Cusworth, Mrs M R, FCLIP, Trainer/Consultant, Tyrrell Wood
Consultants Ltd.
[3525]   02/08/1967   FE26/01/1994
Cutforth, Ms I, MA PCGE, Library Assistant, St Albans Library.
[10020658]   15/03/2012   ME
Cuthbert, Mrs M M C, Senior Customer Services Assistant (PT),
Halstead Library, Essex County Council.
[10022473]   11/03/2013   ME
Cuthbertson, Mrs A B, BA (Hons) MA MSc MCLIP, Head of Learning
Resources, Huntingdonshire Regional College.
[10011785]   13/11/2008   CM18/01/2012
Cuthbertson, Miss J C, MCLIP, Life Member.
[3530]   20/09/1948   CM01/01/1956
Cuthbertson, Ms L, BA MSc, Electronic Records Manager, Foreign &
Commonwealth Office, London.
[61922]   18/11/2002   ME
Cuthell, Miss H, MCLIP, Retired.
[3531]   23/01/1946   CM01/01/1951
Cuthill, Mrs S J, MA MArAd, School Librarian, Clifton High School.
[10034610]   23/07/2014   ME
Cutler, Ms E J, BA (Hons) MSc (Econ), Librarian, Dudley College.
[58288]   14/12/1999   ME
Cutler, Mr N, BSc (Hons) MA MCLIP, Dept Lib. Computer Laboratory,
University of Cambridge.
[53434]   25/06/1996   CM10/07/2002
Cutmore, Mrs R A, MCLIP, Life Member.
[3534]   27/09/1951   CM01/01/1957
Cutts, Ms A L, BA DipLib MCLIP, Librarian, University of Cambridge,
Faculty of Educ.
[37991]   01/01/1985   CM23/03/1993
Cyrus, Mr K K, Student, Aberystwyth University.
[10033880]   08/05/2014   ME

D

Da Costa, Mrs H, BA (Hons), Comm. Librarian, Kent County Council,
Broadstairs Library.
[47487]   02/09/1992   ME
Da Silva, Mr L R, BSc DipLIS MCLIP, Electronic Systems Librarian,
University of Chichester.
[47692]   15/10/1992   CM16/05/2001
Dabbs, Ms R A, LLB (Hons), Deputy Information Centre Manager,
Bristows, London.
[10001638]   06/03/2007   ME
Dada, Mrs A, BA CA Cert MSc, Information Rights Officer, Department
for Communities and Local Government.
[10018047]   08/11/2010   ME
Dade, Mrs P, BA DipLib MCLIP, Ind. Information Specialist.
[21430]   29/10/1973   CM10/10/1977
Dafis, Mr L L, BA Dip Lib, Head of Digitisation, Description and Legacy
Aquisitions, National Library of Wales.
[10031608]   11/09/2013   ME
Dafydd, Mrs M A, BA (Hons) MSc (Econ) MCLIP, Library Service
Manager North, Powys County Council.
[54621]   04/02/1997   CM16/07/2003
Dagger, Mr J R, BA (Hons) MA,
[60862]   13/12/2001   ME

Dagnall, Mrs C, BSc (HONS) MA, Trust Library Services Manager, Trust
Library Wigan, WW&L NHS FT.
[10008608]   11/04/2012   ME
Dahlke, Ms H, BA (Hons) MA MCLIP, Librarian, Wellington College.
[63770]   06/10/2004   RV15/07/2014   CM08/08/2008
Daines, Mr G F, BA DipLib MCLIP FRSA, Director, Policy & Advocacy,
CILIP, London.
[23173]   05/11/1974   CM22/08/1977
Dainton, Mr M, BSc MSc, Lib. University of Wolverhampton.
[61552]   18/09/2002   ME
Dakers, Ms F J G, BA DipIM MCLIP, Libraries Manager, Angus.
[61074]   01/03/2002   CM23/06/2004
Dakers, Mrs H P, MA MSc FCLIP, Independent Researcher – Specialist
in Jewish & South African Genealogy.
[24645]   12/10/1975   FE27/11/1996
Dakin, Miss A E, MCLIP, Retired.
[3548]   09/10/1968   CM01/01/1972
Dale, Mrs K K, MCLIP, Library Group Manager (South), Bristol L. Serv.,
Bristol.
[57415]   03/03/1999   CM29/08/2007
Dale, Mrs R, MCLIP, Resource Acquisitions Librarian, University of
Nottingham.
[41283]   25/10/1987   CM14/11/1990
Dale, Dr S M, DipTransIoL ACIL MCLIP, Retired.
[3557]   06/04/1963   CM01/01/1966
Daley, Mrs M R, BSc DipLib MCLIP, Assistant Librarian, Liverpool City
Library.
[40762]   02/06/1987   CM18/11/1992
Dalgleish, Dr A J, MA DipLib MCLIP, Assistant Head (L. Servs.),
University of South Wales, Pontypridd.
[42827]   09/03/1989   CM16/09/1992
Dallas, Miss S, Unwaged.
[10033157]   07/03/2014   ME
Dallas, Mrs S D, BA,
[10033396]   07/03/2014   ME
Dalley, Mr N M, BA (Hons) DipInfSc, L. Relations Manager, Sirsidynix.
[51817]   06/07/1995   ME
Dalley, Mrs P M, BA DipLib MCLIP, Retired.
[32533]   30/04/1980   CM20/01/1986
Dalling, Miss G M, MSc, Librarian /Cataloguer, University of
Technology, Jamaica.
[10016853]   27/05/2010   ME
Dalling, Mr J M, BSc MSc Econ, Senior Learning Resources Advisor,
University of Wales Trinity Saint David.
[10018991]   07/04/2011   ME
Dallison, Miss D, SCONUL Graduate Trainee Librarian, Glasgow
School of Art.
[10031947]   15/10/2013   ME
Dallison, Mrs L, BSc PGCE, Customer Service Assistant, Croydon
College Library.
[10022479]   11/03/2013   AF
Dallman, Mrs S J, MA DipLib MCLIP, Assistant Librarian, National
Museum of Scotland, Edinburgh.
[34151]   10/10/1981   CM23/06/1986
Dalrymple, Mr I R, Librarian Performance Monitor High Life Highland.
[56378]   01/07/1998   ME
Dalsgaard, Ms L,
[10011836]   20/06/2014   ME
Dalton, Mr A M, MA HDipEd MCLIP, Life Member.
[16692]   29/03/1962   CM01/01/1968
Dalton, Miss K, BA (Hons) MA, Library Manager, Cardinal Newman
College.
[10032953]   30/01/2014   ME

Daly, Mrs A C, Clinical Librarian, NHS.
[59268]   23/01/2001   **ME**
Daly, Mr S A, BA (Hons), Bibl. Serv. Librarian, University of Liverpool,
Sydney Jones Library.
[48232]   16/11/1992   **ME**
Danels, Miss J L, BD DipLib, Unwaged.
[40127]   17/10/1986   **ME**
Danes, Mrs N E, BLIB MCLIP, Advisory Librarian, Essex School Library
Service, Chelmsford.
[28637]   11/01/1978   **CM21/01/1983**
Dang, Miss T L, BLIS, Student, University of Strathclyde.
[10035693]   29/10/2014   **ME**
Daniel, Ms C, BA MA MCLIP, Librarian, Cumbria College of Art &
Design, Carlisle.
[43763]   01/01/1990   **CM18/11/1993**
Daniel, Mrs J H M, BLib, School Librarian, St Augustine's Catholic
College.
[29780]   04/10/1978   **CM05/09/1986**
Daniel, Miss L R, BA (Hons) MSc (Econ) MCLIP, Competition
Researcher, Freshfields, London.
[58305]   04/01/2000   **CM16/07/2003**
Daniels, Mrs A E, BA (Hons), Library Manager, All Saints Junior School
Hampshire.
[10034330]   04/07/2014   **ME**
Daniels, Mr F, BA (Hons) DipLib MCLIP, Retired.
[23440]   01/01/1975   **CM10/11/1978**
Daniels, Mr K, BA MCLIP PGCTHE FHEA, Academic Liaison Librarian,
Media & Biomedical Sciences, University of Bedfordshire.
[40863]   20/07/1987   **CM30/01/1991**
Daniels, Miss R, BA (Hons), Student, Northumbria University.
[10035161]   22/09/2014   **ME**
Daniels, Miss R J, MCLIP, Deputy Head, Barrington Library, Cranfield
University, Defence Academy of the UK.
[63364]   20/04/2004   **CM16/04/2010**
Daniels, Mrs T J, BLib MCLIP, Supp. Serv. -Development Officer,
Torfaen Co. Borough Council, Information Advisor-Cataloguing,
UWIC.
[34315]   20/10/1981   **CM21/11/1985**
Dann, Mr M J, BA (Hons), Learning Resources Manager, New College,
Durham.
[52584]   09/11/1995   **ME**
Danquah, Miss M A, BSc (Hons) MA, Careers Adviser, University of
West London.
[52117]   05/10/1995   **ME**
Dansey, Mr P, BSc MCLIP, Retired.
[60185]   14/10/1971   **CM01/07/1976**
Danskin, Mr A R, Metadata Standards Manager, British Library.
[39355]   19/01/1986   **ME**
Daramola, Mr S O, Pgd MIS MA BEcons (Hons) BSc Adm (Hons),
Financial Advisor / Library Assistant, Citizen Advice Bureau.
[10021919]   01/11/2012   **ME**
Darbyshire, Dr K J, BSc (Hons) PGCRM MSc PhD MIET, Student.
[10032081]   24/10/2013   **ME**
d'Ardenne, Miss S, BMus MA MCLIP, Assistant Librarian (Reader
Services), Royal Northern College of Music, Manchester.
[10009361]   15/05/2008   **CM15/02/2012**
Dare, Mrs J E, BA (Hons) MA MCLIP, Part-time Assistant Lib.
[56124]   03/03/1998   **RV**30/04/2014   **CM29/11/2006**
Dargan, Ms J C, BSc,
[10017569]   08/09/2010   **ME**
Darling, Miss H O, BA (Hons) MCLIP, Relief Senior Library Assistant
Local Studies, Scottish Borders Council.
[35854]   31/01/1983   **CM22/05/1996**

Darling, Ms S L, BA MA MCLIP, Self-employed.
[45436]   04/02/1991   **CM26/05/1993**
Darlington, Mrs N J, BA (Hons) MCLIP, Faculty Team Librarian.,
University of Nottingham.
[51173]   23/11/1994   **CM19/01/2000**
Darlington, Mr P M, MCLIP, Technical Product Manager, Axiell,
Nottingham.
[52578]   08/11/1995   **CM01/04/2002**
Darrah, Mrs N, BA (Hons) MSc (Econ), Unwaged.
[10019467]   12/02/1997   **ME**
Darter, Ms P E, BA MCLIP, Life Member.
[3610]   03/10/1963   **CM01/01/1968**
Dase, Ms A, MA, Sch. Librarian, Trent College, Long Eaton, Notts.
[59138]   23/11/2000   **ME**
Dash, Miss C G J, BA (Hons), School Librarian, Herts and Essex High
School.
[10021453]   17/08/2012   **ME**
Dashfield, Mrs D, BSc (Hons) MLIS, Librarian, Wellington, New
Zealand.
[10006487]   24/10/2007   **ME**
Date, Miss R J, BEd, School Librarian, Bryntirion Comprehensive
School, Bridgend.
[64666]   13/05/2005   **ME**
Datiles, Ms J M, JD MS. LIS, Student, Catholic University of America.
[10032562]   16/12/2013   **ME**
Datson, Mr S, Information Support Administrator, Ministry of Defence.
[10034540]   21/07/2014   **ME**
Dattili, Ms M, BA DipLib MCLIP, L. Resource Centre Manager, North
Lanarkshire C. C.
[37463]   01/10/1984   **CM05/07/1988**
Daubney-Marsden, Ms S, Assistant in Charge, Derbyshire County
Council.
[10033607]   03/04/2014   **ME**
Davenport, Ms L, BA (Hons), Library Assistant, Heartlands High
School.
[10022268]   29/01/2013   **ME**
Davey, Mr A J, BSc MCLIP, L. Manager, Devon County Council, Exeter.
[33283]   27/10/1980   **CM13/12/1983**
Davey, Ms E M, BA, Information Services Manager, University of
Brighton, Aldrich Library.
[46298]   24/10/1991   **ME**
Davey, Mrs G A, Learning Resources Supervisor, Grantham College.
[10032982]   03/02/2014   **ME**
Davey, Mrs N, BA (Hons) PgDipLIS, Senior Library Assistant (Health
Resources), Stockton Borough Council.
[64946]   03/10/2005   **ME**
David, Mrs S J, BA MA MCLIP, Liaison Co-ordinator, St Georges
Hospital, University of London.
[47964]   28/10/1992   **RV**27/09/2005   **CM24/05/1995**
Davidge, Mrs D C, HNC, Student, Aberystwyth University.
[10035323]   08/10/2014   **ME**
Davidson, Mrs A, BA (Hons), Enquiry Officer, Suffolk Libraries.
[39604]   19/03/1986   **CM26/05/1993**
Davidson, Mrs B T, BSc DipLib MCLIP, Assistant Librarian, Capel
Manor College Enfield, Middlesex.
[41653]   05/02/1988   **CM12/12/1990**
Davidson, Ms E, MA MCLIP, Reading Room Assistant (volunteer), The
Morgan Library & Museum.
[10008305]   26/03/2008   **CM29/05/2013**
Davidson, Miss H, BSc (Hons) MSc, Library Assistant, Durham
University Library, Queen's Campus.
[10022759]   16/04/2013   **ME**

Davidson, Mrs J, BSc MCLIP, Research Cataloguer, University of
Worcester.
[32358]   03/03/1980   **CM21/07/1993**
Davidson, Mrs M, Ma MSc, Sch. Librarian, Nairn Academy, Nairn.
[10011869]   22/11/2004   **ME**
Davidson, Mr M J, BA (Hons), Information Assistant, Nottingham Trent
University Notts.
[10017154]   12/07/2010   **ME**
Davidson, Mrs M W, BA DipLib MCLIP, Employment not known.
[28592]   11/01/1978   **CM28/01/1980**
Davidson, Mrs P B, MA MCLIP, Network Librarian, Banchory Acad.,
Banchory, Kincardineshire.
[26368]   11/10/1976   **CM19/01/1979**
Davidson, Mr P C, BA MSc,
[10021795]   16/10/2012   **ME**
Davidson, Mr R, Library Services Coordinator, GLL Middlegate House.
London.
[10031611]   11/09/2013   **ME**
Davidson, Mrs S A, BA (Hons) MA, Liaison Librarian (Education),
University of Wolverhampton, Walsall.
[47676]   14/10/1992   **ME**
Davidson, Mr V, ACLIP, Library Supervisor, North Inch Community
Library, Perth.
[64437]   18/03/2005   **ACL16/04/2008**
Davie, Mrs D E, BA DipLib MCLIP, Community/College Librarian, Notts.
County Council.
[41256]   26/10/1987   **CM18/07/1991**
Davies, Ms A, BA (Hons) MCLIP, Retired.
[22690]   15/08/1974   **CM02/08/1978**
Davies, Ms A E, BA (Hons) MCLIP, Senior Information Assistant,
Universityof Nottingham.
[62392]   22/05/2003   **CM21/03/2007**
Davies, Mrs A E, BSc, Student, Aberystwyth University.
[10032441]   06/12/2013   **ME**
Davies, Miss A M, BA (Hons) PgDipILS MCLIP, Unwaged.
[55187]   05/08/1997   **CM08/12/2004**
Davies, Mr A N, BSc MCLIP, Retired.
[26340]   01/10/1976   **CM12/09/1979**
Davies, Mrs B, BSc, LRC Manager, Harris Academy Beckenham.
[10006318]   10/10/2007   **AF**
Davies, Miss C, Cataloguer, Metadata Team, Natational Library of
Scotland.
[10015770]   25/01/2010   **ME**
Davies, Ms C, BA Cert Ed, Learning Resources Coordinator, Petroc
Library.
[10020468]   20/02/2012   **AF**
Davies, Mr C B, BA MCLIP, Senior Librarian, London Borough of
Camden, Swiss Cottage Library, London.
[31127]   30/08/1979   **CM27/10/1981**
Davies, Mrs C C, ACLIP, Information Unit Manager, CBI, Centre Point,
London.
[62843]   06/11/2003   **ACL04/07/2006**
Davies, Miss D M W, Library Assistant, Victoria University of Wellington,
New Zealand.
[3671]   02/10/1970   **ME**
Davies, Mr D T, MA BA MCLIP, Unwaged.
[21690]   09/01/1974   **CM27/02/1978**
Davies, Mr E, MSCI, Graduate Trainee Librarian, Radcliffe Science
Library.
[10032123]   29/10/2013   **ME**
Davies, Mrs E, BA (Hons), Information Officer, Veale Wasborough
Uizards, Bristol.
[63199]   03/03/2004   **AF**

Davies, Mrs E A, BEd DipLib MCLIP, Librarian, Coldharbour Library,
Royal Borough of Greenwich.
[42142]   03/10/1988   **CM27/07/1994**
Davies, Mrs E I, MCLIP, Housewife & Mother.
[21306]   10/10/1973   **CM19/11/1976**
Davies, Miss E W, BA (Hons) MSc (Econ) MCLIP, Subject Librarian,
Swansea University.
[65439]   23/02/2006   **CM07/07/2010**
Davies, Miss G, MCLIP, Retired.
[3682]   18/10/1945   **CM01/01/1967**
Davies, Mr G E, MCLIP, Retired.
[3687]   31/10/1966   **CM01/01/1970**
Davies, Miss H, BA,
[10006901]   17/12/2007   **ME**
Davies, Ms H J, BA MSc MCLIP, Librarian, Enfield Borough Council.
[43427]   26/10/1989   **CM29/01/1992**
Davies, Ms I J, BA DipLib, Librarian, Essex Sch. L. Serv., Chelmsford.
[36990]   27/01/1984   **ME**
Davies, Miss J, BSc Econ, Education Centre Coordinator.
[64641]   03/05/2005   **ME**
Davies, Mrs J, BA MCLIP, Retired.
[6011]   01/01/1972   **CM06/10/1975**
Davies, Mrs J A, ALIA Tec, Student, Charles Sturt University.
[10035169]   23/09/2014   **ME**
Davies, Dr J E, MA PhD FCLIP FRSA HonFCLIP, Honorary Visiting
Research Fellow, Loughborough University, Centre for Information
Management, School of Business and Economics.
[3705]   25/01/1961   **HFE02/09/2010**
Davies, Mr J I, FCLIP, Life Member.
[3709]   27/02/1958   **FE29/01/1976**
Davies, Miss J L, BA, Student, Aberystwyth University.
[10034148]   10/06/2014   **ME**
Davies, Mr J R M, MA MCLIP, Retired.
[18608]   10/04/1965   **CM01/01/1967**
Davies, Miss K, MA, Enquiry Service Manager, Institute of Chartered
Accountants of England and Wales.
[64983]   06/10/2005   **ME**
Davies, Mr K, Information Strategy & Planning, Ministry of Defence.
[10034302]   02/07/2014   **ME**
Davies, Miss K L, BSc (Hons) MA MCLIP, Faculty Liaison Librarian,
Health & Social Care, Canterbury Christ Church University.
[59050]   06/11/2000   **RV20/02/2014**   **CM15/09/2004**
Davies, Ms K L, MCLIP, Legal Secretary, Ealing, London.
[3666]   01/01/1970   **CM16/07/1973**
Davies, Miss L, MA MCLIP, Access Librarian, Institute of Advanced
Legal Studies, London.
[62776]   22/10/2003   **RV12/09/2012**   **CM29/11/2006**
Davies, Mrs L, BA DipLib MCLIP, Community Librarian, Denbighshire
County Council, Ruthin L.
[43446]   26/10/1989   **CM18/11/1992**
Davies, Mrs L, BA MCLIP, Science & Biomedical Sciences Librarian,
Cardiff University.
[35019]   22/06/1982   **CM30/07/1985**
Davies, Mrs L, Student, Aberystwyth University.
[10033184]   18/02/2014   **ME**
Davies, Miss L C, BA FCLIP, Life Member.
[3717]   01/01/1956   **FE01/01/1961**
Davies, Mrs L I, ACLIP, Information Assistant, St Georges University
Library, London.
[65048]   21/10/2005   **ACL29/03/2007**
Davies, Mrs L J, SDM Children & Young People, Crowby, Liverpool.
[65467]   24/02/2006   **AF**

Davies, Dr M, BA MSc DipLib MBCS, Deputy CIO & Director of Res. & Learning Supp., King's College, London.
[21317] 04/10/1973 CM11/11/1976

Davies, Mrs M, MA BLib, Head of L. & Information Serv., Norton Rose LLP, London.
[35176] 04/10/1982 CM14/11/1989

Davies, Miss M, BA MCLIP, Life Member.
[3720] 19/02/1959 CM01/01/1961

Davies, Mrs M, MCLIP, Life Member.
[3722] 23/06/1954 CM01/01/1958

Davies, Mrs M, MCLIP, Retired.
[3723] 16/02/1969 CM05/12/1972

Davies, Mr M O, BSc MA MCLIP, Senior Indexer, House of Commons Library, London.
[54795] 02/04/1997 CM19/07/2000

Davies, Miss N J, BA (Hons), Library Assistant, Wirral Libraries.
[10020874] 19/04/2012 ME

Davies, Miss N J, Student.
[10016732] 30/04/2010 ME

Davies, Ms P M, BA (Hons) MSc Econ MCLIP, Student, Aberystwyth University.
[10019473] 06/07/2011 CM09/09/2013

Davies, Dr R, PhD BEng, Service Manager – Analytical Services, The Scottish Government.
[10031470] 13/08/2013 ME

Davies, Ms R B, BA MA, Liaison Librarian, Leeds Trinity University College.
[10034679] 30/07/2014 ME

Davies, Mrs R E, BA (Hons) Dip ILM, LRC Manager, Framwellgate School, Durham.
[59424] 12/03/2001 ME

Davies, Mr R R, BA (Hons), Unemployed.
[59809] 04/10/2001 ME

Davies, Miss S, BA (Joint Hons), Information Specialist, National Assembly for Wales.
[10022414] 26/02/2013 AF

Davies, Miss S E, BA PGCE MSC MCLIP, Librarian, Cotham School, Bristol.
[10006432] 19/10/2007 CM27/08/2014

Davies, Mrs S I, MCLIP, Retired.
[3751] 28/09/1950 CM01/01/1956

Davies, Mr T H, Librarian, Central Library, North Lincs.
[10000788] 30/10/2006 ME

Davies, Ms W, BA MCLIP MRTPI, Cultural Manager, Fishguard Library.
[8114] 16/01/1968 CM01/01/1972

Davies, Mr W, FCLIP, Retired.
[3758] 06/01/1948 FE01/01/1970

Davies, Mrs W M, BA MCLIP, Loughborough University.
[18398] 02/10/1972 CM09/09/1974

Davis, Ms A K, BA (Hons) DipILM MCLIP, Subject Librarian, University of Gloucestershire.
[57203] 14/01/1999 CM17/09/2003

Davis, Miss A M, BA MCLIP, Life Member.
[3763] 01/03/1952 CM01/01/1959

Davis, Ms E, Assistant Librarian (Full Time), Office of Gas & Electricity Markets.
[63874] 11/10/2004 ME

Davis, Ms E, BA (Hons) MCLIP, Assistant Librarian, Barnsley Central Library.
[50429] 28/07/1994 CM20/01/1999

Davis, Miss E, BA, Student.
[10035526] 16/10/2014 ME

Davis, Mr H J, BSc FBIS MCLIP, Unemployed.
[60272] 20/09/1977 CM31/07/1980

Davis, Miss J E, BLib MCLIP, Head of Libraries, Wiltshire Council.
[26180] 02/08/1976 CM01/01/1980

Davis, Mr J G, MA FCLIP, Genealogist, Thistle Heritage Services; Giffnock, Glasgow.
[3777] 01/10/1970 FE13/12/1979

Davis, Ms J G, BA (Hons),
[10002306] 09/07/1991 ME

Davis, Mrs J I, Subject Lib. Maths & Physics, Betty & Gordon Moore Library, Cambridge.
[57917] 01/10/1999 ME

Davis, Mr J M, FRSA AMRI, Customer Service Manager, Huddersfield Library.
[10013571] 07/05/2009 AF

Davis, Mrs K Y, Librarian, Fort Pitt Grammar School.
[10021292] 06/07/2012 ME

Davis, Miss M A, PMICS, Library Events Officer, Mapperley Library.
[10031935] 15/10/2013 ME

Davis, Mr P, MCLIP, Life Member.
[3788] 14/03/1951 CM01/01/1963

Davis, Mr S, British Medical Association, London.
[65249] 01/12/2005 ME

Davis, Mrs S, BA (Hons) MA MCLIP, Information Research Officer, EON, Nottingham.
[63937] 18/11/2004 CM29/08/2007

Davis, Mrs S, BA (Hons) PGCE MEd MCLIP, Librarian, Framlingham College.
[10022952] 14/05/2013 CM27/08/2014

Davison, Ms A M, BA (Hons) MCLIP, Strategic Manager Libraries., Durham C. C.
[45180] 02/08/1990 CM23/09/1998

Davison, Mrs P, LLB, Student.
[10019213] 05/05/2011 ME

Davy, Miss A F, MCLIP, Retired.
[3801] 20/09/1969 CM04/08/1972

Davy, Miss J, BA (Hons), Information Assistant, University of Westminster, Harrow Learning Res. Centre for.
[59991] 16/11/2001 ME

Dawes, Ms L, BA (Hons) MPhil MCLIP, Lib. Harlaxton College, Lincolnshire.
[10011670] 11/11/2008 CM12/05/2011

Dawes, Miss P J, BA MCLIP, Systems Librarian, University of Bradford.
[33998] 08/07/1981 CM31/10/1984

Dawes, Mrs R, BA (Hons) MA, Private Music Teacher, Department of Culture Media and Sport.
[49178] 08/10/1993 ME

Dawes, Mrs S, BA MA DipLib MCLIP, Information & QA Manager, PRPArchitects, LLP. Thames Ditton.
[35410] 18/10/1982 CM01/04/2002

Dawes, Mrs S, BLib MCLIP, Senior Librarian, City of London Freemen's School, Surrey.
[33725] 09/02/1981 CM28/09/1984

Dawes, Mr T, MLS EdM, Circulation Services Director, Princeton University.
[10021918] 01/11/2012 ME

Daws, Mr A L, BA MCLIP, Retired.
[3813] 01/04/1967 CM01/01/1970

Dawson, Mr A D, BA MCLIP DLIS MEI, MSc Programme Director, Department of Information Studies, UCL.
[32647] 01/07/1980 CM16/08/1982

Dawson, Miss A H, BA DipLib, Admin. Assistant, Department of the Environment, Belfast.
[35533] 29/10/1982 ME

Dawson, Ms A J, BA CertEd, Information Manager, Watts Group PLC, London.
[32385]   01/01/1972   **CM18/06/1984**

Dawson, Mrs D M, BA MA MCLIP, Arts Librarian, University of Nottingham.
[39034]   29/10/1985   **CM19/06/1991**

Dawson, Miss H S, BA MA DipLib MCLIP, Academic Support Librarian, London School of Economics and Political Science.
[46102]   02/10/1991   **CM26/01/1994**

Dawson, Ms J, MA (Hons) MCLIP, School Library Resource Centre Co-Ordinator., Aberdeen City Council.
[63176]   03/03/2004   **CM22/08/2012**

Dawson, Mr J A, BA MA MCLIP, University of Sheffield, Sheffield.
[39911]   01/10/1986   **RV**17/06/2009   **CM18/04/1990**

Dawson, Mr J D, BLIB MCLIP, Senior Librarian, Arup, London.
[39426]   24/01/1986   **CM15/05/1989**

Dawson, Ms J E, BA MCLIP, Reader Development Librarian, Warwickshire County Council.
[11900]   01/01/1970   **CM25/09/1972**

Dawson, Mrs L, BA (Hons) MSc MCLIP, Retired.
[43960]   05/03/1990   **CM25/01/1995**

Dawson, Mrs M M, BA (Hons) MSc MCLIP, Knowledge Manager, Bradford District Care Trust.
[58271]   01/12/1999   **CM03/10/2007**

Dawson, Miss N J, BA MCLIP, Library Manager Children and Young People – Job Share, Shropshire Council.
[42295]   18/10/1988   **CM25/05/1994**

Dawson, Ms S,
[10000249]   01/07/2008   **ME**

Day, Mrs A A, BA (Hons) MA MCLIP, Lead Librarian, Poole Hospital NHS Foundation Trust.
[47482]   01/09/1992   **RV**08/03/2013   **CM27/11/1996**

Day, Miss E A, BA (Hons) MA MCLIP, Career break.
[51761]   01/07/1995   **CM17/03/1999**

Day, Mrs E V, MCLIP, Retired.
[11726]   26/04/1971   **CM02/08/1974**

Day, Mr M A T, Student, Manchester Metropolitan University.
[10013185]   03/04/2009   **ME**

Day, Mr N J, MCLIP, Life Member.
[3842]   27/09/1951   **CM01/01/1955**

Day, Mr S R, BA MLib MCLIP, Product Manager, OCLC, Birmingham.
[41393]   20/11/1987   **CM01/04/2002**

Day, Mr T G, BA (Hons) PgDip MCLIP, Senior Assistant Lib. (Media), London Borough of Wandsworth, Putney Library.
[48243]   17/11/1992   **CM09/11/2005**

Dayasena, Mr P J U, BSc MCLIP,
[60721]   10/01/1985   **CM10/01/1985**

De Abaitua, Mrs C A, MSc, Student.
[10015563]   07/10/1997   **ME**

de Chazal, Mrs P, MA MCLIP, Research Mgr, Centre for Exercise & Rehabilitation Science, Respiratory Biomedical Research Unit, Glenfield Hospital.
[10000904]   16/11/1992   **CM01/04/2002**

De Jong Lee, Mrs T B H, Student, University of Groningen, Holland.
[10023328]   25/06/2013   **ME**

de Klerk, Mr M E, BSc (Econ) MCLIP, Res. Centre Co-ordinator, Dundee City Council.
[57590]   13/05/1999   **CM14/12/2011**

De Kock, Ms S A M, BLS, Assistant Librarian, NHS Leeds, (Leeds DCT).
[61178]   03/04/2002   **ME**

De Pretto, Mrs A, MCLIP, Systems Librarian National L. of Scotland.
[10016000]   10/02/2010   **CM13/05/2014**

de Silva, Mr D P, BSc MSc, Information Manager, Information Management, Foreign & Commonwealth Office, London.
[46777]   22/01/1992   **ME**

De Simone, Ms M G, MA MCLIP, Library Assistant, Trinity College, Cambridge.
[10017950]   27/10/2010   **CM20/06/2012**

Deacon, Ms A, BA (Hons) MCLIP, LRC Co-ordinator, The Brit School, Croydon.
[62060]   07/02/2003   **CM29/11/2006**

Deacon, Mrs D A, MCLIP, Reader Development Librarian, Newbury Library, West Berkshire.
[22384]   01/04/1974   **CM21/09/1983**

Deacy, Miss M, BA AKC, Student, City University, London.
[10017873]   21/10/2010   **ME**

Deadman, Mrs S, BA,
[35599]   26/10/1982   **ME**

Dean, Mrs D, Distribution Manager, River Island.
[10035303]   25/10/1977   **ME**

Dean, Mrs E J, BA (Hons) MA, Librarian, Ackworth School, Pontefract.
[51743]   12/06/1995   **CM17/05/2000**

Dean, Mrs E J, BA MCLIP, Retired from Civil Service.
[33352]   15/10/1980   **CM26/05/1993**

Dean, Miss H, BA MA, Information Officer.
[10018109]   16/11/2010   **ME**

Dean, Mrs L, MCLIP, Learning Res. Centre Manager, Ashton-on-Mersey School, Sale.
[19847]   02/01/1973   **CM01/09/1975**

Dean, Miss S, BA (Hons), Community Librarian, Luton Central Library.
[10006611]   11/09/2007   **ME**

Dear, Mrs J, MA (Hons) PGDE MSc, Graduate, University Strathclyde, Glasgow.
[10016004]   10/02/2010   **ME**

Dearden, Mrs N L, Branch Manager – Coppull Library.
[10035306]   07/10/2014   **ME**

De'Ath, Miss A F, BA DipLib MCLIP, School Librarian, Eastwood High School.
[43164]   04/09/1989   **CM21/07/1993**

Deaville, Mrs A M, BA PgDipLib MCLIP, Senior Sch. Servs. Officer, School Library Service, Cumbria.
[38455]   03/05/1985   **CM07/09/2005**

Debnam, Ms A, MCLIP, Retired.
[15687]   30/08/1964   **CM07/02/1975**

Deeks, Mr P,
[10034783]   14/08/2014   **ME**

Deeley, Mrs S L, Library and Community Development Officer.
[10022131]   08/01/2013   **ME**

Deen, Ms F, Information Center Coordinator, Organization of the Petroleum Exporting Countries (OPEC).
[10001537]   03/10/1984   **ME**

Deering-Punshon, Ms S E, BLib MCLIP, Semi-retired from West Berkshire Public Libraries Service. Previously Berkshire Education Library Service.
[21506]   27/10/1973   **CM27/02/1980**

Dehavilan, Mr N J, BSc (Hons), Student, Cranfield University.
[10032747]   08/01/2014   **ME**

Del Bono, Mrs M R S, MA DipIS MCLIP, Librarian, London Contemp. Dance School, London.
[52643]   15/11/1995   **CM15/05/2002**

Del Campo Cabezas De Herrera, Mr M, BA, Student, León University.
[10032995]   11/02/2014   **ME**

Delahaye, Ms E, BA, MA Library and Information Studies, Student, UCL.
[10031690]   24/09/2013   **ME**

Delahunty, Miss S, BA (Hons) MCLIP, Library Customer Assistant., Monmouthshire.
[49740]   29/11/1993   **CM15/03/2000**

Delaney, Mrs E A, MCLIP, Casual Library Assistant, RCT Libraries.
[21296]   16/10/1973   **CM02/08/1977**

Delaney, Miss E L, BA (Hons) MCLIP,
[10001723]   31/10/1994   **CM21/01/1998**

Delaney, Mrs G, Information Assistant, University Of Ulster.
[10020450]   20/02/2012   **ME**

Delaney, Ms N, MA M. LIH, Student, Bodleian Libraries.
[10033293]   28/02/2014   **ME**

Delbecque, Ms E, MA MCLIP,
[10019270]   01/06/2011   **CM20/06/2014**

Delderfield, Miss J, BA (Hons) MA MCLIP, Library Systems Manager, The Royal College of Surgeons of England, London.
[64609]   03/05/2005   **CM31/01/2007**

Delgado Caraballo, Mr F J, BA, Assistant Prison Librarian.
[10020016]   25/10/2011   **ME**

Delgal, Miss C, Assistant Librarian, Institution of Civil Engineers, London.
[63541]   17/06/2004   **ME**

Dell, Miss R, Student, Manchester Metropolitan University.
[10022532]   19/03/2013   **ME**

Dellar, Mr G, Retired.
[16715]   28/09/1948   **CM01/01/1951**

Dellar, Mr M G, MA MCLIP, Learning Resources Manager, College of North West London, London.
[39669]   30/04/1986   **CM15/08/1990**

Deller, Ms C S, BA (Hons), Student/Assistant Librarian, Aberystwyth University/The Skinner's School, Tunbridge Wells.
[10013470]   28/04/2009   **ME**

Del-Pizzo, Ms J E, MSc (Econ), Acquisitions Manager, College of Law, London.
[53343]   14/05/1996   **ME**

Delve, Mr B, MCLIP, Retired.
[3881]   12/09/1961   **CM01/01/1970**

Dempsey, Mr L, BA DipLIS MCLIP, Vice President, Research, OCLC.
[41053]   06/10/1987   **CM01/04/2002**

Dempster, Mrs G, Student, University of Brighton.
[10033273]   07/03/2014   **ME**

Dempster, Dr J A H, MA PhD MCLIP, Senior Librarian, Systems, High Life Highland.
[20774]   01/07/1973   **CM08/06/1976**

Dempster, Mrs R E, BSc (Hons) MSc MCLIP, Librarian, Falkirk Community Trust.
[59214]   09/01/2001   **CM08/12/2004**

Denham, Mrs M, MA DipLib MCLIP, Primary School Librarian, Hutchesons Grammar School, Glasgow.
[35161]   23/09/1982   **CM23/11/1986**

Denholm, Mrs V, MA MCLIP, Access and Outreach Officer, National Library of Scotland.
[56727]   07/10/1998   **CM13/06/2007**

Denmead, Mr J, MA, L. Serv. Manager, MoD, London.
[10001420]   04/10/1988   **ME**

Denning, Mr R T W, BA FCLIP, Retired.
[3888]   08/01/1945   **FE01/01/1959**

Dennis, Miss N, BSc (Hons) MA MCLIP, Business Information Specialist, Aston University, Birmingham.
[53740]   18/09/1996   **CM15/11/2000**

Dennis, Ms S E, BA DipLib MCLIP, Head of Information Services, Charles Russell LLP.
[33720]   02/01/1981   **CM26/05/1983**

Dennison, Mr D J, Library Manager, Rainham Library.
[10032110]   28/10/2013   **AF**

Dennison, Mr P J, BA (Hons) MSc, Head of User Services, Institute of Educaction, University of London.
[49467]   03/11/1993   **ME**

Denny, Mr G E, BA (Hons) DipIM MCLIP, Library Services Supervisor, Norfolk Educational Services.
[51085]   14/11/1994   **CM08/12/2004**

Denny, Ms L, BA, Student, Manchester Metropolitan University.
[10021798]   16/10/2012   **ME**

Denoon, Ms C M, MA DipLib MCLIP, L. Serv. Manager, NHS Greater Glasgow & Clyde., Maria Henderson L.
[43561]   08/11/1989   **CM16/12/1992**

Dent, Mr J, BA PgDip, Information Assistant, Kingston University.
[10022957]   14/05/2013   **ME**

Denton, Mr D, BSc MCIEH MCLIP, Retired.
[60456]   06/04/1989   **CM06/04/1989**

Denton, Miss K, Student, Cranfield University.
[10032088]   24/10/2013   **ME**

Deon, Miss K, Library Assistant, Luton Central Library.
[10022801]   23/04/2013   **AF**

Depledge, Miss A J, BA (Hons) DPS MA MCLIP, Archive Assistant, West Yorkshire Archive Service.
[44670]   22/11/1990   **CM21/07/1999**

Derbyshire, Mrs A J S, Student.
[10007560]   13/02/2008   **ME**

Deshmukh, Ms A, Student, University of Brighton.
[10022306]   05/02/2013   **ME**

Deslignères, Ms L, PgDip MCLIP, Librarian, Language Centre., Oxford University.
[63602]   09/07/2004   **RV**20/06/2012   **CM24/10/2008**

Devalapalli, Mrs U M, MSc BLISc MLISc MCLIP, Librarian, West Middlesex University Hospital NHS Trust.
[60891]   20/12/2001   **CM17/09/2003**

Devaney, Ms K R, BA DipLib, Acquisitions Manager, University of Reading Library.
[59890]   29/10/2001   **ME**

Devine, Mrs C E, Student, University of Ulster.
[10018060]   09/11/2010   **ME**

Devine, Ms G, MA HNC, Student, University of Strathclyde.
[10035324]   08/10/2014   **ME**

Devitt, Ms B, BSc (Hons), Know How Officer, Slaughter and May, London.
[55383]   07/10/1997   **ME**

Devlin, Ms L M, DMS MCLIP, Retired.
[10625]   16/01/1968   **CM01/01/1972**

Devlin, Ms N M, BA (Hons) MA MCLIP, Head of Information Res., Nottingham Trent University.
[44224]   16/07/1990   **CM29/01/1992**

Devlin, Mr P, BA DLIS MLIS MA MCLIP, College Librarian, Dublin Institute of Technology (DIT).
[10004709]   01/01/1997   **CM01/04/1999**

Devnally, Mr D K, BA DipLib HonFLA, Resident Bombay.
[39728]   06/07/1956   **HFE13/09/1984**

Devonald, Ms J A, BA (Hons) MA, Project Officer, Race Relations Resource Centre, University of Manchester.
[56889]   02/11/1998   **ME**

Devoy, Mrs F, MA DipLib MCLIP PGDE, Librarian, St Mungos High School, Falkirk.
[36236]   15/08/1983   **CM24/03/1987**

Dewe, Ms A J, BSc FNZLA AALIA MCLIP MArtsMgt, Formerly University Librarian, La Trobe University, Aus.
[60070]   07/03/1978   **CM07/03/1978**

Dewerpe, Ms M, BA MSc, Librarian, UKCBC.
[10026407]   03/10/2014   **ME**

Dewhirst, Mrs A L, BA MSc, Unemployed.
[10020822]   18/04/2012   ME
Dewhurst, Mrs V B, BA (Hons), Head of Library, Queen Elizabeth's
Grammar School, Blackburn.
[63212]   16/03/2004   ME
Dewick, Mrs K, Student, Aberystwyth University.
[10035156]   22/09/2014   ME
Dews, Mrs E, BA (Hons) FCLIP, Retired.
[3921]   26/02/1951   FE01/01/1961
Dexter, Mr S, BSc (Hons),
[10014336]   10/07/2009   AF
Dextre Clarke, Mrs S G, MSc FCLIP, Retired.
[60275]   05/10/1971   FE22/04/1988
Dezurick-Badran, Ms E, UCL MA LIS student and YA Library UK
blogger.
[10017341]   02/03/2011   AF
Dhawan, Ms K, BA, Part time.
[10009719]   31/08/1995   ME
Dholiwar, Miss V, MCLIP, Retired.
[31814]   15/12/1979   CM15/09/1983
Di Cicco, Mrs C F, BSc (Hons) MA LIS, Librarian and Learning
Resources Coordinator, Princess Alice Hospice.
[10035093]   15/09/2014   ME
Di Tillio, Mr C, Funzionario Biblioteche, Roma Capitale – Istituzione
Sistema Biblioteche Centri Culturali.
[58734]   01/07/2000   ME
Diakakis, Mr P, BA MA MA, Student, King's College London.
[10026422]   04/12/2013   ME
Diaper, Mrs P H, BLib MCLIP, Lib & Info Assistant, Fowey Lib & One
Stop Shop, Cornwall Council.
[19874]   01/01/1973   CM28/11/1977
Dibbins, Miss E J C, ACLIP, Senior Lib. Assistant, Dudley Library,
Dudley.
[10017382]   12/08/2010   ACL19/10/2012
Dick, Ms A M, Information Officer, Scottish Envir. Protection Agency,
Heriot Watt Res. Park, Edinburgh.
[45620]   04/04/1991   ME
Dick, Miss B A M, MA DipLib MCLIP, Retired.
[27153]   24/01/1977   CM31/01/1980
Dick, Miss M H, MCLIP, Retired.
[3931]   05/02/1952   CM01/01/1959
Dickenson, Mrs M J, ACLIP, Senior Library Assistant, Chichester
Library.
[10014004]   17/06/2009   ACL20/04/2012
Dickerson, Mrs J, B. BIBL (Hons),
[10034905]   21/08/2014   ME
Dickey, Miss M T, MCLIP, Retired.
[30614]   19/02/1979   CM03/05/1989
Dickinson, Mrs A, MCLIP, Librarian, Netherhall School, Cambridge.
[559]   01/01/1971   CM01/11/1975
Dickinson, Miss E, BA MCLIP, Retired.
[13246]   01/01/1961   CM01/01/1963
Dickinson, Mr S, Volunteer Library Assistant, Samuel Pepys School, St
Neots.
[10020982]   03/05/2012   AF
Dickinson, Mr T, OBE HonFLA Hon ELA, Hon. Fellow.
[46052]   11/09/1991   HFE11/01/1991
Dickinson, Mrs T A, BA MCLIP, Young Peoples Serv. Lib. (Job Share),
Torbay L. Serv., Torquay Central Library.
[46877]   20/02/1992   CM16/11/1994
Dicks, Mrs K L, BA DipLib MCLIP, Chief Library Assistant, European
Collections and Cataloguing, Cambridge University Library.
[42893]   04/04/1989   CM22/04/1992

Dickson, Miss D M, FCLIP, Life Member.
[3944]   17/02/1951   FE01/01/1964
Dickson, Mr E, MA (Hons) Dip Lib DipGerman, Senior Legal Deposit
Librarian, National Library of Scotland.
[10006176]   11/08/1986   ME
Dickson, Mrs K A, MA DipILS, Senior Library Assistant, Aberdeenshire
Council.
[54620]   04/02/1997   ME
Dickson, Mrs S M T, BA DipLib MCLIP, L. Resource Centre Co-Ord.,
City of Edinburgh Council.
[56198]   01/04/1998   CM20/09/2000
Didino, Mr G, Information Support Assistant, Queen Mary University of
London.
[10033067]   07/02/2014   ME
Dienelt, Mr O, DipLib MCLIP, Librarian, Inst. fuer Baustoffe, Tech.
University of Braunschweig, Germany.
[42897]   18/04/1989   CM17/01/2001
Diggle, Mr A H, BSc MBA MCLIP, Consultant, Self-employed, London.
[23176]   02/11/1974   CM05/01/1978
Dighe, Mrs S, BA (Hons) LLB BLS, Librarian, Park High School,
Stanmore.
[65347]   01/01/2006   ME
Dillon, Mrs M, BA DipLib MCLIP, Information Centre Manager., BNP
Paribas., London.
[35902]   02/02/1983   CM14/04/1987
Dillon, Mr M, Team Leader FOI / Open Data Policy Team, DWP.
[10033884]   09/05/2014   ME
Dilly, Mrs V S, BA (Hons), Assistant, Librarian, Ardingly College,
Haywards Heath.
[10016915]   10/06/2010   ME
Dimate Diaz, Mr F, PgDip, Unemployed.
[10032108]   28/10/2013   AF
Dimmock, Mrs G F, BA (Hons) MSc PGCTHE MCLIP FHEA, Head of
Academic Liaison, Library and Learning Services, University of
Northampton.
[58718]   01/07/2000   CM13/03/2002
Dimmock, Miss L M, BA (Hons), Student.
[10015440]   18/11/2009   ME
Dine, Mr D G, MCLIP, Retired.
[3962]   24/08/1951   CM01/01/1956
Dingley, Mrs P O, BA MCLIP, Retired.
[3964]   31/10/1971   CM04/10/1973
Dingwall, Miss S, PgDip, Research Officer, IDOX Information Service,
Glasgow.
[10022785]   23/04/2013   ME
Diprose, Mrs K A, MSc BSc, Information & Support Programme Mngr,
Macmillan Cancer Support, London.
[66044]   08/09/2006   ME
Disalvo, Miss M K, BA, Casual Lib. Assistant /Student, Aberystwyth
University.
[10020884]   19/04/2012   ME
Divall, Mrs P J, BA (Hons) MA MSc MCLIP, Clinical Librarian, University
Hospital of Leicester NHS, Leicester Royal Infirmary.
[59984]   15/11/2001   CM08/12/2004
Dix, Mrs N B, BSc MA MCLIP, Unwaged.
[62088]   12/02/2003   CM03/10/2007
Dixon, Mrs A L, BA (Hons) MA MCLIP, L. Servs. Manager, British
Geological Survey, Nottingham.
[56642]   01/10/1998   CM21/11/2001
Dixon, Mr A T, MA LLM, Knowledge Manager, Turley Associates.
[43395]   19/10/1989   ME
Dixon, Dr D, BA MPhil DipLib PhD MCLIP,
[18636]   18/10/1969   CM01/01/1972

Dixon, Mr G J, Blib (Hons) MLib, Senior Branch Librarian, City of Armadale Libraries, Western Australia.
[10015207]   26/02/1991   ME

Dixon, Miss I L, MCLIP, Retired.
[3981]   30/03/1944   CM01/01/1957

Dixon, Miss J, Res. Development Manager, ICAEW L. &Information Serv., London.
[10016555]   19/11/1993   ME

Dixon, Mr J G, BA (Hons), Senior Learning Advisor, Aberystwyth University.
[10020689]   26/03/2012   ME

Dixon, Mr K A, MA MA, Information Scientist, IOM., Edinburgh.
[38193]   30/01/1985   CM01/04/2002

Dixon, Mrs M L R, MCLIP, Retired.
[3987]   01/10/1945   CM01/01/1957

Dixon, Mr N, MCLIP, Learning and Teaching Librarian, The Open University.
[10011080]   24/09/2008   CM12/09/2012

Dixon, Miss R P, MCLIP, Retired.
[3989]   01/01/1964   CM01/01/1967

Djakov, Mrs G, BSc Librarianship, Library Manager, Didcot Girls School.
[10032594]   18/12/2013   ME

Dobb, Mr C R, BA MCLIP DMS, Development Librarian for Adult Services, Greenwich Leisure Limited.
[29636]   05/10/1978   CM13/01/1984

Dobbins, Mrs D A, BA (Hons) MCLIP, Freelance Indexer/Proofreader (Advanced Member of Society of Indexers).
[41645]   03/02/1988   CM23/07/1997

Dobbins, Mrs J, BA MSc, Library Volunteer, Wiltshire CC.
[56390]   24/09/2013   ME

Dobby, Miss P C, BA MCLIP, HR Records Administrator, UCL.
[4001]   01/01/1967   CM01/01/1971

Dobie, Mrs H D, MA DipLib MCLIP,
[28116]   04/10/1977   CM25/03/1980

Dobie, Mrs L C, Pg Dip MCLIP, Information Officer, Idox Information Serv.
[10011173]   29/09/2008   CM16/05/2012

Dobreva, Prof Dr M, Senior Researcher, CDLR, University of Strathclyde.
[10014609]   19/08/2009   ME

Dobson, Miss E, MA FCLIP, Life Member.
[4005]   02/02/1954   FE01/01/1968

Dobson, Miss G, BA (Hons), Urban Renewal Officer-Housing Choice, Salford Council.
[42050]   19/08/1988   CM24/05/1995

Dobson, Miss H, BA (Hons), Graduate Trainee, Manchester Metropolitan University.
[10032467]   06/12/2013   ME

Dobson, Mrs L, BSc (Hons), Online Learn. Coordinator, Durham C. C.
[58662]   09/05/2000   ME

Dobson, Miss L N, MA (Hons) MCLIP, Technical Services Librarian., Queen's College., Oxford.
[59849]   16/10/2001   CM03/10/2007

Dobson, Mr M L, BBibl (Hons), L. Director, US Embassy Library, Pretoria, South Africa.
[63814]   01/10/2004   ME

Dobson, Mrs P, BA (Hons) MSc MCLIP,
[39354]   13/01/1986   RV22/06/2007   CM17/11/1999

Dobson, Mrs R, BA (Hons) MA MCLIP, Art and Architecture Librarian, Edinburgh College of Art.
[54327]   15/11/1996   CM01/06/2005

Dobson, Miss V J, BA MA MCLIP, Information Services Librarian.
[10020302]   11/01/2012   CM20/06/2014

Docherty, Miss T, MCLIP, Acting Team Leader, Clackmannanshire Library, Alloa.
[64814]   18/07/2005   CM18/12/2009

Dodd, Mr D C, BSc (Hons) MCLIP, Unemployed.
[4018]   01/01/1967   CM01/01/1971

Dodd, Dr R L B, BA MPhil Phd, Research Officer.
[10023203]   18/06/2013   ME

Dodd, Mr S, BA (Hons) MA, Library Services and Learning Centre Manager, County Durham and Darlington NHS Foundation Trust.
[10033087]   10/02/2014   ME

Dodds, Mr I, BSc (Hons) MA MCLIP, Hd. of Cultural Servs., London B. of Richmond upon Thames.
[51464]   24/02/1995   CM22/07/1998

Dodds, Mr J C, FCLIP, Life Member.
[4030]   24/09/1951   FE18/11/1998

Dodson, Mrs E R, BA DipLib MCLIP, Head of L. /Resources, Myton School, Warwick, Warks.
[30152]   17/01/1979   CM16/01/1981

Doe, Mrs B M, BA (Hons) MCLIP, Senior Business Intelligence Analyst, Edwards Wildman Palmer UK LLP, London.
[10006375]   23/10/2007   CM15/01/2013

Doe, Ms S E, DipLib MCLIP, Director of Information & Research, Sidley Austin, London.
[44288]   15/08/1990   CM26/01/1994

Dogterom, Miss M E, MA PgDip MCLIP, Cataloguer, British Library, Boston Spa.
[46198]   10/10/1991   CM08/12/2004

Doherty, Mr A F, MCLIP, Campus Librarian, University College Falmouth (Jobshare).
[22740]   02/09/1974   CM18/08/1977

Doherty, Ms L, MScILS, Assistant Librarian, Royal Irish Academy of Music.
[10021651]   10/02/2004   ME

Doherty, Miss L, Information Manager, Ministry of Defence.
[10034309]   02/07/2014   ME

Doherty, Miss S, BA (Hons) MSc MA, Information Specialist, MHRA, Communications Division, London.
[53970]   16/10/1996   ME

Doherty-Allan, Ms R, BA Dip MA DipIM, Campus Library Manager, Magee Campus, Ulster University.
[54702]   06/03/1997   ME

Doig, Miss C, MA (Hons) DipILS MCLIP, Librarian, Bell Baxter High School, Fife.
[54391]   02/12/1996   CM15/10/2002

Doig, Mr C, BA (Hons) PgDipLIS MCLIP, Post Graduate Student., University of Paisley.
[55485]   15/10/1997   CM15/05/2002

Doig, Mrs F L, MA DipLib MCLIP, Part Time Librarian (Bibliographic Service.), University of Dundee.
[26290]   01/10/1983   CM19/01/1988

Dolan, Mr J, OBE BA MCLIP, Consultant.
[23907]   21/01/1975   CM21/01/1977

Dolan, Rev M J, MA FCLIP, Retired.
[4047]   20/01/1956   FE01/01/1965

Dolben, Ms L, BA DipLib MCLIP, Part-time Assistant Librarian, Tavistock & Portman NHS Trust.
[37097]   14/02/1984   CM06/10/1987

Dolby, Mr C, BA, Prison Library Manager, HMP Birmingham.
[10014565]   15/09/1998   ME

Doleschal, Miss M, MA PgDip,
[10013968]   17/06/2009   ME

Dolitzscher, Mrs A, MA FCLIP, Retired.
[4050]   25/09/1951   FE01/01/1959

Dolman, Miss K, MA PGCE (FE), Senior Assistant Librarian, Manchester Metropolitan University.
[10022555]   26/03/2013   ME

Dombovari, Dr A, PhD, Student, Robert Gordon University.
[10032479]   10/12/2014   ME

Donadello, Mr I, Student.
[10021747]   09/10/2012   ME

Donald, Mrs J, Library Assistant, Perth & Kinross Council.
[10020991]   03/05/2012   ME

Donald, Mr P, BLS PGCHE MCLIP FHEA, Learning and Teaching Librarian, Libraries & Learning Resources, Nottingham Trent University.
[53507]   10/07/1996   **CM17/03/1999**

Donaldson, Mrs J L, MA DipLib MCLIP, School Librarian, Jordanhill School, Glasgow.
[37694]   16/10/1984   **CM07/06/1988**

Donaldson, Dr R, MA PhD, Life Member.
[4070]   23/04/1956   ME

Donaldson, Mrs S A, BSc PgDipLib MCLIP, Adult Library and Information Services Section Leader, Leisure Culture Dundee.
[35600]   10/11/1982   **CM29/03/2006**

Donegan, Mrs C, MCLIP, Retired.
[13550]   22/02/1967   **CM01/01/1970**

Doney, Ms E J, BA (EC) MSc MCLIP, Trials Search Co-ordinator, Cochrane Skin Group, University of Nottingham.
[54268]   12/11/1996   **CM22/09/1999**

Dong, Mr H, Student University of Sheffield.
[10032281]   13/11/2013   ME

Donin, Mrs A L, BA (Hons) MA MCLIP, Assistant Librarian (Accessibility), University of Portsmouth Library.
[10031471]   13/08/2013   **CM20/06/2014**

Donkin, Mrs E, MA MCLIP, Library Manager., Biddick Sch. Washington.
[59198]   19/12/2000   **CM18/09/2002**

Donkor, Mr J E, Student, University of Manchester.
[10022142]   20/05/2013   ME

Donlan, Ms C, BA MSc, Student Information Points Manager, University of Edinburgh.
[10021011]   04/05/2012   ME

Donnelly, Mrs A J, BA (Hons) MCLIP, Visitor welcome supervisor, National Trust.
[50553]   15/09/1994   **CM06/04/2005**

Donnelly, Ms K, BA, Library Manager, Mitchell Library, Glasgow.
[10014143]   07/03/1984   ME

Donnelly, Miss M R, BA DipLib MCLIP, Retired.
[4080]   06/10/1969   **CM13/02/1973**

Donnelly, Mrs S J, BA (Hons) MA, Learning Resource Centre Manager, Library Cheadle, Marple Sixth Form College.
[10011616]   30/10/2008   ME

Donoghue, Mr S, BA (Hons) PgDipLIS MCLIP, Local Studies Librarian, London Borough of Havering, Central Library.
[42834]   14/03/1989   **CM07/09/2005**

Donoghue, Mrs V, BA MSc MCLIP, Learning Resources Manager, Wood Green School, Witney.
[27751]   04/08/1977   **CM18/11/1981**

Donohue, Miss K, Student.
[10032066]   24/10/2013   ME

Donohue, Mr N, BA (Hons) MA MCLIP, Learning & Teaching Services Manager, University of Leicester.
[10010113]   04/07/2008   **RV27/03/2014**   **CM11/06/2010**

Donovan, Mrs A, MA MCLIP, Part-time Student, University College Ferrier Lib., London.
[65276]   25/11/2005   **CM07/07/2010**

Donovan, Mr P, BA, Senior Library Assistant, Northumbia University.
[10022577]   26/03/2013   ME

Doody, Mrs A L, BLS (Hons) MCLIP, Service Development Librarian, Berkshire Education Library Service, Reading.
[33533]   01/01/1981   **CM25/11/1985**

Doogan, Miss A H, MA (Hons) DipLIS, School Librarian, St Peter the Apostle School.
[50860]   24/10/1994   ME

Dooley, Mr T, BA PgDip, Assistant Librarian, Manchester Metropolitan University.
[10022826]   13/08/2013   ME

Dorabjee, Miss S, BSc MCLIP, Information Consultant.
[60278]   06/06/1980   **CM06/06/1980**

Doran, Ms E, BA MCLIP, Life Member.
[24204]   18/04/1975   **CM12/12/1991**

Doran, Ms J D, BA (Hons) MA PGCHE MCLIP FHEA, Subject Librarian for Business, Education and Professional Studies (BEPS) University of Gloucestershire, Cheltenham.
[58214]   18/11/1999   **CM17/09/2003**

Doran, Ms N, MSc, City University.
[10001324]   06/02/2007   ME

Dore, Mrs J D, MCLIP, Information Librarian, Worthing Library, West Sussex County Council.
[22783]   15/10/1974   **CM04/08/1977**

Dormer, Ms D, Unwaged.
[63417]   06/05/2004   ME

Dorney, Mr C G, BA (Hons) MA MCLIP, Principal Librarian For Information, Advice and Digital Services, Northamptonshire County Council.
[61025]   03/02/2002   **CM15/09/2004**

Dorney, Mr P A, BA (Hons) MCLIP, Senior Librarian., School Library Service.
[52358]   26/10/1995   **CM18/11/1998**

Dorsett, Miss R, MSc BA (Hons), Graduated from Northumbria University 2012.
[10018116]   16/11/2010   ME

Dott, Miss E, MA MCLIP, Academic Liaison Librarian, University of Sunderland.
[10018414]   14/01/2011   **CM08/03/2013**

Douce, Mr G O, ICT Technician, Website Manager, Ashley School, Lowestoft.
[10006290]   05/10/2007   AF

Douch, Mr P, BA MCLIP MSocInd, Parish Clerk.
[32922]   25/10/1980   **CM10/05/1988**

Doughty, Mr K A, FCLIP, Retired.
[4103]   27/01/1948   **FE01/01/1957**

Doughty, Miss S J, BA (Hons) PgDipILS MCLIP, Applications Support Officer, University of Aberdeen.
[61097]   28/02/2002   **CM11/03/2009**

Douglas, Ms A M, MCLIP, Head of L. Serv., Tavistock & Portman NHS Foundation Trust, London.
[18644]   25/09/1972   **CM01/01/1975**

Douglas, Miss C E,
[10011283]   07/10/2008   ME

Douglas, Mr J D, BA (Hons) DipIS MCLIP, Director, The National Literacy Trust, London.
[51334]   16/01/1995   **CM22/07/1998**

Douglas, Mrs L, BA (Hons), Information Manager, University of Northumbria, Newcastle.
[62251]   02/04/2003   ME

Douie, Mrs M D P, BBIBL (Hons), Higher Education Librarian, City College Plymouth.
[62101]   17/02/2003   ME

Doulgeris, Mrs P, BA MInfoStud (Lib), Doulgeris, P., BA, MInfoStud(Lib). Metadata Librarian, IAEA.
[10017542]   02/09/2010   ME

Dovey, Miss A H, BA MA,
[65266]   02/12/2005   **ME**

Dovey, Mr M J, BA MSc MBCS MCLIP, Programme Director, JISC Executive, Bristol.
[60464]   05/07/1999   **CM05/07/1999**

Dowding, Ms F S, LLB (Hons) PgD PgDipLIS, Subject Librarian/ Campus Co-ordinator, University of West of England, Bristol.
[55989]   12/01/1998   **ME**

Dowling, Mrs E L, BSc Econ LIS MCLIP, Principal Lib. Assistant, Hartley Library, University of Southampton.
[10013653]   01/06/2009   **CM14/11/2012**

Dowling, Mrs H M, BA MCLIP, Customer Serv. Manager, London Borough of Islington L. Serv., London.
[38182]   24/01/1985   **CM16/02/1988**

Dowling, Mr J H, MCLIP, Retired.
[4126]   18/01/1962   **CM01/01/1966**

Dowling, Ms M E, BA MCLIP, Retired.
[4127]   31/07/1965   **CM01/01/1970**

Dowling, Ms T L, BA (Hons) DipIM MCLIP, Librarian, Swindon Borough Council, West Swindon L.
[55797]   24/11/1997   **CM17/01/2001**

Downard, Mrs K J, BA DipILS MCLIP, School Librarian, Shavington High School, Crewe.
[43659]   20/11/1989   **CM27/11/1996**

Downes, Miss D, BA DipLib MCLIP, Librarian, Lewisham & Southwark College, London.
[35936]   14/02/1983   **CM01/04/1986**

Downes, Ms E, BA MSc, Graduate Trainee, Classical Faculty Library.
[10031702]   14/10/2013   **ME**

Downey, Mrs L D, MCLIP, Consultant, School Library Advisory Service, Kent.
[22792]   10/10/1974   **CM28/09/1977**

Downham, Ms G J, BA DipLib MCLIP PGCAP FHEA, Academic Liaison Librarian, University of Surrey Library, Guildford.
[34261]   08/10/1981   **CM16/11/1994**

Downham, Mrs K M, ACLIP, Senior Library Assistant Local & Family History, Leeds Library, Leeds.
[10006902]   17/12/2007   **ACL09/11/2011**

Downie, Ms C M, BA, Freelance.
[44584]   30/10/1990   **ME**

Downie, Miss R, BA (Hons) MSc MCLIP, Library Development Officer, West Lothian Council.
[10021554]   30/08/2012   **CM13/11/2013**

Downing, Miss E A J, BA MCLIP, Retired.
[16813]   31/08/1945   **CM01/01/1952**

Downing, Miss S, BA (Hons) MA, Knowledge & Information Professional.
[54089]   25/10/1996   **ME**

Dowson, Ms N, BSc (Hons) DipIS MCLIP, Library Services Manager, Open University, Milton Keynes.
[52539]   06/11/1995   **CM13/03/2002**

Doyle, Mr A, MCLIP, Life Member. Retired.
[4152]   24/08/1953   **CM01/01/1960**

Doyle, Mrs G C A, MCLIP, Lib. /Cheltenham College, Cheltenham.
[21493]   09/10/1973   **RV**30/04/2014   **CM11/11/1976**

Doyle, Miss H R, MA,
[10014276]   10/07/2009   **ME**

Doyle, Mrs K M, BA MCLIP,
[30059]   17/10/1978   **CM18/05/1981**

Doyle, Mrs L, MCLIP, Unemployed.
[21353]   17/11/1973   **CM15/11/1976**

Doyle, Ms R A, MBA MCLIP, Head of L. & Heritage Serv., Central Library, London Borough of Islington.
[25730]   11/03/1976   **CM26/07/1978**

Doyle, Ms S M, BA MCLIP, Retired.
[4157]   09/10/1969   **CM01/01/1972**

Doyle, Ms S P, MCLIP, Librarian.
[26717]   07/10/1976   **CM29/12/1980**

Dracup, Miss J B, BSc MCLIP, Lib. Teacher.
[28806]   25/01/1978   **CM13/11/1981**

Dracup, Ms N, Information Specialist, Social Care Institute for Excellence.
[10016980]   01/12/2011   **ME**

Draffin, Ms A M, BA DipLib MCLIP, Information Manager, National Autistic Society London.
[29638]   03/10/1978   **CM23/01/1981**

Draisey, Miss A L, MA (Hons), Library Manager, West Exe School.
[10022568]   26/03/2013   **ME**

Drakard, Mrs H, BA (Hons) MA MCLIP, Library Development Manager, Leicestershire County Council.
[10013525]   27/10/2009   **RV**30/04/2014   **CM08/03/2013**

Drake, Miss C E, MA, Research Support Administrator, University of Bath.
[10035012]   05/09/2014   **ME**

Drakes, Mrs E R R, BA (Hons) MCLIP, Librarian, Cheshire East Council.
[49843]   21/12/1993   **CM17/09/2003**

Draup, Mrs V M, BSc, Lecturer, Bradford College.
[10011367]   19/03/1982   **CM01/03/1982**

Drayton, Mrs A C, BA (Hons), Assistant Librarian, Yeovil District Hospital NHS Foundation Trust.
[60992]   28/01/2002   **ME**

Drayton, Dr S, BA (Hons) MSc DPhil,
[10015540]   02/11/1995   **ME**

Dredge, Mrs M R, MA DipLIS MCLIP, Librarian, Macicie Academy, Aberdeenshire.
[36606]   17/10/1983   **CM17/05/2000**

Dreimann, Mr J, User Experience Manager, University of Sheffield.
[10032148]   29/10/2013   **ME**

Dresser, Mrs I M, BA DipLib MCLIP, Information and E oorvicoo Officer, White Swan Centre, North Tyneside MBC.,
[35435]   01/10/1982   **CM14/04/1987**

Drever, Ms R M, MA DipLib MCLIP, Assistant Head of Library & Information Serv., East Sussex County Council, East Sussex.
[37531]   01/10/1984   **CM18/01/1989**

Drew, Mrs H P, BSc MCLIP MA, Unemployed.
[25080]   11/11/1975   **CM03/10/1978**

Drew, Mrs J, BA (Hons), Library Assistant, Sheffield University.
[10032089]   24/10/2013   **ME**

Drew, Mrs P A, MCLIP, Retired.
[4180]   15/12/1965   **CM01/01/1970**

Drewett, Mrs A J, FCLIP, Information Specialist, National Crime Agency.
[21912]   04/02/1974   **FE07/09/2005**

Driels, Ms J, BA MCLIP, Retired.
[4187]   01/01/1967   **CM01/01/1971**

Dring, Mrs S, MA (Hons) MCLIP, Learning Resources Manager, Ripon Grammar School.
[64176]   31/01/2005   **CM10/03/2011**

Drinkwater, Mr R, BA, Student, UCL.
[10026497]   09/12/2013   **ME**

Driscoll, Ms M C, BA DipLib MCLIP, Family Information Service Co-ordinator, Conwy Family Information Service, Conwy County Borough Council.
[34188]   15/10/1981   **CM16/05/1985**

Driver, Miss K A, BA (Hons), Counter Services Supervisor, Kings College London, University of London.
[40464]   03/02/1987   **ME**

Driver, Ms T, BA DipLib MCLIP, Printed Books Librarian, Religious Society of Friends, London.
[34263]   20/10/1981   **CM08/12/1987**
Drosopoulou, Dr L, BA MA PhD, Student, University of Sheffield.
[10026498]   17/10/2014   **ME**
Drumm, Ms K, MA, Graduate Trainee Information Assistant, City University.
[10031874]   10/10/2013   **ME**
Drummond, Mr G N, MBE MCLIP, Retired.
[4199]   01/01/1957   **CM01/01/1964**
Drummond, Miss L H, MA, Knowledge Specialist, Pennine Care NHS Foundation Trust.
[10015172]   21/10/2009   **ME**
Drummond, Mrs M, BA (Hons) MCLIP, Librarian, Fife Council, Glenrothes.
[22467]   20/05/1974   **CM01/07/1991**
Drummond, Miss S, BA, Student.
[10022525]   19/03/2013   **ME**
Drury, Mrs K E, BA (Hons) MA MCLIP, Liaison Librarian, Reading University Library.
[56868]   29/10/1998   **CM10/07/2002**
Drury, Ms S, MEd BA MCLIP, Life Member.
[4211]   30/01/1961   **CM01/01/1965**
Drust, Mrs W V, BA MCLIP, Principal Lib. -Collections Management, Bibl. Serv., Co. Library, West Sussex.
[32633]   04/06/1980   **CM21/12/1984**
Dryburgh, Mr L, Document Controller (Senior),
[10032125]   29/10/2013   **ME**
Dryburgh, Mrs R F, MA DipLib MCLIP, Assistant Librarian Schools, Midlothian Council.
[30550]   05/02/1979   **CM12/02/1981**
D'Souza, Miss T, BSc (Hons), Library Manager, Woolwich Centre Library.
[10033168]   18/02/2014   **ME**
Du, Mr J, Student, The University of Hong Kong.
[10035574]   20/10/2014   **ME**
Du, Ms M, BSc MA MCLIP, Assistant Librarian, Royal College of Veterinary Surgeons Trust Library, London.
[10001701]   15/03/2001   **CM09/07/2008**
Dua, Mr E D, MCLIP, Life Member.
[4215]   25/02/1958   **CM01/01/1963**
Dubber, Mrs E H S, BA MCLIP,
[4216]   18/11/1971   **CM09/12/1974**
Dubiel, Mrs D, Central Circulating Library Co-ordinator, Polish Library, London.
[10012993]   17/03/2009   **ME**
Duce, Mrs M P, MA MCLIP, Retired.
[12545]   15/09/1967   **CM30/11/1972**
Ducker, Mrs A J, BSc (Hons), Collections Librarian, Liverpool Hope University.
[56706]   01/10/1998   **ME**
Ducker, Mr J M, MA MBCS FCLIP, Retired.
[60767]   24/06/1987   **FE24/06/1987**
Duckett, Mrs P N, BSc MA MSc MCLIP, Retired.
[4223]   13/10/1966   **CM01/01/1969**
Duckett, Mr R J, PhD FCLIP, Retired.
[4224]   03/10/1963   **FE27/05/1992**
Duckworth, Mrs A, BA MCLIP, Faculty Librarian, Liverpool Hope University.
[35829]   17/01/1983   **CM15/08/1989**
Duckworth, Mrs S J, BA (Hons) MCLIP, Prison Librarian, Kent County Council.
[49189]   12/10/1993   **CM17/03/1999**

Dudley, Mr P E, BED (Hons) MA MCLIP, Classroom Teacher, Sybourn Primary School, London.
[10015043]   06/11/1998   **CM21/11/2001**
Dudman, Miss J A, BSc MSc, L. Researcher, Self-emp., London.
[46159]   03/10/1991   **ME**
Dudman, Mr P V, BA (Hons) MSc (Econ), Arch., University of East London, London.
[55112]   15/07/1997   **CM18/09/2002**
Duff, Mr C I R, BA,
[10020467]   20/02/2012   **ME**
Duff, Mrs D J, BA (Hons) MCLIP, Librarian, East Lothian Council, Libraries.
[10010590]   01/11/1994   **CM22/08/2012**
Duff, Mr H A M, MA M LITT MCLIP, Librarian, Gleniffer High School, Paisley.
[28426]   01/12/1977   **CM21/07/1981**
Duffus, Mr I, BA, Student.
[10019998]   20/10/2011   **ME**
Duffy, Mrs A J, BA MCLIP, Retired.
[4236]   03/01/1965   **CM01/01/1969**
Duffy, Mr D A, BA MCLIP, Collections & Central Services. Manager., Calderdale MBC, Halifax.
[34514]   02/10/1981   **CM22/07/1985**
Duffy, Mrs D G, BA MCLIP, Electronic Resource Dev. Librarian, Bradford College.
[31639]   18/10/1979   **CM31/10/1984**
Duffy, Mr J O, BA MSc MCLIP ALAI, Sub- Lib. Bar Council Law L. Dublin.
[58081]   25/10/1999   **CM16/07/2003**
Duffy, Mr K, PGdiplib, Senior Service Manager, Community Libraries, Birmingham.
[10021094]   01/01/1985   **ME**
Duffy, Mr P J, BA (Hons) PgDip, Employed, Squire Sanders UK LLP, Manchester.
[10002207]   01/04/1995   **ME**
Dufty, Ms E, BA (Hons) DipLIS MCLIP, Knowledge Manager.
[48114]   09/11/1992   **CM23/07/1997**
Duggan, Mr A J, Office Manager (2), Ministry of Defence.
[10033916]   12/05/2014   **ME**
Duguid, Mrs A M, BA DipLib MCLIP, Librarian, Mott MacDonald, Croydon.
[29387]   29/06/1978   **CM10/11/1980**
Duley, Mrs M C, BA (Hons) MCLIP,
[10016669]   10/01/1994   **CM06/07/2011**
Dumper, Miss L J, BA DipLib MCLIP, Manager, Information Serv., TWI Ltd, Cambridge.
[26955]   19/01/1977   **CM19/01/1979**
Dunbar, Mr J A, BA (Hons), Librarian, John Laing Integrated Services, Hounslow, London.
[41658]   08/02/1988   **ME**
Duncan, Miss A, BA, Library Assistant Collection Development, Central St Martins College of Art & Design, London.
[10018009]   03/11/2010   **ME**
Duncan, Mr C M, MA (Hons) DipLib MCLIP, Information Serv. Librarian, Inverclyde Library, Greenock.
[40106]   21/10/1986   **CM29/03/2006**
Duncan, Miss H M, BA, Community Services Librarian, Aberdeen City Council.
[33905]   03/05/1981   **CM05/12/1985**
Duncan, Mr J, MA MCLIP, Retired.
[4260]   04/02/1960   **CM01/01/1963**
Duncan, Mr M, MA MSc, Library Adviser, Edinburgh City Council.
[10031619]   11/09/2013   **ME**

Duncan, Mrs S, BA (Hons) MCLIP, Assistant Director, School Library
Association, Swindon, Wiltshire.
[10001867]   13/03/2007   **CM19/03/1980**

Duncan, Mrs S F, BA MCLIP,
[25286]   13/01/1976   **CM18/09/1979**

Duncan, Ms S J, BA DipLib MCLIP, Self-employed.
[36397]   04/10/1983   **CM18/07/1991**

Dundas, Mrs K M, MA MCLIP, Life Member.
[20509]   14/03/1973   **CM01/04/1976**

Dungworth, Mrs N M, BA (Hons) MA MCLIP, Support Services
Librarian/Part-time, Loughborough University, Leics.
[48450]   12/01/1993   **CM22/01/1997**

Dunk, Mrs J, BSc (Pend), Lib. Assistant, Aberystwyth University,
Aberystwyth.
[10008396]   19/03/2008   **ME**

Dunkerley, Mrs L M, BA MCLIP, Retired.
[4267]   27/06/1964   **CM01/01/1968**

Dunkley, Mr M, BA MA, Principal Information Assistant, De Montfort
University, Leicester.
[10009844]   25/06/2008   **AF**

Dunlop, Miss J A, MSc (Econ) BLib MCLIP, Subject Assistant Librarian,
University of Ulster.
[10012331]   21/10/1980   **CM16/01/1986**

Dunmore, Mrs M C, BA MS, LRC Manager for secondary and primary,
Preston Manor All-Through School, Wembley, Middlesex.
[10001325]   07/02/2007   **ME**

Dunmore, Mr T G, BA (Hons) DipLib, Librarian, Royal Automobile Club,
London.
[53958]   16/10/1996   **ME**

Dunn, Mr A, MA MCLIP, Information Librarian, David Wilson Library,
University of Leicester.
[59118]   20/11/2000   **CM29/08/2007**

Dunn, Miss A, BA, Mental Health Specialist Librarian, Sussex Education
Centre, Mill View Hospital, Hove.
[10003284]   23/05/2007   **ME**

Dunn, Miss C I, DIP LOC HIST MCLIP, Retired.
[4275]   09/02/1961   **CM01/01/1969**

Dunn, Mrs E B, BA (Hons) MA MCLIP, Libr., Cheshire E. CC., Cheshire.
[55533]   20/10/1997   **CM02/02/2005**

Dunn, Ms H, BA DipLib MCLIP, Librarian, Higgs & Sons, Brierley Hill.
[31605]   25/10/1979   **CM24/01/1986**

Dunn, Miss J M, BA (Hons) DipIM, Stock Librarian, London Borough of
Barnet, London.
[56563]   25/08/1998   **ME**

Dunn, Mrs K, MA MCLIP, Resident overseas.
[61408]   10/07/2002   **CM04/10/2006**

Dunn, Mrs R J, BA (Hons) MCLIP, Library Assistant, Robinson Library,
Newcastle University.
[47696]   16/10/1992   RV13/11/2013   **CM13/06/2007**

Dunn, Mrs S J, BSc ACLIP, Learning Resource Centre., Herefordshire &
Ludlow College, SY8 1GD.
[10015419]   19/11/2009   **ACL14/03/2012**

Dunn, Miss T, MCLIP, Librarian, Guiseley School.
[55855]   02/12/1997   **CM23/01/2008**

Dunne, Ms G, BBS MSc, Branch Librarian, Kanturk Library.
[10031607]   10/09/2013   **ME**

Dunne, Ms M, MSc Psych MSc ILS, Information Officer, Health
Research Board.
[10009292]   15/05/2008   **ME**

Dunne, Mr M B, BA MA MCLIP, Digital Resources Librarian, IET.
[41153]   16/10/1987   **CM30/01/1991**

Dunne, Ms P, MA Information Services Man., Librarian London Borough
of Lambeth, Streatham.
[61594]   02/10/2002   **ME**

Dunnicliff, Ms J, LRC Manager, Stratford Upon Avon High School.
[59612]   28/06/2001   **ME**

Dunsford, Mrs J B I, MCLIP, Life Member.
[4291]   04/03/1944   **CM01/01/1947**

Dunsford, Mr S F, FCLIP, Life Member.
[4292]   19/01/1950   **FE01/01/1957**

Dunsire, Mr G J, BSc MCLIP, Retired.
[29551]   26/09/1978   **CM29/09/1980**

Dunstan, Mrs R M, BA MCLIP, L. Manager, Oxfordshire County Council.
[25525]   20/01/1976   **CM27/11/1979**

Durber, Mr D M, BA, Unwaged.
[49902]   10/01/1994   **ME**

Durbidge, Mrs D M, MCLIP, Retired.
[4297]   01/01/1947   **CM01/01/1950**

Durcan, Mr A J, BA MCLIP, Head of Culture, L. & Lifel. Learn.,
Newcastle City L.
[26956]   14/01/1977   **CM07/12/1981**

Durham, Mrs F P R, BA DipLib MCLIP, Learning and Teaching
Librarian, Open University Library, Milton Keynes.
[33504]   13/01/1981   **CM23/06/1986**

Durham, Mrs S R, BA DipLib MCLIP, Retired.
[39408]   24/01/1986   **CM19/09/1989**

Durham, Miss W K, Student, City University London.
[10035515]   16/10/2014   **ME**

Durkan, Mrs S K, BA MCLIP, Librarian and Careers Coordinator, John
Port School, Etwall, Derby.
[30607]   16/02/1979   **CM28/10/1981**

Durndell, Ms H M, MA DipLib, University Librarian, University of
Glasgow.
[27344]   08/03/1977   **ME**

Durrani, Mrs C, BA MCLIP, Retired.
[8220]   21/08/1964   **CM01/01/1969**

Duthie, Mrs T, BSc MCLIP, Library & Information Officer, Central Library,
Wellgate, Dundee DD1 1DB.
[10016793]   18/05/2010   **CM14/10/2011**

Dutt, Mr K K, MA MCLIP, Retired.
[4311]   23/01/1967   **CM19/04/1973**

Dutton, Dr A M, DPhi MA MA BA (Hons), Librarian, Upper Shirley High
School, Southampton.
[53756]   01/10/1996   **ME**

Dutton, Dr B G, BSc PhD CChem FRSC FCLIP, Retired.
[60581]   01/01/1965   **FE01/04/2002**

Dutton, Mrs C M, AInstAM MCLIP, Retired.
[4313]   03/02/1958   **CM01/01/1968**

Dutton, Mrs M T A, BA (Hons) DPS MCLIP, Librarian, Cent. Manchester
Child. NHS Trust.
[55506]   16/10/1997   **CM07/09/2005**

Dutton, Ms S H, MA, Knowledge Management Consultant.
[43089]   21/07/1989   **ME**

Duxberry, Mrs M, Team Librarian, Market Drayton Library, Shropshire.
[10019772]   08/09/2011   **AF**

Duxbury, Mrs P J, MA BSc (Hons) PGCE MCLIP, Information Librarian,
University of South Wales.
[61285]   08/05/2002   **CM21/11/2007**

Dwiar, Miss E, MA PGCE DipIS, Full Time Carer.
[43218]   02/10/1989   **ME**

Dwiar, Miss P, BA MSc CertEd DipLib, Library Assistant, Vision RCL,
London.
[32931]   07/10/1980   **CM06/12/1983**

Dwyer, Mr B A, BA DPA MCLIP, Retired.
[18652]   03/02/1953   **CM01/01/1964**

Dwyer, Mrs J M, BA DipLib MCLIP, Senior Library Assistant, Metadata &
eTechnologies Section, University of Sheffield L.
[33141]   05/10/1980   **CM18/06/1985**

Dybkowska, Ms M, Part-time Lib. Assistant, UCL, London.
[10001403] 14/02/2007 ME
Dyce, Mrs S E, MA DipLib MCLIP, L. Systems Officer, Aberdeen C. C., Aberdeen.
[31384] 01/10/1979 CM30/04/1982
Dye, Miss J, Library Services Coordinator, Ravensbourne.
[10022127] 08/01/2013 ME
Dyer, Miss A, BA MCLIP, Information Service Web Manager, University of East Anglia.
[42598] 20/01/1989 CM24/05/1995
Dyer, Mrs C H, BA MCLIP, Head of Service, Nottingham City Council.
[31445] 15/10/1979 CM28/07/1983
Dyer, Miss C M L, BA MCLIP, Bibliographic Servs. Team Mgr, De Montfort University.
[30399] 29/01/1979 CM05/10/1984
Dyke, Mrs L M, BA MCLIP, ICT/Knowledge Team Leader, Staffordshire County Council, Cannock L.
[43655] 20/11/1989 CM22/07/1992
Dykes, Mr A, BEd MA MSc FHEA, Professional Academic Development Tutor, University of Bedfordshire.
[10020223] 30/11/2011 ME
Dykes, Mrs A R, BA, Lib. Adult Serv., East Lothian L. Serv.
[10010657] 19/08/2008 ME
Dykes, Mrs E, BA MCLIP, Child. Serv. Librarian (Job Share), Nottingham City Council.
[22063] 22/01/1974 CM26/07/1977
Dykes, Mrs S, ACLIP, Discovery Centre Assistant, Gosport Discovery Centre.
[10018287] 13/12/2010 ACL27/03/2014
Dymott, Mr E A E, BSc MA MSc MRTPI MCLIP,
[38595] 01/08/1985 CM18/09/1991
Dyos, Mrs G, MCLIP, School Librarian, Putney High School, London.
[20381] 22/02/1973 CM03/11/1976
Dyson, Ms C J, BA (Hons) MSc MCLIP, Career Break.
[39007] 21/10/1985 CM29/10/1985
Dyson, Mrs M, BA GradDip MMus, Library Assistant.
[10022410] 26/02/2013 ME
Dziadyk, Mr N E, Student.
[10032096] 24/10/2013 ME

E

Eacott, Miss C M, BA (Hons) MSc (Econ), Library Assistant, Martial Rose Library, University Winchester.
[64612] 20/04/2005 ME
Eadon, Mrs J M, BA (Hons) MSc, Assistant Librarian, Warwick School, Warwick.
[53565] 24/07/1996 ME
Eagle, Ms K H, BSc (Hons), Student.
[10012559] 23/02/2009 ME
Eagle, Mr P A C, MChem MSc, Quick Information Officer, British Library.
[61847] 18/11/2002 ME
Eagle, Mr R S, MA DPA FCLIP, Life Member.
[4339] 04/02/1950 FE01/01/1959
Eagles, Mrs J, MSc MCLIP, Retired.
[25121] 04/11/1975 CM30/10/1978
Eames, Miss L L, MSc, Assistant librarian, Greenwich School of Management.
[10015516] 09/12/2009 ME
Earl, Mr C, BSc HonFLA, Retired.
[4343] 11/01/1960 HFE01/01/1999

Earl, Mrs G, BA (Hons) MCLIP, L. Serv. Manager, Health Management Library, Edinburgh.
[47522] 25/09/1992 CM17/03/1999
Earl, Mrs J A, BA Pg Dip MCLIP, Academic Support Librarian, The Library, University of Salford.
[66043] 11/08/2006 CM19/12/2008
Earl, Miss R K, ACLIP, L. Assist., Kempston Library, Bedford.
[10019436] 04/07/2011 ACL12/09/2012
Earl, Mr T, BSc, Student, University of Brighton.
[10032873] 23/01/2014 ME
Earl-Ridley, Mr J, BSc PgDip, Research Librarian, Slaughter and May.
[10032564] 16/12/2013 ME
Earls, Mr D, BA MLIS, Campus Support Assistant, Napier University.
[10021734] 08/10/2012 ME
Early, Mrs F, BA (Hons), Library Assistant, St James Catholic Primary, London.
[10001121] 12/01/2007 ME
Earney, Miss S L, BA (Hons) MA MCLIP, Manager, Aberconway L. Services, Cardiff University.
[50694] 12/10/1994 CM21/07/1999
Earnshaw, Mrs D, BA MCLIP, Resident in USA.
[40819] 01/07/1987 CM27/02/1991
Earnshaw, Mrs L C, Customer Serv. Officer, Kirklees County Council, Huddersfield.
[60036] 30/11/2001 ME
Easson, Ms K, MA DipLib MCLIP, Librarian, Literary & Philosophical Society, Newcastle.
[43278] 01/01/1947 CM27/05/1992
East, Miss J, MCLIP, Life Member.
[4353] 12/02/1952 CM01/01/1959
Eastell, Ms C, BA (Hons) MA MCLIP, Head of Libraries, Culture & Heritage, Devon County Council.
[49267] 20/10/1993 CM20/03/1996
Easthope, Miss J S, BA (Hons), Business Support Assistant, Cambridgeshire Libraries.
[10021375] 30/07/2012 ME
Eastoe, Mrs J I, Senior Library Assistant,
[64873] 22/08/2005 AF
Easton, Mr F M J, FCLIP, Retired.
[4362] 16/02/1955 FE01/01/1965
Easton, Mr R, Student, University of Strathclyde.
[10033055] 03/10/2014 ME
Eastwood, Ms E J, BA (Hons) MLIS CLIP, Reference Librarian, Los Alamos Public Library, USA.
[45721] 07/05/1991 CM22/11/1995
Eato, Mrs K A, BA (Hons) DipLib MCLIP, Retired.
[38201] 09/01/1985 CM01/09/1987
Eaton, Miss C, MSc BA (Hons) PgDip PGCE MCLIP, Analyst Team Leader: Knowledge & Records Management team, Care Quality Commission.
[47014] 01/04/1992 CM18/11/1993
Eaton, Mrs S D, BSc,
[64128] 18/01/2005 ME
Eatwell, Mr R F, MA FCLIP, Retired.
[4374] 17/01/1947 FE01/01/1962
Eaves, Miss K E, MA (Oxon) DipILS MCLIP, Unwaged.
[54132] 30/10/1996 CM20/09/2000
Ebenezer, Ms C M, MSc MA (Oxon) STM AKC MCLIP, PhD student, Information School, University of Sheffield.
[47544] 01/10/1992 CM13/06/2000
Ecclestone, Ms B M, MCLIP, Retired.
[32417] 24/03/1980 CM17/04/1986

Ecclestone, Ms K F, MLib MA Management, Learning Centre Manager, Cornwall College St Austell.
[41757] 10/03/1988 ME

Eckford, Ms J A, BSc (Hons) MSc MA, Information Governance Lead (SYB), West and South Yorkshire and Bassetlaw Commissioning Support Unit.
[10032400] 03/12/2013 ME

Economou, Mrs H, LRC Manager, The Latimer Arts College, Kettering.
[10021009] 04/05/2012 AF

Eddisford, Miss R, BA (Hons) MA MCLIP, Member Services Librarian, The London Library.
[10017055] 21/06/2010 CM09/11/2011

Eddison, Mrs S M, MA MCLIP, Libraries Shared Services Manager.
[37669] 17/10/1984 CM14/11/1989

Ede, Mrs E D, ALA MCLIP, Document Controller, Saint Gobain Property Department.
[10022216] 24/02/1975 CM20/09/1979

Eden, Mr R, MCLIP, Retired.
[4390] 01/01/1968 CM01/01/1971

Edgar, Ms J D, MA,
[10018128] 18/11/2010 ME

Edgar, Prof J R, MA FCLIP, Retired.
[4392] 23/05/1947 FE01/01/1964

Edge, Mrs K, BScEcon,
[10007452] 13/02/2008 ME

Edge, Mr T, MA (Hons) PGCE, Student, UCL.
[10035411] 13/10/2014 ME

Edmonds, Miss A J, BA (Hons) DipIS MCLIP, Head Librarian, St Mary's School, Shaftesbury Dorset.
[50395] 15/07/1994 CM19/05/1999

Edmonds, Mrs L, BA MCLIP,
[4402] 04/07/1971 CM01/01/1974

Edmonds, Mr R E, MCLIP, Retired.
[4404] 12/02/1969 CM06/12/1972

Edmunds, Ms A, BA CertEd CertTESOL MCLIP, Employment not known.
[4409] 03/10/1968 CM01/01/1971

Edmunds, Mr G L, BSc (Econ) DipLib MCLIP, Library Manager, West Sussex County Council.
[40358] 22/01/1987 CM15/08/1990

Edwardes, Miss G E, BA (Hons) MCLIP FHEA, Chief Catg. /Information Librarian, Caerleon Campus Library, University of South Wales.
[46675] 06/12/1991 CM08/12/2004

Edwards, Miss A, MA (Hons), Student Library Assistant, University of Essex.
[10031746] 16/09/2014 ME

Edwards, Mrs A E, ACLIP, Lib. Assistant, Potland School, Worksop.
[10015232] 29/10/2009 ACL10/11/2010

Edwards, Mrs A J, BA (Hons) PgDip ILS, Lib. & Arch., Pocklington School, Pocklington, York.
[63748] 29/09/2004 ME

Edwards, Mr A J, BA MCLIP, Retired.
[4415] 09/01/1953 CM01/01/1956

Edwards, Mr A S, BLib (Hons) MCLIP, Head Printed Historical Sources, British Library, London.
[38488] 17/05/1985 CM12/12/1990

Edwards, Ms B C, BSc MCLIP, Information Specialist, OSFI, Canada.
[38436] 25/04/1985 CM03/10/1989

Edwards, Mr C, BA (Hons) DipLib MCLIP, Chief Librarian.
[35127] 01/08/1982 CM06/12/1985

Edwards, Ms C, BLib (Hons) MCLIP, Programme Officer (Self-Employed), Nottingham.
[10004962] 01/07/1980 CM14/08/1985

Edwards, Miss C A, MA MIL MCLIP DipTrans, Head of Information Policy and Practice, Foreign & Commonwealth Office.
[39067] 14/10/1985 CM09/08/1988

Edwards, Ms C E, DipLib MA (Hons) MCLIP, Programme Officer, Civil Society Deptartment, Department for International Development, East Kilbride.
[29643] 11/10/1978 CM16/10/1981

Edwards, Mrs C L, BA (Hons) MSc (Econ) MCLIP, Learning and Development Lead - L., NHS West Midlands, Workforce Deanery, Birmingham.
[51186] 23/11/1994 CM18/03/1998

Edwards, Ms C M, BA DipLib MCLIP, Head of Reader Services, National Library of Wales.
[40006] 15/10/1986 CM22/05/1991

Edwards, Mr D L, MBIOL MSc, Senior Library Assistant, Bournemouth BC.
[10034376] 09/07/2014 ME

Edwards, Mrs E, BA (Hons) DipILM, Evidence Services Manager, Cheshire & Merseyside Commissioning Support Service Chester.
[57424] 15/03/1999 ME

Edwards, Mrs E A, BA (Hons) MA MCLIP, Team Manager: Libraries, Nottinghamshire County Council.
[61870] 22/11/2002 CM09/11/2005

Edwards, Ms E C, MCLIP, Project Librarian, Coleg Sir Gar, Llanelli.
[30156] 17/01/1979 CM27/02/1981

Edwards, Miss G, BA (Hons) MSc MCLIP, Career Break.
[36040] 20/04/1983 CM10/05/1988

Edwards, Mr G B, BA (Hons) MSc (Econ) MCLIP, Local and Family History Librarian, Pembrokeshire CC.
[55494] 15/10/1997 CM18/09/2002

Edwards, Ms H, HonFCLIP, L. Project Manager SKOLKOVO Moscow School of Management.
[10014188] 03/11/2009 HFE13/07/2009

Edwards, Mrs H, L. Systems Manager, County Hall, Aylesbury.
[63537] 17/06/2004 AF

Edwards, Ms H E A, BLib MCLIP, Retired (from 24/11/2011).
[14229] 14/05/1970 CM09/10/1974

Edwards, Mr H J, MCLIP, Life Member.
[4429] 15/03/1951 CM01/01/1960

Edwards, Mrs J, BA MCLIP, Retired.
[4432] 04/03/1959 CM01/01/1961

Edwards, Mr J A, BA MSc PgCertHE MCLIP, Liaison Manager, Middlesex University, London.
[36527] 19/10/1983 CM05/04/1988

Edwards, Ms J E, BA MCLIP, Librarian, Maclay, Murray & Spens, Edinburgh.
[26358] 14/10/1976 CM04/11/1981

Edwards, Mrs J L, MCLIP CTEFLA, Unwaged.
[21261] 17/10/1973 CM31/08/1977

Edwards, Mrs J M, BA (Hons) QTS Education, LLRC Co-Ordinator, St Edmunds Catholic School.
[10032377] 29/11/2013 ME

Edwards, Miss J M, MA MLib, Student.
[39983] 08/10/1986 CM27/02/1991

Edwards, Mr J N, BSc MCLIP, Director, Nick Edwards Consulting Ltd, London, SE3 8SY.
[60315] 10/12/2001 CM10/12/2001

Edwards, Miss K, BSc (Hons) MSc, Knowledge Management Internal Consultant, Department of Health.
[51580] 03/04/1995 ME

Edwards, Miss K, Student, Universty of Strathclyde.
[10021684] 27/09/2012 ME

Edwards, Miss K E, BA MSc MCLIP PGCHE, Humanities Liaison
Librarian, Templeman Library, University of Kent, Canterbury.
[10006329]   10/10/2007   **CM08/09/2010**
Edwards, Mrs K E, BA (Hons) PgCert, Student, Aberystwyth University.
[10019444]   04/07/2011   **ME**
Edwards, Miss K L, BA (Hons) MSc (Econ), Acting Reference Librarian,
Carmarthenshire County Council, Llanelli Regional Library.
[56901]   02/11/1998   **ME**
Edwards, Mrs L, BA MCLIP, Assistant Librarian (Part-time), Drayton
Manor High School, London.
[30686]   13/03/1979   **CM10/11/1983**
Edwards, Mrs L A, BA MCLIP, Sch. Librarian, North Somerset Council,
St Katherine`s Sch. Ham Green, Pill.
[38831]   14/10/1985   **CM15/08/1989**
Edwards, Miss L M, MA BA (Hons) DipLib MCLIP, Director, The
European Library.
[34837]   15/03/1982   **CM01/04/2002**
Edwards, Mr M, BA (Hons), Team Leader, The University of Wales,
Newport.
[62785]   22/10/2003   **ME**
Edwards, Mr P C G, BA MCLIP, Learning Resource Centre Assisant,
Wiltshire College, Lackham.
[23264]   20/11/1974   **CM12/10/1979**
Edwards, Mr P M, BA (Joint Hons), Student, Aberystwyth University.
[10035024]   05/09/2014   **ME**
Edwards, Mr R C, MSc BSc BA Dip Man, Project Manager, Welsh
Government.
[10021681]   27/09/2012   **ME**
Edwards, Mrs R J, BA MCLIP, Senior Librarian, Manchester Library,
Central Library.
[26106]   01/07/1976   **CM10/12/1979**
Edwards, Ms R S, MA DipLib, Stock Reader Dev. Librarian,
Hertfordshire County Council.
[36492]   14/10/1983   **ME**
Edwards, Mrs S E, BSc (Hons) MSc PMP MCLIP, Programme Manager,
Knowledge and Collaboration, UNISYS.
[54454]   09/12/1996   **CM24/10/2001**
Edwards, Miss S J, Student, Robert Gordon University.
[10035561]   20/10/2014   **ME**
Edwards, Mr S M, BA (Hons) MCLIP, Director of Professional Services,
CILIP.
[49122]   06/10/1993   **RV**18/12/2013   **CM26/11/1997**
Edwards, Mrs S P, BA MLS DipLib MCLIP, Comm. Librarian, West
Wilts, District, Wilts.
[30806]   18/04/1979   **CM14/06/1982**
Edwards, Mr S P, DipILS, Outreach Librarian, NHS Salford.
[43743]   15/12/1989   **ME**
Edwards, Mr S W, BA (Hons) MA, Information Specialist, Royal Institute
of British Architects, London.
[54257]   11/11/1996   **ME**
Edwards, Mr S W, BA DipLib MCLIP, Joint Chair, Shelf Free E-Books
Group.
[29510]   11/09/1978   **CM18/11/1981**
Edwards, Mrs W E, BA (Hons) MA MCLIP, Community Librarian, West
Sussex County Council, Horsham L.
[58997]   18/10/2000   **CM16/07/2003**
Edwardson-Hill, Mr P S, BA FCIL, Unemployed.
[10022370]   19/02/2013   **ME**
Egarr, Mrs H E, MCLIP, Lib. i/c., South Glos. Council.
[21039]   01/10/1973   **CM22/09/1976**
Egbuji, Mrs A N, MCLIP, Librarian, Stratford College, Stratford-upon-
Avon.
[66134]   29/09/2006   **CM28/01/2009**

Egerton, Mr F D, BA (Hons) Oxon Dip Est Man, Librarian and Subject
Consultant, Bodleian Latin American Centre Library.
[10023355]   02/07/2013   **ME**
Eggleston, Miss K J, MA MEd MCLIP, Life Member.
[4469]   25/09/1956   **CM01/01/1959**
Egleton, Ms J D, ACLIP, Lib. Assistant, Chichester College Library,
West Sussex.
[10017638]   01/10/2010   **ACL**14/03/2012
Egleton, Miss S, BA MA MCLIP, Head of Systems and User Services,
University of Reading.
[55158]   24/07/1997   **CM17/01/2001**
Egwim, Mr U G, Unwaged.
[10015465]   07/01/2009   **ME**
Ehibor, Mr O, BA MSc, Librarian, UCL Qatar.
[48364]   04/12/1992   **ME**
Eichhorn, Ms R, BA (Hons) PgDipILM, Learning Resources Tutor,
Luther King House Library, Luther King House Educational Trust.
[58785]   20/07/2000   **ME**
Ekin, Mrs S M, BA DipLIS MCLIP, Librarian, NIPEC, Belfast.
[58336]   17/01/2000   **CM15/01/2003**
El Hadidi, Miss M, Student, UCL.
[10033851]   12/05/2014   **ME**
Elder, Mr D B, BA MLib FCLIP, Deputy Head, Knowledge Management
Serv., GCHQ, Cheltenham.
[36547]   10/10/1983   **RV**14/11/2012   **FE**08/12/2004
Elder, Mrs M, BEng (Hons) PgDipLIM, Lis Manager – Warrington
University of Chester.
[62596]   05/09/2003   **ME**
Elder, Mr M A, BA (Hons) DipILS MCLIP, on sabbatical.
[55522]   20/10/1997   **CM03/10/2007**
Elder, Mrs V, BA (Hons), Librarian, Northumbria Healthcare NHS
Foundation Trust.
[41295]   30/10/1987   **ME**
Elderton, Mrs D L, BA DipEd MCLIP, Librarian, Ibstock Place School,
Roehampton, London.
[53647]   13/08/1996   **CM19/07/2000**
Elgar, Mr P G, Retired.
[4488]   29/10/1946   **ME**
Elias Lomba, Mr S, MEd, Student, ISLA Leiria.
[10035445]   14/10/2014   **ME**
El-Jouzi, Ms A, BA (Hons) MSc MCLIP, Liaison Librarian, St Georges'
University of London.
[54998]   19/06/1997   **CM21/03/2007**
Ellery, Dr D A, BSc PhD CPsychol, Research & Information Centre
Supervisor, Blatchington Mill School.
[10033700]   16/04/2014   **ME**
Ellery, Ms J, BSc (Hons) MA MCLIP, Director of Knowledge, Gov. &
Comm., Lewisham Hospital NHS Trust University Hospital Lewisham
L.
[46836]   14/02/1992   **CM15/03/2000**
Elliott, Mrs C, Library Assistant, Plymstock School.
[10032376]   29/11/2013   **ME**
Elliott, Mrs C A, BA MCLIP, Librarian, Newcastle High School for Girls,
Newcastle Upon Tyne.
[22589]   02/07/1974   **CM02/10/1978**
Elliott, Mrs D A, MA (Hons) MCLIP, Area Librarian, East Lothian
Council.
[47552]   01/10/1992   **CM24/07/1996**
Elliott, Mrs D D E, BEd (Hons) PgDipILM MA, Part-time Library
Assistant, University of Durham.
[53046]   19/02/1996   **ME**
Elliott, Miss E M, BA MCLIP, Retired.
[4507]   05/10/1961   **CM01/01/1963**

Elliott, Ms J, Student, Robert Gordon University.
[10033100]   10/02/2014   ME

Elliott, Ms K, BA (Oxon) MSc, Library Assistant, Sidney Sussex College.
[10032087]   24/10/2013   ME

Elliott, Mrs L, Library Assistant, Lambeth Palace Library.
[10031616]   11/09/2013   ME

Elliott, Mrs L, MA FCLIP, Retired.
[4513]   20/01/1965   FE22/05/1991

Elliott, Mrs M, BA (Hons), Library Assistant, Enniskillen Library/Student, University of Ulster.
[10026595]   04/10/2013   ME

Elliott, Mrs M J, BA (Hons) MCLIP, Team Librarian, NottsCC.
[47921]   26/10/1992   CM17/03/1999

Elliott, Mr P, Business Librarian, ESCP Europe, London.
[10013304]   08/10/2009   ME

Elliott, Miss P, BA CertEd MCLIP, Librarian, Westminster Sch. L. Serv., London.
[28948]   07/02/1978   CM05/06/1986

Elliott, Mrs P E, MPhil BA MCLIP, Retired.
[4519]   03/01/1972   CM23/11/1976

Elliott, Mr P J V, BSc MCLIP, Head of Archives, Royal Air Force Museum, London.
[60282]   25/05/1979   CM24/03/1988

Ellis, Dr A C O, MA PhD FCLIP, Life Member.
[4525]   19/01/1950   FE01/01/1964

Ellis, Mrs A W, MCLIP, Retired.
[4527]   22/01/1950   CM01/01/1954

Ellis, Mrs C E, MA BSc (Hons), Head High School Librarian.
[10014907]   23/09/2009   ME

Ellis, Ms E J, Librarian, Lampton School, Middlesex.
[10005895]   02/08/2007   ME

Ellis, Mrs F A, MSc MCLIP, Retired.
[462]   25/10/1966   CM01/01/1970

Ellis, Miss F M, BA MCLIP MSc, Lib. & Web Manager, Marymount Int. Sch of Paris.
[41646]   05/02/1988   CM16/11/1994

Ellis, Mr G J, BA MA MCLIP, L. & Learning Centre Manager, Whitley Bay High School.
[10006907]   17/12/2007   CM18/01/2012

Ellis, Mr J L, BLib HonFCLIP, Retired.
[4536]   01/01/1968   HFE30/09/2014

Ellis, Mrs L, Student, Coleg Llandrillo.
[10032186]   12/12/2013   ME

Ellis, Ms M J, BSc (Hons) DipInfSci MA MCLIP, Senior Information Researcher, Roffey Park Inst., West Sussex.
[34375]   26/10/1981   CM10/10/1983

Ellis, Mrs P, BA MEd MCLIP, Head of Knowledge Managment & E-learning, Health Education, South West.
[8399]   12/10/1971   CM16/10/1974

Ellis, Mr R J, MCLIP, Assistant, Ceredigion County Council.
[21326]   17/10/1973   CM01/01/1978

Ellis, Mr T M, BSc, Assistant Librarian, Basildon Healthcare Library.
[10015218]   27/10/2009   ME

Ellis-Barrett, Mrs L G A, BA (Hons) MA MSc MCLIP, Head of Library, St John's School, Leatherhead.
[56262]   17/04/1998   CM23/06/2004

Ellison, Mrs A C, BA (Hons) MA MCLIP, Head of Servs. to Child, Sch. L. Serv., Dialstone Centre for, Stockport.
[36076]   11/05/1983   CM14/03/1986

Ellison, Miss M J, BA (Hons) MSc, Head Librarian (London Office) – Skadden, Arps, Slate, Meagher & Flom (UK) LLP.
[57413]   04/03/1999   ME

Ellison, Mr S J, BA (Hons), Student studying Archives Administration M. A. At present volunteering at the National Library of Wales in their Sound.
[10032074]   24/10/2013   ME

Ellison, Ms W L, BA (Hons) MA MCLIP, Subject Librarian, University of Chichester.
[48699]   01/04/1993   CM15/05/2002

Ellul, Mr K J, MSc, Director Library Services, University of Malta.
[10014400]   10/08/2009   ME

Ellwood, Mrs F, BA MCLIP, Bookseller, Waterstones.
[27489]   26/04/1977   CM07/12/1984

Ellwood, Mr M P, BA MCLIP, Compliance Manager, Suffolk Libraries.
[26363]   04/10/1976   CM30/10/1979

Ellyard, Mrs J M, BA MCLIP, School Librarian, Glossopdale Comm. College.
[31490]   18/10/1979   CM22/08/1984

Elmasry, Mr A, BA, Student, UCL.
[10032950]   10/02/2014   ME

Elmore, Ms J R, MA MSC, Student, University of Sheffield.
[10035419]   13/10/2014   ME

Elsegood, Ms S A, BSc MCLIP FHEA, Humanities Faculty Librarian, University of East Anglia, Norwich.
[43563]   08/11/1989   RV04/04/2006   CM24/09/1997

Else-Jack, Mrs J, BLib MCLIP,
[40782]   08/06/1987   CM27/03/1991

Elson, Mrs D, BA (Hons) MSc MA, Principal Information Assistant (PT), Leeds Beckett University.
[10034132]   09/06/2014   ME

Elson, Mr D L, BA (Hons),
[10014282]   13/07/2009   ME

Elson, Miss S A, BA MCLIP, Library Project Manager, Milton Keynes Libraries.
[39225]   01/01/1986   CM15/08/1989

Elston, Mr L H, MCLIP, Retired.
[4554]   04/08/1941   CM05/09/1972

Elves, Mr R J, BSc (Hons) MSc MCLIP, Information Specialist, Kingston University.
[47361]   23/07/1992   CM23/09/1998

Elwell, Ms H, BA (Hons) MSc, Assistant Librarian, British Medical Association, London.
[47353]   21/07/1992   ME

Elwen, Miss C L, BA (Hons), Student, Leeds Metropolitan University.
[63966]   22/11/2004   ME

Ely, Mrs H J, MA MCLIP, Retired.
[21457]   12/10/1973   CM10/11/1975

Emerton, Mrs J J, BA (Hons) MA MCLIP AHEA, Subject Librarian, Cardiff University.
[61121]   20/02/2002   CM31/01/2007

Emery, Mr C D, BA MPhil MCLIP, Life Member.
[16845]   12/03/1958   CM01/01/1961

Emery, Mrs L, MA MCLIP, Subject Librarian – Buisiness, University of Strathclyde, Glasgow.
[26526]   17/10/1976   CM09/07/1979

Emery-Wallis, Cllr F, CBE HonFLA, Hon. Fellow.
[53197]   01/01/1996   HFE01/01/1996

Emly, Mr M A, MA MCLIP, Head of Collection Services, University of Leeds Library.
[28427]   01/12/1977   CM19/11/1979

Emmelhainz, Ms C M, MA, Student, Kent State University.
[10031811]   07/10/2013   ME

Emmott, Mrs A J, BSc MCLIP, Librarian, Nicholas & Co., Solicitors, London.
[4581]   01/01/1968   CM10/08/1972

Endicott, Mrs A J, BA (Hons) PgDip, Student.
[10012721]   01/04/1998   **ME**
Engel-Gough, Miss D N, HNC, Student, University of Wales
Aberystwyth.
[10009492]   21/05/2008   **ME**
England, Mrs A J, BA MLS MCLIP, Community Librarian (Local
Studies) Cambridgeshire County Council.
[33036]   08/10/1980   **CM13/12/1982**
England, Miss K J, MA MSc MCLIP, School Librarian, Tiree High
School, Isle of Tiree.
[55342]   01/10/1997   **CM15/01/2003**
England, Ms P M, MA BA MCLIP, Information Advisor (Health), London
South Bank University,
[29165]   05/04/1978   **CM24/11/1980**
England, Miss R L, ACLIP, Site Manager: E-resources, Tunbridge Wells
Hospital Library.
[10002786]   01/05/2007   **ACL16/07/2008**
England, Dr T G, BSc PhD,
[10012618]   19/02/2009   **ME**
Englert, Ms G, MCLIP, Librarian, Wavelengths Library, Lewisham.
[10000572]   16/10/2006   **CM13/07/1973**
English, Mr D J, BA MCLIP, Retired.
[4596]   07/10/1963   **CM01/01/1966**
English, Ms J, BA MA, Deputy Librarian – English Faculty Library,
Oxford University.
[10018071]   20/01/2014   **ME**
English, Mrs L H, BA (Hons) PgDipILM MCLIP, Part-time Learning
Advisor., University of Cumbria.
[52195]   12/10/1995   **CM20/05/1998**
Ennion, Mrs C, BA DipEdTech MCLIP, Retired.
[23560]   20/01/1975   **CM20/01/1977**
Ennis, Mrs A P, BSc MCLIP, Retired.
[19994]   11/01/1973   **CM13/07/1976**
Ennis, Ms K, BA (Hons) DipLib MCLIP, Kathy Ennis.
[35972]   10/03/1983   **CM05/07/1988**
Enright, Ms S, BA DipLib MCLIP, Director Information Services,
University of Westminster, London.
[30831]   17/05/1979   **CM03/09/1982**
Enser, Prof P G B, BA (Econ) MTech PhD MBCS FCLIP, Head of
School, School of Computing, Math. & Information Sci., University of
Brighton.
[60283]   06/01/1981   **FE01/04/2002**
Ensing, Miss R J, FCLIP, Life Member.
[4606]   08/03/1940   **FE01/01/1951**
Ensor, Mr R J, BA, Library Assistant, Leicester College.
[10032570]   17/12/2013   **ME**
Epps, Mrs A T, BSc MCLIP, Tech., Prospect College, Reading.
[60151]   01/07/1979   **CM01/06/1983**
Ereira, Ms K, BA, Student, City University.
[10032121]   29/10/2013   **ME**
Ernestus, Mr H, FCLIP, Life Member.
[16853]   30/01/1956   **FE15/09/1993**
Errington, Mr D J, BSc (Hons), Assistant Librarian, Robinson Library,
Newcastle University.
[10009450]   18/11/2005   **ME**
Erskine, Ms K, MCLIP, Learning Centre Manager at CATS College
Canterbury.
[10007093]   09/10/1987   **CM27/01/1993**
Erskine, Mr S C B, MA MCLIP, Database Integrity Librarian,
Bournemouth L.
[23120]   06/11/1974   **CM10/02/1978**
Escreet, Mr P K, MA MCLIP, Life Member.
[4615]   15/08/1951   **CM01/01/1955**

Eskander, Dr S, HonFCLIP,
[10011429]   20/10/2008   **HFE16/10/2008**
Espitalier-Noel, Mrs C, BA (Hons) MCLIP, Information & Marketing
Manager.
[36693]   03/11/1983   **CM15/03/1989**
Essex, Mrs L, BEd (Hons) DipLIS MCLIP, Senior Team Leader,
Portfolio, Warwickshire County Council, Nuneaton Library.
[47454]   19/08/1992   **CM20/01/1999**
Esslemont, Mr J L, MA MSc MCLIP, Retired.
[60284]   07/11/1975   **CM18/01/1978**
Estall, Miss C J, BA (Hons) PGCE MA, Librarian, Wells Cathedral
School.
[10016608]   16/04/2010   **ME**
Estremadoyro, Dr J, PhD LLM (Law), Information Officer, Blake
Lapthorn, Oxford.
[10021644]   18/09/2012   **ME**
Etheridge, Mr M, BA (Hons) MSc MSc CMIIA MA MCLIP, Football
Referee Development Co-ordinator.
[59783]   02/10/2001   **CM11/03/2009**
Etheridge, Mrs S, BA (Hons), Student, UCL.
[10035506]   16/10/2014   **ME**
Etienne, Mr O, Systems Support Officer, Nottinghamshire CC.
[10033455]   11/06/2014   **ME**
Etkind, Mrs A, BA DipLib MCLIP, Part-time Knowledge Consultant,
University of Herts., Hatfield.
[26876]   28/12/1976   **CM19/01/1979**
Eu Ahara, Mrs S I T, MCLIP, Retired.
[4624]   01/01/1965   **CM01/01/1970**
Euesden, Mr M A, MSc MBA MCLIP, ICT Project Manager, The British
Library, Boston Spa.
[35440]   01/10/1982   **CM01/07/1989**
Eunson, Miss B G, BA FCLIP, Life Member.
[4626]   03/01/1947   **FE01/01/1959**
Evans, Mr A, BA, Account Manager – Academic Libraries – UK, OCLC
UK Ltd, Birmingham.
[39947]   06/10/1986   **ME**
Evans, Ms A, BA MA MCLIP, Assistant Librarian, Swansea Metropolitan
University.
[42325]   12/10/1988   **CM20/10/2005**
Evans, Mrs A, BA (Hons) MSc, Lib. Operations Manager, Health
Library., Cardiff University.
[62471]   08/07/2003   **ME**
Evans, Mr A C, MCLIP, Visiting Research Fellow, Department of
Computing, Goldsmiths College University of London.
[28754]   06/01/1971   **CM12/07/1978**
Evans, Mrs A E, MA BA MCLIP, Head of College & Resource
Description, Bodleian Library, University of Oxford.
[37633]   16/10/1984   **CM14/03/1990**
Evans, Prof A J, BPharm PhD HonFLA FCLIP, Life Member.
[4634]   16/04/1958   **HFE31/03/1990**
Evans, Ms A M, BSc (Hons) MA, Public Services Supervisor, University
of Leicester.
[38960]   15/10/1985   **ME**
Evans, Miss C M S, MSc BA, Service Development Librarian-Inclusion,
Dudley MBC.
[10021166]   14/06/2012   **ME**
Evans, Mr D, MA (Hons) PgDip, Europe Direct Co-Ordinator, Europe
Direct Information Centre.
[10033595]   01/04/2014   **ME**
Evans, Mrs D, Publisher, Ashgate Publishing Ltd, Farnham.
[64343]   07/03/2005   **ME**
Evans, Mr D H, MA DipLis ALCM, Library Assistant, Sevenoaks School.
[10022143]   08/01/2013   **ME**

Evans, Mrs E, BA MA (Dist), Librarian, Coalville Library, Leicestershire County Council.
[58686] 30/05/2000 ME

Evans, Miss E A, MCLIP, Retired.
[4655] 01/01/1955 CM01/01/1969

Evans, Miss E E, BA MCLIP, Retired.
[4657] 09/02/1960 CM01/01/1966

Evans, Miss E J, BA (Hons) BSc (Hons), Assistant Manager, Swansea Central Library.
[10017824] 11/10/2010 ME

Evans, Mrs F M, BLib MCLIP, Librarian, Godstowe Prep. School, Bucks.
[29508] 18/09/1978 CM25/01/1985

Evans, Mrs G, Library & Resources Assistant, ST Michaels C of E.
[10033841] 02/05/2014 ME

Evans, Mr G H, BLib MBA MCLIP, Business dev. Manager, Caerphilly County Borough Council.
[43980] 23/03/1990 CM26/05/1993

Evans, Mrs H J, BA MCLIP, Medical Records Adminstrator.
[39476] 31/01/1986 CM12/12/1991

Evans, Mr H L, BSc DipLib MCLIP, Head of the Libraries Development Team/ Pennaeth Datblygu Llyfrgelloedd, CyMAL, Welsh Government.
[32940] 23/10/1980 CM19/04/1983

Evans, Miss H M D, BLib DipIllus MCLIP, Media Tech. /Assistant Librarian, West Cheshire.
[26719] 03/11/1976 CM16/05/2012

Evans, Mr I W H, MA MA BA (HONS) MCLIP, Systems & Serials Librarian, Knowledge Centre, Redgrave Court, Merton Road, Bootle, Merseyside, L20 7HS.
[62958] 25/11/2003 CM27/01/2010

Evans, Miss J, BA (Hons) DipMus DipLib, Service Development Manager, SCURL, National Library of Scotland, Edinburgh.
[55159] 25/07/1997 ME

Evans, Mr J A, BSc MSc MCLIP, Information Services, National Institute for Biological Standards and Control, South Mimms, Herts.
[51970] 24/08/1995 CM01/04/2002

Evans, Mrs J A, Sch. Librarian, London Metropolitan University.
[63980] 22/11/2004 ME

Evans, Mr J C, BA MA PGCE, Learning Centre Assistant, Strode's College.
[10033910] 12/05/2014 ME

Evans, Mr J C, MA (Oxon) PGCE MSc (Econ) MCLIP, Library & Information Serv. Manager, Kenilworth Sch, Warwickshire County Council.
[54187] 06/11/1996 CM20/11/2002

Evans, Mrs J E, BA MCLIP, Retired.
[18450] 15/10/1972 CM08/06/1976

Evans, Mr J F L, BA, Student, University of Wales Aberystwyth.
[10032636] 23/12/2013 ME

Evans, Miss J M, BA, Research Data Manager, Middlesex University London.
[66009] 25/08/2006 ME

Evans, K, MMath MScEcon MCLIP, Research Analytics Librarian, Bath University.
[65038] 13/10/2005 CM07/07/2010

Evans, Mr L, BA (Hons) PGCE DipLib MCLIP, Previously Senior Educ. Librarian, L. HQ, North East Wales SLS, Mold.
[10013095] 17/06/1994 CM02/05/1998

Evans, Ms L G, MA MSc, Assistant Curator of Rare Books, Bodleian Libraries.
[10006352] 16/10/2007 ME

Evans, Mrs L S, MCLIP, Sharpe Librarian, Giggleswick School, North Yorks.
[31803] 18/01/1980 CM02/02/1983

Evans, Lord M, of Temple Guiting CBE HonFCLIP, Hon. Fellow.
[57252] 04/02/1999 FE01/01/1999

Evans, Mr M, Information Support Administrator, Ministry of Defence.
[10034539] 21/07/2014 ME

Evans, Prof M, BA MBA PhD PGCE FLA FIIntSc FCLIP, Retired.
[10016069] 10/09/1964 FE23/03/1993

Evans, Mrs M, BA (Hons) PGCE, Student, Aberystwyth University.
[10035527] 16/10/2014 ME

Evans, Mrs N, Retired.
[4691] 01/01/1952 ME

Evans, Miss N A, BEd (Hons) DipLIS MCLIP, Art & Design Librarian, University of South Wales, Newport.
[47553] 01/10/1992 CM22/07/1998

Evans, Mrs N N, BA MSc, School Librarian, Knights Templar School, Baldock.
[54437] 09/12/1996 ME

Evans, Mr P J, BA MCLIP, Lib. Assistant, Norbury Library, London Borough of Croydon.
[36855] 11/01/1984 CM15/02/1989

Evans, Ms R A, BA (Hons) MA MCLIP, Head of Collections, Insitute of Education Library, University of London.
[10005122] 12/10/1999 CM12/03/2003

Evans, Miss R A, MCLIP, Information Advisor, Cardiff. Metropolitan University.
[59389] 27/02/2001 CM10/03/2011

Evans, Mrs R F, BA MA, Assistant Librarian, House of Lords Library, London.
[10018216] 09/12/2010 ME

Evans, Mrs S E, BA (Hons), P/+ Children & Young People's Librarian., Aberystwyth.
[62525] 05/08/2003 ME

Evans, Mrs S L, BA (Hons) MSc Econ, Learning and Resources Manager, St Michaels C E High Business & Enterprise Colle.
[10033219] 21/02/2014 ME

Evans, Ms T M, BA (Hons) MSc, Unwaged.
[62319] 01/04/1997 ME

Evans, Mrs T N, BSc (Hons) MA MCLIP, Unwaged.
[52888] 19/01/1996 CM16/05/2001

Evans, Mrs W J, BA (Hons) MCLIP ILTA, Head Librarian, University of St Mark & St John.
[40407] 02/02/1987 CM20/11/2002

Evason, Miss M, MA MCLIP, Retired.
[4710] 01/01/1939 CM01/01/1947

Evenson, Ms S E, BA, Information Servs. Manager, Slaughter and May, London.
[47798] 19/10/1992 ME

Everall, Mrs A, OBE BA (Hons) MCLIP, Director, Authors Aloud UK.
[26365] 12/10/1976 CM19/06/1987

Everest, Mr A R, MA (Hons) PgDIP, Informatics Consultant.
[10006720] 16/10/1991 ME

Everhard, Dr C J, PhD MA DipLib MCLIP, Formerly Foreign Instructor, Aristotle University, Thessaloniki, Greece.
[18329] 12/10/1972 CM23/04/1975

Everist, Mrs J, School Librarian, Holmewood House School, Tunbridge Wells.
[57067] 07/12/1998 ME

Everitt, Ms C E, BA (Hons) CertEd DipLIS MCLIP, Reader Serv. Librarian, Bishop Grossteste University College.
[52330] 30/10/1995 CM18/09/2002

Everitt, Mrs R, MSc MCLIP, Assistant Director, Operations, SOAS University of London.
[59628] 04/07/2001 CM15/09/2004

Everitt, Mrs S M, BSc DipLib MCLIP, Library Assistant, Home Library
Service, Dudley/Wolverhampton.
[30024]   13/11/1978   **CM30/03/1981**
Everson, Mr A D, MA Med MA MCLIP, Retired.
[44034]   01/04/1990   **CM20/03/1996**
Evetts, Mrs L, BA (Hons) MA MCLIP, Librarian, Chiltern Edge School.
[54445]   10/12/1996   **CM15/11/2000**
Ewart, Mrs K, BScEcon, School Librarian.
[10006426]   17/12/2007   **ME**
Ewing, Mr D K, BA (Hons) MCLIP, Senior Development Manager –
Heritage & Information Services.
[46434]   04/11/1991   **CM25/01/2011**
Exton, Miss L S, BSc MSc MCLIP, Information Scientist, Clinical
Standards Unit, British Association of Dermatologists.
[60756]   05/01/1987   **CM12/04/1989**
Eyles, Mr K, Art L. Assistant Vol., Pallant House Gallery, Chichester.
[10018773]   09/03/2011   **AF**
Eynon, Dr A D, BA (Hons) DipLIS MCLIP PhD, Library & Learning
Technology Manager, Grwp Llandrillo Menai.
[45745]   15/05/1991   **CM23/09/1998**
Eynon, Mrs K, BA (Hons) MCLIP, SCL (Wales) Deve Officer.
[44964]   28/01/1991   **CM27/01/1993**
Eyres, Mrs R J, BA (Hons) DipLIS MCLIP, Assistant Librarian,
Manchester Metropolitan University, Sir Kenneth Green Library.
[50864]   24/10/1994   **CM24/09/1997**
Ezzelino, Miss F, BA, Student, Aberystwyth University.
[10033883]   12/05/2014   **ME**

F

Fagg, Mrs S V, BSc (Hons) DipTP MSc (Econ) MCLIP, Information
Librarian, University of Worcester.
[63387]   27/04/2004   **CM27/03/2014**
Fairall, Mrs S A C, Retired.
[27759]   01/08/1977   **ME**
Fairbrother, Mr J V, MCLIP, Life Member.
[4747]   20/01/1961   **CM01/01/1963**
Fairbrother, Mr P, BA (Hons) MSc MCLIP, Drug-related Deaths Review
Coordinator, NHS Lothian.
[50426]   27/07/1994   **CM18/03/1998**
Fairfoul, Ms S, MA MCLIP,
[10005492]   06/08/1997   **CM09/07/2013**
Fairhurst, Miss R S M, BA (Hons) MA, Student.
[10019915]   03/10/2011   **ME**
Fairman, Mr R B, MSc BSc DipLib MCLIP, Research & Development
Librarian, University of Worcester.
[33288]   07/11/1980   **CM01/04/2002**
Fairweather, Mrs K J, BA (Hons), L. Res. Centre Co-ordinator, The
Moray Council, Speyside High School.
[57610]   24/05/1999   **ME**
Fairweather, Mrs P J, MCLIP,
[29111]   27/02/1978   **CM20/08/1981**
Fairweather, Ms S K, BA PgDip MA, Reference Serv. Librarian, House
of Lords Library, London.
[55326]   01/10/1997   **ME**
Falconer, Ms V, MA (Hons) MA, Student, UCL.
[10026690]   11/09/2013   **ME**
Falconer Hall, Mrs A, ACLIP, Librarian, King's High School, Warwick.
[10020704]   27/03/2012   **ACL09/07/2013**
Falla, Mrs J, BA DipLib MCLIP, Head of Serv. to Educ. & Young People
Guille-Alles Library, Guernsey.
[36629]   24/10/1983   **CM25/09/1996**

Falla, Miss M J, BA MA MLib MCLIP, Chief Librarian, Guille-Alles
Library, Guernsey.
[35477]   06/10/1982   **CM08/12/1987**
Fallon, Mrs S A, MA, Principal Editor, ThomsonReuters.
[52770]   11/12/1995   **ME**
Fallone, Mrs E, BA MCLIP,
[31200]   02/10/1979   **CM30/11/1987**
Fang, Mr W, Student, The University of Hong Kong.
[10035577]   20/10/2014   **ME**
Fanner, Mrs D A, BScEcon (Hons) MCLIP, Librarian, Stower Provost CP
School, Dorset.
[10001350]   09/08/2004   **CM16/10/2009**
Fanning, Ms A, BA (Hons), School Librarian, Prince Albert Primary
School.
[10022857]   30/04/2013   **AF**
Farbey, Mr R A, MBE BA DipLib FCLIP, Head of Library & knowledge
Services, British Dental Association, London.
[27965]   13/10/1977   **FE19/03/2008**
Farfort, Mrs S, Learning Res. Assist., Preston College, Preston.
[10018871]   24/03/2011   **AF**
Farley, Mrs E J, BA (Hons), Learning Resources Assistant, Ormiston Six
Villages Academy.
[10021014]   04/05/2012   **AF**
Farmer, Miss V G, MA Msc MCLIP, Liaison Librarian, Robert Gordon
University, Aberdeen.
[59768]   01/10/2001   **CM21/03/2007**
Farncombe, Mrs J C, BA DipLib MCLIP TTAIT, Self-employed Contract
Librarian, Researcher.
[36843]   11/01/1984   **CM18/07/1990**
Farndell, Mrs M, BA (Hons) MCLIP, Employment not known.
[48933]   26/07/1993   **CM27/11/1996**
Farndon, Mr L R, BSc, Digital Res. Officer, City College Norwich.
[10018037]   05/11/2010   **ME**
Farnsworth, Miss L A, BSc MA, Assistant Librarian, Torbay Hospital.
[10015688]   14/01/2010   **ME**
Farooq, Mr M, MLISc, Director Information Services, Riphah
International University.
[10002523]   20/04/2007   **ME**
Farquhar, Mrs D S, Head Librarian, JPGS, Jeddah, Saudi Arabia.
[10019624]   10/08/2011   **ME**
Farquhar, Miss S C, MA DipLib, Retired.
[27966]   20/09/1977   **ME**
Farquharson, Miss V R, MA DipLib MCLIP, Community Librarian, South
Lanarkshire Council.
[31062]   01/08/1979   **CM14/10/1981**
Farr, Mr D J, BA (Hons) MCLIP, Assistant Librarian, Staffordshire
County Council, Stafford, Staffordshire.
[48764]   12/05/1993   **CM21/01/1998**
Farr, Miss J M, BA MCLIP, Assistant Librarian, Aberdeen City Library,
Scotland.
[32721]   24/07/1980   **CM27/01/1984**
Farr, Mrs M F, BA DipLib, Local Studies Librarian, Surrey Heritage,
Surrey History Centre, Woking.
[33289]   16/11/1980   **ME**
Farr, Miss N, BA, Music Librarian, Cardiff Central Library.
[10013451]   27/04/2009   **ME**
Farr, Mr P J, BSc MBCS, Services Assistant (Heritage), Ferens Art
Gallery.
[10032906]   24/01/2014   **ME**
Farr, Mrs R A, MA (Hons) BSc (Hons) DIP LIB, Volunteer Information
Officer, The Alzheimer's Society.
[38103]   16/01/1985   **ME**

Farragher, Ms L E, MLIS MSc, Information Specialist, Health Research Board, Ireland.
[65589] 23/02/2006 **ME**

Farrall, Mrs L, BSc (Hons), Library Assistant, Clinical Studies Library, QEQM Hospital, Margate.
[10000953] 30/11/2006 **ME**

Farrell, Ms A, BCL MSSC, Student.
[10031995] 24/10/2013 **ME**

Farrell, Ms C, L. & Collections Manager, The Kennel Club, London.
[10001209] 02/02/2007 **ME**

Farrell, Ms C, BA PgDipLS, Librarian, Inst. of Intern. Relations, Universityof the West Indies, Trinidad & Tobago.
[10013488] 22/05/2009 **ME**

Farrell, Ms E J, BA (Hons) MCLIP, Senior Information Manager, NICE.
[27490] 01/04/1977 **CM15/09/1983**

Farrell, Miss H P, BA (Hons) DipILS MCLIP, Librarian, Oxfordshire County Council.
[42786] 01/03/1989 **CM21/11/2001**

Farrell, Miss M, BA MA, Library Assistant, Belfast Met College.
[10031333] 23/07/2013 **AF**

Farrelly, Ms C A, BA MCLIP, L Frontline Officer, Northfleet Librarian, Lancs. County Council.
[30833] 28/04/1979 **CM06/10/1982**

Farrow, Mrs A J, MA BA MCLIP, Principal Lecturer, Liverpool John Moores University, Business Sch.
[741] 13/10/1970 **CM01/12/1974**

Farrow, Ms E C, BA (Hons) MA MCLIP, Programme Manager, Library Strengthening, INASP, Oxford.
[49849] 22/12/1993 **CM27/11/1996**

Farruggia, Ms J A, BA (Hons) PgDip, Senior Library Assistant, University of Birmingham.
[10008009] 20/03/2008 **ME**

Farthing, Mr A,
[10032310] 15/11/2013 **ME**

Farthing, Mrs A R, BA (Hons) MCLIP, Acquisitions Manager, Cheshire County Council, Chester.
[10001552] 02/01/1992 **CM25/01/1995**

Farthing, Mrs T, MA MCLIP, Librarian, The Royal Grammar School, Guildford.
[10012911] 20/03/2009 **CM11/04/2013**

Fati, Miss O I, MLIS, System Programmer, University of Jos.
[10035050] 08/09/2014 **ME**

Faughey, Mrs L C, MCLIP, Retired.
[8923] 17/01/1962 **CM01/01/1965**

Faulconbridge, Miss K, BA, Student, Robert Gordon University.
[10032046] 22/10/2013 **ME**

Faulds, Miss H, MA (Hons), Deputy Collections Manager.
[10006361] 15/10/2007 **ME**

Faulknall-Mills, Ms J S, BLS MCLIP, Divisional Librarian, Atherstone L. Warwickshire.
[39227] 01/01/1986 **CM21/07/1999**

Faulkner, Ms K, BA (Hons) MSc MCLIP, Library Invigilator, University of Cambridge.
[54755] 01/04/1997 **CM17/01/2001**

Faulkner, Mr M, BA (Hons), Information Centre Manager, Bank of England. London.
[51982] 30/08/1995 **ME**

Faulkner, Mrs M, BA (Hons) MCLIP, Retired Librarian.
[31608] 09/11/1979 **CM10/09/1984**

Faulkner, Mrs S F, BA MCLIP, Retired.
[22235] 18/03/1974 **CM29/03/1976**

Faulkner, Mr T W A, MCLIP, Retired.
[4799] 29/01/1948 **CM01/01/1950**

Faulkner Gibson, Ms M, MCLIP MSc BA (Hons), Subject Support Librarian, University of the West of England.
[65109] 01/11/2005 **CM15/07/2014**

Faulks, Ms K M, MCLIP, Support Worker, Voluntary Action Leeds.
[23515] 21/11/1975 **CM29/12/1977**

Faux, Mrs J M, BSc (Hons) MSc MCLIP, Liaison Librarian, Newman University, Birmingham.
[59233] 11/01/2001 **RV**17/06/2009 **CM01/06/2005**

Fawcett, Mrs A B, BA, Retired.
[4802] 25/02/1959 **CM01/01/1962**

Fawcett, Mr D J, FInstPet DipTh MCLIP, Life Member.
[4804] 20/08/1948 **CM01/01/1951**

Fawcett, Mrs G M, BA MLS MCLIP, Business Specialist., Capita, Birmingham Business Park.
[29715] 01/10/1978 **CM20/01/1981**

Fawcett, Mrs H, MCLIP, Unemployed.
[12047] 01/01/1970 **CM03/03/1977**

Fawcett, Miss L A, Information Manager, A M E C Environment & Infrastructure UK Ltd, Newcastle upon Tyne.
[56461] 16/07/1998 **ME**

Fay, Mr D, BA, Service Manager: Libraries & Leisure.
[32275] 29/02/1980 **CM10/11/1983**

Fazakerley, Miss M E, BA MCLIP, Life Member.
[4808] 04/10/1945 **CM01/01/1948**

Featherstone, Mr J R, BA DipLib MCLIP, Legal Librarian, Department for Communities & Local Government London.
[39918] 01/10/1986 **CM21/12/1988**

Featherstone, Mr T M, BA FCLIP, Life Member.
[4815] 03/05/1949 **FE01/01/1961**

Feetham, Ms M G, BA DipLib MA FHEA MCLIP PGCHE, Deputy University Librarian (Information Services and Systems), Southampton Solent University.
[39072] 28/10/1985 **CM27/07/1994**

Feggetter, Miss N, BA (Hons) MA MA MCLIP, Librarian, Southbank International School.
[10006715] 21/11/2007 **CM18/12/2013**

Fei, Mrs M E, BA (Hons) Econ, Assistant Librarian, Godolphin and Latymer School, London.
[10007000] 17/12/2007 **AF**

Feiler, Ms J, MSc, Unwaged.
[65299] 14/12/2005 **ME**

Felgate, Mr P R, Library Officer Advice & Assistance, Education Library Service, Reading.
[10020599] 08/03/2012 **AF**

Fell, Miss C, BA DipLib, Librarian, National Offender Management Service, Learning and Development, Rugby.
[37160] 16/02/1984 **ME**

Fell, Mrs R, BA (Hons) PgDip MCLIP, Senior Assistant Librarian, Manchester Metropolitan University.
[61963] 19/12/2002 **RV**20/06/2014 **CM13/06/2007**

Fellah, Mrs E, BA (Hons), Library Assistant, Chislehurst Library.
[10033596] 01/04/2014 **ME**

Fellerman, Ms J B, BA MCLIP, Principal Officer, L. & Information Centre, North Yorks County Council.
[28559] 27/12/1977 **CM17/05/1983**

Felstead, Ms A P, BA PgDipLib MCLIP, Head of Resource Description, Bodleian Library, Oxford University.
[38730] 01/10/1985 **CM19/01/1988**

Feltham, Mrs S, BSc MA MCLIP, School Library Mngr, Priory School, Portsmouth.
[65437] 24/02/2006 **CM12/05/2011**

Felton, Miss A E, BA MA (Ed) MCLIP, retired.
[24943] 22/10/1975 **CM12/03/1980**

Fenerty, Mrs V J, BSc (Hons) MA MCLIP, Academic Liaison Librarian, University of Southampton.
[43515]   06/11/1989   **RV**28/01/2009   **CM25/09/1996**

Fenn, Miss J M, BA DipLib MCLIP, Deputy Website Manager, UK Trade & Investment, London.
[38949]   23/10/1985   **CM15/11/1988**

Fenn, Miss K L, BA MA MCLIP, Dev. Librarian, Leeds Sch. L. Serv.
[59395]   28/02/2001   **CM21/10/2008**

Fennell, Mr G R, MA MCLIP FHEA, Subject Librarian, Anglia Ruskin University.
[63964]   22/11/2004   **CM24/10/2008**

Fenton, Mrs A M,
[10000892]   22/11/2006   **AF**

Fenton, Mrs D E, BA MCLIP, Employed – not in Library & information environment.
[33157]   10/10/1980   **CM05/12/1985**

Fenwick, Ms S E, Library Assistant, Danum Academy.
[10032561]   16/12/2013   **ME**

Ferguson, Mr J B, MBE MA FCLIP, Retired.
[4850]   10/09/1937   **FE01/01/1949**

Ferguson, Miss J M, MCLIP, Retired.
[4851]   11/10/1966   **CM01/01/1970**

Ferguson, Mrs K M, BA MCLIP, Retired.
[7714]   02/10/1969   **CM16/09/1975**

Ferguson, Mrs L J, MA DipLib MCLIP, Unemployed.
[35901]   11/02/1983   **CM06/10/1987**

Ferguson, Mrs L S, BA (Hons) MA FCLIP, Deputy Director of Health L. NW, NW Health Care L. Unit, Wigan.
[31643]   25/10/1979   **RV**15/07/2014   **FE09/09/2009**

Ferguson, Mr M, Student, RMIT University.
[10032080]   24/10/2013   **ME**

Ferguson, Mrs S, BA MCLIP, Library & Information Officer, Dundee District Council.
[33130]   01/10/1980   **CM18/07/1983**

Ferguson, Mrs S R, MA DipLib MCLIP, Media Specialist, USA.
[38967]   22/10/1985   **CM06/09/1988**

Ferguson, Mrs V A, BA FCLIP, Retired.
[4862]   03/10/1957   **FE20/12/1976**

Fernandes, Mr D C, MCLIP, Librarian Enquiries, R. B. of Windsor & Maidenhead.
[22025]   21/02/1974   **CM01/01/1976**

Fernandes, Mrs H, Deputy Librarian & Romance Languages Librarian, Modern & Medieval Languages Library, University of Cambridge.
[10021104]   09/02/2001   **ME**

Fernandes, Mr J, Student, Robert Gordon University.
[10035403]   29/10/2014   **ME**

Fernandes, Miss V, BSc, Communications, Learning and Development Officer, Foreign & Commonwealth Office.
[10033267]   25/02/2014   **ME**

Fernandez, Mr N, BA (Hons) MSc, Librarian, Royal Society of Medicine Library.
[10011049]   18/09/2008   **ME**

Fernando, Mrs A, BSc (Hons) MCLIP, Library Manager, Department for Work and Pensions, London.
[46645]   02/12/1991   **CM09/11/2005**

Ferrar, Mrs L, DipEdTech MCLIP, Unemployed.
[22005]   11/01/1974   **CM01/10/1977**

Ferreira, Miss T, BA, Student, Aberystwyth University.
[10026748]   30/01/2014   **ME**

Ferreira Silva De Castro, Ms J, Senior Librarian, Universidade Federal do Estado do Rio de Janeiro.
[10031791]   04/10/2013   **ME**

Ferris, Mrs P J, Learning Ctr Co-ord., Chelmsford College.
[10020783]   04/04/2012   **AF**

Fetherston, Mrs K A, BA (Hons) MIS MCLIP, Children's Librarian, Warwickshire Libraries.
[63482]   14/05/2004   **CM21/03/2007**

Fewins, Mrs N M, BA (Hons), Area Children & Young People's Librarian, Salisbury Library, Salisbury.
[66028]   29/08/2006   **ME**

Fiander, Mrs W, BSc MA MCLIP, Deputy Director of Learning and Information Services, University of Chester.
[28394]   20/11/1977   **CM24/07/1980**

Fiddes, Mr A J C, BSc (Hons) PhD, Information Assistant, Sheffield Health & Social Care NHS Foundation Trust.
[53444]   01/07/1996   **ME**

Fidegul, Ms J, BA ACLIP, Senior Library Assistant, Putney and Roehampton Libraries, London.
[65229]   16/11/2005   **ACL29/03/2007**

Fidell, Mrs S, BA (Hons), Service Development Officer, NYCC, Scarborough Library.
[10012989]   23/03/2009   **AF**

Field, Mr C R, FCLIP AIMC, Retired.
[4881]   12/02/1959   **FE01/01/1965**

Field, Ms L J, Library Assistant, Queen's College, Cambridge.
[10022750]   16/04/2013   **AF**

Field, Mr M, BA DipLib, Knowledge Management Lead, Department for Education.
[10000830]   17/11/1981   **ME**

Field, Mrs M, Learning Centre Assistant, Eastleigh College, Eastleigh.
[10022369]   19/02/2013   **AF**

Field, Mrs S K, BA (Hons) MA MCLIP, Part-time. Librarian, Hume City Council, Australia, Part-time. lib. Brimbank Council, Australia.
[55861]   04/12/1997   **CM01/06/2005**

Field, Mr T J, BSc MCLIP MISTC MAAT, Employment not known.
[60610]   23/03/1983   **CM15/05/1990**

Field, Ms W E, BA MCLIP, Librarian, William Booth College, London.
[37700]   11/10/1984   **CM18/07/1990**

Fielder, Mrs E M, MCLIP, Retired.
[4888]   12/03/1938   **CM01/01/1940**

Fielding, Mrs C S, BSc (Hons) MA MCLIP, Sch. Lib.
[63298]   08/04/2004   **CM13/11/2013**

Fielding, Mr D J, BSc (Hons) PgDip, Staffing & Customer Support Officer, Bury MBC.
[57469]   29/03/1999   **ME**

Fielding, Mrs M H L, BA (Hons) DipILM MCLIP, Career Break.
[47768]   14/10/1992   **CM31/01/1996**

Fieldsend, Mrs V C, BA (Hons) MCLIP, Retired.
[4893]   11/01/1956   **CM13/04/1962**

Filer, Mr R B, BA MCLIP, Retired.
[4896]   14/03/1971   **CM27/03/1973**

Files, Mr R B, MA MCLIP, Retired.
[4898]   10/03/1966   **CM01/01/1970**

Finch, Miss A M, BA (Hons) MSc (Econ) MCLIP, Principal Librarian Northamptonshire Library and Information Service.
[52053]   02/10/1995   **CM22/07/1998**

Finch, Mrs A M, BA (Hons) DipILM MCLIP, Unemployed.
[56675]   01/10/1998   **CM20/11/2002**

Finch, Ms C, BA MA MSc MCLIP Ass. HEA, Information Advisor, Cardiff Metropolitan University, Llandaff Learning Centre.
[54366]   25/11/1996   **CM21/03/2001**

Finch, Ms D, ACLIP, School Librarian, Wheatfields Jnr. School, St Albans.
[10000909]   18/11/2004   **ACL01/07/2006**

Finch, Mrs D S, LRC Technician, Guilford College, Guilford.
[10019925]   04/10/2011   **AF**

Finch, Mr J R, BA (Hons) MSc (Econ) MCLIP, Business Subject
Librarian, Cardiff Metropolitan University.
[54537]   20/01/1997   RV27/08/2014   CM21/03/2001
Finch, Mr S K W, BA MCLIP, Librarian – Information & Learning Team,
Bexley & Bromley Shared Services.
[29650]   19/10/1978   CM30/11/1984
Finch, Mr T W, MCLIP, Retired.
[4905]   23/01/1966   CM01/01/1970
Findlay, Miss J, BSc PgDip MCLIP, Information and Research
Specialist, Tods Murray LLP, Edinburgh.
[60944]   14/01/2002   RV27/03/2014   CM19/03/2008
Findlay, Mrs S, BA (Hons) MCLIP, Community Information Officer,
Harrogate L. & Information Centre.
[10008003]   14/10/1985   CM24/04/1991
Findlay, Mr S R, BA MCLIP, Librarian, NHS Forth Valley.
[29651]   05/10/1978   CM01/07/1992
Finlay, Mrs D, Librarian, Fife Council.
[63811]   01/10/2004   ME
Finlay, Mr G, BSc MSc ACLIP, Library Supervisor, Ware Library,
Hertfordshire CC.
[10016009]   10/02/2010   ACL12/05/2011
Finlay, Miss J, Student.
[10032147]   29/10/2013   ME
Finlayson, Ms D M, MA MCLIP, Librarian, British College of Osteopathic
Medicine, London.
[21324]   13/10/1973   CM21/07/1976
Finn, Mrs W C, Lib. Manager, Springbourne Library, Bournemouth.
[10017562]   07/09/2010   AF
Finnamore, Mrs J A, BA MA, Head of Collection Care, The London
Library.
[10013700]   22/05/2009   ME
Finnegan, Miss A F, BA (Hons) MA,
[10020381]   10/02/2012   ME
Finney, Mrs P, ACLIP, Library Assistant, Anglia Ruskin University.
[64973]   05/10/2005   ACL17/06/2009
Firby, Miss N K, BA M Phil FCLIP, Retired.
[4920]   12/03/1935   FE01/01/1946
Firebrace, Ms C, MA, Research information specialist.
[55401]   09/10/1997   ME
Firth, Mr G W, BA MCLIP, Retired.
[4924]   22/09/1966   CM01/01/1969
Fishburn, Mrs R K, MCLIP, Retired.
[14047]   09/01/1970   CM05/11/1973
Fisher, Ms B M, OBE MLib FCLIP, Life Member.
[4938]   11/07/1971   FE17/11/1999
Fisher, Mrs C A, BA, Learning Resources Manager, Ormiston Venture
Academy, Gt. Yarmouth.
[64783]   01/07/2005   ME
Fisher, Ms C R, BA (Hons), Trust Librarian, City Hospital Sunderland,
Sunderland Royal Hospital.
[38302]   11/03/1985   ME
Fisher, Mrs D C, MA DipLib MCLIP, Self-employed.
[29633]   10/10/1978   CM12/02/1981
Fisher, Mrs D J G, BA MCLIP, Retired.
[24485]   01/10/1975   CM14/02/1978
Fisher, Mrs E R K, DipLib MCLIP, Manager, L. & Information Serv.,
Rotherham.
[31470]   26/09/1979   CM11/05/1985
Fisher, Ms F M, Not Known.
[10019533]   22/07/2011   ME
Fisher, Mrs H L, Lib. and Information Officer – CRIS, Belfast Health and
Social Care Trust.
[65692]   30/03/2006   AF

Fisher, Mrs H S, MCLIP, Retired.
[33771]   18/03/1961   CM01/01/1965
Fisher, Miss J W, BSc MCLIP, Retired.
[21250]   08/10/1973   CM08/10/1975
Fisher, Mrs K J, BA MSc, Academic Librarian, Leeds Beckett University,
Leeds.
[10016645]   25/11/1998   ME
Fisher, Ms L C, MSLIS,
[10035682]   29/10/2014   ME
Fisher, Miss L J, MA MCLIP, Information Centre Manager, Competition
Commission, London.
[31277]   08/10/1979   CM15/12/1981
Fisher, Mr R K, MLitt MA FCLIP, Retired.
[4950]   02/01/1961   FE16/07/1986
Fisher, Mrs S, BA (Hons) MA MCLIP, Librarian, Gloucestershire.
[61627]   04/10/2002   RV13/11/2013   CM29/03/2006
Fisher, Mrs S, MA, Student, Aberystwyth University.
[10032082]   24/10/2013   ME
Fisher, Ms S G, BA (Hons), Grad. Trainee Librarian, Christ's College
Library, Cambridge.
[10013086]   24/03/2009   ME
Fisher, Mrs T S, School Librarian, The Chafford School.
[10023401]   16/07/2013   AF
Fisher, Mr W E, BA MEd DipLib MCLIP, Lecturer, Chiba Instituteof
Tech., Japan.
[29187]   03/04/1978   CM17/04/1980
Fishleigh, Miss J F, BA MA FCLIP, Librarian, Payne, Hicks, Beach,
London.
[40966]   01/10/1987   FE10/03/2011
Fitt, Mrs C A, BA MCLIP, Children's Reading Enthuser.
[25541]   25/01/1976   CM01/08/1979
Fittall, Ms P S, MA DipLib MCLIP, Records Administrator, Norman
Disney & Young, Australia.
[27672]   08/07/1977   CM18/07/1980
Fitzgerald, Mrs C, MA, Library Assistant/Customer Services Assistant,
Dunstable Library.
[10033983]   15/05/2014   ME
Fitzgerald, Mrs H, BA (Hons) MA MCLIP, Customer Servs. Manager, St
Mary's UniversityCollege.
[61753]   31/10/2002   CM07/09/2005
Fitzgerald, Mrs M T, BLib MCLIP, Librarian, Moberly Library, Winchester
College.
[24152]   10/03/1975   CM23/07/1980
Fitzgerald, Mr P, BA (Hons) MA MSc MCLIP, Information Specialist.
[50231]   11/05/1994   CM16/07/2003
Fitzgerald, Miss S M D, BA (Hons) FLS MCLIP, Retired.
[4963]   12/08/1958   CM01/01/1962
Fitzmaurice, Mrs A M, BA MCLIP, Head of L. R. C., St Marks School,
Hounslow.
[31308]   01/10/1979   CM21/10/1982
Fitzmaurice, Ms D, BA (Hons) MSc Econ,
[10001957]   16/04/2004   ME
Fitzpatrick, Mrs E R, BA (Hons) MCLIP, Assistant Library & Research
Services Manager, Royal Academy of Dance, London.
[62982]   02/12/2003   CM19/03/2008
Flagner, Ms K E, BA, Senior Librarian, Cumbria CC.
[45882]   08/07/1991   ME
Flain, Mrs R M, Part-time Consultant Lib. /Information Sci., Envirotox-
International, Stevenage.
[51278]   16/12/1994   ME
Flanagan, Mrs K D, BA (Hons) MA MCLIP, Special Collections
Librarian, Brunel University.
[60004]   21/11/2001   CM11/03/2009

Flannigan, Miss S, Student, University of Strathclyde.
[10035384]   10/10/2014   **ME**
Flather, Ms K, Fdsc, Senior Learning Technologies and Library Services Coordinator, Petroc.
[10020292]   09/01/2012   **AF**
Flavell-Irving, Miss A, BSc (Hons), Student, Northumbria University.
[10035622]   24/10/2014   **ME**
Fleet, Mrs C J, BA (Hons) MCLIP, Career Break.
[49187]   11/10/1993   **CM24/07/1996**
Fleetwood, Mr R, BA FCLIP, Retired.
[4981]   06/10/1959   **FE01/01/1966**
Fleetwood, Ms S, BA MSc MCLIP, Disability Support Librarian, University of the West of England.
[10008563]   01/04/2008   **CM04/10/2013**
Flegg, Ms S A, BA Dip Lib MSLS MCLIP, Information Resources Manager, Ashfords LLP.
[10014014]   06/08/1991   **CM01/07/1994**
Fleming, Ms C A, BSc (Hons) DipLib FHEA MCLIP, Multimedia Project Officer, EDINA, University of Edinburgh, Warrington Office.
[38159]   15/01/1985   **CM12/03/2003**
Fleming, Mrs J L, BA (Hons) PgDipILS MCLIP, Library Services Co-ordinator, Exeter College.
[10000757]   15/11/1996   **CM19/03/2008**
Fleming, Miss K E, BSc PgDip MCLIP, Children & Young People's Librarian, Milton Keynes Central Library, Milton Keynes.
[10013747]   27/05/2009   **CM15/02/2012**
Fleming, Mrs K E L, BA (Hons) MCLIP, Information Professional, Self-Employed.
[54614]   04/02/1997   **CM15/11/2000**
Fleming, Mrs L C, BSc (Hons) MSc, Library Resources Adviser, City College Norwich.
[57106]   14/12/1998   **ME**
Fleming, Miss L J, DipIM MCLIP, Engineering Librarian, London Underground Ltd.
[56021]   28/01/1998   **CM21/05/2003**
Fleming, Mr W, BA MCLIP, Retired.
[4995]   29/10/1969   **CM14/01/1974**
Fletcher, Miss B J, BA DipLib MCLIP, Information Consultant.
[34460]   04/11/1981   **CM19/09/1989**
Fletcher, Mrs E G, MA MSc MCLIP, Voluntary Librarian, Beacon Park Retirement Village.
[18688]   02/04/1963   **CM21/02/1973**
Fletcher, Mrs H A, BA AKC DipLib MCLIP, School Librarian, Bishop's Stortford High School, Herts.
[35773]   20/01/1983   **CM05/04/1988**
Fletcher, Ms J E, BA (Hons) MA, Legal L., Rosling King Solicitor.
[55346]   29/09/1997   **ME**
Fletcher, Mr J W, BA MA MA MA MCLIP, Liaison Librarian, Nottingham Trent University.
[65909]   04/07/2006   **CM06/05/2009**
Fletcher, Dr M, PhD, Cambridge Theological Federation and Faculty of Philosophy at Cambridge University.
[65731]   06/04/2006   **AF**
Fletcher, Ms M A, MA MIL MCLIP, Retired.
[5005]   25/10/1964   **CM01/01/1968**
Fletcher, Mr P J, BA (Hons) DipILM MCLIP, Wodehouse Lib. Dulwich Coll.
[47770]   14/10/1992   **CM24/09/1997**
Fletcher, Miss S J, MA, Assistant Librarian, St Catharine's College, Cambridge.
[10015016]   06/10/2009   **ME**
Fletcher, Miss S K, BA MA MCLIP, Assistant Librarian, Guille-Alles Library, Guernsey, Channel Islands.
[44875]   04/01/1991   **CM27/05/1992**

Fletcher, Ms S M, MA MCLIP, Retired.
[18692]   07/09/1969   **CM21/09/1972**
Fletcher, Mr T H, BA MCLIP, Library Technology Innovation Manager, Birkbeck, University of London.
[23484]   01/01/1975   **CM30/10/1978**
Flett, Mrs E D, BSc MCLIP, Retired.
[5010]   10/03/1966   **CM01/01/1968**
Flett, Mr J R W, BSc MSc, Senior L. Assistant, Bristol Central Library, Bristol.
[10014826]   18/09/2009   **ME**
Flint, Mrs A M, BSc (Hons) MA, Assistant Librarian, MOD.
[63016]   15/12/2003   **ME**
Flintham, Mrs C H G, MCLIP Hon BA, Retired.
[10921]   08/01/1964   **CM01/01/1967**
Flintoff, Mrs H F, MSc MCLIP, Deputy Learning Res. Centre Manager, Brockenhurst College, Hants.
[58706]   09/06/2000   **CM13/06/2007**
Floate, Rev R C, BA DipLib DipThSt MCLIP, Priest-in-charge, Wool and East Stoke, Diocese of Salisbury.
[34214]   08/10/1981   **CM23/06/1986**
Flood, Mrs D, BA (Hons) ALA DMS, Librarian, Furze Platt Senior School.
[34597]   07/01/1982   **ME**
Flor, Mrs P A I, Senior Librarian, Telemark University College, Skien, Norway.
[5023]   20/09/1967   **CM01/01/1970**
Florence, Miss J, BA MCLIP, Lead Adviser with Hampshire School Library Service.
[39433]   26/01/1986   **CM19/06/1991**
Florin, Ms J, BA (Hons) PgDipLIS MCLIP, Collection Development Manager, Royal College of Nursing.
[10006147]   15/07/1992   **RV**30/04/2014 **CM15/01/2003**
Flower, Ms C S, BA (Hons), Librarian, Gensler, London.
[47805]   19/10/1992   **ME**
Flower, Mr L, DipHE MCLIP, Lead Librarian – Outreach, Swindon Borough Council.
[10017159]   11/07/2010   **CM27/03/2014**
Flower, Mrs M E, BA (Hons) PgDipLib MCLIP, PT Librarian, Newman University.
[39290]   06/01/1986   **CM04/10/1988**
Flowers, Miss G M, MCLIP, Retired. Lifeline Vol. (Family Reading).
[5026]   31/01/1970   **CM19/12/1972**
Floyd, Ms E K, MA MCLIP, Librarian, The Paul Mellon Centre for Studies in British Art, London.
[44408]   05/10/1990   **CM17/11/1999**
Floyd, Mrs S, BA (Hons) DTLLS, Head of Library Services, City College Norwich.
[10015922]   25/01/2010   **ME**
Flude, Mrs E M, MCLIP, Retired.
[5028]   17/03/1944   **CM01/01/1955**
Flynn, Ms B, BA (Hons), Librarian, Imperial War Museum.
[48514]   04/02/1993   **ME**
Flynn, Mr D, Information Literacy Lead.
[10021410]   03/08/2012   **ME**
Flynn, Mrs J, Senior Sch. Lib, Hall Cross School, Doncaster.
[10001688]   22/03/2007   **AF**
Flynn, Mr J M, BA MCLIP, Head of Access, V&A, London.
[28739]   24/01/1978   **CM28/11/1980**
Flynn, Ms P A, BA MCLIP, Reader Svces Librarian, Lib. HQ, Argyll and Bute Library Service.
[29961]   07/11/1978   **CM30/06/1983**
Flynn, Mrs R I, BSc Econ (Hons) MCLIP, Librarian, AECOM, London.
[10000920]   23/11/1994   **CM15/10/2002**

Fodale, Ms F, MSc, Postgraduate Research Student, University of Ulster.
[10021756]   09/10/2012   ME

Foden, Mrs L J, Librarian, Dr Challoners High School 01/04/2014.
[10020147]   11/11/2011   AF

Foden, Miss S, BA (Hons), Information Manager, Kraft Foods, Birmingham.
[40338]   20/01/1987   ME

Fodey, Mr W J, MA DipLib MCLIP, Librarian, Glasgow Caledonian University.
[43580]   09/11/1989   CM26/02/1992

Foe, Mr L S, BA (Hons) DipLib, Learning Support Librarian, Paddington Library, Westminster City Council.
[46266]   21/10/1991   ME

Fogarty, Mr R, BA MA MLIS,
[10032676]   14/01/2014   ME

Fogg, Ms H S, BA MA,
[55333]   01/10/1997   ME

Fogg, Mr N J, DRSAM BA, Library Assistant, The Society of Genealogists, London.
[40791]   15/06/1987   ME

Foister, Miss C, BA, Student, University of Cambridge.
[10031563]   13/10/2014   ME

Foley, Mr M, MA BEd MSc DipLib MCLIP, Cataloguer, Baker and Taylor, YPB Yankee Book Pedler.
[35008]   15/06/1982   CM20/12/1986

Follett, Sir B K, HonFLA, Chairman/Chair, Arts & Humanities Research Board, Strategy Group on Res. L's.
[54736]   19/03/1997   HFE19/03/1997

Fomo, Mrs A E G, MCLIP, Life Member.
[16893]   20/03/1961   CM01/01/1964

Fone, Mrs C H, MA MCLIP, Clinical/ Outreach Librarian Bassetlaw District Gen. Hospital, Worksop.
[30081]   29/11/1978   CM23/04/1982

Foot, Mrs E R, BA MA, Information and Reviews Officer, NFER.
[63105]   30/01/2004   ME

Foote, Mrs L, MCLIP, Library Manager., Yeovil District hospital NHS Foundation Trust., Yeovil.
[8707]   21/11/1969   CM30/03/1973

Footitt, Mrs A C, BSc MSc MCLIP, Information Officer Highlands for The National Autistic Society Scotland, based in Inverness.
[41271]   23/10/1987   CM24/05/1995

Forbes, Mr G S, BA MA MBA MCLIP, Head of Ingest, National Library of Scotland.
[30906]   13/05/1979   CM20/05/1981

Forbes, Miss S A, Student, Manchester Metropolitan University.
[10035544]   17/10/2014   ME

Ford, Ms A, BA DipLib MCLIP, Librarian, Dartford Science and Technology College.
[40828]   03/07/1987   CM21/07/1989

Ford, Ms A M, BLib MCLIP, Information Manager, Careers Service, Aberystwyth University.
[32518]   29/04/1980   CM27/09/1982

Ford, Mrs C E M, MA Dip Lib MCLIP, CMS Project Volunteer, Mr Straw's House, National Trust.
[40907]   11/08/1987   CM29/01/1992

Ford, Ms H E, MA, Information Executive, Enquries & Acquisitions, ICAEW.
[62523]   05/08/2003   ME

Ford, Ms J M, BA, Centre Coordinator, Adult Educ. Service, Birmingham.
[37612]   12/10/1984   ME

Ford, Mrs K M, MA DipLib MCLIP, Retired.
[5047]   16/10/1967   CM26/01/1984

Ford, Mr M, MA BA, KIM Assistant, Office For National Statistics.
[10033806]   01/05/2014   ME

Ford, Mr N, MSc (Econ) MCLIP, Subject Librarian, Bournemouth University.
[62368]   12/05/2003   CM06/05/2009

Ford, Mrs S, Information Professional, Ministry of Defence.
[10034298]   02/07/2014   ME

Ford, Miss S A H, BA MA, Acquisitions and Discovery Officer, King's College London.
[10032699]   06/01/2014   ME

Ford, Miss S L, Purchasing Officer, University of The West of England. Bristol.
[10019491]   11/07/2011   AF

Ford, Miss S M, BA (Hons) MCLIP, Librarian, St Helens & Knowsley Hospital Trust, Whiston, Merseyside.
[46644]   02/12/1991   CM01/06/2005

Forde, Mrs J R, BA PGCE MCLIP, Retired.
[5060]   01/01/1965   CM01/01/1968

Forde, Miss L L, BA DipLib MCLIP, Library Manager, Glasgow Clyde College.
[43478]   27/10/1989   CM19/08/1992

Forder Blakeman, Mr K, BA MCLIP, Life Member.
[1373]   01/01/1953   CM01/01/1962

Fordham, Mrs L E, Student, University of Northampton.
[10035426]   13/10/2014   ME

Ford-Smith, Ms A M, BA (Hons) MA MCLIP, Manager (Communications, Publishing and Archives), Bernard Quaritch Ltd.
[56939]   09/11/1998   CM15/09/2004

Fordyce, Mr D W, BSc MSc, Head of Membership and Information Serv., Brewing Research International, Nutfield.
[56083]   13/02/1998   ME

Foreman, Ms J M, MA DipLib, Head Librarian, Scottish Government Library, Scottish Government, Victoria Quay, Commercial Street, Edinburgh EH6 6QQ.
[37781]   17/10/1984   ME

Foreman, Mrs L R, MA (Hons) MLib MCLIP, Relocated to Switzerland.
[49273]   20/10/1993   CM22/01/1997

Foreman, Dr R L E, PhD MLib FCLIP HonFTCL, Retired.
[5065]   01/01/1961   FE13/06/1972

Forgham-Healey, Mrs N F L, BA (Hons) MSc MCLIP, Library Manager, Western General Hospital., Somerset.
[59578]   05/06/2001   RV30/04/2014   CM13/06/2007

Forrest, Mr A, BA (Hons), Information Officer, University of Stirling, Stirling.
[65708]   28/03/2006   ME

Forrest, Mrs A J, BA DipLib MCLIP, Sch. Lib. - Independent.
[10001722]   26/10/1993   CM22/05/1996

Forrest, Mrs A Y, BA MCLIP, Sutherland Area L. Officer, Highland Reg. L. Serv.
[30842]   20/05/1979   CM04/11/1982

Forrest, Ms E L, BA DIP LIB IS MCLIP, School Library Resource Centre.
[41028]   05/10/1987   CM12/09/1990

Forrest, Mrs M E M, MA MCLIP, Retired.
[5071]   02/10/1971   CM01/04/1974

Forrest, Mrs M E S, MA MSc DipLib FCLIP FSA Scot FHEA, Immediate past President of CILIPS; Academic Liaison Librarian, School of History, Classics & Archaeology, University of Edinburgh.
[36541]   19/10/1983   FE19/05/1999

Forrest, Mrs M V, MCLIP, Life Member.
[5072]   01/01/1955   CM01/01/1961

Forrest, Miss R, BSc (Hons) MCLIP, Ministry of Justice Assistant Librarian. Ministry of Justice., London.
[46634]   29/11/1991   CM24/07/1996

Forrest, Mrs S A, BA DipLib MCLIP, Part-time Assistant Subject
Advisor, University of Derby.
[39569]   04/03/1986   **CM13/06/1990**
Forster, Mrs A E, BA MCLIP, L. &Information Manager, Newcastle City
Libraries.
[30114]   10/01/1979   **CM09/09/1981**
Forster, Miss L, BA MCLIP, Grad. Trainee, Nuffield College, Oxford.
[10015274]   29/10/2009   **CM13/11/2013**
Forster, Ms T D A, MSc, Information Scientist, independent consultant.
[60084]   12/11/1984   **ME**
Forsyth, Miss E M, BSc MCLIP, Retired.
[28951]   10/02/1978   **CM29/02/1980**
Forsyth, Ms S, MCLIP,
[10001563]   20/10/1997   **CM19/11/2008**
Forsythe, Mrs F M, BA MSc (Econ) MCLIP, Self-employed, Fionn
Consultancy, Northumberland.
[38078]   17/01/1985   **CM15/05/1989**
Forsythe, Mrs J E, BA MCLIP, Retired.
[7025]   01/10/1970   **CM23/01/1974**
Foss, Mrs J A, BA (Hons) MSc (Econ) MCLIP, Child. Librarian, Guille-
Alles Library, Guernsey.
[62236]   31/03/2003   **CM10/07/2009**
Foster, Miss A, Student, UCL, London.
[10020009]   25/10/2011   **ME**
Foster, Mr A J, BA FCLIP, Information Industry Consultant & Writer,
Lancashire.
[5094]   21/02/1966   **FE01/04/2002**
Foster, Mrs C E, BA MSc MCLIP, PhD Res. stud., Universityof
Strathclyde.
[10000511]   16/10/2006   **CM11/06/2010**
Foster, Mrs F E, DipPhysEd MCLIP, Life Member, Overseas.
[16897]   01/01/1963   **CM01/01/1963**
Foster, Mrs G, BA MSc PgC MCLIP, Clinical Information Specialist,
HSCIC/ NHS Choices.
[38171]   23/01/1985   **CM01/04/2002**
Foster, Mrs H C, BA (Hons) Msc (Econ) MCLIP, Assistant Librarian –
Special Collections Sydney Jones Library, University of Liverpool.
[51184]   23/11/1994   **CM18/11/1998**
Foster, Mrs J, BA (Hons), Head Librarian, St Albans High School For
Girls.
[10007780]   16/10/1987   **ME**
Foster, Ms J M, MA BA (Hons) MCLIP, Client Services and Support
Manager, University of Southampton.
[65806]   16/05/2006   **CM16/01/2014**
Foster, Mrs K M, BA (Hons) MCLIP, Retired.
[5109]   28/09/1960   **CM01/01/1966**
Foster, Ms L M, BA DipLib MCLIP, Area Manager, Peckham Library,
London.
[40348]   21/01/1987   **CM15/08/1990**
Foster, Mrs P, BA (Hons),
[10013412]   27/04/2009   **AF**
Foster, Mrs R, BA (Hons) MCLIP, Library Services Manager, Chester
Public Library, Chester.
[51717]   25/05/1995   **CM17/11/1999**
Foster, Mr R L, BA DipIM MCLIP, Deputy Counter Supervisor, Kings
College London, Maughan L.
[50807]   19/10/1994   **CM09/11/2005**
Foster, Mrs S M, BLib MCLIP,
[37102]   13/02/1984   **CM02/06/1987**
Foster, Ms W F A, BA (Hons) MCLIP, Business Librarian, City of London
Corporation.
[42950]   04/05/1989   **CM15/11/2000**

Foster, Mrs W J, BA MCLIP, Knowledge Servs. Manager, Hywel Dda
University Health Board.
[28737]   27/01/1978   **CM08/08/1980**
Foster-Jones, Mrs J J, BA (Hons) MCLIP MA ODE FHEA, Part-time
Teaching Fellow, Department of Information Studies, University of
Aberystwyth.
[52590]   09/11/1995   **CM15/05/2002**
Foulis, Ms S, BA (Hons), Part-time Student, City University /House of
Commons Library, London.
[10000952]   30/11/2006   **ME**
Fountain, Mrs K M, MSc (Econ) MCLIP, Part-time School Librarian,
Gunnersbury Catholic School, London Borough of Hounslow.
[22777]   09/10/1974   **CM16/08/1977**
Fourie, Prof I, BBibl MBilb MCLIP, Professor, Department of Information
Science, University of Pretoria.
[60102]   04/10/2000   **CM04/10/2000**
Fowke, Mrs A S, BA MCLIP, Information Librarian, Unitec, New
Zealand.
[45803]   04/06/1991   **CM23/03/1994**
Fowkes, Miss H, MA, Sch. L. Centre Manager, Guille-Alles Library,
Guernsey.
[10012626]   02/11/1998   **ME**
Fowkes, Mr R, MCLIP, Retired.
[5129]   15/08/1938   **CM01/01/1948**
Fowler, Miss A M R, BA MCLIP, Child. & Sch. Librarian, London
Borough of Redbridge.
[32653]   23/07/1980   **CM19/01/1984**
Fowler, Mrs C, MA BSc MCLIP PgCert HE Mgmt, Head of Library
Services & University Librarian, Bournemouth University.
[31228]   08/10/1979   **RV**20/06/2014   **CM15/09/1983**
Fowler, Ms C B, BSc (Hons) MA MCLIP, Subject Librarian for Publishing
and the Creative Arts, Oxford Brookes University Library.
[56739]   12/10/1998   **CM09/11/2005**
Fowler, Mr G, Retired.
[5132]   20/10/1947   **ME**
Fowler, Mr L W, BA (Hons), Student, Aberystwyth University.
[10020235]   02/12/2011   **ME**
Fowler, Miss M K, BA (Hons) MLib (Dist) MCLIP, Team Leader, North
Yorks C. C. Information Serv., Richmond.
[47987]   30/10/1992   **CM18/09/2002**
Fowles, Mrs C, BA PgDip, Librarian, Congleton Library.
[10022139]   08/01/2013   **ME**
Fox, Mr A J, FCLIP, Life Member.
[5141]   27/02/1952   **FE01/01/1959**
Fox, Mr D J, Systems Librarian, Victoria University, Canada.
[62561]   20/08/2003   **ME**
Fox, Mr E S, MSc MPhil FCLIP, Life Member.
[5144]   01/01/1943   **FE01/01/1952**
Fox, Mrs J M, MRSC MIMMM, Retired.
[60582]   11/12/2001   **CM11/12/2001**
Fox, Mrs M, BSc DLIS MCLIP, Press Officer, Duke of Kent School,
Ewhurst.
[27427]   01/04/1977   **CM12/10/1979**
Fox, Mr N J, BA MCLIP, Information Officer, Linklaters, London.
[27972]   06/10/1977   **CM30/10/1979**
Fox, Mr N R, BA FCLIP FRSA, Retired.
[5149]   01/01/1967   **FE27/01/1993**
Fox, Mr R G, BA (Hons), Information Specialist, Qinetiq, Portsmouth,
Hants.
[46344]   29/10/1991   **ME**
Fox, Ms S, BA MCLIP, Librarian, Ardingly College, Haywards Heath,
West Sussex.
[63818]   06/10/2004   **CM21/11/2007**

Fox, Mrs T M, BA (Hons) MCLIP, L. & Resource Centre Manager, Frome Community College.
[10011093]   24/09/2008   **CM19/10/2012**
Fox, Mrs V J, MCLIP, Retired.
[5602]   18/01/1966   **CM01/01/1970**
Fragkos, Mr D, BA MSc MCLIP, Cataloguer, The London Library.
[10014146]   02/07/2009   **CM25/01/2011**
France, Mrs K, BA (Hons) DipILS, Knowledge Management Specialist., Rotherham PCT.
[59372]   21/02/2001   **ME**
France, Mrs R F, MTheol DipLib MCLIP, Librarian, Bradford Girls' Grammar School, Bradford.
[10017048]   22/06/1984   **CM15/11/1988**
Francis, Mrs E J, BSc MSc MCLIP, Cataloguer, University of Aberdeen.
[63100]   28/01/2004   **CM08/08/2008**
Francis, Mr J P E, BA FCLIP, Life Member.
[5175]   16/10/1948   **FE01/01/1961**
Francis, Ms N, Learning Resource Centre Manager, St Benedicts Upper School.
[10018212]   09/12/2010   **ME**
Francis, Ms R, PgDip MCLIP, Academic Services Librarian, University of Greenwich.
[10006247]   26/09/2007   **CM09/07/2013**
Francis, Ms R, BSc, Librarian, Sherfield School.
[10022946]   14/05/2013   **ME**
Francis, Mr S, MA FCLIP, Life Member.
[5180]   24/03/1958   **FE02/03/1965**
Francis, Ms S J, BA (Hons) DipLIB MCLIP, Locality Manager, Dudley MBC.
[43376]   16/10/1989   **CM20/04/2012**
Francis, Miss S L, BA MPhil, Relief Library Assistant, West Sussex CC.
[10031946]   15/10/2013   **ME**
Franck, Ms M E A, MCLIP, Age UK Lindsey, Lincolnshire.
[64448]   30/03/2005   **CM27/03/2014**
Frangeskou, Dr V, BA PhD MA, Assistant Librarian, University of Bristol.
[42217]   03/10/1988   **ME**
Frank, Dr A, BA (Hons) MA PhD, Library Assistant, Brighton & Hove L. Serv., Jubilee L.
[10018849]   22/03/2011   **AF**
Frankland, Mr J M, BA MSc, Service Development Officer.
[10005863]   16/08/2007   **ME**
Franklin, Mr A G, MA MCLIP, Librarian, Manx National Heritage, Douglas, Isle of Man.
[21952]   29/01/1974   **CM14/02/1977**
Franklin, Miss A M, BA MCLIP, School Librarian, Canons High School, Middx.
[33596]   21/01/1981   **CM19/01/1984**
Franklin, Mr A P C, MSc, Indexing Officer, Royal Anthropological Institute, London.
[10000957]   24/11/2006   **ME**
Franklin, Miss C E, BA (Hons) MA MCLIP,
[51441]   14/02/1995   **CM17/09/2003**
Franklin, Mrs F S, BA MCLIP, Child. Librarian, Derby City Council.
[25597]   27/01/1976   **CM22/10/1979**
Franklin, Mrs G, BA MA MCLIP AHEA, Academic Librarian, Loughborough University.
[43332]   20/10/1989   **CM16/11/1994**
Franklin, Ms G, BSc, Librarian, Health Promotion Resources, Northamptonshire NHS Provider Services.
[10010907]   04/09/2008   **ME**
Franklin, Mrs M, BA MCLIP, Retired.
[10044]   13/12/1968   **CM30/03/1976**

Franklin, Mrs S M, BA (Hons), Senior Library Assistant, Woodrow Library, Worcs.
[10011210]   02/10/2008   **AF**
Franks, Mrs D, BSc MSc Sci Soc (Open) MCLIP, L. Serv. Manager, STFC, Daresbury Laboratory, Warrington.
[37756]   23/10/1984   **RV20/06/2014**   **CM12/12/1991**
Franks, Miss K, BA (Hons) MA, Assistant Librarian, Hurstpierpoint College.
[10035082]   07/10/2014   **ME**
Franssen, Mr J, BA (Hons) MA, Head of Research, Travers Smith LLP.
[57628]   02/06/1999   **ME**
Fraser, Mr A, BA, Student, Robert Gordon University, Aberdeen.
[10013633]   18/05/2009   **ME**
Fraser, Mrs B J, DIPL BIBL MCLIP, Assistant Librarian Cataloguing & Metadata Serv., Anglia Ruskin University, Chelmsford.
[10005879]   20/05/2004   **CM06/07/2011**
Fraser, Mrs C L, Collections Officer, Lincolnshire L. Serv., Lincoln.
[65945]   14/07/2006   **AF**
Fraser, Dr D M, BA (Hons) MCLIP, Retired.
[19893]   19/12/1972   **CM21/07/1975**
Fraser, Ms F, BA MCLIP, Community Librarian (Job Share)., Larbert Library, Falkirk Council.
[30618]   19/02/1979   **CM21/12/1981**
Fraser, Dr K, BA MSc MA PhD MCLIP, Senior Librarian, University of Nottingham, Nottingham.
[10001309]   19/01/2007   **CM07/09/2011**
Fraser, Ms K A, MCLIP, Executive Manager, Shetland Islands Council.
[64675]   25/05/2005   **CM10/07/2009**
Fraser, Mr K C, MA BSc MCLIP, Retired.
[5197]   19/10/1966   **CM01/01/1969**
Fraser, Mr K G, BA DMS MCLIP, Librarian, The Robert Gordon University, Aberdeen.
[33932]   22/05/1981   **CM05/12/1985**
Fraser, Mrs M, HNC, Lib. Sup., William Patrick Library, Kirkintilloch.
[10017278]   22/07/2010   **AF**
Fraser, Ms M A, MA MCLIP, Principal Knowledge Coordinator., Department for International Development Library, East Kilbride.
[23251]   15/10/1974   **CM31/08/1977**
Fraser, Mr T, BA MSc, Student, Strathclyde University.
[10031744]   01/10/2013   **ME**
Fraser, Ms V E, BA DipLib MIPD FCLIP, Head of Data Protection, Information Risk Management & CHIP Briefing System, Department of Health.
[5202]   14/04/1972   **FE15/09/2004**
Fraser, Miss V L, BA (Hons) MCLIP, Support Services Librarian, Angus Council.
[51026]   09/11/1994   **CM21/05/2003**
Fratus, Mrs L M, BA (Hons) MSc (Econ) MCLIP, Resident in Australia.
[52504]   02/11/1995   **CM17/11/1999**
Freebury, Mr R, BA DipLib MCLIP PhD, Indexing Manager, House of Commons Library.
[40817]   01/07/1987   **CM14/11/1990**
Freedman, Ms J D, BA (Hons) Dip Lib, LRC Manager Sir George Monoux College, London.
[38091]   08/01/1985   **ME**
Freedman, Mrs S B, Learning Resource Centre Manager The Forest Academy L. B. Redbridge.
[49898]   07/01/1994   **ME**
Freedman, Ms V R, MA, Assistant Librarian, Hebrew & Jewish Studies Librarian, UCL.
[63543]   22/06/2004   **ME**
Freeman, Mrs J H, BA MCLIP, Unwaged.
[28788]   26/01/1978   **CM15/12/1983**

Freeman, Ms L, Library Manager, Samuel Whitbread Academy, Shefford.
[10021102]   29/05/2012   **AF**

Freeman, Mrs L A, BA MCLIP, Library Assistant, Calderdale M. B. C.
[41511]   11/01/1988   **CM27/03/1991**

Freeman, Mrs L M, BA MCLIP, Surestart Librarian, Derbyshire County Council.
[26915]   04/01/1977   **CM01/07/1992**

Freeman, Mr M C E, BA MCLIP, Libraries and Heritage Manager, Stockton on Tees Borough Council.
[31288]   08/10/1979   **CM14/02/1984**

Freeman, Dr M J, BA MEd PhD FCLIP, Retired.
[5216]   30/09/1959   **FE18/04/1989**

Freeman, Miss O J, MLS MCLIP, Retired.
[5217]   27/09/1967   **CM01/01/1970**

Freeman, Mrs S D, MCLIP, Branch Librarian, Stockton Borough Council.
[23217]   15/11/1974   **CM09/08/1977**

Freemantle, Mr D J, BA DipLib MCLIP, Information Analyst, BG Group plc., Reading.
[36404]   08/10/1983   **CM15/02/1989**

French, Miss A C, BA (Hons), Student.
[10032280]   13/11/2013   **ME**

French, Miss C, MA MCLIP, Stock Librarian, West Sussex Library Service.
[62046]   28/01/2003   **CM29/11/2006**

French, Mr G, BA, Student, Institute of Advanced Legal Studies.
[10032497]   10/12/2013   **ME**

French, Mr J M, BA MCLIP, Retired.
[5223]   19/01/1971   **CM24/01/1974**

French, Mrs L M, BSc MCLIP, Part-time Child. Librarian, Bexley Central L.
[50131]   06/04/1994   **CM07/09/2005**

Frenzel, Ms F, Dipl Bibl,
[10021297]   06/07/2012   **ME**

Fretten, Miss C E, MCLIP MBE, Retired.
[5231]   02/10/1968   **CM01/01/1971**

Frey, Mrs L, BA (Hons) DipLib, Assistant Librarian, DFPNI Library, Belfast.
[10006146]   11/09/2007   **ME**

Fricker, Mr A, BSc MSc MCLIP, Library Liaison Manager, King's College London.
[55376]   06/10/1997   **CM12/03/2003**

Fricker, Mrs R, BA MA MCLIP, Freelance legal researcher and abstractor.
[55369]   06/10/1997   **CM20/11/2002**

Friday, Ms K, Res. Student, RGU.
[63180]   03/03/2004   **ME**

Fridman, Ms I, MA MCLIP, Local Studies Librarian, Medway Arch. Centre, Rochester.
[62618]   18/09/2003   **CM21/11/2007**

Friedlander, Ms J R, BA MCLIP, Retired.
[32654]   15/07/1980   **CM21/07/1982**

Friel, Mrs L, Librarian, King Edward VI Grammar School.
[10023113]   11/06/2013   **AF**

Friggens, Ms G L, BA (Hons) MSc (Econ) FHEA MCLIP, Faculty Librarian, Creative and Cultural Industries, University of Portsmouth.
[52529]   06/11/1995   **CM20/01/1999**

Fripp, Mr A J, BA,
[10035053]   08/09/2014   **ME**

Froggatt, Ms S J, Head of L. &Information Serv., Reynolds Porter Chamberlain LLP, London.
[39167]   01/10/1985   **ME**

Frohawk, Mrs T, Learning Resources Centre Manager, Rushden Community College Northamptonshire County Council.
[10035051]   15/09/2014   **ME**

Frontin, Mr H, Library Facilitator., City & Islington College, London.
[10016477]   01/04/2010   **AF**

Frost, Miss A J, BLS MCLIP, Adult Reading & Learning Librarian, Norfolk Library & Information Service.
[29324]   23/05/1978   **CM10/11/1982**

Frost, Miss S M, BA MCLIP, Learning Advisor, University of Cumbria L.
[31826]   18/01/1980   **CM24/01/1985**

Froud, Mr R N, OBE BLib DMS MIMgt FCLIP, Retired.
[21900]   21/01/1974   **FE23/07/1997**

Fry, Mrs A, Student / Assistant Librarian.
[10026893]   **ME**

Fry, Mrs C, MIBC CMC MCIPD BA (Hon) MBA, DES CIO Head, DCSA Directorate strategic Transition – MOD.
[10033962]   14/05/2014   **ME**

Fry, Mrs E M, BLib (Hons), Unwaged.
[43550]   06/11/1989   **ME**

Fry, Ms R, BA HDipLib, Librarian, Peebles High School.
[10006139]   11/09/2007   **ME**

Frydland, Mrs L C, BA (Hons), Librarian, AWE, Aldermaston.
[50796]   18/10/1994   **ME**

Fryer, Ms F A, MA BA (Hons) PG DIP, L. Assistant, Rustington Library, West Sussex County Council.
[10015778]   25/01/2010   **ME**

Fryers, Mrs H R, MA MA MCLIP, Senior L. Assistant, Cheltenham L.
[57494]   06/04/1999   **CM16/07/2003**

Fuchs, Dr H, PhD FRSA, Senior Assistant Librarian, University of Gottingen, Germany.
[39726]   23/05/1986   **ME**

Fudakowska, Miss E, BA MCLIP, Retired.
[5257]   01/01/1953   **CM01/01/1968**

Fuidge, Miss V R, BA MUS MA, Student, University of Sheffield, Department of Information Studies.
[10016186]   23/02/2010   **ME**

Fujiwara, Mr Y, MLS, Associate Profof Librarianship, Chubu Gakuin University, Seki City, Japan.
[57740]   20/07/1999   **ME**

Fulbrook, Mrs L G, BA (Hons) PgDip ILS, Deputy Library Services Manager, Robert Jones & Agnes Hunt Orthopaedic Hospital NHS Foundation Trust.
[10008425]   19/03/2008   **ME**

Fuller, Mr R P, Business Manager, Ministry of Defence.
[10033915]   12/05/2014   **ME**

Fulljames, Mr D R, MSc MCLIP, Retired.
[5264]   16/10/1970   **CM05/01/1973**

Funk, Ms C, HonFCLIP,
[10011431]   16/10/2008   **HFE16/10/2008**

Furderer, Ms E S, MLIS MCLIP, Project Support Officer, University of Kent.
[10008387]   19/03/2008   **CM14/11/2012**

Furlong, Mrs J C, Librarian., Ashlyns School.
[44999]   04/02/1991   **ME**

Furlong, Mr S, Assistant Librarian, Leeds Trinity University.
[10032863]   21/01/2014   **ME**

Furness, Miss E L, Learning Resources Coordinator, Great Yarmouth, Norfolk.
[59302]   31/01/2001   **ME**

Furness, Ms R J, Librarian.
[10017020]   21/06/2010   **ME**

Fynes-Clinton, Mrs A B, BA DipLib MCLIP, Librarian, Haberdashers' Aske's School for Girls, Elstree.
[40152]   09/10/1986   **CM14/02/1990**

G

Gabbatt, Miss J M, BLib MCLIP, Principal Lib. :Literary Development, Learning & Stock, Blackburn with Darwen B. C.
[25535]   29/01/1976   **CM26/06/1979**

Gabriel, Mrs J, Librarian, St Leonards-Mayfield School.
[10015528]   09/12/2009   **ME**

Gabriel, Miss S J, BA (Hons) ACLIP, LR Administrator, Colchester Institute Library.
[10020871]   19/04/2012   **ACL27/08/2014**

Gadd, Ms E A, MSc BA (Hons) MCLIP, Academic Services Manager, Loughborough University.
[10013410]   05/09/2004   **CM22/07/1998**

Gadelrab, Miss M,
[10013145]   02/04/2009   **ME**

Gadsden, Mr S R, MLS MCLIP, Life Member.
[5282]   08/11/1947   **CM01/01/1958**

Gaffiney, Mr M K, BA (Hons), Unwaged, previously Archive Services Manager, BBC Birmingham.
[10033912]   12/05/2014   **ME**

Gaffney, Ms D L, Senior Library Assistant, Queenswood School.
[10035078]   10/09/2014   **ME**

Gaffney, Miss L A, PgDip, Student, Northumbria University.
[10023081]   05/06/2013   **ME**

Gahan, Mr P N, MA, Lib. /Information & Local Studies, Swindon Central Library.
[50364]   01/07/1994   **ME**

Gair, Miss J, BA MCLIP, Library Performance and Resources Section Leader, Central Library, Dundee.
[36019]   04/04/1983   **CM17/04/1985**

Gair, Ms M J, MA DipLib MCLIP, Information Manager MOD, Glasgow.
[39068]   30/10/1985   **RV23/09/2009**   **CM14/09/1994**

Gaj, Mrs L A T, BA MCLIP, Director University of Kurdistan Hewler.
[35914]   07/02/1983   **CM06/10/1987**

Gala, Miss B, MLIS, Student, Department of Library & Information Science, Maharaja Sayajirao University of Baroda, Vadodara, Gujarat, India.
[10032415]   03/12/2013   **ME**

Gale, Mr J R, BA PgDip, Trust Librarian, Mid Cheshire Hospitals NHS Trust.
[10032390]   03/12/2013   **ME**

Gale, Mr M J M, BA (Hons) MLib MCLIP, Librarian, Queens Foundation, Birmingham.
[44858]   01/01/1991   **CM18/11/1993**

Gale, Mrs M T C, DipLib MCLIP, Training Manager, Suffolk Lib. IPS.
[33917]   14/05/1981   **CM23/08/1985**

Gale, Mrs P, MCLIP, Retired.
[5302]   01/01/1958   **CM01/01/1963**

Gale, Mrs S, BSc MSc, Unwaged.
[10018611]   14/02/2011   **ME**

Gall, Ms J A, MA (Hons) DipILS MCLIP, School Librarian, Angus Council, Arbroath High School.
[58030]   19/10/1999   **CM04/02/2004**

Gallacher, Mrs A, BA (Hons) AUDIS, Service Manager Libraries, Maidenhead Library.
[61114]   21/02/2002   **ME**

Gallacher, Mrs K A, MA (Hons) PGDE, Student, Robert Gordon University.
[10035619]   24/10/2014   **ME**

Gallagher, Ms C F, BA (Hons) MA MCLIP, Principal Librarian: Children and Families, Nottinghamshire.
[59348]   13/02/2001   **CM08/12/2004**

Gallagher, Ms J, Special Collections Assistant, Aberystwyth University.
[10016136]   28/05/2012   **ME**

Gallagher, Miss J, BA MA, Student, Robert Gordon University.
[10020454]   20/02/2012   **ME**

Gallagher, Miss K, BEd (Hons) MA, Teacher Librarian, International School of the Sacred Heart, Tokyo.
[10019214]   09/05/2011   **ME**

Gallagher, Mr M T, BA PgCert MA, Director of Learning Resources, William Morris Sixth Form, London.
[61933]   11/12/2002   **ME**

Gallagher, Mr P, MA (Hons) DipLIS MCLIP, School Librarian, King's Park Secondary, Glasgow.
[43488]   30/10/1989   **CM21/05/2003**

Gallagher, Ms S, Student, Aberystwyth University/Executive Officer, Legal Aid Board.
[10031760]   01/10/2013   **ME**

Gallart Marsillas, Ms N, Librarian, University Autonoma de Barcelona, Spain.
[37396]   16/08/1984   **ME**

Gallehawk, Miss R K, BA (Hons) MCLIP, Lib. Thurrock Council, Essex.
[41744]   10/03/1988   **CM27/11/1996**

Galligan, Ms M L, BA, Student.
[10032163]   12/11/2013   **ME**

Galloway, Mr J S, MCLIP, Bib Ser Lib.
[24081]   18/03/1975   **CM07/03/1979**

Galloway, Mrs S E, BA (Hons) DipILS MCLIP, Career Break.
[53976]   15/10/1996   **CM13/03/2002**

Galopin-Dimitriadis, Dr L, BA MA Phd, Bibliothèque Des Chiroux, Belgium.
[10015145]   15/10/2009   **ME**

Galsworthy, Ms J G, FCLIP, Life Member.
[5322]   20/09/1956   **FE01/01/1965**

Galt, Ms C O, BA (Hons) DipILM, Community Librarian, Family History & Heritage, South Tyneside Metropolitan Borough Council.
[54247]   14/11/1996   **ME**

Galt, Ms E, BA MCLIP, Team Librarian, Educ. Resource Serv., Glasgow.
[35568]   18/10/1982   **CM24/02/1986**

Galvin, Mr N D, MA, Student, City University.
[10022332]   11/02/2013   **ME**

Gamage, Dr P, PhD HonFCLIP, Chief Librarian, Institute of Policy Studies, 100/20, Colombo 7, Sri Lanka.
[63102]   05/01/2004   **HFE02/09/2010**

Gamble, Mrs A, BA (Hons) MSc MCLIP, Head of Knowledge Management, Brunswick Group.
[55449]   13/10/1997   **CM15/09/2004**

Gamo-Mckenna, Mrs A, BSc (Hons) MSc, Library Assistant, Highlife Highland.
[10019618]   04/08/2011   **ME**

Gandon, Ms A, BA MCLIP, Retired.
[20882]   10/08/1973   **CM06/05/1977**

Gandour, Ms A, Information Skills Trainer – Tavistock and Portman NHS Foundation Trust.
[10022859]   30/04/2013   **ME**

Gandy, Ms F, MA, Fellow Librarian, Girton College, University of Cambridge.
[9054]   01/10/1966   **CM01/01/1970**

Gannaway, Mrs K, BEd (Hons) MA MCLIP, Librarian: Children, Young People & Families- Oxfordshire Libraries.
[59879]   29/10/2001   **CM17/09/2008**

Gannaway, Mr N M, MCLIP, Retired.
[5334]   07/01/1953   **CM01/01/1961**

Garbacz, Ms S J, BA (Hons) MA MCLIP, Strategic Manager, City of York Council.
[52338]   30/10/1995   **CM20/09/2000**

Garbett, Miss R S, BA (Hons) MCLIP, Team Librarian, Madeley Library.
[10000979]   04/12/2006   **CM15/01/2013**

Garbutt, Mrs L, AMBCS, Senior Library Asisstant, Dumfries and
Galloway Council.
[10031583]   04/09/2013   ME

Garcia, Mrs S, Information Specialist, Durham University, Wolfson
Research Institute.
[10006417]   19/10/2007   ME

Garcia Nombela, R, BA,
[10020590]   05/03/2012   ME

Garcia-Jane, Mr C, BA, Student.
[10023061]   04/06/2013   ME

Garcia-Ontiveros, Ms D M, BA (Hons) MA MCLIP, Head of
Bibliographic Services, London Library.
[58112]   01/11/1999   RV13/11/2013   CM19/11/2003

Garden, Mrs E, MA MCLIP, L. Resource Centre Co-ordinator, Bridge of
Don Academy, Aberdeen.
[29475]   17/08/1978   CM18/08/1980

Gardiner, Mrs C J, BA MCLIP, Librarian, South Wilts Grammar School
for Girls.
[38148]   22/01/1985   CM17/01/1990

Gardiner, Ms D, BA (Hons) MSc MCLIP, Journals Manager/Research
Officer, IDOX Software Ltd.
[64432]   17/03/2005   CM09/07/2008

Gardiner, Miss L J, MA (Hons) MPhil,
[66155]   04/10/2006   ME

Gardner, Mrs C, BA (Hons) MA MCLIP, Development Officer, CILIP.
[66059]   12/09/2006   RV27/08/2014   CM07/07/2010

Gardner, Miss C L, BA MA MCLIP, Stock and Promotions Manager,
London Borough of Richmond upon Thames Libraries.
[59421]   22/03/2001   RV05/10/2007   CM23/06/2004

Gardner, Ms E R, BA, Graduate Trainee Library Assistant, Burlington
Danes Academy.
[10032298]   14/11/2013   ME

Gardner, Mrs H C, BSc MCLIP, L. Manager, Sherwood Forest Hospital
NHS Foundation Trust, King's Mill Hospital.
[31456]   18/10/1979   CM10/10/1985

Gardner, Mr I, BA MA MCLIP,
[65158]   03/11/2005   RV15/01/2013   CM20/04/2009

Gardner, Dr J C, BA (Hons) MA PhD, Library Assistant, Robinson
Library, Newcastle University.
[10033390]   07/03/2014   ME

Gardner, Mrs S, BSc DipLib MLib, Unwaged.
[38920]   16/10/1985   ME

Gardner, Mrs S J, MCLIP, Life Member.
[5361]   19/01/1946   CM01/01/1953

Gardner, Miss S J, BA, Student, Northumbria University.
[10031787]   04/10/2013   ME

Gardner, Mrs V J, Librarian, Learning Resource Centre, John Henry
Newman Catholic College, Birmingham.
[10019970]   13/10/2011   AF

Garea Garcia, Ms N, Student Systems Developer, UCL.
[10022480]   11/03/2013   ME

Garfield, Dr E, BSc MS PhD MIEEE HonFCLIP, Hon. Fellow. Retired.
[60072]   24/07/1958   HFE21/03/1989

Garman, Mrs E A, BA MA, Service Development Officer, Harrogate
Library, North Yorkshire County Council.
[56979]   17/11/1998   CM11/03/2009

Garner, Mr D K, Knowledge Assistant, Nabarro, London.
[10002233]   20/04/2007   AF

Garner, Mrs D M,
[10014372]   21/07/2009   AF

Garner, Ms H J, BA (Hons) DipILM MCLIP, Senior Information Adviser
Cataloguing., Sheffield Hallam university.
[45851]   03/07/1991   CM23/09/1998

Garnett, Mrs J K, BSc MA MBA MCLIP, HEI Librarian, SRUC Barony
Campus, Dumfries.
[51220]   29/11/1994   CM26/11/1997

Garnsworthy, Mr A C, MA, Community L. Serv. Manager, Stoke
Newington Library, London.
[10009775]   06/06/2008   ME

Garraway, Mrs A H, BA (Hons) ELL (Open), Learning Centre Manager,
Thamesmead School.
[10022896]   07/05/2013   ME

Garrett, Mrs M E P, MCLIP, School Librarian, Bishops Stortford College,
Herts.
[27061]   20/01/1977   CM28/08/1979

Garrett, Dr P, BA MSt (Oxon) PhD (Cantab), Research Associate,
Faculty of Asian and Middle Eastern Studies, University of
Cambridge.
[10023205]   18/06/2013   ME

Garrett, Miss P L, BSc (Hons) MA, Macmillan Library Officer,
Portsmouth Central Library.
[61132]   07/03/2002   ME

Garriock, Dr J B, MA PhD FCLIP FRSA, Life Member.
[16195]   01/01/1951   FE01/01/1963

Garside, Miss R L, BA, Library Assistant, Leagrave Library.
[10022943]   14/05/2013   AF

Gartland, Mrs C E L, DipLis MA, Collections Officer, Libraries NI, Newry
and Downpatrick.
[10022145]   08/01/2013   ME

Gartside, Ms E J, BA (Hons) MCLIP, Editor, Career Workshop,
Buckinghamshire.
[42354]   25/10/1988   CM25/05/1994

Gas, Mr Z, BA MA ACIL, Subject Advisor (Modern Languages and
Education), Library Services, University of Birmingham.
[37568]   09/10/1984   CM21/07/1993

Gascoigne, Miss J E, BA (Hons), Know How Officer, Slaughter and
May, London.
[54278]   13/11/1996   ME

Gaston, Mr R S, BA (Hons) MA MCLIP,
[57874]   22/09/1999   CM04/02/2004

Gater, Miss L, BA (Hons), Temporary Library Assistant.
[46812]   04/02/1992   ME

Gater, Miss R M, Library Assistant, Mod.
[10032968]   31/01/2014   ME

Gaterell, Miss H, BA (Hons) CANTAB, Student, University of Brighton.
[10026969]   12/09/2013   ME

Gatti, Dr I M, MA PhD, Lib. St Clare's College, Oxford.
[10008745]   15/04/2008   ME

Gaule, Mrs J, BA (Hons) MCLIP,
[54009]   16/10/1996   CM29/03/2004

Gault, Mrs C, BA MSc Econ, Cultural Services Manager, Belfast
Education & Library Board.
[10021346]   19/05/2002   ME

Gaunt, Mrs F J, BA (Hons) MLib MCLIP, Career Break.
[58188]   15/11/1999   RV13/04/2011   CM28/10/2004

Gavaghan, Miss S H, BA (Hons) DMS PGCE, Learning Resource
Centre Manager, Sir William Turner Learning Resource Centre,
Redcar & Cleveland College.
[49705]   25/11/1993   ME

Gavan, Mrs A, BA, Area Librarian, Haddington Library, East Lothian.
[65960]   21/07/2006   ME

Gavan, Mrs A, BA (Hons), District Manager, Nelson Library.
[10022378]   19/02/2013   ME

Gavillet, Mrs E L, BA (Hons) DipLib MA, Medical Librarian, Walton
Library, Medical School, University of Newcastle upon Tyne.
[49073]   01/10/1993   ME

Gavin, Mrs J S, BA (Hons) DipIM MCLIP,
[52715]   24/11/1995   **CM19/01/2000**
Gavin, Ms W, School Librarian, Edward Peake (C of E) Middle School.
[10033928]   13/05/2014   **ME**
Gaw, Mr P W, BA, Head of Libraries(Archives & Information), Notts CC, Nottingham.
[43645]   15/11/1989   **CM26/01/1994**
Gawali, Mrs K, MCLIP,
[10008231]   12/03/2008   **CM25/01/2011**
Gawne, Ms E, BA (Hons) MA (RCA) RMARA, Librarian, Architectural Association.
[10011753]   23/04/2013   **ME**
Gayle, Miss J, Library & Information Assistant, Saltash Library.
[10033524]   24/03/2014   **ME**
Gayler, Mrs E, MCLIP, Programme Support Officer, West Sussex CC.
[65366]   16/01/2006   **CM14/03/2012**
Gazey, Mrs T L, MA, Librarian, City College Coventry.
[10004945]   18/01/1995   **ME**
Gear, Mr S J, MCLIP, Life Member.
[5413]   27/01/1950   **CM01/01/1956**
Gear, Mrs S J, MCLIP, Retired.
[33788]   01/01/1953   **CM01/01/1957**
Gebbie, Mrs J D, BA (Hons) DipEurHum PgDip ILS, Information &L. Services, Scottish Natural Heritage, Inverness.
[45680]   18/04/1991   **ME**
Geddes, Mrs L H, Lending Services Co-ordinator, Elgin Library, Moray.
[10011475]   21/04/1992   **AF**
Geddes, Ms S J, BLib MCLIP, Lister Community School Temp Library Assistant.
[28662]   10/01/1978   **CM02/11/1982**
Gediking, Miss R, BA (Hons), Children's Library Specialist – GLL (Greenwich Leisure Limited).
[10020813]   18/04/2012   **ME**
Gee, Mr A P, BA DipLib MCLIP, Systems Support Officer, North Yorkshire County Council L. Headquarters.
[25036]   10/11/1975   **CM21/06/1979**
Gee, Mr D R, BA MA DipLib MCLIP, Deputy Librarian, InstituteAdvanced Legal Studies, University of London.
[40939]   07/09/1987   **CM24/04/1991**
Gee, Mrs J, BA MCLIP, Librarian, South Tees Hospital NHS Trust, North Yorks.
[23645]   26/01/1975   **CM29/12/1978**
Geekie, Mrs J, BA (Hons) MCLIP, Information Literacy & Learning Librarian, Aberdeenshire Libraries, Oldmeldrum.
[44706]   30/11/1990   **CM31/01/1996**
Geldard, Mrs D, BA MCLIP, Unemployed.
[25718]   29/02/1976   **CM12/11/1980**
Geldenhuys, Mrs P R, E-Resources Librarian, Exeter Health Library, Royal Devon and Exeter NHS Foundation Trust.
[65902]   26/06/2006   **ME**
Gellatly, Mrs C J, BA MLS MCLIP, Librarian, American School of Doha, Qatar.
[34144]   08/10/1981   **CM24/06/1992**
Gent, Mrs S, BSc (Hons) MCLIP, Retired.
[12804]   04/10/1971   **CM01/10/1974**
George, Mr B S, MCLIP, Retired.
[5436]   08/12/1961   **CM01/01/1966**
George, Mrs J, BA DipLib MCLIP, Retired.
[32959]   06/10/1980   **CM08/11/1982**
George, Ms L, Library Manager, LB of Brent.
[65887]   27/06/2006   **ME**
George, Mrs L K, BA MCLIP, Sch. Librarian, Dover Grammar School for Boys, Dover, Kent.
[26936]   17/01/1977   **CM22/10/1981**

George, Mrs S L, BA MSc MCLIP, Subject Librarian, University Bradford, Bradford.
[63944]   18/11/2004   **CM23/01/2008**
George, Miss S M, BA MCLIP, Librarian, ABM University, Princess of Wales Hospital, Bridgend and Neath Port Talbot Hospital.
[40752]   01/06/1987   **CM24/06/1992**
George, Mr W H, BA DipLib FGS MCLIP, Unwaged.
[27980]   03/10/1977   **CM07/01/1981**
Georgiades, Ms A S, HBA, Student, Aberystwyth University.
[10033911]   12/05/2014   **ME**
German, Mr R N, MSc, Health Sciences Librarian, University of Otago.
[10033999]   09/11/1994   **ME**
Gerrard, Mr A D, BA (Hons) MSc (Econ) MCLIP, Metadata Librarian, University of Cumbria.
[54299]   20/11/1996   **CM21/05/2003**
Gerrard, Mrs A J, BA MCLIP, Deputy Library Services Manager, Francis Costello Library (part-time).
[49549]   09/11/1993   **CM26/11/1997**
Gerrard, Miss K L, Student, Aberystwyth University.
[10017324]   29/07/2010   **ME**
Gerrard, Mrs K S, BA (Hons) MSc (Econ) MCLIP, Senior Library Assistant, Lancaster University.
[53471]   01/07/1996   **CM16/07/2003**
Gerrard, Miss S E, BA (Hons) MA, Information Officer, The Concrete Society, Camberley.
[49929]   25/01/1994   **ME**
Gerritsen, Mrs C L, BA (Hons) MCLIP PRINCE2, Project and Information Management Consultant, GPI Consultants Ltd, Brighton.
[39818]   05/08/1986   **CM11/12/1989**
Gharti, Mr R B, Student.
[10031920]   15/10/2013   **ME**
Ghiggino, Mrs R, BA MCLIP, Housewife.
[35552]   01/11/1982   **CM27/10/1992**
Ghilchik, Mr T C, BA, Unemployed.
[54913]   13/05/1997   **ME**
Ghiotto, Miss A, BA PgDipILS, Librarian, University of Padova, Italy
[57600]   19/05/1999   **ME**
Ghosal, Mr N, BA MCLIP, Life Member.
[5450]   01/09/1961   **CM01/01/1966**
Ghoshray, Mrs A, Assistant Lib, Badminton School, Bristol.
[63370]   21/04/2004   **CM28/01/2009**
Ghumra, Ms I, BA (Hons) MCLIP,
[44778]   19/11/1990   **CM17/01/2001**
Giannakopoulos, Mr T, BSc MA, Acting Head, IAEA Library, Austria.
[10010840]   29/08/2008   **ME**
Giannitrapani, Ms S, Student, Instituteof Advanced Legal Studies.
[10006112]   03/03/2009   **ME**
Gibb, Mrs C E, MA DipLib MCLIP, Retired.
[33887]   10/04/1981   **CM11/04/1985**
Gibb, Mr I P, BA MCLIP, Life Member.
[5453]   05/10/1950   **CM01/01/1954**
Gibb, Mr K, LLB (Hons) MA MSc, Rare Books Cataloguer.
[62810]   24/10/2003   **ME**
Gibb, Mrs T H, MCLIP, Librarian, Young Peoples Serv., Hertfordshire County Council, Hoddesdon.
[23687]   23/01/1975   **CM31/08/1977**
Gibbins, Mrs K J, BA MCLIP, Principal Lib. for Information and Learning, City and County of Swansea, Swansea.
[41544]   12/01/1988   **CM24/06/1992**
Gibbons, Mr A A, HonFCLIP, Author, Self-employed.
[10019468]   09/12/2011   **HFE01/09/2011**
Gibbons, Mr M, PgDipILM MCLIP, Librarian, Halton Lea Library, Cheshire.
[61451]   31/07/2002   **CM20/06/2012**

Gibbons, Ms S J, BA MCLIP, Assistant Mgr, CYPS Fosse Library
Leicester City Library.
[36842]   01/01/1984   CM14/02/1990
Gibbons, Miss S L, BA (Hons) MCLIP, Research Co-Ordinator.
[49405]   21/10/1993   CM12/03/2003
Gibbs, Mrs D, BA MCLIP, Retired.
[5461]   05/08/1950   CM01/01/1955
Gibbs, Mr D W, BA MCLIP, Deputy Director., Derbys. County Council,
Matlock.
[35764]   17/01/1983   CM06/10/1987
Gibbs, Mrs E, ACLIP,
[10010175]   05/03/2012   ACL29/05/2013
Gibbs, Mrs L, BA MA MCLIP, Liaison Librarian, Newman University,
Birmingham.
[10017325]   07/02/1990   CM26/05/1993
Gibbs, Miss S, BA BCom, Student, Aberystwyth University.
[10035518]   16/10/2014   ME
Gibbs, Miss T A, BA MSc MCLIP, Academic Liaison Librarian,
University of Southampton, Hartley Library.
[60008]   21/11/2001   CM21/03/2007
Gibbs-Monaghan, Mrs Z A, BA (Hons), Liaison Librarian., Harold
Cohen University, Liverpool.
[10008512]   02/04/2008   ME
Giblin, Mrs S, Student, Aberystwyth University.
[10013921]   17/06/2009   ME
Gibson, Ms A R, BA DipLib MCLIP, Librarian, Backwell School, North
Somerset.
[36562]   19/10/1983   CM16/12/1986
Gibson, Ms C, BA (Hons), Part-time Student, Manchester Metropolitan
University, University of Central Lancashire.
[10001551]   23/02/2007   ME
Gibson, Ms C, BA MA, Retired.
[38300]   21/02/1985   ME
Gibson, Mrs E A, MCLIP, Retired.
[2538]   25/09/1969   CM06/07/1973
Gibson, Mrs G, BA MA, Assistant Librarian & Literary Events Co-
ordinator, Tolworth Girls School.
[10034251]   24/10/1996   ME
Gibson, Mrs G, MCLIP, Retired.
[22049]   08/01/1974   CM01/01/1977
Gibson, Ms J, BA MA MCLIP, Head of L. & Museums, London Borough
of Enfield.
[35720]   01/01/1983   CM06/10/1987
Gibson, Mr K L, BA DipLib FCLIP, Life Member.
[5478]   01/01/1947   FE01/01/1958
Gibson, Mrs M, MCLIP, retired.
[28300]   10/11/1977   CM29/02/1980
Gibson, Miss M E, LLARM RAMDip MLS MCLIP DHMSA, Retired.
[5483]   11/03/1960   CM01/01/1963
Gibson, Ms M M, BA (Hons) MCLIP, L. Information Serv. Manager,
Northern Ireland Housing Executive, Belfast.
[50273]   25/05/1994   CM16/07/2003
Gibson, Miss R J, MA (Hons), Mobile Coordinator., Action for Blind
People, London.
[57330]   12/02/1999   ME
Gibson, Mr S P, Tech. Serv. Librarian, Falmouth University, Falmouth.
[34942]   14/05/1982   ME
Gick, Dr R C, MA (Oxon) MusM PhD PgDip MCLIP, Search Analyst &
Information Architect (NICE).
[62727]   13/10/2003   CM06/07/2011
Gidman, Mrs J E, BA (Hons) DipLib, Public libraries.
[34742]   13/01/1982   ME
Giesbrecht, Mrs B M, MCLIP, Life Member.
[17387]   30/01/1951   CM01/01/1957

Giffen, Miss S A, BA MCLIP, Retired.
[5491]   01/10/1968   CM01/01/1972
Giggey, Ms S E, MLS MCLIP, Adjunct Lecturer, Vancouver, Canada.
[36539]   23/10/1983   CM11/02/1986
Gilbert, Mrs L, MCLIP, Site Librarian, Rutherford Appleton Laboratory.
[63256]   23/03/2004   CM06/05/2009
Gilbert, Mr L A, MSC HonFLA, Retired.
[36768]   19/09/1983   HFE19/09/1983
Gilbert, Ms S E, MSc MCLIP, Retired.
[23577]   13/01/1975   CM13/06/1989
Gilbert, Mr T, BA MA, Staff, Leicester College.
[10014736]   07/09/2009   ME
Gilchrist, Mr A D B, DLitt FRSA HonFCLIP, Retired.
[5506]   21/04/1961   FE01/04/2002
Gilchrist, Mrs J R, MA DipLib MCLIP, Outside Serv. Coordinator, North
Lanarkshire Council, Motherwell.
[31106]   25/07/1979   CM07/12/1982
Gilchrist, Mr N M, MA DipLIS MCLIP, L. Officer, Edinburgh City Council.
[59044]   07/11/2000   CM04/02/2004
Gildersleeves, Mrs E L P, MA MLib MCLIP, Part-time Lecturer, UCL.
[37489]   01/10/1984   CM18/01/1989
Giles, Mr A, LLB (Hons), Student, City University London.
[10032557]   16/12/2013   ME
Giles, Mr D P, BA MA JD, Student, City University, Northampton.
[10027016]   04/10/2013   ME
Giles, Mrs G, MLib BA MCLIP, Faculty Knowledge Manager., Heart of
England NHS Foundation Trust, Good Hope Hospital, Sutton
Coldfield.
[25349]   05/01/1976   CM11/04/1980
Giles, Mrs J B, MA DipLib MCLIP, Curator (Scottish Communities and
Organisations), National Library of Scotland.
[35463]   15/10/1982   CM05/05/1987
Giles, Mrs M, MSc, Records Information Manager, Statoil.
[63398]   28/04/2014   ME
Giles-Bather, Mrs J D, BSc (Hons) MBA (Open), Lib. Assistant,
Derbyshire County Council.
[10008695]   18/04/2008   AF
Gilham, Ms W, MA (Hons) PgDip ILS, Mobile library coordinator,
Lincolnshire.
[10007760]   04/03/2002   ME
Gilhooly, Miss H L, BA, Student, University of Glasgow.
[10035620]   24/10/2014   ME
Gill, Ms A J, BA MA, Information Officer, Gtr. Manchester Co. Record
Office, Manchester.
[41052]   05/10/1987   ME
Gill, Mrs D, BA DipLib MCLIP, Showroom Manager, Peters Bookselling
Serv., Birmingham.
[39494]   10/02/1986   CM06/09/1988
Gill, Mrs F M, Sr. Assistant, Cataloguing, Devon Libs.
[10000759]   02/09/1996   ME
Gill, Mrs J, BSc ACLIP, Librarian, The Holy Trinity CE Secondary
School, Crawley.
[10013353]   16/04/2009   ACL09/11/2011
Gill, Mrs J, BA MCLIP, Library Assistant, NHS Borders Library Service,
Borders General Hospital, Melrose.
[26102]   30/06/1976   CM28/04/1980
Gill, Mr J S, Library Assistant, South & City College.
[10023077]   04/06/2013   AF
Gill, Mrs K L, BA MCLIP, School Librarian, Learning Resources Centre,
St Chad's Catholic and Church of England High School, Runcorn.
[30520]   08/01/1979   CM05/07/1982
Gill, Mrs L, BSc (Hons) PGDIP MCLIP, Lib. Yorkshire Water Services
Ltd.
[63079]   27/01/2004   CM10/11/2010

Gill, Miss L V, Trainee Librarian, Crawley L.
[64155]   19/01/2005   ME
Gill, Mrs M E, BA MCLIP, Campus Library Manager, Napier University,
Edinburgh.
[5533]   14/01/1970   CM11/06/1973
Gill, Mrs P, Student, John Moores University, Liverpool.
[10017874]   21/10/2010   ME
Gill, Mr P G, FCLIP, Life Member.
[5534]   16/01/1957   FE21/08/1974
Gillam, Mr L A, BD DipSocAdmin MCLIP, Retired.
[5537]   08/01/1968   CM01/01/1971
Gillen, Ms L, BA MA, Information Assistant.
[10013515]   30/04/2009   ME
Gillespie, Miss G C, BA (Hons), Learning Community Librarian,
Garnock Cluster. North Ayrshire Council.
[10016502]   02/12/1996   ME
Gillespie, Mrs M A, BA DipLib MCLIP, Area & Campus Librarian,
University of Stirling, Inverness.
[27189]   06/12/1976   CM25/11/1981
Gillespie, Mrs S M, MCLIP, Life Member.
[5548]   01/01/1950   CM01/01/1956
Gillespie, Mr T S, FCLIP, Retired.
[5549]   10/09/1948   FE01/01/1957
Gillies, Mr A S, MA (HONS) DipLib (LIS), Deputy Head of Information
Service, IDOX Information Solutions, Glasgow.
[48078]   03/11/1992   ME
Gillies, Miss C A, BA PgDip, Library Assistant, University of the West of
Scotland, Hamilton, South Lanarkshire.
[10020005]   25/10/2011   ME
Gillies, Mrs F F, BA MCLIP, Senior Librarian, Service Develpoment and
Support (Acting), Aberdeenshire Council.
[35608]   19/10/1982   CM08/12/1987
Gillies, Mrs R L, MA PGCE, Library Assistant, The Portsmouth
Grammar School.
[10021620]   14/09/2012   AF
Gillies, Mr S, MA, Reference Team Leader, The British Library, London.
[41770]   25/03/1988   ME
Gilliland, Ms G M, BA PGCE DipLIS MCLIP, Stock & User Engagement
Librarian, Pembrokeshire L.
[44661]   20/11/1990   CM28/10/2004
Gillings-Grant, Ms F L A, BSc (Hons) DipLS MBA, L. Manager,
Birmingham City Council, Sheldon & Kents Moat L.
[58855]   07/09/2000   ME
Gillis, Ms H R, Learning & Access Manager, Museums Galleries
Scotland.
[61469]   12/08/2002   ME
Gillis, Mr I R, BSc MCLIP, Records Associate, Financial Serv. Authority,
London.
[5557]   05/10/1968   CM11/11/1974
Gilman, Ms A H E, BA MCLIP, Librarian, Derbyshire County Council,
Derbyshire.
[25037]   14/11/1975   CM09/08/1979
Gilman, Miss L J, MA (Hons) MSc PGDE, Enquiries Assistant, The
Scottish Parliament.
[10015363]   12/11/2009   ME
Gilmour, Miss A, BA MCLIP, Customer Serv. Team Leader.,
Dunfermline Carnegie Library, Fife Council.
[35780]   24/01/1983   CM31/07/1984
Gilmour, Ms A E, BA DipIT MCLIP, Information Strategy Officer, Dundee
City Council.
[60258]   21/10/1996   CM11/01/2001
Gilpin, Mrs B, PgDip, Student, City University.
[10005342]   05/07/2007   ME

Gilroy, Mr D P, BA (Hons) MA MCLIP, Library & Knowledge Service
Manager, Leeds & York Partnership NHS Foundation Trust.
[55282]   15/09/1997   RV11/07/2012   CM16/07/2003
Gilzean, Ms V, Student, City University.
[10001056]   12/12/2006   ME
Gimeno-Sanjuan, Ms A, BA (Hons),
[10027030]   16/07/2014   ME
Gingell, Mr J, Information Manager, Ministry of Defence.
[10034538]   21/07/2014   ME
Ginn, Mr J W, BSc MA MCLIP, Assistant Librarian, Department of Work
and Pensions, London.
[59491]   09/04/2001   CM09/11/2005
Ginn, Mrs S J, MCLIP, Librarian, Holy Cross 6th Form College, Bury.
[64501]   13/04/2005   CM14/12/2012
Girma, Rev A H, PhD, Student.
[10015427]   16/11/2009   ME
Gittins, Miss F R, BA, Student, Aberystwyth University.
[10034149]   10/06/2014   ME
Giurlando, Ms L, BA MCLIP, Librarian., Oundle School, Oundle.
[53452]   01/07/1996   CM23/09/1998
Givan, Mr A M, MA (Hons) MSc MCLIP, Librarian, Children, Young
People and Families Officer, Renfrewshire Council.
[51084]   14/11/1994   CM10/07/2002
Given, Mrs L, Records Management Officer, Northern Ireland Library
Authority, Ballymena.
[65037]   13/10/2005   ACL01/07/2007
Given, Mr R J, BA (Hons) PgDip, Records Operator, Simmons &
Simmons.
[10031648]   17/09/2013   ME
Gkoutsidou, Miss M A, Library Assistant, American Sch. of Classical
Studies, Athens.
[10012365]   23/02/2009   ME
Gladden, Mr N J, BA (Hons) PgDip MCLIP, Acquisition &
Documentation Officer, North West Film Archive, Manchester.
[58906]   03/10/2000   CM12/03/2003
Gladotono, Mr T M, LLB (Hons), Business Information Officer, Institute
of Directors, London.
[51740]   12/06/1995   ME
Glaister, Mr P, BA MA MA, Specialist Librarian: Online Resources.
[10021455]   20/08/2012   ME
Glancy, Mr A, MA (Hons), Information Provison Manager, Home Office
London.
[59171]   05/12/2000   ME
Glancy, Mr M J, BA MCLIP, Information Serv. Manager, National
Museums Scotland.
[32520]   21/05/1980   CM10/08/1982
Glancy, Mr P C, MA (Hons), Senior Information Assistant, De Monfort
University, Leicester.
[42375]   18/10/1988   ME
Glanville, Ms J M, BA PgDipLib MSc MCLIP, Associate Director, York
Health Economics Consortium Ltd, University of York.
[35198]   05/10/1982   CM01/04/2002
Glasby, Mrs J B, BA MCLIP, L. Manager, Leeds College of Music.
[27817]   28/08/1977   CM28/08/1979
Glasgow, Miss C M, MSc MA (Hons), Library Assistant, East
Renfrewshire Council.
[64986]   06/10/2005   ME
Glasgow, Mrs F, ACLIP, Unwaged.
[64740]   14/06/2005   ACL04/03/2009
Glass, Mr N R, BA, Senior Lecturer, Department of Information
&Comm., Manchester Metropolitan University.
[10020101]   01/11/2011   ME
Glasse, Miss H, ACLIP, Lib. Assistant, Leicester College, Leicester.
[10017415]   18/08/2010   ACL17/06/2011

Glayzer, Ms J A, MCLIP, Retired.
[5586]   06/10/1964   **CM01/01/1968**
Glazebrook, Ms D, BSc (Hons) Librarianship, Librarian, Kingsdale
Foundation School.
[10027042]   23/07/2014   **ME**
Gledhill, Miss R, BA (Hons), Librarian, Sodexo Justice Services.
[10022299]   05/02/2013   **ME**
Gledhill, Ms S E, BA DipLib MCLIP, Operations librarian Hertfordshire
County Council.
[39264]   15/01/1986   **CM15/03/1989**
Gledhill, Mrs V C, MA DipLib MCLIP, Assistant Librarian, (Cataloguing) /
Ext. Hours Librarian, Oxford Brookes University Library.
[38704]   01/10/1985   **CM13/06/1989**
Glee, Mr J, BSc (Hons), Library & Digital Assistant, Northern School of
Contemporary Dance, Leeds.
[10023019]   21/05/2013   **AF**
Gleeson, Mrs A, BA MA, Deputy Librarian at Magdalene College,
Cambridge MA in Library and Information Studies.
[10017719]   29/09/2010   **ME**
Gleeson, Miss C, BA MA MCLIP FHEA PgDip, Subject Librarian,
University of Chester, Warrington.
[62724]   13/10/2003   **CM21/03/2007**
Glen, Mrs S M, BA, Deputy Subject Lib. (Science & Engineering),
Swansea University.
[44058]   20/04/1990   **ME**
Glendinning, Mrs H A, BA (Hons), Community Librarian (Acting),
Buckley Library, Flintshire.
[10004964]   06/06/2007   **ME**
Glenn, Miss E S, BLib MCLIP, LR Manager, Belfast Metro Coll,
[10005102]   11/10/1981   **CM10/03/1988**
Glenton, Mrs R, BA, Sure Start Librarian, Derbyshire County Council.
[61924]   04/12/2002   **ME**
Glossop, Miss J C, BA, Student, Manchester Metropolitan University.
[10020310]   11/01/2012   **ME**
Glover, Mrs G A, BA (Hons) MA MCLIP, Unemployed.
[43695]   30/11/1989   **CM24/09/1997**
Gluyas, Mrs J, Locality Team Leader, Liskeard Library.
[10022651]   05/04/2013   **AF**
Godbolt, Mrs L S, BA FCLIP HonFCLIP, Retired.
[13786]   01/10/1965   **HFE23/10/2003**
Goddard, Mr C, BMus (Hons) DipLib MCLIP, Library Service Manager.
[31838]   01/01/1980   **CM25/06/1982**
Goddard, Mrs E L, BA (Hons) ACLIP, Enq. Officer Ipswich Co. Library,
Suffolk C. C.
[56637]   01/10/1998   **ACL06/09/2006**
Goddard, Mr M, MSc BSc (Hons), Information Sci., Medicines and
Healthcare Products Regulatory Agency, London.
[46714]   03/01/1992   **ME**
Goddard, Ms S, BA MA MCLIP AFHEA, Assistant Librarian, University
of Westminster, Marylebone Campus Library.
[58274]   06/12/1999   **CM23/06/2004**
Godfrey, Mrs A J, MCLIP, Lib. (Sunday), Putney Library, London.
[26617]   19/10/1976   **CM20/10/1980**
Godfrey, Mrs J, MCLIP, Principal Library Assistant, Bodleian Libraries.
[15634]   29/05/1969   **CM26/02/1973**
Godfrey, Ms M A, MA ARMIT MCLIP, Life Member.
[5625]   03/03/1970   **CM01/01/1972**
Godfrey, Miss S A B, MA MCLIP, Information Librarian., West Sussex
County Councill. Serv., Chichester.
[62091]   12/02/2003   **CM21/06/2006**
Godrich, Mrs D A, BA (Hons) DipIM MCLIP, Academy Librarian,
Droylsden Academy, Manchester.
[52437]   31/10/1995   **CM19/01/2000**

Godsell, Mrs S, BSc MCLIP, Sci. Subject Librarian, Birkbeck College,
University of London.
[60830]   01/04/1991   **CM23/08/1993**
Godsmark, Mrs R J, BA DipLib MCLIP, Employment not known.
[26986]   10/01/1977   **CM29/01/1979**
Godwin, Mrs K J, BA (Hons) MCLIP, Learning Resource Centre Co-
ordinator, New College Stamford.
[10013349]   16/04/2009   **CM16/01/2014**
Godwin, Mr P, BA MCLIP CLTHE, Retired.
[5632]   03/01/1972   **CM25/01/1974**
Godwin, Mrs S E, BSC (Hons) DPS, Librarian, Herbert Smith Freehills,
London.
[10001912]   22/03/2007   **ME**
Godwin, Mrs S M, BA (Hons) MA MCLIP, Unwaged.
[55360]   03/10/1997   **CM20/11/2002**
Gohil, Miss D, BA MScEcon, Research Analyst, Egon Zehnder
International.
[10011691]   03/02/2009   **ME**
Going, Miss H, BA (Hons) MA, Information Officer, Clyde and Co LLP,
London.
[63970]   22/11/2004   **ME**
Gokce, Mrs C M, BSc (Hons) MSc MCLIP FLS, Project Director,
Electoral Registration Transformation Programme, Cabinet Office.
[35950]   23/03/1983   **CM17/09/2003**
Gold, Miss S E, BA (Hons) DipLib MCLIP, Librarian, Doncaster College.
[40306]   05/01/1987   **CM07/09/2005**
Golden, Mrs S M, BSc (Hons) PGCE, Reading and Literacy Manager,
Kent County Council.
[46158]   03/10/1991   **ME**
Goldfarb, Mr M B, Tower Hamlets Local History Lib. & Archives,
London.
[64849]   28/07/2005   **AF**
Goldfinch, Mrs A M, BSc (Hons) MSc MCLIP, Subject Librarian.
[10000839]   02/03/1981   **CM20/11/1989**
Goldfinch, Mr R G, MSc MCLIP, Information Services Manager, MHRA.,
London.
[33755]   31/01/1981   **CM01/04/2002**
Goldie, Mrs V S, BA DipIS MCLIP, Area Manager:South, Bournemouth
Borough Council.
[30908]   08/06/1979   **CM20/11/2002**
Goldrick, Miss M E, FCLIP, Life Member.
[5644]   05/03/1942   **FE01/01/1954**
Goldsmith, Miss E, BA, Graduate Trainee Library Assistant, Anglia
Ruskin University.
[10031806]   07/10/2013   **ME**
Goldsmith, Dr H A, PhD MA BMus LGSM, Library Assistant – Bank
Staff, Surrey County Council.
[10022526]   19/03/2013   **AF**
Goldsmith, Ms S J, BA MCLIP, Campus Librarian, City College Leeds.
[43698]   28/11/1989   **CM23/06/2004**
Goldstone, Mr J, BSc DipLib MCLIP, Employment not known.
[26967]   11/01/1977   **CM11/04/1979**
Goldstone, Mrs P A, Retired.
[5649]   03/10/1962   **AF**
Goldwater, Mr S J, BA MCLIP, Information Officer, Montagu Evans,
London.
[24492]   21/08/1975   **CM04/08/1978**
Golightly, Mr I C, Student, Robert Gordon University.
[10031968]   16/10/2013   **ME**
Golland, Mr A R L, BA DipLib MCLIP, Retired.
[19839]   10/01/1973   **CM01/01/1975**
Golodnitsky, Ms A, BA MLS, Derials Librarian, Tate Library & Archive.
[10022538]   20/03/2013   **ME**

Gomersall, Mrs R F, BSc (Econ) MCLIP, L. Manager, Cheshire East C., Sandbach & Middlewich L.
[47402]   10/08/1992   **CM21/03/2001**

Gomm, Miss B, MCLIP, Life Member.
[5657]   16/09/1956   **CM01/01/1963**

Gomm, Mrs K, Records Manager, Foreign & Commonwealth Office.
[10033704]   16/04/2014   **ME**

Gommersall, Ms K, BA FCLIP, Knowledge and Information Management Librarian, Department for Work and Pensions, Leeds.
[41566]   28/01/1988   **FE18/01/2012**

Gonzalez Gonzalez, Ms M, BSc Econ, Records Management & Information Analyst, Aberystwyth University.
[10018850]   22/03/2011   **ME**

Gooch, Ms A, BA MA MSc, Library Assistant, University of Essex.
[10022898]   07/05/2013   **ME**

Gooch, Mr P S L, BSc MCLIP, Retired.
[60292]   18/01/1978   **CM18/01/1978**

Good, Ms K, Student, Northunbria University.
[10035447]   23/10/2014   **ME**

Goodall, Mr A, BEng MBA CEng MIET MAPM, Volunteer at Deanshanger Library.
[10027070]   07/03/2014   **ME**

Goodall, Dr D L, MPhil BA PhD MCLIP,
[38792]   07/10/1985   **CM18/09/1991**

Goodall, Ms L, BA (Hons) MA, Cataloguer, University of Leicester.
[54306]   20/11/1996   **ME**

Goodall, Mr N, MA FCLIP, Retired.
[5669]   03/08/1948   **FE01/01/1964**

Goodall, Mrs P A, BA DipTEFL, Subject Advisor, Science & Engineering Team, University of Birmingham.
[37343]   02/07/1984   **ME**

Goodall, Miss W F, MCLIP, Unwaged.
[56396]   01/07/1998   **CM19/03/2008**

Goodchild, Ms G, BA DipLib MCLIP, College Librarian, Colchester Sixth Form College, Essex.
[33810]   10/03/1981   **CM24/01/1986**

Goodchild, Miss L R, BA (Hons) MA MCLIP,
[65424]   24/02/2006   **CM11/06/2010**

Gooden, Miss C, BA (Hons), ICT and Information Co-ordinator.
[10032037]   22/10/2013   **ME**

Goodey, Mrs L F, BA (Hons) MA, Research Serv. Librarian, Slaughter and May, London.
[57023]   26/11/1998   **ME**

Goodfellow, Mrs J A, MA (Hons) MA MCLIP, Career Break.
[53934]   11/10/1996   **CM15/11/2000**

Goodfellow, Mr N J, BA MA MCLIP, Director of L. & Learning Resources, Leeds Trinity University, Leeds.
[42070]   03/10/1988   **CM17/10/1990**

Goodger, Mr C F, MA (Hons), Sr. Researcher, CRA Inter., London.
[50575]   21/09/1994   **ME**

Goodger, Ms G R, BA DipLib, Senior Librarian, Herbert Smith, London.
[37372]   25/07/1984   **ME**

Goodier, Miss R, BA (Hons) DipLib, Faculty Team. Librarian, The John Rylands University Library, University of Manchester.
[10000810]   26/07/1984   **ME**

Goodin, Ms C J, NZLS Cert BSc (Hons),
[10023321]   25/06/2013   **ME**

Gooding, Mr D P, Library Assistant, Medical Library, University of Bristol.
[10022959]   14/05/2013   **ME**

Gooding, Mrs L A, BSc MSc MCLIP, Principal. Lib. Assistant. (Part-time), University of Southampton.
[52754]   05/12/1995   **CM01/04/2002**

Gooding, Mrs R, BA DipLib MCLIP, Liaison. Librarian, Cataloguing Department, University of Reading L.
[43494]   30/10/1989   **CM16/11/1994**

Goodman, Mrs A, BMedSci PgDipLIS, Immanuel College, Herts.
[57672]   01/07/1999   **ME**

Goodman, Mr A D, BA MCLIP, Community Team Leader, West Sussex County Council L.
[35924]   28/02/1983   **CM08/12/1987**

Goodman, Ms C, BEd (HONS) MA, Librarian, Tower Hamlets Schools Library Service.
[10020927]   24/04/2012   **ME**

Goodman, Ms E C, BSc MSc MCLIP MAPM MCLIP, Owner and Principal Consultant, RiverRhee Consulting.
[10015640]   24/03/1984   **CM29/10/1987**

Goodman, Ms H L, BA DipInfSc MCLIP, L. Manager, West London Mental Health NHS Trust.
[45873]   03/07/1991   **CM24/07/1996**

Goodman, Ms S L, BSc MA DipLib, Retired.
[63673]   12/08/2004   **ME**

Goodman, Miss T J, MCLIP, Life Member.
[5695]   17/02/1964   **CM01/01/1969**

Goodman, Mrs T S, BA (Hons) MSc MCLIP, Library Assistant, Hampshire School Library Service.
[54552]   20/01/1997   **CM18/09/2002**

Goodridge, Miss A K, BSc MSc, Assistant Librarian, The Leeds Library, Leeds.
[10020507]   22/02/2012   **ME**

Goodwill, Miss G M, BA MCLIP, Retired.
[5701]   01/01/1969   **CM01/01/1971**

Goodwin, Ms A J, MA DipLib, Crichton Librarian, University of the West of Scotland.
[36485]   18/10/1983   **ME**

Goodwin, Miss C H, Part-time. Student /Senior Learning Res. Centre Assistant, Bridgwater College, Somerset.
[53787]   01/10/1996   **ME**

Goodwin, Mr C J, Librarian.
[51200]   23/11/1994   **ME**

Goodwin, Ms D, BA (Hons), Assistant Librarian, Norwich School.
[10009344]   01/06/2008   **ME**

Goodwin, Mrs K A, BA (Hons) MA, Faculty Liaison Librarian, Canterbury Christ Church University.
[50619]   01/10/1994   **CM19/07/2000**

Goodwin, Mrs R, LRC Assistant, David Young Community Academy, Seacroft.
[10018215]   09/12/2010   **ME**

Goom, Miss N, FCLIP, Retired.
[5706]   30/09/1935   **FE01/01/1946**

Goonatillake, Mrs T P A, MSc, Senior Assistant Librarian, Central Bank of Sri Lanka.
[10010658]   19/08/2008   **ME**

Goose, Mrs M E, BLS MCLIP, Sch. Lib. (JobShare), Hitchin Girl's School, Herts.
[28141]   07/10/1977   **CM29/09/1982**

Gopika Jacob, Mr M J, Student, Thames Valley University, London.
[10013125]   03/04/2009   **ME**

Goram, Mrs R, BA MA MCLIP, Information &Database Officer, Age UK Norfolk.
[59925]   10/09/2001   **CM04/10/2006**

Gordon, Mr A, MA (Hons) DipLib MCLIP, School Librarian, West Dunbartonshire Council.
[46787]   23/01/1992   **CM15/09/1993**

Gordon, Mrs C B, LLB (Hons) ACLIP, Senior L. Assistant, Culloden Library, Inverness.
[10018297]   14/12/2010   **ACL18/01/2012**

Gordon, Mrs C E, BA MCLIP, Teaching Fellow, Library/Database
Manager, Faculty Web Programmer, School of Earth & Environment,
Leeds University.
[38811]   09/10/1985   **CM27/05/1992**

Gordon, Mrs J T, BA DipLib MCLIP, Team Co-ordinator, Surrey Lib.
[43245]   13/10/1989   **CM18/11/1993**

Gordon, Miss L, BA (Hons) MA PgCTLHE FHEA MCLIP, Environment
& Social Sciences Liaison Librarian., Newcastle University.
[62774]   20/10/2003   **CM19/11/2008**

Gordon, Mrs L A, BA (Hons) DipLib MCLIP, Librarian, Paisley Grammar,
Strathclyde Region.
[45780]   28/05/1991   **CM18/11/1993**

Gordon, Ms N, BA (Hons),
[10022049]   19/11/2012   **ME**

Gordon, Mrs P, BA (Hons), Programme Manager, Value for Money Unit,
Home Office.
[10032090]   24/10/2013   **ME**

Gordon, Mrs S E, BA (Hons) DipLis, Information Assistant, Integreon.
[43015]   14/06/1989   **ME**

Gordon, Mr T, MA BA (Hons) PGC, Library Manager, Ardoyne Library.
[10033480]   17/03/2014   **ME**

Gore, Ms H J, Information and Knowledge Management Team Leader.
[10034300]   02/07/2014   **ME**

Gore, Miss N, BSc MA, Lib. and Learning Resources Assistant.
[10015238]   29/10/2009   **ME**

Gorecki, Miss A, BA (Hons), Learning Resources Assistant, Greenwich
School of Management.
[10031812]   07/10/2013   **ME**

Goreham, Miss A L, BLib, Area Manager, Royal Borough of Kensington
& Chelsea, London.
[35200]   01/10/1982   **CM21/04/1986**

Gorman, Mr M J, FCLIP HonFCLIP, University Librarian Emeritus,
California State University, Fresno, USA.
[5725]   28/09/1963   **HFE21/10/2004**

Gorman, Ms S J, BA MCLIP, L. Resource Centre Co-ord., Castlebrae
Community High School, Edinburgh.
[25146]   14/10/1975   **CM31/07/1980**

Gormley, Miss A, PgCert, Gateway Assessor at CAB, Sutton.
[10032083]   24/10/2013   **ME**

Gormley, Mr J S, BA (Joint Hons) MA MCLIP PgCert, Information
Officer, Macfarlanes, London.
[62795]   22/10/2003   **CM09/11/2011**

Gorring, Ms H M, BA (Hons) DipLib MSc FCLIP, Library Services
Manager, Birmingham Solihull Mental Health NHS Foundation Trust.
[58244]   24/11/1999   **FE12/05/2011**

Gosbee, Miss C J, Student, School of Computing, Northumbria
University.
[10020312]   11/01/2012   **ME**

Gosby, Mrs E J, BSc MSc MCLIP, Unemployed.
[37950]   25/11/1984   **CM19/01/1988**

Gosden, Mrs C, BSc MSc MCLIP, Sch, Librarian, London Borough of
Tower Hamlets Sch. L. Serv., London.
[51397]   03/02/1995   **CM16/07/2003**

Gosling, Mrs C H, MPhys (Hons) MCLIP,
[62769]   20/10/2003   **CM23/01/2008**

Gosling, Miss P L, MCLIP, Retired.
[5733]   11/09/1953   **CM01/01/1961**

Gossler, Ms A M, Librarian, Cirencester Kingshill School,
Gloucestershire.
[51479]   27/02/1995   **AF**

Goswami, Mrs L A, BA (Hons) MA MBA MCLIP, Head of LKS
Development, NHS Kent Surrey and Sussex LKS Development
Team.
[45636]   08/04/1991   **CM07/11/1996**

Gotts, Mr S T, BA DipLib MCLIP, Retired.
[33530]   01/01/1981   **CM01/07/1984**

Goudie, Miss L, MA BA, Graduate Library Assistant, Special Collections
and Archives, University of Liverpool.
[10032070]   24/10/2013   **ME**

Gould, Mrs A, BA (Hons) MCLIP, Library Manager Learning Education
and Development Keyll Darree Library, Isle of Man.
[59500]   05/04/2001   **CM13/06/2007**

Gould, Ms A L, Student, NCB Western University.
[10031950]   15/10/2013   **ME**

Gould, Mrs J M L, ACLIP, Library Assistant, Broke Hall Comm. Prim.
School, Ipswich.
[65402]   02/02/2006   **ACL23/09/2009**

Gould, Miss P M, MCLIP, Retired.
[5753]   13/02/1967   **CM01/01/1970**

Gould, Miss R M, MA (Hons), Information Librarian, Aberdeen City
Council.
[10011529]   17/10/2008   **ME**

Gould, Mrs S, BA MCLIP, Retired.
[8258]   11/03/1962   **CM01/01/1967**

Gould, Ms V M, DipED ACLIP, Librarian, Finborough School, Suffolk.
[10019034]   13/04/2011   **ACL29/05/2013**

Goulding, Miss L V, BA DipLib, Information Resources Manager,
Simmons & Simmons LLP, London.
[35464]   19/10/1982   **ME**

Goult, Mr R, MCLIP, Learning Resources Manager, Welbeck Defence
6th Form College.
[5757]   21/09/1966   **CM01/01/1971**

Gourdie, Mrs E, BA MCLIP, Retired.
[3577]   07/02/1954   **CM01/01/1957**

Gourlay, Mrs G L, BA MCLIP, Network Librarian, Westhill Academy,
Westhill.
[35937]   18/02/1983   **CM01/07/1990**

Gover, Miss S A, BA MCLIP, Retired.
[21750]   11/01/1974   **CM19/01/1976**

Gow, Ms H, BA DipLib MCLIP, Early Years Librarian, Kinson Library,
Bournemouth.
[51145]   23/11/1994   **CM21/05/2008**

Gow, Mrs R, BA, Student, Aberystwyth University.
[10032484]   09/12/2013   **ME**

Gowans, Mrs M S, MLIS MCLIP, Network Librarian, High Life Highland.
[57447]   01/04/1999   **CM01/02/2006**

Gower, Miss R J, BA, Assistant Librarian, Gonville & Caius College,
Cambridge.
[10000508]   17/10/2006   **ME**

Goy, Mr J R, BA MCLIP, Retired.
[5766]   01/10/1961   **CM01/01/1963**

Gozutok, Mr E, MSc, Library Loans Service Executive, House of
Commons Library.
[10023413]   16/07/2013   **ME**

Grace, Mr E A, BA (Hons),
[10023357]   02/07/2013   **AF**

Graddon, Mrs P H B, BA (Hons) BA (Hons) MCLIP, Retired.
[10006401]   17/07/1984   **CM17/07/1984**

Grady, Ms H J, BA MA MSc MCLIP, Temporary Inf Worker (Part-time).
[37477]   01/10/1984   **RV07/06/2006**   **CM19/08/1992**

Grafton, Mrs P R, MA MCLIP, Unwaged.
[29734]   03/10/1978   **CM04/03/1983**

Graham, Mrs A, BA (Hons) MSc MCLIP,
[52189]   12/10/1995   **CM23/09/1998**

Graham, Miss C, BSc Honours, Graduate.
[10019765]   07/09/2011   **ME**

Graham, Miss C I, MSc BA MCLIP, Senior Librarian, Isle of Man College, Douglas.
[5776]   01/01/1972   **CM04/02/1975**

Graham, Mr C J, MA MSc, College Librarian, Leeds College of Art.
[10021294]   06/07/2012   **ME**

Graham, Mr D, Student, Dominican University, USA.
[10031785]   04/10/2013   **ME**

Graham, Miss E, MA, Education, Training & Res. Team Leader, Wellcome Trust, London.
[42831]   16/03/1989   **ME**

Graham, Mrs K A, BA (Hons) DipIS MCLIP, Head of Corporate Knowledge, GCHQ, Cheltenham.
[49001]   24/08/1993   **CM22/01/1997**

Graham, Dr M, MA PhD FSA, Retired.
[5787]   03/10/1968   **CM12/10/1972**

Graham, Ms N, MA, Library Academic Liaison Manager, University of Roehampton.
[10008752]   23/07/1998   **ME**

Graham, Mrs S, BA (Hons) MSc (Econ) MCLIP, Information Development, IBM, Hampshire.
[59517]   18/04/2001   **CM21/03/2007**

Graham, Mrs S, BA (Hons) MSc, Library Manager, South Tyneside NHS Foundation Trust.
[57223]   20/01/1999   **ME**

Graham, Mr S I, BA (Hons), Education Cen. Library, Cumberland Infirmary, Carlisle.
[58705]   09/06/2000   **ME**

Graham, Mr S P, BSc (Hons) DipLib MCLIP, Product Stewardship Adviser, Infineum UK Ltd, Abingdon, Oxfordshire.
[34511]   19/11/1981   **CM23/08/1985**

Grainger, Miss H, BA (Hons) MA MCLIP AFHEA, Academic Services Librarian (Procurement), Bath Spa University.
[61675]   17/10/2002   **CM28/01/2009**

Grainger, Ms L J, BA MA, Cataloguing Librarian, Wellcome Library.
[10033632]   07/04/2014   **ME**

Grainger, Mrs S B, MCLIP, Head of Lib. and Heritage Walsll MBC Walsall Central Library.
[16239]   29/12/1971   **CM16/09/1974**

Grajcarek, Mrs J L, MCLIP, Teacher's Assistant, Gilbert Colvin Primary School, Ilford.
[31851]   07/01/1980   **CM25/10/1983**

Grandy, Mr J W A, BA, Librarian, Oxfordshire CC.
[10032607]   20/12/2013   **ME**

Granger, Mrs A M, BLib MCLIP, Sales Assistant, St Paul's Bookshop, Leeds.
[27853]   12/09/1977   **CM11/10/1982**

Gransbury, Miss W, Information Support Assistant, Ministry of Defence.
[10035498]   16/10/2014   **ME**

Grant, Mrs A, MA,
[44043]   17/04/1990   **ME**

Grant, Mrs C, PG Lib,
[10012330]   03/11/1992   **ME**

Grant, Mrs C G, BA DipLib MCLIP, Field Officer /Librarian, City of Edinburgh Council.
[29142]   18/10/1978   **CM18/11/1981**

Grant, Miss C S, Library Assistant, Northumbria University.
[10020661]   15/03/2012   **ME**

Grant, Ms D, Learning Resources Assistant, Forth Valley College.
[10022222]   22/01/2013   **AF**

Grant, Miss D M, MCLIP, Librarian, L. Support, Falkirk Council.
[21956]   12/01/1974   **CM09/02/1977**

Grant, Mrs E, MCLIP, Retired (nee Miss Olive Trickett).
[9110]   01/01/1938   **CM01/01/1942**

Grant, Mr E A, MA (Hons) MSc, Senior Information Assistant, Sir Duncan Rice Library, University of Aberdeen.
[61309]   20/05/2002   **ME**

Grant, Mrs F G T, BA (Hons) MA MCLIP,
[56455]   13/07/1998   **CM16/07/2003**

Grant, Mr J, BSc DipLib MCLIP, Associate Director Information Serv., Quintiles Ltd, Livingston, West Lothian.
[28304]   03/11/1977   **CM12/02/1982**

Grant, Mr J D, BA (Hons) MCLIP, Lending Servs. Manager, Aberdeen City Council, Aberdeen.
[39922]   01/10/1986   **CM18/11/1993**

Grant, Ms J E, BA (Hons) DipIM MCLIP, Librarian, Lewisham Library, London.
[48505]   27/01/1993   **CM15/03/2000**

Grant, Mrs J M, BA MCLIP, Information & Learning Res. Co-ordinator, St Robert of Newminster School, Tyne & Wear.
[46161]   08/10/1991   **CM21/07/1993**

Grant, Mrs K A, BA (Hons) MCLIP, Assistant Librarian, Health & Safety Executive, Information & Advisory Serv., Sheffield.
[40594]   01/04/1987   **CM08/12/2004**

Grant, Ms M, BA, Student, Victoria University of Wellington.
[10032586]   17/12/2013   **ME**

Grant, Ms M J, BA (Hons) MSc, Res. Fellow, Salford University, Manchester.
[10007156]   03/01/1991   **ME**

Grant, Miss M L, BA MA, Acquisitions Services Manager, Wellcome Library.
[10011617]   30/10/2008   **ME**

Grant, Ms M P, MA DipLib MCLIP, Principal Librarian, The Mitchell Library, Glasgow.
[34491]   17/11/1981   **CM26/02/1992**

Grant, Miss R H, MA (Hons), Team Leader: Student Help Point – The Robert Gordon University, Aberdeen.
[54570]   28/01/1997   **ME**

Grant, Mr S J, MA PGCE MCLIP, College Librarian, Reid Kerr College, Paioley.
[40979]   01/10/1987   **CM18/07/1991**

Grantham, Ms J, BA MA, Assistant Librarian, City of London School, London.
[61852]   19/11/2002   **ME**

Gratsea, Mrs A, MSCECON, Bibliographic Project Co-ordinator, Aberystwyth University.
[10014402]   19/02/2002   **ME**

Gravely, Miss C E, Student.
[10018255]   15/12/2010   **ME**

Graver, Ms J F, BSc DipLib MIIS MCLIP, Unwaged.
[21055]   19/09/1973   **CM01/10/1975**

Graves, Mrs R H, MCLIP,
[10012094]   17/12/2008   **CM14/11/2012**

Gravett, Ms K L, MCLIP,
[64462]   31/03/2005   **CM23/01/2008**

Gray, Mr A, BSc MSc, Librarian, British Antarctic Survey.
[10001216]   02/02/2007   **ME**

Gray, Mrs A E, BSc DipLib MCLIP, Knowledge Officer, NHS Greater East Midlands CSU.
[30142]   11/01/1979   **CM11/11/1985**

Gray, Miss A J, MA MCLIP, Librarian, Slough L.
[63129]   11/02/2004   **CM03/10/2007**

Gray, Miss C M, MA MPhil DipLib MCLIP BABE, Learning Servs. Manager, New College Lanarkshire.
[37743]   16/10/1984   **CM08/12/1987**

Gray, Mrs G E, BSc PgDipLIS MCLIP, Assistant Librarian, British Geological Survey, Edinburgh.
[62534]   06/08/2003   **CM03/10/2007**

Gray, Mrs H, MA DLIS MCLIP, Office Manager, Egypt Exploration Society, London.
[26571]   01/10/1976   **CM31/12/1979**

Gray, Miss H C, Student, Aberystwyth University.
[10027123]   10/06/2014   **ME**

Gray, Miss J, MA MCLIP, Life Member.
[5830]   15/09/1954   **CM01/01/1963**

Gray, Miss J M, MCLIP, Retired.
[5834]   17/01/1947   **CM01/01/1954**

Gray, Ms K A, BA (Hons) MCLIP, Retired.
[60295]   10/12/2001   **CM10/12/2001**

Gray, Mrs K A, BSc (Hons), Senior L. Assistant, School of St Helen & St Katharine, Oxon.
[59478]   05/04/2001   **AF**

Gray, Ms K J, BA DipLib MCLIP, Head of Information Resources., Lawrence Graham LLP, London.
[44155]   06/06/1990   **CM21/10/1992**

Gray, Mr P A, BA, Learning Resources Assistant, Southampton Solent University.
[39835]   16/08/1986   **ME**

Gray, Mr P K, BSc (Hons), Librarian, Scottish Government, Edinburgh.
[51853]   13/07/1995   **ME**

Gray, Mrs S A L, BScEcon (Hons) MCLIP, Librarian, Kings School, Canterbury.
[51570]   01/04/1995   **CM23/01/2002**

Gray, Mrs S I, BA (Hons) DipLIS MCLIP, Local Studies Librarian, Warwick L.
[57589]   13/05/1999   **CM23/01/2008**

Gray, Mr T M, DPA FCLIP, Life member.
[5843]   01/03/1941   **FE01/01/1967**

Grayson, Mrs H E, BA (Hons) DipLib MCLIP, Information &Reviews Manager, National Foundation for Educ. Research, Slough.
[45515]   28/02/1991   **CM12/09/2001**

Grayson, Mr J, BA (Hons) MA MCLIP, Racing Analyst, The Sportsman, London.
[55560]   21/10/1997   **CM20/11/2002**

Gray-Williams, Mrs M A M, BA, Student, Robert Gordon University.
[10032425]   18/12/2013   **ME**

Greasley, Miss L, Technical Analyst, Infor Global Solutions.
[10017514]   31/08/2010   **ME**

Greasley, Mrs S, Senior L. Assistant, University College Falmouth, Tremough L.
[10016203]   12/07/1996   **AF**

Greasley, Ms Y, BLib MCLIP, Library Assistant, Concord College.
[10033263]   25/02/2014   **ME**

Greaves, Miss K R, BLib, L. Serv. Manager, Harper Adams University College.
[38545]   17/06/1985   **CM21/12/1988**

Greaves, Miss M A, BA MA FCLIP AI, Life Member.
[16954]   08/03/1954   **FE01/01/1966**

Greaves, Ms P, BSc MCLIP, L. Development Worker, Leicestershire County Council.
[60504]   19/05/2001   **CM19/05/2001**

Greaves, Mrs R M, BA DipLib MCLIP, Learning Res. Centre Manager, Weald of Kent Grammar School.
[35254]   04/10/1982   **CM10/10/1986**

Green, Mr A, BA MLS DMS MCLIP, Head of L. & Heritage Serv., Wandsworth Council.
[31069]   27/07/1979   **CM28/09/1981**

Green, Mr A, MSc MCLIP, Information Advisor, Kingston College, Kingston.
[10018563]   07/02/2011   **CM16/05/2012**

Green, Ms A, BA, Librarian, Bermuda Aquarium Museum.
[10009701]   25/02/2005   **ME**

Green, Miss A M, MCLIP, Retired.
[5864]   13/05/1971   **CM13/02/1975**

Green, Mr A M W, MA MCLIP, Former Librarian, National Library of Wales, Aberystwyth.
[23294]   06/11/1974   **CM30/11/1977**

Green, Mr C, Student, CILIP Scotland.
[10002148]   20/04/2007   **ME**

Green, Dr C A, BA (HONS) MA PhD, Library Assistant, BCOM Library.
[10021578]   03/09/2012   **ME**

Green, Mr D, BA MA MLIS, Rare Books Librarian, University of St Andrews Library, St Andrews.
[10017445]   23/08/2010   **ME**

Green, Mrs D J, BA DipLib MCLIP, Housewife.
[38383]   03/04/1985   **CM10/11/1987**

Green, Ms E C, BA (Hons) MCLIP, Community Librarian, West Sussex County Council, Crawley.
[49727]   25/11/1993   **CM15/05/2002**

Green, Mrs E J, Assistant Librarian.
[10015934]   28/01/2010   **ME**

Green, Miss E V, BA DipLib MCLIP, Librarian, Southampton Reference Library, Southampton City L.
[30172]   10/01/1979   **CM08/02/1982**

Green, Miss G E, MCLIP, Life Member.
[5876]   17/08/1955   **CM01/01/1968**

Green, Miss G M, BA MCLIP, Unwaged.
[24892]   08/10/1975   **CM06/12/1979**

Green, Miss J, MA, Communications Officer, RBKC.
[65332]   06/01/2006   **ME**

Green, Mrs J, BA MCLIP, Stock and Reader Development Librarian, Hoddesdon Library, Herts.
[35640]   23/11/1982   **CM09/08/1988**

Green, Mrs J E, BA MCLIP, Information Manager, Covington & Burling, London.
[24771]   29/09/1975   **CM24/01/1978**

Green, Ms J S, BA (Hons) MSc DipLIS, Knowledge Services Manager, NHS Health Scotland, Scotland.
[63631]   02/08/2004   **ME**

Green, Mrs K A, BA (Hons) DMS MCLIP, Chief Lib. Officer, Barnsley MBC.
[31895]   17/01/1980   **CM20/03/1985**

Green, Mrs L, BA, Student, Victoria University of Wellington.
[10034763]   14/08/2014   **ME**

Green, Ms M, Librarian, Central Library of The European Commission. Germany.
[10019493]   11/07/2011   **ME**

Green, Ms M I, MCLIP, Audience Development Officer, Library Services Ltd, Slough.
[10006464]   19/10/2007   **CM14/12/2011**

Green, Mrs M M, MCLIP, Retired.
[5892]   30/09/1964   **CM01/01/1969**

Green, Mrs N A, BA DipLib, Abstract legal journal articles for a legal database, select keywords from a legal taxonomy and apply indexing criteria.
[44212]   09/07/1990   **ME**

Green, Miss R E, Student, University of Strathclye.
[10033538]   25/03/2014   **ME**

Green, Mrs R J, BA MCLIP,
[34632]   16/01/1982   **CM16/05/1990**

Green, Mr R S, MA MLib MCLIP, Librarian, Howes Percival LLP, Northampton.
[28305]   15/10/1977   **CM27/01/1984**

Green, Mr S, MA MCLIP, Librarian, Cent. Reference Library, Hull City Council.
[18258]   03/10/1972   **CM11/11/1975**

Green, Miss S V, DipLib MCLIP, School Librarian, Camden School for Girls, London.
[34756] 17/02/1982 **CM14/09/1985**

Green, Miss V S M E, BA (Hons), Post Grad Dip.
[10019644] 16/08/2011 **ME**

Greenall, Ms J, MA BA DipCOT, Graduate Librarianship.
[10018965] 01/04/2011 **AF**

Greenall, Mr J, MCLIP, Retired.
[19744] 01/01/1966 **CM01/01/1969**

Greenaway, Mrs H M, BA (Hons) MCLIP, Part-time Information Assistant, RoSPA.
[10022046] 22/11/2012 **CM15/07/2014**

Greene, Ms J L, BA, Student.
[10020405] 11/02/2012 **ME**

Greene, Mrs M, BA (Hons) MRes MSc,
[10015339] 11/11/2009 **ME**

Greenhalgh, Mrs M C, BSc MCLIP, Self-employed.
[60368] 29/01/1970 **CM29/01/1970**

Greenhalgh, Miss S L, BA, Library Graduate Trainee, South Devon Healthcare NHS Foundation Trust.
[10031588] 04/09/2013 **ME**

Greenhead, Mr J D, BA MA, Technical Services Librarian, House of Lords, London.
[62095] 13/02/2003 **ME**

Greenidge, Mrs C, MSc MET, Information Technologist, University of West Indies.
[10009472] 20/05/2008 **ME**

Greenidge-Forsyth, Mrs E, Librarian, Battersea Park School, London.
[65252] 06/12/2005 **ACL01/11/2007**

Green-Morgan, Mrs N E, BA MSc (Econ) MCLIP, Researcher Librarian, Freehills, Sydney.
[52059] 02/10/1995 **CM09/11/2005**

Greenough, Mrs S A, BA (Hons), Librarian, Lancaster School.
[10023322] 25/06/2013 **ME**

Greenslade, Mrs S A, BA (Hons), Patent Information Manager Alder Hey Childrens NHS Foundation Trust, Liverpool.
[58441] 15/02/2000 **ME**

Greenstreet, Mrs J W, BA (Hons) MSc, Library Assistant, Royal Agricultural University.
[62280] 10/04/2003 **ME**

Greenstreet, Miss O E, BA (Hons) MA MCLIP, Student, UCL.
[10019843] 01/10/2011 **CM15/07/2014**

Greenway, Ms J, BA (Hons) ACLIP, L. Technician, Bemrose School, Derby.
[10016068] 10/02/2010 **ACL07/09/2011**

Greenway, Mrs M, Lib. Supervisor, HMP YOI Swinfen Hall, Lichfield.
[10017008] 17/06/2010 **AF**

Greenwod, Mr S, BA MSc, Learning Resource Assistant.
[10006504] 24/10/2007 **ME**

Greenwood, Mr A, BSc MSc, Information Professional.
[65779] 24/04/2006 **ME**

Greenwood, Ms E, BA (Hons) MA MCLIP, Business Librarian, City Business Library.
[56968] 11/11/1998 **CM20/11/2002**

Greenwood, Mr G W, Knowledge and Information Officer, Office For National Statistics.
[10032221] 01/05/2014 **ME**

Greenwood, Mr M J, BA (Hons), Student, Manchester Metropolitan University.
[10032072] 24/10/2013 **ME**

Greenwood, Mrs O, BEd MA MCLIP, Jobshare, Library Manager, Notts. County Council.
[46832] 14/02/1992 **CM15/01/2003**

Gregg, Mr A R, DipLib, Librarian, Clyde & Co., London.
[47289] 03/07/1992 **ME**

Gregory, Mrs A M, MA MCLIP, Hennepin County Library, Minnesota, USA.
[37737] 23/10/1984 **CM19/09/1989**

Gregory, Mrs C M B, BA MA, Senior Info Specialist, Integreon Managed Solutions.
[41326] 02/11/1987 **ME**

Gregory, Mrs J R, BA (Hons), Library Services and First Point Officer, Telford and Wrekin Council.
[10034520] 18/07/2014 **ME**

Gregory, Mrs K L, Cluster Manager, Leeds Libraries.
[10018454] 19/01/2011 **AF**

Gregory, Miss K L, MSc, Student Sheffield University.
[10032275] 13/11/2013 **ME**

Gregory, Miss N, BA PgDip MA, Assistant Librarian, Wigan & Leigh College.
[64375] 14/03/2005 **ME**

Gregory, Mrs R S, BA MCLIP, School Librarian, City of Derby Academy, Derby.
[29591] 29/09/1978 **CM29/09/1980**

Gregory, Mr S F, BSc MA MCLIP, Assistant Librarian, Welsh Government.
[43628] 14/11/1989 **RV**16/06/2010 **CM15/09/1993**

Greig, Ms F, BA MCLIP, E-Strategy and Resources Manager, University of Surrey.
[43862] 05/02/1990 **CM23/03/1993**

Gresser, Dr C, MSc MA PhD, Librarian, Marshall Library, University of Cambridge.
[65339] 17/01/2006 **ME**

Gresty, Miss H G, BA MCLIP, Knowledge ManagementManager, J. P. Morgan Asset Management, Luxembourg.
[30423] 10/01/1979 **CM07/11/1984**

Grewcock, Mr J A, BA ACLIP, Library Assistant, Watford Central Library, Herts.
[10001556] 06/10/2004 **ACL17/06/2009**

Grey, Miss A, Senior Library Assistant, Cardiff University.
[10000852] 13/11/2006 **ME**

Grey, Dr D, BSc (Hons) PhD, Assistant Librarian, Bloomsbury Healthcare Library, London.
[62706] 03/10/2003 **ME**

Grey, Mr O, BSc (Hons) MSc, Reference Librarian, Westminster City Council.
[64771] 16/06/2005 **ME**

Grier, Mrs V C, BA MCLIP, Retired.
[5962] 01/01/1967 **CM01/01/1971**

Grieve, Miss H C, Student.
[10023305] 25/06/2013 **ME**

Grieve, Miss L, Library Assistant, Hartpury College.
[10021505] 24/08/2012 **ME**

Grieve, Mr S, MCIBS, Business Manager, W. J. Grieve, Dumfriesshire.
[49040] 13/09/1993 **ME**

Griffin, Mrs A, BA DipLib PGCE, Sunday Librarian, London Borough of Lewisham, Lewisham L.
[40856] 10/07/1987 **ME**

Griffin, Miss C A, Unwaged.
[45104] 11/07/1990 **AF**

Griffin, Ms M A V, BA, Unwaged.
[40834] 22/07/1987 **ME**

Griffin, Mrs V C, BA (Hons) MSc MCLIP, Head of Indexing and Data Management, Department of Information Serv., House of Commons, London.
[54034] 18/10/1996 **CM17/11/1999**

Griffin, Mrs W, BA MCLIP, Senior Team Officer, Safer & Stronger Comm. Team, Surrey County Council.
[28306]   03/11/1977   **CM07/08/1980**

Griffith, Mr J H, BA (Hons), Information Manager, ARUP.
[47175]   22/05/1992   **ME**

Griffiths, Miss A, BA PGCE, Learning Centre Manager, Wolverley CE Secondary School.
[10015691]   14/01/2010   **ME**

Griffiths, Mrs A A, BA (Hons) MCLIP, Reader Serv. Manager, Liverpool Hope University, Liverpool.
[56605]   15/09/1998   **CM12/09/2001**

Griffiths, Mrs A D, BSc, Community Outreach Officer with Vale of Glamorgan Libraries and loving every minute.
[66086]   01/10/2006   **ME**

Griffiths, Mrs A J, BA (Hons) MSc (Econ) MCLIP, Unwaged – Career Break.
[51167]   23/11/1994   **CM15/03/2000**

Griffiths, Mrs A L, BA (Hons) MA MSc (Econ) MCLIP, Strategy and Policy Officer, Welsh Government, Ceredigion.
[55857]   02/12/1997   **CM01/04/2002**

Griffiths, Mr D J, BA MA MCLIP, Librarian, BMT Group Ltd, Teddington, Middx.
[25878]   01/01/1976   **CM13/06/1989**

Griffiths, Miss F R, BA MSc, Deputy Library Manager.
[10002309]   20/04/2007   **ME**

Griffiths, Mrs G E, BA DipLib MCLIP, Librarian, Shropshire C. Oswestry.
[45451]   11/02/1991   **CM22/11/1995**

Griffiths, Mrs H, BA (Hons) MLib, Cataloguer (Part-time).
[47750]   16/10/1992   **ME**

Griffiths, Miss J A, BA (Hons) MA MCLIP, Operational Manager, Halton L. Serv., Runcorn.
[62764]   20/10/2003   **RV**18/12/2013   **CM10/07/2009**

Griffiths, Mr J M, MCLIP, Life Member.
[5985]   05/09/1959   **CM01/01/1967**

Griffiths, Mrs J M, MA MCLIP, Part-time Library Assistant, Denbighshire County Council.
[26649]   12/10/1976   **CM29/12/1980**

Griffiths, Miss J P W, JP BA MCLIP, Life Member.
[5987]   19/02/1948   **CM01/01/1962**

Griffiths, Ms K A, BD DipLib, Locality Manager, Norfolk & Norwich Millennium Library.
[10023064]   04/06/2013   **ME**

Griffiths, Miss L M, MLS BA MCLIP, Information & Research Officer, Chartered Society of Physiotherapy, London.
[27678]   13/07/1977   **CM20/05/1980**

Griffiths, Miss M, BA MA, Student.
[10032058]   10/12/2013   **ME**

Griffiths, Mrs S N T, BA MA DipLib MCLIP, Retired.
[30757]   11/04/1979   **CM10/12/1981**

Griffiths, Mrs V M, OBE BA MCLIP, Consultant.
[5998]   15/06/1971   **CM26/09/1973**

Griffiths, Dr W R M, MA MLitt DipLib MCLIP, Retired.
[24688]   02/10/1975   **CM07/11/1978**

Grigg, Mrs N A, Site Co-ordinator, Lincoln Central Library, Lincolnshire CC.
[10035511]   16/10/2014   **ME**

Grigoropoulou, Dr E, Library Assistant, Durham University Library.
[10034328]   04/07/2014   **ME**

Grigson, Mrs G, MA MCLIP, Librarian (Training and Information Support), Keele University Health Library.
[40307]   01/01/1987   **CM18/01/1989**

Grimes, Mrs C L, Librarian, Northumbria University.
[10022173]   15/01/2013   **ME**

Grimmond, Mrs M A G, BA (Hons) MCLIP, School Librarian, The High School of Glasgow, Anniesland, Glasgow.
[24483]   16/09/1975   **CM25/07/2001**

Grimshaw, Miss J M, BA, Curator-Social Sciences Collections, British Library, London.
[18218]   01/10/1972   **ME**

Grindlay, Dr D J C, BSc MA PhD MCLIP, Information Specialist, Centre for Evidence-based Veterinary Medicine, University of Nottingham.
[59195]   14/12/2000   **CM21/03/2007**

Grindrod, Ms K J, BA MIL MCLIP, Head of Subsurface & Bus. Data & Doc. Management, Total E & P UK Ltd, Aberdeen.
[60237]   27/10/1988   **CM27/10/1988**

Grinnall, Mr A P, BSc MSc,
[10018018]   09/11/2010   **ME**

Grist, Ms A P, BA (Hons) MA MCLIP, School Librarian, Henbury School, Bristol.
[54757]   01/04/1997   **CM12/03/2003**

Gristwood, Mrs H, BA (Hons) MA MCLIP, Retired.
[94]   01/01/1970   **CM17/08/1973**

Grocott, Mrs G, Lib. Health & Safety Executive, Sheffield.
[10001439]   02/02/1982   **ME**

Grogan, Miss J C, BTEC HND BLib MCLIP, Information Specialist, Civil Service.
[41510]   18/01/1988   **RV**27/11/2007   **CM19/06/1991**

Groom, Mr C, BSc (Hons), Records Manager, Norwich Bioscience Institutes, Norfolk.
[62000]   13/12/2002   **ME**

Groom, Miss C J, MA (Hons) MSc, Learning Tech., Carnegie College, Dunfermline.
[62789]   22/10/2003   **ME**

Groom, Mrs J, Learning Resources Centre Assistant, The RNLI College, RNLI, Dorset.
[10019025]   12/04/2011   **AF**

Groom, Mrs J E C, Legal Information Consultant & Librarian, Self-Employed.
[6021]   27/09/1967   **CM01/01/1972**

Groombridge, Mrs S E A, BA DipLib MCLIP, Knowledge and Information Agent, DSTL, Salisbury.
[31226]   11/10/1979   **CM24/09/1985**

Groome, Mrs C R, Councillor, Borough of Kettering.
[34782]   22/01/1982   **ME**

Groome, Miss G, MSc, Information Compliance and Records Management Assistant.
[10021702]   01/10/2012   **ME**

Grosvenor, Mr J R H, DipLib DipMgmt (Open) MCLIP,
[31304]   01/10/1979   **CM08/11/1982**

Grove, Mrs H, MA, Librarian, London Transport Museum, London.
[56780]   14/10/1998   **ME**

Grover, Ms S M, BA MA DipLib MCLIP,
[27325]   10/03/1977   **CM10/03/1980**

Grove-Smith, Ms P, BA MCLIP, Retired.
[6029]   08/10/1971   **CM31/08/1974**

Gruffydd, Ms N V, BA MCLIP, User Services Manager, Gwynedd Council.
[40205]   06/11/1986   **CM12/09/1990**

Grundy, Ms D L, BA (Hons) MCLIP, Subject Librarian. University of Bolton.
[10006060]   03/09/2007   **CM27/01/2010**

Gryspeerdt, Mr R G P, BA MCLIP, retired.
[20331]   05/03/1973   **CM15/03/1979**

Gschwandtner, Mr M, Faculty Liaison Librarian Health and Social Care, Canterbury Christ Church University.
[10022059]   27/11/2012   **ME**

Gu, Miss L, MA, Student, Kings College.
[10034738] 12/08/2014 ME

Guard, Mrs O, BSc (Econ) MCLIP, Locality Manager, Breckland & South Norfolk. Norfolk County Council Library and Information Service.
[51507] 13/03/1995 CM19/01/2000

Gudgeon, Mrs N J, BSc (Hons), Senior Librarian, Department of Health.
[63912] 26/10/2004 ME

Guedes Pereira Rosa, Mrs A, BA MSc, Postgraduate Research Student.
[10018746] 02/03/2011 ME

Guest, Mrs N, BA (Hons) MA MCLIP, Document Delivery Coordinator, Liaison Librarian and Multimedia Manager, University of Reading.
[62856] 17/11/2003 CM21/11/2007

Guest, Mrs R S, ACLIP, Assistant Manager, Castlepoint Library, Bournemouth.
[61426] 25/07/2002 ACL16/06/2010

Guest, Mr T D, BA, Student, Manchester Metropolitan University.
[10032908] 24/01/2014 ME

Guevara, Ms A P, BA (Hons) MA, Librarian, West Area, East Sussex L. &Information Service.
[61921] 02/12/2002 ME

Guilbert, Ms R, BA (Hons) MA MCLIP, Library and Information Services Manager, CFE library.
[10006323] 10/10/2007 CM13/04/2011

Guiney, Mrs P, BA MCLIP, Learning Res. Manager, Capital City Academy, London.
[30758] 17/04/1979 CM16/07/1982

Guinn, Mrs V, BSc PgDip (InfSc), Housing Customer Advisor, London Borough of Redbridge.
[65348] 13/01/2006 ME

Guite, Miss C J E, MA LTCL MCLIP, Senior Subject Librarian for Law, University of Stirling.
[30174] 17/01/1979 CM23/06/1986

Gulland, Mrs D, MCLIP, Retired.
[6043] 18/01/1957 CM01/01/1963

Gumbrell, Miss A C, BSc, Student, Robert Gordon University.
[10035691] 29/10/2014 ME

Gunard, Mr S R, Student, Northumbria University.
[10027198] 03/12/2013 ME

Gundersen, Mr R, Senior Adviser at BIBSYS, Norway (http://www. bibsys. no/en/).
[10007047] 07/01/2008 ME

Gundry, Mrs D, BSc (Hons) MCLIP, Head of Library Services, Plymouth College of Art.
[10012743] 01/06/2010 ME

Gunewardena, Dr A, BSc MSc PhD MA (ILM), Library Support Assistant, University of Nottingham.
[10018068] 09/11/2010 ME

Gunn, Mrs C S, BSc DipLib MCLIP, Librarian Clackmannanshire Council.
[34558] 13/01/1982 CM14/04/1987

Gunn, Miss F, BSc PGCe,
[10032048] 22/10/2013 ME

Gunn, Mr J, Information Support Officer, Ministry of Defence.
[10027202] 21/07/2014 ME

Gunning, Mr S J, BA (Hons) DipLIS MCLIP, Subject Classifier, Nielsen Bookdata, Stevenage.
[44205] 06/07/1990 CM19/05/1999

Gunther, Ms Y, MA, Head Librarian/Archivist, Nottingham High School (Boys).
[65131] 03/11/2005 ME

Gunton, Mr D H, OBE MA FCLIP, Life Member.
[16970] 07/01/1947 FE05/03/1973

Guo, Ms X, MA,
[10007662] 19/02/2008 ME

Gupta, Mrs C, BLS (Hons), Office Manager, Black kite Ltd.
[10004831] 01/06/1981 ME

Gura, Mrs E, MCLIP, Life Member.
[6054] 28/01/1953 CM01/01/1956

Gurajena, Miss C R, LLB (Hons) MSc MCLIP, Senior Librarian, HM Land Registry, London.
[56964] 13/11/1998 CM21/05/2003

Gurjar, Mr R, PGCE,
[66076] 01/10/2006 ME

Gurnsey, Mr J, FCLIP, Retired.
[6057] 09/07/1966 FE26/09/1977

Gusavac, Ms M, BA, Student, RGU.
[10031879] 10/10/2013 ME

Gutierrez Yunda, Miss A, Student, Robert Gordon University.
[10031910] 14/10/2013 ME

Gutteridge, Mr P J, BA MSC MCLIP, Retired.
[34886] 27/03/1982 CM10/05/1984

Gutteridge, Mr S R, BA, Stock & Web – Central Bedfordshire Council.
[38602] 18/07/1985 CM16/02/1988

Guy, Mrs C A, BA MCLIP, Comm. Librarian, Connahs Quay Library, Deeside.
[50347] 04/07/1994 CM20/03/1996

Guy, Mr J, PgDipILM, Librarian, The ABC International School, Vietnam.
[49904] 10/01/1994 ME

Guy, Mr N G, MA MCLIP, Manager, Information Services, BHR Group, Cranfield.
[60372] 11/12/2001 CM11/12/2001

Guy, Mr R F, BA MA MCLIP, Project Manager.
[6070] 01/07/1971 CM31/01/1974

Guyatt, Miss E J, BA FCLIP, Life Member.
[6071] 04/10/1950 FE01/01/1954

Guyon, Ms A A M, MSc MCLIP, Senior Librarian, Young People's Serv., East Lothian.
[54622] 04/02/1997 CM09/07/2008

Gwilliam, Mrs S M, BLS MCLIP, Librarian, Beau Soleil College, Alpin International, Switzerland.
[30209] 05/12/1978 RV20/02/2014 CM21/06/1983

Gwilt, Ms R V, BA MA MCLIP, Library Manager/Librarian, University for Creative Arts, Maidstone.
[42924] 20/04/1989 CM24/06/1992

Gwinn, Mrs H E, BLib MCLIP, Legal Information Manager, Blake Morgan.
[40757] 29/05/1987 CM14/03/1990

Gwyer, Ms R, BLib MSc FCLIP PgCert PFHEA, University Librarian, University of Portsmouth.
[27187] 12/01/1977 FE09/07/2008

Gwynn, Ms L, BA (Hons), Currently studying for a PhD on library history at Queen Mary University London.
[65230] 24/11/2005 ME

Gyasi-Tetteyfio, Mrs E,
[10023065] 04/06/2013 ME

Gyebi-Ababio, Mr O, BSc (Hons) InfMg, Unwaged.
[58944] 06/10/2000 ME

Gzebb, Miss V, Student, McGill University.
[10019073] 15/04/2011 ME

H

Haardt, Ms M, MA WissDok MCLIP, Deputy Senior Librarian & Cataloguer, The Wiener Library for the Study of the Holocaust & Genocide, London.
[65837]   23/05/2006   RV30/04/2014   CM03/10/2007

Habibi, Ms K, BA (Hons) MA MCLIP, L. Manager, Coulsdon and Bradmore Green L. Croydon.
[53781]   01/10/1996   CM23/01/2002

Hack, Ms J, LRC Manager, Comberton Village College.
[10018734]   01/03/2011   ME

Hackett, Miss D H M, BA MA, Student.
[10032122]   29/10/2013   ME

Hadaway, Mrs K A, BSc (Econ), Principal L. Assistant, University of Southampton.
[65879]   16/06/2006   ME

Haddow, Dr G C, PhD, Senior Lecturer, Curtin University (School of Media, Culture & Creative Arts), Australia.
[10014619]   20/08/2009   ME

Hadfield, Ms E J, BA (Hons) MA MCLIP, Learning Resources Manager, Thomas Rotherham College.
[10005089]   06/06/2007   CM13/10/2010

Hadwick, Mrs K E, BA DipLib, Librarian, Surrey Co. L.
[34688]   25/01/1982   ME

Haerkoenen, Miss S, Dipl Bibl MCLIP, Scholarly Publications Manager, Cardiff University.
[62104]   19/02/2003   CM23/06/2004

Hafeez, Miss S, PG Cert BA MA, Assistant Information Adviser, Aldrich Library, University of Brighton.
[10019532]   22/07/2011   ME

Hagemann, Mrs H C, BA MA, School Librarian.
[10017087]   22/06/2010   ME

Hagen, Ms M, BA MILS,
[10032808]   14/01/2014   ME

Hager, Ms T, BA (Hons) Msc MCLIP, Area Children & Young Persons Librarian, Chippenham Library.
[65247]   25/11/2005   CM19/08/2011

Hagger Street, Mrs E M, BA (Hons) CertEd MCLIP, Retired.
[26023]   25/09/1967   CM23/02/1984

Hagon, Mr N K, BA DipLib ALA, Deputy Project Manager, Foreign & Commonwealth Office.
[10033533]   24/03/2014   ME

Hague, Miss V L, BA MA MSc MCLIP, Librarian, ARUP, London.
[61935]   11/12/2002   CM27/03/2014

Haigh, Miss J, BA, Student, Northumbria University.
[10031807]   02/10/2008   ME

Haigh, Mrs V C, BA MSc MCLIP, L. Manager, Salford Royal NHS Found. Trust.
[41451]   01/01/1988   CM19/06/1991

Haines, Miss C M C, MA BA BSc MSB Mem MBA, Writer/Researcher.
[33238]   30/10/1980   ME

Haines, Ms H, MA MSc, Student, Northumbria University.
[10032428]   03/12/2013   ME

Haines, Mrs J M, MA BLib DipM MCLIP, Head of Service Development and Delivery, Learning Resources Library, Oxford Brookes University.
[24143]   24/03/1975   CM31/08/1979

Haines, Ms M P J, BA MLS FCLIP HonFCLIP, Retired.
[43248]   09/10/1989   HFE01/10/2006

Haines, Miss S, BSc (Hons), Library Assistant (Graduate Trainee), University of Bath.
[10034171]   12/06/2014   ME

Hair, Ms F M, BA DipILM MCLIP ILTM, Assistant Librarian, Sheppard-Worlock Library, Liverpool Hope University College.
[55160]   28/07/1997   CM12/09/2001

Haji Moksin, Mrs N, Student, University of Sheffield.
[10032871]   22/01/2014   ME

Halabura, Miss K J, MA, Community Librarian, Wandsworth Town and Southfields Libraries., London.
[64966]   05/10/2005   ME

Haldane, Mr G C, BD MSc MCLIP, L. & Knowl. Serv. Manager, East Lancashire Hospitals NHS Trust, Blackburn.
[10016308]   12/10/1981   CM31/10/1985

Hale, Miss A, MSc, Librarian, Shrewsbury High School.
[62702]   09/10/2003   ME

Hale, Mrs C J, BA MCLIP, Unwaged.
[27545]   16/05/1977   CM07/08/1980

Hale, Mrs H R, BA MCLIP, Assistant Librarian, The Leys School.
[24597]   01/10/1975   CM14/11/1978

Hale, Miss H S, Library Graduate Trainee.
[10031643]   17/09/2013   ME

Hale, Ms J, BEd MA, Young People`s Services Manager Plymouth City Council.
[58141]   13/02/2003   ME

Hale, Mrs J E, BA, Assistant Librarian, St Hilda's CE High School, Liverpool.
[10021108]   30/05/2012   ME

Hale, Mr P, BSc, Student, University of the West of England, Bristol.
[10009347]   01/06/2008   ME

Hale, Miss S, BA MA, Community Library Assistant, Huntingdon Library.
[10033328]   16/04/2014   AF

Hales, Mrs C A, BA (Hons) MA, Senior Team Officer – Children & Young People Stream, Surrey County Council Libraries.
[35558]   04/11/1982   ME

Haley, Miss A, BA (Hons),
[10027235]   01/10/2013   ME

Haley, Ms B J, Systems Librarian, Department of Printed Books, Imperial War Museum.
[65317]   23/12/2005   ME

Halfhide, Mrs D G, MA DipLib MCLIP, L. Information Serv. Manager, Peterborough & Stamford Hospital NHS Foundation Trust.
[37438]   10/09/1984   CM14/04/1987

Halford, Mrs E D, BA (Hons) MCLIP, Sch. Librarian, St Mary's Catholic School, Bishop's Stortford.
[52321]   26/10/1995   CM06/04/2005

Halfpenny, Mrs K, BA (Hons) MCLIP, Acquisitions Manager, Edge Hill University.
[40132]   17/10/1986   CM13/06/2007

Halfpenny, Mrs S J, BA MA, Teaching and Learning Advisor, University of York.
[10035248]   01/10/2014   ME

Hall, Ms A, BA (Hons), Lib. Manager, Royal Liverpool & Broadgreen University Hospitals NHS Trust, Liverpool.
[46346]   29/10/1991   ME

Hall, Mr A, BSc Phd, Logistician / Student.
[10033769]   25/04/2014   ME

Hall, Mr A C L, MA MCLIP, Semi-retired consultant.
[6118]   21/01/1959   CM01/01/1963

Hall, Miss A J B, BA B MUS FCLIP, Retired.
[16977]   07/03/1961   FE26/11/1997

Hall, Mr A L, BSc Social Sciences, Library Assistant, Battersea Library, London.
[10009449]   28/05/2008   AF

Hall, Miss B P, MCLIP, Retired.
[6125]   16/01/1961   CM01/01/1970

Hall, Mrs C A, BA MCLIP, Retired.
[26797]   11/11/1976   **CM01/11/1979**

Hall, Mr C A, MA MCLIP, Retired.
[26398]   08/10/1976   **CM14/02/1979**

Hall, Ms D M, BA DipLib MCLIP, Bibliographic Service Librarian, Powys Library Service Headquarters, Llandrindod Wells.
[33219]   10/10/1980   **CM02/02/1983**

Hall, Ms D M, BA, Lib. Assistant Map section, Bodleian Lib. Oxford.
[65169]   01/11/2005   **ME**

Hall, Ms E, BA, Student (DL), Aberystwyth University.
[10014454]   31/07/2009   **ME**

Hall, Mrs E A, BA (Hons), Director of Information, I C I S Information For Life.
[58504]   08/03/2000   **AF**

Hall, Mr G, BA DipLib MCLIP, Assistant Librarian, Eastwood Library, Nottinghamshire County Council.
[37813]   22/10/1984   **CM06/09/1988**

Hall, Dr H E, BSc Phd, Student.
[10006700]   21/11/2007   **ME**

Hall, Prof Dr H J R, BA (Hons) MA PhD FCLIP FHEA, Director, Cent for Social Informatics, Edinburgh Napier University, Edinburgh.
[41231]   19/10/1987   **FE01/04/2002**

Hall, Ms J, BA (Hons) DipLib MCLIP DMS, Information &Heritage Manager, London Borough of Lewisham, Lewisham, London.
[31311]   19/10/1979   **CM09/10/1981**

Hall, Mr J, MSc MCLIP, Retired.
[18347]   12/10/1972   **CM07/10/1975**

Hall, Miss J A, BSc, L. & Electronic Res. Assistant, Healthcare Library, Prospect Park Hospital, Reading.
[10019631]   10/10/2000   **ME**

Hall, Mrs J C, BA DipLib, Sch. Librarian, Queen's Park High School Library, Chester.
[41667]   11/02/1988   **ME**

Hall, Ms J F, BA MCLIP, Currently unemployed and seeking work.
[35208]   04/10/1982   **CM16/05/1990**

Hall, Mrs J H, BA (Hons), Librarian, Langley Park Girls School, Beckenham, Kent.
[62645]   01/10/2003   **ME**

Hall, Dr J P, BA (Hons) MA PhD, Assistant Director (Library & Research Support) University of Exeter.
[64087]   13/01/2005   **ME**

Hall, Dr J T D, MA PhD, Emeritus Librarian, Durham University.
[42811]   02/03/1989   **ME**

Hall, Miss K, BA MCLIP AFHEA, Skills Plus Co-ordinator, Northumbria University Lib.
[26103]   12/07/1976   **CM26/09/1980**

Hall, Mrs K, BA (Hons) MCLIP, Subject Librarian, Swansea University.
[46081]   01/10/1991   **CM17/03/1999**

Hall, Ms K E, PgDip, Student.
[10019968]   13/10/2011   **ME**

Hall, Dr L, BA PhD, Careers Advisor.
[60468]   19/10/1999   **ME**

Hall, Miss L N,
[10020186]   15/11/2011   **AF**

Hall, Mr M, MA MCLIP, Content Services Team Leader, Oxford Brookes University.
[62670]   02/10/2003   **CM21/06/2006**

Hall, Mrs N, Trials Search Co-ordinator, University of Liverpool.
[61854]   20/11/2002   **ME**

Hall, Mr R, BLib MCLIP, Knowledge Specialist, Proxima Group.
[30953]   22/06/1979   **CM06/04/1984**

Hall, Mr R E, LLB MA, Senior Librarian, Support, South Tyneside Metropolitan Borough Council, Central Library.
[59004]   20/10/2000   **ME**

Hall, Mrs S, BA (Hons) MCLIP, Academic Skills Tutor (Librarian), Staffordshire University, Beaconside, Stafford.
[31125]   09/09/1979   RV27/03/2014   **CM27/11/1996**

Hall, Miss S, BA MA, Student, Sheffield University.
[10031925]   15/10/2013   **ME**

Hall, Mr S, CBiol PgDip ILS, Unwaged.
[10012727]   20/11/1990   **ME**

Hall, Mrs S A, BLib BA MA PGCE MCLIP, Librarian, Queen Margaret's School, York.
[27579]   18/05/1977   **CM17/11/1980**

Hallam, Miss C M, BA MCLIP, Retired.
[6161]   01/10/1968   **CM11/09/1972**

Hallam, Mrs J H, BA (Hons) MCLIP, Outreach Librarian, Oxford Health NHS Foundation Trust.
[62475]   07/07/2003   **CM13/06/2007**

Hallam, Ms P A, BSc DipLib MCLIP, Team Leader., Library Resources., Northumberland C. C.
[35469]   14/10/1982   **CM18/02/1986**

Hallam, Ms S M, BA MSc, Internet Marketing Consultant, Hallam Internet Ltd, Nottingham.
[60173]   21/03/1989   **ME**

Hallaways, Mrs K, BA MCLIP, Life Member and Chartered.
[18185]   10/10/1972   **CM05/01/1976**

Hallett, Miss A N E, BA (Hons) MSc, Librarian, London.
[52213]   10/10/1995   **ME**

Hallett, Miss L A, BSc MSc MCLIP, Career Break.
[44337]   20/09/1990   **CM20/03/1996**

Hallewell, Prof L, BA PhD FCLIP, Life Member.
[6167]   10/01/1950   **FE01/01/1959**

Halliday, Mrs A, BA DipLIS MCLIP, Chief Librarian, Thurrock Council, Essex.
[46214]   16/10/1991   **CM25/01/1995**

Halliday, Mrs G, DESCIO-Exp-AcctMgr, DCSA Directorate strategic Transition – MOD.
[10033966]   14/05/2014   **ME**

Halligan, Mr C F, MA DipLib MCLIP, Librarian, St Lukes H. S., Barrhead.
[43489]   30/10/1989   **CM24/03/1992**

Hallissey, Mr M H, BA (Hons) DipLIS, Assistant Librarian, Ministry of Justice.
[46623]   28/11/1991   **ME**

Hallman-Lewis, Mrs C, ACLIP, Learning Resources Assistant, Seaborne Library, Univdrsity of Chester.
[10012420]   05/02/2009   **ACL23/09/2009**

Hallworth, Ms L K, MCLIP, Learning Centre Assistant (Curriculum), City & Islington College, London.
[63490]   15/06/2004   **CM21/05/2008**

Hallyburton, Miss E, MA (Hons) PgLIS, Senior Library & Information Officer.
[51086]   14/11/1994   **ME**

Halper, Mrs S D, MCLIP MCMI, Social Science Content & Service Development Manager, British Library, London.
[58140]   08/11/1999   **CM21/05/2008**

Halpin, Prof E F, PhD MA FRSA, Professor of Social and Human Rights Informatics, Leeds Beckett University.
[55140]   23/07/1997   **CM01/04/2002**

Halpin, Mr T D, MA, Library Assistant, New forest Academy.
[10021994]   15/11/2012   **ME**

Halsey, Mrs M, BA MCLIP, Librarian, John Lyon School.
[31372]   15/10/1979   **CM14/08/1985**

Halton, Miss L M, BA (Hons), Senior Library Assistant, Library and Information Service, Preston.
[10023066]   04/06/2013   **AF**

Hambidge, Mrs F A M, BA, Librarian, Swindon B. C.
[35561]   25/10/1982   **CM21/02/1985**

Hambly, Miss M, BA (Hons), Student, University of Strathclyde.
[10035388]   10/10/2014   **ME**
Hambrook, Ms K M P, BA DipLib MCLIP, Audio-Visual Librarian, Oxford Brookes University.
[37110]   09/02/1984   **CM15/08/1989**
Hamer, Mrs A F, ACLIP, Library Manager / H&S Coordinator, St Luke's Science & Sports College.
[65047]   21/10/2005   **ACL06/02/2008**
Hamer, Miss E J, MCLIP, Retired.
[6190]   07/09/1966   **CM01/01/1971**
Hamill-Stewart, Ms N C, BA DipLib MCLIP, Relief Librarian, Cambridgeshire Libraries.
[42485]   23/11/1988   **CM26/05/1993**
Hamilton, Miss A E, BA (Hons), St George School for Girls, Edinburgh.
[57726]   08/07/1999   **AF**
Hamilton, Mrs C E, Librarian, MOD, Ash Vale.
[23181]   05/11/1974   **CM11/12/1978**
Hamilton, Miss D, MTH BA MCLIP, Life Member.
[16985]   27/09/1951   **CM01/01/1957**
Hamilton, Mr G E, FCLIP, Life Member.
[6200]   14/09/1955   **FE01/04/1960**
Hamilton, Miss J, Student, Aberystwyth University.
[10009487]   21/05/2008   **ME**
Hamilton, Mrs J B, BSc (Hons), Student, University of Strathclyde.
[10035385]   10/10/2014   **ME**
Hamilton, Mr J E, FCLIP, Retired.
[6203]   05/03/1963   **FE18/06/1976**
Hamilton, Miss K M, BA MSc MCLIP, Assistant Librarian, FCO, London.
[61337]   30/05/2002   **CM20/04/2012**
Hamilton, Mr P C W, BA (Hons) DipLib MCLIP, Information Researcher, Food Standards Agency, London.
[32076]   11/02/1980   **CM11/05/1984**
Hamley, Miss J, BA DipLib MCLIP, Faculty Librarian, University of the West of England.
[39582]   07/03/1986   **CM18/07/1991**
Hammerton, Mr D, BA MA, Student, London Metropolitan University.
[65197]   17/11/2005   **ME**
Hammond, Mrs D C, BA MCLIP, Adult Librarian, Milton Keynes Library.
[37450]   01/10/1984   **CM30/01/1991**
Hammond, Mrs K M, BSc MSc DipLib MCLIP, Life Member.
[6232]   30/01/1964   **CM01/01/1967**
Hammond, Miss S C, BSc (Hons), Conference Team Support Member, The British Library, Boston Spa.
[10000812]   16/11/2006   **ME**
Hamnett, Miss K L, BA, Senior librarian at a large secondary school in the West Midlands.
[10019536]   22/07/2011   **AF**
Hampshire, Dr M D, BA (Hons) MSc (Econ) PhD MCLIP, Temporary Part-time Cataloguer., The National Archives, Kew.
[52893]   17/01/1996   **CM11/03/2009**
Hampson, Mrs A M, MCLIP, Unwaged.
[1611]   21/02/1968   **CM01/01/1970**
Hampson, Mrs E P, MA (Hons) MCLIP, Retired.
[21283]   12/10/1973   **CM01/11/1976**
Hampson, Mr J P, BSc MSc MRPharmS MCLIP, Public Health Specialist, Cheshire West and Chester Council, HQ, Nicholas Street, Chester, CH1 2HS.
[60443]   07/08/1998   **CM07/08/1998**
Hamwela, Ms V, BLIS, Student, University of Sheffield.
[10035688]   29/10/2014   **ME**
Hancock, Mr D B, Lib. Assist., Brierley Hill L.
[10019903]   30/09/2011   **AF**
Hancock, Miss K M, MCLIP, Retired.
[6249]   01/09/1941   **CM01/01/1948**

Hancock, Mr L J, MCLIP, Librarian, New College Swindon.
[64207]   02/03/2005   **CM09/09/2013**
Hancox, Miss C, MCLIP, Community Librarian, Walsall Council.
[10013582]   08/05/2009   **CM13/11/2013**
Hand, Mrs A A, Information Specialist.
[10000869]   17/11/2006   **ME**
Hand, Mrs J F, BA (Hons) DipLib MCLIP, Unwaged.
[39323]   14/01/1986   **CM18/03/1998**
Handley, Mrs S L, BA MCLIP, Life Member.
[6259]   15/02/1950   **CM01/01/1961**
Hanes, Mrs J, BA (Hons) MSc MCLIP, Learning & Teaching Services Librarian, University of Leicester.
[56829]   20/10/1998   **CM06/04/2005**
Hanes, Mrs S C, BA (Hons) MCLIP, Head of Library and Knowledge Services, Northumberland, Tyne & Wear NHS Trust.
[54251]   13/11/1996   **CM16/07/2003**
Hanford, Mrs A, MCLIP, Life Member.
[6263]   09/09/1954   **CM01/01/1961**
Hanford, Mrs J, MCLIP, Librarian, The Athenaeum, Liverpool.
[10008995]   25/09/1962   **CM01/01/1970**
Hanley, Miss A, BA, Student, City University.
[10027271]   07/10/2013   **ME**
Hanlon, Ms C, BA (Hons) MSc (Econ) MCLIP,
[54642]   05/02/1997   **CM21/11/2001**
Hanlon, Mrs C L, BA (Hons) MCLIP, Knowledge Officer, Veale Wasbrough Vizards, Bristol.
[49853]   07/01/1994   **CM26/11/1997**
Hanlon, Mrs S M, BComm PGCE MA, Senior Lecturer, Northumbria University.
[48119]   09/11/1992   **ME**
Hanna, Miss D A, Information Officer, Law Society of Northern Ireland, Belfast.
[64228]   21/02/2005   **AF**
Hanna, Mrs E E, BA, Area Manager, Libraries NI.
[41155]   14/10/1987   **ME**
Hannaford, Mrs L E, BA (Hons) DipLib, Faculty Librarian, University for the Creative Arts, Rochester.
[45785]   28/05/1991   **ME**
Hannagan, Ms G, Student, University of Sheffield.
[10035195]   29/10/2014   **ME**
Hannah, Miss I, MCLIP, Retired.
[6270]   29/03/1950   **CM01/01/1964**
Hannah, Mrs J, BA (Hons) DipILM MCLIP, Unwaged.
[50499]   22/08/1994   **CM25/07/2001**
Hannah, Mr T, BA (Hons) MCLIP, Learning Centre Facilitator, Swansea College Learning Centre.
[61126]   19/02/2002   **CM23/06/2004**
Hanney, Mrs J B, BSc MSc DIC MCLIP, Employment unknown.
[60375]   14/11/1977   **CM04/10/1982**
Hanney, Ms P M G, BA (Hons) MA, Library Res. Manager, Stafford College.
[50117]   05/04/1994   **ME**
Hannington, Mrs P E, MCLIP, Law & Legal Information Lib. (Freelance).
[17098]   28/09/1967   **CM04/09/1972**
Hannon, Mrs E, Head of Main Issue Desk, UCL.
[62845]   06/11/2003   **ME**
Hannon, Mr M S M, MA DipLSc FRSA MCLIP, Retired.
[6277]   02/10/1969   **CM01/01/1972**
Hanrahan, Miss F M, DipLib MCLIP, Co. Librarian, Wexford County Council.
[25296]   14/01/1976   **CM02/01/1986**
Hanratty, Miss N, BA Grad Dip, Student, Dublin Business School.
[10031796]   04/10/2013   **ME**

Hans, Mrs K A, BSc (Hons) MA MCLIP, School Librarian, St Martin-in-the-Fields High School, London.
[51849]   13/07/1995   **CM21/11/2001**
Hansen, Miss M K H, Student, University of Brighton.
[10034150]   10/06/2014   **ME**
Hanson, Mr D T, BA DipLib MCLIP, Librarian, Bethnal Green Tech. Centre, London.
[22681]   11/08/1974   **CM03/02/1978**
Haran, Mr R A, Account Knowledge Executive, Ernst & Young.
[61785]   07/11/2002   **ME**
Harbour, Mrs C L, MA MCLIP, Subject Librarian: Business, Health & Education, Anglia Ruskin University.
[64820]   20/07/2005   **CM18/01/2012**
Harbour, Miss J, BSc (Hons) MCLIP, Health Information Scientist, NHS Quality Improvement, Scotland.
[62792]   22/10/2003   **CM25/01/2011**
Harcup-McLean, Mrs M R, MA, Student, Manchester Metropolitan University.
[10032465]   06/12/2013   **ME**
Harcus, Ms J, BA (Hons) MA, Library & Information Services Officer, Lucy Cavendish College, University of Cambridge.
[10006760]   17/12/2007   **ME**
Harden, Mr R, BA MCLIP, Retired.
[6293]   12/10/1967   **CM01/01/1971**
Harden, Mrs S K, BA MCLIP, Retired.
[20766]   23/06/1973   **CM17/09/1976**
Hardie, Mrs M C, MA,
[10006952]   17/12/2007   **ME**
Harding, Ms A, MA DipLib MCLIP, Self-employed, Trainer, Specialisms: children's & young people's reading; children's libraries; school libraries.
[30176]   15/01/1979   **CM15/01/1981**
Harding, Mrs A C, MA MSc, Librarian, Ornithology & Rothschild Library, Natural History Museum, Tring.
[35815]   11/01/1983   **CM11/11/1986**
Harding, Ms A R, BA (Hons) MLib MCLIP, Head of Library and Learning Resources: Carmarthen And Lampeter, Universtiy of Wales, Trinity Saint David.
[48278]   20/11/1992   **CM23/07/1997**
Harding, Mr G L, MCLIP, Life Member.
[6304]   14/02/1947   **CM01/01/1962**
Harding, Miss L, Assistant Librarian, LRC, Treloar College, Alton.
[10016928]   14/10/1997   **ME**
Harding, Mrs R, BA (Hons) MA MCLIP, Head Librarian and Archivist, The King's School, Chester.
[58616]   13/04/2000   **CM15/07/2014**
Harding, Ms S, BA (Hons), Librarian, Kirklees Council.
[10009761]   09/06/2008   **ME**
Hardley, Ms E, BA (Hons) FPSNZ AFIAP, Psychology and Forensic Science Subject Librarian, University of Auckland, New Zealand.
[10001847]   08/01/1978   **CM19/02/1981**
Hardman, Mrs K M, Resources Librarian, Bury College.
[62472]   08/07/2003   **ME**
Hardman, Mr S J, BSc (Econ), Library Services Manager., Civic Centre City & County Swansea, Swansea.
[59488]   09/04/2001   **ME**
Hards, Mrs J E, BLib MCLIP, Content Manage. Librarian, CIPD, London.
[27328]   18/02/1977   **CM30/04/1980**
Hards, Mrs S A, Library Assistant, Basildon Health Library.
[10023386]   09/07/2013   **AF**
Hardy, Mrs A D, MCLIP, Retired.
[25694]   12/02/1959   **CM24/01/1979**

Hardy, Dr G C, MChem PhD MA MCLIP FHEA, Information Specialist, Aston University, Birmingham.
[62959]   25/11/2003   RV20/06/2014   **CM05/05/2010**
Hardy, Miss J E, MSc MCLIP, Life Member.
[6326]   28/09/1959   **CM01/01/1965**
Hare, Mrs C E, BA PGCE MCLIP, Retired.
[6333]   01/10/1971   **CM03/09/1975**
Hare, Mr G, OBE MCLIP, Retired.
[6335]   31/08/1954   **CM01/01/1960**
Hare, Miss K L, BA (Hons) MCLIP, Group Manager, Southway Library, Plymouth.
[65378]   06/01/2006   **CM11/11/2009**
Hare, Ms R, BA (Hons),
[10020141]   09/11/2011   **ME**
Harffy, Mrs M T, Student, Northumbria University.
[10019006]   10/12/2013   **ME**
Hargest, Mrs S, BA (Hons) PgDipILM, Serv. Development Co-ordinator Children and Families, Worcestershire County Council.
[61639]   07/10/2002   **ME**
Hargreaves, Mrs A, BSc (Hons) MA, KM Manager, Towers Watson, Surrey.
[58551]   01/04/2000   **ME**
Hargreaves, Ms C, Systems Supp. Librarian, Oxford University, Bodleian Digital Lib Systems & Services.
[46737]   16/01/1992   **ME**
Hargreaves, Mr J A, BA FCLIP, Life Member.
[6347]   17/05/1941   **FE01/01/1958**
Hargreaves, Mr J B G, BA (Hons), Assistant Librarian Law, University of Bristol.
[64241]   22/02/2005   **ME**
Harket, Mrs E J, Retired as Deputy Co-ordinator, Study Centre, Orpington College, Kent.
[47079]   15/04/1992   **ME**
Harkness, Mrs C L, ACLIP, Customer Care Lib. Assit., Newcastle College, Newcastle.
[10015657]   08/01/2010   **ACL20/06/2012**
Harland, Miss E A, BA MA DipLib, Unwaged – Career Break.
[32291]   06/03/1980   **CM05/03/1982**
Harley, Mrs C J, MCLIP, Retired.
[6359]   29/03/1961   **CM01/01/1969**
Harley, Mrs W B, BA (Hons) MCLIP, Retired.
[24312]   01/01/1952   **CM29/09/1977**
Harling, Mrs A M, LLB (Hons) MSc, Senior Assistant Librarian, Calderdale College, Halifax.
[48481]   21/01/1993   **ME**
Harling, Mr B S C, CertEd MCLIP, Retired.
[6362]   05/03/1958   **CM24/09/1974**
Harling, Mr C, MCLIP, Library Development Serives Manager.
[10018315]   26/10/1978   **CM14/11/1984**
Harman, Mr C K, BA DipLib MCLIP, Branch Manager: Kirkham Library, Lancashire County Libraries.
[39040]   27/10/1985   **CM15/02/1989**
Harman, Ms C M, BSc MSc,
[58900]   02/10/2000   **ME**
Harman, Lady E J, MA, Life Member.
[6363]   13/10/1959   **ME**
Harper, Mrs A J, BSc (Hons) MScEcon, Information & Research Consultant.
[10001559]   26/02/2007   **ME**
Harper, Mrs P, BA (Hons) PRINCE 2, Project Manager, BHP Management.
[10007992]   03/03/2008   **ME**
Harper, Miss P, Student, Aberystwyth University.
[10027303]   16/09/2014   **ME**

Harper, Mrs S M, ACLIP, Serv. Development Librarian, Dudley Library, Dudley.
[10019774]   08/09/2011   **ACL09/07/2013**

Harradence, Mrs M, ACLIP, LRA., Sir George Monoux College., London.
[10020720]   29/03/2012   **ACL15/07/2014**

Harries, Mrs C W, MA MEd, Community Librarian, Llangollen L.
[59522]   24/04/2001   **ME**

Harrington, Mrs A B, MCLIP, Retired.
[6390]   22/11/1940   **CM01/01/1946**

Harrington, Mrs B M, BA MCLIP, Retired.
[6393]   23/01/1968   **CM01/01/1971**

Harrington, Ms E, BA MA HDip in Ed HDip in ILS, Library Assistant, University College Cork.
[10021454]   17/08/2012   **ME**

Harrington, Mrs E S, Library & Information Assistant, Queen Victoria Hospital.
[10021560]   30/08/2012   **ME**

Harrington, Mrs F A, MCLIP RLIANZA, Librarian, Southern District Health Board, Southland Hospital, New Zealand.
[10012718]   08/03/1963   **CM01/07/1991**

Harrington, Mrs H L, BSc (Hons) MSc FHEA, Assistant Librarian, Harrow School.
[57632]   04/06/1999   **ME**

Harris, Miss A M, MBChB MSc MCLIP, Senior Library Assistant, Research and Learning Support, Andersonian Library, University of Strathclyde.
[49550]   09/11/1993   **CM16/07/2003**

Harris, Mrs C, BMus MA, Information Services Librarian, Lancashire Care NHS Foundation Trust.
[61798]   13/11/2002   **ME**

Harris, Miss E L, BA MCLIP, Library Development Officer, Leek Library, Staffordshire County Council.
[30429]   25/01/1979   **CM17/10/1985**

Harris, Mrs E L, MCLIP, Subject Librarian, University of Wales, Trinity Saint David Carmarthen Campus.
[36925]   18/01/1984   **CM13/06/2007**

Harris, Mr F A, HonFCLIP, Hon. Fellow.
[62815]   23/10/2003   **HFE23/10/2003**

Harris, Mrs G, BA MA, Learning Resources Adviser, Colchester Institute Library, Essex.
[10016427]   24/03/2010   **ME**

Harris, Ms G R, MA MCLIP, Head of Sch. L. Serv., London Borough of Tower Hamlets.
[26404]   12/10/1976   **CM20/01/1981**

Harris, Mrs J, BA, Librarian & Extended Essay Co-ordinator, King Edwards School.
[10006492]   20/09/1999   **ME**

Harris, Mrs J A, BA DipLib MCLIP, Academic Liaison Librarian, Bournemouth University.
[30838]   02/05/1979   **CM11/12/1981**

Harris, Mrs J B A, BSc DipLib MCLIP, Information Officer, The Moray Council, Elgin.
[29197]   29/03/1978   **CM28/03/1980**

Harris, Mrs J C, DES NAG Business/Information Manager, Ministry of Defence.
[10034531]   18/07/2014   **ME**

Harris, Mr J K, MSc MCLIP,
[51418]   10/02/1995   **CM01/04/2002**

Harris, Mrs K A, Resource Centre Manager, William Farr C. of E. Comprehensive School, Lincoln.
[10019485]   08/07/2011   **ME**

Harris, Mrs L I P, MA DipILS MCLIP, Cataloguer, Coutts Information, Serv., Ingram Content Group.
[51280]   19/12/1994   **CM21/01/1998**

Harris, Mrs L J, BSc,
[10019219]   13/08/2013   **ME**

Harris, Mr L K, BA Dip Lib MA FCLIP, L. Manager, The Queen Elizabeth Hospital, SA Health Library Service, Adelaide, Australia.
[40255]   16/11/1986   **FE18/09/2003**

Harris, Miss L M, MA MLib MCLIP, Subject Advisor, University of Birmingham.
[40291]   15/01/1987   **CM22/04/1992**

Harris, Ms M, BA DipLib MCLIP, Deputy Head of L. & Information Serv., Department of Work and Pensions, London.
[33536]   19/01/1981   **CM02/06/1987**

Harris, Mrs M, MCLIP, Information and Skills Development Manager, Somerset CC Library Service.
[33377]   01/11/1980   **CM27/02/1984**

Harris, Miss M P, BMus, Senior Library Assistant, Goldsmiths, University of London.
[10019779]   13/09/2011   **ME**

Harris, Mr P, BSc MRSC FCLIP, Retired.
[60380]   27/05/1969   **FE03/11/1981**

Harris, Miss R M, BA MCLIP, Life Member.
[6415]   07/02/1965   **CM01/01/1967**

Harris, Ms S, BA MA MCLIP, Assistant Librarian, The Grammar School at Leeds, Leeds.
[39052]   30/10/1985   **CM14/03/1990**

Harris, Miss S, MA DipLib MCLIP, InfManager, Campbell Reith, London.
[28311]   07/11/1977   **CM25/06/1981**

Harris, Miss S, BsocSC, Library Assistant, Aberystwyth University.
[10031795]   04/10/2013   **ME**

Harris, Mr S, MA (Hons) MSc MCLIP, Senior Lib, Penicuik Library, Midlothian Council.
[51281]   19/12/1994   **CM23/07/1997**

Harris, Mrs S E, BLib MCLIP, Sch. Lib.
[38909]   15/10/1985   **CM22/05/1996**

Harris, Ms S E L, MA (Oxon), NHS Healthcare Library Assistant.
[10019405]   24/06/2011   **AF**

Harris, Ms V, BA (Hons), Student.
[10002051]   14/01/2009   **ME**

Harrison, Mrs A A M, Retired.
[5505]   06/10/1969   **CM01/01/1973**

Harrison, Mrs A J, BA, Retired.
[19576]   16/11/1972   **CM14/10/1975**

Harrison, Mrs A P, BSc MSc MCLIP,
[37875]   05/11/1984   **CM15/08/1989**

Harrison, Prof C T, FRSA MIMgt MCLIP, Life Member.
[6424]   01/09/1958   **CM01/01/1965**

Harrison, Miss F, BA, eSystems Team Manager., Nottingham Trent University.
[10020511]   22/02/2012   **ME**

Harrison, Mrs F A, BA (Hons) MPhil MCLIP, Principal Librarian, West Berkshire Council.
[38090]   08/01/1985   **CM01/04/2002**

Harrison, Ms F C, BA MA, Retired.
[36176]   03/07/1983   **ME**

Harrison, Dr J, BA (Hons) Dip PhD, Senior Lecturer, Department of Information Science, Loughborough University.
[10022463]   05/03/2013   **ME**

Harrison, Miss J, BA (Hons), Student, Northumbria University.
[10031572]   11/12/2013   **ME**

Harrison, Mrs J A, BA MCLIP, Part-time Learning Resources Assistant, Birmingham Metropolitan College.
[33454]   09/01/1981   **CM10/10/1984**

Harrison, Mr J A, MA MCLIP, Rare Books Librarian, Senate House
Librarian., London.
[55902] 15/12/1997 **CM10/07/2009**

Harrison, Ms J K, BA DipLib MCLIP, Retired.
[6437] 06/01/1967 **CM01/01/1969**

Harrison, Mrs J M, Library Assistant, Hampshire County Council,
Stubbington L.
[54186] 06/11/1996 **AF**

Harrison, Mrs K, BA DipLib MCLIP, Area Manager, Library and
Information Centres, Kirklees Council.
[39198] 06/01/1986 **CM15/05/1989**

Harrison, Miss K J, BA (Hons) MCLIP, Career Break.
[51091] 14/11/1994 **CM17/11/1999**

Harrison, Mrs L E, BSCS MCLIP, Librarian, Bedford Sch.
[64363] 14/03/2005 **CM07/07/2010**

Harrison, Mrs M M, MA MCLIP, Retired.
[10834] 03/04/1965 **CM01/01/1970**

Harrison, Dr N A, BSc PhD DipLib MCLIP, Information Sci.,
[41657] 09/02/1988 **CM18/11/1992**

Harrison, Mrs N J, BSc PgDip, Technical Librarian.
[10008282] 19/03/2008 **ME**

Harrison, Mrs P A, MCLIP, LRC Manager, Driffield School, Driffield.
[10001083] 12/01/2007 **CM16/05/2012**

Harrison, Ms R E J, BA (Hons) MA, Team Leader: Education and
Research Support, Central Library, Imperial College, London.
[55953] 19/12/1997 **ME**

Harrison, Mr S, MA MCLIP, Manager, Tech Serv & Sys., Holmesglen
Learning Commons, Australia.
[22724] 02/09/1974 **CM20/01/1977**

Harrison, Mrs S, BA (Hons), Medical Librarian, Tameside & Glossop
NHS Trust, Ashton-U-Lyne.
[58450] 15/02/2000 **ME**

Harrison, Mrs S J, BA DipLib MCLIP, Principal Library Adviser, School
Lib. Serv., Essex Education Services, Essex County Council.
[40077] 17/10/1986 **CM14/08/1991**

Harrison- Doyle, Mr B, Quality Information Officer, Methodist Homes
[10033096] 10/02/2014 **ME**

Harriss, Ms E, MA MSc MCLIP, Knowledge Centre Manager and
Outreach Librarian, Bodleian Health Care Library, Oxford.
[10010505] 30/07/2008 **CM14/12/2012**

Harriss, Ms R, BA DipLib MCLIP, Community Librarian, Norfolk Library
& Information Serv.
[36853] 01/01/1984 **CM05/05/1987**

Harrity, Mrs S, MBE BA BPhil, Cert. of Merit.
[50583] 22/09/1994 **ME**

Harrop, Miss D, BA, Student.
[65912] 03/07/2006 **ME**

Harrop, Mr P, BA DipLib MCLIP, Unemployed.
[35861] 03/02/1983 **CM04/08/1987**

Harrow, Mr A J, MA DipLib MCLIP, Retired.
[6461] 10/03/1958 **CM18/01/1989**

Hart, Mr B, MCLIP, Life Member.
[6463] 21/03/1948 **CM01/01/1959**

Hart, Mrs C, BA (Hons) DipLIS MCLIP, Learning Centre Team Leader,
Inverness College.
[45790] 31/05/1991 **RV**16/01/2014 **CM20/09/1995**

Hart, Mr D R, MA MCLIP, Service Delivery Librarian, University of
Dundee.
[28582] 28/12/1977 **CM17/07/1981**

Hart, Miss E M, BA MCLIP, Retired.
[6465] 26/09/1966 **CM01/01/1970**

Hart, Mrs H M, LLB LLM ACLIP, Knowledge Management Lawyer,
LexisNexis UK.
[10021164] 14/06/2012 **ACL20/02/2014**

Hart, Ms K, LLB MSc, Head of Res. & L., Hogan Lovells International
LLP, London.
[65454] 24/02/2006 **ME**

Hart, Ms S, MA MCLIP, Library & Digital Communications Manager,
British Assoc. of Psychotherapists.
[50375] 07/07/1994 **CM06/04/2005**

Hart, Mrs S, MCLIP, Library Manager., Kimbolton School, Kimbolton,
Huntingdon, Cambs.
[26916] 17/12/1976 **CM09/08/1979**

Harte, Mrs K, BA (Hons) MA MCLIP, Development Lib. Communities,
Sneinton Lib, Nottingham.
[48149] 11/11/1992 **CM12/03/2003**

Hartiss, Miss R, BA (Hons) MSc (Dist.) AF HEA, Academic Support
Librarian, University of Greenwich.
[10020684] 26/03/2012 **ME**

Hartley, Ms C, BSc (Hons) PgDipLIS MCLIP, Not currently employed.
[10005513] 11/11/1992 **CM19/03/1997**

Hartley, Mr C M, MA FCLIP, Life Member.
[6486] 10/10/1946 **FE01/01/1958**

Hartley, Miss H M, Admin. Officer, Department for Work & Pensions,
Leeds.
[44769] 14/11/1990 **ME**

Hartley, Prof R J, BSc MLib FCLIP, Emeritus Professor of Information
Science, Manchester Metropolitan University.
[6495] 11/01/1972 **FE01/04/2002**

Hartnup, Dr K, MA (Hons) MSc PhD, Student, University of Strathclyde.
[66124] 01/10/2006 **ME**

Hartshorne, Mr D I, BA DipLib MCLIP, College Librarian, Harrogate
College, Harrogate.
[39055] 31/10/1985 **CM15/03/1989**

Hartshorne, Mr S, BA (Hons) MA, Information and Enquiry Officer,
Bolton Metropolitan Borough Council, Central Library.
[54464] 18/12/1996 **CM07/09/2005**

Hartwell, Mr A, BSc Econ (Hons) LLB MSc, Student.
[63727] 03/09/2004 **ME**

Harty, Ms J, MA PhD, Student, Robert Gordon University.
[10027335] 18/06/2014 **ME**

Harvey, Miss A, LLB, Head of Library & Learning Resources., Swansea
Metropolitan University.
[37634] 14/10/1984 **ME**

Harvey, Mr A P, MCLIP, Retired.
[20873] 07/08/1973 **CM26/11/1982**

Harvey, Mr C, BA PGCE DipCG, Library, Bishop Thomas Grant Sch.
[64702] 01/06/2005 **ME**

Harvey, Mrs G, BSc (Hons) MCLIP, Divisional Manager of Operations,
London Borough of Barnet.
[26550] 01/10/1976 **CM30/11/1979**

Harvey, Mrs J A, MA DipLib MCLIP, Support Serv. Librarian, East
Ayrshire Council.
[29897] 10/10/1978 **CM28/10/1981**

Harvey, Mr M N, BA MA,
[10016196] 23/02/2010 **ME**

Harvey, Mr N, BA (Hons) MCLIP, Community Prog. Officer, London
Borough of Haringey.
[59408] 05/03/2001 **CM15/05/2002**

Harvey, Mr P M, BA (Hons) MA MCLIP, Head of Information
Management & Information Assurance, HMGCC.
[55271] 11/09/1997 **CM21/11/2001**

Harvey, Mr R A M, MA MCLIP, Retired.
[6518] 10/07/1967 **CM01/01/1970**

Harvey, Mr S, Learning Recources Service Manager, Hertford Regional
College.
[10011720] 13/07/2012 **ME**

Harvey, Mrs S M, MBE BA MCLIP, Retired.
[6521]   22/01/1958   **CM01/01/1962**
Harvey, Mrs T R, BSc MCLIP, ICT Librarian, Rutland County Council.
[56046]   30/01/1998   **CM20/11/2002**
Harvey, Mrs V, Admin. /Library Assistant, Buckley Library, Flintshire.
[10022372]   19/02/2013   **AF**
Harvey-Brown, Mrs J, MA MCLIP, Team Librarian, Bracknell Forest.
[33349]   07/11/1980   **CM23/06/1986**
Harwood, Mrs C A, PgDipLib, Team Librarian, Oxfordshire County
Council, Central Library.
[33006]   01/10/1980   **ME**
Harwood, Ms C L, BA, Harwood, Carla, BA(Hons). MLIS student at
Rutgers University, NJ, USA. Fulbright Awardee 2014-15. Joined
28/02/2013.
[10022361]   19/02/2013   **ME**
Harwood, Mrs K F, Library Assistant, Woodgreen School.
[37507]   03/10/1984   **ME**
Hasan, Mr A, BA (MCLIP submitted app. 24/8), Subject Librarian:
Arabic, Politics, Security Studies. University of Exeter.
[10022757]   16/04/2013   **ME**
Hasan, Ms B, MA (Hons) MSc (Econ), Information Specialist, FCO.,
London.
[59254]   18/01/2001   **ME**
Hasker, Mr N A, LLB MCLIP, Retired.
[6529]   17/02/1969   **CM01/01/1971**
Haskins, Mr W T, BSc, Information Specialist, CIMA, London.
[59384]   27/02/2001   **ME**
Haslam-Dockerty, Mrs S, Student, Manchester Metropolitan University.
[65192]   17/11/2005   **ME**
Hasler, Mrs E A, BSc (Econ) (Hons) MCLIP, Information Specialist,
National Collaborating Centre for Cancer, Cardiff.
[58981]   16/10/2000   **CM01/06/2005**
Hasler, Mr K M P, BA (Hons), Library Assistant/Driver, Hertfordshire
County Council.
[10035312]   07/10/2014   **ME**
Hassall, Mrs S, BA (Hons) DipILS, Librarian, Anthony Collins Solicitors
LLP, Birmingham.
[55426]   13/10/1997   **ME**
Hassan, Dr L, PhD,
[10034563]   01/10/2014   **ME**
Hastie, Mrs M E, MCLIP, Head of Learning Res. &Information Centr.,
Horndean Tech. College, Hants.
[5083]   18/01/1971   **CM20/12/1974**
Hastie, Miss S E, BA, Learning Centre Manager, Ashmole School,
Southgate.
[10016043]   26/09/2003   **ME**
Hateley, Miss D M, BSc (Econ), Senior Librarian Priority Groups,
Warwickshire County Council.
[57732]   13/07/1999   **ME**
Hathaway, Ms H M, MA DipLib ILTM, Faculty Team Manager, Sci.,
University of Reading L.
[6542]   01/01/1972   **ME**
Hatton, Dr P H S, PhD MA DipLib MCLIP, Retired.
[24693]   07/10/1975   **CM12/05/1980**
Hauxwell, Mrs H, BA (Hons) MA MSC MCLIP, Resource Centre
Manager, Gloucester Diocese.
[63652]   09/08/2004   **RV22/08/2012**   **CM21/05/2008**
Havard, Mrs L, MLS, Head of Academic Support, Information Services
and Systems, Swansea University.
[59808]   14/05/2001   **ME**
Haward, Mrs J, MCLIP, L. Manager /Coordinator, Richard Lander
School, Cornwall. Retired.
[6554]   29/01/1970   **CM15/03/1974**

Hawes, Mrs B M, MCLIP, Life Member.
[6555]   12/05/1948   **CM01/01/1953**
Hawes, Mr G A, MA (Hons) MPhil, Assistant Academic Liaison
Librarian, University of St Andrews, St Andrews.
[10013338]   16/04/2009   **ME**
Hawke, Mrs J C, MCLIP, L. Supervisor, Pettswood Library, London
Borough of Bromley.
[10006676]   06/03/1995   **CM06/05/2009**
Hawke, Mrs S M, BEd MSc (ECON) ILS MCLIP, Digital Literacy
Librarian, Bath Spa University.
[64376]   14/03/2005   **CM14/10/2011**
Hawker, Ms L, MCLIP, Librarian, Barnet Enfield and Haringey Mental
Health Trust.
[10011473]   21/10/2008   **CM07/09/2011**
Hawker, Mrs S E, BSc (Hons) MSc MCLIP, Self-employed.
[55453]   13/10/1997   **CM12/03/2003**
Hawker, Miss Z P, BA (Hons) MSc, Librarian, Manchester High School
for Girls.
[64915]   16/09/2005   **ME**
Hawkes, Miss C J, MCLIP, E-Resources and Clinical Support Librarian,
Croydon Health Services Library.
[10011791]   13/11/2008   **CM13/05/2014**
Hawkes, Mrs E A, MA MCLIP, Res. Serv. Manager EME, Reed Smith,
London.
[24778]   03/10/1975   **CM01/03/1978**
Hawkes, Mrs J, ACLIP, Library Assistant, Queen Mary's College,
Basingstoke.
[10017968]   28/10/2010   **ACL20/02/2014**
Hawkey-Edwards, Ms S E M, MSc PgDip, Senior Learning
Development Officer, West Dunbartonshire Libraries and Cultural
Services.
[10001304]   16/09/2003   **ME**
Hawkins, Mrs A M, BA DipLib MCLIP, Assistant Librarian, Brooklands
College.
[10006328]   29/10/1980   **CM28/01/1983**
Hawkins, Mrs J M, BA DipLib MCLIP, Library Assistant, Winstanley
College, Billinge, Lancs.
[35808]   17/01/1983   **CM23/01/1986**
Hawkins, Ms S, BA BPhil, Library Manager, Hounslow Library.
[10020455]   20/02/2012   **ME**
Hawkins, Miss Y, BSc (Hons) Grad Dip, Assistant Librarian –
Bibliographic & E-Services, Midlothian Council.
[10017876]   21/10/2010   **ME**
Hawkyard, Mrs L A, Head Librarian, Walker Morris, Leeds.
[56126]   03/03/1998   **ME**
Hawley, Mr G J, BA (Hons) MSc MCLIP, General Collections Manager,
National Library of Scotland, Edinburgh.
[59448]   30/03/2001   **CM01/02/2006**
Hawley, Miss R E, BA MA, Team Librarian, Nottingham City Council.
[10006540]   07/11/2007   **ME**
Haworth, Mrs N A, BA (Hons) PgDip,
[61871]   25/11/2002   **ME**
Hawthorn, Mr T L, BSc (Econ), Senior Library Assistant, Haddon
Library of Archaeology and Anthropology, University of Cambridge.
[53470]   01/07/1996   **ME**
Hawton, Miss S F M, BA, Lib. Assistant, Goldsmiths College Library,
University of London.
[10012513]   23/02/2009   **AF**
Hay, Mrs C, MCLIP, Retired Jan 2012 – (Formerly Chartered Librarian at
Birmingham Central Library, Arts, languages & Literature Dept).
[10001138]   05/01/1976   **CM19/09/1978**
Hay, Ms K J, BA MLIS, Knowledge Manager, The Medical Defence
Union, London.
[66151]   04/10/2006   **ME**

Hayball, Miss S R, BA MCLIP, Retired.
[20613]   30/04/1973   CM20/07/1976
Hayden, Mrs A L C, MA MA, School Librarian, Royal Blind School,
Edinburgh.
[60977]   23/01/2002   ME
Haydock, Mr I, MCLIP, L. Systems Manager, Keele University.
[40488]   12/02/1987   CM12/09/1990
Hayes, Ms B, BA (Hons) MSc MA DipILM MCLIP, Programme Lead L.
Serv., 5 Borough Partnership NHS Foundation Trust, Warrington.
[54004]   17/10/1996   CM23/01/2002
Hayes, Miss B E, BA, School Librarian.
[28827]   03/02/1978   CM26/01/1983
Hayes, Mr D C, BA (Hons) DipLib,
[36143]   01/07/1983   ME
Hayes, Miss E, MA MCLIP, Learning Resource Centre Manager, The
Carlton Academy, Nottingham.
[62905]   18/11/2003   CM13/06/2007
Hayes, Ms L, Student, Aberystwyth University.
[65001]   06/10/2005   ME
Hayes, Mr M A, DipLib MCLIP, County Local Studies Librarian, West
Sussex CC Library Service, Worthing.
[33299]   27/10/1980   CM23/11/1982
Hayes, Mrs R E, BA MCLIP, Part-time Information Officer (Temporary),
Social Care Institute for Excellence (SCIE).
[5292]   05/10/1971   CM05/09/1975
Hayes, Miss V J,
[10015012]   06/10/2009   ME
Hayet, Ms M, MCLIP, Reg. Account Manager, RCUK SSC Ltd, Swindon.
[60148]   15/08/1988   CM20/12/1993
Hay-Gibson, Dr N V, BA MA MSc PhD, Lbrarian.
[65627]   14/03/2006   ME
Hayhurst, Mr G L, BA FCLIP, Life Member.
[6600]   05/01/1954   FE01/01/1960
Hayler, Mr W E F, MCLIP, Retired.
[6604]   01/01/1950   CM01/01/1963
Hayles, Miss J M, BA MCLIP, Assistant Director Customer Services,
Queen Mary University of London.
[25302]   13/01/1976   CM07/02/1979
Hayman, Ms A, MA,
[10034293]   01/07/2014   ME
Haynes, Ms E, BA DipLib, Information & Knowledge Manager.,
Metropolitan Police Serv., London.
[44464]   10/10/1990   ME
Haynes, Miss E M, BSc BA MCLIP, Retired.
[6606]   13/09/1969   CM11/11/1983
Haynes, Mrs H J, BA (Hons) MSc, Information & Content Librarian,
Lowestoft Central Library.
[10012360]   05/02/2009   ME
Haynes, Ms J A,
[10032568]   17/12/2013   ME
Haynes, Mr J D, MSc FCLIP, Director, Aspire Squared Ltd.
[33404]   24/11/1980   FE01/04/2002
Haynes, Mrs W H, MA, Currently not working in library.
[62998]   26/11/2003   ME
Haysman, Miss W F, MSc BH MCLIP, Retired.
[6607]   26/08/1969   CM16/08/1973
Haysom, Mrs D, BA MCLIP, Academic Liaison Librarian, University of
Bedfordshire.
[33869]   07/04/1981   CM17/10/1985
Hayward, Mrs A E, BA MSc (Econ) MCLIP, Community Services
Librarian, Bracknell cent lib, Berkshire.
[55399]   09/10/1997   CM23/01/2002

Hayward, Mr K, BA MCLIP, Librarian, Cent. Reference Library,
Hampshire County Council.
[6614]   24/01/1965   CM01/01/1967
Hayward, Miss L D, BA (Hons), Bibl. Librarian, Peters Bookselling
Serv., Birmingham.
[62254]   02/04/2003   ME
Haywood, Mr E J, MCLIP, Life Member.
[6621]   28/03/1941   CM01/01/1956
Haywood, Miss G, BA MCLIP, Librarian, Thames Water, Reading.
[30764]   23/04/1979   CM06/04/1984
Haywood, Mr G C, MCLIP, Retired.
[21854]   14/02/1974   CM13/03/1978
Haywood, Mrs R J, BA MCLIP, Learning resources Centre Manager,
Kimberley School Nottingham.
[24596]   08/10/1975   CM20/09/1979
Hayworth, Mr R A, MA MPhil DipILS MCLIP, Serials & Electronic
Resources Manager, University of Aberdeen.
[55985]   08/01/1998   CM17/01/2001
Hazle, Mrs L, BA (Hons), Student, Aberystwyth University.
[10017417]   18/08/2010   ME
Hazlehurst, Mrs D J, BSc Econ (Hons), Unemployed.
[62504]   29/07/2003   ME
Hazlewood, Mrs M, BA (Hons) MA MCLIP, Team Librarian,
Bournemouth & Poole College.
[51456]   27/02/1995   CM20/11/2002
Head, Mrs A L, MSc BA MCLIP,
[6631]   13/03/1967   CM05/07/1976
Head, Mr P A, FRSA MCLIP, Retired.
[6634]   01/01/1963   CM01/01/1968
Head, Mrs S R, MCLIP, Life Member.
[6636]   06/03/1950   CM01/01/1956
Heads, Mrs L M, BA MCLIP, Subject Librarian, Hull College.
[31540]   24/10/1979   CM18/10/1982
Healey, Mr T B, BA MA, Unwaged.
[10005240]   29/06/2007   ME
Healy, Mr J, BA (Hons) MA MCLIP, Library Customer Services Officer,
Chipping Barnet Library.
[10020300]   11/01/2012   CM11/04/2013
Healy, Ms L, Student.
[10020626]   13/03/2012   ME
Heaney, Mrs A G, BA (Hons) Dip lib, Team Leader: Community
Libraries.
[10016185]   30/01/1980   ME
Heaney, Mr M, MA FCLIP, Retired.
[22383]   08/04/1974   FE15/03/2000
Heap, Ms A M, BA MCLIP, Freelance.
[36380]   03/10/1983   CM04/10/1988
Heard, Ms S C, Ba (Hons) PGCE MCLIP, Team Librarian, Bedford
Central Library.
[10011444]   21/10/2008   CM05/05/2010
Heard, Mr S C A, BA (Hons) MLib, Librarian, Acquisitions &
Cataloguing, National Maritime Museum, London.
[64112]   17/01/2005   ME
Hearnden, Miss K, BA (Hons), Student, University Campus Suffolk.
[10035162]   22/09/2014   ME
Heaslip, Ms M E, BA MLS, Retired.
[10016880]   01/06/2010   ME
Heath, Miss A K, ACLIP,
[10014346]   10/07/2009   ACL14/03/2012
Heath, Mrs A K E, BA (Hons) MSc, Freelance Information Specialist,
BMJ Publishing Group.
[46619]   26/11/1991   ME
Heath, Mrs C S, BA MCLIP, Subject Librarian, Croydon College.
[28678]   16/12/1977   CM23/11/1982

Heath, Mr D J, Learning Resource Assistant, Coleg Llandrillo Cymru.
[10022135]   08/01/2013   **ME**
Heath, Ms E, MA, Information Executive (LIS Web Services), ICAEW.
[10008010]   04/03/2008   **ME**
Heath, Mrs G M, BA MCLIP, Adult Literacy Tutor, SCOLA, Sutton.
[29824]   17/10/1978   **CM31/07/1984**
Heath, Mrs J M, BA (Hons), College Librarian, St Mary's College, Durham University.
[10017704]   19/10/1989   **ME**
Heath, Mrs N L, BA (Hons), School Librarian, Werneth School, Stockport.
[57503]   12/04/1999   **ME**
Heath, Mrs P L, Lib. Assistant, Cambridgeshire L. Serv., Cambridge.
[10016429]   24/03/2010   **ME**
Heath, Mrs P V, BA (Hons) ACLIP, Assistant Librarian, Anglo European College of Chiropractic Library, Bournemouth.
[10011321]   13/10/2008   **ACL19/08/2011**
Heath, Ms R B, MCLIP, Life Member.
[6664]   20/03/1952   **CM01/01/1956**
Heathcote, Ms K, BA DipLIS MCLIP, Service Delivery Manager, Tameside Metropolitan Borough Council.
[39691]   20/05/1986   **CM18/11/1998**
Heatley, Miss N L, BA DipLib PGCE MCLIP MIfL, Tutor, Hartlepool Adult Education.
[41497]   12/01/1988   **CM18/07/1990**
Heaton, Mrs B C, BA MCLIP, School Librarian, Weaverham High School, Cheshire.
[10001131]   11/01/1978   **CM11/01/1980**
Heaton, Mrs J A, MCLIP, Senior Child. Librarian, Borough Telford and Wrekin Council.
[28002]   05/10/1977   **CM22/09/1981**
Heaton, Mr J M, BA DipLib MCLIP, Operational Manager, Lifelong Learning, Library & Customer Services, Rotherham MBC.
[28236]   12/10/1977   **CM09/01/1981**
Heaton, Miss W, BA (Hons) MCLIP, Operations Manager, Wigan Leisure & Cult. Trust.
[28957]   16/01/1978   **CM19/07/1983**
Heaword, Ms R A, BA MSc MCLIP, Local Museum, Archeology Support Community Education.
[60381]   06/04/1977   **CM13/06/1978**
Hebron, Ms P E, BA (Hons) PgDipLIM PGCE, Senior Information Officer / Part-time lecturer, Coleg Llandrillo Cymru, Conwy.
[49437]   27/10/1993   **ME**
Hedgecock, Mrs C M, ACLIP, Librarian, Portland Comprehensive School, Worksop.
[64407]   15/03/2005   **ACL28/01/2009**
Hedges, Mr G, MCLIP HonFCLIP, Retired.
[22662]   02/08/1974   **HFE29/06/2005**
Heeks, Dr P D, PdD MA FCLIP, Retired.
[6685]   31/01/1941   **FE01/01/1959**
Heeks, Mrs S, BA (Hons), Student, Northumbria University.
[10027382]   16/09/2014   **ME**
Heffer, Mr C M, BA DipLib MCLIP, Customer Serv. Librarian, Beckenham Library, London Borough of Bromley.
[31857]   16/01/1980   **CM18/02/1983**
Heffernan, Mr R C, BA MCLIP, Assistant Librarian, The Institution of Civil Engineers, London.
[28586]   16/01/1978   **CM30/09/1987**
Hegarty, Mr R, BA HDip MLIS, Assistant Librarian, Homerton University Hospital NHS Foundation Trust.
[10027386]   15/09/2014   **ME**
Hegarty, Mr S M, BA (Hons), Student.
[10019725]   31/08/2011   **ME**

Hege, Mr R, Student, Universitaets Bibliothek Der Fu Berlin.
[10032655]   23/12/2013   **ME**
Hegenbarth, Mrs J A, BA (Hons) MA MCLIP, Academic Support Team Manager, University of Birmingham, Barnes Library, Medical School.
[51951]   17/08/1995   **CM17/11/1999**
Heidtmann, Mr R A, Student University of South Africa Pretoria.
[10032286]   13/11/2013   **ME**
Heinecke, Mr P M, BA MCLIP, Retired.
[24697]   06/10/1975   **CM12/10/1977**
Heinrich, Mrs M, BSc (Hons), School Librarian.
[10017050]   21/06/2010   **ME**
Heissig, Mr H N, BA FCLIP, Life Member.
[18764]   15/03/1955   **FE01/01/1965**
Hekim, Mr S, Library Assistant, Tower Hamlets Schools Library Service.
[10033336]   17/03/2014   **ME**
Helgesen, Ms J C, BA (Hons) MA MCLIP, Information Skills Librarian, UniversityEast Anglia, Norfolk.
[58859]   12/09/2000   **CM13/06/2007**
Hellen, Mrs R, MCLIP, Retired.
[8495]   04/04/1972   **CM03/07/1975**
Heller, Ms Z, MITI MCLIP DPSI, Retired.
[60382]   18/05/1972   **CM17/09/1979**
Helliwell, Miss C S, MCLIP BSc, Retired.
[21754]   12/01/1974   **CM13/02/1976**
Helliwell, Mrs J F, Retired.
[45903]   01/07/1991   **AF**
Hellon, Mrs C, BLS MCLIP, Career Break.
[33458]   01/01/1981   **CM10/06/1986**
Hellon, Mrs S J, BA DipLib MCLIP, Librarian, Ilkeston L. Derbys. County Council.
[36323]   01/10/1983   **CM29/01/1992**
Helm, Miss S V, BA MCLIP DipMS, Principal Learning & Development Officer, Dudley Public Library.
[29039]   13/03/1978   **CM30/09/1982**
Helsey, Mr M, L. Executive, BTs Department, House of Commons Library, London.
[10006752]   22/11/1984   **ME**
Hemming, Ms R, BA MusB (Hons) MSc, Head of L., University College School, Hampstead.
[55544]   17/10/1997   **ME**
Hemmings, Mr P M, BLib MCLIP, Central Library Manager, Birmingham City Council, Central Library.
[28314]   07/10/1977   **CM31/07/1980**
Hempshall, Mrs M C S J, L. Res. Co-ordinator (Vol.), Wycliffe Assoc. UK.
[52688]   17/11/1995   **ME**
Hemsley, Mr M K, BA (Hons), Head Librarian, Hampton School.
[61873]   25/11/2002   **ME**
Hemstock, Mr P A, Knowledge manager/Analyst.
[10022865]   30/04/2013   **AF**
Hemsworth, Miss C, BA (Hons) PgDip,
[10015233]   29/10/2009   **ME**
Hemus, Ms E, BA (Hons) PgDip, Information Officer, Linklaters, London.
[55559]   21/10/1997   **CM01/06/2005**
Henczel, Ms S M, BBUS MBUS, Owner & Principal Consultant, Infase Solution.
[10022178]   15/01/2013   **ME**
Henderson, Miss B, MCLIP, Life Member.
[6715]   13/03/1943   **CM01/01/1947**
Henderson, Mrs B E, DipArch (Hons), Learning Resources Manager, Trinity High School.
[10032398]   03/12/2013   **ME**
Henderson, Ms E, Student, University of Cambridge.
[10035753]   **ME**

Henderson, Mrs E A, Rare Books Librarian St Andrews University.
[59947]   09/11/2001   ME
Henderson, Ms E F, BA DipLib MCLIP, Locality Manager, Norfolk L. &
Information Serv., Dereham L.
[27737]   21/07/1977   CM23/10/1980
Henderson, Mrs E R, BEd DipT MEd, Librarian, The UCL Academy.
[10008566]   03/04/2008   ME
Henderson, Miss J, BA (Hons) MA, Information Manager, TUC,
London.
[44407]   04/10/1990   ME
Henderson, Mr J A, MA PgDip MCLIP, LRC Coordinator, St Machar
Academy.
[10019723]   31/08/2011   CM11/04/2013
Henderson, Mrs J P, BA DipLib MCLIP, Customer Service Supervisor,
Wimbledon Library, London Borough of Merton.
[36315]   02/10/1983   CM16/10/1989
Henderson, Mr J T, BSc, Customer Serv. Assistant, Lambeth L. & Arch.
[39089]   01/11/1985   ME
Henderson, Mrs L, Student, Glyndwr University, Wrexham.
[10017522]   01/09/2010   ME
Henderson, Miss M, MA (Hons) MSc, Student, Robert Gordon
University.
[10017853]   15/10/2010   ME
Henderson, Mrs M E, BA DipLib MCLIP, Stock & Online Resources
Librarian, Bath & NE Somerset L.
[29265]   02/05/1978   CM23/05/1980
Henderson, Mrs M M, BA FCLIP, Retired.
[15844]   17/02/1951   FE01/01/1968
Henderson, Mrs S M, MCLIP, Mobile Family Library, Family Library Ltd.
[28621]   11/01/1978   CM15/12/1981
Henderson, Mrs S R, MCLIP, On Career Break.
[29180]   19/04/1978   CM30/07/1980
Henderson Smith, Mr O, Student & Researcher (BIS).
[10020461]   20/02/2012   ME
Hendey, Ms L K, ACLIP, Library Assistant, Bridgewater High School,
Warrington.
[65950]   19/07/2006   ACL29/08/2008
Hendrix, Ms G F, JP BA MBA FCLIP, Retired.
[6728]   13/02/1963   FE18/11/1998
Hendry, Mrs M M, MA MBA DipLib FCLIP, Retired.
[26178]   04/08/1976   FE21/07/1993
Henley, Ms T M, BA MSc MCLIP, Assistant Academic Librarian Teesside
University, Tees Valley.
[37692]   17/10/1984   CM15/02/1989
Henning, Mrs H M E, BA ACLIP, Library Assistant, Lib. NI, Bronte
Library, Rathfriland, Co Down, Northern Ireland.
[48036]   26/10/1992   ACL16/07/2008
Henriette, Mrs L T, Student, University of Seychelles.
[10035166]   23/09/2014   ME
Henry, Mr M W, BA (Hons), MSc Library Science student, City
University London.
[10031915]   14/10/2013   ME
Henshaw, Miss D A, BA (Hons), Research Officer, DLA Piper,
Manchester.
[59093]   14/11/2000   ME
Henshaw, Miss J, BMus (Hons) MA MCLIP, Learning Res. Manager,
Music & Performing Arts, Colchester Institute, Essex.
[57021]   25/11/1998   RV15/07/2014   CM12/03/2003
Henshaw, Miss S, MA DipLib MCLIP, Unwaged.
[37299]   10/06/1984   CM14/11/1990
Henslowe, Ms A E, ACLIP, Locality Team Leader – Face to Face Serv.,
Cornwall Lib. Ser., Truro, Newquay, Perranporth & St Agnes
Libraries, Truro.
[64217]   21/02/2005   ACL17/01/2007

Henty, Mrs S J, BACS PgDip, Community Services Librarian, Bracknell
Library.
[10033425]   11/03/2014   ME
Hepburn, Miss T, MA, School Librarian, Robert Gordon University.
[10033419]   11/03/2014   ME
Heppell, Mrs C, BSc Econ PGCTHE FHEA MCLIP, Library Manager
Random House Group Archive and Library.
[62420]   12/06/2003   CM19/03/2008
Hepplewhite, Mrs K A, BA (Hons) MA, DSTL Records Manager, DSTL
Portsdown West.
[57261]   02/02/1999   CM10/07/2002
Hepworth, Miss A, MSc MCLIP, Information Serv. Librarian, Leeds
Metropolitan University, Leeds.
[10017251]   15/07/2010   CM14/11/2012
Hepworth, Mrs J, BA, Team Leader, North Yorkshire School Library
Service.
[57899]   01/10/1999   ME
Hepworth, Mr M, MA BSc MCLIP, Retired.
[6752]   01/01/1968   CM01/01/1970
Herbert, Mrs C, MPhil MA MA (Cantab), Unwaged.
[63785]   18/10/2004   ME
Herbert, Mrs J S, MCLIP, Life Member.
[6758]   26/05/1950   CM01/01/1956
Herbert, Mrs K E, BA (Hons) DipILS MCLIP, L. &Information Serv.
Manager, Part-time, Hinchingbrooke NHS Healthcare T., Huntingdon.
[49462]   02/11/1993   CM21/01/1998
Herbert, Ms K J, BA (Hons) ACLIP, Library Assistant, Watford Central
Library.
[10001310]   01/10/2004   ACL16/07/2008
Herbert, Mr L, LLB (Hons) MSc, Assistant Library Manager,
Hertfordshire County Council.
[10017944]   27/10/2010   ME
Herbert, Mrs O T, FCLIP, Life Member.
[6759]   07/10/1942   FE01/01/1969
Herbert, Mr P, MA MSc PgDipILS MCLIP, Health Information Scientist,
Healthcare Improvement Scotland.
[63069]   27/01/2004   RV04/08/2010   CM04/10/2006
Herbstritt, Ms B C, BA (Hons) PgDip, School Librarian Abbot Beyne
School Winshill Burton DE15 0JL.
[10014676]   27/08/2009   ME
Herd, Mr D, Prison Librarian, HMP North Sea Camp.
[10034676]   30/07/2014   ME
Herdan, Mr N, Consultant, USA.
[35498]   19/10/1982   ME
Heritage, Mr I, MA MCLIP, Information Manager, Gerald Eve LLP,
London.
[34458]   06/11/1981   CM10/11/1987
Hernandez, Mrs C V, PGD BA (Hons), Nursery & Primary Sch. Advisor,
Staffordshire CC, District Manager for Stafford District Libraries.
[10015278]   29/10/2009   ME
Hernandez, Ms M, Librarian, Mid-State Technical College, Wisconsin,
USA.
[10000874]   15/11/2006   ME
Herne, Mr I M, BA MA MSc (Econ) FAETC MCLIP, Chief Librarian,
South Bank Intl. School, Westminster, London.
[21256]   05/10/1973   CM16/08/1976
Hernik, Mrs S E, BA MA MCLIP, Assistant Librarian for Adult Fiction,
Reading Central Library.
[61588]   02/10/2002   CM19/03/2008
Herniman, Miss J, MCLIP, Unemployed.
[24390]   15/02/1964   CM16/02/1983
Herriman, Mrs M C, BA DipLib MCLIP, Lib Outreach & Comms Area
Apecialist, Milton Keynes Library.
[33757]   25/01/1981   CM01/07/1984

Herring, Mrs P S, BA MLS MCLIP, Librarian, Nuneaton Training Centre.
[21323]   07/10/1973   **CM12/11/1976**
Herring, Mrs R V, BA DipLIS MA MCLIP, Contract.
[50519]   31/08/1994   **CM04/02/2004**
Herring, Mrs S E, MA BA (Ed) MCLIP, Information Specialist, Career
Servs., University of Bristol.
[57010]   24/11/1998   **CM10/07/2002**
Herriot, Mr J M, BSc, Customer Service Manager, LB of Richmond
Upon Thames.
[10021792]   16/10/2012   **ME**
Herrmann, Mrs T S, ACLIP, Senior Library Assistant, Southbourne
Library, Bournemouth.
[10014384]   21/07/2009   **ACL16/06/2010**
Herron, Ms A, MA DipLib MCLIP, Team Leader (Public Libraries).
[36616]   24/10/1983   **RV27/09/2006**   **CM03/03/1987**
Hesketh, Ms C, BCombStud (Hons) DipLib MCLIP, Library Service
Manager : Reading and Inclusion.
[42242]   12/10/1988   **CM15/05/2002**
Hesketh, Mrs J E, BA MCLIP, Foreign & Commonwealth Office.
[27664]   04/07/1977   **CM08/11/1979**
Hesketh, Miss R, BA, Student, University of Greenwich.
[10032369]   09/12/2013   **ME**
Hessey, Ms R C, MCLIP, Senior Learner Support Assistant, The Open
University.
[10018254]   10/12/2010   **CM20/06/2014**
Hester, Mrs P I, MCLIP, Life Member.
[6785]   01/01/1951   **CM01/01/1964**
Hetherington, Mrs N C, BLS MCLIP, School Librarian, Lady Manners
School, Bakewell.
[33457]   01/01/1981   **CM12/03/1986**
Hettiaratchi, Mrs W, BA MCLIP, Life Member.
[6786]   02/01/1968   **CM13/07/1972**
Hevey, Mrs M M, MCLIP, Life Member.
[18766]   15/03/1947   **CM01/01/1952**
Heward, Mrs K, BSc (Hons) MA, Information Officer, Boyes Turner.
[10005029]   06/06/2007   **ME**
Hewerdine, Mrs V, BSc (Hons), Library Assistant, Hertfordshire County
Council.
[57799]   02/08/1999   **ME**
Hewings, Mrs R M, BSc DipLib FCLIP DMS FHEA, Head of Learning
Information Servs., Writtle College, Chelmsford.
[30575]   29/01/1979   **RV27/08/2014**   **FE03/10/2007**
Hewins, Mrs J M, BA MCLIP, Service Engagement Librarian (part-
time), Bournemouth University, Dorset.
[31485]   16/10/1979   **CM23/09/1982**
Hewish, Mr D S, MCLIP, Assistant Librarian, University West of the
England.
[63191]   03/03/2004   **CM21/11/2007**
Hewison, Mrs H, BA MCLIP, Information Serv. Officer, Clarke Willmott
Solicitors., Birmingham.
[27286]   14/02/1977   **CM30/10/1979**
Hewit, Mrs K, BA (Hons), Student, Edith Cowan University.
[10035523]   16/10/2014   **ME**
Hewitt, Mrs K W, Library & LRC Manager, Bilton School.
[10033820]   02/05/2014   **ME**
Hewitt, Mr M, Medical Sciences Librarian, Bristol University.
[45504]   26/02/1991   **AF**
Hewitt, Mrs M, BA, Student.
[10032092]   24/10/2013   **ME**
Hewitt, Ms M J, DipLib MCLIP, Service Manager North West Film
Archchive, Manchester Metropolitan University.
[28830]   07/02/1978   **CM01/12/1982**

Hewitt, Miss P M, BA DipLib MCLIP, Librarian, University of East Anglia,
Robert Sainsbury Library, Norwich.
[29679]   04/10/1978   **CM16/07/1982**
Hewitt, Ms S, MCLIP, Retired, Resident South Africa.
[18943]   27/05/1943   **CM01/01/1954**
Hewitt, Mrs V J, MLS MCLIP, Retired.
[6799]   01/01/1956   **CM01/01/1969**
Hewlett, Miss M A, MA MCLIP, Retired.
[6802]   07/03/1966   **CM01/01/1970**
Hey, Dr J M N, MA MCLIP, Researcher, ECS, University of
Southampton, Southampton, Hants.
[23655]   22/01/1975   **CM13/04/1977**
Heyda, Miss B M, BSc DipLib MCLIP, Assistant Teacher ESOL, West
Sussex CC.
[60733]   30/08/1985   **CM30/08/1985**
Heyes, Miss H, BSc DipILM MCLIP, Repository Manager, University of
Salford.
[59875]   29/10/2001   **CM21/11/2007**
Heyes, Mrs J L, BA (Hons) MCLIP, Self-employed.
[39739]   10/06/1986   **CM12/09/1990**
Heyes, Miss S A, BA (Hons) CertEd MCLIP, Head of Sch. L. Serv.,
West Sussex County Council, Chichester.
[35400]   15/10/1982   **CM22/09/1986**
Heys, Mrs C, BSc,
[10016635]   18/02/2011   **AF**
Heywood, Mrs J M, BA MCLIP, Careers Co-Ordinator, Wootton
Academy Trust.
[18293]   11/10/1972   **CM19/06/1978**
Hibbert, Mr O D, MSc CChem MRSC CertEd MCLIP, Freelance
Scientific Abstractor and Indexer.
[60588]   10/11/1971   **CM28/03/1973**
Hibbert, Ms P C, BA PgDip, Unemployed.
[56147]   05/03/1998   **ME**
Hicken, Mrs M E, MLS MCLIP, Retired.
[6827]   24/01/1951   **CM01/01/1956**
Hickey, Miss E, BA MPHIL MSCECON, ReExercher, Roland
Berger/Distance Learning Student, Aberystwyth.
[10020464]   20/02/2012   **ME**
Hickey, Mr J A, L. Information Systems Specialist, British Medical Ass.,
London.
[56495]   28/07/1998   **ME**
Hickford, Mrs B, MA DipLib MCLIP, Librarian, Our Lady's Abingdon.
[29680]   09/10/1978   **CM27/11/1980**
Hicklin, Miss P N, BSc, Online Publications Assistant, English Heritage.
[37540]   06/10/1984   **ME**
Hickman, Mrs M A, BA (Hons), Library & Knowledge Manager,
Derbyshire Healthcare NHS Foundation Trust, Derby.
[47136]   06/05/1992   **ME**
Hicks, Mx A, MA MSIS MCLIP, Romance Languages Librarian,
University of Colorado, Boulder, USA.
[65201]   17/11/2005   **CM29/05/2013**
Hicks, Miss J, MA BA (Hons), Graduate Library Trainee, University of
Oxford.
[10035112]   15/09/2014   **ME**
Hicks, Mr T J, BA (Hons) MCLIP MA, Academic Res. Librarian – Art &
Design, University of Wolverhampton.
[51443]   10/02/1995   **CM20/03/1996**
Hickson, Mrs C, MA, Librarian, Ellesmere Port L.
[10001451]   14/02/2007   **ME**
Hider, Dr P M, BSc (Hons) MLib PhD FCLIP, Head, School of
Information Studies, Charles Sturt University Australia.
[49277]   20/10/1993   **FE15/09/2004**
Hidson, Mr R, DIP ARCH FCLIP, Retired. (Life Member).
[6844]   01/01/1961   **FE17/10/1990**

Hidson, Mr R A, MA ISM, Senior Database Analyst, Morgan Stanley UK Ltd.
[10035674]   28/10/2014   **ME**

Higgins, Mrs C L, Trainee Librarian., Manchester Metropoltan Univ.
[10020859]   19/04/2012   **ME**

Higgins, Mrs E M, BA DipLib, Librarian, Madras College, Fife, Council Educ. Department.
[28843]   30/01/1978   **ME**

Higgins, Miss J S K, MSc student at The Robert Gordon University; Library Assistant.
[10031632]   04/10/2013   **ME**

Higgins, Miss M M, BA (Hons) MA MCLIP,
[59429]   13/03/2001   **CM14/11/2012**

Higgins, Mrs R J B, MLib MCLIP, Nursery Woman.
[21442]   30/10/1973   **CM18/08/1976**

Higgins, Miss S L, BA (Hons) MLIT, Student, University of Strathclyde.
[10031765]   01/10/2013   **ME**

Higginson, Mrs C E, BA (Hons) MSc MCLIP, Senior Information Officer, National Foundation for Educ. Res., Slough.
[58362]   25/01/2000   **CM03/10/2007**

Higgison, Ms M S, BA, Librarian, Scottish Government., Edinburgh.
[43916]   19/02/1990   **CM16/07/2003**

Higgs, Mrs G M, BA MCLIP PGCE (PCE), Librarian, Cornwall College, Cornwall.
[25533]   28/01/1976   **CM06/09/1979**

Higgs, Mr G P, BSc (Hons) DipILS, LRC Manager.
[48519]   02/02/1993   **ME**

Higgs, Miss J V, BSc MA, Information Services Librarian, Walsall Central Library.
[65570]   28/02/2006   **ME**

High, Mr B, BA (Hons) MA MCLIP, Senior Information Assistant – Special Collections, Kings College, London.
[45781]   28/05/1991   **CM18/09/2002**

Higham, Mrs J K, BA (Hons) MA, Special Collections & Archives Manager, University of Liverpool.
[61301]   16/05/2002   **ME**

Higham, Miss J W, MCLIP, Retired.
[6863]   25/09/1950   **CM01/01/1963**

Higman, Ms R, MSc BA, Graduate Trainee, Said Business School.
[10021912]   30/10/2012   **ME**

Hilditch, Mrs K L, BSc (Hons), Learning Resources Manager., The Redhill Academy.
[63109]   10/02/2004   **ME**

Hiles, Ms L H, BSc, Data Management Specialist, Schlumberger, Reading.
[10016539]   13/04/2010   **ME**

Hill, Miss A J, BA (Hons), Library Assistant, H M Prison Dovegate.
[10033427]   11/03/2014   **ME**

Hill, Mr A J, MCLIP, Retired.
[6871]   20/03/1955   **CM01/01/1962**

Hill, Mrs C, BA PGLIS, Group Librarian, Subsea 7.
[10022512]   19/03/2013   **ME**

Hill, Mrs C, BA MCLIP, Librarian. Capel Manor College, Enfield.
[32207]   15/02/1980   **CM15/08/1984**

Hill, Mrs C J, BA MCLIP, Operations Librarian, East Area, Stevenage.
[36586]   24/10/1983   **CM10/05/1988**

Hill, Mr D, BA (Hons) MCLIP,
[42942]   28/04/1989   **CM23/09/1998**

Hill, Miss J, BA (Hons) MA MCLIP, Book Acquisitions Grp Leader, University of Nottingham.
[10014744]   23/03/2004   **CM11/03/2011**

Hill, Mr J, BSc LLM MCLIP, Retired.
[60226]   01/09/1963   **CM01/04/2002**

Hill, Miss J L, BA (Hons), Student, MA in Information and Library Studies at Aberystwyth University.
[10031971]   16/10/2013   **ME**

Hill, Mrs J M, BA (Hons) MSc (Econ) MCLIP, Subject. Librarian, University of Bath.
[55057]   02/07/1997   **CM28/01/2009**

Hill, Mrs J M A, BA MCLIP, Stock and Reader Development Librarian, Hertfordshire C. C., Watford Library.
[25344]   21/01/1976   **CM06/06/1979**

Hill, Mrs J R, BSc (Hons), Library Assistant, Newbold Community School.
[10031694]   24/09/2013   **ME**

Hill, Ms K A, BA,
[10033597]   01/04/2014   **AF**

Hill, Ms M, BA MCLIP AdvDipEd,
[44025]   02/04/1990   **CM20/03/1996**

Hill, Mrs M L, BSc (Hons) MPhil DipIM MCLIP, Lib. Manager, Stockport NHS Foundation Trust.
[59297]   31/01/2001   **CM21/05/2003**

Hill, Mrs M M, MA (Hons) MLib MCLIP, Early Years Librarian, Central Library, Aberdeen.
[10001411]   04/10/1985   **CM07/06/1988**

Hill, Mrs M M, MCLIP, Retired.
[10006251]   26/09/2007   **CM29/09/1975**

Hill, Mr M W, MA MSc MRSC CChem FCLIP, Life Member.
[6893]   15/02/1965   **FE01/04/2002**

Hill, Mrs P M, BSc MCLIP, Library Manager, Historic Scotland, Edinburgh.
[24827]   10/10/1975   **CM14/12/1978**

Hill, Miss R, BA (Hons) MA MCLIP, Community Librarian, Crawley Library, West Sussex County Council.
[65727]   12/04/2006   **CM27/08/2014**

Hill, Mrs S, BA (HONS) MA PgCert MA, Lib. User Support Advisor., University of Surrey.
[10020873]   10/04/2012   **ME**

Hill, Mrs S, BA (Hons) MCLIP, Management Information Systems Trainer, City of York Council.
[39391]   22/01/1986   **CM26/07/1995**

Hill, Mrs S A, BA MCLIP, Team Leader (Library Support), Falkirk Community Trust.
[30247]   30/12/1978   **CM18/03/1981**

Hill, Mrs S E, MCLIP BA, Retired.
[19536]   26/03/1965   **CM01/01/1968**

Hill, Ms S J, HonFCLIP, Retired.
[40725]   19/05/1987   **HFE17/06/1998**

Hill, Mrs S M, BA (Hons) DipILM MCLIP, L. Manager, Neston Library, Cheshire.
[55513]   16/10/1997   **CM23/06/2004**

Hill, Ms V, BA (Hons) MA DipLIS MCLIP, Reader Development Librarian, London Borough of Havering, Romford.
[50783]   18/10/1994   **CM25/07/2001**

Hille, Ms J J, L. Servs. Assistant, Universityof Birmingham.
[10018125]   18/11/2010   **AF**

Hille, Ms M E, MSc, Unemployed.
[43500]   31/10/1989   **ME**

Hilliar, Miss J L, BA (Hons), Student, University of Sheffield.
[10032517]   11/12/2013   **ME**

Hilliard, Mr R P, BSc (Econ) FCA HonFLA, Formerly L. A. Secretary.
[31110]   29/06/1979   **HFE01/01/1979**

Hillier, Mr R W E, BA MCLIP, Local Studies Librarian, Local Studies & Archives, Central Library, Peterborough.
[24701]   01/10/1975   **CM28/08/1981**

Hillier, Miss S L, BA PGCE MCLIP, Co. Child. Librarian, Westbury
Library, Wilts.
[37292]   07/06/1984   **CM26/02/1992**
Hillman, Ms A L, BA (Hons), Team Leader Data Sharing & Data
Protection Policy, DWP.
[10033636]   07/04/2014   **ME**
Hills, Ms S B, BSc MSc FCLIP,
[60712]   09/03/1984   **FE25/03/1993**
Hills, Mrs T, BA (Hons) MSc, Senior Information Assistant, City
University.
[60958]   21/01/2002   **ME**
Hillyard, Mrs J A, MCLIP, Librarian, North of England Inst. of Mining
and Mechanical Engineers.
[65421]   24/02/2006   **CM20/04/2009**
Hilmer, Miss D, MSc DIPL. BIBL., Assistant Librarian.
[10021725]   04/10/2012   **ME**
Hilsden, Mrs D, ACLIP, Learning Resources Administrator, Colchester
Institute.
[10021794]   16/10/2012   **ACL16/01/2014**
Hilton, Mrs D M, BSc MCLIP FHEA MA, Customer Services Manager,
Anglia Ruskin University, Chelmsford.
[41705]   15/02/1988   **CM19/06/1991**
Hilton, Mr J J, BA (Hons) MA, Information Support Librarian, University
of Liverpool.
[59159]   04/12/2000   **ME**
Hilton, Mrs J J, Library Services Coordiantor, Derby College.
[47261]   29/06/1992   **ME**
Hilton Boon, Ms M L, BA MA MLIS MPH MCLIP, PhD Researcher,
MRC/CSO Social and Public Health Sciences Unit, University of
Glasgow.
[63548]   30/06/2004   **CM21/03/2007**
Hinder, Mrs H P, BA PgDipLib MCLIP, Information Officer, Universtiy of
Law, Guildford.
[27931]   11/10/1977   **CM12/10/1979**
Hindle, Ms J, Information Adv., Careers Centre for, University of Leeds.
[56741]   12/10/1998   **AF**
Hindle, Mrs J L, BA AHEA MCLIP, Quality Assurance Assistant,
University of Exeter.
[59662]   23/07/2001   **CM10/03/2010**
Hindle, Mr J W, BA (Hons), Student.
[10033420]   11/03/2014   **ME**
Hindmarch, Mr A J, BA (Hons), Library Assistant, City Library & Arts
Centre.
[10023406]   16/07/2013   **ME**
Hindson, Miss A, BA (Hons) DipIM MCLIP FHEA, Assistant Faculty
Librarian – Science and Technology, University of Portsmouth.
[57743]   15/07/1999   **CM18/09/2002**
Hine, Mrs R E, BA (Hons) MA, Head of Learning Resources,
Berkhamsted School.
[10005039]   17/01/2000   **ME**
Hinshalwood, Mr K W, MA MCLIP, Life Member.
[6935]   07/03/1961   **CM01/01/1965**
Hinton, Dr B J C, MBE MA MA (OXON) PhD MCLIP, Hon. Librarian,
Julia Margaret Cameron Trust, Freshwater Bay, I. O. W.
[28344]   08/11/1977   **CM04/02/1980**
Hinton, Mrs C N, BA, Resident in New Zealand.
[27979]   06/10/1977   **CM10/08/1982**
Hinton, Mrs S, BA (Hons) MCLIP, Part-time Information Manager,
Sagentia Ltd, Cambridge.
[43878]   07/02/1990   **CM23/03/1994**
Hipkin, Mrs A L, BA DipLib MCLIP, Freelance Indexer.
[26401]   11/10/1976   **CM24/12/1979**

Hipkiss, Mrs L M, BSc (Hons) FibMS ACLIP, Learning Centre Assistant,
Halesowen College, Halesowen, West Midlands.
[65987]   09/08/2006   **ACL05/10/2007**
Hipny, Mrs E S, Student, University of Strathclyde.
[10032249]   11/12/2013   **ME**
Hirano, Mr A, Librarian, Sainsbury Inst., Jap Arts & Cult., Norwich.
[58892]   02/10/2000   **ME**
Hird, Mr S J, BA MCLIP, Retired.
[6949]   12/02/1969   **CM01/01/1971**
Hirsch, Ms D, BA MSLS, Unwaged.
[10010553]   05/08/2008   **ME**
Hirst, Mrs A J, BA MA MCLIP, Res. Lib, Notts.
[36456]   10/10/1983   **CM02/06/1987**
Hirst, Mrs S, Data Analysis Manager, Ministry of Defence.
[10034221]   24/06/2014   **ME**
Hitchcock, Mrs A M, BA (Hons) MCLIP, LRC Systems Manager,
Guildford College.
[51421]   10/02/1995   **CM08/12/2004**
Hitchcock, Mrs N K, BA (Hons) DipILS MCLIP, Area Manager –
Partnerships and Inclusion, Worcester C. C.
[52340]   30/10/1995   **CM21/07/1999**
Hitchen, Miss J, BA (Hons) DipLIS MCLIP, Principal Information Officer,
University of Central Lancashire, Preston.
[45634]   08/04/1991   **CM21/05/1997**
Hitchen, Mrs S E, BA (Hons) MCLIP, L. Resource Centre Manager, St
Margaret's High School, Airdrie.
[49702]   25/11/1993   **CM20/01/1999**
Hitchman, Miss S, Enquiries & Digital Information Officer RBWM
Library.
[63352]   19/04/2004   **AF**
Hixon, Ms B C, BA MA MCLIP, Librarian, Royal Berkshire NHS
Foundation Trust.
[28317]   20/11/1977   **CM21/01/1980**
Ho, Mr A, MSc MSc (ITE) MCLIP, Information Professional specializing
in Teaching and Research Support.
[49219]   14/10/1993   **CM01/04/2002**
Ho, Miss L Y C, BA (Hons), Assistant Librarian, De Montfort University,
Leicester.
[54310]   18/11/1996   **ME**
Ho, Ms W F, BA, Senior Librarian, Sunway College, Austin, Malayasia.
[10022107]   19/12/2012   **ME**
Hoare, Miss C, BA MSc, Library Graduate Trainee, St John's College
Library, Cambridge.
[10031918]   14/11/2003   **ME**
Hoare, Mrs G M, BLib MCLIP, Retired.
[15933]   20/01/1970   **CM04/02/1976**
Hoare, Mr P A, MA DipLib FSA MCLIP HonFLA, Retired.
[6979]   01/01/1960   **HFE10/10/1995**
Hoare, Mrs S, Information Support Officer, Ministry of Defence.
[10035067]   09/09/2014   **ME**
Hoath, Mrs A, Librarian, Salisbury L.
[65143]   03/11/2005   **ME**
Hoban, Ms R, BA (Hons) MCLIP, Divisional Librarian, Durham C. C.
[58238]   24/11/1999   **CM06/07/2011**
Hobart, Mrs J L, BA MCLIP,
[31338]   01/10/1979   **CM15/08/1984**
Hobbs, Mr C, Knowledge and Info Manager, Foreign & Commonwealth
Office.
[10033262]   25/02/2014   **ME**
Hobbs, Mrs F, BA (Hons), Learning Resources Advisor, Central
Bedfordshire College.
[10021891]   25/10/2012   **AF**

Hobbs, Mr G P, BA (Hons) MSc, Information Manager., Scottish Parliament., Edinburgh.
[61268]   09/05/2002   **ME**

Hobby, Mr P A, BA DipLib MCLIP, Collection Support Co-ordinator: Music, British Library, London.
[37501]   01/10/1984   **CM27/11/1996**

Hobson, Mrs A M R, BA DipLib MCLIP, Retired.
[5621]   28/04/1972   **CM22/02/1978**

Hobson, Ms C R, BA MA, Subject Librarian, Birkbeck, University of London.
[59084]   10/11/2000   **ME**

Hobson, Mr J, MBE BA DipLib MCLIP HonFCLIP, Retired, Brockham.
[6994]   01/01/1970   **HFE01/10/2006**

Hockey, Miss M A, BA (Hons) MSc Econ, Librarian, Canford School.
[10010176]   08/07/2008   **ME**

Hockey, Ms R M, BA (Hons) DipLIS MCLIP, L. Res. Manager, Chorlton High School, Manchester.
[42635]   26/01/1989   **CM26/11/1997**

Hocking, Miss K M, MCLIP, Unemployed.
[27647]   08/01/1964   **CM01/01/1968**

Hockley, Mrs J J, BSc (Hons) MCLIP, Library and Information Manager, Herbert Smith Freehills, LLP.
[51690]   15/05/1995   **CM19/07/2000**

Hodder, Ms D K, MA MCLIP, Librarian, Newnham College, Cambridge.
[35182]   06/10/1982   **CM13/05/1986**

Hodds, Mr J, BA (Hons) MCLIP, Subject Librarian, University of Bath.
[56645]   01/10/1998   **CM28/10/2004**

Hodge, Mr G, BLib MCLIP, L. Serv. Manager, North East Surrey College of Tech., Ewell.
[37425]   15/09/1984   **CM07/06/1988**

Hodge, Mrs H M, MCLIP, Subject Librarian, Nescot, Surrey.
[22700]   22/08/1974   **CM01/02/1978**

Hodge, Miss M E, BA (Hons) DipLib, Freelance researcher and copy editor.
[30915]   31/05/1979   **ME**

Hodge, Mrs S L, ACLIP, Librarian at Hillside Primary School, Ipswich.
[10010555]   05/08/2008   **ACL23/09/2009**

Hodgeon, Ms A, BA DipLib MCLIP, Library Assistant, Hebden Bridge L.
[39387]   22/01/1986   **CM09/08/1988**

Hodges, Mrs J S, BA (Hons) MSc MCLIP MIVA, Learning Centre Manager, Coleg Morgannwg, Nantgarw Campus.
[63924]   03/11/2004   **CM29/08/2007**

Hodges, Ms S A, BA MA MCLIP, Director of Libraries and Archives, Bangor University.
[27740]   19/07/1977   **CM19/11/1979**

Hodgkins, Mrs L K, BA FCLIP, Regional Librarian, LIEM.
[29328]   26/05/1978   **FE03/10/2007**

Hodgman, Mr M,
[10034775]   14/08/2014   **ME**

Hodgson, Mrs A J, BA PGCE, Retired.
[65646]   08/03/2006   **ME**

Hodgson, Dr A M, BA (Hons) MA PhD MCLIP, Librarian, St John's College, Nottingham.
[59955]   09/11/2001   **CM06/04/2005**

Hodgson, Miss D A, BA (Hons), Student, City University, London.
[10022061]   27/11/2012   **ME**

Hodgson, Ms J A, BA (Hons), L. Manager, Queens's Campus, Durham University.
[43602]   09/11/1989   **ME**

Hodgson, Mrs J D, BA MA MCLIP, Head of Special Collections, University of Sheffield L.
[31138]   31/08/1979   **CM21/10/1981**

Hodgson, Mr M, BA (Hons) DipLIS MA MCLIP, Subject Liaison Librarian (Arts) Brunel University.
[47351]   20/07/1992   **CM26/07/1995**

Hodgson, Mr R, BA (Hons) MA, Assistant Librarian, Gray's Inn Library, London.
[10008423]   29/10/2002   **ME**

Hodkin, Mrs A F, BA MCIPD ACLIP,
[10012611]   19/02/2009   **ACL13/04/2011**

Hodson, Miss L, BSc MCLIP, Information Specialist, National Assembly for Wales, Cardiff.
[65878]   07/06/2006   **CM25/01/2011**

Hodson, Mrs V J, Library Service Advisor, Newark Library.
[10032115]   12/11/2013   **AF**

Hoffman, Miss J D, BA, Student.
[10018234]   20/12/2010   **ME**

Hoffman, Ms M, HonFLA, Hon. Fellow, Writer.
[56142]   11/03/1998   **HFE11/03/1998**

Hogben, Mr B M, MA MCLIP, Retired.
[20606]   08/05/1973   **CM04/09/1975**

Hogben, Miss R S, L. Manager, Plymstock School, Plymoth.
[65853]   31/05/2006   **ME**

Hogg, Ms C G, BA MCLIP, Retired.
[7044]   02/02/1968   **CM01/01/1972**

Hogg, Mr D, BA MCLIP, School Librarian, Glasgow City Council, Glasgow.
[36707]   11/11/1983   **CM10/11/1987**

Hogg, Mrs L, BA MCLIP, Librarian, Glasgow Life.
[34370]   27/10/1981   **CM03/03/1987**

Hogg, Mrs M, BA, Library Assistant, Alness Library.
[10032326]   19/11/2013   **AF**

Hogg, Miss S E, BA LLM MSc, Community Library Assistant, Cambridgeshire CC.
[10015537]   11/12/2009   **ME**

Hohmann, Ms T, Dipl. -Ing MLIS MCLIP, Deputy Head Information Services. Technische Universität München.
[64724]   03/06/2005   **CM09/09/2009**

Hokimi, Mrs M B, MA, Student, Stanmore College, Harrow, London.
[10009227]   07/05/2008   **ME**

Holborn, Mr G F, MA LLB MCLIP, Librarian, Lincolns Inn Library, London.
[28590]   13/01/1978   **CM26/08/1982**

Holbourn, Mrs C J, MCLIP, Primary School Librarian, Sch. L. Serv., London.
[7977]   05/01/1972   **CM18/08/1975**

Holcombe, Mrs S J, BA, Unemployed (Career Break).
[43709]   07/12/1989   **CM25/05/1994**

Holcroft, Ms C J, Prison Libraries Manager, Doncaster MBC.
[10022524]   19/03/2013   **ME**

Holden, Mrs C, Learning Res. Manager, Loughborough College.
[10001129]   28/07/1994   **ME**

Holden, Miss C A, ACLIP, Information Officer, Hill Dickinson LLP, Liverpool.
[66005]   16/08/2006   **ACL17/06/2009**

Holden, Mrs D M, BEd DipILS MCLIP, Senior Librarian, Cumbria C. C., Penrith L.
[51872]   20/07/1995   **CM18/03/1998**

Holden, Mr D R, BSc (Hons) MSc MCLIP, Faculty Librarian (Engineering and Physical Sciences), Queens University Belfast.
[52246]   18/10/1995   **CM20/05/1998**

Holden, Mrs G M, BA M PHIL DipLib MCLIP, Senior Library Officer, Oldham MBC.
[31865]   11/01/1980   **CM05/04/1989**

Holden, Mrs H, BA, CSA Cultural Serv. Adv.,
[10019335]   08/06/2011   **ME**

Holden, Miss M R, MCLIP, Life Member.
[7061]   01/01/1951   **CM01/01/1960**
Holden, Mrs R E, MCLIP, Librarian Stock/Affiliated, Blackburn Central L.
[10011881]   25/11/2008   **CM14/11/2012**
Holden, Mrs S, BA (Hons), Student, University of Huddersfield.
[10034265]   27/06/2014   **ME**
Holder, Miss A, Student, Elso Rhyno Hall University.
[10027488]   11/12/2013   **ME**
Holdstock, Miss M E, MCLIP, Retired.
[7065]   20/03/1943   **CM01/01/1951**
Holdsworth, Mrs C A, BA (Hons), Student, Aberystwyth University.
[10033876]   08/05/2014   **ME**
Holdsworth, Miss L, BA (Hons) MA,
[10009767]   09/06/2008   **ME**
Holgate, Ms C M, BA DipLib MCLIP, Service Development. Officer,
North Yorkshire County Council Knaresborough L.
[43651]   16/11/1989   **CM16/09/1992**
Holinde, Ms S, LLM, Student, Aberystwyth University.
[10034151]   10/06/2014   **ME**
Holland, Mr A D, BA PgDip, Assistant Informatics Co-ordinator,
Alzheimers Society.
[10020411]   05/10/1995   **ME**
Holland, Mr C J, BA MCLIP, Freelance.
[25309]   05/01/1976   **CM03/03/1978**
Holland, Mrs J, BA MCLIP, Assistant Director Community Services and
Head of L. & Information Serv., Norfolk County Council.
[30419]   08/01/1979   **CM19/07/1983**
Holland, Miss J E, BA (Hons) MCLIP, Retired.
[23198]   01/11/1974   **CM01/12/1976**
Holland, Mr M J, BA DipLib DMS MA MCLIP, Outreach Librarian, North
West Ambulance Service NHS Trust, Bolton.
[10013111]   14/02/1985   **CM01/04/2002**
Holland, Mr M S, BLib MLib MCLIP, Unwaged.
[44481]   03/10/1990   **CM22/11/1995**
Holland, Mr R, KIM Professional, MOD.
[10035260]   02/10/2014   **ME**
Holland, Miss S, BA, L. Executive, House of Commons L.
[36227]   08/08/1983   **ME**
Holland-Bright, Mrs D L, BA, School Librarian, Walsall Academy.
[37037]   31/01/1984   **ME**
Hollands, Mrs A M, BSc MCLIP, Librarian., Outreach., Maidenhead
Library, Royal Borough of Windsor & Maidenhead L.
[38825]   14/10/1985   **CM14/03/1990**
Hollenstein, Miss Y, PgDip MCLIP,
[10012212]   27/01/2009   **CM16/05/2012**
Hollerton, Mr E J, MCLIP, Unwaged.
[7081]   19/02/1969   **CM03/09/1973**
Holliday, Mr G W, MA MCLIP, Information Manager, Clyde & Co LLP.
[22836]   14/10/1974   **CM18/12/1978**
Hollier, Ms C, MLIS, Librarian, University of Nottingham.
[10016974]   16/06/2010   **ME**
Hollingdale, Miss E A, MCLIP, Retired.
[7090]   07/03/1956   **CM01/01/1961**
Hollingsworth, Mr B P, BA (Hons) MA MCLIP, Research & Learning
Support Assistant, Research Services, Manchester University.
[52611]   13/11/1995   **CM10/07/2002**
Hollins, Mr P, BLib MCLIP, Project Officer, The Open University.
[40525]   26/02/1987   **CM11/12/1989**
Hollis, Mrs B M E, MCLIP, Retired.
[7093]   21/03/1941   **CM01/01/1953**
Hollis, Miss C E, Student, Aberystwth University.
[10033588]   01/04/2014   **ME**
Hollis, Ms H, BA MSc, Student, UCL.
[10035427]   13/10/2014   **ME**

Hollis, Mrs M E, MCLIP, Life Member.
[7094]   19/02/1951   **CM04/03/1965**
Hollis, Mr N G, BA DipLib BA MCLIP, Library User Services Manager,
Reading University Library.
[36488]   11/10/1983   **CM15/11/1988**
Hollyfield-Hesford, Mrs A W, BA, School Librarian.
[10005351]   25/07/2007   **ME**
Hollywood, Miss S C, BA (Hons) PgDipILS, Library Supervisor,
Glasgow Clyde College.
[61884]   21/11/2002   **ME**
Holman, Miss A P, MCLIP, Life Member.
[7102]   22/05/1950   **CM01/01/1956**
Holman, Miss M R, BA (Hons) MSc, Information Asst/Assistant
Librarian, University of Ulster., NI.
[10001804]   02/08/1999   **ME**
Holman, Miss S M, BA (Hons) ACLIP, School Librarian, St Christopher's
C. E. High School, Accrington.
[66049]   06/09/2006   **ACL16/04/2008**
Holmes, Mrs C L, BA (Hons) MA MCLIP, School Librarian, The
Venerable Bede C. of E. Secondary School, Sunderland.
[56779]   14/10/1998   **CM19/11/2003**
Holmes, Ms J, BA MCLIP DMS, Principal Librarian: Information
Services, Hertfordshire Libraries & Heritage Services.
[21328]   15/10/1973   **CM13/07/1978**
Holmes, Mrs J C, MA MCLIP, Retired.
[28318]   05/11/1977   **CM29/07/1980**
Holmes, Ms L C, MA, Library Intern, Gladstone's Library.
[10035491]   16/10/2014   **ME**
Holmes, Mr M, MA DipLib, Head of Catalogue Support Serv., Oxford
University Library Serv.
[37490]   04/10/1984   **ME**
Holmes, Ms M M, BA (Hons) DipIS MCLIP, Part-time Library Manager;
Tuckton Library;Bournemouth Libraries.
[45127]   17/07/1990   **CM19/05/1999**
Holmes, Ms N, MA, Student, King's College London.
[62803]   24/10/2003   **ME**
Holmes, Ms N M, MA MCLIP, Information Lib. Notts County Council.
[35356]   13/10/1982   **RV**23/01/2007   **CM21/07/1989**
Holmes, Dr P L, PhD FCLIP, Retired.
[30765]   01/04/1979   **FE14/02/1990**
Holmes, Mr R K, BA MA MCLIP, Academic Liaison Librarian, Durham
University.
[57995]   08/10/1999   **CM19/03/2008**
Holmes, Ms R M, MSc MCLIP, Communities Librarian, Scottish Borders
Library & Information Services.
[62811]   24/10/2003   **CM21/03/2007**
Holmes, Ms S E, BA (Hons) MA MCLIP, Serv. Development Manager,
Dorset County Council.
[51587]   04/04/1995   **CM15/03/2000**
Holmes, Ms S J, Assistant Librarian, Berkhamsted School, Year 2 of MA
Library & Information Studies, UCL.
[65714]   04/04/2006   **ME**
Holmes, Miss V A, BA MCLIP, Retired.
[7125]   30/06/1969   **CM22/08/1972**
Holroyd, Ms I, BA (Hons), Knowledge/Information Management
Consultant.
[62225]   24/03/2003   **ME**
Holt, Miss A, MA, Electronic Serv. Librarian, NESCOT, Surrey.
[58663]   09/05/2000   **ME**
Holt, Ms G A, DipLib BA MCLIP, Consultant.
[34433]   30/10/1981   **CM18/07/1985**
Holt, Mrs M B, MA DipLib MCLIP, Bookstart Co-ordinator, Cardiff
Libraries, Cardiff.
[36467]   08/10/1983   **CM05/07/1988**

Holton, Mr G S, BA DipLib MCLIP FHEA LRAM LTCL, Genealogy Tutor & Consultant, Centre for Lifelong Learning, University of Strathclyde.
[24500]   27/08/1975   **CM26/02/1979**

Home, Miss A, BA, Librarian, Oakbank School.
[10035160]   22/09/2014   **ME**

Home, Mrs M E, BA DipLib MCLIP, Research Skills Librarian, University Library, Academic Services, Northumbria University.
[32986]   02/10/1980   **CM15/02/1983**

Homer, Mrs E A, BA (Hons) MA MCLIP, Associate Director, UEL.
[61831]   14/11/2002   **CM21/06/2006**

Homer, Miss M, MCLIP, Life Member.
[7141]   29/03/1951   **CM01/01/1954**

Homer, Mr S J, BA (Hons) MA, Leader of Learning Resources, St Paul's Catholic College, Burgess Hill, West Sussex.
[10001889]   22/03/2007   **ME**

Homer-Brine, Mrs C L, BA (Hons) MA MCLIP, Unemployed.
[47725]   15/10/1992   **CM31/01/1996**

Hon, Miss Y, BA MLITT, Trainee Liaison Librarian, University of Reading.
[10020442]   21/02/2012   **ME**

Hone, Mrs G, MCLIP, Life Member.
[20796]   21/10/1947   **CM18/08/1982**

Hood, Mr D T, BA (Hons) MSc MCLIP, Librarian, Institute and Faculty of Actuaries.
[10016086]   09/05/2003   **CM12/05/2011**

Hood, Mrs E M, BA MSc MCLIP, Job Seeking, Interested in Pharmaceutical and Health sectors.
[36537]   04/10/1983   **CM16/12/1986**

Hood, Mrs G T, BA MCLIP, Librarian, Wheatley Park School, Oxford.
[23118]   05/11/1974   **CM05/11/1976**

Hood, Miss I Y, BA (Hons) LLB FCLIP, Knowledge Services Assistant, NHS Education for Scotland.
[51957]   21/08/1995   **RV**22/08/2012   **FE07/09/2005**

Hood, Mrs M, MCLIP, Lib. &Information Worker, Central Library, Wellgate, Dundee.
[10007092]   24/01/2008   **CM06/05/2009**

Hood, Mrs M A, DOc DipLib MCLIP, Education Support Officer (Literacy), Angus Council.
[31192]   04/10/1979   **CM08/02/1982**

Hoodless, Miss C L, BA,
[10031882]   10/10/2013   **ME**

Hooker, Miss D J V, BA DipLib MCLIP, Librarian, Harbottle & Lewis LLP (Solicitors), London.
[34147]   09/10/1981   **CM01/04/1986**

Hookway, Sir H T, LLD FCLIP HonFLA, Retired.
[24219]   28/04/1975   **HFE15/06/1982**

Hoole, Miss B R S, Student, Aberystwyth University.
[10032464]   06/12/2013   **ME**

Hoole, Mrs N M, BSc (Hons) MSc MCLIP, Career Break.
[55011]   24/06/1997   **CM21/11/2001**

Hoolihan, Mrs A, BA (Hons) PgDip MCLIP, Librarian, Halton Lea L.
[10011285]   09/10/2008   **CM16/01/2014**

Hooper, Mrs B R, Manager, Child. & Sch., North Yorks. County Council, Library and Community Services.
[2428]   22/04/1971   **CM27/03/1975**

Hooper, Mrs C E M, BA (Hons) MA, Deputy Librarian, Palmers College.
[10035472]   15/10/2014   **ME**

Hooper, Mrs J, BA (Hons), Student, University of the West of England.
[10008697]   22/04/2008   **ME**

Hooper, Ms K J C, MA DipLib, Special Collections Librarian, The University of Liverpool.
[10021080]   29/05/2012   **ME**

Hooper, Mr L, MCLIP, Retired.
[7155]   01/01/1964   **CM01/01/1968**

Hooper, Mrs S B, BSc (Hons) MSc, Secondary School Librarian Greenfield Community School, Dubai.
[10009234]   07/05/2008   **ME**

Hope, Mrs J G, MCLIP, Life Member.
[7166]   13/10/1965   **CM01/01/1969**

Hope, Mrs L H, BSc MSc MCLIP, Consultant Information Sci.
[60389]   05/02/1975   **CM04/07/1977**

Hope, Mrs N J, Data Protection Account Manager, DWP.
[10033637]   07/04/2014   **ME**

Hopes, Mr A, Information Support Administrator, Ministry of Defence.
[10034542]   21/07/2014   **ME**

Hopkin, Mrs L, Librarian, North Oxfordshire Academy.
[10027522]   21/01/2014   **ME**

Hopkins, Mr A, BA (Hons) PgDipIS MCLIP, Hd. of Book, Witt and Conway Libraries, Courtauld Institute of Art.
[52048]   02/10/1995   **CM01/06/2005**

Hopkins, Mr A, Head of Library & Heritage Service, London Borough of Merton.
[10021377]   30/07/2012   **ME**

Hopkins, Mr C G P, Library Manager, Highcliffe Library, Dorset.
[10023210]   18/06/2013   **AF**

Hopkins, Miss E J, BA (Hons) MA MCLIP, Knowledge Service Manager, Pennine Care NHS Foundation Trust.
[64144]   19/01/2005   **RV**16/01/2014   **CM11/11/2009**

Hopkins, Mr M, BA PhD MCLIP, Retired.
[7178]   06/02/1968   **CM01/01/1971**

Hopkins, Mr R L, BA (Hons) MA MSc, Learning & Skills Librarian, University of Wolverhampton.
[10020404]   11/02/2012   **ME**

Hopkinson, Mr A, MA DipLib FBCS, Retired.
[18783]   05/09/1972   **ME**

Hopson, Mrs I, MCLIP, Head of Information Centre, George Abbot School, Guildford.
[6795]   27/10/1971   **CM01/07/1975**

Hopson, Mrs M A, BA MCLIP, School Librarian, Don Valley School & Performing Arts College, Doncaster.
[63196]   03/03/2004   **CM01/02/2006**

Horan, Ms A, BA MA MCLIP, Knowledge Manager, Dept for Education, London.
[60477]   22/05/2000   **CM01/04/2002**

Horan, Miss A, BA (Hons), Libraries & Archives Trainee (HIf), Stockport Metropolitan Borough Council.
[10033862]   07/05/2014   **ME**

Horan, Miss J, BEd (Hons) DipILS, School Librarian, St Aidan's High School.
[10017183]   11/07/2010   **ME**

Horan, Mrs L, BA, Seeking Work.
[10011526]   17/10/2008   **ME**

Horder, Miss B, BA MCLIP, Retired.
[7193]   11/10/1960   **CM01/01/1962**

Hordon, Mrs F M, MA DipLib MCLIP, Child. Librarian, retired; Editor Books for Keeps; Editor IBBYLink.
[90]   01/01/1971   **CM01/10/1974**

Horley, Mr N G B, BA (Hons) MSc (Econ) MCLIP, Unwaged.
[51225]   30/11/1994   **CM16/07/2003**

Horne, Mr C, ACQI,
[10010989]   12/09/2008   **ME**

Horne, Miss C I, Library Assistant, Baker Tilly.
[10012162]   08/01/2009   **ME**

Horne, Miss F, BA (Hons) MA, Information Assistant, Linklaters.
[10022531]   19/03/2013   **ME**

Horner, Miss A A, BA, LInC Manager, Metropolitan Police Serv.
[65305]   19/12/2005   **ME**

Hornung, Dr E, DipBibl MLIS PhD ALAI FCLIP, Librarian, CDETB Curriculum Development Unit/Trinity College Dublin, Dublin.
[61527]   13/09/2002   **RV**30/04/2014   **FE16/05/2012**

Horrigan, Miss M, BA (Hons), Library and Knowledge Service Manager, Liverpool Heart and Chest Hospital, NHS Foundation Trust.
[10001030]   21/06/2001   **ME**

Horrocks, Mrs A C M, BA MSc DipLib MCLIP, Retired.
[22794]   12/10/1974   **CM10/03/1978**

Horsfield, Mrs K, BEd MCLIP MSc, Manager, Resources for Learning.
[61710]   23/10/2002   **CM21/05/2008**

Horslen, Ms J C, BA MCLIP, Subject Librarian for Law, UCL.
[28593]   03/01/1978   **CM07/10/1982**

Horsler, Mr P N, MCLIP, Assistant Librarian, LSE, London.
[63183]   03/03/2004   **CM13/04/2011**

Horsley, Miss J E, MCLIP, Retired.
[7220]   24/09/1968   **CM01/01/1972**

Horsnell, Ms V, BSc MSc FCLIP, Life Member.
[31077]   27/08/1979   **FE01/04/2002**

Horstmanshof, Ms K, BA (Hons) MSc DIC PgDip (LIS), LIS Manager, Chartered Institute of Building.
[66100]   22/09/2006   **ME**

Horth, Ms G B, BA (Hons) MA, Learning Centre Coordinator, Moorside Community Tech. College, Consett.
[10009983]   30/06/2008   **ME**

Horton, Mrs E, MCLIP, Freelance Editor.
[60438]   23/03/1998   **CM01/04/2002**

Horwood, Ms L K, BA MCLIP Associate CIPD MIoEE, Director, Odonata River Ltd, L & D Consultant, Executive Coach.
[38803]   11/10/1985   **CM15/08/1990**

Hosie, Mrs J, BA (Hons) PgDip MCLIP, Librarian, North Lanarkshire C., Bellshill.
[59535]   01/05/2001   **CM28/01/2009**

Hosking, Miss E M, MCLIP, Life Member.
[7238]   03/10/1947   **CM01/01/1953**

Hosking, Mr M G, MCLIP, Retired.
[7239]   19/09/1968   **CM01/07/1972**

Hoskins, Mrs J K, MCLIP, LRC Manager, The Gryphon School.
[63473]   14/05/2004   **CM14/03/2012**

Hoskins, Ms S L, MA MCLIP, Library Services Manager, University of Salford, Salford.
[10013453]   03/08/1990   **CM29/01/1992**

Hou, Mrs C Y, Graduate Student, University of Illinois.
[10033539]   25/03/2014   **ME**

Hough, Mr A M, BA (Hons) MA PGCERT PGDIP PTLLS, Health Librarian.
[10035536]   16/10/2014   **ME**

Houghton, Mr D J, BA MCLIP, Life Member.
[7250]   25/09/1955   **CM01/01/1963**

Houghton, Miss E, BA MSc MCLIP, Deputy School E-Librarian, Eton College.
[10006380]   23/10/2007   **CM19/10/2012**

Houghton, Mrs E A, BA (Lib) MCLIP, Librarian, King's School, Gloucester.
[21835]   31/01/1974   **CM09/08/1978**

Houghton, Mr L P, BA (Hons) MCLIP, Periodicals Acquisition Group Leader, University of Nottingham., Nottingham.
[65948]   19/07/2006   **CM18/01/2012**

Houghton, Mrs R, Library Information Assist, Aberdeen Business School.
[10021412]   03/08/2012   **ME**

Houlton, Ms L,
[10012028]   10/12/2008   **ME**

Hounsome, Mrs L M, BA MCLIP, Volunteer Lib.
[4926]   18/01/1971   **CM01/09/1975**

Hounsome, Miss M E, BA (Hons), Faculty Librarian University of Portsmouth.
[64815]   18/07/2005   **ME**

Hourihan, Mrs J M, BSc BA PgDip, Assistant Librarian, The Maynard School.
[10018072]   09/11/2010   **ME**

Housden, Mr A, BA MA,
[10012722]   05/03/2009   **ME**

House, Mr D E, BA MCLIP, Retired.
[7266]   20/11/1968   **CM01/01/1971**

House, Mrs F L, BA (Hons) DipLIS MCLIP,
[50950]   31/10/1994   **CM19/05/1999**

House, Mrs M E A, MA DipLib MCLIP, Prison Librarian, HMP Onley, CV23 8AP.
[34179]   12/10/1981   **CM13/12/1984**

House, Ms M S, BA (Hons) MA, UCL Library and Information Studies student.
[10032407]   03/12/2013   **ME**

Housego, Ms J, HonFCLIP,
[10035775]   20/09/2014   **HFE20/09/2014**

Houston, Mrs L Y, BLS MBA MCLIP HonFCLIP, Retired. Formerly Chief Librarian with Belfast Education and Library Board and Director of LISC NI.
[27148]   03/02/1977   **HFE02/09/2010**

Houston, Mr P A, BA MA, Library Assistant, Hertfordshire CC.
[10031750]   01/10/2013   **ME**

Houston, Mrs S J, BA MCLIP, Assistant Librarian (Readers' Serv.), Goldsmiths College Library, London.
[32055]   12/02/1980   **CM10/11/1982**

Hovish, Mr J J, BA DipLib MLib MCLIP, Retired.
[21338]   17/10/1973   **CM01/11/1976**

Howard, Mrs A G, BA MCLIP, Development Manager Learning and Information Plymouth Libraries.
[27951]   04/10/1977   **RV**16/07/2008   **CM28/08/1981**

Howard, Mr A G, MA FCLIP, Retired.
[7270]   06/10/1960   **FE01/01/1970**

Howard, Miss A S, BA MCLIP, Information Officer, Royal Institution of Chartered Surveyors, London.
[33303]   20/11/1980   **CM10/04/1986**

Howard, Miss C, MA PgDip BA, Student, Aberystwyth University.
[10020587]   02/03/2012   **ME**

Howard, Ms E C, BA DipLib MCLIP, Librarian, St Helens School, Northwood, Middx.
[34283]   20/10/1981   **CM16/05/1985**

Howard, Mrs E J, BEd MSc, Lib. & Customer Serv. Officer, Blackburn Connected, Scotland.
[10013646]   18/05/2009   **ME**

Howard, Mr E S, Information Services Librarian, Leeds Metropolitan University.
[10000530]   16/10/2006   **ME**

Howard, Mr G, BA DipIS, Executive Officer, House of Commons Library, London.
[47127]   05/05/1992   **ME**

Howard, Ms I C, BA DipLib MCLIP, Local Government – Intellectual Property.
[32989]   16/10/1980   **CM11/01/1987**

Howard, Miss J, BA, Librarian, Museum of the History of Science Library Assistant, UWE.
[10019029]   12/04/2011   **ME**

Howard, Mrs J, BA (Hons) MCLIP, Library Manager, Freeman Hospital, Newcastle upon Tyne.
[52779]   12/12/1995   **CM21/03/2001**

Howard, Ms J E, BA MCLIP, Web Manager, Samuel Whitbread
Community College, Shefford, Beds.
[25762]   10/03/1976   **CM07/06/1978**
Howard, Mr L, BSc MCLIP, Managing Director, XIP Pty Ltd, Australia.
[60106]   07/12/2001   **CM07/12/2001**
Howard, Mr M, BA MCLIP, Unwaged.
[24954]   28/10/1975   **CM21/08/1980**
Howard, Mrs N H, BSc (Hons) MA MCLIP, L. Manager, North East
London NHS Foundation Trust.
[61045]   05/02/2002   **CM15/09/2004**
Howard, Miss P J, BSc MA MCLIP, Deputy Library Manager, Trafford
College, Manchester.
[55787]   19/11/1997   **CM17/05/2000**
Howard, Mr T W, FCLIP, Retired.
[7281]   04/03/1947   **FE01/01/1960**
Howarth, Mr C, BA MCLIP, Retired.
[7283]   29/01/1965   **CM01/01/1969**
Howarth, Mrs C A, MA MCLIP, L. & Information Officer, Central Library,
Reference and Information, Leisure and Culture Dundee.
[37513]   05/10/1984   **CM10/05/1988**
Howarth, Mrs H, BA (Hons) MCLIP,
[64932]   14/09/2005   **CM09/11/2011**
Howarth, Mr J A, BA MA, Assistant Librarian, International Institute for
Strategic Studies London.
[61606]   03/10/2002   **ME**
Howat, Mrs M M, BA MCLIP, Retired.
[7289]   11/02/1957   **CM01/01/1961**
Howden, Ms J S, MA DipLib MCLIP MPhil, University Librarian,
University of the West of Scotland.
[35541]   04/10/1982   **CM08/03/1988**
Howe, Miss C E A, BLS MCLIP, Unwaged.
[28022]   02/10/1977   **CM16/11/1994**
Howe, Mrs G, MCLIP, Retired.
[7884]   24/09/1964   **CM07/02/1973**
Howe, Mr J A, FCLIP, Life Member.
[7295]   06/01/1949   **FE01/01/1957**
Howe, Mrs L C, BA (Hons) MCLIP, Childrens. Librarian, Milton Keynes
City Council.
[48672]   07/04/1993   **CM21/03/2001**
Howe, Mr M P, BA, LRC Manager, Hartlepool College of Further
Education.
[35096]   10/08/1982   **ME**
Howe, Miss P J, BEd, Library Assistant, Connah's Quay Library.
[55752]   12/11/1997   **ME**
Howell, Miss E S, BA MCLIP, Head of Information, Investec, London.
[41005]   01/10/1987   **CM22/07/1992**
Howell, Mrs L M, ACLIP, Community Librarian, Children & Young
People, Luton Central Library, Beds.
[10005222]   29/06/2007   **ACL16/07/2008**
Howell, Ms M F, BA (Hons) MA MCLIP, Learning Resources Centre
Manager, Sutton Centre Community College, Ashfield.
[55077]   09/07/1997   **CM29/11/2006**
Howell, Mr P A, BA (Hons), Clinical Librarian, Archway Healthcare
Library.
[62718]   08/10/2003   **ME**
Howell, Mrs S J, Library Assistant, Frank Curtis Library, Hellesdon
Hospital.
[10021235]   29/06/2012   **ME**
Howes, Miss K, BA (Hons), Student, University of the West of England.
[10032423]   03/12/2013   **ME**
Howes, Mr M G, FCLIP, Retired.
[60388]   08/11/1966   **FE03/11/1981**

Howey, Miss H, BA (Hons) MCLIP, L. Manager Horsham Library, West
Sussex.
[43662]   20/11/1989   **CM14/09/1994**
Howkins, Mr S J, BA MCLIP, Retired.
[26902]   07/01/1977   **CM30/11/1981**
Howland, Mr J, Information Support Assistant,
[10034303]   02/07/2014   **ME**
Howley, Mr P R, BSc PGCE PgDip MCLIP, Subject Librarian, Leeds City
Col.
[47492]   04/09/1992   **CM21/08/2009**
Howley, Mrs S M, BA MA MCLIP, Retired.
[4703]   01/01/1969   **CM01/01/1971**
Howrie, Ms H, BA (Hons), Student, City University London.
[10027554]   20/08/2013   **ME**
Howsam, Miss D C, BA DipLib MCLIP, Principal Lib. Performance,
Northamptonshire County Council.
[38004]   01/01/1985   **CM11/12/1989**
Howse, Ms J, BSc MA, Senior Librarian, Merchant Taylors' School,
Northwood.
[64931]   14/09/2005   **ME**
Hoyle, Mr J N, BA (Hons) DipLib, Senior Manager for Digital Marketing
at London South Bank University.
[44395]   04/10/1990   **ME**
Huang, Mr H C, MSc, Clinical Technologist, The James Cook University
Hospital, Middlebrough.
[10019656]   18/08/2011   **ME**
Huang, Ms Z, MSc MCLIP, Senior Lib. Assistant, Engineering Team,
Central L. Imperial College London.
[54624]   27/01/1997   **CM17/01/2001**
Hubbard, Mr A, BA, Student, Manchester Metropolitan University.
[10032505]   10/12/2013   **ME**
Hubbard, Prof T F, MA DipLib PhD FCLIP, Editor BILC, National
University of Ireland, Maynooth.
[28320]   24/10/1977   **FE04/10/2006**
Hubbard, Mr W J I, BSc MA, Information Scientist, Mary Seacole
Research Centre, De Montfort University.
[61361]   26/06/2002   **ME**
Hubble, Mrs M M, MCLIP, Life Member.
[7346]   01/01/1951   **CM01/01/1955**
Hubschmann, Ms K, MA MA MCLIP, Senior Librarian, Wiener Library,
London.
[53688]   05/09/1996   **CM21/05/2008**
Huckle, Mr C S, MCLIP, Lib. Assistant, Hackney L. s., Hackney.
[62160]   04/03/2003   **CM16/05/2012**
Huckle, Mrs F M, BA MCLIP, Freelance Taxonomist & Information
Specialist.
[24616]   29/09/1975   **CM10/05/1978**
Huckle, Ms M J, BSc (Hons) MCLIP,
[21069]   21/10/1973   **CM13/07/1978**
Huddart, Mr D J, MA MSc MCLIP, Technical Information Specialist
(Patents), Solvay. France.
[60390]   30/04/1980   **CM22/10/1985**
Hudgens, Ms A, MA, Unwaged.
[10019147]   21/04/2011   **ME**
Hudson, Mr A, BSc MCLIP, Retired.
[21226]   10/10/1973   **CM19/01/1977**
Hudson, Miss B P, MA MCLIP, Life Member.
[7354]   29/02/1948   **CM01/01/1956**
Hudson, Mrs C M, MCLIP, Team Leader, Library Customer Services,
University of Nottingham.
[10006631]   11/09/2007   **CM27/03/2014**
Hudson, Ms C M, MChem,
[65224]   18/11/2005   **ME**

Hudson, Mrs G L, MA MPhil MIL MCLIP FHEA, Head of L. Serv.,
University of Bradford.
[18630]   01/01/1972   **CM10/10/1974**
Hudson, Mr J, BA MCLIP, Library Assistant, Royal Wolverhampton
Hospitals NHS Trust.
[38011]   01/01/1985   **CM15/08/1989**
Hudson, Miss J K, BA (Hons), Library Assistant, Lambeth Palace
Library.
[10021223]   29/06/2012   **ME**
Hudson, Mr K, BSc MSc, Mycology Publications Co-ordinator, CABI,
UK.
[35834]   24/01/1983   **ME**
Hudson, Mrs K M, BA MA, Reading & Community Learning Manager,
Dorset County Council.
[58028]   19/10/1999   **ME**
Hudson, Mr M G, BA, Student.
[10011954]   09/12/2008   **ME**
Hudson, Mrs M P, BA (Hons) MCLIP, Information Librarian,
Southampton Solent University.
[40658]   23/04/1987   **CM23/03/1993**
Hudson, Mr P A, BA (Hons) MSc (Econ) MCLIP, Learning & Outreach
Manager, Worcestershire Archive & Archaeology Service.
[54415]   05/12/1996   **CM17/01/2001**
Hudson, Mr R E, BA DipLib MCLIP, Technical Product Specialist.
[42343]   21/10/1988   **CM01/04/2002**
Hudson, Mr T J, MCLIP, Naval & Maritime Res. Consultant;
Photographic Librarian, Narrow Gauge Railway Socirty.
[7368]   04/10/1971   **CM12/08/1974**
Hudspith, Mrs S E, Unwaged.
[64379]   14/03/2005   **ME**
Huggan, Ms A M, BA (Hons) MA MCLIP, Library Services Manager, The
Dudley Group NHS Foundation Trust.
[54249]   14/11/1996   **CM19/07/2000**
Huggins, Mrs D, BA (Hons) MCLIP, unemployed.
[45225]   31/07/1990   **CM21/11/2001**
Hughes, Mrs A, BA DMS MBA PGCE MCLIP, Head of ILT & Learning
Resources, Sandwell College of F. & Higher Education, West
Bromwich.
[25067]   28/10/1975   **CM16/06/1978**
Hughes, Miss A, BA (Hons) MLIS, Head, Digital Operations, UK Trade
& Investment (UKTI), London.
[56580]   28/08/1998   **ME**
Hughes, Mrs A, BSc, Student, Robert Gordon University.
[10032992]   03/02/2014   **ME**
Hughes, Mrs A J, BA, Unwaged.
[27467]   04/04/1977   **ME**
Hughes, Mr A P, BA (Hons) MA, Assistant L., College of Occupational
Therapists, London.
[62286]   17/04/2003   **ME**
Hughes, Mr A V, BSc (Hons), Part-time Student, University of Wales,
Aberystwyth, National Library of Wales.
[10001048]   14/12/2006   **ME**
Hughes, Mrs B J, MCLIP, Retired.
[7377]   02/03/1941   **CM01/01/1950**
Hughes, Ms B M, BA DipLib MCLIP, Reading Serv. Manager,
Denbighshire County Council Library & Information Serv.
[41198]   18/10/1987   **CM14/08/1991**
Hughes, Miss B S, BA, Library Resourcing manager, University of
Exeter.
[44540]   23/10/1990   **ME**
Hughes, Mrs C, BA (Hons) MCLIP, Information Resources Manager,
Edge Hill University, Ormskirk.
[52297]   23/10/1995   **CM18/11/1998**

Hughes, Mrs C A, MCLIP, Accounts, Practice Manager.
[22732]   27/08/1974   **CM21/06/1977**
Hughes, Mrs C E, BA (Hons) MCLIP, Assistant Community Librarian,
Selly Oak Library, Birmingham.
[65776]   01/05/2006   **CM09/09/2009**
Hughes, Ms C E, BA MA MSc MBA FCMI CMGR, Head of Knowledge,
Research and Collaboration, KPMG, London.
[10011118]   07/07/1995   **ME**
Hughes, Mr D R, BSc DipEd MCLIP, Retired.
[7386]   07/02/1972   **CM18/07/1974**
Hughes, Miss E, BSc, Information Officer – Information Services, UK
Health Forum, London.
[10020333]   23/01/2012   **ME**
Hughes, Ms F, MA PgDip MCLIP, Senior Information Officer, Glasgow
CC.
[10010828]   29/08/2008   **CM12/05/2011**
Hughes, Mrs F C M, BA (Hons) MLib FCLIP, Library Services Manager,
Sir Kenneth Green Library, Manchester Metropolitan University.
[44594]   01/11/1990   **FE11/04/2013**
Hughes, Mr G W, BA MCLIP, Retired.
[7393]   28/04/1965   **CM01/01/1970**
Hughes, Mrs J, BA (Hons) MSc ACLIP, School Librarian, The Dawnay
School, Bookham and Library Assistant, Bookham Library.
[10006431]   19/10/2007   **ACL09/07/2013**
Hughes, Miss J, BSc Econ, Senior Library Assistant, Healthcare
Library, Weston General Hospital.
[10027567]   13/11/2013   **ME**
Hughes, Mrs J E, BA (Hons) PgDipILM MCLIP, Librarian, Ellesmere
Port Specialist Sch. of Performing Arts Ellesmere Port.
[57312]   08/02/1999   **CM06/04/2005**
Hughes, Mrs J E, BA DipLib MCLIP, Network Librarian, Fortrose
Community Library. Highlife Highland.
[35425]   01/10/1982   **CM05/04/1988**
Hughes, Mrs J L, BSc MCLIP, Employment not known.
[41236]   20/10/1987   **CM22/05/1991**
Hughes, Ms J M, BA, Student, University of the West of England.
[10018431]   18/01/2011   **ME**
Hughes, Mr M, FCLIP DMS, Life Member.
[7411]   22/09/1954   **FE01/01/1962**
Hughes, Mr M J, BA (Hons), Head of Collections, Swansea University.
[59615]   03/07/2001   **ME**
Hughes, Miss N J, BA MCLIP, Online Serv. Manager, Cheshire East
North Yorkshire County Council.
[43604]   09/11/1989   **CM23/03/1994**
Hughes, Mrs P A, DipIT MCLIP, Life Member.
[7418]   16/08/1955   **CM01/01/1960**
Hughes, Ms P M, BA (Hons) MCLIP, Librarian, National Police Library,
College of Policing.
[58119]   03/11/1999   **CM23/06/2004**
Hughes, Mr R G, BA MSc MCLIP, Systems Librarian, University of the
Highlands and Islands.
[10001151]   12/01/2007   RV27/03/2014   **CM16/04/2010**
Hughes, Miss R L, Student, Glyndwr University Wrexham.
[10032480]   09/12/2013   **ME**
Hughes, Ms S, OBE HonFLA, Hon. Fellow.
[54737]   01/01/1997   **HFE01/01/1997**
Hughes, Miss S E, BA, Library Assistant, Elm Park Library, Essex.
[10019952]   06/10/2011   **AF**
Hughes, Miss S E, BA (Hons), Student, University Sheffield.
[10016003]   11/02/2010   **ME**
Hughes, Mrs S J, MCLIP, Regional Manager, East of England, MLA.
[249]   28/05/1968   **CM07/12/1973**
Hughes, Mrs S M, MA, Consultant, Self-Employed.
[51372]   01/02/1995   **ME**

Hughes, Ms S R, Records & Information Officer, Norfolk County
Council.
[45295]   02/10/1990   AF
Hughes, Mrs V E, ACLIP,
[10012656]   05/03/2009   ACL23/09/2009
Hughesdon, Mrs R F, BA MCLIP, Hon. Librarian, Surrey Archaelogical
Society.
[21153]   06/10/1973   CM01/11/1976
Hughston, Mr D A, BA (Hons), Lib. Assistant, Healthcare Library,
Whiston Hospital, Prescot.
[10015228]   29/10/2009   AF
Huish, Mr A W, BA MA FCLIP, Life Member.
[7425]   21/01/1947   FE01/01/1967
Hukins, Mrs C E, BA (Hons) MCLIP, Retired.
[17072]   01/10/1967   CM01/01/1970
Hull, Miss A E, BA MLIS, Graduate Trainee, Courtauld Institute of Art.
[10035517]   16/10/2014   ME
Hull, Mr R C, MA MCLIP, Research Officer, Liverpool Record Office.
[7429]   17/01/1972   CM27/01/1975
Hulme, Mrs L H, BSc MCLIP, Lib. /Information, Advice & Guidance
Worker, Halton Lea Library, Runcorn.
[10016684]   19/11/2002   CM15/07/2014
Hulse, Mrs H J, Lib. & Records Officer, AHVLA (Animal Health and
Veterinary Laboratories Agency).
[39416]   23/01/1986   ME
Hume, Ms S F, BA, Student, UCL.
[10033589]   01/04/2014   ME
Humfrey, Mr J R, MA BA (Hons) DipLib DipEdMan MCLIP, Head of
Library and Central Services., Myerscough College., Bilsborrow,
Preston, Lancs., PR3 0RY.
[46420]   05/11/1991   CM18/11/1993
Humphrey, Mrs L A, MCLIP, Retired.
[7447]   15/01/1964   CM01/01/1967
Humphrey, Mr M, MCLIP, Life Member.
[7448]   10/01/1961   CM01/01/1966
Humphrey, Miss 9 J, BA DipLib, Documentalist, European Space
Agency, Netherlands.
[40839]   18/07/1987   ME
Humphreys, Miss A, LLB Law MA,
[10001984]   20/04/2007   ME
Humphreys, Mr A R C, BA, Assistant Librarian, Jobs & Pertemps.
[10032859]   21/01/2014   ME
Humphreys, Mrs C E, Library Assistant, Oakham School.
[10035540]   17/10/2014   ME
Humphreys, Miss C L, BA (Hons), Librarian & Head of Careers,
Fulneck School.
[10032629]   21/12/2013   ME
Humphreys, Mr G P, FRSA MCLIP, Retired.
[7454]   29/03/1966   CM01/01/1970
Humphreys, Miss R, BA DipLib MCLIP, Assistant Librarian, Department
for Education, Sheffield.
[34161]   05/10/1981   CM11/11/1986
Humphreys, Mrs S, BA MCLIP, Retired,
[7459]   14/01/1950   CM01/01/1964
Humphries, Mrs C M, BA DipLib MCLIP, Liaison Librarian, Queen
Margaret University, Edinburgh.
[44736]   21/11/1990   CM23/03/1993
Humphries, Dr C R, BSc MSc PhD, Information Specialist (Health).,
Cranfield University.
[61324]   22/05/2002   ME
Humphries, Mrs J, MCLIP, Learning Res. Centre Manager, Coleg
Gwent, Ebbw Vale Campus.
[10001332]   06/02/2007   CM10/11/2010

Humphries, Mrs L C, MCLIP, Unemployed.
[32222]   07/01/1980   CM18/06/1984
Humphries, Ms M E, BA (Hons) MCLIP, Sch. Liaison Officer, Bristol Ls.
[10009488]   21/05/2008   CM08/03/2013
Humphries, Mr N D, FCLIP, Life Member.
[7463]   08/12/1945   FE01/01/1957
Humphries, Miss P K, BA MCLIP, Life Member.
[7464]   04/10/1946   CM01/01/1953
Hung, Ms M W, MAppSc, Assistant Librarian, Hong Kong.
[10019074]   15/04/2011   ME
Hung, Miss M Y Y, BSc MA, Lib. /Student PhD., Tower Hamlets Sch. L.
Serv., London.
[10001353]   20/08/1998   ME
Hunjan, Miss G K, BA (Hons), Comm. Librarian, Spring Hill Library,
Birmingham.
[52377]   30/10/1995   ME
Hunt, Mr C J, BA MLitt FSA MCLIP, Retired.
[18798]   14/09/1959   CM01/01/1963
Hunt, Mrs C S, BA MA,
[10022460]   05/03/2013   ME
Hunt, Mrs E A, MCLIP, Unemployed.
[13210]   04/02/1968   CM03/08/1972
Hunt, Mrs G, BA (Hons), Children's Activities Librarian, Cultural NL Ltd.
[10032380]   29/11/2013   ME
Hunt, Mr G L, BA MA MCLIP, Head of External Engagement, University
of the West Scotland.
[44662]   20/11/1990   CM10/01/1994
Hunt, Ms J M, BA (Hons) DipIM MCLIP, Volunteer Coordinator, Wiltshire
Library Service.
[55367]   03/10/1997   CM20/09/2000
Hunt, Mr M, MSc BSc, Chartered Quality Institute.
[48836]   01/07/1993   ME
Hunt, Mrs M C, BA DipLib MCLIP, Unemployed.
[36656]   31/10/1983   CM15/11/1988
Hunt, Mrs M M, BA MCLIP, Comm. Librarian, Kings Heath L. & Hall
Green Library, Birmingham Public Library.
[32988]   10/10/1980   CM29/07/1983
Hunt, Ms N J, BA MA MCLIP, Academic Liaison Librarian, University of
Southampton.
[38575]   12/07/1985   CM16/05/1990
Hunt, Mrs R, BSc (Hons) MSc MCLIP, Full-Time Mother.
[50526]   01/09/1994   CM18/03/1998
Hunt, Mr R A, FCLIP, Retired.
[7484]   02/09/1954   FE01/01/1967
Hunt, Mrs R A H, BA DipLib MCLIP, Information, Guidance & Supp.
Officer, Stroke Association, Stockport.
[41384]   17/11/1987   CM12/09/1990
Hunt, Miss S, BA (Hons), Helpdesk Assistant., Moray House Library,
Edinburgh.
[10005565]   25/07/2007   ME
Hunt, Dr S E, BA (Hons) MA PhD MCLIP, Subject Support Librarian
(Business and Law), Frenchay Library, University of The West of
England.
[63750]   29/09/2004   CM11/03/2009
Hunt, Miss S J, BA PgDip MA, Assistant Librarian, Durham Cathedral.
[10019328]   02/06/2011   ME
Hunt, Mr S W, BA MA DipLib MA MCLIP, Head of Resource
Development and Delivery, Oxford Brookes University.
[45898]   09/07/1991   CM16/11/1994
Hunter, Mrs A M, BA DipLib MCLIP, Retired.
[33413]   19/11/1980   CM27/01/1984
Hunter, Ms C L, BSc (Hons) MCLIP, Learning Resource Centre
Manager, Titus Salt School, Baildon.
[10014549]   21/03/1983   CM01/01/1983

Hunter, Mrs C M, MLib MA FCLIP, Corporate Services Manager, South
Kent Coast Clinical Commissioning Group, Dover.
[24970]   24/10/1975   **FE15/09/2004**
Hunter, Prof E J, MA AMIET FCLIP, Emeritus Professor of Information
Management, Liverpool John Moores University.
[7494]   16/12/1948   **FE01/01/1966**
Hunter, Mr G, MA MA MCLIP, Librarian, Angus Council, Forfar L. &
Kirriemuir L.
[44335]   19/09/1990   **RV14/11/2012   CM20/09/1995**
Hunter, Mr I D, BA MA MA (CANTAB), Librarian, Reader and Info
Services; Oxford Central Lib.
[10018314]   16/12/2010   **ME**
Hunter, Mr I J, BA (Hons) MSc MCLIP, Shearman & Sterling (London)
LLP, London.
[46741]   14/01/1992   **CM23/07/1997**
Hunter, Mr J C, Student, University of Sheffield.
[10020043]   27/10/2011   **ME**
Hunter, Mr J G, BA MCLIP, Retired.
[7496]   17/01/1969   **CM29/08/1973**
Hunter, Mr P J, BA (Hons), Information Manager, Scottish Government.
[52974]   01/02/1996   **ME**
Hunter, Mr P S, MSc CChem MRSC MCLIP, Retired.
[60392]   01/01/1967   **CM03/06/1970**
Hunter, Miss T C, BA, Library Graduate Trainee at the Royal Botanic
Gardens Kew.
[10031650]   17/09/2013   **ME**
Hunter, Miss V E, BA (Hons) ENG LIT, Library Assistant, Knutsford
Library.
[10035313]   07/10/2014   **ME**
Huntingford, Mrs L, MA (Hons) PgDip (IT) PgDip (LIS), Librarian,
Monifieth Library.
[64664]   18/05/2005   **ME**
Huntington, Mrs S, MCLIP, Librarian, Leicester College.
[63597]   05/07/2004   **CM12/05/2011**
Hunton, Mrs J E, Neighbourhood Librarian, Redcar & Cleveland
Borough Council.
[10010654]   19/08/2008   **ME**
Hunwick, Ms E R, BA (Hons) MA PgDipLIS MCLIP, Lib. : Serv.,
Basildon Healthcare L.
[57042]   30/11/1998   **CM29/03/2006**
Hurcombe, Mrs M, BA MCLIP, Unwaged.
[31465]   15/10/1979   **CM22/10/1981**
Hurley, Ms L, Student.
[10022558]   26/03/2013   **ME**
Hurley, Miss V C, Librarian, Northbury Junior & Infant School.
[10032575]   17/12/2013   **ME**
Hurley, Mrs Z, MA (Hons) (Oxon) MSc, Acquisitions Librarian, University
of Bath.
[10035309]   07/10/2014   **ME**
Hurn, Mr M D, MA MCLIP, Departmental Librarian, Inst. of Astronomy,
University of Cambridge.
[40975]   28/09/1987   **CM16/05/1990**
Hurry, Mr A, DESCIO-Exp-4, Ministry of Defence.
[10033965]   14/05/2014   **ME**
Hurry, Miss P, MA MCLIP, Librarian & Research Secretary,
Congregational History Society.
[7512]   25/05/1970   **CM01/01/1974**
Hurst, Mr A V, MSc,
[10020385]   09/02/2012   **ME**
Hurst, Mrs J, BA (Hons) MA MCLIP, Information Officer, ASH Scotland.
[61646]   11/10/2002   **CM19/10/2012**
Hurst, Mr J, BA DipLib MCLIP, L. Consultant & Trainer, Freelance.
[29691]   01/10/1978   **CM04/12/1981**

Hurst, Ms S, BA (Hons) MA PgDip, Enquiry Services Specialist,
University of Salford.
[10023067]   04/06/2013   **ME**
Hurt, Mrs E H, BA, Assistant Clinical Librarian, Lancashire Teaching
Hospitals NHS Foundation Trust.
[62141]   28/02/2003   **ME**
Husband, Ms K R, BSc DipLib MCLIP, Research Librarian, Glasgow
University.
[42232]   13/10/1988   **CM16/09/1992**
Husbands, Mrs E S, BA DipLib MCLIP, Subject Classifier, Nielsen
Bookdata., Herts.
[19776]   26/11/1972   **CM18/08/1975**
Huse, Mr R J, FCLIP, Life Member.
[7524]   01/10/1946   **FE01/01/1959**
Hussein, Ms S, BA HDip LIS, Student.
[10027616]   16/04/2014   **ME**
Hussey, Mrs N M, MCLIP, Librarian, Peacehaven Comm. School, East
Sussex.
[13665]   04/09/1971   **CM07/03/1975**
Hutchens, Mrs E G, BA (Hons) MA MCLIP, Volunteer museum
assistant, Surrey.
[26421]   14/10/1976   **CM20/09/1995**
Hutcheon, Mr J R, BA MCLIP, Retired.
[7529]   09/02/1968   **CM24/10/1972**
Hutchings, Miss K L, BA (Hons) History, Library Assistant, Staffordshire
County Council.
[10034652]   28/07/2014   **ME**
Hutchins, Miss R Z, BA MSc, Deputy Librarian, New College, Oxford.
[10018540]   03/02/2011   **ME**
Hutchinson, Mr A J, BA (Hons) MCLIP, Head of Library Operational
Services.
[39465]   31/01/1986   **CM12/03/2003**
Hutchinson, Mrs A M, BLib, Assistant Director, Information Services, St
Mary's University College, Twickenham, London.
[47926]   26/10/1992   **ME**
Hutchinson, Mrs E, BSc MCLIP, Head of Services to Education and
Young People, Guernsey.
[59191]   12/12/2000   **CM19/03/2008**
Hutchison, Ms D M E, BA DipLib MCLIP, Under Librarian, Hughes Hall,
Cambridge.
[41001]   01/10/1987   **CM12/09/1990**
Hutchison, Mrs E M, BSc (Econ) (Hons) MCLIP, Information Officer,
CultureNL Limited.
[47162]   18/05/1992   **CM20/11/2002**
Hutchison, Mrs K, MSc, Research and Information Services Manager,
Forestry Commission Library.
[10016139]   26/09/2009   **ME**
Hutchison, Ms M J, BA (HONS) MSc, Library Adviser, Stockbridge
Library.
[10022415]   26/02/2013   **ME**
Hutton, Mr I, BA MA, Unwaged.
[39891]   01/10/1986   **ME**
Hutton, Mrs J I F, MCLIP, Retired.
[7553]   01/01/1951   **CM01/01/1963**
Hutton, Mrs J J, BSc, Librarian, Langley Park School for Boys.
[10035275]   03/10/2014   **ME**
Hutton, Miss L A, BA, Information & Res. Facilitator, NHS Fife.
[10007569]   18/02/2008   **ME**
Huws, Mrs D P, BA (Hons) DipLib MCLIP,
[10020062]   31/10/2011   **CM21/05/1997**
Huws, Mr D R, BA (Hons) PgDipILM, LRC Co-ordinator, Grwp Llandrillo
Menai (Rhyl Campus).
[64813]   12/07/2005   **ME**

Huws, Mr R E, MLib FCLIP, Retired.
[7555]   01/01/1968   FE07/01/1982
Hvass, Miss A, MCLIP,
[62838]   06/11/2003   CM21/03/2007
Hyams, Ms E, HonFCLIP, Contributing Editor, CILIP Update.
[59133]   21/11/2000   HFE01/04/2002
Hyde, Ms J C, BA DipLib, Assistant Library Manager, Cobham Library.
[41285]   28/10/1987   CM18/11/1993
Hyde, Ms K J, MA (Hons), Knowledge Services Coordinator, Chartered
Insurance Institute, London.
[10012889]   19/03/2009   ME
Hyde, Mrs M, BA (Hons), Senior Library Assistant, The Elms Library,
Long Eaton.
[10017761]   05/10/2010   AF
Hyde, Ms S F, MA PGCE BSc, Executive Officer to the Vice-Chancellor,
University of Nottingham.
[59461]   03/04/2001   ME
Hyde, Ms S G, BSc (Hons) DipLib, Information Serv. Manager, Thales
Research & Tech. (UK) Ltd, Reading.
[32601]   30/05/1980   CM04/10/1983
Hyde, Mrs V A, BA MEd MCLIP, Librarian, Blessed Robert Catholic,
College,
[7563]   01/01/1963   CM01/01/1967
Hyett, Mr D J, BSc DipLib MCLIP, Head of Web & Information Services,
Natural Environment Research Council.
[37170]   14/03/1984   CM16/02/1988
Hyland, Ms A, Library Assistant, Hertfordshire Partnership NHS Trust.
[10035558]   20/10/2014   ME
Hyland, Miss J A, BA (Hons) ACLIP, Library Assistant, Hertfordshire
County Council.
[10013133]   02/04/2009   ACL20/02/2014
Hyland, Miss S A, BA MCLIP, Policy & Performance Officer, Bucks.
County Council.
[24707]   09/10/1975   CM11/02/1980
Hymans, Miss N, BA (Hons), Student, University of Sheffield.
[100276351]   08/01/2014   ME
Hynes, Mr A R, BA MCLIP, College Librarian, Longsands Academy, St
Neots, Cambridgeshire.
[33813]   18/02/1981   CM17/07/1984
Hysa, Mrs D F, BA (Hons), Capital Markets Information Advisor,
Linklaters Business Services.
[58060]   21/10/1999   ME

I

Ibberson, Mrs C S, Student, University of Wales Aberystwyth.
[10032646]   23/12/2013   ME
Icke, Miss A, BA MSt MA, Librarian, Wimbledon High School.
[10015603]   17/12/2009   ME
Ifie, Mrs Y O, MSc B. Liss D. Liss, University of Wales Trinity Saint
David, Swansea.
[10008703]   09/04/2008   ME
Iglesias-Dinneen, Mrs G J, Senior Library Assistant, University of
Southampton.
[62157]   04/03/2003   ME
Ignirri, Miss R, Librarian, Teeside High School, Stockton-on-Tees.
[10021243]   29/06/2012   AF
Ike, Prof A O, MA DipLib FNLA, Life Member.
[17084]   14/03/1964   ME
Ikeogu, Mrs C E, BA MSc DMS MCLIP,
[30633]   26/02/1979   CM28/09/1983
Iles, Mrs S, MCLIP, Retired.
[8104]   22/08/1965   CM01/01/1969

Illes, Mr A J, MA MCLIP, Life Member.
[7582]   24/01/1953   CM01/01/1955
Illingworth, Mrs J E, BA (Hons) MCLIP, Self-employed.
[49648]   18/11/1993   CM20/11/2002
Illingworth, Mr M E T, BSc (Hons) DipLib MCLIP, Academic Librarian,
Southampton University.
[45618]   04/04/1991   CM18/11/1993
Imrie, Mr M P, Unwaged.
[63219]   16/03/2004   ME
Inala, Miss P, MSc MCLIP, Senior Assistant Librarian.
[63128]   11/02/2004   CM11/03/2009
Ince, Mr G, BA MSc, Information Librarian, University of Bath, Avon.
[10001826]   08/03/2007   ME
Indran, Mrs N, BA (Hons) PgDip MA, Lib. Children and Young People
Lib. Serv., London Borough of Barnet.
[54516]   15/01/1997   ME
Ingber, Miss L C, BA (Hons), Researcher, Occstrategy, London.
[57026]   26/11/1998   ME
Ingham, Mrs A N, BA PGCE MA, Assistant Information adviser,
University of Brighton.
[10016448]   24/03/2010   ME
Ingham, Mr R A, BA, PURE Content Editor & Cataloguer Lancaster
University.
[50720]   13/10/1994   ME
Inglehearn, Ms A M, BA (Hons) MSc MCLIP, Lib. Manager, Leeds
College of Building,
[51627]   19/04/1995   RV09/11/2011   CM18/09/2002
Ingman, Mrs H, BA (Hons), Assistant Librarian, Kingsthorpe College.
[54078]   24/10/1996   ME
Ingold, Ms M, MA, University of Applied Sciences and Arts
Northwestern Switzerland FHNW, Muttenz / Library.
[64755]   30/06/2005   ME
Ingram, Mrs G A, BA MCLIP, Retired.
[7611]   26/08/1964   CM01/01/1968
Ingram, Ms M, MSc MCLIP, Lib. /Information Officer, Arthritis Research
UK Epidemiology Unit, University of Manchester.
[21774]   11/01/1974   CM01/01/1977
Ingram, Mrs M M, MA (Hons)Geog PgDip MCLIP, Aberdeenshire
Libraries.
[10001401]   14/02/2007   CM10/03/2010
Ingrey, Miss H M, BA (Hons) MA, Super. -Teaching & Learning Supp.,
UCL, London.
[59922]   02/11/2001   ME
Inman, Miss J, BA (Hons) DipLib MCLIP,
[53054]   14/02/1996   CM21/05/1997
Inman, Mrs J L, FCLIP, Retired.
[11692]   04/09/1971   FE29/11/2006
Inness, Mrs J E, MA DipLib MCLIP, Libraries Manager.
[29444]   31/07/1978   CM25/11/1980
Innis, Mrs J, Retired, London.
[23210]   08/11/1974   CM26/07/1979
Innocenti, Miss G, BA,
[10021735]   08/10/2012   ME
Inns, Mrs C M R, BA (Hons) MCLIP, Resources Librarian, House of
Commons Library.
[39452]   08/02/1986   CM12/03/2003
Inskip, Dr C, MSc LIS, Lecturer.
[65303]   19/12/2005   ME
Introwicz, Ms M L A, BSc,
[10016956]   02/10/1988   ME
Iona, Mr J, MCILIP, Librarian, Oasis Academy, Enfield.
[10006097]   26/09/2007   CM13/11/2013
Ions, Ms L, BSc, Learning Centres Manager, Gateshead College.
[10008098]   27/03/1995   ME

Iqbal, Mrs G A, BA DipLib, Team Leader, Hounslow Library, London Borough of Hounslow.
[36837]	09/01/1984	ME

Iqbal-Gillani, Ms N, BA MCLIP, Retired.
[29047]	27/02/1978	CM16/07/1980

Iredale, Miss J, BA (Hons) Dip Im, Languages & Digital Resources Manager, Hampton School, Middex.
[10016006]	03/04/1996	ME

Ireland, Mrs E J, BEd (Hons) DipILM MCLIP, Retired.
[48241]	17/11/1992	CM24/05/1995

Ireland, Mrs H, MA MCLIP, Academic Support Librarian, University of Warwick Library.
[2623]	31/10/1971	CM26/07/1977

Ireland, Mr I B, MCLIP FRSA, Retired.
[7622]	12/02/1968	CM01/01/1971

Ireland, Miss J, BA MCLIP, Unwaged.
[36857]	11/01/1984	CM09/08/1988

Ireland, Miss K J, Student, Aberystwith University.
[10033881]	08/05/2014	ME

Iremonger, Ms L I, BA (Hons), Librarian, Nottingham City Council.
[49593]	19/11/1993	ME

Irish, Ms R H, BA (Hons) ACLIP, L. Manager, St Louis Catholic Middle School, Suffolk.
[10010656]	19/08/2008	ACL18/01/2012

Irvine, Ms G, MCLIP, Access to Services Senior Manager Lancashire County Council.
[65228]	17/11/2005	CM15/01/2013

Irvine, Mr N, BA DipLib MCLIP, Part-time Stock Support Officer, Wokingham BC, Part-time Library Assistant, Oxfordshire BC.
[44823]	07/12/1990	CM21/07/1993

Irving, Ms C M, BA (Hons) MSc MCLIP, Research Fellow, PhD Student & Freelance Information Professional,
[57124]	14/12/1998	CM21/06/2006

Irving, Mr P J, MCLIP, Retired.
[10019327]	01/04/1970	CM01/01/1973

Irwin, Miss J M, ALAA MCLIP, Retired.
[7637]	01/01/1947	CM01/01/1965

Irwin, Miss R, BLib MCLIP, Customer Serv. Manager, Dorset.
[38466]	02/05/1985	CM16/10/1989

Irwin Tazzar, Mrs J L, BA (Hons) MCLIP, Systems Librarian, University of St Mark & St John, Plymouth.
[47205]	03/06/1992	CM18/03/1998

Isaac, Mr D G, BA DipLib MCLIP DMS,
[7640]	01/10/1971	CM26/11/1974

Isaac, Ms K, MCLIP, Information Librarian, London Borough of Sutton.
[26747]	02/11/1976	CM07/08/1981

Isaac, Ms S, MA, Customer Services Manager (Environment & Access), King's College London.
[45276]	01/10/1990	ME

Isaacs, Mr J M, MA FCLIP, Life Member.
[7642]	21/06/1957	FE01/01/1966

Isaksen, Miss K G, BA (Hons) DipLib, Retired.
[7644]	13/07/1971	ME

Ishaaq, Miss H, BA (Hons), Student, Robert Gordon University.
[10035381]	14/10/2014	ME

Ishikawa, Miss N, MA in Librarianship, Student, University of Sheffield.
[10034194]	18/06/2014	ME

Iskandar, Ms F, BA (Economics), Library Customer Services Officer, London Borough of Barnet Libraries & Archives.
[10023396]	16/07/2013	ME

Ismail, Mrs M, Student, University Teknologi Mara.
[10032643]	23/12/2013	ME

Ismail, Mrs N, MCLIP, Children's Services Librarian, West Sussex County Council L. Serv., Horsham.
[63893]	26/10/2004	CM17/09/2008

Itayem, Mr M A, MA FCLIP, Life Member.
[17094]	20/09/1963	FE26/02/1992

Ivanou, Mr I, MA MCLIP, Head of Learning Resources, QAHE.
[63821]	08/10/2004	CM27/01/2010

Iyogun, Mrs B, Student, Greenwich Community College.
[10034191]	18/06/2014	ME

Izzard, Mr D F, BA (Hons) DipIS MCLIP, L. Manager, Golders Green Library, London.
[10008990]	15/01/1992	CM22/09/1999

J

Jablkowska, Miss H M, MCLIP, Unwaged.
[21800]	15/01/1974	CM01/10/1976

Jack, Mr M J, MA, Counter Service Supervisor, King's College London.
[65182]	16/11/2005	AF

Jackson, Ms A, L. and Information Officer, WWF, Godalming.
[10007792]	11/03/2008	ME

Jackson, Miss A, Library Manager, London Borough of Greenwich.
[10033173]	18/02/2014	AF

Jackson, Mr A, BA MCLIP, Principal Assistant Librarian, University Dundee.
[39713]	24/05/1986	CM14/11/1989

Jackson, Ms A B, BA MCLIP, Career Break.
[29667]	05/10/1978	CM11/08/1987

Jackson, Mrs A H, MSc MCLIP, Assistant Librarian, UWE, Bristol.
[10000799]	03/11/2006	CM13/11/2013

Jackson, Mrs C, BSc MAEcl (Open), Learning Resources Manager, Regents Park Community Primary School.
[10032430]	18/02/2014	ME

Jackson, Mrs C, BLib MCLIP, Librarian.
[32859]	13/10/1980	CM30/07/1985

Jackson, Mrs C M, BSc (Econ) MSc PGCE (FE), Managing Editor, Journel of Information Literacy.
[44722]	29/11/1990	ME

Jackson, Miss E, BA, L. &Information Serv. Assistant, CIOB, Ascot.
[10016458]	26/03/2010	AF

Jackson, Mr E, LLB MCLIP, Retired.
[7669]	03/10/1969	CM10/01/1975

Jackson, Miss E A, PgDip, Learning Resources Co-ordinator, LRC Darlington College, Darlington.
[10017407]	18/08/2010	ME

Jackson, Mrs E K, BA (Hons) DipLIS MCLIP, Young Peoples Serv. Librarian, Young Peoples L. Serv., Newport, I. O. W.
[50038]	24/02/1994	CM18/11/1998

Jackson, Mrs J C, BA (Hons), Student, University of Strathclyde.
[10035528]	16/10/2014	ME

Jackson, Mrs L A, BSc, L. Assistant (Technician), Aberystwyth University, Royal Bolton NHS Foundation Trust.
[10016153]	16/02/2010	ME

Jackson, Ms M E, Learning Resource Centre Manager, St Anthony's Girls' Catholic Academy, Sunderland.
[10010357]	22/07/2008	ME

Jackson, Ms M F, MA, Catg., Scottish Parliament Information Centre, Edinburgh.
[40056]	10/10/1986	ME

Jackson, Mrs P A, BA (Hons) MCLIP, Unwaged.
[10540]	19/01/1968	CM02/08/1972

Jackson, Mr P L, MA DipLib MCLIP, Deputy Librarian, Instituteof
Classical Studies Library, London.
[42690]   06/02/1989   CM14/09/1994
Jackson, Ms P S, BA DipEd BEd Grad DipIfs, Information Management
Practitioner Hertfordshire County Council.
[59196]   14/12/2000   ME
Jackson, Mr R A, MA DipLib MCLIP, Systems Development Manager,
Leicestershire County Council.
[36016]   06/04/1983   CM03/03/1987
Jackson, Miss S L, Lib. Manager, JR Knowles, Warrington.
[41424]   09/12/1987   ME
Jackson, Mr S T, MA MCLIP, Dir of Lib & Info Serv Divison., RVC,
Hatfield.
[10020790]   24/10/1989   CM18/11/1992
Jackson-Ross, Mr L A, BA (Hons), Graduate Trainee, Bodleian Social
Science Library.
[10032015]   21/10/2013   ME
Jacob, Miss C H, BSc MCLIP, Information Specialist, NICE.
[66103]   25/09/2006   CM25/01/2011
Jacob, Mrs L, BLib, LRC Librarian, Abraham Moss High School.
[10034635]   25/07/2014   ME
Jacob, Mr T J, MA MCLIP, Senior Library Assistant, Nottingham
University Library.
[46348]   29/10/1991   CM15/10/2002
Jacobs, Ms M, Senior Lib. Assistant, Faculty of Asian & Middle Eastern
Studies, University of Cambridge.
[10007693]   21/02/2008   ME
Jacobs, Mrs S E, BSc (Hons), LMS Training and Support Specialist,
Furlong Business Solutions Ltd.
[10035029]   09/09/2014   ME
Jacobsen, Ms S E, MA BA MLIS MCLIP,
[63824]   08/10/2004   CM10/03/2010
Jacques, Miss E L, BA MA MCLIP,
[10012150]   08/01/2009   CM29/05/2013
Jacques, Mr M O, BA DipLib MCLIP, currently unemployed – made
redundant.
[41041]   06/10/1987   CM25/05/1994
Jacques, Miss S E, Assistant Librarian, North East Wales Schools
Library Service, Mold.
[51328]   12/01/1995   ME
Jacquest, Mr D F, BA (Hons), Student, Manchester Metropolitan
University.
[10035534]   16/10/2014   ME
Jaffray, Mrs K C, BA MCLIP, Senior Librarian, Larbert Library, Falkirk
Community Trust.
[35453]   17/10/1982   CM27/03/1991
Jaiteh, Ms S, BA (Hons), Project Manager, Soutron Limited.
[10007125]   07/01/1981   ME
Jaiyeoba, Ms E J, Work Placement, Wellcome Institute, London.
[10019334]   08/06/2011   AF
Jajjawi, Miss H, PhD, Unwaged.
[10017342]   30/07/2010   ME
Jakes, Mr C R, MCLIP, Local Studies & Information Manager,
Cambridgeshire County Council, Cambridge Central Library.
[21715]   02/01/1974   CM24/01/1977
James, Mrs A, Student.
[10014098]   25/06/2009   ME
James, Ms A C, BA MA, Antiquarian Cataloguer, Regents Park College.
[64108]   17/01/2005   ME
James, Mr A C, BA MCLIP, Assistant Librarian, Society of Antiquaries,
London.
[32602]   19/06/1980   CM31/12/1989
James, Miss A G, Student, Aberystwyth University.
[10033540]   25/03/2014   ME

James, Miss A M, BA DipLib MCLIP,
[49062]   28/09/1993   CM26/07/1995
James, Mrs B, BSc DipInf, TA, St Thomas More School, Letchworth.
[59239]   15/01/2001   ME
James, Ms B E, BSc (Hons) MCLIP, Information Resources Assistant,
London South Bank University, Perry L.
[50448]   03/08/1994   RV14/10/2011   CM13/06/2007
James, Mrs B R, BA MCLIP, Life Member.
[3215]   07/09/1955   CM01/01/1961
James, Mrs B S, BA Lib Dip MCLIP, Senior Librarian, Wellington
School, Somerset.
[55034]   01/07/1997   CM15/11/2000
James, Mrs C A L, BA (Hons) PgDipILS, Librarian, Guille-Alles Library,
Guernsey.
[44476]   11/10/1990   ME
James, Miss C F, Library Assistant, Aberystwyth University.
[10023001]   21/05/2013   ME
James, Ms D, BSc (Hons) MSc DipLib, Editorial Co ordinator, Calibre
Audio Library.
[41997]   14/07/1988   ME
James, Ms E, MA DipLib, Librarian, National Art Library, London Senior
Librarian, Victoria and Museum, London.
[36318]   01/10/1983   ME
James, Miss E A, BA DipLib, Technical Librarian, Liverpool Victoria,
Bournemouth.
[10011114]   09/01/1984   ME
James, Mr H, BA DipLib MCLIP, Principal Librarian, Cyngor Gwynedd,
Caernarfon.
[29985]   31/10/1978   CM04/01/1982
James, Mrs H R, Assistant Librarian, Dame Alice Owen's School,
Potters Bar.
[64157]   19/01/2005   ME
James, Mrs J M, BA MCLIP, Student.
[26924]   11/12/1976   CM12/02/1981
James, Miss J T, BA (Hons) MSc (Econ) MCLIP, Learning Resource
Centre Manager, Morriston Comprehensive School.
[52840]   02/01/1996   CM19/05/1999
James, Ms P, BA MCLIP, Information Officer, Stephenson Harwood,
London.
[30192]   10/01/1979   CM16/12/1982
James, Mr P M, MSc MIIS CertEd MCLIP, Head of L. &Learning Res.,
Maryvale Institue, Birmingham.
[7719]   01/11/1969   CM01/07/1974
James, Mr R S, MA MCLIP, Assistant Under Librarian, Cambridge
University Library, Cambridge.
[10008948]   23/04/2008   CM18/12/2013
James, Mrs S, BSc MCLIP, Employment not known.
[60707]   07/11/1973   CM07/11/1973
James, Dr S, DUniv BA FCLIP, Retired.
[7723]   26/10/1965   FE22/07/1992
Jameson, Ms T, BA (Hons) DipILM MCLIP, Sch. Librarian, Woodcroft
College, Adelaide, S-Australia.
[46617]   25/11/1991   CM16/11/1994
Jamie, Mrs E J, MA MSc, Chief Librarian, International Institute for
Strategic Studies London.
[55790]   24/11/1997   ME
Jamieson, Mr I M, FCLIP CertEdFE, Retired.
[19503]   27/09/1955   FE01/01/1961
Jamieson, Mrs J, Assistant Librarian, Erith School.
[40054]   16/10/1986   ME
Jamieson, Ms S, BA (Hons) MSc DipLIS MCLIP, Librarian, Royal
College of Physicians, London.
[55447]   13/10/1997   CM20/09/2000

Jamieson, Mrs S L, BA MCLIP, Library Services Manager, Aberdeenshire.
[37663]   15/10/1984   **CM21/07/1989**

Jamieson, Mrs S V, MCLIP, Life Member.
[8613]   23/11/1967   **CM14/08/1974**

Jamnezhad, Miss B, BA (Hons) MA,
[51882]   24/07/1995   **CM29/03/2004**

Janda, Ms B K, BA, Assistant Area Librarian, Walsall Council.
[65496]   08/02/2006   **ME**

Janes, Mr A C, BA DipLib MCLIP, Library Assistant LB of Havering, LB of Havering.
[38136]   21/01/1985   **CM16/09/1992**

Janes, Miss C L, Arch. Researcher, ITN, London.
[52501]   02/11/1995   **ME**

Janes, Mrs F E, BA MSc (Econ) MCLIP, Career break.
[38847]   14/10/1985   **CM18/04/1989**

Janota, Mrs H, BA (Hons) MA, Labour market information manager – Futures Advice, Skills and Employment.
[56822]   23/10/1998   **CM16/07/2003**

Janta-Lipinski, Mrs P M, MCLIP, Librarian Advisor, Library Services for Education, Glos County Council.
[24333]   01/07/1975   **CM01/01/1978**

Jap, Mrs Y S, MCLIP, Senior Assistant, Cultural Community Solutions.
[61813]   13/11/2002   **CM19/11/2008**

Jara De Sumar, Ms J, Liaison Librarian, McGill University Montreal, Canada.
[22781]   19/10/1974   **ME**

Jarbur, Ms R C, BSc, Student, University of Strathclyde.
[10033864]   07/05/2014   **ME**

Jardine, Ms S, BSc PgLib MCLIP, Information Manager, SCIE, London.
[10008035]   11/09/1986   **CM01/07/1993**

Jardine-Willoughby, Miss S, BA (Hons) MCLIP, Retired.
[26423]   18/10/1976   **CM25/01/1980**

Jarman, Mrs J, BA, Student, Brunel University.
[10035502]   16/10/2014   **ME**

Jarrett, Ms C E, BA (Hons) DipLib, Subject Librarian, Health & Applied Sciences, University of the West of England, Bristol.
[10001444]   27/06/1988   **ME**

Jarvis, Miss A E, BA MCLIP, Librarian, Newport City Council.
[32095]   25/01/1980   **CM06/09/1985**

Jarvis, Mrs A M, BA (Hons) MA MCLIP,
[58962]   10/10/2000   **CM27/01/2010**

Jarvis, Mr K A, MA FCLIP, Retired.
[17110]   14/03/1955   **FE29/05/1974**

Jary, Mrs C V, BA (Hons), Collection Dev. Manager, East Area, Lancashire.
[65998]   11/08/2006   **AF**

Jay, Miss M E, MA MCLIP, Enquiry and Information Manager, Derby City Lib.
[26749]   11/10/1976   **CM11/10/1982**

Jazosch, Ms K, BA (Hons) Phil MA, L. Assistant, Biomedical Sci. Library, Southampton.
[10010322]   18/07/2008   **AF**

Jeal, Ms S M, BA MA, Unwaged.
[10014789]   10/11/2009   **ME**

Jeal, Mrs Y A, MA DipInfLib FCLIP, Customer Support Manager, University of Salford, Information Serv. Div.
[44388]   03/10/1990   **FE03/10/2007**

Jeeves, Mr J, BA MCLIP, Reader Development Specialist, Harrow & Ealing Library Services.
[31871]   03/01/1980   **CM28/07/1983**

Jeeves, Mrs S J, BA MCLIP, Service Development Specialist, Harrow Libraries.
[31627]   29/10/1979   **CM29/07/1983**

Jeffcock, Ms C, Customer Serv. Librarian, Fire Serv. College, Moreton in Marsh.
[64331]   04/03/2005   **ME**

Jefferson, Mrs C E, BA (Hons) MA MCLIP, Senior Researcher, Hogan Lovells, London.
[56409]   01/07/1998   **CM21/06/2006**

Jefferson, Dr G, BSc MA PhD FCLIP PGCE, Life Member.
[7764]   30/04/1948   **FE01/01/1953**

Jeffery, Mrs H, BA DipLib MCLIP, Assistant Librarian, Surrey Archaeological Society.
[31306]   17/10/1979   **CM10/09/1982**

Jeffery, Mrs L C, BA (Hons) MSc MCLIP, Assistant Librarian, (Enquiries), University of Portsmouth.
[53878]   07/10/1996   **CM09/07/2008**

Jefford, Ms M J, BA MCLIP, ICT Systems Librarian, South Ayrshire Council, Carnegie L.
[39762]   01/07/1986   **CM18/04/1990**

Jeffrey, Mrs L K S, BA (Hons) MSc MCLIP, Career Break.
[62963]   25/11/2003   **CM08/08/2008**

Jeffries, Mrs L J, Lib. Manager, Winton Library, Bournemouth.
[10017560]   07/09/2010   **AF**

Jeffries, Mrs S L, BSc (Hons) MSc MCLIP, Admin. Assistant.
[51444]   10/02/1995   **CM24/07/1996**

Jeffs, Miss K, BA MA PgDip, Network Librarian/Library Assistant, Dingwall Sch & Comm Lib.
[10020980]   03/05/2012   **ME**

Jefkins, Mrs H J, MCLIP, Unemployed.
[28646]   12/01/1978   **CM08/10/1981**

Jelfs, Mrs K J, BA (Hons) MLITT, Librarian, Cains.
[10031828]   08/10/2013   **ME**

Jelleyman, Ms S, BA MCLIP PGCE, Extended Services Development Officer, Shropshire Council.
[23419]   13/01/1975   **CM05/07/1978**

Jellis, Miss S, FCLIP, Life Member.
[7786]   21/09/1944   **FE01/01/1971**

Jenkin, Mr J, BA (Hons) MA, Assistant Librarian – Trainee, Anglia Ruskin University, Cambridge.
[10022376]   19/02/2013   **AF**

Jenkin, Ms S M, BA (Hons) MA MCLIP, Comm. Librarian, Medway Council., Kent.
[62024]   20/01/2003   **CM09/07/2008**

Jenkings, Mrs M E, BA MCLIP, Dev. Librarian, Notts City Libraries.
[29143]   05/04/1978   **CM08/02/1982**

Jenkins, Miss A C, BA DipLib MA MCLIP, Head of Information and Communications, Alcohol Concern, London.
[29695]   30/09/1978   **CM11/11/1983**

Jenkins, Mr D R, BA (Hons) MCLIP, Assistant Librarian, Manchester Metropolitan University.
[10006991]   17/12/2007   **CM18/01/2012**

Jenkins, Miss E W, BA (Hons) PgDipLib, Assistant Library Promoter, Gwynedd Council, Blaenau Ffestiniog Library Gwynedd.
[42483]   23/11/1988   **CM17/09/2003**

Jenkins, Miss H, BScEcon, Graduate, Aberystwyth University.
[10032679]   03/01/2014   **ME**

Jenkins, Mr M, BSc MCLIP ILTM MEd FHEA NTF, Academic Developer (Digital Literacy), Coventry University.
[38160]   24/01/1985   **CM10/05/1988**

Jenkins, Miss N, BA FCLIP, Retired.
[7800]   01/02/1964   **FE11/04/1973**

Jenkins, Mrs N G, BA DipLib MCLIP, Librarian, Conwy & Denbighshire NHS Trust, Glanclwyd Hospital.
[46084]   18/09/1991   **CM19/01/2000**

Jenkins, Ms R, BA (Hons) MCLIP, Retired.
[31040]   26/09/1962   **CM24/02/1986**

Jenkins, Ms R, Student, University of Wales Aberystwyth.
[10032874]   22/01/2014   **ME**
Jenkins, Miss R, MA MCLIP,
[10022084]   04/12/2012   **CM13/05/2014**
Jenkins, Mrs R M, BA MCLIP, Library Assistant, Bridgend.
[33733]   11/02/1981   **CM11/01/1987**
Jenkinson, Miss C M, MCLIP, Retired.
[7805]   15/09/1970   **CM21/11/1973**
Jenkinson, Mrs E M, MCLIP, Life Member.
[7806]   01/01/1956   **CM01/01/1970**
Jenkinson, Ms S, BSc DipLib MCLIP, Local Access Officer, Surrey Hist.
Serv., Woking, Surrey.
[43074]   11/07/1989   **CM18/09/1991**
Jennings, Mrs A, BA MA MSc, Librarian, The Metanoia Institute.
[10021772]   09/10/2012   **ME**
Jennings, Ms B J, BA DipLib MCLIP, Unemployed.
[31872]   13/12/1979   **CM10/09/1982**
Jennings, Ms D M, BA MSc DipLib MCLIP, Collection Development
Librarian, Catawba Co. Library, Newton., North Carolina, USA.
[26145]   12/07/1976   **CM01/01/1978**
Jennings, Mrs E, BA (Hons) MSc MCLIP, Technical Data Officer,
University of Bath.
[58027]   19/10/1999   **RV**27/08/2014   **CM19/03/2008**
Jennings, Miss R, BSc Econ Info Mgmt MCLIP, Forum Library
Supervisor, University of Exeter.
[10014097]   25/06/2009   **CM27/03/2014**
Jennings, Ms S C, BTh (Cantab) MA MCLIP, Faculty Librarian, Faculty
of Architecture & History of Art, University of Cambridge.
[10001966]   29/03/2007   **CM27/01/2010**
Jennings, Mrs S L, MCLIP, Clinical Evidence Specialist – Warrington &
Halton NHS Foundation Trust.
[49064]   01/10/1993   **CM30/04/2014**
Jennings, Ms S L, BSc (Hons) MA, Director of Digital & Community
Engagement, CapacityGrid Knowledge Hub.
[10007200]   27/08/1996   **ME**
Jennings-Young, Mrs S, BA (Hons) MA, Unemployed.
[35528]   29/10/1982   **ME**
Jeorrett, Mr P W, BA PgDip MCLIP, University Librarian, Glyndwr
University, Wrexham.
[26825]   19/11/1976   **CM17/07/1981**
Jeromson, Mrs C G, BA (Hons) MSc, Senior Library Assistant,
Shetland Library.
[10020315]   12/01/2012   **ME**
Jervis, Mrs B, BSc (Hons) MA MCLIP, Sch. L. Consultant.
[55410]   10/10/1997   **CM15/05/2002**
Jervis, Mrs J M, BA MCLIP, Part-time Assistant Worthing Library, West
Sussex County Council, Worthing.
[22087]   28/01/1974   **CM14/11/1978**
Jervis, Mr M, BA BA MA PgDip PhD, Archive Assistant, Durham C. C.
[10034327]   04/07/2014   **ME**
Jeskins, Miss L J, BA (Hons) MSc MCLIP, Freelance Trainer.
[58732]   01/07/2000   **CM10/07/2002**
Jesmont, Mrs C J, MA (Hons) DipLib MCLIP, Jackton Library, Police
Scotland, East Kilbride.
[33445]   01/01/1981   **CM01/07/1990**
Jesper, Ms S, MA, HYMS Library Service Assistant and Teaching &
Learning Assistant, University of York.
[10019613]   05/08/2011   **ME**
Jess, Mr D, BA DipLib MLS CDipAF MCLIP, Assistant Chief Librarian,
Belfast Education & Library Board, Northern Ireland.
[10002011]   22/10/1973   **CM21/09/1977**
Jesson, Rev A F, TD MA MLS FCLIP, Retired; formerly Bible Society's
Librarian.
[7830]   26/01/1966   **FE27/03/1991**

Jewell, Mr E E, BA (Hons) MA MScEcon MCLIP, Chief Librarian, Jersey
Library.
[56510]   30/07/1998   **CM16/05/2001**
Jewell, Mr K B, MA MCLIP, Information Services Manager. Chartered
Institute of Marketing, Cookham, Berkshire.
[10018582]   02/10/1986   **CM01/07/1993**
Jewell, Miss R E, BSc (Hons) Maths Stats Comp, Knowledge
Management Team Leader and Intranet Administrator, IoD, London.
[10001399]   14/02/2007   **ME**
Jewell, Miss S, BA (Hons), Library Assistant, UWE, Bristol.
[10018272]   10/12/2010   **ME**
Jhavary, Mr A C, BA DipLib, PT Librarian, Dept of Neuroradiology,
National Hospital for Neurology & Neurosurgery, London.
[41754]   11/03/1988   **ME**
Jin, Mrs H, MSc, Library Assistant, Mary Seacole Library, University of
C. England, Birmingham.
[65921]   06/07/2006   **ME**
Job, Mr D E V, MCLIP, Life Member.
[7841]   01/01/1950   **CM01/01/1953**
Job, Ms D M, MA DipLIS, Director of Library Services, The University of
Birmingham.
[51905]   03/08/1995   **ME**
Jobey, Ms A, BA MCLIP, Central and Collections Manager.
[31078]   01/06/1977   **CM24/09/1980**
Jocys, Mr T,
[10007718]   21/02/2008   **ME**
Jodrell, Miss C L, Student / Part-time Library Assistant.
[10022560]   26/03/2013   **ME**
Joglekar, Mr P L, BSc DipLib MISTC MCLIP, Retired.
[26118]   01/02/1973   **CM15/07/1976**
John, Ms K A, MCLIP, Community Dev. Manager, Caerphilly Libraries.
[32430]   21/03/1980   **CM29/04/1983**
John, Mrs L J, BLib MCLIP, Library Services Manager, South
Leicestershire College.
[30917]   28/06/1979   **RV**22/09/2010   **CM22/10/1982**
John Watson, Mr R D, MA PGCE PgDipILS, Administration Assistant.
[54291]   13/11/1996   **ME**
Johns, Ms E, Student.
[10033713]   16/04/2014   **ME**
Johns, Mrs J M, BSc (Econ), Retired.
[7859]   26/05/1971   **CM31/12/1973**
Johns, Mr M, MLIB MGNT, Reference Librarian, University of South
Australia.
[10031723]   27/09/2013   **ME**
Johnsen, Mrs J, MCLIP, Retired.
[7860]   19/02/1960   **CM01/01/1965**
Johnson, Ms A, Office & Quality Manager, Skelly & Couch.
[10013092]   24/03/2009   **ME**
Johnson, Mrs A M, BA (Hons) QTS, Library Assistant, Worthing Library,
West Sussex.
[10019769]   08/09/2011   **ME**
Johnson, Mr A R I, BA (Hons) ECDL, Library Assistant, Donald Mason
Library, Liverpool Sch. of Tropical Medicine.
[61493]   22/08/2002   **ME**
Johnson, Miss B L, BSc Econ, Agency staff.
[54336]   20/11/1996   **ME**
Johnson, Mrs C, Librarian, Kineton High School, Kineton, Warwick.
[10022271]   29/01/2013   **AF**
Johnson, Mr D, BA DipLib MCLIP, Cataloguer, British Library Boston
Spa, West Yorkshire.
[37948]   28/11/1984   **CM08/03/1988**
Johnson, Mrs D S, Senior Library Assistant (Part Time), University of
the West of England, Frenchay Campus, Bristol.
[10013652]   18/05/2009   **ME**

Johnson, Mrs G, MA MCLIP, Retired.
[7885]   04/02/1964   **CM01/01/1968**
Johnson, Miss H, Librarian, Tobago House of Assembly, L. Serv.
Department, West Indies.
[61035]   05/02/2002   **ME**
Johnson, Ms H F, BA MA MSc MCLIP PGCAP FHEA, Digital
Resources Manager., University of Bedfordshire, Bedford.
[53530]   09/07/1996   **CM16/05/2001**
Johnson, Prof I M, BA FCLIP FCMI, Senior Editor, 'Libri: international
journal of libraries and information services'.
[7889]   06/03/1963   **FE26/01/1994**
Johnson, Ms J M, BA DipLib MCLIP, Due Diligence Researcher,
Executive Profiles Ltd, London.
[26426]   23/10/1976   **CM12/06/1980**
Johnson, Miss K C, BA (HONS) PgDip MCLIP, Knowledge Centre
Analyst., J R Knowles Ltd, Warrington.
[10009809]   12/06/2008   **CM16/01/2014**
Johnson, Mrs K C, MA MCLIP, Librarian, Herbert Smith Freehills LLP,
London.
[61013]   01/02/2002   **CM04/10/2006**
Johnson, Ms K F, BA MSc, Retired.
[58075]   25/10/1999   **ME**
Johnson, Ms K M, MSc, Resource Centre Coordinator, Info Service,
Heriot Watt University.
[10017140]   14/07/2010   **ME**
Johnson, Mrs L, MA, Student, Robert Gordon University.
[10035608]   23/10/2014   **ME**
Johnson, Ms L C, MLS MCLIP, Unwaged.
[25326]   15/01/1976   **CM06/06/1980**
Johnson, Miss L H, MA BA (Hons) MCLIP, Librarian.
[10020637]   14/03/2012   **CM13/05/2014**
Johnson, Dr L M, BA MA PhD, Library Assistant / Student.
[10033843]   02/05/2014   **ME**
Johnson, Ms M, BA (Hons) DipLib LLA MCLIP, Learning Resources
Manager, Treloar's (College & School), Alton.
[34089]   06/10/1981   **CM07/09/2005**
Johnson, Mrs M, ACLIP, Lib. Supervisor, Devon CC.
[10019477]   07/07/2011   **ACL09/09/2013**
Johnson, Mrs M, BA MCLIP, Retired.
[46716]   02/01/1992   **CM21/07/1993**
Johnson, Ms M S, MA (Hons) MA MCLIP, Head of Member Services,
IDOX plc., Glasgow.
[62090]   12/02/2003   **CM21/05/2008**
Johnson, Mrs N, MCLIP, Senior L. Customer Care Assistant, Newcastle
College L.
[63320]   13/04/2004   **CM09/07/2008**
Johnson, Mr P, BA MCLIP, Retired.
[43280]   02/02/1964   **CM01/01/1967**
Johnson, Mrs P A, MCLIP, Head of Library and Leanrer SUpport,
University of Derby.
[20298]   29/01/1973   **CM10/08/1976**
Johnson, Mr P B, BA MA MCLIP, Head of Collections and Space,
University of Reading.
[61839]   15/11/2002   **CM31/01/2007**
Johnson, Mr P J, BA MCLIP, Historical Researcher.
[36474]   15/10/1983   **CM04/12/1987**
Johnson, Ms R, BA MSc, Resources & InformationWorker, Football
Unites, Racism Divides; Weekend Co-ordinator, University of
Sheffield.
[51700]   22/05/1995   **ME**
Johnson, Miss R A, School Librarian, Shoreham Academy, Shoreham-
by-Sea, West Sussex.
[60979]   22/01/2002   **ME**

Johnson, Mrs R D A, BA MCLIP, Sch. Librarian, Maidwell Hall School,
Northamptonshire.
[26223]   12/08/1976   **CM16/09/1980**
Johnson, Dr R E, MA MCLIP, Retired.
[23689]   23/01/1975   **CM25/05/1978**
Johnson, Dr R N, BA MA PhD MCLIP, Part-time (Non-LIS).
[43199]   03/10/1989   **CM20/03/1996**
Johnson, Dr S P, PhD MA BA (Hons), Keeper of the Abbey Archives
and Library, Downside Abbey.
[10034222]   24/06/2014   **ME**
Johnson, Ms W, MLIS, Information Advr., Linklaters, London.
[10007866]   26/02/2008   **ME**
Johnson, Mrs Y K, BEd MCLIP, Freelance Law Lib.
[39632]   07/04/1986   **CM12/12/1990**
Johnson, Mrs Z, BA (Hons) MA MCLIP FHEA, Subject Librarian.,
Huddersfield University.
[58929]   06/10/2000   **CM23/06/2004**
Johnston, Miss A, BA (Hons) MCLIP, Resident in South Africa.
[26978]   03/10/1976   **CM17/08/1988**
Johnston, Miss A G, BA MCLIP, School Librarian, Dunbar Grammar
School, Dunbar.
[22631]   03/07/1974   **CM26/08/1980**
Johnston, Mr A R, BA FSA SCOT MCLIP, Retired.
[7922]   01/04/1970   **CM09/07/1974**
Johnston, Mrs F E, BLS, Career Break.
[39429]   19/01/1986   **CM22/05/1996**
Johnston, Dr J O D, DipMgmt (OU) AKC BSc MSc MCMI MCLIP,
Retired.
[60401]   03/10/1972   **CM12/10/1973**
Johnston, Miss L A, BA (Hons) MA, Information Serv. Librarian,
London College of Fashion Library, London.
[63407]   05/05/2004   **ME**
Johnston, Mrs M, BA, Librarian, Falkirk Council.
[28337]   27/10/1977   **ME**
Johnston, Mr N E, BA PgDip, Higher Library Executive, House of
Commons Library, London.
[61036]   01/02/2002   **ME**
Johnston, Mrs R A, BA MA MCLIP, Librarian, Manor Lodge School,
Hertfordshire.
[37399]   09/08/1984   **CM04/10/1988**
Johnston, Mrs S, BA, Library Liaison Officer, Northumbria University.
[10022345]   11/02/2013   **ME**
Johnston, Mrs S M, BSc MSc FCLIP, Retired.
[60402]   19/12/1972   **FE01/03/1986**
Johnston, Mr W C P, BA, Customer Service Bibliographer, Yankee
Book Peddler Ltd.
[41846]   17/03/1988   **ME**
Johnstone, Mr G T, BA (Hons) MCLIP, Librarian, Bo'ness Library,
Falkirk Community Trust.
[61401]   09/07/2002   **CM29/03/2006**
Johnstone, Mrs J A, BA MSc, Librarian, Scottish Poetry Librarian,
Edinburgh.
[61144]   11/03/2002   **ME**
Johnstone, Mrs J M, BA (Hons) MSc, Information Professional, Ministry
of Defence.
[10001300]   26/01/2007   **ME**
Joint, Mr N C, BA MA, Head of Reference & Information, University of
Strathclyde, Andersonian Library, Glasgow.
[38275]   15/02/1985   **ME**
Jolley, Mrs M A, Lib. Assistant.
[10017280]   22/07/2010   **AF**
Jolliffe, Mr A, MA, Student, University of Northumbria, Newcastle.
[10022960]   14/05/2013   **ME**

Jolly, Ms E, BA (Hons) DipILS FCLIP FRSA, Director, L. and Information
Serv., Teesside University, Middlesbrough.
[43745]   14/12/1989   **FE03/10/2007**

Jones, Mrs A, MLib MCLIP, Libraries Museums and Arts Manager
Monmouthshire County Council.
[27315]   03/03/1977   **CM05/02/1981**

Jones, Mrs A, FCLIP, Life Member.
[7950]   22/01/1952   **FE05/05/1980**

Jones, Mr A, MCLIP, Life Member.
[7947]   26/02/1947   **CM01/01/1956**

Jones, Mrs A, BLib, Unemployed.
[28123]   23/09/1977   **CM31/08/1982**

Jones, Mrs A, MSc Econ,
[10032709]   07/01/2014   **ME**

Jones, Mr A C, MCLIP, Retired.
[61240]   08/09/1983   **CM01/04/2002**

Jones, Miss A E, BA (Hons) MCLIP FRSA, Senior Librarian, Telford &
Wrekin Council.
[61021]   01/02/2002   **CM31/01/2007**

Jones, Miss A E N, BA (Hons) MSc (Econ) MCLIP, Lib. Arch., Glasgow
Museum Res. Centre.
[36683]   07/11/1983   **CM19/06/1991**

Jones, Dr A G, BA MA PhD, Chief Executive & Librarian, National
Library of Wales.
[10033475]   17/03/2014   **ME**

Jones, Mrs A H, MA (Oxon) MA MPhil, Libr, Whipple Lib, Dpt of History
& Philosophy of Science, Cambridge.
[54024]   23/10/1996   **ME**

Jones, Mrs A J, BLib MSc MCLIP, Assistant Commissioner, Information
Commissioners Office, Wilmslow.
[21126]   12/10/1973   **CM01/01/1981**

Jones, Mrs A J, BA, Prep Librarian, St Catherine's School, Twickenham.
[43023]   21/06/1989   **ME**

Jones, Miss A K, BA (Hons) ACLIP, L. Assistant, Leicester College.
[10015775]   25/01/2010   **ACL16/06/2010**

Jones, Mrs A M, MA MCLIP, Life Member.
[7954]   24/02/1955   **CM01/01/1956**

Jones, Mrs A M, BA MCLIP, Part-time. Information Librarian, Kingston
University, Kingston upon Thames.
[28694]   13/01/1978   **CM07/10/1981**

Jones, Mrs A M A, BA DipLib MCLIP, Assistant Subject Librarian,
(Business)/Information Manager (Careers), Cardiff University.
[40170]   06/11/1986   **CM27/02/1991**

Jones, Mr A P, Student / Library Research Assistant.
[10027839]   03/10/2014   **ME**

Jones, Mr A R, BA MCLIP, Res. Centre Co-ordinator, National Stem
Centre, York.
[43513]   01/11/1989   **CM17/05/2000**

Jones, Mr A W, BA (Hons) PgDip, Information Serv. Librarian, Dolgellau
Library, Gwynedd.
[10010854]   02/09/2008   **ME**

Jones, Mrs B, Librarian, Joseph Chamberlain Sixth Form College.
[41264]   21/10/1987   **CM05/05/2010**

Jones, Mr B, BA MUSM PgDip, Student, University of the West of
England.
[10027813]   10/06/2014   **ME**

Jones, Mrs B M, BSc, Research Repository and Information Officer,
University of Lincoln.
[63979]   22/11/2004   **ME**

Jones, Mr B P, BA DipLib FCLIP, Life Member.
[7966]   01/01/1960   **FE01/01/1968**

Jones, Mrs C, DipLib, Retired.
[42800]   01/03/1989   **ME**

Jones, Mr C F, DIPAD BA (Hons) MA MA, Learning & Teaching
Librarian, University for the Creative Arts.
[10011010]   12/09/2008   **ME**

Jones, Miss C L, MA (Hons) DipILS MCLIP, Manager, Information &
Learning Resources, City of Edinburgh Council.
[41748]   01/03/1988   **CM15/08/1990**

Jones, Mrs C M, BSc (Hons) MCLIP, Information Skills Trainer, King's
College Hospital NHS Foundation Trust.
[61915]   03/12/2002   **CM21/03/2007**

Jones, Mrs C M, BSc (Hons) DipIM MCLIP, Information Systems Project
Manager, Scienfic Computing Department, Science & Technology
Facilities Council.
[52932]   25/01/1996   **CM12/03/2003**

Jones, Mrs C M, BA MCLIP, Life Member.
[7979]   07/01/1964   **CM01/01/1967**

Jones, Mr C M, BA MSc MCLIP,
[10000645]   23/10/2006   **CM10/03/2010**

Jones, Mr D, BA (Hons), Graduate Trainee, Reader Services, Bodleian
Library.
[10034212]   15/09/2014   **ME**

Jones, Ms E, Graduate Library Trainee, Jesus College.
[10031876]   10/10/2013   **ME**

Jones, Mrs E L, BA (Hons) MCLIP, Cent. Manager/Library Serv.
Manager, Swansea Psychiatric Educ. Cent. Cefn Coed Hospital.
[49578]   19/11/1993   **CM22/09/1999**

Jones, Miss E M, MCLIP, Retired.
[8010]   01/01/1970   **CM08/09/1976**

Jones, Mr G, BSc (Econ), Outreach Services Librarian University of
Wales Trinity Saint David.
[10016413]   03/12/2013   **ME**

Jones, Mrs G H, BLib MCLIP, Sch. Lib. Assistant, Ysgol Glan Clwyd.,
Denbighshire C. C.
[27088]   19/01/1977   **CM20/08/1981**

Jones, Miss G S L, Library Resources Officer, The Manchester College.
[10034730]   12/08/2014   **ME**

Jones, Mr G T, BA MSc, Savills Plc, London.
[60403]   02/07/1981   **ME**

Jones, Mr G W, BLIB MCLIP, Assistant Librarian, Ammanford Library
Dyfed County Council.
[40799]   26/06/1987   **CM27/02/1991**

Jones, Mr G W, BA (Hons) DipILS MCLIP, L. & Information Centre
Manager, Islay High School, Isle of Islay.
[52450]   02/11/1995   **CM13/03/2002**

Jones, Mrs H, School Librarian, Our Lady of Sion School, Worthing.
[10006125]   11/09/2007   **AF**

Jones, Mrs H C, MCLIP, Learning Resources Serv. Manager, Bedford
College.
[24092]   19/04/1975   **CM06/12/1979**

Jones, Miss H E, BA, Classifier, Nielsen BookData.
[56915]   04/11/1998   **ME**

Jones, Mrs H J, BA MCLIP, Mimas Services and Projects Support, Jisc.
[30767]   04/04/1979   **CM10/10/1983**

Jones, Mrs H M, BSc (Hons)MSc DipEd MCLIP, Librarian, Freelance.
[19870]   01/01/1973   **CM21/04/1975**

Jones, Dr I, BA MPhil PhD, Student.
[10020867]   19/04/2012   **ME**

Jones, Mrs J, Learning Centre Assistant, Coleg Gwent.
[10032068]   24/10/2013   **ME**

Jones, Mrs J, BA MCLIP, Senior Branch Librarian, Neath & Port Talbot
L. & Information Serv., Neath L.
[24302]   07/06/1975   **CM02/02/1978**

Jones, Mrs J, BA, Student, Glyndwr University Wrexham.
[10032804]   14/01/2014   **ME**

Jones, Mrs J, MCLIP, Team Librarian, Bedford Central Library.
[12570]   01/01/1970   **CM16/01/1974**
Jones, Mrs J A, BSc (Econ) (Hons), Bookstart Development Officer,
Hertfordshire County Council.
[51196]   23/11/1994   **ME**
Jones, Mr J E, BA MCLIP, Liaison Librarian, University of Reading.
[10014431]   30/07/2009   **CM08/03/2013**
Jones, Ms J M, BA (Hons) MBA MCLIP, Head of Information
Management & Practice, The National Archives.
[21823]   07/02/1974   **CM05/07/1979**
Jones, Mrs J S, MA (OXON), Librarian\Distance Student.
[10021595]   06/09/2012   **ME**
Jones, Mrs J S, BLib MCLIP, Library Manager, Hereford Sixth Form
College.
[27219]   11/01/1977   **CM08/08/1980**
Jones, Miss K E, Student.
[10000472]   09/10/2006   **ME**
Jones, Mrs K J, BA PGCE Dip Lib, Library Skills Trainer, Smallwood
Library, Birmingham.
[10023208]   01/07/1997   **ME**
Jones, Ms K L, MAppSc MCLIP, Head of Research Services., University
of Bath L.
[64929]   13/09/2005   **CM17/09/2008**
Jones, Mrs K M, BA MA MCLIP, Senior Library Assistant, Swansea
Uiniversity, Swansea.
[43596]   09/11/1989   **CM26/05/1993**
Jones, Mrs L, BA (Hons), Learning Centre Manager, The Green School,
Isleworth.
[10018952]   01/04/2011   **ME**
Jones, Mrs L I, BA DipLib FCLIP, Subject Lib. (Law and Criminology),
University of Portsmouth.
[26935]   10/01/1977   **FE12/05/2011**
Jones, Miss L M, BA MLIS, Head of Lib. and Research Centre.
[10001206]   02/02/2007   **ME**
Jones, Miss L M, BA (Hons) MA,
[10023207]   18/06/2013   **ME**
Jones, Mrs M, DESCIO-Prog-Mgr, DCSA Directorate strategic Transition
– MOD.
[10033968]   14/05/2014   **ME**
Jones, Miss M, BA (Hons), Masters Student, Aberystwyth University.
[10034718]   05/09/2014   **ME**
Jones, Mr M, MCLIP, Retired.
[8051]   01/01/1965   **CM01/01/1969**
Jones, Mrs M, Student, Coleg Llandrillo.
[10032516]   11/12/2013   **ME**
Jones, Mr M, BA (Hons),
[10031914]   14/10/2013   **ME**
Jones, Mr M A, BA (Hons) DipILS MCLIP, Marketing Intelligence
Executive, Scottish Power, Glasgow.
[54545]   17/01/1997   **CM26/11/2001**
Jones, Miss M A, BA (Hons) PgDip,
[48821]   09/06/1993   **ME**
Jones, Mrs M E, Student, Coleg Llandrillo.
[10032680]   03/01/2014   **ME**
Jones, Mrs M F, BA (Hons) MCLIP, Life Member.
[30322]   23/01/1979   **CM08/10/1981**
Jones, Mrs M H, MLIS, Head of Library & Learning Lounge.
[10033549]   25/03/2014   **ME**
Jones, Mrs M H, MA BSc (Hons) PGCE, Systems Librarain, Hadlow
College, Tonbridge.
[62652]   01/10/2003   **ME**
Jones, Mrs M P, Branch Librarian.
[10023307]   25/06/2013   **ME**

Jones, Mrs M S, BA, Samye Ling Librarian.
[10032278]   24/12/2013   **ME**
Jones, Miss M T, BA (Hons) MA, Student, Aberystwyth University.
[10035531]   16/10/2014   **ME**
Jones, Ms N, BA MA, Information Manager, Cushman & Wakefield LLP.
[10002673]   05/03/2001   **ME**
Jones, Miss N W, BLib MCLIP, Community Librarian, Mold Library,
Flintshire County Council.
[33943]   04/06/1981   **CM06/07/1987**
Jones, Mr P, BA (Hons) Dip, Information Services Specialist, TWI Ltd.
[10022171]   15/01/2013   **ME**
Jones, Ms P, BA MCLIP, Reading & Learning Serv. Manager, Knowsley
Metropolitan Borough Council, Page Moss L.
[27688]   01/07/1977   **CM30/06/1980**
Jones, Mr P E, MCLIP, Retired.
[8076]   06/03/1957   **CM01/01/1962**
Jones, Mr P F, BA MCLIP, Retired.
[8077]   06/10/1970   **CM16/07/1975**
Jones, Mr P H, MA FCLIP, Retired.
[8078]   02/01/1968   **FE16/08/1977**
Jones, Dr R, BA MCLIP, School Librarian, Malvern St James.
[47525]   01/10/1992   **CM20/09/1995**
Jones, Mr R A, DipLib MCLIP, Head of L. & Arch., Denbighshire County
Council.
[33009]   20/10/1980   **CM19/01/1984**
Jones, Mr R B, BA MCLIP, Management Information Officer, Cult. &
Comm. Serv. Department, Derbyshire County Council.
[28438]   07/12/1977   **CM05/02/1980**
Jones, Mr R F, BA MA,
[10016538]   13/04/2010   **ME**
Jones, Miss R J H, BA (Hons) PgDip, Deputy Lib. Serv. Manager,
Manchester Metropolitan University.
[61726]   29/10/2002   **ME**
Jones, Mr R L, GradDipMus DipLib MCLIP, Music Librarian, The
Barbican Music Library, London.
[45567]   15/03/1991   **CM27/07/1994**
Jones, Mr R M, BA MLS MCLIP, British Medical Association Library,
London.
[34413]   05/11/1981   **CM02/06/1987**
Jones, Mr R S, BA (Hons), Information & E-Services Manager,
Reference & Information Serv., London Borough of Richmond upon
Thames.
[32668]   01/07/1980   **ME**
Jones, Mrs S, BA DipLib MCLIP, Head of Non-Welsh Legal Deposit
Monographs Unit.
[35328]   08/10/1982   **CM14/11/1991**
Jones, Miss S, Information Manager Acas, London.
[10008090]   30/07/2008   **AF**
Jones, Mrs S, MCLIP, Information Resources Officer, Wirral
Metropolitan College, Birkenhead.
[29420]   18/07/1978   **CM18/07/1980**
Jones, Mr S, BA MA, IRC Graduate Trainee, E. ON New Build &
Technology.
[10032347]   21/11/2013   **ME**
Jones, Mr S, BA (Hons) ACILIP, Librarian, Herefordshire Libraries.
[10016456]   26/03/2010   **ACL07/09/2011**
Jones, Mr S, BA DipLib MCLIP, Principal Lib. -Information, Serv. &
Reference, Jersey L.
[41405]   25/11/1987   **CM12/12/1990**
Jones, Mrs S, MCLIP, Retired.
[8103]   01/01/1955   **CM01/01/1963**
Jones, Mr S, BA,
[10014627]   25/08/2009   **ME**

Jones, Miss S A, BSc MA, Circulation Librarian, Regents College
Library, London.
[64635] 27/04/2005 ME

Jones, Miss S A, BA DipLib MCLIP, Retired.
[36561] 18/10/1983 RV01/10/2008 CM15/11/1988

Jones, Miss S A, BSc DipLib MCLIP, Unemployed.
[37909] 15/11/1984 CM09/08/1988

Jones, Miss S D, BA DipLib MCLIP,
[39221] 01/01/1986 CM15/02/1989

Jones, Miss S E, BA (Hons) MSc Econ, Graduate, Aberystwyth
University 2012.
[10009716] 03/06/2008 ME

Jones, Miss S E, BA MCLIP, Librarian, Mansfield College, University of
Oxford.
[63082] 27/01/2004 CM05/05/2010

Jones, Mrs S E, BA MA MCLIP, Retired.
[41305] 01/01/1962 CM23/08/1966

Jones, Ms S L, Business Information Officer at the Inst of Dir, Pall Mall,
London.
[62874] 17/11/2003 ME

Jones, Mrs T, BA MCLIP, Stock Spec., Halton Borough Council.
[42707] 10/02/1989 RV27/03/2014 CM21/07/1993

Jones, Ms T A, ACLIP, Library Manager, Blaina Library, Gwent.
[10015911] 27/01/2010 ACL10/11/2010

Jones, Mrs T H, BSc MSc, Independent researcher.
[54295] 15/11/1996 ME

Jones, Mrs V, JP BSc (Econ) MCLIP, Site Librarian, Bridgend College
(Pencoed Campus), Mid Glam.
[45571] 06/03/1991 CM12/03/2003

Jones, Ms V L, DipILM MSc MCLIP, Acquisitions Representative, Better
World Books.
[58842] 25/08/2000 CM09/07/2008

Jones, Mrs W A, BScEcon (Hons) MCLIP, Joint Digital Content
Manager & Metadata Librarian, Oxford Brookes University.
[45229] 21/08/1990 CM23/01/2002

Jones, Mr W O, BSc DipLib MCLIP, Faculty Librarian, University of East
Anglia, Norwich.
[37732] 10/10/1984 CM15/08/1989

Jones-Davis, Mrs D, BSc, Library Adviser (Inter Library Loans and
Administration), University of Gloucestershire.
[10023209] 18/06/2013 ME

Jones-Evans, Dr A, BLib (Hons) PGCED PhD MCLIP, Independent L.
Consultant, Enlli Associates, Cardiff.
[39175] 04/12/1985 CM14/11/1990

Jones-Williams, Mrs S, Library Assistant, Coleg Menai Llangefru Site.
[10022133] 08/01/2013 ME

Jordan, Mrs A A, MSc MCLIP, Consultant.
[11767] 01/09/1970 CM01/07/1975

Jordan, Mrs A M, BA MCLIP, Head of Swindon Library, Swindon
Borough Co.
[24627] 03/10/1975 CM14/02/1979

Jordan, Dr A T, BA MCLIP ARCM MLS DLS (Col), Life Member,
Resident Trinidad.
[17134] 01/01/1951 CM01/01/1955

Jordan, Ms C, BA PgDip LIS,
[10016322] 08/03/2010 ME

Jordan, Mrs J L, BSc MSC MA, Information Specialist & Systematic
Reviewer at Arthritis Research UK Primary Care Centre, Keele
University.
[10014986] 14/04/1999 ME

Jordan, Mr M, BSc (Hons) MA MCLIP, Programme Manager, Health &
Social Care Integration, NHS Connecting for Health, Leeds.
[51094] 15/11/1994 CM20/01/1999

Jordan, Mrs N J, BA (Hons) MCLIP, Librarian, Library Services for
Educucation, Leicestershire.
[52322] 26/10/1995 CM12/03/2003

Jordan, Mr P, MPhil BSc FCLIP, Retired.
[8122] 16/03/1954 FE01/01/1961

Jordan, Mr S, ACLIP, Customer Services Manager, Library &
Information Services, University of Gloucestershire, Cheltenham.
[64967] 05/10/2005 ACL14/11/2012

Jordan, Miss V, ACLIP, Acting Librarian, Countess of Chester Hospital.
[10019906] 30/09/2011 ACL13/11/2013

Joseph-McFarlane, Mrs C, Librarian, Library Micoudst.
[10027854] 20/12/2013 ME

Josh, Mrs H, BA (Hons) MA MCLIP,
[61793] 08/11/2002 CM01/02/2006

Joshevska, Ms E, HR Speacialist.
[10032647] 23/12/2013 ME

Joshi, Ms C, School Librarian, Southbank International School, London.
[10012073] 24/04/2009 ME

Jost, Mrs L, ACLIP,
[10001671] 16/05/2003 ACL04/03/2009

Joyce, Mrs E M, BA DipLib MCLIP, Unemployed.
[41376] 16/11/1987 CM22/05/1991

Joyce, Mrs L, BEd MSc PGCHE MCLIP FHEA, Academic Librarian,
Leeds Metropolitan University.
[49851] 07/01/1994 CM15/05/2002

Joyce, Miss L, BA (Hons) MCLIP, School Librarian.
[47825] 14/10/1992 CM19/11/2003

Joykin, Ms A, Student, University of Strathclyde.
[10035386] 10/10/2014 ME

Judge, Ms A, BAgrSc DipLIS ALAI PGCE-PCET, The Education
Partners.
[46979] 16/03/1992 ME

Judge, Mr D, BA, KM Project Manager, DLA Piper UK LLP.
[10032798] 14/01/2014 ME

Judson, Mrs J E, MCLIP, Information Officer, Nottingham Health NHS
Trust County Health Partnerships
[18103] 01/10/1972 CM07/07/1975

Julien, Miss C H, Student, Aberystwyth University.
[10035277] 03/10/2014 ME

Jung, Mrs I, DipLIng MSc, Solihull College.
[59267] 23/01/2001 ME

Juskaityte, Ms J, LRC Manager, Sion-Manning RC School, London.
[10016917] 10/06/2010 ME

Justice, Miss J, MLIS, Library Assistant (Summer Relief), Aberdeen
City Council.
[10031871] 10/10/2013 ME

Jutson, Ms A L, BA, Student, Victoria University of Wellington.
[10032815] 14/01/2014 ME

K

Kaczmarek, Miss M A, BA, Shelving Assistant (Part Time), Durham
University.
[10022109] 18/12/2012 ME

Kahn, Ms R, MA, Student, King's College London.
[10032401] 18/12/2013 ME

Kainth, Mrs R, BSc (Hons) Assoc CIPD, Student, Cranfield University.
[10033541] 25/03/2014 ME

Kale, Ms A, BA (Hons) MCLIP, Community Information Officer, North
Yorkshire County L.
[58315] 10/01/2000 CM31/01/2007

Kalhorzadeh, Miss N, Student.
[10032145] 29/10/2013 ME

Kalsi, Miss B K, Student.
[21227]   08/10/1973   ME
Kamen, Mrs R H, MBE FCLIP HonFRIBA FRSA, Retired.
[23454]   01/01/1975   FE15/09/1993
Kane, Mrs A D, BA DipLib MCLIP,
[36452]   02/10/1983   CM29/08/1986
Kane, Mrs G A, BA (Hons) MCLIP, Bibl. Serv. Man. Halton Borough Council, Cheshire.
[33547]   08/01/1981   RV27/03/2014   CM15/01/1985
Kane, Miss S M, MCLIP, Retired.
[8161]   28/09/1968   CM18/12/1972
Karagianni, Miss F,
[10031997]   18/10/2013   ME
Karakasidou, Ms C, MA, Student, Northumbria University.
[10032996]   03/02/2014   ME
Kargianioti, Mrs E, BA MA, Senior Officer, Records and Information, Black Sea Bank, Thessaloniki, Greece.
[53876]   07/10/1996   ME
Karn, Miss J C, BA (Hons) MA MSc MCLIP, Library Manager, Blaenau Gwent Co. Borough, Tredegar.
[37617]   15/10/1984   CM16/10/1989
Karnik, Mrs A, BSc BLIB MLISC, Student, University of Mumbai.
[10032248]   10/11/2013   ME
Karwat, Miss A, BA (Hons) MCLIP, Principle Librarian, Customer Services.
[39673]   07/05/1986   CM15/05/2002
Kasaey Fard, Mrs H, BA, LRC Counter Assistant, College of North West London.
[65596]   24/02/2006   ME
Kassir, Ms L, Academic Support Librarian, University of the Arts London.
[61416]   12/07/2002   ME
Katny, Mrs M, DipIS MA MCLIP, Senior Media Manager, BBC.
[46330]   28/10/1991   CM01/04/2002
Kattan, Mrs L B, MCLIP, Head Librarian, Private Library of His Royal Highness Prince Talal bin Mohammad.
[21531]   24/10/1973   CM01/11/1977
Kattuman, Mrs M P, BA MA DipLIS, Cataloguer, Cambridge University Library.
[46313]   28/10/1991   ME
Katz, Mr D, MA, Library Assistant, Hastings Library.
[10022653]   05/04/2013   ME
Kaune, Ms H, BA (Hons) DipLib, Information Advisor, Institute of Materials, Minerals and Mining, London.
[10013171]   17/01/1985   ME
Kaung, Mr T, BA (Hons) DipLib HonDLitt HonFLA, Librarian, University Central Library, Rangoon, Burma.
[17154]   01/01/1960   HFE12/06/1984
Kaur, Mrs H, MCLIP, School Librarian, Aldridge School, Aldridge.
[65933]   30/06/2006   CM09/11/2011
Kaur, Mrs P, MPhil MLib, Learning Resource Manager, St John Fisher High School.
[10032583]   17/12/2013   ME
Kaur, Miss S, Def Comrcl-Comms-IM-1a, Ministry of Defence.
[10034747]   12/08/2014   ME
Kaur Bhoda, Mrs M, BSc LIS MCLIP, Indexer, Chartered Institute of Marketing, Maidenhead, Berkshire.
[10001812]   15/03/2007   CM25/01/2011
Kavanagh, Mrs C H, BA MA, Assistant Librarian, Nuffield College.
[53753]   01/10/1996   ME
Kay, Ms C, BA MA DipLib MCLIP, Head of Planning and Resources, University of Liverpool.
[10002657]   01/01/1974   CM01/07/1988

Kay, Mr C H, BA MCLIP, Retired.
[24722]   01/10/1975   CM02/12/1977
Kay, Ms E A, College Librarian, Brasenose College, Oxford.
[59288]   29/01/2001   AF
Kay, Mr J, MA BA (Hons), Subscriptions & Document Delivery Librarian, University of Derby.
[63670]   12/08/2004   ME
Kay, Ms J K, BA, Student, City University London.
[10035434]   14/10/2014   ME
Kay, Mrs P M, MCLIP, Retired.
[60591]   07/07/1970   CM01/09/1978
Kay, Mrs S, BA (Hons) DipIM MCLIP, Managing Director, The Professionalism Group.
[48469]   18/01/1993   CM23/09/1998
Kaye, Mr D, BA MSc FCLIP, Life Member.
[8179]   07/01/1954   FE01/01/1969
Kaye, Mrs G M, MCLIP, Assistant Librarian, Sheffield Children's Hospital.
[65045]   14/10/2005   CM28/01/2009
Kaye, Miss J, BA (Hons) MCLIP, Part-time Assistant Librarian, Tameside College, Ashton-under-Lyne.
[49360]   28/10/1993   CM25/01/2011
Kaye, Mr J, BA (Hons), Student, Loughborough University.
[10018730]   01/03/2011   ME
Kaye, Miss R, BA MCLIP, Senior Library Manager (SLM), Bolsover Cluster, Derby C. C.
[18374]   22/10/1972   CM11/08/1976
Kazi, Mrs B, MSc, Information Specialist (Science), MHRA, London.
[10020575]   01/03/2012   ME
Kazmierczak, Mr P, BSc (Hons) PGCE MA MCLIP, Senior Librarian for Heritage & Older People, Bournemouth Libraries.
[61437]   19/07/2002   CM23/01/2008
Kealey, Ms G E, MA PG DIP, Cultural Assistant.
[10020470]   20/02/2012   ME
Kean, Ms A, BA (Hons) MA, Library Services Manager, North Middlesex University.
[10007566]   18/02/2008   CM06/07/2011
Kean, Mr G, MSc, Student, University of Strathclyde.
[10015561]   15/12/2009   ME
Keane, Mr I, BA (Hons) PgDip Lib, Librarian (Voluntary)., Woodmill High School, Fife.
[10012560]   23/02/2009   ME
Keane, Ms M P, BA (Hons) DipLib MCLIP, Collections Access Manager, Bolton Library & Museum Services.
[35405]   13/10/1982   CM27/07/1985
Keane, Mrs P, MCLIP, Retired.
[8190]   12/04/1962   CM01/01/1966
Kearley, Miss V L, BA MA, Assistant Library Manager, Chandlers Ford Library.
[10022623]   05/04/2013   ME
Kearney, Ms C, BA MEd DipLib DipEdTech MCLIP, Director, CILIP Scotland.
[37871]   09/11/1984   CM10/02/1987
Kearney, Mr J A, Student.
[10035685]   29/10/2014   ME
Kearns, Mr T G, BA DipLib MCLIP,
[43841]   06/02/1990   CM21/07/1993
Keary, Mrs M, MPhil FCLIP, IM/KM Consultant, London.
[8195]   12/03/1962   FE31/07/1974
Keat, Mrs L P S, BSc MA MA, Librarian, Danes Hill Sch.
[64908]   08/09/2005   ME
Keates, Mr P J, BA (Hons) MA, Library assistant, University of Cambridge.
[10020400]   11/02/2012   ME

Keating, Mrs C, BA DipLib MCLIP, L. Resource Centre Manager, Jack
Hunt School, Peterborough.
[30465]   29/01/1979   **CM02/10/1981**

Keating, Mrs L M, MCLIP FHEA, Liaison Librarian, Newcastle
University.
[49044]   13/09/1993   **CM22/05/1996**

Keating, Mr R F, Chief Executive, British Library.
[10021797]   16/10/2012   **ME**

Keay, Mrs J M, BA MCLIP, I. T. & Systems Librarian, South Lanarkshire
Council.
[29665]   13/10/1978   **CM16/03/1984**

Keddie, Ms C A, BA (Hons) MA MCLIP, Senior Assistant Librarian, De
Montfort University, Leicester.
[54462]   16/12/1996   **CM17/01/2001**

Keddie, Mrs J, BA MCLIP, Resources Manager /Senior Library
Executive, House of Commons Library, London.
[41652]   06/02/1988   **CM16/10/1991**

Keefe, Mrs J H, BA MCLIP, Community Outreach Librarian, Calgary
Public Library, Alberta, Canada.
[34716]   30/01/1982   **CM17/07/1985**

Keelan, Mr P J, BSc DipLib MCLIP MSc, Head of Special Collections,
Cardiff University.
[29708]   04/10/1978   **CM07/12/1981**

Keeler, Mrs E, MA (Hons) PGC Info Sci, Learning Resource Centre
Manager, LVS Ascot.
[61116]   21/02/2002   **ME**

Keeling, Mr D, FCLIP, Retired.
[8204]   12/03/1956   **FE01/01/1964**

Keeling, Miss D J, ACLIP, Neighbourhood Librarian Ormesby Library.
[10010634]   19/08/2008   **ACL03/11/2010**

Keeling, Dr D M, BA (Hons) MA PhD MCLIP, Retired.
[8205]   19/03/1957   **CM01/01/1963**

Keen, Miss L, BSc Econ, Student, Aberystwyth University.
[10018069]   09/11/2010   **ME**

Keenan, Ms J, Project Manager.
[10000764]   13/10/1992   **ME**

Keenan, Ms S, MPhil FCLIP, Retired.
[18956]   12/03/1951   **FE01/04/2002**

Keene, Dr J A, BSc DipLib MCLIP, University Librarian and Assistant
Director, ILS, University of Worcester.
[42259]   13/10/1988   **CM19/07/2000**

Keevil, Mr D, MCLIP, Part-time Consultant, Aluminium Federation.
[8213]   09/09/1958   **CM01/01/1964**

Kehoe, Miss A, ALAI MCLIP, Retired.
[8215]   01/01/1949   **CM30/08/1984**

Keiller, Mrs H C, BA (Hons) MA, Career Break.
[55680]   04/11/1997   **ME**

Keir, Mrs K, BA (Hons) DipLIS MCLIP, Local and Family History
Librarian, Manager, Glos. Archives, Gloucester.
[10001992]   01/07/1984   **CM15/05/2002**

Kelby, Mrs S E, BA MCLIP, Sch. Librarian, Irthlingborough Junior Sch.
[20299]   02/02/1973   **CM23/08/1977**

Kell, Mrs N J, BSc, Health Lib, NHS.
[65595]   24/02/2006   **ME**

Kelland, Mr N E, BSc (Econ), Information Serv. Librarian, Treorchy
Library, Rhondda-Cynon-Taff C. B. C.
[58626]   18/04/2000   **ME**

Kellas, Mr S D, MA (Hons), Governance Manager, The Physiological
Society, London.
[54729]   12/03/1997   **ME**

Kelleher, Mrs C G, BA (Hons) DipII MCLIP, LRC Manager, Herne Bay
High School, Kent.
[56863]   29/10/1998   **CM12/03/2003**

Kelleher, Mr M D, BA (Hons) MSc MCLIP, Bibl. Serv. Librarian,
University of Liverpool.
[56474]   23/07/1998   **CM29/03/2004**

Kelleher, Mrs R A, BSc PGCE, Subject Supp. Assistant, Swansea
University.
[10018326]   16/12/2010   **ME**

Kellet, Mrs K J, BSc (Hons) MSc PgDip, Site Operations Co-ordinator
(Job Share), University of Salford, Information Serv. Div.
[10000961]   02/11/2001   **ME**

Kelley, Mrs L, BA (Hons) DipIM MCLIP MSc, Librarian, St Paul's Girls'
School, London.
[50911]   31/10/1994   **RV05/10/2007**   **CM19/01/2000**

Kelly, Mrs A B M, BA (Hons), School Librarian, St Swithun's School,
Winchester.
[53278]   12/04/1996   **ME**

Kelly, Mrs A F, BLS MCLIP, Life Member.
[30350]   30/01/1958   **CM23/09/1980**

Kelly, Mrs C, MCLIP, Retired.
[15850]   29/08/1968   **CM08/05/1974**

Kelly, Mrs C, BA (Hons) PgDip,
[65984]   07/08/2006   **AF**

Kelly, Mr D B, BA BSc MSc, Customer Serv. Officer, Culture and
Leisure Serv., Kirklees.
[63796]   06/10/2004   **ME**

Kelly, Mr D G, MSc MCLIP, Director of Libraries & Archives, National
Institutions of the Church of England.
[36557]   19/10/1983   **CM01/04/2002**

Kelly, Mrs E M, BSc DipLib MCLIP, Employment not known.
[37152]   16/02/1984   **CM06/09/1988**

Kelly, Mr G I, BA MCLIP, Hist. Res. Consultant, Norwich.
[8233]   01/06/1964   **CM01/01/1970**

Kelly, Mrs I, Life Member.
[8235]   07/01/1962   **ME**

Kelly, Ms J B M, BA (Hons) MA, Children & Young People's Librarian
part-time, North Lincolnshire Central Library.
[63886]   14/10/2004   **ME**

Kelly, Ms L C, BA (Hons) PgDip DipLIS MCLIP, Team Leader, L.
Operations, Northumberland County Council.
[36692]   07/11/1983   **CM11/11/1986**

Kelly, Ms M A, DipLib MCLIP, Interim Libraries & Information Services
Manager, Perth & Kinross Council.
[33014]   03/10/1980   **CM31/01/1983**

Kelly, Miss S, MA (Hons),
[10032303]   15/11/2013   **ME**

Kelly, Mrs S A, MCLIP, Assistant Librarian, House of Lords.
[10717]   21/02/1972   **CM15/12/1975**

Kelly, Mr T, BA MSc,
[10014057]   20/10/2010   **ME**

Kelly, Dr W, MA MA PhD FCLIP, Hon. Research Fellow, Scottish Centre
for the Book, Edinburgh Napier University.
[8246]   19/10/1966   **FE15/03/1983**

Kelly-Keightley, Mrs J Y, MA Lib Sci, LAIS NVQ Assessor.
[10007132]   04/10/1989   **ME**

Kelsall, Ms L, BA (Hons), Cataloguer, The Angus Library and Archive;
student, Aberystwyth University.
[10032970]   31/01/2014   **ME**

Kelsey, Mrs A,
[65329]   22/12/2005   **ME**

Kemp, Miss C, BA MA, Assistant Librarian, Coventry City Council.
[10027935]   25/07/2014   **ME**

Kemp, Mrs H J, BA MA MCLIP, Librarian, Angmering School, West
Sussex.
[38925]   21/10/1985   **CM15/09/1993**

Kemp, Mrs J, Outreach & Events Officer, Royal Borough of Windsor & Maidenhead.
[10021715]   03/10/2012   **ME**
Kemp, Ms L, BA MA MCLIP, Research Associate.
[61578]   02/10/2002   **CM09/09/2009**
Kemp, Mrs L E, BA (Hons) MScEcon, Learning Resources Adv., Colchester Institute, Colchester.
[63724]   03/09/2004   **ME**
Kemp, Miss S, BA (Hons), Information Librarian, Sutton Central Library.
[65320]   23/12/2005   **ME**
Kempling, Mr H K, DipLib MCLIP, Retired.
[30668]   10/03/1979   **CM11/05/1981**
Kempshall, Mrs J R, BA MCLIP, Retired.
[6933]   28/09/1970   **CM07/11/1972**
Kempster, Mrs G D, OBE BA (Hons) MLib MCLIP FRSA, Customer and Library Services Manager.
[27333]   21/02/1977   **CM27/07/1981**
Kendall, Mrs A J, MSc (Hons) BSc (Hons), Unwaged.
[57854]   10/09/1999   **ME**
Kendall, Mrs J H, BLib (Hons), Librarian, Reader Services:Children, Young People and Families Team, Oxfordshire County Council.
[10002304]   26/02/1990   **ME**
Kendall, Miss M, MA MCLIP, Librarian, Churchill College, Cambridge.
[8262]   02/04/1972   **CM28/02/1974**
Kendall, Ms M A, MA MPhil FHEA MCLIP, Senior Assistant Librarian, Manchester Metropolitan University.
[29993]   02/10/1978   **CM20/11/1980**
Kendall, Ms S, BA DipLib MCLIP, Lib/Info Services Manager., Mills & Reeve, Birmingham.
[40901]   14/08/1987   **CM17/10/1990**
Kendrick, Miss L, BA (Hons) PgDip MCLIP, Knowledge & L. Servs. Manager, Queen Elizabeth Hospital, Norfolk.
[61618]   03/10/2002   **CM13/11/2013**
Kenna, Mrs S, MA FCLIP HonFCLIP, Retired.
[20786]   02/07/1973   **HFE02/09/2010**
Kennaway, Mrs M, FCLIP FSA Scot, Life Member.
[8266]   31/03/1939   **FE13/02/1975**
Kenneally, Mr J, BA (Hons) PGCE, School Teacher, Oslo International School, Norway.
[10031798]   04/10/2013   **ME**
Kennedy, Mrs C M, BA MCLIP, Part-time Comm. Librarian, Malmesbury, Cricklade & Purton Ls. Wilts. County Council,
[32689]   16/06/1980   **CM30/07/1982**
Kennedy, Mr J, MA FCLIP, Retired.
[8273]   01/01/1962   **FE29/04/1975**
Kennedy, Mr J, MA (Hons) MSc,
[57314]   10/02/1999   **ME**
Kennedy, Miss J L, MA MCLIP, Gallery Records Manager, Tate.
[39018]   28/10/1985   RV07/06/2006   **CM15/11/1988**
Kennedy, Mrs M L, MA BSc PgDip MCLIP, Subject Librarian, Heriot Watt University Library, Edinburgh.
[48769]   17/05/1993   **CM28/01/2009**
Kennedy, Miss N J, BA (Hons) MA, Senior Library Assistant. Lending Services Supervisor, University of Oxford.
[10032501]   10/12/2013   **ME**
Kennedy, Mrs R, BA (Hons) MCLIP, Development Librarian, Redbridge Central Library.
[30432]   29/01/1979   **CM01/01/1981**
Kennedy, Mr S, Information/Knowledge Assistant, Royal College of Psychiatrists, London.
[65371]   12/01/2006   **ME**
Kennedy, Mrs S A, BA DipLib MSc MCLIP PGHE, Retired.
[13447]   08/06/1971   **CM09/05/1975**

Kennedy, Miss Y M, MCLIP, L. Officer, City of Edinburgh Council.
[26430]   05/10/1976   **CM25/08/1983**
Kennerley, Mr F C, FCLIP, Life Member.
[8284]   24/04/1935   **FE01/01/1949**
Kennerley, Mrs S J, BA (Hons) MA MCLIP, Unwaged.
[47701]   19/10/1992   **CM20/03/1996**
Kennett, Miss L, Information Support Officer, Ministry of Defence.
[10034536]   21/07/2014   **ME**
Kenny, Ms N, MA LPC LLB MSc, Student.
[10001201]   03/02/2007   **ME**
Kensler, Ms E, BA (Hons) DipLib, Customer Serv. Manager, Aberystwyth University.
[50168]   20/04/1994   **CM27/11/1996**
Kenssous, Mr N, Assistant Librarian, Luton and Dunstable University Hospital.
[63451]   12/05/2004   **ME**
Kent, Mrs E C, ACLIP, Assistant Librarian, St Edwards School, Oxford.
[63791]   06/10/2004   **ACL22/06/2007**
Kent, Ms E J, Retired.
[22915]   07/10/1974   **ME**
Kent, Ms G L, BA (Hons) MA, Graduate Trainee, Student Library Assistant, Albert Sloman Library.
[10022654]   05/04/2013   **ME**
Kent, Ms J, MA MCLIP, Library System Manager, Royal Institute of British Architects, London.
[38667]   09/09/1985   **CM25/01/1995**
Kent, Mrs J M, MCLIP, Retired.
[12598]   23/09/1968   **CM05/02/1973**
Kent, Mrs M E, MA (Oxon), Reader Services Officer, Bodmin Librarian, Cornwall C.
[63586]   01/07/2004   **ME**
Kent, Miss N, BA MA MA, Library Assistant, Inner Temple Library.
[10020188]   15/11/2011   **ME**
Kent, Miss S, Library Assistant, Hertfordshire County Council.
[10022226]   22/01/2013   **AF**
Kent, Ms W, BA (Hons) MCLIP, Comm. & Information Officer, North Yorks. County Council, Knaresborough Library & Information Centre.
[36415]   11/10/1983   **CM20/05/1998**
Kent-Sutton, Mrs J, BA MA PgDip MCLIP, School Librarian, Belmont Academy, Ayr.
[10015816]   28/01/2010   **CM20/06/2012**
Kenvyn, Mr D B, BA MCLIP, Retired.
[30323]   17/01/1979   **CM29/12/1981**
Kenward, Miss H E, MA, Librarian: Children, Young People & Families, Oxfordshire CC.
[64062]   15/12/2004   **ME**
Kenwright, Miss C E, BA (Hons) DipInf MCLIP, Head of Knowledge and Learning Services, Irwin Mitchell.
[45411]   09/01/1991   **CM25/01/1995**
Kenyon, Ms R, BA MCLIP, Retired.
[35923]   26/02/1983   **CM21/06/1984**
Keogh, Mr M, BA (Hons) DipIM MCLIP, Assistant Librarian, Ealing Hospital NHS Trust, Southall.
[55690]   04/11/1997   **CM12/03/2003**
Kerameos, Ms A,
[41019]   02/10/1987   **ME**
Kerby, Ms S, MCLIP MIL Cert Ed Dip HE, Site Librarian, Brinsbury.
[14827]   14/01/1972   **CM02/07/1975**
Kernan, Miss M, BM, Student, UCL.
[10033417]   11/03/2014   **ME**
Kernot, Mr A E, BA (Hons) MA, Senior Information Librarian, University of Oxford.
[57085]   04/12/1998   **ME**

Kerr, Mrs C, BA MCLIP, SLRCC, City of Edinburgh, Council.
[32798]   24/09/1980   **CM09/10/1986**
Kerr, Miss D S, MA DipLib MCLIP, Digital Services Manager, the City of
Edinburgh Council.
[38209]   28/01/1985   **CM08/03/1988**
Kerr, Mrs J, Children's Librarian, Peters Bookselling Servs.
[10009277]   15/01/1973   **CM07/09/1976**
Kerr, Ms L, BA DipLib MCLIP, Head of Learning Resources, Regent's
College, Regent's Park, London.
[42097]   01/10/1988   **CM24/06/1992**
Kerr, Mr M W C, BA (Hons) PgDip MCLIP, Clinical Librarian, East Kent
Hospitals NHS trust.
[50310]   15/06/1994   **CM30/04/2014**
Kerr, Mr P, Student, University of Strathclyde.
[10032491]   10/12/2013   **ME**
Kerr, Ms S V, PgDipLib BA (Hons) MCLIP, Learning Res. Centre
Manager, Army Foundation College, Harrogate.
[53596]   01/08/1996   **RV**20/02/2014   **CM23/06/2004**
Kerridge, Mrs E J, BA, Housewife.
[35657]   06/12/1982   **ME**
Kerrins, Ms L, BA MSocSC, Student.
[10022141]   08/01/2013   **ME**
Kerry, Mr D A, MA DipInf, College Librarian, Union Theological College,
Belfast.
[48700]   07/04/1993   **ME**
Kerry, Mr J A, BSc (Hons) MCLIP, Site Librarian, Leeds Teaching
Hospitals NHS Trust.
[62499]   29/07/2003   **CM10/07/2009**
Kerry, Mrs J C, BSc MCLIP, Teaching Assistant.
[38049]   10/01/1985   **CM21/07/1989**
Kerry, Mrs R M, BA MCLIP, Unwaged.
[38809]   09/10/1985   **CM14/11/1990**
Kersey, Mrs M, MCLIP, Retired.
[8316]   23/09/1955   **CM01/01/1964**
Kersey, Mrs S, MCLIP, Senior Librarian, Reader Serv., Bournemouth L.
[21370]   13/11/1973   **CM03/11/1976**
Kershaw, Mrs H, BA DipLib MCLIP,
[33769]   16/02/1981   **CM01/07/1984**
Kershaw, Mrs S C, BSc MA MSc,
[10034295]   01/07/2014   **ME**
Kerslake, Mrs S E, BA (Hons) MA MCLIP, Customer Services Manager,
The Library, The Royal Society of Medicine.
[48292]   01/01/1993   **CM22/07/1998**
Kesse, Mr E, MSLIS PrA, Unwaged.
[10015781]   26/01/2010   **ME**
Kettel, Ms B, Library Assistant, University of St Andrews University
Library.
[10019740]   02/09/2011   **ME**
Kettle, Mr S J, BA DipLib MCLIP GDipMan, Dev. Manager, Leics. L.
Serv.
[34531]   02/12/1981   **CM18/07/1985**
Kettles, Mr N J, MA MLIS, JCSP Librarian, St Kevin's College.
[10034612]   23/07/2014   **ME**
Kettlety, Mrs J, BA MCLIP, Service Development Manager, Manchester
City Council.
[31942]   08/01/1980   **CM28/07/1983**
Kettlewell, Mrs J D, ACLIP, Senior Library Advisor, Customer Services,
University of Nottingham.
[10007658]   18/02/2008   **ACL23/09/2009**
Kettlewell, Mr P, MSM ALA, Retired.
[8329]   08/03/1961   **CM01/01/1966**
Kettlewell, Miss R, BSc, Student, Robert Gordon University.
[10035504]   16/10/2014   **ME**

Keup, Mr J, MLIS MA, Specialist / Librarian, Menwith Hill School.
[10014882]   21/09/2009   **ME**
Kevill, Ms S, BA (Hons) MSc (Econ) MCLIP, Subject Librarian,
University of Stirling.
[62897]   18/11/2003   **RV**20/06/2014   **CM19/03/2008**
Key, Mrs J, BA MCLIP, Literature Searcher, Royal College of Nursing,
London.
[34722]   19/01/1982   **CM14/04/1987**
Key, Ms J A, School Librarian, Devonport High School for Girls.
[10022514]   19/03/2013   **ME**
Key, Mr O, ACLIP, Lib. User Support Advisor., UniversityLibrary,
University of Surrey.
[10018034]   05/11/2010   **ACL11/04/2013**
Key, Miss P J, Library Service Advisor, Arnold Library.
[10031354]   29/07/2013   **AF**
Keyton, Mr T S J, BA (Hons),
[10019789]   13/09/2011   **ME**
Kgosiemang, Ms R T, MSc, Coordinator, Humanities, Subject Librarian,
University Botswana.
[51436]   14/02/1995   **ME**
Khan, Mr A, BA (Hons) FCLIP MBE, Head of Face to Face Services,
Warwickshire County Council, L. & Information Serv.
[44888]   08/01/1991   **FE15/09/2004**
Khan, Ms A, BA (Hons), Information Specialist, British Film Institute.
[10032660]   24/12/2013   **ME**
Khan, Mr K, BA (Hons),
[10035672]   28/10/2014   **ME**
Khan, Mr M, MSc (Oxon) FBCS CITP FIAP, Director, Technology and
Software Development.
[10022264]   29/01/2013   **ME**
Khayi, Ms N, BA (Hons) Mst MA, Librarian, St Hugh's College, Oxford
University, Oxford.
[10018438]   18/01/2011   **ME**
Khorshidian, Mrs M, BA DipLIS MCLIP, Campus Library Manager,
Ulster University, Belfast.
[45066]   03/07/1990   **CM22/07/1998**
Khouri, Mrs M, ACLIP, Senior Library Assistant, UCL Institute of
Orthopaedics.
[10021682]   27/09/2012   **ACL15/07/2014**
Khurshid, Mr S, MA Library and Information Science, Instructor
(Library), Jubail Industrial College.
[10034634]   25/07/2014   **ME**
Kidd, Mr A J, MA MCLIP, Retired.
[23153]   08/10/1974   **CM29/11/1976**
Kidd, Ms E, MA (Hons) DipLIS MCLIP, Senior Librarian, Buckie Library,
The Moray Council.
[46174]   09/10/1991   **CM22/05/1996**
Kidd, Mrs E, BA,
[10019755]   06/09/2011   **ME**
Kidson, Mrs J A, Head of KIM, Home Office.
[10031672]   19/09/2013   **ME**
Kiehl, Dr C A, MA MCLIP PhD, Dean of University Library, University of
Southern Mississsippi.
[24559]   19/08/1975   **CM30/10/1978**
Kieliszek, Mr J, MA, Senior Advisor, University for the Creative Arts.
[10033711]   16/04/2014   **ME**
Kielt, Miss H, BA (Hons) PgDip, Outreach & Information Officer (Health
in Mind project), Libraries NI.
[10020406]   11/02/2012   **ME**
Kiely, Mrs C M, BA (Hons) DipILS MCLIP, Consultant, research &
information, media planning and bookeeping.
[40822]   01/07/1987   **CM01/04/2002**

Kift, Mrs K L, BA (Hons) MSc MCLIP, Academic Liaison Manager, Coventry University.
[53877]   07/10/1996   **CM01/02/2006**
Kift, Ms S M L, BA MCLIP, Senior Lib. Lending – North Somerset.
[37032]   30/01/1984   **CM11/12/1989**
Kilbride, Mrs S, MA (Hons) DipILS PGCE, Child. & Young People's Librarian, North Lanarkshire Council.
[46839]   13/02/1992   **CM20/03/1996**
Kilgallon, Mrs I J, MCLIP, Information Specialist, Faculty of Tech., University of Portsmouth.
[13794]   01/10/1971   **CM11/12/1989**
Kilgour, Ms A E, BA (Hons) DipLib MCLIP, Liaison Librarian, Queen Margaret University, Edinburgh.
[46120]   02/10/1991   **CM20/09/1995**
Killean, Mrs E J, BA MCLIP, Volunteer Librarian.
[41092]   07/10/1987   **CM25/05/1994**
Killen, Miss C, BA (Hons) MSc, Information Officer, Voice of Young People in Care, Northern Ireland.
[10015105]   13/10/2009   **AF**
Killington, Ms V J, BA (Hons) (Oxon) MA MLIS, Trainee Librarian, Falkirk Community Trust.
[10032816]   14/01/2014   **ME**
Killoran, Mrs P A, College Librarian.
[61003]   29/01/2002   **ME**
Killoran, Ms S A, BA MA (Oxon) DipLib MCLIP, Fellow Librarian, University of Oxford, Harris Manchester College.
[34965]   18/05/1982   **CM11/04/1985**
Kilmartin, Ms O, Student.
[65804]   12/05/2006   **ME**
Kilmurray, Miss L, MCLIP, Retired.
[8358]   17/03/1960   **CM09/03/1982**
Kilner, Mrs A, BA (Hons) MA MCLIP, Assistant Director, Library & Information Services, Teesside University.
[51529]   01/04/1995   **RV**27/08/2014   **CM10/07/2002**
Kilvington, Mrs L M, BA MCLIP, Housewife.
[24335]   08/07/1975   **CM10/08/1977**
Kim, Ms S Y, MA, Student, The iSchool at UBC.
[10032133]   29/10/2013   **ME**
Kimber, Mrs C E, MA (Oxon) MA MCLIP, Career break.
[57580]   12/05/1999   **CM29/03/2004**
Kinahan, Mr H O, MSc, Knowledge and Information Manager, Foreign & Commonwealth Office.
[10032983]   03/02/2014   **ME**
Kindness, Mrs F, BA MCLIP, School Librarian, Govan High School.
[40103]   21/10/1986   **CM19/08/1992**
King, Ms A B, BA (Hons) ACLIP, Lib. Assistant, Holy Cross 6th Form College, Bury.
[10017642]   20/09/2010   **ACL14/03/2012**
King, Mrs A C, BA MCLIP, Advisory Librarian, School Library Service, Chelmsford.
[30164]   15/01/1979   **CM01/07/1991**
King, Miss D R, BA (Hons) MSc MCLIP, L. & Information Manager, Winckworth Sherwood, London.
[47160]   20/05/1992   **CM27/07/1994**
King, Ms E,
[10010123]   26/06/2008   **ME**
King, Miss E J, BA (Hons) MSc MCLIP, Head of Research Solutions, PriceWaterhouseCoopers, London.
[56279]   20/04/1998   **CM25/07/2001**
King, Mrs F E, BA MCLIP, Partnership Librarian, Banbury School Partnership.
[29455]   03/08/1978   **CM30/06/1981**
King, Mrs J, BA MCLIP, Librarian, Reaseheath College, Cheshire.
[40514]   27/02/1987   **CM21/07/1993**

King, Mrs J, Part-time Librarian, Warrington Borough Council.
[39721]   22/05/1986   **ME**
King, Mrs J C, BA (Hons) MA MCLIP, Information Advisor, Sheffield Hallam University.
[43834]   25/01/1990   **CM26/05/1993**
King, Ms K, BA (Hons) MCLIP, Information & Learning Resources Manager, Oakbank School, West Yorkshire.
[46028]   06/09/1991   **CM01/04/2002**
King, Mrs M, MCLIP, Retired.
[8391]   24/01/1963   **CM01/01/1971**
King, Mr M B, MCLIP FIMgt FRSA, Retired.
[8393]   03/02/1961   **CM01/01/1967**
King, Mr M C, BA (Hons) ILTHE MCLIP, Society & Health Faculty Librarian, Buckinghamshire New University.
[10001130]   20/01/1975   **CM18/08/1986**
King, Ms N C S, BA (Hons) MA (Hons) PGCE MCLIP, Scholarly Publications Assistant, Northumbria University.
[57041]   27/11/1998   **CM10/07/2009**
King, Ms P A, BLS DipHE MCLIP, Librarian, Brigidine School, Windsor.
[28040]   13/10/1977   **CM19/10/1982**
King, Mr P M, MA DipLib, Deputy Information Serv. Manager, Holman, Fenwick Willan, London.
[35670]   10/01/1983   **ME**
King, Mr R J, MSc, Joint Librarian.
[10019953]   06/10/2011   **ME**
King, Mrs S, BA (Hons) MCLIP FRSA, Head of Information Serv., Health and Safety Executive, Bootle.
[38197]   17/01/1985   **CM04/08/1987**
King, Mrs S, MA MCLIP, Retired, House of Lords.
[8403]   01/01/1969   **CM02/10/1972**
King, Mrs S A, BSc (Hons) MBA, Librarian, Hemel Hempstead Library.
[10014788]   18/09/2009   **ME**
King, Mr S A, BA (Hons) MA (Lib), School Librarian, Duke of York's Royal Military School, Dover, Kent.
[63866]   11/10/2004   **ME**
King, Miss S D, BA (Hons) MCLIP, Librarian and CDD Library Advisor, Northern School of Contemporary Dance.
[48676]   08/04/1993   **CM01/02/2006**
King, Mrs S H, BA (Hons) DipILS MCLIP, Archive Manager, MOD.
[49034]   07/09/1993   **CM22/07/1998**
King, Mrs S J, DipLib MCLIP, Information Advisor, Student Careers & Skills Serv., University of Warwick.
[33240]   27/10/1980   **CM12/04/1983**
King, Miss T, MA (Hons) MSc, Senior Knowledge Management Officer, NHS Health Scotland.
[62737]   15/10/2003   **ME**
Kingma, Miss M A, Librarian, the British Library, London.
[65974]   09/08/2006   **ME**
Kings, Ms P A, BA MCLIP, Freelance Lib. Children/Youth. Trainer, consultant, resources creation: Reading for pleasure.
[32309]   05/03/1980   **CM09/12/1982**
Kingsbury-Barker, Mrs T C, BA MCLIP, Librarian, Blackfen School for Girls.
[41964]   04/07/1988   **CM18/11/1992**
Kingsmill, Mrs P J, ACLIP, Librarian, Crawley L.
[65471]   24/02/2006   **ACL01/11/2007**
Kinnear, Ms K A, BSc MSc, Senior Researcher, Hogan Lovells International LLP, London.
[10002924]   30/01/1992   **ME**
Kinnear, Miss K E, BA (Hons) MA MCLIP, Property & Environment Lead (Libraries), Surrey County Council.
[59382]   23/02/2001   **CM21/06/2006**
Kinnish, Mr M, Library Assistant, IRBY Library, Wirral.
[10022537]   19/03/2013   **AF**

Kirby, Mrs C E, BA PgDipLib MCLIP, HE & Cannington Services Co-ordinator, Bridgwater College, Somerset.
[33016]   01/10/1980   **CM08/02/1983**
Kirby, Ms V, Bsc (Ecom), Student, Aberystwyth University.
[10032600]   20/12/2013   **ME**
Kirk, Mr A, MA MSc, IS Helpdesk Supervisor, University of Edinburgh.
[10032867]   30/01/2014   **ME**
Kirk, Mrs L, BA (Hons) PgDip RLP, Directorate Support Manager, Aberdeen City Council.
[10033930]   13/05/2014   **ME**
Kirk, Mr R W, BA MCLIP HonFCLIP, Retired.
[8434]   21/03/1966   **HFE24/10/2002**
Kirk, Ms S A M, BA (Hons) MCLIP, Senior Librarian, Halton Lea Library, Runcorn.
[43623]   13/11/1989   **CM25/05/1994**
Kirk, Mrs S C, BA Lib, Assistant Librarian, Banchory Library.
[10007785]   12/11/1981   **ME**
Kirk, Miss W, BA (Hons) MSc, Librarian, Glasgow City Council.
[61767]   05/11/2002   **ME**
Kirkby, Mrs E, BA MCLIP, Retired.
[8436]   01/01/1966   **CM01/07/1973**
Kirkham, Miss B D, BA (Hons) DipLIS MCLIP, Assistant Librarian, Denbighshire County Council.
[46441]   06/11/1991   **CM31/01/1996**
Kirkham, Mr N A, LLB MA, Assistant Librarian (Bibliographic Serv.), Gonville & Caius College, Cambridge.
[64925]   12/09/2005   **ME**
Kirkham, Mrs V E, BA DipLib MCLIP, Tourist Assistant (Part Time).
[38106]   15/01/1985   **CM14/02/1990**
Kirkpatrick, Mrs A S, BA, ICT Technician, All Saints' CE (VA) Primary School, Peterborough.
[37707]   10/10/1984   **ME**
Kirkpatrick, Mrs S D, BLS MCLIP, Senior Manager Dorset County Council.
[32327]   03/03/1980   **CM21/06/1983**
Kirtley, Mrs S, MA (Hons) MSc. Res. Information Specialist, Centre for Statistics in Medicine, University of Oxford.
[56740]   12/10/1998   **ME**
Kirton, Ms J, Librarian, Wollongbar Primary Industries Institute, Australia.
[10000796]   03/11/2006   **ME**
Kirton, Miss M H, BA MA MCLIP, Information Serv. Advisor, Napier University, Edinburgh.
[36484]   18/10/1983   **CM05/05/1987**
Kirwan, Mrs P, MCLIP DipPsych, Retired.
[9158]   01/01/1967   **CM01/01/1971**
Kisiedu, Prof C O, Librarian, Catholic University College of Ghana, Ghana.
[20906]   28/08/1973   **ME**
Kistell, Mr T J, BA (Hons) PgCert MA, Information Adviser, Sheffield Hallam University.
[10015676]   13/01/2010   **ME**
Kitch, Mrs P W, MLib MCLIP, Retired.
[34104]   01/01/1960   **CM07/09/1966**
Kitchen, Miss J A, BA MCLIP, Law Librarian & Information Manager, Hugh James, Cardiff.
[28613]   04/01/1978   **CM07/10/1981**
Kitchin, Mrs E, MCLIP, Life Member.
[8453]   27/02/1947   **CM01/01/1957**
Kitchin, Miss S, BA (Hons) MSc (Econ) MCLIP PgCert FHEA, Research Support Librarian, Northumbria University Library.
[62783]   22/10/2003   **CM29/08/2007**
Kite, Ms K, BA MA MS, Self-employed.
[10033612]   03/04/2014   **ME**

Kleinknecht, Miss D I, MSc Econ, Librarian, Oxford Central Library, Oxford.
[10000980]   04/12/2006   **ME**
Klien, Miss C, MSc,
[10021589]   05/09/2012   **ME**
Klijn-Passant, Mrs S, ACLIP, Development Officer – Cultural Services.
[64575]   06/05/2005   **ACL05/10/2007**
Klungthanaboon, Miss W, MA, PhD Research Student, University of Glasgow.
[10033586]   01/04/2014   **ME**
Kluttz, Ms K, MLIS,
[10018946]   18/06/2013   **ME**
Kmet, Mrs C M, BEd MEd, Teacher Librarian, Thomas's London Day School, London.
[10015059]   15/10/2009   **ME**
Knee, Mrs J D, Dip Lib BA MA MCLIP, Library Assistant at West Dean College, Edward James Foundation, West Dean, Chichester.
[10015673]   09/10/1987   **CM30/01/1991**
Kneebone, Mrs C, MCLIP, Retired.
[8468]   09/02/1960   **CM01/01/1965**
Kneebone, Mr W J R, BSc MCLIP, Retired.
[8469]   23/01/1961   **CM01/01/1964**
Knight, Miss A, Information Assistant, Kimberlin Library.
[10033633]   07/04/2014   **AF**
Knight, Mrs A H, BSc (Hons) MSc MCLIP, Head of Content, Digital & Client Services, Cranfield Library & Information Service, Cranfield University.
[48139]   11/11/1992   **CM15/10/2002**
Knight, Dr G A, PhD FCIL FIAP MCLIP MBCS, Consultant Patent Analyst.
[60535]   29/05/1979   **CM29/05/1979**
Knight, Mrs J E, BA PgDip ACLIP, L. Assistant, Oxford Brookes University.
[10010965]   10/09/2008   **ACL23/09/2009**
Knight, Mr J F, BA, Student, UCL (Lib. Assist., Haldow College, Tonbridge)
[10019606]   03/08/2011   **ME**
Knight, Mr J I, BA (Hons), Lib. & Information Assistant, Exeter Central Library, Devon.
[10005569]   25/07/2007   **AF**
Knight, Miss J L, MSc (Econ) MCLIP, Deputy Chief Librarian, Guille-Alles Library, St Peter Port, Guernsey.
[56524]   10/08/1998   **CM23/01/2002**
Knight, Miss R, PGDip BA (Hons), Librarian, Sherborne School for Girls.
[10013651]   18/05/2009   **ME**
Knight, Mr R, Retired.
[8489]   10/01/1950   **ME**
Knight, Ms R, Student, Northumbria University.
[10035525]   16/10/2014   **ME**
Knight, Mr R F E, MA FRSA FCLIP, Life Member.
[8488]   14/03/1952   **FE01/01/1969**
Knight, Mr R G, BA MCLIP, Retired.
[23804]   31/01/1975   **CM12/09/1977**
Knight, Mrs T, MA MA MCLIP, Director of L. & Information Serv., Royal College of Surgeons of England.
[29054]   01/03/1978   **CM17/07/1981**
Knock, Mr D, BA (Hons) MSC MCLIP DHMSA, L. & K. Serv Manager, Princess Royal Hospital, King's College Hospital NHS Foundation Trust.
[58830]   22/08/2000   **CM10/11/2010**
Knott, Mrs J F, BA (Hons) MSc MCLIP, School Librarian, The Norton Knatchbull School, Ashford, Kent.
[35252]   01/10/1982   **CM16/02/1988**

Knowles, Mrs C P, MA MCLIP, Libraries, Museums and Arts Manager, Calderdale MBC, Halifax.
[31144]   29/08/1979   CM14/10/1981

Knowles, Mrs G A, BA MA MCLIP, Branch Manager, Lancashire County Council.
[43607]   09/11/1989   CM21/07/1993

Knowles, Mrs R A, BSc (Hons) MSc MCLIP, Information Specialist, Cranfield University, Swindon.
[58230]   22/11/1999   CM20/04/2009

Knowlson, Mrs A, BA MCLIP, College Librarian, City of Sunderland College.
[32886]   06/10/1980   CM30/07/1985

Knox, Mrs A M, BA MCLIP, Unwaged.
[57375]   26/02/1999   CM28/10/2004

Knox, Ms E B, BA (Hons) PgDip MCLIP, School Librarian, St John's RC High School.
[39540]   19/02/1986   ME

Knox, Mrs J, MA MCLIP, Assistant Librarian, University of Ulster at Jordanstown, Newtownabbey.
[33421]   23/11/1980   CM02/01/1988

Knutson, Mrs B, BA (Hons) MCLIP, L. R. C. Manager, The Kings of Wessex Academy, Cheddar.
[45355]   24/10/1990   CM20/11/2002

Kobzeva, Mrs I, MSc MCLIP, Librarian, Leeds City Council.
[10009771]   05/06/2008   CM13/10/2010

Koch, Mrs C J, MA MCLIP, Virtual Support & eServices Developer, University of Surrey, Guildford.
[59850]   16/10/2001   CM12/05/2011

Koenig, Miss G R N, BA, Audience Development Officer, Slough Libraries.
[62647]   01/10/2003   ME

Kohli, Mr G, BA BSc DipLib MCLIP, Retired.
[8517]   02/02/1966   CM01/01/1968

Kohlwagen, Ms J, DipLib MCLIP, Resident in Germany.
[52148]   06/10/1995   CM19/07/2000

Kohn, Ms A K E, NULL.
[10021625]   14/09/2012   ME

Kohnen-Zuelzer, Ms U, LRC Coordinator, Harris Academy At Peckham.
[10034743]   12/08/2014   ME

Kolawole, Mrs B O, BA (Hons) PgDIPILS, Intranet Editor., Ministry of Defence., Whitehall, London.
[62043]   28/01/2003   ME

Koltsova, Miss M, Student, University of Glasgow.
[10035570]   20/10/2014   ME

Kondylis, Mr D, BSc PgDipHRM MA HRM MBA, Archivist – Librarian, HR Professional Ministry of National Education and Religious Affairs, General State Archives of Greece.
[64794]   04/07/2005   ME

Kong, Mr P Y, MCLIP AALIA, Resident in Australia.
[18394]   19/10/1972   CM29/12/1980

Kong, Ms W S E, MA, Student, The University of Hong Kong.
[10035611]   23/10/2014   ME

Kontou, Miss V, Student.
[10032085]   24/10/2013   ME

Koopman, Ms M M, BA MSc HDip LIS, Library Manager, Percy Fitzpatrick Institute of African Ornithology.
[10021605]   11/09/2012   ME

Kopec, Miss K,
[10019265]   01/06/2011   ME

Kopecky, Mrs B J, MCLIP, Kopecky, Mrs B J, Sixth Form Librarian, Northampton School for Girls.
[30267]   09/01/1979   CM28/10/1981

Koper, Mrs E H, BA MA PGCE MCLIP, Reader Serv. Librarian, Royal Horticultural Society, Lindley Library, London.
[54604]   27/01/1997   CM16/07/2003

Kosinski, Mrs Z E, BA CNAA Dip MCLIP, Librarian, Adams Grammar School, Telford & Wrekin C. C.
[23762]   10/01/1974   CM01/03/1977

Koster, Mr C, BA FRSA MCLIP, Life Member.
[8524]   17/02/1959   CM01/01/1963

Koster, Miss F S C, BSc, Student, University of Sheffield.
[10035565]   20/10/2014   ME

Kostiw, Mr J M, Collections Support Librarian University of the West of England.
[10018559]   07/02/2011   ME

Kowalczuk, Mr F, BA (Hons) DipILM FCLIP, Knowledge Management Coordinator, Kings College London.
[52480]   02/11/1995   FE13/11/2013

Kowalski, Mrs R H, BSc Econ, Library & Resources Manager, St Michaels CE High School.
[10033601]   01/04/2014   ME

Kowalski, Mrs R Z, BA (Hons) MSc MCLIP, Career Break, unwaged.
[57506]   14/04/1999   CM23/06/2004

Koyama, Mr N, DipLib MCLIP, Under-Librarian, Cambridge University Library.
[32671]   03/07/1980   CM25/03/1985

Koziel, Ms M A, MSc, Information Assistant, City University, London.
[10020934]   24/04/2012   ME

Kozlowska-Wolodkowicz, Mrs A, MA, Library Manager/Information Professional.
[63469]   14/05/2004   ME

Krajewski, Mrs E, BSc (Econ) ACLIP, Librarian, The Hemel Hempstead School.
[64948]   03/10/2005   ACL28/01/2009

Krajewski, Miss H, Lib. Assistant, Durham Clayport L.
[10012831]   19/03/2009   ME

Kreinberga, Miss I,
[10021220]   29/06/2012   ME

Krieger, Miss C, BA, Student, Robert Gordon University.
[10035610]   23/10/2014   ME

Kroebel, Ms C, BA MSc MA,
[44227]   17/07/1990   ME

Krumbach, Ms M, MA, Librarian, RPSGB, London.
[10001460]   26/02/2007   ME

Kruse, Mrs H C, BA (Hons) MCLIP,
[49890]   12/01/1994   CM22/07/1998

Kumiega, Miss L U, BA MA DipLib MCLIP, Retired. *IN QUERIES FOLDER*.
[28999]   10/02/1978   CM12/05/1980

Kumra, Miss A, MA, Assistant Librarian (Cataloguing), Goldsmiths, University of London.
[10015429]   16/11/2009   ME

Kumuyi, Ms B O, BA (Hons) MSc LIS (Merit), L. Executive, Department of Information Servs., House of Commons, London.
[64713]   01/06/2005   ME

Kunderan, Mrs M, MA (Hons), Children's Activities Librarian, North Lanarkshire Council. Motherwell.
[10000913]   15/10/2003   ME

Kundu, Dr D K, MSc MA MLibSc PhD, Student, West Bengal State University.
[10035699]   ME

Kurzeja, Miss A, MA MRes, Student, UCL, London.
[10023329]   25/06/2013   ME

Kvebekk, Mrs M D, BA MCLIP, Retired.
[17207]   07/02/1956   CM01/01/1960

Kvrivishvili, Dr G, MA, Student.
[10002345]   01/05/2007   **ME**
Kwabla-Oklikah, Mrs G, BA MCLIP, Retired.
[8535]   01/01/1955   **CM01/01/1959**
Kwan, Ms I C L, DipLib MLib MCLIP, Senior Academic Liaison Librarian,
University of Westminster, London.
[44725]   27/11/1990   **CM25/01/1995**
Kybird, Mrs C L, MCLIP, L. Manager Khartoum International Community
School.
[1002]   18/01/1970   **CM01/02/1974**
Kyffin, Ms E, BA (Hons) MA DipIS MCLIP, Senior Academic Liaison
Librarian, University of Westminster, Harrow.
[52244]   18/10/1995   **CM19/05/1999**
Kyriakides, Mrs C, BA MCLIP, Part-time Information Officer, Child. Aid
to Ukraine, London.
[8539]   01/01/1966   **CM14/08/1967**

L

Labacevic, Mr I A, MA STB, Student, St Catherine's University.
[10034732]   12/08/2014   **ME**
Laban, Mrs R A, BA (Hons) MSC, Assistant in Charge, Derbyshire
County Council.
[10032724]   07/01/2014   **ME**
Lacey, Mr C S, L., F. C. O. Serv., London.
[48259]   18/11/1992   **ME**
Lacey, Ms E, BA (Hons), Graduate Trainee Librarian, Newnham Library
Company Limited.
[10031489]   28/08/2013   **ME**
Lacey Bryant, Mrs S M J, BA DipLib MSc, Associate Director of GP
Consortia Development/Chief Knowledge Officer.
[28615]   16/01/1978   **CM17/03/1980**
Lack, Mr S J, BA (Hons) DipLib MCLIP,
[37932]   16/11/1984   **CM07/06/1988**
Lackey, Ms A, BA (Hons) DMS PGCE, Associate L. Serv. Manager,
Brighton & Sussex University Hospital, NHS Trust, East Sussex.
[37619]   09/10/1984   **ME**
Lacy, Miss C P, BSc MCLIP, Unwaged.
[28047]   05/10/1977   **CM13/11/1979**
Ladd, Miss L D, MCLIP, Life Member.
[8548]   13/01/1948   **CM10/09/1975**
Ladizesky, Mrs K A, BA FCLIP, Retired.
[28745]   22/01/1978   **FE22/07/1998**
Ladjevardi, Miss A M, Sch. Librarian, TASIS The American School in
England, Thorpe, Surrey.
[63590]   30/06/2004   **ME**
Ladva, Mr M, L. &Sixth Form Study Centre, Cranford Comm. College.
[10018939]   31/03/2011   **AF**
Lafif, Mr E A, BA (Hons), MSc. Information Science Graduate from UCL.
[10032132]   29/10/2013   **ME**
Lai, Miss H N H, Student, The University of Hong Kong.
[10035671]   28/10/2014   **ME**
Lai, Miss S F, MSc MCLIP Chartered Marketer,
[61689]   21/10/2002   **CM31/01/2007**
Lai Sheung, Ms F, Head of Knowledge Centre, Arup, Hong Kong.
[10007193]   25/01/2008   **ME**
Laidlaw-Farmer, Mrs A W, MLS BA MCLIP, Retired.
[16868]   23/05/1966   **CM01/01/1971**
Lainchbury, Mrs A C, BA MCLIP, Librarian & Archivist, The Leys
School, Cambridge.
[36696]   31/10/1983   **CM16/05/1990**
Laine, Miss K, BA (Hons),
[10034465]   15/07/2014   **ME**

Laing, Mr C J, BA (Hons) MCLIP, Senior Assistant Librarian, De
Montfort University, Leicester.
[52476]   02/11/1995   **CM01/06/2005**
Laing, Mrs F, ACLIP, Senior Curator, National Library of Scotland,
Edinburgh.
[64785]   04/07/2005   **ACL24/04/2009**
Laing, Mrs R, BA (Hons) DipIM MCLIP AFHEA, Academic Librarian,
Loughborough University.
[54032]   21/10/1996   **CM23/01/2002**
Laird, Ms A, BA PgDipLib, Senior Information Executive, ICAEW.
[44498]   16/10/1990   **ME**
Laite, Mrs N, Learning Support Centre Manager/Leader, Wath
Comprehensive School.
[10033609]   03/04/2014   **ME**
Lake, Mr J B, BA HonFCLIP, Self-employed.
[22774]   11/10/1974   **HFE01/09/2011**
Lake, Miss N J, BA (Hons) MA MCLIP, L. Relations Manager, Sirsidynix.
[55748]   13/11/1997   **CM21/03/2001**
Lake, Miss R K, BA (Hons), Library Assistant, Bodleian Music Faculty
Library.
[10019911]   03/10/2011   **ME**
Laker, Mr K, MCLIP, Retired.
[8572]   01/05/1969   **CM23/01/1974**
Laker, Miss S C, BA DipLib MCLIP, Deputy Chief Librarian, Priaulx
Library, St Peter Port, Guernsey.
[37861]   14/10/1984   **CM30/01/1991**
Lakin, Mrs J E, Student.
[10033715]   16/04/2014   **ME**
Lale, Mrs J M, BLib MCLIP, Library Manager, West Suffolk College,
Bury St Edmunds.
[21284]   12/10/1973   **CM12/09/1977**
Lalic, Ms M M, BA GradDipLIS, Librarian, House of Commons Library,
London.
[64123]   17/01/2005   **ME**
Lally, Mrs P, MCLIP, Retired.
[8199]   01/04/1971   **CM04/03/1975**
Lam, Miss C H, MA, Graduate Trainee Library Assistant, The Courtauld
Institute Book Library.
[10015125]   15/10/2009   **ME**
Lam, Miss H Y, Student Aberystwyth University.
[10032262]   12/11/2013   **ME**
Lam, Mr K F G, MSc MA MLitt PGAS BSSc, Archivist, Legislative
Council, Hongkong.
[10008594]   02/04/2008   **ME**
Lam, Miss W Y W, BBus MA MCLIP FHKLA, Senior Assistant Librarian,
CPCE.
[62558]   20/08/2003   **CM17/06/2011**
Lamb, Mrs B, MCLIP, Life Member.
[8575]   09/02/1955   **CM01/01/1966**
Lamb, Mrs C, Student, Northumbria University.
[10032417]   03/12/2013   **ME**
Lamb, Mrs J M, BA (Hons), L. Assistant, Brooklands College, Ashford.
[10018286]   13/12/2010   **AF**
Lamb, Mr K D I, BA (Hons) DipLib MA, Head of Evidence Services,
Cheshire & Merseyside Commissioning Support Unit.
[44406]   05/10/1990   **ME**
Lamb, Ms K M, MA, Student, Northumbria University.
[10031866]   10/10/2013   **ME**
Lamb, Mrs R, MA MCLIP, Retired.
[20896]   01/10/1958   **CM01/01/1961**
Lambe, Miss L, BSc PgDip, Open Access Support Assistant, Imperial
College London.
[10022422]   26/02/2013   **ME**

Lambe, Ms M, BA DLIS DAS MA MSc (Econ), Librarian, Marino Inst. of Educ., Dublin.
[58596]   07/04/2000   **ME**

Lambe, Ms S E J, BA (Hons) MA, Student, UCL.
[10033608]   03/04/2014   **ME**

Lambert, Mrs A, BA (Hons) MCLIP,
[47782]   14/10/1992   **CM13/03/2002**

Lambert, Mrs C, BA (Hons) MCLIP, Principal Librarian- Children's Services (Part-time), West Sussex County Council.
[40579]   02/04/1987   **CM24/05/1995**

Lambert, Ms C, BA MA, Senior Library Assistant, University of Leicester L.
[44614]   06/11/1990   **ME**

Lambert, Mr D D, BA MCLIP, Team Librarian, Bedfordshire County Council, Leighton Buzzard.
[62414]   03/06/2003   **CM21/06/2006**

Lambert, Mrs J, BSc MA FCLIP, Retired.
[12665]   01/01/1970   **FE23/01/2008**

Lambert, Mrs J J, BA DipLib MCLIP, Librarian, London Borough of Sutton, Cent. L.
[35794]   20/01/1983   **CM13/05/1986**

Lambie, Ms L T, MA DipLib MCLIP DipLEDQ, Economic Development Team Leader, Inverclyde Council.
[39936]   01/10/1986   **CM15/08/1989**

Lamble, Mr W H, RFD BA AALIA MCLIP, Retired.
[17225]   21/02/1949   **CM01/01/1959**

Lambon, Mrs A R, BLib MCLIP MA, Lending Serv. Lib. (Job-share), University of Centre England, Birmingham.
[36129]   02/06/1983   **CM16/12/1986**

Lamming, Mr J D, BA DipLib MCLIP, Information Executive, Instituteof Chartered Accountants, London.
[31346]   30/09/1979   **CM11/01/1984**

Lamusse, Mrs F M, BA DipLib, Clinical Outreach Librarian, Portsmouth Hospital NHS Trust, Queen Alexandra Hospital.
[58966]   10/10/2000   **ME**

Lamyman, Miss J E, MCLIP, Life Member.
[24959]   28/10/1975   **CM19/02/1979**

Lancaster, Mr A, MCLIP, Assistant Headteacher/Librarian Monk's Walk School.
[63787]   18/10/2004   **CM13/06/2007**

Lancaster, Mr F W, FCLIP, Retired, Resident USA.
[27649]   13/01/1950   **FE01/01/1969**

Lancaster, Prof J M, MPhil, Retired.
[10020459]   04/12/1967   **CM25/10/1972**

Lancey, Mrs A, BNurs DPS (m) MA, L. and Knowledge Serv. Manager, Isle of Wight NHS PCT, Newport.
[49075]   01/10/1993   **ME**

Land, Mr A J, Msc BA PgDipIM MCLIP MBCS, Electronic L. Infrastructure Manager, University of Manchester.
[60493]   07/02/2001   **CM07/02/2001**

Lander, Miss K N, BA MCLIP, L. Manager, BAE Systems – Munitions, Glascoed.
[48074]   04/11/1992   **CM24/09/1997**

Lander, Mrs S A I, Retired.
[17229]   30/09/1968   **ME**

Landry, Mr P, MA MLS, Management Support Officer, Swiss National Library, Switzerland.
[10013166]   26/03/2009   **ME**

Landrygan, Ms R, BA, Apprentice Library Technician, Schools Library Service, Mountain Ash Library.
[10022799]   23/04/2013   **ME**

Lane, Mrs J, ACLIP, Information Assistant, Mansfield Library, Notts.
[65624]   15/03/2006   **ACL09/01/2007**

Lane, Mrs R A, BA (Hons), Sch. Librarian, Pangbourne College, Berks.
[34826]   15/03/1982   **ME**

Lane-Gilbert, Mrs P, MCLIP, Retired.
[8625]   02/05/1969   **CM10/11/1972**

Lang, Mr K, BSc (Eng) PGCE DipHE MSc (Econ), Liaison Librarian, Richmond upon Thames College.
[58218]   18/11/1999   **ME**

Langdon, Ms K, BSc (Hons) MA, Librarian, Radcliffe Science Library, Oxford.
[59545]   02/05/2001   **ME**

Langdon, Miss L E, BA (Hons) MSc MCLIP, Centre Manager, Exeter Central Library, Devon County Council, Exeter.
[64701]   01/06/2005   **CM06/05/2009**

Langdown, Mrs C H L, BSc MA MCLIP,
[41216]   19/10/1987   **CM14/11/1990**

Langella, Dr M L, DPhil, Assistant Librarian, Oxford Centre for Islamic Studies.
[10032111]   28/10/2013   **ME**

Langford, Ms R C, MA MCLIP, Unwaged.
[38170]   25/01/1985   **CM03/10/1991**

Langham, Mr M, BA DipLib MCLIP, Retired.
[27692]   06/07/1977   **CM18/07/1980**

Langley, Mrs L R, BA (Hons), Student, Aberystwyth University.
[10032044]   22/10/2013   **ME**

Langley, Mr M, MA MSc MCLIP, Intellectual Property Librarian, Queen Mary, University of London.
[56903]   02/11/1998   **CM29/03/2004**

Langley-Fogg, Mrs L A, Local Studies Libr., Derbyshire CC.
[42507]   22/11/1988   **ME**

Langman, Mrs C, BSc MSc, Information Specialist, Aston University, Birmingham.
[63006]   28/11/2003   **ME**

Langrish, Miss E, MCLIP, Information Specialist, Civil Service.
[63267]   23/03/2004   **CM13/04/2011**

Langrish, Mr T M, BA DipLib AIL MCLIP FETC, Principal Library Assistant, Bodleian K B Chen China Centre Library, University of Oxford.
[34045]   01/08/1981   **CM18/08/1983**

Langstaff, Miss H, Student.
[10006622]   11/09/2007   **ME**

Lanney, Mrs S F, BLS (Hons) MCLIP, Librarian, Basildon & Thurrock University Hospitals NHS Foundation Trust, Basildon Hospital.
[58575]   04/04/2000   **CM12/09/2001**

Lannon, Mrs I J, MA MCLIP, Retired.
[4288]   16/10/1964   **CM20/01/1975**

Lantry, Ms M, MA MA (Lib) HDipEd MCLIP, Information Services, Research, Data management, ROI.
[43675]   22/11/1989   **CM01/04/2002**

Lantz, Ms M A, BA DipLib MCLIP, Sch. Librarian, Montsaye Community College.
[33215]   27/10/1980   **CM07/03/1985**

Laogun, Mrs J, MA Lib Stud, Learning and Teaching Librarian, Open University, Milton Keynes.
[10013126]   31/03/2009   **ME**

Lapa, Ms A L S, Assistant Lecturer, Faculade de Letras, Universidade de Coimbra.
[50471]   12/08/1994   **ME**

Lara, Ms E J, BA MA DipLib, Librarian, University of the West Indies.
[36373]   07/10/1983   **ME**

Larbey, Mrs M A, BA MCLIP, Tech. Librarian, TWI, Granta Pk., Cambridge.
[29600]   01/10/1978   **CM19/11/1979**

Larbi, Mr K, BA MA MSc MCLIP, Subject Librarian, University of East London, Stratford.
[8646]   07/07/1971   **CM01/07/1989**

Lardner, Miss A E, MA, Knowledge Manager, The MDU, London.
[62808]   24/10/2003   **ME**

Lardner, Mrs L R, Res. Centre Manager, Blackheath High School, London.
[39461]   10/01/1986   **ME**

Lardner, Mr M D, BA MCLIP, Head of Information, Worklife Support Ltd, London.
[38005]   01/01/1985   **CM16/02/1988**

Larkin, Ms G, BA MA MSc, Student RGU.
[10032259]   12/11/2013   **ME**

Larkin, Mr J R W, BA DipLib MCLIP, Library Assistant (part time) London Brough of Southwark.
[31539]   16/10/1979   **CM30/04/1982**

Larkins, Miss A, BA PgDipIS MCLIP, Electronic Resources & Journals Manager, University of Huddersfield.
[48506]   01/02/1993   **CM07/09/2005**

Laskey, Miss A E, Performance and Improvement Manager., London Borough of Barking & Dagenham, Essex.
[45162]   31/07/1990   **ME**

Lass, Mr D M, MA DipLib MCLIP ALAI, Hon. Secretary ARLG – London & South East Region Committee. Currently seeking suitable posts in cataloguing/higher education.
[24514]   01/10/1975   **CM27/02/1985**

Lassam, Miss C, Retired.
[8663]   04/01/1967   **CM01/01/1971**

Last, Ms A, BSc MSc, Information Architect, Health & Social Care Information Centre, Leeds.
[10023123]   11/06/2013   **ME**

Last, Mrs L, ACLIP, Trust L., L. &Information Centre, West Suffolk Hospital NHS Foundation Trust.
[65940]   11/07/2006   **ACL04/03/2009**

Last, Mrs R A, MLS MCLIP, Consultant for L. in Sch. & Educ. Rosemary Last L. Serv.
[847]   09/02/1960   **CM01/01/1966**

Latham, Ms C E, MA (Hons) PGCE MSc ILS MCLIP, Part-time Children Librarian, Luton Cultural Services Trust.
[63383]   27/04/2004   **CM28/01/2009**

Latham, Ms S, BA (Hons) MA, Assistant Librarian, Univeersity of South Wales.
[10012888]   18/05/2005   **ME**

Latham, Mr S J, BA MA MPhil MSc MCLIP, Head of Knowledge, Transparency and Resilience, DEFRA.
[43719]   04/12/1989   **CM29/01/1992**

Lathrope, Mr D, BSc MCLIP DMS MBE, Retired.
[21996]   15/01/1974   **CM30/03/1976**

Latimer, Mrs K, MA DipLib FCLIP, Med L., Queens University, Belfast.
[9482]   01/01/1970   **FE05/05/2010**

Lattimore, Dr M, MA FCLIP, Retired.
[8675]   14/07/1958   **FE01/01/1965**

Latulip, Ms L, MCS MCLIP, Secondary School Libarian.
[10006221]   26/09/2007   **CM08/03/2013**

Lauder, Mrs J, BSc (Hons) MSc, Librarian.
[10001974]   28/03/2007   **ME**

Launder, Mr C, BA (Hons) MA MCLIP, Senior Library Supervisor Exmouth Library.
[56791]   23/10/1998   **CM15/05/2002**

Launder, Mrs J S, BA (Hons) MA MCLIP, Information & Learning Librarian, Exeter Central Library.
[53993]   14/10/1996   **CM12/03/2003**

Laundy, Mr P A C, FCLIP, Retired.
[17236]   22/03/1948   **FE27/09/1976**

Laurence, Mrs M T, MCLIP, Nursery Teacher.
[12164]   06/10/1967   **CM03/04/1975**

Laurence, Mrs S, BA (Hons) DipLib MCLIP, Head of Library Services. Glos. C. C.
[46387]   31/10/1991   **CM31/01/1996**

Laurenson, Ms J, BA (Hons), Graduate Trainee Library Assistant, The Courtauld Institute of Art, London.
[10020169]   15/11/2011   **ME**

Lauriol, Mrs C, MA MSc (Econ) MCLIP, Library Manager, Harcourt Hill Library Oxford Brookes University, Oxford.
[58933]   06/10/2000   **CM07/09/2005**

Lavender, Mrs G A, ACLIP, Support Serv. /Reader Development, Dudley L.
[10009970]   24/06/2008   **ACL09/11/2011**

Lavender, Ms S, LRC Manager, Calderdale College, Halifax.
[10014519]   27/08/2009   **ME**

Laver, Miss S L, MA, KM Systems Manager, Slaughter and May, London.
[52023]   15/09/1995   **ME**

Laverick, Mr D, FCLIP, Life Member.
[8688]   13/03/1948   **FE01/01/1961**

Laverick, Ms S J, BA, Part-time Librarian, De Montfort University, Leicester.
[36681]   04/11/1983   **CM05/07/1988**

Lavery, Mrs S M, MA MCLIP, L. Media Technician., Carlsbad Unified School District, Carlsbad, California, USA.
[27405]   22/03/1977   **CM26/03/1984**

Law, Prof D, DUniv FCLIP FKC HonFCLIP FRSE, Professor Emeritus, University Strathclyde, Glasgow.
[8690]   21/10/1969   **FE18/01/1989**

Law, Miss M, BA FCLIP, Life Member.
[17237]   05/06/1951   **FE22/09/1975**

Law, Ms W A, BA (Hons), Area Library Manager, Cambridgeshire County Council, South Cambridgeshire North.
[61614]   03/10/2002   **AF**

Lawal, Prof O O, BA MA PhD FCLIP, Information Manager, Ibadan, Nigeria.
[17238]   19/09/1971   **FE21/11/2001**

Lawler, Ms S, MSc PgDip,
[10011499]   22/10/2008   **ME**

Lawler, Ms U R E, MLS MCLIP, Unwaged.
[8107]   18/08/1967   **CM01/01/1970**

Lawrence, Mrs A R, BA MSc MCLIP, Executive Officer, University of Winchester.
[59858]   17/10/2001   **CM29/03/2004**

Lawrence, Mr B, BMUS (Hons), Children & Young People's Library Officer: Early Years, Central Library, Halifax.
[10016911]   08/06/2010   **ME**

Lawrence, Mrs C S, MA MSc MCLIP, Retired.
[21665]   24/12/1973   **CM11/11/1976**

Lawrence, Mrs H, BA (Hons), Assistant Academic Liaison Librarian, University of Sunderland.
[10010489]   30/07/2008   **ME**

Lawrence, Miss J, BA, Community Library Assistant, Cambridgeshire CC.
[10028188]   05/09/2014   **ME**

Lawrence, Ms K, BA (Hons) MA, Assistant Librarian, The Knights Templar School.
[52941]   29/01/1996   **ME**

Lawrence, Mrs L, BA (Hons) MSc Econ, Clinical Librarian, Royal Derby Hospital.
[64614]   20/04/2005   **ME**

Lawrence, Miss L L, BA, Child. Librarian, Ashburton Library, Croydon.
[52930]   25/01/1996   **ME**

Lawrence, Mrs P, Sr. Team Officer, Chertsey Library, Surrey.
[10012729]   25/02/2009   **AF**
Lawrence, Mr R, BA MCLIP, Retired.
[8713]   01/01/1964   **CM01/01/1967**
Lawrence, Mr S, BA BSc MSc MCLIP, Retired.
[60537]   22/10/1974   **CM22/10/1974**
Lawrence, Dr V J, BA PhD MA PGCHE, Acting Librarian, Goldsmiths,
University of London.
[44642]   13/11/1990   **ME**
Lawrence, Mrs Y T, MLS MCLIP, Retired., Kingston Jamaica.
[25194]   23/03/1962   **CM01/01/1970**
Laws, Mrs A E, BA Lib, Lead Literacy Support – Askham Bryan College
of Agriculture and G. T. A Librarian, Schools, NYCC and ERCC.
[39819]   31/07/1986   **ME**
Laws, Miss A M, BSc MSc MCLIP, Librarian, Ponteland High School.
[62132]   25/02/2003   **CM09/11/2011**
Laws, Ms E L E, BA (Hons) MSc (Econ) MA MCLIP, Curator, Childrens
Literature, V&A Museum.
[53419]   20/06/1996   **CM15/11/2000**
Lawson, Mrs A M, BA (Hons) MCLIP, Research and Open Access
Librarian, University of the West of England.
[10006396]   19/10/2007   **CM07/09/2011**
Lawson, Mrs D, BA DipLib MCLIP, Weekend Services Librarian, Leeds
Beckett University.
[40850]   08/07/1987   **CM14/03/1990**
Lawson, Miss K, BSc MSc MBA MCLIP, Head, Market Information &
Promotion, Tun Abdul Razak Res. Centre for, Hertford.
[60720]   23/10/1984   **CM01/02/1986**
Lawson, Mrs K J, BSc, Resource Co-ordinator, Shawfield Primary
School, Surrey.
[10021057]   28/05/2012   **AF**
Lawson, Mrs L J, BSocSc MA, Assistant Librarian, Kidderminster
College, Kidderminster.
[52413]   30/10/1995   **ME**
Lawson, Miss M, MA DipLib MCLIP, Resource Centre Manager, History
of Art, Resource Centre, Manager, University of Glasgow.
[31351]   15/10/1979   **CM23/12/1982**
Lawson, Mrs M, BA (Hons), Student, Bodleian Libraries.
[10031779]   03/10/2013   **ME**
Lawson, Mr M J, BA (Hons) MA MCLIP, Deputy Site Manager, Kings
College London, Information Serv. Centre.
[56588]   04/09/1998   **CM15/05/2002**
Lawson, Miss S, BSc (Hons) DipILM MCLIP, Librarian, Queen Square
Library, Institute of Neurology, UCL.
[50715]   12/10/1994   **CM19/05/1999**
Lawson, Ms S, BA PgDip, Service Development Co-ordinator,
Manchester City Council.
[10021824]   22/02/1999   **ME**
Lawson, S,
[10017447]   23/08/2010   **AF**
Lawton, Ms A, MLIS BA, System Librarian, Health Services Executive
Ireland, Dublin.
[10008271]   11/03/2008   **ME**
Lawton, Miss A P, BSc MSc MCLIP, Information Officer, Royal Institute
of British Architects.
[39678]   06/05/1986   **CM06/05/1986**
Lay, Mrs J, BA, Lib. Manager, Winton Library, Bournemouth.
[10017176]   26/05/1995   **AF**
Lay, Miss L, BSc (Econ) PgDip MCLIP, Librarian, Truro & Penwith
College, Cornwall.
[64593]   20/04/2005   **CM09/09/2009**
Lay, Mr S J, GTCL LTCL DipLib MCLIP, Area Manager, Oxfordshire
Library Service.
[45941]   26/07/1991   **CM27/07/1994**

Laycock, Mrs V A, MCLIP, Sch. Librarian, Central Lancaster High
School, Lancaster.
[10005380]   25/07/2007   **CM04/10/2013**
Layton, Ms C, BSc (Econ) MCLIP,
[57394]   03/03/1999   **CM20/04/2009**
Layzell Ward, Prof P J, MA PhD FCLIP, Life Member.
[8732]   01/01/1954   **FE01/01/1963**
Lazim, Ms A, BA MA MCLIP, Librarian, Centre for Literacy in Prim.
Educ., London.
[21862]   08/02/1974   **CM16/04/1981**
Le Bihan, Mrs K J, Beng Bcom, Systems Librarian.
[10015295]   30/10/2009   **ME**
Le Bourgeois, Ms S, MSc BA (Hons), Unwaged.
[10033638]   07/04/2014   **ME**
Le Boutillier, Miss F, MCLIP, Life Member.
[17243]   12/09/1959   **CM01/01/1964**
Le Breton, Mrs W, Student, Charles Sturt University.
[10035670]   28/10/2014   **ME**
Le Chat, Mrs S A, BA DipLib MCLIP,
[33831]   24/03/1981   **CM15/08/1984**
Le Cheminant, Mrs M, MCLIP, Retired.
[12409]   08/09/1971   **CM16/02/1976**
Le Lannou, Mrs M, School Librarian, CFBL.
[10031926]   15/10/2013   **ME**
Le Page, Mrs R J, Senior Library Assistant, Manchester Metropolitan
University.
[10032631]   21/12/2013   **ME**
Le Sadd, Mr W, Public Libraries.
[52870]   02/01/1996   **ME**
Lea, Miss E, BA (Hons) MSc (Econ), Assistant Librarian, New College,
Swindon.
[52451]   02/11/1995   **ME**
Lea, Mrs E S, BSc DipLIS MCLIP,
[43333]   20/10/1989   **CM14/09/1994**
Lea, Mr R A, BSc Dip Lib,
[37990]   01/01/1985   **ME**
Leach, Mr A, BA DPA FCLIP, Life Member.
[8745]   08/03/1948   **FE01/01/1959**
Leach, Mr C, BA MA DipLib MCLIP, Systems Librarian, University of
Lincs.
[29722]   05/10/1978   **CM06/11/1980**
Leach, Miss P R,
[38758]   06/10/1985   **ME**
Lead, Miss L, BA (Hons), Student, Aberystwyth University.
[10031809]   07/10/2013   **ME**
Leader, Mrs L M, BA MCLIP, Head of Library Business Planning &
Quality, University of Salford.
[31927]   17/12/1979   **CM05/08/1983**
Leak, Miss A R, BA (Hons) MA MCLIP, Subject Librarian, Arts
University Bournemouth, Poole.
[46011]   22/08/1991   **CM08/12/2004**
Leake, Miss A, MA (Hons) MSc, Senior Researcher, Hogan Lovells
International LLP.
[10001423]   12/10/1998   **ME**
Leather, Mrs C, Senior L. Officer, Educ. L. Serv., Reading.
[61566]   02/10/2002   **AF**
Leavy, Ms C, Project Manager – Library relocation specialist/consultant.
[10021087]   29/05/2012   **ME**
Lebeter, Mr I, BA MCLIP, School Librarian, Hillpark Secondary School,
Glasgow.
[63981]   22/11/2004   **CM19/11/2008**
Lecky-Thompson, Mrs J E, BA (Hons) MA MCLIP, Librarian, Faculty of
Philosophy, University of Cambridge.
[55504]   16/10/1997   **RV**30/04/2014 **CM15/01/2003**

Ledson, Mrs J E, BA MCLIP, Retired.
[17245]   01/01/1967   **CM01/10/1971**
Lee, Mrs A, Liaison Librarian – Enquiry Services, Birmingham City University.
[10009078]   08/01/2013   **ME**
Lee, Mrs A S, BA (Hons) DipILM MCLIP PGCE, Learning Centres Manager., Rotherham College., Sheffield.
[58512]   06/03/2000   **CM29/03/2004**
Lee, Mrs B, BA MSc, Cultural Services Officer, Neath Port Talbot., Co. Borough Council., Neath Port Talbot.
[59399]   05/03/2001   **ME**
Lee, Mrs B, MCLIP, Retired.
[8772]   31/01/1947   **CM01/01/1953**
Lee, Ms D T, MA (Oxon) MMus MA,
[60876]   18/12/2001   **ME**
Lee, Mrs E, BA MCLIP, Unemployed.
[25346]   13/01/1976   **CM23/11/1979**
Lee, Mrs G M, BA (Hons) MLS DipLib MCLIP, Health Information Specialist, Tribal Education Ltd, Sheffield.
[34199]   12/10/1981   **CM06/12/1985**
Lee, Miss H A, Information Specialist, FERA, York.
[52628]   14/11/1995   **ME**
Lee, Mrs J, MCLIP, Operations Mgr, Caerphilly Co. Borough Council, Ty Penallta, Tredomen, Ystrad Mynach.
[22826]   08/10/1974   **CM10/08/1977**
Lee, Mrs J, BA (Hons) DMS MCLIP, Service Development Officer, Barnsley Library and Information Service.
[28065]   13/10/1977   **CM11/09/1981**
Lee, Mr J D, FCLIP, Retired.
[8781]   05/09/1955   **FE01/01/1960**
Lee, Mr K S, MA, Research Assistant, Department of Cultural Studies.
[10034130]   09/06/2014   **ME**
Lee, Miss M, BA (Hons), Senior Library Assistant, Aberbargoed Library.
[10022559]   26/03/2013   **ME**
Lee, Miss R A, MA DipILS MCLIP, Unwaged.
[50686]   10/10/1994   **CM17/03/1999**
Lee, Mr S J, BA MCLIP, Part-time Senior Information Librarian, Tower Hamlets, London.
[38856]   17/10/1985   **CM24/04/1991**
Lee, Mrs S K, BSc (Hons) PGCE ACLIP, Customer Service Assistant and Business Support, Exeter Library, Exeter.
[10013955]   15/06/2009   **ACL03/11/2010**
Lee, Mrs S M, BA MCLIP, Unemployed.
[31203]   14/10/1979   **CM05/10/1984**
Lee, Miss S M Y, BA (Hons), Information Officer, Sidley Austin LLP.
[65290]   25/11/2005   **ME**
Leech O'Neale, Ms C A S, BSc MCLIP, Retired.
[17254]   26/02/1968   **CM01/01/1971**
Lees, Ms A, MA MCLIP, Senior Information Manager, Knowledge Serv. Group, NHS Education for Scotland, Glasgow.
[31352]   15/10/1979   **CM10/11/1981**
Lees, Miss J, BA (Hons) MScEcon MCLIP, Library Resources Manager, Wolverhampton Girls' High School.
[10008791]   18/04/2008   **CM16/01/2014**
Lees, Mr N G, MSc MCLIP, Unemployed.
[60540]   21/01/1980   **CM06/11/1989**
Lees, Miss R K, MA (Hons), Learning Resource Centre Manager, St Margaret's Academy, Livingston.
[10006546]   30/10/2007   **ME**
Leeson, Miss D C, BA MCLIP, Content and Access Team Leader, Brynmor Jones Library, University of Hull.
[35598]   11/11/1982   **CM09/08/1988**

Leet, Mrs J H, BA (Hons) MA MCLIP, Deputy Librarian, St Andrews Hospital, Northampton.
[48177]   11/11/1992   **CM20/01/1999**
Leeves, Ms J, BA MCLIP, L. Systems Consultant, Farnham, Surrey.
[8807]   22/06/1971   **CM15/12/1974**
Lefebvre, Mrs C J, BA MSc HonFCLIP, Independent Information Consultant, Lefebvre Associates Ltd, Oxford, UK: consultancy and teaching in info retrieval.
[37226]   01/04/1984   **HFE12/12/2007**
Lefebvre, Ms M J, MA MLS MA AALIA FCLIP, Chief Librarian, Ryerson University, Toronto, Canada.
[18790]   30/09/1972   **FE16/07/2003**
Leftley, Mr C P, BA BSc MCLIP, Librarian, Wycliffe Hall, University of Oxford; Assistant Librarian, Wolfson College, University of Oxford.
[30463]   29/01/1979   **CM05/02/1981**
Legg, Mrs E A, BA DipLib MCLIP, Unwaged.
[33026]   10/10/1980   **CM01/11/1982**
Legg, Mrs J C, BA (Hons) MCLIP, Part-time Information Researcher, Thales Res. & Tech. Ltd, Reading.
[41328]   03/11/1987   **CM27/07/1994**
Legge, Mrs K E, BLib MCLIP, Unwaged.
[29847]   06/10/1978   **CM14/02/1984**
Leggett, Mrs D, BA (Hons) MCLIP, Librarian, Discover North Tyneside Co-ordinator, North Tyneside Council.
[49992]   08/02/1994   **CM25/07/2001**
Lehmann, Mrs J, MBE BA MCLIP HonFCLIP, Retired.
[8817]   23/04/1967   **HFE01/09/2011**
Leibowitz, Miss Y, BA (Hons) MA,
[59631]   05/07/2001   **ME**
Leifer, Mrs J E, BA DipLib MA MCLIP, School Librarian, Immanuel College, Bushey.
[42009]   19/07/1988   **CM27/03/1991**
Leigh, Miss B,
[10012309]   27/01/2009   **ME**
Leighton, Mrs E, Lib. Admin., Central Bedfordshire College, Dunstable.
[10016987]   16/06/2010   **ME**
Leinster, Mrs A H, BA (Hons) MA MCLIP, Librarian, Wirral University Teaching Hospital NHS Found. Trust.
[58786]   20/07/2000   **CM29/03/2006**
Leith, Mrs A, BA DipLib MSc MCLIP, Part-time library assistant, Haberdashers' Aske's Boys School.
[32108]   06/02/1980   **CM25/01/1983**
Lelong, Miss S, BA, Student, Surrey County Council.
[10032876]   22/01/2014   **ME**
Lemonidou, Ms M, BA MA MCLIP, Unemployed.
[49173]   08/10/1993   **CM19/05/1999**
Lempinen, Mr A, MA, Student, Robert Gordon University.
[10032528]   12/12/2013   **ME**
Lendon, Mr J W, FCLIP, Life Member.
[8830]   01/01/1951   **FE01/01/1968**
Lenihan, Ms D F, BA (Hons) DipLib MCLIP, Assistant Subject Librarian, Wheatley Library, Oxford Brookes University.
[50798]   18/10/1994   **CM01/02/2006**
Lenihan, Mr M A, BSc DipLib MCLIP, Reference Librarian., Lewisham Library Lewisham.
[30464]   26/01/1979   **CM09/07/1981**
Lennox, Mrs S, BA MSc MCLIP, Unwaged.
[32230]   09/02/1980   **CM07/02/1985**
Lenti, Ms H, MA, Knowledge Services Co-Ordinator, Chartered Insurance Institute.
[10028240]   03/02/2014   **ME**
Leo, Miss M, DTLLS, Learning Resource Centre Facilitator, City of Westminster College.
[10034026]   21/05/2014   **ME**

Leonard, Mrs K, BA (Hons) MCLIP, Community Librarian, Flintshire.
[52418]   26/10/1995   **CM14/12/2012**

Leonard, Mrs L E, BSc (Econ) MCLIP, Librarian, Department of
Veterinary Medicine, Cambridge.
[52231]   16/10/1995   **CM12/03/2003**

Leonard, Ms M B, BA DipLib MCLIP FICA, Compliance Systems
Manager, Slaughter and May, London.
[28328]   24/10/1977   **CM09/12/1980**

Leonard, Mr P A L, Assistant Librarian, Science Library, UCL, London.
[10008570]   01/04/2008   **ME**

Lepley, Mrs D J, BA (Hons) MCLIP, Library Manager, Mid Essex
Hospital Trust, Chelmsford.
[44816]   03/12/1990   **CM17/03/1999**

Leppington, Mr C E, BA (Hons) MA MCLIP, Knowledge & Librarian,
Serv. Manager, Bromley Hospital NHS Trust, Edu. Centre L.
[53947]   15/10/1996   **CM21/07/1999**

Leslie, Miss A E, BA (Hons) MCLIP, Library Assistant, National Library
of Scotland, Edinburgh.
[56902]   02/11/1998   **CM08/08/2008**

Leslie, Mrs A H, MA DipLib MCLIP, Res. Development Officer, Educ.
Development Serv., Dundee.
[31243]   15/10/1979   **CM02/11/1982**

Leslie, Mr R, MCLIP, Retired.
[8843]   12/09/1967   **CM01/01/1969**

Lester, Dr R G, BSc PhD FCLIP FLS, Retired.
[33852]   01/04/1981   **FE25/03/1993**

Leszczynska, Ms M A, BA BSc MCLIP, Departmental Analyst
Programmer, IT Services, London Borough of Merton, Morden.
[32672]   15/07/1980   **CM05/08/1983**

Letellier, Mr P L, Student.
[63678]   12/08/2004   **ME**

Letendrie, Mrs F E, BA (Hons) Dip Inf Sci,
[10005499]   09/07/1990   **ME**

Lethaby, Miss B, BA MSc, The University of the West of England.
[10032688]   14/01/2014   **ME**

Letton, Miss C R, MA FSA SCOT MCLIP, Retired.
[19623]   10/10/1972   **CM21/01/1975**

Levay, Mr P, BA (Hons) MA MCLIP, Information Specialist, National
Institute for Health and Care Excellence.
[58185]   15/11/1999   **CM21/05/2003**

Levene, Mrs A, BA MCLIP, Retired.
[10217]   20/04/1969   **CM01/01/1972**

Levenson, Mrs J, Library Assistant, North London Collegiate Jnr.
School, Edgware.
[57811]   16/08/1999   **AF**

Leventhall, Mr A M, BA (Hons) DipLib MCLIP, Community Librarian,
Fakenham Library, Norfolk County Council.
[35762]   01/11/1982   **CM07/07/1987**

Levett, Ms S E, BA CertED MCLIP, Retired.
[29518]   23/09/1978   **CM27/10/1980**

Levey, Miss C, MCLIP, Senior Assistant Librarian, Goldsmiths College
Library, New Cross, London.
[10013469]   20/06/1980   **CM27/08/1982**

Levey, Mrs D, DipLib MCLIP, L. Development Manager, West Herts.
NHS Trust, Hemel Hempstead Hospital.
[27615]   25/05/1977   **CM14/08/1981**

Levi, Miss R, Unwaged.
[50889]   27/10/1994   **ME**

Levin, Mrs A J T, FCLIP, Life member.
[8859]   11/10/1933   **FE01/01/1948**

Levingstone, Mrs C, ACLIP, L. Manager, Dunstable Library, Beds.
[64184]   31/01/2005   **ACL07/12/2005**

Levy, Ms R, BA (Hons) MA, Principal L. Manager, Sutton Central L.
[61543]   10/09/2002   **ME**

Lewandowski, Ms S, BFA MCLIP, Learning Support, Northumbria
University, Newcastle Upon Tyne.
[10013152]   11/07/2010   **CM13/11/2013**

Lewendon, Miss C, ACLIP, Senior Library Assistant, Keele University
Library.
[10021737]   08/10/2012   **ACL09/07/2013**

Lewent, Mrs J A, BSc DipLib MCLIP, unwaged.
[33815]   26/02/1981   **CM04/10/1983**

Lewin, Miss H, BA MA MCLIP,
[64190]   31/01/2005   **CM13/11/2013**

Lewington, Dr R J, BSc PhD MCLIP, Retired.
[60541]   22/10/1974   **CM06/11/1978**

Lewis, Mr A I, BSc DipLib MCLIP, Librarian, Moore Stephens LLP,
London.
[31887]   14/01/1980   **CM21/01/1982**

Lewis, Ms C, LLB, Library Assistant, University of Buckingham.
[10035060]   09/09/2014   **ME**

Lewis, Ms C, BSc (Hons) PgDip MCLIP, LLS Head of Gateway
Services, University for the Creative Arts, Epsom, Surrey.
[58771]   17/07/2000   **CM10/07/2002**

Lewis, Mrs C E, Library Coordinator/Manager, RAKESS – BC, UAE.
[10021465]   22/08/2012   **AF**

Lewis, Mr D, BSc MBA BA CBiol FSB MCLIP, Writer & Translator.
[60725]   30/04/1980   **CM26/03/1985**

Lewis, Ms F R, BA PGCE,
[10015564]   15/12/2009   **ME**

Lewis, Mr H M, BA (Hons) PgDipILS MCLIP, Librarian, Bracknell Forest
Council.
[58187]   15/11/1999   **CM01/06/2005**

Lewis, Ms J M, MA (Oxon) MSc MBA, Service Development Supervisor
(PT), Fife Council.
[10031577]   03/09/2013   **ME**

Lewis, Mrs J R, MAPD PgDip MCLIP, Advisor, CyMAL; Museums,
Archives and Libraries Wales.
[10020654]   16/03/2012   **CM20/02/2014**

Lewis, Ms K A, BA (Hons)DipLib, Head of Knowledge Management,
Department of Health, London.
[35871]   26/01/1983   **ME**

Lewis, Ms L, BA (Hons), Business Information Coord., Arup, Sydney.
[61095]   28/02/2002   **AF**

Lewis, Ms M D, Student, Victoria University of Wellington.
[10032548]   13/12/2013   **ME**

Lewis, Mrs M J, Student, University of Wales Aberystwyth.
[10032652]   23/12/2013   **ME**

Lewis, Mrs M P, BSc (Hons) Dip Psych (OU) MCLIP MA, Learning
Resource Facilitator, Coleg Cambria, North Wales.
[10002763]   27/04/2007   **CM05/05/2010**

Lewis, Mr P R, MA HonFLA FCLIP, Life Member.
[8894]   23/03/1949   **HFE01/10/1989**

Lewis, Mr R W, BA DipLib MLS MBA MCLIP, Head, Corporate Science
Unit, Health & Safety Executive, Bootle.
[34581]   01/01/1982   **CM16/05/1985**

Lewis, Ms S J, BEd MLIS MCLIP, Comm. Librarian, Biggar Library,
South Lancs.
[41468]   01/01/1988   **CM06/04/2005**

Lewis, Ms S J I, MCLIP, Retired.
[8900]   09/07/1969   **CM01/07/1972**

Lewis, Ms S M, BA (Hons) MA MCLIP, Clinical Outreach Librarian,
Buckinghamshire Healthcare NHS Trust, Wilfred Stokes Library.
[53737]   20/09/1996   **CM21/11/2001**

Lewis, Ms W J, MA Phd, Cataloguer, Dr Williams' Library.
[10017762]   06/10/2010   **ME**

Lewis, Ms Y, BA MA, Assistant L. Curator, The National Trust, London.
[42181]   05/10/1988   **ME**

Lewsey, Miss S W, MCLIP, Life Member.
[17264]   11/06/1950   CM01/01/1955
Ley, Mrs A K, Online Support Officer, Unit 17, Threemilestone, Truro,
TR4 9LD, Cornwall.
[64414]   15/03/2005   AF
Leyland, Mr T P, BSc (Hons) PGCE PgDipILM, Learning Centre /
Support Services Coordinator. Exeter College.
[61953]   17/12/2002   ME
Li, Miss J, MLIS MBA, Student, The University of Tennessee.
[10033925]   13/05/2014   ME
Li, Mr K Y, Student, The University of Hong Kong.
[10035696]   29/10/2014   ME
Li, Miss O Y, Student, The University of Hong Kong.
[10032469]   09/12/2013   ME
Liang, Ms M, BA ALAA,
[10001252]   18/11/1988   ME
Libbey, Miss J P, BA MSc (Econ), Information Assistant, Brunel
University, Uxbridge.
[61776]   04/11/2002   ME
Licence, Miss S, BA (Hons), Student, Manchester Metropolitan
University; Administrator Guidance Information Services, NICE.
[10033707]   10/10/2014   ME
Lichfield, Mrs L M, BA MCLIP, Learning Resources Manager, Luton VI
Form College.
[37896]   15/11/1984   CM10/05/1988
Lichtenstern, Ms J, MSC BA (Hons), Librarian, Metanoia Inst., London.
[10017650]   21/09/2010   ME
Lickley, Mr D, BA (Hons) DipLib MA, Consultant, Sue Hill Recruitment,
London.
[44453]   09/10/1990   ME
Liddle, Miss M O, MCLIP, Life Member.
[8912]   02/03/1950   CM07/01/1976
Ligocka, Mrs M M, Team Assistant, Guildford Libary.
[10031789]   04/10/2013   ME
Lill, Ms F S, Electronic Services Manager, The British Library.
[41035]   06/10/1987   ME
Lilley, Dr G, MA PhD DipLib FCLIP, Life Member & Senior Research
Fellow in Bibl., Department of English, University of Wales.
[8927]   06/10/1961   FE01/01/1970
Lilley, Mrs M, BA LTCL MCLIP, Retired.
[8930]   03/02/1960   CM01/01/1962
Lilliman, Mrs K, BA (Hons) MA, Learning Resources Manager,
Freelance.
[10022751]   16/04/2013   ME
Lim, Ms S H, BSocSc MCLIP, Director, Library, Universiti Tunku Abdul
Rahman.
[22989]   08/10/1974   CM09/09/1977
Limb, Miss C H, BA (Hons), Student, John Port School.
[10035573]   20/10/2014   ME
Limper-Herz, Dr K, MA, Curator, The British Library, London.
[59481]   09/04/2001   ME
Lin, Ms Y J, Library Assistant, UCL.
[10028284]   12/05/2014   AF
Linacre, Ms C E, BA DipLib MCLIP, Head of Reference Services, RICS,
London.
[37597]   09/10/1984   CM08/03/1988
Lincoln, Mrs J M, BA MCLIP, Relief Work(Part-time), Highland Council
Library Department.
[19685]   30/10/1972   CM04/08/1976
Lindau, Mrs A, BA MA, Assistant Librarian, Chesterfield Royal Hospital,
Chesterfield.
[10012286]   21/06/2010   ME
Lindley, Mr D, MCLIP,
[8938]   19/02/1965   CM01/01/1969

Lindley, Mrs J M, BA (Hons) MCLIP, Librarian.
[48164]   11/11/1992   RV27/08/2014   CM22/03/1995
Lindsay, Mrs C A, BLib MCLIP DMS, Library Manager, Tuckton Library-
Bournemouth.
[32913]   01/10/1980   CM02/09/1986
Lindsay, Mr D, BA DipLib MCLIP, Knowledge ManagementConsultant,
Northamptonshire.
[28442]   28/11/1977   CM22/06/1981
Lindsay, Miss D, MA DipLib MCLIP, Retired.
[28058]   01/10/1977   CM20/10/1980
Lindsay, Ms G M, BEd BA (Hons) CertLS MCLIP, Library Volunteer,
Sussex Archaeological Society.
[57911]   01/10/1999   CM19/11/2003
Lindsay, Mr J W, BA MCLIP, Bibliographic & Support Manager, North
Lanarkshire Council, Motherwell.
[25589]   02/02/1976   CM16/07/1980
Lindsay, Dr M, BA MPhil PhD RGN MCLIP, Retired.
[8942]   19/07/1971   CM03/09/1979
Lindsey, Mrs P, MCLIP, Life Member.
[8945]   25/10/1945   CM01/01/1969
Lindsey-Tolley, Miss C M, BA, Student, University of the West of
England.
[10032500]   10/12/2013   ME
Linford, Ms R, MA (Hons) PgDip ILS MCLIP MSocInd, Freelance
indexer & website consultant.
[52649]   15/11/1995   CM19/11/2003
Lingard, Mrs K L, Librarian, Silcoates School, Wakefield.
[10017406]   17/08/2010   AF
Linnane, Mr C, BA, L. Officer, Edinburgh.
[65102]   01/11/2005   ME
Linton, Ms A M, BA (Hons) Dip IT MSc MCLIP, Bibliographic & User
Services Librarian, CCCU Library, Canterbury Christ Church
University.
[42238]   06/10/1988   CM20/05/1998
Linton, Mr W D, BSc BLS CBiol MIBiol ALAI FLA HonFLA, Life Member.
[0905]   23/09/1965   HFE21/05/1992
Linwood, Ms S, BSc MA, Lib. & Learning Resource Centre Manager,
the Highfield School, Letchworth.
[10012878]   23/10/2000   CM29/03/2004
Linwood, Ms S, BA, Research Services Librarian, Slaughter and May.
[10028302]   16/12/2013   ME
Lionel, Mr M, BSc, LRC (Library) Assistant Esher College Library.
[10021253]   02/07/2012   ME
Liquorice, Miss M E, FCLIP, Retired.
[8969]   01/01/1942   FE01/01/1955
Lisle, Mr P E, BA MSc MCLIP, Lib. Roy Graham Library, Newbold
College of Higher Education.
[46718]   08/01/1992   CM24/09/1997
Lisle, Mrs S J, BA, Student, Open Polytechnic of New Zealand.
[10033225]   21/02/2014   ME
Lister, Ms J, MA PgDipILS MCLIP, Dept. Librarian, Architecture & Bldg.
Sci., University of Strathclyde.
[54335]   21/11/1996   CM17/09/2003
Lister, Mrs K, MCLIP, Customer Serv. Librarian, Leicestershire County
Council.
[64183]   31/01/2005   CM13/08/2010
Lister, Ms M, BA MSc MIMgt MILAM MCLIP, Retired.
[8975]   28/03/1966   CM01/01/1971
Lister, Mr M J, BA MCLIP, Area Library Manager, Cumbria County
Council, Carlisle Library.
[24520]   03/09/1975   CM29/12/1978
Litchfield, Mrs M, BA (Hons) MCLIP, Retired.
[8978]   10/01/1966   CM01/01/1969

Litchmore, Miss F N, BA PgDip, Volunteer, Carers Lewisham.
[10034907]   21/08/2014   ME
Little, Mr B, MPhil FCLIP, Retired.
[8979]   18/02/1963   FE02/11/1973
Little, Mr D R T, MCLIP, L. Serv. Manager, Shrewsbury & Telford Hosps.
[50718]   13/10/1994   CM13/10/1994
Little, Miss J H, BA MBA MCLIP, Retired Head of Liverpool Libraries &
Information Services.
[8984]   30/06/1970   CM05/07/1973
Little, Mr N, BA ACLIP, Community Librarian, Norfolk&Norwich
Millennium L.
[10013922]   17/06/2009   ACL30/04/2010
Littledale, Mrs F J, MA (Hons) MA MCLIP, Liaison Librarian, St
Georges, University of London.
[57353]   17/02/1999   CM29/03/2004
Littler, Ms A R, BA (Hons) MLS MCLIP, Career Break.
[31503]   19/10/1979   CM18/02/1986
Littler, Miss J, MCLIP, Retired.
[8992]   11/02/1963   CM01/01/1970
Litwin-Roberts, Mrs M L, BSc (Econ) MA MCLIP, Librarian, Southfields
Comm. College, London.
[53146]   01/04/1996   CM01/02/2006
Liu, Mrs C, MSc MCLIP, Systems Advisor, Library & Learning Support
Services, University of Surrey.
[64797]   04/07/2005   CM09/09/2009
Liu, Miss L, BEng (Hons) MSc, Assistant Librarian, North West London
Hospitals NHS Trust, Central Middlesex Hospital.
[57868]   23/09/1999   ME
Liu Yew Fai, Mrs M, Senior Librarian, Municipality of Port-Louis,
Mauritius.
[52392]   31/10/1995   ME
Livesey, Mr D, BA (Hons) MA MCLIP, Health Information and Resources
Library Supervisor, Manchester Mental Health & Social Care NHS
Trust.
[10020685]   26/03/2012   CM20/06/2014
Livesey, Rev L J, FCLIP, Life Member.
[9000]   19/03/1951   FE01/01/1957
Llewellyn, Mrs M I, BSc (Hons) DipLib MCILIP,
[10020505]   21/02/2012   CM16/11/1994
Llewellyn-Jones, Ms F D W, BA MCLIP, Part-time Lecturer/Tutor,
Further Education Suffolk County Council, Lowestoft.
[16015]   01/01/1971   CM10/12/1974
Lloyd, Mrs A E, MA PGCE, Student.
[10031464]   13/08/2013   ME
Lloyd, Mrs A M, BA PgDipIM MCLIP, Early Years Librarian, Stoke on
Trent C. C.
[59820]   10/10/2001   CM08/12/2004
Lloyd, Mrs C E, BA MCLIP, SELMS Coordinator.
[37643]   12/10/1984   CM15/05/2002
Lloyd, Ms C S, BA MA MCLIP, Associate Director – Library & Research
Services, Goldsmiths, University of London.
[47638]   09/10/1992   CM31/01/1996
Lloyd, Ms D, BA DipLib MCLIP, Records and Information Services Team
Leader, Natural Resources Wales/ Cyfoeth Naturiol Cymru.
[33312]   06/10/1980   CM21/11/1983
Lloyd, Mr D R, BA, Mgr:Learning Partnerships, Coventry City Council.
[54068]   22/10/1996   ME
Lloyd, Mrs E, BA MEd MCLIP, Retired. Malta.
[31002]   10/07/1979   CM13/06/1989
Lloyd, Mr G K, MCLIP MA, Life Member.
[18888]   21/10/1968   CM01/01/1971
Lloyd, Mr H G, MSc BSc HND MCLIP, Assistant Librarian, National
Library of Wales, Ceredgion.
[60901]   21/12/2001   CM28/01/2009

Lloyd, Mr P, MCLIP, Employment not known.
[9021]   23/09/1969   CM04/09/1973
Lloyd, Mrs S, BA (Hons), 502 Army and Library Information Service,
Headquarters Land Forces.
[10008655]   09/11/1986   ME
Lloyd, Mrs S A, BA MSc, Librarian – Access Services, School of
Foreign Service, Qatar.
[10033102]   10/02/2014   ME
Lloyd, Mrs V, BA MCLIP, Author.
[24509]   01/09/1975   CM30/10/1979
Lloyd-Evans, Ms B, BA (Hons) DipLIS MCLIP, Metadata Co-ordinator,
The Wellcome Trust, London.
[44889]   09/01/1991   CM15/03/2000
Lloyd-Wiggins, Mrs A, BA MCLIP, Junior School Librarian, Robert
Gordon's College, Aberdeen.
[30559]   08/01/1979   CM30/09/1982
Loach, Miss K S, BA (Hons) MA, PhD student at Manchester
Metropolitan University, researching the sustainability of independent
libraries.
[10019950]   01/10/2011   ME
Loake, Miss C, MCLIP,
[10012003]   09/12/2008   CM15/07/2014
Loarridge, Mrs C, BA, Unemployed.
[2724]   01/01/1972   CM21/07/1975
Loat, Ms S M, BA MA MCLIP,
[36881]   11/01/1984   CM16/05/1990
Lobban, Miss M, MA MSc DipLib MCLIP, Assistant Director, Information
Services, Edinburgh Napier University.
[28060]   08/10/1977   CM28/11/1980
Lobban, Miss R, BA MCLIP, Retired.
[9030]   03/01/1963   CM01/01/1966
Lobo, Mrs A, Library Assistant, Aston University.
[10009226]   07/05/2008   ME
Loche, Mr G, Knowledge Coordinator, HayGroup, London.
[10032272]   12/11/2013   AF
Lochhead, Mrs A, BA MCLIP, Resource Assistant (Bibliographic),
Edinburgh Napier University.
[22542]   22/06/1974   CM01/08/1977
Lochhead, Ms I R, BA DipLib MCLIP, Liaison Librarian, Norwich City
College.
[36351]   04/10/1983   CM13/06/1989
Lochore, Mr S, BA (Hons) MA MSc MCLIP, Project Manager, Idox
Knowlege Exchange., Glasgow.
[62217]   19/03/2003   CM21/05/2008
Lochrie, Dr E A, Phd, Student, University of Strathclyde.
[10035562]   20/10/2014   ME
Lock, Ms E, BSc, Information Specialist.
[52123]   05/10/1995   ME
Lock, Ms M A, BA (Hons) MPhil MCLIP, Retired.
[24434]   25/07/1975   CM26/09/1978
Locke, Mr D W, BA MSc MCLIP, Manager, BBC, London.
[20050]   15/01/1973   CM26/07/1977
Locker, Mrs A, MA (Hons) MA, Acting Library and Archives Manager,
Institute of Mechanical Engineers.
[10033268]   25/02/2014   ME
Lockett, Miss K J, BA (Hons) MA MCLIP, Librarian, Wellington Library,
Wellington City Library, New Zealand.
[60963]   18/01/2002   CM29/03/2006
Lockley, Mrs U K, BSc MSc (Econ) MCLIP, Librarian-in-Charge, Oxford
Union Society, Oxford.
[29806]   06/10/1978   CM17/03/1982
Lockwood, Miss A T, MA, Librarian, Taunton School.
[52318]   26/10/1995   ME

Lockwood, Miss J A, BA (HONS) MA, Community Engagement Officer, University of Warwick.
[10021303]   10/07/2012   AF

Lockwood, Mrs J M, Retired.
[59579]   05/06/2001   ME

Lockyer, Mrs D, FCLIP, Life Member.
[9049]   09/09/1955   FE30/01/1978

Lodge, Mrs A J, BA (Hons) DipInf MCLIP, Lib. (part-time) Hertfordshire Children, Schools & Families L.
[44371]   02/10/1990   CM24/05/1995

Lodge, Miss E E, BLib MCLIP, Librarian, Serious Fraud Office, London.
[39568]   06/03/1986   CM17/10/1990

Lodge, Miss H A, BLib MCLIP MSc, Knowledge & Communications Manager., London Health Observatory.
[35272]   01/10/1982   CM13/06/1990

Lodge, Mrs M, LRC Manager, St Dunstan's College, London.
[65487]   10/02/2006   ME

Loewenstein, Mr P, BA MSc CQSW FCLIP, Retired; formerly worked Leicestershire Libraries; Nottinghamshire Probation Service & National Youth Agency.
[37007]   19/01/1984   FE23/09/1998

Loft, Mr T, Maps & Geographic Information, Foreign & Commonwealth Office.
[10033422]   11/03/2014   ME

Lofthouse, Mrs A, BA (Hons) MA DipEd MCLIP, Freelance English Tutor.
[1554]   23/09/1970   CM12/09/1973

Logan, Ms J, DipLib MCLIP, Dev. Lib, London Borough of Havering, Storytelling Trainer. Expertise – Children's Reading Development & Literacy.
[37005]   30/01/1984   CM01/09/1987

Lomas, Mrs A M, ACLIP, Senior L. Manager, Swadlincote Library, Derbyshire.
[65188]   17/11/2005   ACL29/03/2007

Lomas, Miss T,
[10014349]   17/07/2009   ME

Lomas, Mr T C, BA MSc MCLIP, Retired.
[21516]   01/01/1969   CM21/10/1975

Lomax, Mrs S M, BA MCLIP, Information Assistant, Bolton University Library.
[25904]   01/04/1976   CM11/04/1979

Londero, Ms S, BA (Hons) MSc, Assistant Librarian (Biblliographic Serv.), Gonville & Caius College, University of Cambridge.
[63148]   12/02/2004   ME

Lonergan, Mrs G F, BA MCLIP PgDip FSocInd, Head of Heritage Resources, Co-operative Heritage Trust, Manchester.
[30401]   15/01/1979   CM27/04/1984

Long, Mrs C A, MCLIP, Information Specialist, Aston University.
[64457]   31/03/2005   CM14/09/2011

Long, Mrs H M, Student/Library Assistant, University of the West of England, Bristol.
[65572]   28/02/2006   ME

Long, Mr M T, MCLIP BA DMS, Retired.
[10006900]   17/10/1977   CM01/07/1991

Long, Mr N, BA (Hons), Library Assistant, Calderdale MBC, Central Library.
[10035249]   01/10/2014   ME

Long, Mr N W, BLib MBA MCLIP, Library Services Consultant, OCLC, Western Canada.
[29731]   20/10/1978   CM21/02/1984

Long, Ms S L, BA (Hons) MSc, Senior Lib. Resource Development Department of Health Library, Leeds.
[58094]   29/10/1999   ME

Long, Mrs T, BA MCLIP, Library Services MGR., Dorset CC.
[37983]   01/01/1985   CM27/05/1992

Long, Mr T N, BA DipLib MCLIP CertNatSci, Knowledge & Information Officer, Clifford Chance LLP, London.
[36312]   02/10/1983   CM01/04/2002

Longbottom, Mr P R, BSc (Hons) MA MCLIP DipLIS, Library Team Leader, Scottish Natural Heritage.
[43251]   11/10/1989   CM22/09/1999

Longmulr, Ms S J, BA (Hons) MCLIP, Information Specialist, NBS, Newcastle.
[54266]   11/11/1996   CM20/11/2002

Lonsdale, Mr B W, Student.
[10021733]   08/10/2012   ME

Lonsdale, Mr D, MA (Hons) MSc MCLIP, Learning Resource Centre Coordinator, Coatbridge College, Lanarkshire.
[48079]   03/11/1992   CM26/11/1997

Lonsdale, Miss D J, Community Librarian, Brotton L.
[10012562]   24/02/2009   AF

Lonsdale, Ms J M, BLib MCLIP, Community Information Officer – West & Community Information Officer – Children and Schools.
[28331]   01/11/1977   CM09/10/1981

Looney, Ms L C, MA MSc Econ, Research Serv. Librarian, Slaughter and May, London.
[61486]   19/08/2002   ME

Lopez-Boronat, Miss L, MA,
[10015692]   14/01/2010   ME

Lord, Ms S C, Senior Library Assistant, Kings Mill Hospital.
[10020972]   03/05/2012   ME

Lorenz, Mrs L, MCLIP, Prison Library Service Development Manager, StaffordshireLibrary Service.
[135]   01/01/1970   CM10/09/1973

Loth-Hill, Mrs J M, MA PgDipLIS, Learning Res. Librarian, William Howard School, Brampton, Cumbria.
[38082]   11/01/1985   ME

Louden, Mrs J A, MA MSc MCLIP MSc, Head of Libraries and Learning Technologies, City of Glasgow College, Glasgow.
[41745]   01/03/1988   CM18/04/1990

Loudon, Mrs K J, MSc BSc (Hons) PGCe, Research Student, University of Strathclyde.
[10021685]   27/09/2012   ME

Loudon, Ms L, Unwaged.
[10015356]   11/12/2009   ME

Loughbrough, Mrs T J, BSc MCLIP, Information Management Specialist, Unilever R&D, Colworth, Beds.
[60501]   23/04/2001   CM23/04/2001

Loughead, Miss R A, BA (Hons), Postgraduate Student in Libraries & Information Studies, UCL.
[10032075]   24/10/2013   ME

Loughlin, Mrs A L, BA (Hons) MCLIP, Cust. Serv. Assistant /Assistant Registrar/Lib. Assistant, Broadford Cust. Service, Isle of Skye.
[46823]   11/02/1992   CM19/07/2000

Loughnane, Mr C J, MA MSc, Acquisitions Assistant, University of Edinburgh.
[10017933]   26/10/2010   ME

Loughridge, Mrs J I, BA MCLIP, Retired.
[6204]   25/10/1966   CM01/01/1969

Louison, Ms P, BA MCLIP DMS, Subject Librarian, Thames Valley University, London.
[34703]   11/02/1982   CM07/06/1988

Love, Miss J I, MCLIP, Life Member.
[9102]   16/04/1943   CM01/01/1952

Lovecy, Dr I C, MA PhD HonFLA FCLIP, Information Consultant.
[20617]   01/05/1973   HFE01/01/1993

Loveland, Mr A, BA (Hons) MA MCLIP, Senior Librarian, The British Museum.
[55837]   21/11/1997   **CM07/09/2005**

Lovell, Mrs J R, BA FCLIP, Life Member.
[9106]   04/10/1945   **FE01/01/1965**

Lovelock, Mr W, MCLIP, Retired.
[9105]   07/02/1949   **CM01/01/1951**

Lovely, Mrs A E, BA (Hons) MCLIP, Principal Lib. Kettering L.
[27008]   13/01/1977   **CM02/11/1984**

Lovern, Mrs L A, MCLIP, Community Librarian, Walsall Council.
[10013581]   08/05/2009   **CM13/11/2013**

Love-Rodgers, Mrs C R, MA MA MCLIP FHEA, Liaison Librarian, College of Humanities & Social Science, Edinburgh University Library.
[53151]   01/04/1996   **RV**03/12/2008   **CM17/03/1999**

Loverseed, Mrs K, ACLIP,
[10019550]   27/07/2011   **ACL09/11/2011**

Lovett, Mr J H, FCLIP, Life Member.
[9116]   06/02/1951   **FE01/01/1959**

Lovett, Mrs S, BA (Hons) MA MCLIP, Group Leader, Editorial Processing, Nielsen Book.
[50625]   01/10/1994   **CM19/05/1999**

Low, Ms Y M, MSc, Employment not known.
[50341]   01/07/1994   **CM19/07/2000**

Lowe, Mrs A H, BA MCLIP, Senior Lib. -Equal Access & Comm., Nottinghamshire Ls., Beeston, Nottinghamshire.
[33128]   10/10/1980   **CM14/10/1983**

Lowe, Mrs C E, Leeds Community Healthcare NHS Trust.
[25053]   04/11/1975   **CM28/09/1979**

Lowe, Mrs D J, BA (Hons) MCLIP, LRC Manager, Bemrose Comm. School, Derby.
[64839]   03/08/2005   **CM11/11/2009**

Lowe, Miss J, Administrator/Information Officer, University of Exeter Medical School, Exeter.
[10021674]   27/09/2012   **AF**

Lowe, Miss J, Head of Knowledge Management, Ward Hadaway, Newcastle upon Tyne.
[36927]   12/01/1984   **ME**

Lowe, Ms R, BA (Hons) MA ACLIP, Library & Information Assistant, Leeds College of Art, Leeds.
[10016606]   14/04/2010   **ACL18/01/2012**

Lowe-Michael, Mrs J, BSc, Study Supp. Facilitator, Epping Forest College, Essex.
[10017188]   11/07/2010   **AF**

Lowen, Mrs T B, BLib (Hons), Sure Start Children's Centre for Librarian, Eckington Library, Derbyshire County Council.
[37324]   02/07/1984   **CM25/09/1996**

Lower, Mrs S B, DipLib MCLIP, Learning Services Manager, Penwith College (part of Truro & Penwith College), Penzance.
[34486]   12/11/1981   **CM11/11/1986**

Lowery, Miss J, Library Assistant, Perth & Kinross Council, Perthshire.
[10021103]   29/05/2012   **AF**

Lowes, Mrs M, MA BA (Hons), Learning Res. Centre Manager, Kenton School, Newcastle-upon-Tyne.
[47852]   21/10/1992   **ME**

Lowis, Mr D R, BA MCLIP, Cultural Serv. Adviser, Lincolnshire County Council.
[20986]   03/09/1973   **CM08/12/1976**

Lowry, Mr J, BA MCLIP, Life Member.
[9143]   25/03/1958   **CM01/01/1969**

Lowther, Mr S R, BA (Hons) DipLib, Cataloguing Librarian, Wellcome Library, London.
[38111]   20/01/1985   **ME**

Loy, Mr J A, BA MA PgDip, Learning Resources Manager, Avon & Wiltshire Mental Health Partnership NHS Trust.
[53918]   10/10/1996   **ME**

Lubarr, Ms K, BA, College Librarian, Maitland Robinson Library Downing College, University of Cambridge.
[59328]   07/02/2001   **ME**

Lubbock, Ms L A, BA (Hons) QTS, Sch. Librarian, Reepham High School.
[10018647]   18/02/2011   **ME**

Lubrun, Mr M, BA, Librarian.
[10032047]   22/10/2013   **ME**

Luc, Mrs D L, MSc MCLIP, Librarian, Craigholme School, Glasgow.
[42723]   13/02/1989   **CM24/06/1992**

Lucas, Ms C, BSc MSc MCLIP, Research Information Officer, Alzheimer's Research UK.
[60860]   12/12/2001   **CM12/12/2001**

Lucas, Mr J M, BA MSc MCLIP, Head of Information Resources & Content, St Mary's University Twickenham.
[63972]   22/11/2004   **CM16/10/2009**

Lucas, Mrs M A, MSc MCLIP, Data Analyst, National Trust, Swindon.
[57706]   05/07/1999   **CM21/06/2006**

Lucas, Mrs N, MCLIP, Life Member.
[9157]   30/03/1954   **CM01/01/1963**

Lucas, Mrs R M A, MCLIP, Library Systems Officer West Sussex County CouncilL. Serv.
[20095]   21/01/1973   **CM10/08/1976**

Lucas, Mr S T, MA FRSA FCLIP JP, Life Member.
[9161]   01/10/1953   **FE23/11/1965**

Luckett, Mrs P Y, BA (Hons) ACLIP, Lending & Operations Supervisor Oxford Brookes University.
[58574]   04/04/2000   **ACL27/09/2005**

Lucy, Mrs C M, BA MCLIP, Keeper of the Arch., Dulwich College, London.
[34579]   01/01/1982   **CM01/04/1986**

Luddington, Ms S C, BA DipLib MCLIP, Volunteer Cataloguer.
[34170]   05/10/1981   **CM01/04/2002**

Ludford, Miss J, MCLIP, Life Member.
[9166]   30/01/1958   **CM01/01/1963**

Ludgero-Newlove, Mrs S, PGCE BSc, L. & Learning Res. Assistant, Preston College, Preston, Lancs.
[10019942]   06/10/2011   **ME**

Ludlam, Mr R M, BA (Hons) DipLib, LRC Manager, Gorseinon College, Swansea.
[43144]   22/08/1989   **ME**

Lumsden, Mr I G, MA MSC, Information Management Librarian Wood Group PSN.
[10020194]   16/11/2011   **ME**

Lumsden, Mr J, MCLIP, Retired.
[9180]   12/10/1967   **CM01/01/1971**

Luna, Mrs C, BA, Senior L. Assistant, Judge Business School Library, Cambridge.
[10010668]   19/08/2008   **ME**

Lundstrom, Mr T E, BA MSL,
[10002022]   28/03/2007   **ME**

Lungu, Miss A, Unemployed.
[10035097]   15/09/2014   **ME**

Lunt, Mr M W, FCLIP, Life Member.
[9191]   04/09/1955   **FE01/01/1962**

Lunt, Mr R, BA MCLIP, Unemployed.
[9192]   13/10/1970   **CM24/09/1973**

Lunt, Mrs T L, BA (Hons) MSc, Information Services Manager BDP, Sheffield.
[49521]   10/11/1993   **ME**

Lupton, Miss M, MCLIP, Retired.
[9195] 14/01/1963 **CM01/01/1967**
Lusted, Ms C A, BA (Hons) MA MCLIP, Service Development Team Leader, LB of Barnet.
[57635] 07/06/1999 **CM10/07/2002**
Lustigman, Ms A I, BA MCLIP, Knowledge Officer, Nabarro, London.
[10006592] 23/10/2007 **RV**15/07/2014 **CM12/05/2011**
Luther, Ms L M, BSc (Hons) MSc, Student, University of the West of England.
[10022146] 08/01/2013 **ME**
Luxton, Mrs J E, BEd MSc, Academic Support Manager, University of Plymouth.
[57856] 10/09/1999 **ME**
Luxton, Mr T J, BA MCLIP, Retired.
[21551] 23/10/1973 **CM28/09/1976**
Lyden-Milwain, Miss H, BA, Student.
[10028405] 16/04/2014 **ME**
Lyle, Mr R M, MCLIP, Life Member.
[9208] 01/01/1945 **CM01/01/1963**
Lynas, Mrs H M, MCLIP, Retired.
[9210] 14/08/1954 **CM01/01/1959**
Lynch, Mrs B, MA Librarianship, Community Information Assistant, Sheffield City Council.
[10034326] 04/07/2014 **ME**
Lynch, Miss C A, BA (Hons) MA MCLIP, Information Literacy Specialist, Royal College of Nursing, London.
[47296] 06/07/1992 **CM17/01/2001**
Lynch, Mr C J, BA DipILM MCLIP, Knowledge Management Specialist, The Rotherham NHS Foundation Trust.
[49765] 06/12/1993 **CM19/05/1999**
Lynch, Ms G, BHum DipLib, Librarian, Hammersmith Library, London Borough of Hammersmith & Fulham.
[33038] 03/10/1980 **CM10/05/1986**
Lynch, Prof M F, BSc PhD CChem HonFCLIP, Hon. Fellow.
[60593] 11/12/2001 **HFE30/09/2000**
Lynch, Mr N T, BA (Hons), Head of Information Srvcs., The Scottish Gov , Edinburgh.
[10006560] 30/10/2007 **ME**
Lynch, Mrs S M, BA (Hons) MCLIP, Archive Assistant, Staffordshire County Council.
[42953] 08/05/1989 **CM27/11/1996**
Lyngdoh, Miss A, MLISc MSc IS, Assistant Librarian BMA.
[10008558] 03/04/2008 **ME**
Lynn, Miss I T P, BA MLitt DipLib MCLIP, Librarian, The London L.
[42658] 31/01/1989 **CM16/09/1992**
Lynn, Mr M, BA (Hons) DipIM MCLIP, Area Manager Libraries NI, North East Education and Library Board.
[57403] 16/03/1999 **CM10/07/2002**
Lynwood, Ms W J, BA (Hons) MA MCLIP, Subject Lib. (Law), Birkbeck College.
[55249] 09/09/1997 **RV**27/06/2006 **CM13/03/2002**
Lyon, Mrs P G, MA MCLIP, Retired.
[17311] 27/09/1967 **CM02/10/1978**
Lyon, Ms W G, BA MSc (Econ) MCLIP, School Librarian, Fettes College, Edinburgh.
[51544] 01/04/1995 **CM12/09/2001**
Lyons, Miss D, MCLIP, Retired.
[19294] 26/08/1972 **CM04/08/1975**
Lyons, Miss R, Student, Manchester Metropolitan University.
[10035508] 16/10/2014 **ME**
Lysford, Ms M, BA, Student, University of Strathclyde.
[10035438] 14/10/2014 **ME**
Lyth, Miss M, BA MCLIP, Retired.
[9221] 22/01/1962 **CM01/01/1968**

Lythgoe, Miss C L, Librarian, HR Wallingford & Information Specialist, NHS Blood and Transplant.
[10015180] 21/10/2009 **ME**
Lyus, Mrs T, B. I. S,
[10034523] 18/07/2014 **ME**

M

Ma, Miss F, MA, Student, Loughborough University.
[10033185] 18/02/2014 **ME**
Ma, Ms L K, BA PGCE MLib MCLIP, Hospital Librarian, Caritas Medical Centre, Hong Kong.
[42512] 22/11/1988 **CM25/05/1994**
Ma, Dr Y, PhD MCLIP, Health Care Assistant, Cambridge University Hospital.
[64021] 02/12/2004 **CM08/08/2008**
Mabbott, Ms C, PhD Candidate at University of Illinois.
[10033414] 11/03/2014 **ME**
MacAri, Mrs A E, BSc MCLIP, School Librarian, Fife Council.
[59553] 16/05/2001 **CM15/09/2004**
MacArthur, Mr C M, BA MSc MCLIP, Retired.
[19821] 20/11/1972 **CM08/10/1975**
MacArthur, Mrs F M, MA DipLib MCLIP, Cultural Development Team Leader, East Dunbartonshire Council.
[35562] 01/11/1982 **CM05/04/1988**
Macartney, Mrs J E, BA (Hons) MCLIP, Borough Librarian, Henry Bloom Noble Library, Douglas, Isle of Man.
[39161] 26/11/1985 **CM24/07/1996**
Macartney, Mr N S, MA DipLib MCLIP, Retired.
[9230] 21/08/1968 **CM01/01/1972**
MacColl, Mr J A, MA MEd DipLib MCLIP, UniversityLib. & Director of L. Servs., Universityof St Andrews.
[10008430] 29/09/2010 **CM14/04/1987**
MacCormack, Mr J A D, BSc IEng MIAgrE MCLIP, Retired.
[60228] 25/01/1972 **CM21/06/1976**
MacCorquodale, Ms M A, MA (Hons) DipLib MCLIP, IS Manager., Hants.
[46698] 16/12/1991 **CM24/09/1997**
MacDermott, Mrs L K, BA (HONS) QTLS, LIS Student, Aberystwyth University.
[10021302] 10/07/2012 **ME**
MacDermott, Mr P D, BA DipLib MCLIP, Retired.
[34090] 08/09/1981 **CM20/01/1986**
MacDiarmaid-Gordon, Mrs J, FCLIP, Life Member.
[9311] 28/10/1935 **FE01/01/1943**
MacDonald, Mrs A, Development Manager (Technical Services), Plymouth Library Service.
[10014388] 21/07/2009 **AF**
MacDonald, Mr B I, MBE MA MCLIP, Retired.
[9317] 12/03/1962 **CM12/07/1966**
MacDonald, Mr C N, MA DipLib, Arch. Assistant, North Devon Record Office, Barnstaple.
[35537] 28/10/1982 **ME**
MacDonald, Ms E, MA (Hons) DipILS, Information Management Team Leader., The Scottish Parliament, Edinburgh.
[56114] 23/02/1998 **ME**
MacDonald, Mrs E M T, MA DLIS, Enquiry Services Manager, National Library of Scotland.
[39210] 01/01/1986 **ME**
MacDonald, Miss I M, BSc (Hons), Student, Robert Gordon University.
[10019902] 30/09/2011 **ME**

MacDonald, Mrs K, BA (Hons) DipILS MCLIP, Sr. Development
Manager, Sefton B. C.
[40258]   11/11/1986   **CM25/07/2001**
MacDonnell, Mrs R D M, BA MCLIP, Zero Waste Officer, Scottish
Borders Council.
[31804]   09/01/1980   **CM13/11/1984**
Mace, Miss C, BA (Hons) MSc, Senior Library Assistant (Acq. & Cat.),
Winchester School of Art Library.
[10031539]   12/11/2013   **ME**
Mace, Mrs K E S F, BA (Hons) PgDip,
[63663]   12/08/2004   **ME**
MacEachen, Mr A J, BA MCLIP, Librarian, Glasgow Life.
[24436]   07/08/1975   **CM15/11/1979**
Macey, Mr I R, MCLIP, National Police Library.
[23261]   20/11/1974   **CM26/03/1979**
MacFarlane, Ms S J, BA MSc, Information Officer, Scottish CILT.
[59949]   09/11/2001   **ME**
MacGlone, Miss E M C M, MSci (Hons) MSc, Web Archivist, National
Library of Scotland, Edinburgh.
[63986]   22/11/2004   **ME**
Macgregor, Mr G R W, BA (Hons) MSc PgCert LTHE MCLIP, Lecturer,
Liverpool Business School, Liverpool John Moores University.
[59946]   09/11/2001   **CM29/08/2007**
Machell, Ms F E, BA (Hons) MA MCLIP, Head of Collection
Management, University of Birmingham.
[58005]   12/10/1999   **CM29/03/2004**
Machell, Mrs J, MBE MCLIP, Life Member.
[9405]   21/03/1955   **CM01/01/1959**
MacInnes, Mr A, MA MSc MCLIP, Automated Systems Librarian,
Central Library, Aberdeen.
[61553]   18/09/2002   **CM20/04/2009**
MacInnes, Mr N C, Head of Libraries, Information and Archives,
Manchester City Council.
[61494]   19/08/2002   **AF**
MacIntyre, Miss C M, BA MScEcon MCLIP, Library Resource Centre
Manager. Taylor High School.
[31892]   08/01/1980   **CM01/08/1984**
MacIsaac, Mrs C M, MA (Hons) DipILS, Customer Serv. Manager,
University of Glasgow L.
[58812]   07/08/2000   **ME**
Mack, Ms C S, BA (Hons) DiP, Head of Legal Knowledge and
Information Section, Foreign & Commonwealth Office, London.
[49966]   01/02/1994   **ME**
MacKay, Mr A, BA (Hons), Information Analyst, Cairn Energy PLC.
[10028432]   11/06/2014   **ME**
MacKay, Mr D M, MA (Hons) MA MCLIP, Head of Health Care Library,
Bodleian Library.
[48410]   05/01/1993   **CM23/07/1997**
MacKay, Mr H, BA (Hons) MCLIP, Retired.
[9433]   20/03/1958   **CM01/01/1969**
Mackay, Miss K, ACLIP, Library Assistant, Breadalbane Community
Library, Aberfeldy.
[10020992]   03/05/2012   **ACL29/05/2013**
Mackay, Miss K, Student, Robert Gordon University.
[10032969]   31/01/2014   **ME**
MacKechnie, Mr J W, MA MCLIP, Retired.
[19523]   16/10/1970   **CM09/01/1973**
MacKenzie, Mr D, MA (Hons) MA MCLIP, Public Serv. Manager, City
University Library, London.
[52838]   02/01/1996   **CM01/06/2005**
MacKenzie, Ms F M, MA DipLib DipEdTech MCLIP, L. Director, Christ's
Hospital, Horsham.
[39321]   13/01/1986   **CM06/09/1988**

MacKenzie, Mr J A, MA (Hons) PgDip Lib MCLIP, Information Analyst (
part-time), Subsea 7, Aberdeenshire.
[10022745]   14/07/1977   **CM30/06/1985**
MacKenzie, Mrs J C, BA MCLIP, Librarian, Fachbibl. Engl. Garten.,
University Munich. (retired).
[19309]   16/08/1972   **CM28/01/1975**
MacKenzie, Ms J M, BA MA MCLIP, Team Leader, Scottish
Government.
[31365]   15/10/1979   **CM16/03/1982**
MacKenzie, Miss K, BA (Hons), Student, University of Strathclyde.
[10032139]   29/10/2013   **ME**
MacKenzie, Miss R, BSc MSc MCLIP, Cent. Enquiries QA Manager,
British Geological Survey, Nottingham.
[51695]   19/05/1995   **CM17/01/2001**
Mackey, Ms A, MA BA Grad DipEd, PA at Daring and Mighty.
[10006254]   26/09/2007   **ME**
Mackie, Mr A, MA (Hons) MSc MCLIP, Careers Information Manager,
University of Aberdeen.
[55250]   28/08/1997   **CM04/10/2006**
Mackie, Miss A, BA (Hons),
[10012096]   17/12/2008   **ME**
Mackin, Mrs H D, BA DipLib MCLIP, LIS Manager, Barnardos Library,
Ilford, Essex.
[29415]   01/07/1978   **CM22/09/1981**
MacKinnon, Ms A M, BA (Hons) MCLIP, Information Manager, Scottish
Environment Protection Agency, Stirling.
[28627]   12/01/1978   **CM24/07/1996**
MacKinnon, Mr N A, MA DipLib MCLIP, Assistant Librarian (Systems),
Goldsmiths, University of London.
[21646]   18/12/1973   **CM11/04/1979**
MacKintosh, Mrs A M, ACLIP, Senior Library Assistant, Kirriemuir
Library, Angus.
[64496]   06/04/2005   **ACL04/04/2006**
MacKintosh, Mrs J, BA, Operations Co-Ordinator, Perth & Kinross
Council.
[10001115]   12/01/2007   **ME**
Mackle, Ms R D, BA (Hons) MCLIP, Subject Librarian, Faculty of Health,
Social Care and Education, Anglia Ruskin University, Essex.
[50185]   26/04/1994   **CM13/05/2014**
MacKwell, Miss C, MA B LITT MCLIP, Retired.
[9483]   09/10/1970   **CM14/01/1974**
Mackworth, Mrs A, BSc, Student, Aberystwyth University.
[10033882]   08/05/2014   **ME**
MacLachlan, Ms E A, MA DipLib FCLIP HonFCLIP, Retired.
[24749]   08/10/1975   **HFE07/12/2007**
MacLachlan, Mr H C, MA FCLIP, Life Member.
[9486]   15/02/1956   **FE01/01/1967**
Maclean, Mrs A D B, BA MSc DIPeurhum DIPpm MCLIP, Information
Serv. Directorate, Directorate Administrator., University of
Strathclyde.
[28503]   23/11/1977   **CM13/11/1980**
MacLean, Mr C C, BSc DipLib MCLIP, Liaison Librarian, Robert Gordon
University Library, Aberdeen.
[38860]   17/10/1985   **CM15/03/1989**
MacLean, Mr D, MA (Hons) DipILS MCLIP, Librarian, Perth College,
Scotland.
[55476]   17/10/1997   **CM20/09/2000**
MacLean, Mrs H, MCLIP, Librarian (Stock Services), East Kilbride
Central Library.
[10001145]   12/01/2007   **CM13/11/2013**
MacLean, Mr R, BSc MSc, Assistant Librarian, Special Collections,
University of Glasgow, Scotland.
[10001983]   28/03/2007   **ME**

MacLellan, Miss F, BA (Hons) DPS PGCTHE FHEA, Academic Librarian, University of Northampton.
[61799]   13/11/2002   **ME**

MacLennan, Dr A, MA MSc PhD, Lecturer, Robert Gordon University.
[46744]   14/01/1992   **ME**

MacLeod, Miss A A, BA (Hons) MA, Librarian, Brora Cultural Centre & Library, Brora.
[10011874]   25/11/2008   **AF**

MacLeod, Mrs C, MA MCLIP, Senior Information Specialist, for and on behalf of, CMS Cameron mckenna LLP.
[38434]   25/04/1985   **CM10/05/1988**

MacLeod, Ms C M E, BSc MSc MCLIP,
[40465]   02/02/1987   **CM14/03/1990**

MacLeod, Mrs E K, MA MCLIP, Retired.
[27416]   10/02/1958   **CM01/01/1962**

MacLeod, Mrs J, BA (Hons) MCLIP, Reading & Learning Librarian., Dorset Library Service.
[44828]   10/12/1990   **CM26/07/1995**

MacLeod, Mr N G, BA DipIT, Res. Centre Coordinator, Dundee City Council.
[42546]   06/12/1988   **CM27/11/1996**

MacLeod, Mr R A, MA DipLib MCLIP, Retired.
[25377]   07/01/1976   **CM05/07/1985**

Macleod, Miss R L, MA (Hons) PgDip LIS, Information Manager.
[62866]   17/11/2003   **ME**

MacLeod, Mr R W, BA, Student, Robert Gordon University.
[10035690]   29/10/2014   **ME**

MacMahon, Ms J, BSc (Hons) DIP RIM, Information Manager/Student, Cranfield University.
[10033108]   11/02/2014   **ME**

MacMahon, Mr T M, BA DipLib, Librarian, Herbert Smith, London.
[45516]   28/02/1991   **ME**

MacMaster, Mr T, MA (Hons) DipILS MCLIP, Head of ICT, Digital and Library Services Carnegie College, Dunfermline.
[44740]   21/11/1990   **CM19/05/1999**

MacMullen, Miss R, BA (Hons) MA, Systems Support and Library Compliance Officer, York St John University.
[10019304]   01/06/2011   **ME**

MacNab, Mrs C, MA, Librarian, The Oratory School, Oxon.
[10022657]   05/04/2013   **AF**

MacNaughtan, Mr A, BA DMS MCMI MCLIP, Retired.
[9544]   16/10/1969   **CM17/07/1972**

MacPhail, Mrs J C, MCLIP, Unemployed.
[27051]   22/01/1977   **CM01/10/1986**

MacPherson, Miss F, MA DipLib MCLIP, Children's Library & Information Services Section Leader, Leisure & Culture Dundee.
[34124]   01/10/1981   **CM08/11/1984**

Macpherson, Mrs L M, BA (Hons) MA MA MCLIP, Assistant Librarian, Royal Academy of Arts Library, London.
[57931]   04/10/1999   **CM16/07/2003**

MacPherson, Mr S, BA (Hons) MSc, School Librarian, Glasgow Life.
[10011766]   11/11/2008   **ME**

MacPherson, Mrs T, BSc MA, Librarian, North Tyneside L. Serv.
[58414]   04/02/2000   **ME**

MacRae, Miss J, BA DipEdTech MCLIP, Retired.
[9570]   17/02/1959   **CM01/01/1969**

Macrae-Gibson, Miss R, BA (Hons) MA MCLIP PG Cert FHEA, Head of Library Academic Services.
[47062]   09/04/1992   **CM17/05/2000**

MacRitchie, Mr D J, BA MCLIP, Local Studies Librarian, Manly Publi Library, Sydney, Australia.
[28333]   04/11/1977   **CM28/10/1981**

Madden, Miss A R, MSc BA (Hons), Student.
[10015038]   07/10/2009   **ME**

Madden, Dr J L, CBE HonFCLIP MA, Hon. Fellow.
[9590]   04/10/1962   **FE01/01/1964**

Madden, Mrs M J, MA BMus HDE, Part-time Cataloguer, University lib.
[65585]   23/02/2006   **ME**

Maddison, Mrs G, BA MA, Relief Cover, Coleg Llandrillo Library,
[10001303]   01/07/1988   **ME**

Maddock, Mrs S R, BA (Hons) MA MSc, Library Services Manager, Warneford Libray, Warneford Hospital, Oxford.
[61109]   22/02/2002   **ME**

Madeira, Mr J,
[10033879]   08/05/2014   **ME**

Madelin, Miss L, MCLIP, Retired.
[9604]   14/01/1965   **CM01/01/1968**

Madge, Mr B E, DHSMA FCLIP PGCERT, Comm. Director, London Upright MRI Centre, London.
[27193]   27/01/1977   **FE16/07/2003**

Madida, Miss M, Student, University of KwaZulu-Natal.
[10033547]   25/03/2014   **ME**

Madin, Mrs A, BA (Hons) MA LLB (Hons) DipApSS Eur. Hum ACLIP, Senior L. Manager, Chesterfield L.
[10006687]   21/11/2007   **ACL04/03/2009**

Madley, Mrs R C, BA (Hons) MA MCLIP, Senior Business Information Specialist (Library), London Business School.
[54031]   21/10/1996   **CM21/05/2003**

Madni, Mr S N, BSc, Unwaged.
[10013162]   02/01/1997   **ME**

Maguire, Mr M L G, MCLIP, Service Development Manager, Devon County Council, Exeter.
[9615]   14/01/1969   **CM13/07/1972**

Mahon, Miss C L, Part-time Customer Serv. Librarian, University of Wolverhampton.
[56999]   19/11/1998   **ME**

Mahsud, Ms K, BA, Student, UCL Qatar.
[10035439]   14/10/2014   **ME**

Mahurter, Miss S J A, BA (Hons) MA MCLIP, Manager, University Arch. & Special Collections Centre, University of the Arts London.
[43260]   13/10/1989   **CM15/09/1993**

Mahy, Miss R M, BA Dip Lib, Schools Library Liaison Officer, Guille Alles Library.
[66050]   07/09/2006   **ME**

Maiden, Mr C I, BA MSc MCMI MCLIP, Director of Knowledge Management, Appleby, Bermuda.
[10000550]   02/05/2002   **CM02/05/2002**

Maiden, Mr D L, BA (Hons) MSc, Team Librarian, Madeley Library.
[65413]   24/02/2006   **ME**

Maidment, Mr M, DipLib MCLIP, Transparency Publishing Team Lead, Defra, London.
[31658]   12/11/1979   **CM03/03/1987**

Main, Mr D, BA (Hons) MA MCLIP, Knowledge and Resources Librarian, Aberdeen City Libraries.
[10001862]   13/03/2007   **CM14/11/2012**

Main, Mrs J R, BA DipLib MCLIP, L. Assistant, Ongar, Essex L.
[36206]   18/07/1983   **CM06/10/1987**

Main, Mrs L V, MCLIP, Librarian, Twickenham Prep. School, Middlesex.
[26794]   26/10/1976   **CM11/08/1980**

Mainds, Mr G R, MA MCLIP, Service Development Leader, City of Edinburgh Council.
[53422]   17/06/1996   **CM19/01/2000**

Mainwaring, Mrs L M, BEd (Hons),
[10007235]   25/01/2008   **AF**

Mainzer, Mr H C, MA DPhil, Retired.
[39830]   20/08/1986   **ME**

Mair, Miss A E, BA PG Cert MCLIP, Retired.
[18129]   02/10/1972   **CM04/07/1975**

Maitland-Cullen, Mr P S, BD PhD DipLIS MCLIP, Communications Officer, NHS Quality Improvement Scotland, Edinburgh.
[45992]   12/08/1991   **CM22/09/1999**

Mak, Dr S, BA (Econ) (Hons) MA (Econ) PhD ACLIP, Records Manager, Public Health England.
[10020979]   03/05/2012   **ACL19/10/2012**

Makeham, Miss J C, BSc (Hons) MSc (Econ) MCLIP, L. & Ind. Serv. Project Officer, Leeds Teaching Hospital Trust.
[56855]   27/10/1998   **CM16/07/2003**

Makepeace, Mr C, BA FSA MCLIP, Retired.
[9640]   15/10/1965   **CM01/01/1968**

Makin, Miss L, PgDip BA (Hons) MCLIP, Avril Roberts Library, Liverpool John Moores University.
[10005825]   12/12/1998   **CM10/07/2002**

Makljenovic, Mrs J, BA, Junior Library Assistant, Aberystwyth University.
[10021833]   19/10/2012   **ME**

Malcolm, Mrs C, BA, Librarian, Sir William Perkins's School, Chertsey.
[25716]   23/02/1976   **CM26/09/1980**

Malcolm, Mrs L, MCLIP, Prison Librarian, HMP Kilmarnock, Premier Prisons.
[61124]   19/02/2002   **CM19/03/2008**

Malcomson, Mrs V, DIP IT PGC, Lib. Assistant, Bangor Academy & Sixth Form College, Bangor.
[10006755]   10/12/2007   **ME**

Malde, Mrs N, BSc MCLIP, Senior Information Sci., Corp. Intellectual Property, GlaxoSmithKline, Brentford.
[48325]   25/11/1992   **CM16/05/1983**

Males, Mrs B, BA MCLIP, Retired.
[9648]   01/10/1968   **CM01/01/1971**

Malin, Mrs J, DMS MCLIP, Retired from Prison & Public Libraries.
[29505]   21/09/1978   **CM13/07/1981**

Malinova, Dr T, MSc (Eng) MSc (Econ) PhD, Associate Member.
[66101]   01/10/2006   **ME**

Malinowski, Ms R J, BA (Hons) PgDipLIS, Librarian, Oxfordshire County Council Oxford.
[48030]   04/11/1992   **ME**

Mallen, Miss S L, BSc (Hons) DipILS MCLIP, Information Manager, Careers Serv., University of Manchester.
[52484]   02/11/1995   **CM20/05/1998**

Mallett, Mr C J, MA MCLIP,
[43250]   06/10/1989   **CM15/09/1993**

Mallett, Ms D L, BSc (Hons) MA MCLIP,
[55502]   16/10/1997   **CM21/11/2001**

Mallett, Mrs S, MCLIP, Retired.
[9657]   11/01/1953   **CM01/01/1965**

Mallon, Mrs S M, BA MCLIP, Audio-Visual Librarian, North Ayrshire Council, Ardrossan.
[31427]   15/10/1979   **CM14/10/1983**

Malone, Mrs E A, BA DipLib MCLIP, Co-Director Library & Learning Services / Head of Content Development, Kingston University Library, Surrey.
[39200]   01/01/1986   **CM18/07/1991**

Malone, Mrs E M, LLB DipLIS MCLIP, Area Community Manager, Hinckley Library, Leicestershire.
[49390]   21/10/1993   **CM22/07/1998**

Malone, Miss K, BA (Hons) MSc MCLIP, Library Assistant, The Bodleian Libraries, University of Oxford.
[64637]   27/04/2005   **CM04/10/2013**

Malone, Dr N, BA PhD ma, Currently Unemployed.
[10033705]   16/04/2014   **ME**

Maloney, Mrs C A, BLib MCLIP, Principal Librarian Information Stock & Quality, Warwickshire County Council.
[32553]   21/05/1980   **CM20/09/1985**

Maloney, Ms F M, BA (Hons) MA, Children's Librarian, West Sussex L.
[56812]   23/10/1998   **ME**

Maloney, Miss M J, BA MCLIP, Learning Res. Manager, Basingstoke College of Tech.
[38827]   14/10/1985   **CM27/01/1993**

Maloney, Miss S L, Student.
[10033716]   17/04/2014   **ME**

Maltby, Mrs J P L, BA (Hons) MA MCLIP, Librarian (Teaching & Learning), University of Nottingham.
[61368]   01/07/2002   **CM13/06/2007**

Mandelstam, Mr C, BA MCLIP, Retired.
[9668]   07/10/1948   **CM01/01/1960**

Manders, Miss J, Learning Resource Advisor, BMETC.
[10028507]   12/05/2014   **ME**

Manecke, Dr U, MA PhD MCLIP, Clinical Supp. Librarian, Milton Keynes NHS Foundation Trust.
[10012988]   17/03/2009   **CM08/09/2010**

Manghani, Mr P, BA (Hons) MCLIP, Service Manager, Libraries, Sutton Library Service.
[52012]   11/09/2013   **CM17/09/2003**

Mangold, Ms E M, BLib MLib, Global Knowledge Management Lead, Syngenta Crop Protection AG, Basel, Switzerland.
[33043]   01/10/1980   **ME**

Manin, Mr M, MA MCLIP, Librarian.
[10022252]   29/01/2013   **CM27/03/2014**

Manjil, Mr M, BA MA DLSC FCLIP, Life Member.
[9921]   03/01/1958   **FE18/04/1989**

Manley, Mrs D A, BA (Hons) PgDipLib MCLIP, L. Manager, St Pauls Catholic School, Milton Keynes.
[32807]   23/09/1980   **CM31/08/1982**

Manley, Dr K A, DPhil FRSA HonFCLIP FSA, Retired.
[9677]   30/09/1969   **HFE12/12/2007**

Manley, Mr W S, MA ACIB MinstLM MLIA (dip), Library Manager, Derbyshire County Council, Pinxton Libr'y, Matlock Libr'y.
[10006520]   15/11/2007   **ME**

Manlow, Mr J C, MA BA (Hons), Library Manager, Castlepoint Library.
[10031651]   17/09/2013   **ME**

Mann, Miss J, Student. Northumbria University.
[10031837]   08/10/2013   **ME**

Mann, Mrs J M, MSc MCLIP, Retired.
[10006071]   31/10/1997   **CM12/01/1998**

Mann, Ms K, BA (Hons) MA, Information Specialist, Aston University.
[10033943]   13/05/2014   **ME**

Mann, Mrs M K, MCLIP, Information Specialist, Cardiff University.
[60466]   26/08/1999   **CM29/08/2001**

Mann, Ms R Y, BA MPhil DipIS, Outreach & Engagement Manager, ICAEW, London.
[44188]   25/10/1990   **ME**

Mann, Ms W, BSc (Hons) MCLIP, Service Development Officer, Barnsley MBC.
[33425]   17/12/1980   **CM27/03/1985**

Mann, Ms W,
[10006104]   27/01/2009   **AF**

Mann, Miss W P, BSc Psychology (HONS), Library Assist., University of Ulster.
[10020758]   03/04/2012   **ME**

Manners, Mrs J, DipLib MCLIP, Principal Librarian Community, West Sussex County Council Library Service.
[38113]   18/01/1985   **CM04/08/1987**

Manners, Miss L C, BA MA DipLib MCLIP, Librarian, Acton High School.
[38765]   04/10/1985   **CM27/03/1991**

Manning, Mr C, BA MA MCLIP, Systems Librarian, London School of
Hygiene & Tropical Medicine.
[64556]   11/05/2005   **CM03/10/2007**
Manning, Miss H M, BA MA MCLIP, L. Serv. Development Manager,
Child. & Young People., Putney Library.
[34078]   23/09/1981   **CM16/12/1986**
Manning, Ms Y, MA DipLib MCLIP, Principal Librarian, L. Support,
Falkirk Council.
[36463]   11/10/1983   **CM19/01/1988**
Manning, Mrs Y A, BSc (Hons) MSc MCLIP, Senior Library Assistant,
Warwickshire College, Moreton Morrell College part of Warwickshire
College Group.
[53919]   10/10/1996   **CM21/05/2008**
Mannion, Miss M, BSc (Open), Student, Manchester Metropolitan
University.
[10032419]   03/12/2013   **ME**
Manoharan, Mr P, MBA, Arts Heritage and Libraries Manager, London
Borough of Ealing.
[10022471]   20/06/1997   **ME**
Manoli, Miss T, MA MCLIP, Library Assistant, The Royal Agricultural
University., Cirencester.
[55001]   19/06/1997   **CM08/12/2004**
Mansell, Mrs F J M, ACLIP, Senior Library Assistant, Colchester Sixth
Form College.
[10009972]   24/06/2008   **ACL12/09/2012**
Mansfield, Ms S, BA (Hons) MSc,
[10012400]   20/04/1989   **ME**
Manson, Ms H J, MA (Hons) PgDipLeIS, Team Leader, Currie Library,
Edinburgh.
[56788]   15/10/1998   **CM15/09/2004**
Manson, Mr P D, BA PgDip, Liaison/Clinical Librarian, NHS, Aberdeen.
[10018066]   21/02/2005   **ME**
Manson Smith, Mr R, MA MPhil PgDip, Library Assistant: Renfrewshire
village libraries.
[10033909]   12/05/2014   **ME**
Mantle, Mrs S J, MCLIP, Idea Store Co-ordinator, Idea Store Bow, Tower
Hamlets.
[21675]   03/01/1974   **CM30/10/1979**
Manuel, Dr A L, LLB MA MSc MEd ACA PhD, Lib+Archivist and Head of
Information Services, Somerville College, Oxford University.
[10010592]   08/08/2008   **ME**
Manuel Viejobueno, Miss L, Student, Llanbadarn Campus,
Aberystwyth University.
[10033542]   25/03/2014   **ME**
Manuell, Mrs E C, MA, L. /Information Serv. Manager, Mills &. Reeve,
Norwich.
[58937]   09/10/2000   **ME**
Mapasure, Mr S, HND MA MCLIP, Library & Knowledge Services
Manager., London NHS.
[60041]   03/12/2001   **CM10/07/2009**
Marais, Ms D J, BSc (Hons) PgDipLIS, Branch Manager, Oswestry
Library.
[48883]   08/07/1993   **ME**
Maranti, Mrs E, BA MA MA, Student.
[10012698]   25/02/2009   **ME**
Marcella, Prof R C, MA (Hons) DipLib DipEd FCLIP Ph, Dean of
Faculty, Robert Gordon University, Aberdeen.
[35650]   21/11/1982   **FE19/01/2000**
Marcelline, Ms F, BA (Hons) MA, Librarian, Cardinal Newman Cath.
School, Hove.
[58973]   13/10/2000   **ME**
March, Mrs B, Librarian., King's School, Bruton, Somerset.
[63569]   08/07/2004   **AF**

March, Ms M, BA MA MCLIP, Assistant Director, Academic Services,
Anglia Ruskin University, Chelmsford.
[40395]   30/01/1987   **CM19/09/1989**
Marchand, Mrs D, MCLIP BA (Hons), Branch Assistant, Essex County
Library, Kingsville, Canada.
[63147]   12/02/2004   **CM06/05/2009**
Marchant, Mr A S, BA MCLIP, Web Designer.
[38395]   16/04/1985   **CM14/02/1990**
Marchant, Mr P C, BH (Hons) MA MCLIP, Head of L. Serv., Knowsley
Metropolitan Borough Council.
[36294]   03/10/1983   **CM21/12/1988**
Marchant, Mrs S D, BA MCLIP, College Librarian. Lancing College,
West Sussex.
[27131]   01/02/1977   **CM30/11/1981**
Marchesan, Ms C, BA (HONS) PgCert PgDip, Librarian & Tutor, The
Prince's Foundation & Prince's School of Traditional Arts.
[10021586]   26/10/2004   **ME**
Marcuccilli, Mrs E C, MSc BA (Hons) MCIL,
[59280]   25/01/2001   **ME**
Mardakis, Mr N, Student.
[10032210]   12/11/2013   **ME**
Marett, Mrs L, BEd MA, Librarian / Learning Resources Manager, Christ
the King RC Maths & Computing College, Preston, Lancashire.
[65917]   04/07/2006   **ME**
Margerison, Mr M A, BA (Hons) PgDipILM, School Librarian, The
Elmgreen School.
[61139]   12/03/2002   **ME**
Marigliano, Ms E, BA (Hons), Librarian, The Portico Library,
Manchester.
[10019930]   07/11/2011   **ME**
Marillat, Mrs I T, School Librarian, Tolworth Girls' School.
[65963]   26/07/2006   **AF**
Marin, Ms A, MSc (Econ) BA DipLIS CIM MCLIP, Information &
Learning Manager, Shared Library Service (Bexley & Bromley).
[40755]   01/06/1987   **CM23/03/1994**
Marinor, Miss L, BA (Hons) MA MCLIP, Assistant Librarian, Poetry
Library, London.
[52972]   06/02/1996   **CM21/03/2001**
Mark, Miss R J, BSc MSc,
[49198]   12/10/1993   **ME**
Marke, Mrs K A, BA (Hons) MA MCLIP, Career break, House of
Commons Library, London.
[52232]   16/10/1995   **CM18/11/1998**
Marker, Mrs B C B, BA PgDipLIS, Retired.
[46048]   01/01/1963   **ME**
Markham, Mrs J A, MA DipLib MCLIP, Librarian, Newbury Weekly
News.
[32929]   08/10/1980   **CM01/07/1992**
Markham, Mrs R, BA DipLib MCLIP, Team Librarian, Information &
Lifelong Learning, Morpeth Library, Northumberland County Council.
[28225]   12/10/1977   **CM26/09/1980**
Markless, Ms S, HonFCLIP,
[10000814]   20/11/2006   **HFE01/10/2006**
Marks, Dr S, BA DPhil, Student University of Liverpool.
[10032420]   03/12/2013   **ME**
Marks, Mrs S M, Private tutor and researcher in English and French.
[64707]   01/06/2005   **ME**
Markus, Ms A, MCLIP, Retired.
[940]   30/07/1959   **CM17/11/1975**
Marley, Ms E A, MA MSc, Thesaurus Editor, House of Commons
Library, London.
[10001988]   11/11/1992   **ME**
Marlowe, Mrs M R,
[10008373]   19/03/2008   **ME**

Marney, Miss R M, BA MCLIP, L. Mgr, Institution Civil Engineers,
London.
[33047]   11/10/1980   **CM20/11/1986**
Marr, Ms C F, BA DipLib MCLIP, Lib. Officer, City of Edinburgh Council,
Central L.
[41054]   06/10/1987   **CM16/05/1990**
Marrable, Dr D M, BSc PhD MCLIP, Career Break.
[60820]   02/12/1986   **CM02/12/1986**
Marriott, Mrs F E, BA (Hons) MCLIP, Strategy and Development
Manager, Luton Culture.
[10005358]   29/10/1986   **CM16/10/1989**
Marriott, Miss H, MCLIP, Life Member.
[9758]   01/01/1951   **CM01/01/1959**
Marriott, Mr J R, BA (Hons) MA MCLIP, L. &Information Co-ordinator,
University of Derby.
[57980]   08/10/1999   **CM18/09/2002**
Marrison, Miss H E, BA (Hons), Library Events Officer, Mansfield
Library.
[10023002]   21/05/2013   **AF**
Marsden, Ms C J, BA MA PgDipLib MCLIP, Library Outreach Team,
Hants L. Service.
[30218]   11/01/1979   **CM21/06/1983**
Marsden, Mr T S, BA (Hons) MA MCLIP AIfL, Learning Centre Co-
ordinator, Washington Learning Centre, Sunderland College, Stone
Cellar Road, Washington.
[56237]   14/04/1998   **CM21/11/2001**
Marsh, Mrs A C, MA MCLIP, Retired.
[29755]   09/10/1978   **CM14/10/1981**
Marsh, Mrs B L, BA DipLib MCLIP, Unemployed.
[24854]   21/10/1975   **CM05/12/1977**
Marsh, Ms E A, BA MCLIP, Part-time Learning Support Librarian, City of
Westminster, London.
[25355]   14/01/1976   **CM11/09/1979**
Marsh, Miss J, BA (Hons) MCLIP, Retired (Previously LOcal Heritage
Librarian, Bournemouth Library.
[45281]   01/10/1990   **CM12/03/2003**
Marsh, Mrs J L, BA (Hons) MSc MCLIP, Repository Dev. Officer,
Lanchester Library, Coventry University.
[59598]   26/06/2001   **CM21/06/2006**
Marsh, Mrs S, BA MSc MCLIP, Hd. of Lib. & Knowledge Servs., North
Cumbria., Informatics Service., Carlisle.
[37012]   28/01/1984   **CM20/01/1987**
Marsh, Miss S J A, BA DipLib MCLIP, Career break.
[38387]   10/04/1985   **CM22/11/1995**
Marsh, Ms S L, BA MA MCLIP, Director of Information Services.,
University of Bradford.
[41489]   08/01/1988   **CM14/08/1991**
Marshall, Dr A, BA MA PhD, Additional Library Support Services
Coordinator, University of Bristol.
[10034741]   12/08/2014   **ME**
Marshall, Mrs A F, MCLIP, Librarian, Marlborough School, Oxon.
[1224]   15/03/1972   **CM14/05/1975**
Marshall, Mr A J, BA DipLib MCLIP, Lib. (Local Studies), Hounslow
Community Services Limited, London Borough of Hounslow.
[38230]   07/02/1985   **CM27/03/1991**
Marshall, Ms A L, BA (Hons) PgDip, Senior Customer Services
Assistant, University of Sheffield.
[10002158]   30/03/2007   **ME**
Marshall, Ms A M, MA DipLib MCLIP, Senior Lecturer, University of
Brighton.
[25476]   05/02/1976   **CM24/10/1978**
Marshall, Mrs C J, BA DipLib MCLIP, Lib. (Job Share), St George's
School, Herts.
[40930]   01/09/1987   **CM18/04/1989**

Marshall, Mrs C L, BA MCLIP, Senior Lib. (job share), L. Headquarters,
Area Library, West Yorks.
[25369]   14/01/1976   **CM01/07/1988**
Marshall, Mrs C M, BA MBA MCLIP, Retired.
[5622]   01/10/1971   **CM08/11/1973**
Marshall, Mrs D, BA MCLIP, Information Centre Manager, Portakabin
Ltd, York.
[44640]   13/11/1990   **CM15/09/1993**
Marshall, Mr D, BSc MA MCLIP, Sheffield City Council.
[65494]   08/02/2006   **CM10/07/2009**
Marshall, Mr D N, Professor Emeritus, University of Bombay Library,
India.
[17357]   20/05/1953   **ME**
Marshall, Miss E J, BA (Hons) DipLib MCLIP, Academic Engagement
Librarian.
[46545]   19/11/1991   **CM26/07/1995**
Marshall, Miss F L, BA, Library Administrator, nplaw, Norfolk County
Council.
[60014]   23/11/2001   **ME**
Marshall, Mrs G P, MA DipLib MCLIP, L. Res. Centre Co-ordinator,
Aberdeen City Council, Educ. Department.
[31362]   16/10/1979   **CM30/03/1984**
Marshall, Mr G T C, BA MCLIP, Retired.
[9794]   01/04/1967   **CM01/01/1970**
Marshall, Miss H, BA, Senior Librarian, Glasgow Caledonian University.
[10011478]   23/10/1995   **ME**
Marshall, Mrs H M, BA MCLIP, Child. L. Serv. Manager, Derby City L.
[23145]   06/11/1974   **CM15/08/1978**
Marshall, Ms J, BLib MCLIP, Head of Serv., Birmingham City Council.
[34324]   10/10/1981   **CM01/07/1986**
Marshall, Mrs J A, BA, Part-time Public L.
[39486]   04/02/1986   **ME**
Marshall, Dr J D, PhD, Rare Books Librarian, Edinburgh University
Library.
[59792]   03/10/2001   **ME**
Marshall, Mrs K, BA (Hons) MA MSc FHEA MCLIP, Student Information
Services Manager, Grantham College.
[55421]   06/10/1997   **RV30/10/2009   CM09/11/2005**
Marshall, Mrs L A, BA (Hons) MSc, Unwaged-Career Break,
[57508]   14/04/1999   **ME**
Marshall, Mr P, MCLIP, Retired.
[9805]   23/01/1963   **CM01/01/1967**
Marshall, Mrs P M, MCILIP, Adult Librarian, Milton Keynes Library.
[21115]   09/10/1973   **CM15/09/1976**
Marshall, Mrs R C, BA MA MCLIP, Part-time Librarian, Chilwell
Comprehensive School, Notts. County Council.
[38861]   17/10/1985   **CM22/05/1991**
Marshall, Mrs R J, MSc (Econ) BA (Hons) MCLIP, Sixth Form Leader,
Lipson Cooperative Academy, Plymouth.
[57895]   01/10/1999   **CM16/01/2014**
Marshall, Mr R L, BA (Hons) MA MCLIP, Information Manager, Imperial
College, London.
[55658]   30/10/1997   **CM19/11/2003**
Marshall, Mr S N, FCLIP, Life Member.
[9806]   17/09/1949   **FE01/01/1963**
Marshall, Mrs T M, BA MA MCLIP, Academic Librarian, Loughborough
University, Leicestershire.
[52401]   30/10/1995   **CM29/11/2006**
Marshall, Mrs V, BA MA, Librarian, Queen Elizabeth Grammer School,
Penrith, Cumbria.
[44817]   03/12/1990   **ME**
Marsland, Mrs A, Assistant Librarian, St Martin-In-The-Fields High
School, London.
[63271]   24/03/2004   **AF**

Marsland, Mr I K, BA MA, Subject Librarian, Bournemouth University.
[10012510]   23/02/2009   **ME**

Marsterson, Mrs K M, BSc (Hons) MSc MCLIP, Assistant Librarian, Berkhamsted School.
[57016]   24/11/1998   **CM21/03/2007**

Marsterson, Mr W, MA MCLIP, Retired.
[9812]   23/10/1967   **CM01/01/1970**

Martell, Miss H, MA BA MCLIP, Author and publisher.
[9814]   28/09/1967   **CM01/01/1971**

Martin, Ms A, BA, Senior Learning Centre Assistant, City College, Southampton.
[10018650]   10/03/2011   **AF**

Martin, Mr A H, BA MCLIP, Enquiry Assistant, Southend on Sea Borough Council, Southend Central Library.
[23249]   14/11/1974   **CM30/11/1976**

Martin, Miss A J, MSc (Econ), Information Officer, Simmons & Simmons, London.
[52447]   02/11/1995   **ME**

Martin, Mr A V, MA MCLIP, Clerk to Parish Council, Down St Mary, Devon.
[25600]   27/01/1976   **CM24/03/1978**

Martin, B, Acquisitions Librarian (Print), UCL.
[61727]   29/10/2002   **ME**

Martin, Dr B P, BA MA PhD, Library Assistant, The Library, St Mary's University College.
[10020641]   14/03/2012   **ME**

Martin, Mr C A, BSc (Hons) PgDipILS PgDipEd, e-Learning Manager, Suffolk One.
[57373]   01/03/1999   **ME**

Martin, Mr D, FCLIP, Retired.
[9823]   28/03/1960   **FE18/03/1985**

Martin, Ms D, BA MCLIP, Unwaged.
[60201]   23/04/2001   **CM23/04/2001**

Martin, Ms E, MA MCLIP, Librarian, Nuffield College, Oxford.
[28074]   02/10/1977   **CM28/11/1980**

Martin, Ms F, Schools Librarian, Southampton School Library Service.
[10011108]   24/03/2014   **ME**

Martin, Ms F C, MA BA DipLib MCLIP, Academic Liaison Librarian, University of Westminster.
[34755]   17/02/1982   **CM20/01/1986**

Martin, Mrs F S, BA DipLib MCLIP, Librarian, Special Projects, Wellcome Trust, Cambridgeshire.
[31745]   21/11/1979   **CM04/11/1982**

Martin, Miss G M, BA MCLIP, Head Librarian, Johns Hopkins University, S. A. I. S, Bologna, Italy.
[31367]   08/10/1979   **CM26/05/1983**

Martin, Mrs H, MA (Hons) DipLib MCLIP, School Librarian, East Dunbartonshire Council.
[29753]   09/10/1978   **CM22/01/1981**

Martin, Ms J, BA MSc MCLIP, Hd of Information Services, School of Tropical Medicine, Liverpool.
[33622]   29/01/1981   **CM07/01/1987**

Martin, Mrs J, MCLIP, Retired.
[46606]   01/01/1968   **CM01/01/1971**

Martin, Mrs L G, MA MCLIP, Librarian, Culford School, Bury St Edmunds.
[38883]   18/10/1985   **CM08/12/1987**

Martin, Mrs L M, MCLIP, Operations and Development Manager, Cambridgeshire County Council.
[7481]   02/01/1969   **CM01/01/1973**

Martin, Mr M, BA DipLIS MCLIP,
[48833]   28/06/1993   **RV**12/09/2012   **CM31/01/1996**

Martin, Mrs N, BA (Hons), Employed in Library Sector.
[10001775]   20/12/1996   **ME**

Martin, Miss P J, BA MCLIP, Life Member.
[9854]   04/11/1963   **CM01/01/1971**

Martin, Mr R, BA (Hons) MA, Know How Officer, Slaughter & May, London.
[10015570]   01/01/2010   **ME**

Martin, Mr S, BA,
[10034779]   14/08/2014   **ME**

Martin, Mrs S E, BA MCLIP, Senior Assistant Librarian, De Montfort University, Leicester.
[28532]   05/01/1978   **CM06/03/1981**

Martin-Bowtell, Mrs A E, BA (Hons) MA MCLIP, Learning & Teaching Librarian, University for the Creative Arts.
[55298]   19/09/1997   **CM15/03/2000**

Martindale, Mr C R, BA DipLIS, Faculty Suport Manager, Business, Computing & Law, University of Derby.
[33505]   13/01/1981   **ME**

Martindale, Miss P, BA (Hons) DipLib MCLIP, Member of CILIP Professional Registration & Accreditation Board.
[32888]   21/10/1980   **RV**30/04/2014   **CM12/10/1983**

Martinez Ortiz, Ms M I, MSc, Knowledge, Skills and System Librarian, Surrey and Sussex NHS Trust, Crawley.
[10005088]   06/06/2007   **ME**

Martinez-Roura, Ms S, MSc PgDipl, Assistant Librarian, BMA Library, London.
[10002519]   20/04/2007   **ME**

Martino, Mrs A, BA (Hons) MA, Student.
[10022003]   16/11/2012   **ME**

Martland, Ms K W, BA MCLIP, Life Member.
[9874]   08/03/1955   **CM08/09/1976**

Martzoukou, Dr K, MA MSc PhD, Lecturer, Robert Gordon University.
[10032382]   29/11/2013   **ME**

Marvin, Miss J H L, BA (Hons) MSc (Econ), User Services Manager, St George's, University of London.
[10009210]   07/05/2008   **ME**

Maryon, Mr A W, BSc DipLib MCLIP, Senior L Manager, Woolwich Library, London.
[30648]   18/02/1979   **CM18/02/1981**

Maseide, Mr K E, BA (Hons), Assistant Cataloguer, Guildhall School of Music & Drama, London.
[64684]   25/05/2005   **ME**

Maskell, Ms A, MCLIP, Assistant Librarian – eResources, House of Lords.
[10014906]   01/04/2010   **CM15/02/2012**

Mason, Mrs C F, BA (Hons) PgDip, HE Library Development Manager, Cleveland College of Art and Design.
[47775]   14/10/1992   **ME**

Mason, Mrs F, BA MCLIP, Children & Family Manager, Shared Library Services (Bexley & Bromley).
[27755]   01/08/1977   **CM14/08/1981**

Mason, Mrs J, BA (Hons) MCLIP, Sch. Learning Res. Centre for Manager, St Gregory's Catholic High School, Warrington.
[30355]   24/01/1979   **CM21/09/1982**

Mason, Miss J E, BA MA, Web Coordinator, East Sussex County Council.
[58681]   18/05/2000   **ME**

Mason, Miss J V, BA (Hons) DipLIS MCLIP, Reader Services Manager: Adults, Oxfordshire County Council.
[47509]   16/09/1992   **CM31/01/1996**

Mason, Mrs L A, BA MCLIP, School Librarian, Belmont School, London.
[9849]   07/01/1969   **CM15/12/1972**

Mason, Mr M, MCLIP, Retired.
[9897]   20/09/1971   **CM16/07/1975**

Mason, Mrs N, BSc (Hons) ACLIP, LRC Manager, Wilmslow High School, Wilmslow, Cheshire.
[10013718]   22/05/2009   **ACL13/04/2011**

Massey, Mrs A E, MA (Hons) DipLIS MCLIP, Archives Assistant, Orkney Library and Archive.
[49633]   16/11/1993   **CM23/07/1997**

Massey, Mr G J, Librarian, London School of Theology.
[10010457]   30/07/2008   **ME**

Massey, Mrs S J E, BLib MCLIP, Librarian, Illingworth Library, Sheffield Child. NHS FoundationTrust.
[34245]   10/10/1981   **RV**04/03/2009   **CM12/12/1984**

Massil, Mr S W, BA DipLib FCLIP FSA FRAS, Retired.
[9906]   12/01/1970   **FE13/06/1990**

Masson, Dr A J, BSc (Hons) PhD PGCE,
[10013179]   03/04/2009   **ME**

Masson, Mrs A M, Information L. Assistant, Highland Council(Lochaber High School), Fort William.
[10003258]   23/05/2007   **ACL01/07/2008**

Masterman, Miss C, BA (Hons), Librarian, Co. Durham & Darlington Foundation Trust, Darlington.
[51130]   23/11/1994   **ME**

Masterman, Mrs T J, BA MA MCLIP, Librarian., Teignmouth Community School, Devon.
[43758]   01/01/1990   **CM25/07/2001**

Masters, Miss F L, BA (Hons) MA MCLIP, Community Librarian, Chichester L.
[10006459]   19/10/2007   **CM11/11/2009**

Masters, Ms S, BSc MCLIP, Multi-Media Res. Manager, Thomas Deacon Academy, Peterborough.
[44880]   08/01/1991   **CM22/11/1995**

Masters, Mr T, MCLIP, Retired.
[9913]   17/03/1958   **CM01/01/1961**

Masztalerz, Ms S L, BA (Hons), Student, Aberystwyth University.
[10021951]   05/11/2012   **ME**

Mateer, Miss H E, BA MA MCLIP, Acquisitions and Metadata Manager, Birkbeck Library, University of London.
[54408]   04/12/1996   **CM12/09/2001**

Matheson, Ms C M, BSc MCLIP, Librarian, Highland Council, Glenurquhart Comm.
[25076]   29/10/1975   **CM09/03/1979**

Matheson, Ms F M, MA MCLIP, Resource Centre Librarian, Vale of Leven Academy, Alexandria, G83 0BH.
[44525]   22/10/1990   **CM12/03/2003**

Matheson, Ms J, BA MCLIP, Career Counsellor.
[33049]   08/10/1980   **CM12/02/1986**

Matheson, Miss J C, BSc (Hons), Admin. Assistant, Lorn Medical Centre, Oban, Argyll.
[61984]   10/01/2003   **ME**

Matheson, Ms L A, BA (Hons) DipLib, Information Specialist, Aston University.
[50029]   23/02/1994   **ME**

Mathew, Mrs J, Student, University of Northampton.
[10035440]   14/10/2014   **ME**

Mathias, Mrs A, ACLIP, LRC Manager, Holbrook High School, Holbrook.
[10011654]   30/10/2008   **ACL23/09/2009**

Mathias, Ms G M, MLib DipLib CertEd CertInfSc, Retired.
[25990]   05/05/1976   **ME**

Mathie, Ms A E, MCLIP MPhil, Retired.
[17364]   15/09/1967   **CM01/01/1970**

Mathieson, Miss A, MCLIP, Life Member.
[9927]   22/09/1951   **CM01/01/1962**

Mathieson, Mrs J E, MA BA MCLIP, Reg. Reader Development Coordinator, Time To Read, Manchester.
[21464]   16/10/1973   **CM01/10/1980**

Mathieson, Mrs S E, BA (Hons) MA MCLIP, Librarian, St Columba's College, St Albans.
[58814]   07/08/2000   **CM29/03/2004**

Matkin, Mrs C A, BA (Hons) MCLIP, Access & Inclusion Manager, Derbyshire County Council Cultural & Community Services Department.
[55582]   21/10/1997   **CM29/11/2006**

Matovu, Ms S, MScEcon ILS (AW), Information and Documentation Officer TASO – The AIDS Support Organisation (TASO).
[10019754]   17/03/2014   **ME**

Matsuki, Ms M, MSc, Librarian, The United Nations University, Tokyo, Japan.
[42394]   17/10/1988   **ME**

Matta, Mr P O, Student, University of Strathclyde.
[10035441]   14/10/2014   **ME**

Matthews, Ms B F, BA (Hons) DipTchg MLIS,
[10023118]   11/06/2013   **ME**

Matthews, Mrs B S, MCLIP, Senior Librarian, Tonbridge School, Kent.
[13503]   13/09/1969   **CM02/10/1972**

Matthews, Mrs D, Local Studies Librarian, Dudley Archive & Local History Service, West Midlands.
[10002043]   21/10/1993   **ME**

Matthews, Mr G, BA DipLib PhD MCLIP, Prof. of Information Management, Dept of Information Science, Loughborough University.
[25077]   10/11/1975   **CM14/11/1977**

Matthews, Ms G, MA,
[10032117]   29/10/2013   **ME**

Matthews, Miss H V, BA (Hons) MSc, Assistant Librarian.
[10019927]   04/10/2011   **ME**

Matthews, Miss J, BA (Hons) MCLIP, Senior Librarian, York Hospitals NHS Foundation Trust.
[10001589]   27/01/1979   **CM01/07/1989**

Matthews, Mrs K, Learning Centre Manager, Ridgewood High Sch, West Mids.
[10020647]   14/03/2012   **ME**

Matthews, Mrs N, MA MCLIP, Head of Information Services, Cains Advocates Ltd.
[40050]   13/10/1986   **CM15/11/1988**

Matthews, Miss S A, BA MCLIP, Tenbury Wells Manager, Worcs. C. C., Tenbury Wells.
[27699]   04/07/1977   **CM19/05/1982**

Matthews, Mr S A, BEd MSc MCLIP, Unwaged.
[40776]   04/06/1987   **CM17/05/2000**

Matthews, Mrs S E, BA (Hons) DipLib, Prison Lib. & Children's & Young People's Coord., City of York Council.
[42524]   30/11/1988   **ME**

Matthews, Mrs S J, BSc DipLib MCLIP, School Librarian, Pinewood School, Swindon.
[35619]   16/10/1982   **CM18/02/1986**

Mattock, Mrs S, BA (Hons) MA (Inf & Lib Mgmnt) MCLIP, Senior Information Assistant, De Montfort University, Leicester.
[64568]   11/05/2005   **CM10/03/2010**

Mauger, Ms A J, BA (Hons) MCLIP MBA, Chief Executive, CILIP.
[37571]   03/10/1984   **RV**27/03/2014   **CM01/09/1987**

Maughan, Mr G, MCLIP, Life Member.
[9957]   24/04/1947   **CM01/01/1955**

Maughan, Mrs L, BSc MSc, Digital Collections Librarian, Teesside University.
[10017416]   18/08/2010   **ME**

Maville, Mr A J, BA MA MCLIP, Business Adviser.
[60210]   17/05/1999   **CM24/05/1999**

Mavin, Mrs H I, BSc Econ,
[64939]   03/10/2005   **ME**

Mawhirt, Mrs A G, BA (Hons) MSc, Student.
[10018032]   05/11/2010   ME
Mawson, Ms M B, BA MA MCLIP, Faculty Librarian, University of
Sheffield.
[35462]   20/10/1982   **RV**27/03/2014   **CM18/02/1986**
Maxim, Mrs A J, CertEd MCLIP, Life Member.
[9970]   22/03/1950   **CM01/01/1963**
Maxim, Mr G E, MA FCLIP, Life Member.
[9971]   01/01/1959   **FE01/01/1965**
Maxwell, Mrs C, BSc MCLIP,
[60670]   11/12/2001   **CM11/12/2001**
Maxwell, Mrs H, PgDipLIS, Library Assistant, IDOX PLC, Glasgow.
[48061]   03/11/1992   ME
Maxwell, Mr L, MLIS, Librarian, Glenthorne High School, Sutton.
[10023333]   25/06/2013   ME
Maxwell, Mr N, FCLIP, Life Member.
[9977]   29/02/1960   **FE01/01/1967**
Maxwell, Mrs P, BSc, Retired.
[60846]   01/08/1990   ME
May, Mr H M H, MA MCLIP, Retired.
[17368]   24/09/1953   **CM01/01/1968**
May, Ms J A, BA (Hons) MA, Policy Officer, Policy, CILIP.
[54405]   03/12/1996   ME
May, Miss L, BA (Hons) Oxon, Research and Learning Support
Assistant, University of Manchester. Student, Manchester
Metropolitan University.
[10032559]   16/12/2013   ME
May, Mr T, Student, Cardiff Council.
[10032683]   03/01/2014   ME
May, Ms T G, BScEcon (Hons) MSc MCLIP, Subject Librarian, Anglia
Ruskin University, Cambridge.
[47531]   01/10/1992   **CM26/07/1995**
Mayanobe, Miss C A, MA English MA Information St, Head Librarian,
Brighton College, Brighton.
[10001577]   26/02/2007   ME
Maybury, Mrs T A, BA MA, Assistant Library Services Manager, Library,
Edward Llwyd Centre, Glyndwr University Wrexham.
[10031542]   28/08/2013   ME
Mayers, Mrs A, BSc (Hons) MA MCLIP, Librarian, Liverpool Medical
Institution (part-time) & Assistant Librarian, Cheshire & Wirral
Partnership NHS Found. Trust (part-time).
[55890]   16/12/1997   **CM13/06/2007**
Mayers, Mr R O, MCLIP, Life Member.
[19335]   01/01/1955   **CM01/01/1970**
Mayes, Mrs A L, BScEcon MCLIP, College Librarian, Queen Mary's
College, Basingstoke.
[61859]   21/11/2002   **CM23/01/2008**
Mayes, Miss G D, BA (Hons) MSc, Librarian, Queen's School, Chester.
[59316]   02/02/2001   ME
Mayor, Mrs F E, BA MCLIP, Learning Resource Centre, Bridgwater
College, Somerset.
[22403]   07/05/1974   **CM05/03/1979**
Mayor, Miss L A, BA MSc MCLIP, Senior Assistant Librarian, Branch
Manager, Bamber Bridge Library, Preston.
[65926]   07/07/2006   **RV**27/08/2014   **CM07/07/2010**
Mazer, Mrs C, BA (Joint Hons) MCLIP, Academic Liaison Librarian,
Brunel University Library, Uxbridge.
[49568]   19/11/1993   **CM06/04/2005**
Mbasera, Miss S F, Student, University of Kwazulu-Natal.
[10035170]   23/09/2014   ME
Mbuthia, Mrs R D, MEd, Part-time L. Assistant, Durham University
Library.
[10012593]   19/02/2009   ME

Mc Keown, Mr A T, BA MA MSc, Fulltime PHD Student at The
University of Ulster.
[10016162]   17/02/2010   ME
McAdam, Mr D, BSc, Student, Robert Gordon University.
[10035567]   20/10/2014   ME
McAdams, Mr A C, LLB DipAcc, L. Information Officer, MacRoberts,
Glasgow.
[49989]   10/02/1994   ME
McAinsh, Mr A, BA (Hons) MSc, Information Officer, Royal College of
Physicians and Surgeons of Glasgow.
[10017884]   22/10/2010   ME
McAinsh, Mrs C M, MA (Hons) DipLib MCLIP, Librarian., East Kilbride
Central Library, Glasgow.
[31631]   15/10/1979   **CM20/07/1982**
McAllister, Mrs A M, BA (Hons) MCLIP, Systems & Support Officer,
North Ayrshire Information & Culture.
[38389]   15/04/1985   **CM14/08/1991**
McAllister, Mr D, PhD, Student, Drexel University.
[10031945]   15/10/2013   ME
McAllister, Mrs M S, BA (Hons), Librarian, The Laytmer School.
[10010949]   15/05/2014   ME
McAlpine, Mr I K, MA,
[49641]   16/11/1993   ME
McAra, Mrs V E M, MCLIP, Community Librarian, Bridge of Allan,
Stirling Council L.
[64583]   13/04/2005   **CM10/11/2010**
McArdle, Mrs C, BA DipLib MCLIP, Deputy Librarian, Lincoln's Inn
Library, London.
[38131]   19/01/1985   **CM09/08/1988**
McArthur, Ms C A, Assistant Library Manager, Southend Borough
Council, Leisure, Culture & Amenity Serv.
[59289]   29/01/2001   AF
McAulay, Miss A M N, BA FCLIP, Life Member.
[9237]   24/08/1950   **FE01/01/1957**
McAulay, Dr K E, BA MA LTCL DipLib FCLIP, Music & Academic
Services. Librarian/Postdoctoral Researcher, Royal Conservatoire of
Scotland.
[36433]   11/10/1983   **FE05/05/2010**
McAuley, Miss S, MLIS, Librarian, Allen & Overy LLP.
[10013437]   29/04/2009   ME
McBain, Mr H, BA (Hons) MLIH MSc, Unwaged.
[10018285]   13/12/2010   ME
McBride, Mrs V J, BA MCLIP, Library Manger Northumbria University,
Newcastle.
[35800]   25/01/1983   **CM01/04/1986**
McBurnie, Miss L C, BA (Hons), Student, University of Brighton.
[10032412]   03/12/2013   ME
McCabe, Mrs T L, BA BFA MLS, Knowledge Exchange Fellow,
University of Strathclyde.
[63319]   13/04/2004   ME
McCafferty, Ms C, BA (Hons) MSc, Manager.
[10006561]   11/10/1982   ME
McCaffrey, Mrs K E,
[10014082]   25/06/2009   ME
McCaig, Miss L, BSc (Hons) DipILS MCLIP, Assistant Project Manager,
Transport Scotland, Glasgow.
[52191]   12/10/1995   **CM16/07/2003**
McCalley, Mrs M, BA (Hons) MSc MCLIP, Support Worker, Learning
Disabilities, Sense Scotland, Glasgow.
[37118]   27/02/1984   **CM21/12/1988**
McCallum, Ms A J, Records & Information Officer, Li. Countryside
Council for Wales.
[59290]   29/01/2001   AF

McCallum, Miss F, MSc, Volunteer – Collections Management.
[10022871]   30/04/2013   **ME**

McCallum, Mr J, BA (Hons) MSc, School Librarian, Dunoon Grammar School, Argyll and Bute Council.
[61700]   14/10/2002   **ME**

McCallum, Miss M M, Student, University of Strathclyde.
[10033465]   14/03/2014   **ME**

McCann, Miss J E, BA MCLIP, Resources & Performance Manager, Sunderland City Council.
[31660]   05/11/1979   **CM05/10/1984**

McCargar, Ms T J, MA MCLIP, Librarian, Latymer Upper School.
[63691]   01/10/2004   **CM22/02/2010**

McCarney, Mr E, BA MA HDip Lis, Head of Collection Services, University College Dublin.
[10016394]   08/10/2013   **ME**

McCarren, Ms J F, BA PgDip MCLIP ILT,
[46880]   20/02/1992   **CM25/05/1994**

McCarron, Ms L, BA (Hons) DipILS, Reader Services Manager, National Library of Scotland.
[57233]   15/01/1999   **ME**

McCart, Miss A M, BA DipLS, Communities, Learning & Access Manager, Armagh.
[27620]   13/12/2004   **ME**

McCarthy, Mrs A P, BA DipLib MCLIP, Information & Training Project Officer, Somerset Library Service.
[28301]   15/11/1977   **CM28/11/1980**

McCarthy, Mrs E, MA MSt (Oxon) BA (Hons) MCLIP, Comms. & Social Media Officer, Bodleian Libraries / Special Collections Librarian, U of Reading.
[10011204]   02/10/2008   **CM27/03/2014**

McCarthy, Mrs L, Student – Cranfield University.
[10033961]   14/05/2014   **ME**

McCarthy, Mr P J, BA MCLIP, Bibl. Serv. Manager, City of Bradford Metropolitan District Council, Central Library.
[34803]   26/01/1982   **CM21/07/1989**

McCaul, Miss L C, BA (Hons) MA, Principal L. Assist. Cataloguing, University of Essex, Colchester.
[10001365]   01/07/2000   **ME**

McChrystal, Ms M M, BLib (Hons) MCLIP, Acting Libraries and Information Services Manager, City of Edinburgh Council.
[10010528]   31/10/1983   **CM17/10/1990**

McChrystal Plimmer, Miss N J, BA (Hons), Student, Children's Literature & Culture MA.
[58226]   19/11/1999   **ME**

McClean, Mrs S A C, BA DipLib MCLIP, Part-time Librarian, Stockport M. B. C & part-time Librarian, AECOM.
[26712]   12/10/1976   **CM19/01/1979**

McClellan, Mrs J A, MCLIP, Unemployed.
[29062]   13/03/1978   **CM16/02/1982**

McClelland, Mrs A, BA MCLIP,
[10031335]   23/07/2013   **CM27/11/1996**

McClintock, Ms E A, BSc MSc, Information Officer, Westminster CC., London.
[65110]   01/11/2005   **ME**

McCloskey, Mr P C M, BAHons DipLib MCLIP, Lib. Dev. Officer, Edinburgh City L. & Information Serv.
[34906]   27/03/1982   **CM18/06/1985**

McClure, Mr C J, MA MLib MCLIP, Retired.
[39814]   28/07/1986   **CM18/07/1990**

McCluskey, Miss C, Student, University of Strathclyde, Glasgow.
[10021384]   31/07/2012   **ME**

McCluskey, Miss C J, BA (Hons) MSc PgCert MCLIP FHEA, Academic Liaison Librarian, York St John University.
[61782]   06/11/2002   **RV**27/08/2014   **CM21/06/2006**

McCluskey, Miss F J, BA MCLIP, Volunteer cataloguer.
[18318]   16/10/1972   **CM14/08/1975**

McCoid, Mrs S L, BA (Hons) MA MCLIP, Associate Lecturer/PhD Student.
[33084]   08/10/1980   **CM15/12/1983**

McColl, Miss F M, BA (Hons), LRC Co-ordinator., Cambridgeshire Regional College, Cambridge.
[62200]   13/03/2003   **ME**

McCombe, Miss S A, MA MSc, Library & Research Manager, Allen & Overy LLP.
[54709]   06/03/1997   **ME**

McComiskey, Miss K L, BA (Hons), Student.
[10020021]   25/10/2011   **ME**

McConkey, Ms B, BA, Managing Editor / Student at RGU.
[10033631]   07/04/2014   **ME**

McConnachie, Mrs S L E, BA MCLIP, Librarian, Douglas Academy, East Dunbartonshire.
[32116]   28/01/1980   **CM20/03/1985**

McConnell, Miss L, BA (Hons), Student.
[10020018]   25/10/2011   **ME**

McConnell, Mr M R A, MA MSc MCLIP MBCS CITP, Business Apps. Manager, University of Aberdeen.
[60249]   21/06/1994   **CM14/03/2000**

McConnell, Mr W, Senior Learning Assistant, New College Lanarkshire.
[10032770]   21/01/2014   **ME**

McConville, Ms J,
[10012468]   22/02/2005   **ME**

McConville, Mrs K, BA (Hons) MCLIP,
[56187]   01/04/1998   **CM20/11/2002**

McCormick, Mr E A, MA DipLib MCLIP, Team Leader, Edinburgh City Ls., McDonald Road L.
[45473]   14/02/1991   **CM23/03/1993**

McCormick, Miss K, BA (HONS) PgDip, Librarian, The Mitchell Library, Glasgow.
[10020619]   16/03/2012   **ME**

McCorry, Miss M C I, DipLib MCLIP, Assistant Librarian, Dublin Public Library Headquarters, Eire.
[27498]   26/04/1977   **CM07/06/1984**

McCoskery, Mrs W R, BA MCLIP, Unwaged.
[27067]   24/01/1977   **CM20/07/1979**

McCourt, Mrs D, MA RCA MCLIP, Librarian, University for the Creative Arts.
[64725]   07/06/2005   **CM11/06/2010**

McCracken, Mrs H, BSc MCLIP, Derby City Council Libraries.
[40062]   16/10/1986   **CM12/12/1990**

McCracken, Mr I G, BA MCLIP, Unemployed.
[26776]   26/10/1976   **CM27/09/1982**

McCrea, Mr R, MA (Hons) MSc MCLIP, Information Officer, Scottish Health C., Glasgow.
[61765]   05/11/2002   **CM01/02/2006**

McCready, Mrs A, BA MCLIP, Librarian, Cheshire Co. L.
[26420]   01/10/1976   **CM13/12/1978**

McCready, Mrs E C, BA (Hons),
[10031751]   01/10/2013   **ME**

McCree, Mr M, BSc (Hons) MA MCLIP, Collections Access Manager, Stamford Library, Stamford, Lincs.
[55135]   16/07/1997   **CM15/05/2002**

McCrossan, Ms J, BA MA, Library Assistant/Graduate Trainee, E. ON Technologies (Ratcliffe) Limited.
[10031630]   29/10/2013   **ME**

McCrudden, Mrs P A, MCLIP, Information Manager & Researcher., Hawkins & Associates., Cambridge.
[32657]   02/07/1980   **CM27/08/1985**

McCue, Mrs J, MSc, Network Librarian, Aberdeenshire Council.
[10000711]   25/10/2006   ME
McCulloch, Miss C J, MA (Hons), Library Graduate Trainee, Anglia Ruskin University.
[10035387]   10/10/2014   ME
McCulloch, Mr D, BA MCLIP, Retired.
[25372]   31/12/1975   CM16/09/1980
McCulloch, Mr E, MA (Hons) MSc ECDL, Part-time Cultural Assistant, William Patrick Library, East Dunbartonshire Cultural and Leisure Trust.
[55820]   26/11/1997   ME
McCullough, Mrs D, MCLIP, Assistant Librarian, Central Sussex College.
[10022071]   03/12/2012   CM16/01/2014
McCullough, Miss J E, Information Services Librarian, Library & Surgical Information Services, Royal College of Surgeons of England.
[10022301]   28/08/2001   ME
McDonald, Prof A C, BSc FCLIP, Retired.
[18403]   18/09/1972   FE19/07/2000
McDonald, Mr A H, MA,
[58676]   15/05/2000   ME
McDonald, Mr A J, MSc LRSM BMus, Senior Library Assistant, Westminster City Council.
[10035096]   15/09/2014   ME
McDonald, Mrs E, BA (Hons) MSc MCLIP,
[10006462]   24/10/2007   CM07/09/2011
McDonald, Miss E L, MA, SLA, WSCC Public Libraries.
[65200]   17/11/2005   ME
McDonald, Mrs E M, ACLIP, Senior Library Assistant, Perth & Kinross Council.
[10020994]   03/05/2012   ACL13/11/2013
McDonald, Mrs F C, BA, Community Librarian, North Lanarkshire Council.
[34513]   20/11/1981   CM15/08/1983
McDonald, Ms G A, MA MCLIP MBA, Retired.
[31373]   16/10/1979   CM05/11/1981
McDonald, Mrs H E, BA, Learning Resources Assistant, LRC, Kingston College.
[10015568]   15/12/2009   AF
McDonald, Ms L M, BA (Hons) MA, Librarian, Leicester College Library, Leicester.
[10001715]   01/07/1998   ME
McDonald, Mr R, BA PgDip ILS, Librarian, Victoria College, Belfast.
[10022227]   22/01/2013   ME
McDonald, Mrs R A, BA, Library Graduate Trainee, St John's College.
[10022335]   11/02/2013   ME
McDonald, Mr V, BA MCLIP MCIPR, Retired. Author of 'Honey from Dorabjees; a volunteer in India'.
[9336]   01/01/1971   CM24/10/1973
McDonnell, Mrs D, Dep Head of KIM, HM Passport Office, London.
[10031668]   19/09/2013   ME
McDonnell, Miss G, BA BA MCLIP, Retired.
[9339]   04/10/1967   CM21/09/1972
McDougall, Ms A, MCLIP, Network Librarian, Highlife Highland.
[10006408]   19/10/2007   CM19/10/2012
McDowall, Mrs R A C, BEd PgDipILS MCLIP, L. and Information Worker, Whitfield Library, Dundee.
[62266]   07/04/2003   CM30/11/2009
McDowell, Mrs B A, Retired.
[56380]   01/07/1998   ME
McDowell, Mrs J, BA (Hons) MA MCLIP, Information Serv. Advisor, Napier University, Edinburgh.
[62329]   29/04/2003   CM11/03/2009

McEachern, Miss K L, BA MCLIP, Librarian, Mearns Castle High School,
[42380]   28/10/1988   CM23/03/1993
McElligott, Mrs M E, BA DipLib, Unwaged.
[34210]   12/08/1981   ME
McElmurray, Ms H E, Student, University of Ulster.
[10031824]   08/10/2013   ME
McElroy, Mrs M H, MBA MRPharmS MCLIP, Life Member.
[26120]   01/07/1976   CM24/09/1979
McElroy, Prof R, MA MBA DipLib FCLIP, Life Member.
[9352]   12/10/1967   FE18/04/1989
McEvoy, Miss E M, BA (Hons) MSc MCLIP, Global Knowledge Manager, Ernst & Young.
[58829]   17/08/2000   CM15/09/2004
McEvoy, Ms H, BA (Hons) DipILM MCLIP, Repository Manager, Collections and Digital Developments, The Library, University of Salford.
[58661]   09/05/2000   CM27/08/2014
McEwan, Mrs A J, BA (Hons), Graduate Trainee Library Assistant, Royal College of Surgeons, London.
[10021621]   14/09/2012   ME
McEwan, Mr C W, MA BA (Hons), Information Assistant (Graduate Trainee), Kingston College.
[10032009]   21/10/2013   ME
McEwan, Mr K, MCLIP, Retired.
[9359]   01/01/1957   CM01/01/1968
McFarlane, Ms C J, DipEd DipLib MCLIP, School Library Advisor, Babcocks LDP.
[43871]   02/02/1990   CM16/09/1992
McFarlane, Ms I, MA (Hons) MSc, School Librarian, High School of Dundee.
[10020876]   19/04/2012   ME
McFarlane, Ms J, BA MCLIP, Head of Partnerships & Professional Adviser, National Library of Scotland.
[30890]   21/05/1979   CM10/07/1981
McFarlane, Mr J, MCLIP,
[63963]   22/11/2004   CM21/11/2007
McFarlane, Mrs J A, BA MCLIP, Acting Library Manager, Renfrewshire Council.
[23408]   09/01/1975   CM26/09/1979
McFarlane, Ms K, LIS Manager, Last, Cawthra, Feather Solicitors, Bradford.
[56806]   19/10/1998   ME
McFarlane, Mrs K A, CMG BA MLib FCLIP, Government Head of Profession For Knowledge & Information Management, Q A Ltd.
[28245]   10/10/1977   FE23/10/2008
McFetridge, Mrs D, BA (Hons) MSc (Econ), Senior Information Officer, Law Society of Northern Ireland, Belfast.
[52844]   09/01/1996   ME
McFie, Ms J E, BA MA,
[10014350]   01/07/2001   ME
McGarrigle, Mrs H P, MCLIP, Prison Librarian, Oakham Library, Rutland.
[25319]   05/01/1976   CM05/12/1978
McGarrity, Mr J, BA MCLIP, Information Serv. Co-ordinator, South Lanarkshire Council, Hamilton Town House L.
[26476]   01/10/1976   CM09/09/1981
McGarry, Ms D, MLS, Retired.
[44630]   12/11/1990   ME
McGarry, Ms M, MA DipLib MCLIP, Local Studies Librarian, North Lanarkshire Council.
[35253]   01/10/1982   CM26/02/1992

McGarvey, Mrs V, BA (Hons) DipILS MED MCLIP, Senior E-Learning Developer, Nottingham Trent University, Dryden Centre.
[52489]   02/11/1995   **CM19/05/1999**
McGavin, Mr S, MA PgDip, Student, Cranfield University.
[10035114]   16/09/2014   **ME**
McGee, Ms S, BSc, Library Assistant, Dublin City Public Libraries.
[10012361]   03/02/2009   **ME**
McGeechan, Mrs F, BA BSc (Hons) MA, Student.
[10032067]   24/10/2013   **ME**
McGettigan, Mrs E, BA MCLIP MBILD ACMI, Head of Ls. &Information Servs., Edinburgh City Council.
[9649]   05/11/1970   **CM01/07/1975**
McGhee, Ms W, MA MSc, Archivist, North Lanarkshire Council Archives, Cumbernauld.
[57985]   08/10/1999   **ME**
McGhie, Ms J, MSc,
[65064]   24/10/2005   **ME**
McGill, Miss J C, BA (Hons) DipILS MCLIP, Librarian, Auchinleck Acad., Auchinleck, Ayrshire.
[52845]   09/01/1996   **CM20/11/2002**
McGinty, Mr S, Student, Strathclyde University.
[10021727]   05/10/2012   **ME**
McGlamery, Ms S, BA MLS, Senior Product Manager, OCLC.
[10017062]   21/06/2010   **ME**
McGlen, Miss H E, BSc MCLIP, Information Advisor, Shell U. K. Exploration, Aberdeen.
[33058]   20/10/1980   **CM17/07/1985**
McGlew, Ms C K, MA (Hons) MSc, Career break as a full-time mother.
[53956]   16/10/1996   **ME**
McGlinn, Miss C, BA (HONS) MSc, Sch. Librarian, Mitchell Library, Glasgow.
[10008414]   27/11/2003   **ME**
McGovern, Mrs M, MCLIP, Unwaged.
[10000170]   01/05/1975   **CM11/11/1985**
McGowan, Mr A K, BA MA MCLIP, Student.
[10000798]   03/11/2006   **CM16/12/2010**
McGowan, Mr I D, BA, Retired.
[44953]   22/01/1991   **ME**
McGowan, Mr S, BA (Hons) DipLIS DipMUS, Liaison Librarian, Keele University Library.
[55121]   16/07/1997   **ME**
McGrath, Mrs A J, MSc, Unwaged.
[49756]   02/12/1993   **ME**
McGrath, Dr B, BA (Mod) MLitt PhD DLIS, Information Consultant, lecturer, trainer, researcher, Ireland.
[10008379]   19/03/2008   **ME**
McGrath, Mrs C M, BA MCLIP, School Librarian, Bucksburn Academy, Aberdeen.
[46402]   01/11/1991   **CM19/03/1997**
McGrath, Ms F M, BA, Senior Research Specialist, SPICe, Edinburgh.
[38875]   16/10/1985   **ME**
McGrath, Mr M I, BA (Hons), Editor Interlending & Document Supply.
[62145]   28/02/2003   **ME**
McGregor, Ms H M, MA (Hons) PgDipILS, Library and Information Manager, Marine Scotland Marine Laboratory, Aberdeen.
[57812]   13/08/1999   **ME**
McGregor, Mr I, BA MCLIP AALIA, Lending Services Librarian, Monash University.
[9398]   22/09/1968   **CM08/08/1972**
McGregor, Mr R, BA (Hons) MLITT PgDipILS MCLIP, Librarian, Heritage Services Officer, Burns Monument Centre, East Ayrshire Council.
[61313]   17/05/2002   **CM07/09/2005**

McGrimmond, Miss J, BA MCLIP, Business & Enterprise Librarian, Aberdeen City Libraries.
[28080]   11/10/1977   **CM16/02/1982**
McGuffin, Ms T M M, BA (Hons) MA MSc PgDip NVQL3, School Librarian, Wellington College.
[63761]   29/09/2004   **ME**
McGuigan, Miss H J, Graduate Trainees, London Library.
[10021997]   15/11/2012   **ME**
McGuinness, Mrs J A, BLib MCLIP, Team Leader, Library Learning, Resources and Researcj Team., University of Abertay Dundee., Dundee.
[36128]   27/05/1983   **CM05/07/1988**
McGuinness, Miss R, BA (Hons), Student, Manchester University.
[10019545]   26/07/2011   **ME**
McGuire, Mr D, FInstPa QPL, Principal Rare Books Modern & Antiquarian and printed Ephemera Researcher.
[10031545]   28/08/2013   **ME**
McGurk, Miss G R, MCLIP, Weekly volunteer work at Chained Library, Hereford Cathedral, Cathedral Reference Library.
[19753]   23/09/1967   **CM01/01/1972**
McHarazo, Dr A A S, BA MA PhD HonFCLIP FCLIP, Lib. /Head of Department, University College of Lands & Arch. Studies, Dar es Salaam, Tanzania.
[47548]   01/10/1992   **HFE07/12/2007**
McHugh, Ms E A, MA (Hons) DipILS MCLIP, Electronic Resources Manager, University of the Highlands and Islands.
[52836]   02/01/1996   **CM23/09/1998**
McHugh, Mr J, Information Officer, Milbank Tweed, London.
[10012867]   17/03/2009   **ME**
McHugh, Miss L F M, Senior Library Assistant, Chichester Library, West Sussex CC.
[10034729]   12/08/2014   **ME**
McHugh, Mrs M, MCLIP, LIRC Manager., London Fire Brigade.
[19968]   04/01/1973   **CM25/07/1977**
McIlroy, Miss A J, BSc (Hons) MLIS MCLIP, Borrower Servs. Librarian, Queen's University of Belfast Medical Library, Belfast.
[58222]   12/11/1999   **CM13/06/2007**
McIlveen, Mrs M, BA (Hons) DipLib MCLIP, Unemployed.
[10035503]   03/10/1980   **CM19/09/1984**
McIlwaine, Prof I C, BA PhD FCLIP FSA, Prof. Emeritus, Dept of Inf Studies., UCL.
[9414]   01/01/1958   **FE01/01/1962**
McIlwaine, Prof J, BA MCLIP, Prof. Emeritus of the Bibl. of Asia & Africa, Dep of Information Studies., UCL.
[9415]   05/10/1961   **CM01/01/1965**
McInnes, Mrs A, BA (Hons), Lib. Officer Young People 0-18, Cornwall L. Serv., Truro.
[10005997]   13/05/2005   **ME**
McInnes, Mrs A M, BA DipLib MCLIP, Young Peoples Serv. Librarian, East Ayrshire Council, Kilmarnock, Ayrshire.
[34745]   05/02/1982   **CM21/12/1988**
McIntosh, Miss O C, MA, Student, Robert Gordon University.
[10034024]   21/05/2014   **ME**
McIntosh, Mrs S, BA MSc MCLIP, Learning Resources Manager, Heanor Gate Science College.
[57524]   20/04/1999   **CM23/01/2002**
McIntyre, Mr A, BSc DipLib MCLIP, Retired.
[9423]   30/03/1966   **CM01/01/1972**
McIntyre, Miss F R, MCLIP, Community Heritage Manager, Nelson Library, Lancashire.
[64410]   15/03/2005   **CM19/12/2008**
McIntyre, Ms R, BA (Hons) MA MCLIP, Facilities Coordinator, Children's Mobile Library, North Shields Central Library.
[62932]   20/11/2003   **CM05/05/2010**

McKay, Miss A L, BA (Hons), Librarian, Corby Business Academy,
Northamptonshire.
[10002933] 10/05/2007 ME

McKay, Mr D J, FCLIP, Retired.
[22838] 04/10/1974 FE01/04/2002

McKay, Mrs E, BA LTCL DiplLS MCLIP, Information and Local Studies
Librarian, Argyll & Bute Council, L. Headquarters, Dunoon.
[36706] 03/11/1983 CM15/08/1990

McKay, Mrs E L, BA Dip Lib MCLIP, Stock Manager, Trafford Library,
Manchester.
[10007734] 14/12/1983 CM22/03/1995

McKay, Mr I S H, BA MA MA MLitt PgCert FHEA, Subject Librarian / LIS
Copyright Manager.
[10007233] 01/02/2008 AF

McKay, Mr M J, MA PgDip, L. & Information Assistant, Dundee C. C.
[65786] 18/04/2006 ME

McKay, Mrs S H C, BA MCLIP, Librarian, Aberdeenshire L. &
Information Serv.
[33417] 29/09/1980 CM06/03/1986

McKay, Miss V S M, BEd DipLib MCLIP, Retired.
[36464] 11/10/1983 CM16/10/1991

McKean, Miss M B, MA MSc, Lead Learning Resource Centre
Assistant, SRUC – Elmwood College.
[10021257] 02/07/2012 ME

McKean, Mrs P E, MCLIP, Retired.
[27378] 01/03/1977 CM02/07/1980

McKeating, Mrs S F, MSc MCLIP, Academic Services Manager,
Loughborough University, Pilkington Library.
[42588] 13/01/1989 CM13/01/1989

McKee, Mrs K J, BA MSc MCLIP, Sub. Librarian, St John's College,
Cambridge.
[42110] 01/10/1988 RV08/09/2005 CM16/11/1994

McKee, Miss T, MA (Hons) MSc MCLIP, Serv. Librarian, NHS Greater
Glasgow & Clyde.
[63940] 18/11/2004 CM11/06/2010

McKeeman, Mrs R L, DA (Hons) MLib MCLIP, Sch. Library Assistant,
Foundry Lane Prim. School, Southampton City Council.
[43766] 05/01/1990 CM22/03/1995

McKeen, Mr M S, DipEarthSci BSc DMS MCLIP, Unemployed.
[31086] 08/08/1979 CM05/03/1984

McKeever, Ms C M, BA MSc, Sch. Librarian, North Eastern Education
and Library Board (NEELB),
[10018246] 11/12/2010 ME

McKellar, Ms J, Serv. Coordinator, Lib. & Learning, Brimbank C. C.,
Victoria, Aus.
[64577] 17/05/2005 ME

McKellar, Mrs K, Learning and Skills Assistant at Cardiff and Vale
College and Distance Learner at Coleg Llandrillo.
[10032470] 09/12/2013 ME

McKellar, Miss R, MCLIP, Children & Families Development Officer,
East Dunbartonshire Leisure & Culture Trust.
[10000826] 28/02/2002 RV13/11/2013 CM09/07/2008

McKellen, Ms C L, BSc FCLIP, Retired.
[60543] 06/02/1978 FE11/12/2001

McKelvey, Mrs C J, BA ACLIP, Library Assistant, Hertford L.
[63907] 26/10/2004 ACL17/01/2007

McKelvie, Ms J, Student, Telford College, Edinburgh.
[10008535] 06/05/2008 ME

McKenna, Mrs E A V, BA (Hons), Student, University of Brighton.
[10032619] 20/12/2013 ME

McKenna, Mr G, MA FCLIP, Retired.
[9445] 13/09/1966 FE01/06/2005

McKenzie, Mr A D G, BSc PGCE (Secondary), Information Support
Officer, Ministry of Defence.
[10034527] 18/07/2014 ME

McKenzie, Mrs H E M, BSc MLS MCLIP MA, Librarian, Cardinal
Wiseman Catholic School, Greenford. Middx. UB6 9AW.
[55278] 12/09/1997 CM04/02/2004

McKenzie, Mr J M, LLB (Hons) DipLIS MCLIP, Faculty Librarian, Royal
Faculty of Procurators in Glasgow.
[54013] 17/10/1996 CM23/06/2004

McKenzie, Ms K R, BA (Hons), Acquisitions Librarian, The National
Archives.
[10022635] 05/04/2013 ME

McKeown, Ms C M, Part-time Branch Library Manager, Moira Library –
Student.
[10022350] 12/02/2013 ME

McKichan, Miss F, MA, Information Librarian, Southampton Solent
University, Hants.
[63757] 29/09/2004 ME

McKinney, Miss D, MCLIP, Life Member.
[9474] 09/05/1956 CM01/01/1964

McKinney, Mrs P A, BA (Hons) MSc, Lecturer (part time), University of
Sheffield Information School.
[59928] 06/11/2001 ME

McKirgan, Mrs K, LRC Manager, BBG Academy.
[10022573] 26/03/2013 AF

McKnight, O M, MMath MA, Librarian, Jesus College, Oxford.
[56885] 03/11/1998 ME

McKrell, Dr L, BA MSc PhD MCLIP, Community Librarian (City), Stirling
Council.
[43521] 01/11/1989 CM22/04/1992

McLachlan, Mrs K N, BA (Hons) MA MCLIP, Senior Information Officer,
Macfarlanes, London.
[55427] 07/10/1997 CM19/11/2003

McLaney, Mr J D, BA MCLIP, Life Member.
[9489] 02/04/1953 CM01/01/1959

McLaren, Miss C M, DA (Hons) MCLIP, L. Serv. Manager, George Elliot
Hospital, Nuneaton.
[61994] 16/01/2003 RV09/07/2013 CM19/11/2008

McLarty, Mrs E, MA (Hons) MSc, Librarian, Solicitor's Legal Information
Centre, Scottish Government Legal Directorate, Edinburgh.
[10005007] 06/06/2007 ME

McLaughlin, Mrs A J, BA MCLIP, Lib. Serv. Manager, Jones Day,
London.
[33935] 28/05/1981 CM06/02/1986

McLaughlin, Mr J F E, MA DLIS, Retired.
[10001732] 07/03/2007 ME

McLaven, Miss T J, BA (Hons) MA, Deputy Librarian, Education Centre
Library, Glenfield Hospital, University Hospitals of Leicester.
[47792] 27/02/1997 ME

McLean, Ms F, BSc MSc RGN RMN NDN, career break.
[55412] 08/10/1997 ME

McLean, Mrs L R, BSc, Senior Information Assistant, University of
Ulster.
[10032043] 22/10/2013 ME

McLean, Prof N, BA DipEd DipLib MCLIP, Retired.
[9505] 03/01/1972 CM18/12/1978

McLean, Miss P, MA (Hons), Learning Services Librarian, Inverclyde
Libraries.
[10020058] 28/10/2011 AF

McLean, Mr R J, BSc (Hons) DipLib, Retired.
[10019494] 07/01/1979 CM10/12/1981

McLellan, Miss E L, Senior Library Assistant, HMP Belmarsh Library.
[10020475] 20/02/2012 AF

275

McLelland, Dr D, EdD MA MSc FCLIP, Life Member.
[15695]   01/01/1956   **FE01/01/1966**
McLeod, Prof J, PhD MSc BSc PGCutl MCLIP, Prof. in Records Mgmnt, Sch. of Computing, Engineering & Information Sci., Northumbria University Newcastle upon Tyne.
[60167]   27/01/1982   **CM25/07/1989**
McLeod, Mrs J, BA (Hons) MSc MCLIP, Senior Librarian, Dentons UKMEA LLP.
[60871]   18/12/2001   **CM29/05/2013**
McLeod, Mr M, IT Instructor/Librarian, Aberdeen College.
[40541]   06/03/1987   **ME**
McLoughlin, Mrs A M, BA MCLIP, Strategic Librarian, Bebington Central Adults Library, Wirral.
[39805]   29/07/1986   **CM14/11/1990**
McLoughlin, Mrs R S, BA (Hons) Soc Sci PgDip, Library Systems Assistant, Exeter College.
[59330]   08/02/2001   **ME**
McLoughlin, Mrs U M, BA (Hons) PgDip MA, Library Manager, H M Prison.
[58963]   10/10/2000   **ME**
McLullich, Mrs J J, BA MCLIP, Career Break.
[34507]   19/11/1981   **CM18/09/1991**
McMahon, Mrs S J, MCLIP, Information Librarian, Worthing Library, West Sussex County Council.
[22790]   21/10/1974   **CM02/09/1977**
McMahon, Ms S T A, BA DipLib MCLIP, Head of Libraries & Information Services., Brighton & Hove City Council.
[31731]   23/11/1979   **CM16/08/1982**
McManamon, Miss C M, MA BA (Hons) MCLIP, Manchester Metropolitan University.
[10020231]   02/12/2011   **CM15/07/2014**
McManus, Ms F M, BA (Hons) MA Post Grad Dip, Student.
[10035280]   03/10/2014   **ME**
McManus, Miss P A, BA MCLIP, Semi-retired (Working from home), Otley, West Yorkshire.
[10001755]   04/10/1988   **CM04/10/1988**
McMaster, Mrs C, BLib MCLIP, Academic Services Manager, Anglia Ruskin University, Chelmsford.
[23265]   18/11/1974   **CM10/09/1979**
McMaster-Mason, Mrs P A, BA MSc, Head Librarian, St Vincent and the Grenadines Community College.
[10033176]   18/02/2014   **ME**
McMeekan, Mr I, MA FCLIP, Life Member.
[9526]   07/02/1956   **FE15/02/1989**
McMenemy, Mr D, BA (Hons) MSc MCLIP FHEA FRSA, Lecturer., Department of Computer & Information Sciences., Universityof Strathclyde.
[53830]   03/10/1996   **CM20/09/2000**
McMillan, Mrs B M, BA MCLIP, School Librarian, King Edward VI School, Suffolk.
[18371]   21/10/1972   **CM01/01/1976**
McMillan, Ms E, BA, Libraries Manager Library Services (Slough) Ltd.
[10007756]   31/08/1982   **ME**
McMillan, Ms J E, BA (Hons) MCLIP, Senior Librarian – Resources, High Life Highland.
[52507]   02/11/1995   **CM17/11/1999**
McMillan, Mr T, BEd, Vol. Librarian, Irish Centre, London.
[63047]   26/01/2004   **ME**
McNally, Mrs A M, MCLIP, Retired.
[19754]   18/08/1964   **CM01/01/1967**
McNally, Mrs L E, MA (Hons) DipILS MCLIP, Faculty Librarian (MBA), University of Strathclyde.
[55821]   26/11/1997   **CM12/03/2003**

McNally, Ms R C, BSocSci DipLIS MSc MCLIP, Outreach Librarian, Manchester Mental Health & Social Care Trust.
[44060]   20/04/1990   **RV**20/06/2014   **CM16/11/1994**
McNally, Miss S, BA, Librarian, Welsh Assembly Gov.
[10009725]   23/02/2012   **ME**
McNamara, Mr S, BA MCLIP, CILIPS Policy and Digital Officer.
[10008816]   21/04/2008   **CM10/03/2010**
McNeil, Ms F J, BA MCLIP, Online Content Adviser (Registry), Institute and Faculty of Actuaries, Oxford.
[41586]   21/01/1988   **CM14/11/1990**
McNeill, Miss E, BA DLS ATCL MCLIP, Life Member.
[9554]   07/03/1957   **CM01/01/1967**
McNeill, Mrs J, Quality Documentation Coordinator, Northumbria University.
[10031794]   04/10/2013   **ME**
McNeill, Mrs J I, BLib MCLIP, Information Officer, Healthwatch Cambridgeshire.
[34097]   01/10/1981   **CM12/12/1990**
McNichol, Mrs K A, MA DipLib MCLIP, Force Records Manager, HQ, Merseyside Police.
[34183]   09/10/1981   **CM18/11/1992**
McNicol, Miss F E, BA (Hons) DipILS MCLIP, Unwaged.
[53021]   31/01/1996   **CM12/03/2003**
McPhail, Mrs R J, BA (Hons) MCLIP,
[44600]   05/11/1990   **CM21/07/1999**
McPhail-Smith, Ms Z C, MA (Hons) MSc, Serials Librarian, National Library of Scotland.
[10000520]   10/12/2006   **ME**
McPherson, Miss M, BA MCLIP, Comm. Librarian, South Lanarkshire Leisure & Culture.
[29463]   14/08/1978   **CM14/08/1980**
McPhie, Miss J C, MA M Phil, Student, UCL, MA Library and Information Studies.
[10032478]   09/12/2013   **ME**
McQueen, Mr G J, BA (Hons) DipIM MCLIP, Librarian (Stock & Promotions), London Borough of Richmond.
[53276]   12/04/1996   **CM13/03/2002**
McQuilkin, Miss J M, MSc (Econ), Assistant Librarian for Social Science and Business, University of Ulster, Magee Campus, Londonderry.
[51402]   06/02/1995   **ME**
McRae, Mr J A, BSc MCLIP, Info & Knowledge Manager, IMarEST, London.
[64862]   09/08/2005   **CM04/10/2006**
McRobbie, Mr J D, MA (Hons) MCLIP, School Librarian, Newbattle Community High School.
[10006709]   21/11/2007   **CM10/11/2010**
McRoberts, Mrs J N, BA MA, News Reference Specialist, The British Library.
[10021985]   12/11/2012   **ME**
McRoy, Mrs C, BA (Hons) MCLIP, Staff Library., Birmingham Children's Hospital NHS Foundation Trust.
[31184]   03/10/1979   **CM11/11/1986**
McShane, Mrs L, BSc MSc, Information Manager, Newcastle NHS.
[10022262]   29/01/2013   **ME**
McTaggart, Mr A, BA (Hons), L. Officer, Sighthill Library, Edinburgh.
[10010871]   02/09/2008   **ME**
McTaggart, Mr W J, MA, Cataloguing & Access Assistant, North West Film Archive, Manchester Metropolitan University.
[65765]   05/05/2006   **ME**
McVeigh, Ms G F, BA MCLIP, Retired.
[29122]   01/01/1962   **CM17/10/1990**
McVey, Mr D M, BSc (Hons) MSc MCLIP, Unemployed.
[51213]   25/11/1994   **CM08/11/1999**

McWalter, Mr I B, ND:LIS NHD:LIP BTECH:LIS, Finance, The Royal Opera House, London.
[10011877]   25/11/2008   **ME**

McWhirter, Ms M, MA PgDip, Knowledge and Information Support Officer, DFID – Department for International Development.
[10032855]   21/01/2014   **ME**

McWilliam, Mrs R, BA (Hons) MCLIP, Deputy Site Librarian, Woodlands Centre.
[52128]   05/10/1995   **CM15/03/2000**

Meachem, Mrs L V M, MCLIP, Unemployed.
[32079]   28/01/1980   **CM25/02/1986**

Mead, Mrs B J, BA MSc, Community Engagement Librarian, Cambridgeshire CC.
[10002312]   01/03/2002   **ME**

Mead, Dr D K, BSc (Hons) MSc PhD CELTA FCLIP, Deputy National Librarian, National Library of Scotland.
[10019497]   11/07/2011   **FE27/03/2014**

Mead, Mr W D, BA (Hons) MCLIP, Legal Advisers Branch Librarian and Copyright Manager., Home Office, London.
[50755]   17/10/1994   **CM17/09/2003**

Meaden, Miss K, BA (Hons) PgDip MCLIP, Marketing & Communications Specialist, Cranfield University.
[56102]   17/02/1998   **CM20/11/2002**

Meades, Mr G J, BA (Hons) DipInfSc, Library Services Manager, Northamptonshire Healthcare NHS Foundation Trust, Northampton.
[53204]   09/04/1996   **ME**

Meadows, Prof A J, MA MSc DSc DPhil FCLIP, Emeritus Professor, Loughborough University.
[38903]   18/10/1985   **FE13/06/1989**

Meadows, Mr P, BA MCLIP, Retired.
[10018]   01/10/1968   **CM01/01/1971**

Meadows, Mrs S K, BA MA, Student, Robert Gordon University.
[10035201]   24/09/2014   **ME**

Meale, Mrs J, BSc, Senior Information Assistant, Teesside University.
[10028762]   19/11/2013   **ME**

Mealey, Mr A J, MCLIP, Retired.
[10027]   20/03/1961   **CM26/11/1982**

Mears, Miss A M, BSc, Unwaged.
[10006499]   30/10/1996   **ME**

Mears, Mr J A, Student, Northumbria University.
[10021345]   18/07/2012   **ME**

Mears, Miss S J, MA BSc DipLib MCLIP, Child. Serv. Dev. Manager, Essex County Council L.
[41050]   08/10/1987   **CM14/02/1990**

Mears, Ms W E, BA (Hons) MA MCLIP, Learning and Teaching Librarian, Open University, Milton Keynes.
[44824]   07/12/1990   **CM20/11/2002**

Medcalf, Mr J P, BA (Hons) DipLib MCLIP, Area Manager, Calderdale MBC Northgate Halifax.
[38035]   15/01/1985   **CM14/03/1990**

Medd, Miss K S, BLib MCLIP, Senior Library & Information Assistant, HMP Kirklevington Grange Library.
[41132]   07/10/1987   **CM16/10/1991**

Meddaugh, Ms G,
[10033272]   25/02/2014   **ME**

Medina, Mr V, BA (Hons), Librarian, Brighton College.
[10033921]   13/05/2014   **ME**

Medley, Miss L, MCLIP, Librarian, Lancashire C. C Home L. Serv., Preston.
[10038]   16/01/1968   **CM01/01/1971**

Medlock, Miss J, BSc MSc MCLIP, Pharmaco Vigilance Compliance Mgr, PPD Cambridge.
[60859]   01/09/1983   **CM09/07/1991**

Medway, Mr A, BLib MCLIP, Service Development Manager: Learning and Resources, Staffordshire County Council.
[31379]   20/10/1979   **CM31/03/1986**

Meechan, Mr T M D, BA, Press Office, Department for Business, Innovation & Skills, London.
[41773]   22/03/1988   **ME**

Meera Muhiadeen, Mr R, MLS BSc AGSC (Hons), University Librarian, University of Sri Lanka.
[10033553]   25/03/2014   **ME**

Meeson, Mrs P L, BA (Hons), Knowledge Skills Librarian, University Hospitals Coventry & Warwickshire NHS Trust.
[10012370]   08/02/1981   **ME**

Mehdi, Ms D, BSc, IT Technician, Hadleigh Junior School.
[10021910]   30/10/2012   **AF**

Meier, Mrs V, BA (Hons) MA MCLIP, Deputy Lib. Serv. Manager, University Hospital Lewisham.
[63600]   09/07/2004   **CM23/01/2008**

Meijueiro, Miss L, BA MA, Library Services Graduate Trainee, Manchester Metropolitan University.
[10031877]   10/10/2013   **ME**

Meineck, Mrs J, ACLIP, Information Assistant, Kingston University, Surrey.
[61449]   31/07/2002   **ACL01/10/2006**

Meldrum, Miss D A, MA (Hons) MA (PG) PgCert, Student, Robert Gordon University.
[10035624]   24/10/2014   **ME**

Melgosa, Mrs A A D, BSc MA MCLIP, Associate Librarian, Walla Walla University, USA.
[52220]   16/10/1995   **CM20/11/2002**

Melia, Ms K M, BA (Hons) DipIS MCLIP,
[47810]   19/10/1992   **CM23/07/1997**

Mellenchip, Mrs S, BA (Hons) DipLIS MCLIP, District Manager, Staffordshire County Council.
[48313]   25/11/1992   **CM31/01/1996**

Meller, Mr P J, BSc MSc, Student, Manchester Metropolitan University.
[10032481]   09/12/2013   **ME**

Melling, Miss M A, MCLIP, Retired.
[10052]   21/08/1966   **CM20/02/1973**

Melling, Miss R H, BA MCLIP, Life Member.
[10054]   08/11/1957   **CM01/01/1961**

Mello Bertao, Mrs D, Student, Federal University of Rio de Janeiro.
[10035173]   23/09/2014   **ME**

Mellor, Miss C, BSc DipLib MCLIP, General Manager L. North Yorks County Council.
[35403]   01/10/1982   **CM16/12/1986**

Mellor, Mrs E M, BA MCLIP, Librarian, Young People, North Somerset.
[36486]   18/10/1983   **CM05/07/1988**

Mellors, Mrs M J, DipLib MCLIP, Early Years Librarian, Hertfordshire Library Service.
[37605]   10/10/1984   **CM13/06/1989**

Melmoth, Mrs A, BA MCLIP MBA, Customer Services Manager, Bolton MBC.
[40015]   09/10/1986   **CM13/06/1989**

Melrose, Ms E A, MA DipLib MCLIP, Retired.
[10065]   12/11/1964   **CM31/10/1978**

Melton, Ms M R, BA (Hons) PgDipIS MLitt, Librarian, Queen Ethelburga's College.
[57163]   05/01/1999   **ME**

Melville, Mrs Y M, BA MCLIP, Adult Services Coordinator, Lib & Museum HQ, Kirkaldy.
[10020875]   19/04/2012   **CM15/02/1989**

Memmott, Mrs A L, BA (Hons) PgDip, Information Resources Manager, Foreign & Commonwealth Office, London.
[54368]   25/11/1996   **ME**

Menary, Mr A J, BSc PgDip,
[10032003] 21/10/2013 ME

Mendham, Mrs C M, BA DipLib MCLIP, Unwaged.
[30284] 04/01/1979 **CM10/08/1981**

Mends, Ms S J, BA (Hons) MSc (Econ) PgDip FHEA, Unwaged.
[54395] 03/12/1996 ME

Menendez-Alonso, Dr E, BSc (Hons) PhD MCLIP, Information Designer, University of Plymouth L.
[64922] 12/09/2005 **CM15/01/2013**

Mengu, Mr M D, BSc MSc MGIP MCLIP, Director, International Centre, Danish Technological Institute.
[60054] 07/12/2001 **CM07/12/2001**

Mennie, Mr H J, BA MCLIP DMS, Performance and Operations Manager, L. Central Bedfordshire Council.
[19890] 01/01/1973 **CM04/09/1975**

Menown, Miss C A, BA MSc, Assistant Librarian Trainee – Anglia Ruskin University.
[10032499] 10/12/2013 ME

Mensch, Mr H C, Student.
[10033846] 02/05/2014 ME

Menzies, Miss M D, BA MLib MCLIP, Lib. & Information Services Manager, Scottish Borders Council, Library Headquarters, St Mary's Mill, Selkirk.
[29749] 09/10/1978 **CM02/10/1981**

Mercer, Ms A I, BLS, Head of Library and LSS, Stranmillis University College, Belfast.
[33110] 17/10/1980 **CM21/01/1985**

Mercer, Miss E K, BSc (Econ) MCLIP, Stock Development Officer and Service Design Officer Somerset County Council.
[51304] 16/01/1995 **CM16/05/2001**

Mercer, Miss J, Student, The Royal High School.
[10034450] 14/07/2014 ME

Mercer, Mrs L, MSc BSc MA, Client Services Manager, Victoria University of Wellington.
[10006511] 24/10/2007 ME

Merchan-Hamann, Dr C A, BSc MA PhD, Deputy Librarian, Leopold Muller Memorial Library, Oxford Centre for Hebrew & Jewish Studies, Oxford.
[10018321] 01/01/2011 ME

Merchant, Mr A J, MA, Unwaged.
[57012] 20/11/1998 ME

Mercy, Mrs A R, BA (Hons), Project Management.
[10034910] 09/09/2014 ME

Meredith, Mrs C H, BA (Hons) MSc MCLIP, Head of Indexing and Data Management Section, House of Commons Library, Westminster.
[57532] 23/04/1999 **CM15/09/2004**

Meredith Galley, Mrs K, BA MA, PhD Research Student, Department of Information Science, Loughborough University.
[10018840] 21/03/2011 ME

Merillat, Ms S, MLIS,
[10033706] 16/04/2014 ME

Merison, Mrs S F, BSc MLib MCLIP, Part-time Librarian, Education L. Serv., Winsford Cheshire.
[43961] 05/03/1990 **CM14/09/1994**

Meriton, Mr J C, BA (Hons) MA DipLib FCLIP FRSA, Book historian.
[55956] 22/12/1997 **FE04/10/2006**

Merner, Miss S, BLib MCLIP, Deputy Head of Library & Knowledge Services, Surrey & Sussex Healthcare Trust.
[37094] 02/02/1984 **CM14/11/1990**

Merricks, Mrs H J, MCLIP, Business Support Manager, Northamptonshire County Council.
[20370] 13/02/1973 **CM05/09/1975**

Merrill, Miss R C, BA MCLIP, Librarian., Staff Library, Education Centre.
[32607] 21/05/1980 **CM21/05/1982**

Merriott, Miss S, BA (Hons), Libraries Officer (Stock Management). Lib. Serv., Reading.
[10012956] 19/03/2009 AF

Messenger, Mrs G S, MA MCLIP, Information Serv. Librarian, Royal Horticultural Society, London.
[35502] 12/10/1982 **CM29/07/1986**

Messenger, Mr M F, OBE FCLIP, Life Member.
[10091] 13/09/1954 **FE01/01/1964**

Messenger, Mr S P, BSc MA (Lond),
[10015019] 07/10/2009 ME

Messer, Mrs C J, BA (Hons) Msc MCLIP, Librarian In Charge, Musselburgh Library.
[10015921] 05/11/2002 **CM25/01/2011**

Messer, Mr I M, BA (Hons) MSc, Customer Services Assistant, Essex Libraries.
[10006403] 23/10/2007 ME

Messere, Mrs A P, BA MCLIP, L. Manager, Hendon Library, London Borough of Barnet.
[43299] 16/10/1989 **CM09/07/2008**

Messum, Mrs A P, BA (Hons) DipLib, Academic Subject Librarian, Plymouth College of Art.
[44502] 16/10/1990 ME

Mestre Lampreia, Ms E, Post-Graduate, Librarian/Documentation Manager.
[10035049] 08/09/2014 ME

Metcalf, Miss J R, MA (Hons), Acquisitions Assistant, University of Edinburgh.
[10022417] 26/02/2013 ME

Metcalf, Ms S M, BA MCLIP, Retired.
[23723] 14/01/1975 **CM30/03/1977**

Metcalfe, Mrs P A, MCLIP, Life Member.
[15551] 14/02/1961 **CM01/01/1965**

Metcalfe, Mrs V L, BA (Hons), Information Resources Assistant, University of Huddersfield.
[10035505] 16/10/2014 ME

Methold, Mrs D M, MCLIP, Learning Res. Centre Manager, Woking College.
[18166] 01/10/1972 **CM02/07/1976**

Methven, Mrs M, MCLIP, Retired.
[9388] 08/09/1969 **CM11/08/1972**

Mewies, Mr T A, BA (Hons), Information Support Officer, Defence Equipment & Support, MOD.
[10022746] 16/04/2013 AF

Mexi-Jones, Ms D, BSc MSc MCLIP, Information specialist.
[51032] 09/11/1994 **CM21/01/1998**

Michael, Ms A, BA (Hons) MA, Business Information Executive, London Chamber of Commerce.
[62401] 30/05/2003 ME

Michael, Mr D A, BSc DipLib MCLIP, L. Assistant, Islington Council.
[32320] 12/02/1980 **CM05/04/1982**

Michael, Miss H, Student, University of Brighton.
[10028787] 29/10/2013 ME

Michaud, Ms F, BA PGCE MSc MCLIP, Library and Information Services Manager. The Geological Society.
[10003041] 25/05/2007 **CM12/09/2012**

Michell, Mr M L, L. Executive, House of Commons Library, London.
[62097] 13/02/2003 ME

Michon-Bordes, Mrs H J M, GradDip MA, Researcher Executive Search & database administrator.
[10011128] 25/09/2008 ME

Middle, Miss S M, MA, Senior Library Assistant, Scott Polar Research Institute.
[10023075] 04/06/2013 ME

Middleton, Ms A, BSc (Hons) PgDip MSc MCLIP, Head of Customer Services, Robinson Library, Newcastle University Library.
[54195]   28/10/1996   **CM12/03/2003**

Middleton, Mrs C, BSc (Hons) MSc MIMechE MCLIP, Associate Director (Collections Management), University of Nottingham.
[49561]   12/11/1993   **CM23/07/1997**

Middleton, Miss C E, BA, Graduate Trainee, University of Surrey.
[10021993]   15/11/2012   **ME**

Middleton, Mrs H, BA (Hons), Student, Aberystwyth University.
[10011104]   24/09/2008   **ME**

Middleton, Mr I A, BSc MSc PgDip MCLIP, Web Devel. - Career Break.
[60267]   01/07/1999   **CM01/07/1999**

Middleton, Miss S L, Resources Manager, Bristol Brunel Academy.
[10013607]   12/05/2009   **ME**

Midgley, Ms C M, BA MA MCLIP, Unemployed.
[35354]   08/10/1982   **CM03/07/1996**

Midgley, Mrs E A, BA (Hons) DMS MCLIP PGCM MCMI M, Service Manager, Customer First, Blackpool. Council.
[38701]   01/10/1985   **CM18/04/1989**

Midgley, Mrs L, BSc DipLib MCLIP, Librarian, Leicester Grammar School.
[38852]   14/10/1985   **CM21/12/1988**

Midgley, Ms N J, MSc, Reference and Information Assistant, Calderdale MBC.
[10034463]   15/07/2014   **ME**

Miehe, Ms D, MA MLib MCLIP, Curator – German Section, The British Library, London.
[48332]   27/11/1992   **CM16/11/1994**

Milby, Ms C L, BA DipLib MCLIP, Freelance Library & Translation Work.
[34828]   15/03/1982   **CM16/05/1985**

Mildren, Mr K W, BSc MCLIP, Retired.
[10128]   29/08/1968   **CM01/01/1971**

Miles, Mr P G, BA MCLIP, Retired.
[10131]   25/10/1967   **CM01/01/1970**

Miles, Mr S E, BA (Hons), Information Resources Assistant, Perry Library.
[10033984]   15/05/2014   **ME**

Miles, Ms S J, BA MCLIP, Bibl. & Metadata Advisor, Kingston University, Kingston.
[35346]   12/10/1982   **CM18/04/1990**

Milford-Dickson, Ms M R, BA MS (LIS), Branch Librarian, Thornaby Library, Stockton-on-Tees.
[10006197]   18/09/2007   **ME**

Millar, Mrs A L, BSc, Area Development Librarian (Reader Development), Leeds City Council.
[10017875]   21/10/2010   **ME**

Millar, Ms K, MA MSc, Information Officer, The Scottish Parliament, Edinburgh.
[43346]   24/10/1989   **ME**

Millar, Ms M S, BSc DipLib MCLIP, Subject Librarian, Stirling UniversityL.
[37144]   01/03/1984   **CM01/09/1987**

Millar, Mrs N, BA (Hons) Dip Lib MCLIP, Front Line Serv. Manager, SEELB, Co Down.
[10014571]   23/10/1978   **CM31/12/1981**

Millard, Mr R E, BA (Hons) DipLib MCLIP MAPM, Project Manager, MOD, Bristol.
[29752]   04/10/1978   **CM26/02/1981**

Miller, Mrs A, MA MCLIP, Life Member.
[10141]   20/10/1953   **CM01/01/1959**

Miller, Mrs A, Stream Lead Children & Young People Stream, Surrey County Council.
[65905]   29/06/2006   **AF**

Miller, Mrs A E, BA DipLib MCLIP, Library Officer, Bibl. Serv., Edinburgh Central Library.
[33066]   19/09/1980   **CM30/11/1982**

Miller, Mrs C, BA (Hons) MSc MCLIP, Health Information Scientist, Healthcare Improvement Scotland.
[10015266]   29/10/2009   **CM11/04/2013**

Miller, Mrs C, BA DipLib MCLIP, Part-time Learning Res. Assistant, City of Liverpool College.
[10001677]   05/07/1977   **CM16/10/1979**

Miller, Miss C A, BA MCLIP, Retired.
[10146]   27/02/1969   **CM01/01/1972**

Miller, Mrs C L, BA DipLib MCLIP, Tax Information Officer, Allen & Overy LLP, London.
[44538]   23/10/1990   **CM24/05/1995**

Miller, Mrs C M, BA DipLib MCLIP, Information & Local Studies Librarian, William Patrick Library, East Dunbartonshire L.
[35752]   10/01/1983   **CM16/12/1986**

Miller, Mr D, PgDip MA (Hons), Digitisation Officer, Scottish Football Museum.
[10031820]   08/10/2013   **ME**

Miller, Miss D, BA (Hons) MA (Dunelm) MA MCLIP, Senior Information Officer, Lawrence Graham, Solicitors, London.
[56088]   02/02/1998   **CM12/03/2003**

Miller, Miss J, Campus Support Assistant, Napier University, Edinburgh.
[10021004]   04/05/2012   **ME**

Miller, Mrs J, Life Member.
[26778]   04/11/1976   **ME**

Miller, Mr J P, BA MCLIP, Librarian, African Law Library, Geneva.
[20790]   06/07/1973   **CM24/01/1977**

Miller, Mrs K A, BSc (Hons), Institutional Support Officer, Digital Curation Centre, University of Edinburgh.
[59071]   07/11/2000   **ME**

Miller, Miss L, MA MSc, Support Liaison Librarian, St George's, University of London.
[10006387]   23/10/2007   **ME**

Miller, Mrs M D, MCLIP, Life Member.
[10162]   28/09/1946   **CM01/01/1949**

Miller, Ms M L, BA MCLIP, Senior Lib. Res. Manager, Glasgow Caledonian University.
[26907]   10/01/1977   **CM31/01/1980**

Miller, Ms M M, BA (Hons) PgDip MCLIP, L. Collections Manager, Tate L. & Arch., London.
[37718]   16/10/1984   **CM09/08/1988**

Miller, Mr P, BA (Hons) MSc, Information Professional.
[10017035]   18/06/2010   **ME**

Miller, Mrs S, BA (Mod) (Hons) HDipLIS, Head of Library Services, Church of Ireland College of Education.
[62376]   16/05/2003   **ME**

Miller, Ms S M, MCLIP, Retired.
[22733]   22/08/1974   **CM04/08/1977**

Millerchip, Mr J J G, BLib MA FCLIP MCMI, Retired.
[18392]   16/10/1972   **FE18/11/1998**

Millership, Ms K L, MA BA, Children's Librarian, Roehampton Library.
[10018296]   14/12/2010   **ME**

Milligan, Miss D E, MA (Hons) PgDipILS MCLIP, Senior Librarian (Digital Assets), National Library of Scotland., Edinburgh.
[61322]   22/05/2002   **CM21/06/2006**

Milligan, Mr E H, BA MCLIP, Life Member.
[10171]   08/03/1940   **CM01/01/1950**

Milligan, Ms J, BA MA, Full-time, L. Society of Friends, London.
[10001856]   22/04/1997   **ME**

Milligan, Miss L B, BEd MSc (Econ) DipLib MCLIP, Chief Librarian, Guille-Alles Library, Guernsey.
[31904]   16/01/1980   **CM05/05/1982**

Milligan, Ms M A T, MA DipLib MCLIP, Retired.
[23221]   08/11/1974   **CM13/10/1977**
Milligan, Ms T J, MA DipLIS MCLIP, Senior Librarian, Larbert Library,
Stenhousemuir, Larbert.
[10002993]   04/10/1996   **CM20/01/1999**
Milliken, Mrs C, BA (Hons) MSc, Northern Ireland Assembly.
[10000465]   09/10/2006   **ME**
Milliken, Miss R J, Unemployed.
[20572]   28/04/1973   **ME**
Millington, Ms J M, BA MSc MCLIP, Systems/I. T. Support Librarian,
Uni of Chester.
[10020458]   20/02/2012   **CM26/11/1997**
Millington, Ms K J, BSc MSc, Evening Librarian, Birkbeck College,
London.
[51319]   10/01/1995   **ME**
Million, Miss A R, BA MCLIP, Freelance Law Lib.
[44197]   04/07/1990   **CM16/11/1994**
Millis, Mrs A J, BSc (Hons) PGCE DIPHEILS MCLIP, Training &
Outreach Manager, Tunbridge Wells Hospital Library, Pembury.
[10008501]   30/01/1998   **RV30/04/2014** **CM07/07/2010**
Millman, Mrs S M, MCLIP, Retired.
[2029]   04/03/1954   **CM01/01/1960**
Mills, Mr A, BA, Customer Service Assistant, Croydon College Library.
[10021774]   10/10/2012   **ME**
Mills, Mr C, BA MA DipLib MCLIP FLS, Head of L. Art & Archives, The
Royal Botanic Gardens, Kew.
[31664]   05/11/1979   **CM18/11/1981**
Mills, Mrs C E L, BA (Hons) MA MCLIP, Stock Services Manager,
County Hall Matlock, Derbys County Council.
[59011]   24/10/2000   **CM21/06/2006**
Mills, Mr G J, MSc BA DipLib MCLIP, Retired.
[20191]   06/02/1973   **CM01/01/1976**
Mills, Miss H E, BA (Hons) DipLib MCLIP, Assistant Librarian, Homerton
University Hospital NHS Foundation Trust, London.
[47129]   05/05/1992   **CM12/03/2003**
Mills, Mrs J A, BA DipLib MCLIP, Academic Liaison Librarian,
Roehampton University, London.
[31701]   25/10/1979   **CM17/11/1981**
Mills, Mrs J S, BA MCLIP, Retired.
[10179]   12/09/1957   **CM01/01/1960**
Mills, Mrs K, MCLIP, Senior Acquisitions Assistant, Lancashire Library
Headquarters, Bowran Street, Preston.
[23787]   08/01/1975   **CM19/12/1977**
Mills, Miss K M, Digital Servs. Development Officer, The Open
University Library, Milton Keynes.
[56030]   28/01/1998   **ME**
Mills, Mr R A, MA MCLIP, Retired.
[10185]   02/04/1970   **CM05/10/1972**
Mills, Mrs S, BA (Hons) MA MCLIP, LRB Manager, Middleton Tech.
School, Greater Manchester.
[63104]   30/01/2004   **CM18/12/2009**
Mills-Paton, Miss S, BA, Graduate Document Controller, AECOM.
[10035272]   03/10/2014   **ME**
Milne, Mr C, BA (Hons) DipIA MCLIP, Information Manager, University of
Abertay, Dundee.
[48063]   04/11/1992   **CM17/05/2000**
Milne, Mr D C, BA (Hons) DipLib PgDip MCLIP, Information Sci., Yell
Ltd, Reading.
[49262]   19/10/1993   **CM19/03/2008**
Milne, Miss H, MA (Hons) PgDip, School Librarian, Prestwick Academy.
[10035056]   08/09/2014   **ME**
Milne, Mr I A, MLib MCLIP, Librarian, Sibbald Library, Royal College of
Physicians, Edinburgh.
[32446]   11/04/1980   **CM23/04/1982**

Milne, Mr J, MA FCLIP, Life Member,
[10194]   25/08/1947   **FE01/01/1966**
Milne, Miss J R, MA (Hons) DipILS MCLIP, L. Development Officer, East
Neighbourhood, Edinburgh.
[56878]   29/10/1998   **CM13/03/2002**
Milne, Mr J R, BA MCLIP, Librarian, Robert Gordon University,
Aberdeen.
[44814]   04/12/1990   **CM15/05/1997**
Milne, Ms K, BASocSci PgDipLIS MA MCLIP, Eilean Siar.
[57723]   09/07/1999   **CM04/10/2006**
Milne, Mr R R, MA FRSE FCLIP FRSA,
[34100]   02/10/1981   **FE21/03/2001**
Milne, Mrs S, BA MCLIP, Life Member.
[10201]   16/09/1960   **CM01/04/1996**
Milne, Mrs S A, MA DipLib MCLIP, Information Serv. Librarian, Scottish
Borders Council, L. Serv.
[44777]   21/11/1990   **CM21/10/1992**
Milne, Mrs S L T, BA, Senior Lib. Assistant, University College
Falmouth, Penryn.
[10017402]   17/08/2010   **AF**
Milner, Mrs J A, BA MCLIP, Metadata Specialist, University of
Northampton.
[24480]   01/09/1975   **CM23/05/1979**
Milns, Ms A V L, BSc (Hons) MCLIP, EO, Home Office, London.
[54058]   24/10/1996   **CM23/01/2002**
Milroy, Mrs M P, BA DIP LIB MCLIP, Librarian, Outwood Academy City,
Sheffield.
[33068]   06/10/1980   **CM02/11/1984**
Milton, Mrs C M, BA MCLIP, Life Member.
[10212]   05/09/1953   **CM01/01/1956**
Milton, Dr F S, BA (Hons) PhD MCLIP, Senior Library Assistant, Teeside
University.
[10018417]   14/01/2011   **CM08/03/2013**
Milton, Mr H R, BA DipLib MCLIP, Retired.
[10213]   29/01/1969   **CM01/01/1971**
Milton, Mrs M B, BA (Hons) DipLIS MCLIP, Career break.
[50631]   01/10/1994   **CM22/09/1999**
Minde, Mrs D, BA (Hons), Team Leader (Information Resources),
Liverpool John Moores University.
[43904]   14/02/1990   **ME**
Minkova, Miss M, Library Assistant, University of Boras.
[10032021]   21/10/2013   **ME**
Minns, Mrs A E, BA DipLib FCLIP, Retired.
[18419]   17/10/1972   **FE20/03/1996**
Minta, Mrs L V, MSc MCLIP, Resource Librarian, Millennium Library,
Bury College.
[62950]   21/11/2003   **CM21/03/2007**
Minter, Mrs E C, BA (Hons) DipISM MCLIP, Librarian, Bryanston
School.
[54818]   11/04/1997   **CM17/05/2000**
Minter, Mrs S M, BA (Hons) DipLIS MCLIP, Senior Librarian, Young
Peoples Services, Herts County Council.
[48465]   19/01/1993   **CM22/01/1997**
Minto, Miss N H, BA (Hons), Minto, Miss N H, BA (Hons). Membership
LRC Assistant, CILIP.
[10031740]   15/11/2013   **ME**
Minton, Mrs C, BA MCLIP, Relief Librarian, W Berks.
[9029]   16/07/1967   **CM01/01/1971**
Minty, Mrs W L F, MTheol MA, Head of Acquisitions Management,
Bodleian Library, University of Oxford.
[42023]   25/07/1988   **ME**
Miranda, Mrs M A, BSc (Hons) MCLIP,
[53305]   25/04/1996   **CM17/11/1999**

Mircic, Ms A A, BA DipLib MCLIP, Team Leader, North Yorkshire County Council.
[40513] 02/03/1987 CM11/12/1989

Mires, Miss E, BA (Hons) MA MCLIP, Academic Liaison Librarian, University of Westminster.
[59874] 29/10/2001 CM01/02/2006

Mishra, Mrs M, BLIS, Student, Indira Gandhi National Open University.
[10032526] 12/12/2013 ME

Missaggia, Miss L, Librarian.
[10007038] 17/12/2007 ME

Mitchell, Ms C M, BA MCLIP, Librarian, Epping Forest College.
[33441] 08/01/1981 CM16/10/1984

Mitchell, Mrs C M, BA MCLIP, Teaching Assistant, Millbrook Junior School, Kettering, Northamptonshire.
[29205] 07/04/1978 CM20/08/1981

Mitchell, Mrs D, MCLIP, Life Member.
[17388] 01/01/1952 CM01/01/1957

Mitchell, Mr D J D, BA MA PgDipELM MBA FCLIP AFHEA, Librarian, Wales Evangelical School of Theology.
[32129] 28/01/1980 RV04/10/2013 FE26/11/1997

Mitchell, Miss E, BA (Hons) MSc FHEA, Edcuation Support Manager, Imperial College London.
[65686] 31/03/2006 ME

Mitchell, Mrs G A, BA DipLib MCLIP, Librarian, Millfield Library, Belfast Metropolitan College.
[31665] 12/11/1979 CM01/07/1990

Mitchell, Mr G D, BA MCLIP, Library Staff and Volunteer Officer, Milton Keynes Council.
[28859] 31/01/1978 CM17/01/1984

Mitchell, Mrs H F, MA MCLIP, Retired.
[3697] 04/10/1967 CM01/01/1971

Mitchell, Ms J, Library Assistant Barbican Music Library, City of London.
[45901] 01/07/1991 AF

Mitchell, Mr J E, BA (Hons) DipTP MSc, Information Adviser, South Lanarkshire Council.
[10009710] 03/06/2008 ME

Mitchell, Mr J L, BMus MMus LIT (Dip) MLIS MCLIP, Rare Book Curator, National Library of Scotland, Edinburgh.
[55728] 10/11/1997 CM18/12/2009

Mitchell, Mrs K J, BLib MCLIP, Volunteer Service Coordinator, Wokingham Libraries, Wokingham Borough Council.
[26112] 16/07/1976 CM14/09/1979

Mitchell, Miss L, BSc (Hons) DipLib MCLIP, Head of Library Services, Royal Botanic Garden Edinburgh.
[48453] 13/01/1993 CM31/01/1996

Mitchell, Miss L A, MA (Hons) MSc DipLib MCLIP, School Librarian, Stewarton Academy, Stewarton.
[35932] 20/02/1983 CM20/01/1987

Mitchell, Ms M, M. I. St., Learning Services Librarian, UBCO Library.
[10034543] 21/07/2014 ME

Mitchell, Mrs R E, BSc (Hons), Student, Northumbria University.
[10031784] 04/10/2013 ME

Mitchell, Ms S, BSc PgDip, Business Analyst, DWP Change Programme.
[50235] 12/05/1994 ME

Mitchell, Mrs S E, Library Manager, Dorset County Council.
[10033931] 13/05/2014 AF

Mitchell, Mrs T, BA MCLIP, Contractor, TFPL, London.
[42237] 13/10/1988 CM18/11/1992

Mitcheson, Mrs E A, BA DipLib MCLIP, Retired.
[26131] 30/07/1976 CM02/10/1979

Mitlin, Ms J A, BSc Phd DMS, Head of L., Arts & Archives, Bexley L. Serv., London.
[10007540] 13/02/2008 ME

Miura, Miss S, Student, University of Tsukuba.
[10034914] 21/08/2014 ME

Mizzi, Mr R, MSc (ILS) Aber DipLIS, Manager Knowledge Services at GANADO Advocates.
[62069] 07/02/2003 ME

Mlynarczyk, Mrs J M, MA, Senior Information Assistant, City University Library.
[10034140] 10/06/2014 ME

Moar, Ms T J, Student, Robert Gordon University.
[10035582] 21/10/2014 ME

Mobbs, Mr E A, MCLIP, Retired.
[10264] 20/02/1968 CM01/01/1971

Mochan, Ms E L, MA (Hons) PGCE MSc, School Librarian, The Mitchell Library, Glasgow.
[10001595] 26/02/2007 ME

Mochrie, Mrs D, MCLIP, Life Member.
[10265] 19/03/1955 CM01/01/1960

Modak, Mrs R D, BA (Hons) MA, Deputy Service Owner – Corporate Applications and Collaboration Services, Department of Health, London.
[55735] 10/11/1997 ME

Moeller, Mrs J C, Cluster Manager, Storrington Library.
[10035480] 15/10/2014 ME

Moffat, Ms E C, BSc (Econ) MCLIP, Comm. Outreach Librarian, Stirling Libraries.
[49315] 18/10/1993 CM21/03/2001

Moffat, Ms S H, BSc MSc DMS MCLIP AFHEA, Information Services Advisor, Edinburgh Napier University, Edinburgh.
[36551] 21/10/1983 CM24/03/1992

Moffatt, Mrs L K, MCLIP, Stock Team Leader, Library Headquarters, Cornwall.
[64237] 22/02/2005 RV27/08/2014 CM27/01/2010

Moger, Mr D, BA DipLib MCLIP, Community Librarian, North Somerset.
[38399] 17/04/1985 CM19/09/1989

Mogg, Ms R J, BA (Hons) MA MCLIP, Senior Subject Librarian, Cardiff University, Cardiff.
[58885] 01/10/2000 CM08/12/2004

Mohammad Salleh, Miss N, BA, Student, City University London.
[10031735] 08/10/2013 ME

Mohammadi, Mr E, Student, University of Wolverhampton.
[10032294] 14/11/2013 ME

Mohammed, Ms K, BA (Hons) MSc,
[10017194] 13/08/2010 ME

Moho Din, Miss N B, BSc Econ, Student, Aberystwyth University.
[10032136] 29/10/2013 ME

Moise, Mr C A,
[10033555] 25/03/2014 AF

Molesworth, Mr W, MA MLitt, Student, City University London.
[10035507] 16/10/2014 ME

Moll, Mr C, Academic Liaison Librarian, Brynmor Jones Library, University of Hull.
[30011] 30/10/1978 ME

Moll, Mrs E, BLib MCLIP, Lib. Hull History Centre, Kingston-Upon-Hull C. C.
[28063] 04/10/1977 CM11/05/1982

Mollard, Mr T W, MCLIP, Life Member.
[19526] 01/10/1948 CM01/01/1957

Molloy, Miss C A L, BA (Hons) DipILS MCLIP, Information Consultant., University of Aberdeen.
[55687] 04/11/1997 CM21/05/2003

Molloy, Ms M, BA MSc, Senior Librarian, Mayo Co Library, Ireland.
[10019212] 05/05/2011 ME

Molloy, Mr M J, OBE BA DipLib MCLIP, Strategic Director Cult. and Community Serv., Derbyshire County Council, Matlock.
[29465]   28/07/1978   **CM25/07/1980**

Molloy, Mrs S, BA MA, Research Support Manager.
[62166]   05/03/2003   **ME**

Molloy, Mrs S J, ACLIP, Information & Research Officer, The Chartered Society of Physiotherapy, London.
[10001180]   03/02/2007   **ACL16/05/2012**

Molloy, Mr S P, BA (Hons) DipILM MCLIP, Librarian, Liverpool Womens NHS Foundation Trust.
[55606]   24/10/1997   **CM21/01/2009**

Moloney, Mrs E J L, BA (Hons) MA, Librarian, Hunton & Williams, London.
[54070]   21/10/1996   **CM12/03/2003**

Monaghan, Mrs G, Library Assistant.
[10033590]   01/04/2014   **ME**

Monaghan, Ms J T, MA (Hons) MA, Librarian, King Alfred School.
[64990]   06/10/2005   **ME**

Monagle, Miss H M, BA (Hons), Student.
[10020258]   14/12/2011   **ME**

Monahan, Mr C, BA (Hons) MA, Graduate Information Trainee, Barnet Centre for Independent Living.
[10032681]   03/01/2014   **ME**

Monds, Mrs J M, BLib MCLIP, Director of Learning Resources, Sarum College.
[31475]   15/10/1979   **CM08/11/1982**

Monem, Mrs I C, Librarian, St George's College, Addlestone.
[65288]   28/11/2005   **ME**

Moneta, Ms C, BA (Hons), Head of Knowledge and Information Management., Veale Wasbrough Vizards LLP, Bristol.
[40800]   26/06/1987   **ME**

Monk, Mr G C, BA (Hons) MCLIP, Head of Resources and Capability, Department Work and Pensions, London.
[26780]   25/10/1976   **CM08/10/1981**

Monk, Mrs L A, BA (Hons) MCLIP, Children's Services Manager, Birmingham City Council.
[42248]   13/10/1988   **CM17/09/2003**

Monks, Mr G F, BSc (Hons) MCLIP, Retired.
[30072]   27/11/1978   **CM02/03/1981**

Monro, Mr N, Student.
[10016686]   30/04/2010   **ME**

Monsef, Miss S R, MSc, Senior Consultant, Deloitte MCS Limited.
[10032865]   21/01/2014   **ME**

Montague, Mr C, BA MSc, LMS Librarian, Trinity College Library Dublin.
[10035512]   16/10/2014   **ME**

Montague, Miss M B, BEd (Hons) DipLib MSc MCLIP, Assistant Director Business Support, Queen Mary, University of London.
[31385]   03/10/1979   **CM10/05/1983**

Montague, Ms R, MA, Library Assistant, LGMA.
[10033526]   24/03/2014   **ME**

Montenegro, Ms E, Student, Universita Degli Studi Di Parma.
[10032494]   20/12/2013   **ME**

Montgomery, Mrs A, BA DipLib MCLIP, Librarian, Bury Grammar School Boys, Bury.
[32777]   25/08/1980   **CM19/04/1983**

Montgomery, Miss F G, BEd (Hons) DipLib MCLIP CPSRIM, TLSS Assistant, UCL LIbrary Services.
[31667]   02/11/1979   **CM15/12/1983**

Moodie, Miss E B, BA (Hons) MCLIP, Retired.
[25079]   11/11/1975   **CM19/09/1978**

Moody, Mrs J M, BA (Hons) MSc PGCE MCLIP, Information Specialist, University of Plymouth.
[59953]   09/11/2001   **CM21/06/2006**

Moody, Mrs K B, BLib MCLIP, School Librarian, Herts. C. C.
[20442]   05/12/1972   **CM16/10/1975**

Moody, Mrs P H, MCLIP, LRC Manager, John Taylor High School, Barton-under-Needwood, Staffordshire DE13 8AZ.
[24999]   18/11/1975   **CM01/02/1979**

Moon, Mr C, BA (Hons), Student.
[10020709]   27/03/2012   **ME**

Moon, Miss G J, Learning Zone Assistant, Preston's College.
[10019878]   07/10/2011   **AF**

Mooney, Ms C A, BSocSci MA ACLIP, Library Co-ordinator Openshaw Campus, The Manchester College.
[10016673]   23/04/2010   **ACL22/08/2012**

Moorcroft, Mrs C R, BA MCLIP, Access & Inclusion Librarian, Chesterfield Library, Derbyshire County Council.
[40558]   20/03/1987   **CM25/05/1994**

Moore, Mr A, BA (Hons) MA PgDipMUS LIS, Library Assistant, National Galery of Ireland.
[10028889]   25/07/2014   **ME**

Moore, Ms C A, BSc MA MCLIP, Chartered Institute of Personnel & Development (CIPD).
[30223]   10/01/1979   **CM06/04/1981**

Moore, Mr C C, BA DipLib MCLIP, Area Manager, Lewisham Library.
[31906]   20/12/1979   **CM13/10/1982**

Moore, Mr C J K, BA (Hons) MSc MCLIP, Library Operations Manager, Wiltshire County Council.
[55501]   16/10/1997   **CM20/09/2000**

Moore, Mrs D, Head of Library Resources Centre, Caterham School.
[10022535]   15/10/2014   **ME**

Moore, Mr D R, BA, Temporary Administrative Assistant.
[58795]   31/07/2000   **ME**

Moore, Mr G R, Librarian, Lancashire Teaching Hospitals NHS Foundation Trust.
[10033800]   30/04/2014   **ME**

Moore, Mrs H, BA MA MCLIP, Medical Education Manager, Queen Victoria Hospital, East Grinstead.
[10009026]   28/04/2008   **CM09/09/2009**

Moore, Mrs J C, BA MCLIP, Retired.
[2511]   19/01/1966   **CM01/01/1970**

Moore, Miss J E, BSc, Service Support Manager, Dawson Books.
[41858]   29/04/1988   **ME**

Moore, Mrs J M, BA MCLIP, Freelance Hist. Researcher/Genealogist, Manchester.
[24341]   12/07/1975   **CM05/05/1981**

Moore, Mrs J R, BA MSLS MBA PhD, Retired, Resident USA.
[17405]   26/07/1961   **ME**

Moore, Miss K M H, BSc,
[10021252]   **ME**

Moore, Miss L, BA,
[10000656]   25/10/2006   **ME**

Moore, Mr M A, BSc (OPEN), Library Assistant, Norwich School.
[10035295]   07/10/2014   **ME**

Moore, Mr N F, FCLIP, Retired.
[10353]   30/03/1960   **FE01/01/1969**

Moore, Miss P, BA (Hons), Student, Aberyswyth University.
[10021901]   25/10/2012   **ME**

Moore, Mr P G, Data Analyst, Glasgow Dental Hospital & School.
[10021838]   16/09/1996   **AF**

Moore, Miss S, Local History & Reference Librarian, West Dunbartonshire County Council, Glasgow.
[10006368]   16/10/2007   **CM09/11/2011**

Moore, Miss S E, BA, Student, Sheffield University.
[65041]   12/10/2005   **ME**

Moore, Mr S R, BA MCLIP, Head of Records. Mgmnt & Buisness Continuity, London Ambulance Serv. NHS Trust, London.
[19527] 07/10/1968 **CM31/07/1972**

Moore, Mrs T A, BA MA, Principal Library Assistant, Manchester Metropolitan University.
[10012168] 15/12/2003 **ME**

Moors, Mrs R M, BSc DipLib MCLIP, College Librarian, Greenhead College, Huddersfield.
[30328] 19/01/1979 **CM17/07/1981**

Moralee, Ms S, Student, Newcastle University.
[10032404] 03/12/2013 **ME**

Moreau, Mrs L, Local Studies Librarian, Aberdeen City Council Central Library.
[10034425] 11/07/2014 **ME**

Morgan, Mr A C, MA (Hons) BSc PgDip, Prison Librarian, HMP Whitemoor, Cambridgeshire.
[10001322] 15/06/2004 **ME**

Morgan, Ms C, BEd (Hons) DipIS MCLIP, Assistant Director Library Services, University of Brighton.
[53474] 01/07/1996 **CM15/05/2002**

Morgan, Miss C, ACLIP, Library Assistant Cornish Studies, The Cornwall Centre – Kresenn Kernow.
[10001103] 12/01/2007 **ACL27/11/2007**

Morgan, Miss C, BSc Econ, Unwaged.
[10018708] 25/02/2011 **ME**

Morgan, Ms E R, MCLIP, Prison Librarian, HMP Whatton, Notts.
[10014455] 22/07/1992 **CM18/11/1993**

Morgan, Mr G, MCLIP, Managing Director, Ferret Information Systems, Cardiff.
[60753] 04/07/1986 **CM04/07/1986**

Morgan, Mr G J A, BSc (Hons) MSc Econ AFHEA, Academic Liaison Librarian for Architecture, Construction and Real Estate Management, Oxford Brookes University.
[59576] 04/06/2001 **ME**

Morgan, Miss H E, MCHEM, Student, Robert Gordon University.
[10022408] 26/02/2013 **MF**

Morgan, Miss H L, Database Development Librarian, Department of Health, Leeds.
[58397] 01/02/2000 **ME**

Morgan, Mr H T C,
[10020129] 08/11/2011 **ME**

Morgan, Mr J H D, BA MLib (Wales) MCLIP, Assistant Librarian, Library & Learning Resources, Birmingham City University.
[41838] 18/04/1988 **CM23/03/1994**

Morgan, Mr J L, BA MCLIP, Life Member.
[10403] 21/10/1950 **CM01/01/1954**

Morgan, Ms J L, BA, Senior Information Services Librarian Leeds Metropolitan University.
[61579] 02/10/2002 **ME**

Morgan, Miss J R R, BA MCLIP, Life Member.
[10404] 20/09/1948 **CM01/01/1964**

Morgan, Mrs K B, BA MCLIP, Head Lib. /Arch., North London Collegiate School, Edgware.
[18379] 09/10/1972 **CM08/03/1978**

Morgan, Mrs K L, BSc (Hons) MSc MCLIP, Library and Knowledge Manager, Southend University Hospital.
[49597] 19/11/1993 **CM17/03/1999**

Morgan, Miss L P, BA MCLIP, Stock Specialist, Cheshire Library, Crewe.
[24910] 16/10/1975 **CM31/10/1978**

Morgan, Mr M G, BA DipLib MCLIP, Librarian, Heythrop College, University of London.
[39631] 03/04/1986 **CM12/09/1990**

Morgan, Mrs N, BA MCLIP, Museum Ed. Policy Adviser, Museums L. & Archives Council, London.
[27590] 24/05/1977 **CM04/07/1979**

Morgan, Mr N J, MA BA (Hons) DipLib MCLIP FHEA, Subject Librarian, Cardiff University.
[43457] 26/10/1989 **CM17/05/2000**

Morgan, Mrs P M, MCLIP, Retired.
[329] 31/10/1955 **CM01/01/1963**

Morgan, Mrs S, BLib MCLIP, Lending Librarian, Carmarthen Public Library, Carmarthen.
[10002099] 17/05/1976 **CM26/11/1982**

Morgan, Mrs S L, BA (Hons) DipLIS, Performance & Personnel Librarian, Conwy Library, Conwy Co. Borough Council.
[49949] 28/01/1994 **CM22/01/1997**

Morgan, Mrs U M, MCLIP, Life Member.
[2869] 03/09/1948 **CM01/01/1953**

Morgan-Bindon, Ms M E, Manager Lib. Serv. & Cultural Dev., Gold Coast C. C., Australia.
[63185] 03/03/2004 **ME**

Morgan-Daniel, Ms J, Student.
[10020730] 29/03/2012 **ME**

Morgan-Green, Mr J A, PgDipLIM MCLIP, Senior L. Officer, Halesowen College, West Midlands.
[57306] 05/02/1999 **CM19/07/2011**

Morgan-James, Miss K A, BA (Hons), School Librarian, Hagley Catholic High School.
[39232] 01/01/1986 **ME**

Morgan-Jones, Ms J, Student, Coleg Llandrillo.
[10028903] 03/12/2013 **ME**

Morgan-Lodge, Miss E, BA (Hons), Student, Aberystwyth University.
[10015814] 29/01/2010 **ME**

Morgans, Mrs C, MCLIP, Welsh/Children's Librarian, Cardiff Council.
[22803] 09/10/1974 **CM08/12/1978**

Morita, Dr Y, BA MA MA PhD MCLIP, Senior Library Assistant, King's College London.
[66153] 04/10/2006 **CM29/05/2013**

Morland, Mrs M, MA, Librarian, Boston University.
[10032328] 17/06/2009 **ME**

Morley, Mrs J E, MA DipLib MCLIP, Lib. (Job Share), Hyndland Secondary School, Glasgow.
[40196] 27/10/1986 **CM14/03/1990**

Morley, Miss S A, Information specialist, Integron, Bristol.
[61282] 08/05/2002 **ME**

Moron, Miss A B, MA, Systems Librarian, Bishop Grosseteste University, Lincoln.
[10022303] 05/02/2013 **ME**

Moroney, Ms M S, MA MSc MCLIP, Strategy Manager, Hertfordshire County Council.
[41538] 14/01/1988 **CM19/06/1991**

Morrey, Ms E E, BA (Hons) MSc, Librarian, Wilmslow Library, Cheshire East Council.
[10009316] 04/09/2013 **ME**

Morrill, Mrs L M, ACLIP, Lib. Assistant, Roedean School, Brighton.
[10013120] 05/05/2009 **ACL16/06/2010**

Morris, Mrs B G, BA (Hons), Deputy Librarian, Southport & Ormskirk NHS Trust.
[58036] 18/10/1999 **ME**

Morris, Ms D, MA BA MLib MCLIP, Academic Liaison Librarian, Hartley Library, University of Southampton.
[39026] 28/10/1985 **CM14/11/1991**

Morris, Mrs D, BA MCLIP, Retired.
[29519] 12/09/1978 **CM16/10/1980**

Morris, Ms D L, BA (Hons) MCLIP, Lib. Systems Team Manager, Leeds Metro. University.
[48454]　　　　13/01/1993　　**RV**28/01/2009　　**CM13/03/2002**

Morris, Ms E, BA ACLIP, Senior Librarian, Worth School.
[10022951]　　　　　　　　14/05/2013　　　　　**ME**

Morris, Mrs E L, BA DipLib MCLIP, Learning and Development Officer, East Dunbartonshire Leisure and Culture Trust.
[33083]　　　　　　　　03/10/1980　　**CM26/01/1984**

Morris, Mr G, BA DipLib MCLIP, Retired.
[60321]　　　　　　　　21/10/1992　　**CM21/10/1992**

Morris, Mrs G L, BA (Hons) DipILS MCLIP, Nee Gill White. Had a career break to bring up my children. Now working part time as a library assistant.
[51175]　　　　　　　　23/11/1994　　**CM15/03/2000**

Morris, Ms H, BA (Hons) MCLIP, Assistant Librarian, International Institute for Strategic Studies (IISS).
[29198]　　　　　　　　17/04/1978　　**CM29/08/1980**

Morris, Mrs I G, BA (Hons) PgDip, Community Library Assistant, Cambridgeshire Libraries (City).
[10011174]　　　　　　　29/09/2008　　　　　**ME**

Morris, Mrs J C, BA DipLib MCLIP, Librarian, Reader & Information Services, Oxford Central Library.
[37027]　　　　　　　　30/01/1984　　**CM14/04/1987**

Morris, Mrs J M, BA DipLib MCLIP, Assistant Librarian, Sibthorp Library, Bishop Grosseteste University College.
[32437]　　　　　　　　07/04/1980　　**CM27/09/1982**

Morris, Miss J M, BA DipLib MCLIP,
[30490]　　　　　　　　29/01/1979　　**CM27/02/1981**

Morris, Mr J T, Unwaged.
[57002]　　　　　　　　19/11/1998　　　　　**ME**

Morris, Ms L A, DipLib, Head of Records and Information Governance Services, Western Health & Social Care Trust.
[31391]　　　　　　　　04/10/1979　　　　　**ME**

Morris, Mr L D, BA (Hons) MSc Econ MCLIP, Academic & Information Services Librarian, Leeds Beckitt University.
[10013647]　　　　　　　18/05/2009　　**CM15/07/2014**

Morris, Ms M, MSc, Information Centre Manager, Bevan Brittan, Bristol.
[46982]　　　　　　　　25/03/1992　　　　　**ME**

Morris, Ms M E, BA MCLIP, Retired.
[20208]　　　　　　　　29/01/1973　　**CM27/07/1977**

Morris, Mrs M L, MCLIP, Retired.
[10455]　　　　　　　　01/01/1941　　**CM01/01/1944**

Morris, Ms R E, LLB (Hons) LLM, Researcher, Freshfields Bruckhaus Deringer, London.
[62137]　　　　　　　　28/02/2003　　　　　**ME**

Morris, Mrs S J, BSc (Hons) MSc MCLIP, Team Lib.
[55553]　　　　　　　　21/10/1997　　**CM13/11/2013**

Morris, Mrs V H, BA, Europe PubMed Central Service Support Officer, British Library.
[10014563]　　　　　　　17/08/2009　　　　　**ME**

Morris, Mrs W D, BSc MCLIP, Senior Information Advisor, Kingston University.
[28704]　　　　　　　　12/01/1978　　**CM26/08/1982**

Morris, Mrs W J, Enquiry Assistant, Newbury Central Library.
[65723]　　　　　　　　06/04/2006　　　　　**ME**

Morris, Miss Y, MA MCLIP, Policy Officer, CILIP, London.
[65484]　　　　　　　　24/02/2006　　**CM09/09/2009**

Morris Powley, Mrs C, BA, Library and Information Officer, Clinical Library, Sandwell General Hospital.
[10021630]　　　　　　　14/09/2012　　　　　**AF**

Morrison, Mrs A E, BA DipLib MCLIP, Team Leader, Fine Art and Music Collections, Central Library, Edinburgh.
[33248]　　　　　　　　28/10/1980　　**CM07/03/1985**

Morrison, Mr A J, BLib MCLIP, Business Support Manager, London Borough of Lewisham.
[29405]　　　　　　　　01/07/1978　　**CM22/10/1981**

Morrison, Mrs D, MA DipLib MCLIP, Librarian, University of Edinburgh Business School, Edinburgh.
[26067]　　　　　　　　10/06/1976　　**CM03/10/1979**

Morrison, Mr D A, MA (Hons) BSc (Hons) DipLib MBPs FHEA MCLIP, Technology Tutor, Glasgow.
[38708]　　　　　　　　01/10/1985　　**CM16/02/1988**

Morrison, Dr D J, BA MA PhD, Lib. /Arch., Worcester Cathedral Library, Worcester.
[61448]　　　　　　　　22/07/2002　　　　　**AF**

Morrison, Miss J C, MCLIP, Retired.
[10476]　　　　　　　　09/03/1962　　**CM01/01/1966**

Morrison, Ms L J, MA (Hons) MSc MCLIP, Research Executive, Scottish Enterprise.
[10006481]　　　　　　　24/10/2007　　**CM13/11/2013**

Morrison, Mrs P S, BA (Hons) MCLIP, Outreach Librarian, Aberdeenshire L. & Information Serv., Oldmeldrum.
[52633]　　　　　　　　16/11/1995　　**CM06/04/2005**

Morrison, Mrs R A L, MCLIP, Retired.
[1778]　　　　　　　　08/02/1962　　**CM01/01/1966**

Morrison, Mr V R, MCLIP, Retired.
[60555]　　　　　　　　22/10/1975　　**CM14/09/1981**

Morrisroe, Ms K L, BA (Hons) DipILS, Business Librarian, Wrexham L.
[61879]　　　　　　　　20/11/2002　　　　　**ME**

Morrissey, Miss S, BSc, Student, Robert Gordon University.
[10032795]　　　　　　　10/06/2014　　　　　**ME**

Morris-Spicer, Mrs T M, BSc (Hons), Student.
[66082]　　　　　　　　01/10/2006　　　　　**ME**

Morsi, Miss T, BA, Coordinator, Research & Development Unit, Arabic Bibliographic Standards Department, Bibliotheca Alexandrina.
[10022782]　　　　　　　20/10/2014　　　　　**ME**

Morter, Mr G M B, BA (Hons) MSc, Librarian, Planning Inspectorate Library, Bristol.
[10007219]　　　　　　　27/07/2012　　　　　**ME**

Mortimer, Ms J R, BA DMS DipLib MCLIP, Head of Academic Liaison and Administration, De Montfort University, Leicester.
[39400]　　　　　　　　22/01/1986　　**CM16/02/1988**

Mortimer, Ms M A, MCLIP,
[10015949]　　　　　　　21/03/1962　　**CM01/01/1966**

Mortimer, Mrs Z C, CertEd, Lib. (Sch.), Bryanston School, Blandford, Dorset.
[53135]　　　　　　　　01/04/1996　　　　　**AF**

Morton, Mrs A R, ECDL ACLIP,
[10016957]　　　　　　　10/06/2010　　**ACL13/04/2011**

Morton, Mr B, Information Professional, Ministry of Defence.
[10034297]　　　　　　　02/07/2014　　　　　**ME**

Morton, Ms E A, BA (Hons) MCLIP, Librarian, Falkirk Public Library.
[39960]　　　　　　　　04/10/1986　　**CM26/07/1995**

Morton, Mrs J, BA (Hons) MCLIP, Comm. Information Officer, North Yorks. County Council, Ripon Library & Information Centre.
[55607]　　　　　　　　24/10/1997　　**CM06/04/2005**

Morton, Ms J, MA MCLIP FHEA, Library Learning Advisor, University of Leeds.
[25485]　　　　　　　　27/01/1976　　**CM29/09/1983**

Morton, Mr J C, BA Dip IM, Acquisitions Manager, National Art Library, V&A Museum, London.
[10017090]　　　　　　　27/10/1982　　　　　**ME**

Morton, Mr N J, BA PgDipILM, Learning Resource Manager, Manchester Enterprise Academy, Manchester.
[57446]　　　　　　　　01/04/1999　　　　　**ME**

Morton, Miss S L, MA (Hons) MCLIP, School Librarian, John Paul
Academy, Glasgow.
[64156]   19/01/2005   **CM17/09/2008**

Moses-Allison, Mrs L L, BA (Hons) PgDip MSc, Learning Enhancement
Advisor, University of Cumbria.
[10001097]   12/01/2007   **ME**

Moss, Mrs C, MSc, Learning Resources Centre Manager, Thirsk School
& Sixth Form College.
[10028925]   05/09/2014   **ME**

Moss, Ms K, BA (Hons) PGCE PgDip, Library CS Administrator/
Supervisor, University of Manchester.
[10032905]   24/01/2014   **ME**

Moss, Mrs L R, MSc,
[10015813]   29/01/2010   **ME**

Moss, Mrs S G, BA LLB FCLIP, Retired.
[17413]   01/01/1958   **FE01/07/1969**

Moss, Miss T C, BA MCLIP, Info Services Librarian, Hertfordshire P L.
Serv., St Albans.
[29199]   01/04/1978   **CM21/08/1980**

Moss, Mr W, BA MCLIP, Retired.
[10516]   11/01/1965   **CM01/01/1967**

Moss-Gibbons, Ms C A, BLib (Hons) PGCE, Research Officer and
Lecturer in Information Studies, University of Brighton.
[32131]   21/01/1980   **ME**

Moug, Mrs C M, BA (Hons) MCLIP, Resource Centre Coordinator, St
Paul's RC Academy.
[10007131]   27/02/1981   **CM10/10/1985**

Moulden, Miss J, BA FCLIP, Life Member.
[10528]   21/01/1950   **FE01/01/1958**

Moulton, Ms J, BA DipIM MCLIP, Children & Young Persons Librarian,
London Borough of Lewisham.
[53873]   07/10/1996   **CM20/01/1999**

Mount, Ms R J, BA (Hons) PhD DipIS MCLIP, School Librarian, Upper
Shirley High School.
[51118]   16/11/1994   **CM18/03/1998**

Mountford, Ms B A, BA DipLib MCLIP, Service Administrator,
Alzheimer's Society.
[38248]   10/02/1985   **CM14/04/1987**

Mountford, Mrs S J, BA (Hons) MSc (Econ) MCLIP, Comm. Child.
Librarian.
[59014]   25/10/2000   **CM15/09/2004**

Mourad, Mrs R, MCLIP, Academic Liaison Librarian, Glasgow
Caledonian University.
[10000670]   27/10/2006   **CM14/12/2012**

Mousavi-Zadeh, Mrs M S, MA MCLIP, Librarian, Worth Sch.
[59173]   05/12/2000   **CM19/11/2003**

Mousley-Metcalfe, Mrs N, BA (Hons) MSc PgDip MCLIP PgDip,
[62065]   07/02/2003   **CM19/11/2008**

Mowat, Miss M W, BA MLib MCLIP, Senior Librarian, Rowett Res. Inst.,
Aberdeen.
[29077]   25/03/1978   **CM26/08/1982**

Mowbray, Mr J A, Student, University of Strathclyde.
[10034155]   11/06/2014   **ME**

Moxham, Mrs K, ACLIP, Information Officer, Simmons & Simmons,
London.
[10016231]   26/05/2010   **ACL16/01/2014**

Moye, Mrs B F, BSc MSc MCLIP, Healthcare Librarian Barkshire
Healthcare Foundation Trust.
[49632]   15/11/1993   **CM14/03/2012**

Moynagh, Mrs J M, MA DipLib MCLIP, Associate Director Operational
Services, Robert Gordon University, Aberdeen.
[36477]   14/10/1983   **CM27/03/1991**

Mudau, Ms N K, Relief Assistant Lib. /Student, West Sussex County
Council, Chichester.
[10001143]   12/07/2005   **ME**

Muddiman, Mr D J, MSc BA DipLib MCLIP,
[33450]   01/01/1981   **CM16/05/1985**

Muharrem, Ms C, BA (Hons) PgDip, Information Officer, College of Law,
London.
[59027]   23/10/2000   **ME**

Muir, Dr A, MA MSc PhD PgDip FHEA MCLIP, Sr. Lecturer,
Loughborough University.
[45606]   02/04/1991   **CM05/01/1994**

Muir, Mrs H A, BA (Hons) MCLIP, Research Supp. Librarian, Queen
Margaret University, Edinburgh.
[47950]   27/10/1992   **CM31/01/1996**

Muirhead, Mrs A M, BA DiP Lib, Assistant Librarian, Latymer Upper
School.
[10032880]   22/01/2014   **ME**

Mulhern, Mr N P, MA MA DipLIS MCLIP, Librarian, ACU, London.
[50174]   22/04/1994   **CM20/11/2002**

Mulholland, Ms C N, MRPharmS, Unwaged.
[10016218]   05/03/2010   **ME**

Mulholland, Ms E, MA MSc MCLIP, University Library.
[64515]   27/04/2005   **CM11/03/2009**

Mullan, Mr J P, BA (Hons) MCLIP, KM Systems Manager, Field Fisher
Waterhouse.
[49852]   07/01/1994   **CM22/09/1999**

Mullen, Miss J L, BA (Hons), Deputy Library and Information Services
Manager, Newcastle Hospital NHS Trust, Newcastle upon Tyne.
[57366]   26/02/1999   **ME**

Muller, Mr M, BA, Graduate Trainee Librarian, Royal Botanic Gardens.
[10022404]   26/02/2013   **ME**

Mulvenny, Mrs K A, MA MPhil, Student, University of Strathclyde.
[10035026]   05/09/2014   **ME**

Mumford, Mrs H A, BSc (Hons) PgDipLib MCLIP, Training, Information
& Marketing Manager, ERA Technology. Leatherhead Surrey KT22
7SA.
[33085]   03/10/1980   **CM19/06/1985**

Munasinghe, Mrs A I, BA MCLIP, Retired.
[20148]   25/01/1973   **CM30/12/1977**

Munday, O, Student, UCL, London.
[10028947]   16/10/2013   **ME**

Mundill, Mrs E, MA DipLib MCLIP, Part-time School Librarian,
Glenalmond College, Perth.
[33775]   23/02/1981   **CM14/02/1984**

Mungur, Mrs L R,
[10020320]   19/01/2012   **ME**

Muniz, Mr T, BA MSc MCLIP, Unwaged.
[63304]   08/04/2004   **CM31/01/2007**

Munks, Miss E J, BA (Hons) DipLib MCLIP, Academic Support
Librarian, York St John University, Fountains Learning Centre.
[42244]   13/10/1988   **CM23/09/1998**

Munks, Miss S L, BA PgDip, Liaison Librarian, Leeds Trinity University.
[59680]   31/07/2001   **ME**

Munn, Mrs S, Student, Robert Gordon University.
[10035442]   14/10/2014   **ME**

Munns, Mrs K, BLib MCLIP, Librarian: Reader Services Adults,
Oxfordshire.
[34975]   24/05/1982   **CM12/02/1985**

Munro, Mr C, Student, University of Strathclyde.
[10035547]   17/10/2014   **ME**

Munro, Mrs C H, BA (Hons) MCLIP, Unemployed.
[34470]   16/11/1981   **CM16/10/1991**

Munro, Miss E, BA MA PGCE MPhil, Library Assistant, Reading
Borough Council.
[10033165]   18/02/2014   ME
Munro, Ms G, Pg Dip LIS, Information Officer, Scotland's Commissioner
for Children and Young People.
[10012179]   11/01/1996   ME
Munro, Mr J A J, MCLIP, Retired.
[10576]   22/05/1950   CM01/01/1953
Munro, Ms J H, MSc MBA ARCS MCLIP, Head, University Library &
Collections Services, and University Librarian, University of Reading.
[60556]   16/11/1977   CM19/05/1980
Munro, Mrs J M, BA MCLIP, Retired.
[10577]   17/07/1956   CM01/01/1963
Munro, Mr N, DESCIO-Exp-2, Ministry of Defence.
[10033964]   14/05/2014   ME
Munro, Mrs R J, MCLIP, Life Member.
[10581]   12/02/1943   CM01/01/1945
Munsey, Ms S C, Student, David Young Community Academy.
[10032991]   03/02/2014   ME
Munslow, Mrs A, Student, Cranfield University.
[10034157]   11/06/2014   ME
Munslow, Miss A M, MCLIP, Retired.
[10586]   20/01/1965   CM01/01/1969
Murariu, Miss M, BA, Librarian, LSBF, London.
[10020260]   11/09/2012   ME
Murawski, Mrs M,
[10017389]   13/08/2010   AF
Murch, Miss K A, BA (Hons), Librarian, Transport for London.
[10008498]   02/04/2008   ME
Murdoch, Mrs J F, MA DipLib MCLIP, Network Librarian, Aberdeenshire
Council, Ellon Academy.
[36505]   11/10/1983   CM04/08/1987
Murdoch, Mrs J M, BA MCLIP, Network Librarian, Nairn High Life
Highland.
[39562]   04/03/1986   CM19/06/1991
Murdoch, Mrs S A, BSc, Librarian & Careers Co-ordinator, Fernhill
School & Language College., Hants.
[63561]   14/06/2004   ME
Murdoch, Mr S G, BSc (Hons) MCLIP, Community Librarian,
Bloomsbury Library, Birmingham City Council.
[25179]   04/12/1975   CM19/04/1979
Murgatroyd, Ms D C, BA MCLIP, Head of Knowledge and Intranet
Services, Foreign & Commonwealth Office, London.
[35465]   22/10/1982   CM22/10/1985
Muris, Mr C, MA FCLIP, Retired.
[10594]   21/03/1952   FE01/01/1957
Murphy, Miss A M, Team Leader Ctr. for the Child, Birmingham Central
L.
[65403]   24/02/2006   AF
Murphy, Mr B, BA MCLIP, Retired.
[10601]   08/04/1970   CM26/10/1973
Murphy, Mr B P, BA MA MCLIP, Retired.
[35141]   30/09/1982   CM10/10/1983
Murphy, Mrs C, MSc (Econ) BA (Hons), Stock Development Project
Officer, Somerset Libraries Centre.
[10000194]   14/11/2008   ME
Murphy, Ms C A, BA (Hons) MCLIP, Intelligence Officer, Leicestershire
Police.
[28863]   16/01/1978   CM29/04/1986
Murphy, Ms E J, BA DipLIS, Assistant Librarian – General Collections &
Finance, The Library, Maynooth University, Maynooth, Co. Kildare,
Ireland.
[48746]   05/05/1993   ME

Murphy, Miss E L, BA MA MCLIP, Academic Liaison Librarian,
University of Westminster.
[65056]   24/10/2005   CM14/11/2012
Murphy, Mrs H, BSc MSc, Assistant Academic Librarian, Teesside
University, Middlesbrough.
[53479]   01/07/1996   ME
Murphy, Ms H E, MA MTh MThRes MSc (Econ) MCLIP, Assistant
Librarian.
[10020462]   20/02/2012   CM20/02/2014
Murphy, Miss I, MA (Hons), Student The University of Strathclyde.
[10032285]   13/11/2013   ME
Murphy, Miss J C, Student, The London Library.
[10035614]   23/10/2014   ME
Murphy, Mr J J, BA MCLIP, Reg. Librarian, Ministry of Justice,
Liverpool.
[19673]   30/10/1972   CM07/01/1976
Murphy, Mr K, Student, Aberystwyth Uni, Wales.
[10016175]   17/02/2010   ME
Murphy, Miss K A, BA (Hons) ACLIP, Information Services Librarian,
East Area Hertfordshire.
[10017097]   23/06/2010   ACL13/04/2011
Murphy, Miss L A, BSc (Econ) MCLIP, Res. Editor, Good Practice,
Edinburgh.
[54504]   02/01/1997   CM15/05/2002
Murphy, Mrs M, ACLIP, Librarian, Islamic College, Willesden, London.
[10012838]   19/03/2009   ACL14/10/2011
Murphy, Mrs M, BA (Hons) MSc MCLIP, Senior Librarian, Denton
UKMEA LLP, London.
[57128]   17/12/1998   CM21/05/2008
Murphy, Mr M, MLIS,
[10034761]   14/08/2014   ME
Murphy, Miss M E, BA (Hons) DipLib MCLIP, Principal Librarian:
Customers & Communities.
[43313]   18/10/1989   CM23/03/1993
Murphy, Mrs M K, MCLIP, Retired.
[10604]   19/03/1956   CM01/01/1962
Murphy, Mr P, BA LLB MA PGDE, Student, Aberystwyth University.
[10032622]   20/12/2013   ME
Murphy, Miss P C, BA (Hons) MA DipLib PGCE MCLIP,
[37920]   17/10/1984   CM15/11/1988
Murphy, Miss S, BA (Hons) MA MCLIP, L. Executive, House of
Commons, London.
[59964]   12/11/2001   CM11/03/2009
Murphy, Ms Y, MSSc BA DipEd, College Librarian, Keble College,
Oxford.
[42128]   05/10/1988   ME
Murr, Mrs S L, MCLIP, Branch Librarian, Churston, Devon.
[25364]   07/01/1976   CM26/02/1981
Murray, Miss A M, BLib MCLIP,
[31910]   21/01/1980   CM16/08/1982
Murray, Mrs A R, BA MCLIP, Service Support Officer, East
Dunbartonshire Council.
[10017563]   03/11/1981   CM05/12/1985
Murray, Ms C, MA, Librarian at Queen Elizabeth's School for Boys,
Barnet.
[10021977]   08/11/2012   ME
Murray, Mrs L, MA (Hons), Student, University of Glasgow.
[10034755]   13/08/2014   ME
Murray, Mr N F, MA (Hons) MCLIP, Information Specialist, Librarian,
European Parliament, Brussels.
[50309]   14/06/1994   CM19/11/2003
Murray, Mrs P, BA, Student, University of Ulster.
[10034911]   21/08/2014   ME

Murray, Mrs R A, BA MA MCLIP, Retired.
[7590]   07/01/1957   **CM01/01/1965**
Murray, Ms S, BSc DipLib MCLIP MA, Head of Library Service,
Liverpool Hope University.
[42305]   17/10/1988   **CM21/07/1993**
Murray, Dr S J, Research Assistant, Queen Margaret University,
Edinburgh.
[54681]   19/02/1997   **ME**
Murray, Miss V L, BA (Hons), Business Intelligence Services Manager,
Edwards Wildman Palmer UK LLD.
[59980]   15/11/2001   **ME**
Murrell, Mrs J L, BA (Hons) DipLib MCLIP, Librarian., Bromley High
School GDST.
[37265]   21/05/1984   **CM03/03/1987**
Mussell, Ms J, BA DipLib MCLIP,
[44433]   08/10/1990   **CM21/07/1993**
Mustafa, Ms E, BA (Hons) PgDipInfSc,
[46105]   01/10/1991   **ME**
Mustard, Miss C A, BEd PgDip MCLIP, Subject Liaison Librarian,
Brunel University.
[59516]   18/04/2001   **CM21/06/2006**
Mustieles-Salvador, Miss M, Student, Aberystwyth University.
[10034160]   11/06/2014   **ME**
Muszynski, Mrs M C, BA, Library Services Co-ordinator, NHS Fife.
[10000622]   20/10/2006   **ME**
Mutch, Mrs L K, BSc (Econ), Library Officer, Moray College UHI, Elgin.
[58220]   16/11/1999   **ME**
Muyawala, Miss C T, BA LIS, Knowledge Management Coordinator,
National HIV/AIDS/STI/TB Council.
[10021573]   10/07/1995   **ME**
Mwanga, Mr R L, BA, Business Information Officer, Malawi Investment
& Trade Centre.
[10022902]   07/05/2013   **ME**
Mwangi, Mr A M, Student, Robert Gordon University.
[10032079]   24/10/2013   **ME**
Mwangi Muritu, Mr J, Director, Express Management Services.
[10034731]   12/08/2014   **ME**
Mwangola, Mrs H M, Custoemr Service Assistant (Library), Croydon
College.
[10031445]   06/08/2013   **ME**
Myall, Mrs N J, BA (Hons), Knowledge & Information Agent, Sevenoaks,
Kent.
[58377]   26/01/2000   **ME**
Myall, Mr R, BA MA MCLIP, Library Manager, Haywards Heath Library,
West Sussex County Council. RH16 1BN.
[43233]   10/10/1989   **CM19/06/1991**
Myatt, Mrs E J, BA MCLIP, PT Lib. & House Tutor at The Royal Hospital
School, Ipswich.
[28777]   23/01/1978   **CM18/07/1991**
Mycock, Miss J V, BA (Hons) PgDip,
[10018456]   21/01/2011   **ME**
Mydrau, Mr N F, BA MCLIP, Retired.
[10641]   29/02/1972   **CM19/09/1977**
Myer, Mrs S, BA MA PGCLTHE MCLIP FHEA, Learning Hub Manager,
Teesside University.
[10013013]   03/11/1986   **CM15/11/1988**
Myers, Mrs C E, BA (Hons) MA MCLIP, Outreach Officer, London
Borough of Lewisham.
[54815]   08/04/1997   **CM15/05/2002**
Myers, Miss S, BA, Assistant Subject Librarian (Life & Social Sciences),
University of Chester.
[10016121]   18/02/2010   **ME**

Myford, Miss M A, Lib. Assist., Aiglon College Library, Chesieres,
Switzerland.
[10019692]   25/08/2011   **ME**
Myhill, Mrs J L, BA (Hons) DipLIS MCLIP ILTHE, Hd. of Academic
Liaison, University of Beds.
[47888]   22/10/1992   **CM13/03/2002**
Myhill, Mrs L F, BA DipLib MCLIP, School Librarian, Chatham &
Clarendon Grammar School, Ramsgate.
[41910]   17/05/1988   **CM19/06/1991**
Myhill, Mr R P, BA,
[10016478]   09/11/1982   **ME**
Mylles, Mr M, MCLIP, Information Manager, University of Hertfordshire,
Hatfield.
[38928]   17/10/1985   **CM15/05/1990**

N

Nadaj, Ms D M, MA, Self-employed+F9560.
[10006694]   21/11/2007   **ME**
Nagle, Ms M E, PT Library Assistant, York Minster Library, The Old
Palace, York.
[10020659]   15/03/2012   **AF**
Naglls, Ms S, BA PhD, Library Assistant, Royal Faculty of Procurators.
[10011557]   27/10/2008   **ME**
Nahal, Mrs H C, BLib MCLIP, Senior Lib. Digital and Information Serv.,
Telford & Wrekin Libraries.
[35097]   09/08/1982   **CM03/03/1987**
Nail, Mr M, MA DipLib MCLIP, Unemployed.
[19985]   08/01/1973   **CM15/01/1975**
Nair, Mrs R, BA MCLIP, Library Services Manager(Job Share).,
Tameside Hospitals, NHS Foundation Trust.
[12837]   01/01/1966   **CM01/01/1969**
Nairn, Mr W K, MSc MCLIP, Senior Librarian – Adult Services., Scottish
Borders L. & Information Servs., Selkirk.
[10001331]   22/02/2007   **CM11/03/2009**
Naish, Mr P J, BA MLib MCLIP, Acquisitions Manager, University of
Bedfordshire.
[39630]   11/04/1986   **CM12/09/1990**
Naismith, Mrs R, BLib MCLIP, Part-time. Learning Resource Assistant
for Sixth Form Study Ctr. /Library.
[40601]   05/04/1987   **CM14/11/1991**
Nakane, Mr K, Retired.
[51661]   01/01/1995   **ME**
Nakayama, Mr C, Assistant Professor, Tokiwa University.
[10034218]   24/06/2014   **ME**
Namponya, Mr C, BInf MPhil, Director, University of the Free State
Library, South Africa.
[10009329]   25/08/1967   **ME**
Nangle, Mrs S, MA (Hons) PgDip ILS, Academic Liaison Librarian.
[64433]   18/03/2005   **ME**
Nankivell, Ms A M P, BA (Hons) MA, Student Charles Sturt University
NSW.
[10032282]   13/11/2013   **ME**
Nankivell, Mr B, BSc (Hons) DipILS MCLIP, Community Librarian,
Trowbridge Library, Wiltshire.
[53875]   07/10/1996   **CM17/05/2000**
Nanthakumar, Mrs K, MSc, Library Service Manager, London Borough
of Lambeth.
[10021775]   10/10/2012   **ME**
Napier, Mrs P E N, BA, Retired.
[30017]   30/10/1978   **CM29/07/1983**
Napper, Mr C J, BA DipLib MCLIP, Retired.
[30857]   10/05/1979   **CM07/02/1985**

Napper, Mrs J, BA MCLIP, Team Librarian, Adult & Comm. Serv., Beds. Co. L., Biggleswade.
[30091]　　　　　　　　　　05/01/1979　　**CM07/09/1981**

Nash, Mrs J L, BA (Hons), Post-Graduate Student, Manchester Metropolitan University, Manchester.
[10032297]　　　　　　　　14/11/2013　　　　　**ME**

Nash, Mrs V R, BA MCLIP, Retired.
[17435]　　　　　　　　　　17/01/1966　　**CM01/01/1969**

Nashwalder, Mrs K, MSc (Econ), Librarian, Salisbury Library, Wiltshire.
[10014058]　　　　　　　　01/07/2009　　　　　**ME**

Nason, Mrs G, BSc MSc MCLIP MRSC CChem CSci, Programme Manager, MRC.
[52371]　　　　　　　　　　26/10/1995　　**CM15/09/2004**

Nason, J, Student Digital Library and information Science Masters Programme University of Boras Sweden.
[10032406]　　　　　　　　03/12/2013　　　　　**ME**

Nathan, Miss A R, Information Centre Assistant, DSTL Portsdown West, Fareham.
[63583]　　　　　　　　　　23/06/2004　　　　　**AF**

Nathan, Miss O R, MA PgCert Ed,
[10033599]　　　　　　　　01/04/2014　　　　　**ME**

Nattriss, Mr J B, BA FCLIP, Life Member.
[10672]　　　　　　　　　　15/03/1953　　**FE01/01/1958**

Naylor, Dr B, MA DipLib FRSA MCLIP, Retired.
[10680]　　　　　　　　　　23/10/1963　　**CM01/01/1969**

Naylor, Mrs C A, MCLIP, Retired Librarian.
[23582]　　　　　　　　　　13/01/1975　　**CM11/01/1978**

Naylor, Mr G, BA (Hons), Group Manager (Central – Information)., Plymouth Central Library.
[10013394]　　　　　　　　27/11/2002　　　　　**ME**

Naylor, Miss J, Resources Management Librarian, Teesside University.
[10010375]　　　　　　　　21/03/2012　　　　　**ME**

Naylor, Ms L, BA (Hons) MA, L. Assistant (Business L.), Nottingham Central Library, Notts.
[10005114]　　　　　　　　13/06/2007　　　　　**ME**

Naylor, Mr M A, MA MCLIP, School Librarian, Thornhill Community Academy, Thornhill.
[65362]　　　　　　　　　　27/01/2006　　**CM11/06/2010**

Neal, Mr G P, Employment not known.
[38445]　　　　　　　　　　03/05/1985　　　　　**ME**

Neal, Mrs J M, ACLIP, L. Serv. Adv., Hucknall Library, Nottingham.
[10018276]　　　　　　　　10/12/2010　　**ACL14/03/2012**

Neal, Miss R, Partnership Librarian, Castle Manor Academy.
[10033904]　　　　　　　　12/05/2014　　　　　**AF**

Nealon, Ms L A, DipLib MCLIP, Sch. L. Resource Centre for Coordinator, Edinburgh Council/St Thomas of Aquins School, Edinburgh.
[37657]　　　　　　　　　　15/10/1984　　**CM15/11/1988**

Neath, Mrs C Y, BA (Hons) MA MCLIP, Customer Service Librarian, Loughborough Library, Leicestershire County Council.
[59967]　　　　　　　　　　13/11/2001　　**CM04/10/2006**

Neck, Miss E, BA PDip, Senior Librarian, Aberdare Library.
[10013511]　　　　　　　　08/05/2009　　　　　**ME**

Neenan, Mrs J, BA (Hons) MA MCLIP, Information Advisor., UWIC, Cardiff.
[54397]　　　　　　　　　　03/12/1996　　**CM10/07/2002**

Neeve, Mrs M P, BLib MCLIP, Teaching Assistant, Essex County Council.
[2507]　　　　　　　　　　17/03/1970　　**CM18/12/1974**

Negueruela, Miss M J, BA,
[10019860]　　　　　　　　29/09/2011　　　　　**ME**

Negus, Mr A E, MA FCLIP, Retired.
[10714]　　　　　　　　　　20/07/1964　　**FE01/04/2002**

Neill, Miss G H, Student, University of Strathclyde.
[10035488]　　　　　　　　15/10/2014　　　　　**ME**

Neill, Mr M, MA, Unwaged.
[10021161]　　　　　　　　13/06/2012　　　　　**ME**

Neilson, Mr D T, MA (Hons) DipLib MCLIP, Retired.
[10010128]　　　　　　　　30/09/1977　　**CM10/07/1981**

Neilson, Ms S, BA (Hons) MA, Business Subject Librarian.
[10019934]　　　　　　　　05/10/2011　　　　　**ME**

Nelmes, Mrs D A, BA (Hons), Senior Service Development Assistant.
[10020291]　　　　　　　　09/01/2012　　　　　**AF**

Nelson, Mrs G J, BA DipLib MCLIP, Schools & Library Advisor, Dorset School Library Service.
[35420]　　　　　　　　　　01/10/1982　　**CM17/01/1990**

Nelson, Ms M, BA MSc, Health Research Board, Dublin, Ireland.
[10022743]　　　　　　　　16/04/2013　　　　　**ME**

Nelson, Mrs P E, BA MCLIP, Information Manager., Business Intelligence., Savills plc.
[25587]　　　　　　　　　　29/01/1976　　**CM10/09/1982**

Nelson, Mr S A, BA DipLib MCLIP, Learning Centre Assistant Manager, City & Islington College, London.
[40808]　　　　　　　　　　22/06/1987　　**CM09/09/2009**

Nelson, Mrs S E, MCLIP, Retired.
[23420]　　　　　　　　　　07/01/1975　　**CM12/08/1977**

Nelson, Mrs S T, BA MCLIP, Retired.
[20658]　　　　　　　　　　01/01/1973　　**CM21/11/2001**

Nemanyte, Miss L,
[10032107]　　　　　　　　28/10/2013　　　　　**ME**

Nemeth, Miss Z, Senior Librarian Assistant WRF.
[10019421]　　　　　　　　29/06/2011　　　　　**ME**

Nephin, Ms E L, BA (Hons)PGCHE MSc MCLIP FHEA, Library Academic Support Team Manager, Leeds Beckett University.
[61807]　　　　　　　　　　11/11/2002　　**CM19/11/2008**

Nesaratnam, Mrs J A, BA MCLIP, Senior Reader Serv. Librarian, Herefordshire Libs.
[35021]　　　　　　　　　　09/06/1982　　**CM01/10/1986**

Nesta, Dr F, PhD, Senior Lecturer, MA LIS Programme, UCL, Qatar.
[10034580]　　　　　　　　22/07/2014　　　　　**ME**

Nesterovic, Mrs G, PgDip, Senior Library Assistant, University of Strathclyde.
[64077]　　　　　　　　　　15/12/2004　　　　　**ME**

Nettleton, Mrs S J, BA (Hons), Librarian, - Moreton Morrell Centre, Warwicks. College, Warwick.
[33653]　　　　　　　　　　19/01/1981　　　　　**ME**

Nevard, Ms K, BA, Information Specialist, NSPCC.
[34639]　　　　　　　　　　22/01/1982　　**CM13/06/1989**

Nevill, Mr C D, BA (Hons), Learning Resources Manager, St James School, Exeter.
[10018757]　　　　　　　　07/03/2011　　　　　**ME**

Neville, Miss K E, BA DipLib MCLIP, Stock Serv. Manager, Derbyshire County Council.
[36374]　　　　　　　　　　04/10/1983　　**CM05/05/1987**

Neville, Ms L S C, BA (Hons), Assistant Librarian, Royal College of Art, London.
[46113]　　　　　　　　　　01/10/1991　　　　　**ME**

Newall, Ms E, BA (Hons) MA MCLIP, Senior Librarian (Teaching and Learning Support), University of Nottingham.
[52171]　　　　　　　　　　10/10/1995　　**CM20/01/1999**

Newbold, Mrs F M, BLib (Hons) MCLIP, Head of Res. & Information Serv., Presdales School, Ware.
[28373]　　　　　　　　　　01/10/1977　　**CM04/12/1982**

Newbold, Mrs G, BA (Hons) MA MCLIP, Head of Information Serv., Astrium Ltd.
[63913]　　　　　　　　　　26/10/2004　　**CM17/06/2011**

Newbury, Mrs J I, MCLIP, Retired.
[10745] 13/10/1964 **CM01/01/1969**
Newell, Mr G G, BA, Higher Library Executive, House of Commons.
[41158] 09/10/1987 **ME**
Newgass, Mrs O R, MCLIP, Information Consultant, Dartmouth.
[40737] 22/05/1987 **CM01/04/2002**
Newham, Ms H, MCLIP, Management Consultant, HNA, Windrush, The
Ridgeway, Enfield.
[16036] 25/08/1964 **CM01/01/1970**
Newiss, Miss J, MA MCLIP, Hon. Librarian, Thoresby Society.
[10755] 23/01/1960 **CM01/01/1962**
Newlove, Mrs C, BA MCLIP, Part-time Librarian, Taylor Vinters
Solicitors, Cambridge.
[32999] 01/10/1980 **CM20/03/1987**
Newman, Mr C, BA DipLib MCLIP, Assistant Librarian, City of London
Library, Information Services Section, Guildhall Library.
[37923] 19/11/1984 **CM18/04/1990**
Newman, Mrs L E, FCLIP, Retired.
[60564] 11/12/2001 **FE01/04/2002**
Newman, Miss L J M, MA BA (Hons), Librarian, BSix Sixth Form
College, London.
[10022517] 19/03/2013 **ME**
Newman, Mrs L M, BA PhD MCLIP, Retired.
[10765] 06/01/1964 **CM01/01/1968**
Newman, Mr M, MCLIP BSc MBCS MIfA FSA FRSA, Datasets Dev.
Manager, English Heritage, Swindon.
[10018375] 20/05/2011 **CM11/04/2013**
Newman, Miss M K, BA (Hons) MCLIP, Assistant Learning Resource
Manager, Lewisham College, London.
[63899] 26/10/2004 **CM07/09/2011**
Newman, Mrs N B, BA (Hons) DipInf MCLIP, Head Librarian, St
Andrews Hospital, Northampton.
[47690] 15/10/1992 **CM31/01/1996**
Newman, Mrs S, BA DipLib MCLIP,
[37786] 26/10/1984 **CM18/04/1990**
Newsome, Miss J, Subject Librarian., Doncaster College.
[56439] 13/07/1998 **ME**
Newson, Mr B A R, MCLIP, Retired.
[10775] 17/04/1956 **CM01/01/1969**
Newton, Miss A J, BA (Hons) MA MCLIP, Library Learning Adviser.
[55772] 18/11/1997 **CM10/07/2002**
Newton, Mrs C J, BA MA FRSA, Former Director of Collections &
Research, National Library of Scotland, Edinburgh.
[21288] 14/10/1973 **ME**
Newton, Mrs J M, MCLIP, Retired.
[2325] 22/06/1970 **CM16/07/1973**
Newton, Mrs K, BSc (Hons) ACLIP, Hub Services Manager, Sunderland
Public Libraries.
[45188] 06/08/1990 **ACL05/05/2005**
Newton, Ms M, BA MCLIP, Lib. & Archivist, Mount St Mary's College.
[44913] 14/01/1991 **CM18/11/1993**
Newton, Mrs R, BA MCLIP, Staff Resources Co-ordinator, Imperial
College, London.
[10012856] 23/10/1987 **CM01/07/1994**
Newton, Miss V B, BSc DipLib MCLIP, Library & Knowledge Services
Manager, Exeter Health Library, Royal Devon & Exeter NHS
Foundation Trust.
[26996] 19/01/1977 **CM07/02/1979**
Ng, Mr J, Student, Nanyang Technological University.
[10032811] 14/01/2014 **ME**
Ngabia MBE, Mrs A P, BA (Hons) MCLIP, Founder, Kidslibs Trust.
Kenya; School Librarian Grangemouth High School.
[33060] 14/10/1980 **CM11/01/1984**

Nguyen, Ms H A, Student.
[10005972] 18/02/2008 **ME**
Nguyen, Mrs M D, BA, Senior L. Information Officer, Coventry L. &
Information Serv.
[61863] 22/11/2002 **ME**
Ni Chearuil, Ms L, BA MA MLIS,
[10032131] 29/10/2013 **ME**
Nicholas, Miss H, BA, Graduate Trainee Library Support Adviser, Anglia
Ruskin University.
[10035689] 29/10/2014 **ME**
Nicholas, Mr J R, BA MCLIP, Retired.
[10794] 18/09/1963 **CM01/01/1969**
Nicholas, Miss K, BA (Hons), Health Information and Resources Library
Assistant, Manchester Mental Health & Social Care NHS Trust.
[10031792] 15/01/2014 **ME**
Nicholas, Dr R O, PhD MA MSc, Senior Information Scientist, Zoetis,
Sandwich, UK.
[10018697] 21/11/2000 **ME**
Nicholls, Mr D A, BA (Hons) MSc MCLIP, Assistant Information
Specialist, National Institute of Health & Care Excellence.
[62793] 22/10/2003 **CM05/05/2010**
Nicholls, Mrs G, BA MCLIP, Information Specialist, Bucks. County
Library, Bucks.
[33142] 03/10/1980 **CM02/11/1982**
Nicholls, Mrs H T, BA DipLib MCLIP, Lib. /Copyright Manager, AQA,
Manchester.
[23605] 16/01/1975 **CM02/02/1979**
Nicholls, Mrs S, MCLIP, Librarian, Calthorpe Park School, Fleet.
[8330] 22/04/1971 **CM20/11/1974**
Nichols, Mr R M, MCLIP, Retired.
[10812] 12/01/1969 **CM22/07/1975**
Nichols, Ms S J, LIS Manager, Bircham Dyson Bell, London.
[35042] 05/07/1982 **ME**
Nicholson, Ms A, BSc MSc MSc, Graduated.
[10000534] 18/10/2006 **ME**
Nicholson, Miss A, MA (Hons), Network Librarian, High Life Highland
[64733] 08/06/2005 **ME**
Nicholson, Ms A K, BA, Student, Victoria University of Wellington.
[10032490] 17/12/2013 **ME**
Nicholson, Mrs C A, Customer Service Assistant, Central Bedfordshire
Council.
[10033932] 13/05/2014 **AF**
Nicholson, Mr H D, MA hLLD (Hon) MCLIP FRSA, Retired.
[25379] 05/01/1976 **CM11/04/1979**
Nicholson, Ms J, BA MA, Surestart Librarian, Derbyshire County
Council.
[40138] 17/10/1986 **ME**
Nicholson, Miss M, BA MCLIP, Retired.
[10822] 01/01/1961 **CM01/01/1965**
Nicholson, Miss M S, BA (Hons) MA MCLIP, Academic Subject
Librarian, University of Lincoln.
[51877] 24/07/1995 **CM17/09/2003**
Nicholson, Mr N T, MA DipLib, Metadata Manager (Purchases,
Donations and Standards), National Library of Scotland.
[31519] 15/10/1979 **CM12/04/1983**
Nicholson Arnott, Ms D, BA (Hons) MSc, Enquiries Assistant.
[10021678] 27/09/2012 **ME**
Nickell, Mrs C, Student, MSc Information Science. City University
London.
[10035443] 14/10/2014 **ME**
Nicklen, Mr J E, BA (Hons) DipLib MCLIP, Retired.
[28348] 31/10/1977 **CM30/10/1979**
Nicol, Miss A M, MA Pdip, School Librarian, School Library Outreach.
[10015205] 23/10/2009 **ME**

Nicolaides, Ms E, BA DipLib MCLIP, Employment not known.
[35760]   24/01/1983   **CM02/09/1986**
Nicoll, Miss F L, MA DipLIS MCLIP, Senior Development Officer,
Glasgow City Council.
[41639]   05/02/1988   **CM01/12/1994**
Nicolson, Mrs M A S, BA DipLib, YPS Librarian, Shetland Islands
Council, Lerwick.
[27986]   03/10/1977   **CM03/10/1979**
Nicolson, Mr M S, BA MA MCLIP, LRC Manager Havant College,
Hampshire.
[54253]   11/11/1996   **CM19/11/2008**
Nief, Ms R, BA PgDip, Assistant Librarian, Wellcome Trust Library,
London.
[41702]   22/02/1988   **ME**
Nielsen, Ms J, Bibliotekar D. B., Enquiries and Services Team Leader,
Welcome Library, London.
[57860]   13/09/1999   **ME**
Nielsen, Mrs J C, BA (Hons) MA, Administrator.
[55512]   16/10/1997   **ME**
Nielsen, Mrs M E, BA MLib MCLIP, Retired.
[34625]   19/01/1982   **CM12/10/1986**
Nieto Arco, Miss N,
[10035153]   22/09/2014   **ME**
Nieuwold, Ms L, BA MA MCLIP, Self-employed.
[39003]   28/10/1985   **CM15/02/1989**
Niewiadomska, Ms E, MA MCLIP, Information Serv. Manager, British
American Tobacco, Southampton.
[62926]   20/11/2003   **CM09/11/2005**
Nijhoff, Ms A, MLIS BA,
[10019126]   21/04/2011   **ME**
Nik Hussin, Ms N N T, ACLIP, Information Servis. Adv., Queen Margaret
University, Edinburgh.
[10012056]   15/12/2008   **ACL12/02/2010**
Nikoi, Dr S K, PhD MA BLS, Academic Services Librarian, Aberystwyth
University.
[10034728]   12/08/2014   **ME**
Nirasawa, Miss M, PgDip LOMA, Unwaged.
[10018007]   03/11/2010   **ME**
Nisco, Mrs S L, BSc (Hons) MCLIP, Analyst, Knowledge Management.
[49569]   19/11/1993   **CM20/11/2002**
Nitti, Miss C J, BA MA, Access and Inclusion Librarian, Matlock Library,
Derbyshire.
[10015364]   09/11/2009   **ME**
Niven, Ms A S, MA (Hons) DipLib MCLIP, Stock Development Co-ord.,
Mitchell L. Glasgow.
[32137]   10/01/1980   **CM08/12/1982**
Niven, Ms E S, MA (Hons) DipLib MCLIP, School Librarian, Dingwall
Academy, Highland Council.
[32811]   29/09/1980   **CM27/01/1984**
Nixon, Mrs L A, BLib MCLIP, Information Officer, Child. Centre for, City
Hospital, Nottingham.
[23624]   15/01/1975   **CM25/01/1979**
Nixon, Miss M C, BA MA DipLib MCLIP, Librarian, Goldsmiths College,
London.
[21110]   08/10/1973   **CM31/12/1989**
N'Jie, Ms I, BA Honours DPS, Clinical Librarian, Barts Health NHS
Trust, London, United Kingdom.
[58373]   28/01/2000   **ME**
Noake, Ms C, BA MA, Learning Support Librarian, Durham University
Library.
[65545]   24/02/2006   **ME**
Noakes, Mr P,
[10020724]   28/03/2012   **AF**

Noall, Miss C A F, MCLIP, Branch Librarian, Cardiff Library Services.
[10857]   03/03/1972   **CM16/07/1975**
Noble, Ms A, BA DipLib MCLIP, Principal Librarian, Sch. L. Serv.,
Monmouthshire County Council.
[38241]   12/02/1985   **CM22/04/1992**
Noble, Miss A D, MA FCLIP, Retired.
[10858]   27/09/1943   **FE01/01/1965**
Noble, Mrs A H, BA MCLIP, Greenwood Centre Librarian., Greenwood
Centre for, Irvine.
[32271]   24/01/1980   **CM21/03/1984**
Noble, Mrs C J, BA (Hons), Senior Librarian, Technip UK Ltd, Westhill,
Aberdeenshire.
[46063]   10/09/1991   **ME**
Noble, Mrs J, BA MCLIP, Network Lib. at Westhill Academy,
Aberdeenshire L. & Information Serv.
[32500]   13/05/1980   **CM18/08/1983**
Noble-Harrison, Mrs A, BSc MSc MCLIP, Lead Librarian, Swindon
Central Library, Swindon.
[10016925]   16/06/2010   **CM08/03/2013**
Noblett, Mr W A, MA MCLIP, Head Official Publications, Cambridge
University Library.
[21517]   11/10/1973   **CM13/02/1984**
Nock, Miss J, BSc Econ (Hons), Information and Library Studies
Graduate.
[10018853]   23/03/2011   **ME**
Nock, Mr J A, MSc, Student, Robert Gordon University.
[10021582]   04/09/2012   **ME**
Nockels, Mr K H, MA (Hons) DipLib MCLIP FHEA, Learning and
Teaching Services Librarian, University of Leicester.
[39975]   08/10/1986   **CM21/07/1999**
Noel, Miss L M A, Senior Library Assitant.
[10020412]   11/02/2012   **AF**
Nolan, Miss A F, MSocSc hDLIS ALAI, Librarian, Woodfarm High
School Glasgow.
[65928]   10/07/2006   **ME**
Nolan, Mrs C A, BA (Hons) MA MCLIP, Assistant Librarian, The
Ravensbourne School, Bromley.
[56356]   11/06/1998   **CM23/01/2002**
Nolan, Mrs H J, MCLIP, Information Management Librarian, Department
for Work & Pensions, Leeds.
[61156]   15/03/2002   **CM11/03/2009**
Nolan, Miss J, BA (Hons) MA, Community Library Officer, St Helens
Council.
[65671]   07/03/2006   **ME**
Nolan, Miss L, MA, Librarian, The Daily Mail, London.
[10019417]   28/06/2011   **ME**
Nolan, Miss S, BA (Hons) DipLIS MCLIP, Senior Liaison Librarian,
Middlesex University.
[55139]   23/07/1997   **CM07/09/2005**
Nolan, Mrs S R, BA (Hons), Librarian, STV.
[51437]   14/02/1995   **ME**
Nolan, Mr T M, Information Assistant, ICAEW Library, London.
[10007004]   17/12/2007   **ME**
Nonhebel, Ms L, MSc Information Science,
[10031700]   23/07/2014   **ME**
Noon, Mrs G E, BA (Hons) MA, Customer Services Manager, Calgary
Public Library, Canada.
[10019348]   13/06/2011   **ME**
Noon, Mr L, BA, Senior Library Assistant, Central Library, Leeds City
Council.
[10029094]   08/09/2014   **ME**
Noorani, Miss Y, BA MSc MA, Academic Support Officer, Library
Services, Bangor University.
[10021966]   23/11/1994   **AF**

Norbury, Mrs L, BSc MPhil MCLIP, Academic Support Consultant, University of Birmingham, Main Library.
[43001]   02/06/1989   CM15/12/1997
Norman, Mrs G, BA (Hons) MCLIP, Stock & Support Services Manager, Bracknell Forest BoroughCouncil, Bracknell, Berks.
[27573]   18/05/1977   CM24/11/1980
Norman, Ms J, BLib MCLIP, Unwaged.
[38140]   11/01/1985   CM16/09/1992
Norman, Mr J F, BSc DipLib MCLIP, Librarian, National Inst. for Medical Res., London.
[32138]   29/01/1980   CM17/02/1982
Norman, Mr M A, BA (Hons) MCLIP, Strategic Library Manager, Nottinghamshire County Council.
[52365]   26/10/1995   CM19/05/1999
Norman, Ms S A, BA DipLib FCLIP HonFCLIP, Retired.
[32451]   01/04/1980   HFE29/06/2005
Noronha, Miss A P, B Bus MCLIP, Senior Librarian, Edith Cowan University, Western Australia.
[17468]   06/01/1969   CM01/01/1971
Norquay, Ms S, BSc MSc, Assistant Librarian, SIRCC, University of Strathclyde, Glasgow.
[58073]   25/10/1999   ME
Norris, Mrs H E, MA DipLib MCLIP, Librarian, Queen Anne's School, Caversham, Reading.
[32894]   02/10/1980   CM22/12/1982
Norris, Mrs J, Library Assistant, Poole High School.
[10022179]   15/01/2013   AF
Norris, Miss K A, MA (Hons), Student.
[10020853]   19/04/2012   ME
Norry, Miss J, BA MA DipLib FCLIP FHEA, Director of Libraries & Learning Innovation, Leeds Beckett University.
[39205]   01/01/1986   FE07/07/2010
North, Mrs R, BA, Student.
[10006298]   10/10/2007   ME
North, Mr S A, BA (Hons) ACLIP, LRC & ICT Assist., East Surrey College.
[10020042]   27/10/2011   ACL14/03/2012
North, Mrs S L, BA (Hons), Information Advisor, Careers Bradford Ltd.
[56333]   20/05/1998   ME
Northam, Miss J, BA (Hons) MA MCLIP.
[56689]   05/10/1998   CM15/09/2004
Nortje, Mrs C A, BA (Hons) DipIM MCLIP, Unemployed.
[49645]   17/11/1993   CM19/01/2000
Norton, Mr I C, BLIB MCLIP, Information Assstant, Plymouth University.
[21585]   29/10/1973   CM14/02/1977
Norton, Miss J, BSc Econ MCLIP, Librarian, Wilmslow Cheshire.
[10016919]   10/06/2010   CM27/03/2014
Noyes, Mrs K, BSc (Hons) PGCE PgDip, Library Assistant, Derbyshire County Council.
[10029113]   10/02/2014   ME
Nugent, Mr G T, BA (Hons) DipILM MCLIP, Collections Access Team Leader (Libraries), Economy & Culture, Lincolnshire County Council.
[47781]   14/10/1992   CM22/11/1995
Nugent, Miss M C R, MCLIP, Retired.
[10930]   09/09/1957   CM01/01/1962
Nunn, Miss A, Hogan Lovells.
[10020321]   19/01/2012   ME
Nunn, Mrs T A, Business Information Specialist, Cranfield University.
[10033885]   09/05/2014   ME
Nurcombe, Mrs V J, BA MCLIP, Freelance Information Consultant, Cheshire.
[1591]   18/09/1969   CM16/03/1973
Nurse, Mr E B, MA FSA MCLIP, Retired.
[10934]   19/01/1970   CM01/01/1972

Nurse, Mr R A, BA MA MCLIP, Head of Digital Services Development, Open University.
[36443]   14/10/1983   CM16/12/1986
Nuttall, Mr B S, BA MCLIP, Life Member.
[10937]   01/10/1960   CM01/01/1963
Nuttall, Ms P A, BA MLS MCLIP, Unemployed.
[30783]   04/04/1979   CM18/05/1982
Nutting, Mrs D E, BA MCLIP, Retired.
[6196]   08/08/1967   CM01/07/1990
Nwajei, Mrs E F, BA DipComp (Open), Admin. Assistant, H. M. Revenue & Customs, St Austell.
[15177]   01/01/1968   CM01/01/1971
Nwokike, Mr O A, Student, Babcock University, Ilisham Remo, Nigeria.
[10034339]   07/07/2014   ME
Nye, Ms N, BA (Hons) ACLIP, Library Services Coordinator, Exeter College, Exeter.
[64243]   22/02/2005   ACL02/03/2010
Nylinder, Ms A M, BA MA, Librarian, Rivers Academy West London.
[55411]   10/10/1997   ME

O

Oakford, Mrs A, BSc (Hons) MA MCLIP, Systems & Applications Support Advisor, Network Rail.
[10006436]   19/10/2007   CM09/11/2011
Oakley, Mrs A E, BA DipLib MCLIP, Part-time School Librarian, Dame Allans School, Newcastle upon Tyne.
[30387]   08/02/1979   CM09/02/1981
Oakley, Ms H J, BA (Hons) MA MCLIP, Learning Resources Manager, Hillcroft College, Surrey.
[44389]   03/10/1990   CM20/09/1995
Oakley, Mrs J E, BA MCLIP, County Information Librarian, Worthing Library, West Sussex.
[36278]   01/10/1983   CM10/05/1988
Oakley, Dr T C, BA MSt MA MCLIP PhD, Academic Librarian
[49592]   19/11/1993   CM21/07/1999
Oates, Ms J L, BA (Hons) MA MCLIP, Law Lib. &Manager, Research Information Servs. (St Lucia), University of Queensland.
[49233]   14/10/1993   CM22/07/1998
Oates, Mrs M, MCLIP, Life Member.
[10946]   26/03/1944   CM01/01/1949
Obasi, Mr J U, MA MCLIP, Retired.
[10000683]   01/01/1962   CM01/01/1970
O'Beirne, Mr R, BA (Hons) MEd FCLIP SFHEA FRSA, Director Learning Development & Research, Bradford College.
[47150]   12/05/1992   FE23/01/2008
O'Boyle, Mr J, BSc MSc MCLIP, Information Consultant.
[60618]   06/05/1986   CM06/05/1986
Obradovic, Ms C L, BA MA MSc, Information Professional.
[62660]   26/09/2003   ME
O'Brien, Mr B, Student.
[10018316]   01/01/2011   ME
O'Brien, Ms B M, BSc DipLib MCLIP, Street Naming and Property Addressing, Birmingham City Council.
[33735]   09/02/1981   CM23/08/1985
O'Brien, Ms C P, BA DipLib MCLIP, Assistant Librarian – Monograph Acquisitions, University College Cork, Ireland.
[40038]   06/10/1986   CM14/11/1990
O'Brien, Mrs E, BA MCLIP, Life Member.
[10952]   20/02/1960   CM01/01/1963
O'Brien, Miss E C, BA MA MCLIP, Information Specialist, Bazian Ltd (an Economist Intelligence Unit business).
[10012367]   05/02/2009   RV20/06/2014   CM12/09/2012

O'Brien, Mrs E K, MSc BA (Hons), R&D Library & Archives Supervisor, Reckit Benchiser Healthcare UK, Hull.
[10019969]   12/10/2011   ME
O'Brien, Ms F G, MA, Academic Liaison Manager.
[36644]   27/10/1983   CM23/03/1993
O'Brien, Ms G M, MLIS, Sales Assistant, John Morrisons Kiltmakers.
[10035732]   31/10/2014   ME
O'Brien, Mrs I, Lic. Phil. Hist MA, Early Printed Collections Cataloguing & Processing Manager, British Library.
[66056]   11/09/2006   ME
O'Brien, Mrs J A, BA MCLIP DTLLS, Learning Resource Co-ordinator, Kidderminster College, Worcs.
[39386]   21/01/1986   CM14/03/1990
O'Brien, Mrs M P G, BA MCLIP DipHA, Retired.
[11789]   07/11/1970   RV19/10/2006   CM06/08/1975
O'Brien, Mrs P, BA (Hons), Library Manager/Community Librarian, Bognor Regis Library, West Sussex CC.
[29905]   24/10/1978   ME
O'Brien, Mr R A, BA,
[10006360]   23/10/2007   ME
O'Brien, Ms S, BCom MSc, Clerical Assistant/Student, Robert Gordon University.
[10021509]   13/08/2013   ME
O'Brien, Miss S, BSc, Student, University of Sheffield.
[10035489]   16/10/2014   ME
O'Brien-Barden, Mr T, BSc (Hons) MBCS CITP, Information and Knowledge Manager, Northumbria University.
[10032302]   15/11/2013   ME
O'Byrne, S, MCLIP, Information Specialist, Ontario Ministry of the Environment, Canada.
[60093]   04/03/1991   CM16/12/1999
O'Callaghan, Miss E M, BA DipLib MCLIP, Library and Knowledge Services, Kent & Medway Public Health Observatory.
[22944]   01/10/1974   CM03/03/1978
O'Carroll, Ms V C, MCLIP, Stock & Reader Development Librarian, Mid Area2, Herts L. Serv.
[63916]   26/10/2004   CM06/05/2009
Ochigbo, Ms M, MA, Student.
[10003900]   10/10/2007   ME
Ocock, Mr K F, MCLIP, Reference Librarian, Customer Contact Centre, Christchurch City Library, New Zealand.
[10960]   05/10/1970   CM09/07/1973
O'Connor, Ms C, Lib. & Learning & Information Co-ordinator, Islington L. & Heritage Serv., North Library, London.
[10001054]   06/12/2006   ME
O'Connor, Mrs C L, BA (Hons) DipIM MCLIP, Deputy Library Services Manager., Gloucestershire Hospitals NHS Foundation Trust., Gloucester.
[55782]   17/11/1997   CM10/07/2002
O'Connor, Mr D J, BA (Hons), Senior Library Assistant., Newsam Library, London.
[10019630]   10/08/2011   AF
O'Connor, Ms E, DipLIS, Consultant, Metataxis Ltd, London.
[58815]   07/08/2000   ME
O'Connor, Miss E, BA MSc, Information Officer, Weil, Gotshal & Manges.
[65679]   31/03/2006   ME
O'Connor, Miss E, BA MA, Student, Aberystwyth University.
[10016439]   23/03/2010   ME
O'Connor, Mrs G, BA MCLIP, Librarian, Swindon Borough Council.
[35919]   17/01/1983   CM27/02/1991
O'Connor, Miss J, MA, Universtiy College School.
[10019783]   13/09/2011   ME

O'Connor, Mr K, Librarian, NBS, Newcastle upon Tyne.
[47784]   14/10/1992   ME
O'Connor, Dr M, BA MA PhD PGCE, Student, University of Ulster.
[10034632]   25/07/2014   ME
O'Connor, Mr M D, MA PgDip MCLIP, Retired.
[10020145]   22/03/1976   CM26/11/1982
Oda, Prof M, BEd MA, Professor, Department of Education, Aoyama Gakuin University, Tokyo.
[50501]   22/08/1994   ME
Oddy, Ms E, BA (Hons) MSc MCLIP, Head of Learning and Research Support Services, Newcastle University.
[42270]   13/10/1988   CM15/10/2002
Oddy, Mrs J M, BA MCLIP, Life Member.
[11100]   24/03/1954   CM01/01/1956
O'Dell, Mr F J, BSc (Hons), L. Assistant, Northamptonshire Primary Care Trust.
[65766]   03/05/2006   ME
O'Dell, Mr T, MA* MCLIP, Development Librarian, London Borough of Lambeth.
[62692]   17/10/2003   CM08/09/2010
O'Deorain, Mr F A, BSc DipLib, Assistant Librarian, University of Ulster, Derry.
[33235]   10/10/1980   CM21/12/1984
O'Deorain, Mrs S, BLib MCLIP, Archives & Business Support Co-ordinator Library, University of Ulster.
[34640]   19/01/1982   CM20/09/1985
Odie, Mrs T, BA (Hons), School Librarian, Anderson High School. Lerwick, Shetland.
[10032617]   20/12/2013   ME
O'Donnell, Mrs E M, BA DipLib, Librarian, Alleyn's School, London.
[10001032]   25/11/2003   ME
O'Donnell, Mr J, BA (Hons), Student, Northumbria University.
[10021773]   10/10/2012   ME
O'Donnell, Miss J R, BA, Student.
[10035281]   03/10/2014   ME
O'Donnell, Mrs K H, BA Lic Ed. MCLIP, Librarian, Balfron High School, Balfron.
[62745]   09/10/2003   CM02/02/2005
O'Donnell, Mrs M E, BA DipLib, School Librarian, West Dunbartonshire Council.
[10003071]   22/10/1991   ME
O'Donnell, Mrs M L, MCLIP, Librarian, Thomas Bennett Comm. College, Crawley.
[19944]   15/01/1973   CM19/07/1976
O'Donnell, Dr P, BA MPhil PhD, Student.
[10018987]   04/04/2011   ME
O'Donnell, Mrs W A, BSc (Hons) MCLIP, Librarian, Balwearie Jigh School, Kirkcaldy, Fife.
[10010360]   22/07/2008   CM25/01/2011
O'Donoghue, Ms K M, BA DipLib MCLIP, Part-time School Librarian, Harrytown Catholic High School, Stockport.
[26000]   03/04/1976   CM19/03/1979
O'Donohoe, Miss A, BA, Graduate Trainee, The London Library.
[10035499]   16/10/2014   ME
O'Donovan, Mrs A, MA MCLIP, Sch. Development Librarian, Bucks C. C. L. Sev.
[10009763]   09/06/2008   CM12/05/2011
O'Driscoll, Mrs C A, BA MCLIP, Director, Archer Search Limited.
[38040]   17/01/1985   CM04/08/1987
O'Driscoll, Miss D, BA PGDE,
[10021903]   29/10/2012   ME
Oduntan, Mrs O O, Student, University of Strathclyde.
[10031810]   07/10/2013   ME

O'Farrell, Mrs R E, BA (Hons) MSc, Information Manager.
[10019549] 26/07/2011 ME
Offord, Mrs A, Group Manager L., Maldon Library, Essex.
[10009343] 01/06/2008 AF
Offord, Mrs J D, BEd (Hons) DipLib MCLIP, Advisory Librarian, Suffolk Schools Library Service.
[36744] 25/11/1983 CM08/03/1988
Offord, Mrs W, Learning Resource Coordinator, East Bergholt High School.
[10034526] 18/07/2014 ME
O'Flynn, Miss H Y, BA MCLIP, Head of Information Policy & Strategy, Deaprtment for Business, Innovation & Skills.
[41031] 03/10/1987 CM15/09/1993
Ogba, Mrs C, MSc, Law Librarian, Ekiti State University Library.
[10034175] 12/06/2014 ME
O'Grady, Mrs J A, MLIS, Unemployed.
[10032105] 28/10/2013 ME
O'Grady, Mrs J M K, BSc (Hons) (Econ) MCLIP, Senior Librarian – Information Services, The Jersey Library.
[53022] 06/02/1996 CM16/05/2001
Ogundipe, Mr A, MSc BSc, Assistant Librarian, Princess Alexandra Hospital, Harlow.
[62121] 21/02/2003 ME
O'Hanlon, Miss B, BA (Hons) PGCE,
[10014184] 02/07/2009 ME
O'Hara, Mrs A, MSc MCLIP, Librarian, Milton Keynes Council.
[58040] 20/10/1999 CM29/11/2006
O'Hare, Miss R, MA PgDipILS MCLIP, Principal Librarian, The Mitchell Library, Glasgow.
[56787] 15/10/1998 CM17/09/2003
O'Hora, Ms N, MSc BMus MCLIP, Information Services Librarian, Borough of Poole Libraries.
[10017722] 29/09/2010 CM27/03/2014
O'Kane-Walls, Mrs M, LMis, Senior Assistant Learning Resource Officer, Castlereagh Colllege Library.
[10004961] 06/06/2007 MF
O'Keefe, Ms J, BA MLIS, ARLG London & South East committee member.
[10022413] 26/02/2013 ME
O'Kelly, Ms J L, BA MCLIP, p. /t Sch. Librarian, Aylesbury.
[22651] 29/07/1974 CM01/10/1976
Okure, Miss C, BLS MCLIP,
[49925] 24/01/1994 CM19/07/2000
Oladjins, Mrs E, MA DipILS MCLIP, Resource Procurement Librarian., Aberdeenshire Libraries, Oldmeldrum.
[57098] 09/12/1998 CM18/09/2002
Olayanju, Mr L, BSc MSc, Student, Coventry University.
[10034156] 11/06/2014 ME
Olden, Dr E A, BA MLS PhD FCLIP MCIPR, Academic Lead for Research Students & Associate Professor, University of West London.
[17512] 23/07/1972 FE12/09/2001
Oldfield, Ms C, District Manager/Cultural Service Advisor, Lincolnshire Ls., Lincolnshire.
[65886] 27/06/2006 AF
Oldfield, Mrs C A, BA (Hons) MCLIP,
[39190] 06/01/1986 CM18/01/1989
Oldfield, Mrs D M, FCLIP, Life Member.
[7358] 08/03/1940 FE01/01/1954
Oldfield, Ms J M, BSc MCLIP MA, Oxfam Bookshop Manager.
[30859] 27/04/1979 CM10/05/1984
Oldham, Miss C A, BA MA DipLib MCLIP, Retired.
[33330] 20/11/1980 CM04/04/1984

Oldman, Mrs H, MA MA MCLIP, Head of Learning Resources., Grammar School, Leeds.
[53848] 04/10/1996 CM19/07/2000
Oldridge, Mr P, BSc (Hons) AMINSTP ACLIP, Customer Serv. Librarian, East Herts & Broxbourne District, Herts.
[64306] 25/02/2005 ACL06/02/2008
Oldridge, Mrs R V, BA (Hons) MSc, Digital Resource Manager, University of Bedfordshire.
[57633] 03/06/1999 ME
Oldroyd, Mrs M E, BA MLib HonFCLIP, Retired.
[13811] 01/10/1970 HFE16/10/2008
Oldroyd, Mr R E, BA MA DipLib FCLIP, Retired.
[30344] 15/02/1968 FE25/05/1994
O'Leary, Mr I G, MA DLIS, National Physical Laboratory, Middlesex.
[10022435] 05/03/2013 ME
O'Leary, Miss R, BA (Hons) MSc MCLIP, Digital Content Manager, RIBA Enterprises, Newcastle Upon Tyne.
[48271] 20/11/1992 CM16/11/1994
Olga, Ms R, BSc, Student.
[10035282] 03/10/2014 ME
Olive, Mrs M D B, MCLIP, Librarian, Charterhouse School.
[56307] 06/05/1998 CM21/05/2008
Oliveira, Mr F G J, Information Professional.
[10008661] 18/04/2008 ME
Oliver, Mrs J, BSc MCLIP MCMI, Customer Serv. Manager, Teeside University, Middlesbrough.
[47344] 17/07/1992 RV15/07/2014 CM09/11/2005
Oliver, Mrs J M, BSc (Hons) MCLIP, Performance & Office Services Librarian., London Borough of Bexley, Sidup.
[49732] 25/11/1993 CM22/05/1996
Oliver, Miss K M, BA MCLIP, Retired.
[19055] 09/12/1963 CM01/01/1967
Oliver, Miss L S, MSc MA, L. & Information Serv. Manager, Ashridge.
[51385] 01/02/1995 ME
Oliver, Mrs S N, BSc (Hons), Lib. Assistant, Trust Library, Queen Elizabeth Hospital, Gateshead.
[10015219] 27/10/2009 AF
Ollerenshaw, Mrs H E, BA (Hons) MSc DMS MCLIP, Faculty Librarian for Arts, Social Sciences and Law and Joint Head of Academic Engagement, University of Bristol.
[56165] 01/04/1998 CM08/01/2002
Olney, Ms S D, MA DipLib MCLIP, Unwaged.
[35220] 07/10/1982 CM06/10/1987
O'Loughlin, Ms M J, BA HDipEd HDipLIS MLIS,
[10032329] 19/11/2013 ME
Olsen, Mr A J, BA (Oxon) MCLIP, Retired. Formerly Head of Libraries and Adult Education, London Borough of Southwark.
[11009] 01/04/1970 CM26/01/1973
Olulode, Ms A S, BA (Hons) MA MCLIP, Development Librarian, Literacy, Skills, Employment and Business London Borough of Lambeth, London.
[59904] 31/10/2001 CM08/09/2010
O'Mahony, Ms M M, BA MA HDipLIS MCLIP, Library & Knowledge Service Manager, Southport & Ormskirk Hospitals Trust.
[10009364] 25/04/2002 CM11/07/2012
Omar, Mrs D J, BA (Hons) MSc MCLIP, Information Specialist, Kingston University Library.
[59656] 07/11/2001 CM08/12/2004
Omissi, Mrs L, BA (Hons) MA MCLIP, Senior Librarian, Young Readers Department., Jersey Library, St Helier.
[55019] 01/07/1997 CM17/11/1999
Omopupa, Mr K T, MLIS CLN, Doctoral Student, University of KwaZulu-Natal, Pietermaritzburg Campus South Africa.
[10020057] 28/10/2011 ME

Omordia, Mrs A N, Assistant Librarian, Ministry of Defence.
[66060]   06/09/2006   **ME**
Omorogbe, Ms J O, BA MA PGCE, Resource Assistant, Aldrich Library.
[10000641]   18/10/2006   **ME**
Omotayo, Mrs M, BA (Hons) PgCert PgDip, Customer Services Officer,
MHRA, London.
[61052]   01/02/2002   **ME**
Onatola, Mr A D, BSc (Hons) PGDE MLS, Librarian & Learning Centres
Supervisor, Abingdon & Witney College, Oxfordshire.
[64737]   09/06/2005   **ME**
O'Neil, Miss K J, BA MCLIP, Central Library and Service Development
Manager, Bedford Borough Libraries.
[41726]   24/02/1988   **CM17/10/1990**
O'Neill, Ms A M, BA PgDip MA MCLIP, Director of Learning and
Information Services, University of Chichester.
[55698]   04/11/1997   **CM04/02/2004**
O'Neill, Miss C J, MCLIP, Life Member.
[11016]   18/03/1959   **CM01/01/1970**
O'Neill, Mr D J, MCLIP, Head of Learning Res., Anglo European College
of Chiropratic, Bournemouth.
[27202]   14/01/1977   **CM01/01/1981**
O'Neill, Mrs G C, BA MCLIP, Unemployed.
[30116]   14/01/1979   **CM30/06/1982**
O'Neill, Ms H A, BA (Hons) MSc MCLIP, Head of Reader Serv., London
Library, London.
[46456]   07/11/1991   **RV**09/11/2011   **CM16/07/2003**
O'Neill, Ms K, BA (Hons), Open Access Assistant, University of
Sheffield.
[10006322]   16/10/2007   **ME**
O'Neill, Ms K M, MA MSc MPHIL, Assistant Librarian, Sotheby's
Institute of Art.
[10006548]   17/11/2003   **ME**
O'Neill, Mrs R, ACLIP BSc (Hons), Subject Librarian., Croydon College.
[10006199]   18/09/2007   **ACL03/12/2008**
O'Neill, Mr T K W, BA (Hons), Student, Manchester Metropolitan
University.
[10032411]   03/12/2013   **ME**
Onwudike, Miss O C, PhD MSc BTech, Student, Loughborough
University.
[10035448]   14/10/2014   **ME**
Onwughara, Miss L, MSc, Team Member, Barking Learning Centre.
[10032330]   19/11/2013   **ME**
Oparinde, Mr S A, BSc (Hons) MSc DipIM DMS, Branch Librarian,
Battersea Park Library, Wandsworth Council.
[47518]   22/09/1992   **ME**
Oppenheim, Prof C, BSc PhD FCLIP HonFCLIP, Retired Prof.
Information Sci., Loughborough University, Leics.
[46639]   29/11/1991   **HFE14/09/1997**
Oram, Mrs M A, MCLIP, Retired.
[6191]   31/01/1969   **CM20/07/1972**
Orbell, Mrs D J, BA (Hons), Student, Aberystwyth University.
[10034176]   13/06/2014   **ME**
Orchard, Mrs C, BA, Librarian, PAA Ecology Library, Buxton,
Derbyshire.
[10001961]   22/03/2007   **ME**
Ord, Miss S, BA MCLIP, Unemployed.
[42169]   06/10/1988   **CM18/09/1991**
O'Regan, Mr J A, BA MCLIP,
[28353]   03/11/1977   **CM10/11/1982**
O'Reilly, Ms B, MA BPhil, Catalogue Support Librarian, The Bodleian
Library, Oxford.
[10016518]   01/12/2010   **ME**
O'Reilly, Miss M C A, BA (Hons), Library Assistant, Bodleian Libraries.
[10020600]   08/03/2012   **AF**

O'Reilly, Mr P, BA (Hons), Faculty Librarian – Systems, Heart of
England NHS Foundation Trust.
[10035107]   15/09/2014   **ME**
O'Reilly, Mr P E, MA, DIKTI Scholarship Co-Ordinator: Managing
programme for Indonesian lecturers to study for PhDs at UK HEIs.
[10032258]   29/09/2003   **ME**
Orford, Mrs K J, BA MA MCLIP,
[10013975]   17/06/2009   **CM14/11/2012**
Orford, Ms M, Library Assistant, Swansea University.
[10022132]   08/01/2013   **ME**
Organ, Mrs C H, MA DipLib MCLIP, Subject Librarian, Cornwall Health
Library, RCH, Truro.
[36753]   21/11/1983   **CM19/08/1992**
Orlandi, Mrs A, MA, UCL Alumna.
[10009222]   06/05/2008   **ME**
Orlygsson, Mr O I, BSc (HONS) MSc, Student, City University London.
[10031497]   19/08/2013   **ME**
Orme, Mrs S P, MSc BSc MCLIP, Unwaged.
[47288]   20/09/1977   **CM20/05/1980**
Ormiston, Ms T M, BA MA MSc MCLIP, Data Serv. Director, IMS Health,
London.
[60507]   10/06/2001   **CM10/06/2001**
Orpen, Mrs A, MCLIP BSc, Information Specialist, St Andrew's School
for Girls.
[20275]   21/02/1973   **CM02/09/1976**
Orr, Mr A J, BMus PgDip MCLIP, Lib. : Children's & Early Years,
Blackburn with Darwen Borough Council. Blackburn.
[59970]   14/11/2001   **CM17/09/2008**
Orr, Mr C A, MCLIP, School Librarian.
[66122]   01/10/2006   **CM16/01/2014**
Orr, Mrs P, BA (Hons) DipILS MCLIP, Knowledge Supp. Librarian, North
Cumbria University Hospitals NHS Trust, Carlisle.
[46673]   06/12/1991   **CM19/03/2008**
Ortega, Ms M, BA (Hons) MLib PGCE MCLIP, Senior Academic Subject
Librarian – Research, University of Lincoln.
[48093]   06/11/1992   **CM24/07/1996**
Orton, Mr G I J, BA MSc MBA FRSA MCLIP CiLCA, Parish Clerk:
Burley Parish Council.
[11046]   25/01/1968   **CM01/01/1973**
Orton, Mr R, MA (Hons) MSc MCLIP, Information Researcher.,
Chartered Management Institute, Northamptonshire.
[57216]   20/01/1999   **CM09/09/2009**
Osadzinski, Mr H R, Search Executive / Information Management
Student.
[10031916]   14/10/2013   **ME**
Osafo, Mrs L, BA MA, Senior Librarian, Bristol Grammar School.
[61563]   02/10/2002   **ME**
Osborn, Ms H, MLib MCLIP, Director of Library Services, Libraries NI.
[33497]   13/01/1981   **CM16/05/1984**
Osborn, Mr R M, BA AKC DipLib, London Strategic Lead for Library
Services & eLearning, Health Education North Central & East
London.
[37413]   30/08/1984   **ME**
Osborne, Dr A, EdD MSc BA (Hons) FHEA MCLIP, Academic Librarian,
University of Huddersfield.
[10016280]   27/10/1989   **CM18/07/1991**
Osborne, Ms E S, BA (Hons) PGCE MA MCLIP, Outreach & Enquiry
Service Manager, Bodleian Healthcare Lib. University of Oxford.
[50803]   18/10/1994   **CM20/11/2002**
Osborne, Mrs H, BA (Hons) MA, Student.
[10016415]   22/03/2010   **ME**
Osborne, Mrs J, MA DipLib MCLIP, Life Member.
[30021]   05/11/1978   **CM04/01/1983**

Osborne, Mrs S L, BA (Hons) MCLIP, Senior Library Advisor, University of Nottingham.
[50882] 26/10/1994 **CM15/03/2000**
O'Shaughnessy, Mr P E, BA (Hons) DipInfLib, Subject Support Librarian, University of the West of England.
[47447] 18/08/1992 **ME**
O'Shea, Ms B E, BA, Student, Robert Gordon University.
[10032002] 21/10/2013 **ME**
O'Shea, Ms M, BA MA PgDip, Student, Robert Gordon University.
[10031370] 30/01/2014 **ME**
Osman, Miss E A, MA (Oxon) MA, College Librarian, Homerton College, Cambridge.
[63767] 06/10/2004 **ME**
Osman, Ms S J, MA MSc MCLIP, Senior Information Adv., Kingston University, Kingston Upon Thames.
[42955] 03/05/1989 **RV**27/08/2014 **CM12/12/1990**
Osman-Weyers, Mrs I, MSc, Sch. Lib.
[65739] 10/04/2006 **ME**
O'Sullivan, Miss C, ACLIP, Library Assistant, Animal Health and Veterinary Laboratories Agency.
[10008275] 23/06/2009 **ACL15/01/2013**
O'Sullivan, Mr K M C, BA (Hons) MA MSc (Econ) MCLIP, Sr. Rare Books Librarian, University of Aberdeen.
[52814] 18/12/1995 **CM19/07/2000**
O'Sullivan, Mrs V M, MCLIP, Librarian, Bournemouth BC.
[21886] 20/01/1974 **CM07/07/1976**
Oswald, Mr D,
[10019742] 02/09/2011 **ME**
Oswald, Mr N, BA DipLib, Unemployed.
[39016] 24/10/1985 **ME**
Othick, Ms J, BA (Hons) LLM, Head of KIM Policy, Profession and Compliance, Home Office.
[10034032] 21/05/2014 **ME**
O'Toole, Miss T, ACLIP, Currently not working in libraries.
[10002055] 28/03/2007 **ACL16/07/2008**
Ottaway, Ms J, BA MCLIP, Retired.
[36411] 06/10/1983 **CM05/04/1988**
Oulamara, Ms A, MLIS, Student, University College Dublin.
[10034737] 12/08/2014 **ME**
Ovenden, Miss E, BA (Hons) DipIM MCLIP, Unemployed.
[53580] 02/08/1996 **CM25/07/2001**
Ovenden, Mr R, BA DipLib MA, Keeper of Special Collections, Bodleian Library, Oxford.
[39917] 02/10/1986 **ME**
Ovens, Mr J P, BA (Hons) MCLIP, L. Mgr, Royal United Hospital Hosp, Bath.
[49605] 19/11/1993 **CM24/07/1996**
Overend, Mrs S A, BA Oxon DipILIS, Reader Services Librarian, Oxford Health NHS Foundation Trust, Oxford.
[35265] 05/10/1982 **ME**
Overfield, Mr N, MSc BA, Library Supervisor, Scottish Borders Library Service.
[65923] 06/07/2006 **ME**
Overington, Mr M A, MA PhD FCLIP, Life Member.
[17530] 19/09/1955 **FE01/01/1967**
Overton-Jones, Mrs J, BA (Hons) MA,
[10012398] 03/02/2009 **ME**
Owen, Mrs A, BA (Hons), Knowledge, Skills & Systems Librarian, Surrey & Sussex Healthcare Trust.
[59903] 26/10/2001 **ME**
Owen, Mr D, OBE BA DipLib MCLIP, Consultant.
[11089] 10/10/1965 **CM01/01/1968**
Owen, Mrs D E, BA MCLIP, L. Manager, Chester Library, Cheshire C. C.
[40386] 26/01/1987 **CM27/07/1994**

Owen, Mrs K, BA FCLIP, Chair of CILIP Professional Registration and Accreditation Board. Retired senior manager in public services.
[33332] 03/11/1980 **FE13/06/2007**
Owen, Mr K, BSc (Econ), Librarian, International School of Dusseldorf.
[10035146] 23/09/2014 **ME**
Owen, Miss K A, BA (Hons) DipILS MCLIP, Information Serv. Librarian, Vale of Glamorgan Pub. Ls., Barry.
[49302] 20/10/1993 **CM17/11/1999**
Owen, Mrs M, Law Librarian, Bangor University.
[45253] 06/09/1990 **ME**
Owen, Mr M, BA MCLIP, Life Member.
[19234] 14/09/1956 **CM01/01/1963**
Owen, Mrs T J, BSc (Hons) MCLIP, Library Resources Manager, North West Commisioning Support Unit, Liverpool.
[55579] 21/10/1997 **CM19/03/2008**
Owen-McGee, Mr D J, BA (Hons) MA MCLIP FHEA, IT Advisor & Dev., LIS University of Derby.
[57670] 01/07/1999 **CM07/09/2005**
Owens, Ms A J, BA MCLIP, Children's Services Librarian, City of London.
[32530] 24/04/1980 **CM24/10/1983**
Owens, Miss J, MA, Librarian, University of Sheffield.
[10015025] 07/10/2009 **ME**
Owens, Ms M, Student, McGill University Library.
[10035686] 29/10/2014 **ME**
Owen-Strong, Mrs M, MA, Student, Aberystwyth University.
[10015779] 25/01/2010 **ME**
Owston, Ms F C, BA MCLIP, Market Analyst, British Telecommunications Group PLC.
[29782] 05/10/1978 **CM11/11/1980**
Owston, Mr J A, BA MCLIP, Retired.
[21819] 19/09/1953 **CM23/08/1963**
Owusu, Mrs P A, BA DipLib, Stockport Council Libraries.
[30986] 03/07/1979 **CM21/09/1982**
Oxborrow, Miss K M, BA (Hons) MA MCLIP ALIANZA, Senior Tutor, Information Studies Programmes, Victoria University of Wellington, New Zealand.
[10011341] 09/10/2008 **RV**27/08/2014 **CM14/03/2012**
Oxford, Miss S A, BA (Hons), Academic Liaison Librarian, Institute for Education, University of Worcester.
[63720] 09/09/2004 **ME**
Oyedoh, Mrs M, BSc MSc MCLIP, Librarian, St Edward's School, Oxford.
[61142] 08/03/2002 **CM09/11/2011**
Oza, Ms H, MA, Post Processing, Royal Mail Group Plc.
[10010232] 01/02/2010 **AF**
Ozmen, Mrs N C, BSc (Hons) MSC, Community Librarian – Children and Young People, North Somerset Council.
[10006337] 15/10/2007 **ME**

P

Pacey, Mrs G K, BA DMS MCLIP, Retired.
[11123] 14/10/1968 **CM01/01/1972**
Pachent, Ms G J, BA DLIS FRSA MCLIP MCMI, Retired.
[24770] 01/10/1975 **CM31/10/1977**
Pacht, Miss D, BA (Hons) MA, Electronic Services Support Manager, British Library, London.
[10002629] 20/04/2007 **ME**
Pachuca, Ms E J, Customer Account Advisor, Manchester Metropolitan University, Manchester.
[10016126] 18/02/2010 **ME**

Pacitti, Mrs M K, BA (Hons) MCLIP, Unwaged.
[55665] 07/11/1997 **CM13/03/2002**
Packard, Mrs S A, BSc (Hons) MCLIP, Digital Resources & Depository Coordinator, Anglia Ruskin University, Chelmsford.
[54740] 01/04/1997 **CM15/09/2004**
Packwood, Mrs A, MCLIP, Subject Librarian, Anglia Ruskin University, Cambridge.
[47018] 01/04/1992 **CM11/03/2009**
Padalino, Ms V, BA (Hons) MSc, L. Manager, Highgate Library, London.
[10006534] 01/06/2005 **ME**
Paddon, Ms T C, BSc (Hons) MSc Dip AppSS MCLIP, Area Librarian, Newport Central Library, South Wales.
[57700] 01/07/1999 RV30/04/2007 **CM19/11/2003**
Padgham, Mrs S, BA (Hons) MCLIP,
[33203] 13/10/1980 RV27/08/2014 **CM27/07/1983**
Padley, Miss B, MCLIP, Retired.
[20083] 28/03/1955 **CM01/01/1960**
Padley, Ms W A, MCLIP, Research Assistant, De Montfort University, Leicester.
[63496] 15/06/2004 **CM09/11/2011**
Page, Ms A C, BA (Hons) MSc MCLIP, Clinical Support Librarian, Wrightington, Wigan & Leigh NHS Foundation Trust.
[47916] 26/10/1992 **CM10/03/2010**
Page, Mr B F, FCLIP, Retired.
[11136] 17/01/1950 **FE01/01/1968**
Page, Mrs C L, BA MCLIP, Senior Library Officer, Pinsent Masons LLP.
[30579] 14/02/1979 **CM03/09/1981**
Page, Mrs H, MCLIP, Librarian, Knutsford Academy, Cheshire.
[25025] 29/10/1975 **CM02/10/1978**
Page, Mrs I, MCLIP, Retired.
[11140] 20/02/1961 **CM01/01/1966**
Page, Ms N, BA (Hons) PgDip, Community Librarian, Luton Libraries.
[62955] 25/11/2003 **ME**
Page, Mr T, BA MA MSc, Librarian, Central College Nottingham & Treasurer, East Midlands Branch of CILIP.
[10017086] 22/06/2010 **ME**
Paine, Ms K P, BA (Hons) MA MCLIP, Senior Library Assistant, LSE, London.
[54663] 12/02/1997 **CM03/10/2007**
Painter, Mrs M J, BLib MCLIP, Community History Librarian & ICT, Darwen L. Manager.
[33982] 30/06/1981 **CM14/10/1985**
Palavinskaite, Mrs J, Student, Robert Gordon University.
[10032868] 21/01/2014 **ME**
Palethorpe, Mrs R S, ACLIP, Information Assistant, Djanogly LRC, University of Nothingham.
[10020371] 26/03/2012 **ACL11/04/2013**
Palfrey, Ms M, BA (Hons) MA MCLIP, Team Librarian, Reading Borough Council.
[59992] 16/11/2001 **CM21/05/2008**
Palka, Mrs J B, BA DipLib MCLIP, Librarian.
[26587] 12/10/1976 **CM18/03/1980**
Pallister, Mrs S M, BA MCLIP, Unwaged.
[20530] 04/04/1973 **CM16/11/1977**
Palmer, Ms B, E-Learning Mentor, Tresham College.
[10020807] 18/04/2012 **AF**
Palmer, Ms B, BMus DipLib MCLIP,
[29784] 06/10/1978 **CM04/03/1982**
Palmer, Mrs C, BA (Hons) MA MCLIP, Head of Information Mgmnt, Charltons, Hong Kong.
[55750] 13/11/1997 RV01/10/2008 **CM12/03/2003**
Palmer, Mrs D M, MBE HonFLA, Freelance Consultant.
[11169] 06/02/1969 **HFE16/06/1978**

Palmer, Dr J, BA (Hons) MA DPhil PgDip MCLIP, Information consultant and researcher.
[10014751] 05/02/1977 **CM01/07/1994**
Palmer, Dr J M P, BSc DipLib PhD MCLIP FCLIP, Retired.
[17540] 23/03/1972 **FE21/05/1997**
Palmer, Mrs J S, BA MCLIP, Serv. Manager, Saffron Walden Public Library, Essex.
[25709] 29/02/1976 **CM22/08/1980**
Palmer, Mrs J T, BA MA, Intranet Editor, MOD, London.
[64134] 19/01/2005 **ME**
Palmer, Ms K, BA (Hons) FCLIP, Senior Information Officer, Simmons & Simmons LLP, London.
[41739] 02/03/1988 **FE16/01/2014**
Palmer, Mrs M, MCLIP, District Manager, Ribble Valley, Lancashire County Council, Preston.
[26139] 21/06/1976 **CM29/08/1980**
Palmer, Ms M, MBibl MSc MCLIP, Head Library and Archive Services & Dept. Records Officer, Welsh Gov., Cardiff.
[10011436] 23/11/1998 **CM23/11/1998**
Palmer, Mr M E, MA (Cantab) MSc, Content Editor, CAB International, Wallingford.
[51450] 15/02/1995 **ME**
Palmer, Mr M J, BA (Hons) MA, Information Officer, Institute of Directors, London.
[10020947] 27/04/2012 **ME**
Palmer, Mr N D, BA MCLIP, Retired.
[11184] 14/10/1966 **CM01/01/1968**
Palmer, Mr R, BA (Hons) MSc, Information Officer, Scottish Library and Information Council, South Lanarkshire.
[10001307] 07/02/2007 **ME**
Palmer, Mr S J, BA (Hons) DipLib, Children's, Young People & Learning Librarian, Solihull Central Library, Solihull.
[37831] 28/10/1984 **ME**
Palmer, Ms S L, BA (Hons) MA MCLIP, Media Manager, Newsnight, BBC.
[52257] 18/10/1995 **CM01/06/2005**
Pang, Miss K M, BA, Student, University of Brighton.
[10017961] 27/10/2010 **ME**
Pang, Mr L P, MSc, Acting Librarian, Hong Kong Central Library, Hong Kong.
[10022655] 05/04/2013 **ME**
Pankhurst, Mrs R J, MA FCLIP, Retired.
[17543] 03/06/1959 **FE15/09/1993**
Pankiewicz, Miss A M,
[65157] 03/11/2005 **ME**
Pankiewicz, Mrs S J, BA (Hons) MSc MCLIP, Manager, National Meteorological Library, Exeter.
[39201] 01/01/1986 **CM21/07/1998**
Panomereva, Mrs A, MPhie MA,
[10007949] 20/03/2008 **ME**
Pantry, Mrs S, BA OBE FCLIP, Director, Sheila Pantry Assoc. Ltd.
[11204] 23/03/1953 **FE18/01/1989**
Papadakou, Miss E, Student.
[10022360] 19/02/2013 **ME**
Papadimitriou, Miss M,
[10035291] 15/10/2014 **ME**
Pape, Mrs G, BA (Hons), Libr., Dumfries & Galloway College.
[64359] 07/03/2005 **ME**
Parcell, Ms E J, MA, Senior E Learning Advisor, Swansea University.
[38973] 24/10/1985 **ME**
Pardoe, Mrs A, DipLib MCLIP, Librarian, King Edward VI College – Stourbridge.
[33315] 23/10/1980 **CM26/08/1983**

Parfitt, Mr M J, BA (Hons) ACLIP, Learning Resources Coordinator, Coleg Powys.
[10017714] 29/09/2010 **ACL30/04/2014**

Parfitt, Mrs S T, BSc (Hons) MCLIP, Assistant Librarian, Tanglin Trust School, Singapore.
[46003] 19/08/1991 **CM25/09/1996**

Paris, Mrs F, BA PG CELTD, Student, CILIP Scotland.
[10035269] 03/10/2014 **ME**

Paris, Mr K R, BA PgDipLib, Senior Research Procurement Officer, DLA Piper, UK, LLP London.
[43217] 04/10/1989 **ME**

Parish, Mrs P L, BSc (Hons) DipLib MCLIP, Freelance Project Management and Author Events for Libraries, Schools, Literature Festivals and the Arts.
[10033905] 12/05/2014 **ME**

Parish, Mr R H, MCLIP, Retired.
[11216] 06/09/1956 **CM01/01/1966**

Park, Mrs A, MCLIP, Academic Librarian, Leeds Metropolitan University.
[59338] 09/02/2001 **RV27/03/2014 CM19/03/2008**

Park, Mrs A K, BA MCLIP, Sch. Lib.
[21656] 05/01/1974 **CM01/08/1977**

Park, Mrs M, MA DipLib MCLIP, Research Data Librarian, University of St Andrews, Fife.
[35694] 14/01/1983 **CM26/10/1985**

Park, Ms M A, BA (Hons) MA MSc MCLIP, Unwaged.
[60050] 06/12/2001 **CM11/03/2009**

Park, Mr R D M, MA (Hons), Subject Librarian, Universityof The West of Scotland.
[46551] 14/11/1991 **ME**

Parke, Mr J T E, BA (Hons) DipIM MCLIP, Administrator, Centre for Theoretical Cosmology, University of Cambridge.
[55363] 03/10/1997 **CM28/10/2004**

Parker, Mr A D, MA DipLib MCLIP, Higher Library Executive, House of Commons Library, London.
[33473] 07/01/1981 **CM20/01/1986**

Parker, Miss A M, MBE HonFLA, Life Member.
[11222] 26/08/1949 **HFE01/01/1994**

Parker, Miss A S, BA (Hons), Learning Centre Manager, Birkenhead Sixth Form College, Wirral.
[56225] 07/04/1998 **ME**

Parker, Miss B J, BA (Hons) MCLIP DipEngLit, Life Member.
[19802] 03/10/1972 **CM25/08/1982**

Parker, Mrs C, BSc (Hons) MCLIP, Library Manager, Barton Peveril College.
[10000762] 06/11/2006 **CM20/06/2014**

Parker, Mrs D F, Assistant Librarian, The Grammar School at Leeds.
[10007228] 25/01/2008 **ME**

Parker, Mr D F, MCMI FCLIP, Life Member.
[19236] 28/02/1954 **FE01/01/1959**

Parker, Miss E, BSc, Student, UCL.
[10017940] 26/10/2010 **ME**

Parker, Ms E K, BA MCLIP, Senior Network Librarian, Highland Council, Inverness.
[54284] 15/11/1996 **CM20/11/2002**

Parker, Mr F N, FCLIP, Retired, Life Member.
[11232] 10/09/1952 **FE01/01/1966**

Parker, Mrs G D, BA (Hons) MCLIP, Unwaged.
[22747] 06/09/1974 **CM29/01/1979**

Parker, Miss H L, Information Assistant, Ward Hadaway, Newcastle Upon Tyne.
[10023068] 04/06/2013 **AF**

Parker, Mrs J E, BA (Hons) MCLIP, IS Project Manager, Sanctuary Group, Worcester.
[52591] 10/11/1995 **CM24/10/2001**

Parker, Ms J E, BA (Hons) MA MCLIP, Library Services Manager (Information Literacy).
[52062] 02/10/1995 **CM21/07/1999**

Parker, Mrs J E, MCLIP, Volunteer at Corby Libraby.
[27517] 14/05/1977 **CM23/02/1983**

Parker, Mrs J M, BA MCLIP, Operations Manager, Learning Centres New College Nottingham.
[28683] 13/01/1978 **CM10/11/1981**

Parker, Mr J S, Retired.
[19237] 26/09/1952 **FE10/08/1978**

Parker, Mrs L, ACLIP, Senior L. Assistant, Worksop Library, Notts.
[10003418] 23/05/2007 **ACL28/01/2009**

Parker, Mrs M, Library Assistant.
[10033227] 17/04/2014 **ME**

Parker, Mrs M J, MA BA MCLIP, RDSM\Children's Librarian.
[65622] 07/03/2006 **CM16/01/2014**

Parker, Mr N M, BSc DipLib MCLIP, Operations Manager, Chartered Management Inst., Corby.
[35702] 17/01/1983 **CM13/05/1986**

Parker, Mrs P C, BA DipLib MCLIP, Unemployed.
[32891] 20/10/1980 **CM08/04/1983**

Parker, Miss P E, MCLIP, Retired.
[11244] 10/10/1968 **CM19/12/1972**

Parker, Mr R J, BSocSc BInfoSci MCLIP, Head of Library and Knowledge Services, Derby Hospitals Foundation Trust.
[55099] 08/07/1997 **CM21/05/2008**

Parker, Miss S A, BA FCLIP, Retired.
[25386] 12/01/1976 **RV20/02/2014 FE03/10/2007**

Parker, Miss S M, BA DMS FCLIP, Retired.
[11251] 01/03/1962 **FE25/01/1995**

Parker-Dennison, Mrs D, DipLib MCLIP,
[58632] 20/04/2000 **CM17/06/2011**

Parkes, Dr D, BA (Hons) MSc MA MCLIP, Librarian, FSULSC.
[52897] 17/01/1996 **CM19/01/2000**

Parkes, Mr D J, BA (Hons) DipLib MCLIP, Head of Learning Support, StaffordshireUniversity, Thompson Library, Stoke on Trent.
[46795] 28/01/1992 **CM26/07/1995**

Parkhill, Ms S, BA (Hons) MA MCLIP, School and Community Librarian, Hurlingham and Chelsea School.
[63925] 03/11/2004 **CM16/12/2010**

Parkin, Mrs C M, BA (Hons) Msc, Academic Librarian, Leeds Metropolitan University.
[58263] 30/11/1999 **ME**

Parkin, Miss E R, BA (Hons) DipIS MCLIP, Team Librarian, Norfolk L., Kings Lynn.
[48903] 15/07/1993 **CM22/09/1999**

Parkin, Mr S, MA, Curator (Italian Printed Collections), The British Library, London.
[10018250] 15/08/1991 **ME**

Parkinson, Mrs A L, MCLIP, Lib. Assistant, Ramsbottom Library, Bury.
[2722] 06/10/1971 **CM13/09/1974**

Parkinson, Mrs C M, BA BSc MA, Senior Library Assistant, Vaughan College.
[63208] 16/03/2004 **ME**

Parkinson, Mrs D, BA (Hons) MCLIP,
[59594] 21/06/2001 **CM19/11/2008**

Parkinson, Mrs F, BLS MCLIP, Senior Manager, Business Analysis.
[28197] 13/10/1977 **CM28/02/1983**

Parkinson, Mr J K, BA DipLib MCLIP, Librarian, Serco (for Cabinet Office)/Emergency Planning College, York.
[26502] 20/10/1976 **CM26/06/1979**

Parkinson, Mrs S A, MCLIP, Life Member.
[11273] 01/01/1957 **CM01/01/1962**

Parkinson, Ms V S, BA (Hons), Student, Institute of Advanced Legal Studies.
[10032615]   20/12/2013   **ME**
Parkinson, Miss W H, MCLIP, Retired.
[11276]   13/02/1947   **CM01/01/1966**
Parkinson-Hardman, Mrs L A, BA (Hons) MSc, The Hysterectomy Assoc., Dorchester.
[53255]   17/04/1996   **ME**
Parks, Mrs J, MCLIP, Retired.
[11660]   09/01/1964   **CM01/01/1967**
Parlain, Ms K, BA (Hons) MA MCLIP, Librarian, Trinity School, Croydon.
[42695]   25/01/1989   **RV**13/05/2014   **CM22/05/1996**
Parmiter, Mr T M, BA MCLIP, Retired.
[36918]   14/01/1984   **CM16/10/1989**
Parr, Mrs N R, BA (Hons) DipILM,
[55584]   21/10/1997   **CM25/07/2001**
Parr, Ms S C, BA DipLib MA MCLIP, Librarian, Brentside High School, Hanwell, London.
[35545]   01/11/1982   **CM18/07/1985**
Parratt, Mrs J P, BA MCLIP, User Serv. Librarian, University of Brighton, Queenwood L.
[40359]   21/01/1987   **CM22/05/1991**
Parris, Ms J, MSc, Subject Support Librarian.
[10014941]   01/11/2010   **ME**
Parrott, Mrs R P L N, BSc, Senior L. Assistant, Wellcome Library, London.
[65592]   23/02/2006   **AF**
Parry, Ms C M, BA MA MCLIP, Team Mgr (Systems, Subs & Licencing), LSBU.
[42346]   24/10/1988   **CM07/10/1997**
Parry, Miss J, BA (Hons) MLIS, L. Serv. Manager, Powys Teaching Health Board, Bronllys, Nr. Brecon.
[56441]   10/07/1998   **ME**
Parry, Mrs J S, BA (Hons) PGCL MCLIP HonFCLIP, Retired. Previous job – Information & Relationship Manager, Hillsborough Independent Panel Secretariat, Home Office, London.
[42183]   10/10/1988   **HFE30/09/2013**
Parry, Mrs K, BA (Hons), Student, Aberystwyth University.
[10014988]   01/10/2009   **ME**
Parry, Mrs K M, BA (Hons), Student, Aberystwyth University.
[10033946]   13/05/2014   **ME**
Parry, Mr M, BA, Senior Library Assistant, Aberystwyth University.
[10031645]   17/09/2013   **ME**
Parry, Ms S T, BLib MCLIP, Web Content Manager., Metropolitan Police Services., London.
[41756]   10/03/1988   **CM18/09/1991**
Parry, Mr V T H, MA (Oxon) FCLIP FRSA FRAS, Life Member.
[11302]   29/09/1950   **FE01/01/1959**
Parry, Mrs W, BA (Hons) PgDipLIS DTLLS, College Librarian, Heart of Worcestershire College.
[45211]   13/08/1990   **ME**
Parsley, Ms S, BEng BA, Part-time Student, City University, LSHTM, London.
[10000699]   15/11/2006   **ME**
Parsonage, Ms H L, BA (Hons) MA MCLIP PGCHE, Liaison Librarian, Barckenhurst Campus Library, Southwell.
[61844]   18/11/2002   **CM09/09/2009**
Parsons, Mrs A, KIM Strategy, Policy and Compliance Engagement.
[66069]   14/09/2006   **ME**
Parsons, Mr A J, BA (Hons) MPhil MCLIP, Academic Liaison Librarian, University of Westminster.
[38310]   04/03/1985   **CM10/11/1987**

Parsons, Mrs C, BLib MCLIP, Principal Librarian, Bracknell Forest Borough Council, Berks.
[33075]   01/10/1980   **CM30/07/1985**
Parsons, Miss L D, BSc MCLIP, Retired.
[60735]   22/10/1985   **CM22/10/1985**
Partington, Miss J, BA DipLib MCLIP, Senior Assistant Librarian, Goldsmiths, University of London.
[33333]   07/11/1980   **CM27/07/1983**
Parton, Mrs G, BA (Hons) MCLIP, Librarian, Northbrook College Sussex, Worthing.
[49114]   06/10/1993   **CM21/07/1999**
Parton, Mr S, BA MA MCLIP, Clinical Effectiveness Librarian, University of North Staffordshire Hospital at Keele University Health Library.
[61024]   05/02/2002   **CM28/01/2009**
Partridge, Mr D A, FCLIP, Life Member.
[11320]   10/02/1950   **FE01/01/1969**
Partridge, Mr G A, BA (Hons), R&D Director, Soutron LTD, Derbyshire.
[49845]   21/12/1993   **ME**
Partridge, Mrs J E, BA (Hons), Cataloguer, University of Lincoln.
[63905]   26/10/2004   **ME**
Partridge, Mr K A, MCLIP, Marketing Manager, UK Trade & Investment, London.
[61904]   28/11/2002   **CM13/06/2007**
Partridge, Mr R A, BA (Hons) PgDipLIS, Head of User Experience, Library and Learning Services, De Montfort University, Leicester.
[52669]   20/11/1995   **ME**
Pascoal Rodrigues, Mrs V C, PgDip, Retail Operative, Primark.
[10032333]   19/11/2013   **ME**
Paskova, Miss J, Student.
[10031883]   10/10/2013   **ME**
Patalong, Mrs S L, BA FHEA MCLIP, Subject Librarian, Coventry University.
[31034]   02/07/1979   **CM19/08/1981**
Patchett, Mrs G W, MCLIP, Unemployed.
[3314]   26/08/1969   **CM20/09/1972**
Patel, Miss J, BSc MA, L. Executive, House of Commons, London.
[57581]   12/05/1999   **ME**
Patel, Mrs R, BSc (Hons) MSc, Information Specialist, Midlands.
[62373]   16/05/2003   **ME**
Pateman, Mr J P, BA DipLib MBA FCLIP, Chief Librarian and Chief Executive Officer, Thunder Bay Library Service, Ontario, Canada.
[32146]   01/02/1980   **FE26/11/1997**
Paterson, Miss A, BA DipILS MCLIP, Volunteer Librarian, Glasgow Women's Library.
[58011]   12/10/1999   **CM16/07/2003**
Paterson, Miss C L, BA (Hons) MCLIP, Assistant Librarian (Systems), Goldsmiths, London.
[43163]   05/09/1989   **CM16/07/2003**
Paterson, Mrs D W, MA (Hons) MCLIP, Examination Invigilator.
[42133]   05/10/1988   **CM12/12/1991**
Paterson, Mrs E A, MCLIP, Retired.
[11338]   02/03/1962   **CM01/01/1965**
Paterson, Mrs M, MCLIP,
[10014151]   01/07/2009   **CM11/04/2013**
Paterson, Mr N J, MCLIP, Lifelong Learning Librarian, Aberdeen City Libraries.
[10006914]   17/12/2007   **CM11/02/2010**
Paterson, Mr R, Lib. Assistant f. /t., St Albans Central Library, Hertfordshire.
[10005991]   11/09/2007   **ME**
Paterson, Mrs S E, MA DipLib, Curator F, Lib., Department of Printed Books, Imperial War Museum.
[38364]   01/04/1985   **ME**

Paterson, Mrs S M, BA MCLIP, Librarian, Fortrose Library,
[23248]   15/11/1974   **CM18/10/1977**
Paton, Ms K L, BA (Hons), Student, Manchester Metropolitan University.
[10021363]   25/07/2012   **ME**
Patrick, Mr D, MCLIP, Librarian, Community Libraries Network,
Glasgow.
[10017115]   23/06/2010   **CM27/03/2014**
Patrick, Dr S, Gilead Sciences Lit. Resources, Foster City, CA, USA.
[35977]   11/02/1983   **ME**
Patten, Mrs J, Information Services Manager, Libraries NI.
[56412]   06/07/1998   **ME**
Patten, Mr J, BA MA, Library Assistant.
[58023]   14/10/1999   **ME**
Patterson, Mrs F C, Assistant Librarian, Monk's Walk School.
[10021074]   29/05/2012   **ME**
Patterson, Ms L C, BA (Hons) MA MCLIP, Prison Librarian, HMP
Sudbury.
[49595]   19/11/1993   **CM26/11/1997**
Patterson, Mrs M C, BA MCLIP, Young Peoples Serv. Librarian, East
Ayrshire Council, Kilmarnock.
[30360]   08/02/1979   **CM11/02/1985**
Patterson, Mrs R A, Lib. Ass. University of York.
[63894]   26/10/2004   **ME**
Patterson, Mr S J, LVO MA MA MCLIP, Head of Collections &
Information, Management, Royal Collection, Buckingham Palace.
[39374]   17/01/1986   **CM27/01/1993**
Pattinson, Mrs K F, Managing Director, Askews L. Serv., Preston.
[10018443]   18/01/2011   **AF**
Pattison, Miss S J, MSc MCLIP, Senior Library Assistant (Biomedical
Sciences), UCL, London.
[10019047]   13/04/2011   **CM13/11/2013**
Paul, Ms A E, BSc (Econ) MCLIP, Deputy Manager., Library &
Knowledge Services., Ashford & St Peter's Hospitals NHS Trust.
[54644]   06/02/1997   **CM23/06/2004**
Paul, Mrs H E, BA DipLib MCLIP, Systems Manager, Guilles-Alles
Library, Guernsey.
[33226]   23/10/1980   **CM18/09/1991**
Paul, Mrs J E, MA MCLIP, Retired.
[11368]   01/01/1959   **CM01/01/1962**
Pavey, Mrs M, BA PgDip MCLIP, Education Consultant – Libraries.
[10122]   01/01/1966   **CM16/09/1974**
Pavey, Mrs S J, BSc MSc FCLIP, Independent trainer / consultant for
schools.
[60802]   12/12/2001   **FE31/01/2007**
Pavlik, Mrs D, FCLIP, Retired.
[11376]   28/02/1971   **FE29/10/1976**
Pawley, Miss J, BA (Hons), Senior Library Assistant, Musgrove Park
Hospital.
[10034131]   09/06/2014   **ME**
Paxman, Miss C, Information Exploitation and iHub Manager, Ministry of
Defence.
[10034316]   02/07/2014   **ME**
Paxton, Ms G, BA (Hons), Bury Archives, Local & Family History
Service, Moss Street, Bury, Greater Manchester.
[10016431]   01/10/2002   **ME**
Payne, Miss C S, PgDip, Outreach Librarian, Mersey Care NHS Trust.
[10015090]   15/10/2009   **ME**
Payne, Mr D, BA MLS, Branch Manager, Free Library of Philadelphia,
USA.
[41475]   01/01/1988   **ME**
Payne, Mrs D M, BA DipLib MCLIP, Librarian, Ministry of Defence, Army
Library and Information Service.
[40040]   07/10/1986   **CM12/09/1990**

Payne, Ms E A, BA DipLib MCLIP, Student.
[44489]   15/10/1990   **CM18/11/1993**
Payne, Mr I C, MA CertEd DipLib MCLIP,
[35732]   04/01/1983   **CM06/09/1988**
Payne, Miss J M, ACLIP, Service Development Specialist, Harrow
Libraries.
[64412]   15/03/2005   **ACL10/01/2006**
Payne, Mrs K A, MCLIP, Unwaged.
[63994]   01/12/2004   **CM10/07/2009**
Payne, Miss L, BA (Hons) MA, Enquiries & Digital Officer, Royal
Borough of Windsor & Maidenhead.
[10006762]   17/12/2007   **ME**
Payne, Mrs L, BA MA, Library Manager, Lady Eleanor Holles School.
[64553]   10/05/2005   **ME**
Payne, Mrs L M E, MA MCLIP, Assistant Head of Serv. – Development,
Norfolk L. & Information Serv., Norwich.
[33212]   28/10/1980   **CM15/02/1983**
Payne, Mr M, BA DipLib MCLIP, Senior Librarian, Penarth Library, Vale
of Glamorgan.
[37794]   26/10/1984   **CM14/04/1987**
Payne, Mrs N A, BA, Student, Manchester Metropolitan University.
[10032714]   07/01/2014   **ME**
Payne, Mr P M, BA MCLIP HonFCLIP, Retired.
[11394]   20/01/1972   **HFE29/06/2005**
Payne, Ms S E, BA MA MCLIP AMIRMS, Dept Records Officer, DCMS,
London.
[43541]   02/11/1989   **CM18/11/1993**
Payne, Mrs T P, BA (Hons), Trainee Librarian, Conwy County Borough
Council.
[10022257]   29/01/2013   **ME**
Payne, Ms V J, BA MLIS DipLib MCLIP ALAI, Aquisitions and
Periodicals Librarian; National University of Ireland, Maynooth.
[30784]   03/04/1979   **CM19/05/1982**
Paynter, Mr D F, MCLIP, Unwaged.
[11398]   10/01/1968   **CM01/01/1971**
Peace, Ms A M, BA (Hons) MA ILS MCLIP, Head of Development &
Research, The Chartered Society of Physiotherapy.
[49616]   19/11/1993   **RV**13/11/2013   **CM06/04/2005**
Peach, Ms M, LRC Manager, Park View, London.
[10018218]   09/12/2010   **ME**
Peach, Mrs S P, BA MCLIP, Local Studies Librarian, Derbys. County
Council.
[23395]   14/01/1975   **CM14/01/1977**
Peacock, Ms E,
[10007022]   28/02/1995   **ME**
Peacock, Mrs J A, MCLIP, Retired.
[12486]   30/09/1968   **CM15/12/1972**
Peaden, Mrs A M, BA MCLIP, Area Manager, Culture & Leisure
Services, Kirklees Council, Huddersfield.
[33167]   07/10/1980   **CM03/02/1986**
Peagram, Miss E P, BSc (Hons) MSc MCLIP, Librarian, Dr J H
Burgoyne and Partners LLP, London.
[62630]   01/10/2003   **CM07/07/2010**
Peake, Mrs H M, BSc (Hons) MCLIP, Knowledge Interchange
Information Executive, Cranfield School of Management, Cranfield
University.
[55737]   10/11/1997   **CM29/03/2004**
Peake, Mr H S, BA MCLIP, Life Member.
[11412]   23/09/1954   **CM01/01/1957**
Peake, Miss S T, BA MCLIP, Senior Librarian, Educ. L. Serv., Berks.
[39392]   22/01/1986   **CM15/08/1990**
Pearce, Mr D, Information Professional, Ministry of Defence.
[10035065]   09/09/2014   **ME**

Pearce, Mr J K, BA (Hons) PgDipLIS, Deputy Librarian, Royal Military
    Academy Sandhurst.
    [46781]   22/01/1992   ME
Pearce, Mrs L A, BEd (Oxon), Resource Ctre. Manager, Kendrick
    School, Reading, Berks.
    [57922]   05/10/1999   ME
Pearce, Mrs L M, BSc MSc MCLIP, Unwaged.
    [60836]   01/06/1990   CM11/03/2009
Pearce, Ms M, BA (Hons) ACLIP, Librarian, Penrith Library, Cumbria
    County Council.
    [65264]   08/12/2005   ME
Pearce, Mr M, BA (Hons) MA MCLIP,
    [55294]   18/09/1997   CM07/09/2005
Pearce, Mrs P, BA MCLIP, Librarian Tewkesbury Group, Glos. County
    Council.
    [32033]   11/02/1980   CM21/02/1985
Pearce, Mrs P, BA MSc (Econ) MCLIP, Retired.
    [12311]   27/01/1966   CM01/01/1969
Pearce, Mr R, BA MCLIP, Performance officer, ccs ltd.
    [38822]   10/10/1985   CM14/11/1990
Peare, Mr J D T, BA MSc FLAI FCLIP, Keeper (Readers' Services),
    Trinity College Library, Dublin.
    [18999]   02/10/1972   FE07/09/2005
Pearl, Mr C J, BA MCLIP, Retired.
    [11432]   25/05/1970   CM22/03/1974
Pearlman, Mrs D P, BA MCLIP, Librarian, Freelance.
    [20003]   12/01/1973   CM02/10/1978
Pearse, Mrs E M, MCLIP, Life Member.
    [11461]   19/09/1947   CM01/01/1954
Pearson, Mr B, DMA MILAM FCLIP, Retired.
    [11439]   06/02/1957   FE13/06/1990
Pearson, Ms C A, BA DipLib MCLIP, Team Leader, East Area, North
    YorkshireCounty Library Service.
    [27704]   04/07/1977   CM31/01/1980
Pearson, Mr D R S, MA PhD DipLib FCLIP, Director, Culture, Heritage &
    Libraries, City of London.
    [33163]   01/10/1980   FE25/07/2001
Pearson, Mrs J V, BTech DipLib MCLIP, Retired.
    [11447]   25/04/1968   CM01/01/1970
Pearson, Mrs M, BSc (econ) MA, Database Manager., Henley Business
    School, University of Reading.
    [10016949]   19/04/2012   ME
Pearson, Mr N T, BA (Hons), Library Assistant, Royal Marsden NHS
    Foundation Trust, London.
    [10018450]   19/01/2011   ME
Pearson, Mr P J, BSc MA MCLIP, Assistant Librarian, Courtauld
    Institute of Art.
    [43273]   09/10/1989   CM24/03/1992
Pearson, Dr P M, BTh MTh PhD MA MCLIP, Director & Arch., Thomas
    Merton Centre, Bellarmine University, Louisville.
    [52093]   03/10/1995   CM15/03/2000
Pearson, Mr R F M, MCMI MIMS MCLIP, Retired.
    [11451]   05/02/1964   CM01/01/1971
Pearson, Miss T, MCLIP, Stock Officer.
    [10001669]   02/10/2000   CM20/04/2012
Pearson, Mr W D, MCLIP, Retired.
    [19244]   20/01/1965   CM01/01/1970
Peasley, Mr M E, MA (Oxon) DipLib MCLIP, Area Manager, Devon
    Libraries.
    [35633]   19/11/1982   CM18/02/1986
Peat, Mrs R A, BA (Hons) MCLIP, Network Librarian, Wick High School,
    Wick/Caithness.
    [42613]   18/01/1989   RV27/03/2014
    CM12/09/2001

Peat, Mrs S A, BSc (Econ) MCLIP, Knowledge Design Officer, College
    of Law, York.
    [57194]   12/01/1999   CM29/11/2006
Peattie, Mr P R, MCLIP, Retired.
    [26648]   26/10/1976   CM08/10/1979
Peck, Mrs J E, BA MCLIP, Librarian, Cheshire County Council, Chester.
    [22026]   01/01/1974   CM21/10/1976
Pecout, Mr R, MCLIP, Senior Librarian for Information and Online
    Services, Hertfordshire.
    [63460]   12/05/2004   CM07/07/2010
Peddie, Mr C, BA MSc MCLIP,
    [10000878]   16/11/2006   RV20/06/2014
    CM10/11/2010
Peddlesden, Ms K K, BA (Hons) MCLIP, Information Scientist, MOD,
    London.
    [39752]   16/06/1986   CM20/01/1999
Peden, Miss A M, MCLIP, Retired.
    [11462]   01/08/1967   CM01/01/1970
Peden, Mrs J E, BLib BA (Hons) MSc MCLIP FHEA, University
    Librarian, University of Ulster.
    [44368]   01/10/1990   CM13/03/2002
Pedersen, Mr V B, BA (Hons) MA MCLIP, L. Manager, Civil Aviation
    Authority, Gatwick.
    [55744]   12/11/1997   CM29/03/2004
Pedley, Mrs A J M, MA MCLIP, Retired.
    [40402]   05/02/1987   CM16/02/1988
Peebles, Ms E, MA (HONS) PGDE PgDipILS, School Librarian.
    [10020838]   18/04/2012   ME
Peel, Mrs J D, BSc MCLIP, Life Member.
    [22576]   08/07/1974   CM11/06/1987
Peel, Miss M, BA (Hons) MA MCLIP, Information Manager, Transport for
    Greater Manchester.
    [62406]   02/06/2003   CM19/03/2008
Peet, Mrs E, BA (Hons) MA MCLIP, Senior Assistant Librarian,
    Manchester Metro. University.
    [58586]   05/04/2000   CM19/11/2003
Pelekanou, Dr A, BA MA PhD, Librarian, George Green Library,
    Greenfield Medical Library, James Cameron Gifford, University of
    Nottingham.
    [10008623]   04/04/2008   ME
Pellett, Mrs G R, BA (Hons), Librarian., Willingdon Community Sch.
    [59298]   31/01/2001   ME
Pemberton, Mrs M M, MA BA (Hons) MCLIP, Freelance School Library
    Adviser, Growing your library.
    [16022]   16/06/1971   CM22/07/1975
Pemberton, Mr R, Community Librarian., Medway Libraries.
    [63812]   01/10/2004   ME
Pemberton, Miss S J, BA DipLib MCLIP, Librarian, Continuing
    Education Library, University of Oxford.
    [30025]   23/11/1978   CM07/04/1982
Pemberton Jewitt, Ms T, DESCIO-InfoSkills-Dev-AsstHd, MoD.
    [10032158]   14/05/2014   ME
Penfold, Dr D W, PhD DIC BSc ARCS MCLIP CEng MB, Senior
    Lecturer/Consultant/Editor, London College of Comm., Edgerton
    Publishing Serv.
    [60572]   30/12/1981   CM30/12/1981
Penfold, Mrs K A, BA MCLIP, Cataloguer, University of Edinburgh, Main
    Library.
    [18144]   07/10/1972   CM13/01/1975
Penn, Ms E A, BA (Hons) MA MCLIP, Librarian, Notts. County Council.
    [51584]   03/04/1995   CM23/09/1998
Penn, Mrs L, BA (Hons) MCLIP, Head of Resources & Technology,
    University of West London.
    [44842]   13/12/1990   CM22/07/1998

Penn, Miss L, Information Manager, Civil Service.
[10034317]   02/07/2014   ME
Penn, Mrs S J, BEd DipLib MCLIP, Librarian, Hewitsons, Cambridge.
[31441]   27/09/1979   CM23/03/1982
Penn, Mr S W, BA (Hons) DipLib MCLIP, Product Solutions Specialist, Axiell Ltd, Nottingham.
[28355]   14/11/1977   CM12/11/1980
Penney, Mrs B M, MCLIP, Life Member.
[28998]   23/08/1950   CM01/01/1955
Penney, Miss C L, BA DipLib MCLIP, Hon. Hurd Librarian, Hartlebury Castle.
[11503]   01/01/1966   CM01/01/1969
Penney, Miss V R, MCLIP, Life Member.
[11505]   10/01/1945   CM01/01/1964
Pennick, Mrs K P, BA MA MCLIP, Librarian, Royal Botanic Gardens, KEW.
[42205]   05/10/1988   CM22/11/1995
Pennie, Mr D A, MA MCLIP, Retired.
[11507]   14/10/1970   CM01/03/1973
Pennington, Mr N J, BEng, Patent Searcher, EIP Europe LLP, London.
[10023080]   04/06/2013   ME
Pennock, Mrs L, Learning Resource Centre Manager, Redden Court School.
[10034337]   01/10/2014   ME
Penny, Mr A, BA MCLIP, Customer Services Agent. Argyll and Bute Council.
[43454]   26/10/1989   CM18/09/1991
Penny, Mrs M E, MA (Hons) DipLIS MCLIP, Records Management Officer, Scottish Fire and Rescue Service.
[49647]   18/11/1993   CM19/01/2000
Penny, Mrs S, MA DipLib MCLIP, School Librarian, Tobermory High School, Argyll & Bute.
[43420]   26/10/1989   CM18/09/1991
Penny, Mrs S J, ACLIP, Library Assistant., Southmead Hospital, Bristol.
[10020610]   27/03/2012   ACL13/11/2013
Penrose, Mrs D, BA MCLIP, Head of Academic Support, Ealing, Hammersmith & West London College.
[10011296]   13/10/2008   CM18/12/2009
Pensaert, Ms A, Head of Music (Collections), University of Cambridge, University Library.
[10023088]   05/06/2013   ME
Pentelow, Miss G M, MCLIP, Life Member.
[11514]   13/01/1955   CM01/01/1958
Pentney, Mrs S J, BSc (Econs) MCLIP, Service Manager (Delivery), Plymouth County Council.
[55153]   24/07/1997   CM19/11/2003
Peoples, Miss M A, BA HonFCLIP DMS, Retired.
[21175]   01/10/1973   HFE12/12/2007
Pepin, Miss S, BA DipLib MCLIP, Reader's Advisor, House of Commons Library, London.
[36938]   18/01/1984   CM15/05/1989
Peppard, Ms C, BA, Liaison Support Librarian, St George's, University of London.
[10020313]   11/01/2012   ME
Percival, Mr D, MA, Learning and Engagement Manager Portsmouth CC.
[61420]   15/07/2002   ME
Percival, Miss L, BA (Hons),
[10021584]   04/09/2012   ME
Percival, Dr N, MA MA PhD,
[10012166]   08/01/2009   ME
Percival, Ms S, Library Assistant, Department of Engineering, University of Cambridge.
[10031878]   25/04/2014   ME

Pereira, Ms M J, BA MCLIP MA CTESL, Consultant, Infoman Inc., Canada.
[26509]   21/10/1976   CM07/02/1980
Pere-West, Mrs V, MA,
[10033482]   17/03/2014   ME
Perez, Mrs A, BSc, Unwaged.
[10020229]   02/12/2011   ME
Perfitt, Ms M T, FCLIP, Volunteer Librarian/ Reading Help, Highbury Quadrant Primary School.
[11538]   01/01/1961   FE29/10/1976
Perham, Mrs L, JP BA MCLIP HonFCLIP FRSA, Director, Various Charities and Non-Departmental Public Bodies.
[11539]   01/01/1969   HFE23/10/2003
Perkins, Mr C A E, BA, Library Assistant, Jesus College, Cambridge.
[41299]   01/11/1987   ME
Perkins, Mr D, MA, Unwaged.
[10001318]   31/03/2005   ME
Perkins, Mrs L J, BScEcon (Hons) MCLIP, P. A Shropshire Primary Health Trust.
[54349]   14/11/1996   CM18/09/2002
Perkins, Mrs S A, School Librarian, Beauchamps High School, Wickford.
[65341]   18/01/2006   ME
Perrett, Mrs C H J, BA DipLib MCLIP,
[36620]   24/10/1983   CM14/03/1990
Perrin, Miss P M, FRSA BA MCLIP, Retired.
[11556]   17/02/1949   CM01/01/1956
Perrott, Mrs M, BA HDipEd MA MCLIP, Sch. Lib, Cedars Upper School.
[47575]   02/10/1992   CM12/09/2001
Perry, Mrs A, BSc DipLib MCLIP, Information Manager.
[42279]   13/10/1988   CM27/07/1994
Perry, Ms E, BA,
[10029413]   11/02/2014   ME
Perry, Mrs G E, BA MCLIP, Information and Signposting Officer Healthwatch East Riding of Yorkshire.
[25804]   20/02/1970   CM27/04/1982
Perry, Miss N E, BA (Hons) MA, Library Systems Manager, University of Roehampton.
[63946]   18/11/2004   ME
Perry, Mr P, MCLIP, Unwaged.
[11563]   07/02/1955   CM01/01/1960
Perry, Miss R K, BA MCLIP, L. Serv. & E – Learning Manager, Royal Berks, NHS FT, Reading.
[42596]   18/01/1989   CM22/07/1992
Perry, Mrs S A, MA MCLIP, Librarian, Institute of Education.
[63458]   12/05/2004   CM08/08/2008
Perry, Mrs V, CQSW, Student, Bridgwater College.
[10033229]   21/02/2014   ME
Person, Ms A, LLB (Hons) DTTLS, Librarian, De La Salle College.
[10032396]   03/12/2013   ME
Pert, Ms R J, BA (Hons) MA, Library Assistant, Cardiff University.
[10032395]   03/12/2013   ME
Pester, Mr D R, BA, Cataloguer, London Metropolitan University, London.
[10019727]   20/02/1984   CM24/03/1987
Peters, Mrs A E, MCLIP, Life Member.
[11569]   03/03/1960   CM01/01/1966
Peters, Mrs B, BSc (Hons) MCLIP, Library Services Co-ordinator.
[10018415]   14/01/2011   CM14/11/2012
Peters, Mrs C, BSc MCLIP, Team Librarian, Surrey County Council.
[33366]   26/10/1980   CM13/05/1986
Peters, Mrs E J, MCLIP, School Librarian.
[26418]   01/10/1976   CM04/09/1980

Peters, Mr J, LRC Manager, City & Islington College, London.
[10013687]   21/10/2009   ME
Peters, Mrs J M, BA MLS FHEA MCLIP FRSA, Director of Library
Services & University Librarian, Cardiff University.
[34208]   12/10/1981   CM07/07/1987
Peters, Dr L J, BSc (Hons) MSc (Econ) MCLIP PhD, Sub. Lib. for Law,
Learning & Information Serv., University of Chester.
[53495]   04/07/1996   CM15/09/2004
Peters, Mrs N A, BA MA MCLIP, Part-time Librarian, Redditch Library,
Worcs. County Council.
[35301]   01/10/1982   CM05/05/1987
Peters, Mrs R, BSc, Admin Assistant, Southport & Ormskirk NHS Trust.
[10006484]   24/10/2007   ME
Petersen, Miss C L, BA (Joint Hons) MCLIP, Children's Librarian,
Alfreton Librarian, Derbyshire.
[10001947]   01/04/1995   CM14/10/2011
Petersen, Mrs L A, Part-time Student /Assistant Librarian, University of
Central England, Birmingham, Lordswood Boys Sch. & 6th Form
Cent.
[59021]   27/10/2000   AF
Peterson, Ms C, Student, City University London.
[10022305]   05/02/2013   ME
Peterson, Mrs J, MA, Student, King's College London.
[10032493]   10/12/2013   ME
Peterson, Dr M F, BA (Hons) DipLib PhD, Knowledge Manager, South
Australia Health Library Service, Adelaide.
[64094]   14/01/2005   ME
Pethers, Ms H J, BA (Hons), Reader Services Librarian, Natural History
Museum, London.
[57577]   06/05/1999   ME
Peto, Mrs G, BA DipLib MCLIP, Prison Librarian, HMP Whatton.
[26307]   01/10/1976   CM23/10/1979
Petrie, Mrs H M, BA (Hons) MSc MCLIP, Open Learning Officer,
CultureNL, Motherwell.
[51126]   17/11/1994   CM16/07/2003
Petrou, Dr A, PhD (LIS), Consultant and Information Management
Educator, Freelance.
[10021559]   30/08/2012   ME
Pett, Mrs S C, BA, Learning Resources Centre Manager, De Stafford
School, Surrey.
[10011311]   13/10/2008   ME
Pettitt, Miss J M, MCLIP, Life Member.
[11586]   31/03/1938   CM01/01/1953
Pexton, Mr M J, MA, Library Assistant at Herbert Smith Freehills LLP.
[10017684]   23/09/2010   ME
Peyn, Ms O B, MA MA, Head of L. Cataloguing, Society of Antiquaries
of London, Piccadilly, London.
[10015206]   07/10/1982   ME
Phelps, Mrs S H, MCLIP, Retired.
[31684]   05/11/1979   CM27/07/1983
Phenix, Mr A P, LLB (Hons) PGC, Library & Information Services
Manager, Wilsons Solicitors LLP.
[61078]   04/03/2002   ME
Philip, Mrs H R, BA MCLIP, Network Librarian., Millburn Academy,
Inverness.
[20945]   11/09/1973   CM04/08/1976
Philip, Mrs K, BA DipSW, Library Assistant, Culloden Library.
[10022850]   30/04/2013   AF
Phillips, Mrs A J, BA (Hons) MCLIP, Career break.
[48661]   02/04/1993   CM22/05/1996
Phillips, Mr C, BA DipLib MCLIP, Retired.
[29791]   08/10/1978   CM31/03/1981

Phillips, Mr C J, BA DipLib MCLIP, Retired; previously Area Manager
Surrey County Council Libraries; available for public library
management consultancy.
[25392]   09/01/1976   CM08/06/1978
Phillips, Ms C J, BA (Hons) MA, Student, UCL.
[10013421]   16/10/2014   ME
Phillips, Mr D, Graduate Library Trainee, Institute of Historical
Research.
[10029444]   29/10/2013   ME
Phillips, Mrs D J, BSc (Hons) MA, Senior Library Assistant: Faculty
Support, Imperial College London.
[10033702]   16/04/2014   ME
Phillips, Mrs D J, BA MCLIP,
[28118]   01/10/1977   CM01/10/1979
Phillips, Miss E, BA (Hons), Student, City University London.
[10035444]   14/10/2014   ME
Phillips, Mrs H M, MA MSc MCLIP, Unwaged.
[52548]   08/11/1995   CM13/03/2002
Phillips, Mrs I,
[10017517]   01/09/2010   ME
Phillips, Mrs J, BSc (Hons), Raising Reading Co-ordinator & Library
Manager, Alec Reed Academy.
[10033832]   02/05/2014   ME
Phillips, Mrs J C S, BA (Hons) MSc MCLIP, Community Librarian,
Wootton Bassett, Cricklade & Purton Libraries, Wiltshire.
[64838]   02/08/2005   CM21/05/2008
Phillips, Ms K E, BA MA MCLIP, Lib, Imperial War Museum.
[33743]   16/02/1981   CM14/10/1983
Phillips, Miss K L, BA (Hons) MCLIP, Assistant Librarian, GCHQ,
Cheltenham.
[51864]   18/07/1995   CM19/07/2000
Phillips, Miss L, BA MCLIP, Retired.
[11625]   30/01/1968   CM01/01/1972
Phillips, Ms L A, BA (Hons), Unemployed.
[50824]   20/10/1994   ME
Phillips, Mr M E, MA MA MCLIP, Head of Digital and Bibliographic
Services, Durham University.
[50672]   07/10/1994   CM16/05/2001
Phillips, Mrs M E, MCLIP, Stock & Distribution Librarian,
Carmarthensire C. C.
[21595]   16/10/1973   CM31/08/1978
Phillips, Miss M H, BA MCLIP, Retired.
[11626]   08/02/1967   CM01/01/1971
Phillips, Mrs M S, MA MCLIP, Information Services Manager,
Queenwood Library, Universtiy of Brighton.
[31759]   30/11/1979   CM16/09/1982
Phillips, Mr R, BA (Hons) MPhil DipLib, Assistant Archivist, The
National Library of Wales, Aberystwyth.
[10006059]   03/09/2007   ME
Phillips, Mr R, DipIM, Head of Information Serv., King's Fund, London.
[56713]   07/10/1998   CM21/11/2001
Phillips, Mr R, MA FCLIP, Life Member.
[11631]   05/10/1960   FE01/01/1967
Phillips, Miss R, BA (Cantab), MA student, University of Sheffield.
[10031790]   04/10/2013   ME
Phillips, Miss R, User Serv. Lib, Archway Healthcare Library, Highgate.
[10015769]   27/09/2000   ME
Phillips, Mrs S, BL FCLIP, Retired.
[17564]   22/01/1958   FE13/06/1990
Phillips, Mr S, BA DipLib MCLIP,
[11636]   02/03/1965   CM01/01/1968
Phillips, Mrs S E, BA (Hons) MCLIP, School Librarian, Royal Blind
School, Edinburgh.
[57028]   26/11/1998   CM17/09/2003

Phillips, Ms S E, BA (Hons) MA, Surestart Children's Centre Librarian,
Derbyshire County Council.
[10033556]   25/03/2014   ME
Phillips, Mr S J, BLib MCLIP, Executive Director, Morgan Stanley,
London.
[40788]   06/06/1987   CM14/11/1991
Phillips, Ms S L, BA, Unemployed.
[35699]   17/01/1983   ME
Phillips, Dr V M, BA (Hons) MPhil PhD, Junior Library Assistant,
University of Cambridge.
[10035262]   02/10/2014   ME
Phillips, Mr W T, BA DipLib MCLIP, Reg. Library Manager,
Carmarthenshire County Council, Carmarthen Library.
[35191]   04/10/1982   CM30/01/1991
Phillipson, Mrs E A, BA (Hons) PGCE,
[65899]   27/06/2006   ME
Phillpotts, Ms C E, BA (Hons) MA MCLIP, Director of Library Services,
London Metropolitan University.
[43276]   10/10/1989   CM25/09/1996
Philp, Mr G J, BMus Dip Lib MPhil ARIM MCLIP, Records &
administration Manager, Ashburton District Council, New Zealand.
[10019075]   01/10/1979   CM08/10/1981
Philpot, Mrs F L, BA MA, Unwaged.
[60475]   11/12/2001   CM04/02/2004
Philpott, Mr S J, BLib MSc MCLIP, Freelance Business Consultant.
[36222]   01/08/1983   CM06/04/1999
Physick, Miss H M, BA MCLIP, Library Customer Svces Manager,
London Borough of Harrow L.
[33956]   17/06/1981   CM30/07/1985
Pickard, Dr A J, BA (Hons) MA Phd, Head of Information & Comm. Mnt,
School of Computing, Engineering & Information Sciences,
Northumbria University.
[10008126]   24/01/1994   ME
Pickard, Mrs M, Office Manager, MOD.
[10033162]   12/05/2014   ME
Pickard-Brace, Mr A, MA BA (Hons), Libr., University Nottingham.
[55908]   12/12/1997   ME
Pickering, Mrs A J, BA (Hons) MCLIP, Assistant Manager, Customer
Services, Brotherton Library, University of Leeds.
[52687]   20/11/1995   CM20/01/1999
Pickering, Mrs C B, BA (Hons) MA PgDipls MCLIP DMS, L. Officer,
Wakefield Libraries, Wakefield.
[59358]   14/02/2001   CM02/02/2005
Pickering, Mrs O M, BA MA MPhil MCLIP, Assistant Librarian, Oxford
Health NHS Foundation Trust.
[57876]   20/09/1999   CM16/07/2003
Pickering, Miss P L, MCLIP, Life Member.
[11662]   31/03/1955   CM01/01/1961
Pickett, Mrs K P, BA (Hons) MCLIP, NEMS Co-ordinator & Mid Day
Supervisor.
[42445]   09/11/1988   CM14/09/1994
Pickstone, Ms M E, BSc DipLib MCLIP, Research Support Librarian,
Manchester Metropolitan University.
[34325]   23/10/1981   CM10/02/1987
Pickton, Dr M, BA MSc PhD MCLIP, Research Support Librarian,
University of Northampton.
[63166]   02/03/2004   CM21/03/2007
Pickup, Mr P W H, FCLIP, Life Member.
[11672]   23/02/1950   FE01/01/1959
Pierce, Mr J D, BA BSc MLIS, Office Manager, University of Aberdeen.
[10014813]   16/09/2009   ME
Pierce, Dr K F, BA (Hons) MPhil MSc PhD, Cataloguing Librarian,
Cardiff University.
[61197]   08/04/2002   ME

Pieris, Mrs K S, BA MCLIP, Retired.
[19947]   15/01/1973   CM21/10/1975
Pieroni, Mrs W J, Learning Res. Coordinator, Blairgowrie High School,
Perth.
[65105]   01/11/2005   ME
Pietsch, Ms A, Academic Development Manager, University of
Roehampton, London.
[64858]   03/08/2005   ME
Piggott, Mr R L, Self-employed researcher.
[10016452]   30/07/1974   CM22/08/1977
Pigott, Mrs F C, BA (Hons), Unwaged.
[43324]   19/10/1989   ME
Pigula, Mrs E D, MA, Assistant Librarian, The College of Law, Guildford,
Surrey.
[57379]   22/02/1999   ME
Pike, Ms D L, MA MLITT, Student, Robert Gordon University.
[10033186]   18/02/2014   ME
Pike, Mrs J A, BA MCLIP, Librarian., Southborough High School,
Surbiton.
[32892]   15/10/1980   CM10/10/1983
Pike, Mr R, BA MSc, Knowledge and Information Agent, Ministry of
Defence.
[10032805]   14/01/2014   ME
Pike, Mrs R A, BA (Hons) DipLib MCLIP, School Librarian, Bishops
Stortford College, Junior Sch.
[34418]   05/11/1981   CM16/05/1985
Pilfold, Mrs J J, ACLIP, Retired.
[64651]   13/05/2005   ACL16/04/2008
Pilkington, Mrs C A, BA (Hons) DIPCeD, Unwaged.
[53616]   12/08/1996   ME
Pilkington, Mrs G H, BSc, Media Centre Admin., British Sch. in the
Netherlands.
[46516]   15/11/1991   ME
Pill, Dr T J H, MA MLib MA PhD, Assistant Professor, Department of
English, American University of Beirut, Lebanon.
[47740]   10/10/1992   ME
Pillans, Mrs H A, BA MCLIP, School Librarian, Barrhead High School,
East Renfrewshire.
[27604]   15/06/1977   CM12/06/1979
Pilling, Mr J C, MA MCLIP, Reader Services Manager: Children, Young
People & Families, Holton, Oxfordshire County Council.
[35556]   27/10/1982   CM05/05/1986
Pilling, Mrs S, BA MBA DipMus MCLIP,
[1350]   22/02/1969   CM01/01/1971
Pillok, Miss E, BSc (Hons), Senior Resources Assistant, University of
West London.
[10020797]   11/04/2012   ME
Pilmer, Mr A C, BA MA MCLIP, Librarian, National Aerospace Library,
Royal Aeronautical Society.
[58869]   14/09/2000   RV27/08/2014   CM09/11/2005
Pilmer, Ms S J, BSc MSc MCLIP, L. Manager., NSPCC, London.
[48884]   12/07/1993   CM19/05/1999
Pilsel, Miss L J, Customer Services Team Leader (Headington Library),
Oxford Brookes University.
[10006308]   10/10/2007   ME
Pimperton, Mrs L, BA (Hons) MA DipIS MCLIP, Assistant Librarian,
Lancaster University, Lancaster.
[44879]   08/01/1991   CM18/11/1998
Pinder, Mrs E, MCLIP, Retired.
[9248]   25/03/1943   CM01/01/1948
Pinder, Ms M J, BA (Hons) MA MCLIP, Collections Officer – Cdm Team,
University of Leeds.
[47928]   26/10/1992   CM21/05/1997

Pinfield, Dr S J, MA MCLIP, Senior Lecturer, University of Sheffield.
[44397]   04/10/1990   **CM18/11/1992**
Pinfold, Ms D, BA DipLib MCLIP, Head of L. and Information Serv., UniversityCollege Falmouth.
[31924]   07/01/1980   **CM03/03/1982**
Pinion, Miss C F, BA FRSA HonFLA FCLIP, AV Consultant, Sheffield.
[11711]   12/03/1961   **HFE20/09/2000**
Pink, Mr T, Student, City University London.
[10034514]   18/07/2014   **ME**
Pinnegar, Ms S V, BA DipLib MCLIP, School Librarian, St Catherine's British Embassy School, Athens, Greece.
[39322]   12/01/1986   **CM14/11/1991**
Pinnell, Mrs J, BA (Hons) PgDip, Business Intelligence Manager, CTPartners.
[10017452]   23/08/2010   **ME**
Pinnock, Mr A C, MA MCLIP, Retired.
[19581]   16/11/1972   **CM30/06/1976**
Pipe, Mr C C, BA DipLib MCLIP, Freelance. Watermark, Norfolk.
[11715]   01/07/1969   **CM01/07/1993**
Pir, Ms S E, LLB (Hons), Senior Librarian, Wandsworth.
[10005494]   25/07/2007   **ME**
Pirie, Ms A, BSc (Hons) DipILS MCLIP, Development Librarian, Perth & Kinross Council, Perth.
[51144]   23/11/1994   **CM06/04/2005**
Pirwitz, Ms H, MA DipLib MCLIP, Retired.
[30785]   20/01/1979   **CM18/12/1981**
Pitman, Mrs A J, BA MCLIP, career break.
[29181]   06/04/1978   **CM20/08/1981**
Pitman, Ms C, BA (Hons) MA DipLib MCLIP, Idea Store Development Manager, Idea Store, London Borough of Tower Hamlets.
[10000886]   02/12/1981   **CM24/09/1985**
Pitman, Mrs H, ACLIP, Yourspace Proj. Manager, Lancs Lib. & Information Serv.
[63312]   08/04/2004   **ACL04/03/2009**
Pitman, Miss N J, BA MCLIP, LRC / ILT Manager, Norton Radstock College, Radstock.
[43688]   28/11/1989   **CM23/03/1994**
Pivnenko, Mrs N, MA, Information &L. Assistant, Judge Business School Library, Cambridge University.
[64334]   04/03/2005   **ME**
Plaice, Ms C J, BLib (Hons) MA MCLIP, Faculty Lib. for Health & Life Science, University of the West of England.
[34174]   07/10/1981   **CM10/02/1987**
Plain, Mr W A, BA (Hons), School Librarian, Knox Academy, East Lothian.
[48314]   25/11/1992   **ME**
Plaister, Miss J M, OBE BSc FCLIP, Life Member.
[11732]   01/01/1947   **FE01/01/1955**
Plater, Mrs L A, BA (Hons) DIPIS MCLIP, Senior Information Advisor, Kingston University.
[10022940]   02/07/1991   **CM26/05/1993**
Platt, Ms A, MSc, Unwaged.
[10021230]   29/06/2012   **ME**
Platt, Ms G S, BA DipLib MCLIP, Retired.
[22707]   16/09/1974   **CM28/01/1977**
Platt, Mrs M J, BSc DipLib MCLIP,
[35691]   19/01/1983   **CM26/02/1992**
Platts, Mrs H J, MA DipLib MCLIP, Health Information Librarian, Suffolk County Council.
[31854]   09/01/1980   **CM17/05/1983**
Platts, Mrs J K, MCLIP, Principal Library Assistant, Manchester Metropolitan University.
[64143]   19/01/2005   **CM28/01/2009**

Playforth, Ms C, BA, Library Assistant – Cataloguing, University of Sussex Library.
[10020899]   17/04/2014   **ME**
Plowman, Mrs P A, MCLIP, Learning Res. Manager, Guilsborough School, Northamptonshire.
[62390]   21/05/2003   **CM14/11/2012**
Pluess, Mrs S, BA MSc, Independent English Teacher.
[65687]   31/03/2006   **ME**
Plum, Mrs S M, BA MCLIP, Assistant Librarian, Priory School Library, Hitchin.
[28630]   03/01/1978   **CM17/08/1982**
Plumb, Mr D W, MA MCLIP, Retired.
[11754]   30/01/1972   **CM28/08/1975**
Poad, Mrs J E, BA MCLIP, Head of L., Bedford Borough C. C.
[24127]   13/03/1975   **CM21/09/1978**
Poingdestre, Mrs K, Library & Resources Officer, HMP LA Moye, Jersey.
[10020882]   19/04/2012   **AF**
Pointer, Ms R J, BA MCLIP, Locality Manager (South), Leicestershire County Council – Communities & Wellbeing.
[31545]   19/10/1979   **CM31/10/1984**
Poku, Miss M, MCLIP, Librarian, Financial Serv. Authority, London.
[64084]   15/12/2004   **CM11/11/2009**
Pol, Mrs A, Assistant Librarian.
[10033397]   07/03/2014   **ME**
Polchow, Ms S U, BA MA MCLIP FRSA, Literacy & Library Adviser, Microlibrarian Systems MLS.
[44647]   14/11/1990   **CM17/11/1999**
Polding, Mrs G M, MCLIP, Community Librarian, Schools' Library Service, Luton Cultural Services Trust.
[21254]   17/10/1973   **CM12/12/1977**
Polfreman, Dr M J, MA Phd, Unwaged.
[10018951]   09/11/1994   **ME**
Politowski, Mr B, MA MLitt, Enquiry Executive, House of Commons Library.
[10032468]   06/12/2013   **ME**
Polkinghorne, Mrs A S M, BA (Hons) MCLIP, Librarian, Truro School, Truro.
[10022797]   21/10/1986   **CM21/07/1993**
Pollard, Mrs N J A, MCLIP, Sch. Librarian, St John Fisher Catholic High School, Harrogate.
[38439]   26/04/1985   **CM14/11/2012**
Pollard, Mr W, BSc (Econ), System Librarian, Anglia Ruskin University, Chelmsford.
[61276]   09/05/2002   **ME**
Pollecutt, Ms N A, BA MA MCLIP, L. Systems Officer, Wellcome Library, London.
[55853]   02/12/1997   **CM17/01/2001**
Pollitt, Mr M J, BA MA, E-Services Librarian, Nottinghamshire CC.
[64855]   02/08/2005   **ME**
Pollitt, Miss M L, MCLIP, Unemployed, Essex.
[11786]   14/02/1972   **CM20/12/1974**
Pond, Dr C, OBE MA PhD HonFCLIP, Councillor, Essex CC & Epping Forest DC.
[62818]   23/10/2003   **HFE23/10/2003**
Pond, Miss F M, BA DipLib MCLIP, Deputy Information Manager, Birmingham City University, Birmingham. Library Manager, Royal College of Organists.
[32610]   04/05/1980   **CM20/05/1982**
Ponka, Mrs J A, MA BA (Hons) BA MCLIP, Assistant Library Manager, Holy Cross 6th Form College, Bury, Lancashire.
[23147]   31/10/1974   **CM31/08/1977**

Ponniah, Mrs G V, BA MCLIP, Corporate Information Government
Manager.
[40376]　　　　　　　　　23/01/1987　　**CM24/03/1992**
Ponsonby, Miss S E, BA MCLIP, Researcher, ITN, London.
[31926]　　　　　　　　　09/01/1980　　**CM07/11/1984**
Pool, Miss E R, Life Member.
[11798]　　　　　　　　　25/09/1948　　　　**ME**
Pool, Mr M, MCLIP, Retired.
[11800]　　　　　　　　　03/12/1969　　**CM02/09/1975**
Poole, Mr K, BA (Hons) MCLIP, Retired. Formerly: Senior Tutor
Librarian, Stevenage College, Herts.
[11802]　　　　　　　　　12/02/1952　　**CM01/01/1956**
Poole, Miss K, BA MSc MCLIP,
[61106]　　　　　　　　　25/02/2002　　**CM03/10/2007**
Poole, Miss L, BA, Student, UCL.
[10021724]　　　　　　　04/10/2012　　　　**ME**
Poole, Mrs L E, BA MCLIP, Life Member.
[11803]　　　　　　　　　16/01/1950　　**CM01/01/1955**
Pooley, Miss A K, BA (Hons) MA, Information Adv., Linklaters.
[66088]　　　　　　　　　21/09/2006　　　　**ME**
Poolton, Mrs K E, BA MCLIP, College Lib, St Bede's College,
Manchester.
[33888]　　　　　　　　　30/04/1981　　**CM15/08/1984**
Poon, Miss Y M A, Student.
[10022561]　　　　　　　26/03/2013　　　　**ME**
Poore, Mrs H M, BA (Hons) MA MCLIP, Assistant Librarian, UWE,
Bristol.
[57976]　　　　　　　　　07/10/1999　　**CM01/02/2007**
Pope, Miss A, MA, Student, City University London.
[10032777]　　　　　　　14/10/2014　　　　**ME**
Pope, Mr A G, BA (Hons) MLIS CELTA, Senior Digital Librarian, ARUP,
London.
[10014173]　　　　　　　23/06/2003　　**CM13/10/2010**
Pope, Mrs A J, BA LLB DipLib MCLIP FHEA, Learning and Information
Services Manager StaffordshireUniversity, Leek Road Library, Stoke
on Trent.
[35207]　　　　　　　　　05/10/1982　　**CM06/09/1900**
Pope, Mrs A V, BA (Hons) MA MCLIP, Knowledge Serv. Programme
Manager, West Midlands Deanery, NHSWM, St Chads Court.
[47349]　　　　　　　　　20/07/1992　　**CM27/01/2010**
Pope, Mrs N A, BA MA MSc,
[10012381]　　　　　　　30/01/2009　　　　**ME**
Pope, Miss S A, BA (Hons), Community Librarian.
[10021419]　　　　　　　06/08/2012　　　　**ME**
Pope, Miss S D, BSc, Library Assistant at Cardiff Universitys Trevithick
Library.
[10010615]　　　　　　　19/08/2008　　　　**ME**
Popham, Miss V, BA,
[10032129]　　　　　　　29/10/2013　　　　**ME**
Popp, Ms G, Head of Collections & Information., British Film Institute.
[44982]　　　　　　　　　24/01/1991　　　　**ME**
Poppleston, Mr M, MCLIP, Life Member.
[11817]　　　　　　　　　07/02/1961　　**CM01/01/1964**
Porritt, Ms F H, BA (Hons) MSc PgDipLib MCLIP, Academic Librarian,
Library & Information Services, Teesside University, Middlesborough.
[10013918]　　　　　　　24/02/1989　　**CM16/05/2012**
Porteous, Ms L D, BA MA MCLIP, Senior Information Advisor, Kingston
University.
[39978]　　　　　　　　　07/10/1986　　**CM18/04/1990**
Porter, Mrs A K, BA MCLIP, Relief Librarian.
[20972]　　　　　　　　　31/08/1973　　**CM01/11/1976**
Porter, Miss C E, BA MLib MCLIP, Director of L. & Learning Servs.,
Newman University, Birmingham.
[10014273]　　　　　　　14/10/1986　　**CM14/09/1994**

Porter, Mr D, BA (Hons), Aberystwyth University.
[10022810]　　　　　　　23/04/2013　　　　**ME**
Porter, Mrs E B, BA MCLIP OBE, Retired.
[23273]　　　　　　　　　25/11/1974　　**CM31/08/1978**
Porter, Mr G J, BA MA MCLIP, Network Manager, Lincolnshire Co. C.,
Sleaford.
[40300]　　　　　　　　　18/01/1987　　**CM23/03/1993**
Portokalidis, Mr S, BA,
[10032684]　　　　　　　03/01/2014　　　　**ME**
Posner, Ms K, MA, Part time Librarian and Archivist, East India
Club/Naval & Military Club; Chair, Association of Pall Mall Libraries.
[10012034]　　　　　　　10/12/2008　　　　**ME**
Postlethwaite, Mrs F D, BA (Hons) Cert Ed MCLIP, Children & Young
People's Librarian, Explore York Libraries and Archives Mutual Ltd.
[31802]　　　　　　　　　06/12/1979　　**CM22/10/1985**
Postma, Miss C A W, MA, Informationprofessional/librarian, University
Maastricht.
[10033241]　　　　　　　24/02/2014　　　　**ME**
Poston, Mr T D V, BA (Hons) MSc, Director &Head of Res., Kreab Gavin
Anderson, London.
[53855]　　　　　　　　　07/10/1996　　**CM07/10/1996**
Pote, Ms G F, BA MA MCLIP, Principal Librarian, Barbican L. City of
London.
[34028]　　　　　　　　　02/07/1981　　**CM20/11/1986**
Pothecary, Miss J C, BA (Hons) (Cantab), Learning Centre Coordinator,
South Essex College.
[10021591]　　　　　　　06/09/2012　　　　**AF**
Potter, Mrs J C, BA (Hons) MCLIP, Learning Resources Assistant – JET
Library, Leighton Hospital.
[44617]　　　　　　　　　07/11/1990　　**CM27/07/1994**
Potter, Mrs J H, BSc MCLIP, Unwaged.
[60577]　　　　　　　　　02/03/1976　　**CM07/03/1980**
Potter, Mr J M, BA MCLIP, Life Member.
[19535]　　　　　　　　　26/02/1959　　**CM01/01/1964**
Potter, Mrs L, BA DipLib MCLIP, Primary Care/eLearning Librarian,
Milton Keynes Hospital L.
[31571]　　　　　　　　　04/11/1979　　**CM23/02/1982**
Potter, Mr N, BA MA MSc, Life-share Prospect Officer, University of
Leeds.
[10012966]　　　　　　　17/03/2009　　　　**ME**
Potter, Mrs S P, BA DipLib MCLIP PGCHE FHEA, Research Support
Librarian, Nottingham Trent University.
[37515]　　　　　　　　　02/10/1984　　**CM05/04/1988**
Potton, Mr D M, MA DipLib MCLIP, Head of L. Serv., Derby City
Council.
[29795]　　　　　　　　　22/10/1978　　**CM28/10/1981**
Potton, Mrs J K, BA (Hons) MCLIP, Children's Service Manager,
Derbyshire County Council.
[32880]　　　　　　　　　09/10/1980　　**CM17/12/1985**
Poulter, Mr A J, BA MA MSc MCLIP, Lecturer, Department of Comp. &
Information Sci., Glasgow.
[33117]　　　　　　　　　20/10/1980　　**CM01/07/1990**
Poulton, Ms A J, BA (Hons) MA DMS PGDSM PgCertHE FCLIP,
Academic Team Manager – Learning and Skills Development – De
Montfort University.
[52236]　　　　　　　　　17/10/1995　　**FE12/09/2012**
Poulton, Mrs M, BA MA MEd DipLib MCLIP, Retired.
[25630]　　　　　　　　　26/01/1976　　**CM26/01/1978**
Pouton, Mrs S, Senior LRC Assistant, Aberystwyth.
[10032124]　　　　　　　29/10/2013　　　　**ME**
Powell, Mrs A F, BA (Hons) MscEcon, Librarian Children, Young People
and Families.
[10007321]　　　　　　　13/02/2008　　　　**ME**

Powell, Mrs C L, BA (Hons) DipILM MCLIP, Deputy Library Manager, Coleg Llandrillo.
[58146] 08/11/1999 **CM06/04/2005**

Powell, Miss E, BA MSc, Assistant Librarian, National Police Library, College of Policing.
[63957] 22/11/2004 **ME**

Powell, Miss E C, BA (Hons) DipLib MCLIP, Medical Librarian part-time.
[35286] 09/10/1982 **CM30/03/1999**

Powell, Mrs H D, BA MCLIP, School Librarian, Claremont High School, Kenton, Harrow.
[31298] 05/10/1979 **CM11/12/1989**

Powell, Mr H G, BA, Library Assistant, Holton, Oxford.
[10019846] 23/09/2011 **ME**

Powell, Ms I F, BSc MSc, Advisory Librarian, Coventry Schools Library & Resource Service, Coventry.
[62151] 03/03/2003 **ME**

Powell, Mrs J, BA MCLIP, Deputy District Librarian, High Peak, Derbys. County Council.
[28801] 02/02/1978 **CM05/02/1981**

Powell, Mr J C, FCLIP, Life member.
[11867] 01/01/1941 **FE01/01/1954**

Powell, Mrs J R, BA (Hons) DipLib MCLIP, IP Formalities & Information Officer, Foseco Intl. Ltd, Tamworth.
[43518] 31/10/1989 **CM21/07/1993**

Powell, Miss L A, MCLIP, Community Librarian, East Ayrshire Council.
[64387] 14/03/2005 **CM16/10/2009**

Powell, Mr L B, BA M DIV MCLIP, Pastor, Covenant Baptist Church, Toronto, Ontario, Canada.
[17588] 18/09/1953 **CM01/01/1960**

Powell, Mrs M, MCLIP MSc BA (Hons) Dip EngLit, CILIP Policy Officer, Wales.
[64894] 09/09/2005 **CM21/11/2007**

Powell, Mr P E, MCLIP, Retired.
[60497] 09/04/2001 **CM09/04/2001**

Powell, Mr S, BA (Hons) MCLIP, Team Librarian – Children & Young People. Nottinghamshire County Council.
[42943] 28/04/1989 **CM26/01/1994**

Power, Mr G N, BA DipLib MCLIP, Research Specialist, IFS University College.
[43193] 01/10/1989 **CM15/10/2002**

Power, Miss L C, ACLIP, Senior Library Assistant, Littlehampton Library.
[10022147] 08/01/2013 **ACL27/08/2014**

Power, Mrs V R, BA (Hons) MSc MEd, Graduate Tutor in Information Management, UWE, Bristol.
[10000750] 01/02/1995 **ME**

Powis, Mr C M, BA MA MLib FCLIP HEA, Head of Library & Learning Services, University of Northampton.
[42381] 21/10/1988 **FE03/10/2007**

Powles, Mrs J C, BA MA MCLIP, Librarian, Spurgeons College, London.
[22916] 08/10/1974 **CM04/11/1976**

Powling, Mrs K T Z, BA MAEd MS, High School Librarian, ACS Hillingdon International School.
[10029538] 23/07/2013 **ME**

Powling, Mr T J, BA (Hons) Cert ED PGCE, Learning Resource Manager, Northbrook College, Worthing.
[10005983] 21/08/2007 **ME**

Pownall, Miss R L, BA MA PgDipILS MCLIP, Senior Information Advisor, Kingston University.
[59370] 19/02/2001 **CM29/03/2006**

Powney, Mrs A, ACLIP, Library Assistant, Luton Culture.
[10022787] 23/04/2013 **ACL27/03/2014**

Powrie, Ms G, MA ACLIP, Prison and Lending Library Assistant.
[10020494] 21/02/2012 **ACL27/03/2014**

Prada, Mrs J A, BSc (Hons) MCLIP, Head of Metadata Team, Senate House Library, University of London.
[42727] 13/02/1989 **CM26/07/1995**

Prady, Mrs N L, BA (Hons) MCLIP, Subject Librarian, Anglia Ruskin University, Cambridgeshire.
[60957] 18/01/2002 **CM30/11/2009**

Prangnell, Mr R D, BSc MCLIP, Retired.
[60624] 25/09/1964 **CM21/03/1967**

Pratchett, Ms T L, BA (Hons) MSc MCLIP, Clinical Librarian, Lancaster Infirmary, Lancs.
[10005107] 13/06/2007 **CM11/04/2013**

Pratt, Ms F H, MA, Stock Serv. Officer, London Borough of Southwark.
[61572] 02/10/2002 **AF**

Pratt, Mrs J, BSc (Hons) DipIM MCLIP, Librarian – Partnership and Outreach, LB of Richmond Upon Thames.
[48626] 19/03/1993 **CM06/04/2005**

Pratt, Ms L A, BA DipLib MCLIP, Senior Systems Administrator.
[24259] 03/05/1975 **CM19/08/1977**

Pratt, Mrs P K, BA MCLIP, Retired.
[10030] 09/02/1953 **CM01/01/1963**

Preater, A J, BSc MSc, Team Leader Systems and Innovation Support Services, Imperial College London.
[10014448] 31/07/2009 **ME**

Preciado Rodriguez, Mr J, Commis Waiter, Floridita.
[10022444] 05/03/2013 **ME**

Precious, Ms A J, BA, Business Development, M O D.
[41627] 05/02/1988 **ME**

Precious, Mrs H, BA (Hons) MSc, Career Break.
[61736] 30/10/2002 **ME**

Preece, Ms B A, MSc, Librarian, EMW Law LLP.
[64864] 09/08/2005 **ME**

Preece, Ms L J, BA NZLSc MCLIP RLIANZA, Community Librarian, Mercury Bay Library, New Zealand.
[10017608] 12/12/2000 **CM18/09/2002**

Preest, Ms K J, BA PgDipILM MA MCLIP, Librarian, Murray Edwards College.
[55049] 01/07/1997 **CM25/07/2001**

Prentice, Mrs K M, BLib MCLIP, Group Manager, Loughton & Brentwood Group, Essex County Council,
[39436] 22/01/1986 **CM26/02/1992**

Prescott, Mr A R, BA (Hons) DipILS, Operations Manager, Newport City Council.
[54761] 01/04/1997 **ME**

Prestage, Mrs L R, MA BA MCLIP, Service Improvement Manager – Reading and Literacy, Kent County Council.
[41070] 01/10/1987 **CM13/06/1990**

Preston, Mr D G W, BSc, Hospice Volunteer.
[10035052] 08/09/2014 **ME**

Preston, Ms I F, BA MA MCLIP, Manager-Systems and Support, Northumberland CC.
[10012596] 19/02/2009 **CM10/11/2010**

Preston, Miss K A, BA (Hons) MSc MCLIP, Senior Information Librarian, Wiltshire Libraries.
[62735] 15/10/2003 **CM21/03/2007**

Preston, Mr M, BA (Hons) MLib MCLIP, Subject Librarian (Education & English), Goldsmiths College, London.
[48592] 25/02/1993 **CM06/04/2005**

Preston, Mr S, MA PG/Dip ILS, Local Studies Assistant, North Lanarkshire Council.
[63293] 07/04/2004 **ME**

Prestwood, Mrs D A, ACLIP, Lib. Assistant, Skegby Library, Mansfield, Notts.
[10012664] 01/03/2009 **ACL11/12/2009**

Preuss, Mrs R J, BA MCLIP, Child. Librarian, West Berks. Council, Newbury Library.
[36908]   13/01/1984   **CM02/06/1987**
Prevost, Miss A, BA (Hons) MSc, Supervisor, Lush Retail Ltd.
[10033567]   03/04/2014   **ME**
Prew, Miss C L, Graduate Library Trainee, Public Health England, London.
[10031443]   06/08/2013   **ME**
Price, Mrs A N, BA (Hons) MA MCLIP, Librarian, Lincs County Council Directorate of Public Health, Lincs. Knowledge & Resource Service.
[49967]   31/01/1994   **RV**22/08/2012   **CM17/03/1999**
Price, Ms C, BA PgDip PG Cert, Student, University of the West of England.
[10031758]   08/10/2013   **ME**
Price, Mrs C L, BA (Hons) MA FCLIP, E-Strategy & Res. Manager, University of Surrey, Guildford.
[51038]   09/11/1994   **FE13/11/2013**
Price, Mr D, BSc (Econ) MCLIP, Branch Librarian, Treorchy, Rhondda Cynon Taff County Borough Council, Treorchy, Mid Glamorgan.
[56367]   18/06/1998   **CM15/11/2000**
Price, Mrs E, MCLIP, Retired.
[11938]   10/01/1965   **CM01/01/1969**
Price, Miss F E M, BA DipLib, L. Technician/Researcher, ITN, London.
[33823]   02/03/1981   **ME**
Price, Mr G D, BA DipLib MCLIP, Acquisitions and Metadata Librarian, University of Brighton.
[32153]   30/01/1980   **CM09/02/1982**
Price, Mrs H J, BA (Hons) PgDip, Library Assistant, Aylesbury Central Library.
[10022464]   05/03/2013   **ME**
Price, Mrs K M, MCLIP, Life Member.
[11948]   14/02/1953   **CM01/01/1958**
Price, Mrs L, MSc, Student, Glamorgan University.
[64541]   09/05/2005   **ME**
Price, Miss L W S, BA (Hons), Student.
[10021360]   24/07/2012   **MF**
Price, Mr M, BA, Student, City University London.
[10029563]   20/12/2013   **ME**
Price, Miss P, BA PGCE MSc (Econ) MCLIP FHEA, Assistant Librarian, UWTSD Swansea.
[62748]   01/10/2003   **CM06/05/2009**
Price, Mrs S, BLS MPhil PGCHE FHEA MCLIP, Library Learning and Teaching Team Manager, Nottingham Trent University.
[42008]   17/07/1988   **CM01/04/2002**
Price, Miss S D, BA BTEC, Principal Library Assistant, Birmingham Conservatoire.
[43373]   09/10/1989   **ME**
Price, Miss S E, BSc MSc, Information Professional, MOD.
[65367]   16/01/2006   **ME**
Price, Mrs S E, BA (Hons) MA MCLIP, Knowledge Manager RJAH Orthopaedic Hospital. Oswestry.
[56313]   29/04/1998   **CM02/02/2005**
Price, Miss S T, BA (Hons) MCLIP, Branch Libraian Welshpool Library, Powys County Council.
[57025]   26/11/1998   **CM11/03/2009**
Price, Ms T A, BLS MSc MCLIP, Information Specialist, NICE, Manchester.
[33459]   01/12/1980   **CM24/02/1986**
Prichard, Mr J A, FCLIP, Life Member.
[11959]   15/02/1943   **FE01/01/1957**
Priddey, Mrs D J, BA (Hons) MSc (Econ) MCLIP, Senior Editor BNI, Proquest.
[49826]   10/11/1993   **CM19/01/2000**

Priddey, Mrs E J, MCLIP,
[11367]   04/01/1972   **CM03/09/1975**
Pridham, Mrs J P, MCLIP, Life Member.
[11966]   01/01/1954   **CM01/01/1969**
Pridmore, Ms J, BA DipLib MCLIP, Librarian, GWP Consultants.
[32154]   24/01/1980   **CM04/03/1983**
Priest, Mr D C, BSocSc RMN, Information Specialist, BSI Group, London.
[10016636]   20/04/2010   **AF**
Priest, Mrs R E, BA DipLib MCLIP, College Librarian, Shetland College UHI/NAFC Marine Centre.
[10002653]   02/12/1981   **CM18/07/1985**
Priestley, Mrs J, BA MCLIP, Learning Services Manager. Fife College.
[30791]   03/04/1979   **CM23/02/1983**
Priestley, Ms M J, BA, Librarian, G4S, HMP Altcourse, Liverpool.
[28129]   03/10/1977   **CM18/10/1979**
Prime, Ms K B, Student, University of Wales Aberystwyth.
[10033208]   20/02/2014   **ME**
Prince, Ms A, BA (HONS) MCLIP, Web Manager, Bodleian Libraries, Oxford.
[10021016]   04/05/2012   **CM09/09/2013**
Prince, Ms H K, BA MA, L. Serv. Manager, Princess Alexandra Hospital NHS Trust, Harlow, Essex.
[57991]   08/10/1999   **ME**
Prince, Miss R J, MA MCLIP, Bibl. Serv. Co-ordinator, South Glos. L. Serv., Yate.
[41108]   12/10/1987   **CM17/01/1990**
Pringle, Miss L A, BA (Hons) DipInf, Senior Assistant Librarian, Wirral Borough Co., West Kirby L.
[44447]   09/10/1990   **ME**
Pringle, Mrs M C, BSc MSc MCLIP, Director, Vital Information Ltd, Bucks.
[37106]   09/02/1984   **CM22/04/1992**
Prior, Miss D E, MA (Hons), Student, Strathclyde University.
[64265]   22/02/2005   **ME**
Prior, Miss H I, BA MCLIP, Child. Serv. Librarian, London Borough of Harrow, Middlesex.
[32334]   06/03/1980   **CM14/11/1985**
Prior, Mrs M R, BA MA MCLIP, Retired.
[11986]   04/03/1954   **CM01/01/1963**
Prior, Ms S D, BA (Hons) MA MCLIP, Librarian (PT) & Community, Learning and Outreach Assistant (PT), Bexley C., Footscray Offices, Sidcup.
[48823]   09/06/1993   **CM25/07/2001**
Pritchard, Mrs L C, MCLIP, L. Asst, L. & Information Serv., University of Wales, Swansea.
[25060]   22/10/1975   **CM29/05/1979**
Pritchard, Mr O J, BA (Hons) MA (Labhist) MA MCLIP, Assistant Director (Services), Student and Learning Support, University of Sunderland.
[45562]   07/03/1991   **CM26/01/1994**
Pritchard, Mrs S E, BA (Hons) DipLib MCLIP, Branch Librarian, Newtown Library, Powys.
[43751]   01/01/1990   **CM15/09/1993**
Pritchatt, Ms D J, BLS (Hons) DipLib MCLIP, Learning Resources Coordinator, NHS Blood & Transplant., Birmingham.
[29797]   15/09/1978   **CM22/06/1984**
Privetti, Mrs P A, BA (Hons) DipMus MCLIP, Librarian, Royal Sch. Haslemere.
[231]   07/10/1968   **CM22/02/1993**
Procter, Miss H, BA, Student, Manchester Metropolitan University.
[10035450]   14/10/2014   **ME**

Procter, Mr J, BA, Graduate Trainee, Avon & Wiltshire Mental Health
Partnership NHS Trust.
[10034772]   14/08/2014   ME
Proctor, Ms B L, ACLIP, Health & Safety Executive, Knowledge Centre,
1. G Redgrave Court, Merton Road, Bootle, Merseyside L20 7HS.
[64510]   27/04/2005   ACL22/06/2007
Proctor, Mrs J L, BA MA MCLIP, Librarian, Richmond L. NHFT,
Northamptonshire.
[63456]   12/05/2004   CM21/03/2007
Proctor, Mr J M, FCLIP, Retired.
[19263]   01/01/1949   FE01/01/1968
Prosser, Mrs J, MA MCLIP, Lib. Adult Serv., Hendon Library, London
Borough of Barnet.
[59832]   15/10/2001   CM29/03/2006
Prosser, Mr R J, BA (Hons) MCLIP, L. Customer Serv. Manager,
Chipping Barnet Library, London Borough of Barnet.
[43879]   07/02/1990   CM21/07/1999
Prosser, Mrs R M, Senior Librarian, Cumbria Lib. Serv.
[61358]   24/06/2002   ME
Prosser, Ms S, BA DILS MSc MCLIP, Library Services Manager, ABMU
Health Board, Singleton Hospital, Swansea.
[40538]   16/02/1987   CM18/04/1989
Protheroe, Mrs A E, L. Assistant, House of Lords Library, London.
[10015927]   12/02/2010   AF
Prowse, Mrs K E, BSc MSc, Librarian, Ifield Community College.
[40807]   01/07/1987   ME
Prowse, Mr S W, Retired.
[10016114]   11/02/2010   ME
Prud'Homme, Ms R,
[10020304]   11/01/2012   ME
Prue, Mr A J, BA (Hons) MA DipLib, Web Development Librarian, KSS
Library.
[10006602]   19/04/1995   ME
Pryce-Jones, Mrs J E, BSc MCLIP, Retired.
[20221]   31/10/1973   CM20/10/1975
Pryce-Jones, Ms L, MA, PhD Student, Oxford Brookes University.
[10020852]   19/04/2012   ME
Pryer, Mr P L A, MA MCLIP, Life Member.
[12019]   01/01/1957   CM01/01/1965
Pryor, Miss H E, MCLIP, Retired.
[19993]   11/01/1973   CM16/02/1976
Ptolomey, Mrs J, BSc DipLIS, Freelance Information Worker.
[54080]   24/10/1996   ME
Publicover, Mr J R, BEM MCLIP, Life Member.
[12022]   25/07/1938   CM01/01/1949
Publicover, Mrs M, BSc MCLIP MA, Information Officer/Journal Editor,
Springdale College.
[10022866]   12/01/1982   CM24/11/1983
Pudner, Mr B G, BA (Hons) PgDip, LRC Officer, Pembrokeshire
College, Haverfordwest.
[10015418]   16/11/2009   ME
Pugh, Miss H J, BA (Hons) BA MCLIP, School Librarian, Kings College
School, London.
[28401]   22/11/1977   CM30/10/1979
Pugh, Miss K E, BA (Hons) MCLIP,
[10012075]   14/11/1991   CM22/07/1998
Pujadas Bartes, Miss M, BA MA, Student, University of Sheffield.
[10032424]   03/12/2013   ME
Puligari, Mrs P, MLISc MCLIP, Outreach & E-Resources Librarian,
Heart of England NHS Foundation Trust.
[59459]   30/03/2001   CM21/05/2008
Pullen, Mr A D, MA, Student, Northumbria University.
[10017999]   01/11/2010   ME

Pullen, Mrs H, BSc, Librarian, University Hospitals Bristol NHS
Foundation Trust.
[55313]   01/10/1997   ME
Pullen, Mrs S F, Bsc MCLIP, Business & Development Manager –
Shared Services (Face to Face) – Libraries, Registration & One Stop
Shops.
[57255]   02/02/1999   CM19/03/2008
Pullinger, Mr D J, BA MA MSc AFHEA, Learning Services Team
Leader, Leeds University Library, University of Leeds.
[10022563]   26/03/2013   ME
Pullinger, Mr J J, National Statistician, UK Statistics Authority.
[64348]   07/03/2005   ME
Punter, Miss C L, School Librarian, Sheldon School Wilts.
[61461]   12/08/2002   ME
Puplett, Mr D, MCLIP, Drill Hall Library Manager, University of
Greenwich.
[63186]   03/03/2004   CM13/06/2007
Purcell, Mrs C W, MTheol MA MLitt MCLIP, Academic Liaison Librarian,
Durham University.
[28383]   08/11/1977   CM19/11/1983
Purcell, Mr J, BA MBA DipLib DMS MCLIP, University Librarian,
Durham University.
[31092]   15/08/1979   CM15/08/1981
Purchase, Mr S W F, BN (Hons), Assistant Librarian, Child. Hospital
NHS Trust, Birmingham.
[56975]   17/11/1998   AF
Purchon, Mrs K M, BA MA, School Librarian, St Francis College,
Letchworth.
[35779]   24/01/1983   CM18/02/1986
Purdy, Mrs D J, BA DMS MCLIP, Lib. at Leicester College.
[37460]   01/10/1984   CM08/12/1987
Purkiss, Miss J, SLRC Assistant, Sir George Monoux College, London.
[10015521]   29/03/2012   AF
Purkiss, Ms T L, MA, Learning Advisor, University of Cumbria.
[58430]   11/02/2000   ME
Purvis, Mr B S, BA MSc MCLIP, Retired.
[12058]   05/02/1969   CM01/01/1971
Puscas, Miss I, BLib MCLIP, Lib. /Knowledge Manager, Public Health
Wales Observatory, Cardiff.
[22089]   22/01/1974   CM10/11/1978
Puskas, Ms S E, Dipl, Librarian, Paedagogische Hochschufe Heidelberg
University of Education.
[10013618]   13/05/2009   ME
Puxley, Mrs N A, BA DipLib MCLIP, Secretary, Amphlett Lissimore,
London.
[32181]   23/01/1980   CM17/05/1983
Puzey, Miss S L, BA MCLIP, Subject Librarian – Social Sciences,
Cardiff University.
[10000773]   07/11/2006   CM06/07/2011
Pyant, Mr A F, Dip MA MCLIP, Retired.
[42611]   16/01/1989   CM29/04/1994
Pycock, Mr L R, BA (Hons) MCLIP, Assistant Manager., London
Borough of Southwark., E. St. L.
[50788]   18/10/1994   CM01/06/2005
Pye-Smith, Ms H M E, MA MCLIP, Head of L., The National Arch., Kew.
[40191]   04/11/1986   CM19/03/2008
Pyle, Mrs B D, MCLIP, Life Member.
[12067]   16/10/1943   CM01/01/1955
Pyves, Mrs I H, MCLIP, Life Member.
[12070]   01/01/1955   CM01/01/1959

Q

Quarmby Lawrence, Mrs E A, BLib, Assistant Rare Books Librarian Edinburgh University Library.
[40517]   23/02/1987   **ME**

Quaye, Ms K C, BA MSc MCLIP, Assistant Librarian, The Restaurant School at Walnut Hill College, Philadelphia, PA, USA.
[10017429]   19/08/2010   **CM29/05/2013**

Queen, Miss C R, MA ACLIP, Information Officer, Mitchell Library.
[10021908]   29/10/2012   **ACL27/03/2014**

Quenby, Miss S F, BA, Student, Aberystwyth University.
[10032473]   09/12/2013   **ME**

Quibell, Mr J R C, BA MCLIP, Retired. Volunteer, National Museum for Royal Navy Library, Portsmouth.
[19272]   02/10/1972   **CM07/10/1974**

Quigley, Ms A, MLIS, Library Assistant, Dublin Business School.
[10022362]   19/02/2013   **ME**

Quigley, Ms C S, Student, Loughborough University.
[10019553]   27/07/2011   **ME**

Quigley, Miss S K, School Librarian, Bonneville Primary School.
[10021776]   10/10/2012   **AF**

Quilty, Ms L, MSc, Assistant Child. Librarian, Bristol Central Lending Library.
[59504]   18/04/2001   **ME**

Quinlan, Mrs H E, BA (Hons) MA MCLIP, Neighbourhood Library Manager., City of Salford.
[59848]   16/10/2001   **CM08/12/2004**

Quinn, Mr D, BSc MSc, Assistant Asset Manager, Libraries NI.
[10022409]   26/02/2013   **ME**

Quinn, Miss H F, BA DipLib MCLIP, Librarian, Ramboll Whitbybird Limited.
[37009]   14/01/1984   **CM07/07/1987**

Quinn, Mrs W, BA PGCE MCLIP, Learning Resources Manager, Parkfield Community School.
[10020261]   15/12/2011   **CM04/10/2013**

Quinney, Mrs L, MA (Hons) MA MCLIP, Maps Reading Room Manager, National Library of Scotland (part-time).
[59800]   03/10/2001   **CM29/03/2004**

R

Rabbitt, Miss K, BA (Hons) MCLIP, Librarian, The Morley Academy, Leeds.
[10013089]   09/01/2001   **CM09/07/2013**

Rabbitt, Mr P, BA LLB DipLib, Senior Exec. Lib, Galway Co. L. Galway.
[28132]   06/10/1977   **ME**

Rabindranath, Mr A, PgDip,
[10035697]   29/10/2014   **ME**

Raby, Ms A S, BA (Hons) DipIS MCLIP, LRC Manager, Whitcliffe Mount School, Cleckheaton.
[48239]   17/11/1992   **CM21/05/2003**

Racey, Mrs J A, BA Lib MCLIP, Community Librarian and Area Volunteer Co-ordinator, Ramsey Library, London.
[10022230]   22/01/2013   **CM18/03/1993**

Rackley, Mrs A L, MCLIP, Sch. L. Serv. Manager, Blackburn with Darwen Borough, Blackburn, Lancs.
[13034]   26/01/1972   **CM10/02/1975**

Radcliffe, Ms P R, BA MSc, L. & Information Manager, Northern Ireland Court Serv., Belfast.
[63054]   27/01/2004   **ME**

Radevski, Miss R, Student.
[10020481]   21/02/2012   **ME**

Radford, Ms K, MA MCLIP, Academic Liaison Librarian, University of York.
[49227]   14/10/1993   **CM15/05/2002**

Radford, Mrs S M, BA (Hons) MA, Resource Centre Manager, The Third Age Trust, Bromley.
[65514]   11/02/2006   **ME**

Rae, Miss C T, BA (Hons) MA, Libraries Development Manager, LB of Waltham Forest, London.
[65803]   15/05/2006   **ME**

Rae, Mrs E, MA (Hons) MSc MCLIP, Sch. Lib. /Assistant Librarian, Hunter High School, East Kilbride, Med. Library, Western Information, Glasgow.
[65391]   01/02/2006   **CM09/09/2009**

Rae, Dr N G D, BSc (Hons) PhD, Student, University of Strathclyde.
[10035524]   16/10/2014   **ME**

Raffan, Miss A K, BA MCLIP, Stock Assistant, Cultural Community Services / Carillion, for London Borough of Ealing.
[35770]   12/01/1983   **CM27/07/1994**

Rafferty, Ms E P F, BA MSc MCLIP, Sunday Librarian, London College of Communication, University of the Arts.
[26521]   16/09/1976   **CM01/07/1990**

Rafferty, Dr P M, MA MSc PhD MCLIP, Senior Lecturer, University of Wales, Aberystwyth.
[40240]   13/11/1986   **CM01/07/1992**

Rafter, Mr D, Acquisitions Support Officer, Sound, British Library, London.
[10013466]   13/07/2001   **ME**

Ragab, Mrs L A, BA MCLIP, Librarian, CABI, Egham, Surrey.
[30412]   25/01/1979   **CM31/10/1983**

Ragaller, Miss I, MCLIP, Koordinatorin Wissensvermittlung, Zürcher Hochschule der Künste.
[10011095]   24/09/2008   **CM09/11/2011**

Raghunanan, Mrs A E D, BScEcon, Student, Aberystwyth University.
[63288]   30/03/2004   **ME**

Rahaman, Mrs C, BScEcon MCLIP, Librarian, The Regis School, Bognor Regis.
[04380]   14/03/2005   **CM09/11/2011**

Raine, Miss D, BA MA, Librarian, Ampleforth College, North Yorkshire.
[42333]   24/10/1988   **ME**

Raine, Mrs M, MCLIP, Retired.
[12118]   13/01/1956   **CM01/01/1961**

Rainton, Miss A, BSc MA MCLIP, Service Support Librarian, County Hall, Norfolk County Council.
[10001014]   07/12/2006   **CM14/03/2012**

Raisin, Mrs A, BA DipLib MLib FCLIP, Group Information Manager, Department for Business, London.
[25399]   05/01/1976   **FE15/09/2004**

Raistrick, Mr C J, MCLIP, Previously L. Serv. Manager, Procter & Gamble, Newcastle upon Tyne.
[38807]   10/10/1985   **CM18/04/1994**

Rajacic, Ms V, BA (Hons) PgDipILS MCLIP, Team Leader – Central Library, Edinburgh City Libraries and Information Service.
[59385]   27/02/2001   **CM13/06/2007**

Rajendran, Miss M Y, BSc MLib DipEd, Knowledge Manager, Health Insurance Commission, Australia.
[44492]   15/10/1990   **ME**

Rakotoarivony, Ms L G,
[10029633]   01/10/2013   **ME**

Ralls, Mrs M C, BD MSc MCLIP, Retired.
[12125]   25/04/1972   **CM01/12/1982**

Ram, Mr S, MPhil, PhD Student.
[10031936]   29/10/2013   **ME**

Ramalingam, Ms R, LLB (Hons) MCLIP, Retired.
[17609]   14/08/1969   **CM21/09/1976**

Ramlal, Miss K A, Student, University of Wales Aberystwyth.
[10033099]   10/02/2014   **ME**
Ramm, Mr A, ACLIP, Senior Library Assistant, Leeds Central Library.
[10021356]   24/07/2012   **ACL15/07/2014**
Ramos Gamazo, Miss A, MA, Librarian (Level 2), Air Balloon Hill
Primary School.
[10035016]   05/09/2014   **ME**
Rampersad, Ms S, BSc, Systems and Stock Manager, Greater London
Authority.
[10007931]   20/03/2008   **ME**
Ramphal, Mr R, BA MLIS, Librarian, Cipriani College of Labour and
Cooperative Studies.
[10032903]   18/02/2014   **ME**
Rampling, Ms C, Assistant Librarian, Lincoln's Inn Librarian, London.
[62648]   01/10/2003   **ME**
Ramsbottom, Miss R J, BA, Assistant Librarian, House of Lords
Library, London.
[10006501]   24/10/2007   **ME**
Ramsden, Mrs A, MSc, Senior Information Officer (Law subject &
Researcher support), University of Central Lancashire.
[10005993]   21/08/2007   **ME**
Ramsden, Ms I, BA (Hons),
[10031763]   01/10/2013   **ME**
Ramsden, Mr M J, BA MSOCSC FALIA FCLIP, Retired.
[17618]   10/03/1958   **FE01/01/1971**
Ramsden, Mr P A, BA CertEd MCLIP, Partnering for Talent Project
Officer, MOD.
[27210]   01/01/1977   **CM31/07/1981**
Ramsey, Mrs J, Student, Coleg Llandrillo.
[10032511]   11/12/2013   **ME**
Ramstead, Miss E J, BA PGCE MCLIP, Student, Manchester
Metropolitan University.
[10010239]   16/07/2008   **CM13/11/2013**
Rana, Mr D, BSc MSc MCLIP, Service Development Librarian, Dudley
Metropolitan Borough Council.
[10015498]   08/10/2003   **CM29/05/2013**
Ranahan, Mr T, BA (Hons) MSc, Assistant Community Librarian,
Hawthorn House Library, Birmingham.
[10017327]   29/07/2010   **ME**
Randall, Mrs A, BA (Hons) MA MCLIP, Subject Librarian, University of
Roehampton.
[58924]   04/10/2000   **CM29/03/2004**
Randall, Mrs J B, ACLIP, Vision Manager, Outwood Academy Valley,
Worksop.
[10000714]   25/10/2006   **ACL01/10/2008**
Randall, Ms L, BA (Hons) MCLIP, Senior L. Assistant, Wandsworth
Town Library, London.
[64841]   29/07/2005   **CM09/09/2009**
Randell, Mrs C M, MCLIP, Bookshop Manager, Norfolk Child. Book
Centre.
[324]   01/01/1969   **CM27/03/1973**
Randewich, Mrs C M, BA (Hons), Library Assistant (Part-time) Tadley
Library, Hants.
[10022105]   17/12/2012   **ME**
Randhawa, Mrs P K, ACLIP, Assistant Librarian, Lampton School,
Hounslow.
[65268]   07/12/2005   **ACL17/06/2009**
Randle, Ms C L, MCLIP, Retired.
[28927]   25/01/1974   **CM07/09/1979**
Rankin, Dr C E M, PhD MA BSSc DipLib FHEA MCLIP, Visiting Fellow,
Faculty of Arts, Environment & Technology, Leeds Beckett University.
[28661]   01/11/1977   **CM06/07/1981**

Rankin, Miss R C, MA (Hons) DipILS MCLIP, School Librarian, Hillhead
High School, Glasgow.
[61027]   11/02/2002   **CM15/09/2004**
Ransom, Mrs N, BSc (Econ), Data Quality Librarian, University for the
Creative Arts.
[65434]   23/02/2006   **ME**
Ranson, Mr M C, MCLIP, Retired.
[12152]   15/02/1949   **CM01/01/1955**
Rao, Miss Y, BSc (Hons), Library Assistant, Cambridge University
Library.
[10033416]   11/03/2014   **ME**
Rapson, Mr B, BSc (Econ) DipLib, Library Manager, Digital &
Information. Shropshire Libraries.
[10020399]   16/02/1989   **ME**
Rasdall, Mr M, BA (Hons) MSc, Managing Director, Burwell Web
Communications Ltd.
[10001356]   11/03/1993   **ME**
Raseroka, Ms H K, BSc MA HonFCLIP, Director, University of Botswana
Library, Gaborone.
[53168]   01/04/1996   **HFE21/10/2004**
Rashbrook Cooper, Ms A C, BA (Hons), Library Assistant, BFI Reuben
Library.
[10011714]   06/11/2008   **ME**
Rashidah Begum, Madam F M, BA MCLIP, Chief Librarian, Kolej
Disted.
[18908]   11/08/1972   **CM01/01/1975**
Rasmussen, Miss M L, BA, Library Assistant, NHS Direct.
[10000731]   31/10/2006   **ME**
Rastall, Mrs D M, MCLIP, Life Member.
[12156]   01/01/1951   **CM01/01/1956**
Rastrick, Mrs E F, MCLIP, Advisory Librarian, L. Archives & Information,
Suffolk.
[18180]   10/10/1972   **CM23/04/1976**
Ratcliffe, Mrs D J, Student, Aberystwyth University.
[10033863]   07/05/2014   **ME**
Ratcliffe, Dr F W, CBE JP HonFLA MA PhD, Life Member.
[12159]   12/03/1962   **HFE06/01/1987**
Ratcliffe, Mr J, MCLIP, Retired.
[12161]   21/09/1960   **CM01/01/1964**
Ratcliffe, Miss S A, BA (Hons) PgDip MCLIP, Senior Information
Assistant – Serials (Electronic), University of Aberdeen.
[54623]   04/02/1997   **CM11/03/2009**
Ratnasamy, Ms T, BA MCLIP, Senior Librarian, NUS Library, National
University of Singapore.
[34054]   01/08/1981   **CM11/11/1985**
Rattigan, Mrs G, ACLIP, Lib. Assistant, Invergordon Library,
Invergordon, Ross-shire.
[10001962]   19/03/2007   **ACL16/07/2008**
Raub, Ms C, BA MA, Student, The Catholic University of America.
[10032596]   18/12/2013   **ME**
Raven, Ms D M, BA DipLib MCLIP, Information Standards Knowledge
Manager, Health & Social Care Information Centre, Leeds.
[10012018]   11/10/1983   **CM10/11/1987**
Raven, Miss N A, BA (Hons) ACLIP, Learning Facilitator, The Library,
Northampton College.
[10018956]   01/04/2011   **ACL20/06/2012**
Raven Conn, Mrs C M, BSc (Econ) MCLIP, Part-time Lib, Nottingham
Central Library.
[48726]   27/04/1993   **CM17/09/2003**
Ravenwood, Mrs J C F, Student.
[10007122]   22/01/2008   **ME**
Raw, Mrs A, MCLIP, Unemployed.
[10112]   17/09/1969   **CM03/02/1978**

Rawes, Mrs P M, BA (Hons) MCLIP, Unemployed.
[34997]   08/06/1982   **CM11/03/1984**
Rawles, Miss M, BA (Hons), Community and Literacy Development
Officer, Central Library, Plymouth.
[10034030]   21/05/2014   ME
Rawling, Mrs D A, Lower LRC Manager, Lower Graham School,
Scarborough.
[62928]   20/11/2003   ME
Rawling, Mrs H, BA MA, Unwaged.
[10011669]   12/11/2008   ME
Rawlings, Mr J F, BA MCLIP, Retired.
[21706]   01/01/1974   **CM04/08/1977**
Rawlings, Mrs S J, BA MCLIP, Cent. Operations Librarian, Norfolk LIS.
[1593]   10/01/1966   **CM01/01/1970**
Rawlinson, Miss K A, MCLIP, Retired.
[17624]   17/04/1962   **CM01/01/1966**
Rawls, Mrs A, Library Technician.
[10034424]   11/07/2014   ME
Rawson, Miss J L, BA (Hons) MA MCLIP, Librarian, Vere Harmsworth
Library, University of Oxford.
[61823]   12/11/2002   **CM21/05/2008**
Rawsthorne, Mr L, MLib FCLIP, Co. Librarian, Flintshire County
Council, Mold.
[25095]   05/11/1975   **FE20/05/1998**
Ray, Mrs A, MSc, Student, Maharaja Sayajirao University of Baroda.
[10032654]   23/12/2013   ME
Ray, Mr A K, MA MCLIP, Life Member.
[17626]   06/01/1956   **CM01/01/1962**
Ray, Ms C, Student, Aberystwyth University.
[10005990]   11/09/2007   ME
Ray, Mrs E, Assistant Librarian/Teacher, College Beau Soleil,
Switzerland.
[10019665]   19/08/2011   ME
Ray, Mrs E R, MCLIP, Retired.
[12188]   13/09/1966   **CM01/02/1972**
Ray, Mrs S G, BA MPhil HonFLA FCLIP, Life Member.
[12191]   21/09/1951   **HFE01/01/1990**
Raybould, Ms S J, BA MCLIP, Information Centre Manager.
[24445]   10/08/1975   **CM26/08/1980**
Raymont, Mr D M, BA, Librarian., Institute& Faculty of Actuaries.
[41549]   18/01/1988   ME
Rayner, Mrs G E, BA (Hons), Student.
[10033718]   17/04/2014   ME
Raynor, Mrs J M, MCLIP, Not employed.
[21004]   03/10/1973   **CM17/10/1975**
Rea, Mrs M E, BA MCLIP, School Librarian, Merchant Taylors' Boys'
School, Liverpool.
[27011]   10/01/1977   **CM19/01/1979**
Read, Miss C A, MA MCLIP, Life Member.
[12200]   07/10/1971   **CM31/07/1975**
Read, Mrs C R, Retired.
[47373]   27/07/1992   ME
Read, Ms F M A, LLB DipLP DipInf, Unwaged.
[10017012]   17/05/2002   ME
Read, Ms K J, BA MA MCLIP, Principal L. Asst, Academic Services,
IALS, London.
[43599]   09/11/1989   **CM22/05/1996**
Read, Miss L A, MA BA MCLIP, College Librarian, Robinson College,
Cambridge.
[25401]   18/01/1976   **CM13/09/1979**
Read, Ms M, MA, Self-employed.
[43562]   08/11/1989   ME
Read, Mrs M A, Librarian, Morrab Library, Penzance, Cornwall.
[57105]   14/12/1998   ME

Reade, Mrs J, BA MLS MCLIP, Retired.
[12210]   01/01/1966   **CM01/01/1970**
Reader, Mr D K, MCLIP, Retired.
[12211]   01/10/1971   **CM01/08/1974**
Ready, Ms K W, BEd DipLib MCLIP, Subject Librarian, Anglia Ruskin
University, Cambridge.
[38557]   01/07/1985   **CM10/11/1987**
Ready, Ms S E, BSc, Librarian, Bassingbourn Village College, South
End.
[66025]   24/08/2006   AF
Reardon, Dr M, PhD MA, Business Intelligence Assistant, Edwards
Wildman Palmer LLP, London.
[10006107]   03/07/2008   ME
Reason, Mrs C, DipLS, Retired.
[36034]   19/04/1983   ME
Redfearn, Mrs J, MCLIP, Part-time Prison Librarian, Leyhill Open
Prison, South Glos. L.
[22879]   01/10/1974   **CM20/09/1977**
Redgate, Ms J L, Student, University of Brighton/Learning centre
Assistant, Sussex Downs College.
[10022458]   05/03/2013   ME
Redhead, Mr M K, MA MCLIP, Retired.
[20773]   02/07/1973   **CM15/12/1975**
Redican, Ms H, MA, Unwaged.
[42518]   21/11/1988   ME
Redman, Miss F L, BSc MSc,
[10017674]   23/09/2010   ME
Redman, Mr G C, MA ARCO MCLIP, Information Librarian, Chichester
L. West Sussex. County Council.
[61037]   11/02/2002   **CM29/11/2006**
Redman, Ms J, BSc (Hons) MSc PGCE MCLIP CMALT, Technology
Enhanced Learning (TEL) Librarian, UWE, Bristol.
[57093]   07/12/1998   **CM23/01/2002**
Redman, Miss P, BA (Hons) MCLIP, Research & Information Advisor,
Lifetime Development N. E. LTD Barnsley, Doncaster & Rotherham.
[48739]   30/04/1993   **CM25/01/1995**
Redpath, Ms A E, BA MCLIP, Acquisitions Manager, Napier University
Learning Information Services.
[53346]   20/05/1996   **CM11/03/2009**
Redrup, Mrs R M J, BA MLib MCLIP, Marketing Co-ordinator, University
of Reading L.
[40997]   02/10/1987   **CM25/05/1994**
Reed, Mrs D J, BA, Assistant Librarian, Ardingly College.
[10008809]   21/04/2008   ME
Reed, Mr D M, BA, Community Learning & Engagement Manager,
Solihull Metropolitan Borough Council.
[40484]   12/02/1987   **CM30/01/1991**
Reed, Mrs J F, BA MCLIP, Information Specialist, England.
[64251]   22/02/2005   **CM28/01/2009**
Reed, Mrs J M, BA (Hons) MCLIP, Prison Library Service Development
Manager/Advisor, Staffordshire County Council.
[25419]   16/12/1975   **CM01/07/1992**
Reed, Miss L C, BSc (Hons) MSc,
[10012464]   10/02/2009   ME
Reed, Mr M W, BA, Unwaged.
[46895]   28/02/1992   ME
Reed, Mr R A, LLB DipLib MCLIP, Assistant Librarian, Royal Institute of
British Architects, London.
[43224]   05/10/1989   **CM24/06/1992**
Reed, Mr R T, BSc Econ, Area Librarian, RCT Libraries.
[10018712]   01/03/2011   ME
Reed, Mrs S, BA FCLIP, Learning Resources and Feedback Manager,
South Downs College.
[28965]   06/02/1978   **FE28/01/2009**

Reed, Miss S E, BA (Hons) MA MCLIP, Assistant Librarian, Collection Management.
[56730]   07/10/1998   **CM13/04/2011**

Reed, Miss S J, BA (Hons) MSc Econ, Community Library Assistant, Cambridgeshire CC.
[10031575]   03/09/2013   **ME**

Reedie, Mrs S P, BA MA DipLib MCLIP, Stock Supervisor (job share) Dorset County Libraries.
[29557]   07/10/1978   **CM24/10/1980**

Reedy, Mrs K J, BA MA MCLIP PG Cert AP FHEA, Information Literacy Specialist, Open University Library, Milton Keynes.
[38724]   01/10/1985   **CM24/03/1992**

Reekie, Dr C S, MSc (Econ) MCLIP, Federation Librarian, Cambridge Theological Federation.
[22560]   01/07/1974   **CM03/07/1978**

Rees, Mr A D W, BA MCLIP, Learning Resources Manager, Coleg Menai, Bangor.
[38022]   16/01/1985   **CM30/01/1991**

Rees, Mr A G, BSc MIBiol MCLIP, Retired.
[60627]   27/05/1969   **CM18/11/1971**

Rees, Mrs F A, BLib (Hons) MCLIP, Librarian, South StaffordshireHealthcare NHS Trust, Stafford.
[28864]   23/01/1978   **CM10/07/2002**

Rees, Ms H A, BA MEd MCLIP, Retired.
[17632]   29/09/1969   **CM12/04/1973**

Rees, Ms S, Planning & Compliance Librarian, Ministry of Justice.
[10021225]   29/06/2012   **ME**

Rees-Jones, Mrs E A, BA MCLIP, Principal Librarian, Community Devel & Partnerships., Staffordshire County Council.
[26702]   29/10/1976   **CM29/02/1980**

Rees-Jones, L, BA MCLIP FRSA, Mind Mapping | Life management – from chaos to clarity | Remote collaboration | Organising things | Transitioning.
[26594]   26/10/1976   **CM16/05/1988**

Reeve, Mrs S, MCLIP, Assistant Information Advisor, University of Brighton.
[64191]   31/01/2005   **CM14/11/2012**

Reeves, Mrs C C, BA (Hons), Info Specialist Foreign & Commonwealth Office (F. C. O).
[10005251]   11/11/1992   **ME**

Reeves, Mrs S, BA (Hons) MCLIP, Relief Assistant Librarian, West Sussex Library Serv.
[49790]   08/11/1993   **CM04/02/2004**

Reeves, Miss T L, BA (Hons) MA AKC MCLIP, Information Specialist, Foreign & Commonwealth Office, London.
[59978]   15/11/2001   **CM13/11/2013**

Regan, Mrs E A, MA DipLib MCLIP, Part-time Information Librarian, Pwllheli Library, Gwynedd.
[32926]   04/10/1980   **CM16/05/1984**

Regan, Mr T, BA (Hons) DipILS, Senior Lib. -E. Area, Dalkeith L.
[51621]   18/04/1995   **ME**

Regelous, Mr P, BA MSc,
[10022528]   19/03/2013   **ME**

Regnault, Miss C, BA, Librarian, LB of Camden.
[10032578]   17/12/2013   **ME**

Regulski, Dr C, MA PhD, Information Assist., King's College, London.
[10019905]   30/09/2011   **AF**

Reid, Mr A, MA MCLIP, Retired.
[22822]   04/10/1974   **CM31/08/1977**

Reid, Mrs A J, Librarian, Alleyn's Junior School.
[10006296]   10/10/2007   **ME**

Reid, Ms A M, MA DipInfSc MCLIP, Procurement and Access Manager (Job Share), London School of Economics and Political Science Library, London.
[60650]   15/06/1982   **CM14/07/1988**

Reid, Mr B J, BA AALIA MCLIP, Retired.
[38965]   23/10/1985   **CM13/06/1989**

Reid, Mrs C A, BSc (Hons) MSc MCLIP, Librarian, University of Cambridge, Lucy Cavendish College.
[47377]   28/07/1992   RV30/04/2014   **CM22/05/1996**

Reid, Miss C D, BA MA FCLIP FRSA,
[12270]   01/07/1972   **FE01/04/2002**

Reid, Ms C J, MA (Hons) DipLib MCLIP, Unwaged.
[46302]   25/10/1991   **CM20/09/1995**

Reid, Mrs E, MA MCLIP, HR Officer, Banff & Buchan College.
[60318]   28/07/1992   **CM28/07/1992**

Reid, Miss F, BSc (Hons), Information Manager, Aquamarine Power, Edinburgh.
[10001950]   22/03/2007   **ME**

Reid, Mrs F S, BSc, Learning Resource Assistant.
[10006608]   11/09/2007   **ME**

Reid, Miss J, BA PgDip MCLIP, Children's Librarian, Dundee City Council.
[64658]   18/05/2005   **CM21/05/2008**

Reid, Miss J L H, BA MCLIP, School Librarian, Grange Acad., Kilmarnock, East Ayrshire.
[37890]   11/10/1984   **CM22/05/1996**

Reid, Ms K, BSc (Hons) MSc, Library Manager, Royal College of Physicians, London.
[10001854]   15/07/1999   **ME**

Reid, Ms L C, BA (Hons) MA, Head of Library and eLearning Services.
[53760]   01/10/1996   **ME**

Reid, Ms L C, BA MCLIP, Service Development Assistant, West Lothian Council.
[33122]   01/10/1980   **CM17/07/1984**

Reid, Mrs L J, BLS MCLIP, Assistant Librarian, University of Ulster, Belfast.
[41736]   29/02/1988   **CM06/05/2009**

Reid, Mr M A, MCLIP, Clinical/Management Librarian, Hospital NHS Foundation Trust, Blackpool Teaching.
[52003]   06/09/1995   **CM23/09/1998**

Reid, Prof P H, BA (Hons) PhD FSA (Scot), Head of Department, Robert Gordon University, Aberdeen.
[48679]   13/04/1993   **ME**

Reid, Mr R, BA (Hons) PGdip MSc MCLIP, Lib. Data Creator, Highland Libraries, Inverness.
[10006757]   10/12/2007   **CM15/01/2013**

Reid, Mrs R J, BA, Subject Librarian(Media, Arts and Technology) Humanities), University of Gloucestershire, Cheltenham.
[59497]   11/04/2001   **ME**

Reid, Mr S, BSc Econ, Assistant Librarian, The Bar library, Belfast.
[10032580]   17/12/2013   **ME**

Reid, Mrs S D, BA (Hons) MA PGCE MCLIP, Academic Librarian, Pilkington Library, Loughborough University.
[62312]   23/04/2003   **CM13/06/2007**

Reid, Mrs S E R, BEd, Library Manager, Collingwood College.
[10023074]   04/06/2013   **ME**

Reid-Smith, Dr E R, BA MEd FCLIP MEdAdmin MBus Dip, Life Member.
[12283]   01/01/1947   **FE01/01/1967**

Reilly, Mrs J, BA (Hons) PGdip, Student, Robert Gordon University.
[10032706]   07/01/2014   **ME**

Reilly, Mr L J, BA DipLib MCLIP, Arch. & L. Manager, London Borough of Lambeth.
[39084]   29/10/1985   **CM15/02/1989**

Reilly, Mrs N H, BA (Hons), Branch Library Manager, Garvagh Library.
[10016529]   01/04/2010   **ME**

Reilly-Cooper, Mrs P, BSc DipLib MCLIP, L. Serv. Manager, Halton Borough Council.
[34607]   11/01/1982   **CM21/12/1985**

Relph, Mr T R, BA (Hons) MCLIP, Community Librarian: Health, Wellbeing and Employment, Hebburn Library, South Tyneside Metropolitan Borough Council.
[43721]   01/12/1989   **CM24/07/1996**

Relton-Elves, Mrs D, Library and Information Services Manager, STW – STC.
[10008400]   19/03/2008   **ME**

Relves, Miss V J, BA (Hons) DipLib MCLIP, Librarian, ARUP.
[44449]   09/10/1990   **CM20/05/1998**

Rendell, Mrs F J, BA (Hons) MSc MCLIP, Information Specialist.
[62765]   20/10/2003   **RV**25/01/2011 **CM03/10/2007**

Rendle, Miss A E, BSc MCLIP, Retired.
[26025]   07/10/1974   **CM15/10/1976**

Rendle, Mrs L C, BA (Hons) MSc Econ, Information Assistant, Integreon, Bristol.
[10011885]   26/11/2008   **ME**

Renfrew, Ms F, MCLIP, L. Co-ordinator, South Lanarkshire Council, Hamilton Town House L.
[10001565]   10/10/1987   **CM18/07/1990**

Renfrew, Mr K, Student, Strathclyde University.
[10032120]   29/10/2013   **ME**

Rennie, Mr C, MA DipLib, Systems Librarian, School of Oriental & African Studies, London.
[10016475]   26/04/1994   **ME**

Rennie, Mr I S, BA MA, Knowledge, Library & Information Manager, Fulbourn Library.
[10021249]   02/07/2012   **ME**

Rennison, Mrs S, BA FCLIP, Life Member.
[4013]   19/03/1957   **FE29/09/1986**

Renshaw, Mrs S L, BA (Hons) PgDip MCLIP, Deputy Librarian, University of Winchester.
[10014999]   01/10/2009   **RV**13/05/2014 **CM11/07/2012**

Renson, Ms H A, BA DipLib MCLIP, Library Manager, Jubilee Library, Brighton.
[34424]   30/10/1981   **CM16/05/1985**

Renwick, Mrs S, MLIS MPhil FCLIP, Faculty Liaison Librarian, Science and Agriculture, University of the West Indies.
[64886]   09/09/2005   **FE31/01/2007**

Rex, Mr S P, BLib (Hons), Information Services Manager, Building Societies Association., London.
[55184]   04/08/1997   **ME**

Rey, Mrs P B L, BA MCLIP, L. Serv. Manager, Queen Vic. Hospital NHS Trust., East Grinstead, West Sussex.
[29351]   14/06/1978   **CM19/02/1981**

Reyner, Mr R J,
[57112]   11/12/1998   **ME**

Reynish, Mr P E, Senior Lib. Assistant, Legal Practice Library, Cardiff.
[10014091]   01/07/2009   **ME**

Reynolds, Mrs A W, ACLIP,
[10016310]   08/03/2010   **ACL15/02/2012**

Reynolds, Ms J A, MSc MCLIP, Arts and Social Sciences Library and Special Library Services Manager.
[66008]   23/08/2006   **RV**30/04/2014 **CM18/01/2012**

Reynolds, Miss J E, BA MSc DipLib MCLIP, Training Development Librarian, West Herts. Hospital NHS Trust.
[42372]   20/10/1988   **CM24/06/1992**

Reynolds, Mr J G, BA (Hons), Information Officer, Clarke Willmott.
[10001558]   24/02/1983   **ME**

Reynolds, Ms L, BA (Hons) MCLIP, Executive Assistant, Homes and Communities Agency.
[52429]   01/11/1995   **CM23/01/2002**

Reynolds, Mr P C, BA DipLib MCLIP, Information Exec. Royal Institution of Chartered Surveyors, London.
[35072]   01/07/1982   **CM01/04/1986**

Reynolds, Mr P R, MA MCLIP, University Librarian, Keele, Staffordshire.
[41834]   14/04/1988   **CM18/07/1991**

Reynolds, Mrs R, Research Librarian. Reedsmith LLP, lONDON.
[10013190]   27/03/2009   **ME**

Reynolds, Miss T, MCLIP, Senior Information Officer, Clifford Chance, London.
[10007007]   17/12/2007   **RV**27/03/2014 **CM11/07/2012**

Reynolds Taylor, Mrs K, BA LLB LLM, Library Assistant (Part-time), Durham University.
[10020491]   21/02/2012   **AF**

Rhodes, Mrs C A, BA MA MCLIP, Faculty Librarian, University of Liverpool.
[44917]   14/01/1991   **CM18/11/1992**

Rhodes, Mr C J, MA, Subject specialist (Industries and businesses), House of Commons, London.
[65966]   31/07/2006   **ME**

Rhodes, Ms H J, BSc (Hons) MSc MCLIP, Management Subject Librarian.
[53244]   19/04/1996   **CM15/05/2002**

Rhodes, Miss J, MCLIP, Life Member.
[12317]   24/11/1960   **CM01/01/1969**

Rhodes, Ms L A, BA (Hons) DipLib MCLIP, Local Studies Librarian, Valence House Museum, Dagenham.
[33124]   09/10/1980   **CM26/05/1983**

Rhodes, Mrs S, BLib (Hons), Relief Library Assistant, Somerset County Council.
[38502]   15/05/1985   **ME**

Rhodes, Miss S A, BSc (Hons) MA MCLIP, Librarian – Children & Young People, North Lincs. Ctr. Library, North Lincs.
[59681]   31/07/2001   **RV**04/02/2000 **CM15/09/2004**

Rhys-Jones, Miss R H, BSc MCLIP, Retired.
[12327]   07/10/1970   **CM06/02/1974**

Riboloni, Miss V, BA, Student, University Carlos Iii Madrid.
[10029740]   16/12/2013   **ME**

Riccalton, Ms C L, Overseas.
[40261]   21/11/1986   **ME**

Ricci, Ms C, BA (Hons) MA, Russian Cataloguer and Acquisition Specialist, The London Library.
[59383]   27/02/2001   **ME**

Rice, Mrs J J, MA MCLIP, Librarian, Copthall School, London Borough of Barnet.
[39853]   05/09/1986   **CM19/09/1989**

Rice, Mrs L E, BA (HONS) DipILM ALA MCLIP, Librarian., West Kirby Library.
[10021054]   11/10/1996   **CM20/09/2000**

Rice, Mr S A, MBA, Unwaged.
[25639]   27/01/1976   **ME**

Richards, Mr A, BSc FCA MCLIP, Retired.
[60687]   12/01/1982   **CM12/01/1982**

Richards, Mrs A C, MA DipLib MCLIP, Information Specialist, Swithon Associates Ltd.
[31428]   01/10/1979   **CM14/10/1981**

Richards, Miss A L, MA (Hons) MA, Trainee Liaison Librarian, University of Reading.
[10018017]   09/11/2010   **ME**

Richards, Mr D F, FCLIP, Life Member.
[12336]   23/09/1949   **FE01/01/1964**

Richards, Mr E L, MCLIP, Assistant Librarian, Ceredigion Co. L.
[12338]   01/01/1970   **CM25/01/1974**

Richards, Ms J, Manager, Central West Library, Orange, Australia.
[10014386]   30/07/2010   **ME**

Richards, Miss K, BA, Student, Loughborough University.
[10032618]   20/12/2013   **ME**

Richards, Mrs K P, BA MCLIP, Teaching Assistant Coopers Tech.
College, Kent.
[35473]   14/10/1982   **CM10/11/1987**

Richards, Miss L, Student, Christ Church College Library.
[10032716]   07/01/2014   **ME**

Richards, Mrs N C, BA (Hons) DipLib MCLIP, Central Library Manager,
Cardiff Central Library.
[47455]   19/08/1992   **CM12/09/2001**

Richards, Mrs R, BSc (Hons), Information Adviser, Linklaters.
[10022530]   19/03/2013   **ME**

Richards, Ms S, BA, Student, University of the West of England.
[10031698]   29/10/2013   **ME**

Richards, Ms S,
[10023130]   12/06/2013   **ME**

Richardson, Mrs A, MA, eLibrary Co-ordinator, National STEM Centre.
[10013147]   23/04/2009   **ME**

Richardson, Mr A G, MCLIP, Lib. & e-Learning Lead, Colchester
Hospital University NHS Foundation Trust, Colchester.
[25402]   04/12/1975   **CM01/08/1978**

Richardson, Miss D M E, BA MCLIP, Life Member.
[12358]   07/01/1952   **CM01/01/1958**

Richardson, Ms F B, BA MSc MCLIP, Librarian, Linacre College Oxford.
[1866]   14/01/1969   **CM01/01/1972**

Richardson, Mr G, MCLIP, Retired.
[19282]   24/03/1965   **CM01/01/1969**

Richardson, Ms J, MA, Assistant Librarian, Northumbria Healthcare
NHS Trust.
[61624]   04/10/2002   **ME**

Richardson, Ms J C, DipHE, Data & Information Process Officer,
Environment Agency, Bristol.
[58647]   28/04/2000   **ME**

Richardson, Mrs J C, Peak Relief Employee for Essex L.
[61442]   18/07/2002   **AF**

Richardson, Mrs J M, BLIB MCLIP, Retired.
[22689]   15/08/1974   **CM19/11/1979**

Richardson, Miss K J, BA (Hons), Systems Librarian, Home Office,
London.
[54043]   22/10/1996   **ME**

Richardson, Ms M J, BA (Hons) DipIM, Web Manager, City of London,
Guildhall.
[51973]   29/08/1995   **ME**

Richardson, Mrs S, BSc DipLib MCLIP, Retired.
[27776]   22/07/1977   **CM01/07/1984**

Richardson, Mrs S E, MCLIP, Sch. Librarian, Gumley House Convent
School, Middlesex.
[10009306]   15/05/2008   **CM25/01/2011**

Richardson, Mrs V M, BA (Hons) MCLIP, Community Engagement
Librarian, Cambridgeshire Libraries.
[10009971]   14/05/1982   **CM29/07/1986**

Richens, Ms E J, BSc (Hons) MSc, Assistant Librarian, Wellcome
Library, London.
[62762]   20/10/2003   **ME**

Richens, Ms H, BA (Hons) DipILM MCLIP, Principal Lib. :Child. & Youth,
London Borough of Barnet.
[52670]   20/11/1995   **CM20/05/1998**

Riches, Mrs J L, Sch. Librarian, Stoke High School, Ipswich.
[10018715]   28/02/2011   **AF**

Richmond, Mrs H J, BSc MSc, E-Resources, Cheadle & Marple 6th
Form College, Stockport.
[10016309]   05/03/2010   **ME**

Richmond, Mr S, BA, Student, City University London.
[10035694]   29/10/2014   **ME**

Richmond, Mrs S E, BA DipLib MCLIP, Principal Librarian, Hull Central
Library.
[31817]   02/01/1980   **CM13/12/1984**

Richter, Mr T E, PG Cert, Student, Robert Gordon University.
[10033075]   07/05/2014   **ME**

Rickard, Mrs A T, BA MA DipLib MCLIP, School Librarian, St George's
RC Primary School, Harrow, Middlesex.
[10020126]   07/04/1989   **CM01/07/1992**

Rickard, Dr K, BA (Hons) PhD,
[10032077]   24/10/2013   **ME**

Rickers, Mrs C M, MCLIP, Volunteer, Rural Housebound Serv., Warks.
Co. L. /Age Concern.
[38]   01/01/1961   **CM01/01/1967**

Ricks, Miss A E, BA MCLIP, Retired.
[12393]   12/07/1967   **CM01/01/1971**

Ridall, Mrs C, LIS Portfolio Manager, Sheffield Hallam University.
[10034616]   23/07/2014   **ME**

Ridd, Mrs A, Library Assistant, The Piggott School.
[10032260]   12/11/2013   **AF**

Riddell, Miss A M, LLB DipLP MSc,
[10015197]   23/10/2009   **ME**

Riddell, Mrs L M, BA (Hons) DipILM MCLIP, Senior Librarian (Children
& Young People).
[58939]   09/10/2000   **CM29/03/2004**

Riddick, Ms A, BA, Library Assistant, London Borough of Haringey.
[10018376]   09/03/2011   **AF**

Riddington, Mrs L, BA (Hons) MSc MCLIP, Library Services Manager,
Gloucestershire Hospitals NHS Foundation Trust.
[10000463]   10/10/2006   **CM10/11/2010**

Riddle, Miss J S, BSc MA, Senior Information Officer, Ward Hadaway,
Newcastle.
[65422]   24/02/2006   **ME**

Rider, Mr P, BA MA PGCE, Teacher/Librarian, Strothoff International
School Germany.
[10016878]   01/06/2010   **ME**

Ridgeway, Miss Y L, BA MSc, Student, Aberystwyth University (MA
Information and Library Studies, distance learning).
[10035111]   15/09/2014   **ME**

Ridgill, Mrs J, ACLIP, Library Assistant 17 years. Some Schools
experience.
[10005138]   20/06/2007   **ACL28/01/2009**

Ridout, Mrs E M, BA MCLIP, Assistant Librarian, Sotheby's Institute of
Art.
[10032696]   06/01/2014   **CM20/06/2014**

Ridsdale, Mr J, BA PgDip, Acquisitions Librarian, Royal Institute of
British Architects.
[10008386]   25/03/2008   **ME**

Rigby, Ms K I, BA (Hons) MSc MCLIP, L. and Information Serv.
Manager, Hinchingbrooke Healthcare Library, Hinchingbrooke
Hospital, Cambridgeshire.
[60035]   29/11/2001   **CM06/04/2005**

Rigglesford, Mr D N, BA MCLIP, Retired.
[12416]   01/10/1964   **CM01/07/1989**

Rikowski, Mrs R L, BA DipLib MSc MA MCLIP CLTHE AHEA, Lecture,
London South Bank University.
[28194]   20/10/1977   **CM16/04/1981**

Riley, Mrs C, MA MSc,
[66157]   04/10/2006   **ME**

Riley, Ms E A, BA DipLib MCLIP, Group Manager, Stroud Library.
[10022904]   07/05/2013   **CM22/05/1991**
Riley, Mrs E H, MA MCLIP, Law Librarian, University of Warwick Library,
Coventry.
[30456]   25/01/1979   **CM12/03/1981**
Riley, Mrs H, BA (Hons) MCLIP, Principal Librarian, Adult Serv., Dudley
L.
[10007732]   11/12/1979   **CM14/11/1985**
Riley, Miss H J, Graduate Trainee, Bodleian Library.
[10031762]   01/10/2013   **ME**
Riley, Mrs P J, BA (Hons) MSc CertEd PGCE, Learning Resources
Centre Coordinator, East Norfolk Sixth Form College, Gorleston.
[10017665]   22/09/2010   **AF**
Riley, Mr T J, BA MA MSc, Library Supervisor, Lib. Serv., Education
Library Grad. Sch, Wills Mem. Librarian, University of Bristol.
[10021349]   19/07/2012   **ME**
Riley-Smith, Mrs P A, BA (Hons) MSc, School Librarian, Fulneck
School, Pudsey.
[56373]   01/07/1998   **ME**
Rimmer, Mrs S E, MA AI MCLIP, Cataloguing and Metadata Librarian.
[10002096]   19/11/1993   **CM16/12/2010**
Rinaldi, Mrs A M, BA (Hons) PgDip MSc MCLIP, Stock Dev. Officer,
Dumfries & Galloway Council, Scotland.
[10019495]   08/11/1999   **CM12/03/2003**
Ring, Ms V J, BA (Hons) DipIM MCLIP, Librarian, Falkirk Council, Denny
L.
[49894]   07/01/1994   **CM22/09/1999**
Ringrose, Mrs L F, BA (Hons), Library Assistant, Calne Library.
[10020407]   11/02/2012   **AF**
Ripley, Mr J, BA BFA MLIS PhD (ABD), Student, University of Western
Ontario.
[10029780]   03/02/2014   **ME**
Ripp, Mr J, BA MSLS, Librarian, Heinz Archive & Library, National
Portrait Gallery, London.
[63317]   13/04/2004   **ME**
Rippon, Miss A, BA MA, Student, University of Surrey.
[10035117]   16/09/2014   **ME**
Risberg Kane, Mrs E I M, BS MA, Librarian.
[10033896]   12/05/2014   **ME**
Riste, Mr J R, BA (Hons) MCLIP, Library Services Manager., The
Hillingdon Hospitals NHS Foundation Trust, Uxbridge.
[44049]   10/04/1990   **CM19/01/2000**
Ristic, Mrs N, Unwaged.
[10018091]   16/11/2010   **ME**
Ritchie, Mr J S, MCLIP, Information Officer, University of Glasgow.
[60246]   25/04/1993   **CM10/12/2001**
Rivers, Mrs S, BA, Student, University of Brighton.
[10033231]   07/03/2014   **ME**
Rivers-Moore, Miss A R, BA DipLib MCLIP, Chief Librarian, Hanover
Public Library, Canada.
[35035]   13/07/1982   **CM01/08/1991**
Rix, Mr D W, MCLIP, Unemployed.
[26240]   17/09/1976   **CM11/11/1980**
Rix, Mrs R S, MCLIP, Retired.
[12444]   02/04/1959   **CM01/01/1961**
Road, Mr J R, Stock Performance, Analysis & Monitoring Stock
Management Team PEST Libraries, Surrey County Council, Based
at Ewell library.
[39990]   09/10/1986   **ME**
Robb, Mrs A J, MA (Hons) DipILS MCLIP, Local Studies Librarian, East
Renfrewshire Council.
[51600]   06/04/1995   **CM23/07/1997**
Robb, Mr C I, BA (Hons) DipILS, Unemployed.
[58740]   03/07/2000   **ME**

Robb, Mrs F M, ACLIP, L. Assistant, Monifieth High School, Scotland.
[10016127]   16/02/2010   **ACL09/12/2010**
Robb, Mrs H D, BA DipLib MCLIP FHEA, Academic Liaison Librarian,
Durham University Library.
[38788]   09/10/1985   **CM07/06/1988**
Robbins, Mr A T, BA, Outreach Services Supervisor, Hertfordshire CC.
[10032954]   30/01/2014   **ME**
Robbins, Mrs R M, BA (Hons) PgDipLib, Senior Librarian, Ministry of
Justice, London.
[43289]   16/10/1989   **ME**
Roberts, Mrs A, BA (Hons) MA, Information Assistant, University of
Chichester Bognor Regis campus.
[10031574]   03/09/2013   **ME**
Roberts, Ms A, BA MA MCLIP PhD, Library Operations Manager, Barts
Health NHS Trust.
[10006439]   19/10/2007   **CM10/11/2010**
Roberts, Miss A, BA Dip MSc, School Librarian, St Margaret's Bushey,
Herts.
[10020209]   23/11/2011   **ME**
Roberts, Miss A C, BA PgDip, Outreach Librarian, Warrington and
Halton Hospitals NHS Foundation Trust.
[10020656]   15/03/2012   **ME**
Roberts, Miss A L, PGCE MSc BA (Hons) MCLIP, Liaison Librarian,
Queen Margaret University, Edinburgh.
[61131]   07/03/2002   **CM28/01/2009**
Roberts, Ms A M, BA (Hons) PGCE, Coordinator, Calderdale Schools
Library Service, Northgate.
[10006776]   12/10/1982   **ME**
Roberts, Mrs A M, BLib MCLIP, Customer Serv. Manager, University of
Warwick L.
[22007]   19/01/1974   **CM01/08/1977**
Roberts, Ms A S E, BA (Hons), Student, Robert Gordon University.
[10035681]   29/10/2014   **ME**
Roberts, Mr B F, CBE MA PhD HonFLA, Retired Librarian, National
Library of Wales.
[39278]   06/01/1086   **HFE01/01/1994**
Roberts, Ms C, MA DipIS MCLIP, Information Literacy Librarian, City of
Glasgow College, Glasgow.
[55240]   08/09/1997   **CM12/03/2003**
Roberts, Mr C, MA (Hons) MSc MCLIP, Reader Services Librarian,
University of Bath.
[59818]   10/10/2001   **RV**27/08/2014 **CM23/06/2004**
Roberts, Mrs C A H, BSc DipLib MCLIP, Part-time Librarian, The
Queen's Sch. Chester.
[17126]   04/04/1972   **CM16/09/1975**
Roberts, Mrs C L, MA DipLib MCLIP, Network Librarian, Peterhead
Academy.
[33069]   08/10/1980   **CM27/10/1983**
Roberts, Ms D, BLib MCLIP, Knowledge Management Team lead,
Evidence Service, Public Health Wales.
[27458]   01/04/1977   **CM01/07/1990**
Roberts, Mrs D, BA MSc MCLIP, Librarian, Burnetts Solicitors.
[5472]   29/01/1968   **CM01/01/1971**
Roberts, Mrs D, MCLIP, Retired.
[15095]   29/03/1963   **CM01/01/1971**
Roberts, Mr D A W, BA, Customer Service Advisor, Capita CRB,
Liverpool.
[10007553]   13/02/2008   **ME**
Roberts, Mr D W, Student, King's College London.
[10032410]   18/12/2013   **ME**
Roberts, Ms E, BA MA, Subject Specialist for Art & Music/Rare Books,
Los Angeles Public Library, USA.
[10014382]   22/10/1997   **ME**

Roberts, Mrs E C, BA (Hons) MA MCLIP, Schools Library Consultant, Walsall Schools Library Support Service.
[50952]   31/10/1994   **CM21/05/2003**

Roberts, Ms E H, BSc, School Librarian, The Ravensbourne School, Bromley.
[49489]   05/11/1993   **ME**

Roberts, Mrs E J, BSc (Hons) MA, Academic Liaison Librarian, University of Surrey.
[55710]   06/11/1997   **ME**

Roberts, Miss E K, BA DipLib MCLIP, Serv. Development Librarian, Cirencester Bingham Library, Gloucestershire City Council.
[41713]   20/02/1988   **CM22/05/1991**

Roberts, Ms F M, BA MSc, Librarian.
[10006921]   17/12/2007   **ME**

Roberts, Mrs H M, BTECH, Strategy Manager for Information, Advice and Guidance, Lea Valley High School.
[63904]   26/10/2004   **ME**

Roberts, Mrs H R, BSc, LRC Operations Manager, The City of Liverpool College, 52 Roscoe Street, Liverpool L1 9DW.
[63324]   16/04/2004   **ME**

Roberts, Miss I M B, MCLIP, Retired.
[12483]   20/03/1964   **CM01/01/1972**

Roberts, Miss J, BA (Hons) PgDip ILM DMS MA, Team Leader, Liverpool Libraries & Information Service.
[10021690]   07/03/2002   **ME**

Roberts, Miss J E, BA (Hons) MA, Outreach Librarian, Salford Royal NHS Foundation Trust.
[10006662]   21/11/2007   **ME**

Roberts, Ms J L, BA (Hons) MScIS, Assistant Librarian FE&HE.
[55840]   21/11/1997   **ME**

Roberts, Mrs K, MCLIP, Information Librarian (Chartered) – Acquisitions, University of Bath.
[10007119]   18/01/2008   **CM07/07/2010**

Roberts, Ms K, MBA BA (Hons),
[10033878]   08/05/2014   **ME**

Roberts, Miss K L, BA MA, Subject Librarian. Anglia Ruskin University Library, Chelmsford, Essex.
[10009992]   30/06/2008   **ME**

Roberts, Mrs L M, BA MCLIP, Information Officer (Job Share), Child. Information Bureau, Wrexham L. & Arts Centre for.
[28451]   04/11/1977   **CM06/03/1981**

Roberts, Miss M, BA (Hons), Business Intelligence, Oxford Innovation.
[62270]   07/04/2003   **ME**

Roberts, Mr M, MA MA MCLIP, Retired.
[21828]   15/02/1974   **CM03/11/1976**

Roberts, Mrs M A F, MCLIP, Life Member.
[12498]   01/01/1957   **CM01/01/1961**

Roberts, Mr M J, MCLIP, Director, Infodoc Serv. Ltd, London.
[12502]   09/08/1961   **CM01/01/1965**

Roberts, Mr M V, MA MCLIP, Retired.
[12505]   01/01/1964   **CM01/01/1967**

Roberts, Mr N R, BA (Hons), Assistant Librarian, University of Glamorgan.
[54125]   30/10/1996   **ME**

Roberts, Ms N W, BA (Hons) MSc (Econ), Knowledge Centre, Bodleian Health Care Libraries.
[56867]   29/10/1998   **ME**

Roberts, Mrs P J, BA MCLIP, Div. Manager, IPC Group, St Ives.
[26306]   01/10/1976   **CM07/07/1980**

Roberts, Mrs R, BA (Hons) MCLIP, Learning Centre Coordinator., Wolverhampton College.
[43082]   25/07/1989   **CM25/05/1994**

Roberts, Mrs R A, Senior Library Assistant, AK Bell Library, Perth, Scotland.
[10020503]   21/02/2012   **AF**

Roberts, Mrs R E, BSc (Hons) MA Ed MSc MCLIP, Unwaged.
[61255]   29/04/2002   **CM21/11/2007**

Roberts, Mrs S, BA (Hons) MA MCLIP, Librarian, Nottinghamshire Healthcare NHS Trust.
[59635]   09/07/2001   **CM28/10/2004**

Roberts, Dr S A, MA MA PhD MCLIP, Senior Lecturer, Centre for for Information Management, Thames Valley University.
[12516]   29/08/1969   **CM01/01/1972**

Roberts, Miss S M, BA (Hons) MCLIP, Knowledge Centre Manager, HEFCE, Bristol.
[51123]   17/11/1994   **CM08/12/2004**

Roberts, Mr W D, MA MCLIP, Senior Advisor, National Library of New Zealand, Wellington.
[10008012]   03/03/2008   **CM11/11/1980**

Roberts Cuffin, Mrs T L, BA (Hons) MCLIP, Head of Library & Knowledge Services; University Hospitals of Morecambe Bay NHS Foundation Trust.
[40664]   28/04/1987   **CM04/02/2004**

Robertshaw, Ms J, MA DipLib MCLIP, Lib. Development Manager, Department of Collections Access, Imperial War Museum, London.
[39378]   23/01/1986   **CM16/05/1990**

Roberts-Maloney, Mrs L M, BA (Hons) MA, Digital Resources and Collections Assistant, Liverpool School of Tropical Medicine.
[64532]   09/05/2005   **ME**

Robertson, Mrs A C, BA (Hons) DipLib MAppSc (LIM) MCLIP, Academic Liaison Librarian, University of Bedfordshire.
[35534]   21/10/1982   **CM21/05/2003**

Robertson, Miss A J, BA (Hons) DipLib, Part-time. Medical records Clerk, NHS, Caithness Gen. Hospital.
[41777]   08/04/1988   **ME**

Robertson, Miss A K, MA MCLIP, Quality Control and Documentation Librarian, Fife Cultural Trust.
[57785]   14/08/1999   **CM11/07/2012**

Robertson, Mr B G, Student, Robert Gordon University.
[10035341]   14/10/2014   **ME**

Robertson, Mrs C A, BA MCLIP, Freelance Proofreader & Library Research Worker.
[12527]   17/05/1965   **CM01/01/1970**

Robertson, Mr D, MA (Hons), Sr. Lib. Assistant, Arbroath.
[64214]   21/02/2005   **ME**

Robertson, Mr D B, BA (Hons), Student, Glasgow Kelvin College.
[10035266]   02/10/2014   **ME**

Robertson, Mrs D K, FCLIP, Life Member.
[12529]   05/03/1940   **FE01/01/1968**

Robertson, Ms F, BA DipLib, Sub-Librarian, British Medical Assoc., London.
[42163]   07/10/1988   **ME**

Robertson, Ms F M, BA MCLIP, Network Librarian, Aberdeen Lib. & Information Serv.
[37829]   29/10/1984   **CM11/12/1989**

Robertson, Miss I M, MCLIP, Life Member.
[12536]   06/09/1955   **CM01/01/1962**

Robertson, Mrs J A, MA (Hons) DipILS MCLIP, Lib. Technical Serv. Manager.
[51067]   10/11/1994   **CM21/11/2001**

Robertson, Ms J M, BA MCLIP, Librarian, Evalueserve.
[42560]   03/01/1989   **CM26/05/1993**

Robertson, L, BSc (Hons) MSc MCLIP, Librarian, Shepherd and Wedderburn LLP, Edinburgh.
[49607]   19/11/1993   **RV27/03/2014**
CM20/11/2002

Robertson, Mrs L A, PgDip, Knowledge Management Executive, Scottish Enterprise.
[65027]   13/10/2005   ME

Robertson, Miss L J, BA (Hons) MSc, Sch. Librarian, Uddingstom Grammar School, Glasgow.
[10010638]   29/08/2008   ME

Robertson, Mrs L M, MA MSc MCLIP, Liaison Librarian, Biological Sciences and Preclinical Medicine University of Southampton.
[26141]   01/07/1976   CM01/07/1989

Robertson, Ms M, BA (Hons) MSc, Freelance Information Professional.
[63391]   28/04/2004   ME

Robertson, Ms P, BA PgDip MCLIP, Learning Resources Adviser, Jisc.
[57275]   26/01/1999   CM02/02/2005

Robertson, Mrs P, BA (Hons) MCLIP, Librarian, Alloa, Clackmannanshire.
[62713]   09/10/2003   CM05/05/2010

Robertson, Mrs P A C, BSc (Hons) DipILS MCLIP,
[51747]   14/06/1995   RV11/12/2009
CM22/09/1999

Robertson, Miss S, BA (Hons) MA MCLIP, Student (MA Librarianship), University of Sheffield, Sheffield.
[10001475]   26/02/2007   CM19/08/2011

Robertson, Mrs S E, BLib MCLIP, Library Services Manager, Wilfred Stokes Library, Buckinghamshire healthcare NHS trust.
[34584]   01/01/1982   CM02/01/1986

Robertson, Ms S J, BA (Hons), Information Assistant, Riverside Library.
[10035482]   15/10/2014   ME

Robertson, Miss V, BA (Hons) MSc MCLIP, Reader Services Librarian, UCL.
[48299]   25/11/1992   RV20/04/2012
CM22/07/1998

Robertson, Mrs V A A, BA FCLIP, Co-ordinator, Bromley Home Library Service.
[5007]   03/11/1971   RV27/03/2014
FE14/03/2012

Robertson, Mrs V R, MCLIP, Part-time. Senior Library Assistant, Napier University, Edinburgh.
[22859]   03/10/1974   CM04/07/1977

Robin, Ms S C, BA (Hons), Student, Aberystwyth University.
[10014423]   12/08/2009   ME

Robins, Mrs E M, MCLIP, Partner-Engineering Consultancy, Dove Thermal Engineering Ltd, Uttoxeter, Staffordshire.
[12548]   01/01/1959   CM01/01/1964

Robins, Miss S E, BA (Hons) MCLIP, Librarian, CWMTAF Health Board, Royal Glamorgan Hospital.
[62882]   18/11/2003   CM11/06/2010

Robinson, Miss A, BA (Hons), Lib. Officer, Pinsent Masons, London.
[50977]   04/11/1994   ME

Robinson, Miss A, BA (Hons) MA, Programme Manager (Digital Curation), University for the Creative Arts.
[10018986]   08/10/2003   ME

Robinson, Ms A L, BA (Hons) MLib MCLIP, Academic Liaison Librarian, University of Bedfordshire.
[47949]   27/10/1992   CM13/03/2002

Robinson, Miss B E, MCLIP, Retired.
[12554]   08/10/1941   CM01/01/1952

Robinson, Mr C, BA (Hons), Student / Customer Team Manager, Manchester Metropolitan University.
[10032073]   24/10/2013   ME

Robinson, Miss C J, Student, New College.
[10032627]   20/12/2013   ME

Robinson, Mrs D, BA DipLib MCLIP, Librarian, Dallam School, Cumbria.
[38867]   16/10/1985   CM19/06/1991

Robinson, Mr E D G, JP DL MA FRSA MCLIP, Life Member.
[12562]   28/09/1950   CM01/01/1958

Robinson, Dr E J, BSc MCLIP PHD, Independent Heritage Libraries, Research and Consultancy.
[30523]   01/02/1979   CM16/09/1981

Robinson, Mrs G A, BA (Hons) MCLIP, Librarian, Education Centre Library, Hexham.
[10017329]   08/02/1979   CM01/07/1987

Robinson, Mr G A, BA (Hons) DipLIS, Library Manager, Barnet & Chase Farm Hospitals NHS Trust.
[41260]   25/10/1987   ME

Robinson, Ms H, LLB (Hons) DipILS MCLIP, Reader Services Librarian., Advocates Library., Edinburgh.
[53614]   12/08/1996   CM21/05/2003

Robinson, Mrs H J, BA (Hons) PgDipLib, Knowledge & Information Manager, Veale Wasbrough Vizards, Bristol.
[41289]   30/10/1987   ME

Robinson, Mrs J, BA (Hons) MA, Senior Librarian, Service Delivery, South Tyneside Libraries.
[10020655]   10/01/2000   ME

Robinson, Mrs J, Student.
[65931]   10/07/2006   ME

Robinson, Ms J, BA (Hons) DipIS MCLIP,
[57716]   02/04/1960   CM02/04/1960

Robinson, Mr J A, HNC BA, Research & Information Officer, DLA Piper UK LLP, Manchester.
[62465]   08/07/2003   ME

Robinson, Mr J D, BA MA, Director of L. and Information Serv., SOAS, London.
[10013426]   24/04/2009   ME

Robinson, Mrs J L, MCLIP, Retired.
[20365]   15/02/1973   CM10/08/1976

Robinson, Mrs J M, Central Library Manager, Doncaster Council.
[10022162]   15/01/2013   ME

Robinson, Ms K, BA (Hons) MA, Learning Resource Librarian, City of London Academy, Islington.
[61586]   02/10/2002   ME

Robinson, Ms K J, BA MSc, Librarian, Library Support Services, Oxford.
[10021084]   29/05/2012   ME

Robinson, Ms K M, JP MA FCLIP FRSA, University Librarian, University of Bath.
[44072]   30/04/1990   RV20/06/2014   FE16/05/2012

Robinson, Mrs L, BSc ACLIP, Consumer Science & Consumer Law Teesside University 2007.
[10013632]   18/05/2009   ACL27/03/2014

Robinson, Mrs L, BA (Hons), Library Assistant, Highfields School.
[10035479]   15/10/2014   ME

Robinson, Mr L H, BA MCLIP, Retired.
[12574]   05/03/1964   CM01/01/1967

Robinson, Ms M, BSc MSc MLIS MCLIP, Research Evaluation Manager, Arthritis Research UK.
[10002939]   09/05/2007   CM10/03/2010

Robinson, Ms M, BA DipLib MCLIP,
[36940]   20/01/1984   CM09/08/1988

Robinson, Mr N, Res. Officer, Marylebone Cricket Club.
[63334]   16/04/2004   ME

Robinson, Mrs S F, BA (Hons) MCLIP, Subject Librarian, Hull College, Hull.
[49505]   08/11/1993   CM12/03/2003

Robinson, Ms S M, BA, Weekend site Manager, Leeds University Libraries.
[28262]   26/10/1977   CM27/11/1979

Robinson, Mrs T, BA DipLib MCLIP, Retired.
[31361]   03/10/1979   **CM09/12/1982**
Robinson, Mrs V A, Librarian, North Lincs. Council.
[47297]   06/07/1992   **ME**
Robson, Miss A, Student, University of Teeside,
[10019437]   04/07/2011   **ME**
Robson, Ms A,
[10032149]   29/10/2013   **ME**
Robson, Mrs J, College Librarian, Palmers College, Essex.
[10021876]   24/10/2012   **ME**
Robson, Mrs L T, MCLIP, Principal Librarian:Inclusion and Health.,
   Dudley Metropolitan Borough Council.
[49419]   21/10/1993   **CM12/09/2012**
Robson, Mr M S, BA MCLIP, Retired.
[12599]   12/01/1965   **CM01/01/1969**
Roby, Mrs T A, BA (Hons) MCLIP, Retired.
[10006646]   06/10/1987   **CM21/07/1993**
Rocchi, Mrs S J, BA (Hons), Librarian, St Louis High School, Italy.
[10021286]   06/07/2012   **ME**
Roche, Mrs C M L, MA MCLIP, Librarian, Eltham College, London.
[56636]   24/09/1998   **CM31/01/2007**
Roche, Ms K C, BA MLib, LRC Manager, West Thames College,
   Middlesex.
[41129]   11/10/1987   **CM12/12/1990**
Roche, Ms M N, BA MA, Retired.
[43337]   23/10/1989   **ME**
Rochelle, Miss S F, BA MCLIP, Librarian, Telford & Wrekin Authority,
   Shropshire.
[39509]   11/02/1986   **CM14/03/1990**
Rochester, Ms E, BSc (Hons) MSc MCLIP, Web Content Editor
   (Ireland).
[47027]   02/04/1992   **CM07/11/1996**
Rock, Ms C J W, BA MA MCLIP, Director of Library & Learning Support
   Services, University of Surrey.
[40929]   05/08/1987   **CM24/04/1991**
Rocke, Ms S, BA (Hons) MA FDSC BSc, Library Assistant/Study Skills
   Tutor, Glyndwr University.
[10017515]   31/08/2010   **ME**
Rockliff, Ms J A, BSc Pgd, Deputy Information Manager, TUC.
[46237]   18/10/1991   **ME**
Rodda, Mrs S J M, BA MSc (Econ), Collections Librarian, Bishop
   Grosseteste University, Lincoln.
[61440]   29/07/2002   **ME**
Rodenhurst, Mrs F H, BLib MCLIP, Librarian, Oswestry Library,
   Shropshire.
[41545]   20/01/1988   **CM14/11/1991**
Roderick, Mrs K, BSc (Econ) PgDip MCLIP, Information Officer, Poole
   Library.
[10006897]   23/04/2013   **CM11/12/1989**
Rodger, Mrs E A, MA MSc MCLIP, Lib. -IT & Systems (Educ.
   Resources), South Lanarkshire Council, Hamilton.
[57455]   01/04/1999   **CM23/01/2002**
Rodger, Miss E M, BSc MCLIP, Life Member.
[12608]   12/07/1965   **CM01/01/1967**
Rodger, Mrs J, MCLIP, Retired.
[9473]   10/10/1963   **CM01/01/1967**
Rodger, Mrs J H, MA DipLib MCLIP, Unwaged.
[21318]   26/09/1973   **CM07/02/1978**
Rodgers, Mrs E G, BA DipLib MCLIP, Part-time Learning Centre Officer,
   South Tyneside College.
[30582]   15/02/1979   **CM19/01/1983**
Rodriguez, Mr E, Student.
[10032041]   22/10/2013   **ME**

Rodriguez, Miss G M, Researcher, Medellin, Colombia.
[41631]   05/02/1988   **ME**
Rodriguez-Lopez, Miss R, Information Specialist, University of York.
[10033985]   15/05/2014   **ME**
Roe, Miss A, BA, LRC Manager, Belmont Community School, Durham.
[63643]   09/08/2004   **ME**
Roe, Mr J, BA MA FCLIP, Retired.
[12621]   05/09/1949   **FE01/01/1958**
Roe, Mr N W, BA MCLIP, Bibl. Serv. Officer, North East Wales Institute
   of Higher Education, Wrexham.
[12625]   27/02/1972   **CM31/10/1974**
Roe, Mrs S, BA DipLib MCLIP, Child. Librarian, Bebington Central
   Library, Metropolitan Borough of Wirral.
[31336]   15/10/1979   **CM16/02/1983**
Rogers, Mrs B, BA, School Librarian, Notts. C. C., Notts.
[31835]   18/01/1980   **CM15/08/1984**
Rogers, Mrs D C, BA MCLIP, Retired.
[12638]   04/08/1960   **CM01/01/1963**
Rogers, Mrs J, BSc MCLIP, School Librarian, The King's School,
   Peterborough.
[9072]   09/11/1971   **CM31/08/1974**
Rogers, Mrs J A, BA MA MCLIP, Employment not known.
[37814]   29/10/1984   **CM05/07/1988**
Rogers, Mrs L E, FCLIP, Retired.
[7327]   17/02/1936   **FE01/01/1949**
Rogers, Mr M, PgDip, Information Specialist, Home Office, London.
[10019008]   07/04/2011   **ME**
Rogers, Mrs N B, BA (Hons) MA MCLIP, Area Manager, Libraries West,
   Lincolnshire County Council.
[49361]   28/10/1993   **CM19/03/1997**
Rogers, Mrs P, BA (Hons) MCLIP, Senior Assistant Librarian, University
   of Bristol.
[43499]   31/10/1989   **CM21/08/2009**
Rogers, Mrs S, BA MCLIP, Information Resources Manager, Atkins,
   Epsom.
[10018693]   01/04/1974   **CM24/03/1992**
Rogers, Mrs S, BSc NNEB RSH, Library Manager & Post16 Study Skills
   Coordinator @ Helston Community College Cornwall.
[10014088]   01/07/2009   **ME**
Rogers, Mrs S J, BA (Hons) MA MCLIP, Head of Library Service,
   Institute of Mechanical Engineers.
[52902]   22/01/1996   **CM18/09/2002**
Rogerson, Prof I, MLS PhD DLitt FCLIP, Hon. Res. F., John Rylands
   Institute, University of Manchester.
[12658]   13/03/1948   **FE12/03/1982**
Roland, Mr J B, BA DipLib MCLIP, Head of Customer Experience,
   University of West London.
[39136]   12/11/1985   **CM14/11/1990**
Rolfe, Mrs K J E, BSc (Hons) DipIM, Assistant Librarian – User Serv.,
   National Oceanographic Library, University of Southampton.
[52656]   16/11/1995   **CM21/03/2001**
Roll, Mrs M J, BA MCLIP MCMI, Retired.
[14298]   07/01/1971   **CM05/12/1974**
Rollo, Mr D A T, MCLIP, Retired.
[12667]   19/10/1971   **CM03/10/1973**
Rolls, Dr J J, BA MA MA (LIS) PhD, L. Administrator, The Warburg
   Institute, The University of London.
[58408]   07/02/2000   **ME**
Rone-Clarke, Mr D, MRSC MCLIP, General Assistant, Tesco
   Supermarkets, Basingstoke.
[12672]   01/04/1971   **CM08/07/1974**
Ronson, Mrs A R, BA PgDip, Lifelong Learning Assistant, Crosby
   Library, Liverpool.
[61774]   06/11/2002   **ME**

Ronson, Mrs J S, BA (Hons) MA, Development Officer, Mimas, University of Manchester.
[62859]   17/11/2003   ME

Rooke, Mrs E A, BA DipLib MCLIP, Reader Services Manager, Information & Technology.
[31969]   04/01/1980   CM16/07/1982

Rooney, Ms C M, BA, Librarian, Nursing and Midwifery Board of Ireland.
[39598]   09/03/1986   ME

Rooney, Ms E, MA MSc Econ, Librarian, Westminster Reference Library, London.
[10014806]   18/09/2009   ME

Roos, Mrs J, BA (Hons) ACLIP, Senior Library Assistant, Newnham College Library, Cambridge.
[58330]   11/01/2000   ACL29/08/2008

Roots, Mr D, Info Resource Centre Staff, E. ON New Build & Technology.
[10029872]   10/02/2014   ME

Rooza, Mrs J, BA (Hons) DipILM MCLIP, Librarian.
[55441]   13/10/1997   CM15/01/2003

Roper, Miss A L, MA BMus MMus AKC MCLIP, College Librarian, Christ's College Cambridge.
[59785]   02/10/2001   CM03/10/2007

Roper, Mr C T, BA DipLib MCLIP, Primary Care Librarian, West Sussex Knowledge & Libraries.
[31433]   15/10/1979   CM24/05/1995

Roper, Miss L B, BSc (Hons) Cert HE ACILIP, Digital Rsource Manager, CEM.
[10021731]   08/10/2012   ACL27/03/2014

Roper, Mr V D P, BSc MA FCLIP, Life Member.
[12680]   25/09/1951   FE01/01/1965

Roscelli, Miss R M, Student, City University.
[10020299]   11/01/2012   ME

Rose, Mr A D, MSc BA (Hons) MCLIP, Librarian., Wroxton College.
[65508]   13/02/2006   CM21/08/2009

Rose, Mr D A, BA (Hons) DipLib MCLIP, Senior Librarian, City of London School.
[31435]   13/02/2003   CM13/02/2003

Rose, Miss E H, BA (Hons) MA MCLIP, Child. Librarian, Selsdon Library.
[55706]   05/11/1997   CM23/01/2002

Rose, Mrs G, Site Librarian, Stoke Mandeville, Aylesbury Hospital, Bucks.
[53671]   28/08/1996   CM29/11/2006

Rose, Mr G B K, BLib MCLIP, Information Officer, CMS Cameron McKenna, London.
[41615]   05/02/1988   CM27/07/1994

Rose, Miss H L, BA MA, Academic Librarian, University of Northampton.
[63775]   06/10/2004   ME

Rose, Mrs J E, MCLIP, Retired.
[15232]   06/11/1971   CM13/08/1975

Rose, Mr K W, BSc MSc MCLIP, Senior Information & Records Management Analyst, Department for Business, Innovation & Skills, London.
[42368]   25/10/1988   CM24/03/1992

Rose, Mrs L M, BA (Hons) MSc (Econ) MCLIP, Lib. -Performing Arts, Hertfordshire Libraries.
[55988]   13/01/1998   CM12/09/2001

Rose, Miss P, BA (Hons) MA PGCHE, Deputy Librarian.
[10029878]   24/10/2013   ME

Rose, Miss S L, BA (Hons) MSc, Library Frontline Assistant, Lancashire County Council.
[61658]   14/10/2002   ME

Rose, Mr T J, BA MCLIP, Assistant Librarian (Saturdays), Evesham Library, Evesham, Worcester.
[40178]   05/11/1986   CM13/03/2002

Rosen, Miss J A, BA (Hons) DipLib MCLIP, Librarian, Imperial War Museum, Departmentof Printed Books.
[59900]   30/10/2001   CM08/12/2004

Rosenberg, Ms D B, MBE MA FLA HonDSc HonFLA FCLIP, Life Member.
[12688]   06/10/1964   HFE01/01/1991

Rosenberg, Mr S, BSc (Econ) MCLIP, Library Services Manager, Francis Costello Library, RJAH.
[59368]   20/02/2001   CM28/01/2009

Rosenvinge, Mr P J L, MA DipLib MCLIP, Knowledge Manager, DSTL, Porton Down.
[34073]   02/09/1981   CM09/07/2008

Rosie, Miss A S, MCLIP, Retired.
[21313]   03/10/1973   CM27/07/1976

Ross, Mr J M, BSc MSc MILog MCLIP, Brokbourne Solution, Hoddesdon.
[60633]   17/05/1977   CM01/12/1979

Ross, Miss J M, BA, Subsurface Data Technician, Total E & P UK, Aberdeen.
[33133]   02/10/1980   ME

Ross, Mrs K, BA (Hons) MCLIP, School Library Support.
[10020202]   20/10/1980   CM26/10/1982

Ross, Mrs K A, BA MBA MA (Ed) MCLIP TEFL, Unwaged.
[35646]   18/11/1982   CM16/02/1988

Ross, Miss M, Researcher, FENS Information.
[10031675]   15/01/2014   ME

Ross, Mrs N, Manager, Learning Resource Centre, Queen's College, Taunton.
[59815]   10/10/2001   AF

Ross, Mr N J, BA (Hons) DipIS MSc MCLIP, Gateway Services Manager, University for the Creative Arts.
[52760]   07/12/1995   CM19/07/2000

Ross, Mr P D S, BA (Hons) MCLIP, Paul specialises in Social Care Information & Advice.
[10014618]   20/08/2009   CM29/05/2013

Rossall, Mr D K, BSc (Hons) MCLIP, Information Systems Architect, The Institution of Engineering & Technology., Stevenage.
[10005268]   12/03/1982   CM24/03/1988

Rossell, Mrs D J, BA MA MCLIP, Senior Learning Centre Manager.
[49102]   01/10/1993   CM27/11/1996

Rosset, Mr R W, BA (Hons) DipLib MCLIP, Freelance Information Professional currently working in Medical Records for The London North West Healthcare NHS Trust.
[37687]   17/10/1984   CM14/09/1994

Rossiter, Mrs S M, BA MCLIP, Retired.
[12711]   23/03/1965   CM01/01/1969

Rotar, Ms A, Student, RMITUniversity.
[10029896]   24/10/2013   ME

Roth, Mrs K M, BA MCLIP, Library Manager, St Aidan's C of E High School, Harrogate.
[27263]   15/02/1977   CM24/09/1981

Rothera, Ms H M, BA (Hons) MA MCLIP, Academic Development Team Leader and Subject Librarian (Education), Oxford Brookes University.
[52424]   30/10/1995   RV16/01/2014   CM17/03/1999

Rothman, Mrs C, BA ACLIP, L. Manager, Southbourne Library, Bournemouth.
[10016137]   05/09/2003   ACL14/11/2012

Rothwell, Mrs J, BA DipLib MCLIP, Travelling.
[32135]   21/01/1980   CM24/06/1983

Rouki, Miss M, BA (Hons), Information Professional.
[10032659] 24/12/2013 ME
Roulstone, L H, MCLIP, Assistant Librarian/VLE Administrator.
[20169] 29/01/1973 **CM11/11/1975**
Round, Mrs U M, CertEd BA (Hons) MCLIP, Part-time Cataloguer,
Roehampton University, London.
[29028] 26/03/1978 **CM15/04/1982**
Rounsevell, Mrs H J, Library Assistant, Truro Library, Truro.
[64465] 31/03/2005 AF
Rouse, Ms K A, BSc (Hons) MSc, Libraries Resources Manager,
Brighton & Hove City Council Libraries Service.
[65790] 01/05/2006 ME
Routledge, Mrs E, BA (Hons) MA MCLIP, Assistant Librarian, Marie
Curie, Newcastle upon Tune.
[10006938] 17/12/2007 **CM09/07/2013**
Rowan, Miss E, Librarian, Calderglen High School.
[10019308] 01/06/2011 ME
Rowan, Miss E I S, MCLIP, Retired.
[12729] 28/08/1953 **CM01/01/1963**
Rowan, Ms E S, MSc, Acquisitions & Metadata Services Manager,
Edinburgh University Library.
[40671] 30/04/1987 ME
Rowdon, Mr J I, PGD PGD BSc HND, Information Assistant, City of
Glasgow College.
[10021809] 16/10/2012 ME
Rowe, Mrs J P, BA (Hons) PgDip ILM MCLIP, Retired. Living in Portugal.
[10001008] 15/10/1997 **CM22/08/2012**
Rowe, Miss L D, BA, Unemployed.
[41703] 24/02/1988 ME
Rowe, Mrs O F, FCLIP, Retired, Jamaica.
[16605] 01/01/1956 **FE01/01/1966**
Rowe, Miss R M, MA MCLIP, Smuts Librarian for South Asian &
Commonwealth Studies, University of Cambridge.
[37628] 09/10/1984 **CM06/09/1988**
Rowell, Mrs R, BA MCLIP, Project Manager, Ciuica, Newcastle Upon
Tyne.
[38128] 23/01/1985 **CM07/06/1988**
Rowing, Ms E J, BA (Hons) MA, Part-time School Librarian, Dulwich
College.
[62667] 01/10/2003 ME
Rowland, Mr A P, Learning Resource Centre Manager, The Sixth Form
College, Solihull.
[60962] 18/01/2002 **CM11/03/2009**
Rowland, Mrs B, BA MA, Student.
[10022035] 20/11/2012 ME
Rowland, Ms D E, BLib MSc MCLIP, Retired.
[25101] 01/11/1975 **CM28/01/1980**
Rowland, Mrs H, BA MCLIP, Life Member.
[12740] 22/02/1952 **CM01/01/1958**
Rowland, Ms H L, BA MCLIP, Head of Library & Collections, Society of
Antiquaries of London.
[34102] 01/10/1981 **CM11/08/1986**
Rowland, Ms J A B, BSc (Hons) MA, Subj. Lib. IComputing, Media,
Optometry, Psychology, J. B. Priestley Library, University of
Bradford.
[55391] 07/10/1997 ME
Rowland, Mr J S, BSc MCLIP, Information and IP Specialist, Monier
Technical Centre, Crawley.
[52379] 30/10/1995 **CM12/07/2000**
Rowland, Ms L, BA (Hons), Senior Learning Resources Assistant
(Children's Literature Specialism), University of Brighton.
[10032022] 21/10/2013 ME

Rowlands, Ms A M, DipInfMan, Library Manager, Regent's University
London.
[50473] 11/08/1994 ME
Rowlatt, Ms M E, BA MSC, Freelance.
[23708] 08/01/1975 **CM30/07/1979**
Rowles, Mr J, MA, Student, UCL, London.
[65639] 15/02/2006 ME
Rowley, Mrs A M, BSc MA MCLIP, Head of Knowledge Management,
Worcs. Health ICT Serv., Rowlands L.
[12750] 01/01/1968 **CM01/01/1971**
Rowley, Mrs B M, BA DipLIS MCLIP, Lead Adv., SLS.
[44733] 27/11/1990 **CM25/01/1995**
Rowley, Mrs F M, BEd, Teacher, Thomas's Day School.
[10014894] 16/04/2014 AF
Rowley, Mr T D, BA (Hons) ACLIP, Lib. Assistant, Sandbach Library,
Cheshire.
[10015392] 10/11/2009 **ACL09/11/2011**
Rowley, Miss V, BA MA, Library Assistant, Heythrop College, London.
[66127] 29/09/2006 ME
Rowney, Mrs C L, BSc (Hons) MSc MA, Staffordshire University.
[65433] 23/02/2006 ME
Rowntree, Mr M E, BA (Hons) MA MCLIP, Not working.
[49014] 31/08/1993 **CM26/11/1997**
Roy, Mr J V, BA DipEdTech MCLIP, Director, J. V Roy Ltd.
[32165] 17/01/1980 **CM19/08/1988**
Roy, Mrs S, Student City University London.
[10032283] 13/11/2013 ME
Royal, Miss M C, Graduate Trainee, Newnham College.
[10021983] 09/11/2012 ME
Royan, Prof B, BA MBA FSA (Scot) HonFCLIP, Retired.
[29808] 02/10/1978 **HFE29/06/2005**
Royce, Mr J R, BA MLib MCLIP, Freelance consultant, workshop leader,
and more.
[29216] 13/04/1978 **CM31/10/1984**
Ruane, Ms J B, BA (Hons) MA MCLIP, Operations Co-ordination
Manager (Design & Production), The University of Law.
[53687] 05/09/1996 **CM12/09/2001**
Ruberry, Ms C S, BA MA,
[47682] 13/10/1992 ME
Rudd, Mrs S, Student, City University London.
[10034246] 14/10/2014 ME
Ruddock, Ms B A, BA (Hons) MA MCLIP, Content Development Officer
L. & Archive Servs., Mimas, University of Manchester.
[10010589] 07/08/2008 **RV27/03/2014** **CM05/05/2010**
Rudkin, Miss A, BA (Hons), Information & Estates Administrator, HJ
Banks & Co. Ltd, Durham.
[54150] 07/11/1996 ME
Ruehlmann, Ms A, MA MCLIP, Librarian, Institution of Civil Engineers,
London.
[61750] 01/11/2002 **CM13/04/2011**
Rughoo, Mrs S D, BLib MCLIP, Senior Librarian, Municipal Council of
Vacoas-Phoenix, Mauritius.
[32103] 22/01/1980 **CM26/08/1987**
Rule, Mrs R M, BA MCLIP, Retired.
[10716] 08/05/1970 **CM13/11/1974**
Runciman, Miss R J, MCLIP, Arch., Cameron Mackintosh, London.
[28994] 22/02/1978 **CM17/11/1983**
Rundell, Mr K J, MCLIP, Retired.
[20021] 01/01/1969 **CM01/01/1972**
Rush, Mrs C S, BSc DipLib MCLIP, Retired.
[27927] 10/10/1977 **CM05/07/1985**
Rush, Mrs J L, BA (Hons) CertEd MA, Faculty Liaison Librarian,
Templeman Library, Uni of Kent.
[53755] 01/10/1996 ME

Rush, Mr N P, LLB (Hons) MA MCLIP, Assistant Librarian, De Montfort University, Leicester.
[59410]   06/03/2001   **CM29/03/2004**

Rushbrook, Mrs A J, BA (Hons) MA, Acquisitions Manager, House of Commons Library, Lib. Resources Section, London.
[58390]   28/01/2000   **ME**

Rushton, Mr J D, BA DipLib MCLIP, Section Head Libraries & Information Services, West Dunbartonshire Council.
[29810]   05/10/1978   **CM31/12/1981**

Russell, Mr A, BA (Hons), Digital Coordinator, Foreigh & Commonwealth Office, London.
[10019481]   07/07/2011   **AF**

Russell, Mr A D, BA DipLib AMA, Library Manager, Society of Analytical Psychology, London NW3 5BY (Part-time post).
[34441]   06/11/1981   **CM12/12/1991**

Russell, Mrs C, MA DipLib, L. Cataloguer, Warburg Institute, London.
[47503]   09/09/1992   **ME**

Russell, Miss E, Student, Northumbria University.
[10032018]   21/10/2013   **ME**

Russell, Mrs J A, MA DipLib MCLIP, Information and Learning Services Manager, Libraries NI.
[29812]   10/10/1978   **CM11/02/1981**

Russell, Ms L, Student.
[10020019]   25/10/2011   **ME**

Russell, Mr M R, BA (Hons) DipILS MCLIP, School Librarian, Kirkland High School & Comm. College, Methil.
[55887]   16/12/1997   **CM16/05/2001**

Russell, Mrs S, MSc BEd (Mus), Library Adviser, Edinburgh City Libraries.
[10022091]   07/12/2012   **ME**

Russell, Ms S, BA (Hons) DipLib MCLIP, Operations Manager, Book Aid International.
[52658]   16/11/1995   **CM21/08/2009**

Russell, Ms S A, MA BA (Hons), Rare Books Reference Specialist at The British Library.
[10018147]   05/05/1989   **ME**

Russell-Smith, Ms M, BA MA, Frontline Servs. Manager, Gedling Community & Vol. Servs.
[65611]   28/02/2006   **ME**

Russo, Mrs C, ACLIP, Academy Librarian, Oasis Academy.
[10031640]   17/09/2013   **ACL15/07/2014**

Russon, Mr D, BSc FCLIP, Retired.
[44350]   01/10/1990   **FE09/04/1991**

Ruthven, Miss J C, BA (Hons) MA, Assistant Librarian, Hartley Library, University of Southampton.
[33736]   04/02/1981   **ME**

Ruthven, Ms L, MA MCLIP, Special Collections & Music Librarian at Goldsmiths, University of London.
[10006744]   10/12/2007   **CM13/11/2013**

Ruthven, Mr R A, MA DipLIS MCLIP, Director of Library Services, Glasgow Caledonian University.
[44069]   01/05/1990   **CM21/05/1997**

Rutland, Mrs J D, BSc DipLib MCLIP, Library Manager, Public Health & Social Care Library, Kent County Council.
[32885]   17/10/1980   **CM09/12/1982**

Rutledge, Dr H R, BA (Hons) DipLib MCLIP MA PhD, Retired.
[40668]   14/04/1987   **CM18/09/1991**

Rutt, Ms J C, BA (Hons) MCLIP MSc, Knowledge Manager, Yorkshire and Humber Commissioning Support.
[36879]   12/01/1984   **CM22/05/1996**

Rutter, Mrs M R J, BSc, Learning Resource Manager, East Sussex County Council.
[53355]   23/05/1996   **ME**

Ryan, Mrs A M, Part-time Student, UWE, Aberconway Library, Cardiff University.
[10000704]   23/10/2006   **ME**

Ryan, Ms B M, BA (Hons) MSc MCLIP, Systems & Servs. Manager, Library Services, University of South Wales.
[49421]   21/10/1993   **CM21/11/2001**

Ryan, Ms D C, BA MCLIP, unemployed.
[35560]   26/10/1982   **CM22/06/1987**

Ryan, Mr G M, MA (Hons) LLB DipILS MCLIP, Faculty Librarian, Andersonian Library, University of Strathclyde, Glasgow.
[58092]   27/10/1999   **CM15/09/2004**

Ryan, Mrs J, MA (Hons) PgDipILS MCLIP, Assistant Librarian, Andersonian Library, University of Strathclyde.
[61270]   09/05/2002   **CM15/09/2004**

Ryan, Ms J, BA MA, Robert Gordon University.
[10032045]   22/10/2013   **ME**

Ryan, Mrs J H, BA DipLib, L. Manager, Royal Australian College of G. P. s, Melbourne, Australia.
[32213]   08/02/1980   **CM17/02/1982**

Ryan, Ms K A, BA DipLIS MSc, College Librarian, St Andrew's College.
[42065]   21/09/1988   **ME**

Ryan, Mr M A, BA MCLIP, Retired.
[12821]   13/10/1970   **CM01/01/1976**

Ryan, Mrs S E, MCLIP, Medical Secretary, Horton Hospital, Banbury.
[10006532]   01/10/1972   **CM03/10/1975**

Ryder, Miss E, MA, Librarian, Bury Grammar School Girls.
[10006178]   18/09/2007   **ME**

Ryder, Ms J A, MCLIP AGRA Associate Member, Retired/Casual Library Assistant, Hants County Council.
[12872]   06/03/1971   **CM01/01/1975**

Ryder, Mrs J C, BA MCLIP, L. & Information Sector Consultant, Julie Ryder Associates, Witley.
[12830]   01/10/1965   **CM01/01/1969**

S

Sabovic, Ms Z, BA, Head of College Management, The Wellcome Library, London.
[46640]   02/12/1991   **ME**

Sach, Mrs V W, MA MCLIP, Life Member.
[12836]   24/01/1954   **CM01/01/1959**

Sacre, Mr J F, MCLIP, Hon. Archivist & Librarian, Supreme Council 33, London.
[12842]   19/03/1968   **CM06/07/1972**

Sadeghi, Mrs S, MA ACLIP, Senior Library Assistant, University of Nottingham.
[62454]   03/07/2003   **ACL09/11/2011**

Sadler, Mr E, BA (Hons) MSc, Student.
[10020604]   12/03/2012   **ME**

Sadler, Ms R W, BA (Hons), Library Information Services Co-ordinator and Digital Library Management student, University of Sheffield.
[10029945]   25/02/2014   **ME**

Sahari Moghaddam, Mrs S, BSc, Library Customer Service Officer, London Borough of Barnet.
[10022261]   29/01/2013   **ME**

Saich, Mrs B P, BA MCLIP, Life Member.
[12861]   01/01/1954   **CM01/01/1958**

Saich, Mr M J, FCLIP, Life Member.
[12862]   18/03/1950   **FE01/01/1964**

Sainsbury, Mr I M, BA MCLIP, Reading.
[12868]   04/12/1967   **CM01/01/1970**

Sainsbury, Mr M A, BA MA MLIS, Borrower Services Librarian, Saskatchewan Polytechnic.
[10022447]   05/03/2013   **ME**
Sainsbury, Mrs W V, BLib MCLIP, Retired.
[20065]   18/01/1973   **CM21/04/1980**
Saint-Smith, Mrs L, BA MA,
[10029960]   17/12/2013   **ME**
Saiyeed, Mrs G, BSc (Hons) MA, Learning Centre Co-ordinator, Harrow College.
[10002725]   01/05/2007   **ME**
Saks, Mrs H, BA PgDip, School Librarian, Strathallan School.
[10021432]   10/08/2012   **ME**
Saksida, Mr M, HonFCLIP, Hon. Fellow.
[60751]   20/03/1986   **HFE01/03/1986**
Saletes, Mrs D L, BA DipLib MCLIP, Customer Serv. Librarian, Watford Central Library, Hertfordshire County Council.
[32471]   01/04/1980   **CM11/01/1985**
Salha, Dr S,
[10032613]   20/12/2013   **ME**
Salinie, Mrs F, MBE HonFLA, Assistant Director – France, Global Business Manager, British Library Serv., Paris.
[41993]   01/07/1988   **HFE01/01/1993**
Salisbury, Ms J P, BLib (Hons) MCLIP, Library Locality Manager, Essex County Council.
[31095]   14/08/1979   **CM21/07/1989**
Salisbury, Mrs R M, DipLib MCLIP, Life Member.
[29876]   16/10/1978   **CM14/12/1981**
Salisbury, Mr S, Learn Centre Assistant, Grace Academy Coventry.
[10033935]   13/05/2014   **AF**
Salkeld, Mrs D A, BA (Hons)DipLib MCLIP, Retired. Formerly North Yorkshire Schools Library Service, then Independent Consultant.
[28765]   28/09/1957   **CM01/05/1978**
Salmoiraghi, Mrs M P, BA, Librarian.
[10033557]   25/03/2014   **ME**
Salmon, Mrs B, BA DipLib MCLIP, Head of L. & Information Serv., C. I. P. D., London.
[31151]   30/08/1979   **CM30/08/1981**
Salt, Mr D P, BSc FCLIP, Retired.
[12885]   03/05/1967   **FE25/01/1995**
Salt, Mrs F J, BA (Hons) MCLIP, Experienced Information Professional.
[55509]   16/10/1997   **CM15/11/2000**
Salter, Mrs D J, BA (Hons) MA, Essex Library Service.
[54986]   03/06/1997   **ME**
Salter, Ms E, BA DipLib MLib FCLIP, Lib. Manager, University of Westminster.
[35225]   07/10/1982   **FE29/03/2006**
Salter, Mrs N E, BSc PGCE DipILM MCLIP, B. Sc., P. G. C. E., P. G. Dip. ILM., MCILIP.
[53903]   09/10/1996   **CM16/07/2003**
Sambrook, Miss C J, BA (Hons) MA MA MCLIP, Special Collections Librarian, Kings College London.
[47042]   06/04/1992   **CM14/09/1994**
Samm, Mr A M, MEng, Search Manager, EIP, London.
[10021085]   29/05/2012   **ME**
Samman, Miss M J, BA MCLIP, Retired.
[12898]   10/10/1966   **CM01/01/1969**
Sampson, Mr A A, NDD ATD ACP FRSA MCLIP, Life Member.
[12899]   02/01/1965   **CM01/01/1968**
Sampson, Ms J, BA MCLIP MInstLM, Knowledge, Library & Information Services Manager, Doncaster & Bassetlaw Hospitals NHS Foundation Trust.
[50354]   04/07/1994   **CM18/03/1998**
Samson, Mrs J M, BA MCLIP, Lib. Assistant, Fife Council.
[31642]   22/10/1979   **CM07/09/1984**

Samson-Bunce, Mrs S, ACLIP BLit (Hons), Stock & Reader Development Librarian, St Albans Library.
[10016863]   27/05/2010   **ACL25/01/2011**
Sanati Nia, Mrs A, MLIS,
[10009324]   15/05/2008   **ME**
Sanchez, Miss M, Unwaged.
[10035298]   07/10/2014   **ME**
Sanchez-Gonzalez, Mrs S, BA MA, School librarian & Reader development consultant.
[10010194]   10/07/2008   **AF**
Sandell, Ms J E, MA DipLib MCLIP, Senior Librarian: Young People's Services, Moray Council.
[43338]   23/10/1989   **CM19/08/1992**
Sander, Ms L V, MCLIP, Unwaged.
[50968]   03/11/1994   **CM03/11/1994**
Sanders, Mr K J, BA (Hons) MSc, Information Librarian (E-Resources), University of Bath.
[10015565]   15/12/2009   **ME**
Sanderson, Mrs J, BA DipLib MCLIP, Admin. Assistant, Lichfield Library, Staffs County Council.
[34500]   18/11/1981   **CM18/06/1985**
Sanderson, Miss J B, BA MCLIP,
[29282]   25/04/1978   **CM31/07/1980**
Sanderson, Miss S, BSc (Hons), Student, Northumbria University.
[10010110]   03/07/2008   **ME**
Sandford, Mr A M, MCLIP, Catg., Bury Public Library, Lancashire.
[23869]   10/02/1975   **CM30/07/1980**
Sandhu, Mrs G K, BSc MSc MBA MCLIP, Associate Director Lib. & Learning Services, University of East London.
[47994]   30/10/1992   **CM22/11/1995**
Sandison, Mr P E C, MA DipLib MCLIP, Manager L. Serv. & Information Systems, Scottish Borders Campus, Heriot-Watt University, Galashiels.
[35317]   01/10/1982   **CM20/11/1986**
Sandison, Mrs S M I, MA MCLIP, Sch. Lib. (Job Share), Galashiels Academy, Selkirkshire.
[35756]   10/01/1983   **CM21/08/1986**
Sandles, Mr P M, BSc MA, Assistant Librarian, The Supreme Court of the United Kingdom.
[65049]   20/10/2005   **ME**
Sands, Mrs A, BA (Hons), Stock Services Librarian, Bracknell Library.
[54847]   17/04/1997   **ME**
Sands, Mrs P, BA (Hons), Academic Liaison Librarian, University of Southampton.
[47924]   26/10/1992   **ME**
Sandys, Mrs J, HonFLA, Life Member.
[13272]   31/01/1952   **HFE01/01/1996**
Sangha, Mrs H, BA (Hons) DipLIS MCLIP, Assistant Reference Librarian, Birmingham Library Serv., Sutton Coldfield Library.
[47650]   09/10/1992   **CM19/03/1997**
Sansby, Miss E J, BA (Hons) MA MCLIP, Head of Library Services, Bishop Grosseteste University.
[50268]   26/05/1994   **CM27/11/1996**
Sansom, Miss A J C, BA FCLIP, Retired.
[12935]   07/03/1950   **FE01/01/1966**
Sansom, Mrs S E, BA MCLIP, Librarian, Edgbaston High School, Birmingham.
[39508]   30/01/1986   **RV14/10/2011**   **CM10/05/1988**
Sant, Mr D, BA DipLib MCLIP,
[30248]   07/12/1978   **CM06/01/1982**
Santer, Mrs M A, MCLIP, Part-time Library Assistant, Devon County Council.
[24200]   23/04/1975   **CM06/12/1977**

Sardena, Miss S, Medical Librarian, Gibralter H. A., St Bernards
Hospital.
[10001127]   20/10/1995   **ME**
Sarfo-Adu Amankwah, Mr K, MA,
[10007957]   20/03/2008   **ME**
Sarfraz, Mr M, Student.
[64043]   06/12/2004   **ME**
Sargeant, Mrs R, BLib DMS MCLIP, Author and Learning Resource
Centre Manager.
[38559]   01/07/1985   **CM04/10/1988**
Sargent, Mrs C D, MA MCLIP, Head of Archives, Radley College.
[40507]   26/02/1987   **CM18/11/1993**
Sari, Mr B, Library Asistant, London School of Commerce.
[10014368]   20/07/2009   **AF**
Saribi, Mrs C, MA, Librarian, Kirkby-in-Ashfield Library, Nottinghamshire
County Council.
[10001299]   03/09/2004   **ME**
Sarif, Mrs E B, Librarian, Sydney.
[31123]   14/09/1979   **ME**
Sarkar, Ms L, BLISc, Student.
[10031913]   14/10/2013   **ME**
Sarony, Miss A R, BA (Hons), Library Assistant, Faculty of Architecture
and History of Art, University of Cambridge.
[10021946]   05/11/2012   **AF**
Sarre, Ms N, MInstF MCLIP,
[63858]   04/10/2004   **CM09/07/2008**
Sarris, Ms A, Business Development, Frank Hirth.
[10032027]   22/10/2013   **ME**
Sartin, Mrs C I, MCLIP, Hon. Librarian, Kennedy Grant Library, Halsway
Manor, National Centre for the Folk Arts, near Crocombe, Somerset.
TA4 4BD.
[6194]   01/01/1964   **CM01/01/1967**
Sarvilahti, Miss M, BA (Hons) MA, Librarian, University of Art & Design,
Helsinki, Finland.
[57664]   01/07/1999   **ME**
Satchwell, Mrs C E, BA MCLIP, L. Manager, University of Westminster.
[30548]   28/01/1979   **CM14/06/1982**
Satterley, Ms R, MLIS, Deputy Librarian, Honourable Society of the
Middle Temple. Chair, Library & Information History Group.
[65510]   24/09/2013   **ME**
Satterthwaite, Mrs I C, BA (Hons) MA MCLIP, Clinical Librarian, Health
Library, Rotherham NHS Trust, Rotherham Hospital.
[55191]   07/08/1997   **CM10/07/2002**
Sauer, Mr R, APMI MCLIP, Retired.
[12958]   05/12/1967   **CM01/01/1971**
Saunders, Mr D G, BA MA (Oxon), Student.
[10018093]   15/11/2010   **ME**
Saunders, Mr G, MSc MCLIP, Gerald Saunders.
[10016670]   23/04/2010   **CM24/03/1988**
Saunders, Mrs H C, MA DipLib MCLIP, Assistant Librarian, Cardiff
University.
[36405]   05/10/1983   **CM15/02/1989**
Saunders, Mr J C, BA MBA MCLIP, Head of Serv., Educ. L. Serv.,
Berkshire.
[21975]   17/01/1974   **CM01/07/1976**
Saunders, Mr S C, MA, L. Customer Serv. Manager, Barnet L.
[10007692]   21/02/2008   **ME**
Sauron, Dr V, MA (Hons) PhD DipTrans, Senior Service Development
Assistant, Thirsk Library.
[10035283]   03/10/2014   **ME**
Sauvary, Miss L K, BA (Hons) MCLIP, Children's Serv. Librarian,
Rustington Library, Littlehampton.
[10018302]   26/10/1989   **CM20/09/1995**

Savage, Mrs C L, BA (Hons) MA DipILM MCLIP, Head of Regional
Fundraising, Macmillan Cancer Support.
[54220]   05/11/1996   **CM07/09/2005**
Savage, Miss E M, MLS MCLIP, Life Member.
[12978]   24/08/1957   **CM01/01/1964**
Savage, Ms J M, BA (Hons) PG (Dipl), Library Services Co-ordinator,
University of Salford.
[51787]   01/07/1995   **ME**
Savidge, Ms J C, MA MCLIP, Director of L. & Learning Support Serv.,
Surrey University.
[34156]   06/10/1981   **CM18/07/1985**
Savill, Miss R A, ACLIP, Community Librarian, Chichester Library,
Chichester.
[10012784]   03/03/2009   **ACL13/11/2013**
Saville, Miss A J, MA MCLIP, Librarian, The Queens College, Oxford.
[38907]   18/10/1985   **CM15/11/1988**
Savin, Mr J A, MA (Oxon) DipLib, Tax Know How Professional,
Slaughter & May, London.
[40950]   01/10/1987   **ME**
Sawers, Mrs C G L, MSc FCLIP, Retired.
[12986]   07/01/1955   **FE26/05/1993**
Sawers, Mr C J, BA (Hons) DPS MInstLM MCLIP, Team Leader:
Learning Resources, Vision West Nottinghamshire College.
[53551]   16/07/1996   **RV30/04/2014 CM04/10/2006**
Sawhney, Mr S C, MA MCLIP, Life Member.
[12987]   14/02/1968   **CM01/01/1972**
Sawyer, Mrs I A, MA (Hons) MSc MCLIP, Unwaged.
[61014]   01/02/2002   **CM29/08/2007**
Sawyer, Mrs V B, BLS MCLIP, Principal Librarian, Education Library
Service, Nottinghamshire County Council.
[33464]   01/01/1981   **CM06/05/1986**
Saxby, Ms D, BSocSc (Hons) PgDip, Librarian and Digital Literacy
Coordinator, Kingham Hill School, Oxfordshire.
[50786]   18/10/1994   **CM07/09/2005**
Saxby, Miss H J, BLS MCLIP, Self-employed.
[30250]   05/12/1978   **CM05/04/1983**
Saxby, Mrs J M, BA MA MCLIP, e Library. Assistant, National Stem
Centre.
[65999]   11/08/2006   **CM05/05/2010**
Sayed, Mrs S, FCLIP, Life Member.
[12993]   17/03/1950   **FE01/01/1958**
Sayer, Mr A M, BA (Hons), Serials Librarian, University of Central
England, Birmingham.
[52423]   30/10/1995   **ME**
Sayers, Ms K A, BA (Hons) MA MSc MCLIP, Assistant Archivist,
University of Leeds.
[54138]   01/11/1996   **CM21/11/2001**
Sayers, Mrs S J, BSc MCLIP, Unwaged.
[44441]   08/10/1990   **CM26/05/1993**
Scales, Mr R P, MA DipLib MCLIP, Academic Liaison Librarian, Bucks.
Chilterns University College, Chalfont St Giles.
[32725]   23/07/1980   **CM16/09/1985**
Scallon, Miss R, BA, Student, University of the West of England, Bristol.
[10015764]   22/01/2010   **ME**
Scally, Mr J, BA (Hons) PhD (Cantab) Dip ILS, National Librarian &
Chief Executive, National Library of Scotland.
[10009843]   25/06/2008   **ME**
Scalpello, Ms M, MA MA MCLIP, Librarian, City of Glasgow College,
Riverside Campus.
[38726]   01/10/1985   **CM21/12/1988**
Scanlon, Mrs A J, BA (Hons) MCLIP, Deputy Head of Library &
Learning Resources., Swansea Metropolitan University.
[51824]   07/07/1995   **CM17/03/1999**

Scanlon, Mr M J, BA (Hons) MCLIP, Intelligence Hub Consultant, Defra, London.
[34052]   13/08/1981   **CM13/08/1985**

Scanlon, Ms R, MSc, Student, University of Strathclyde.
[10020290]   09/01/2012   **ME**

Scantlebury, Mrs N L, Library Services Manager, The Open University.
[10012997]   14/05/2013   **ME**

Scarborough, Mrs D M, BA MCLIP MBA, District Manager, Chorley and South Ribble, Lancs.
[38125]   12/01/1985   **CM15/08/1989**

Scarce, Mrs M, BScEcon (Hons) MCLIP, Clinical Librarian.
[63915]   26/10/2004   **CM11/04/2013**

Scarlett, Mrs C A E, BA FCLIP, Life Member.
[10828]   17/01/1960   **FE01/01/1964**

Scarman, Dr M, PhD, PhD Student, UCL, London.
[10021686]   27/09/2012   **ME**

Scarpa, Mrs G J M, BA MLS MCLIP, Housewife.
[25048]   10/11/1975   **CM12/01/1979**

Scarrott, Mr M, BA DipLib MCLIP ILTM, Assistant Director – L. Serv., St Mary's College, Twickenham.
[41238]   13/10/1987   **CM12/12/1991**

Schachter, Ms D, MBA, Director, Learning Res., Douglas College, New Westminster, British Columbia, Canada.
[10018266]   10/12/2010   **ME**

Schaeper, Ms S D E, Dipl Libr MLS, Hebraica bibliographer, Cataloguer (Antiquarian, Special Collections, Retrospective, Foreign Language).
[10015984]   03/02/2010   **ME**

Schaffnit Woodland, Mrs L K, BA MA, Casual Library Assistant, Aberystwyth University.
[10021191]   21/06/2012   **AF**

Scharlau, Mrs F, MA MCLIP, Local Studies Lib. /Arch., Angus Council-Cultural Serv., Angus Arch.
[37681]   15/10/1984   **CM15/11/1988**

Scherr, Miss J M S, BA MCLIP, Retired.
[13008]   25/09/1968   **CM01/01/1971**

Schlackman, Mrs E, BA MSc MCLIP AFHEA,
[10006402]   17/10/2007   **CM07/09/2011**

Schlenther, Mrs E C, BA DipLib MCLIP, Retired.
[35852]   01/02/1983   **CM05/04/1988**

Schlesinger, Mr J T, BA (Hons) DipLIS MCLIP, Senior Library Assistant, Birmingham City University.
[44815]   03/12/1990   **CM27/11/1996**

Schneider, Miss C, Dipl. -Bibl. (FH) MCLIP AFHEA, Language Zone Manager, University of Leeds.
[66123]   01/10/2006   **RV**18/12/2013   **CM11/04/2013**

Schofield, Mrs D, Information & Online Team Leader Cornwall Council.
[10013164]   27/03/2009   **AF**

Schofield, Mrs D T, BA (Hons) PgDipLIS MCLIP, Academy Library Manager, University Hospital of South Manchester NHS Foundation Trust, Manchester.
[41074]   05/10/1987   **CM17/09/2003**

Schopflin, Dr K, MA (Hons) MA MCLIP PhD, Knowledge Manager.
[56760]   09/10/1998   **RV**15/07/2014   **CM18/09/2002**

Schots, Mrs S, Senior L. &Information Manager, Herbert Smith Freehills LLP, London.
[10001501]   01/07/1995   **ME**

Schroeder, Miss A, MA, Librarian, Federal Maritime and Hydrographic Agency, Rostock, Germany.
[64390]   14/03/2005   **ME**

Schulkins, Mr J A, BA MA MCLIP, Systems Librarian University of Liverpool.
[63126]   11/02/2004   **CM19/11/2008**

Schultz, Mr C H N, MLIS MA FHEA,
[10032818]   15/01/2014   **ME**

Schulz, Mrs N G, BA GradDipLibSci, Systems Analyst, University Oxford.
[62037]   28/01/2003   **ME**

Schwartz, Ms S, Student, San Jose State University.
[10035059]   08/09/2014   **ME**

Schwenk, Ms K, BSc,
[10013912]   15/06/2009   **ME**

Sciberras, Dr L, PhD MA AIL FCLIP, Retired.
[17701]   21/09/1967   **FE23/07/1997**

Scobie, Mr C J, BA MA, Student, City University London.
[10030069]   24/10/2014   **ME**

Scolari, Mr A, PhD, Library System Director – Università di Genova – Italy.
[45938]   26/07/1991   **ME**

Scoones, Miss J, BA DipLib MCLIP, Director of Information & KM., Trowers & Hamlins, London.
[36451]   06/10/1983   **CM08/08/1986**

Scothern, Miss C, BA (Hons) MA, Head of Library Services, Trent College.
[56899]   02/11/1998   **ME**

Scotland, Mrs C J, MLib MCLIP, Librarian, Featherstone High School, Middx.
[38531]   31/05/1985   **CM10/05/1988**

Scott, Mrs B, BLib MCLIP, Librarian, Cheshire County Council, Chester Library.
[29529]   22/09/1978   **CM15/03/1984**

Scott, Mrs C, BA MCLIP, Librarian, Princethorpe College, Rugby, Warwickshire.
[38407]   21/04/1985   **CM14/03/1990**

Scott, Mrs C, BA MSc, Senior Library Assistant, Vale of Glamorgan Council.
[61018]   04/09/2013   **ME**

Scott, Mrs C L, BA (Hons) MA MCLIP FHEA, Faculty Lib. for the Arts & Humanities, University of Sheffield.
[46582]   20/11/1991   **CM18/11/1998**

Scott, Mrs C S, BA MCLIP, Freelance Indexer.
[22483]   12/06/1974   **CM20/08/1976**

Scott, Mr D, Head of Learning Centres and Support, Kirklees college, Huddersfield.
[10020079]   05/11/2013   **ME**

Scott, Mrs D, MA, Librarian, Mayfield School.
[10012136]   16/07/2014   **ME**

Scott, Mrs D A, BA (Comb Hons), Clerical Assistant & MSc Student, Aberdeenshire Council/Robert Gordon University.
[10031761]   01/10/2013   **ME**

Scott, Mr E, MA (Hons) MCLIP, Community Librarian, Aberdeen City Council.
[10012891]   19/03/2009   **CM04/10/2013**

Scott, Mrs E, School Librarian, Queen's Gate School, London.
[10006393]   23/10/2007   **ME**

Scott, Miss E L, BA MCLIP, Stock and Reader Development Librarian, Heartfordshire Libraries.
[63738]   03/09/2004   **CM10/03/2011**

Scott, Miss E S, BA FCLIP, Learning Resources Centre Coordinator, Menzieshill High School, Dundee.
[13047]   04/01/1972   **FE15/10/2002**

Scott, Miss F A, MCLIP, Life Member.
[13048]   12/02/1951   **CM16/02/1979**

Scott, Mrs F J, BA MCLIP, Senior L. & Information Officer, Central Library, Dundee.
[27916]   09/10/1977   **CM18/12/1981**

Scott, Ms H V, BA (Hons) MSc MCLIP, Film Studies Subject Con., Oxford University Library Serv.
[51415]   10/02/1995   **CM22/07/1998**

Scott, Mrs J, BA MA MCLIP, Sr. Librarian, Chesterfield Library, Derbyshire County Council.
[46786] 23/01/1992 **CM25/09/1996**

Scott, Mrs J, Support Assistant, FDI Solutions, Sheffield.
[44273] 07/08/1990 **ME**

Scott, Mrs J, MA (Hons) MSc MCLIP,
[61989] 06/01/2003 **CM01/02/2006**

Scott, Miss J A, BA (Hons) DipLib MCLIP, Learning Res. Officer, Lurgan & Banbridge Campuses, Southern Region College & Portadown Campus.
[33145] 02/10/1980 **CM07/02/1986**

Scott, Mrs K M, MCLIP, Legal L. Consultant, Self-Employed, Kingston, Surrey.
[13882] 18/02/1972 **CM26/09/1975**

Scott, Miss L B, BA (Hons), Arch., University of Gloucestershire, Cheltenham.
[41569] 21/01/1988 **ME**

Scott, Ms N R, BA MA PgDip Ed MCLIP, CM for Learning Centre/Resource Based Learning.
[31696] 02/11/1979 **CM08/02/1983**

Scott, Miss O D, FCLIP, Life Member.
[13066] 11/10/1944 **FE01/01/1961**

Scott, Mr P J, BLS (Hons) MCLIP, Community, Learning, & Information Librarian, Chesterfield L.
[36795] 01/01/1984 **CM20/09/2000**

Scott, Miss P K, BA (Hons) MCLIP, Chief Librarian and Head of Library & Information Services, Ministry of Justice.
[33558] 19/01/1981 **CM09/10/1986**

Scott, Mrs R, MSc MCLIP, Not Known.
[10031888] 15/11/1995 **CM15/03/2000**

Scott, Mrs R, BA, Student, UCL.
[10033453] 05/09/2014 **ME**

Scott, Miss R E, MA (Hon), Student, Robert Gordon University.
[10032304] 15/11/2013 **ME**

Scott, Miss R J, Electronic Acquisitions Co-ordinator Reading University Library.
[10016096] 16/02/2010 **ME**

Scott, Ms S, MSc, L. Assistant, Andersonian Library, Strathclyde.
[10010887] 05/09/2008 **ME**

Scott, Dr V, BSc PhD, Assistant Librarian, The King's School, Chester.
[10015082] 12/10/2009 **ME**

Scott, Mrs V P, ACLIP, Information Co-ordinator, Aston University, Birmingham.
[65028] 13/10/2005 **ACL19/10/2006**

Scott Cree, Mr J A, MA FCLIP, Retired.
[35101] 03/09/1982 **FE23/09/1998**

Scott-Denness, Miss H, BSc (Hons) MCLIP, Head of Information Centre., Knight Frank LLP, London.
[48872] 07/07/1993 **CM18/11/1998**

Scotting, Mrs R, BLib MCLIP, Lib. :Child & Young Peoples Serv., North Lincs. Council, Riddings L.
[34694] 30/01/1982 **CM16/02/1988**

Scott-Picton, Ms L S, BA (Hons) MLib MCLIP, Librarian, Downe House School, Thatcham, Berks.
[44404] 05/10/1990 **CM24/05/1995**

Scoulding, Miss S J, BA (Hons) PgDip ILS, Assistant Librarian, University of Wales Trinity Saint David.
[64255] 22/02/2005 **ME**

Scown, Mr J M, BA MCLIP, LibrariesWest Development Officer.
[37566] 02/10/1984 **CM16/10/1991**

Scragg, Mr A D R, MPhil LLB DipHE MCLIP, Liaison Librarian, Collection Development, Birmingham City University.
[30255] 06/12/1978 **CM06/07/1981**

Scrimshaw, Mr N, BA MSc, Assistant Librarian, University of Buckingham.
[10012417] 23/03/2010 **ME**

Scrivener, Miss H L, BA MA, Library Manager, Suffolk County Council.
[10000805] 08/11/2006 **ME**

Scrogham, Mr M A, BA (Hons) MA MCLIP, Library Specialist: Information and Digital.
[61687] 21/10/2002 **CM24/10/2008**

Scull, Mrs N, BSc (Hons) PgCert, Head of Learning Resources and Libraries, ifs University College.
[53431] 19/06/1996 **ME**

Scully, Mr E R, BA MA MCLIP, Classifier, Medicines and Healthcare Products Regulatory Agency, London.
[35628] 09/11/1982 **CM10/05/1988**

Scutchings, Ms L, BA (Hons) MSc MCLIP, Assistant Site Manager, Edward Boyle Library, University of Leeds.
[53959] 16/10/1996 **CM01/02/2006**

Scutt, Mrs C E, BA MCLIP, Information Consultant/Freelance Librarian, Self-employed, Loughborough, Leics.
[25185] 23/11/1975 **CM19/10/1979**

Scutt, Ms C S, MA MSc MCLIP, Bodleian Education Librarian, University of Oxford.
[58314] 10/01/2000 **CM19/11/2008**

Scutt, Ms E M, BA DipLib CertEd CMS MCLIP, Unwaged.
[25208] 05/01/1976 **CM05/01/1978**

Seabourne, Miss J, BA (Hons) DipLIS MCLIP, Guild Admin. & Librarian, Dyslexia Action, Egham, Surrey.
[43240] 12/10/1989 **CM15/03/2000**

Seale, Miss L J,
[61458] 02/08/2002 **ME**

Sealey, Miss M M T, MCLIP, Life Member.
[13087] 13/01/1947 **CM01/01/1953**

Seals, Ms E, BA, Student.
[10020835] 18/04/2012 **ME**

Sealy, Miss A M, MCLIP, Library Assistant, London Borough of Greenwich.
[20127] 14/02/1973 **CM01/08/1976**

Sealy, Mr C P, BSc, Library Assistant, The Kennel Club, London.
[10010424] 24/07/2008 **AF**

Seaman, Mr G, MSc, Library Systems Officer, Royal Holloway, University of London.
[10022148] 08/01/2013 **ME**

Seaman, Miss J M, BA MCLIP, Retired.
[13090] 03/01/1970 **CM12/03/1973**

Seamark, Mrs S J, BA (Hons) MA MCLIP, Outreach and Partnership Manager, Medway Council, Strood L.
[55489] 15/10/1997 **CM29/03/2004**

Searle, Mrs C, MA, Senior Indexer, Indexing & Data Management Section, House of Commons Library, London.
[62213] 17/03/2003 **ME**

Searle, Mr M, MA MCLIP, Head of Collection Serv., Radcliffe Sci. Library, Oxford.
[28902] 31/01/1978 **CM31/12/1989**

Searson, Mrs K P, BLib MCLIP, Unemployed.
[27977] 07/10/1977 **CM10/11/1981**

Sebire, Mr L, PgDip MCLIP, Subject Support Librarian, UWE, Bristol.
[10001557] 07/02/2007 **CM27/01/2010**

Secker, Dr J L, BA (Hons) PhD, Copyright and Digital Literacy Advisor., London School of Economics.
[54369] 25/11/1996 **ME**

Seddon, Ms J A, BA MCLIP DipLib, Tech. Author, OCLC(UK) Sheffield.
[37101] 21/02/1984 **CM18/01/1989**

Seddon, Mrs S L, BA (Hons) DipLib CMS, Librarian, The Piggott School.
[10003009]   28/11/1988   **ME**

Seeley, Ms M A, BA MA MCLIP, Subject. Librarian, SOAS (University of London).
[63865]   11/10/2004   **CM27/08/2014**

Seemann, Miss I, BA (Hons), Library Assistant, Stevenage Central Library.
[10032032]   22/10/2013   **ME**

Segal, Mr K, BA, Sr. Systems Officer, Middlesex University.
[38072]   17/01/1985   **ME**

Segall, Mr P H, MSc, Information Assistant, Kingston University.
[10006395]   23/10/2007   **ME**

Selby, Miss C L, BA MA, Information Specialist.
[10021921]   01/11/2012   **ME**

Self, Mrs R A, BA (Hons) ACLIP, Cultural Serv. Adv., Kirton Library, Kirton.
[10018894]   25/03/2011   **ACL04/10/2013**

Sellar, Mrs L D, BA DipLib MCLIP, Subject Librarian, Oxford Brookes University.
[22851]   03/10/1974   **CM12/01/1977**

Sellens, Mr R, BA (Hons) DUNELM, Graduate Trainee, The Library, St John's College.
[10034739]   12/08/2014   **ME**

Sellers, Rev J M, BA MCLIP, Retired Methodist Minister.
[13112]   24/08/1968   **CM05/02/1973**

Sellwood, Miss R, BA MA PGCHE FHEA, Academic Liaison Librarian.
[10008735]   10/12/2008   **ME**

Selwyn, Mrs P M, BA MCLIP, Retired.
[1332]   24/07/1961   **CM01/01/1964**

Semple, Miss A M, Learning Resource Assistant, Coleg Powys.
[10022129]   08/01/2013   **ME**

Semple, Miss A M C, BA, Student, Coleg Llandrillo.
[10032534]   12/12/2013   **ME**

Semple, Mrs G, Retired.
[22894]   01/10/1974   **ME**

Semple, Mrs H, BLib MCLIP, Head of L. and Information Serv., Law Society of Northern Ireland, Belfast.
[43638]   13/11/1989   **CM19/08/1992**

Semugabi, Mr J A, BA (Hons) PgDip MSc, Chief Librarian, Law Development Centre.
[10021147]   13/06/2012   **ME**

Sen, Dr B A, BA (Hons) MA MCLIP PhD, Senior Lecturer, Information School, University of Sheffield.
[46578]   19/11/1991   **CM21/05/1997**

Sen Gupta, Miss B D, MA (Hons) PgDip, Head of Library & Information Services, GSM London.
[10016200]   23/02/2010   **ME**

Senadhira, Dr M A P, FCLIP PhD, Life Member.
[17714]   04/10/1963   **FE01/01/1974**

Senior, Mr C M, BA DipLib MCLIP FHEA, Project Manager, Brotherton Library, University of Leeds.
[41974]   01/07/1988   **CM16/12/1992**

Senior, Mrs K W, BA MCLIP MLib, Retired, Ex Head of Library, University of Bolton.
[13129]   03/10/1968   **CM02/07/1972**

Sentinella, Ms E, Student, Aberystwyth University.
[10031585]   04/09/2013   **ME**

Seok Kwan, Ms Y, MLib BA, Head, Library, NIE, Singapore.
[46385]   01/11/1991   **ME**

Sephton, Mr R S, BA FCLIP LTCL CertEd, Life Member.
[13133]   03/04/1945   **FE01/01/1965**

Seraphina, Mrs C, ACLIP, L. Advisor, Perth College.
[10016039]   10/02/2010   **ACL25/01/2011**

Serbutt, Mr C L, BA (Hons), Student.
[10019730]   31/08/2011   **ME**

Sergeant, Mrs C A, BA MCLIP, School Librarian, Falkirk Council, Falkirk.
[28571]   10/01/1978   **CM10/08/1982**

Serjeant, Mr F P, BA DipLib, Tri-Borough Reference and Information Services.
[33880]   05/04/1981   **ME**

Sermon, Mrs K M, BA MSc MCLIP, Information Governance Manager.
[42980]   15/05/1989   **CM21/07/1993**

Serrano, Mr D G, Information Specialist, British Standards Institution.
[10012357]   03/02/2009   **ME**

Service, Mr D J, MA (Hons) DipLIS MCLIP, Evidence Manager, Scottish Intercollegiate Guidelines Network, Healthcare Improvement Scotland.
[49190]   12/10/1993   **CM19/03/1997**

Sevier, Miss A H, BA MCLIP, Librarian, RAFC Cranwell, Lincs.
[43894]   12/02/1990   **CM07/09/2005**

Seward, Miss H, BA, Student, City University.
[10032322]   18/11/2013   **ME**

Sewell, Mrs A M, MA FCLIP, Retired.
[7070]   25/09/1953   **FE01/01/1966**

Sewell, Miss C E, BA MSc MCLIP,
[10017088]   22/06/2010   **CM13/05/2014**

Sewerniak, Ms A T, BSc (Hons) DipLIS MCLIP, Unwaged.
[43321]   19/10/1989   **CM19/01/2000**

Sexton, Ms C T, BA (Hons) DipLib, Collections Development Librarian, Royal College of Physicians, London.
[10015682]   13/01/2010   **ME**

Sexton, Ms T J, PgDipLib, Librarian, Geldards LLP, Nottingham. Derby.
[44308]   23/08/1990   **ME**

Seymour, Mr A J, BA (Hons) MA MCLIP, L. &Information Officer, The National Autistic Society, London.
[59693]   08/08/2001   **CM09/11/2005**

Shackleton, Miss K E, BA MCLIP,
[35830]   28/01/1983   **CM24/04/1991**

Shackleton, Mrs S M, MCLIP, Life Member.
[13158]   05/09/1951   **CM01/01/1957**

Shafe, Mr M, BSc (Econ) MCLIP, Life Member.
[13160]   02/06/1959   **CM01/01/1963**

Shah, Ms A T, MA (Hons) DipLIS MCLIP, Senior L & Information Officer, Dundee City C., Cent. L.
[55791]   24/11/1997   **CM12/03/2003**

Shah, Mr G J, Student.
[10030120]   17/04/2014   **ME**

Shah, Mrs L, BA MA,
[10012476]   10/02/2009   **AF**

Shah, Mrs P, HND CELTA ACLIP, Library Resources Officer, East Barnet School, London.
[10010191]   09/07/2008   **ACL23/09/2009**

Shah, Mrs P, Research Services Librarian, Science Museum, London.
[10012120]   13/01/2010   **ME**

Shah, Mr T A, MLIS, Student, University of Kashmir.
[10032413]   03/12/2013   **ME**

Shahid, Mrs S H, Mphil Phd, Student, University of Sheffield.
[10032518]   11/12/2013   **ME**

Shaikh, Mrs L M, BA (Hons), Librarian, Jones Day, London.
[37562]   01/10/1984   **ME**

Shakeshaft, Miss G C, BA MA, Lower College Librarian, The Cheltenham Ladies College, Glos.
[50647]   06/10/1994   **ME**

Shakespeare, Mr A D, BSc MCLIP, Academic Liaison, University of Westminster.
[55886]   09/12/1997   **CM01/02/2006**

Shakespeare, Ms K, BA (Hons) MA MCLIP, Assistant Librarian (Loans), Library, University of Portsmouth.
[48178]   11/11/1992   CM20/03/1996
Shallcross, Mrs E, BSc (Hons) MSc ILS, Information Consultant, University of Aberdeen.
[53114]   13/03/1996   ME
Shamsuddin, Ms D, BA MSc MA MCLIP, Senior Librarian, National L. Board, Singapore.
[64057]   13/12/2004   CM13/12/2004
Shanks, Mr J C, Student, Liverpool John Moores University.
[10008812]   21/04/2008   ME
Shannon, Mrs J, Prison Lib. & Information Co-ordinator, Albany Library, HMP Isle of Wight.
[10012977]   20/03/2009   AF
Shaper, Mrs S A, DipLib MA (Ed) FCLIP HonFCLIP, Directorof Library Resources, The Broxbourne School, Herts.
[23706]   01/01/1975   HFE30/09/2012
Share, Mrs L, Librarian, Kellett School, Hong Kong.
[10013708]   22/05/2009   ME
Sharkey, Miss G, PgDip, Graduate Information Assistant, Linklaters.
[10030130]   07/01/2014   ME
Sharman, Ms A J, BSc MSc FHEA MCLIP PGCE, Academic Librarian for the Business School and School of Computing and Engineering, University of Huddersfield.
[42157]   06/10/1988   CM19/06/1991
Sharman, Miss J, MCLIP, Retired.
[13175]   07/02/1953   CM01/01/1964
Sharp, Ms A, BLS (Hons) MCLIP, Currently unemployed.
[36113]   07/02/1983   CM12/03/2003
Sharp, Ms C, BSc (Hons) MSc MCLIP, Early Years Librarian, Falkirk Council.
[56810]   23/10/1998   CM10/07/2002
Sharp, Mrs C A, MSc MCLIP, Retired.
[13179]   05/02/1968   CM09/09/1974
Sharp, Mrs C H, BA MCLIP, Librarian, Montrose and Brechin L. ibraries, Angus Council.
[27836]   30/08/1977   CM01/07/1990
Sharp, Mr D J, BSc (Hons) MSc MCLIP, Information Specialist, British American Tobacco, Southampton.
[10000429]   10/10/2006   CM13/11/2013
Sharp, Ms H M, BA ALA,
[10012938]   20/03/1980   ME
Sharp, Mrs J, Library Assistant.
[10035032]   09/09/2014   ME
Sharp, Mrs R E A, BA MCLIP,
[41518]   11/01/1988   CM18/09/1991
Sharpe, Mrs R W, MCLIP, Enquiry Services Manager, Chesterfield Library.
[10001132]   02/02/1987   CM18/11/1998
Sharples, Mr C, BA MA MCLIP, Information Specialist, Browne Jacobson Sols, Notts.
[59983]   15/11/2001   CM03/10/2007
Sharrock, Mrs M I, BA MCLIP, Librarian, Gateways School, Harewood Leeds.
[38547]   18/06/1985   CM15/08/1989
Shaughnessy, Miss M, BA DipLib MCLIP, Unwaged.
[33698]   12/01/1981   CM31/01/1989
Shaw, Mrs A, ACLIP, L. Serv. Adv., Mansfield Woodhouse Library, Notts.
[10019609]   04/08/2011   ACL18/01/2012
Shaw, Mrs A E, BA (Hons) MCLIP, Res. Librarian, Ely College, Cambridgeshire.
[35624]   16/11/1982   CM21/07/1999

Shaw, Ms C, BA (Hons) MA, Cataloging Manager, British, London.
[53861]   08/10/1996   ME
Shaw, Mrs C M, MA MCLIP, Freelance Editor & Indexer.
[13207]   09/01/1970   CM01/01/1972
Shaw, Mr D, MA MCLIP, Retired.
[13208]   24/10/1966   CM01/01/1969
Shaw, Mrs D A, BA (Hons) PGCE MCLIP, Academic Liaison Assistant, Oxford Brookes University.
[36632]   30/10/1983   CM26/07/1995
Shaw, Mr D E, Information Skills, Career, Support to Head Profession.
[54746]   01/04/1997   ME
Shaw, Miss H A, BA (Hons) DipILS FHEA, Learning and Teaching Librarian, Nottingham Trent University, Nottingham.
[49440]   27/10/1993   ME
Shaw, Ms H R, MCLIP, Information Services Manager.
[10022461]   06/12/1975   CM24/07/1979
Shaw, Mrs I A, BSc MPhil MCLIP, Retired.
[11914]   20/10/1967   CM14/10/1969
Shaw, Mrs I W, BSc MCLIP, Editor of 'Families London – Surrey Borders' Magazine.
[60332]   30/06/1993   CM30/06/1993
Shaw, Mrs J G, BSc M PHIL, Retired. Hon. Research Officer for Partnerships in Health Information (registered charity no. 1031674).
[33149]   01/10/1980   ME
Shaw, Mrs J R, BA (Hons) MSc, Student, Leeds Metropolitan University.
[10015221]   27/10/2009   ME
Shaw, Ms K, Network Lib. (PT) & Cust. Supp. Supervisor, Aberdeenshire City Council & Robert Gordon University.
[10008002]   05/10/1990   ME
Shaw, Miss K M, Student, Northumbria University.
[10022374]   19/02/2013   ME
Shaw, Mrs L E, MCLIP, Learning Res. Centre Team Leader, Nelson & Colne College, Lancs.
[22305]   21/02/1974   CM29/03/1977
Shaw, Ms M, Student, UCL.
[10031863]   10/10/2013   ME
Shaw, Mr M A, BA DipLib MCLIP, Library Service Development Manager, Derbys. County Council.
[31943]   21/01/1980   CM21/01/1982
Shaw, Ms P A, MA BA (Hons), Assistant Librarian, University of the West of England, Bristol.
[61224]   15/04/2002   ME
Shaw, Mrs S, Assistant librarian, Radley College Library, Oxfordshire.
[10020698]   27/03/2012   AF
Shaw, Miss S L, BA (Hons) PgDip MCLIP, Learning Resources Manager, Ashton Sixth Form College.
[10014214]   07/07/2009   RV27/03/2014   CM09/11/2011
Shaw, Mr T, BA (Hons) MSc, Clinical Information Manager, NHS Direct, Bristol.
[64329]   04/03/2005   ME
Shawcross, Miss J, BA (Hons), Academic Liaison Librarian, University Hospitals of Morecambe Bay NHS Trust.
[61703]   22/10/2002   ME
Shawcross, Mrs R, Information Specialist, Integreon.
[59897]   30/10/2001   ME
Shaw-Howells, Mrs G H, BA DMS MCLIP, Retired.
[13213]   29/08/1962   CM01/01/1968
Shea, Miss E, BA, Student, University of Ulster.
[10031896]   21/01/2014   ME
Sheard, Mrs K, MCLIP HonFCLIP, Retired.
[13237]   25/03/1969   HFE02/09/2010
Shearer, Mrs C M, BA MCLIP, Employment not known.
[31672]   16/10/1979   CM30/11/1984

Shearing, Mrs A, Dip HE, Schools Librarian, Southampton School
Library Service.
[10019148]   24/03/2014   ME
Shearman, Miss N J, Deputy Head of KIM, Office For National
Statistics.
[10033805]   01/05/2014   ME
Shearring, Mrs J A, BA MCLIP, Group Manager (East), Orpington
Library, London Borough of Bromley.
[10762]   01/01/1970   **CM25/02/1974**
Shedwick, Ms L A, BA (Hons) DipLib, Retired Library Manager.
[31446]   01/10/1979   ME
Sheehan, Mr K J, BA (Hons) MA MCLIP, School Librarian, Loreto High
School, Chorlton, Manchester.
[10001387]   01/10/1998   **CM28/01/2009**
Sheekey, Mr N, Graduate Library Trainee, St Hilda's college, Library,
Oxford.
[10022102]   12/12/2012   ME
Sheerin, Mrs C E, BA DipLib MCLIP, School Librarian, MOD.
[34272]   21/10/1981   **CM24/09/1985**
Sheffield, Mrs V C, BA MCLIP, Unwaged.
[31250]   09/10/1979   **CM19/10/1982**
Shehata, Mr A M K, MA, PhD Student.
[10021973]   24/10/2013   ME
Sheikh, Mrs J, Student, Coleg Llandrillo.
[10032514]   11/12/2013   ME
Shelley, Miss J, BSc (Hons) MA PG Cert MCLIP, Subject Librarian.
(Health, SocialCare & Education), Anglia Ruskin. University,
Chelmsford.
[48152]   11/11/1992   **CM20/09/1995**
Shelley, Mr K M, BA (Hons) MCLIP, Chartered Member.
[55929]   11/12/1997   **CM16/07/2003**
Shelton, Ms A, BA (Hons) MA MCLIP, Customer Services Manager, St
Mary's University, Twickenham.
[58766]   13/07/2000   **CM07/09/2005**
Shenton, Dr A K, BA (Hons) MSc PhD PGCE, Curriculum and
Resource Support, Monkseaton High School, Tyne and Wear.
[43657]   20/11/1989   ME
Shenton, Mr D E, FCLIP, Retired.
[13256]   10/02/1958   **FE06/10/1977**
Shenton, Miss L D, LLB, Student, University of Sheffield.
[10031570]   10/10/2013   ME
Shenton, Miss S K, BA (Hons) MA MCLIP, Senior Assistant Librarian,
Manchester Metropolitan University.
[56725]   07/10/1998   **CM15/09/2004**
Shepherd, Mr A, BA DMS MIMgt MCLIP, Carer & Story-Teller, London.
[13262]   12/10/1965   **CM01/01/1969**
Shepherd, Ms A M, MA BA (Hons), Lib. Assistant, Sion Hill Library,
Bath.
[10012672]   02/03/2009   ME
Shepherd, Miss D, BA PgDipIS, Unwaged.
[64975]   05/10/2005   ME
Shepherd, Mrs H, MCLIP, Information Centre Manager, Department for
Communities and Local Government.
[19901]   01/01/1973   **CM16/09/1975**
Shepherd, Ms J L, BA MCLIP, Archivist, Wellington College,
Crowthorne, Berkshire.
[24963]   20/10/1975   **CM24/06/1980**
Shepherd, Mrs R, BA, Team Librarian, Bridgnorth Library.
[10031653]   17/09/2013   ME
Sheppard, Mr G D, Information Services Librarian, Vale of Glamorgan
Library Service.
[65083]   01/11/2005   ME
Sheppard, Mrs M, Library Assistant & Student.
[10033770]   25/04/2014   ME

Sheridan, Miss J, BA (Hons) MSc MCLIP, Assistant Learning
Resources Manager, Sparsholt College.
[59103]   15/11/2000   **CM29/03/2004**
Sheridan, Mrs S A, BA MA MCLIP, District Manager, Canterbury
Library, Kent Libraries & Archives.
[40248]   19/11/1986   **CM18/04/1990**
Sherington, Ms J O, MA DipLib MCLIP, Information Serv. Librarian,
Clydebank Librarian, West Dunbartonshire.
[40243]   10/11/1986   **CM15/08/1989**
Sherlock, Mr C J A, BA (Hons), Senior Researcher, Hogan Lovells
International LLP, London.
[49177]   08/10/1993   ME
Sherlock, Dr D, BA MA PhD Diploma ILS, Assistant Librarian, Queens
University.
[10033175]   18/02/2014   ME
Sherlock, Mr I, BA, Student.
[10020174]   15/11/2011   ME
Sherman, Mrs E A, BA MA MCLIP, Strategic Commissioning Officer.
[63900]   26/10/2004   **CM28/01/2009**
Sherman, Mrs G, BSc (Open) MCLIP, Relief Librarian, Devizes Library,
Wiltshire County Council.
[13293]   25/03/1968   **CM01/01/1971**
Sherratt, Miss A B, BA MCLIP, Life Member.
[13294]   15/01/1951   **CM01/01/1953**
Sherriff, Miss E L, BSc (Hons), Development Manager (Literacy),
Central Library, Plymouth.
[66015]   31/08/2006   ME
Sherriffs, Mr G I F, MA (Hons) DipILS MCLIP, Acquisitions Librarian,
Royal Botanic Garden, Edinburgh.
[53776]   01/10/1996   **CM15/03/2000**
Sherrin, Miss P A, MCLIP, Life Member.
[13295]   29/02/1960   **CM01/01/1969**
Sherry, Mrs W, Librarian & Resources Manager, Henlow Church of
England Academy, Henlow.
[10022910]   07/05/2013   AF
Sherwell, Mr J R, MLib FCLIP MRSC, Retired.
[18193]   02/10/1972   **FE18/04/1989**
Sherwin, Miss K, BA (Hons) MA (Dist) MCLIP, Senior Librarian &
Knowledge Specialist, Arup, Australia.
[58792]   26/07/2000   **CM09/11/2005**
Sherwood, Miss A, BA, Senior Library Assistant, University of Teesside.
[10015973]   03/02/2010   ME
Shieh, Miss L Y I, BA DipLib MA MCLIP, Sub-Librarian, University of
Hong Kong Ls., Pokfulam, Hong Kong.
[41006]   02/10/1987   **CM19/06/1991**
Shiel, Ms K A, BSc DipILM PgDipRM CertEd, Librarian, Records
Manager.
[10006149]   04/09/1991   ME
Shields, Ms E, MCLIP, Deputy Library Services Manager, Manchester
Metropolitan University.
[10019780]   18/04/2000   **CM18/09/2002**
Shiell, Ms L M, BA (Hons) MCLIP, Indexer, British Film Institute, London.
[41899]   15/05/1988   **CM27/07/1994**
Shiels, Mrs E C, MCLIP, Retired.
[13302]   31/07/1962   **CM01/01/1967**
Shiels, Mr S M, BSc (Hons) PgDip MCLIP, L. Officer, Edinburgh City
Council.
[61304]   20/05/2002   **CM04/10/2006**
Shimmon, Mr R M, OBE HonFLA FCLIP,
[13305]   14/04/1961   **HFE01/01/2000**
Shine, Ms C R, BA DipLIS MCLIP, School Librarian, The Forest School,
Winnersh.
[40049]   08/10/1986   **CM15/09/2004**

Shinewi, Mr A, MSc, Student.
[10031463]   13/08/2013   **ME**

Shipley, Mrs M, BA MCLIP, Children & Young People's Coordinator, Coventry.
[42818]   01/03/1989   **CM15/09/1993**

Shippey, Miss I J, BA (Hons), Bibliographic Librarian, RNIB National Library Serv., Peterborough.
[42579]   10/01/1989   **ME**

Shipsey, Ms F M, Acquisitions & Serials Librarian, Institute of Education.
[39937]   06/10/1961   **ME**

Shire, Mrs S A, MCLIP B SC (Joint Hons), Retired.
[21248]   06/10/1973   **CM11/06/1976**

Shoemark, Mr H K, BSc MCLIP, Retired.
[22685]   12/08/1974   **CM01/07/1989**

Shoemark, Mrs M L, BA MCLIP, Retired.
[23715]   17/01/1975   **CM16/05/1978**

Shoesmith, Miss C B, MCLIP, Retired.
[19199]   01/10/1972   **CM16/07/1975**

Shomade, Miss G, BSc (Hons) MSc, Information Scientist, ELI LILLY & Co.
[10033558]   25/03/2014   **ME**

Shone, Mrs S E, MCLIP, Retired.
[3036]   16/01/1968   **CM14/08/1972**

Short, Miss A, BA (Hons) MSc, Assistant Librarian, MOD.
[65032]   13/10/2005   **ME**

Short, Mrs B, MA DipLIS, Enquiry Team Librarian, Welwyn Garden City Central Library & Information Service, Hertfordshire County Council.
[64668]   17/05/2005   **ME**

Short, Mr D L, ACLIP, Assistant Library Manager, West Bridgford Library.
[10019924]   04/10/2011   **ACL09/07/2013**

Short, Mr P J, BA MCLIP, Retired.
[13325]   26/07/1967   **CM13/08/1975**

Short, Mrs P M, MCLIP, Retired academic librarian.
[50181]   25/04/1994   **CM09/09/2013**

Shorthouse, Miss E, MA (Hons),
[10033803]   30/04/2014   **ME**

Shovlin, Mrs C L, BA DipLib, School Librarian, Barnard Castle School, Co. Durham.
[48236]   16/11/1992   **ME**

Showell, Mrs C, BA DipLib MCLIP, Librarian, British Trust for Ornithology, Thetford.
[30030]   13/11/1978   **CM29/01/1982**

Showunmi, Mrs J, BSc MCLIP, School Librarian, Phoenix High School, London.
[58952]   10/10/2000   **CM19/11/2008**

Shrigley, Mr R M, BA MCLIP, Retired.
[13330]   03/10/1966   **CM01/01/1970**

Shrive, Mr M A, BA MCLIP,
[45437]   06/02/1991   **CM23/03/1994**

Shukla, Miss N, BA, Student, Aberystwyth University.
[10033959]   14/05/2014   **ME**

Shute, Miss A J, BA MCLIP, Retired.
[13336]   26/01/1961   **CM01/01/1964**

Sibson, Mr M F D, LLB (Hons) BA (Hons) MCLIP, Medical Librarian, Eastbourne District Gen. Hospital, East Sussex.
[36182]   04/07/1983   **CM14/11/1989**

Sicken, Miss E P, BA, Student, Kent State University.
[10032520]   11/12/2013   **ME**

Siddall, Miss G E, BA (Hons) MA PGCTHE MCLIP FHEA, Academic Librarian, University of Northampton.
[10006244]   26/09/2007   **CM18/01/2012**

Siddall, Miss M F, BA (Hons), Assistant Cent. Manager, Sheffield College.
[61912]   02/12/2002   **ME**

Siddall, Ms P M, MSc MCLIP, Independent Consultant.
[13344]   16/03/1972   **CM29/10/1975**

Siddiqi, Mrs T, BA (Hons) DipLIS, Librarian, Burntwood School, London.
[40451]   25/01/1987   **ME**

Siddiqui, Mr A,
[10012449]   11/02/2009   **ME**

Siddiqui, Mr A R, BA LLB MCLIP, Retired.
[13345]   20/03/1964   **CM01/01/1967**

Siddiqui, Mr I, BA MA MSc, Information Assistant, Kingston University.
[10032033]   14/12/2011   **ME**

Sidebottom, Miss M, MCLIP, Retired.
[13348]   30/09/1942   **CM01/01/1956**

Sidgreaves, Mr I, BA DipEd DipLib FCLIP, Retired.
[13349]   03/10/1966   **FE23/07/1997**

Siemaszko, Ms A M, BA DipLib MCLIP, Unwaged.
[34032]   25/07/1981   **CM11/04/1985**

Siemaszko, Mrs W M, MA DipLib MCLIP, Customer Services Manager, Dulwich Library, London Borough of Southwark.
[29341]   25/05/1978   **CM17/03/1981**

Siemsen, Ms A M A, BA DipLib MCLIP, Retired.
[18152]   11/10/1972   **CM04/05/1976**

Sig, Ms H, BSc, Unemployed seeking work.
[61325]   22/05/2002   **ME**

Sihra, Mrs S, BA, Assistant Librarian, King Edward's School, Birmingham.
[37086]   16/01/1984   **ME**

Silburn, Mrs R E, BSc (Econ) MCLIP, Public Serv. Manager, Suffolk Record Office, Lowestoft.
[59685]   31/07/2001   **CM29/08/2007**

Silcocks, Mrs S J, BA DipLib MSc, Information /Knowledge Manager, URS Infrastructure & Environment UK Limited.
[31307]   29/09/1979   **RV08/03/2013**   **CM03/09/1982**

Silk, Miss K A, BA (Hons), Student.
[10019995]   20/10/2011   **ME**

Silman, Mrs R G, Faculty Team Librarian, John Rylands Library, Manchester.
[33152]   01/10/1980   **ME**

Silver, Mrs M V, BA (Hons) DipIM MCLIP, Prison Librarian, Medway Council.
[52441]   31/10/1995   **CM17/11/1999**

Silvester, Mrs S C, MA PgDipHist MCLIP, Self-employed.
[13356]   27/10/1966   **CM01/01/1970**

Silvester, Mrs S M, BSc BA MCLIP, Young People & Sch. Officer, Scarborough Central Library, North Yorkshire County Council.
[33785]   02/03/1981   **CM16/04/1984**

Silvey, Miss E C M, BA MA, Assistant Librarian.
[10021255]   02/07/2012   **ME**

Sim, Miss J A, BA (Hons), Student, Manchester Metropolitan University.
[10032515]   11/12/2013   **ME**

Sim, Mrs L A, BA MCLIP, Acting Head of Libraries, West Sussex County Council.
[27881]   05/10/1977   **CM01/01/1979**

Sime, Mrs A J, BA MCLIP, School Librarian, Fife Reg. Council, Glenrothes.
[29531]   02/08/1978   **CM16/09/1980**

Sime, Mr W C, BSc (Econ) FCLIP, Director of Library Services, Royal Society of Medicine, London.
[53224]   04/04/1996   **FE09/09/2009**

Siminson, Ms N J, BA (Hons) MA MCLIP, Jorum Community Enhancement Officer, University of Manchester, Manchester.
[49067]   27/09/1993   **CM19/01/2000**

Simkin, Mr D, BA, Subscription & Access Assistant, King's College.
[10022033]   20/11/2012   **ME**
Simm, Ms J, MCLIP,
[10022855]   30/04/2013   **CM01/07/1987**
Simm, Mrs J R, BA MCLIP, Assistant Librarian, Early Years Librarian,
Sunderland City Library.
[37339]   04/07/1984   **CM10/11/1987**
Simmonds, Mr G, BSc (Hons) MA MCLIP, Librarian, Southend Library,
Essex.
[59624]   03/07/2001   **CM20/04/2012**
Simmonds, Ms P A, BA DipLib AMIPD MCLIP, Unwaged.
[34897]   15/04/1982   **CM16/05/1985**
Simmons, Ms A L, BA (Hons) MSc MCLIP, Senior Librarian, Luton
Culture.
[58865]   18/09/2000   **CM04/10/2006**
Simmons, Ms L, BSc MA PgDip ALA, Head of Library Customer
Services Development, London Metropolitan Uni.
[10021826]   01/07/1988   **CM01/07/1991**
Simmons, Mrs M M, MCLIP, Retired.
[13374]   18/01/1961   **CM01/01/1965**
Simmons, Mr N A, MA MA (LIB) MCLIP DMS, Life Member.
[13375]   02/04/1972   **CM03/01/1975**
Simmons, Ms S, BA DipSoc MCLIP, Information Management
Consultant.
[55004]   12/06/1997   **CM04/09/1989**
Simoes, Ms M J, BA (Hons) MA, Library Manager, Calderdale & Hudds.
NHS F. Trust /Enquiry Team Supervisor (Equality & Accessibility),
University of Bradford.
[10017894]   21/10/2010   **ME**
Simon, Mrs C, BA (Hons) MSc (Econ) MCLIP, Child. & Sch. Librarian,
Llanelli Area Library, Carmarthenshire County Council.
[55344]   02/10/1997   **CM21/11/2001**
Simon, Ms L H, BA (Hons) MA MCLIP, Library Systems Officer,
Wellcome Library.
[43230]   01/10/1989   **CM20/09/1995**
Simons, Ms P A, BA DipLib MCLIP, Deputy Director, Student Services,
Queen Mary University of London.
[29477]   20/08/1978   **CM07/01/1982**
Simpson, Mr A G, School Librarian, Strood Academy, Strood.
[53064]   21/02/1996   **ME**
Simpson, Mr A J, BSc (Hons) MScEcon MCLIP, Associate University
Librarian, University of Portsmouth.
[54146]   07/11/1996   **CM15/11/2000**
Simpson, Mrs C A, BA (Hons) MA, Cataloguer, Sothebys, London.
[52097]   03/10/1995   **ME**
Simpson, Miss C R, BA (Hons), Student, Manchester Metropolitan
University.
[10035492]   16/10/2014   **ME**
Simpson, Mrs C S, library resources advisor, Stafford College.
[10018208]   08/12/2010   **ME**
Simpson, Miss D E B, MCLIP, Life Member.
[13391]   11/10/1944   **CM01/01/1964**
Simpson, Mr D J, BSc (ECON) FCLIP, Retired, formerly Librarian &
Director of Media Resources, Open University.
[13393]   22/03/1946   **FE01/01/1954**
Simpson, Ms E A, BA (Hons) DipLIS MCLIP, Royal College of
Physicians of Edinburgh.
[50154]   13/04/1994   **CM22/05/1996**
Simpson, Mrs E J, MCLIP, Community Librarian, Norfolk County
Council, Norfolk & Norwich Millennium L.
[19982]   09/01/1973   **CM01/01/1976**
Simpson, Ms E M, BA (Hons) MA MCLIP AFHEA, Subject Librarian,
University of Roehampton.
[10006493]   24/10/2007   **CM09/11/2011**

Simpson, Mr E W M, DipEdTech MCLIP, Retired.
[19205]   26/02/1964   **CM01/01/1968**
Simpson, Mrs J, L. Manager, Christchurch Library, Christchurch.
[65939]   07/07/2006   **AF**
Simpson, Mrs J M, BA MCLIP, Unwaged.
[23250]   13/11/1974   **CM29/10/1979**
Simpson, Ms K, BA, Deputy Supervisor of the Self-Access Area,
University of Leeds.
[10031701]   12/05/2014   **ME**
Simpson, Mr N A, MA MCLIP, Life Member.
[13406]   25/01/1963   **CM01/01/1966**
Simpson, Mrs P D, MA MCLIP, Student, P. H. D.
[22317]   01/04/1974   **CM28/12/1977**
Simpson, Miss P H, MCLIP, Retired.
[13408]   06/01/1968   **CM18/10/1973**
Simpson, Mr R, Assistant Librarian, HM Treasury & Cabinet Office
Library, London.
[65978]   09/08/2006   **AF**
Simpson, Mr S A, BA PgDipIT MCLIP, Systems Manager, Arts,
Learning & Libraries, East Renfrewshire Council.
[44136]   29/05/1990   **CM22/11/1995**
Simpson, Mrs S H, BA DipLib MCLIP, Arch. Assistant, Angus Council,
Montrose.
[33154]   07/10/1980   **CM19/10/1982**
Simpson, Ms S J, BA (Hons) PGCE MSc, School Librarian, Forest
School.
[10013716]   22/05/2009   **ME**
Sims, Mrs A M, BA MCLIP, Retired.
[1651]   12/01/1972   **CM01/09/1974**
Sims, Mrs D E, BSc DipInfSc MCLIP, Librarian, English Heritage,
Swindon.
[40549]   06/03/1987   **CM18/11/1992**
Sims, Mr P S, BSc MCLIP, Patent Search Information Ltd, Chester.
[60354]   13/07/1995   **CM13/07/1995**
Simsova, Mrs S, MPhil FCLIP, Retired.
[13418]   07/03/1952   **FE01/01/1957**
Simspon, Ms M, Community Development & Information Librarian.
[63910]   26/10/2004   **ME**
Sinai, Mr A, BA DLS MCLIP, Retired.
[17735]   28/08/1963   **CM01/01/1967**
Sinclair, Mr A, MA, Library Assistant, Goldsmiths University of London.
[10032783]   01/07/2014   **ME**
Sinclair, Mr C A, BA MCLIP, Library Content Manager, University of
Stirling.
[38530]   05/06/1985   **CM18/04/1990**
Sinclair, Mrs F, BA MCLIP, School Librarian, Orkney Islands Council,
Stromness Academy.
[41102]   05/10/1987   **CM24/05/1995**
Sinclair, Miss H, BA PgDip MCLIP, Information Officer, Glasgow.
[10001725]   03/10/2003   **CM15/07/2014**
Sinclair, Miss H A, BA (Hons) MA MCLIP, Deputy Operations Librarian,
Watford Central Library, Watford.
[53809]   02/10/1996   **CM17/05/2000**
Sinclair, Mrs J M, ACLIP, Library and e-Resources Advisor, Highbury
College, Portsmouth.
[62455]   01/07/2003   **ACL14/06/2005**
Sinclair, Ms S C, Learning Centre Manager.
[10011405]   16/10/2008   **ME**
Sinclair, Miss V M, BA DipInf, Assistant Librarian, Wellcome Library,
London.
[56950]   13/11/1998   **ME**
Sinclair-Giardini, Dr B V, BA MA PhD ACIM, Student, Aberystwyth
University.
[10032809]   14/01/2014   **ME**

Sinden-Evans, Ms R, BA MA BMus MMus MCLIP, Liaison Librarian, Media and Performing Arts., Middlesex University.
[35660]   13/11/1982   **CM14/04/1987**

Singer, Ms H J, BA (Hons) MA MCLIP PGDIP FHEA, Information Manager, University of Hertfordshire.
[52818]   19/12/1995   **CM12/09/2001**

Singh, Miss M, BA (Hons) MCLIP, Electronic Serv. Co-ordinator, Electronic Knowledge Access Team, London.
[61517]   29/08/2002   **CM07/09/2005**

Singleton, Miss H L, BA (HONS) MSc, Assistant Librarian Trainee.
[10020866]   19/04/2012   **ME**

Sinkinson, Mr J V, BA MCLIP, Civil Servant.
[24139]   04/04/1975   **CM19/09/1978**

Sinnott, Mr A J, BA (Hons), Reading & Learning Adviser, Explore Acomb Library Learning Ctr.
[10021097]   29/05/2012   **AF**

Sippings, Mrs G M, MLib FCLIP, Head of Knowledge and Information Management, The MDU.
[24895]   14/10/1975   **FE24/02/1997**

Siriwardena, Miss P L, MLS, Librarian.
[10034286]   30/06/2014   **ME**

Sisson, Miss F, BA (Hons) MA MCLIP, Senior Information Advisor, Kingston University, Kingston-upon-Thames.
[51461]   24/02/1995   **CM19/11/2003**

Sisson, Ms M, ACLIP, Learning Resource Centre Assistant.
[10009711]   03/06/2008   **ACL30/04/2010**

Sissons, Miss J T, BA (Hons) MA MCLIP, Study Centre Assistant/Liaison Librarian, Heart of Worcestershire College.
[53559]   22/07/1996   **RV23/09/2009**   **CM20/09/2000**

Siswell, A, BA DipLib MCLIP, Deputy Director, Bath Spa University, Bath.
[28162]   11/10/1977   **CM06/12/1979**

Siwek, Mrs G R, MA DipLib MCLIP, Community Librarian, Portree Community Library, Isle of Skye.
[32918]   08/10/1980   **CM18/07/1983**

Siwela, Mrs M, BSc (Hons), Library Assistant, Ashford & St Peter's Hospitals NHS FoundationTrust.
[10034192]   18/06/2014   **ME**

Skakle, Mrs S M, MA (Hons) MLib MCLIP, Head of Enquiries, Scottish Parliament Information Centre, Edinburgh.
[47746]   16/10/1992   **CM06/04/2005**

Skander, Mrs J R, Senior Library Assistant, Cheshire E. Council, Hurdsfield & Prestbury L.
[21674]   03/01/1974   **ME**

Skawinska, Mrs A, MA, Unemployed.
[10023004]   21/05/2013   **AF**

Skea, Mrs J R, MCLIP, Retired.
[13437]   07/03/1934   **CM01/01/1937**

Skeet, Ms V, BA (Hons), Student, Aberystwyth University.
[10033107]   11/02/2014   **ME**

Skelly, Rev O D G, BA MCLIP STB, Parish Priest, Diocese of Meath, Ireland.
[26557]   12/10/1976   **CM15/10/1980**

Skelton, Ms H C, MSc, Information Manager.
[41498]   04/01/1988   **ME**

Skelton, Miss S A, BA (Hons) MCLIP, Senior Knowledge and Information Manager.
[49622]   18/11/1993   **CM13/08/2010**

Skene, Mrs S, BA MCLIP, Library Assistant, Robinson College, Cambridge.
[30461]   02/02/1979   **CM19/10/1982**

Skerrow, Mr C J D, MA (Hons) DipLib MCLIP, eResources Librarian, Hull College.
[48055]   03/11/1992   **CM13/06/2007**

Skiffington, Mrs M, BA MCLIP, Life Member.
[17739]   01/01/1954   **CM01/01/1956**

Skimming, Mrs J, MCLIP, Retired.
[998]   22/01/1972   **CM04/11/1974**

Skinner, Mr B J, BSc (Hons) MA MCLIP, Knowledge Management Librarian, Brighton & Sussex University Hospital NHS, Brighton Gen. Hospital.
[56486]   21/07/1998   **CM28/01/2009**

Skinner, Miss J B, BLib MCLIP, Librarian, Valuation Office, PSD:TSS, London.
[21406]   06/11/1973   **CM01/10/1979**

Skinner, Mrs P A, BA MCLIP, Library Development Officer, West Lothian Council.
[40111]   21/10/1986   **CM27/05/1992**

Skinner, Mrs S M, BA MCLIP, Network Librarian, Aberdeenshire L. & Information Serv.
[38981]   24/10/1985   **CM18/11/1992**

Skipp, Miss D F, Student, Robert Gordon University.
[10035453]   14/10/2014   **ME**

Skipp, Miss M, MCLIP, Life Member.
[13468]   16/02/1956   **CM01/01/1964**

Skipper, Miss C D, BSc Econ (Hons) MSc Econ, Student.
[10009707]   02/06/2008   **ME**

Skirrow, Mrs I H, Cert Ed MA MSc Econ ILS, International Schools Lib Consultant; IB workshop leader & school visitor for PYP and Libraries; IB Online facilitator.
[59569]   26/06/2001   **ME**

Skoyles, Miss A, BA (Hons) MA, Assistant Librarian, Chichester College.
[65053]   17/10/2005   **ME**

Skoyles, Miss R, BSc, Information Assistant, L. & Learning Serv., Northumbria University, Newcastle upon Tyne.
[10012101]   17/12/2008   **ME**

Slade, Mr I C, Information Manager, MOD, Bristol.
[10023089]   05/06/2013   **ME**

Slade, Ms S M, BA (Hons) Dip Lib, Academic Support Manager, The Library, University of Salford.
[10018609]   02/10/1978   **CM01/10/1989**

Slark, Mrs A M, MCLIP, Retired, Life Member.
[13480]   03/07/1965   **CM01/01/1970**

Slasor, Miss A, BA MA MCLIP,
[27022]   12/01/1977   **CM17/06/1980**

Slater, Mrs B G, MCLIP, Unwaged.
[20156]   27/01/1973   **CM11/09/1975**

Slater, Ms J A, MA (Hons), Principal Library Assistant.
[51971]   24/08/1995   **ME**

Slater, Miss K, BA MCLIP, Senior Lib. Primary, Cheshire Educ. L. Serv., Cheshire.
[34642]   20/01/1982   **CM05/05/1987**

Slater, Mr M K, BA MCLIP, Support Services. Manager. John Onslow House., London Borough of Tower Hamlets.
[35384]   19/10/1982   **CM07/06/1988**

Slaughter, Mr R M, BA DipLib MCLIP, Local Studies Librarian, Sandwell Metropolitan Borough C.
[34508]   19/11/1981   **CM18/01/1985**

Slavic, Dr A,
[57683]   01/07/1999   **ME**

Sleap, Miss S E, BA DipLib MCLIP, Life Member.
[31155]   07/09/1979   **CM07/09/1981**

Sleat, Mr A J F, BA (Hons) DipLib MCLIP, Subject Librarian, Faculty of Environment & Technology, University of the West of England, Bristol.
[36821]   01/01/1984   **CM26/07/1995**

331

Slee, Ms T, Loughborough University, 2012.
[10012043]   06/01/2012   ME
Sleeman, Miss R A, BA PgDip MA, Academic Support Librarian,
University of West London.
[10014849]   21/09/2009   ME
Sliney, Ms M T, MSocSc DipLib MCLIP ALAI, Retired.
[33347]   16/11/1980   **CM08/06/1987**
Sliwinska, Miss K E, MSc,
[10014048]   23/06/2009   ME
Sloan, Miss T E, BSc (Hons) MSc, Learning Resource Centre Assistant,
Edinburgh College.
[10022625]   05/04/2013   ME
Slough, Mr N S J, BA (Hons) MA MCLIP, Assistant Librarian,
Corporation of London, Guildhall Library.
[44467]   10/10/1990   **CM23/09/1998**
Sludden, Miss P A, BSc (Hons),
[10019917]   03/10/2011   ME
Small, Miss C, BA (Hons) MA, Student.
[10019993]   19/10/2011   ME
Small, Mr G S, BA (Hons) DipLib MCLIP, Learning Resources Manager,
Churchfields Academy, Swindon.
[36830]   01/01/1984   **CM21/07/1989**
Smalley, Mrs R, BMus (Hons) PG CE, Community Librarian, LiveWire
Warrington.
[10020140]   09/11/2011   ME
Smart, Dr D, BSc (Hons) PhD MCLIP, Lead Manager, Libraries, West
Sussex County Council.
[10013745]   27/05/2009   **CM15/07/2014**
Smart, Mrs T, BA (Hons) MA, Rare Books Cataloguer, Hereford
Cathedral Library, Hereford.
[58121]   03/11/1999   ME
Smears, Mrs C, BA (Hons), Librarian (Volunteer), The Library at BABEL,
Grenoble.
[10032180]   05/11/2013   ME
Smeaton, Miss M, Life Member.
[20529]   22/01/1973   ME
Smedley, Miss A, BA (Hons) MA MCLIP, Assistant Librarian, Lancashire
County Council, Ansdell Library.
[56804]   19/10/1998   **CM21/05/2008**
Smedley, Miss O G, BA (Hons), Library Assistant (Casual), Cheshire
County Council.
[10034174]   12/06/2014   ME
Smelova, Dr N, PhD, Student.
[10032071]   24/10/2013   ME
Smethurst, Mr R, BA (Hons) LRAM, Deputy Director, Head of
Knowledge & Information, The Cabinet Office.
[10033797]   30/04/2014   ME
Smith, Mr A, BSc AIMgt MCLIP, Retired.
[13522]   19/10/1966   **CM01/01/1970**
Smith, Mrs A H, BA MCLIP, LRC Coordinator, Aberdeen City Council,
Aberdeen.
[35772]   10/01/1983   **CM07/07/1987**
Smith, Dr A J M, PhD, Student, Aberystwyth University.
[10013504]   08/05/2009   ME
Smith, Mrs A M, BA MCLIP, Adult Literacy Teacher, Self-employed.
[36191]   01/07/1983   **CM20/01/1987**
Smith, Ms A M H, BA (Hons) MSc, Academic Librarian, Vaughan
Memorial Library, Canada.
[48781]   21/05/1993   **CM17/11/1999**
Smith, Mr A P, BSc (Hons) PGCE DipIM MCLIP, Librarian, Cent.
Ecology and Hydrology, Oxon.
[52197]   12/10/1995   **CM20/01/1999**
Smith, Mr A R, MCLIP, Life Member.
[13530]   29/06/1948   **CM01/01/1951**

Smith, Mr A W, BLib MCLIP ARCM, Retired. Formerly: The University of
Law 2003-2014; The British Library 1980-2003; Wakefield MD
Libraries 1974-1979.
[13533]   20/10/1971   **CM08/10/1976**
Smith, Mr B B, DMS MCMI MCLIP, Retired.
[13537]   13/01/1954   **CM01/01/1960**
Smith, Mrs B M, BA MCLIP, Learning Resource Centre Manager, Esher
Coe Hi. School, Surrey.
[31681]   25/10/1979   **CM15/09/1983**
Smith, Mrs C, BA MSc MCLIP, Assistant Librarian, Universityof
Cambridge.
[10002616]   01/05/2007   **RV**27/03/2014   **CM14/11/2012**
Smith, Ms C, BLib MCLIP, Collection Development Manager, University
of Bolton.
[30792]   08/04/1979   **CM26/07/1982**
Smith, Miss C, BSc (Hons), Knowledge and Information Officer, Energy
Institute.
[10031620]   11/09/2013   ME
Smith, Mr C, BA MCLIP, Library Services Officer, City College Norwich.
[35367]   11/10/1982   **CM16/02/1988**
Smith, Mrs C A, BA (Hons) MScEcon, Cataloguer, Coutts Information
Services.
[10022220]   22/01/2013   ME
Smith, Ms C A, BSc (Hons) DipLib MCLIP, Librarian, Bevan Library,
Bedford Hospital.
[10005448]   19/03/1979   **CM22/12/1982**
Smith, Mr C A, MA DipLib MCLIP, Student, Strathclyde University,
Glasgow.
[43534]   06/11/1989   **CM18/11/1993**
Smith, Miss C B, BA (Hons), L. & Information Serv. Manager, Lancs.
Care NHS Trust.
[47122]   05/05/1992   ME
Smith, Mrs C E, MA (Cantab) DipLib MCLIP, Housewife.
[36453]   05/10/1983   **CM10/05/1988**
Smith, Mrs C E, Library Assistant, Haberdashers' Aske's School for
Girls.
[10033923]   13/05/2014   ME
Smith, Mr C J, Retired.
[13548]   08/01/1958   **CM01/01/1967**
Smith, Mrs C M, MA DipLib MCLIP, Information Manager., RTC North
Ltd. Sunderland.
[27918]   01/10/1977   **CM22/12/1979**
Smith, Mrs C M B, BA PgDip MCLIP,
[10020289]   18/10/1988   **CM25/05/1994**
Smith, Mrs C P, BLib MCLIP, Unwaged.
[39472]   30/01/1986   **CM21/10/1992**
Smith, Mr D, BA MA, Graduate Trainee Library Assistant, Stanmore
College.
[10031862]   10/10/2013   ME
Smith, Mr D, BA (Hons) MScEcon MCLIP, Librarian for the Ministry of
Defence, Bedfordshire.
[10000538]   16/10/2006   **CM17/09/2008**
Smith, Mr D A, MA MCLIP, Assistant Director – Corporate Info
Assurance & Records Management Serv., Dept for Communities &
Local Government, London.
[34206]   13/10/1981   **CM20/01/1986**
Smith, Mr D A, DipLib MCLIP, Information & Local Studies Officer,
William Patrick Library, East Dunbartonshire.
[38937]   16/10/1985   **CM21/07/1993**
Smith, Dr D F, MA DPhil MCLIP, Librarian, St Annes College Library,
Oxford.
[33427]   30/11/1980   **CM16/12/1986**

Smith, Mr D J, BA (Hons) DMS MCLIP FInstLM, Corporate Information & Customer Services Manager, Conwy County Borough Council.
[41578]   20/01/1988   **CM27/01/1993**

Smith, Mr D L, Graduate Trainee-Library, Aberystwyth University.
[10033902]   12/05/2014   **ME**

Smith, Mr D P, MLS, Director, Albuquerque Public Library.
[57805]   10/08/1999   **ME**

Smith, Mrs E, BA (Hons), Student, Aberystwyth University.
[10033466]   14/03/2014   **ME**

Smith, Mr E, MCLIP, Unwaged.
[13563]   08/01/1967   **CM01/01/1970**

Smith, Mrs E A, BA (Hons) DipILM MCLIP, School Librarian, Pembroke School, Wales.
[43633]   13/11/1989   **CM18/11/1993**

Smith, Mrs E B, MCLIP, Retired.
[754]   18/01/1972   **CM10/02/1975**

Smith, Mrs E M A, BA (Hons), Librarian, Franconian Inter. School, Erlangen, Germany.
[10006336]   10/10/2007   **ME**

Smith, Miss F, Library Assistant/Student.
[10022450]   05/03/2013   **ME**

Smith, Mrs F J, MA (Hons) PgDipLib, Library Assistant, Cults Library.
[10033897]   12/05/2014   **ME**

Smith, Ms G, BA MCLIP, Career Break.
[36684]   03/11/1983   **CM19/08/1992**

Smith, Mrs G, BA MA GDipl LPC, Information Adv., Sheffield Hallam University.
[10018054]   09/11/2010   **ME**

Smith, Mr G, BA DipLib FCLIP, Retired.
[26560]   03/10/1976   **FE20/09/2000**

Smith, Ms G A, ACLIP, Training Facilitator., Royal Naval College, Devon.
[64416]   15/03/2005   **ACL13/11/2013**

Smith, Miss G D, BA (Hons) PgDip,
[10013973]   18/06/2009   **AF**

Smith, Mr G E, OBE FCLIP, Consultant/Life Member.
[13579]   11/01/1948   **FE01/01/1956**

Smith, Miss G F, BA (Hons) MSc (Econ) MCLIP, Learning & Teaching Librarian, The Open University Library, Milton Keynes.
[52531]   06/11/1995   **CM20/09/2000**

Smith, Mr G H R, BA MCLIP, Retired.
[13581]   23/02/1966   **CM01/01/1969**

Smith, Mrs G M, MCLIP, Greeting Cards Website Proprietor.
[8679]   25/01/1970   **CM05/07/1988**

Smith, Mrs H, BA DMS MCLIP, Career break.
[39617]   01/04/1986   **CM24/06/1992**

Smith, Mrs H, BA MCLIP, Team Leader (Service Development), North Yorkshire County Council Skipton.
[40512]   24/02/1987   **CM12/12/1991**

Smith, Mrs H A, BA (Hons) PGCE PgDipILS, Learning Resources Supervisor, Gloucestershire College, Gloucester.
[52313]   25/10/1995   **ME**

Smith, Miss H E, BA MCLIP, Branch Manager, Borough of Poole.
[37882]   01/11/1984   **CM18/04/1989**

Smith, Ms H R, MSc MCLIP, Legal Librarian/Knowledge Coordinator.
[39825]   09/08/1986   **CM14/11/1989**

Smith, Ms H S, Head Librarian, Ashurst LLP, London.
[49581]   19/11/1993   **ME**

Smith, Mr I M, BA MSc DipLib MCLIP, Librarian (Part-time).
[35204]   05/10/1982   **CM16/05/1990**

Smith, Ms J, MA BA (Hons) MCLIP, Assistant Librarian, Guildhall Library, London.
[10016644]   27/10/1998   **CM07/09/2011**

Smith, Mr J, BA (Hons) MPHIL, Graduate Trainee Librarian, Christ's College Library.
[10022292]   05/02/2013   **ME**

Smith, Mrs J, ACLIP, LRC Information Assistant, Guilford College, Worplesdon.
[10016794]   18/05/2010   **ACL07/09/2011**

Smith, Dr J, BA MA MSc PhD, Open Access Assistant, University of Sheffield; Researcher, Sheffield Hallam University.
[10020195]   16/11/2011   **ME**

Smith, Miss J, BSc MBA MScEcon (Distinction), PhD Student, Aberystwyth University.
[10032507]   11/12/2013   **ME**

Smith, Mrs J, ACLIP, Team Leader, Halfway Library, South Lanarkshire.
[10012527]   24/02/2009   **ACL16/06/2010**

Smith, Mrs J A, MA MCLIP, Freelance trainer/consultant/cataloguer/internet researcher.
[25665]   21/01/1976   **CM17/01/1978**

Smith, Mr J A, BSc (HONS), Librarian, Sunderland City Council, Schools Library Service, Sandhill Centre.
[10010363]   01/11/2012   **ME**

Smith, Mr J A, Stock & Info Librarian, Brighton & Hove Council.
[10001066]   12/01/2007   **ME**

Smith, Ms J B, BA (Hons) MCLIP, Systems Librarian, Newman University, Birmingham.
[33158]   20/10/1980   **CM01/07/1989**

Smith, Mrs J B,
[10000646]   24/10/2006   **AF**

Smith, Ms J E, BA, Academic Liaison Librarian, Saltire Centre, Glasgow.
[10022465]   05/11/1990   **ME**

Smith, Ms J E, Head of Library & Archives, Natural History Museum, London.
[39592]   14/03/1986   **ME**

Smith, Ms J E, BA MCLIP, Retired.
[31156]   16/09/1979   **CM21/06/1984**

Smith, Mrs J L, BEd (Hons), Learning Resource Assistant, Truro College.
[10033600]   01/04/2014   **ME**

Smith, Ms J M, BA (Hons) MCLIP, Research Services Manager, Squire Patton Boggs (UK) LLP, Leeds.
[43593]   09/11/1989   **RV27/11/2007**   **CM24/07/1996**

Smith, Miss J M, MCLIP, Retired.
[13611]   01/01/1965   **CM01/01/1970**

Smith, Rev J S, MA FCLIP, Retired.
[13619]   12/03/1954   **FE01/01/1968**

Smith, Mr K, PDip, Librarian, Mitchell Library, Glasgow.
[10020939]   24/04/2012   **ME**

Smith, Mrs K, BA (Hons), Library Assistant, Thatcham Library, Berks.
[10021981]   09/11/2012   **ME**

Smith, Mrs K, BA (Hons) MA MCLIP, Serv. Manager, Northumbria University, Newcastle.
[42366]   24/10/1988   **CM20/03/1996**

Smith, Ms K A M, MCLIP, Library Resource Centre Co-ordinator, St Augustine`s RC High School, Edinburgh.
[62044]   28/01/2003   **CM11/03/2009**

Smith, Mr K C, Libr., OFGEM, London.
[50122]   05/04/1994   **ME**

Smith, Mrs L, BSc DipLib MCLIP, Information Officer, SIGN, NHS QIS, Glasgow.
[60302]   14/03/2000   **CM14/03/2000**

Smith, Ms L, PhD Research Student, University of Strathclyde.
[10015786]   25/01/2010   **ME**

Smith, Ms L A, MCLIP, Business Information Manager, City Business Library, City of London.
[23094] 28/10/1974 **CM22/05/1979**

Smith, Ms L A E, BA MA, School Librarian, Prior Park College.
[10015812] 29/01/2010 **ME**

Smith, Miss L M, MCLIP, Retired.
[13631] 01/10/1971 **CM19/09/1974**

Smith, Mrs L M, MCLIP, School Librarian, Ecclesbourne School, Derbys.
[8049] 02/01/1970 **CM24/07/1973**

Smith, Mrs L M, BSc, Unwaged.
[47247] 01/07/1992 **ME**

Smith, Miss L M R, MCLIP, Life Member.
[13632] 01/01/1955 **CM01/01/1963**

Smith, Ms L N, BA (Hons) MSc, Senior Information Assistant – Acquisitions, BPP University Ltd.
[10001064] 12/01/2007 **ME**

Smith, Mrs M, MCLIP, Central Librarian, Aberdeen City Council.
[15241] 01/10/1971 **CM18/10/1976**

Smith, Ms M, ALA, College Librarian, Royal College of Surgeons of Edinburgh.
[13642] 21/09/1967 **ME**

Smith, Mrs M, BTh MSc, Group Library Manager, Subsea 7, Global Corporate Library.
[60251] 10/12/2001 **CM01/04/2002**

Smith, Ms M, Information Specialist, Engineering/Research Support Coordinator, Cranfield University.
[10006453] 19/10/2007 **ME**

Smith, Ms M, BA (Hons), Library and Information Manager, Cripps LLP.
[28367] 07/11/1977 **ME**

Smith, Mrs M A, BA MCLIP, Learning Resource Centre Manager, The Holt School, Wokingham.
[38785] 08/10/1985 **CM18/01/1989**

Smith, Mr M J, MPhil MSc BA (Hons) MCLIP, Information Specialist, RIBA Enterprises, Newcastle upon Tyne.
[54683] 19/02/1997 RV30/04/2014 **CM20/11/2002**

Smith, Dr M J, BSc (Hons) MSc MCLIP, Library Collection Manager, Natural History Museum.
[47968] 28/10/1992 **CM20/05/1998**

Smith, Ms M J, MCLIP, Senior Librarian, Cambridgeshire County Council Cambridge.
[26195] 18/08/1976 **CM01/01/1978**

Smith, Mrs M N E, BA MA,
[10010957] 15/09/2008 **ME**

Smith, Mrs M R, BA MCLIP, Exeter Health Library, Royal Devon & Exeter Foundation NHS Trust, Exeter.
[34554] 01/01/1982 **CM16/01/1986**

Smith, Mrs M S, FCLIP, Retired.
[13656] 15/09/1950 **FE01/01/1968**

Smith, Ms N C, Encore Assistant, Hull Central Library.
[10021989] 12/11/2012 **ME**

Smith, Mr N J, BA (Hons) MPhil MSc (Econ), Library and information professional.
[10013988] 27/09/1999 **ME**

Smith, Mrs N N, MA DipLib MCLIP, Director of Research, Right Management, London.
[29437] 18/08/1978 **CM26/10/1981**

Smith, Mr P, MSc MCLIP, Information Adviser, Sheffield Hallam University.
[61608] 03/10/2002 RV27/03/2014 **CM19/03/2008**

Smith, Mr P, BA DipLib MCLIP DMS MA, Retired.
[26806] 05/11/1976 **CM02/02/1979**

Smith, Mrs P J, MCLIP, Librarian, Alloa Academy, Clackmannanshire.
[65096] 01/11/2005 **CM10/11/2010**

Smith, Miss P L, BA MLS MCLIP, Retired.
[17747] 16/01/1950 **CM01/01/1954**

Smith, Mrs P M, BA (Hons) DipILM MCLIP FHEA, Academic Liaison Librarian, Liverpool John Moores University, Liverpool.
[53988] 14/10/1996 **CM10/07/2002**

Smith, Mr P M, BA (Hons) MSc (Econ) MCLIP, Librarian, Blackpool Aspire Academy, Blackpool.
[59573] 04/06/2001 **CM15/01/2003**

Smith, Ms R, MA MSc MCLIP, Head of Collections and Interpretation, National Library of Scotland.
[10020403] 23/02/2012 **CM20/03/1992**

Smith, Mr R A, MA MCLIP,
[32180] 28/01/1980 **CM17/05/1983**

Smith, Mr R F, MCLIP, Life Member.
[13680] 03/05/1937 **CM01/01/1947**

Smith, Ms R J, BA (Hons) DipIS MCLIP, Information Skills Adviser, London South Bank University.
[52196] 12/10/1995 **CM20/11/2002**

Smith, Miss R L, BA (Hons) MCLIP, Communications and Marketing Officer, Durham University Library and Heritage Collections.
[10016633] 01/05/2010 RV30/04/2014 **CM09/07/2013**

Smith, Mr R L, MA, Student, UCL.
[10035595] 22/10/2014 **ME**

Smith, Mrs S, Librarian, William Ellis School, London.
[10000697] 15/11/2006 **ME**

Smith, Mrs S, BA PGCE MCLIP, Retired.
[13690] 08/10/1969 **CM01/01/1972**

Smith, Ms S, BA (Hons), Student.
[10023408] 16/07/2013 **ME**

Smith, Miss S A L, BA, Assistant Librarian, Featherstone High School, Ealing.
[10010694] 26/08/2008 **ME**

Smith, Miss S E, BA MLS MCLIP, Learning Support Coordinator/Liaison Librarian, University of Reading.
[33160] 04/10/1980 **CM24/06/1983**

Smith, Mrs S E, BA (Hons) DipILM MCLIP, Librarian, Queen Elizabeth High School, Northumberland.
[47822] 14/10/1992 **CM18/03/1998**

Smith, Mr S G, MSc BA (Hons) PgDip, IT Instructor.
[61054] 19/02/2002 **ME**

Smith, Mr S J, BA (Hons) MCLIP, Group Library Manager, Library Services (Slough) Ltd, Slough Library.
[53720] 16/09/1996 **CM12/09/2001**

Smith, Mrs S J, BA MCLIP, Lifelong Learning & Local Studies Librarian, Herts County Council.
[41725] 22/02/1988 **CM26/05/1993**

Smith, Mrs S L, BA MCLIP, Borough Librarian, Telford Library, Shropshire.
[25579] 22/01/1976 **CM01/07/1994**

Smith, Mr S M, Lib. Assist., NERLRC, North Shields.
[10019615] 05/08/2011 **AF**

Smith, Miss S M, BA, Student, City University London.
[10033183] 18/02/2014 **ME**

Smith, Mr S P, BSc DipLib MCLIP, Academic Services Librarian Hugh Owen Library, Aberystwyth University.
[30266] 30/12/1978 **CM08/02/1982**

Smith, Miss S R R, BSc MA MCLIP, L. Development Manager, London Borough of Brent, L. Arts & Heritage.
[42989] 26/05/1989 **CM27/01/1993**

Smith, Ms S W, BSc MSc (Econ) MCLIP, Senior Librarian, Jet L. Leighton Hospital, Crewe.
[64961] 04/10/2005 **CM19/11/2008**

Smith, Mrs V, BSc (Econ) MCLIP MInstLM, Campus Support Manager (Library & IT), Edinburgh Napier University.
[50983]   07/11/1994   **CM17/05/2000**

Smith, Mrs V E, Part-time Student, Leicester City Library, University of Wales, Aberystwyth.
[64751]   28/06/2005   **ME**

Smith, Mrs W J, BA (Hons) MA MCLIP, Information Adviser, University of Wales Institute, Cardiff.
[46382]   30/10/1991   **CM21/05/1997**

Smith, Mrs W J, FCLIP, Life Member.
[1149]   22/02/1937   **FE01/01/1948**

Smith, Miss Y M, MA MCLIP, Academic Liaison Librarian, Edge Hill University.
[62884]   18/11/2003   **CM29/08/2007**

Smithson, Mrs D, MCLIP, Retired.
[13711]   23/08/1968   **CM01/01/1972**

Smithson, Mr D P R, BA (Hons) MSc MCLIP, Senior Information Advisor – E learning, Kingston College, Kingston-upon-Thames.
[56627]   23/09/1998   **CM15/01/2003**

Smithson, Ms H, MA, Business Information Officer, Institute of Directors, London.
[59606]   27/06/2001   **ME**

Smithson, Mrs H R, BA MA MSc MCLIP, Knowledge Officer, Oxford University. Careers Serv.
[10015951]   28/01/2010   **CM14/11/2012**

Smithson, Mrs L E, BA MA MCLIP, Team Leader Acquisitions and ILLs, University of Surrey Library.
[59255]   19/01/2001   **CM21/06/2006**

Smyth, Mrs A V, BA MLS MCLIP, Life Member.
[13720]   01/01/1970   **CM26/09/1977**

Smyth, Ms D M, BA MCLIP CMS CertEd, Retired.
[13721]   03/10/1967   **CM01/01/1971**

Smyth, Mrs J E, BSc PhD MSc, Assistant librarian, Scottish Government.
[39782]   17/07/1986   **CM29/03/2004**

Smyth, Mr N T, BA MSc (Econ) MCLIP, Arts Faculty Team Leader, Hallward Library, Nottingham.
[56472]   23/07/1998   **CM06/04/2005**

Smyth, Ms S, MSc, Assistant Subject Librarian, University of Ulster.
[10019746]   02/09/2011   **ME**

Snaith, Miss K, MA, Librarian, University of Nottingham.
[10017328]   29/07/2010   **ME**

Sneddon, Mrs L J, BA (Hons) PGCE MCLIP, Children's & Youth Services Librarian.
[10003004]   10/05/2007   **CM06/07/2011**

Snell, Mrs C, BSc, Employment not known.
[40701]   05/05/1987   **ME**

Snell, Miss H L, BA MCLIP, Outreach Librarian, University Hospital of North Staffordshire, Stoke on Trent.
[63908]   26/10/2004   **CM20/04/2009**

Snelling, Mrs C A, BA DMS MSc MCLIP, Librarian: Darwen Library, Blackburn with Darwen B. C., Lancs.
[34629]   19/01/1982   **CM24/03/1986**

Snelling, Mrs H R, BSc MCLIP, Assistant Librarian, Pendlebury Library of Music, University of Cambridge.
[31479]   12/10/1979   **CM13/09/1984**

Snelling, Ms J R, BA (Hons) MA MCLIP, Librarian, Corpus Christi College, Oxford.
[50138]   08/04/1994   **CM21/03/2001**

Snelling, Mr M W, BA DMS MCLIP, Resource Delivery Manager, University of Manchester Library, University Manchester.
[34563]   13/01/1982   **CM19/09/1984**

Snelling, Mrs P, Library Team Leader, Bucks New University.
[62530]   06/08/2003   **ME**

Snelling, Mrs S M, BSc DipLib MCLIP, Senior Information Advisor, Kingston University, Kingston.
[25210]   02/01/1976   **CM01/12/1977**

Snoad, Mrs N J, BA History, Information Officer, Norton Rose Fulbright.
[10001389]   14/02/2007   **ME**

Snow, Miss K, BA MSc MCLIP, Senior Research Librarian, University of Bristol.
[58810]   04/08/2000   **CM11/03/2009**

Snow, Miss R, BA, Knowledge Assistant, Veal Wasbrough Vizards.
[10022183]   15/01/2013   **AF**

Snowden, Mr A, BSc MSc MCLIP, Consultant, Fujitsu Serv., Bracknell.
[60647]   11/12/2001   **CM01/04/2002**

Snowden, Mr C W, MCLIP, Life Member.
[13746]   18/03/1946   **CM01/01/1955**

Snowley, Mr I R, BA MBA FCLIP, University Librarian, University of Lincoln.
[35753]   11/01/1983   **FE15/09/2004**

Socha, Miss L A, BA (Hons) MSc MCLIP, Senior Information Officer, Trowers & Hamlins, London.
[62442]   25/06/2003   **CM29/11/2006**

Softley, Ms K, BA MCLIP, Lib. Dev. Officer, North Neighbourhood, Edinburgh City L.
[33838]   14/03/1981   **CM27/09/1984**

Soley Barton, Mrs C F, MSc,
[37319]   02/07/1984   **ME**

Solinas, Mrs M, Library Assistant.
[10034163]   11/06/2014   **ME**

Solomon, Mrs E, DESCIO-InfoSkills-Del-1, DCSA Directorate strategic Transition – MOD.
[10033967]   14/05/2014   **ME**

Solomonsz, Ms F T, BA MCLIP, Retired.
[13755]   28/08/1961   **CM01/01/1968**

Somerville, Ms A, MA, Search Analyst, House of Commons.
[65175]   09/11/2005   **ME**

Somerville, Mr J H B, BA MA MCLIP, Unemployed.
[40051]   16/10/1986   **CM18/07/1990**

Somovilla, Miss C L, MA, Records & Information Manager, Financial Ombudsman Serv., London.
[56756]   08/10/1998   **ME**

Son, Miss J, BA, Student, University of Sheffield.
[10032319]   18/11/2013   **ME**

Sonley, Mrs V, BA MCLIP PgCLTHE FHEA, Academic Librarian, Teesside University, Middlesbrough.
[10014950]   16/10/1977   **CM18/09/1981**

Sooriasegaram, Mr A, BA (Hons), Library Assistant, British Architectural Library (Royal Institute of British Architects).
[10031906]   14/10/2013   **ME**

Soprano, Mrs M, BA DipLib MCLIP, Special Projects Archivist, California Institute of Technology, Pasadena, CA 91125, USA.
[39886]   06/10/1986   **CM22/05/1991**

Sorrell, Mrs L J, BA ACLIP, Senior Lib. Assistant, Nairn Library, Nairn.
[10019535]   22/07/2011   **ACL20/04/2012**

Soukup, Mrs D, ACLIP, Information Assistant, Kings College London.
[59525]   25/04/2001   **ACL17/05/2009**

Souter, Mrs F E, MA (Hons) PgDip, Community Librarian, Scone Library.
[10030338]   22/10/2013   **ME**

Souter, Ms J, BA DIPMAN MCLIP, Libraries Service Development Manager, Fife Cultural Trust.
[10021545]   19/01/1984   **CM15/03/1989**

South, Mrs A J, BSc DipLib, Assistant Librarian, Merchant Taylors' School, Northwood, Middlesex.
[42373]   24/10/1988   **ME**

South, Ms H L, BSc DipLib MCLIP, Faculty Librarian, University of Bath.
[47594]   05/10/1992   **CM27/11/1996**
South, Mrs S, BA DipLib MCLIP, Head of L., Bradford Grammar School.
[40796]   15/06/1987   **CM06/04/2005**
Southall, Mrs H V, BA MCLIP, Learning Res. Manager, Colston's Girls'
School, Bristol.
[32212]   25/01/1980   **CM27/01/1993**
Southard, Miss K, BA MPhil, Graduate Trainee, Newnham College
Library.
[10022269]   29/01/2013   **ME**
Southern, Mrs A J, BA (Hons) MA, Librarian, Djanogly City Academy,
Nottingham.
[10011640]   30/10/2008   **ME**
Southern, Ms K, Senior Librarian, Herbert Smith Freehills, London.
[10007886]   26/02/2008   **ME**
Southern, Mrs L M, Assistant Librarian, Bideford College.
[10034418]   11/07/2014   **ME**
Southgate, Mrs D, DipHE BA MCLIP, Head of Knowledge, Chartered
Institute of Marketing, Maidenhead.
[39247]   01/01/1986   **CM23/03/1993**
Southgate, Miss G D, BA (Hons), Senior Library Assistant, IT Support,
Arts and Social Studies Library, Cardiff.
[10021110]   30/05/2012   **AF**
Southwell, Ms J, BA (Hons) Dip Lib, Library Service Manager, Oxford
Central Library, Oxfordshire CC.
[10014855]   03/11/1977   **ME**
Sowerbutts, Mr D L, BA MCLIP, Retired.
[13780]   14/01/1963   **CM01/01/1966**
Sowman, Ms S, BA MCLIP, Content Services Officer, CIPD, London.
[28573]   13/01/1978   **CM17/02/1983**
Sowood, Ms Y, ACLIP, Library Manager Skelmersdale.
[10010716]   18/09/2008   **ACL17/06/2009**
Spacey, Dr R E, BA (Hons) MA PhD MCLIP, Research Fellow, School of
Education, University of Lincoln.
[59230]   09/01/2001   **CM21/03/2007**
Spackman, Mrs K, BLib MCLIP, Lead Librarian Information Services,
Oxfordshire County Council.
[37187]   22/02/1984   **CM13/06/1989**
Spalding, Mrs C J, BA (Hons) MCLIP, Unwaged.
[28119]   04/10/1977   **CM20/09/1995**
Spalding, Mrs M A, BSc MCLIP, Research associate, centre for digital
scholarship; UCA.
[38224]   04/02/1985   **CM15/03/1989**
Spalding, Ms M P, BA (Hons) DipLib, Web Editor, Department of Health,
London.
[44409]   05/10/1990   **ME**
Sparham, Mrs S E, BA (Hons) MCLIP, Librarian, Schools Lib. Serv.,
Northumberland.
[50148]   11/04/1994   **CM23/09/1998**
Sparks, Miss H T, BA MCLIP, Retired.
[33162]   08/10/1980   **CM30/08/1985**
Sparrow, Mr D A, BA (Hons) MA MCLIP, Library& Information Services
Manager, Equality & Human Rights Commission.
[38924]   18/10/1985   **CM15/03/1989**
Sparrow, Mrs G M, BA MCLIP, Retired.
[37939]   16/11/1984   **CM15/11/1988**
Sparrow, Mr K T, BA DipLib MCLIP, Library Assistant, Sch. of Oriental &
African Studies, University of London.
[34788]   16/02/1982   **CM13/12/1988**
Speake, Ms R A, BA (Hons) DipLIS MCLIP, Operational Manager,
Coventry City Council.
[49560]   12/11/1993   **CM19/05/1999**
Spears, Mr K G, OBE BSc MBA MCLIP, Librarian, Wells Cathedral.
[13790]   08/05/1965   **CM01/01/1968**

Speed, Ms J L, BA (Hons) MCLIP, Senior Systems Librarian, Cheshire
Shared Serv.
[38147]   23/01/1985   **CM16/11/1994**
Speedling, Ms K L, BA, Student, City University, London.
[10032006]   21/10/2013   **ME**
Speight, Mr T D, MA (Oxon) MSc (Econ) MCLIP, L. Manager, Berwin
Leighton Paisner, London.
[52497]   02/11/1995   **CM18/03/1998**
Speller, Ms E A, BA (Hons) MSc FHEA, Library Systems and User
Education Manager, Trinity Laban Conservatoire of Music and
Dance.
[63686]   24/08/2004   **ME**
Spellman, Miss J F, BA MCLIP, Librarian, Queen Elizabeth Sixth Form
College, Darlington.
[35032]   02/07/1982   **CM08/03/1988**
Spence, Mr D J F,
[10020380]   10/02/2012   **ME**
Spence, Mrs G M, BA DipLib, Retired.
[44593]   01/11/1990   **ME**
Spence, Ms H P, BEd (Hons) MA MCLIP, Knowledge Manager, Enfield
P. C. T.
[47578]   02/10/1992   **CM22/11/1995**
Spence, Mrs S A, BA (Hons) MCLIP, L. &Information Service Manager,
Swinton L.
[29083]   06/03/1978   **CM01/07/1988**
Spencer, Ms B, Student, University of Strathclyde.
[10035460]   14/10/2014   **ME**
Spencer, Mr J, Departamental records Officer, Office For National
Statistics.
[10033804]   01/05/2014   **ME**
Spencer, Mrs J, MBE BA MBA MCLIP, Head of Library & Museum
Services, Bolton Libraries, Bolton County Council.
[28237]   03/10/1977   **CM09/07/1981**
Spencer, Ms K L, BA, Student, Victoria University of Wellington.
[10033187]   18/02/2014   **ME**
Spencer, Miss L A, BA DipLib MCLIP DMS MIMgt, Retired.
[28174]   18/10/1977   **CM17/12/1980**
Spencer, Ms L O, Mgmt Consultant, Stafford.
[16038]   19/02/1970   **CM29/07/1974**
Spenser, Mrs E J, BA (Hons) MCLIP, Librarian, Bridgnorth Library,
Shropshire.
[52686]   21/11/1995   **CM25/07/2001**
Sperring, Mr D, MSc, Librarian, Digital Library Support, University of
Nottingham.
[64964]   05/10/2005   **ME**
Spezi, Ms V, MA, Research Associate, LISU, Centre for Information
Management, School of Business & Economics, Loughborough
University.
[10021096]   29/05/2012   **ME**
Spiby, Mrs J N, MA DipLib MCLIP, Unwaged.
[29462]   14/07/1978   **CM13/08/1981**
Spickernell, Mrs M P, MCLIP, Retired.
[16235]   05/02/1949   **CM01/01/1954**
Spiers, Mr D L, AdvDipEd MCLIP, LRC Co-ordinator, Craigroyston
Comm. High School, Edinburgh.
[23161]   07/11/1974   **CM17/11/1977**
Spiller, Miss L Z, BA (Hons), Assistant Information Specialist, Baker &
McKenzie, London.
[10007883]   08/04/2004   **AF**
Spina, Mrs R B, BA MA DipLib MCLIP MSocInd, Hd. of Teaching &
Research Support, School of Oriental & African Studies, University
of London (retired).
[26424]   01/01/1976   **CM25/03/1985**

Spink, Mr P J, BA MCLIP,
[21958]   22/01/1974   **CM22/09/1980**
Spink, Ms R E, MLS, Unwaged.
[10006255]   28/09/2007   **ME**
Spink, Mrs W T, BA MCLIP, Res. Officer – Resources (Job Share), Age UK, London.
[13829]   06/10/1971   **CM29/09/1980**
Splaine, Mrs J, MCLIP, Acting Arts Co-Ordinator, Manchester City Council, Manchester Central Library.
[55534]   20/10/1997   **CM08/08/2008**
Spong, Miss A, BA, Grad. Trainee Librarian, East Surrey College, Surrey.
[10015134]   14/10/2009   **ME**
Spooner, Mrs D L, ACLIP, Sr. Lib. Assistant, Thornton Library, Lancs.
[10013139]   02/04/2009   **ACL11/12/2009**
Sprawling, Mrs J E, BA MCLIP, School Librarian, Bolton Metropolitan Borough Council, Turton Media Arts College.
[35007]   15/06/1982   **CM21/08/1986**
Spreadbury, Ms H E, BSc (Hons) MA MCLIP, Unwaged.
[54154]   07/11/1996   **CM29/03/2004**
Spreull, Mrs G S, ACLIP BA (Hons), Sch. Librarian, Blackbourne Middle School, Bury St Edmunds.
[10010827]   28/08/2008   **ACL23/09/2009**
Spring, Ms H C, BA (Hons) MCLIP, Senior Lecturer/Clinical Librarian, York St John University, York.
[52307]   25/10/1995   **CM16/05/2001**
Spring, Miss L, BA PGCE ADTLLS, Student, City College, Plymouth.
[10031593]   29/10/2013   **ME**
Springer, Mrs A, ACLIP, Librarian, Balcarras School, Cheltenham.
[65289]   28/11/2005   **ACL01/10/2008**
Springer, Mrs J, BA (Hons) MA, Career Break.
[56232]   14/04/1998   **ME**
Springer, Mrs J M, BA DipLib MCLIP, Acquisitions/Periodicals Librarian, University of Southampton.
[27914]   12/10/1977   **CM30/04/1981**
Springham, Miss S A, BLib MCLIP, Deputy Head of Library Serv., Brighton & Sussex University Hospital, NHS Trust, East Sussex.
[41603]   26/01/1988   **CM29/01/1992**
Sproat, Miss A E, BA (Hons) MA DipLib MCLIP, Librarian, Henry Moore Institute, Leeds.
[47995]   30/10/1992   **CM18/03/1998**
Sproston, Mr G F, BA MCLIP, Retired.
[13839]   14/02/1967   **CM01/01/1970**
Sproston, Miss S V, BA (Hons) MCLIP, Learning Resources Manager., West Notts. College, Mansfield.
[46469]   08/11/1991   **CM03/10/2007**
Spruce, Mrs W J, BA MCLIP, Retired.
[13842]   28/01/1957   **CM01/01/1961**
Spurgin, Miss C B, MA (Hons), School Librarian, Kilgraston School, Bridge of Earn, Perth.
[52050]   02/10/1995   **ME**
Spurrell, Mrs L, BA (Hons), Library Assistant, Shenley Brook End School.
[10023072]   04/06/2013   **AF**
Squire, Miss K, BA PGdip MCLIP, Academic Liaison Librarian University of Westminster.
[10019951]   06/10/2011   **CM27/08/2014**
Squire, Mrs L, Learning Resources Centre Manager, Christ's College Guildford.
[10034169]   20/06/2014   **ME**
Squire, Mr P A, DES SMAP – Information Manager, Ministry of Defence.
[10032800]   14/01/2014   **ME**

Squire, Mrs S C, BA MA, Library & Information Manager, St Crispin's School, Berkshire.
[59795]   03/10/2001   **ME**
Squires, Ms D, BA (Hons) RSA DipESP, Learning Resource Manager, Isleworth & Syon School for Boys, Isleworth.
[10022802]   23/04/2013   **ME**
St Aubyn, Miss P, MSc Econ, Librarian, SPSA Scottish Police College, Kincardine, Fife.
[29832]   02/10/1978   **CM22/10/1982**
St John, Ms S A, BA MA MCLIP, Tourist Information Support Assistant, East Cambridgeshire District Council.
[44941]   23/01/1991   **CM23/03/1994**
St. John-Coleman, Mrs M A, BSc MCLIP, Retired.
[14285]   14/10/1971   **CM11/10/1973**
Stables, Mrs L, BA (Hons), Senior Information Librarian, Barnsley Central Library.
[10013613]   15/05/2009   **ME**
Stacey, Ms A, BA DipLib MCLIP, Business Analyst, Capita Libraries, Birmingham.
[38129]   21/01/1985   **CM06/10/1987**
Stacey, Mr D J, BA (Hons) MA MCLIP FHEA, Faculty Librarian, University of Bath.
[64803]   15/07/2005   RV15/07/2014   **CM17/09/2008**
Stacey, Mrs M C, BA MCLIP, Retired.
[13854]   02/10/1964   **CM01/01/1967**
Stacey, Mr M J, MA MCLIP, Retired.
[13855]   22/04/1964   **CM01/01/1967**
Stacey, Mr R W, FCLIP, Life Member.
[17771]   12/02/1952   **FE01/01/1959**
Stackley, Ms T, MSc LIS, Student, City University, London.
[10030374]   07/10/2013   **ME**
Stadler, Mrs D E, MCLIP, Life Member.
[10007087]   16/03/1941   **CM01/01/1947**
Stafford, Mr C J, MCLIP, Retired.
[13858]   04/11/1965   **CM01/01/1970**
Stafford, Mr G A, MA AALIA FCLIP, Life Member.
[17772]   10/03/1953   **FE01/01/1960**
Stagg, Ms E J, Project Manager (conserving Local Communities Heritage), Glamorgan Arch., Cardiff.
[10011893]   26/11/2008   **ME**
Staines, Mrs E, BSc (Eng) ACLIP, Lib. Supervisor, Bradford on Avon. Wiltshire.
[10012325]   27/01/2009   **ACL14/11/2012**
Stains Coldwell, Mrs H J, Information Assistant, Health & Safety Executive.
[10020297]   10/01/2012   **ME**
Stairmand-Jackson, Mrs A C, BSc (Hons) DipLib, Assistant Liaison Librarian, Mary Seacole Library, Birmingham City University.
[10013724]   22/05/2009   **ME**
Stallard, Ms V M, BMus (Hons) MA MCLIP, Assistant Librarian, ASSL, Cardiff University, Cardiff.
[59082]   09/11/2000   **CM04/02/2004**
Stanbury, Mrs S C, BA MA MCLIP, Head of Libraries & Archive, Haberdashers' Aske's Boys School.
[35088]   26/07/1982   **CM13/09/1984**
Stancombe, Mrs S, BA MCLIP, Sch. Lib. La Sante Union Secondary School, Highgate Road, London.
[35928]   14/02/1983   **CM25/10/1984**
Standen, Mrs A J, BA (Hons), Senior Librarian, Moira House Girls School, Eastbourne.
[63187]   03/03/2004   **ME**
Stanfield, Mrs K B, BSc MCLIP, Head of Knowledge Management, CMS Cameron McKenna, London.
[38646]   26/08/1985   **CM16/02/1988**

Stanford, Ms E, BA, Graduate Library Trainee, BDLSS.
[10031881]   10/10/2013   **ME**

Stanforth, Ms J M, MCLIP, CYP Services Development Manager 6-11s
Lancs County Council.
[20302]   05/02/1973   **CM01/01/1977**

Staniforth, Mrs S C, BA MCLIP, School Library Consultant.
[27431]   02/04/1977   **CM09/10/1980**

Stanistreet, Mrs J E, MA MCLIP, Retired.
[13885]   25/11/1968   **CM01/01/1972**

Stanley, Mr M, Student, Defence Academy.
[10032011]   11/07/2014   **ME**

Stanley, Ms T S, BA (Hons) MSc, Deputy University Librarian, Cardiff.
[50481]   18/08/1994   **ME**

Stannard, Mrs P, BA (Hons) MCLIP, Unwaged.
[54510]   09/01/1997   **CM15/10/2002**

Stanney, Mr P J, BA MA, Learning Resources Centre Facilitator.,
Salford City College, Worsley.
[10019037]   13/04/2011   **ME**

Stansbury, Ms C T, BLib MCLIP, Secretary.
[38554]   01/07/1985   **CM21/12/1988**

Stanton, Mrs C S, Senior Lib. Assistant, Haywards Heath Lib.
[10009460]   21/05/2008   **AF**

Stanton, Mrs J R, MCLIP, Housewife.
[20552]   04/04/1973   **CM06/09/1978**

Stanton, Mr T M, BA MA MCLIP, Information Librarian, West Sussex L.
Serv., Crawley L.
[55268]   11/09/1997   **CM15/01/2003**

Stanton, Mrs W J, BA MCLIP, Medical Librarian, University of
Nottingham, Queens Medical Centre, Notts.
[23718]   01/01/1975   **CM29/01/1979**

Staples, Mr F D, MCLIP, Retired.
[13900]   09/02/1954   **CM01/01/1958**

Staples, Mrs K J, BMus MSc MCLIP, Subj. Librarian, Health & Social
Care, Oxford Brookes University Librarian, Oxford.
[58162]   10/11/1999   **CM19/11/2003**

Staples, Mrs L M, MCLIP, Life Member.
[13902]   26/09/1949   **CM01/01/1961**

Starbuck, Mrs F A, BA DipLib MCLIP, Senior Information Librarian,
Leeds Metropolitan University Library, Leeds.
[40447]   31/01/1987   **CM30/01/1991**

Starbuck, Mrs S R, LLB DipLib MA MCLIP, Information Officer, Faculty
of Arts & Human Sciences., University of Surrey.
[39912]   01/10/1986   **CM01/07/1991**

Starkie, Miss S, Student, Coleg Llandrillo.
[10032513]   11/12/2013   **ME**

Starks, Mr P, BSc BTh GradDipInfoMan,
[10022449]   05/03/2013   **ME**

Starr, Mr S R, Driver/Assistant, School Library Service, Hampshire
County Council.
[62388]   21/05/2003   **ME**

Statham, Mr M H W, MA FCLIP, Life Member.
[13912]   01/01/1953   **FE01/01/1959**

Statham, Mr M S, BA (Hons) MA, College Librarian, Gonville & Caius
College, Cambridge.
[49164]   08/10/1993   **CM27/11/1996**

Staunton, Ms M T, BA DipLib MCLIP, Head of Library and Archive,
Harrow School.
[39605]   01/04/1986   **CM15/05/1989**

Stavrinides, Ms N, BA MA LPC, Library Assistant, University of Bath.
[10032708]   07/01/2014   **ME**

Stead, Ms M, BA (Hons) DipLIS,
[50624]   01/10/1994   **ME**

Steadman, Mrs A, BA (Double Hons), Head of Libraries and Learning
Resources, British School of Brussels.
[10020633]   14/03/2012   **ME**

Stearn, Mr R R, BA MCLIP, Young Persons Library Worker, Heywood
Library RMBC.
[30878]   22/05/1979   **CM13/07/1981**

Stebbings, Mrs A C, BA MLib MCLIP, Head of Member Services at The
London Library.
[45445]   06/02/1991   **CM16/12/1992**

Stedman, Mrs E, Student, Coleg Llandrillo Menai.
[10035733]   31/10/2014   **ME**

Stedman, Mr R, FCLIP, Life Member,
[13923]   05/02/1956   **FE01/01/1971**

Steel, Miss L, BA MA, Information Officer, University of Law, London.
[10010831]   28/08/2008   **ME**

Steel, Mrs M, MCLIP, Team Librarian, Norfolk Sch. L. Serv., Norwich.
[10015966]   02/10/1973   **CM01/08/1977**

Steel-Bryan, Mrs N J, Student, University of Sheffield.
[10032640]   23/12/2013   **ME**

Steele, Miss A E, BA PgDip, Assistant Researcher, Hogan Lovells
International LLP.
[10032964]   31/01/2014   **ME**

Steele, Miss C L, ACLIP, Administration Assistant, Library HQ, Mold.
[10022314]   05/02/2013   **ACL20/06/2014**

Steele, Mr C R, MA FALIA FCLIP, Emeritus Fellow, Australian National
University.
[13925]   14/01/1966   **FE22/07/1998**

Steele, Mr G, BA (Hons) MA MCLIP, Library Systems Manager, Glasgow
Caledonian University, Glasgow.
[66158]   04/10/2006   **CM07/09/2011**

Steele, Mrs H, BSc MA, Librarian, Mental Health Library, Leeds and
York Partnerships NHS Foundation Trust.
[10021300]   09/07/2012   **ME**

Steele, Mr H F, BA FCLIP, Life Member.
[17777]   21/10/1944   **FE01/01/1951**

Steele, Mr P, MA Msc PGCE,
[10031752]   01/10/2013   **ME**

Steele, Ms R E, BA MA MSc MCLIP, Clinical/Site Librarian, Tees, Esk &
Wear Valleys NHS Foundation Trust.
[10006613]   11/09/2007   **CM19/10/2012**

Steemson, Mr M J, Principal, The Caldeson Consultancy, Wellington,
New Zealand.
[60100]   21/07/1998   **ME**

Steer, Mrs M J, BA (Hons) DipLIS MCLIP, Subject Librarian, University
of Bristol, Bristol.
[46498]   12/11/1991   **CM16/11/1994**

Stefanzzi, Mr A, BA (Hons), Student, Robert Gordon University.
[10031973]   16/10/2013   **ME**

Stein, Mrs H, BA (Hons) MSc Econ, Assistant Librarian, Wodehouse
Library, Dulwich College.
[10006256]   26/09/2007   **ME**

Stein, Mrs L, BA (Hons) PgDipLS MCLIP, School Librarian, Alness
Academy, Ross-Shire.
[65166]   01/11/2005   **CM11/03/2009**

Steiner, Ms K, MMathPhil, Student, Department of Information Studies,
UCL.
[10031743]   01/10/2013   **ME**

Steinhaus, Mrs E R, BA DipLib MCLIP, Part-time School Librarian,
Menorah Primary School, London.
[28055]   06/10/1977   **CM14/01/1980**

Stekis, Miss S J, MCLIP, Life Member.
[17781]   22/02/1954   **CM01/01/1958**

Stemp, Ms J, BA (Hons) PgDipILM MCLIP, Librarian, Trust Library,
Clinical Skills, Queen Elizabeth Hospital, Gateshead.
[51753]   21/06/1995   CM19/03/2008

Stennett, Ms R E, MA DipInf, Bibl. Serv. Assistant Librarian, Canterbury
Christ Church University.
[47600]   05/10/1992   ME

Stepan, Mrs S M, BA, Content Creation Officer, Leeds City Council.
[41738]   28/02/1988   ME

Stephan, Ms K, BS (History) MA MCLIP, Academic Liaison Librarian,
Liverpool John Moores University.
[65754]   04/05/2006   CM03/10/2007

Stephen, Mrs C E D, MSc PgDip MA (Hons) MCLIP FHEA, Head of
Library and Learning Skills, Coventry University London Campus.
[62697]   09/10/2003   CM13/06/2007

Stephen, Ms H E, MSc MCLIP, Subject Librarian for Sociology and
Social, Therapeutic and Community Studies, Goldsmiths, University
of London.
[44030]   03/04/1990   CM25/07/2001

Stephen, Mrs R A R, MA DipLib MCLIP, Systems & Support Librarian,
The Moray Council.
[36357]   01/10/1983   CM14/02/1990

Stephens, Mr A R C, OBE BSc MCLIP, Board Secretary and Head of
International Engagement, British Library.
[10007773]   20/11/1977   CM01/07/1987

Stephens, Mrs E R, BScEcon MCLIP, Circulation Services Supervisor,
Information Services, Senate House Library, University of London.
[62435]   25/06/2003   CM17/09/2008

Stephens, Mrs K D, BEd (Hons) ACLIP, Young People's Serv. Librarian,
Hemel Hempstead Library, Herts.
[10015954]   03/02/2010   ACL12/05/2011

Stephens, Mrs L B, Resource Librarian, Telford Learning Centre,
Telford.
[48438]   08/01/1993   ME

Stephens, Miss S V, BA DipLib, Librarian, Bird & Bird LLP, London.
[37404]   20/08/1984   ME

Stephenson, Ms A, MCLIP, Child. Serv. & Reader Development
Manager, North Tyneside L. & Museum, Wallsend Library.
[53299]   26/04/1996   CM21/11/2007

Stephenson, Mrs D, Career Break.
[62682]   02/10/2003   ME

Stephenson, Mrs J, BLib MCLIP, Head of Health Serv. L., University of
Southampton, Southampton.
[29769]   09/10/1978   CM30/06/1983

Stephenson, Mrs J T, BA (Hons) MCLIP, Information & Comm.
Development Manager, Durham C. C., Culture & Leisure.
[51346]   25/01/1995   CM23/07/1997

Stephenson, Mrs K D, BA PGLIS FHEA, Southampton Solent
University.
[46250]   18/10/1991   ME

Sterling, Ms D M, Admin Officer, Foreign & Commonwealth Office.
[10035483]   15/10/2014   ME

Stevens, Ms A J, BA MCLIP, Resources Team Leader.
[35771]   19/01/1983   CM15/02/1989

Stevens, Dr B E S, BA PhD MCLIP, Retired.
[13980]   01/04/1957   CM01/01/1963

Stevens, Miss C, BSc (Hons), Deputy Head of Library, University of St
Mark & St John.
[10001778]   06/07/2004   ME

Stevens, Miss E, BA (Hons) PGCE MCLIP, LRC Manager, Hartpury
College.
[56445]   10/07/1998   RV02/03/2010   CM29/03/2004

Stevens, Miss E A, MCLIP,
[43014]   12/06/1989   CM01/04/2002

Stevens, Mrs J, BA (Hons) MCLIP, Site Librarian, Manchester L. &
Information Serv.
[49686]   25/11/1993   CM09/11/2005

Stevens, Miss K E, BA (Hons), Children's Librarian., Wandsworth Town
Library.
[44228]   18/07/1990   ME

Stevens, Miss L A, MCLIP, Site Librarian, Shrewsbury & Telford
Hospital NHS Trust – Princess Royal Hospital, Telford.
[58383]   24/01/2000   CM11/07/2012

Stevens, Mr P J, BA (Hons), Librarian and Archivist, Repton School.
[10035108]   15/09/2014   ME

Stevens, Miss P M, MCLIP, Retired.
[13991]   04/09/1964   CM01/01/1971

Stevens, Mrs S J, DipLib, Information Officer, Bank of England.
[52717]   24/11/1995   ME

Stevens, Miss S R, MCLIP, Research Support Librarian, University of
Wolverhampton.
[62669]   02/10/2003   CM28/01/2009

Stevenson, Ms A, MA (Hons) Msc, Head of Learning Resources,
Glasgow School of Art.
[10035698]   31/10/2014   ME

Stevenson, Mr B G, BA DMS MCLIP, Retired.
[14001]   02/04/1966   CM01/01/1971

Stevenson, Mr C C, MCLIP, Retired.
[14004]   01/01/1958   CM01/01/1965

Stevenson, Mr D J, BA, Senior Area Lib. (West), Midlothian District
Library, Bonnyrigg Library.
[30546]   09/02/1979   CM08/07/1982

Stevenson, Ms F, BA MCLIP, Unwaged.
[23693]   13/01/1975   CM02/07/1979

Stevenson, Ms H A, BLib MCLIP, Assistant Librarian, Lancing College.
[21925]   01/02/1974   CM18/12/1978

Stevenson, Mr M A, BA MCLIP, Life Member.
[14009]   09/09/1957   CM01/01/1961

Stevenson, Dr M B, BSc PhD MA, Retired.
[45871]   01/07/1991   ME

Stevenson, Mr P, BSc (Hon) MSc, Senior Health Information Specialist,
Airedale NHS Foundation trust.
[10016225]   10/12/2010   ME

Stevenson, Mrs P, BA (Hons) MCLIP RLIANZA, Unwaged.
[55569]   21/10/1997   CM15/05/2002

Stevenson, Miss R, Student, University of Sheffield.
[10032940]   30/01/2014   ME

Stevenson, Mrs S V, BA MCLIP, Faculty. Librarian, University of
Portsmouth.
[26641]   26/10/1976   CM30/01/1979

Stevenson, Miss V, BA MSc, Student.
[10012558]   23/02/2009   ME

Stevenson, Ms V E, BA (Hons), Head of Research and Learner
Support, Liverpool John Moores University.
[33165]   14/10/1980   ME

Steward, Ms A K, ACLIP, Lib. Assistant, Sheringham high School,
Sheringham.
[10015555]   14/12/2009   ACL13/04/2011

Stewart, Mrs C, MCLIP, Librarian, Northwest Area, Glasgow.
[10015107]   13/10/2009   CM14/11/2012

Stewart, Ms C H, BA (Hons) MA, Specialist Systems Librarian, NHS
Greater Glasgow & Clyde.
[53833]   03/10/1996   RV02/03/2010   CM17/03/1999

Stewart, Mr C J, MCLIP,
[10021238]   08/06/1968   CM18/09/1973

Stewart, Mr D C, BA DipLib FCLIP, Director of Health L. N. W., NHS
Reg.
[33528]   14/01/1981   FE06/07/2011

Stewart, Miss D J, BA (Hons), Student.
[10033413]   11/03/2014   ME
Stewart, Miss F, Student.
[10032141]   29/10/2013   ME
Stewart, Miss H M, MA DipLib, School Librarian, Breechin High School.
[10001956]   03/11/1992   ME
Stewart, Mrs J, BLib MLib MCLIP, Retired.
[23770]   04/02/1975   CM26/09/1977
Stewart, Mrs J A, BA MCLIP, Service Development Librarian, Fife
Cultural Trust.
[39419]   19/01/1986   CM18/09/1991
Stewart, Ms J E D, BLib MA MCLIP, Learning Res. Centre Manager,
Yale College of Wrexham.
[42997]   31/05/1989   CM19/11/2003
Stewart, Mr J M, BA (Hons) DipIS, Assistant Librarian, Ministry of
Justice, London.
[46317]   24/10/1991   ME
Stewart, Mrs L J M, BSc MCLIP, Senior Library Assistant, Monifieth
Library, Angus Council.
[10001069]   12/01/2007   CM13/11/2013
Stewart, Mrs L M, BA MCLIP, Team Librarian, Aberdeen CC.
[40201]   06/11/1986   CM16/09/1992
Stewart, M A, MA, Subject Librarian., University of the West of
Scotland., Ayr Campus.
[44238]   23/07/1990   ME
Stewart, Mrs M C, BA AKC DipLib MCLIP, Librarian, Rydens School.
[24715]   03/10/1975   CM03/10/1977
Stewart, Miss M J, BA MCLIP, School Librarian, Clydeview Academy,
Inverclyde.
[28686]   27/11/1977   CM30/04/1982
Stewart, Mrs O, MCLIP, Life Member.
[14036]   22/02/1962   CM01/01/1968
Stewart, Dr R M, BA MCLIP, Comm. Librarian, Wishaw Library, North
Lanarks.
[31160]   28/08/1979   CM22/11/1995
Stewart, Ms S A, MSc BSc, Information Assistant/Student, City
University.
[10018090]   15/11/2010   ME
Stewart, Dr S M, MA (Hons) PhD MCLIP, Librarian, Broxburn Academy,
West Lothian.
[60866]   13/12/2001   CM15/09/2004
Stewart, Mr W J, BA (Hons) MA, Unwaged.
[56353]   08/06/1998   ME
Sticpewich, Mrs S A, MBA, Librarian, St Catherine's prep School,
Bramley.
[10019920]   04/10/2011   ME
Stiles, Mr D E, MCLIP, Retired.
[17790]   19/10/1942   CM01/01/1949
Stiles, Mrs T A, BA (Hons) MCLIP PGCE, NHS Lib.
[41477]   07/01/1988   CM23/03/1994
Still, Mr J G, MA FCLIP, Life Member.
[14050]   16/10/1947   FE01/01/1965
Still, Mrs M, MSc ACLIP, Librarian, North Tees &Hartlepool Nhs Trust,
University Hospital of North Tees.
[10011804]   14/11/2008   ACL14/03/2012
Stimpson, Mrs F H, BA MA DipLib MCLIP, Freelance rare books
librarian and researcher with a particular interest in the history of
reading.
[24730]   10/10/1975   CM12/09/1977
Stirling, Miss C S, BA (Hons) PgDip, Senior Library Assistant,
Edinburgh University Main L.
[59292]   31/01/2001   ME

Stirling, Ms I E, BA MLitt MCLIP FHEA, HaSS Faculty Librarian,
University of Strathclyde.
[19554]   20/11/1972   CM29/12/1978
Stirrat, Mrs E G, Collections Officer, Scottish Parliament.
[10013945]   18/06/2009   ME
Stirrup, Ms A J, BA (Hons) MCLIP, Ops. Manager, Richmond upon
Thames Lib.
[34952]   14/05/1982   CM14/12/1984
Stitson, Miss C A, BA DipLib MCLIP, Lead Librarian, Reader Services:
Adults, Oxfordshire L.
[38891]   15/10/1985   CM27/05/1992
Stitt, Ms D E, BA, Sr. Researcher, Hogan Lovells International LLP,
London.
[61117]   21/02/2002   ME
Stobo, Miss V, BA (Hons) MSc, PhD Student, University of Glasgow.
[10032374]   29/11/2013   ME
Stock, Ms E J, Sch. L. Serv. Co-ordinator, Salford City Council, Salford.
[47567]   02/10/1992   ME
Stock, Ms E R, Liaison Librarian, University of Sheffield.
[65071]   24/10/2005   ME
Stock, Mr N M, DipLib MCLIP, Assistant Librarian, Ministry of Justice,
London.
[40005]   09/10/1986   CM16/10/1989
Stockbridge Bland, Mrs S C, BA MA MCLIP, Retired.
[14063]   01/01/1970   CM28/09/1973
Stockdale, Miss J H, MCLIP, Customer Service Officer, Kirklees
Council., Huddersfield.
[14064]   24/01/1969   CM24/09/1973
Stocker, Miss H, MA, Librarian, Nazarene Theological College.
[10031843]   06/01/2014   ME
Stocks, Miss M Y, MCLIP CertEd, Life Member.
[14071]   17/03/1941   CM01/01/1946
Stocks, Mr P J, MSc, Academic Support Librarian (The Media School
and the Faculty of Science and Technology), Bournemouth
University.
[10014589]   18/08/2009   ME
Stockwell, Mrs A P, MCLIP, Sch. Librarian, St Augustines Catholic High
School, Redditch.
[32742]   01/08/1980   CM02/08/1982
Stockwell, Mrs C A, BA MCLIP, Casual Shop Assistant Marks and
Spencer.
[37556]   07/10/1984   CM18/07/1991
Stoddard, Mrs K, BA (Hons) MSc, Researcher, Guardian News &
Media, London.
[10016626]   01/05/2010   ME
Stoddart, Miss A, BA DipLib MCLIP, Employment not known.
[36564]   21/10/1983   CM10/11/1987
Stoker, Mrs A H, BA MCLIP, Unwaged.
[18325]   07/10/1972   CM20/07/1976
Stokes, Mrs K, BA (Hons) MSc MCLIP, Business Information Specialist,
Cranfield School of Management, Cranfield University, Bedfordshire.
[55792]   24/11/1997   CM12/03/2003
Stokes, Dr P J, PhD MSc BA (Hons) BSc, Subject Librarian, Anglia
Ruskin University.
[57178]   04/01/1999   CM19/01/2000
Stone, Mrs A F, MCLIP, Unemployed.
[19575]   14/11/1972   CM08/07/1976
Stone, Mrs A L, BA MSc, Library Information Administrator, University of
the West of England.
[10006262]   26/09/2007   ME
Stone, Mr G, BSc DipILS MCLIP, Information Resources Manager,
University of Huddersfield.
[49528]   10/11/1993   CM31/01/1996

Stone, Ms G, BA MLS, L. S. A., Western Primary School, Winchester.
[38652] 02/09/1985 ME

Stone, Mr M B, DipLib MCLIP, Sector Libraries Manager, Royal Greenwich Libraries, Greenwich Leisure Limited.
[30549] 31/01/1979 CM16/02/1981

Stone, Mrs M I, BA MA MCLIP, Assistant Librarian, UCL.
[55798] 26/11/1997 CM21/03/2001

Stone, Mr M L, MCLIP, Assistant Librarian, Bradford Teaching Hospitals NHS FT.
[65872] 12/06/2006 CM27/08/2014

Stone, Mr M P, BA MCLIP HonFCLIP, Co. Secretary, Guinevere Hotels Ltd.
[27371] 18/03/1977 HFE24/10/2002

Stone, Mr N H F, MCLIP, Retired.
[14091] 24/01/1952 CM01/01/1961

Stone, Mrs P A, Teaching Assistant.
[10010169] 09/07/2008 ME

Stone, Miss R G, BA (Hons), Student, Sheffield University.
[63990] 22/11/2004 ME

Stone, Mr R N, BA MArAd MCLIP, Records Manager – Global Policy & Oversight, Royal Bank of Scotland, London.
[60430] 07/10/1997 CM07/10/1997

Stone, Mr S A M, BA (Hons) MPA, Student, UCL.
[10006441] 22/10/2007 ME

Stonebanks, Mrs J, BA (Hons) MCLIP, Reader Services Manager.
[28685] 06/01/1978 CM06/11/1981

Stones, Mrs S J, BA (Hons) MCLIP, Library and Knowledge Service, King's Mill Hospital, Sutton-in-Ashfield, Notts.
[40411] 03/02/1987 CM24/09/1997

Stopforth, Mr N P, ACLIP, Head of Libraries and Culture, Doncaster Metropolitan Borough Council.
[65787] 24/04/2006 ACL16/04/2008

Stoppani, Ms J M, BA (Hons) MCLIP, Deputy L. Manager, Medway NHS Trust., Kent.
[50124] 05/03/1994 CM23/01/2008

Stopper, Miss J, BA (Hons) MCLIP, Assistant L. and Information Serv. Manager, North Lincolnshire Council, Scunthorpe.
[32613] 29/05/1980 CM04/10/1983

Stores, Mr M, BA DipLib MCLIP, Librarian.
[42060] 30/08/1988 CM19/06/1991

Storey, Miss A, BA, Student.
[10020456] 20/02/2012 ME

Storey, Mrs A V, BA MCLIP, Part time contract at ICAEW.
[18316] 13/10/1972 CM20/08/1975

Storey, Dr C, BA MPhil PhD FCLIP HFHKLA, Retired Dec. 2012 (Chinese University, Hong Kong).
[14105] 29/09/1971 FE25/09/1996

Storey, Ms I N J, BSc MSc MCLIP,
[32705] 01/07/1980 CM25/01/1983

Storey, Mrs J, BA MCLIP ACIM DipMkt, Subject & Liaison Manager., Northumbria University, Newcastle.
[25581] 28/01/1976 CM19/12/1978

Storey, Ms M, BA, Career Break.
[60982] 23/01/2002 ME

Storey, Mrs N S, L. Assistant, Aiglon College, Switzerland.
[10019719] 30/08/2011 AF

Storey, Mrs S C, MSc MCLIP, Head of L. Customer Serv., University of Nottingham.
[49901] 10/01/1994 CM10/01/1994

Storey, Mr S M, BSc DipLib, Subject Librarian for Colleges of Medicine and Human & Health Sciences, Swansea University.
[33654] 03/02/1981 ME

Storey, Mrs T, BA (Hons) MCLIP, Widening Participation Officer, School Of Healthcare. University of Leeds.
[48423] 14/05/1993 CM20/11/2002

Story, Mrs B A, BSc MCLIP, Information Officer, Arts and Heritage Team, Windsor Library, Royal Borough of Windsor & Maidenhead.
[20931] 17/09/1973 CM01/11/1976

Stoter, Mr A P, BSc, Learning Support Librarian, Victoria Library, London.
[64444] 30/03/2005 ME

Stott, Mrs F, MA BA MCLIP, Unemployed.
[8749] 01/01/1971 CM04/07/1974

Stout, Mr R W, MA MCLIP, Retired.
[17800] 23/10/1963 CM01/01/1967

Stovin, Mrs K A, BA DipLib MCLIP, Learning Resource Centre Manager, Priory School, Hitchin.
[33609] 22/01/1981 CM16/05/1985

Stovold, Ms E M, BSc (Hons) MA MCLIP, Information Scientist, Cochrane Airways Group, London.
[57977] 07/10/1999 CM28/10/2004

Stower, Mrs E, Archive Manager, Henry Moore Foundation.
[10035300] 07/10/2014 ME

Strachan, Mr A D, MA (Hons) DipLib, Director IT, UK Trade & Investment, London.
[42219] 11/10/1988 ME

Strachan, Miss C E, MA (Hons), Information Assistant.
[10019739] 02/09/2011 AF

Strachan, Mrs E, MA MCLIP, Librarian, Education Library, William Harvey Hospital, Ashford.
[58819] 09/08/2000 CM06/05/2009

Strachan, Ms K V, BA (HONS) PgDip, Historical Records Appraisal Manager (Archivist), Welsh Government.
[10020886] 19/04/2012 ME

Strachan, Mrs M, BA MA MCLIP, Writer.
[28459] 15/01/1969 CM14/06/1978

Strachan, Mrs M E, FCLIP, Librarian, Supreme Courts, Edinburgh.
[26808] 04/11/1976 FE07/04/1986

Stradling, Mr B, MBE FCLIP LRPS FRSA, Life Member.
[14129] 17/02/1947 FE01/01/1966

Stradling, Ms J, BA (Hons) DipLib MCLIP, Lending Librarian, Southampton Central Library.
[49329] 22/10/1993 CM21/11/2001

Strafford, Mrs L, BA (Hons) MCLIP, Library & Knowledge Services Manager., Ashford & St Peter's NHS Trust Chertsey.
[60471] 11/12/2001 CM31/01/2007

Strain, Mrs M H, BA MA MCLIP, Life Member.
[39541] 29/09/1954 CM14/10/1960

Strain, Mr W M, MA FCLIP ACP, Life Member.
[14131] 22/03/1958 FE01/01/1968

Straker, Miss A C, BA (Hons), Digital Resources Officer, City College Norwich.
[10012655] 05/03/2009 ME

Stranders, Mrs A E, BA (Hons) MA MCLIP, Astrande@havering-college. ac. uk.
[43668] 21/11/1989 CM16/11/1994

Strasburger, Mrs H A, BA DipLib MCLIP, Strategic Library Manager, West Bridgford Library. Nottinghamshire County Council.
[36495] 12/10/1983 CM20/01/1987

Stratton, Ms B, BA (Hons) MSc MCLIP, Copyright & Licensing Consultant – Libraries, Archives & Museums.
[30274] 17/01/1979 CM12/05/1981

Stratton, Ms N L, MA (Hons) PgDip, Monographs & Media Manager, National Library of Scotland, Edinburgh.
[10012885] 17/03/2009 ME

Strauss, Mrs S M, BA FCLIP, Life Member.
[14140]   09/03/1965   **FE01/01/1966**
Streather, Ms S K, BA DipLib, Res. & Learner Support Office.
[29840]   09/10/1978   **CM20/10/1981**
Street, Mrs M S, BSc MA MCLIP, Bookstart Development Office,
Hertfordshire County Council (jobshare).
[43196]   02/10/1989   **CM18/11/1993**
Strike, Mr A, BA, Faculty Liasion Assistant, University Campus Suffolk.
[10022541]   20/03/2013   **AF**
Stringer, Mr I M, MCLIP HonFCLIP, Retired & Chair ILIG.
[14150]   01/02/1968   **HFE13/07/2009**
Stringer, Mrs L H, BA PgCert MCLIP, Business Information, Audience
Dev. Officer, Essex L.
[39265]   07/01/1986   **CM12/12/1991**
Stringer, Mr R D, BA DipLib MBA MCLIP, Publishing consultant (self-
employed), TextPertise, Zimbabwe.
[19094]   24/09/1972   **CM12/02/1976**
Stringfellow, Ms S, BA (Hons) MA (Hons), Learning Resource Co-
ordinator, North Bristol Post 16 Centre.
[10031682]   24/09/2013   **ME**
Strong, Mrs C J, BA (Hons) MA ACLIP, Library Service Advisor, Arnold
Library.
[10022407]   26/02/2013   **ACL13/11/2013**
Strugnell, Mr M, BA DipLib, Library Manager, Thames Valley University,
Reading.
[33801]   30/01/1981   **ME**
Stuart, Mrs C A, MCLIP, Director /Company Secretary, CARISS, Kent.
[30018]   01/11/1978   **CM02/08/1982**
Stuart, Mr D W K, PgDip LIS MA, Learning Resource Centre Manager,
Our Ladys High School.
[10012100]   11/09/2013   **ME**
Stuart Edwards, Mrs E L, BA (Hons) MSc MCLIP, Subject Librarian,
University of Bath.
[10015950]   29/01/2010   **CM04/10/2013**
Stuart-Jones, Mr E A L, MCLIP MA, Retired.
[14169]   29/07/1966   **CM01/01/1969**
Stubbings, Ms R E, BA MA, Deputy University Librarian: Information
Resources & Planning, Nottingham Trent University.
[40462]   12/02/1987   **ME**
Stubbs, Prof E A, Librarian, UNLP Facultnd & Bellas Artes Bibliotecs.
[58638]   25/04/2000   **ME**
Stubbs, Mr M, BTH DipLib MA MCLIP, Customer Services Assistant
(Part-time), Dunstable Library, Central Bedfordshire Council.
[41480]   11/01/1988   **CM17/10/1990**
Stuckey, Mrs G V, BA MCLIP, Stock Supply Manager, Wiltshire Council.
[14181]   25/03/1971   **CM24/05/1977**
Stuckey, Miss J, BSc, Library Assistant, Oakham School.
[10035543]   17/10/2014   **ME**
Sturdy, Mr W, CChem MRSC MCLIP, Semi-retired.
[60604]   25/03/1971   **CM01/04/1984**
Sturges, Prof R P, MA PhD FCLIP OBE, Retired.
[14191]   24/11/1966   **FE27/03/1991**
Sturgess, Mrs S A, MCLIP, Retired.
[15573]   11/03/1969   **CM30/07/1972**
Sturm, Mr J A, School Librarian/Marketing & Publicity Officer, Astley
Community High School.
[10016705]   28/04/2010   **ME**
Sturt, Mrs F, FCLIP, Life Member.
[14193]   16/01/1952   **FE01/01/1960**
Sturt, Mr N F, BA (Hons) MCLIP, Librarian, HMS Sultan, Gosport.
[41254]   24/10/1987   **CM21/03/2001**
Styan, Mrs S, BA (Hons) MA MCLIP, L. Manager, Black & Veatch Ltd,
Redhill.
[52828]   17/10/1997   **CM08/03/2013**

Stych, Mr F S, PH D MA FCLIP, Bagno Alla Villa, Bagni Di Lucca Villa,
Italy.
[14195]   08/08/1933   **FE01/01/1960**
Styles, Miss C, BA (Hons) MSc (Econ) MCLIP, Arts and L. Consultant.
[51152]   23/11/1994   **CM17/03/1999**
Suckle, Mr Z, BA MA, Librarian, Capital City Academy, London.
[10010983]   25/09/2008   **ME**
Suckley, Ms J B, BLib,
[28180]   01/10/1977   **ME**
Suddaby, Miss K M, MCLIP, Retired Life Member.
[14200]   25/02/1955   **CM01/01/1959**
Suddell, Mrs G, MSc, Information Serv. Librarian, South Glos. Council,
Winterbourne L.
[61151]   15/03/2002   **ME**
Sudic, Ms A, BSc (Hons) PgDip, Librarian / Documentalist, International
Association of Universities, Paris.
[10021389]   31/07/2012   **ME**
Sudworth, Mrs R A, BA MCLIP, Area Manager, East, Lancashire
County Council.
[31845]   10/01/1980   **CM15/09/1983**
Suga, Ms C, BA MLIS, Lecturer, Keio University.
[61478]   14/08/2002   **ME**
Sugden, Mr P V, MA DipLib MCLIP, Lead Manager, Library Service,
West Sussex County Council.
[32467]   17/04/1980   **CM22/06/1982**
Sugden, Mr T, Student.
[10020469]   20/02/2012   **ME**
Suggitt, Mrs A M, MSc, Library Information Administrator, University of
the West of England.
[10018692]   24/02/2011   **AF**
Sukal, Mrs R, BA MA DipIM MCLIP, Liaison. Librarian, Richmond-upon-
Thames College Library, Surrey.
[55352]   03/10/1997   **CM15/05/2002**
Sullivan, Ms J, BA (Hons) MCLIP, Part-time Arch., Roedean School,
Brighton.
[46950]   09/03/1992   **CM22/03/1995**
Sulston, Mrs D E, MA, Retired.
[50288]   01/06/1994   **ME**
Summers, Mr D, BA (Hons) MA MCLIP, Deputy Librarian, Lancaster
University Library.
[34123]   06/10/1981   **CM07/02/1985**
Summers, Mrs J, BA (Hons) MA MCLIP, Freelance Lib.
[58452]   11/02/2000   **CM29/03/2004**
Summers, Miss P A, BA DipLIS MCLIP, Librarian, Invergordon
Academy.
[53324]   07/05/1996   **CM19/05/1999**
Summers, Miss S, School Librarian, Glasgow Life., Mitchell Library.
[10020869]   19/04/2012   **ME**
Sumpter, Mrs S L, BA (Hons) MCLIP, Independent Consultant.
[46480]   12/11/1991   **CM31/01/1996**
Sunderland, Mrs J C, BSc (Hons) MA MCLIP,
[58911]   03/10/2000   **CM12/03/2003**
Sunley, Miss J, BA, Information Trainee Manager, BSRIA.
[10031922]   15/10/2013   **ME**
Sunley, Mr J W, MCLIP, Life Member.
[14226]   10/08/1950   **CM01/01/1959**
Surman, Miss R E,
[10011054]   17/09/2008   **ME**
Surridge, Dr C, BSc PhD, Assistant Registrar, Head of Timetabling and
Awards Group, Brunel University.
[64041]   06/12/2004   **ME**
Surridge, Mr R G, MA FRSA HonFLA FCLIP, Freelance Consultant,
Surrey.
[14232]   10/03/1947   **HFE11/10/1988**

Sutcliffe, Mrs K L, BChD MSc, Assistant Librarian, Salford Royal NHS Foundation Trust.
[10022126]   08/01/2013   **ME**

Sutcliffe, Mr M R, MCLIP, Librarian, Central Library, Oxford.
[10019741]   02/09/2011   **CM16/01/2014**

Suter, Mrs A J, BA DipLib MCLIP, Librarian, CEB School, London.
[41557]   21/01/1988   **CM18/09/1991**

Suter, Mr M, BA, Assistant Librarian, Kingston College, Kingston.
[35641]   25/11/1982   **ME**

Sutherland, Ms A J, BA (Hons) MCLIP, Library Manager, Mitchell Library.
[43620]   14/11/1989   **CM27/07/1994**

Sutherland, Miss A M, MA DipLib MCLIP, Career break.
[34328]   23/10/1981   **CM09/11/2005**

Sutherland, Mr A P, BA MCLIP, Retired.
[25119]   13/10/1975   **CM30/01/1978**

Sutherland, Miss C J, BA, Deputy Librarian, Pepys Library, Magdalene College.
[65680]   31/03/2006   **ME**

Sutherland, Mr J G, BA MCLIP, Unemployed.
[28692]   13/01/1978   **CM08/12/1987**

Sutherland, Miss K A, MA (Hons) MSc, Assistant Librarian, Sherborne School.
[10011347]   09/10/2008   **ME**

Sutherland, Miss L, BA (Hons), Information Officer, The Mitchell Library, Glasgow.
[10020620]   16/03/2012   **ME**

Sutherland, Miss L M, MA DipLib MCLIP Msoc Ind, Freelance Lib. & Indexer.
[26247]   02/09/1976   **CM25/01/1979**

Sutherland, Ms N M, BA (Hons) DipInf, Reader's Adviser, House of Commons Library, London.
[58387]   31/01/2000   **ME**

Suto, Mrs J C, MCLIP ALAA, Retired.
[17848]   29/09/1943   **CM01/04/1949**

Sutton, Miss A J, BA (Hons) MA MCLIP, Information Resources Group Manager/Senior Information Specialist.
[59010]   24/10/2000   **CM19/11/2008**

Sutton, Mrs A M, BA MA DipLib MCLIP, Institutional Repository Manager, Library, University of Reading.
[41140]   13/10/1987   **CM18/09/1991**

Sutton, Dr A M, MA (Hons) DipLib PhD MCLIP,
[10013966]   17/10/1983   **CM01/07/1987**

Sutton, Mrs D E, BSc (Hons) MA, School Librarian, Withington Girls School.
[55103]   14/07/1997   **ME**

Sutton, Miss E, FCLIP, Life Member.
[14257]   21/03/1941   **FE01/01/1951**

Sutton, Mr I W, BA (Hons) MCLIP, Learning & Information Manager, Rochdale Metropolitan Borough Council.
[29097]   16/01/1978   **CM09/07/1981**

Sutton, Mr J H, Reference Team Leader, British Library, Asian & African Studies, London.
[31709]   13/11/1979   **ME**

Sutton, Mrs K, BA MCLIP, Service Manager, Libraries, Heritage and Art.
[28813]   18/01/1978   **CM25/06/1982**

Sutton, Mrs L, MSc, Information Officer, College of Law, Guildford.
[10003975]   23/05/2007   **ME**

Sutton, Mr L, BA MCLIP, Retired.
[22877]   01/10/1974   **CM07/07/1977**

Sutton, Mrs M, ACLIP, Senior Library Assistant, Castle College Nottingham.
[10031612]   10/09/2013   **ACL15/07/2014**

Sutton, Miss N, BA, Assistant Librarian, Westfield Academy.
[10034162]   11/06/2014   **ME**

Suzuki, Mr H, Life Member.
[17849]   01/01/1970   **ME**

Swain, Ms B, BSc DipInfSc MCLIP, Self-employed.
[60654]   11/12/2001   **CM11/12/2001**

Swain, Miss C O M, Student, University of Sheffield.
[65326]   15/12/2005   **ME**

Swain, Ms K M D, Student, Red River College.
[10032653]   23/12/2013   **ME**

Swain, Miss M, BA, Retired.
[14262]   04/02/1952   **ME**

Swainson, Miss J, Student, Northumbria University.
[10021996]   15/11/2012   **ME**

Swainson, Miss N J, BA DipLib MCLIP, Learning Resources Mgr, Barton Peveril College.
[33168]   11/10/1980   **CM16/05/1985**

Swaisland, Mrs C A, MCLIP BSc (Hons) MSc MAUA IIHHT, Executive Assistant (Governance and Records Management), Liverpool John Moores University.
[56948]   09/11/1998   **CM21/05/2003**

Swales, Mrs B J, BA MCLIP MSc, Career Break.
[34891]   15/04/1982   **CM03/02/1986**

Swales, Ms G E, BA (Hons) DipLib, Senior Librarian, Scottish Borders Council.
[29287]   23/04/1978   **ME**

Swales, Mrs H J, BA (Hons) MSc MCLIP, Librarian, Leeds P. C. T. (maternity leave).
[49746]   29/11/1993   **CM22/05/1996**

Swales, Mr R J, BA (Hons) MA, Faculty Lib. for Fashion & Management, University for the Creative Arts.
[10018644]   18/02/2011   **ME**

Swamy-Russell, Mrs J A, MLib, Retired.
[45893]   10/07/1991   **ME**

Swanick, Mrs V P, MCLIP, Retired.
[20861]   26/02/1959   **CM06/09/1973**

Swann, Mr A, MA (Hons) MLITT, Library Stock Assistant, Glasgow University Library, Glasgow.
[10021967]   06/11/2012   **AF**

Swann, Miss A, BA MA, Student, University of Sheffield.
[10035463]   14/10/2014   **ME**

Swann, Mrs K A, BA (Hons) MA, Librarian, Nantwich Library, Cheshire East.
[10006338]   15/10/2007   **ME**

Swann, Miss K L, BA (Hons) MA MCLIP, Team Leader, City of Edinburgh Council, Central Library.
[54634]   27/01/1997   **CM18/09/2002**

Swann, Mrs M J, BA MCLIP, Retired.
[590]   16/03/1965   **CM01/01/1969**

Swann, Ms S E, BA (Hons) MCLIP, Librarian, Bloxham School, Banbury.
[33170]   26/09/1980   **CM26/09/1983**

Swanney, Mrs S, BA MA, Lib. Stock Manager, Central Library, Rotherham.
[10008702]   18/04/2008   **ME**

Swanson, Mrs C A, BA (Hons) MA MCLIP, School Librarian / Literacy Co-ordinator, Theale Green School Theale, Reading.
[52713]   24/11/1995   **CM21/11/2001**

Swart, Ms M A, BA MA, Knowledge Systems Officer, Nabarro LLP.
[10015792]   20/01/2010   **ME**

Sweeney, Mr J M, MSc MCLIP, Retired.
[60653]   05/06/1975   **CM27/04/1981**

Sweeney, Mr R, BA FCLIP, Retired.
[14284]   01/01/1950   **FE01/01/1964**

Sweet, Mrs K L, BSc MCLIP, Information Resources Executive, Contractor.
[60800]   01/10/1979   **CM10/07/1985**

Sweetland, Ms J M, BA (Hons) MSc MCLIP, Neurosciences Librarian, North Bristol NHS Trust, Frenchay Hospital.
[29323]   17/06/1978   **CM16/07/1980**

Sweetman, Mr P B, BA MCLIP, Retired.
[22970]   24/09/1974   **CM01/11/1976**

Sweetman, Mr R, BSc MA ACLIP, Senior Language Learning Advisor, King's College London.
[10023071]   04/06/2014   **ACL27/03/2014**

Swietlik, Mr P, Secretary, Frome Community Hospital.
[10021414]   03/08/2012   **ME**

Swift, Ms A J, BA (Hons) MCLIP, School Librarian, Welshpool High School, Powys.
[37251]   11/05/1984   **CM17/11/1999**

Swift, Ms K, BA,
[10035274]   03/10/2014   **ME**

Swift, Mr R A, BA DipLib MCLIP, Faculty Support Team Manager., University of Derby.
[34678]   01/02/1982   **CM22/04/1992**

Swindells, Mr R J, MSc MCLIP, Retired.
[14295]   24/05/1965   **CM01/01/1969**

Swinyard, Miss J K F, MCLIP, Life Member and Chartered.
[14296]   25/03/1958   **CM01/01/1963**

Swyny, Ms L, BA (Hons) MA MCLIP, Legal Librarian, HM Land Registry.
[55408]   08/10/1997   **CM29/08/2007**

Syder, Mrs C H M, BA DipLib MCLIP, Area Librarian, Cheshire West & Chester.
[29789]   05/10/1978   **CM12/11/1981**

Syed, Mr M,
[10007570]   18/02/2008   **ME**

Sykes, Mrs E, Librarian, Oldham Hulme Grammar Schs., Oldham.
[46775]   22/01/1992   **ME**

Sykes, Mrs E, MA MSc, School Librarian, The Mitchell Library, Glasgow.
[10001404]   14/02/2007   **ME**

Sykes, Mr H G, BA MCLIP, Stock Librarian, Bristol Central Library, Reference Library.
[27373]   07/03/1977   **CM24/05/1984**

Sykes, Mrs J, BSc (Hons) PGCE MA,
[10012778]   03/03/2009   **ME**

Sykes, Mr P, BA DipLib MCLIP, Librarian, University of Liverpool, Sydney Jones L.
[40628]   06/04/1987   **CM18/04/1990**

Sykes, Mrs P A, BA (Hons) MCLIP, Information Specialist, GCHQ, Cheltenham.
[49577]   19/11/1993   **RV**12/09/2012   **CM19/03/1997**

Sykes, Miss R A, BA (Hons) DipILM MCLIP, LRC Team Leader, Canterbury College.
[47788]   14/10/1992   **CM15/01/2003**

Sykes, Mr T, BA MA, Deputy Librarian, Trinity Hall, Cambridge.
[10022041]   20/11/2012   **ME**

Sylph, Ms E A, BSc MSc MCLIP, Part-time Librarian, Zoological Society of London.
[60691]   01/12/1982   **CM10/03/1987**

Syme, Mrs J, BA MA MCLIP, Sch. Librarian, Simon Balle Sch. Hertford.
[41304]   01/11/1987   **CM22/07/1992**

Symes, Mrs M R, BA MCLIP, Part-time Assistant Librarian, University of Brighton.
[42663]   07/02/1989   **CM27/07/1994**

Symon, Mrs S, MA Librarianship, Library and Research Analyst, Kent CC.
[10034329]   04/07/2014   **ME**

Symonds, Miss K, MA (Hons) MLitt, Graduate Trainee, Institute of Classical Studies.
[10031927]   15/10/2013   **ME**

Symonds, Mr K M, Lib. & Information Serv. Manager, MRC Cognition & Brain Sci. Unit, Cambridge.
[51198]   23/11/1994   **ME**

Symons, Mrs A C, DipLIS MCLIP, Retired.
[45347]   19/10/1990   **CM19/07/2000**

Symons, Miss E, BA MA, Inter-Library Loans & Acquisitions Assistant, York St John University.
[10021231]   29/06/2012   **ME**

Szczyglowski, Mr W L, BSc MSc, Library Manager.
[34172]   08/10/1981   **ME**

Szpytman, Miss T M, BSc MSC MCLIP,
[41397]   20/11/1987   **CM18/04/1990**

Szubarczyk, Miss E, BA, Student, UCL.
[10035449]   14/10/2014   **ME**

Szurko, Mrs M M, BA DipLib MRes MCLIP, Librarian, Oriel College, Oxford University.
[31955]   21/01/1980   **CM21/01/1982**

T

Tabone, Mr G, BEd DEAM PG Cert Maths MSc, Teacher Librarian.
[10033543]   25/03/2014   **ME**

Taggart, Mrs C, BA MCLIP,
[14323]   22/08/1967   **CM01/01/1970**

Tailby, Mrs A P, BA (Hons), Librarian, Department for Work & Pensions (DWP).
[41301]   01/11/1987   **ME**

Tailor, Mr R, BLS, Assistant Librarian, De Monfort University.
[10020396]   11/02/2012   **ME**

Tait, Ms D, BA (Hons), L. and Information Assistant, Newcastle L. and Information Serv.
[64129]   18/01/2005   **AF**

Tait, Mrs H E, Library Supervisor, Ardnamurchan Library.
[10021611]   12/09/2012   **AF**

Tait, Mrs J M, MA MCLIP, Head of Arch. and Library, The Tank Museum, Dorset.
[28697]   12/01/1978   **CM16/01/1980**

Tait, Mrs L, BA (Hons) MCLIP, Librarian, Scottish Water, Edinburgh.
[54374]   28/11/1996   **CM15/05/2002**

Tait, Mr M H, BA, Retired.
[10033393]   07/03/2014   **ME**

Talbi, Mr H, BA MA LIS, Director of Library, University of Bahrain.
[42012]   14/07/1988   **ME**

Talbot, Mrs A L, BA (Hons) MA MCLIP,
[56765]   08/10/1998   **CM13/03/2002**

Talbot, Miss B, BLib MCLIP, Retired.
[26809]   23/10/1976   **CM06/11/1980**

Talbot, Mrs H D, MCLIP, Life Member.
[14333]   01/01/1957   **CM01/01/1962**

Talbot, Mr R G, Data Protection Officer, Dorset.
[54585]   11/02/1997   **AF**

Tales, Mrs A, BA MCLIP, Librarian, Berrywood Library, NHS Northamptonshire Healthcare NHS Foundation Trust.
[20410]   03/03/1973   **CM15/09/1977**

Tam, Ms C Y, MAAppISC BA DipLib, Manager.
[10034906]   21/08/2014   **ME**

Tamblyn, Mrs K L, BA DipLib MCLIP, Medical Records Clerk, Maidstone & Tunbridge Wells Hlth. Tr Pembury Hospital.
[44440]   08/10/1990   **CM18/11/1993**

Tamby, Miss Z, B EC MCLIP, Project Librarian, Inst. of South East Asian
Studies, Singapore.
[22156]   30/01/1974   **CM12/02/1980**

Tan, Ms C L A, MA, Librarian, Singapore Institute of Management.
[10032861]   21/01/2014   **ME**

Tanker, Mrs A C, BA (Hons) MCLIP, Librarian, Sheffield Primary Care
Trust.
[10009977]   30/06/2008   **CM10/11/2010**

Tanna, Mrs A M, BA (Hons) DipLib MCLIP, Retired.
[28805]   07/02/1978   **CM01/07/1993**

Tanner, Mr M E, BA DipLib MCLIP, Senior Librarian, Torfaen Ls.,
Pontypool.
[39168]   04/11/1985   **CM09/08/1988**

Tansley, Mr I P, MCLIP, Retired Group Librarian, North West Devon,
Devon Library & Information Serv.
[14343]   11/03/1968   **CM01/01/1971**

Tansley, Mrs U M, MA MCLIP, Librarian, Wellington, New Zealand.
[66117]   01/10/2006   **CM11/11/2009**

Taplin, Mr B K, BA (Hons) DipIM, Licensing Manager, JISC Collections,
London.
[51013]   09/11/1994   **CM17/05/2000**

Taplin, Mrs S V, Assistant Law Library & Information Manager, Hugh
James Solicitors, Cardiff.
[10007552]   13/02/2008   **AF**

Tapping, Ms A J, BA (Hons) MSc, Librarian & Information Officer, MRC
Laboratory of Molecular Biology.
[10011786]   13/11/2008   **ME**

Tarling, Mr M R, MCLIP, Retired.
[14348]   01/08/1971   **CM02/07/1974**

Tarrant, Ms A, MSc Econ BA, Librarian; Cambourne Village College;
Cambridgeshire.
[10015058]   08/10/2009   **ME**

Tarrant, Miss G A, Bsc (Hons) MSc MCLIP, Senior Taxonomy
Specialist.
[62719]   08/10/2003   **CM13/11/2013**

Tarrant, Mrs S E, BA MCLIP, Retired.
[14352]   12/01/1967   **CM01/01/1970**

Tarrier, Miss S P, Student, University of Sheffield.
[10032475]   09/12/2013   **ME**

Tarron, Mrs M P, BA DipIS PGCLTHE FHEA, Academic Liaison
Librarian, University of Surrey, Guildford.
[55472]   14/10/1997   **ME**

Tate, Ms J, BA (HONS) MSc, Proj & Dev Manager, The London Sch of
Economics & Political Science.
[10006584]   23/10/2007   **ME**

Tate, Mrs J M, BA (Hons) MSc (Econ) MCLIP, Unwaged.
[58318]   07/01/2000   **CM16/07/2003**

Tatem, Ms S, MCLIP, Retired.
[14359]   01/10/1971   **CM26/02/1982**

Tatham, Ms S, BScEcon MA MCLIP, Teaching & Learning Support
Librarian, University of Sussex.
[58533]   22/03/2000   **CM25/01/2011**

Tattersall, Mr S, MSc MCLIP, ICT Development Manager, Bristol City
Council.
[29536]   18/09/1978   **CM05/09/1980**

Tatton, Mrs H D, PgDipLib, School Librarian, Ilford Ursuline High
School, Ilford.
[36832]   01/01/1984   **ME**

Tawn, Mrs H V, BA (Hons) DipLib MCLIP, Subject Librarian, Leeds City
College Keighley Campus.
[44343]   01/10/1990   **CM25/01/1995**

Taylor, Ms A C, MA MCLIP, Librarian, King Fahad Academy, London.
[10014875]   18/09/2009   **CM08/03/2013**

Taylor, Ms A E, BSc MCLIP,
[30868]   29/04/1979   **CM26/02/1982**

Taylor, Mr A J, BA (Hons) MA MCLIP, Assistant Librarian, Manchester
Metropolitan University.
[10017379]   12/08/2010   **CM11/04/2013**

Taylor, Mrs A M, BA MA, Acquisitions Team Leader, University of
Reading Library.
[62910]   18/11/2003   **ME**

Taylor, Miss A P, BA MA, Information and Skills Development Officer,
Somerset CC.
[43653]   16/11/1989   **ME**

Taylor, Miss C, BSc (Hons) MA MCLIP, Information Serv. Subscriptions
Manager, Field Fisher Waterhouse, London.
[52951]   26/01/1996   **CM18/09/2002**

Taylor, Ms C J, BA DipLib MCLIP, University Librarian, University of
Leicester.
[34727]   05/02/1982   **CM29/07/1986**

Taylor, Miss C M, BA, Liaison Assistant, Newcastle University,
Newcastle.
[10013634]   18/05/2009   **ME**

Taylor, Mr C V, BA (Hons) MA MCLIP, International Collections
Manager, National Library of Scotland, Edinburgh.
[47731]   15/10/1992   **CM25/09/1996**

Taylor, Mrs D A, BA (Hons) MCLIP, Service Development Librarian,
Young People, Dudley MBC.
[40781]   06/06/1987   **CM16/05/2012**

Taylor, Miss D E, MSc MCLIP M I BIOL MA, Storyteller.
[25120]   15/11/1975   **CM07/06/1978**

Taylor, Mr D N, BA MCLIP, Unwaged.
[34643]   30/01/1982   **CM14/11/1989**

Taylor, Ms E, MA MCLIP, Learning & Information Specialist, RCN
Scotland Learning Hub, Edinburgh.
[59587]   11/06/2001   **CM13/04/2011**

Taylor, Miss E, BA, Lib Assist., Central Library, Croydon.
[10020726]   29/03/2012   **AF**

Taylor, Miss E, BA (Hons) MA MCLIP, Nursery Assist., St Johns Nursery
Group, Worcester.
[50115]   05/04/1994   **CM22/11/1995**

Taylor, Mrs E, BA (Hons) MSc PGDE MCLIP, Teacher.
[59420]   07/03/2001   **CM29/03/2004**

Taylor, Miss E J, BA MA MCLIP, Lib. -Support Serv., Lincs. County
Council.
[43392]   19/10/1989   **CM18/11/1992**

Taylor, Mrs F M, Young People's Area Librarian, Kendal Library,
Cumbria.
[35160]   24/09/1982   **ME**

Taylor, Mrs G, Bibliographical Services Manager, Bibliographical
Services Unit, Westbrook Library, Warrington.
[10022789]   04/02/2000   **ME**

Taylor, Mr G A, BA (Hons) MA MCIPR MCLIP, Public Relations Officer,
West Yorkshire Combined Authority, Leeds.
[58321]   05/01/2000   **CM29/03/2004**

Taylor, Ms H, BA MLS MCLIP, Development Officer (Member Services),
CILIP, London.
[28184]   14/10/1977   **CM01/10/1979**

Taylor, Miss I J, BA (Hons) DipILM MCLIP, Information Co-ordinator,
Careers and Employment Service, Northumbria University.
[10019135]   18/09/1995   **CM09/07/2013**

Taylor, Mrs J, BA MA MCLIP, Clinical Librarian, NHS Foundation Trust,
Lancashire.
[10009445]   01/12/2004   **CM08/03/2013**

Taylor, Mrs J, BLib MCLIP, Librarian, Stockport Sch. L. Serv.
[28136]   12/10/1977   **CM08/08/1980**

Taylor, Ms J, MA BA DipLib MCLIP, Librarian, Working Class Movement
  Librarian, Salford.
  [39363]   16/01/1986   **CM15/02/1989**
Taylor, Mrs J A, MLS MCLIP, Retired.
  [3440]   16/10/1969   **CM17/07/1972**
Taylor, Mrs J C, BSc (Hons) MA MCLIP, Library Assistant, Lancashire
  County L. Serv., Preston.
  [55587]   22/10/1997   **CM01/02/2006**
Taylor, Mrs J D, MCLIP, Cathedral Librarian, Lincoln Cathedral.
  [10032565]   04/04/1984   **CM01/07/1991**
Taylor, Mr J R, BA (Hons), Information Sci., DSTL, Knowledge Serv.,
  Salisbury.
  [65393]   30/01/2006   **ME**
Taylor, Mr J R H, MA FRCO ARCM, Retired.
  [63311]   08/04/2004   **ME**
Taylor, Mr J W, BA MCLIP, Retired.
  [19110]   20/03/1957   **CM01/01/1961**
Taylor, Mrs K E, MA DipM MCLIP,
  [10344]   07/01/1971   **CM22/04/1974**
Taylor, Ms L, MA, Biblographic Services Librarian, British Museum.
  [40947]   25/09/1987   **ME**
Taylor, Ms L, BA, Student, Bodleian Libraries.
  [10032487]   10/12/2013   **ME**
Taylor, Mr L H, BA (Hons) MA MCLIP, Management Co-Ordinator –
  East, Scarborough Library, North Yorkshire.
  [46636]   29/11/1991   **CM24/09/1997**
Taylor, Mrs L J, MEd BA ILTM MCLIP, Acting Clinical Librarian, Wirral
  University Teaching Hospital NHS Foundation Trust.
  [29145]   16/04/1978   **CM07/12/1981**
Taylor, Mr L J, BA FCLIP, Retired, Tamarisk Books, Hastings, East
  Sussex.
  [14426]   28/08/1958   **FE14/11/1991**
Taylor, Mr L S, BA (Hons) MA MCLIP, Librarian, British Library, London.
  [55801]   24/11/1997   **CM25/01/2011**
Taylor, Mr M, BA MCLIP, Head of L., Arts & Heritage Serv., Royal
  Borough of Windsor & Maidenhead.
  [29842]   03/10/1978   **CM22/08/1984**
Taylor, Mr M, BA (Hons), Student, University of Ulster.
  [10018467]   24/01/2011   **ME**
Taylor, Mr M J, BA MCLIP, Retired.
  [14435]   07/08/1957   **CM01/01/1960**
Taylor, Mr M R, BA MPhil MCLIP, Research Assistant, Cent. & North
  West London Mental Hlth. NHS Trust.
  [39246]   01/01/1986   **CM09/08/1988**
Taylor, Mrs P J, Student, Aberystwyth University – Library Assistant
  Cardigan Library.
  [10014532]   12/08/2009   **ME**
Taylor, Ms R C, BA (Hons) MA, Classifications Editor Ringgold Inc.
  [42263]   13/10/1988   **ME**
Taylor, Mrs R S, BA (Hons) MA MCLIP, Research Match Support
  Officer, University of Warwick Library.
  [64847]   28/07/2005   **CM11/04/2013**
Taylor, Mrs S, MCLIP, Life Member.
  [14461]   01/02/1955   **CM01/01/1959**
Taylor, Mrs S, ACLIP, Study Ctr. Manager, Jubilee High School,
  Addlestone.
  [10006489]   24/10/2007   **ACL04/03/2009**
Taylor, Miss S, ACLIP, Subject Librarian, Croydon College L.
  [10010698]   29/08/2008   **ACL07/08/2009**
Taylor, Mr S C, BA, Bookshop Assistant (part-time), Wells, Somerset.
  [24966]   13/10/1975   **ME**
Taylor, Mrs S E, BA (Hons) MPhil PgDip MCLIP, Electronic Resources
  Librarian, University of Bolton.
  [62922]   20/11/2003   **CM21/11/2007**

Taylor, Miss S E C, MA (Hons) DipILS MCLIP, Librarian, Archives and
  Special Collections, Glasgow Life, Glasgow.
  [53974]   15/10/1996   **CM20/09/2000**
Taylor, S H, BA (Hons) MA MCLIP, Information & Records Manager,
  New College Durham.
  [56311]   01/05/1998   **RV**06/02/2008   **CM18/09/2002**
Taylor, Mrs S L, Library Assistant, Wakefield L.
  [65196]   17/11/2005   **AF**
Taylor, Mrs S M, BA (Hons) PGCE, Assistant Librarian, Swansea
  Metropolitan University.
  [10033582]   31/03/2014   **ME**
Taylor, Mrs S M, BA (Hons) MA MCLIP, Information Officer, The
  National Autistic Society, London.
  [59923]   02/11/2001   **CM01/02/2006**
Taylor, Ms S M, BSc (Hons) DipLIM MCLIP, Learning Res. Centre Co-
  ordinator, Bicton College, Devon.
  [51376]   01/02/1995   **CM29/03/2006**
Taylor, Ms S M, ACLIP, Network Librarian Highlife Highland.
  [10019790]   13/09/2011   **ACL27/03/2014**
Taylor, Mr T, BA (Hons) DipILS MCLIP, Retired.
  [48125]   10/11/1992   **CM25/09/1996**
Taylor, Mrs V L, MSc BA MILAM MCLIP, Retired.
  [1229]   07/10/1965   **CM01/01/1970**
Taylor-Bradshaw, Mrs L, Retired.
  [10015456]   25/11/2009   **ME**
Taylor-Roe, Mrs J L, MA MCLIP, Deputy Librarian & Head of Planning &
  Resources, Newcastle University Library.
  [35137]   13/09/1982   **CM20/01/1986**
Taylor-Roome, Mrs D, BSc MCLIP AdvDipEd, Retired – Volunteer: Mine
  of Information(Community Resource Centre), Tuxford,
  Nottinghamshire.
  [14470]   24/01/1962   **CM01/01/1968**
Taylor-Smith, Mrs C L, Sch. Lib.
  [65121]   01/11/2005   **ME**
Teague, Mr S J, BSc (Econ) FCLIP FRSA, Retired.
  [14474]   02/01/1940   **FE01/01/1950**
Tearle, Miss B M, LLB MSt MCLIP, Retired.
  [15583]   18/02/1967   **CM01/01/1970**
Teasdale, Mrs F S, BSc (Hons) DipIS MCLIP, Head of Collections and
  Discovery, University for the Creative Arts, Farnham.
  [51892]   31/07/1995   **CM01/04/2002**
Teather, Miss J K, BA MCLIP, Career Break.
  [35872]   31/01/1983   **CM11/12/1989**
Tedeschi, Mr A M, MA MLS, Deputy Curator, Special Collections
  Baillieu Library, University of Melbourne.
  [64574]   05/05/2005   **ME**
Teglu, Mrs G K, MSc, Unwaged.
  [10021246]   02/07/2012   **ME**
Teijken, Ms A, BA (Hons), Retired.
  [45914]   19/07/1991   **ME**
Tejura, Ms P, BSc MA ACLIP, Library Assistant, Cheam Library.
  [10031537]   01/10/2013   **ACL27/03/2014**
Telfer, Ms R A, BA DipLib,
  [10035476]   15/10/2014   **ME**
Telfer, Miss R L, BA, Graduate Trainee, Lincoln's Inn Library.
  [10030580]   24/10/2013   **ME**
Templar, Mrs A, BA (Hons) MCLIP, Locality Librarian, Dudley M. B. C.
  [61545]   10/09/2002   **CM20/04/2012**
Temple, Ms E, MSc MCLIP, Information Manager, West Sussex County
  Council, Chichester.
  [60856]   07/08/1998   **CM07/08/1998**
Templeton, Ms J, BA (Hons) MSc MCLIP, Information Assist.,
  Edinburgh Napier University, Edinburgh.
  [10015293]   30/10/2009   **CM07/09/2011**

Tenebe, Miss R V, Student, University of Sheffield.
[10035537]   16/10/2014   ME
Terras, Prof M M, MA MSc DPhil, Professor of Digital Humanities, UCL.
[10032393]   03/12/2013   ME
Terrell, Mrs J M, BSc DipLib MCLIP, Support Services Manager,
Cambridgeshire.
[41649]   01/02/1988   CM15/05/2002
Terry, Ms J V, BA DipLib MCLIP, Retired.
[21301]   11/10/1973   CM11/12/1975
Terzi, Ms P, Intern, Welcome Trust, International Dunhuang Project
Erasmus.
[10030589]   06/05/2014   ME
Tester, Miss C J, ACLIP, Cluster Manager., Burgess Hill PL
[65380]   04/01/2006   ACL27/09/2006
Tew, Mr C S, BEd, Librarian, Brooklands College, Weybridge.
[41454]   01/01/1988   ME
Thacker, Mrs S J, BA (Hons) MCLIP, CEIAG. Co-ordinator, Prospects
Black Country, Oldbury.
[52632]   16/11/1995   CM23/01/2008
Thackeray, Mrs E, BMus (Hons) MMus MA MCLIP, Acting Clinical
Librarian, Royal Preston Hospital.
[64394]   14/03/2005   CM09/07/2013
Thain, Ms A E, BA MCLIP, Head of Knowledge Based Practice Team,
NHS Education for Scotland, Glasgow.
[25431]   18/12/1975   CM26/01/1983
Thanigasalam, Mrs M, BA (Hons) LIS, Library Assistant.
[10022338]   11/02/2013   ME
Thebridge, Mrs S W, BA DipLib MCLIP, Principal Librarian: schools and
reading, Warwickshire L (incl SLS Manager).
[29788]   02/10/1978   CM26/02/1982
Theis, Miss A, BA (Hons), Student, Manchester University.
[10031832]   08/10/2013   ME
Thickins, Mr J O T, BA (Hons) MA MCLIP, Academic Liaison Librarian,
University of Westminster.
[57966]   06/10/1999   CM23/06/2004
Thies, Ms A M, BA MLib MCLIP FCIPD, Participation Manager., Co. L.
Headquarters, Lancs. County Council.
[39981]   03/10/1986   CM16/10/1989
Thirsk, Mr J W, FCLIP, Life Member.
[14515]   20/06/1933   FE01/01/1947
Thivend, Mr L, MA, Student Manchester Metropolitan University.
[10032418]   03/12/2013   ME
Thom, Mrs T L, BA MA MCLIP, Librarian, The Hon. Society of Grays Inn
Library, London.
[26576]   07/10/1976   CM08/10/1979
Thomas, Ms A, BA (Hons) MCLIP, Librarian, Conwy County Borough
Council.
[29099]   27/02/1978   CM18/09/2002
Thomas, Mrs A, BLib, Principal Lib. (Development), Pembrokeshire
Library, Wales.
[10001746]   09/10/1982   CM08/12/1987
Thomas, Mrs A E, BA MA MCLIP, Information & Enquiry Services
Librarian Warwickshire County Council.
[41179]   14/10/1987   CM27/01/1993
Thomas, Mr A R, MA FCLIP, Life Member.
[14525]   01/07/1947   FE01/01/1958
Thomas, Mr C, Student, Manchester Metropolitan University.
[10033954]   13/05/2014   ME
Thomas, Mrs C E, BA (Hons) MA MCLIP FHEA, Head of Learning
Support Serv., University of Chester, Cheshire.
[10004060]   07/03/1986   CM26/01/1994
Thomas, Mrs C K, BLib MCLIP, Principal Lib. Powys Co. L. Serv.,
Llandrindod Wells.
[31248]   07/10/1979   CM08/03/1985

Thomas, Miss C M, BA (Hons) DipLib MCLIP, Information Advisor,
Linklaters, London.
[31163]   12/09/1979   CM28/09/1983
Thomas, Mrs D, Corporate Records Officer, Foreign & Commonwealth
Office.
[10032803]   14/01/2014   ME
Thomas, Mrs D, PgDip, Outreach Librarian, St Helens & Knowsley
Teaching Hospitals NHS Trust.
[10010118]   17/01/2000   ME
Thomas, Ms D G, BSc (Hons) MSc MCLIP, Sr. L. Executive, National
Assembly for Wales, Cardiff.
[54088]   25/10/1996   CM17/01/2001
Thomas, Mr D R, MA DipLib MCLIP, Product Specialist UK, SirsiDynix.
[24831]   01/10/1975   CM18/10/1978
Thomas, Mrs E, MCLIP, Community Librarian, Gwynedd Council,
Caernarfon L.
[29234]   10/04/1978   CM17/06/1982
Thomas, Miss E J, BA MCLIP,
[25124]   14/11/1975   CM09/07/1980
Thomas, Mrs F, MCLIP, Retired.
[14547]   01/01/1939   CM01/01/1946
Thomas, Miss F, BA (Hons) MA ODE DipLib MCLIP, Ships L. Officer,
Ministry of Defence, Portsmouth.
[40633]   03/04/1987   CM15/12/1992
Thomas, Mrs G, BA (Hons) MSc (Econ), Library Assistant, Prince Philip
Hospital, Llanelli.
[10002683]   27/04/2007   ME
Thomas, Mr G, BA FCLIP, Life Member.
[14548]   21/09/1951   FE01/01/1961
Thomas, Miss G, MLib BA DipLib PGC MCLIP, Unwaged.
[33941]   01/06/1981   CM09/03/1989
Thomas, Mr G C G, BA MA MCLIP, Retired.
[14551]   05/04/1971   CM15/05/1979
Thomas, Mrs G N, BA DipIS MCLIP,
[44109]   16/05/1990   CM21/07/1999
Thomas, Ms H, BA MSc MCLIP, Central Services Librarian, Cardiff
Metropolitan University.
[59954]   09/11/2001   CM07/09/2005
Thomas, Mr H, BMus DipRCM DipLIS, Library Manager, City of
Westminster.
[49366]   29/10/1993   ME
Thomas, Ms I J, BA (Hons), Career Break.
[49407]   21/10/1993   ME
Thomas, Ms J, BA MCILIP, Programme Manager, Woking Library,
Surrey County Council.
[33173]   08/10/1980   CM30/11/1984
Thomas, Dr J A, MA DipLib DipLA MCLIP PhD, Customer Services
Librarian, University of Wolverhampton.
[22938]   01/10/1974   CM09/11/1976
Thomas, Mrs J E, BA (Hons) MLitt MSc (Econ), Community Librarian,
Moray Council.
[57900]   01/10/1999   ME
Thomas, Mrs J H, BA MCLIP, School Librarian, St Bartholomews
School, Newbury.
[14562]   29/04/1972   CM31/08/1974
Thomas, Mrs J M, MCLIP, District Manager, Lancashire County L. Serv.
[10009346]   01/06/2008   CM10/03/2011
Thomas, Mrs K L R, Study Support Worker, Southfields Library.
[10033906]   12/05/2014   ME
Thomas, Mrs K M, BA MCLIP, School Librarian, Bishopbriggs Academy,
Bishopbriggs, Glasgow.
[36860]   10/01/1984   CM03/03/1987

Thomas, Miss L, BA (Hons) DipLIS MCLIP, Assistant Librarian, Library, University of South Wales.
[44321]   07/09/1990   **CM17/11/1999**

Thomas, Mrs M, MCLIP, Community Librarian, Wrexham Co. Borough Council.
[21536]   11/10/1973   **CM13/09/1977**

Thomas, Mrs M, BA (Hons) DipLis,
[63280]   24/03/2004   **ME**

Thomas, Mrs M, BA DipLib MCLIP,
[44229]   18/07/1990   **CM26/01/1994**

Thomas, Mrs M G, MA MCLIP, Retired.
[14570]   10/08/1954   **CM01/01/1957**

Thomas, Mr M H, BA DipLib MCLIP, Retired.
[14571]   10/09/1971   **CM21/10/1974**

Thomas, Mrs M J, BA (Hons) DipLIS, Assistant Area Sch. Librarian, South Ham Library, Hampshire County Council.
[46727]   03/01/1992   **ME**

Thomas, Mr N R, BLib (Hons) DPLM MCLIP, Serv. Delivery Manager, Leics. C. C., Leicester.
[30689]   28/02/1979   **CM30/12/1983**

Thomas, Mr O C, DipHE BA (Hons) DipIS MCLIP, Assistant Librarian, De Montfort University, Leicester.
[50214]   05/04/1994   **CM16/07/2003**

Thomas, Miss P, Student.
[10016927]   16/06/2010   **ME**

Thomas, Mrs P A, MCLIP, Learning Centre Coordinator, Coleg Y Cymoedd – Ystrad Mynach Campus, Hengoed.
[10006765]   17/12/2007   **CM09/07/2013**

Thomas, Mr P D, ACIB MCLIP, Life Member.
[23968]   25/02/1975   **CM25/09/1978**

Thomas, Mr R E, BA MCLIP, Library Manager, The Institution of Structural Engineers.
[39500]   07/02/1986   **CM22/07/1992**

Thomas, Mr R H, BA (Hons) DipLib MCLIP, General Manager Town Hall, Reading Borough Council,
[41357]   11/11/1987   **CM13/06/1990**

Thomas, Mrs S, BA (Hons) MA MCLIP, Learning & Teaching Librarian, The Open University.
[56864]   29/10/1998   **CM15/10/2002**

Thomas, Ms S J, BA DipLib MCLIP, Health Promotion Library, Public Health, Cardiff, Wales.
[33845]   01/04/1981   **CM07/03/1985**

Thomas, Mrs S M, BA MWeldI MCLIP MBCS, Weldasearch Manager, TWI Ltd, Cambridge.
[60657]   29/11/1979   **RV27/03/2014**   **CM29/11/1979**

Thomas, Mrs S W, BA (HONS) MSc Econ, Senior Library Assistant, Staff Library, Duncan Macmillan House, Nottinghamshire Healthcare NHS Trust.
[10021290]   06/07/2012   **ME**

Thomas, Mrs V, MCLIP, Community Librarian, Services to Children & Young People.
[8597]   01/01/1970   **CM01/01/1975**

Thomas, Miss Z, BA (Hons), Information Services Support Librarian, UCL Medical Library.
[64277]   23/02/2005   **ME**

Thompson, Ms A, Community Librarian, Medway L.
[66032]   04/09/2006   **ME**

Thompson, Mrs A, BA (Hons) MA PGCE MLitt PgDip MCLIP, Consultant Librarian, Sydney PLUS International Library Systems (Lucidea).
[10015735]   19/01/2010   **CM11/07/2012**

Thompson, Mrs A E, BSc (Hons) PgDip, Retired.
[59426]   12/03/2001   **ME**

Thompson, Dr A H, MA FCLIP HonFCLIP, Retired;Chairman CILIP Multimedia Information & Tech Group.
[14593]   26/02/1957   **HFE23/10/2003**

Thompson, Mr A J, BA (Ed), LRC Manager, Laisterdyke Business & Enterprise College, Bradford, West Yorkshire.
[10021221]   29/06/2012   **ME**

Thompson, Mrs B A, BSc DipLib MCLIP MA, Retired.
[14595]   01/01/1969   **CM01/01/1972**

Thompson, Mrs C A, MCLIP, Children's Centre Outreach Worker & Library Consultant, Achieving for Children (London Borough of Richmond & Royal Borough of Kingston).
[18282]   03/10/1972   **CM06/10/1976**

Thompson, Mr D, Digital Curator, Wellcome Library, London.
[62971]   01/12/2003   **ME**

Thompson, Mr D J, MA MCLIP FHEA, Academic Subject Librarian, University of Gloucestershire.
[53678]   04/09/1996   **CM17/01/2001**

Thompson, Mrs G, BA MCLIP, Data Controller, RM Education.
[18406]   25/10/1972   **CM04/02/1976**

Thompson, Mrs G M, MCLIP, Unwaged.
[10891]   10/02/1972   **CM19/01/1976**

Thompson, Mrs H, BA (Hons), Group Manager, Durham C. C.
[46310]   28/10/1991   **ME**

Thompson, Mr H, FCLIP, Retired.
[14616]   05/10/1936   **FE01/01/1951**

Thompson, Ms I J R, MA DipLib MCLIP, Career Break.
[25433]   05/01/1976   **CM26/09/1978**

Thompson, Ms J, BA (Hons) MCLIP, Consultant – Self-employed.
[10019611]   26/01/1978   **CM11/08/1980**

Thompson, Mr J, BA FCLIP, Life Member.
[14618]   18/02/1949   **FE01/01/1963**

Thompson, Mrs J, BA (Hons) QCG CertSocSci, Student, University of Brighton.
[10031687]   24/09/2013   **ME**

Thompson, Mr J E, BA DipLib MCLIP, Development & Quality Manager., Edinburgh City Libraries.
[33383]   21/11/1980   **CM27/07/1983**

Thompson, Mrs J M, MCLIP, Retired.
[41505]   01/01/1966   **CM05/04/1989**

Thompson, Miss K, BSc MA, Unemployed.
[57208]   18/01/1999   **ME**

Thompson, Ms K E, BA (Hons) PgDipLIS MCLIP, Liaison Librarian, Imperial College, London.
[55907]   12/12/1997   **CM19/11/2003**

Thompson, Mrs L, BSc (Hons), Library Services Assistant, Leeds Metropolitan University.
[10033710]   16/04/2014   **ME**

Thompson, Ms L A, MA (Hons) MLIS, Unwaged.
[10019768]   01/04/1997   **ME**

Thompson, Mrs L M, BA (Hons) MCLIP, Academic Subject Librarian, University of Lincoln.
[52652]   16/11/1995   **CM19/11/2003**

Thompson, Mrs M, Business Res., London.
[52427]   26/10/1995   **AF**

Thompson, Miss M, BA MSc, Public Library Librarian.
[40709]   09/05/1987   **ME**

Thompson, Mrs M K N, MCLIP, Life Member.
[14626]   01/01/1940   **CM01/01/1943**

Thompson, Ms R E A, BA (Hons), Information Manager, University of Strathclyde, Careers Serv.
[39132]   10/11/1985   **ME**

Thompson, Mr R H, FSA MCLIP, Retired.
[14630]   03/02/1963   **CM06/11/1972**

Thompson, Mrs S L, BA (Hons) MSc MCLIP, L. Serv. Manager, Frimley Park Hospital, Surrey.
[49617]   19/11/1993   **CM22/01/1997**

Thompson, Mrs S M, BA MCLIP, Retired.
[32386]   01/01/1956   **CM24/07/1980**

Thompson, Mrs V E, BA MCLIP, Retired university librarian with 10 years Middle East experience. Available for consultancy work.
[14640]   17/03/1967   **CM19/07/2000**

Thompson, Mrs W J, BA DipLib MCLIP, Senior Res., UBS Investment Bank, London.
[43557]   07/11/1989   **CM29/01/1992**

Thomson, Ms A, LLB MA, Deputy Librarian, Ashurst, London.
[52033]   02/10/1995   **ME**

Thomson, Ms A J, BA (Hons) MCLIP, Part-time Cataloguer, Society of Genealogists, London.
[18212]   05/10/1972   **CM13/07/1976**

Thomson, Mrs D M, MCLIP, Adult Services Reader Development Librarian, Aberdeenshire Library & Information Services, Aberdeenshire.
[21016]   01/10/1973   **CM15/09/1976**

Thomson, Mrs E M, BA, Branch Librarian, West Loan Library, East Lothian Council.
[28224]   26/10/1977   **CM19/11/1979**

Thomson, Mr G, L. Systems Manager, Royal College of Surgeons of England, London.
[10015323]   16/11/2009   **ME**

Thomson, Ms H, School Library Service Advisor, Warwickshire.
[10008696]   29/04/2008   **CM10/03/2011**

Thomson, Mrs I, MSc MCLIP, Unemployed.
[61243]   01/04/2002   **CM23/06/2004**

Thomson, Miss K S, BSc (Hons) MSc MCLIP FHEA, Subject Librarian, Heriot-Watt University.
[58925]   05/10/2000   **CM21/11/2007**

Thomson, Mrs L, Volunteer Library Assistant.
[10022640]   05/04/2013   **AF**

Thomson, Miss L A, BSc, Student.
[10020937]   24/04/2012   **ME**

Thomson, Mrs M M, BA MCLIP, Vol. Lib. & Counselling Co-ordinator, Grampian Racial Equality Council, Aberdeen.
[30050]   26/10/1978   **CM07/08/1981**

Thomson, Mr R J, MA (Hons) DipLIS, Unwaged.
[50290]   31/05/1994   **CM15/05/2002**

Thomson, Mr T, BA (Hons) MSc, Enquiries Assistant, Natural Library of Scotland.
[10018950]   01/04/2011   **ME**

Thorburn, Mr D, BA (Hons) MA PgDipIS MCLIP, Information Executive, Royal Institution of Chartered Surveyors, London.
[51460]   27/02/1995   **CM01/02/2006**

Thorn, Mrs L, BSc PgDip MCLIP,
[60474]   02/02/2000   **CM02/02/2000**

Thornborow, Mr P, MSc MA BA DipLib MCLIP, Liaison Officer for Methodist Archives Methodist Church.
[29851]   02/10/1978   **CM04/06/1981**

Thorne, Mrs A A, MSc BA (Hons) MCLIP, Information Manager & PA, Society of Motor Manufacturers & Traders Ltd, London SW1P 2BN.
[43999]   01/04/1990   **CM19/11/2003**

Thorne, Miss A M, BLib MCLIP, Comm. Lib, Norfolk County Council, Dersingham Library.
[41604]   26/01/1988   **CM24/03/1992**

Thorne, Mrs G E, Information Assistant, St George's, University of London.
[10023216]   18/06/2013   **ME**

Thorne, Mrs M F, ACLIP, L. S. A., Central Library, Sutton in Ashfield.
[65203]   17/11/2005   **ACL05/10/2007**

Thorne, Mrs S M, BA MA MCLIP, Accounts Assistant, AWM International, Worthing.
[33178]   06/10/1980   **CM20/12/1982**

Thorne, Miss V M, BA MCLIP, Customer Serv. Manager, London Borough of Barking & Dagenham.
[40350]   21/01/1987   **CM18/11/1992**

Thorner, Miss J, BA MA MCLIP, Retired.
[29852]   11/10/1978   **CM14/10/1981**

Thornes, Miss S L, BSc (Hons) MSc MCLIP, Faculty Team Librarian, University of Leeds.
[59801]   03/10/2001   **CM04/10/2006**

Thornhill, Ms B J, JP DipSoc DipPsych MCLIP, Life Member.
[14670]   27/09/1952   **CM01/01/1967**

Thornhill, Mrs M A, MPhil FCLIP, Life Member.
[17859]   12/02/1941   **FE01/01/1954**

Thornley, Dr C V, MA MSc PhD, Lecturer (PT) & Research Consultant.
[10022642]   05/04/2013   **ME**

Thornton, Mrs C A, BA MCLIP, Team Leader., Shrewsbury College of Arts & Tech.
[34674]   01/02/1982   **CM06/10/1987**

Thornton, Mrs D, MCLIP, Knowledge and L. Services Mngr, Blackpool Victoria Hospital.
[33702]   06/02/1981   **CM08/09/2010**

Thornton, Ms D K, BA (Hons) MCLIP, Community Information Officer, Knaresborough Library, Yorks.
[34737]   03/02/1982   **CM21/02/1984**

Thornton, Ms I, BA, Comm. Librarian, Aston Library, Birmingham.
[38053]   17/01/1985   **ME**

Thornton, Mrs T J, BA (Hons) MCLIP, LRC Manager, Hazelwick Sch. West Sussex.
[48251]   18/11/1992   **CM23/09/1998**

Thorp, Dr R G, MA MSc DPhil CChem MRSC MCIL MCLIP, Retired.
[60616]   09/11/1984   **CM02/12/1986**

Thorpe, Miss A, BSc, Student.
[10021793]   16/10/2012   **ME**

Thorpe, Ms C M, BSc (Hons) MSc MCLIP, Senior Information Adviser (Web Services), Sheffield Hallam University SLS.
[00424]   27/11/1980   **CM22/07/1998**

Thorpe, Ms D, BA (Hons) MCLIP, School Librarian, New Charter Academy, Tameside.
[52567]   06/11/1995   **CM13/03/2002**

Thorpe, Ms H M, PGCE MA MCLIP, Teacher, Lincolnshire.
[30723]   01/01/1973   **CM01/01/1977**

Thorpe, Mr P, BSc FCLIP, Retired.
[14694]   12/03/1971   **FE01/04/2002**

Thorpe, Mr P, Search Engine Visitor Serv. Assistant, National Railway Museum, York.
[10015394]   12/11/2009   **AF**

Thow, Mrs J A, MCLIP, Retired.
[22392]   12/03/1951   **CM01/01/1957**

Thow, Miss L R, BA (Hons) PgDip/CPE, Library Resource Co-ordinator, Portobello High School, Edinburgh.
[10016169]   18/02/2010   **ME**

Thresh, Mrs P A, BA (Hons) MCLIP, School L. Serv. Manager., Leeds.
[30061]   06/11/1978   **CM18/11/1980**

Thrift, Mrs H, BMus MA MCLIP MInstLM, Director of Library Services, Liverpool John Moores University.
[39021]   28/10/1985   **CM09/08/1988**

Throwgood, Mrs H,
[10013969]   17/06/2009   **ME**

Thurley, Mr N M, BA (Hons) MA MCLIP, Outreach Librarian, University of Oxford.
[54461]   16/12/1996   **CM29/03/2004**

Thursfield, Mrs J, MCLIP, Principal Lib. ; Serv. Delivery, Stoke on Trent
L. I. A.
[22980]   01/10/1974   **CM24/02/1978**
Thwaite, Ms N, MA, Assistant Lib. Curator, National Trust.
[42136]   07/10/1988   **ME**
Thwaites, Ms M E, BA (Hons) DipILS MCLIP, Librarian, Nottinghamshire
County Council, Education Library Service.
[46584]   20/11/1991   **CM27/11/1996**
Tibbitts, Mrs G M, MCLIP, Part-time Bookshop Assistant.
[31118]   20/08/1979   **CM16/07/1982**
Tidswell, Miss J, BA (Hons) MSc MCLIP, Assistant Librarian, De
Montfort University.
[10006595]   06/02/2007   **CM09/07/2013**
Tiernan, Mr J J, MA FCLIP FRSA, Retired.
[19810]   01/12/1972   **FE14/08/1991**
Tierney, Miss C, BA PgDip,
[10020377]   09/02/2012   **ME**
Tiley, Mr S D, BA (Hons) MA DipLIM MCLIP, Librarian, St John's
College, Oxford.
[55578]   21/10/1997   **CM16/05/2001**
Tilke, Dr A, BA MEd FRSA FCLIP ATCL, Head of Library, International
School, Amsterdam, The Netherlands.
[26582]   23/10/1976   **FE24/09/1997**
Tilley, Mrs B J, MCLIP, Life Member.
[14721]   01/01/1948   **CM18/02/1974**
Tilley, Mr D, Unwaged.
[64662]   12/05/2005   **ME**
Tilley, Mrs E A, BA (Hons) MSc (Econ) MCLIP, Engineering Faculty
Librarian, University of Cambridge.
[58942]   05/10/2000   **CM01/06/2005**
Tilley, Ms J, BSc MCLIP, Senior Assistant Subject Librarian, Teesside
University Library, Tees Valley.
[10017043]   21/06/2010   **CM14/12/2012**
Tilley, Ms J E, BA MA DipLaw, Legal and Business Researcher, Lewis
Silkin.
[10032582]   02/10/1987   **ME**
Tilly, Mr N J, MCLIP, Life Member.
[14726]   14/03/1954   **CM01/01/1960**
Timlin, Miss H E, BA (Hons) MA, Bibliographic Data Assistant, Bertram
Books.
[10019054]   13/04/2011   **ME**
Timmins, Ms G, BA PGCE MA, Collections Officer, Tennyson Research
Centre, Lincoln.
[10020628]   16/03/2012   **ME**
Timmons, Mr A, BA (Hons) DipLIS MCLIP, Desk Officer for the Digital
Library, FCO. London.
[49995]   07/02/1994   **CM22/09/1999**
Timms, Mr D B, MCLIP, Retired.
[14730]   17/03/1953   **CM01/01/1962**
Timms, Mrs J A, BA MCLIP, Cataloguer, Derbyshire L. & Heritage,
Matlock.
[28908]   18/01/1978   **CM15/09/1983**
Timms, Mr M G, BA MCLIP, Retired.
[18448]   23/10/1972   **CM26/09/1975**
Timothy, Mrs C M, BA MA, Public Health & Commissioning Librarian.
[58083]   25/10/1999   **ME**
Timothy, Mrs W, BA MLib MCLIP, Senior Librarian, Managment
Information, Staffordshire County Council.
[43896]   13/02/1990   **CM22/07/1992**
Timpson, Miss H, BA MSc, Acquisitions Librarian, Ministry of Justice.
[10022176]   15/01/2013   **ME**
Timson, Ms J, BA MA,
[10011483]   12/01/1995   **ME**

Tindale, Mr J W, BA (Hons) MA MCLIP, Information Manager,
Department for Work & Pensions, London.
[54990]   12/06/1997   **CM13/03/2002**
Tiney, Mrs P C, DipLib MCLIP, Cataloguer, The British Library, Boston
Spa.
[29955]   23/11/1978   **CM24/01/1984**
Tinker, Dr A J, BA (Hons) MSc PhD MCLIP FHEA, Part-time Academic
Skills Coordinator/Senior Lecturer, University of Huddersfield.
[53582]   01/08/1996   **CM08/11/1999**
Tinkler, Mrs F E, MA (Hons) (Edin) MSc (Bris),
[64242]   22/02/2005   **ME**
Tinson, Miss S L, BA (Hons) MCLIP, Cent. Manager, Plymouth Sch. L.
Serv.
[49420]   21/10/1993   **CM20/05/1998**
Tinto, Miss F, BA (Hons), Student, University of Strathclyde.
[10021689]   27/09/2012   **ME**
Tipple, Mr A, ACLIP, Librarian, Adult Services; London Borough of
Barnet Libraries.
[10003948]   23/05/2007   **ACL04/03/2009**
Tirimanne, Mrs G S, DipLib MCLIP, Unwaged.
[27010]   10/01/1977   **CM25/05/1988**
Titcombe, Mrs J M, MPhil FCLIP, Retired.
[3367]   25/09/1968   **FE18/07/1990**
Tither, Mrs J M, BA MCLIP, Retired.
[5810]   05/01/1971   **CM03/08/1973**
Titley, Mr G D C, BA (Hons) MCLIP, Information Specialist & Copyright
Advisor., Plymouth University.
[34141]   05/10/1981   **CM17/09/1986**
Titterington, Mrs S F, MCLIP, Community Development Manager,
Leeds City Council.
[36619]   24/10/1983   **CM19/01/1988**
Tivey, Ms G P, BA MA MCLIP, Lib. & Information Mgr, Science & Advice
for Scottish Agriculture (SASA), Edinburgh.
[36723]   04/11/1983   **CM15/08/1989**
To, Ms M Y V, BA (Hons) LLB BAR, Librarian, Mayer Brown JSM, Hong
Kong.
[10017604]   10/01/1986   **CM15/09/1993**
Toase, Mr C A, HonFLA, Retired.
[14747]   09/02/1946   **HFE01/01/1993**
Toase, Mrs S A, BA MCLIP, Cust. Serv. Manager, Central Library,
Oxfordshire County Council.
[33779]   06/02/1981   **CM07/10/1986**
Tobin, Mrs C M, MA MCLIP, Team Manager, Partnerships & Volunteers-
Newark & Sherwood Locality, Notts. County Council.
[52078]   02/10/1995   **CM20/11/2002**
Todd, Mr C P, Librarian, Sutton.
[65453]   24/02/2006   **AF**
Todd, Miss E, Data Protection Manager, DWP.
[10033591]   01/04/2014   **ME**
Todd, Mrs M E, BSc (Econ) MCLIP, Principal Librarian, Belfast Educ. &
L. Board.
[54494]   02/01/1997   **CM15/10/2002**
Todd, Mr P, BA, Library Assistant, Leeds City Council.
[10034519]   18/07/2014   **ME**
Todd, Miss R E, BA (Hons) MA,
[57482]   06/04/1999   **ME**
Todd, Mrs S, BA MA (Ed) MCLIP FRSA, School Archivist St Johns
School, Leatherhead.
[1310]   21/09/1970   **CM01/11/1972**
Todd, Mrs S C, BSc MCLIP, Metadata Librarian, Oxford Brookes
University.
[36444]   13/10/1983   **CM10/11/1987**

Todd-Jones, Mr M J, MCLIP, Deputy Librarian, University of Cambridge, Department of Chemisty.
[28705]   17/01/1978   **CM07/04/1981**

Toerien, Mr D, BA (Hons) MA PDC, Head of L. and Information Serv., Oakham School.
[63772]   06/10/2004   **ME**

Toffoli, Miss O, Student.
[10020465]   20/02/2012   **ME**

Toft, Miss S D, BA PgDip MScEcon, Training Librarian, Royal Derby Hospital.
[10009978]   27/06/2008   **ME**

Togia, Dr A, Lecturer In Library Science, Alexander Technological Educational Institute (ATEI) of Thessaloniki.
[10035664]   28/10/2014   **ME**

Tokwe, Mr H, HND LIS, Chief Library Assistant, Midlands State University, Zimbabwe.
[61664]   14/10/2002   **ME**

Tomblin, Mrs J M, MA MCLIP, Life Member.
[17865]   22/03/1966   **CM01/01/1971**

Tomes, Mrs J, FCLIP, Life Member.
[14768]   10/04/1953   **FE01/01/1964**

Tomes, Mr P C, BLib MCLIP, Librarian, Salisbury L.
[42463]   14/11/1988   **CM22/05/1996**

Tomkinson, Ms G M, MA MCLIP, Resource Discovery and Innovation Metadata Librarian, NTU Library, Nottingham Trent University.
[38659]   17/09/1985   **CM16/07/2003**

Tomlinson, Miss J A, BA MA MCLIP, Cataloguing and Metadata Servs. Manager, Wellcome Library, London.
[34485]   12/11/1981   **CM18/06/1985**

Tomlinson, Mrs S, MA DMS MCLIP, Librarian\LRC Manager, Hymers College.
[10022005]   07/05/1974   **CM22/07/1977**

Tomos, Dr Y, BA MA PhD, Student, Aberystwyth University.
[10034217]   24/06/2014   **ME**

Toms, Miss A L, BA (Hons) DipILM MCLIP, Reader Serv. Officer, RNIB National Lib. Serv.,
[58874]   20/09/2000   **CM23/06/2004**

Tong, Miss L, MA MCLIP,
[42280]   19/10/1988   **CM27/07/1994**

Tong, Mr R K L, Library Assistant, European Sch. of Osteopathy, Maidstone.
[62977]   02/12/2003   **AF**

Tonge, Mrs C, Library Resource Assistant, Preston College.
[10022333]   11/02/2013   **AF**

Tongue, Mrs J C, BA (Hons), Library Assistant, Thurrock Council.
[10033240]   24/02/2014   **ME**

Tonkiss Cameron, Mrs R, BA (Hons) MA MCLIP, Archivist, The Burke Library, Columbia University Libraries, New York, NY, USA.
[22081]   01/01/1974   **CM12/06/1979**

Tonks, Mr J D M, BA DipLib MCLIP, Information Librarian, NorthamptonshireL. & Information Serv., Wellingborough L.
[38333]   15/03/1985   **CM14/11/1989**

Tonner, Mrs N C, BA (Hons) PgDipLib MCLIP, Team Leader, Edinburgh Council, Edinburgh.
[48976]   12/08/1993   **CM20/03/1996**

Toon, Mr J E, MCLIP MA, Life Member.
[14797]   29/08/1957   **CM01/01/1960**

Toop, Mr S, BSc, Communications Officer, Connexions Shropshire, Shrewsbury.
[10006660]   05/05/1992   **CM17/01/2001**

Toor, Miss N, LLB (Hons) LPC, Information Manager, Arnold & Porter, London.
[10017574]   08/09/2010   **AF**

Tooth, Mrs G M, MCLIP, Retired.
[14802]   06/02/1961   **CM01/01/1967**

Topping, Mrs D, BLib MCLIP, Assistant Librarian (Part-time), De Montfort University, Leicester.
[34995]   08/06/1982   **CM09/04/1987**

Topping, Mrs K J, BA DipLib MCLIP, Information Officer, Neurosupport, Liverpool.
[39676]   07/05/1986   **CM14/03/1990**

Topping, Mrs P R, BA (Hons) BEd MEd, Network Librarian, Kingussie.
[57761]   28/07/1999   **ME**

Toribio, Mrs M, PgCert, Student, Robert Gordon University.
[10031919]   14/10/2013   **ME**

Torley, Mr G, BA MSc MCLIP, Supply and Acquisitions Officer, Mitchell Library, Glasgow.
[34815]   12/03/1982   **CM11/11/1986**

Torpey, Mrs S L, BA (Hons), Career Break.
[56071]   06/02/1998   **ME**

Torrero, Mr C L, BA MCLIP,
[53600]   06/08/1996   **CM04/05/1993**

Toscani, Mrs D, BA MA, Training Consultant + Coach. Essex.
[10007758]   22/04/2002   **ME**

Toth, Mr G, Collections Librarian.
[10016566]   16/04/2010   **ME**

Totham, Mrs P, BA (Hons) MCLIP, Self-employed, Snodland, Kent.
[26554]   01/10/1976   **CM16/07/1981**

Totty, Miss J T, MA BA (Hons) PGCE MCLIP, Lib. Servs. Manager, Middlesbrough College.
[56081]   12/02/1998   **CM11/04/2013**

Tout, Ms F, MSc MCLIP, Community Librarian, North Somerset Public Libraries.
[10008377]   19/03/2008   **CM16/01/2014**

Tovell, Mr P J, BA (Hons) MA MCLIP, District Manager: Lichfield District Libraries, Staffordshire County Council.
[63065]   27/01/2004   **RV**27/08/2014   **CM29/11/2006**

Towers, Ms H, BA DipLib MCLIP, Reader Dev. and Stock Manager, Cumbria County Council.
[36334]   04/10/1983   **CM21/07/1989**

Towers, Miss H S, BA (Hons) MA MCLIP, Young Peoples Serv. Librarian, St Albans Central Library, Herts.
[58439]   14/02/2000   **CM29/03/2004**

Towey, Mrs C, MA, Senior Assistant Librarian, House of Lords.
[10017949]   27/10/2010   **ME**

Towler, Mr J W, MA MCLIP, Retired, (Member of friends of Sydenham Community Library).
[14820]   07/09/1964   **CM01/01/1968**

Towlson, Ms K B, BSc (Hons) MA FHEA MCLIP, Senior Assistant Librarian, De Montfort University, Leicester.
[41078]   08/10/1987   **CM12/12/1990**

Town, Mr J S, MA DipLib FCLIP, Director of Information & University Librarian, University of York.
[29350]   02/06/1978   **FE22/05/1991**

Towner, Mr S, MCLIP, Retired.
[14821]   01/01/1949   **CM01/01/1966**

Townsend, Miss A C, BA MA MCLIP, Team Leader, Adult Services & Acquisitions.
[44112]   18/05/1990   **CM21/07/1993**

Townsend, Miss C, BA MScEcon MCLIP, Information Advisor, Kingston University.
[10000473]   09/10/2006   **CM08/03/2013**

Townsend, Mrs W A, BA (Hons) MSc MCLIP, Library Services Manager, Coventry & Warwickshire Partnership Trust.
[63666]   12/08/2004   **CM29/11/2006**

Townsley, Mrs J, BA (Hons) ACLIP, L. Mgr, Nottingham C. C.
[10019447]   04/07/2011   **ACL**18/01/2012

Townson, Mrs A, MA, Unwaged.
[55161]   28/07/1997   **CM25/07/2001**
Towsey, Mr M A, MA MCLIP, Retired.
[23652]   20/01/1975   **CM04/02/1977**
Toyne, Miss J, BSc (Econ) MCLIP, Information Services Librarian.,
Welwyn Garden City Library, Hertfordshire.
[54393]   02/12/1996   **CM07/09/2005**
Toyne, Miss L M, BA (Hons), Student.
[10019726]   31/08/2011   **ME**
Tozer, Miss C J, BA (Hons) MSc, Assistant Librarian, Cardiff Council.
[10012843]   13/03/2009   **ME**
Tozer-Hotchkiss, Dr G, MA PhD, Freelance Chemical Information
Specialist.
[60717]   25/08/1984   **ME**
Trafford, Mrs D M, BA (Hons) PGCE ACLIP, School Librarian, Thomas
Clarkson Academy, Cambridgeshire.
[62379]   19/05/2003   **ACL18/01/2012**
Train, Mrs J P, BSc PhD, Librarian, Dorridge Junior School, Solihull,
West Mids.
[10004922]   06/06/2007   **AF**
Trainor, Mrs E, BEd (Hons) MA, Student, University of Ulster.
[10034762]   14/08/2014   **ME**
Tramantza, Mrs E, BA MSc MCLIP, Academic Liaison Librarian, Faculty
of Engineering & Physical Sciences, University of Surrey, Guildford.
[10001713]   15/03/2007   **CM05/05/2010**
Tran, Ms A B, BA (Hons) MSc MCLIP, Knowledge and Evidence
Manager, Public Health England, London.
[10001784]   22/11/1999   **CM30/11/2009**
Trant, Ms H A, BA MBA, LIS MA Student, UCL.
[10020811]   18/04/2012   **ME**
Traue, Miss S I,
[64038]   06/12/2004   **ME**
Travis, Mrs K L, BA (Hons) MCLIP, Unwaged.
[55414]   08/10/1997   **CM25/07/2001**
Traynor, Miss E M, MA DipLib MCLIP, Assistant Director (Information
Services) Queens University Belfast.
[37494]   01/10/1984   **CM07/07/1987**
Treadway, Mrs V J, MA, Clinical Librarian, Wirral University Teaching
Hospital NHS Found. Trust.
[63266]   23/03/2004   **ME**
Treadwell, Mrs H M, BA (Hons) MSc MCLIP, Web Editor, Hartpury
College.
[58975]   13/10/2000   **CM21/06/2006**
Treadwell, Mrs N, ACLIP, Librarian, The Nuneaton Academy, Nuneaton.
[10018645]   18/02/2011   **ACL09/09/2013**
Treder, Mrs K, BA,
[10020295]   11/01/2012   **ME**
Tree, Mrs L, BA MCLIP, Community Librarian (Kings Lynn Library),
Information Librarian (Norfolk & Norwich Millennium Library).
[25160]   11/12/1975   **CM19/11/1979**
Treeves, Mrs C, BSc MA ACLIP, Senior Library Assistant (Cataloguing
and Preservation), University of Reading.
[10018857]   23/03/2011   **ACL14/03/2012**
Trench, Mrs S G, MCLIP, Director Research & Dev., AIG, London.
[10012918]   06/01/1975   **CM03/10/1977**
Trenchard, Mrs S M, MCLIP, Retired. Now carrying out part time
genealogy research.
[491]   04/10/1967   **CM01/01/1971**
Trevett, Ms P A, BA FCLIP, Retired.
[14861]   01/01/1956   **FE01/01/1964**
Trevor, Mrs R W, BA (Hons) MCLIP, School Librarian City of London
School for Girls.
[32101]   05/02/1980   **CM06/06/1984**

Trevor-Allen, Mr J A V, BA (Hons) MSc (Econ) MCLIP, Information
Services Librarian, Oxfordshire County Council.
[10019901]   30/09/2011   **CM16/01/2014**
Trickey, Mrs H F, BA (Hons) MA, Information Centre Manager,
Wilsthorpe Community School.
[63489]   15/06/2004   **ME**
Trickey, Mr K V, BA MA FCLIP MCIM, Trainer, Consultant, Mentor and
Coach.
[21882]   28/01/1974   **FE23/09/1998**
Triggol, Mr G J, MCLIP, Retired.
[14866]   01/01/1966   **CM01/01/1970**
Trimming, Mrs F J, BA (Hons) MCLIP, Children's Services Librarian,
Crawley, West Sussex.
[47883]   23/10/1992   **CM21/07/1999**
Trinder, Miss V M, BEd FCLIP LTCL, Retired.
[31100]   13/08/1979   **FE20/05/1998**
Tring, Mr T J, BA MSc MCLIP, Librarian, Castle College, Nottingham.
[61015]   01/02/2002   **CM23/06/2004**
Tripathi, Mrs U, MA MCLIP, Life Member. (Retired Librarian).
[14870]   11/09/1962   **CM01/01/1965**
Troake, Mr J, MCLIP, Retired.
[14876]   01/01/1948   **CM01/01/1960**
Tromans, Miss E H C, BA (Hons) MCLIP, L. & Learning Res. Mgr,
Halesowen College.
[49694]   25/11/1993   **RV**01/10/2008   **CM12/03/2003**
Trott, Mrs A, BA DipLib MCLIP, Retired.
[34660]   18/01/1982   **CM21/01/1986**
Trott, Mrs F J, BA MCLIP, ISLEC East Administrator.
[27078]   26/01/1977   **CM01/10/1982**
Trotter, Mr R R, BA FCLIP, Retired.
[14882]   01/01/1966   **FE24/09/1997**
Trout, Mr E A R, BA DipLib, Manager Information Serv., The Concrete
Society, Camberley.
[38385]   03/04/1985   **CM15/05/2002**
Trowsdale, Mrs J M, BEd (Hons) MCLIP, Library Development Officer
Lincolnshire and Schools Library Service Professional Consultancy
Service Louth Library.
[65830]   22/05/2006   **CM09/09/2009**
Truelove, Ms M, MCLIP, Unwaged.
[28707]   13/01/1978   **CM02/04/1982**
Trueman, Mrs G R, MA MCLIP, Librarian, Peasedown St John Primary
Sch.
[41939]   22/05/1988   **CM27/11/1996**
Truran, Mrs J E, BA ACLIP, School Librarian, Francis Coombes School,
Watford.
[59051]   06/11/2000   **ACL29/03/2006**
Truslove, Mrs E J, BSc (Hons) MA MCLIP, Unemployed.
[57040]   27/11/1998   **CM17/09/2003**
Tryner, Miss J, BA ACLIP, Library and Information Manager, Manor
Academy.
[10023409]   16/07/2013   **ACL20/06/2014**
Tsang, Mr C L A, Assistant Library Officer, Fong Sum Wood Library,
Hong Kong.
[10031340]   23/07/2013   **ME**
Tsang, Ms P K Y, MCLIP, Senior Tech., Map Library, Department of
Geography, University of Hong Kong.
[52782]   12/12/1995   **CM20/11/2002**
Tsang, Ms S S Y, BA MLib MCLIP, Section Head-Information Services,
Hong Kong Polytechnic University Library.
[39932]   03/10/1986   **CM30/01/1991**
Tsang Phillips, Mrs L, BA (Hons) MA MA MCLIP,
[61575]   02/10/2002   **CM01/02/2006**

Tse, Miss T L P, BA (Hons) MA, Senior Librarian, Herbert Smith, London.
[52950]   26/01/1996   **ME**

Tuck, Mrs J, LLB (Hons), Information and Resources Co-ordinator St Catherine's Hospice, Crawley.
[64200]   03/02/2005   **ME**

Tuck, Mr J P, MA MCLIP, Director of Librarian, Royal Holloway, London.
[30799]   10/04/1979   **CM11/12/1981**

Tuck, Miss N, MCLIP, Retired.
[14897]   01/01/1948   **CM01/01/1958**

Tucker, Ms C, BA (Hons) MA, Assistant Librarian, BMA Library, London.
[55860]   04/12/1997   **ME**

Tucker, Ms C, MA, Assistant Librarian, Procurement and Access, LSE.
[10022088]   05/12/2012   **ME**

Tucker, Mrs C L, BA DLS, Unwaged.
[34386]   21/10/1981   **ME**

Tucker, Mr E S J, Student, UEL.
[10031756]   02/10/2013   **ME**

Tucker, Ms K F, BA (Hons) MSc MCLIP, Child. Serv. Librarian, West Sussex.
[63124]   11/02/2004   **CM19/11/2008**

Tucker, Miss S J F, MCLIP, Retired.
[14906]   01/01/1964   **CM01/01/1969**

Tuckerman, Miss L, Graduate Trainee, Institute of Advanced Legal Studies.
[10020398]   11/02/2012   **ME**

Tuckwell, Mr G C, BA MCLIP, Not Working.
[28709]   11/01/1978   **CM07/07/1980**

Tugwell, Mr A C, BPharm MSc MPS MCLIP, Sr. Director Pharm., Barts. & the London NHS Trust, The Royal London Hospital.
[60736]   22/10/1985   **CM22/10/1985**

Tulasiewicz, Mr E, MA, Director of Communication, Westminster, London.
[61193]   08/04/2002   **ME**

Tulip, Ms J, BA (Hons), EMEA Information Manager.
[10001878]   13/11/1999   **ME**

Tumelty, Ms N, BA HDipEd MScEcon MCLIP,
[10011527]   17/10/2000   **CM27/08/2014**

Tumilty, Miss A M, MCLIP, Retired.
[14917]   01/01/1964   **CM01/01/1968**

Tunesi of Liongam, Mrs J E M, MSc MCLIP, Specialist Administrator.
[38329]   20/03/1985   **CM16/05/1990**

Tunks, Mrs D C, BA DipLib MCLIP, Unemployed.
[42365]   24/10/1988   **CM14/08/1991**

Tunley, Mr M F, MA FCLIP, Life Member.
[14920]   01/01/1954   **FE01/01/1963**

Tunley, Mrs S A V, FCLIP, Retired.
[14921]   26/03/1957   **FE01/01/1965**

Tunnicliffe, Mr N W, BSc MCLIP, Retired.
[14923]   01/01/1967   **CM01/01/1969**

Tuomey, Mrs S, CIPD, Librarian, Lambrook School.
[10034143]   10/06/2014   **ME**

Turek-Odushote, Mrs A L, Unwaged.
[10018568]   07/02/2011   **ME**

Turley, Mrs P J, BSc (Econ) (Hons), Subject Librarian, House of Commons Library, London.
[45157]   27/07/1990   **ME**

Turnbull, Ms B, BSc PgDip Msc, Digital Development Librarian, Livewire Libraries.
[65775]   01/05/2006   **ME**

Turnbull, Mr G T, BA MCLIP, Retired.
[14932]   01/01/1968   **CM27/07/1972**

Turnbull, Ms S E, BLib MCLIP MSc, International Tax Information Manager, PricewaterhouseCoopers, London.
[24840]   01/10/1975   **CM10/04/1981**

Turner, Mr A, Information Specialist, Foreign & Commonwealth Office.
[10022454]   05/03/2013   **ME**

Turner, Mrs A E, BA (Hons) ACLIP, Prison Library Manager, HMP & YOI New Hall, Wakefield MDC.
[53467]   01/07/1996   **ACL16/07/2008**

Turner, Mrs A F, BA MCLIP, Archivist, Liberal Judaism.
[27889]   04/10/1977   **CM10/10/1982**

Turner, Mrs A H, BA MCLIP, Young Peoples Serv. Manager, Lancashire Co. Libs.
[37867]   08/11/1984   **CM15/11/1988**

Turner, Mr A R, BA MCLIP, Tech. Enhanced Learning Manager, University of West London, London.
[35987]   17/03/1983   **CM07/07/1987**

Turner, Mrs C, BA (Hons) LPC, MSc Student.
[10032140]   29/10/2013   **ME**

Turner, Miss C E, BA (Hons), Information Resource Centre Assistant, E. ON.
[10021738]   08/10/2012   **AF**

Turner, Mrs C V, BA PgDip, Librarian, University of Reading.
[10033181]   18/02/2014   **ME**

Turner, Mrs D, BA (Hons) MSc PgCLTHE MCLIP, Subject Librarian, Teesside UniversityL.
[10013148]   06/02/1981   **CM30/08/1985**

Turner, Mrs E J, MA MCLIP, Info Specialist for Aerospace & Automotive., Kings Norton Lib, Cranfield Univ, Bedford.
[10020649]   14/03/2012   **CM19/07/2000**

Turner, Ms G C, MA MCLIP, Head of Acquisitions &, Spanish Acq. Library, The London L.
[49957]   31/01/1994   **CM21/01/1998**

Turner, Miss H, BA, Local and Family History Officer, Leigh Local Studies, Leigh.
[10019043]   13/04/2011   **ME**

Turner, Mrs I, MA DipLib MCLIP, Network Librarian, Aberdeenshire Council, Banff Academy.
[22663]   01/06/1974   **CM23/03/1993**

Turner, Mrs J, MCLIP, Retired.
[2968]   01/01/1968   **CM01/01/1972**

Turner, Ms J F, BA (Hons) DipLIS MCLIP MSc (Econ), Library services manager., East Sussex Healthcare NHS Trust.
[41780]   08/04/1988   **CM17/03/1999**

Turner, Mrs J R, BA (Hons) MCLIP, Lead Bookseller, Waterstones, Lincoln.
[50370]   07/07/1994   **CM22/07/1998**

Turner, Mr J W S, MA MCLIP, Life Member.
[14962]   01/01/1960   **CM01/01/1965**

Turner, Ms K, MA (Hons) MA MCLIP, Senior Librarian: ICT & Technical Services, Somerset C. C.
[55409]   08/10/1997   **CM23/01/2002**

Turner, Mrs K E, MSc Econ MCLIP, Information Serv. Librarian, Leeds Beckett University, Leeds.
[58979]   16/10/2000   **CM29/05/2013**

Turner, Mrs K J, BA DipLib MCLIP, Information Partnership Co-ordinator, Suffolk County Council.
[41441]   06/01/1988   **CM15/08/1990**

Turner, Miss K L, BSc MSc MCLIP, Ministry of Justice Librarian, MoJ.
[61728]   29/10/2002   **CM23/01/2008**

Turner, Mrs L M, BA MCLIP, Team. Manager,
[20983]   22/07/1973   **CM01/10/1976**

Turner, Mrs M, BA (Hons) MCLIP, Retired.
[35581]   06/10/1982   **CM25/01/1995**

Turner, Mr N D W, BA (Hons) MA MCLIP, Learning & Teaching Librarian, University for the Creative Arts, Epsom / Farnham.
[54580]   27/01/1997   **CM19/07/2000**

Turner, Mr N W, LLB FCMI MCLIP FSA Scot, Retired.
[14969]   01/01/1968   **CM01/01/1971**

Turner, Mrs P M, MCLIP, Retired.
[14974]   01/01/1969   **CM21/08/1972**

Turner, Mr P N, FCLIP, Life Member.
[14975]   01/01/1952   **FE01/01/1961**

Turner, Mr R, Information Professional, London.
[10008381]   19/03/2008   **ME**

Turner, Mr R J, BA DipLib MA MCLIP,
[41947]   08/06/1988   **CM26/02/1992**

Turner, Miss S, BLib MCLIP, Senior Information Adviser, University of Gloucestershire.
[44597]   02/11/1990   **CM27/07/1994**

Turner, Mrs T, BA (Hons), Unemployed.
[10035311]   07/10/2014   **ME**

Turpin, Ms C M, MA (Oxon) MA MCLIP, Self-employed, Ranociel Publishing Serv., Perthshire.
[41121]   02/10/1987   **CM21/11/2001**

Turrell, Mrs K H, BA, Librarian., The Beacon School, Amersham.
[60760]   02/03/1987   **ME**

Turrell, Mrs S A, BA DipLib MCLIP, Resource Ctr. Manager, Sir Roger Manwoods School, Sandwich.
[35497]   25/10/1982   **CM04/08/1987**

Turriff, Dr A, BA MEd PhD FCLIP, Now living in France, maintaining an interest in CPD and school libraries. Researcher and academic proofreader.
[24388]   04/07/1975   **RV**20/02/2014   **FE22/05/1996**

Turtle, Mrs K M, BA MSc MCLIP, Retired.
[22132]   15/02/1974   **CM06/05/1976**

Tutill, Mrs A, Community Information Officer, Sherburn L.
[10016934]   10/06/2010   **AF**

Tutin, Miss P D, BA MCLIP, Life Member.
[14991]   01/01/1954   **CM01/01/1962**

Tuttle, Ms C, BA MSc, Senior Information Assistant (Customer Services), City University London.
[10033642]   08/04/2014   **ME**

Tweed, Mrs J E, BLib MCLIP, Part-time Library Assistant, NILA.
[25953]   09/05/1976   **CM03/03/1980**

Tweedy, Miss J A, BA (Hons) MCLIP, Library Resources Manager, Middlesborough Council.
[38228]   09/02/1985   **CM14/11/1991**

Twiddy, Mr P, BA BSc DipLib MCLIP, Lib. &Information Serv. Manager, Leeds Teaching Hospital NHS Trust.
[34706]   02/02/1982   **CM18/06/1985**

Twine, Mr T J, BA DipLib, Managing Director, EOS International, London.
[38929]   21/10/1985   **ME**

Twinn, Ms R D T, BA Dip Lib, Part-time. Librarian, BBC Television Library, Plymouth.
[39335]   16/01/1986   **ME**

Twist, Mrs M, BA MCLIP, Retired.
[8534]   01/04/1967   **CM01/01/1969**

Twomey, Dr C E J, BSc (Hons) MA PhD MCLIP, Associate Director (Volunteer), Partnerships in Health Information.
[55171]   29/07/1997   **CM12/09/2001**

Tye, Miss L S, MA (Hons), Graduate Library Trainee, South Devon Healthcare NHS Foundation Trust.
[10035027]   05/09/2014   **ME**

Tye, Miss M M, MCLIP BA, Life Member.
[15008]   01/01/1951   **CM01/01/1956**

Tyers, Mrs M K, BA, Part-time Student /Library Assistant, Harold Bridges Library, Lancaster.
[59570]   04/06/2001   **ME**

Tylee, Ms C, BA (Hons) MA MCLIP, Bibl. Serv. Librarian, University of Bath.
[50793]   18/10/1994   **CM17/03/1999**

Tyler, A, MCLIP, Retired.
[15012]   07/08/1963   **CM26/10/1981**

Tyler, Mrs L J, MSc BSc, Lib. Supervisor – Young People's Services, East Dunbartonshire L.
[10015534]   20/11/1991   **ME**

Tyler, Mr S C, BA MSc MCLIP, Systems Admin., University Reading.
[61708]   23/10/2002   **CM19/03/2008**

Tyrell, Ms A, BA (Hons) PgDipLIS MCLIP, LUP Librarian & Academic Program Coordinator, University of Notre Dame (USA) in England.
[55845]   25/11/1997   **CM19/11/2003**

Tyrer, Mrs J A, BA DipLib MCLIP, Bib. Serv. Officer, North Yorkshire County Council.
[42836]   28/03/1989   **CM19/08/1992**

Tyrrell, Ms F, BA (Hons) MCLIP, Assistant Librarian.
[43799]   15/01/1990   **CM23/07/1997**

Tyrrell, Mrs S, BA MA LIS MCLIP, Records Manager, HSBC.
[63848]   01/10/2004   **CM19/03/2008**

Tyson, Ms A, BA,
[10020372]   14/03/2012   **ME**

U

Ullersperger, Miss K A, BA (Hons) DipLIS MCLIP, Trilborough Reference Manager Royal Borough of Kensington & Chelsea.
[47956]   27/10/1992   **CM19/03/1997**

Umansky, Ms G, MA,
[10015925]   03/02/2010   **ME**

Unamboowe, Ms S, MCLIP, Senior Lib. Assistant, Harefield Hospital Medical Lib.
[64045]   06/12/2004   **CM11/11/2009**

Underwood, Mrs A F, MA DipLib MCLIP, Librarian, St Gregorys High School, London Borough of Brent.
[27036]   26/01/1977   **CM31/01/1979**

Underwood, Mr G M, BA MCLIP, Retired.
[15037]   21/08/1958   **CM01/01/1964**

Underwood, Mr J, BSc, Site Librarian, Science Museum, Wroughton.
[10012121]   11/11/2009   **ME**

Underwood, Prof P G, MBA MIIS FCLIP, Emeritus Professor, University of Cape Town / Senior Associate, Knowlead Consulting and Training.
[19134]   15/10/1966   **FE11/07/1977**

Undrill, Miss H, School Librarian, Eastbury Comprehensive School.
[10030746]   25/06/2014   **ME**

Unwin, Mrs K E, BA MCLIP, School Librarian, Mark Rutherford Upper School, Bedford.
[30304]   15/01/1979   **CM17/07/1984**

Unwin, Miss L J, BA (Hons) MSc, Support Consultant, Talis Education Ltd.
[61811]   12/11/2002   **ME**

Unwin, Mrs R C, BA (Hons) MA, Senior Academic Administrator, New College, Oxford.
[58371]   31/01/2000   **CM08/12/2004**

Upton, Dr D, BSc (Hons) PhD MSc, Librarian, Millfield Sch. Library, Somerset.
[36181]   05/07/1983   **ME**

Upton, Mr J C, Deputy Director Library Services, University of St Andrews.
[39888]   03/10/1986   **ME**

Ure, Miss L J, BA (Hons) MLIS, Faculty Liaison Librarian, Humanities and Social Sciences, Queen Mary, University of London.
[58571]   04/04/2000   **ME**

Uren, Dr V S, MSc MCLIP, Lecturer, Aston University, Birmingham.
[60794]   09/01/1989   **CM11/08/1994**

Urrestarazu, Mrs F, BSc, Librarian., International Sch. of London.
[62231]   24/03/2003   **ME**

Urwin, Ms J P, MEd BA (Hons), Senior Lecturer, Northumbria University, Newcastle.
[34928]   19/04/1982   **ME**

Usher, Mr J A, BSc DipLib, ICT Mangager, Islington Council Library and Heritage Service, London.
[39462]   01/02/1986   **ME**

Usher, Mrs J M, BA MCLIP, Co. Information Librarian, Worthing Library, West Sussex.
[40543]   03/03/1987   **CM16/10/1991**

Usher, Mrs K P H, MCLIP HonFCLIP, Librarian, South Hunsley School, East Riding of Yorkshire.
[13628]   12/10/1971   **HFE01/10/2006**

Usher, Mrs P J, BA DMS MCLIP, L. Serv. Manager, Southwark.
[31450]   12/10/1979   **CM06/11/1981**

Usherwood, Prof R C, BA PhD HonFLA FRSA FCLIP, Emeritus Prof. of Lib, Department of Information Studies, University of Sheffield.
[15049]   19/02/1962   **HFE01/01/1992**

Ustun, Mrs A J, LRC Co-ordinator, Harlaw Academy.
[10015271]   29/10/2009   **ME**

Uta, Prof J J, MLS PhD FCLIP, University Librarian, Mzuzu University, Mzuzu, Malawi.
[17894]   24/08/1967   **FE17/11/1999**

Utting, Mrs S J, MCLIP, Life Member.
[16665]   06/03/1953   **CM01/01/1957**

V

Vaananen, Mrs R J, BA (Hons) MCLIP, Knowledge & Resource Specialist, Leeds.
[56105]   17/02/1998   **CM21/03/2001**

Vaisey, Mr C R, BSc DipLib MCLIP, Freelance Consultant, Self-employed.
[26593]   07/10/1976   **CM01/05/1979**

Valcarce Liermo, Miss B, Sales Assistant, Zara.
[10034184]   16/06/2014   **ME**

Vale, Mr P, Information Management Consultant, Arup, London.
[10013398]   23/04/2009   **ME**

Valentine, Ms A B, BA MCLIP, Librarian, North Lanarkshire Council.
[23199]   19/10/1974   **CM22/05/1978**

Valentine, Mrs M, MCLIP, Trust Librarian, Freeman Hospital, Newcastle-upon-Tyne Hospital NHS Foundation Trust.
[9413]   09/01/1968   **CM01/01/1972**

Valentine, Mrs S A, BA MCLIP, Head of Stock Reader Development & Customer Serv., Hertfordshire L.
[27840]   15/09/1977   **CM17/07/1981**

Valla, Miss F, MA, Student, Robert Gordon University.
[10031998]   18/10/2013   **ME**

Vallance, Ms D, BA (Hons) PgDipLIS MCLIP, Reader Development/Information Officer, The Dick Inst., Kilmarnock.
[50457]   04/08/1994   **CM31/01/1996**

Valouchova, Miss I, BA,
[64065]   15/12/2004   **ME**

Van De Weyer, Mr J, PG Cert, Student, Cranfield University.
[10034459]   15/07/2014   **ME**

Van Der Wateren, Mr J F, MA FCLIP FRSA Hon FRIBA, Retired.
[15064]   25/04/1967   **FE22/11/1995**

Van Dort, Mr C, BSc (Hons) MSc, Intelligence Hub Consultant, Defra, London.
[57263]   02/02/1999   **ME**

Van Dort, Mrs K L, MA BA (Hons) MCLIP, High School Librarian, ACS Cobham international School, Cobham.
[10001946]   10/11/1998   **CM15/01/2013**

Van Loo, Mrs N S, MA BA MCLIP, Librarian, New College, Oxford.
[20738]   15/06/1973   **CM29/03/1976**

Van Montfort-Van Der Beek, Mrs S, MSc, Library Services Manager, Animal Health and Veterinary Laboratories Agency.
[10032375]   29/11/2013   **ME**

Van Niekerk, Mrs J M, BA (Hons) MA MCLIP, Head of Library and Media Centre.
[55315]   01/10/1997   **CM13/08/2010**

Van Noorden, Mr A, BSc (ECON) MA MCLIP, Life Member.
[15068]   29/03/1962   **CM01/01/1965**

Van Ochten, Ms J, BA (Hons) MSc (Econ), KM Team Leader., Instituteof Directors, London.
[55817]   28/11/1997   **ME**

Van Riel, Ms R,
[10000716]   19/10/2006   **ME**

van Strien, Mr D, Student, City University London.
[10031371]   24/10/2014   **ME**

Van Tol, Mrs L, BA MCLIP, Co-ordinator Corporate Initiatives, Royal HaskoningDHV, Peterborough.
[23240]   08/11/1974   **CM05/10/1978**

Van Welsenes, Mrs C A, Senior Assistant Librarian, The Third Age Trust.
[10020865]   19/04/2012   **ME**

Vanes, Ms A, BA MCLIP, Learning Resource Centre Manager, David Young Community Academy, Leeds.
[10015026]   01/10/1977   **CM19/11/1979**

Vargues, Miss M M, Librarian, Universidade do Algarve, Faro, Portugal.
[40811]   30/06/1987   **ME**

Varley, Mr A, FCLIP, Life Member.
[15071]   18/02/1950   **FE01/01/1968**

Varley, Mrs D L, DipRSA MCLIP, Retired Head of Learning Resource Centre, Sponne School, Towcester, Northants.
[59924]   01/01/1967   **CM21/03/2007**

Varol, Miss E, MBA PgDip BA (Hons), Electronic Resources Assistant, University of Lincoln Library.
[10019544]   26/07/2011   **ME**

Vaughan, Mr G A, BA, Cataloguer, The Stationery Office, London.
[41729]   26/02/1988   **ME**

Veal, Dr D C, BSc PhD FRSC FCLIP, Hon. Fellow.
[60660]   19/11/1981   **FE25/03/1993**

Veale, Mr T, BA MSc H Dip MCLIP, Information Specialist, Leeds Institute of Health Sciences, University of Leeds.
[10012369]   29/01/2009   **CM18/01/2012**

Veevers, Mr R A, Library Assistant, Burnley Campus Library.
[10021851]   22/10/2012   **ME**

Veitch, Mrs R, BA (Hons) MCLIP, Community Engagement Librarian Cambridgeshire.
[10007744]   08/10/1980   **CM01/07/1989**

Velluet, Mrs E, BA MCLIP, Retired.
[842]   08/10/1966   **CM01/01/1970**

Verlander, Mrs S, MA MCLIP, Information Officer, University of Law, Chester.
[62326]   29/04/2003   **CM13/06/2007**

Vernon, Miss E A, MA (Hons) DipLib MA MCLIP, Area Librarian, North Ayrshire Council.
[56716]   07/10/1998   **CM02/02/2005**

Versaggi, Mrs N T, Student.
[10035284]   03/10/2014   **ME**

Verth, Mrs M, BA MCLIP, EMEA KM CRM Manager, IBM Global Business Services, Edinburgh.
[39255]   13/01/1986   **CM25/01/1995**

Vespa, Mrs C, MLIS, Community Librarian, Childrens Services, Burlington Public Library.
[10032697]   06/01/2014   **ME**

Vicente Tsarouhis, Mrs E, Senior Library Assistant, SOAS Library, London.
[10021397]   31/07/2012   **ME**

Vicinanza, Ms G, Library Information Assistant, Institute of Chartered Accountants of England and Wales.
[10032573]   17/12/2013   **ME**

Vickerman, Mrs H J, BA (Hons), Principal Libraries Officer, Sandwell MBC.
[30694]   22/02/1979   **CM26/08/1982**

Vickers, Miss L J, BA (Hons), KIM Specialist Desk Officer, Foreign & Commonwealth Office.
[46755]   14/01/1992   **ME**

Vickers, Mr P H, FCLIP, Librarian, Prince Consort's Library, Aldershot.
[20555]   03/04/1973   **FE03/10/2007**

Vickers, Dr R W, Enquiry Serv. Specialist, University of Salford, Greater Manchester.
[10001096]   12/01/2007   **ME**

Vickery, Mr J E, MA FCLIP, Retired.
[15118]   01/03/1972   **FE20/05/1998**

Vidgen, Mr G A, BLib MCLIP, Business Consultant, Capita Business Serv., Cardiff.
[40917]   20/08/1987   **CM01/12/1995**

Viegas, Ms G, MA, Student, Robert Gordon University.
[10022263]   29/01/2013   **ME**

Vieitez, Mrs H L, LLB (Hons) Dip LP MSc, Senior Information Assistant, City University London.
[10022916]   07/05/2013   **ME**

Vigour, Ms L, BA (Hons) MA, Student, UCL.
[10033018]   16/10/2014   **ME**

Vijayaganesh, Ms S, ILMS, Faculty Knowledge Assistant, Library / Goodhope Hospital.
[58478]   23/02/2000   **ME**

Villa, Mrs D J, BA MCLIP, Library and Knowledge Services Manager, North Bristol NHS Trust, Bristol.
[3767]   27/10/1970   **CM20/07/1976**

Vincent, Mr G D, BSc MCLIP, Applications Consultant, Accent on Systems Ltd, Burnham.
[60659]   21/03/1972   **CM01/07/1979**

Vincent, Mrs H F, BA (Hons) DipILM MCLIP, Principal Business Systems Analyst, London Borough of Hillingdon.
[50645]   06/10/1994   **CM17/05/2000**

Vincent, Mr I W, BA MCLIP, Retired.
[15130]   17/03/1963   **CM01/01/1966**

Vincent, Mr J C, HonFCLIP, Networker, The Network – Tackling Social Exclusion.
[15131]   10/10/1966   **HFE30/09/2014**

Vinnicombe, Mr R A J, DMA MCLIP, Retired.
[15139]   10/09/1964   **CM01/01/1969**

Virgo, Mrs A J, BA (Hons) PGCE, Librarian Stamford High School.
[10007029]   13/12/1979   **ME**

Virnes, Mrs H, MSc, Career Break.
[58363]   26/01/2000   **ME**

Visser, Mrs C, BSc, L. Manager, Accrington & Rossendale College, Accrington.
[10005111]   06/06/2007   **AF**

Vitai, Mrs J G T, FCLIP, Life Member.
[17911]   26/05/1952   **FE01/01/1963**

Vittles, Miss K, Suffolk Libraries Innovation and Development Manager.
[10020631]   13/03/2012   **ME**

Vodden, Ms G J, BSc (Hons) DipIS MCLIP, Knowledge Officer, Nabarro LLP., London.
[46334]   28/10/1991   **RV**15/07/2014   **CM21/05/2003**

Voisey, Ms J, ACLIP, Lending L. Supervisor, Bristol Central Library, Bristol.
[65770]   24/04/2006   **ACL06/02/2008**

Vollmer, Mr P M, LLB LLM, Head of Research Services, House of Lords.
[10022870]   30/04/2013   **ME**

Voy, Mr E, MCLIP, Life Member.
[15150]   01/01/1954   **CM01/01/1963**

Voyce, Mr P D, BA MCLIP, Comm. L. Manager, Wednesbury Town, Sandwell Metropolitan Borough Council.
[35649]   01/12/1982   **CM13/12/1984**

Voysey, Ms J D, BA, Student, University of Brighton.
[10033210]   20/02/2014   **ME**

Voysey, Miss J P, MCLIP, Life Member.
[15152]   02/09/1949   **CM01/01/1959**

Vraca, Mrs M,
[10013352]   16/04/2009   **ME**

Vriend, Mrs A K, ACLIP, Library Supervisor, Epping, North Weald & Chipping Ongar Libraries, Essex Libraries, Essex County Council.
[10020448]   20/02/2012   **ACL04/10/2013**

Vyas, Mrs M, BA (Hons) MCLIP, Learning Res. Centre Manager, Sir Jonathan North Comm. College, Leicester.
[10000809]   10/01/1985   **CM04/10/1988**

W

Waddilove, Ms K, MA MCLIP, Head of Learning Res., JFS School, Harrow.
[15155]   13/02/1970   **CM16/10/1972**

Waddington, Mrs A E F, BA (CNAA) MCLIP, Librarian, HMP Ranby.
[65673]   23/03/2006   **CM11/11/2009**

Wade, Ms L, BA (Hons) MSc, Senior Information Specialist, Integreon Managed Solutions, Bristol.
[58953]   10/10/2000   **ME**

Wade, Mr M J, BA MLib MCLIP, Independent Library Professional.
[23782]   22/01/1975   **CM10/11/1978**

Wadee, Miss S, BA (Hons), Student, Manchester Metropolitan University.
[10035101]   15/09/2014   **ME**

Wafer, Mr R A, MCLIP, Life Member.
[19374]   10/03/1947   **CM01/01/1950**

Wagg, Mrs S, BSc (HONS) Econ, Part-time MA student in Librarianship at the University of Sheffield Interested in children/youth and health libraries.
[10020710]   27/03/2012   **ME**

Wagner, Mrs M J, MLIS, Unemployed.
[10022316]   05/02/2013   **ME**

Wagstaff, Mrs D A, Part-time Assistant Library Manager, Birmingham City Council.
[63178]   03/03/2004   **ME**

Wagstaff, Mr D J, BA MMus FCLIP, Resident in USA.
[44195]   04/07/1990   **FE21/05/2003**

Wainman, Mrs E, PgDip, Student, Aberystwyth University.
[10032538]   12/12/2013   **ME**

Wainwright, Miss E, BA (Hons), Librarian, Sprowston Community High School & College of Arts.
[10034095]   04/07/2014   **ME**

Wainwright, Mrs J M, OBE BA FCLIP, Retired.
[60661]   01/01/1979   **FE01/03/1986**
Waite, Miss C G, BA (Hons) PgDipLib, Information Development
Manager, Cultural Services, Lancashire County Council., Preston.
[10008284]   26/10/1989   **ME**
Waite, Mrs J A, MCLIP, Head of L. & Information Serv., Arts univ.
College, Bournemouth.
[15178]   18/06/1969   **CM20/11/1972**
Waite, Mrs M H, BA MCLIP, Prison Librarian, Leeds L. & Information
Serv., HMP Wealstun.
[15458]   21/01/1969   **CM01/01/1973**
Waites, Mr R, ACLIP, Library Assistant/Assistant Administrator, OVE
ARUP & Partners, London.
[10013926]   22/01/2013   **ACL13/11/2013**
Waithe, Mr H L, Library Clerk, Aberystwyth University.
[10032301]   15/11/2013   **ME**
Wake, Mrs M C, BA (Hons) MA, Head L. and Information Serv., The
School of Pharmacy, University of London.
[46254]   21/10/1991   **CM19/03/1997**
Wake, Mr R L, MA MA MCLIP, Deputy Librarian, University of
Southampton.
[32353]   20/02/1980   **CM25/11/1982**
Wakeham, Mr M W, MA DipLib FCLIP, Retired.
[39820]   30/07/1986   **FE09/09/2009**
Walaitis, Miss C J, BLib MCLIP, Librarian, Greenhills Library, South
Lankashire.
[30289]   09/01/1979   **CM09/01/1981**
Waldhelm, Mr R J, BA DipLib MCLIP, Head of Solicitors Legal
Information Centre, Scottish Government Legal Directorate, Victoria
Quay, Edinburgh EH6 6QQ.
[29859]   10/10/1978   **CM17/07/1984**
Wale, Miss E L, Library Assistant, University of Reading.
[10032864]   21/01/2014   **ME**
Wales, Mrs C M, BA MCLIP, Lending Serv. Manager, North Lanarkshire
Council.
[31472]   16/10/1979   **CM25/10/1983**
Wales, Mrs J, MCLIP, School Librarian, Glasgow City Council.
[14416]   06/06/1072   **CM15/12/1976**
Wales, Mr T B, BA (Hons) MSc MCLIP FHA, Director of Library
Services, The University of West London.
[55082]   09/07/1997   **CM12/09/2001**
Walford, Mrs J E, FCLIP, Retired.
[15199]   19/11/1942   **FE01/01/1954**
Walke, Ms P, BSc MCLIP, Deputy L. Serv. Manager, Health Science
Library, Frimley Park Hospital NHS Trust.
[10009923]   02/07/1998   **CM25/01/2011**
Walker, Mrs A, BA (Hons) MCLIP, Cataloguer, Jersey Archive.
[43389]   06/10/1989   **CM23/07/1997**
Walker, Mrs A, MCLIP, Unemployed.
[15204]   25/02/1960   **CM01/01/1966**
Walker, Mrs A F, BA MCLIP, Resource Centre for Coordinator,
Lossiemouth High School.
[26010]   04/05/1976   **CM18/07/1979**
Walker, Mr A J, BA MCLIP, Development Librarian, Operations, Isle of
Wight L. Serv.
[36587]   21/10/1983   **CM11/11/1986**
Walker, Miss A M, MA DipLib MCLIP, Library Assistant, LB of Havering
L. Serv., Hornchurch.
[38723]   01/10/1985   **CM21/07/1989**
Walker, Ms A R, BA MCLIP, Librarian, Turcan Connell, Solicitors,
Edinburgh.
[38057]   10/01/1985   **CM18/09/1991**

Walker, Mrs C, MCLIP, Learning Resource Centre Manager, Aylsham
High School, Norfolk.
[65625]   13/03/2006   **CM09/11/2011**
Walker, Mr C A, MCITP MCP, knowledge Info manager, Ministry of
Defence.
[10032941]   30/01/2014   **ME**
Walker, Dr C G, BA (Hons) PGCE MA MCLIP PhD, Assistant
Lecturer/Researcher, Leeds Metropolitan University & Information
Officer University of Law, York.
[47929]   26/10/1992   **CM31/01/1996**
Walker, Mrs C M, BA (Hons) MSc MCLIP, Resource Assistant,
Halesowen College, Halesowen.
[62273]   07/04/2003   **CM09/07/2008**
Walker, Mrs D, MA MCLIP, Reference Specialist, British Library,
London.
[10005097]   26/10/2010   **CM14/12/2012**
Walker, Miss D, Student, Robert Gordon University.
[10031584]   04/09/2013   **ME**
Walker, Mrs F, BA MCLIP, Library & Information Services Manager.
[10022343]   11/02/2013   **CM09/07/1981**
Walker, Miss F E M, ACLIP, Assistant Librarian, All Nations Christian
College, Ware.
[10016424]   24/03/2010   **ACL09/11/2011**
Walker, Dr G P M, MA PhD FCLIP, Retired.
[15220]   30/06/1964   **FE24/12/1980**
Walker, Mrs H S, Retired.
[15221]   01/09/1950   **ME**
Walker, Mrs J, LLM, Head of Casework, FOI & DPA Team, Foreign &
Commonwealth Office.
[10033531]   24/03/2014   **ME**
Walker, Mr J, BA (Hons) MA, Library Assistant, The Hereford Academy,
Herefordshire.
[10017449]   27/11/1995   **ME**
Walker, Ms J, BA MCLIP, Retired.
[3181]   01/01/1962   **CM26/10/1978**
Walker, Ms J, MA, Student, The University of Sheffield.
[10031759]   01/10/2013   **ME**
Walker, Miss J, MCLIP,
[10013576]   07/05/2009   **CM13/05/2014**
Walker, Miss J A, BSc MCLIP, Director of Operations, South of England,
The Stroke Assoc.
[60715]   29/06/1984   **CM29/06/1984**
Walker, Mrs J E, LRC Manager, Sandbach High School, Sandbach.
[10000872]   17/11/2006   **AF**
Walker, Mr J R A, FCLIP, Retired.
[15235]   25/10/1946   **FE04/06/1965**
Walker, Mr K, MA (Hons) PgDipILS MCLIP, Information Serv. Advisor,
Napier University, Edinburgh. Current Chair of the Business
Librarians Association (www. blalib. org).
[57033]   27/11/1998   **CM07/09/2005**
Walker, Mrs K E, BA DipLib MCLIP, Senior ICS Consultant Infor, Bristol.
Library Division – Customer consultation, Training and Project
management.
[39107]   04/11/1985   **CM18/04/1989**
Walker, Mrs K J, BA MCLIP, Senior Information & Research Officer,
Evangelical Alliance.
[33564]   17/01/1981   **CM16/02/1988**
Walker, Miss K M B, BA MA MCLIP, Retired.
[15238]   15/01/1968   **CM01/01/1970**
Walker, Ms L E, MA BA BSc,
[58072]   25/10/1999   **ME**
Walker, Mr M, BA (Hons) LLB (Hons) MSc, Information & Research
Manager – London & Desks, Linklaters.
[52937]   29/01/1996   **ME**

Walker, Mrs M L, ACLIP, Library Assistant in Charge., West Mill Street
Library, Perth, Scotland.
[10020499]   21/02/2012 **ACL13/05/2014**
Walker, Mrs M L, Research Support Librarian, Northumbria University,
Newcastle.
[59012]   24/10/2000   **ME**
Walker, Mrs P, BA (Hons) ACLIP, Lib. Assistant, Mansfield Library,
Notts.
[10002966]   10/05/2007 **ACL16/04/2008**
Walker, Mrs P, BA (Hons) MA MCLIP, Service Development Officer, with
responsibility for Stokesley Library, North Yorkshire Libraries.
[58211]   17/11/1999 **CM11/03/2009**
Walker, Miss P, BA MCLIP, Unwaged.
[29861]   10/10/1978 **CM23/09/1985**
Walker, Mr R B, Student, University of Strathclyde.
[10033949]   13/05/2014   **ME**
Walker, Miss R C, MPhys, Student, University of Aberystwyth.
[10019833]   19/09/2011   **ME**
Walker, Mrs R F M, MA (Hons), Library Assistant, Okehampton L.
[65019]   07/10/2005   **ME**
Walker, Mrs R M, BSc (Hons) MCLIP, Unwaged.
[48147]   11/11/1992 **CM24/09/1997**
Walker, Mrs S A, Student, New College Stamford.
[10030860]   03/02/2014   **ME**
Walker, Mrs S L, BA (Hons) MCLIP AFHEA, Assistant Librarian, The
Orkney Library & Archive.
[46459]   07/11/1991 **CM21/01/1998**
Walker, Mrs S M, HNC MCLIP, Medical Information Sci., Sharon Walker
Medical Information Serv., Newmarket.
[60831]   01/03/1990 **CM01/03/1990**
Walker, Mrs S M, BSc MCLIP, Retired.
[13260]   09/10/1968 **CM24/08/1972**
Walker, Mrs S M, MLitt MA MCLIP, Retired.
[29340]   06/06/1978 **CM12/09/1980**
Walker, Miss V, MTheol (Hons) MSc MCLIP, Head of Information &
Research, Watson, Farley & Williams, London.
[50600]   29/09/1994 **CM21/05/1997**
Walker, Mrs V L, MCLIP, Retired.
[19967]   09/01/1973 **CM01/01/1975**
Walker, Ms V M, MCLIP, Retired.
[10583]   01/01/1967 **CM01/01/1971**
Walker, Mrs W E, BA MCLIP, Resource Area Manager, Glyn School,
Surrey.
[31767]   10/12/1979 **CM23/01/2008**
Walker-Roberts, Mrs K A, BA (Hons) PgDip, LRC Manager, St Nicholas
Catholic High School.
[10007177]   24/01/2008   **ME**
Walkington, Ms E, BA DipLib MCLIP, L. & Resource Centre Assistant,
Halesowen College.
[44435]   08/10/1990 **CM21/07/1993**
Walkinshaw, Mr B R, BA MCLIP, Retired.
[15263]   10/02/1965 **CM01/01/1968**
Walkley, Mrs R J,
[61716]   25/10/2002   **ME**
Wall, Mr C J, MCLIP, Researcher at health care chartered surveyors,
Carterwood Ltd.
[42387]   27/10/1988 **CM15/09/1999**
Wall, Mr M D, BSc DipLib MCLIP, Assistant Director (Library Services),
University of Bristol.
[39970]   07/10/1986 **CM21/07/1989**
Wall, Dr R A, PhD FCLIP HonFCLIP HonMAslib, Life Member.
[15266]   24/01/1942 **FE01/01/1950**

Wallace, Ms A, BA MCLIP, Learning Res. Manager., Buxton Comm.
School, Derbys. County Council.
[36588]   26/10/1983 **CM15/11/1988**
Wallace, Mrs C A, MCLIP, Coordinator Business & Learning Library of
Birmingham.
[31370]   19/10/1979 **CM07/09/1982**
Wallace, Miss E J, BA (Hons) MCLIP,
[62663]   01/10/2003 **CM21/11/2007**
Wallace, Miss E M, Area Children's Librarian (PT), Salisbury Library,
Wiltshire.
[10006614]   11/09/2007   **ME**
Wallace, Miss J, MA (Hons) DipLib TQFE CELTA, College Lecturer, City
of Glasgow College.
[10033907]   12/05/2014   **ME**
Wallace, Mrs J, MCLIP, Librarian, Technical Information, Ctr. Royal
Engineers, MoD.
[64276]   22/02/2005 **CM24/10/2008**
Wallace, Mrs K M, BA MCLIP, Lead Manager. Library Service, West
Sussex County Council.
[35316]   11/10/1982 **CM11/06/1986**
Wallace, Ms L G, BSc MSc PgDip, Librarian, HMP Forest Bank.
[62767]   20/10/2003   **ME**
Wallace, Miss M, MCLIP, Retired.
[15275]   08/03/1964 **CM01/01/1970**
Wallace, Mrs M G, BA MCLIP DPA, Part-time Librarian, Falkirk Council
L.
[23590]   21/01/1975 **CM12/03/1980**
Wallace, Mr N E, Student, Defence Academy of the UK.
[10034615]   23/07/2014   **ME**
Wallace, Mrs S, BA (Hons) MSc, Senior L. Assistant, Sackler Library,
Oxford University.
[66140]   02/10/2006   **ME**
Wallace, Miss S A, BSc MCLIP, Retired.
[22840]   01/10/1974 **CM01/10/1976**
Wallace, Mrs S M, BLib PGCE MCLIP, Casual Librarian, Norfolk County
Council.
[37194]   01/04/1984 **CM16/02/1988**
Wallace, Mrs T R, DipLib MA MCLIP, Communications and Information
Officer, Learning & Teaching Scotland, Dundee.
[32956]   03/10/1980 **CM18/08/1983**
Wallace, Mr W, MA MCLIP, Retired.
[21896]   17/02/1974 **CM01/01/1976**
Waller, Mrs S, MCLIP, L. Res. Manager, Kent College, Pembury, Kent.
[22196]   18/02/1974 **CM01/01/1977**
Wallis, Ms C, BA,
[10031520]   03/09/2013   **ME**
Wallis, Ms K, BA MCLIP, Cust. Serv. Librarian, Oadby Library, Leics.
County Council.
[37358]   10/07/1984 **CM16/10/1991**
Wallis, Mrs K, BSc PgDip, Student, Aberystwyth University.
[10021025]   21/02/2014   **ME**
Wallis, Mrs K M, BA (Hons) MA MCLIP, Learning Resource Manager,
Kesteven and Sleaford High School Selective Academy.
[59043]   07/11/2000 **CM04/10/2006**
Wallis, Ms M K, BA DipLib MCLIP, Retired.
[20602]   24/04/1973 **CM11/11/1975**
Walmsley, Mr A J, BA MA DipLib MCLIP, Community Heritage Manager,
St Annes Library, Lancashire CC.
[42197]   10/10/1988 **CM27/07/1994**
Walmsley, Ms S J, BA MA, ICT Project Manager, UK Trade &
Investment.
[10008650]   03/10/2001   **ME**
Walne, Mrs L R, BA (Hons) MA MCLIP, Retired.
[15300]   08/02/1952 **CM01/01/1958**

Walne, Mr M J, BA (Hons) MCLIP, Librarian, Stenhouse Library, Kingston Hospital NHS Trust, Kingston upon Thames.
[58872]   20/09/2000   **CM23/06/2004**

Walpole, Mr J M, BA MCLIP AIL, Life Member.
[17926]   29/10/1948   **CM01/01/1953**

Walsh, Mr A, BSc MSc MCLIP, Academic Librarian and Teaching Fellow, University of Huddersfield. Trainer and publisher, Innovative Libraries Ltd+F120.
[62927]   20/11/2003   **CM31/01/2007**

Walsh, Mrs A C, MA (Hons) DipILS MCLIP, Library Educational Services Manager, Culture NL.
[56872]   27/10/1998   **CM15/11/2000**

Walsh, Mr A D, MA, Metadata & Systems Librarian, Durham University.
[10022057]   27/11/2012   **ME**

Walsh, Mrs B V, BSc, Assistant Librarian, West Suffolk Hospital NHS Foundation Trust.
[65942]   11/07/2006   **ACL05/10/2007**

Walsh, Miss C, MA (Hons),
[10018783]   21/03/2011   **ME**

Walsh, Ms C J, BA MA PG DIP LIB SFHEA, Director of Library and Learning Services, University of East London.
[10015771]   19/02/1986   **ME**

Walsh, Mrs E K, MA (Hons) MSc (Econ) MCLIP, Site Librarian, Warrington Campus, University of Chester.
[51197]   23/11/1994   **CM06/04/2005**

Walsh, Mrs J, Student, Aberystwyth University.
[10019224]   09/05/2011   **ME**

Walsh, Mrs J A, BA MCLIP, Management Coordinator North Yorks. County Council.
[29396]   18/06/1978   **CM17/07/1981**

Walsh, Mrs J A, BA (Hons) MA MCLIP, Senior Library Assistant, University of Nottingham.
[54392]   02/12/1996   **CM16/07/2003**

Walsh, Miss K M, PT Lib. Assistant, Accrington Library, Accrington.
[10014852]   18/09/2009   **AF**

Walsh, Mrs L, BA MA, Faculty Training Librarian, Heartlands Hospital Library, Birmingham.
[10018089]   14/12/2010   **ME**

Walsh, Ms N J, BA (Hons) MCLIP, Senior Information Manager, Guidance Information Services, National Institute for Health and Care Excellence (NICE).
[50955]   31/10/1994   **CM22/07/1998**

Walsh, Mrs S, BA DipLib MCLIP, Manager Sch. L. Serv., Plymouth C. C.
[35454]   18/10/1982   **CM15/02/1989**

Walsh, Mrs S A, BSc HDLS MCLIP, Information Serv. Manager, Burgoyne Management Ltd, London.
[48350]   01/12/1992   **CM03/07/1996**

Walsh, Miss T, BA MA,
[10014292]   14/07/2009   **AF**

Walters, Mr J, BA MCLIP, Retired.
[15322]   23/02/1954   **CM01/01/1962**

Walters, Mrs K O, BA DipLib MCLIP, Librarian, The Athenaeum, London.
[33678]   09/02/1981   **CM17/02/1987**

Walters, Mr L, Student, Cardiff University.
[10032902]   24/01/2014   **ME**

Walters, Mr R J, MBE MA B PHIL MCLIP, Retired.
[18228]   06/10/1972   **CM25/10/1974**

Walters, Dr W H, PhD FCLIP, Executive Director, O'Malley Library, Manhattan College, NY, USA.
[62143]   28/02/2003   **FE13/06/2007**

Walters-Smith, Mrs K, BA HONS PG DIP, Learning Community Librarian, North Ayrshire Council.
[10021585]   04/09/2012   **ME**

Walther, Ms J, BSc Econ, Librarian.
[10033708]   16/04/2014   **ME**

Walton, Ms E L, BA (Hons) MA FHEA, Head of Academic Services, Loughborough University Library.
[10007746]   01/11/1996   **ME**

Walton, Dr G L, BA (Hons) MA PGCHPE PhD MCLIP FHEA, Lecturer Information Sciences, Fac. of Engineering & Environment, Northumbria University.
[47672]   13/10/1992   **CM25/09/1996**

Walton, Mrs H M, BA MCLIP, Area Sch. Librarian, Sch. L. Serv., Hampshire County Council.
[38037]   08/01/1985   **CM18/04/1990**

Walton, Mrs I C, MA Dip Inf Sci, Retired.
[49996]   07/02/1994   **ME**

Walton, Ms J, BA MCLIP FCIPD, Education Consultant.
[34683]   26/01/1982   **RV**04/04/2006   **CM14/11/1985**

Walton, Dr J G, BSc MA MBA FETC MCLIP, Head of Planning & Res., Loughborough University.
[26599]   01/10/1976   **CM31/10/1978**

Walton, Miss N, MA ILM, Learning Res. Manager, Poynton High School, Stockport.
[10014853]   04/03/2003   **ME**

Walton, Miss V A, Student.
[10006307]   10/10/2007   **ME**

Walworth, Dr J C, MA PhD, Fellow Librarian, Merton College, Oxford.
[47108]   01/05/1992   **ME**

Walwyn, Ms O, MA MCLIP, Student.
[10012728]   25/02/2009   **CM10/03/2011**

Wan, Mr K, MSci MA, Business Information Assistant, John Lewis.
[10022365]   19/02/2013   **ME**

Wan, Miss L T, BSc (Hons) MCLIP, Senior Librarian, Singapore Polytechnic.
[22159]   25/01/1974   **CM05/09/1977**

Wan, Ms V, MA BSc, Subject Classifier, Nielsen Bookdata, Herts.
[10012974]   19/03/2009   **ME**

Wan, Dr Y C, BA MPhil PhD MCLIP FHKLA, Deputy. Librarian, University of Hong Kong L.
[41864]   26/04/1988   **CM19/08/1992**

Wan Cheung, Mrs M Y A, Chief Librarian, Hong Kong Public Library.
[41865]   26/04/1988   **ME**

Wang, Ms M L, Prof., National Cheng-Chi University, Taiwan.
[52083]   22/09/1995   **ME**

Wann, Miss L S, BA (Hons) MCLIP, Assistant Librarian, West Middlesex University Hospital NHS Trust, Isleworth.
[56744]   08/10/1998   **CM23/01/2002**

Wannop, Miss S, BA DipLib MCLIP, User Support Manager, EUMETSAT Germany.
[42601]   17/01/1989   **CM12/12/1991**

Warburton, Mr J, BA MSc, Prison Lib. & Res. Manager, HMPS Young Offenders Inst., Littlehey Cambridgeshire.
[63732]   09/09/2004   **ME**

Warburton, Mr M K, BSc (Hons), Unemployed.
[10022364]   19/02/2013   **AF**

Warburton, Miss S J, BA (Hons), Weekend Library Assistant, Norton Library.
[10032211]   24/12/2013   **ME**

Ward, Mrs A, BA MA MCLIP, Head of Academic Services, Sheffield Hallam University.
[29675]   02/10/1978   **CM14/05/1981**

Ward, Ms A D, BA (Hons) MA, Reader Serv. Dev. Manager, Essex Libraries.
[57769]   29/07/1999   **ME**

Ward, Mrs A L, MA (Hons) MSc MCLIP, Libraries, Museum and Archives Manager, Inverclyde C., Greenock.
[59937]   08/11/2001   **RV**27/11/2007   **CM29/03/2004**

Ward, Ms B J, HE Learning Resource Advisor, University Centre Yeovil.
[61084]   01/03/2002   **AF**

Ward, Miss C E, BAHons BAHons DipMS PGCE QTLS, Librarian, Luton Culture.
[35486]   19/10/1982   **ME**

Ward, Mrs D M, MCLIP, Retired.
[11858]   26/09/1969   **CM15/07/1972**

Ward, Mrs F, Student, Aberystwyth University.
[10031808]   07/10/2013   **ME**

Ward, Mrs G, BA, Branch Manager, Lancashire County Council.
[39420]   23/01/1986   **ME**

Ward, Mrs G, BA, Senior Lib. & Independent Studies Manager, Fortismere School, London.
[10009294]   13/05/2008   **ME**

Ward, Mr G B J, BA (Hons) PGCE MEd MSc MCLIP, Senior Library Assistant, University of Sheffield.
[57644]   09/06/1999   **CM20/11/2002**

Ward, Mrs H A, BSc (Hons) DipILM MCLIP, L. Manager, Xaverian College, Manchester.
[48857]   02/07/1993   **CM19/03/1997**

Ward, Mrs H J, BA MSc MCLIP,
[53989]   14/10/1996   **CM08/12/2004**

Ward, Ms J L, BA MSc, Learning Zone Team Leader, Transport for London.
[56696]   05/10/1998   **ME**

Ward, Mrs J M, FCLIP, Retired.
[15353]   18/09/1940   **FE01/01/1946**

Ward, Mrs K M, BA MCLIP, Librarian, Thompsons Solicitors, Manchester.
[16205]   25/04/1969   **CM09/09/1974**

Ward, Mrs L M, BSc (Hons) MSc MScHSR MCLIP, L. Serv. Manager, University Hospital of Leicester NHS Trust.
[52672]   17/11/1995   **CM15/03/2000**

Ward, Mr M, MSc, House of Commons Library.
[10022185]   15/01/2013   **ME**

Ward, Mr M S, Serials Librarian, National Art Library, V&A Museum, London.
[47313]   10/07/1992   **ME**

Ward, Mr N J, BA MA DMS MCLIP, Retired.
[28201]   04/10/1977   **CM25/02/1981**

Ward, Ms N R, BA MCLIP, Sr. Assistant Librarian, Manchester Metropolitan University, All Saints L.
[61261]   10/05/2002   **CM11/03/2009**

Ward, Mrs P, BLS MBA MCLIP, Assistant Chief Librarian, Western Education & Library Board, Central Library.
[34740]   20/01/1982   **CM03/05/1989**

Ward, Mrs P A, BA MCLIP, Lib. Manager, Robert Mays School, Odiham, Hants.
[36077]   26/04/1983   **CM07/07/1987**

Ward, Miss P L, BA DipLib MCLIP, Senior Assistant L., House of Lords.
[36545]   21/10/1983   **CM15/11/1988**

Ward, Mr R, BA MCLIP FBIS, Retired.
[15363]   01/01/1965   **CM01/01/1970**

Ward, Mrs R H, BA (Hons) MCLIP, Locality Manager, Leicestershire County Council.
[26491]   06/10/1976   **CM12/03/1979**

Ward, Ms S, MA CertEd AHEA MCLIP, Subject Team Leader, University of Bolton.
[21938]   01/02/1974   **CM06/10/1979**

Ward, Mr S, MA (Hons) MSc MSc MCLIP,
[65612]   28/02/2006   **CM25/01/2011**

Ward, Dr S E, BSc PhD CertEd FCLIP HonFCLIP, Principal Consultant, Beaworthy Consulting, Senior Associate Consultant TFPL, TFPL Ltd, London.
[60663]   06/12/1973   **FE02/04/1987**

Ward, Mr T, BLib MCLIP, Head of Library and Information. Services, Prince Consort's Library, Aldershot.
[24306]   07/06/1975   **CM19/09/1980**

Wardill, Mrs I N, BSc (Hons), Volunteer, Eltham College.
[10035113]   15/09/2014   **ME**

Wardlaw, Ms J, BA (Hons) MA MCLIP,
[51301]   01/01/1995   **CM23/01/2002**

Wardle, Ms C M, BA MA, Assistant Librarian, Whittington Health Library.
[10017678]   13/04/2004   **ME**

Wardle, Mr R J, BA DipLib MCLIP, Corps Librarian, CTCRM.
[36364]   05/10/1983   **CM01/01/1987**

Wardrope, Miss A, Unemployed.
[35750]   14/01/1983   **ME**

Wardsell, Miss C, Student Leeds Metropolitan University.
[10032403]   03/12/2013   **ME**

Ward-Smith, Ms I T, BSc, Student, University of Exeter.
[10035157]   22/09/2014   **ME**

Ware, Ms C H, BA BLS MIIS, Retired.
[42007]   18/07/1988   **ME**

Ware, Mr P T, BA MCLIP, Senior Group Manager, Bexley L. Serv, London.
[23105]   08/10/1974   **CM02/10/1978**

Wareham, Mrs A, BA (Hons) FCLIP, Library Information and Enquiries Manager, NMRN, Portsmouth.
[37825]   06/11/1984   **FE18/09/2003**

Wareing, Miss A, Information Assistant, User Experience, Kimberlin Library, De Montfort University, Leicester.
[10019089]   18/04/2011   **AF**

Wares, Mr C, BA (Hons) MA MCLIP, Head of Library & Learning Resources, Pearson Higher Education Awards.
[52029]   02/10/1995   **CM20/01/1999**

Warhurst, Ms C M, BA (Hons) MCLIP, L. & Information Serv. Manager, London's Transport Museum, Transport for London.
[25276]   05/01/1976   **CM04/02/1980**

Wark, Mr A, MA (Hons) PgDip MCLIP, Reading Room Assistant, National Library of Scotland, Edinburgh.
[62184]   10/03/2003   **CM21/03/2007**

Wark, Mr P P, MCLIP HonFCLIP, Library Services Manager, Midlothian Council, Loanhead.
[21511]   22/10/1973   **HFE30/09/2014**

Warmington, Mr J, MA DipLib MCLIP, Retired.
[15379]   07/09/1966   **CM01/01/1969**

Warmoth, Mrs K M, BA DipLib, Librarian, Fladgate LLP., London.
[41141]   08/10/1987   **ME**

Warne, Mr P, MA MCLIP, Life Member.
[15380]   13/02/1960   **CM01/01/1962**

Warner, Miss A R, BA MCLIP, Assistant Librarian, DCLG Library, London.
[23535]   05/01/1975   **CM25/04/1979**

Warner, Mrs F M, BA (Hons) DipLib MCLIP, Customer Services Development Officer, East Dunbartonshire Leisure & Culture Trust.
[35307]   10/10/1982   **CM22/05/1996**

Warner, Mr T, BA MA, Librarian, Notts. County Council.
[40326]   21/01/1987   **CM21/10/1992**

Warnock, Mr A P, MA DipLib, Acquisitions Librarian, Department for Work & Pensions.
[29865]   19/10/1978   **ME**

Warr, Dr W A, MA DPhilCChem FRSC FCLIP,
[60615]   25/09/1984   **FE09/04/1991**

Warren, Miss B M, MCLIP, Life Member.
[15392]   14/03/1952   **CM01/01/1958**
Warren, Miss C E, BA, Student, New College Stamford.
[10032986]   03/02/2014   **ME**
Warren, Ms C E, MA MCLIP,
[10012557]   23/02/2009   **CM22/08/2012**
Warren, Mr C J, MSc BA (Hons), Library Assistant – academic.
[10018945]   01/04/2011   **ME**
Warren, Miss D, BA (Hons) PgDipLib, Information Manager, Bevan
Brittan, Bristol.
[41779]   08/04/1988   **ME**
Warren, Miss E J, BA (Hons), Student, Loughborough University.
[10032320]   18/11/2013   **ME**
Warren, Mrs G E, BA (Hons) MScEcon MA MCLIP, Librarian, Norwich
Cathedral.
[54098]   28/10/1996   **CM20/01/1999**
Warren, Mrs J, BA CILIP, Retired.
[15088]   17/11/1971   **CM16/10/1974**
Warren, Ms S, BA MCLIP, Information Servs. Manager, Keoghs LLP,
Bolton.
[41531]   14/01/1988   **CM12/12/1991**
Warren, Mrs Y E, BA MCLIP, Lib. Manager & Info Supervisor, Upper
School Library, Mcauley Catholic High School.
[29288]   15/05/1978   **CM03/11/1981**
Warriner, Ms K P, MSc, Information Services Librarian, Calderdale
Metropolitan Borough Council, Northgate.
[58396]   01/02/2000   **ME**
Warwick, Mrs J, MCLIP, Retired.
[10818]   15/10/1966   **CM01/01/1970**
Washington, Mrs J K, BSc (Hons) MSc (Econ) MCLIP, Unwaged.
[55466]   13/10/1997   **CM20/11/2002**
Washington, Dr L, BA MA MCLIP, Librarian, University of Cambridge.
[42571]   03/01/1989   **CM27/05/1992**
Wason, Mr J, Student, Strathclyde University, Glasgow.
[10017887]   21/10/2010   **ME**
Wassell, Mrs R, Library Assistant, Bond Dickinson LLP, Devon.
[64671]   24/05/2005   **ME**
Wasson, Dr L, MA PhD, Library Assistant, Belfast Central Library,
Heritage Department, Libraries NI.
[10023411]   16/07/2013   **ME**
Waterhouse, Mrs A, BA MSc, Research Admnistrator, DSRU.
[64205]   09/02/2005   **ME**
Waterhouse, Ms C, Information Manager, Foreign & Commonwealth
Office.
[10032707]   07/01/2014   **ME**
Waterhouse, Miss J, BA (Hons) MSc FHEA, Subject Librarian for
Music, University of Huddersfield.
[54267]   11/11/1996   **ME**
Waterhouse, Mr N, BA (Hons) MA, National Information Serv. Assistant
Manager, Baker Tilly Management Ltd, Bromley.
[59838]   16/10/2001   **ME**
Waterman, Mrs M, Library Assistant, Rickmansworth Library.
[10031594]   22/10/2013   **AF**
Waters, Mr B J, Unwaged.
[64816]   13/07/2005   **ME**
Waters, Ms C J, MA MCLIP, MoD, Army Library Service: Head of
Services Central Library.
[46649]   02/12/1991   **RV**13/05/2014   **CM23/06/2004**
Waters, Mrs C L, BA (Hons) DipLIS MCLIP, Learning Resource Centre
Co-ordinator, Stirling C., Stirling.
[48084]   03/11/1992   **CM23/07/1997**
Waters, Mrs J S, BA DipLS MCLIP, Head of Learning Resources.
Centres Wiltshire College, Salisbury.
[36049]   01/05/1983   **CM04/02/2004**

Waters, Mrs K B, MA, Librarian, Poole Hospital Foundation Trust.
[10032036]   22/10/2013   **ME**
Waterson, Mr E S, MA FCLIP, Life Member.
[15424]   06/10/1949   **FE01/01/1958**
Waterson, Ms S, BA MCLIP, Volunteer, Zima Hub Library, Sakhalin
Energy Investment Company, Sakhalin Island, Russian Federation.
[21258]   14/10/1973   **CM05/12/1977**
Waterton-Duly, Mrs T C, BA (Hons) MA MCLIP, E-resources librarian.
[55516]   16/10/1997   **CM21/03/2007**
Watford, Mrs L C, LLB (Hons), L. R. C Support Tutor, Loughborough
University.
[10023116]   11/06/2013   **ME**
Wathan, Dr J, BSc MA MA (Econ) PhD PgDip, Research Fellow, CCSR
SoSS, University of Manchester.
[10031444]   06/08/2013   **ME**
Watkins, Mrs A E, MA MCLIP, Retired.
[15427]   19/09/1967   **CM01/01/1972**
Watkins, Mrs F R, MCLIP, Volunteer Librarian, RHS Wisley, Surrey.
[24120]   08/04/1975   **CM19/09/1978**
Watkins, Mrs J, Bsc (Hons) Librianship, LRC Co-ordinator,
Herefordshire and Ludlow College, Hereford.
[10001568]   22/02/2007   **AF**
Watkinson, Mrs J, BA MCLIP, Area Manager, Brighouse Library, East
Calderdale, Calderdale Library, Halifax.
[35539]   29/10/1982   **CM23/09/1985**
Watkinson, Ms N J, BSc MCLIP FHEA, Deputy University Librarian,
Glyndwr University, Wrexham.
[58588]   06/04/2000   **CM15/05/2002**
Watling, Mrs P C, MCLIP, Retired.
[31043]   01/01/1957   **CM01/01/1963**
Waton, Mrs S, LRC Manager, Sir Robert Woodward Academy, West
Sussex.
[10019081]   18/04/2011   **ME**
Watson, Mrs A, LRC Manager, The St Lawrence Academy, Scunthorpe.
[10015436]   18/11/2009   **ME**
Watson, Mrs A J, MSc MCLIP, Part-time Literature Searcher, Royal
College of Nursing, London.
[37755]   23/10/1984   **CM14/11/1991**
Watson, Mr D, MA (Hons), Researcher, Watson, Farley and Williams
LLP, London.
[10015736]   19/01/2010   **ME**
Watson, Mrs D A H, MCLIP, Library Assistant, Chandlers Ford Library,
Hampshire.
[5852]   04/01/1971   **CM05/03/1974**
Watson, Mrs D E, PgDip MCLIP, Librarian, NHS Fife, Kirkcaldy.
[10013679]   18/05/2009   **CM19/08/2011**
Watson, Mr D J, BA MCLIP, Knowledge Mgr, Knowledge Servs.,
Derbyshire C. PCT.
[40937]   05/09/1987   **CM30/01/1991**
Watson, Mr D T, MA DipLib MCLIP, Network Librarian, The Gordon
Schools, Aberdeenshire.
[41761]   07/03/1988   **CM14/08/1991**
Watson, Mrs E, BA (Hons) MA MCLIP, Career break.
[58935]   09/10/2000   **CM23/01/2008**
Watson, Miss F, BA (Hons) MA, Library Supervisor, Royal College of
General Practitioners.
[10021283]   06/07/2012   **ME**
Watson, Mr G L, PgDip MCLIP, Retired.
[63630]   02/08/2004   **CM04/10/2006**
Watson, Ms H, BA (Hons) MA MCLIP, Knowledge & Information
Manager., Michelmores.
[48829]   16/06/1993   **CM24/05/1995**
Watson, Mrs H M, MCLIP, Retired.
[15450]   19/01/1940   **CM01/01/1943**

Watson, Miss J, BLib MCLIP, Cust. Servs. Librarian, Fife Council, Kirkcaldy Central Library.
[23074]   21/10/1974   **CM30/09/1977**

Watson, Mr J, DMS MCLIP, Retired.
[15451]   28/04/1967   **CM01/01/1970**

Watson, Ms L J, BA (Hons) PgDip MCLIP, Systems and Performance Librarian, Aberdeen City Council.
[52015]   12/09/1995   **CM21/01/1998**

Watson, Mrs L S, MCLIP, Library Assistant, Hertfordshire County Council, St Albans.
[18110]   04/10/1972   **CM15/03/1978**

Watson, M, MA DipLib MCLIP, Academic Services Librarian, Bodleian Law Library, Oxford.
[35181]   06/10/1982   **CM07/06/1988**

Watson, Mrs M, BSc MCLIP, Retired.
[9616]   01/01/1964   **CM01/01/1969**

Watson, Mrs M A, BA MA FCLIP HonFCLIP, Retired.
[15456]   21/09/1966   **HFE01/10/2006**

Watson, Ms R K, BA DipLib MCLIP, Librarian, Jesus College, Cambridge.
[42064]   18/09/1988   **CM15/09/1993**

Watson, Mr R L, MA BA (Hons) Dip Eur Mum, Knowledge and Information Services Manager, Scottish Government.
[10018772]   03/05/2012   **ME**

Watson, Mrs S E, MCLIP, Dev. & Performance Officer, Nottingham.
[22583]   11/07/1974   **CM16/05/1978**

Watson, Mrs S J, BA MCLIP, Librarian, Derbyshire County Council.
[34774]   12/02/1982   **CM30/08/1985**

Watson, Mr T, BA (Hons), Technical Support Officer, Gosforth Junior High Academy.
[10031473]   07/06/2012   **ME**

Watson, Mr W M, DAES FCLIP, Life Member.
[15468]   09/08/1950   **FE01/01/1958**

Watson-Bore, Mrs J, BA CertEd MCLIP, Retired.
[27230]   04/02/1977   **CM05/02/1979**

Watt, Mr A, Cataloguer, Met Office, Exeter.
[63184]   03/03/2004   **ME**

Watt, Mrs A J, BA MCLIP, Young Person's Officer, Halton Borough Council, Runcorn, Cheshire.
[39597]   14/03/1986   **RV20/02/2014**   **CM26/02/1992**

Watt, Ms D M, BSc MA MCLIP,
[61629]   09/10/2002   **CM13/06/2007**

Watt, Miss F N, BA (Hons), Library Assistant / Student.
[10032069]   24/10/2013   **ME**

Watt, Mr I, MA (Hons) MSc (Econ) MBA MCLIP, Chief, Dag Hammarskjöld Library, United Nations, New York.
[35873]   04/02/1983   **CM11/11/1986**

Watt, Mrs S J, BA MCLIP, Assistant Librarian, Queen Margaret University.
[42671]   07/02/1989   **CM26/01/1994**

Watt, Mrs S M, BA MCLIP, L. & Information Officer, Newcastle City L.
[33295]   16/10/1980   **CM14/10/1985**

Wattam, Mrs Y J, BA MSc, Assistant Librarian, Record Office (Arch.), Leicester.
[56917]   04/11/1998   **ME**

Watters, Mrs S J, BA (Hons) MCLIP, LRC Manager/Librarian.
[60015]   26/11/2001   **CM19/12/2008**

Watts, Miss G, MCLIP, Retired.
[15481]   04/02/1935   **CM01/01/1942**

Watts, Mrs L J, BLib MCLIP, Librarian, King Edward VI School, Stratford Upon Avon.
[10011226]   19/03/1975   **CM10/12/1979**

Watts, Miss N J, BSc MSc MCLIP, Medical Information Contractor, Boehringer-Ingelheim.
[60706]   12/12/2001   **CM12/12/2001**

Watts, Miss S, Business Information Services Manager, Institute of Directors.
[10008042]   21/01/2014   **ME**

Watts, Mr S D, MCLIP, Retired.
[15484]   01/10/1966   **CM01/01/1970**

Watts, Mr S L, BA DipLib, Retired.
[30060]   26/10/1978   **ME**

Waudby, Mr A D, MCLIP, Life Member.
[17938]   01/01/1939   **CM01/01/1948**

Waugh, Mrs J D, BA DipLib MCLIP, Audience Development Manager, Essex County Council, Chelmsford Library.
[33502]   12/01/1981   **CM24/09/1985**

Wawa, Mr J N O, Student, UCL.
[64074]   15/12/2004   **ME**

Way, Mr D J, MA FCLIP, Life Member.
[15492]   24/01/1951   **FE01/01/1958**

Weare, Mrs J, MA BA MCLIP, Hist. Researcher.
[15496]   13/03/1964   **CM01/01/1968**

Wearing, Mrs C, BA MCLIP, Knowledge Services Manager, East Kent Hospitals University NHS Foundation Trust, Canterbury.
[35001]   08/06/1982   **CM12/09/2001**

Weatherall, Mr P, MA MCLIP, Library & Archive Services Officer, Manx National Heritage.
[15498]   01/01/1970   **CM23/06/1975**

Weatherburn, Ms J, Student, RMIT University.
[10031818]   08/10/2013   **ME**

Weatherly, Miss K, MCLIP, Retired.
[15501]   13/01/1967   **CM01/01/1970**

Weaver, Mrs E A, BA MCLIP MSc, Librarian, Alexandra House School, Mauritius.
[38058]   08/01/1985   **CM18/07/1990**

Weaver, Mrs M L, BA MCLIP MSc FHEA, Head of Library and Student Services., University of Cumbria.
[44022]   05/04/1990   **CM14/11/1991**

Webb, Mr A A P, BA (Hons) Dip Ed, Service Development Librarian, Kingston Library.
[10023023]   14/05/1998   **ME**

Webb, Ms A E, MBA DipIM, L. Operations Manager, The Christie NHS Foundation Trust, Withington.
[59704]   14/08/2001   **ME**

Webb, Dr C J M, FCLIP, School Librarian, Forest Hill School, London.
[37905]   07/11/1984   **FE21/03/2007**

Webb, Mr D R, BA FCLIP, Life Member.
[15513]   10/03/1962   **FE28/01/1975**

Webb, Miss H, MA, Collections Manager, Royal College of Surgeons, London.
[55897]   15/12/1997   **ME**

Webb, Ms H J, BA (Hons), Student, Brighton University.
[10000715]   19/10/2006   **ME**

Webb, Ms J M, MA MLib MBA FCLIP FHEA FRSA, Director of Library and Learning Services, De Montfort University, Leicester.
[42399]   27/10/1988   **FE03/10/2007**

Webb, Mrs K J W, BA (Hons) MA DipHE MCLIP FHEA, Arts & Humanities Liaison Team Manager / Course Support Co-ordinator, University of Reading Library.
[60867]   13/12/2001   **RV19/10/2012**   **CM09/11/2005**

Webb, Ms K M, Library Systems Officer, Middlesex University, London.
[10009542]   02/06/2008   **AF**

Webb, Miss R, BA, Student, Manchester Metropolitan University.
[10030953]   10/12/2013   **ME**

Webb, Ms S, BA (Hons) PgDip, Assistant Librarian & Senior Library Assistant, Manchester Metropolitan University.
[65079] 01/11/2005 AF

Webb, Miss S, Enquiry Officer, Essex Libraries, Essex.
[10015952] 28/01/2010 ME

Webb, Mrs S P, BA (Hons) FCLIP, Life Member.
[9175] 30/01/1957 FE22/05/1987

Webb, Ms Y, BSc (Hons), Unknown.
[55209] 15/08/1997 ME

Webber, Mrs E, MCLIP, Retired.
[12158] 01/10/1967 CM01/01/1971

Webber, Dr N A, MA PhD FCLIP, Life Member.
[15535] 27/07/1950 FE01/01/1962

Webber, Ms S A E, BA FCLIP, Senior Lecturer, Information School, University of Sheffield.
[28718] 16/01/1978 FE01/04/2002

Webster, Ms D C F, MA MCLIP, Retired.
[19068] 19/09/1972 CM04/11/1974

Webster, Miss E, MA, Library Officer, Pinsent Masons LLP.
[10020725] 29/03/2012 ME

Webster, Mr G J, BSc DipLib FCLIP, Retired.
[27039] 17/12/1976 FE22/05/1987

Webster, Mrs H L, Self-employed.
[15540] 01/07/1971 ME

Webster, Mr H T I, Life Member.
[15541] 23/02/1953 ME

Webster, Mr J M, LLB (Hons) MA, Student, University of Sheffield.
[10003359] 13/11/2001 ME

Webster, Mr K G, BSc (Hons) MLib FCLIP HonFCLIP, Dean of University Libraries.
[36428] 06/10/1983 FE01/04/2002

Webster, Mrs M, LLB MA MCLIP, L. & Information Serv. Manager, Browne Jacobson, Nottingham.
[49750] 01/12/1993 CM12/02/2001

Webster, Mrs M, BA MCLIP, Leader of the Learning Resource Centre., The Becket School, Nottingham.
[36637] 27/10/1983 CM16/02/1988

Webster, Mr S A H, MA MCLIP MSc, Information Officer, MS Trust, Letchworth.
[10001036] 01/10/1987 CM14/11/1991

Wodlake, Mrs C K, BSc MA, Team Librarian., Oxfordshire County Council.
[59891] 29/01/2001 ME

Weech, Mr E J P, BA (Hons) MA MPhil FRSA MCLIP, Librarian, Royal Asiatic Society.
[10007748] 21/02/2008 CM04/10/2013

Weedon, Mr P D, BSc Econ, Unwaged.
[10014539] 12/08/2009 ME

Weedon, Mr R L, BA MA, Information Governance & Compliance Manager, University of Strathclyde.
[60305] 15/11/2000 AF

Weeks, Mrs J, BSc, Student.
[10020245] 09/12/2011 ME

Weerasekera, Mrs D C, Student, Resource Centre.
[10032523] 11/12/2013 ME

Weetman Dacosta, Ms J D, BA DipLib MBA MCLIP, Library Academic Services Manager, University of Derby.
[37022] 30/01/1984 CM09/08/1988

Weighell, Mrs E A, BA MCLIP, L. Manager, Hampshire County Council.
[39163] 25/11/1985 CM21/12/1988

Weightman, Dr A L, BSc PhD DipLib, Head of L. Serv. Development, Information Serv., Cardiff University.
[48543] 11/02/1993 ME

Weinel, Dr M L, BA (Hons) MA PhD ACLIP, Libraries Stock Manager, Bath & North East Somerset Council.
[10018325] 16/12/2010 ACL14/03/2012

Weir, Mrs H E, BSc PgDipLib MCLIP, Library Manager, Harrogate & District NHS Foundation Trust.
[43754] 01/01/1990 CM17/09/2003

Weir, Mrs H W, BA MCLIP, Life member.
[33428] 17/10/1980 CM03/05/1988

Weir, Ms L J, BSc (Hons) MSc MCLIP, Content Manager, MWH Ltd, Edinburgh.
[56350] 04/06/1998 CM15/10/2002

Weir, Mrs S, Network Librarian, Tain Royal Academy, Tain.
[10014542] 01/10/1982 ME

Weir, Mrs S D, MSc BEd (Hons), Academic Liaison Librarian, University of Bedfordshire; Library Assistant Gloucestershire Hospitals NHS Foundation Trust.
[10006249] 28/09/2007 ME

Weist, Ms A H, BA (Hons) MSc MCLIP, Education Manager, NICE Evidence Services.
[42214] 10/10/1988 CM20/09/1995

Weisz, Ms G, Temporary, Sue Hill Recruitment.
[65106] 01/11/2005 ME

Welby, Mrs J P, BA (Open) MCLIP, College Librarian, Shebbear College.
[22749] 04/09/1974 CM01/10/1977

Welch, Ms B N, Msc, Careers Information and Publications Officer, City University London.
[10020754] 02/04/2012 ME

Welch, Ms C A, MCLIP, Chartered Librarian, Bramcote Park School, Nottingham.
[38274] 03/02/1985 CM20/01/1987

Welch, Mr D H, FCLIP, Life Member.
[15571] 22/03/1956 FE01/01/1964

Welch, Mr P E, OBE CIPD MSc, Departmental Records Officer, Head of Profession KIM.
[10021344] 18/07/2012 ME

Wella, Mr K, MSc, PhD Student, Information School, University of Sheffield.
[10013692] 22/05/2009 ME

Wellard, Ms E K, BA (Hons) DipILS MCLIP, Lead Librarian, North Somerset Council.
[10010616] 07/11/1995 CM21/03/2001

Wellburn, Mr P, BA MCLIP, Retired.
[17942] 21/09/1965 CM01/01/1969

Weller, Ms J A, BA, Senior Stock Supply Assistant, Wiltshire Council.
[10033182] 18/02/2014 AF

Weller, Ms J C, BA (Hons) DipLib MCLIP, Secretary, Reference & Information Services Section (RISS), IFLA & ISG National Committee Web Editor.
[23340] 20/11/1974 CM28/02/1977

Wellings, Mrs K M, MCLIP, Business Specialist, Axiell, Nottingham.
[30032] 24/11/1978 CM25/11/1982

Wells, Mrs G, BSc MA MCLIP, Information Assistant, Teeside University.
[10008269] 20/03/2008 CM11/04/2013

Wells, Mrs H J, BSc MSc MCLIP, Head of User Services, The Library, University of East Anglia.
[29367] 10/07/1978 CM17/11/1980

Wells, Ms J, BA (Hons) MBA MCLIP, Customer Services Manager, Anglia Ruskin University, Cambridge and Peterborough.
[42126] 03/10/1988 CM14/08/1991

Wells, Miss J M, MCLIP, Life Member.
[15588] 25/07/1949 CM03/09/1954

Wells, Miss J T, BA DipLib MCLIP, Librarian, London Borough of Bexley.
[33606] 24/01/1981 CM18/04/1989

Wells, Mr P, BSc (Hons) MSc MCLIP, Assistant Lib, University of the West of England, Bristol.
[10000949]   04/12/2006   **CM20/04/2012**

Wells, Ms P, Senior Library Assistant, Buckie Library, Moray.
[10012008]   18/12/2012   **ME**

Wells, Mrs R E, BA (Hons) MCLIP, Learning Advisor, Isle of Wight College.
[56890]   02/11/1998   **CM19/11/2003**

Wells, Mr S L M, BA MCLIP, Information & Assurance & Security Manager.
[60423]   15/05/1997   **CM15/05/1997**

Welsby, Miss E R, BA MA, Student.
[10018323]   16/12/2010   **ME**

Welsh, A, MA MSc (Econ) PGCLTHE FHEA, Lecturer in L. & Information Studies, UCL.
[49026]   03/09/1993   **ME**

Welsh, Mrs L J, BSc, School Librarian, Jedburgh Grammar School.
[63578]   08/07/2004   **ME**

Welsh, Ms S B, BSc (Open) MCLIP, Assistant Librarian, Bournmouth University, Poole.
[66021]   25/08/2006   **CM14/11/2012**

Welsh, Miss S M, PhD DipLib MCLIP, Digital Resources Discovery Officer, Liverpool John Moores University Library Serv.
[30293]   12/01/1979   **CM10/12/1981**

Welsher, Miss A D, MCLIP, Retired.
[15602]   15/09/1967   **CM01/01/1971**

Wemyss, Mrs E M, BSc DipLib MCLIP, Local Studies Lib., Aberdeen L. & Information Serv.
[28137]   08/10/1977   **CM19/11/1979**

Wenham, Mrs J, FCLIP, Retired.
[15606]   01/01/1952   **FE01/01/1959**

Wentworth, Ms S F, BA DipLib MCLIP, Librarian, Reader & Information Services (Local & Family History)., Oxon County Council.
[32767]   12/08/1980   **CM03/09/1982**

Wentzell, Mr C, BA MCLIP, Academic Support Librarian, Bournemouth University.
[65653]   02/03/2006   **CM14/10/2011**

Werb, Mrs S L, ACLIP, Lib. Assistant, Sidmouth L.
[10016563]   14/04/2010   **ACL17/06/2011**

Werndly, Mrs H, BA MCLIP, Unwaged.
[33190]   30/09/1980   **CM14/10/1982**

West, Ms A, BA DipLib MCLIP,
[42819]   08/03/1989   **CM31/01/1996**

West, Mrs C A, BA (Hons) MA MCLIP, Cross College Manager – Library Services, South City College, Birmingham.
[41218]   12/10/1987   **CM16/11/1994**

West, Mr C B, BA DipLib MCLIP, Retired.
[15612]   04/10/1962   **CM01/01/1972**

West, Mr G, BSc MLIS, Unwaged.
[10033709]   16/04/2014   **ME**

West, Mr J, BA DipLib MCLIP, Area Librarian, North Ayrshire Council.
[44166]   18/06/1990   **CM16/10/1991**

West, Mrs K, BSc (Hons) MSc MCLIP, Head of Library, Norwich Bioscience Institutes, Norfolk.
[56977]   17/11/1998   **CM02/02/2005**

West, Mr L E, BSc MCLIP, Retired.
[60666]   21/03/1972   **CM04/07/1977**

West, Mrs L S, ACLIP, Library Supervisor, Ivybridge Library.
[10013400]   23/04/2009   **ACL16/06/2010**

West, Mrs M, MSc, Adult Services Librarian, Shetland Library.
[10007942]   03/11/2005   **ME**

West, Mrs M J, BA DipLib MCLIP, North Ayrshire Council.
[41582]   21/01/1988   **CM11/12/1989**

West, Miss N H, BA (Hons) MCLIP, Unwaged.
[56892]   02/11/1998   **CM08/12/2004**

West, Mr N J M, BA (Hons) DipLIS MCLIP, Unwaged.
[43018]   23/06/1989   **CM20/03/1996**

West, Mr R W C, BA MCLIP, Life Member.
[15618]   14/01/1963   **CM01/01/1965**

Westbrook, Mrs K B, BA MA (Hons) MTh MCLIP, Post Grad. Student, University of Edinburgh.
[27794]   05/11/1965   **CM01/01/1970**

Westbury, Ms M, MLIS MA,
[10018258]   10/12/2010   **ME**

Westcott, Miss E L, BA MCLIP, Life Member.
[15624]   11/01/1958   **CM01/01/1960**

Westcott, Ms J, BLib MCLIP, Reading & Access Librarian, Poole Libraries.
[38999]   24/10/1985   **CM27/03/1991**

Westcott, Miss M R, MA MCLIP, Life Member.
[15625]   19/09/1958   **CM01/01/1962**

Westcott, Ms S R, MA DipLib FCLIP, Team Leader, Department for Communities and Local Government.
[43264]   10/10/1989   **FE29/03/2004**

Westgate, Mrs S, BEcon MCLIP, Lib. & Information Officer, Dundee C. C.
[57509]   14/04/1999   **CM21/06/2006**

Westgate, Mrs V J D, MCLIP, Reading Room Supervisor, Bodleian Library.
[64950]   03/10/2005   **RV**11/04/2013   **CM20/04/2009**

Westhead, Mrs S, PgCert, Student, Robert Gordon University.
[10031797]   04/10/2013   **ME**

Westland, Mrs A C, MScLIS, Librarian, Surbiton High School, Kingston.
[47734]   16/10/1992   **ME**

Westley, Mr D D, BA MA MCLIP, Librarian (Bibliothekar), University of Heidelberg, Germany.
[40921]   25/08/1987   **CM26/05/1993**

Westmancoat, Mrs H T, MCLIP, Deputy University Librarian, York St John University.
[9719]   19/10/1971   **CM07/10/1976**

Weston, Mr C G H, BEng MIET MCLIP, Retired.
[15630]   05/10/1969   **CM22/10/1974**

Weston, Mr M K, BA MCLIP, Knowledge Management Specialist, URS Corporation, 6-8 Greencoat Place, London SW1P 1PL.
[24851]   17/10/1975   **CM12/01/1982**

Weston, Mr N, BA MA MCLIP, Lib. i/c., South Glos. Council, Yate, nr. Bristol.
[43849]   31/01/1990   **CM18/11/1993**

Weston, Mr P G, MA, Professor, Universityof Pavia, Italy.
[10018934]   27/07/1987   **ME**

Weston, Mrs R E, BLib MCLIP, Admin Assistant, (residential home), High Wycombe.
[26685]   26/10/1976   **CM14/10/1981**

Weston, Ms S A, BA (Hons) MSc MCLIP FHEA,
[66072]   20/09/2006   **CM17/06/2011**

Westwood, Miss C A, BA MA, Team Librarian.
[10015081]   12/10/2009   **ME**

Westwood, Ms E M, BA PGCE, Librarian, Internation School of Toulouse, France.
[10017677]   23/09/2010   **ME**

Westwood, Miss J, BSc (Econ) MSc MCLIP, Information Assistant, University of Wales, Aberystwyth.
[55636]   30/10/1997   **CM21/11/2001**

Wetenhall, Mrs M C, MLib BA (Hons) DipLib MCLIP, Retired.
[36776]   08/09/1967   **CM23/08/1985**

Wetherill, Mrs H C, BA (Hons) MA MCLIP, Information Serv. Officer, DPPLLP, Bedford.
[42670]   07/02/1989   CM19/03/1997

Wetherill, Mr J, BA MA MCLIP, Research Cons., Futuresource Consulting, Dunstable.
[42495]   23/11/1988   CM19/06/1991

Weyman, Miss M, BA MCLIP, Life Member.
[15645]   26/09/1957   CM01/01/1963

Whaite, Mrs K C, BA,
[10012530]   19/02/2009   ME

Whale, Mrs H A, MCLIP, Retired.
[2373]   08/02/1966   CM01/01/1970

Whalley, Mr J H, BLib, Senior Assistant Librarian, Manchester Metro. University, Cheshire.
[30570]   28/01/1979   CM31/12/1989

Whapham, Miss E B G, MCLIP, Life Member.
[15650]   27/02/1940   CM01/01/1944

Wharram, Mr S, BSc (Open), DES CIO, Ministry of Defence.
[10033963]   14/05/2014   ME

Wharton, Mrs J, DESCIO-Exploitation-DepHd, Ministry of Defence.
[10034152]   10/06/2014   ME

Wharton, Miss J C, BA DipLib PhD MCLIP, Senior Librarian, Collections & Metadata, University of Nottingham.
[40010]   14/10/1986   CM24/07/1996

Whatley, Mr H A, MA FCLIP, Life Member.
[15654]   02/03/1931   FE01/01/1937

Whayman, Miss C, MSc Econ, Freelance Information Professional.
[10001004]   01/07/1996   ME

Wheatcroft, Mrs A V, BSc MA DMS MCLIP, Freelance.
[47560]   01/10/1992   CM19/07/2000

Wheater, Mrs E A, BEd DipLib MCLIP, Retired.
[42290]   12/10/1988   CM21/07/1993

Wheatley, Mrs C E, BA (Hons) MCLIP, Unemployed.
[51473]   20/02/1995   CM16/07/2003

Wheatley, Mrs G F M, BA (Hons) MCLIP, Lib. Manager, Wimborne Library, Dorset.
[50816]   19/10/1994   CM16/05/2001

Wheatley, Mr G W J, FCLIP DipFE, Life Member.
[15661]   22/03/1943   FE01/01/1966

Wheatley, Mrs J F, FCLIP, Life Member.
[15662]   10/03/1941   FE01/01/1950

Wheeldon, Mrs C, MCLIP, Company Secretary, ERW Consulting Ltd, Bedfordshire.
[15486]   06/02/1969   CM20/12/1972

Wheeler, Mrs A R, PG Celt Mgnet MCLIP, General Manager, Suffolk County Council.
[28393]   25/10/1977   CM24/08/1981

Wheeler, Mr A T F,
[65614]   17/03/2006   ME

Wheeler, Miss E C, Student, University of Sheffield.
[10031814]   07/10/2013   ME

Wheeler, Mrs E L, BSc (Hons) MSc (Econ) MCLIP, Unwaged.
[57521]   15/04/1999   CM20/11/2002

Wheeler, Miss P C, MCLIP BA (Hons), Retired.
[15668]   29/01/1962   CM01/01/1964

Wheeler, Miss S, MA, Wheeler, Miss S, Assistant Librarian, Lincoln's Inn Librarian, London.
[10006155]   27/08/2010   ME

Wheeler, Mr W G, MA DipLib FCLIP, Life Member,
[15669]   29/10/1954   FE01/01/1960

Whelan, Mr D A, BA (Hons), E-Learning Centre Manager, St Philip Howard Catholic School, Derbys.
[58197]   16/11/1999   ME

Whelan, Mr R M, Student, Aberystwyth University.
[10035025]   05/09/2014   ME

Whelehan, Mr B M, BA (Hons) MCLIP, Senior Library Assistant, Acquisitions & Access, Central Library, Imperial College, London.
[46450]   07/11/1991   CM23/07/1997

Whibley, Mr V, MA FRSA MCMI FCLIP, Retired.
[15672]   21/09/1959   FE01/07/1972

Whincup, Mrs P E, MCLIP, Retired.
[15677]   08/09/1955   CM01/01/1961

Whitaker, Mr D H, OBE BA, Chairman, J. Whitaker & Sons, London.
[40257]   11/11/1986   ME

Whitaker, Mr R, BA MA, Retired.
[52599]   10/11/1995   ME

Whitcombe, Mrs A C, MSc MCLIP FRSPH, Lecturer, Robert Gordon University.
[60231]   29/01/1983   CM29/01/1983

Whitcombe, Mrs J M, RN (Dip) MCLIP, Assistant Clinical Librarian, Pennine Acute Hospitals, NHS Trust.
[10014808]   16/09/2009   CM20/06/2014

White, Miss A M, BEd (Hons) DipLIS MCLIP, Team Librarian, Oxfordshire County Council.
[45730]   03/05/1991   CM20/05/1998

White, Mrs B, HonFCLIP FCLIP, Retired.
[15691]   29/08/1955   HFE06/04/1992

White, Miss C E, Msc, Collection Development Manager, Information, University of York.
[56271]   27/04/1998   ME

White, Dr C E, BA (Hons) MA PhD MCLIP, Researcher.
[62208]   17/03/2003   CM21/06/2006

White, Miss C E, BA MCLIP, Schools Library Service Manager, Schools Libraries Support Service, Walsall.
[22301]   21/02/1974   CM31/10/1978

White, Mrs C J, BA (Hons) MSc MCLIP, Information Specialist, Ministry of Defence.
[59140]   28/11/2000   ME

White, Mr D A, BA (Hons), eSystems Technical Officer, Nottingham Trent University.
[10033478]   17/03/2014   ME

White, Mrs E, BEd Information & Events Co-Ordinator, Keele. Studying at Manchester Metropolitan University.
[10020810]   18/04/2012   ME

White, Miss E, BA (Hons), Information Specialist, Transport Research Laboratory Ltd, Wokingham.
[64342]   07/03/2005   ME

White, Mrs G, BA (Hons) MA MCLIP, Self-employed.
[27515]   13/05/1977   CM29/12/1980

White, Mr G J, BA (Hons) PGCe, Student, University of Brighton.
[10023356]   02/07/2013   ME

White, Miss G M, BA (Hons)PgDipLib, Head of Remote Serv., National Art Library, Word & Image Department, Victoria & Albert Museum.
[34653]   19/01/1982   ME

White, Miss H, BA (Hons), Senior Library Assistant, Dudley Metropolitan Borough Council.
[10016622]   01/05/2010   AF

White, Mrs J A, BA (Hons) MA, Knowledge support librarian, Hampshire Healthcare Library, Basingstoke.
[57615]   28/05/1999   ME

White, Mrs J C, BA MCLIP, Librarian- (Children and Young People), Northumb. County L.
[35754]   10/01/1983   CM15/11/1988

White, Mr J M, BA MA, Learning Facilitator., Walsall College.
[57476]   01/04/1999   ME

White, Mrs J M E, MSc MCLIP, Retired.
[10612]   02/10/1968   CM01/01/1972

White, Mrs J M O, MLib AMus TCL MCLIP, Unwaged.
[25824]   01/03/1976   CM07/03/1980
White, Mr J P, BA MA, Subject Librarian, University of Derby.
[65029]   13/10/2005   ME
White, Mrs J S, BA (Hons) MScEcon, Public Sector.
[64393]   14/03/2005   ME
White, Mr L, FCLIP, Life Member.
[15714]   28/09/1950   FE01/01/1968
White, Mrs L A, MCLIP, Sch. Lib.
[10010838]   28/08/2008   CM29/05/2013
White, Miss M, BSc (Hons), Library Assistant, Tenby Library.
[10033908]   12/05/2014   ME
White, Mr M S, BSc HonFCLIP FRSC FRSA MBCS, Managing Director,
    Intranet Focus Ltd, Horsham and Visiting Professor, Information
    School, University of Sheffield.
[60667]   11/12/2001   FE01/04/2002
White, Miss R K, BSc (Hons) MSc, Senior Library Assistant, Imperial
    College, royal Brompton Campus Lib.
[56879]   29/10/1998   ME
White, Mrs S A, BA DipLib FCLIP, Head of L. Serv., University of
    Huddersfield.
[32693]   11/07/1980   FE08/09/2010
White, Mrs S A, MSc MCLIP,
[24384]   02/07/1975   CM30/03/1981
White, Mr S J, BA (Hons), Library Assistant, West Sussex CC.
[10035250]   01/10/2014   ME
White, Mrs S K, BLib MCLIP, LRC/ILT Manager, Swindon College.
[42745]   21/02/1989   CM21/10/1992
White, Mrs T, MSc MCLIP PGCE, Learning Resources Advisor,
    Colchester Institute.
[10031009]   10/10/1996   RV20/06/2014   CM10/07/2002
White, Ms W H, BA (Hons) MA DipLib MCLIP, Head of Scholarly
    Communications, University of Southampton.
[51201]   23/11/1994   CM18/11/1998
White, Mrs W J, BA DipLib MCLIP, Lib. Clark Smith Partnership.
[39489]   08/02/1986   CM15/05/1989
Whitehead, Miss K, BA, Assistant Library Manager/Library Assistant,
    Nottinghamshire County Council.
[10034335]   28/07/2014   ME
Whitehead, Mrs P, FCLIP, Life Member.
[15741]   02/09/1942   FE01/01/1949
Whitehead, Mrs V E, BA MCLIP, Librarian, Gordon's School, Woking.
[27636]   27/06/1977   CM23/07/1979
Whitehouse, Miss D M, BA (Hons), Student.
[10022868]   30/04/2013   ME
Whitehouse, Miss H C, BA MSc, Library Assistant, Oldham Council.
[10032802]   14/01/2014   ME
Whitehouse, Mrs H D, BSc DipInfSc, Head of Information Resources,
    Aston University, Birmingham.
[40940]   08/09/1987   ME
Whitehouse, Miss J C, BA (Hons) MA, Librarian, Lanna International
    School, Thailand.
[65238]   25/11/2005   ME
Whitehouse, Mrs S A, BA MSc MCLIP, Business Intelligence Services
    Manager, Edwards Wildman Palmer UK LLP.
[57766]   29/07/1999   CM21/03/2007
Whitehouse, Mrs S E, BA MCLIP, Locality Librarian, Dudley Public
    Library.
[33196]   02/10/1980   CM28/01/1985
Whitelegg, Ms K L, ACLIP, LRC Manager. Dronfield Henry Fanshawe
    School, Derbyshire.
[62468]   08/07/2003   ACL27/06/2006

Whitelock, Dr J, MA MPhil PhD MA MCLIP, Head of Special
    Collections, Cambridge University Library.
[55976]   07/01/1998   CM17/01/2001
Whiteside, Ms J M, MA MCLIP FRSA, Retired.
[21898]   24/01/1974   CM07/07/1976
Whitethread, Mrs E A, BSc (Hons) MA MCLIP, Senior Researcher,
    Hogan Lovells International LLP, London.
[51217]   28/11/1994   CM22/07/1998
Whitfield, Mrs R, BA MA, WHELF Development Officer.
[10003069]   08/12/1998   ME
Whiting, Mr A D, BA MCLIP, Life Member.
[19412]   06/01/1958   CM01/01/1961
Whiting, Mr D J, BA (Hons), Student, University of the West of England.
[10032004]   21/10/2013   ME
Whiting, Mrs J P, MCLIP, Retired.
[10001522]   04/10/1971   CM07/07/1976
Whitmore, Miss J M, BA MCLIP, Life Member.
[15771]   26/09/1962   CM01/01/1965
Whitmore, Miss K B, MCLIP, Retired.
[15773]   06/02/1953   CM01/01/1959
Whitsed, Mrs N J, MSc FCLIP, Director, L. Serv., Open University,
    Milton Keynes.
[786]   14/09/1970   FE16/09/1992
Whittaker, Miss B A, BA (Hons) MA MCLIP, Library and Information
    Assistant, Norfolk and Norwich Millennium Library.
[43398]   19/10/1989   CM02/02/2005
Whittaker, Mr K A, MA FCLIP, Life Member.
[15779]   20/02/1950   FE01/01/1957
Whittaker, Mr S, BA (Hons), Student, Manchester Metropolitan
    University.
[10033545]   25/03/2014   ME
Whittaker, Ms S R, BMus (Hons) MA, Senior Information Assistant,
    Leicester Royal Infirmary, Clinical Sci. L.
[56715]   07/10/1998   ME
Whittaker, Mrs V I, BA, Service Development Officer Sherburn Library,
    North Yorks.
[39556]   28/02/1986   CM25/05/1994
Whittall, Mr G K, Subject Librarian at the University Centre, Doncaster
    College.
[62023]   20/01/2003   ME
Whittingham, Mrs C, BA (Hons) MCLIP PgCLTHE, Academic Librarian,
    Teesside University, Middlesbrough.
[43856]   02/02/1990   CM14/09/1994
Whittingham, Miss C F, BA DipLib MCLIP, Lib. /Learning Res. Manager,
    Walford & North Shropshire College, Oswestry.
[38569]   05/07/1985   CM14/02/1990
Whittington, Miss R E L, BSc MA, Assistant Librarian, Christie's
    Education.
[10018781]   10/03/2011   ME
Whittle, Ms V E, BHort MLIS, Assistant Librarian, Department for Work
    & Pensions (DWP).
[62358]   09/05/2003   ME
Whittock, Mrs S R, Self-employed as a school library consultant.
[38444]   18/04/1985   ME
Whitton, Mr J B, MA MCLIP, Retired.
[15789]   16/08/1967   CM19/03/1971
Whitton, Miss M, BA MSt MA, Assistant Librarian, London School of
    Hygiene & Tropical Medicine.
[10018308]   14/12/2010   ME
Whitton, Mr M J, MA MChem MCLIP, Academic Liaison Librarian,
    University of Southampton, Hartley Library.
[59148]   28/11/2000   RV20/06/2014   CM04/10/2006

Whitty, Mrs D A, BA (Hons), Assistant Librarian, Thompsons Solicitors, Manchester.
[59238]   12/01/2001   ME

Whybrow, Mrs K M, MCLIP, Life Member.
[15790]   01/01/1948   CM09/10/1959

Whyles, Mrs K, BA (Hons), Learning Centre Supervisor, New College Nottingham, Nottingham.
[10019932]   05/10/2011   ME

Whyte, Ms S M, MA DipLis, Library Customer Services Team Leader, University of Abertay, Dundee.
[63354]   20/04/2004   ME

Whyte, T N, BA (Hons), Learning Centre Supervisor.
[10032661]   24/12/2013   ME

Wickenden, Mr J A, FCLIP, Biomedical Information Sci., Eli Lilly & Co. Ltd, Windlesham, Surrey.
[15795]   01/10/1971   FE28/01/2009

Wickens, Mr S C, BA (Hons) PgDip MA MCLIP, Learning Centre Manager, Kent.
[60872]   18/12/2001   CM29/03/2006

Wicks, Miss H, Gateway Services Manager, University of Arts, London.
[10031025]   05/11/2013   ME

Wicks, Mr J D, BEd (Hons) MA MCLIP, Audience Development Officer, Essex County Council, Braintree, Essex.
[47830]   15/10/1992   CM22/05/1996

Widdicombe, Ms K, BA (Hons) MA MSc MCLIP, Head of Learning Enhancement and Support, University for the Creative Arts.
[63717]   08/09/2004   CM19/11/2008

Widdows Doughty, Mrs C D, MSc BSc (Hons) MCLIP, Senior Library Assistant, Hemel Hempstead.
[48584]   22/02/1993   CM15/02/2012

Widdowson, Miss J H L, BA MA MSc,
[10018947]   01/04/2011   ME

Wleczorek, Mrs J A, MCLIP, Community Engagement Librarian, Cambridgeshire Libraries.
[19079]   02/10/1972   CM04/08/1976

Wiener, Miss S J,
[10011806]   14/11/2008   AF

Wiggans, Mrs E L, MCLIP, Life Member.
[22599]   03/07/1974   CM30/12/1977

Wiggins, Mr S H, MA (Cantab) MA (Shef) MCLIP, Student, University of Sheffield 2011
[10016197]   23/02/2010   RV15/07/2014   CM14/11/2012

Wigglesworth, Ms G S S, BA, Librarian, Immanuel College.
[31979]   04/01/1980   CM23/09/1998

Wiggs, Ms H B Z, BA, Team Librarian.
[10015808]   27/01/2010   ME

Wight, Mrs K, BA (Hons) MCLIP, Outreach & e-resources Librarian, Birmingham & Solihull Mental Health Trust.
[60460]   24/05/1999   CM24/05/1999

Wight, Ms M, Student, Coleg Llandrillo.
[10032721]   07/01/2014   ME

Wightman, Mr A, Information Knowledge Management Senior Leader, Ministry of Defence.
[10034537]   21/07/2014   ME

Wigley, Mrs J E, BLib MCLIP, Learning resources manager, Stonar School, Wiltshire.
[39145]   12/11/1985   CM21/07/1989

Wigmore, Mr M A, MSc,
[10008015]   20/03/2008   ME

Wignall, Mrs J, MCLIP, Unwaged.
[60018]   26/11/2001   CM28/01/2009

Wijesundara, Mrs C J, BA MSc, Student, University of Colombo.
[10032521]   11/12/2013   ME

Wijnstroom, Ms M, FCLIP, Retired.
[41389]   06/01/1987   FE06/01/1987

Wilcock, Mrs J, BSc MSc MCLIP, Employment not known.
[60703]   12/12/2001   CM12/12/2001

Wilcock, Mrs S L, BSc PgDip, Library Assistant, The King's School Boys' Division.
[10031745]   01/10/2013   ME

Wilcock, Mr T R, Literacy, Learning & Engagement Officer, Schools Library Service.
[10021915]   30/10/2012   AF

Wilcox, Miss H L, BScEcon MA, Support Worker, Transform Housing and Support.
[10034902]   21/08/2014   ME

Wilde, Mrs L J, Learn. Centre Manager, Ealing, Hammersmith & West London College.
[26817]   02/11/1976   AF

Wilde, Mr N C, BA MCLIP, Retired.
[15822]   28/09/1962   CM01/01/1967

Wildman, Mrs A R, BA MA, Assistant Librarian, Peterborough Regional College.
[62997]   25/11/2003   ME

Wildman, Ms G M, MLIS BA, Senior Library Assistant, Charing Cross Campus Library, Imperial College.
[10020382]   10/02/2012   ME

Wildman, Miss G R, Pre-Prep Librarian, The Beacon School.
[10035243]   01/10/2014   ME

Wildsmith, Ms S M, MCLIP Dip MLIS, Retired.
[4149]   14/02/1969   CM01/01/1972

Wiley, Ms M E, BA MA MSc, Acting Head of Information Services, Careers Service.
[10011319]   13/10/2008   ME

Wilkes, Mrs F E, BA (Hons) MA DipLib MCLIP, Librarian, Wolfson College Oxford.
[44967]   28/01/1991   CM16/11/1994

Wilkes, Mrs L D, MCLIP, Trust Librarian, West Suffolk NHS Trust.
[65292]   14/12/2005   CM17/09/2008

Wilkes, Mrs R J, BSc MA MCLIP, Retired.
[46594]   21/11/1991   CM26/07/1995

Wilkie, Mrs E A, BSc (Hons) MCLIP, Library Officer, Hampshire County Council.
[56371]   22/06/1998   CM19/11/2008

Wilkie, Mrs S, BLib MCLIP, Freelance Consultant.
[26263]   24/09/1976   CM24/09/1979

Wilkins, Mrs F M, BA MCLIP, L. Res. Manager, Swanmore College of Technology School, Hants.
[21210]   29/09/1973   CM15/09/1975

Wilkins, Miss J, Information Manager.
[10034315]   02/07/2014   ME

Wilkins, Miss J A, BA MCLIP, Head of Learner Services and Safeguarding Wakefield College, West Yorks.
[33623]   30/01/1981   CM25/10/1983

Wilkins, Mrs J A, BA (Hons) MCLIP,
[28210]   01/10/1977   CM24/06/1981

Wilkins, Mrs J I, BA (Hons) MCLIP, Head of Serv. (Strategy), Dudley L.
[33529]   13/01/1981   CM31/07/1984

Wilkins, Ms K S, MA MLIS, Unwaged.
[10033106]   11/02/2014   ME

Wilkins, Ms L A, BA MCLIP, L. Manager, Croydon Library, Surrey.
[41560]   28/01/1988   CM20/03/1996

Wilkins, Ms N, Librarian (School), Coventry City Council.
[10021138]   11/06/2012   ME

Wilkins-Jones, Dr C, BA MCLIP, Retired.
[7971]   01/01/1970   CM01/01/1972

Wilkinson, Ms A M, MCLIP, Librarian, Buxton Library, Derbyshire County Council.
[20322]   07/03/1973   **CM23/08/1976**

Wilkinson, Mrs D, BA MCLIP, Life Member.
[10940]   12/03/1963   **CM01/01/1966**

Wilkinson, Mr E G, BA, Lib. Assistant, North Somerset Council.
[10033261]   25/02/2014   **ME**

Wilkinson, Mrs E M H, MCLIP, Learning Support AssistantTeaching Assistant, part-time.
[29501]   10/01/1974   **CM30/10/1979**

Wilkinson, Mrs K, ACLIP,
[10001649]   06/03/2007   **ACL17/06/2009**

Wilkinson, Miss M E, FCLIP, Life Member.
[15863]   14/09/1943   **FE01/01/1957**

Wilkinson, Mrs R, BSc (Hons) MCLIP, Information Servives Coordinator, NBS, Newcastle-upon-Tyne.
[64653]   22/04/2005   **RV**15/07/2014   **CM21/03/2007**

Wilkinson, Ms S A, BA DipLib MCLIP, Head of Barrington Library, Cranfield University.
[39059]   28/10/1985   **CM16/12/1992**

Wilkinson, Mrs S J, Information Officer, Isaac Newton Institutefor Math. Sci., University of Cambridge.
[51650]   27/04/1995   **AF**

Wilkinson, Mrs S M, FCLIP MBE FRSA, Events & Engagement Manager, Library of Birmingham.
[20273]   22/02/1973   **FE13/06/2007**

Wilkinson, Mrs Z A, BSc (Hons), School Librarian.
[52389]   26/10/1995   **ME**

Wilkinson-Graham, Mrs V L, MA, Head of L. & R. Centre for, Lewis Silkin, London.
[56451]   14/07/1998   **ME**

Will, Dr L, BSc PhD MCLIP MInstP MBCS CITP, Retired.
[24855]   26/09/1975   **CM28/11/1977**

Will, Dr S, PhD,
[64186]   31/01/2005   **ME**

Willans, Mrs S J, MCLIP, Library Manager, Orpington Library, LB Bromley.
[14585]   01/01/1972   **CM24/11/1975**

Willcox, Dr D R, BA MA PhD PGCHE PgDip, Student, Northumbria University.
[10021342]   18/07/2012   **ME**

Willetts, Mr A J, MSc, School Librarian.
[10015336]   10/11/2009   **ME**

Willetts, Ms S J, MA MSc BA DipLib MCLIP, Senior Library Assistant, Inst. of Classical Studies, Hellenic & Roman Society, London.
[33371]   27/11/1980   **CM16/05/1984**

Williams, Mrs A, MSc (Econ), Information Officer, St Michael's College, Cardiff.
[59629]   05/07/2001   **ME**

Williams, Ms A, BA (Hons) MA, L. Manager, Bromsgrove Library, Worcester CC.
[59251]   17/01/2001   **ME**

Williams, Miss A, BA,
[10013198]   03/04/2009   **ME**

Williams, Miss A, BA MSc,
[10006382]   23/10/2007   **ME**

Williams, Ms A D, BA, Student, University of Strathclyde.
[10035535]   16/10/2014   **ME**

Williams, Mr A F, BA, Unwaged.
[55990]   12/01/1998   **ME**

Williams, Miss A J, BA (Hons) MA MSc MCLIP, Clinical Evidence Specialist, Warrington & Halton Hospitals NHS Foundation Trust.
[10017689]   28/09/2010   **CM04/10/2013**

Williams, Ms A J, BA (Hons), Curriculum Centre Co-ordinator, Universityof Brighton.
[10015487]   09/12/2009   **AF**

Williams, Mr A J A, BA MCLIP, Trainer, Speaker, Storyteller.
[15885]   20/10/1967   **CM01/01/1972**

Williams, Miss A K, MCLIP, Assistant Librarian, Royal Glamorgan Hospital, Cwm Taf Health.
[64463]   31/03/2005   **CM16/05/2012**

Williams, Mr A W, Student, Sheffield University.
[10033873]   07/05/2014   **ME**

Williams, Mrs B, Assistant Librarian, Teddington School.
[10033452]   13/03/2014   **ME**

Williams, Mrs C A, BA (Hons) MSc (Econ) MCLIP, Acquisitions Librarian, Buckinghamshire New University, High Wycombe.
[51206]   23/11/1994   **CM17/01/2001**

Williams, Mrs C A, BA (Hons) PGCE MSc, Head of Collections Knowledge, The National Archives.
[53971]   15/10/1996   **ME**

Williams, Ms C A, BA DipLib MCLIP, School Librarian, The Fernwood School, Nottingham.
[29869]   02/10/1978   **CM15/12/1980**

Williams, Mr C C, DMA MCLIP, Retired.
[15896]   03/06/1961   **CM01/01/1964**

Williams, Miss C M, BSc (Hons) DipLib, Tourist Information Assistant South Lakeland District Council.
[41541]   11/01/1988   **ME**

Williams, Miss C R, BA FCLIP, Life Member.
[15899]   24/09/1958   **FE01/01/1965**

Williams, Mr C R G, Lib. /Researcher, CS Associates, London.
[48924]   23/07/1993   **ME**

Williams, Mrs C S, BA (Hons) MA MCLIP, Librarian, Borough of Lewisham, London.
[59099]   14/11/2000   **CM08/12/2004**

Williams, Mrs D E, BA MA MCLIP, Librarian, Salendine Nook High School Academy.
[41211]   15/10/1987   **CM15/09/1993**

Williams, Mr D G, BA (Hons) PgDipIM, Public Health Knowledge Manager, Portsmouth City Council.
[10002531]   03/10/1994   **ME**

Williams, Miss D M, BA (Hons) MA, Library Assistant, Royal College of Physicians.
[10001497]   11/03/2002   **ME**

Williams, Dr E, BA MA PhD, Subject Librarian.
[10014354]   17/07/2009   **ME**

Williams, Miss E A, BSc, Information Librarian.
[62196]   13/03/2003   **ME**

Williams, Miss E M, BA MLIS Prof Cert Mgmt, Deputy Librarian, Royal Agricultural University, Cirencester.
[10002965]   10/05/2007   **ME**

Williams, Miss E M, BA MCLIP, Information Assistant Harrow Libraries.
[34804]   18/02/1982   **CM02/02/1987**

Williams, Ms F C, BA (Hons) DipLib MCLIP, Head of L. & Heritage, City of York Council.
[10001560]   15/02/1988   **CM27/05/1992**

Williams, Mr G, Student, Coleg Llandrillo.
[10035500]   16/10/2014   **ME**

Williams, Mr G A, BA (Hons), Information Officer, Simmons & Simmons, London.
[59482]   09/04/2001   **ME**

Williams, Mr H A, MA, Librarian, Oxford & Cambridge Club, London.
[58991]   12/10/2000   **ME**

Williams, Ms H A K, BSc MSc PgDip MCLIP, Metadata Consultant, currently working in geosciences; previous experience includes law, education, emergency planning.
[31497]   07/10/1979   **CM22/06/1982**

Williams, Mrs H F, BA (Hons) MCLIP, Electronic Services Librarian, Hampshire Hospitals Foundation NHS Trust, Royal Hampshire County Hospital.
[52355]   26/10/1995   **CM21/11/2001**

Williams, Miss H K R, MA MCLIP, Discovery and Metadata Manager, Collections Services Group, LSE, London.
[59494]   09/04/2001   **CM01/02/2006**

Williams, Mrs H M, BA MCLIP, Stock Development Manager (Job Share), Coventry Libraries.
[23977]   27/02/1975   **CM26/09/1979**

Williams, Mrs H M J, MSc Econ ILS MCLIP, Information Specialist, Integreon. Bristol.
[37184]   28/03/1984   **CM11/07/2012**

Williams, Mrs H S, MA MPhil MCLIP, Freelancer.
[34110]   30/09/1981   **CM13/05/1986**

Williams, Dr I A, MA PhD CChem FRSC MCLIP, Retired.
[60676]   12/12/2001   **CM12/12/2001**

Williams, Mr J, Information Assistant, Scottish Government., Edinburgh.
[63478]   14/05/2004   **AF**

Williams, Ms J, BA (Hons) DipLib MCLIP, L. Manager, Croydon Health L. & Resource Serv., Croydon.
[10008466]   01/01/1969   **CM29/04/1975**

Williams, Ms J, LRC Manager, Caerphilly Co. Borough Council, Blackwood.
[63930]   03/11/2004   **ME**

Williams, Mrs J, MCLIP, Retired.
[17967]   28/01/1961   **CM01/01/1966**

Williams, Mr J, BA, Sconul Trainee, University of Surrey.
[10020693]   26/03/2012   **ME**

Williams, Ms J, BA DipLib MCLIP,
[35358]   11/10/1982   **CM16/10/1989**

Williams, Mrs J E, BA DipLib MCLIP, Librarian, Shropshire C. Bridgnorth.
[27265]   12/02/1977   **CM20/09/1979**

Williams, Miss J L, Student.
[10021228]   29/06/2012   **ME**

Williams, Miss K, BA, Evening & Weekend Supervisor, Cass Business School.
[10022539]   20/03/2013   **ME**

Williams, Ms K, BA (Hons) MSc,
[10014278]   18/11/2003   **ME**

Williams, Miss L, BA (Hons) MA, Media Manager, BBC.
[10017967]   28/10/2010   **ME**

Williams, Mrs L M, Stock Manager, Cardiff C. C., Cardiff, retired.
[4681]   10/03/1970   **CM02/07/1973**

Williams, Mr M, Assistant Librarian, MOD, London.
[60042]   03/12/2001   **ME**

Williams, Mrs M, BA MCLIP, Retired.
[15955]   01/01/1965   **CM01/01/1968**

Williams, Mr M A, BSc MSc, Head of Storage & Logistics, Bodleian Libraries, University of Oxford.
[59072]   07/11/2000   **ME**

Williams, Mrs M A, BA DipLib, Librarian, Concord College.
[10033065]   07/02/2014   **ME**

Williams, Mrs M A M, BA DipLib MCLIP, Senior Lib. Assistant, Cardiff University.
[34594]   01/01/1982   **CM20/01/1986**

Williams, Miss M G, BA FCLIP, Retired.
[15958]   17/09/1953   **FE01/01/1963**

Williams, Mrs N, Student, University of Aberystwyth.
[10009335]   01/06/2008   **ME**

Williams, Mrs N M J, BA DipLib MCLIP, Subject Librarian, University of Gloucestershire.
[41675]   10/02/1988   **CM16/12/1992**

Williams, Mr N R, BA MCLIP, Retired.
[21571]   30/10/1973   **CM19/11/1979**

Williams, Mrs P, BSc DipLib MCLIP, Curator, Maps, Mountaineering & Polar Collections, National Library of Scotland, Edinburgh.
[43642]   15/11/1989   **CM23/03/1993**

Williams, Mrs P, BA (Hons) MCLIP, Education Faculty Librarian (Education Studies, PGCE, School Direct, Masters & Research)., Liverpool Hope University.
[49434]   27/10/1993   **CM18/09/2002**

Williams, Mr P, BA MMUS MCLIP,
[10021335]   18/07/2012   **CM21/07/1989**

Williams, Miss P C, MCLIP, Retired.
[15970]   08/03/1961   **CM01/01/1964**

Williams, Mr P J, Student, Liverpool John Moores University.
[10020303]   11/01/2012   **ME**

Williams, Miss P J, BA, Unemployed.
[39987]   08/10/1986   **ME**

Williams, Mrs P L, BA (Hons) MA MCLIP, Research & Business Development.
[52168]   11/10/1995   **CM19/01/2000**

Williams, Mrs P M, BLib MCLIP, Information Officer, Univrsity of Law, Bristol.
[2414]   18/01/1972   **CM14/10/1975**

Williams, Ms R, BA (Hons) MA MCLIP, Development Librarian, Nottingham County Council.
[64175]   07/01/2005   **CM23/01/2008**

Williams, Mr R, BA MCLIP, Senior Branch Librarian, Cardiff C. C.
[33974]   30/06/1981   **CM05/12/1985**

Williams, Dr R G, MA MPhil PhD MCLIP, Information Tech. Trainer/Lib. /Arch., London & Quadrant Housing Trust, Mapledurham & Hendred House.
[15978]   27/01/1968   **CM01/01/1971**

Williams, Mr R G, BA (Hons) MCLIP, Retired.
[15977]   22/02/1962   **CM01/01/1967**

Williams, Mrs R L, BA (Hons) MA MCLIP, L. and Information Resources Manager, Bradford District Care Trust.
[58833]   23/08/2000   **CM08/12/2004**

Williams, Mr R N, BA (Hons) MA MCLIP, Head of Library Services, UCL – Qatar.
[52077]   02/10/1995   **CM20/05/1998**

Williams, Miss S, BA (Hons) MSc MCLIP, Assistant Librarian.
[58711]   01/07/2000   **CM21/05/2003**

Williams, Mrs S, BA (Hons) BSC (Hons) MSC (RES), Liaison Serv. Manager, Queen Margaret University Edinburgh.
[10006790]   11/10/1983   **ME**

Williams, Mrs S C, MSc MLS MCLIP, Retired.
[19034]   07/10/1966   **CM01/01/1971**

Williams, Ms S F, BSc (Hons) MCLIP, Librarian, South Wales Miners' Library, University of Wales, Swansea, Swansea.
[45623]   04/04/1991   **CM27/07/1994**

Williams, Mr S R, BA (Hons) FBCS, Deputy Director, Information Services and Systems, Swansea University.
[10022459]   05/03/2013   **ME**

Williams, Mrs T, MCLIP, Assistant Librarian, The Portico Library.
[10019439]   04/07/2011   **CM16/01/2014**

Williams, Mr T D, BTh (Hons) DipLib MCLIP, Business and Legal Intelligence Analyst, Pinsent Masons, London.
[59480]   09/04/2001   **CM25/01/2011**

Williams, Mr T G, PgDipLib, Lib. /Information Officer, Roskill Information Serv., London.
[37900]   20/10/1984   **ME**

Williams, Ms T L, BA (Hons) MSc (Econ) MCLIP, Information Officer, DWF LLP, Manchester.
[59205]   08/01/2001   **CM31/01/2007**

Williams, Ms V, Student.
[10021913]   30/10/2012   **ME**

Williams, Miss V, BA (Hons), Student, Robert Gordon University.
[10031083]   16/10/2014   **ME**

Williams, Mr W G, OBE HonFLA MInstAM FRSA, Former – Director of Lib. & Info Serv, Clwyn 1982 – 1996. Head of Cultural Serv., Denbighshire County Council 1996–2000. Director Education & Culture, Denbighshire 2000–2001.
[15993]   12/06/1964   **HFE01/12/1993**

Williamson, Mr A R, BA MA, Technical Services Librarian, South Tyneside Libraries.
[42185]   11/10/1988   **ME**

Williamson, Mr B, BA (Hons), Student, University of Sheffield.
[10031089]   14/10/2014   **ME**

Williamson, Mrs H M, BA MSc MCLIP, Librarian, Horniman Museum.
[10020484]   23/10/2007   **CM27/03/2014**

Williamson, Mr M G, JP BA MCLIP MCMI LCGI DL, Information Director /Consultant, Cambridgeshire Arts & Training Serv.
[15999]   03/02/1962   **CM01/01/1966**

Williamson, Mrs M J, BA MCLIP, Assistant Librarian, Rutherford Appleton Laboratory, Oxfordshire.
[20652]   20/05/1973   **CM23/11/1976**

Williamson, Mrs S L, MA MCLIP, Head of Library Services, St Helens MBC.
[63408]   05/05/2004   **CM17/09/2008**

Williamson, Mrs T H, BA (Hons) PgDip, Assistant Librarian, Lancaster University.
[65432]   23/02/2006   **ME**

Willing, Ms J A, BA MCLIP, Senior Librarian, Glasgow L, Mitchell L.
[16004]   24/10/1969   **CM05/08/1974**

Willis, Miss A L, MCLIP, Retired.
[16007]   10/09/1968   **CM09/01/1973**

Willis, Miss E A, BA, Student, City University London.
[10032947]   30/01/2014   **ME**

Willis, Miss H G, MCLIP, Retired.
[17971]   29/01/1957   **CM01/01/1961**

Willis, Mrs M A, BA (Hons) MCLIP, Head of Library Services., Walter Scott & Partners Ltd, Edinburgh.
[62999]   27/11/2003   **CM15/07/2014**

Willis, Miss N D, ACLIP, Senior Library & Information Worker, Grays Library.
[10021916]   30/10/2012   **ACL08/03/2013**

Willis, Mr P J, MCLIP, Life Member.
[16013]   01/01/1957   **CM01/01/1964**

Willis, Mrs S, MCLIP, ERC Co-ordinator, University of Brighton.
[56132]   03/03/1998   **CM03/03/1998**

Willison, Mr I R, CBE HonFLA, Hon. Fellow.
[44039]   30/09/1988   **HFE30/09/1988**

Willmott, Miss E M, MA MCLIP, Life Member.
[16018]   14/03/1959   **CM01/01/1961**

Willox, Miss N P, MA MCLIP, Life Member.
[16024]   27/09/1953   **CM01/01/1958**

Wills, Mr A, BA MCLIP, Head of Libraries & Information Services, Leicester Libraries.
[19926]   16/01/1973   **CM15/08/1978**

Wills, Mr A L, MCLIP, Hon. Ed. Northern Librarian, Kendal.
[16025]   03/03/1951   **CM01/01/1957**

Willshaw, Mr G, Digital Curator, The University of Edinburgh.
[10021779]   10/10/2012   **ME**

Wilman, Mrs L, MCLIP, Retired.
[24458]   21/07/1975   **CM28/08/1981**

Wilmot, Miss C, MA (Hons) MA MCLIP, Deputy Librarian, Arts University College, Bournemouth.
[59083]   10/11/2000   **CM09/11/2005**

Wilmot, Mr R S, BA DipLib, Librarian, King Edward VI Five Ways School, Birmingham.
[42165]   11/10/1988   **ME**

Wilshaw, Mrs K, BA FCLIP, Knowledge Services Lead Health Education Yorkshire and the Humber.
[35430]   04/10/1982   **FE04/10/2006**

Wilsher, Mr R F, MA DipLib, Retired Information Specialist.
[37074]   23/01/1984   **ME**

Wilshere, Mrs J P, BA, Librarian, Notts. Science & Bus. L.
[41409]   26/11/1987   **ME**

Wilson, Mrs A M, MA MCLIP, Deputy Librarian, Bromley College of F. & Higher Education, Kent.
[23595]   22/01/1975   **CM12/03/2003**

Wilson, Ms A M, MA MSc DipLib MCLIP, Life Member.
[35682]   26/09/1966   **CM30/06/1983**

Wilson, Mr C, Librarian, Motherwell Library, Motherwell.
[65906]   01/07/2006   **ME**

Wilson, Miss C A, MA MCLIP, Retired.
[16050]   20/02/1959   **CM01/01/1965**

Wilson, Miss C E, BA (Hons) PGCE MA MCLIP, Deputy L. Serv. Manager, Manchester Metro. University L.
[48881]   09/07/1993   **CM22/09/1999**

Wilson, Mrs C H, BA (Hons) MA MCLIP, Library Assistant. Durham University Lib.
[55949]   23/12/1997   **CM25/07/2001**

Wilson, Mr C J, BA (Hons) DipLib MA MCLIP, Senior Assistant Lib. - Information Servs., London School of Economics.
[48289]   24/11/1992   **CM22/11/1995**

Wilson, Miss C S, BA (Hons) MCLIP, Librarian, Bromsgrove Library, Worcs. County Council.
[43387]   13/10/1989   **CM20/05/1998**

Wilson, Mr C W J, FCLIP, Life member.
[16055]   01/01/1941   **FE01/01/1950**

Wilson, Ms D, BSc (Hons), Senior LRC Information Assistant, Middlesbrough College.
[10001316]   16/01/2007   **AF**

Wilson, Mrs D, MCLIP, Young People Servs. Librarian, Borehamwood Library, Herts.
[12845]   01/10/1971   **CM30/01/1985**

Wilson, Miss D A, MA (Hons) MLitt MCLIP, Retired.
[55959]   22/12/1997   **CM21/03/2001**

Wilson, Mr D A G, MA MCLIP, Life Member.
[16056]   15/09/1948   **CM01/01/1951**

Wilson, Mrs E, BA (Hons), Student, Liverpool John Moores University.
[65719]   15/03/2006   **ME**

Wilson, Mrs E F, MCLIP, Senior Library Assistant, Sheffield University, Main L.
[30300]   02/01/1979   **CM23/02/1983**

Wilson, Mrs E M, MCLIP, Retired.
[16063]   30/01/1964   **CM01/01/1968**

Wilson, Dr F C, MA MSc PhD, Head of Assessment, Bodleian Libraries, Oxford.
[59308]   01/02/2001   **ME**

Wilson, Miss F M, BSc (Hons) MSc BWYDip, Librarian, Bournemouth Borough Council, Bournemouth.
[57219]   20/01/1999   **CM16/07/2003**

Wilson, Ms G, Special Collections Manager, Lancashire Library Service.
[62730]   20/10/2003   **AF**
Wilson, Mrs G M, BA DipLib MCLIP, Senior Lib. Literacy Development,
Blackburn with Darwen B. C., Blackburn Central Library.
[24237]   01/05/1975   **CM13/07/1977**
Wilson, Mrs H V, BSc MA MCLIP, Information Manager, Lloyds TSB,
Bristol.
[10014089]   06/04/1990   **CM24/07/1996**
Wilson, Mr J, BA (Hons) MSc MCLIP, Assistant Librarian, Health
Management Library, Scottish Health Serv. Centre, Edinburgh.
[66131]   02/10/2006   **CM25/01/2011**
Wilson, Mr J, BA, Physics Laboratory Technician, Strathallan School.
[10016473]   01/04/2010   **ME**
Wilson, Mrs J, BA, School Librarian, Marshalls Park School.
[33198]   01/10/1980   **ME**
Wilson, Mrs J, BA MCLIP, SHEQ Manager, DNV, Aberdeen.
[39859]   19/09/1986   **CM21/07/1993**
Wilson, Miss J,
[10006789]   13/12/2007   **ME**
Wilson, Mrs J E, BA (Hons) MCLIP, Career Break.
[40866]   23/07/1987   **CM16/10/1991**
Wilson, Ms J E S, BA MCLIP, Sch. Lib. /Webmaster.
[25105]   28/10/1975   **CM20/07/1979**
Wilson, Ms J M, MCLIP, Liaison & Planning Manager, ISD, University of
Salford.
[10001312]   15/08/1988   **CM30/01/1991**
Wilson, Ms K, BSc (Hons) MSc DipLIS MCLIP, Information Officer,
British Association for Adoption and Fostering (BAAF), London.
[53796]   01/10/1996   **CM19/05/1999**
Wilson, Mr K, BA FCLIP HonFCLIP AssocCIPD, Tech. Information
Director, RIBA Enterprises Ltd, Newcastle upon Tyne.
[16078]   19/01/1972   **RV**16/01/2014   **FE04/10/2006**
Wilson, Mr K H, BA MSc, Assistant Librarian, Goldsmiths College.
[10022905]   07/05/2013   **ME**
Wilson, Miss K J, BA (Hons), Learning Res. Assistant, Middlesex
University.
[62650]   01/10/2003   **ME**
Wilson, Mrs L, MA (Hons) MSc, Unwaged.
[63284]   26/03/2004   **ME**
Wilson, Mrs M, Assistant Librarian, Farnborough Hill School.
[10032383]   29/11/2013   **ME**
Wilson, Mrs M B, MCLIP, Retired.
[12082]   26/09/1958   **CM01/01/1963**
Wilson, Mrs M E, MA (Hons) DipILS MCLIP, School Librarian, Northfield
Academy, Aberdeen.
[54320]   18/11/1996   **RV**30/04/2014   **CM21/03/2001**
Wilson, Miss M E, MA (Hons) PgDip MCLIP, Trainee Librarian, Falkirk
Council L. Serv.
[61526]   13/09/2002   **CM08/09/2005**
Wilson, Miss M H, OBE MSc MCLIP, Life Member.
[16086]   08/03/1963   **CM01/01/1968**
Wilson, Mr M P, BA (Hons) MA, Assistant Librarian, Selwyn College,
Cambridge.
[54332]   21/11/1996   **ME**
Wilson, Miss N, ACLIP, L. Assistant, Clay Cross Library, Clay Cross.
[10019529]   22/07/2011   **ACL16/05/2012**
Wilson, Mr P A, Knowledge and Information Officer, Slaughter and May.
[10019027]   12/04/2011   **ME**
Wilson, Mr P R, BA MA, College Librarian, Fakenham College, Norfolk.
[10015438]   01/08/2002   **ME**
Wilson, Ms R J, BA MCLIP, Senior Continuous Improvement
Practioner., Home Office, London.
[32360]   02/02/1980   **CM20/09/1984**

Wilson, Mrs S, MA, Community Librarian.
[62437]   18/06/2003   **ME**
Wilson, Miss S, BSc (Hons) MSc PgCert MCLIP, Senior Information
Scientist, Healthcare Improvement Scotland.
[63942]   18/11/2004   **CM19/03/2008**
Wilson, Mr S, BA (Hons) DipLib MCLIP, Tribunal Information Officer &
Librarian, Traffic Penalty Tribunal, Wilmslow, Cheshire.
[43885]   08/02/1990   **CM20/01/1999**
Wilson, Miss S A, MCLIP, Life Member.
[16098]   28/02/1950   **CM01/01/1956**
Wilson, Ms S B, BA, Student.
[10032094]   24/10/2013   **ME**
Wilson, Mrs S J, Head of Library, National Assembly for Wales, Cardiff.
[39763]   01/07/1986   **ME**
Wilson, Mrs S J, BA DipLib MCLIP, Information Professional at Wilson
Research.
[32973]   01/10/1980   **CM08/12/1983**
Wilson, Mr S J, BEng (Hons) (Open) MSc MCLIP, Staff Information
Scientist, DePuy International. Ltd, Leeds.
[53783]   01/10/1996   **CM22/09/1999**
Wilson, Ms S J, BA PgDip, Unwaged.
[10017405]   17/11/1995   **ME**
Wilson, Prof T D, BSc (Econ) PhD PhD (h. c.) HedDr (h. c.) FCLIP
HonFCLIP, Senior Professor (PT), Swedish School of Library and
Information Science, Boras, Sweden.
[16101]   24/01/1952   **HFE25/03/1993**
Wilson-Whalley, Mrs K C, MA (Hons) MLitt MSc MCLIP, Librarian,
James Young High School, West Lothian.
[61761]   06/11/2002   **CM21/06/2006**
Wilton, Mrs S E, MA MCLIP, Development Team Librarian, Redhill
Library, Surrey County Council.
[59212]   08/01/2001   **CM11/03/2009**
Wiltshire, Miss P J, IOP Publishing.
[64293]   23/02/2005   **AF**
Wimpenny, Miss M, MA BA (Hons), Senior Librarian, University
Campus Oldham.
[62502]   29/07/2003   **ME**
Windle, Mrs E J, BA (Hons) MScEcon, Research & Information Officer,
DLA Piper UK LLP, London.
[56571]   01/09/1998   **ME**
Winfield, Mrs J A, BA (HONS) MCLIP, Early Years Manager,
Blagreaves Library, Derby City Council.
[33670]   04/02/1981   **CM24/04/1986**
Wing, Mr H J R, MA MCLIP, Retired.
[16125]   01/01/1957   **CM01/01/1970**
Winkworth, Mrs L T, MCLIP, School Librarian, Headington School,
Oxford.
[45405]   03/01/1991   **CM03/10/2007**
Winning, Miss M A, BSc (Hons) MSc MCLIP, Senior Health Information
Scientist, NHS Quality Improvement Scotland.
[57058]   02/12/1998   **CM16/07/2003**
Winstanley, Mrs J V, BA MCLIP, L. Assistant, Beech Green Primary
School, Gloucester.
[23563]   21/01/1975   **CM13/12/1978**
Winstanley, Mr L A,
[65800]   03/05/2006   **ME**
Winter, Mrs D, BA (Hons), Principal Lib. Officer, Central Library, West
Bromwich.
[10012874]   21/10/1993   **ME**
Winter, Mr E C, MA FCLIP HonFLA, Secretary, CILIP Benevolent Fund,
London.
[19435]   10/03/1953   **HFE10/10/1995**
Winter, Ms S, BSc (Hons) MSc (Dist) MCLIP, Managing Director.
[60669]   23/06/2000   **CM23/06/2000**

Winterbotham, Miss D, MBE FCLIP, Life Member.
[19436]   23/03/1953   **FE01/01/1963**
Winter-Burke, Miss B S, Library Assistant, Courtauld Institute of Art.
[10031123]   17/09/2013   **ME**
Winterman, Dr V, BSc MSc PhD MCLIP, Knowledge and Information
Specialist, Independent Consultant.
[40330]   08/01/1987   **CM01/04/2002**
Wintersgill, Mr I, BA DipLib MCLIP, Retired.
[16140]   25/01/1972   **CM21/06/1974**
Wintle, Mrs E M, LLB DipLib MCLIP, Librarian, Blackstone Chambers,
London.
[27376]   24/02/1977   **CM16/07/1979**
Winton, Mr S R, BA DipLib MCLIP, Senior Lib. -Information & Systems
Support, Midlothian Council L.
[33430]   29/11/1980   **CM16/08/1985**
Wiper, Mr C K, BA (Hons) DipLib MCLIP LLM, Senior Policy Officer
ICO.
[31984]   07/01/1980   **CM30/04/1982**
Wisdom, Mr J J, MA FSA MCLIP, Assistant Librarian /Librarian,
Guildhall Library/St Paul's Cathedral.
[30302]   11/12/1978   **CM19/06/1981**
Wisdom, Mrs S, BA (Hons) MA MCLIP, Digital Curator, The British
Library, London.
[54489]   08/01/1997   **CM29/03/2006**
Wise, Mrs C M, BA (Hons) MA Dip Lib MCMI MCLIP CMgr, Associate
Director, Historic Collections & Keeper of Special Collections, Senate
House Libraries, University of London.
[36234]   09/08/1983   **CM24/04/1991**
Wise, Miss H, BA (Hons), Student, University of Surrey.
[10034782]   14/08/2014   **ME**
Wiseman, Miss H, BSc MSc, Clinical Sci., Guys & St Thomas NHS
Trust, Medical Toxicology Unit, London.
[60682]   12/12/2001   **ME**
Wiseman, Mrs L K, BA (Hons) MLib MCLIP, Librarian/Learning Support
Co-ordinator., All Nations Christian College, Ware, Hertfordshire.
[39956]   09/10/1986   **CM14/03/1990**
Wiseman, Ms R, BA (Hons) MA MISt,
[10022954]   14/05/2013   **ME**
Wisher, Mrs E L, BA (Hons) MA MCLIP, Assistant Librarian
(Humanities), Albert Sloman Library, University of Essex, Colchester.
[58235]   23/11/1999   **CM15/10/2002**
Witherick, Mrs T K, BA (Hons) MSc MCLIP, Lead Librarian. North
Somerset C., Town Hall.
[61135]   07/03/2002   **CM13/06/2007**
Witkin, Mr O T, BA MA, Avery Hill Campus Library, Universityof
Greenwich.
[65610]   28/02/2006   **ME**
Witkowski, Mr S F, BA MCLIP, Unwaged.
[36700]   14/11/1983   **CM24/04/1991**
Wittenberg, Ms J V, MBS, Student, Science University of Illinois At
Urbana-Champaign.
[10033207]   20/02/2014   **ME**
Witton, Mrs S A J, Library Assistant, Mod.
[10032966]   31/01/2014   **ME**
Witts, Ms N, MA, Currently on maternity leave.
[10019088]   18/04/2011   **ME**
Wlliams, Miss S, Student.
[10032289]   13/11/2013   **ME**
Wlliams, Miss S, Student.
[10032289]   **ME**
Wojnar, Miss M, MA, Sch. L. Resources Centre Co-ordinator (job share).
[10006343]   10/10/2007   **ME**
Wolf, Mrs C A, MA (Hons) MA, Sch. Librarian, Hele's School, Plymouth.
[53780]   01/10/1996   **ME**

Wolf, Mr M J, BA (Hons) MA MCLIP, Research Support Lead, Sydney
Jones Library, Liverpool University.
[58442]   16/02/2000   **RV**16/01/2014   **CM19/11/2003**
Wolfenden, Mrs S, MCLIP, Wolfenden, Sarah, BA (Hons) MA MCILIP.
[65958]   21/07/2006   **CM20/04/2012**
Wolff, Miss M E, DipLib MCLIP, Community Librarian, Selly Oak,
Stirchley, Druids Heath and Yardley Wood Libraries, Birmingham.
[28725]   07/01/1978   **CM04/09/1981**
Wolffsohn, Miss P J, BA (Hons) MCLIP, Knowledge Services Manager.,
Nabarro., London.
[46520]   15/11/1991   **CM17/05/2000**
Wolpert, Prof L, DIC PhD FRS HonFCLIP, Hon. Fellow.
[60743]   12/12/2001   **HFE29/03/1999**
Wong, Ms F, Student, University of Strathclyde.
[10035521]   16/10/2014   **ME**
Wong, Miss L, Bsc MSc, Journals & Subscriptions Co-ordinator, Royal
Holloway, University of London.
[10011340]   09/10/2008   **ME**
Wong, Mrs R, BA MCLIP, Retired.
[22802]   11/10/1974   **CM11/10/1976**
Wong, Ms W M, BSc FCLIP, Library, The Open University of Hong
Kong.
[36446]   10/10/1983   **FE12/03/2003**
Wontner Osborne, Mrs E M J, BA (Hons) MSc MCLIP, Information
Manager – Export Control Org., BIS, London.
[56723]   07/10/1998   **CM02/02/2005**
Woo, Mr T Y L, BSocSc DipLib MCLIP, Library Consultant, Zambia.
[31725]   02/11/1979   **CM23/02/1983**
Wood, Mrs A, BA (Hons), L. Manager Lending Serv., L's. & Heritage,
Walsall Metropolitan Borough Council.
[56035]   28/01/1998   **ME**
Wood, Miss A, BA, Retired.
[16171]   02/01/1969   **CM03/04/1973**
Wood, Mr A F, BA MCLIP, Life Member.
[16172]   21/08/1960   **CM01/01/1963**
Wood, Dr A J, PhD MA BA FCLIP MITOL AssocCIP, Marketing &
Development.
[21783]   04/02/1974   **FE21/06/2006**
Wood, Mrs A K A, MSc BSc (Hons), Unwaged.
[45714]   01/05/1991   **ME**
Wood, Miss A M, BA, Librarian, Campden BRI, Chipping Campden.
[35823]   21/01/1983   **ME**
Wood, Mrs C A, BA HDE DSE (Media Sc) MCLIP, Head Librarian,
Norwich School, Norfolk.
[58671]   16/05/2000   **CM23/01/2002**
Wood, Mrs D, MCLIP, Retired.
[16178]   01/01/1959   **CM01/01/1963**
Wood, Miss D, MA Cert GSMD (P), Student, Aberystwyth University.
[10009214]   07/05/2008   **ME**
Wood, Ms F C, MA, Subject Librarian, UCL Library Services.
[10001317]   16/01/2007   **ME**
Wood, Mrs G A, BMus, Head of Learning Resources, Chethams' School
of Music.
[62107]   19/02/2003   **ME**
Wood, Miss H, BA, Student, Loughborough University.
[10032042]   22/10/2013   **ME**
Wood, Miss H J, BA (Hons) MCLIP, Librarian, Lamport Bassitt,
Southampton.
[46609]   25/11/1991   **CM22/01/1997**
Wood, Mr I J, BSc (Hons) AMInst LM, Library. Assistant, Bill Bryson
Library, Durham University.
[59958]   12/11/2001   **ME**
Wood, Mrs J, MA Pg Dip ILS MCLIP, Librarian, Cafcass.
[62885]   18/11/2003   **CM23/01/2008**

Wood, Mrs J, Librarian, Toynbee School, Hampshire.
[61580] 02/10/2002 ME
Wood, Ms J, Prison Librarian, HMP Morton Hall, Lincoln.
[65658] 14/03/2006 AF
Wood, Mrs J, Service Development Librarian, Dudley Library.
[10022906] 07/05/2013 AF
Wood, Mrs J, MA, Subject Librarian., Sch of Oriental & African Studies.
[10020762] 22/10/2008 ME
Wood, Mrs J H, MA (Cantab) DipLIS, Lib. & Resource Centre Manager, Farnborough Hill Farnborough.
[40001] 06/10/1986 ME
Wood, Mr J M, MA FCLIP, Life Member.
[16199] 07/08/1957 FE01/01/1961
Wood, Ms K, MA HonFIInfSc HonFLA FCLIP, Retired.
[16217] 01/01/1959 HFE01/01/2002
Wood, Dr M, BA MA PhD MCLIP, Special Collections & Archives Librarian, Newcastle University, Robinson Library.
[59798] 03/10/2014 RV16/01/2014 CM21/11/2007
Wood, Mrs M E, MA (Oxon) MSc PGCE, Information Researcher and Content Developer Chartered Management Institute.
[10001535] 13/12/1993 ME
Wood, Mrs M E, MCLIP, Retired.
[9236] 01/01/1969 CM11/01/1973
Wood, Ms N, BA (Hons) DipLIM MSc, Information Officer, Police Federation of England & Wales.
[53904] 09/10/1996 ME
Wood, Miss N, BA (Hons) MCLIP, Librarian: Collection Development, Royal Society of Medicine. Library, London.
[41506] 13/01/1988 CM22/07/1998
Wood, Mr N V, ACIL MCLIP, Retired.
[16215] 08/02/1964 CM01/01/1968
Wood, Mrs P L, BA (Hons) MSc, Senior Information Servcies Librarian, Leeds Beckett University.
[61087] 04/03/2002 ME
Wood, Ms S, BA (Hons), School Librarian, Holy Cross Preparatory School.
[33819] 24/09/2013 ME
Wood, Mrs S M, BA MCLIP, Product Manager.
[24297] 20/05/1975 CM17/01/1979
Wood, Miss S S, BA DipLib MCLIP, Metadata Co-ordinator/Liaison Librarian, University of Reading.
[38934] 15/10/1985 CM07/06/1988
Woodall, Mr A S, BA (Hons), Assistant Locality Librarian, Brierley Hill Library.
[10017042] 21/06/2010 ME
Woodbridge, Ms S, MA MCLIP, Employment not known.
[44420] 08/10/1990 CM31/01/1996
Woodburn, Mrs S, MCLIP, District Manager, Lancashire Library Service.
[63169] 02/03/2004 CM21/11/2007
Woodcock, Mr J, BSc (Hons), Senior Library Assistant, Franklin Wilkins Library, Kings College.
[10020232] 02/12/2011 ME
Woodcock, Ms L, BA (Hons) MA MCLIP, Assistant Registrar Learning, University of Sheffield.
[55785] 17/11/1997 CM19/01/2000
Woodcock, Mrs R E, BSc (Hons) DipLib, Knowledge & Resources Librarian, Doncaster Royal Infirmary.
[28004] 11/10/1977 ME
Woodcock, Miss S F, Library Services Coordinator, Petroc, Barnstable.
[10022852] 30/04/2013 AF
Woodcraft, Mrs L, MA (Hons) MSc MCLIP, Global Portal Content Manager, Hay Group.
[58087] 26/10/1999 CM06/04/2005

Woodfield, Mr J D, Information Librarian, University of Bath.
[10019284] 24/05/2011 AF
Woodfine, Mr B, BA (Hons), Team Librarian, Bedford Central Library, Bedford.
[10022110] 18/12/2012 ME
Woodforde, Mrs S E, MCLIP, Senior Librarian, Grangemouth Library, Stirlingshire.
[23211] 14/11/1974 CM01/01/1977
Woodhall, Mrs S, BA (Hons) MA MCLIP, Assistant Librarian, Lancashire Teaching Hospitals NHS Foundation Trust.
[10007743] 21/02/2008 CM12/05/2011
Woodhead, Mrs E M, BA (Hons) MA, Unwaged.
[10033900] 12/05/2014 ME
Woodhouse, Mr B W, MA DipLib MCLIP, School Librarian, Smithycroft School, Glasgow C. Co. Educ. Department.
[43134] 10/08/1989 CM23/03/1994
Woodhouse, Mrs D E, MCLIP, Retired.
[7988] 18/03/1948 CM01/01/1953
Woodhouse, Mr R G, BA MA PGCE MCLIP, Life Member.
[16245] 20/07/1959 CM01/01/1964
Woodland, Mr A N, MCLIP, Life Member.
[18000] 23/01/1948 CM01/01/1961
Woodland, Mrs J K, BA (Hons) MCLIP, Sunday Librarian, Bishop's Stortford Public L.
[49572] 19/11/1993 CM18/03/1998
Woodley, Miss H C, BA (HONS) MST MA, Student.
[10020864] 23/07/2013 ME
Woodley, Mrs S, BEd (Hons), Learning Services Team Leader (Resources), Kenwyn Learning Centre, Truro & Penwith College,
[10031646] 17/09/2013 ME
Woodman, Mrs A, BA, Student, University of Dundee.
[10032807] 14/01/2014 ME
Woodman, Mr A J, Business Manager, Ministry of Defence.
[10034296] 01/07/2014 ME
Woodman, Mr G D, BA DipLib MCLIP, Retired.
[24861] 07/10/1975 CM15/01/1979
Woodman, Mrs M C, BSc ACIL, Librarian, Gorseland Primary School, Martlesham Heath.
[10011001] 12/09/2008 ACL23/09/2009
Woodman, Ms R M, BA MLS, Reader Development Adviser, Educ. L. Res. Centre, Reading.
[33431] 01/11/1980 ME
Woodman, Miss S M, BA MCLIP, Librarian, Building Research Establishment, Watford.
[36012] 08/04/1983 CM15/11/1988
Woodman, Ms Z, School Librarian, ISCA College of Media Arts, Exeter.
[10007544] 13/02/2008 ME
Woodmansey, Mrs J, BA (Hons) MCLIP, Librarian, HMP Wolds, Everthorpe.
[10011621] 30/10/2008 CM14/11/2012
Woodroffe, Ms J E, BA MCLIP, Retired.
[35996] 01/01/1964 CM27/03/1985
Woodroofe, Mr S R, BA (Hons) PgDipInfMgt, Assistant Prison Librarian, HM Prison Pentonville, London.
[49380] 01/11/1993 ME
Woodrow, Miss G L, BA (Hons) MCLIP, Learning Resources Assistant.
[42666] 06/02/1989 CM19/07/2000
Woodruff, Mrs E T C, BSc MCLIP, Retired.
[33802] 11/03/1981 CM15/02/1989
Woods, Mr A D, BSc MCLIP, Electronic Services Development Officer, National Museums Scotland, Edinburgh.
[62066] 07/02/2003 CM09/07/2008
Woods, Ms C M, Student, University of Wales Aberystwyth.
[10032625] 20/12/2013 ME

Woods, Mrs D, BA MCLIP, Manager :SLS, Sch. L. Serv., Worcestershire
County Council.
[31947]   05/01/1980   **CM29/01/1985**
Woods, Miss D M, FCLIP, Life Member.
[16257]   28/01/1951   **FE01/01/1963**
Woods, Mr D N, BA (Hons) MCLIP, Retired.
[20035]   15/01/1973   **CM21/07/1976**
Woods, Miss E L, BA MA MCLIP AHEA, Information Consultant, Royal
Holloway, University of London.
[63991]   22/11/2004   **CM21/11/2007**
Woods, Mrs G A, BA, Deputy Librarian, L. of the European Court of
Human Rights, Council of Europe, Strasbourg. France.
[35174]   06/10/1982   **ME**
Woods, Ms H B, BA (Hons) MSc MCLIP FHEA, Information Specialist,
School of Health & Related Research., Uni of Sheffield.
[56481]   22/07/1998   **CM15/09/2004**
Woods, Ms L, Subject Librarian, University of Huddersfield.
[10008139]   11/03/2008   **ME**
Woods, Ms M, BSc PGD, Head of Information and Research.
[10032109]   24/01/1992   **ME**
Woods, Dr N J, BA MPhil DPhil, Library Assistant, West Sussex County
Council.
[10035509]   16/10/2014   **ME**
Woods, Mr P G, MA DipLib, Head L. Information Centre., Treasury
Solicitors Department, London Support Services Treasury Solicitors.
[41938]   31/05/1988   **CM12/12/1991**
Woods, Ms R, BA DipLib, Librarian, North Lanarkshire Council, Wishaw.
[44134]   25/05/1990   **ME**
Woods, Mr R G, MA DipLib MCLIP, Life Member.
[16264]   10/10/1951   **CM01/01/1957**
Woods, Mr S, BA (Hons) MCLIP,
[10012477]   10/02/2009   **CM11/07/2012**
Woods, Mr S R, MCLIP, Retired.
[22704]   17/09/1974   **CM03/08/1977**
Woods, Mrs V L, BA (Hons) MCLIP, Seeking freelance work.
[33682]   16/01/1981   **CM06/12/1983**
Woolcock, Miss K, Student, Aberystwyth University.
[10015780]   26/01/2010   **ME**
Wooldridge, Miss C, BA MA, UMASCS Graduate Trainee Library
Assistant, University of Reading.
[10031873]   10/10/2013   **ME**
Woolf, Mr J, MA BA MCLIP, Assistant Librarian, Wanstead Library
London.
[39890]   06/10/1986   **CM21/05/2008**
Woolf, Miss J L A, BA (Hons) MScEcon, Information Assistant, Harrison
Learning Centre, University of Wolverhampton.
[10015942]   29/01/2010   **ME**
Woolfries, Mrs H, Information Advisor, Kingston University, London.
[10006601]   21/11/2007   **ME**
Woolgar, Mr T, MCLIP, Library Operations & Commissioning Manager,
London Borough of Bromley.
[32476]   01/04/1980   **CM10/09/1984**
Woolhouse, Miss L, BA (Hons) MA, Studying MA Librarianship at the
University of Sheffield whilst working in the University libraries.
[10031159]   14/10/2013   **ME**
Woollard, Mrs C J, BA (Hons) MSc MCLIP, Career Break.
[50352]   04/07/1994   **CM21/05/1997**
Woollard, Mr S J, MCLIP, Retired.
[10001109]   12/01/2007   **CM28/02/1975**
Woollatt, Miss J, MCLIP, Life Member.
[16285]   11/07/1961   **CM01/01/1970**
Woolley, Mrs C A, BLib (Hons) MCLIP, Independent Consultant.
[36978]   24/01/1984   **CM05/04/1988**

Woolley, Mrs D, BSc MSc MCLIP, Lib. in the NHS Fife Public Health
Library, Cameron Bridge.
[26219]   14/08/1976   **CM31/08/1979**
Woolley, Mr M, BA MCLIP, University Librarian.
[35837]   14/01/1983   **CM04/08/1987**
Woolley, Mrs S E, BA (Hons) DipLIS MCLIP, Academic Librarian
Teesside University Middlesbrough.
[49415]   21/10/1993   **CM23/07/1997**
Woolridge, Mrs E A, BA MCLIP, Retired.
[21771]   07/01/1974   **CM05/01/1977**
Woolven, Ms G B, BA MCLIP, Retired from post at Assoc. of
Commonwealth University, London.
[16290]   01/01/1959   **CM01/01/1967**
Woolven, Mrs J, Group Manager, Maldon & Witham, Essex County
Council.
[62152]   03/03/2003   **AF**
Woosley, Mrs T, BA (Hons) ACLIP, Senior Library Assistant, Guille Alles
Library, Guernsey.
[10019418]   28/06/2011   **ACL22/08/2012**
Wootton, Ms A M, BA (Hons) DipLib MCLIP, Senior Librarian,
Department of Collections Access, Imperial War Museum.
[16295]   08/01/1971   **CM11/01/1974**
Wootton, Ms C B, MSc BEd, Librarian, Doncaster College, Doncaster.
[59065]   01/11/2000   **ME**
Worden, Ms A E, MA MCLIP, Faculty Lib. Humanities and Social
Sciences, University of Portsmouth.
[42203]   11/10/1988   **CM17/10/1990**
Worden, Miss K E, BA (Hons) MA MCLIP, Academic Support Librarian,
University of Greenwich.
[43353]   25/10/1989   **CM22/03/1995**
Workman, Dr H M, BSc MA MBA PhD MCLIP, Director of Learning Res.
/University Librarian, Oxford Brookes University.
[28216]   12/10/1977   **CM30/09/1980**
Workman, Mrs M, MCLIP, Librarian.
[61531]   16/09/2002   **CM23/01/2008**
Worley, Ms J, Student, University of Brighton.
[10034161]   11/06/2014   **ME**
Worley, Ms L M, BA MCLIP, Director of EMEA Library Operations, Reed
Smith LLP, London.
[27100]   24/01/1977   **CM25/04/1979**
Wormald, Mr J H, ISO BSc (Econ) MCLIP, Life Member.
[16305]   12/09/1951   **CM01/01/1962**
Worrall, Mrs C B E, BA MCLIP, Outreach Librarian, Oxford Health NHS
Foundation Trust.
[35433]   01/10/1982   **CM15/05/1989**
Worrall, Miss S, BA (Hons) MCLIP, Information Librarian, West Sussex
County Council, Horsham Public Library.
[54169]   04/11/1996   **CM15/05/2002**
Worron, Mr A J, DIP LIS, Desk Officer for Geographical Information
Policy, Foreign and Commonwealth Office.
[10016755]   15/05/2010   **ME**
Worthington, Mrs G R A, BSc (Econ) MCLIP, Librarian, Children's
Team Cambs. Ls. & Information Serv., Cambridge.
[54692]   05/03/1997   **CM08/12/2004**
Worwood, Mr G, BA PGCE, Student, Aberystwyth University.
[10032489]   10/12/2013   **ME**
Wotton, Mrs R, LLM, Information Auditor, Foreign & Commonwealth
Office.
[10020572]   29/02/2012   **ME**
Wraight, Miss A, MA, Unwaged.
[10031167]   08/04/2014   **ME**
Wraith, Mrs E, MCLIP, Librarian, Norwich High School For Girls,
Norwich.
[56080]   12/02/1998   **CM23/01/2008**

Wray, Mrs B, MCLIP, Retired.
[16323] 01/01/1957 **CM01/01/1964**
Wray, Miss D C, BA MCLIP, Office Manager, IVAR, London.
[30305] 02/01/1979 **CM19/03/1985**
Wray, Mrs S J, BA MCLIP, Assistant Librarian, Royal United Hospital
NHS Trust, Bath.
[32106] 28/01/1980 **CM20/02/1987**
Wray, Mrs S J, BA MCLIP, Director of Libraries and Learning
Resources, Uppingham School.
[34215] 07/10/1981 **CM10/05/1986**
Wreghitt, Ms V, PgDip, Electronic Res. Officer, Careers Centre,
University of Warwick, Coventry.
[10013722] 22/05/2009 **ME**
Wren, Mrs D J, BA MCLIP, School Librarian, Beeslack High School,
MidLothian.
[38664] 14/09/1985 **CM18/07/1991**
Wren, Miss L A, BSc, Unwaged.
[62476] 07/07/2003 **ME**
Wride, Mrs P L, BA MCLIP, Collection Officer, Seven Stories,
Newcastle-upon-Tyne.
[31609] 17/10/1979 **CM28/07/1983**
Wright, Miss A, BLib MCLIP, Team Leader, Edinburgh City L.
[29542] 24/08/1978 **CM14/08/1985**
Wright, Mr A B, BA MSc MCLIP, Librarian, Falkirk library.
[56339] 27/05/1998 **CM29/03/2004**
Wright, Mrs A C, BSc (Hons) MCLIP, Librarian, Cadbury Heath
Librarian, South Glos.
[46352] 30/10/1991 **CM24/09/1997**
Wright, Ms A C, BA (Hons) MCLIP, Librarian, University of Law:
Birmingham.
[42303] 07/10/1988 **CM04/10/2006**
Wright, Mr A C, BMus (Hons) PgDipLib, Libraries & Information Service
Development Manager, Wakefield.
[54843] 14/04/1997 **ME**
Wright, Mrs A E, BA MA MCLIP, Librarian, Royal Northern College of
Music, Manchester.
[31452] 07/10/1979 **CM28/10/1981**
Wright, Miss A J, BA (Hons) PgDip MA MCLIP, Reader Development
and Stock Management Librarian, Derbyshire County Council,
[10018175] 01/12/2010 **CM11/04/2013**
Wright, Miss B A, LVO MA DipLib MCLIP, Bibl., Royal Library, Windsor
Castle, Berksshire.
[26619] 11/10/1976 **CM03/03/1982**
Wright, Ms C, BA ACLIP, L. Assistant, North Watford L.
[10016198] 19/02/2010 **ACL15/01/2013**
Wright, Mrs C A, MA MCLIP, Innovative Information Research Services
& Technologies for Libraries, European Commission, Brussels.
[18223] 01/10/1972 **CM21/08/1975**
Wright, Mrs C E, MSc, HE Librarian, Hull College.
[10001266] 14/02/2007 **ME**
Wright, Mrs D J, BA DipLib MCLIP, Child. Librarian, Rutland County
Council, Oakham.
[36242] 01/08/1983 **CM27/11/1996**
Wright, Mr D J, BA (Hons) MCLIP, School Librarian, Stewarts Melville
College, Edinburgh.
[55670] 07/11/1997 **CM13/03/2002**
Wright, Mrs D J, BA, Unwaged.
[6274] 04/10/1971 **CM03/06/1975**
Wright, Ms D W, BA MCLIP, Senior Librarian, Children & Young People,
Berwick Library, Walkergate.
[38438] 16/04/1985 **CM14/02/1990**
Wright, Mrs E A, BA MA MCLIP, Sub. Librarian, Doncaster College.
[59350] 13/02/2001 **RV**30/04/2014 **CM10/07/2009**

Wright, Mr E W, MA B SOC B PHIL MCLIP, Library Development
Officer, Milton Keynes Council.
[25191] 15/12/1975 **CM05/01/1978**
Wright, Mrs F J, MCLIP, Life Member.
[16342] 01/01/1945 **CM01/01/1951**
Wright, Mr G, Information Advisor, Linklaters LLP.
[64562] 11/05/2005 **ME**
Wright, Mrs G J, BA (Hons), Senior Library Assistant, Bodleian Library,
University of Oxford.
[63388] 27/04/2004 **ME**
Wright, H L, BA (Hons) MSc MCLIP, Assistant, L. NSPCC, London.
[65381] 03/01/2006 **CM11/06/2010**
Wright, Miss H M, MA MCLIP, Retired.
[16346] 24/11/1965 **CM01/01/1968**
Wright, Miss J, BA (Hons) MCLIP, Liaison Lib. (Learning and Teaching),
Birmingham City University.
[46977] 17/03/1992 **CM20/03/1996**
Wright, Mrs J M, BA, Stock Development Manager., GLL Libraries
Royal Borough of Greenwich, Plumstead Library.
[10021053] 04/10/1979 **ME**
Wright, Ms K E, BA MA, Information Services Manager, Centre for
Reviews & Dissemination, University of York.
[10006728] 03/10/1977 **CM01/10/1979**
Wright, Miss L D, ACLIP, Career Break.
[65599] 27/02/2006 **ACL17/10/2006**
Wright, Mr M G H, MA FCLIP, Life Member.
[16365] 23/03/1953 **FE01/01/1967**
Wright, Miss N, MCLIP, Life Member.
[16367] 17/09/1948 **CM01/01/1953**
Wright, Mrs P, BA (Hons) MA MCLIP, Content Services Deputy Head,
Defence Communications, Ministry of Defence, London.
[55651] 31/10/1997 **CM23/01/2002**
Wright, Mr P, BA (Hons) MA PGCE MCLIP, Librarian., Foyle College., N
Ireland.
[10016445] 26/03/2010 **CM14/03/2012**
Wright, Mrs R J, BA MCLIP, Librarian, Truro School, Cornwall.
[40578] 02/04/1987 **CM22/04/1992**
Wright, Mrs S, BA (Hons), Acquisitions Co-Ordinator, Edge Hill
University.
[10035510] 16/10/2014 **ME**
Wright, Mrs V, BA DipLib, Assistant Head of L., Customer Serv., East
Sussex County Council.
[35076] 08/07/1982 **ME**
Wright, Ms Z, MA, Research & Information Manager, DLA Piper,
Manchester.
[53928] 11/10/1996 **ME**
Wrighting, Mr A M, BA MCLIP, Employment not known.
[35345] 14/10/1982 **CM02/06/1987**
Wrigley, Mrs G J, Librarian, Thompsons Solicitors, Newcastle upon
Tyne.
[44966] 28/01/1991 **ME**
Wurm, Mr J T, Graduate, Master of Information Management, RMIT
University, Melbourne, Australia.
[10032005] 21/10/2013 **ME**
Wyatt, Miss A, Student, University of Sheffield.
[10017326] 29/07/2010 **ME**
Wyatt, Miss A M E, BA (Hons) MA, Senior L. & Information Assistant,
Jubilee Cres. Library, Coventry.
[62956] 25/11/2003 **ME**
Wyatt, Ms C A, BA DipLib MCLIP, Departmental Security Officer.
Department of Health, London.
[28729] 16/01/1978 **CM16/02/1981**
Wyatt, Miss M, DipHE BA, Librarian, MS Society.
[58715] 01/07/2000 **ME**

Wyatt, Mr M A, BA DipLib MCLIP, Unwaged.
[39824]   10/08/1986   **CM21/07/1993**
Wyatt, Mr N J, BA, L. Manager, Science Museum, London.
[34978]   24/05/1982   **ME**
Wyles, Ms C, Student, University of Arizona.
[10035723]   31/10/2014   **ME**
Wylie, Miss K, RGN, Senior Information Officer, Manchester Royal Infirmary.
[44764]   14/11/1990   **ME**
Wylie, Ms S J, BTh (Oxon), Unemployed.
[51707]   23/05/1995   **ME**
Wyness, Mrs E A, MA MCLIP, Assistant Librarian Part-time, De Montfort University, Leicester.
[57083]   04/12/1998   **CM21/05/2003**
Wynne, Mr B B L, MSc BA DLIS MCLIP DMS, Deputy University Librarian, University of Leicester.
[39475]   01/02/1986   **CM13/06/1990**
Wynne, Mr P, BA MLiH DipLib FRSA MCLIP, Quality Enhancement Officer, Centre for Academic Standards and Quality Enhancement, Manchester Metropolitan University.
[10013055]   21/01/1985   **CM06/09/1988**
Wynn-Jones, Mrs J B, BEd (Hons) MA, Resources Centre for Manager, Hounsdown School, Southampton.
[62712]   03/10/2003   **ME**
Wynton-Doig, Mrs S T, BA MCLIP, Unwaged.
[32718]   01/07/1980   **CM23/12/1983**

X

Xavier, Ms A C, BA MA DipEd Tech Dip Inf MCLIP, Head of Library Central Services, University of Roehampton.
[10010572]   21/10/1991   **CM18/11/1993**
Xu, Mr T, MA, Senior School Library Assistant, Dulwich College Shanghai.
[10031191]   27/09/2013   **ME**

Y

Yam, Mr J K C, BA MSc, Librarian, TAFE, NSW, Australia.
[40104]   16/10/1986   **ME**
Yandle, Miss A C, BA (Hons) PgDipPhil, Head of Faculty, Westfield Comm. School, Yeovil.
[49126]   06/10/1993   **ME**
Yang, Ms D, MSc (Econ), Subject Librarian, University of Wales Trinity Saint David, Lampeter, Ceredigion.
[59024]   25/10/2000   **ME**
Yao, Miss L L, Librarian, China Europe International Business School.
[10021421]   07/08/2012   **ME**
Yarde, Ms M, BA DipLib MCLIP, Service Development Manager, Lewisham MBS.
[33673]   05/02/1981   **CM06/04/1984**
Yardley, Mr A K, BA MCLIP, Music Librarian, Guildhall Sch. of Music & Drama, London.
[22795]   15/10/1974   **CM01/11/1976**
Yardley, Ms C A, BA (Hons) DipILS MCLIP, Senior Lib. -Systems & Cataloguing, Stoke-on-Trent Ls., Information & Arch.
[49678]   25/11/1993   **CM17/11/1999**
Yardley Jones, Miss A, BLib MCLIP, Community Librarian, Gwynedd.
[39879]   01/10/1986   **CM16/10/1991**
Yates, Mrs C A, BA (Hons) MCLIP, Head of Lib. Services, M. O. D.
[53628]   19/08/1996   **CM15/03/2000**

Yates, Miss C J, BLib MCLIP, Local Studies Librarian, Walsall Metropolitan Borough Council.
[36179]   05/07/1983   **CM17/03/1999**
Yates, Mrs K, BA (Hons) MA MCLIP, Librarian, Macclesfield Library, Cheshire County Council.
[59825]   10/10/2001   **CM21/06/2006**
Yates, Mrs P J, BA MCLIP, Librarian, Van Dyke Upper School, Leighton Buzzard.
[32040]   07/02/1980   **CM12/10/1984**
Yates, Mrs S J, BA MCLIP, Life Member.
[16419]   01/01/1951   **CM01/01/1954**
Yates-Mercer, Dr P A, BSc MSc PhD FCLIP, Retired/Hon. Visiting Fellow, City University, London.
[60806]   12/12/2001   **FE01/04/2002**
Yeates, Mr A R, BA MA MCLIP, E-L. Systems Officer, London Borough of Barnet.
[26657]   25/10/1976   **CM09/10/1979**
Yeates, Mrs V P, MA PgDip BA (Hons),
[10019084]   18/04/2011   **ME**
Yellin, Miss J, BA MA MA, Academic Liaison Librarian, University of Westminster.
[10021841]   19/10/2012   **ME**
Yen, Ms Y, MLIM, School Librarian, The International Montessori School.
[10023218]   18/06/2013   **ME**
Yeoh, Dr J M, BA MEd PhD FCLIP, Retired.
[19089]   01/01/1972   **FE29/03/1904**
Yeoman, Mrs F A, MA MCLIP, Site Librarian, Merrist Wood College.
[42252]   13/10/1988   **CM14/08/1991**
Yeoman, Ms K R, MA DipLib MCLIP, School Librarian, Aberdeen City Council, Dyce Academy.
[42236]   18/10/1988   **CM24/06/1992**
Yeomans, Mrs J, BSc MA, Professional Support Officer, IFLA, Netherlands.
[10014164]   07/07/2009   **ME**
Yeomans, Mrs J J, ACLIP, Library Assistant, Houghton Regis Library.
[10016935]   10/06/2010   **ACL12/09/2012**
Yeomans, Mrs K H, BA (Hons), District Manager, Staffordshire County Council, Cannock/Stafford.
[44748]   15/11/1990   **CM25/01/1995**
Yeung Doran, Mrs C Y, Lib. Assistant, William Hulme's Grammar School.
[10001762]   29/03/2007   **ME**
Yewdall, Mrs A J, BA (Hons) MA MCLIP, Assistant Librarian, Department for Education.
[47576]   02/10/1992   **CM17/11/1999**
Yiend, Mrs P, BA (Hons) ACLIP, Yiend, Mrs P A BA (Hons) School Librarian. James Allen's Girls' School since 01. 09. 2014. Membership 04. 12. 2006.
[65769]   24/04/2006   **ACL01/12/2006**
Yip, Ms S Y, BA (Hons) MA, Assistant Acquisitions and Metadata Librarian, University of the Arts London.
[61781]   05/11/2002   **ME**
Yogeswaran, Miss C, MA MLitt,
[10021600]   07/09/2012   **ME**
Young, Ms A J, LLB MSc, Falkirk Community Trust / Heriot Watt University /East Dunbartonshire Leisure & Culture Trust.
[10023388]   09/07/2013   **ME**
Young, Miss C A, BA, Library Officer, Wilberforce College.
[10032813]   14/01/2014   **ME**
Young, Mrs D, MCLIP, Life Member.
[9443]   01/03/1964   **CM01/01/1969**
Young, Mrs G, MCLIP, Lib. Resource Assistant, Stafford College.
[62952]   25/11/2003   **CM19/08/2011**

Young, Mr G, FCLIP, Retired.
[16452]   23/04/1949   FE01/01/1957
Young, Mrs G R, BA (Hons) PgDip LIS MSc HRM, CPD &
Partenerships Manager, NW Health Care Libraries Unit.
[50008]   18/02/1994   FE13/05/2014
Young, Ms H, BA (Hons) MSc Econ, Information Librarian: Law &
Human Sciences, Southampton Solent University.
[64997]   06/10/2005   ME
Young, Mrs H B, BA (Hons) DipIM MCLIP, L. Officer :Child. & Learning,
The Bournemouth Library, Bournemouth Borough Council,
[51318]   10/01/1995   CM20/01/1999
Young, Mrs H M, BA (Hons) MA MCLIP, Academic Librarian,
Loughborough University.
[50771]   18/10/1994   CM18/09/2002
Young, Mr I W, MA (Hons) PgDip ILS MCLIP, Librarian, Heriot-Watt
University Library, Edinburgh.
[54668]   17/02/1997   CM07/09/2005
Young, Mrs J, BA (Hons) MA, Information Specialist, Charles Russell,
London.
[62202]   13/03/2003   ME
Young, Ms J, BA MCLIP, Retired.
[22557]   01/07/1974   CM22/09/1980
Young, Miss J E, MCLIP, Life Member.
[16461]   05/09/1942   CM01/01/1946
Young, Miss K, LLB (Hons) PgDip MSc, Careers Information Adviser,
University of Edinburgh.
[10032078]   24/10/2013   ME
Young, Ms L, BA (Hons) MA MCLIP, Distance Services Librarian, St
Peter's Library, University of Sunderland.
[10001816]   22/06/2005   CM16/01/2014
Young, Ms L A, BA DipLib MCLIP, Information Res. Manager, Instituteof
Advanced Legal Studies.
[36171]   11/07/1983   CM20/03/1985
Young, Mrs P O, MCLIP, Retired.
[16472]   17/10/1944   CM06/06/1952
Young, Mr R, BA, Level 2 Teaching & Learning Assistant, Tupton Hall
School.
[10035557]   20/10/2014   ME
Young, Mrs R S, MCLIP, Information Specialist, ESR, Porirua, NZ,
[36732]   16/11/1983   CM02/06/1987
Young, Miss S, Registration Officer, Registers of Scotland, Edinburgh.
[57125]   14/12/1998   ME
Young, Mrs Z L, BSc (Hons) MSc (Econ), Subject Librarian, Cardiff
University.
[58912]   03/10/2000   ME
Younger, Miss M C, BLib, Lib. Supreme Court of the UK, London.
[10002026]   01/07/1976   CM24/11/1980
Younger, Ms P M, PGCE MA MCLIP, Faculty Librarian Medicine Health
and Life Sciences, Queen's University Belfast.
[52680]   20/11/1995   CM10/07/2002
Younger, Mr S, BSc, MSc Student, City University.
[10032146]   29/10/2013   ME
Youngman, Dr F, BSc MSc DPhil MCLIP, Student, Oxford University.
[60728]   12/12/2001   CM12/12/2001
Yu, Dr Y N R, BEd (Hons) MA EDD MCLIP, Cataloguing, Hong Kong
Polytechnic University.
[54577]   14/01/1997   CM23/09/1998
Yuan, Miss X, BA, Student, The University of Hong Kong.
[10035612]   23/10/2014   ME
Yuen, Miss L W, BSc MLib MCLIP, Librarian, Hong Kong Govt.
[58537]   01/04/2000   CM16/07/2003
Yuen, Miss S W R, Library Assistant, Hong Kong UniversityL.
[64642]   03/05/2005   ME

Yuen, Ms S Y, BSc, Student, The University of Hong Kong.
[10035684]   29/10/2014   ME
Yuen, Mr T K, MCLIP, Retired.
[19867]   01/01/1973   CM12/01/1982

Z

Zado, Dr V Y, BSc MSc MPhil PhD, Employment not known.
[36000]   15/04/1983   AF
Zaforemska-Pawelek, Mrs T Z, MSc,
[10032606]   19/12/2013   ME
Zahid, Mr A, BSc GDL, Student, City University.
[10032010]   21/10/2013   ME
Zaliene, Mrs L, BA, Student.
[10022406]   26/02/2013   ME
Zanelli, Mr P, BA (Hons), Customer Services Manager, London Borough
of Enfield.
[10001694]   26/02/1999   ME
Zarywacz, Mrs S G, BA MCLIP, Archive Clerk, RGP Architects,
Barnstaple.
[38876]   14/10/1985   CM15/03/1989
Zazani, Ms E, BA (LibSci) MCLIP, Learning Support Adv., Birkbeck
College, London Website:zazani. info.
[10012832]   13/03/2009   CM13/11/2013
Zebian, Mrs S, BA, Information Officer, Parliamentary and Health
Service Ombudsman.
[10015988]   03/02/2010   ME
Zehtabi, Mr A F, PgDip, Career Break.
[58958]   10/10/2000   ME
Zeimbekis, Dr M, BA MA PhD, Senior Branch Superviser, The Wills
Library.
[10019855]   26/02/2013   AF
Zelinger, Mr A J, BA (Hons) DipIM, Resources & Collections Librarian,
House of Lords, London.
[55928]   11/12/1997   ME
Zerafa, Mr L, Overseas.,
[49895]   07/01/1994   ME
Zessimedes, Mrs J A, BSc (Hons) MCLIP, Operations Manager,
Saltash Library.
[57542]   28/04/1999   CM28/10/2004
Zhang, Mr I, MMgt, Student, Victoria University of Wellington.
[10032546]   13/12/2013   ME
Zhang, Mrs Y, MA, Information /E-Learning Officer, Information Serv.,
University of Nottingham, Ningbo, China.
[55711]   06/11/1997   ME
Zhaodong, Mr L I U, HonFCLIP, Hon. Fellow.
[60088]   07/12/2001   HFE01/04/1987
Zinn, Dr K, PhD MA Diploma, Lecturer for Egyptian Archaeology &
Heritage (Museums, Archives) University of Wales.
[10007676]   29/08/2008   ME
Zisi, Miss K, BSc, Student, University of Strathclyde.
[10032878]   22/01/2014   ME
Zohn, Ms N, Student, City University London.
[10035461]   14/10/2014   ME
Zorba, Dr I, PhD, Library Univerisity of Thessaly; Greece.
[58621]   19/04/2000   ME
Zorgani, Mr A, Senior Technical Mgr, Home Office.
[10031673]   19/09/2013   ME
Zumpe, Mr M, BA MA MCLIP, Information & Stock Librarian, Portsmouth
City L. Serv.
[59665]   24/07/2001   CM02/02/2005

Organisation Members

A

A. Bilbrough & Co., London	01/11/2014	10035602
Aberystwyth University, Aberystwyth	01/01/1965	8000007
Angus Council, Forfar	01/01/1930	8000014
Aquinas College, Stockport	15/11/2002	8001447
Ashcroft Technology Academy, London	13/08/2001	8001419
Aston University, Birmingham	03/12/2002	8001449
Auckland City Libraries, Auckland 1140, New Zealand	01/01/1922	9000213

B

Bar-Ilan University, Ramat Gan 52900, Israel	20/02/2014	9000635
Barnsley College, Barnsley	15/05/2014	10033988
BBC, London	21/06/1985	8001021
Bilkent University, Ankara 06800, Turkey	23/12/2013	9000705
Birkbeck, University of London, London	09/08/1996	8001277
Birmingham City University, Birmingham	30/11/1976	8000065
Bishopsgate Institute, London	01/01/1952	8000432
Blue Coat School Library, Oldham	02/07/2014	8001472
Bodleian Libraries, Oxford	31/07/2013	10011636
Bolton MBC, Bolton	01/01/1986	8000081
Book Industry Communication, London	05/11/2013	10011376
Borough of Poole Libraries, Poole	29/04/2014	10003003
Brighton and Hove Council, Brighton	21/10/2010	8001308
British Library, London	01/01/1966	8001103
Britten-Pears Library, Aldeburgh	03/03/1999	8001348
Browns Books for students, Hull	04/06/2013	10023050
BSix Brooke House Sixth Form College, London	02/07/2014	8001489
Bury MBC, Bury	01/01/1901	8000121

C

Calderdale MBC, Halifax	25/07/2007	10005483
Cardiff Metropolitan University (formerly UWIC), Cardiff	24/04/1996	8001265
Cats College, Cambridge	19/11/2013	10011856
Cayman Islands National Archives, Grand Cayman, Cayman Islands	31/01/1990	9000695
Christchurch City Libraries, Auckland, New Zealand	01/01/1935	9000215
Cirencester College Library, Cirencester	06/11/2012	8001517
City of Armadale Libraries, Armadale WA 6992, Australia	01/04/2011	9000751
City of Cockburn Public Library & Information Service, Bibra Lake DC, Australia	11/03/2014	10015542
City of Westminster College, London	15/05/2014	10009216
City University London, London	01/01/1966	8000444
Commonwealth Secretariat, London	15/08/2012	10008062
Cork CC, Cork, Ireland	31/05/1983	9000623

D

Dartford and Gravesham NHS Trust, Dartford	17/08/1990	8001106
De Montfort University, Leicester	01/01/1970	8000400
Denstone College, Uttoxeter	20/11/2013	10032337
Department of Languages, Information and Communications, Manchester	06/11/2012	10021856
Derby City Council, Derby	18/07/1997	8001310
Derwentside College, Consett	09/12/2004	8001486

Donegal County Council, Letterkenny, Ireland	10/01/2014	9000701
Dr Williams's Library, London	01/01/1897	8000448
Drayton Manor High School, London	16/12/2003	8001464
Dublin Business School, Dublin 2, Ireland	11/02/2014	10022363
Dublin City Public Libraries, Dublin 7, Ireland	01/01/1935	10011257
Dunedin Public Library, Dunedin 9058, New Zealand	01/01/1934	9000218

E

East Carolina University, Greenville, USA	14/02/2002	9000753
East Riding of Yorkshire Council, Skirlaugh	01/01/1926	8000235
East Sussex County Council, Hailsham	11/02/2011	8000237
EBSCO Publishing Ipswich, Ipswich, USA	01/05/2010	10016764
Edge Hill University, Ormskirk	16/03/1998	8001328
Epsom College in Malaysia, Negeri Sembilan, Malaysia	31/10/2014	10035734
Eton College, Windsor	14/01/1993	8001165
European Central Bank, Frankfurt am Main, Germany	23/10/2013	10007213
European School of Osteopathy, Maidstone	25/04/1985	8001016

F

Falmouth University/FX Plus, Penryn	07/04/2014	10008030

G

Godalming College, Godalming	20/02/2001	8001404
Goethe-Institut London, London	19/02/1973	8000829
Gorkana Group, London	16/04/2007	10002452
Great North Museum: Hancock, Newcastle upon Tyne	14/04/2010	10016597
Greenwich Community College, London	18/05/2006	8001514
Guille-Alles Library, St Peter Port	22/04/1987	8001043

H

Hartlepool Borough Council, Hartlepool	28/05/1996	8001268
Headingley Library, Leeds	01/01/1947	8000396
Hereford Cathedral School, Hereford	17/02/2003	8001450
Highgate School, London	15/04/2014	10003070
Highlands College, St Saviour	21/10/2008	10011489
HMP Forest Bank, Manchester	30/10/2014	10006466
Hong Kong Public Libraries, Central, Hong Kong	01/01/1960	9000140
House of Commons, London	01/01/1963	8000455
House of Lords, London	29/02/1996	8001263
Houses of the Oireachtas, Dublin 2, Ireland	12/05/2006	9000772

I

Imperial College London, London	14/12/2000	8001401
Imperial War Museum, London	01/01/1949	8000458
Inner Temple Library, London	19/02/1996	8001261
Institute of Development Studies, Brighton	09/05/1995	8001232
Institute of Education, London	01/01/1960	10006865
Institute of Technology Carlow, Carlow, Ireland	11/03/1998	9000733
Irwin Mitchell LLP, Sheffield	14/03/2013	10001237

J

Jamaica Library Service, Kingston 5, **Jamaica**	01/01/1950	9000416
JCS Online Resources Ltd, Oxford	18/09/2013	10031663

K

Kent CC, Aylesford	01/01/1926	8000371
Key Note Ltd, Teddington	15/05/2009	10013431
King Abdullah University of Science and Technology (KAUST), Jeddah, **Saudi Arabia**	11/02/2014	10015627
King's College London, London	18/06/2014	8001151
King's Fund, London	28/02/1991	8001116
Kingston University, Kingston upon Thames	01/01/1962	8000377
Kirklees Council, Huddersfield	01/01/1898	8000346

L

Leeds Beckett University, Leeds	03/10/2008	10011241
Leeds Trinity University, Leeds	01/01/1966	8000342
Leyton Sixth Form College (Library), London	15/05/2014	10033991
Libraries NI, Craigavon	11/11/2014	10002890
Library, Universiti Malaysia Kelantan, Petaling Jaya, **Malaysia**	21/06/2013	10023248
Lincoln's Inn Library, London	01/01/1974	8000849
Literary and Philosophical Society, Newcastle upon Tyne	01/01/1947	8000569
Liverpool Institute For Performing Arts, Liverpool	11/12/1995	8001253
London Borough of Hackney, London	01/01/1929	8000306
London Borough of Islington, London	01/01/1905	8000363
Longford CC, Longford, **Ireland**	17/02/1989	9000683

M

Macmillan Cancer Support, London	24/01/2000	8001368
Manchester Metropolitan University, Manchester	04/10/2012	8000539
Marie Curie Cancer Care, Glasgow	10/01/2014	10032776
Marlborough College, Marlborough	03/05/2007	10002925
Massey University, Palmerston North, **New Zealand**	31/01/1990	9000696
Memorial University of Newfoundland, St John's, **Canada**	01/01/2010	10016400
Middlesex University, London	01/01/1971	8000253
Moulton College, Northampton	15/12/2011	10000942

N

National Acquistions Group, Wakefield	25/01/2010	10015916
National Library, Georgetown, **Guyana**	18/07/2013	9000138
National Library of Ireland, Dublin 2, **Ireland**	14/10/2013	9000111
National Library of Wales, Aberystwyth	01/01/1921	8000005
National Museum Wales, Cardiff	14/07/2010	10017221
National University of Ireland, Galway, Galway, **Ireland**	29/08/2014	9000117
Newham College of Further Education, London	15/05/2014	10002902
Newquay Tretherras School, Newquay	29/01/1996	8001256
Nexen Petroleum UK Ltd, Aberdeen	09/01/2012	10020280

NIPR, The National Collection of Northern Ireland Publications, Belfast	31/10/2005	8001507
Norfolk and Suffolk NHS Foundation Trust, Norwich	09/04/2009	10013270
North East Lincolnshire Council, Grimsby	17/02/1975	8000894
North West University, Potchefstroom, **South Africa**	25/11/1974	9000498
Northern Ireland Assembly Library, Belfast	20/09/2001	8001420
Northumbria University, Newcastle upon Tyne	15/04/2014	8000563
Norwich University of the Arts, Norwich	22/04/1986	8001030
Nottingham Trent University, Nottingham	16/02/1993	8001166

O

Oaklands College, St Albans	29/09/2010	10007082
Office of Public Works, Co. Meath, **Ireland**	26/01/2012	10020354
Oldham Council, Oldham	01/01/1931	8000604
Oldham Sixth Form College, Oldham	11/01/2010	10012793
Orkney Islands Council, Kirkwall	19/03/2008	10005690
Oxford Brookes University, Oxford	03/03/1995	8001229
Oxford High School, Oxford	19/03/1993	8001173
Oxford University Press, Oxford	18/06/2008	10002237
Oxfordshire County Council, Oxford	01/01/1929	8000613
Oxfordshire History Centre, Oxford	14/12/2011	10020254

P

Polytechnic of Namibia, Windhoek, **Namibia**	21/10/2010	10017889

R

Regent's University London, London	15/04/2014	8001036
Richmond American International University In London, Richmond	18/04/2013	10021786
RMIT University, Melbourne, **Australia**	16/10/2009	10015122
Rowman & Littlefield, Lanham, **USA**	23/10/2013	10032056
Royal Academy of Dance, London	08/06/1995	8001240
Royal College of Art, London	01/07/2005	8001505
Royal Veterinary College, Hatfield	16/01/2007	10001295

S

Sabanci University, Istanbul, **Turkey**	11/05/2013	10014649
Sandwell MBC, West Bromwich	01/01/1937	8000781
School of Oriental and African Studies (SOAS), London	05/02/1997	8001297
Science Museum, London	01/01/1971	8000506
Scottish Borders Council, Selkirk	01/05/1976	8000937
Sir George Monoux College, London	09/06/2004	8001478
Sixth Form College Farnborough, Farnborough	21/03/2014	10012050
South Dublin CC, Dublin, **Ireland**	01/01/1964	9000108
South Thames College, London	01/06/1993	8001175
St George's, University of London, London	17/07/2002	8001440
St Peter's RC School, Solihull	11/05/2013	10022929
Stanmore College, Stanmore	17/04/2013	10002178
State Library of Ohio, Columbus, **USA**	01/11/1999	9000738
State Library of South Australia, Adelaide, **Australia**	01/01/1969	9000000
State University of NY at Binghamton, Binghamton, **USA**	01/01/2014	9000308

Stockport MBC, Stockport	01/01/1909	8000727
Stockton on Tees Borough Council, Stockton-on-Tees	01/01/1914	
8000746		
Strode College, Street	24/01/2013	10001727
Surrey County Council, Kingston upon Thames	01/01/1965	10001616
Surrey Heritage, Woking	01/01/1999	8001346

Tamaki Makaurau Library, Auckland, **New Zealand** 03/11/2014
  10035668

Teesside University, Middlesbrough	21/01/2009	10002872
Temasek Polytechnic, Singapore, **Singapore**	19/03/1993	9000720

The Chinese University of Hong Kong, Shatin, **China** 17/06/2008
  10008424

The Goldsmiths' Company, London	01/01/1948	8000518

The Hong Kong Polytechnic University, Kowloon, **Hong Kong**
  01/08/1973   9000465

The National Maritime Museum, London	21/01/2009	10002910
The Oldham College, Oldham	24/09/2013	10008341
The Open University, Milton Keynes	01/01/1970	8000077
The University of Manchester, Manchester	18/09/2013	8000543
Trinity College – Bristol, Bristol	30/06/1980	8000989

U

Universiteitsbibliotheek KU Leuven, 3000 Leuven, **Belgium**
  29/04/1974   9000484

University Campus Oldham, Oldham	09/05/2013	10022926
University College Dublin, Dublin 4, **Ireland**	17/01/1977	9000556
University College of Cork, Cork, **Ireland**	16/09/2010	10005969
University of Aberdeen, Aberdeen	01/01/1928	8000004
University of Alberta, Edmonton, **Canada**	01/01/1967	9000053
University of Auckland, Auckland, **New Zealand**	01/01/1971	9000214
University of Bath, Bath	01/01/1956	8000042
University of Birmingham, Birmingham	25/06/2008	10001764
University of Brighton, Brighton	01/01/1862	8000104

University of British Columbia, Vancouver, **Canada** 07/07/2014
  9000082

University of Cambridge, Cambridge	01/01/1968	8000132
University of Dundee, Dundee	01/01/1946	8000224
University of East Anglia, Norwich	01/01/1963	8000591
University of Edinburgh, Edinburgh	01/01/1947	8000249
University of Exeter, Exeter	24/01/2013	8000262
University of Georgia, Athens, **USA**	07/07/2014	9000301
University of Greenwich, Chatham Maritime	27/05/2009	10002164
University of Hawaii, Honolulu, **USA**	23/09/2013	9000345
University of Huddersfield, Huddersfield	01/01/1952	8000345
University of Kent, Canterbury	24/11/2003	8001463
University of Liverpool, Liverpool	01/01/2008	10001857
University of Malta, Msida MSD 2080, **Malta**	03/11/2014	10000927
University of Maryland, College Park, **USA**	01/01/1968	9000327
University of Michigan, Ann Arbor, **USA**	01/01/1935	9000299

University of Plymouth, Plymouth	01/01/1972	8000626
University of Portsmouth, Portsmouth	01/01/1956	8000639
University of Reading, Reading	01/01/1929	8000652
University of Salford, Salford	01/01/1957	8000686
University of Sheffield, Sheffield	01/07/2010	10000438
University of Stirling, Stirling	01/01/1967	8000725
University of Strathclyde, Glasgow	01/01/1953	8000287
University of Surrey, Guildford	01/01/1963	8000305
University of Sussex, Brighton	01/01/1961	8001352
University of Texas at Austin, Austin, **USA**	07/07/2014	9000303
University of the Highlands and Islands,		
Inverness	21/10/2005	8001506
University of the West Indies – Jamaica,		
Kingston 7, **Jamaica**	24/09/2013	9000504
University of the West of England, Bristol	03/04/1987	8001042
University of Toronto, Faculty of Information,		
Toronto, **Canada**	01/01/1972	9000078
University of Wales, Bangor, Bangor	01/01/1937	8000029
University of Warwick, Coventry	19/05/2005	8001499
University of York, York	01/01/1962	8000823

V

Victoria and Albert Museum, London	31/07/1986	8001035

W

Walsall Council, Walsall	01/01/1893	8000766
Wellingborough School, Wellingborough	17/06/2008	10008785
Wellington City Libraries, Wellington,		
New Zealand	01/01/1930	9000226
Welsh Ambulance Service NHS Trust,		
Swansea	19/11/2013	10016461
Welsh Government, Cardiff	21/05/2003	8001458
West Thames College, Isleworth	11/02/2011	8000361
Western University, London, **Canada**	24/12/2013	10031951
Westminster School, London	15/05/2014	10007507
Weston College, Weston-super-Mare	17/02/1983	8000999
Wexford CC, Carricklawn, **Ireland**	30/01/2012	10005803
Wicklow CC, Bray, **Ireland**	21/11/2007	10005805
Wigan and Leigh College, Wigan	30/04/2000	8001379
Wigan Leisure and Culture Trust, Wigan	01/01/1919	8000802
Winstanley College, Wigan	05/05/2006	8001513
Wolverhampton City Council, Wolverhampton	01/01/1888	8000810

Y

Yew Chung Community College, Kowloon Bay, **Hong Kong**
  30/06/2014   10034306

Part 5
HISTORICAL INFORMATION

A short history of the Institute of Information Scientists

The Institute of Information Scientists (IIS) was born in response to rapid advances in science and technology. Fittingly, it was thanks to convergence in technology, and increasingly generalised access to the applications of some of the technology, that IIS has joined forces with the library community once more, after a schism lasting more than 40 years.

Although it was not set up until 1958, the IIS can trace its history back to 1923. In that year a meeting was organised by Professor Hutton of Oxford University and Ben Fullman of the British Non-Ferrous Metals Research Association to discuss issues arising from the rapid growth of scientific research and publication after WW1. The Library Association declined to take part in that meeting, and as a result the Association of Special Libraries and Information Bureaux was set up in 1924. Jumping forward to 1948 Fullman presented proposals to the Aslib Annual Conference for a syllabus for the education of information professionals to cope with the even more rapid growth of science after the Second World War. This visionary approach was not adopted, and for the next few years progress towards professional education and standards for information work (rather than librarianship) was minimal.

The final straw for scientific information officers was the defeat of some revised proposals at the Aslib Conference in 1957 and on 23 January 1958 a meeting was held at the IEE to discuss proposals for a new professional association. The meeting was chaired by Dr G. Malcolm Dyson. Jason Farradane and Chris Hanson made the opening speeches to a motion: 'that a professional body be, and is hereby set up, to promote and maintain high standards in scientific and technical information work and to establish qualifications for those engaged in the profession'. There were 125 people at this first meeting. At a subsequent meeting on 23 May 1958 at the Royal Society of Arts the Constitution of the Institute of Information Scientists was approved. Dr Dyson was elected as President, Chris Hanson as Vice President, Gordon Foster as Hon. Treasurer and Jason Farradane as Hon. Secretary. By the end of the year around 100 Members had joined the Institute.

The first issue of the *Bulletin* was written by Farradane and published in April 1959. Although slightly outside the scope of a history of the IIS it is important to record the establishment in 1963 of the first full-time post-graduate course in information science at what was then the Northampton College of Advanced Technology (now City University). In 1964 the IIS held its first conference at Merton College, Oxford, at which there were 60 delegates. A notable event in 1965 was the first Salary Survey, developed by Dr Malcolm Campbell.

The first issue of *The Information Scientist*, the direct forerunner of the *Journal of Information Science*, was published in 1967. Peter Vickers and John Williams were the initial Editors, until Alan Gilchrist took over in the mid-1970s, continuing as Editor of JIS until 2002.

Widening the scope

As the Institute grew in size in the late 1960s and early 1970s it became clear that the use of the phrase 'scientific and technical information work' was too limiting. At the 1972 AGM there was a motion to widen the scope, but there was also concern that this would mean rewriting the Memorandum of Association, so the proposals were withdrawn. Subsequently Council found that there was no need to change the Memorandum, and they could construe the phrase as they wished, which they then proceeded to do.

Inform was launched in 1975 to complement *The Information Scientist*. Also in 1975 another major change in the structure of the IIS took place. At the AGM Martin White, together with Charles Oppenheim, decided that it was time that Associate Members were represented on Council, rather than just Members and Fellows. To the surprise of Council the motion was passed.

In 1978 the publishing activities of the Institute expanded further with the publication of the first of the celebrated Monograph series of books on information science, managed by John Campbell. The year was also notable for a very lively discussion at the Annual Conference about the future of the Institute as it neared its 21st Anniversary with around 1400 Members. This was to a significant extent the result of an informal meeting of the STIR group of younger members (the Steering Team for Institute Reform). That year had already marked the creation of Special Interest Groups which could accept non-Members of the IIS. The first to be set up was the Online User Group (now Ukolug), followed soon after by the Patent and Trade Marks Group.

1979 was quite a year, and not only because the IIS office moved out to Reading. For the first time the Annual Conference was held at a hotel, the Imperial Hotel, Torquay, and ended up making a very substantial profit for the Institute in its 21st year. Discussions were also taking place to heal the differences between the IIS, The Library Association and Aslib through the creation of the first Tripartite Conference, to be held in Sheffield in 1980. Further cooperation with The Library Association resulted in the first combined Salary Survey.

By 1980 Council had approved a radical reshaping of the membership and committee decision-making structures of the Institute. This made it much more welcoming and open to younger people and to those from outside traditional scientific and technical information backgrounds. New entrants to the profession could now participate fully in the activities and governance of the Institute, and make their voices heard.

A sign that the Institute had become much more open and informal was its launch of the Infotainers. There were four major shows in 1980, 1983, 1985 and 1990, and several smaller ones, all in the best tradition of satirical review.

Acquiring a secretariat

The Silver Jubilee Conference took place in 1983 at St Catherine's College, Oxford, though Council were not exactly concentrating on the papers as there was a very real chance that the IIS had fallen foul of VAT legislation over its charitable/educational status. Luckily the danger passed. The problems did highlight the need for a full-time employee running the IIS office, and the IIS was very fortunate to be able to appoint Sarah Carter, a Member of the Institute, to the post of Executive Secretary in 1984, by which time the membership had reached almost 2000.

From 1985 the IIS had a central focus for its activities with a central London base. Its administrative structure was developed, but it continued to be very dependent on its Members for organising events and conferences, drafting and agreeing professional standards, and accreditation activities in universities and colleges offering courses in information science. Lobbying and advocacy, and all the Branch and Special Interest Group activities, also depended on volunteers from the membership. In addition to Ukolug and PATMG, the IIS set up the City Information Group, the Computerised Information Management Special Interest Group (it was later disbanded), the Small Business Group for consultants et al. (which lasted into the early 1990s), and ALGIS (the Affiliation of Local Government Information Specialists). At least three of these groups became significant organisations within their own specialisations, due entirely to the hard work and enthusiasm of their members.

During this period the Branch structure was revised, and the Midlands Branch disappeared, mainly because the road and public transport links did not make it easy for members from both East and West Midlands to attend any meeting. There were also Local Groups in Reading, Oxford and elsewhere that thrived for a time. The number of branches was a tribute to the energy of Members, given the comparatively small size of the IIS as a whole.

Significant activities organised and developed by members for members included the very successful series of annual Text Retrieval Conferences, and the IIS Evening Events. These were short, affordable professional development workshops and seminars conceived by Martin White when he was IIS President. They attracted many younger members. They came to learn from eminent senior members who were generous in offering their time for professional development opportunities.

The second tripartite conference was held in 1985, as a five-way multipartite event in Bournemouth. The third and final multipartite conference was held in 1990, also in Bournemouth.

1990 was a momentous year for the Institute. After a series of exploratory discussions with the Charity Commissioners, the Institute was granted charitable status. This conferred considerable tax advantages, and enabled the IIS to make the best use of a generous bequest from an early member, John Campbell. Part of the bequest was used to set up the John Campbell Trust, which was to be used for the provision of scholarships, prizes, travel grants or research fellowships. Its work continues today.

1990 also marked the first serious effort by The Library Association, Aslib and the IIS to move closer together with a view to merger. Although support for the merger was not strong enough for formal moves to be made, the discussions (marked by the Saunders Report), and a second series of discussions (the Tripartite discussions) did result in some fundamental reviews of the similarities and differences between the organisations.

For the Institute, the 1990s were dominated by two significant factors:

- Changes in work, cultures and attitudes, that resulted in members having much less time to devote to running the Institute and its activities.
- Increasing use of electronic sources of information, increased availability and ease of use of information resources by non-specialists, and from 1995 onwards, the development of the world wide web and its prospects of freely available information.

These developments led to uncertainties about the long-term future of the Institute, its role, its name and who should form its core membership – their background, qualifications, and what the criteria for Information Science should be. Until then, the IIS had been a group of specialists with fairly clearly defined skills. Once the specialist focus had been lost, it became harder to sustain the IIS network. It was at this point that I succeeded Sarah Carter with a much wider brief: to represent and promote the IIS externally.

By this time, the opportunities for information professionals to attract publicity were enormous. But so was the logic of increased collaboration. The IIS, working with The Library Association and supported by the Association for Geographic Information, launched the Coalition for Public Information. This was a broad-based, cross-sectoral body of organisations with an interest in 'public information' – information generated by government in the course of conducting its business. With some success, CoPI lobbied the government on issues associated with 'the information society' – a term then only beginning to find common currency.

It was not only on grounds of a shared platform for advocacy that the IIS was moving closer to The Library Association. Advances in technology and much more generalised use of electronic resources, together with much more widespread adoption of information management techniques in industry and the public sector, was making it increasingly difficult to distinguish between those who were clearly information scientists, and librarians who used the techniques of information science.

Informal talks on greater collaboration, and a proposal by Dr Ray Lester at the IIS's AGM in 1996 suggesting more of the same, led to more formal talks, and, eventually to unification in April 2002.

In the meantime, and without prejudice to attempts at unification, a joint working party of senior Library Association and IIS members (led by Kate Wood, and Professor Peter Enser) aligned the criteria of both organisations for accrediting academic courses in information science and library management. And IIS celebrated its 40th anniversary with its Ruby Conference in Sheffield in 1998.

In its heyday the IIS's membership reached nearly 2750 members. In proportion to its size, its profile was high, thanks to the personal commitment and direct involvement of many eminent senior members. In the end, the logic of convergence (in academic criteria and technologies and the practice of both professional bodies) on the one hand, and of the need for advocacy from a shared platform on the other, made unification the only logical option.

Compiled with information from and the generous help of a number of IIS members, including most notably Martin White, Sarah Carter, Diana Clegg and Charles Oppenheim.

Elspeth Hyams
Editor, *Library & Information Update*

The Library Association 1877–2002

'We have only to hope that the Library Association of the United Kingdom will flourish and that it will justify itself in public estimation by assisting libraries to become what they ought to be, efficient instruments of national education.' With these words, The Athenaeum welcomed the newly established association in 1877.

Foundation

The Association was founded at an international conference held at the London Institution, attended by over 200 delegates from Australia, Belgium, Denmark, France, Germany, Greece, Italy and the USA, in addition to those from the UK. Melvil Dewey, later to become famous as the author of the Decimal Classification, was there as Secretary of the American Library Association, founded the previous year. Some of the topics discussed at the conference sound familiar 125 years later: Sunday opening, the application of the latest technology (in the shape of the telephone) and salaries of librarians were among them. The organiser of the conference, Edward Nicholson, librarian of the host institution, was moved to describe the salaries then on offer as an 'insult to the liberality and intelligence of our great towns.'

Purpose

The Association was born in the great Victorian tradition of mutual self-improvement, with the intention of promoting the role of libraries and librarians by the exchange of information on good practice, visits to interesting libraries, publishing a journal and manuals, the holding of conferences and, in due course, the running of training courses and holding examinations. Its original object was to 'unite all persons engaged or interested in library work, for the purpose of promoting the best possible administration of existing libraries and the formation of new ones...'

Advocacy

The first President was John Winter Jones, Principal Librarian of the British Museum. Most of those closely involved in the early development of the association were librarians of university and research libraries. However, the fledgling Association devoted a great deal of time and effort in campaigning for the abolition of the restrictions on the amount local councils could spend on their public libraries (they were prevented at that time from spending more than the product of a penny rate on the value of property in their areas) and in persuading councils to establish such libraries under the legislation, which was enabling rather than compulsory. Thus began a long tradition of working to influence public policy, which would be described these days as advocacy and lobbying. Because so much of this has to be conducted behind closed doors and because the final decisions cannot usually be firmly attributed to the Association's efforts, its Members have probably given it less credit for success in this activity than it has deserved. The Association continued its interest in the relationship between local government and public libraries until the present day. After the First World War, the association worked with the Carnegie United Kingdom Trust (CUKT) to persuade the Government finally to lift the restrictions on the amount councils were permitted to spend on public libraries. This resulted in legislation in 1919, which not only did that, but also allowed county councils to provide public libraries for the first time. A large network in rural areas of branch and mobile libraries and collections in village halls and similar locations gradually emerged as a result. At about same time, the Association proposed the establishment of a national library of science and technology, as part of a plan to establish technical and commercial services in public libraries, and pleaded for greater cooperation between public libraries and specialised libraries. After the Second World War, the Association also actively encouraged the development of regional technical and commercial library services by cooperation between different kinds of libraries and Government agencies. It was not until the successful Russian space shot in the sixties prompted greater investment in scientific research that the Government set up the National Lending Library of Science and Technology (NLLST) in Boston Spa, Yorkshire, which eventually became the Document Supply Centre of the British Library.

Public policy

The Association gave firm evidence to the Dainton Committee in 1968, stressing the need for a UK national library. The Committee's findings led directly to the formation of the British Library, by bringing together the National Central Library, the NLLST, the British Museum Library, the National Reference Library of Science and Invention and the British National Bibliography (BNB). The latter had been established by cooperation between a number of groups representing libraries and the book trade, with an initial financial guarantee by the Association.

Another area of public policy that the Association can be fairly said to have influenced is the allocation of public library responsibilities to local councils. Since the publication in 1942 of its own radical report on the subject, prepared by Lionel McColvin, it fairly consistently supported larger authorities, as more able to provide comprehensive services. This approach inevitably led to great controversy within the profession and the establishment from time to time of breakaway

groups representing those working in smaller councils.

The Association also took a great interest in copyright legislation, both within the UK and the European Union, undoubtedly influencing the 1988 Copyright, Designs and Patents Act, especially the inclusion of the concept of fair dealing exceptions for libraries and for the purposes of research and private study. The fight still goes on to ensure that the implementation of the European Directive does not abolish this provision in the UK.

Among the many areas of public policy which have engaged the attention of the Association were postage rates for materials for the visually impaired, public lending right, taxes on publications, the national school curricula, freedom of information legislation, and the provision of libraries in prisons, hospitals and other institutions.

A recent success story, which the Association initiated, is the People's Network, linking every public library to the internet and providing electronic content and training for public library staff. Although it was a report by the former Library and Information Commission (LIC) that persuaded the government to adopt the idea, it was the Association's earlier bid for National Lottery funding which established the desirability of such a project. The Library Association campaigned, with several other organisations, for a government advisory body on library and information matters, which finally came into existence as the LIC. The Commission recently merged with a similar body for museums to become Resource: the Council for Museums, Archives and Libraries.

The Association developed its contacts with politicians and civil servants over the years and was instrumental in the establishment of the All-Party Parliamentary Group on Libraries, which ensures that a wide range of library and information issues are drawn to the attention of MPs and peers.

Education and training

The education and training of library staff was a constant concern of the Association. Its first move, in 1885, was to hold examinations leading to certificates in English and European literature, classification and cataloguing and library administration. Few sat these tests and fewer passed. But summer schools began in 1894. The first lasted three days attracting 45 students. The summer schools increased in length and attendance, the examinations broadened in scope, eventually leading to formal qualifications and Fellowship of the Association. Correspondence courses were set up, to be handed over later to the once independent Association of Assistant Librarians (AAL), after it came within The Library Association's fold as a specialist section. The first full-time library school was established in 1919, at University College London, with the help of the CUKT. In the inter-war period many part-time day and evening classes developed to prepare candidates for the Association's examinations held at several centres around the country. After World War Two, education and training of returning servicemen became a priority for the Government. A number of full-time library schools were set up in colleges of technology under this programme, as the result of negotiations by The Library Association. They were intended to be temporary arrangements, but demand was such that the schools developed along with their institutions, which later became polytechnics and eventually universities. New schools were also set up in the 1960s in a few universities and one, the College of Librarianship Wales, Aberystwyth, was established as a separate institution, only becoming a part of the University of Wales much later. These schools gradually developed systems of internal examining, followed by their own syllabuses, recognised by the Association and, in the case of those in polytechnics, validated by the former Council for National and Academic Awards (CNAA). These developments, not without controversy, eventually led to an all-graduate entry to the profession, and

a great variety of courses at undergraduate, post-graduate and master's levels. The Association gave up its own examinations in the 1970s, in favour of accrediting courses, latterly often as a joint exercise with the Institute of information Scientists (IIS).

The Royal Charter

The Association acquired a Royal Charter in 1898, with revised objects. At the same time, its name became simply The Library Association, which it retained, despite some attempts in the 1980s to change it to include 'information', until unification with the IIS under the title Chartered Institute of Library and Information Professionals (CILIP). The professional register was introduced after the Second World War. Those who completed the newly introduced registration examination, followed by a period of approved employment in a library, could describe themselves as 'Chartered Librarians'. They were also entitled to use the post nominal letters 'ALA' (Associate of the Library Association). After a further period of employment, they could progress, by means of a final examination, to become Fellows (FLA). When the undergraduate and postgraduate courses replaced the registration examination, Fellowship could be obtained by means of a thesis, later replaced by a variety of routes, leading to proof of attainment of a high standard of professional achievement. Discussions took place over a long period on the possibilities for introducing a system of validating continuing professional development. A voluntary scheme was introduced in the 1990s. The possibility of developing in due course a compulsory 're-licensing' requirement, similar to those coming into vogue in other professions was discussed, but never agreed. The possession of the Royal Charter gave the Association status comparable to professional bodies in other spheres, and was the source of much pride. The centenary of the granting of the Charter by Queen Victoria was celebrated in style at the new British

Library building at St Pancras in 1998, in the presence of the Princess Royal and the Secretary of State for Culture, Chris Smith. The Princess presented centenary medals to one hundred Library Association Members representing the thousands who had worked for the profession over the century.

Awards

One way to encourage high standards in any field is to present awards. The Library Association's first initiative in this area was the Carnegie Medal for the best children's book. Awarded for the first time in 1937 to Arthur Ransome for *Pigeon Post* and occasionally not awarded at all for a lack, in the opinion of the judges, of a suitable winner, it has become established as a coveted honour. It was joined in 1955 by the Kate Greenaway Medal for the best illustrated children's book. The Youth Libraries Group judges the nominations for both medals, which have attracted significant sponsorship in recent years and increasing publicity in the national press, aided by a 'shadow' judging process organised in schools. Other awards introduced over the years recognise excellence in published indexes (jointly with the Society of Indexers), bibliographies and reference works, as well as best practice in publicity and public relations.

Publications

The publication of a journal is a basic function of most professional bodies. The Library Association's first initiative in this area was to decide at its inaugural meeting to adopt the *American Library Journal* as its official organ (without the first word in its title). This had obvious drawbacks, exacerbated when Melvil Dewey became its editor and introduced his simplified spelling. In 1880, *Monthly Notes of the Library Association of the United Kingdom*, published commercially on behalf of the Association, took

over the role. It was itself succeeded by *The Library Chronicle* in 1884 and *The Library* in 1888. The latter was the personal property of John MacAlister, at that time Honorary Secretary of the Association, an unsatisfactory arrangement. Ten years later *The Library Association Record* was established as the official organ of the Association, the property of the Association and 'under the control of Council'. It continued until 2002, celebrating its centenary in 1998. For most of that time it was edited by a series of Honorary Editors, until the appointment in 1976 of the first full-time professional Editor, Roger Walter. One of the first publications of the Association in book form was the *Yearbook*, first published in 1891, which, despite its title, did not become a regular annual, until 1932. For many years the financing of publications caused concern to the Association's Council. Various arrangements were made for the sale and distribution of a growing range of titles, including manuals, textbooks and guidelines to standards of service. At first contracts were made with commercial publishers, at other times the responsibilities were carried out in-house and, for a while in the 1970s and 80s, a wholly-owned company was responsible. Eventually all the business units of the Association (Library Association Publishing; INFOmatch, the recruitment agency; the *Record* and conferences and continuing education) were brought together under the title Library Association Enterprises. At the time of unification, approximately 30 new titles were published a year, with a backlist of over 200.

Branches

In common with many membership organisations in the UK, the Association exhibited tensions between those based in London and those elsewhere in the country. This tension was emphasised by the fact that, in the public library sphere at least, development was much slower in London in the early days than in other major cities. It was also not helped by the fact that most of the early meetings were held in London. Long working hours and poor salaries combined to prevent many from outside the capital taking part in the affairs of the Association. This led to the establishment of several independent regional Associations, for example the Birmingham and District and the North Midlands Library Associations. They amalgamated with The Library Association in 1928–9. The Scottish Library Association, formed in 1908, also affiliated under special conditions in 1931 and new Branches were formed to cover Wales and Monmouthshire and Northern Ireland. However, complete coverage of the UK by a network of Branches was not achieved until after the Second World War.

Sections and Groups

A characteristic of most professional bodies is the need to cater for specialisms within the overall discipline. It was gradually recognised that The Library Association had to cater for different types of library, or client groups, and specialist materials and skills. In 1932, two sections were established to reflect the interests of those working in county libraries and those in university and research libraries. The union with the independent AAL, which had taken place in 1930, provided a section designed to provide for those at an early stage in their careers. It was to prove a useful training ground for future leaders of the profession. Sections, later renamed 'Groups', were gradually added to reflect such diverse interests as prison libraries, information technology and library history.

Headquarters

As early as 1888, the Association identified the need for permanent premises. Its first home was in Hanover Square in London, which it rented from 1890 to 1898. This was followed by a series of other rented premises, one shared with the trade union NALGO, another with Association of Special Libraries and Information Bureaux (Aslib) and the

CUKT. Eventually the CUKT provided a more permanent solution with the offer of a derelict property in what was to become Malet Place. Opened in 1933 by Lord Irwin, deputising for the then Prime Minister, Stanley Baldwin, it was named Chaucer House. The refurbished building provided offices, a members' room and a council chamber, with spare floors which were rented to other organisations. One of the initial tenants was the Museums Association. Chaucer House served until 1965, when the present purpose-built headquarters in Ridgmount Street was completed. The Association was fortunate in that the University of London offered to build the Ridgmount Street building in exchange for the acquisition of Chaucer House, which it required to cater for the needs of the rapidly expanding institution. The new building was considerably larger and contained many highly desirable new facilities. From time to time there were discussions on the desirability of moving the headquarters to a location outside London. During the 1980s the most concrete proposal, to move to the University of Liverpool campus, was considered and rejected. The transport routes of the UK, which radiate from London, rendered such proposals unviable. The Ridgmount Street building was recently refurbished and extended.

International developments

Given that the Association was born at an international conference, it is not surprising that it has often been involved in international developments. At its fiftieth anniversary Conference, held in Edinburgh in 1927, a resolution, which led to the establishment of the International Federation of Library Associations and Institutions (IFLA), was adopted. K. C. Harrison was inaugurated as the first President of the Commonwealth Library Association (COMLA) at its formation in Lagos, Nigeria, in 1972. He became Library Association President in the same year. During the 1987 IFLA Conference in Brighton talks were started in London, which led to the formation of the European Bureau of Library, Information and Documentation Associations (EBLIDA) in The Hague in 1992. George Cunningham, Chief Executive of The Library Association from 1984 to 1992, played a leading role in identifying the need for such a body to ensure that the profession's views were heard the European Union's institutions. Ross Shimmon, Library Association Chief Executive from 1992 to 1999, was its founder President.

Unification

The Association was, at times with some justification, more recently with none, criticised for being primarily a public library association. Received wisdom suggests that it was this bias that led to the establishment of the Aslib to cater for those working in specialist libraries in industry. W. A. Munford, the Association's official historian for its first century, argued that the Library Association Council 'could hardly have done more to make [such a move] unnecessary.' Nevertheless, Aslib was established in 1926. After the Second World War, alleged lack of flexibility on the part of the Association is said to have led to the establishment of the Institute of Information Scientists in 1958. The existence of several bodies representing different elements of the profession was thought by many to be unhelpful in the task of influencing government and other decision makers. Various moves were made to try to bring the organisations together, including the organisation of joint conferences. The Library Association Council, on behalf of all three organisations, commissioned Professor Wilfred Saunders, a former president of both the Association and the Institute, to write a pamphlet exploring the pros and cons of unification. In the pamphlet, published in 1989, he recommended the establishment of a new organisation, representing the broad spectrum of library and information professionals. The Association's Council approved the proposal in principle. But Aslib pulled out of the subsequent talks and the IIS soon followed suit. However, his efforts proved not to have been entirely in vain. Informal talks between representatives of the Association and the Institute began in 1998, which eventually led to the unification of the two bodies to form CILIP in 2002. This satisfactorily closed an era in professional history which had lasted exactly 125 years.

The main sources used in the preparation of this article were:

Munford, W. A. (1977) *A History of The Library Association 1877–1977*, London, The Library Association.

Plumb, Philip (1977) *Libraries by Association: The Library Association's first century*, London, The Library Association.

Ross Shimmon
Former Chief Executive,
The Library Association

Presidents of the Institute of Information Scientists

2001–02	P. Enser		1985–86	Sir R. Clayton
2000–01	P. Enser		1984–85	M. Aldrich
	Director, M. Shearer (started)			Director, S. A. Carter (started)
1999–2000	B. Clifford		1983–84	A. R. Haygarth Jackson
1998–99	P. Brophy		1982–83	J. Dukes
1997–98	S. E. Ward		1981–82	R. K. Appleyard
1996–97	B. Hatvany		1980–81	C. W. Cleverdon
1995–96	M. F. Lynch		1979–80	M. Hyams
1994–95	C. Oppenheim		1978–79	J. W. Barrett
	Director, E. Hyams (started)		1977–78	Dr J. W. Barrett
1993–94	B. A. Lang		1975–76	H. T. Hookway
1992–93	M. White		1974–75	H. T. Hookway
1991–92	M. Saksida		1973–74	H. T. Hookway
1990–91	B. White		1972–73	Sir James Tait
1989–90	P. Laister		1968–69	Prof. Sir H. Thompson
1988–89	K. Cooper		1960–61	Dr M. Dyson
1987–88	T. Aitchison		1958–59	Dr M. Dyson
1986–87	Prof. L. Wolpert			

Presidents of The Library Association

Year	President		Year	President
2001	Mr B. Naylor		1962	Prof. W. B. Paton OBE
2000	Rev. G. P. Cornish		1961	Sir Charles Snow CBE
1999	Mrs V. Taylor		1960	Dr B. S. Page
1998	Prof. R. C. Usherwood		1959	The Rt Hon. The Earl Attlee KG PC OM CH
1997	Mr J. D. Hendry			
1996	Ms S. M. Parker		1958	Prof. Raymond Irwin
1995	Mr M. P. K. Barnes OBE		1957	Dr J. Bronowski
1994	Dr G. A. Burrington OBE		1956	Mr E. Sydney MC
1993	Mr R. G. Astbury		1955	Sir Philip Morris KCMG Kt CBE
1992	Mr P. W. Plumb		1954	Mr C. B. Oldman CB CVO
1991	Mr T. M. Featherstone		1953	Sir Sidney C. Roberts Kt
1990	Prof. M. B. Line		1952	Mr L. R. McColvin CBE
1989	Mr A. G. D. White		1951	Mr J. Wilkie MC
1988	Miss Jean M. Plaister OBE		1950	His Royal Highness The Prince Philip, Duke of Edinburgh Kg Kt Com GBE PC
1987	Mr E. M. Broome OBE			
1986	Mr A. Wilson CBE			
1985	Sir Harry Hookway Kt		1949	Sir Ronald Forbes Adam Bt KCE GCB CB DSO OBE
1984	Mr R. G. Surridge			
1983	Dr N. Higham OBE		1948	Mr C. Nowell
1982	Mr K. A. Stockham		1947	Mr R. J. Gordon
1981	Mr A. Longworth OBE		1946	Mr H. M. Cashmore MBE
1980	Prof. W. L. Saunders CBE		1939–45	Mr A. Esdaile CBE
1979	Mr W. A. G. Alison		1938	Mr W. C. Berwick Sayers
1978	Mr G. Thompson		1937	The Most Rev. & Hon. Wm. Temple
1977	The Lord Dainton		1936	Mr E. A. Savage
1976	Mr D. J. Foskett OBE		1935	Mr E. S. Davies CBE
1975	Mr E. V. Corbett		1934	Mr S. A. Pitt
1974	Mr E. A. Clough		1932–3	Sir Henry A. Miers Kt DSC
1973	Mr K. C. Harrison OBE		1931	Lt Col J. M. Mitchell OBE MC
1972	Dr Donald J. Urquhart		1930	Mr L. Stanley Jast
1971	Mr G. Chandler		1929	The Lord Balniel MP
1970	Mr D. T. Richnell CBE		1928	Mr A. D. Lindsay CBE
1969	Prof. W. Ashworth		1927	The Rt Hon. The Earl of Elgin and Kincardine Kt CMG
1968	Mr T. E. Callander			
1967	Mr F. G. B. Hutchings OBE		1926	Mr H. Guppy CBE
1966	Miss Lorna V. Paulin OBE		1925	Sir Charles Grant Robertson Kt CVO
1965	Sir Frank Francis KCB		1924	Sir Robert Sangster Rait Kt CBE
1964	Mr F. M. Gardner CBE		1923	The Most Honourable The Marquis of Hartington MP MBE
1963	Mr J. N. L. Myres OBE			

1922	Sir John Ballinger KBE	1898	The Rt Hon. The Earl of Crawford Kt
1921	Alderman T. C. Abbott JP	1897	Mr H. R. Tedder
1920	The Rt Hon. Sir John H. Lewis PC GBE	1896	Alderman H. Rawson
		1895	The Lord Windsor
1919	Mr G. F. Barwick	1894	The Most Honourable the Marquess of
1915–18	Sir J. Y. W. MacAlister		Dufferin and Ava KP GCB
1914	Mr F. Madan	1893	Mr R. Garnett
1913	The Rt Hon. The Earl of Malmesbury	1892	Mr A. Beljame
1912	Mr F. J. Leslie CC	1891	Mr R. Harrison
1911	Sir John A. Dewar Bt MP	1890	Sir E. Maunde Thompson
1910	Sir Frederic G. Kenyon	1889	Mr R. Copley Christie
1909	Alderman W. H. Brittain JP Chairman, Sheffield Public Libraries Committee	1888	Prof. W. P. Dickson
		1887	Mr G. J. Johnson
1908	Sir C. Thomas-Standford	1886	Sir Edward A. Bond KCB
1907	Mr F. T. Barrett	1885	Mr E. James
1906	Sir William H. Bailey	1884	Prof. J. K. Ingram
1905	Mr F. J. Jenkinson	1883	Sir James Picton
1904	Dr T. Hodgkin	1882	Mr Henry Bradshaw
1902–3	Prof. W. Macneile Dixon	1881	His Honour Judge Russell
1901	Mr G. K. Fortescue	1879–80	Mr H. O. Coxe
1900	The Rt Hon. Sir Edward Fry PC	1877–78	Mr J. Winter Jones
1899	Sir James W. Southern JP		

Honorary Secretaries of the Institute of Information Scientists

2001–02	K. G. Webster		1984–85	P. Brown
2000–01	K. G. Webster		1983–84	P. J. Brown
1999–2000	K. G. Webster		1982–83	J. M. Pope
1998–99	K. G. Webster		1981–82	J. M. Pope
1997–98	K. G. Webster		1980–81	J. M. Pope
1996–97	K. G. Webster		1979–80	Mrs S. A. Carter
1995–96	K. G. Webster		1978–79	Mrs S. A. Carter
1994–95	K. G. Webster		1977–78	M G. Howes,
1993–94	A. J. Wood		1975–76	Mrs M. Siddiqui,
1992–93	P. Griffiths		1974–75	Mrs M. Siddiqui
1991–92	D. Clegg		1973–74	Mrs M. Siddiqui
1990–91	D. Clegg		1972–73	S. P. Cooper
1989–90	D. Clegg		1970–71	R. W. Prior
1988–89	D. Edmonds		1968–69	J. Farradane
1987–88	D. Edmonds		1960–61	J. Farradane
1986–87	D. Edmonds		1958–59	J. Farradane
1985–86	P. Brown			

Secretaries of The Library Association

1999–2002	Dr R. McKee
1992–99	Mr R. Shimmon
1984–92	Mr G. Cunningham
1978–84	Mr K. Lawrey
1974–78	Mr R. P. Hilliard
1959–74	Mr H. D. Barry
1931–59	Mr P. S. J. Welsford
1928–31	Mr G. Keeling

Honorary Secretaries of The Library Association

1961	Honorary Secretary appointments discontinued
1955–61	Mr W. B. Paton
1952–55	Dr W. A. Munford
1934–51	Mr L. R. McColvin
1933–34	Mr E. A. Savage and Mr L. R. McColvin

1928–33	Mr E. Savage
1919–28	Mr F. Pacy
1918–19	Mr F. Pacy and Mr G. F. Barwick
1915–18	Mr F. Pacy (Acting Secretary)
1905–15	Mr L. S. Jast
1902–05	Mr L. Inkster (Mr L. S. Jast, Acting Secretary 1904–1905)
1902	Mr B. Soulsby
1898–1901	Mr F. Pacy
1892–98	Sir J. Y. W. MacAlister
1887–90	Sir J. Y. W. MacAlister and Mr T. Mason
1882–87	Mr E. C. Thomas and Mr J. Y. W. MacAlister
1880–82	Mr E. C. Thomas and Mr C. Welch
1878–80	Mr H. R. Tedder and Mr E. C. Thomas
1877–78	Mr E. B. Nicholson and Mr H. R. Tedder

Library Association honorary awards

Dates below apply to the year the award was made.

Honorary Vice-Presidents

1995	Prof. J. Meadows
1993	Dame E. Esteve-Coll
1991	Dr H.-P. Geh
1990	Baroness David of Romsey
	Mr D. Whitaker
1988	Alexander Macmillan, The Earl of Stockton
1987	Miss M. Wijnstroom
1973	Mr H. Liebaers
	Mrs J. L. Robinson
1969	Mr Bengt Hjelmqvist
1967	Miss M. O'Byrne

Honorary Fellows

2002	Ms M. J. Auckland
	Mr R. Craig
	Mr R. W. Kirk
	Mr M. P. Stone
	Ms K. Wood
2001	Dr M. Clanchy
2000	Miss M. E. Going
	Mr E. Moon
	Miss C. F. Pinion
	Mr R. Shimmon
1999	Mr R. Collis
	Mr C. Earl
	Mr M. Evans
	Mr G. Pau
1998	Mr C. Batt
	Mr B. C. Bloomfield
	Mr P. R. Craddock
	Ms M. Hoffman
	Dr N. Horrocks
1997	Sir Brian Follett
	Ms S. Hughes
	Dr B. Lang
	Ms E. Simon
1996	Ms L. A. Colaianni
	Cllr F. Emery-Wallis
	Mr D. Jones
	Miss J. Shepherd
1995	Mr E. M. Broome
	Mr P. A. Hoare
	Ms M. Segbert
	Mr E. C. Winter
1994	Mr P. Blunt
	Prof. R. Bowden
	Mr M. Bragg
	Miss A. M. Parker
	Mr B. Roberts
1993	Dame C. A. Cookson
	Dr I. Lovecy
	Ms F. Salinie
	Mr C. A. Toase
	Mr W. G. Williams
1992	Mr P. Bryant
	Mr G. Cunningham
	Mr J. Gattegno
	Mr W. D. Linton
	Dr R. C. Usherwood
1991	Mr T. Dickinson
	Mr P. H. Mann
	Ms D. B. Rosenberg
	Mr B. J. S. Williams
1990	Prof. G. W. A. Dick
	Prof. A. J. Evans
	Mrs S. G. Ray
	Mr J. W. Sumsion
	Mr A. L. van Wesemael

1989	Mr W. R. H. Carson		Dr W. A. Munford
	Mr E.Dudley		Mr P. H. Sewell
	Mr P. R. Lewis	1976	Prof J. D. Pearson
	Dr G. Pflug	1975	Mr E. A. Clough
1988	Mr D. Harrison		Mr S. W. Hockey
	Mrs B. Ruff	1974	Mr D. J. Foskett
	Mr R. G. Surridge		Mr F. W. Jessup
	Mr I. R. Willison		Mr T. Kelly
1987	Mr D. Mason		Mr B. I. Palmer
	Prof. M. B. Line	1973	Mr H. D. Barry
	Dr F. W. Ratcliffe		Mr A. D. Jones
1986	Prof. R. C. Alston		Mr W. B. Paton
	Mr C. H. Bingley	1972	Mr H. Coblans
	The Lord Dainton		Dr A. J. Walford
	Prof. P. Havard-Williams		Mr A. J. Wells
1985	Mrs H. Anuar	1971	Miss E. H. Colwell
	Mrs E. Granheim		Mr W. S. Haugh
	Dr H. Wallis		Mr S. H. Horrocks
1984	Mrs D. Anderson	1970	Mr A. H. Chaplin
	Mr D. K. Devnally		Miss A. S. Cooke
	Mr M. C. Fessey		Mr W. R. LeFanu
	Mr T. Kaung		Mr R. D. Macleod
	Mr A. Wilson		Mr W. Tynemouth
1983	Mr L. J. Anthony	1969	Mr T. Besterman
	Mr L. A. Gilbert		F. N. Withers
1982	Mr H. Faulkner Brown	1968	Mr S. W. Martin
	Sir Harry Hookway		Mr E. F. Patterson
	Mr P. E. Morris		Mr N. F. Sharp
	Mr C. L. J. O'Connell	1966	Mr E. Austin Hinton
1981	Mr R. Brown		Miss F. E. Cook
	Mr J. C. Downing		Mr F. M. Gardner
	Mr A. C. Jones	1965	Miss E. J. A. Evans
1980	Prof R. C. Benge		Mr W. J. Harris
	Miss L. V. Paulin	1964	Sir Sydney Roberts
	Mr K. W. Humphreys		Mr E. Sydney
	Mr P. A. Larkin	1963	Mr R. Irwin
1979	Mr R. Buchanan		Mr C. B. Oldman
	Mr E. Coates	1962	Mr E. J. Carter
	Mr R. P Hilliard		Sir Frank Francis
	Mr D. T Richnell	1961	Mr L. R. McColvin
1978	Mrs D. M. Palmer		Mr B. S. Page
	Mr H. Holdsworth	1959	Mr J. D. Stewart
1977	Mr P. Kirkegaard		Mr P. S. J. Welsford
	Sir Robin Mackworth Young		

1948	Mr R. J. Gordon
1947	Mr W. C. Berwick Sayers
	Mr H. M. Cashmore
1946	Mr Arundell Esdaile
	Mr Albert Mansbridge
1938	Mr Wilson Benson Thorne
1935	Mr H. Tapley-Soper
1933	Rt Hon. Stanley Baldwin
	Mr Ernest A. Savage
1932	Rt Hon. Earl of Elgin and Kincardine
	Mr J. M. Mitchell
1931	Mr W. W. Bishop
	Mr George H. Locke
1929	Sir John Ballinger
1924	Mr A. W. Pollard
	Mr W. E. Doubleday
1915	Mr L. S. Jast
1914	Mr J. Potter Briscoe
	Mr R. K. Dent
1913	Mr James Duff Brown
1909	Mr T. C. Abbott
	Mr H. W. Fovargue
1908	Mr J. J. Ogle
1907	Rt Hon. Earl of Plymouth
1906	Mr Henry D. Roberts
1905	Mr Lawrence Inkster
1903	Mr Henry Guppy
1902	Mr W. Macneile Dixon
	Mr Frank Pacy
1901	Mr Thomas Greenwood
1899	Rt Hon. Lord Avebury
	Marquess of Dufferin and Ava
	Mr Samuel Timmins
	Rt Hon. Lord Windsor
1898	Mr J. Y. W. MacAlister
1896	Mr James Bain
	Conte Ugo Balzani
	Prof. Alexander Beljame
	Mr J. S. Billings
	Mr R. R. Bowker
	Mr C. W. Bruun
	Mr Andrew Carnegie
	Mr C. A. Cutter
	Mr Leopold Delisle

	Mr Melvil Dewey
	Sir George Grey
	Mr Justin Winsor
	Mr C. Dziatzko
	Mr J. Passmore Edwards
	Mr S. S. Green
1896	Mr P. G. Horsen
	Rt Hon. Sir John Lubbock
	Sir Henry Tate
	Baron O. de Watteville

Certificates of Merit

2002	Mrs P. Bonnett
	Mr D. R. Butcher
	Ms D. Dixon
	Mr B. M. Hall
	Mr D. N. Rigglesford
2001	Mr R. S. Eagle
	Ms A. Edmunds
	Dr J. Harvey
2000	Mrs V. Nurcombe
1999	Mr M. Stacey
1998	none
1997	Mr I. M. Jamieson
	Mrs J. Machell
1996	Dr H. Fuchs
	Ms F. M. M. Redfern
1995	Miss V. A. Fea
	Mr R. Sweeney
1994	Mr F. Chambers
	Mrs L. Elliott
	Mrs S. Harrity
	Mr J. Pyle
	Mr J. Merriman
1993	Mr A. Chadwick
	Mr D. F. Keeling
1992	Mr P. Thomas
1991	Mr R. Phillips
1990	Mr T. C. Farries
1989	Mr E. Frow
	Mrs R. Frow
1985	Dr F. A. Thorpe

Institute of Information Scientists Award winners

Jason Farradane Award winners

2001   Professor Bruce Royan for SCRAN
2000   Jill Foster for her pioneering work in establishing the Mailbase discussion and distribution list
1999   Michael Keen for his Lifetime's Work in Information Retrieval
1998   Norman Wood and the EIRO Team of the European Foundation for the Improvement of Living and Working Conditions Dublin, for their outstanding and original work on the European Industrial Relations Observatory (EIRO)
1997   Newcastle University Library for the Development and Administration of the Newcastle Electronic Reference Desk – NERD
1996   The Higher Education Funding Council's Electronic Libraries Programme for innovation in the exploitation of IT in Higher Education Libraries
1995   Dennis Nicholson and the BUBL team for the development of the Bulletin Board for libraries
1994   Rita Marcella and colleagues at the School of Librarianship and Information Studies at Robert Gordon University for the development of their innovative Postgraduate Course in Information Analysis
1993   Peter Ingwersen in recognition of his services to Information Science
1992   European Foundation for the Improvement of Living and Working conditions, Dublin, for developing the series of European and Industrial Relations Glossaries

1991   Arnold Myers, Information Scientist, for contribution to information services with the international oil and gas industry
1990   Scottish Science Library, setting up of an important new library for Scotland
1989   Patricia Baird, Blaise Cronin, Noreen MacMarrow, academics, University of Strathclyde, work in the field of hypertext on producing an electronic conspectus on the life and times of the City of Glasgow
1988   No award – no nomination received before closing date
1987   Sandra Ward, Information Scientist, work in raising the profile of industrial information services
1986   Phil Williams, academic and businessman, contributions to making online searching more readily accessible to users
1985   Phil Holmes, achievements in applying technological advances to library development especially in the development of BLAISE (British Library), and PEARL (Blackwell Technical Services)
1984   Jacqueline Welch, librarian at Wessex Medical Library, contributed to promotion of information science particularly within the field of medical information
1983   Karen Sparck-Jones, academic, information science research, eg automation classification and indexing, methods of testing and evaluation, weighting and relevance feedback
1982   Monty Hyams, businessman, Derwent Publictaion Ltd. Developed Central Patents Index for patent searching

1981	William Wisswesser (USA), work with chemical notation, giving his name to Wisswesser line notation (WLN)
1980	Michael Lynch, academic, Sheffield University, expert in chemical structure handling
1979	Jason Farradane, founder of the IIS and a cornerstone of information science teaching and research

Tony Kent Strix Award winners

2002	Malcolm Jones
2001	Professor Peter Willett.
2000	Dr Martin Porter
1999	Dr Donna Harman
1998	Professor Stephen Robertson

These awards are now administered by UKeiG.

Library Association Medal and Award winners

Carnegie Medal winners

Please note that the year refers to when the book was published rather than when the medal was awarded i.e. the 1999 winner was announced and the medal presented in July 2000.

2000 Beverley Naidoo, *The Other Side of Truth*, Puffin

1999 Aidan Chambers, *Postcards From No Man's Land*, Bodley Head

1998 David Almond, *Skellig*, Hodder Children's Books

1997 Tim Bowler, *River Boy*, OUP

1996 Melvin Burgess, *Junk*, Andersen Press

1995 Philip Pullman, His Dark Materials: Book 1 *Northern Lights*, Scholastic

1994 Theresa Breslin, *Whispers in the Graveyard*, Methuen

1993 Robert Swindells, *Stone Cold*, H Hamilton

1992 Anne Fine, *Flour Babies*, H Hamilton

1991 Berlie Doherty, *Dear Nobody*, H Hamilton

1990 Gillian Cross, *Wolf*, OUP

1989 Anne Fine, *Goggle-eyes*, H Hamilton

1988 Geraldine McCaughrean, *A Pack of Lies*, OUP

1987 Susan Price, *The Ghost Drum*, Faber

1986 Berlie Doherty, *Granny was a Buffer Girl*, Methuen

1985 Kevin Crossley-Holland, *Storm*, Heinemann

1984 Margaret Mahy, *The Changeover*, Dent

1983 Jan Mark, *Handles*, Kestrel

1982 Margaret Mahy, *The Haunting*, Dent

1981 Robert Westall, *The Scarecrows*, Chatto & Windus

1980 Peter Dickinson, *City of Gold*, Gollancz

1979 Peter Dickinson, *Tulku*, Gollancz

1978 David Rees, *The Exeter Blitz*, H Hamilton

1977 Gene Kemp, *The Turbulent Term of Tyke Tiler*, Faber

1976 Jan Mark, *Thunder and Lightnings*, Kestrel

1975 Robert Westall, *The Machine Gunners*, Macmillan

1974 Mollie Hunter, *The Stronghold*, H Hamilton

1973 Penelope Lively, *The Ghost of Thomas Kempe*, Heinemann

1972 Richard Adams, *Watership Down*, Rex Collings

1971 Ivan Southall, *Josh*, Angus & Robertson

1970 Leon Garfield & Edward Blishen, *The God Beneath the Sea*, Longman

1969 Kathleen Peyton, *The Edge of the Cloud*, OUP

1968 Rosemary Harris, *The Moon in the Cloud*, Faber

1967 Alan Garner, *The Owl Service*, Collins

1966 Prize withheld as no book considered suitable

1965 Philip Turner, *The Grange at High Force*, OUP

1964 Sheena Porter, *Nordy Bank*, OUP

1963 Hester Burton, *Time of Trial*, OUP

1962 Pauline Clarke, *The Twelve and the Genii*, Faber

1961 Lucy M. Boston, *A Stranger at Green Knowe*, Faber

1960 Dr I. W. Cornwall, *The Making of Man*, Phoenix House

1959 Rosemary Sutcliff, *The Lantern Bearers*, OUP

1958 Philipa Pearce, *Tom's Midnight Garden*, OUP

1957   William Mayne, *A Grass Rope*, OUP
1956   C. S. Lewis, *The Last Battle*, Bodley
        Head
1955   Eleanor Farjeon, *The Little Bookroom*,
        OUP
1954   Ronald Welch (Felton Ronald Oliver),
        Knight Crusader, OUP
1953   Edward Osmond, *A Valley Grows Up*
1952   Mary Norton, *The Borrowers*, Dent
1951   Cynthia Harnett, *The Woolpack*, Methuen
1950   Elfrida Vipont Foulds, *The Lark on the
        Wing*, OUP
1949   Agnes Allen, *The Story of Your Home*,
        Faber
1948   Richard Armstrong, *Sea Change*, Dent
1947   Walter De La Mare, *Collected Stories for
        Children*
1946   Elizabeth Goudge, *The Little White
        Horse*, University of London Press
1945   Prize withheld as no book considered
        suitable
1944   Eric Linklater, *The Wind on the Moon*,
        Macmillan
1943   Prize withheld as no book considered
        suitable
1942   'BB' (D. J. Watkins-Pitchford), *The Little
        Grey Men*, Eyre & Spottiswoode
1941   Mary Treadgold, *We Couldn't Leave
        Dinah*, Cape
1940   Kitty Barne, *Visitors from London*, Dent
1939   Eleanor Doorly, *Radium Woman*,
        Heinemann
1938   Noel Streatfield, *The Circus is Coming*,
        Dent
1937   Eve Garnett, *The Family from One End
        Street*, Muller
1936   Arthur Ransome, *Pigeon Post*, Cape

Kate Greenaway Medal winners

Please note that the year refers to when the book was published rather than when the medal was awarded i.e. the 1999 winner was announced and the medal presented in July 2000.

2000   Lauren Child, *I Will Not Ever Never Eat a
        Tomato*, Orchard Books
1999   Helen Oxenbury, *Alice's Adventures in
        Wonderland*, Walker Books
1998   Helen Cooper, *Pumpkin Soup*,
        Doubleday
1997   P. J. Lynch, *When Jessie Came Across
        the Sea*, Walker Books
1996   Helen Cooper, *The Baby Who Wouldn't
        Go To Bed*, Doubleday
1995   P. J. Lynch, *The Christmas Miracle of
        Jonathan Toomey*, Walker Books
1994   Gregory Rogers, *Way Home*, Andersen
        Press
1993   Alan Lee, *Black Ships Before Troy*,
        Frances Lincoln
1992   Anthony Browne, *Zoo*, Julia MacRae
1991   Janet Ahlberg, *The Jolly Christmas
        Postman*, Heinemann
1990   Gary Blythe, *The Whales' Song*,
        Hutchinson
1989   Michael Foreman, *War Boy: a Country
        Childhood*, Pavilion
1988   Barbara Firth, *Can't You Sleep Little
        Bear?*, Walker Books
1987   Adrienne Kennaway, *Crafty Chameleon*,
        Hodder & Stoughton
1986   Fiona French, *Snow White in New York*,
        OUP
1985   Juan Wijngaard, *Sir Gawain and the
        Loathly Lady*, Walker Books
1984   Errol Le Cain, *Hiawatha's Childhood*,
        Faber
1983   Anthony Browne, *Gorilla*, Julia MacRae
1982   Michael Foreman, *Long Neck and
        Thunder Foot* and *Sleeping Beauty and*

Other Favourite Fairy Tales, Kestrel and Gollancz

1981 Charles Keeping, *The Highwayman*, OUP

1980 Quentin Blake, *Mr Magnolia*, Cape

1979 Jan Pienkowski, *The Haunted House*, Heinemann

1978 Janet Ahlberg, *Each Peach Pear Plum*, Kestrel

1977 Shirley Hughes, *Dogger*, Bodley Head

1976 Gail E. Haley, *The Post Office Cat*, Bodley Head

1975 Victor Ambrus, *Horses in Battle* and *Mishka*, OUP

1974 Pat Hutchins, *The Wind Blew*, Bodley head

1973 Raymond Briggs, *Father Christmas*, H Hamilton

1972 Krystyna Turska, *The Woodcutter's Duck*, H Hamilton

1971 Jan Pienkowski, *The Kingdom under the Sea*, Cape

1970 John Burningham, *Mr Gumpy's Outing*, Cape

1969 Helen Oxenbury, *The Quangle Wangle's hat* and *The Dragon of an Ordinary Family*, Heinemann

1968 Pauline Baynes, *Dictionary of Chivalry*, Longman

1967 Charles Keeping, *Charlotte and the Golden Canary*, OUP

1966 Raymond Briggs, *Mother Goose Treasury*, H Hamilton

1965 Victor Ambrus, *The Three Poor Tailors*, OUP

1964 C. W. Hodges, *Shakespeare's Theatre*, OUP

1963 John Burningham, *Borka: the Adventures of a Goose with No Feathers*, Cape

1962 Brian Wildsmith, *A.B.C.*, OUP

1961 Antony Maitland, *Mrs Cockle's Cat*, Constable

1960 Gerald Rose, *Old Winkle and the Seagulls*, Faber

1959 William Stobbs, *Kashtanka* and *A Bundle of Ballads*, OUP

1958 Prize withheld as no book considered suitable

1957 V. H. Drummond, *Mrs Easter and the Storks*, Faber

1956 Edward Ardizzone, *Tim All Alone*, OUP

1955 Prize withheld as no book considered suitable

Libraries Change Lives Award winners

2001 Merton Libraries Refugee Resources Collection and Service

2000 Kensal Library's Community Action Initiative

1999 The Ad Lib Project, Sheffield

1998 Pontefract's Readers Group

1997 Horley's Local History Centre

1996 Liverpool 8 Law Centre

1995 Sunderland Libraries Bookstart Project

1994 Petersburn Community Library and Teenage Drop in Centre

1993 Wandsworth Prison and Springfield Psychiatric Hospital

1992 Annex Community Centre, Hartlepool

Library Association/ESU Travelling Librarian Award Winners

2001 Robert Atkinson
2000 Paul Anderson
1999 Not awarded
1998 Fiona Hooper
1994–97 Not awarded
1993 Julie Scott (Cully)
1983–92 Not awarded
1982 Kirsten Bax

1981	Stephen Roberts
1980	Ian Johnson
1979	Joe Hendry
1978	David Ferro
1977	Peter Smith
1976	Carol Buxton
1975	Catherine Pinion
1974	Peter R. Brodnax Moore
1973	David Horn
1972	John Chapman
1971	Gillian Clegg
1970	Simon Francis
1969	Antonia Bunch
1968	David Bromley
1967	Janet Hunt
	Frances Anderson (Burgess)
1966	Not awarded
1965	Carol Ashcroft
	Kathleen Asbery (Smith)
	Ivan G. Sparkes
	Marion Wilden-Hart

	Education, Arts and Libraries
1991	Ann-Marie Parker, Hertfordshire Libraries, Arts and Information Service
1990	Max Broome, Library Association President 1987
1989	Peter Grant, City Librarian, Aberdeen
1987	Sue Broughton, Hungerford Branch Library, Berkshire County Libraries
1986	Liz Weir, Belfast Education and Library Board
1985	Joe Hendry, Renfrew District Libraries
1984	Ron Surridge, Library Association President 1984

Public Relations and Publicity Awards

Personal PR Achievement winners

2001	June Turner, Essex Libraries
2000	Jim Jackson, Library Association Affiliated Members National Committee
1999	Desmond Heaps, Warwickshire County Council Libraries and Heritage
1997	The Awards programme for 1997–8 did not run
1996	Dominic Bean, Southwark Library and Information Service
1995	Annie Everall, Centre for the Child, Birmingham City Library
1994	Maggie Goodbarn, Gateshead Libraries and Arts Service
1993	John Stafford, Northamptonshire Libraries and Information Service
1992	Gill Whitehead, Brent Department of

Reference Award winners

The Library Association Reference Awards comprised the Besterman/ McColvin Medals, the Walford Award and the Wheatley Medal.

Besterman/McColvin Medal winners

Electronic category

2001	*The World Shakespeare Bibliography Online* by James L. Harner. The Folger Shakespeare Library www-english.tamu.edu/wsb/
1999/2000	*The British 1881 Census Index on CDROM.* Church of Jesus Christ of the Latter Day Saints

Printed category

2001	*The Encyclopedia of Ephemera* by Maurice Rickards / Michael Twyman (Ed.). The British Library
1999/2000	*The Oxford Companion to Food* by Alan Davidson. OUP

Previously, a Besterman Medal was awarded for bibliography and a McColvin Medal for an outstanding reference work – hence the two lists below.

Besterman Medal winners

1998   *The Victoria and Albert Museum – a Bibliography and Exhibition Chronology 1852–1996* by Elizabeth James. Fitzroy Dearborn

1997   *Handbook for British and Irish Archaelogy* by Cherry Lavell. Edinburgh University Press

1996   *The World Shakespeare Bibliography 1990–1993 on CD/ROM* by Professor James L. Harner. Cambridge University Press

1995   *A Football Compendium: a comprehensive guide to the literature of Association Football* by Peter J. Seddon. The British Library

1994   *Bibliography of Printed Works on London History to 1939* by Heather Creaton. Library Association Publishing

1993   *Africa: A Guide to Reference Material* by John McIlwaine. Hans Zell

1992   Award witheld.

1991   *A Short-title Catalogue of Books Printed in England, Scotland, Ireland and English Books Printed Abroad 1475–1640...* volume 3 by Katherine Pantzer. Oxford University Press/The Bibliographical Society

1990   *British Architectural Books and Writers 1556–1785* by Eileen Harris and Nicholas Savage. Cambridge University Press

1989   *Bibliography and Index of English Verse Printed 1476–1558* by William Ringler Jnr. Mansell

1988   *T E Lawrence: a bibliography* by Philip O'Brien. St Paul's Bibliographies

1987   *Dickens Dramatized* by Philip H. Bolton. Mansell

1986   *English Poetry of the Second World War: a bibliography* by Catherine W. Reilly. Mansell

1985   *Employee Relations Bibliography and Abstracts* by Arthur Marsh. Employee relations bibliography and abstracts

1984   *A Bibliography of the Kelmscott Press* by William S. Peterson. Clarendon Press

1983   *London Illustrated, 1604–1851: a survey and index to topographical books and their plates* by Bernard Adams. Library Association Publishing and *Ted Hughes: a bibliography, 1946–1980* by Keith Sagar and Stephen Tabor. Mansell

1982   *Walford's Guide to Reference Material* 4th edition. Vol. 2: *Social and Historical Sciences, Philosophy and Religion* edited by A. J. Walford. Library Association Publishing

1981   *British and Irish Architectural History: a bibliography and guide to sources of information* by Ruth H. Kamen. Architectural Press

1980   *Alchemy: a bibliography of English-language writings,* by Alan Pritchard. Routledge and Kegan Paul jointly with The Library Association

1979   *Knowhow: a guide to information, training and campaigning materials for information and advice workers* compiled by G. Morby, edited by E. Kempson. Community Information project
and
South Asian Bibliography: a handbook and guide compiled by the South East Asia Library Group, general editor J. D. Pearson. Harvester Press

1978   Award withheld.

1997   *A Bibliography of Cricket* compiled by E. W. Padwick. Library Association Publishing for the Cricket Society

1976   *Guide to Official Statistics*, No 1, 1976 by Central Statistical Office. HMSO

1975   *Printed Maps of Victorian London* by Ralph Hyde. Dawson

1974   *Agriculture: a bibliographical guide* by E. A. R. Bush. Macdonald and Jane's

1973   Award withheld.

1972   *A Bibliography of British and Irish Municipal History* Vol. 1: *General Works.* by Dr G. H. Martin and Sylvia McIntyre. Leicester University Press

1971   *Sourcebook of Planning Information: a discussion of sources of information for use in urban and regional planning; and in allied fields* by Brenda White. Bingley

1970   *English Theatrical Literature 1559–1900* by J. F. Arnott and J. W. Robinson. Society for Theatre Research

McColvin Medal winners

1998   *Parrots* by Tony Juniper and Mike Par. Pica Press

1997   *Ancestral Trails* by Mark D. Herber. Sutton Publishing/ Society of Genealogists

1996   *Who's Who 1897–1996 on CD/ROM* by Christine Ruge-Cope and Roger Tritton. A & C Black and Oxford University Press.

1995   *The Tithe Maps of England and Wales* by Roger Kain and Richard Oliver. Cambridge University Press

1994   *Dictionary of British and Irish Botanists and Horticulturists* by Ray Desmond. Taylor and Francis

1993   *History of Canal and River Navigation* edited by Edward Paget-Tomlinson. Sheffield Academic Press

1992   *The New Grove Dictionary of Opera* edited by Stanley Sadie. Macmillan

1991   *The Cambridge Encyclopedia of Ornithology* by Michael Brooke and Tim Birkhead. Cambridge University Press

1990   *William Walton: a catalogue* by Stewart Craggs. 2nd edition. Oxford University Press.

1989   *The Oxford English Dictionary* 2nd edition edited by John Simpson and Edmund Weiner. Oxford University Press

1988   *The Encyclopaedia of Oxford* edited by Christopher Hibbert. Macmillan

1987   *Fermented Foods of the World: a dictionary and guide* by Geoffrey Campbell- Platt. Butterworths

1986   *The British Musical Theatre* by Kurt Ganzl. Vol 1: *1865–1914*; Vol 2: *1915–1984*. Macmillan

1985   *The Artist's Craft: a history of tools, techniques and material* by James Ayres. Phaidon

1984   *The History of Glass* general editors Dan Klein and Ward Lloyd. Orbis

1983   *Dictionary of British Book Illustrators: the twentieth century* by Brigid Peppin and Lucy Micklewait. Murray

1982   *The Dictionary of Blue and White Printed Pottery, 1780–1880* by A. W. Coysh and R. K. Henrywood. Antique Collectors' Club

1981   *The New Grove Dictionary of Music and Musicians* edited by Stanley Sadie. Macmillan

1980   *Guide to the Local Administrative Units of England*, Volume 1: *Southern England* by Frederic A. Youngs Jr. Royal Historical Society

1979   Award withheld.

1978   Award withheld.

1977   Award withheld.

1976   *A Manual of European Languages for Librarians* by C. G. Allen. Bowker

1975   *Folksongs of Britain and Ireland* by Peter Kennedy. Cassell

1974   *Reviews of United Kingdom Statistical Sources* Volumes 1 to 3. edited by W. F. Maunder, Heinemann Educational Books published for the Royal Statistical Society and the Social Science Research Council

1973   Award withheld.

1972   *Music Yearbook 1972/3* edited by Arthur Jacobs. Macmillan

1971   *Shepherd's Glossary of Graphic Signs and Symbols* by Walter Shepherd. Dent

1970   *Councils, Committees and Boards: a handbook of advisory, consultative, executive and similar bodies in British political life.* CBD

Walford Award winners

2001   Professor John McIlwaine

1999/2000   Charles Toase HonFLA

1998   George Ottley FLA

1997   Barry Bloomfield MA FLA HonFLA

1996   Professor Ian Rogerson MLS PhD Dlitt FLA

1995   Magda Whitrow BA ALA

1994   Professor S W Wells

1993   Professor D F McKenzie

1992   Professor Robin C Alston OBE MA PhD FSA HonFLA FLA

1991   Professor James Douglas Pearson MA HonFLA

Wheatley Medal winners

2001   Crystal, David and Crystal, Hilary for index to *Words on Words*. Penguin Books

1999/2000   Hird, Barbara for index to *The Cambridge History of Medieval English Literature*. Cambridge University Press

1998   Sheard, Caroline, for the index to *Textbook of Dermatology*. 6th ed. 4 vols. Blackwell Science

1997   Ross, Jan, for the index to *Rheumatology*. Mosby International

1996   Levitt, Ruth and Northcott, Gillian, for the index to *Dictionary of Art*. Macmillan

1995   Richardson, Ruth and Thorne, Robert, *The Builder Illustrations Index*. Hutton and Rostron

1994   Matthew, Professor H G C, for the index to *The Gladstone Diaries*. Clarenden Press

1993   Merrall Ross, Janine, for the index to *Encyclopedia of Food Science, Food Technology and Nutrition*. Academic Press

1992   Nash, Paul, for the index to *The World Environment 1972–1992*. London, Chapman and Hall (on behalf of the United Nations Environment Programme)

1991   Moys, Elizabeth, for the index to *British Tax Encyclopedia*. Sweet and Maxell

1990   Award withheld as no index considered suitable.

1989   Raper, Richard, for the index to *The Works of Charles Darwin*. Pickering and Chatto

1988   Burke, Bobby, for the index to *Halsbury's Laws of England*. 4th edition. Butterworths

1987   Fisk, Neil R., for the index to *A Short History of Wilson's School*. 3rd edition. Wilson's School Charitable Trust

1986   Award withheld as no index considered suitable.

1985   Gibson, John, for the index to *Brain's Diseases of the Nervous System*. 9th edition. Oxford University Press

1984   Award withheld as no index considered suitable.

1983   Hewitt, A. R., for the index to *The Laws of Trinidad and Tobago*. Government of Trinidad and Tobago and Latham, Robert, for the index to *The Diary of Samuel Pepys*. Bell and Hyman

1982   Blayney, Peter W. M., for the index to *The Texts of King Lear and their Origins*. Volume 1: *Nicholas Okes and the First Quarto*. Cambridge University Press

1981   Holmstrom, J. Edwin. *Analytical Index to the Publications of the Institution of Civil Engineers. January 1975–1979*. Institution of Civil Engineers

1980   Taylor, Laurie J., for the index to *The Librarian's Handbook*. Vol. 2. Library Association Publishing

1979   Bakewell, K. G. B., for the index to *Anglo-American Cataloguing Rules*. 2nd edition. Library Association Publishing
and
Surrey, A., for the index to *Circulation of the Blood*. Pitman Medical

1978   Prize withheld as no index considered suitable.

1977   Pavel, T. Rowland, for the index to *Archaeologia Cambrensis 1901–60*. Cambrian Archaeological Association

1976   Vickers, John A., for the index to Vol 11 of *The Works of John Wesley: the appeals to men of reason and religion and certain related open letter*. Oxford, Clarendon Press

1975   Anderson, M. D., for the index to *Copy-editing*. Cambridge University Press.

1974   Banwell, C. C., for the index to Encyclopaedia of Forms and Precedents. 4th ed. Butterworths

1973   Boodson, K., for the index to *Non-ferrous Metals*. Macdonald Technical and Scientific
and
Harrod, L. M. Index to *History of King's Works*. Vol. 6. HMSO

1972   Prize withheld as no index considered suitable.

1971   Prize withheld as no index considered suitable.

1970   Mullins, E.L.C., for the index to *A Guide to the Historical and Archaeological Publications of Societies in England and Wales, 1901–1933*. Athlone Press

1969   Thornton, James, for the index to *The Letters of Charles Dickens*. Vol 2. Oxford, Clarendon Press

1968   Blake, Doreen and Bowden, Ruth E. M. for the index to the *Journal of Anatomy, first 100 years, 1866–1966*. Cambridge University Press

1967   Knight, G. Norman, for the index to *Winston S. Churchill*. Vol. 2. Heinemann

1966   Prize withheld as no index considered suitable.

1965   Quinn, Alison, for the index to *The Principall Navigation Voyages and Discoveries of the English Nation* by R. Hakluyt. Cambridge University Press, for the Hakluyt Society and Peabody Museum of Salem

1964   Parsloe, Guy, the index to *The Warden's Accounts of the Worshipful Company of Founders of the City of London, 1497–1681*. Athlone Press

1963   Dickie, J. M. for the index to *How to Catch Trout*. 3rd ed. W & R Chambers

1962   Maclagan, Michael, for the index to *Clemency Canning*. Macmillan

Robinson Medal winners

1999   Margie Mason for Battling with books, a guide for new library staff.

1997   Janet Audain for the design, development and delivery of library services to users with disabilities.

1995 (Award re-launched) Beverley Britton for online submission of off-print database for a reading list database.

1994 Award withheld

1992 Award withheld

1990 JANET Users Group for Libraries for their work in promoting the Joint Academic Network, and plescon limited for the development of the DISCOSAFE and VIDEO TAG electronic security devices.

1988 Award withheld

1986 Prof Nick Moore for the production of guidelines for conducting library and information manpower surveys.

1984 Renfrew district libraries for the inauguration of the Johnstone Information and Leisure Library (JILL).

1982 Award withheld

1980 London Borough of Sutton for innovation in library marketing.

1978 Award withheld

1976 Award withheld

1974 Award withheld

1972 University of Lancaster library research for the development of simulation games in education for library management.

1970 Mr Frank Gurney, of Automated Library Systems Limited for book-charging.

1968 Mansell Information Publishing Limited, of London, for their development of an automatic abstracting camera for use in producing book catalogues from library cards or other sequential material.

Index